# TAXES
## of
# HAWAII
# 2019

❖

## A Comprehensive Guide for Taxpayers and Tax Professionals

❖

### For Tax Year 2018

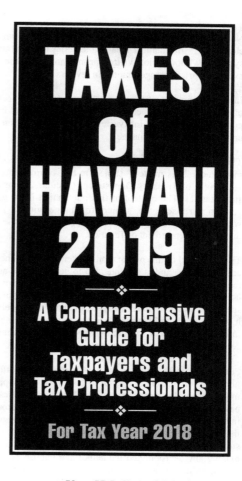

# TAXES of HAWAII 2019

A Comprehensive Guide for Taxpayers and Tax Professionals

For Tax Year 2018

Alan M.L. Yee, CPA
Kurt K. Kawafuchi
Duane Akamine

**WATERMARK**
PUBLISHING

In the preparation of this book, every effort has been made to offer the most current, correct, and clearly expressed information possible. Nonetheless, inadvertent errors can occur, and tax rules and regulations often change.

The information herein is not "written advice concerning one or more Federal tax matters" subject to the requirements of section 10.37(a)(2) of Treasury Department Circular 230 or applicable state statutes. The content of this publication is for general discussion purposes only, subject to change without notice, and without binding effect on either the Internal Revenue Service or the Hawaii Department of Taxation.

The main goal of this publication is intended to enhance the reader's knowledge and is not intended to be applied to any specific reader's particular set of facts. Although we endeavor to provide accurate and timely information, there can be no guarantee that such information is accurate as of the date it is received or that it will continue to be accurate in the future. Applicability of the information to specific situations should be determined through consultation with your tax adviser.

Further, the information in the text is intended to afford general guidelines on matters of interest to taxpayers. The application and impact of tax laws can vary widely, however, from case to case, based upon the specific or unique facts involved. Accordingly, the information in this book is not intended to serve as legal, accounting or tax advice. Readers are encouraged to consult with professional advisors for advice concerning specific matters before making any decision, and the author and publishers disclaim any responsibility for positions taken by taxpayers in their individual cases or for any misunderstanding on the part of readers.

ISBN 978-1-948011-12-9

Library of Congress Control Number: 2019933007

Published and marketed by:
Watermark Publishing
1000 Bishop Street, Suite 806
Honolulu, Hawai'i 96813
Telephone (808) 587-7766
www.bookshawaii.net

Design by Gonzalez Design Co.

Production by Angela Wu-Ki

Printed in the United States

*Special thanks to
Deanna Awa, Rebecca Yuen, and
Jennifer Cordaro for their assistance
and contributions*

# CONTENTS

# INTRODUCTION

This edition of *Taxes of Hawaii* was updated by the partners, managers and consultants of KMH LLP, one of Hawaii's largest locally-owned public accounting firms. KMH LLP follows in the footsteps of Ernst & Young LLP, which updated the editorial content for more than 40 years. Consistent with that tradition, this book is designed as a comprehensive reference tool on Hawaii state taxes for both tax professionals and taxpayers. For the current year, this book follows the general structure and organization of previous editions. Any suggestions to improve the usefulness and functionality of future editions are welcome.

Most of the book is devoted to income taxes.The Hawaii income tax rules generally follow the pattern of the federal tax, but there are some differences. An assumption is made that the reader has some familiarity with federal income taxes and has access to a source of information on the federal tax rules. Special attention was devoted to subjects peculiar to the Hawaii law, such as residence status, income tax credits, allocation of income of multi-state operations and various other areas. A check list is also provided to show the differences between federal and Hawaii rules. In addition to income taxes, the general excise (gross income) tax and related use tax, estate tax, property and unemployment tax are explained in some detail to give a general picture of their nature and impact. All references are based on the Hawaii Revised Statutes and federal laws as they stood as of December 31, 2018 and December 31, 2017, respectively.

A special feature of the book is the inclusion of many filled-in specimen returns. As shown in the table of contents, there are numerous income tax forms, in addition to a franchise tax return, general excise tax returns and an estate tax return, with accompanying schedules where required. The facts on which the returns are based are presented in each case, except where the facts are obvious from the return itself.

Throughout this book, reference is made to Opinions of the Attorney General, Hawaii Administrative Rules, and Tax Information Releases of the Department of Taxation. Some of these published releases provide detailed examples or provide an analysis of the income, excise or use tax laws as they relate to specific matters. As such, included in Chapter 14 are some of the more pertinent administrative releases that hopefully will be beneficial to our readers.

This book is designed as a quick reference course on Hawaii's state taxes. The information in the text is intended to afford general guidance on matters of interest to taxpayers. It is not intended to eliminate the necessity of referring to the law, administrative rules or court decisions for answers to difficult or complicated problems. Nor is this book meant to serve as legal, accounting or tax advice. Tax laws change often, after all, and the application and impact of tax laws vary widely depending on the specific or unique facts involved. Readers should consult with professional advisers on specific matters before making tax decisions.

We are honored to update and maintain this guide on Hawaii taxes, and look forward to continuing this work for many years to come. A heartfelt appreciation is extended to the many friends and associates who have rendered valuable assistance in writing this edition.

**Alan M.L. Yee**
**Kurt Kawafuchi**
**Duane Akamine**

## ABOUT KMH LLP

KMH LLP was established in August 2002 to be the successor organization of Arthur Andersen's Hawaii operations. The partners created KMH based on the belief that Hawaii organizations needed an accounting and business consulting firm with deep skills and the ability to deliver a wide variety of services, and be owned and controlled locally. Our success has attracted national recognition with the invitation and acceptance of KMH into two different premier international accounting and business consulting firm networks: The RSM McGladrey network and The Leading Edge Alliance.

Over the past several years, this vision has been reaffirmed numerous times with the addition of senior accounting and business consulting executives, including four partners, who joined KMH from other international accounting firms.

# DIRECTORY OF HAWAII STATE TAX OFFICES

## MAIN OFFICE—OAHU DISTRICT OFFICE

Princess Ruth Keelikolani Building
830 Punchbowl Street
Honolulu, Hawaii 96813-5094

Telephone ..................................... 587-4242
Fax.............................................. 587-1488

## OFFICE OF THE DIRECTOR

Linda Chu Takayama, Director ..................................................... 587-1540
Damien A. Elefante, Deputy Director ............................................. 587-1540
Jaysen Y Morikami, Taxpayer Advocate ......................................... 587-1791
Adriane Aarona, Administrative Appeals Officer.............................. 587-1446
Deborah Kwan, Chief Communications Officer................................ 587-1540

## STAFF OFFICES

Ted Shiraishi, Rules Officer...................................................... 587-1530
Denise Inouye, Supervising Income Tax Specialist............................587-1577
Seth Colby, Research and Planning Officer.................................... 587-1440
Robert Su, Information Technology Services Officer ........................ 587-1755
Dexter Suzuki, Administrative Services Officer............................... 587-1500
Dean Arashiro, Acting, Dept. Human Resources Officer ....................587-1512

## OPERATIONS STAFF

### Tax Services & Processing Division

Nicki Ann Thompson, Taxation Services Administrator.................................. 543-6811
Todd Kuromoto, Document Processing Operations Manager........................... 543-6813
Jennifer Oshiro, Revenue Accounting Branch Chief...................................587-1790
John Pacheco, Taxpayer Services Branch Chief........................................ 543-6812

### Compliance Division

Kevin Wakayama, Taxation Compliance Administrator ................................ 587-1611
Madelaina Lai, Oahu Field Audit Branch Chief.......................................... 587-1700
Donald Kuriki, Oahu Office Audit Branch Chief......................................... 587-1622
Janessa Bonifacio, Oahu Collection Branch Chief ..................................... 587-1719
John Higgins, Maui District Tax Manager ............................................... 984-8500
Duquesne Hulihee, Hawaii District Tax Manager ...................................... 974-6321
Erin Tsuda, Kauai District Tax Manager.................................................. 274-3456

## BRANCH OFFICE—MAUI DISTRICT OFFICE

State Office Building
54 S. High Street, #208
Wailuku, HI 96793-2198

John Higgins, Maui District Tax Manager
Telephone ..................................... 808-984-8500
Fax.............................................. 808-984-8522

## BRANCH OFFICE—HAWAII DISTRICT OFFICE

State Office Building
75 Aupuni Street, #101
Hilo, HI 96720-4245

Duquesne Hulihee, Hawaii District Tax Manager
Telephone .....................................808-974-6321
Fax.............................................. 808-974-6300

## BRANCH OFFICE—KAUAI DISTRICT OFFICE

State Office Building
3060 Eiwa Street, #105
Lihue, HI 96766-1889

Erin Tsuda, Kauai District Tax Manager
Telephone ..................................... 808-274-3456
Fax.............................................. 808-274-3461

# WEBSITE REFERENCES

The following are important state and county website references.

### City & County of Honolulu

HOME PAGE
http://www.honolulu.gov

REAL PROPERTY ASSESSMENT DIVISION – PROPERTY SEARCH DATABASE
http://qpublic9.public.net/hi_honolulu_address.php

### County of Kauai

HOME PAGE
http://www.kauai.gov/

REAL PROPERTY ASSESSMENT DIVISION – PROPERTY SEARCH DATABASE
http://qpublic9.qpublic.net/ga_address_dw.php?county=hi_kauai

### County of Maui
*(including the islands of Kahoolawe, Lanai, Maui and Molokai)*

HOME PAGE
http://www.mauicounty.gov

REAL PROPERTY ASSESSMENT DIVISION – PROPERTY SEARCH DATABASE
http://qpublic9.qpublic.net/hi_maui_address.php

### County of Hawaii

HOME PAGE
http://www.hawaiicounty.gov

REAL PROPERTY ASSESSMENT DIVISION – PROPERTY SEARCH DATABASE
http://qpublic9.qpublic.net/hi_hawaii_address.php

### Department of Taxation

HOME PAGE
http://www.hawaii.gov/tax/ or http://www.state.hi.us/tax/

SEARCH THE GENERAL EXCISE TAX LICENSES
https://dotax.ehawaii.gov/tls/app

HAWAII STATE GOVERNMENT HOME PAGE
http://www.portal.ehawaii.gov/index.html

DEPARTMENTS AND AGENCIES
http://stayconnected.hawaii.gov/

THE VIRTUAL RULES CENTER (*Administrative Rules for all Departments and Agencies*)
http://ltgov.hawaii.gov/the-office/administrative-rules/

FORMS CENTRAL (*Forms for all Departments and Agencies*)
http://hawaii.gov/forms/

HAWAII STATE LEGISLATURE –
LEGISLATIVE DOCUMENTS (*Includes Current Hawaii Revised Statutes*)
http://www.capitol.hawaii.gov/

# WEBSITE REFERENCES

## Department of Commerce and Consumer Affairs

HOME PAGE
cca.hawaii.gov

BUSINESS NAME SEARCH
http://hbe.ehawaii.gov/documents/search.html

PROFESSIONAL AND VOCATIONAL LICENSING SEARCH
http://pvl.ehawaii.gov/pvlsearch/

CAPTIVE INSURANCE BRANCH
cca.hawaii.gov/captive/

## Department of Business, Economic Development and Tourism

HOME PAGE
dbedt.hawaii.gov

ENTERPRISE ZONES
invest.hawaii.gov/business/ez

## Department of Budget and Finance

HOME PAGE
budget.hawaii.gov

## Other Sites of Interest

FEDERATION OF TAX ADMINISTRATORS
(*Organization of State Tax Administrators, Including the Hawaii Dept. of Taxation*)
http://www.taxadmin.org/

INTERNAL REVENUE SERVICE HOME PAGE
http://www.irs.gov/

INTERNAL REVENUE SERVICE – FEDERAL FORMS, INSTRUCTIONS, AND PUBLICATIONS
www.irs.gov/Forms-&-Pubs

MULTISTATE TAX COMMISSION (*Joint Agency of State Governments, Including Hawaii*)
http://www.mtc.gov/

TAX FOUNDATION OF HAWAII
http://www.tfhawaii.org

TAX TALK TODAY
http://www.taxtalktoday.com

U.S. CENSUS BUREAU
http://www.census.gov/

# PART I

## Income Tax

# 2018 Tax Rate Schedules

CAUTION — If your taxable income is less than $100,000, you MUST use the Tax Table.

## Schedule I

### SINGLE TAXPAYERS AND MARRIED FILING SEPARATE RETURNS

Use this schedule if you filled in Filing Status Oval 1 or 3 on Form N-11

| If the amount on Form N-11, Line 26 is: | Your tax is: |
|---|---|
| Not over $2,400 | 1.40% of taxable income |
| Over $2,400 but not over $4,800 ............... $ | 34 plus 3.20% over $2,400 |
| Over $4,800 but not over $9,600 ............... $ | 110 plus 5.50% over $4,800 |
| Over $9,600 but not over $14,400 ............... $ | 374 plus 6.40% over $9,600 |
| Over $14,400 but not over $19,200 ............... $ | 682 plus 6.80% over $14,400 |
| Over $19,200 but not over $24,000 ............... $ | 1,008 plus 7.20% over $19,200 |
| Over $24,000 but not over $36,000 ............... $ | 1,354 plus 7.60% over $24,000 |
| Over $36,000 but not over $48,000 ............... $ | 2,266 plus 7.90% over $36,000 |
| Over $48,000 but not over $150,000 ............... $ | 3,214 plus 8.25% over $48,000 |
| Over $150,000 but not over $175,000 ............... $ | 11,629 plus 9.00% over $150,000 |
| Over $175,000 but not over $200,000 ............... $ | 13,879 plus 10.00% over $175,000 |
| Over $200,000 ............... $ | 16,379 plus 11.00% over $200,000 |

## Schedule II

### MARRIED TAXPAYERS FILING JOINT RETURNS AND CERTAIN WIDOWS AND WIDOWERS

Use this schedule if you filled in Filing Status Oval 2 or 5 on Form N-11

| If the amount on Form N-11, Line 26 is: | Your tax is: |
|---|---|
| Not over $4,800 | 1.40% of taxable income |
| Over $4,800 but not over $9,600 ............... $ | 67 plus 3.20% over $4,800 |
| Over $9,600 but not over $19,200 ............... $ | 221 plus 5.50% over $9,600 |
| Over $19,200 but not over $28,800 ............... $ | 749 plus 6.40% over $19,200 |
| Over $28,800 but not over $38,400 ............... $ | 1,363 plus 6.80% over $28,800 |
| Over $38,400 but not over $48,000 ............... $ | 2,016 plus 7.20% over $38,400 |
| Over $48,000 but not over $72,000 ............... $ | 2,707 plus 7.60% over $48,000 |
| Over $72,000 but not over $96,000 ............... $ | 4,531 plus 7.90% over $72,000 |
| Over $96,000 but not over $300,000 ............... $ | 6,427 plus 8.25% over $96,000 |
| Over $300,000 but not over $350,000 ............... $ | 23,257 plus 9.00% over $300,000 |
| Over $350,000 but not over $400,000 ............... $ | 27,757 plus 10.00% over $350,000 |
| Over $400,000 ............... $ | 32,757 plus 11.00% over $400,000 |

## Schedule III

### UNMARRIED HEADS OF HOUSEHOLD

Use this schedule if you filled in Filing Status Oval 4 on Form N-11

| If the amount on Form N-11, Line 26 is: | Your tax is: |
|---|---|
| Not over $3,600 | 1.40% of taxable income |
| Over $3,600 but not over $7,200 ............... $ | 50 plus 3.20% over $3,600 |
| Over $7,200 but not over $14,400 ............... $ | 166 plus 5.50% over $7,200 |
| Over $14,400 but not over $21,600 ............... $ | 562 plus 6.40% over $14,400 |
| Over $21,600 but not over $28,800 ............... $ | 1,022 plus 6.80% over $21,600 |
| Over $28,800 but not over $36,000 ............... $ | 1,512 plus 7.20% over $28,800 |
| Over $36,000 but not over $54,000 ............... $ | 2,030 plus 7.60% over $36,000 |
| Over $54,000 but not over $72,000 ............... $ | 3,398 plus 7.90% over $54,000 |
| Over $72,000 but not over $225,000 ............... $ | 4,820 plus 8.25% over $72,000 |
| Over $225,000 but not over $262,500 ............... $ | 17,443 plus 9.00% over $225,000 |
| Over $262,500 but not over $300,000 ............... $ | 20,818 plus 10.00% over $262,500 |
| Over $300,000 ............... $ | 24,568 plus 11.00% over $300,000 |

# ESTATE AND TRUSTS TAX RATES FOR 2018

### Schedule below for use by:
### Estates and Trusts

**If the taxable income is:**                              **Your tax is:**

| | | |
|---|---|---|
| Not over $2,000 | 1.40% of taxable income | |
| Over $2,000 but not over $4,000 | $ 28 | plus 3.20% over $2,000 |
| Over $4,000 but not over $8,000 | $ 92 | plus 5.50% over $4,000 |
| Over $8,000 but not over $12,000 | $ 312 | plus 6.40% over $8,000 |
| Over $12,000 but not over $16,000 | $ 568 | plus 6.80% over $12,000 |
| Over $16,000 but not over $20,000 | $ 840 | plus 7.20% over $16,000 |
| Over $20,000 but not over $30,000 | $ 1,128 | plus 7.60% over $20,000 |
| Over $30,000 but not over $40,000 | $ 1,888 | plus 7.90% over $30,000 |
| Over $40,000 | $ 2,678 | plus 8.25% over $40,000 |

When computing the tax for estate or trusts, taxpayers with no taxable net capital gains should determine the tax using the table above. If the estate or trust has both net capital gains and taxable income, Schedule D (Form N-40) Part VI should be used to compute the taxes.

## Exemptions
Personal Exemptions:

Individual (see Note A below) ...........................................  
Additional for individuals over 65 .....................................  }  $1,144
Dependent ........................................................................

Blind, deaf, or disabled persons (in lieu of all other
personal exemptions) ................................................................................... $7,000
Estate ....................................................................................................................... $400
Trust distributing all income currently ................................................................. $200
All other trusts ......................................................................................................... $80
No exemption is allowed on the final return of an estate or trust.

**Note A:** Exemption for husband and wife is double the amount allotted to an individual.

## Corporate Income Tax Rates
a)  On ordinary taxable income of up to $25,000 .................................... 4.4 %
b)  On ordinary taxable income in excess of $25,000 up to
    $100,000 ............................................................................5.4 % less $250
c)  On ordinary taxable income in excess of $100,000 ...........6.4 % less $1,250
d)  On net capital gain, tax will be the lesser of:
    1)  net capital gains at a 4% rate, plus
        if taxable income exceeds the net capital gain, the excess is taxed at the rates
        in a, b, and c above, or
    2)  compute the tax on all taxable income using the rates on a, b, or c above.

## Franchise Tax Rates

On banks, building and loan associations, development companies, financial corporations, financial services loan companies, trust companies, mortgage loan companies, financial holding companies and qualifying subsidiaries and small business investment companies. The franchise tax rate is:

| | |
|---|---|
| Net income from all sources | 7.92% |
| Net capital gains are taxed at | 4.0% |

# -2018 Hawaii Tax Table

Based on Taxable Income
For persons with taxable
incomes of less than
$100,000

**Example:** Mr. & Mrs. Brown are filing a joint return. Their taxable income on line 26 is $23,275. First, they find the $23,250 - 23,300 income line. Next, they find the column for married filing jointly and read down the column. The amount shown where the income line and filing status column meet is $1,010. This is the tax amount they must write on line 27 of their return.

| At least | But less than | Single or Married filing separately * | Married filing jointly | Head of a house-hold |
|---|---|---|---|---|
| 23,250 | 23,300 | 1,301 | 1,010 | 1,136 |
| 23,300 | 23,350 | 1,305 | 1,013 | 1,139 |
| 23,350 | 23,400 | 1,309 | 1,016 | 1,143 |

**If line 26 (taxable income) is — / And you are —**

| At least | But less than | Single or Married filing separately * | Married filing jointly | Head of a house-hold |
|---|---|---|---|---|
| | | Your tax is — | | |
| 0 | 50 | 0 | 0 | 0 |
| 50 | 100 | 1 | 1 | 1 |
| 100 | 150 | 2 | 2 | 2 |
| 150 | 200 | 2 | 2 | 2 |
| 200 | 250 | 3 | 3 | 3 |
| 250 | 300 | 4 | 4 | 4 |
| 300 | 350 | 5 | 5 | 5 |
| 350 | 400 | 5 | 5 | 5 |
| 400 | 450 | 6 | 6 | 6 |
| 450 | 500 | 7 | 7 | 7 |
| 500 | 550 | 7 | 7 | 7 |
| 550 | 600 | 8 | 8 | 8 |
| 600 | 650 | 9 | 9 | 9 |
| 650 | 700 | 9 | 9 | 9 |
| 700 | 750 | 10 | 10 | 10 |
| 750 | 800 | 11 | 11 | 11 |
| 800 | 850 | 12 | 12 | 12 |
| 850 | 900 | 12 | 12 | 12 |
| 900 | 950 | 13 | 13 | 13 |
| 950 | 1,000 | 14 | 14 | 14 |
| **1,000** | | | | |
| 1,000 | 1,050 | 14 | 14 | 14 |
| 1,050 | 1,100 | 15 | 15 | 15 |
| 1,100 | 1,150 | 16 | 16 | 16 |
| 1,150 | 1,200 | 16 | 16 | 16 |
| 1,200 | 1,250 | 17 | 17 | 17 |
| 1,250 | 1,300 | 18 | 18 | 18 |
| 1,300 | 1,350 | 19 | 19 | 19 |
| 1,350 | 1,400 | 19 | 19 | 19 |
| 1,400 | 1,450 | 20 | 20 | 20 |
| 1,450 | 1,500 | 21 | 21 | 21 |
| 1,500 | 1,550 | 21 | 21 | 21 |
| 1,550 | 1,600 | 22 | 22 | 22 |
| 1,600 | 1,650 | 23 | 23 | 23 |
| 1,650 | 1,700 | 23 | 23 | 23 |
| 1,700 | 1,750 | 24 | 24 | 24 |
| 1,750 | 1,800 | 25 | 25 | 25 |
| 1,800 | 1,850 | 26 | 26 | 26 |
| 1,850 | 1,900 | 26 | 26 | 26 |
| 1,900 | 1,950 | 27 | 27 | 27 |
| 1,950 | 2,000 | 28 | 28 | 28 |
| **2,000** | | | | |
| 2,000 | 2,050 | 28 | 28 | 28 |
| 2,050 | 2,100 | 29 | 29 | 29 |
| 2,100 | 2,150 | 30 | 30 | 30 |
| 2,150 | 2,200 | 30 | 30 | 30 |
| 2,200 | 2,250 | 31 | 31 | 31 |
| 2,250 | 2,300 | 32 | 32 | 32 |
| 2,300 | 2,350 | 33 | 33 | 33 |
| 2,350 | 2,400 | 33 | 33 | 33 |
| 2,400 | 2,450 | 35 | 34 | 34 |
| 2,450 | 2,500 | 36 | 35 | 35 |

**If line 26 (taxable income) is — / And you are —**

| At least | But less than | Single or Married filing separately * | Married filing jointly | Head of a house-hold |
|---|---|---|---|---|
| | | Your tax is — | | |
| 2,500 | 2,550 | 38 | 35 | 35 |
| 2,550 | 2,600 | 40 | 36 | 36 |
| 2,600 | 2,650 | 41 | 37 | 37 |
| 2,650 | 2,700 | 43 | 37 | 37 |
| 2,700 | 2,750 | 44 | 38 | 38 |
| 2,750 | 2,800 | 46 | 39 | 39 |
| 2,800 | 2,850 | 48 | 40 | 40 |
| 2,850 | 2,900 | 49 | 40 | 40 |
| 2,900 | 2,950 | 51 | 41 | 41 |
| 2,950 | 3,000 | 52 | 42 | 42 |
| **3,000** | | | | |
| 3,000 | 3,050 | 54 | 42 | 42 |
| 3,050 | 3,100 | 56 | 43 | 43 |
| 3,100 | 3,150 | 57 | 44 | 44 |
| 3,150 | 3,200 | 59 | 44 | 44 |
| 3,200 | 3,250 | 60 | 45 | 45 |
| 3,250 | 3,300 | 62 | 46 | 46 |
| 3,300 | 3,350 | 64 | 47 | 47 |
| 3,350 | 3,400 | 65 | 47 | 47 |
| 3,400 | 3,450 | 67 | 48 | 48 |
| 3,450 | 3,500 | 68 | 49 | 49 |
| 3,500 | 3,550 | 70 | 49 | 49 |
| 3,550 | 3,600 | 72 | 50 | 50 |
| 3,600 | 3,650 | 73 | 51 | 51 |
| 3,650 | 3,700 | 75 | 51 | 52 |
| 3,700 | 3,750 | 76 | 52 | 54 |
| 3,750 | 3,800 | 78 | 53 | 56 |
| 3,800 | 3,850 | 80 | 54 | 57 |
| 3,850 | 3,900 | 81 | 54 | 59 |
| 3,900 | 3,950 | 83 | 55 | 60 |
| 3,950 | 4,000 | 84 | 56 | 62 |
| **4,000** | | | | |
| 4,000 | 4,050 | 86 | 56 | 64 |
| 4,050 | 4,100 | 88 | 57 | 65 |
| 4,100 | 4,150 | 89 | 58 | 67 |
| 4,150 | 4,200 | 91 | 58 | 68 |
| 4,200 | 4,250 | 92 | 59 | 70 |
| 4,250 | 4,300 | 94 | 60 | 72 |
| 4,300 | 4,350 | 96 | 61 | 73 |
| 4,350 | 4,400 | 97 | 61 | 75 |
| 4,400 | 4,450 | 99 | 62 | 76 |
| 4,450 | 4,500 | 100 | 63 | 78 |
| 4,500 | 4,550 | 102 | 63 | 80 |
| 4,550 | 4,600 | 104 | 64 | 81 |
| 4,600 | 4,650 | 105 | 65 | 83 |
| 4,650 | 4,700 | 107 | 65 | 84 |
| 4,700 | 4,750 | 108 | 66 | 86 |
| 4,750 | 4,800 | 110 | 67 | 88 |
| 4,800 | 4,850 | 111 | 68 | 89 |
| 4,850 | 4,900 | 114 | 69 | 91 |
| 4,900 | 4,950 | 117 | 71 | 92 |
| 4,950 | 5,000 | 120 | 73 | 94 |

**If line 26 (taxable income) is — / And you are —**

| At least | But less than | Single or Married filing separately * | Married filing jointly | Head of a house-hold |
|---|---|---|---|---|
| | | Your tax is — | | |
| **5,000** | | | | |
| 5,000 | 5,050 | 122 | 74 | 96 |
| 5,050 | 5,100 | 125 | 76 | 97 |
| 5,100 | 5,150 | 128 | 77 | 99 |
| 5,150 | 5,200 | 131 | 79 | 100 |
| 5,200 | 5,250 | 133 | 81 | 102 |
| 5,250 | 5,300 | 136 | 82 | 104 |
| 5,300 | 5,350 | 139 | 84 | 105 |
| 5,350 | 5,400 | 142 | 85 | 107 |
| 5,400 | 5,450 | 144 | 87 | 108 |
| 5,450 | 5,500 | 147 | 89 | 110 |
| 5,500 | 5,550 | 150 | 90 | 112 |
| 5,550 | 5,600 | 153 | 92 | 113 |
| 5,600 | 5,650 | 155 | 93 | 115 |
| 5,650 | 5,700 | 158 | 95 | 116 |
| 5,700 | 5,750 | 161 | 97 | 118 |
| 5,750 | 5,800 | 164 | 98 | 120 |
| 5,800 | 5,850 | 166 | 100 | 121 |
| 5,850 | 5,900 | 169 | 101 | 123 |
| 5,900 | 5,950 | 172 | 103 | 124 |
| 5,950 | 6,000 | 175 | 105 | 126 |
| **6,000** | | | | |
| 6,000 | 6,050 | 177 | 106 | 128 |
| 6,050 | 6,100 | 180 | 108 | 129 |
| 6,100 | 6,150 | 183 | 109 | 131 |
| 6,150 | 6,200 | 186 | 111 | 132 |
| 6,200 | 6,250 | 188 | 113 | 134 |
| 6,250 | 6,300 | 191 | 114 | 136 |
| 6,300 | 6,350 | 194 | 116 | 137 |
| 6,350 | 6,400 | 197 | 117 | 139 |
| 6,400 | 6,450 | 199 | 119 | 140 |
| 6,450 | 6,500 | 202 | 121 | 142 |
| 6,500 | 6,550 | 205 | 122 | 144 |
| 6,550 | 6,600 | 208 | 124 | 145 |
| 6,600 | 6,650 | 210 | 125 | 147 |
| 6,650 | 6,700 | 213 | 127 | 148 |
| 6,700 | 6,750 | 216 | 129 | 150 |
| 6,750 | 6,800 | 219 | 130 | 152 |
| 6,800 | 6,850 | 221 | 132 | 153 |
| 6,850 | 6,900 | 224 | 133 | 155 |
| 6,900 | 6,950 | 227 | 135 | 156 |
| 6,950 | 7,000 | 230 | 137 | 158 |

*This column must also be used by qualifying widow(er)

Continued on next page

## 2018 Hawaii Tax Table (continued)

| If line 26 (taxable income) is — | | Single or Married filing separately | Married filing jointly * | Head of a household |
|---|---|---|---|---|
| At least | But less than | Your tax is — | | |
| **7,000** | | | | |
| 7,000 | 7,050 | 232 | 138 | 160 |
| 7,050 | 7,100 | 235 | 140 | 161 |
| 7,100 | 7,150 | 238 | 141 | 163 |
| 7,150 | 7,200 | 241 | 143 | 164 |
| 7,200 | 7,250 | 243 | 145 | 167 |
| 7,250 | 7,300 | 246 | 146 | 170 |
| 7,300 | 7,350 | 249 | 148 | 173 |
| 7,350 | 7,400 | 252 | 149 | 176 |
| 7,400 | 7,450 | 254 | 151 | 178 |
| 7,450 | 7,500 | 257 | 153 | 181 |
| 7,500 | 7,550 | 260 | 154 | 184 |
| 7,550 | 7,600 | 263 | 156 | 187 |
| 7,600 | 7,650 | 265 | 157 | 189 |
| 7,650 | 7,700 | 268 | 159 | 192 |
| 7,700 | 7,750 | 271 | 161 | 195 |
| 7,750 | 7,800 | 274 | 162 | 198 |
| 7,800 | 7,850 | 276 | 164 | 200 |
| 7,850 | 7,900 | 279 | 165 | 203 |
| 7,900 | 7,950 | 282 | 167 | 206 |
| 7,950 | 8,000 | 285 | 169 | 209 |
| **8,000** | | | | |
| 8,000 | 8,050 | 287 | 170 | 211 |
| 8,050 | 8,100 | 290 | 172 | 214 |
| 8,100 | 8,150 | 293 | 173 | 217 |
| 8,150 | 8,200 | 296 | 175 | 220 |
| 8,200 | 8,250 | 298 | 177 | 222 |
| 8,250 | 8,300 | 301 | 178 | 225 |
| 8,300 | 8,350 | 304 | 180 | 228 |
| 8,350 | 8,400 | 307 | 181 | 231 |
| 8,400 | 8,450 | 309 | 183 | 233 |
| 8,450 | 8,500 | 312 | 185 | 236 |
| 8,500 | 8,550 | 315 | 186 | 239 |
| 8,550 | 8,600 | 318 | 188 | 242 |
| 8,600 | 8,650 | 320 | 189 | 244 |
| 8,650 | 8,700 | 323 | 191 | 247 |
| 8,700 | 8,750 | 326 | 193 | 250 |
| 8,750 | 8,800 | 329 | 194 | 253 |
| 8,800 | 8,850 | 331 | 196 | 255 |
| 8,850 | 8,900 | 334 | 197 | 258 |
| 8,900 | 8,950 | 337 | 199 | 261 |
| 8,950 | 9,000 | 340 | 201 | 264 |
| **9,000** | | | | |
| 9,000 | 9,050 | 342 | 202 | 266 |
| 9,050 | 9,100 | 345 | 204 | 269 |
| 9,100 | 9,150 | 348 | 205 | 272 |
| 9,150 | 9,200 | 351 | 207 | 275 |
| 9,200 | 9,250 | 353 | 209 | 277 |
| 9,250 | 9,300 | 356 | 210 | 280 |
| 9,300 | 9,350 | 359 | 212 | 283 |
| 9,350 | 9,400 | 362 | 213 | 286 |
| 9,400 | 9,450 | 364 | 215 | 288 |
| 9,450 | 9,500 | 367 | 217 | 291 |
| 9,500 | 9,550 | 370 | 218 | 294 |
| 9,550 | 9,600 | 373 | 220 | 297 |
| 9,600 | 9,650 | 376 | 222 | 299 |
| 9,650 | 9,700 | 379 | 225 | 302 |
| 9,700 | 9,750 | 382 | 228 | 305 |
| 9,750 | 9,800 | 385 | 231 | 308 |
| 9,800 | 9,850 | 388 | 233 | 310 |
| 9,850 | 9,900 | 392 | 236 | 313 |
| 9,900 | 9,950 | 395 | 239 | 316 |
| 9,950 | 10,000 | 398 | 242 | 319 |

| If line 26 (taxable income) is — | | Single or Married filing separately | Married filing jointly * | Head of a household |
|---|---|---|---|---|
| At least | But less than | Your tax is — | | |
| **10,000** | | | | |
| 10,000 | 10,050 | 401 | 244 | 321 |
| 10,050 | 10,100 | 404 | 247 | 324 |
| 10,100 | 10,150 | 408 | 250 | 327 |
| 10,150 | 10,200 | 411 | 253 | 330 |
| 10,200 | 10,250 | 414 | 255 | 332 |
| 10,250 | 10,300 | 417 | 258 | 335 |
| 10,300 | 10,350 | 420 | 261 | 338 |
| 10,350 | 10,400 | 424 | 264 | 341 |
| 10,400 | 10,450 | 427 | 266 | 343 |
| 10,450 | 10,500 | 430 | 269 | 346 |
| 10,500 | 10,550 | 433 | 272 | 349 |
| 10,550 | 10,600 | 436 | 275 | 352 |
| 10,600 | 10,650 | 440 | 277 | 354 |
| 10,650 | 10,700 | 443 | 280 | 357 |
| 10,700 | 10,750 | 446 | 283 | 360 |
| 10,750 | 10,800 | 449 | 286 | 363 |
| 10,800 | 10,850 | 452 | 288 | 365 |
| 10,850 | 10,900 | 456 | 291 | 368 |
| 10,900 | 10,950 | 459 | 294 | 371 |
| 10,950 | 11,000 | 462 | 297 | 374 |
| **11,000** | | | | |
| 11,000 | 11,050 | 465 | 299 | 376 |
| 11,050 | 11,100 | 468 | 302 | 379 |
| 11,100 | 11,150 | 472 | 305 | 382 |
| 11,150 | 11,200 | 475 | 308 | 385 |
| 11,200 | 11,250 | 478 | 310 | 387 |
| 11,250 | 11,300 | 481 | 313 | 390 |
| 11,300 | 11,350 | 484 | 316 | 393 |
| 11,350 | 11,400 | 488 | 319 | 396 |
| 11,400 | 11,450 | 491 | 321 | 398 |
| 11,450 | 11,500 | 494 | 324 | 401 |
| 11,500 | 11,550 | 497 | 327 | 404 |
| 11,550 | 11,600 | 500 | 330 | 407 |
| 11,600 | 11,650 | 504 | 332 | 409 |
| 11,650 | 11,700 | 507 | 335 | 412 |
| 11,700 | 11,750 | 510 | 338 | 415 |
| 11,750 | 11,800 | 513 | 341 | 418 |
| 11,800 | 11,850 | 516 | 343 | 420 |
| 11,850 | 11,900 | 520 | 346 | 423 |
| 11,900 | 11,950 | 523 | 349 | 426 |
| 11,950 | 12,000 | 526 | 352 | 429 |
| **12,000** | | | | |
| 12,000 | 12,050 | 529 | 354 | 431 |
| 12,050 | 12,100 | 532 | 357 | 434 |
| 12,100 | 12,150 | 536 | 360 | 437 |
| 12,150 | 12,200 | 539 | 363 | 440 |
| 12,200 | 12,250 | 542 | 365 | 442 |
| 12,250 | 12,300 | 545 | 368 | 445 |
| 12,300 | 12,350 | 548 | 371 | 448 |
| 12,350 | 12,400 | 552 | 374 | 451 |
| 12,400 | 12,450 | 555 | 376 | 453 |
| 12,450 | 12,500 | 558 | 379 | 456 |
| 12,500 | 12,550 | 561 | 382 | 459 |
| 12,550 | 12,600 | 564 | 385 | 462 |
| 12,600 | 12,650 | 568 | 387 | 464 |
| 12,650 | 12,700 | 571 | 390 | 467 |
| 12,700 | 12,750 | 574 | 393 | 470 |
| 12,750 | 12,800 | 577 | 396 | 473 |
| 12,800 | 12,850 | 580 | 398 | 475 |
| 12,850 | 12,900 | 584 | 401 | 478 |
| 12,900 | 12,950 | 587 | 404 | 481 |
| 12,950 | 13,000 | 590 | 407 | 484 |

| If line 26 (taxable income) is — | | Single or Married filing separately | Married filing jointly * | Head of a household |
|---|---|---|---|---|
| At least | But less than | Your tax is — | | |
| **13,000** | | | | |
| 13,000 | 13,050 | 593 | 409 | 486 |
| 13,050 | 13,100 | 596 | 412 | 489 |
| 13,100 | 13,150 | 600 | 415 | 492 |
| 13,150 | 13,200 | 603 | 418 | 495 |
| 13,200 | 13,250 | 606 | 420 | 497 |
| 13,250 | 13,300 | 609 | 423 | 500 |
| 13,300 | 13,350 | 612 | 426 | 503 |
| 13,350 | 13,400 | 616 | 429 | 506 |
| 13,400 | 13,450 | 619 | 431 | 508 |
| 13,450 | 13,500 | 622 | 434 | 511 |
| 13,500 | 13,550 | 625 | 437 | 514 |
| 13,550 | 13,600 | 628 | 440 | 517 |
| 13,600 | 13,650 | 632 | 442 | 519 |
| 13,650 | 13,700 | 635 | 445 | 522 |
| 13,700 | 13,750 | 638 | 448 | 525 |
| 13,750 | 13,800 | 641 | 451 | 528 |
| 13,800 | 13,850 | 644 | 453 | 530 |
| 13,850 | 13,900 | 648 | 456 | 533 |
| 13,900 | 13,950 | 651 | 459 | 536 |
| 13,950 | 14,000 | 654 | 462 | 539 |
| **14,000** | | | | |
| 14,000 | 14,050 | 657 | 464 | 541 |
| 14,050 | 14,100 | 660 | 467 | 544 |
| 14,100 | 14,150 | 664 | 470 | 547 |
| 14,150 | 14,200 | 667 | 473 | 550 |
| 14,200 | 14,250 | 670 | 475 | 552 |
| 14,250 | 14,300 | 673 | 478 | 555 |
| 14,300 | 14,350 | 676 | 481 | 558 |
| 14,350 | 14,400 | 680 | 484 | 561 |
| 14,400 | 14,450 | 684 | 486 | 564 |
| 14,450 | 14,500 | 687 | 489 | 567 |
| 14,500 | 14,550 | 691 | 492 | 570 |
| 14,550 | 14,600 | 694 | 495 | 573 |
| 14,600 | 14,650 | 697 | 497 | 576 |
| 14,650 | 14,700 | 701 | 500 | 580 |
| 14,700 | 14,750 | 704 | 503 | 583 |
| 14,750 | 14,800 | 708 | 506 | 586 |
| 14,800 | 14,850 | 711 | 508 | 589 |
| 14,850 | 14,900 | 714 | 511 | 592 |
| 14,900 | 14,950 | 718 | 514 | 596 |
| 14,950 | 15,000 | 721 | 517 | 599 |
| **15,000** | | | | |
| 15,000 | 15,050 | 725 | 519 | 602 |
| 15,050 | 15,100 | 728 | 522 | 605 |
| 15,100 | 15,150 | 731 | 525 | 608 |
| 15,150 | 15,200 | 735 | 528 | 612 |
| 15,200 | 15,250 | 738 | 530 | 615 |
| 15,250 | 15,300 | 742 | 533 | 618 |
| 15,300 | 15,350 | 745 | 536 | 621 |
| 15,350 | 15,400 | 748 | 539 | 624 |
| 15,400 | 15,450 | 752 | 541 | 628 |
| 15,450 | 15,500 | 755 | 544 | 631 |
| 15,500 | 15,550 | 759 | 547 | 634 |
| 15,550 | 15,600 | 762 | 550 | 637 |
| 15,600 | 15,650 | 765 | 552 | 640 |
| 15,650 | 15,700 | 769 | 555 | 644 |
| 15,700 | 15,750 | 772 | 558 | 647 |
| 15,750 | 15,800 | 776 | 561 | 650 |
| 15,800 | 15,850 | 779 | 563 | 653 |
| 15,850 | 15,900 | 782 | 566 | 656 |
| 15,900 | 15,950 | 786 | 569 | 660 |
| 15,950 | 16,000 | 789 | 572 | 663 |

*This column must also be used by qualifying widow(er)

Continued on next page

## 2018 Hawaii Tax Table (continued)

| If line 26 (taxable income) is — | | Single or Married filing separately | Married filing jointly * | Head of a household |
|---|---|---|---|---|
| At least | But less than | Your tax is — | | |
| **16,000** | | | | |
| 16,000 | 16,050 | 793 | 574 | 666 |
| 16,050 | 16,100 | 796 | 577 | 669 |
| 16,100 | 16,150 | 799 | 580 | 672 |
| 16,150 | 16,200 | 803 | 583 | 676 |
| 16,200 | 16,250 | 806 | 585 | 679 |
| 16,250 | 16,300 | 810 | 588 | 682 |
| 16,300 | 16,350 | 813 | 591 | 685 |
| 16,350 | 16,400 | 816 | 594 | 688 |
| 16,400 | 16,450 | 820 | 596 | 692 |
| 16,450 | 16,500 | 823 | 599 | 695 |
| 16,500 | 16,550 | 827 | 602 | 698 |
| 16,550 | 16,600 | 830 | 605 | 701 |
| 16,600 | 16,650 | 833 | 607 | 704 |
| 16,650 | 16,700 | 837 | 610 | 708 |
| 16,700 | 16,750 | 840 | 613 | 711 |
| 16,750 | 16,800 | 844 | 616 | 714 |
| 16,800 | 16,850 | 847 | 618 | 717 |
| 16,850 | 16,900 | 850 | 621 | 720 |
| 16,900 | 16,950 | 854 | 624 | 724 |
| 16,950 | 17,000 | 857 | 627 | 727 |
| **17,000** | | | | |
| 17,000 | 17,050 | 861 | 629 | 730 |
| 17,050 | 17,100 | 864 | 632 | 733 |
| 17,100 | 17,150 | 867 | 635 | 736 |
| 17,150 | 17,200 | 871 | 638 | 740 |
| 17,200 | 17,250 | 874 | 640 | 743 |
| 17,250 | 17,300 | 878 | 643 | 746 |
| 17,300 | 17,350 | 881 | 646 | 749 |
| 17,350 | 17,400 | 884 | 649 | 752 |
| 17,400 | 17,450 | 888 | 651 | 756 |
| 17,450 | 17,500 | 891 | 654 | 759 |
| 17,500 | 17,550 | 895 | 657 | 762 |
| 17,550 | 17,600 | 898 | 660 | 765 |
| 17,600 | 17,650 | 901 | 662 | 768 |
| 17,650 | 17,700 | 905 | 665 | 772 |
| 17,700 | 17,750 | 908 | 668 | 775 |
| 17,750 | 17,800 | 912 | 671 | 778 |
| 17,800 | 17,850 | 915 | 673 | 781 |
| 17,850 | 17,900 | 918 | 676 | 784 |
| 17,900 | 17,950 | 922 | 679 | 788 |
| 17,950 | 18,000 | 925 | 682 | 791 |
| **18,000** | | | | |
| 18,000 | 18,050 | 929 | 684 | 794 |
| 18,050 | 18,100 | 932 | 687 | 797 |
| 18,100 | 18,150 | 935 | 690 | 800 |
| 18,150 | 18,200 | 939 | 693 | 804 |
| 18,200 | 18,250 | 942 | 695 | 807 |
| 18,250 | 18,300 | 946 | 698 | 810 |
| 18,300 | 18,350 | 949 | 701 | 813 |
| 18,350 | 18,400 | 952 | 704 | 816 |
| 18,400 | 18,450 | 956 | 706 | 820 |
| 18,450 | 18,500 | 959 | 709 | 823 |
| 18,500 | 18,550 | 963 | 712 | 826 |
| 18,550 | 18,600 | 966 | 715 | 829 |
| 18,600 | 18,650 | 969 | 717 | 832 |
| 18,650 | 18,700 | 973 | 720 | 836 |
| 18,700 | 18,750 | 976 | 723 | 839 |
| 18,750 | 18,800 | 980 | 726 | 842 |
| 18,800 | 18,850 | 983 | 728 | 845 |
| 18,850 | 18,900 | 986 | 731 | 848 |
| 18,900 | 18,950 | 990 | 734 | 852 |
| 18,950 | 19,000 | 993 | 737 | 855 |

| If line 26 (taxable income) is — | | Single or Married filing separately | Married filing jointly * | Head of a household |
|---|---|---|---|---|
| At least | But less than | Your tax is — | | |
| **19,000** | | | | |
| 19,000 | 19,050 | 997 | 739 | 858 |
| 19,050 | 19,100 | 1,000 | 742 | 861 |
| 19,100 | 19,150 | 1,003 | 745 | 864 |
| 19,150 | 19,200 | 1,007 | 748 | 868 |
| 19,200 | 19,250 | 1,010 | 751 | 871 |
| 19,250 | 19,300 | 1,013 | 754 | 874 |
| 19,300 | 19,350 | 1,017 | 757 | 877 |
| 19,350 | 19,400 | 1,021 | 760 | 880 |
| 19,400 | 19,450 | 1,024 | 763 | 884 |
| 19,450 | 19,500 | 1,028 | 767 | 887 |
| 19,500 | 19,550 | 1,031 | 770 | 890 |
| 19,550 | 19,600 | 1,035 | 773 | 893 |
| 19,600 | 19,650 | 1,039 | 776 | 896 |
| 19,650 | 19,700 | 1,042 | 779 | 900 |
| 19,700 | 19,750 | 1,046 | 783 | 903 |
| 19,750 | 19,800 | 1,049 | 786 | 906 |
| 19,800 | 19,850 | 1,053 | 789 | 909 |
| 19,850 | 19,900 | 1,057 | 792 | 912 |
| 19,900 | 19,950 | 1,060 | 795 | 916 |
| 19,950 | 20,000 | 1,064 | 799 | 919 |
| **20,000** | | | | |
| 20,000 | 20,050 | 1,067 | 802 | 922 |
| 20,050 | 20,100 | 1,071 | 805 | 925 |
| 20,100 | 20,150 | 1,075 | 808 | 928 |
| 20,150 | 20,200 | 1,078 | 811 | 932 |
| 20,200 | 20,250 | 1,082 | 815 | 935 |
| 20,250 | 20,300 | 1,085 | 818 | 938 |
| 20,300 | 20,350 | 1,089 | 821 | 941 |
| 20,350 | 20,400 | 1,093 | 824 | 944 |
| 20,400 | 20,450 | 1,096 | 827 | 948 |
| 20,450 | 20,500 | 1,100 | 831 | 951 |
| 20,500 | 20,550 | 1,103 | 834 | 954 |
| 20,550 | 20,600 | 1,107 | 837 | 957 |
| 20,600 | 20,650 | 1,111 | 840 | 960 |
| 20,650 | 20,700 | 1,114 | 843 | 964 |
| 20,700 | 20,750 | 1,118 | 847 | 967 |
| 20,750 | 20,800 | 1,121 | 850 | 970 |
| 20,800 | 20,850 | 1,125 | 853 | 973 |
| 20,850 | 20,900 | 1,129 | 856 | 976 |
| 20,900 | 20,950 | 1,132 | 859 | 980 |
| 20,950 | 21,000 | 1,136 | 863 | 983 |
| **21,000** | | | | |
| 21,000 | 21,050 | 1,139 | 866 | 986 |
| 21,050 | 21,100 | 1,143 | 869 | 989 |
| 21,100 | 21,150 | 1,147 | 872 | 992 |
| 21,150 | 21,200 | 1,150 | 875 | 996 |
| 21,200 | 21,250 | 1,154 | 879 | 999 |
| 21,250 | 21,300 | 1,157 | 882 | 1,002 |
| 21,300 | 21,350 | 1,161 | 885 | 1,005 |
| 21,350 | 21,400 | 1,165 | 888 | 1,008 |
| 21,400 | 21,450 | 1,168 | 891 | 1,012 |
| 21,450 | 21,500 | 1,172 | 895 | 1,015 |
| 21,500 | 21,550 | 1,175 | 898 | 1,018 |
| 21,550 | 21,600 | 1,179 | 901 | 1,021 |
| 21,600 | 21,650 | 1,183 | 904 | 1,024 |
| 21,650 | 21,700 | 1,186 | 907 | 1,027 |
| 21,700 | 21,750 | 1,190 | 911 | 1,031 |
| 21,750 | 21,800 | 1,193 | 914 | 1,034 |
| 21,800 | 21,850 | 1,197 | 917 | 1,037 |
| 21,850 | 21,900 | 1,201 | 920 | 1,041 |
| 21,900 | 21,950 | 1,204 | 923 | 1,044 |
| 21,950 | 22,000 | 1,208 | 927 | 1,048 |

| If line 26 (taxable income) is — | | Single or Married filing separately | Married filing jointly * | Head of a household |
|---|---|---|---|---|
| At least | But less than | Your tax is — | | |
| **22,000** | | | | |
| 22,000 | 22,050 | 1,211 | 930 | 1,051 |
| 22,050 | 22,100 | 1,215 | 933 | 1,054 |
| 22,100 | 22,150 | 1,219 | 936 | 1,058 |
| 22,150 | 22,200 | 1,222 | 939 | 1,061 |
| 22,200 | 22,250 | 1,226 | 943 | 1,065 |
| 22,250 | 22,300 | 1,229 | 946 | 1,068 |
| 22,300 | 22,350 | 1,233 | 949 | 1,071 |
| 22,350 | 22,400 | 1,237 | 952 | 1,075 |
| 22,400 | 22,450 | 1,240 | 955 | 1,078 |
| 22,450 | 22,500 | 1,244 | 959 | 1,082 |
| 22,500 | 22,550 | 1,247 | 962 | 1,085 |
| 22,550 | 22,600 | 1,251 | 965 | 1,088 |
| 22,600 | 22,650 | 1,255 | 968 | 1,092 |
| 22,650 | 22,700 | 1,258 | 971 | 1,095 |
| 22,700 | 22,750 | 1,262 | 975 | 1,099 |
| 22,750 | 22,800 | 1,265 | 978 | 1,102 |
| 22,800 | 22,850 | 1,269 | 981 | 1,105 |
| 22,850 | 22,900 | 1,273 | 984 | 1,109 |
| 22,900 | 22,950 | 1,276 | 987 | 1,112 |
| 22,950 | 23,000 | 1,280 | 991 | 1,116 |
| **23,000** | | | | |
| 23,000 | 23,050 | 1,283 | 994 | 1,119 |
| 23,050 | 23,100 | 1,287 | 997 | 1,122 |
| 23,100 | 23,150 | 1,291 | 1,000 | 1,126 |
| 23,150 | 23,200 | 1,294 | 1,003 | 1,129 |
| 23,200 | 23,250 | 1,298 | 1,007 | 1,133 |
| 23,250 | 23,300 | 1,301 | 1,010 | 1,136 |
| 23,300 | 23,350 | 1,305 | 1,013 | 1,139 |
| 23,350 | 23,400 | 1,309 | 1,016 | 1,143 |
| 23,400 | 23,450 | 1,312 | 1,019 | 1,146 |
| 23,450 | 23,500 | 1,316 | 1,023 | 1,150 |
| 23,500 | 23,550 | 1,319 | 1,026 | 1,153 |
| 23,550 | 23,600 | 1,323 | 1,029 | 1,156 |
| 23,600 | 23,650 | 1,327 | 1,032 | 1,160 |
| 23,650 | 23,700 | 1,330 | 1,035 | 1,163 |
| 23,700 | 23,750 | 1,334 | 1,039 | 1,167 |
| 23,750 | 23,800 | 1,337 | 1,042 | 1,170 |
| 23,800 | 23,850 | 1,341 | 1,045 | 1,173 |
| 23,850 | 23,900 | 1,345 | 1,048 | 1,177 |
| 23,900 | 23,950 | 1,348 | 1,051 | 1,180 |
| 23,950 | 24,000 | 1,352 | 1,055 | 1,184 |
| **24,000** | | | | |
| 24,000 | 24,050 | 1,356 | 1,058 | 1,187 |
| 24,050 | 24,100 | 1,360 | 1,061 | 1,190 |
| 24,100 | 24,150 | 1,364 | 1,064 | 1,194 |
| 24,150 | 24,200 | 1,367 | 1,067 | 1,197 |
| 24,200 | 24,250 | 1,371 | 1,071 | 1,201 |
| 24,250 | 24,300 | 1,375 | 1,074 | 1,204 |
| 24,300 | 24,350 | 1,379 | 1,077 | 1,207 |
| 24,350 | 24,400 | 1,383 | 1,080 | 1,211 |
| 24,400 | 24,450 | 1,386 | 1,083 | 1,214 |
| 24,450 | 24,500 | 1,390 | 1,087 | 1,218 |
| 24,500 | 24,550 | 1,394 | 1,090 | 1,221 |
| 24,550 | 24,600 | 1,398 | 1,093 | 1,224 |
| 24,600 | 24,650 | 1,402 | 1,096 | 1,228 |
| 24,650 | 24,700 | 1,405 | 1,099 | 1,231 |
| 24,700 | 24,750 | 1,409 | 1,103 | 1,235 |
| 24,750 | 24,800 | 1,413 | 1,106 | 1,238 |
| 24,800 | 24,850 | 1,417 | 1,109 | 1,241 |
| 24,850 | 24,900 | 1,421 | 1,112 | 1,245 |
| 24,900 | 24,950 | 1,424 | 1,115 | 1,248 |
| 24,950 | 25,000 | 1,428 | 1,119 | 1,252 |

*This column must also be used by qualifying widow(er)

Continued on next page

## 2018 Hawaii Tax Table (continued)

| If line 26 (taxable income) is — | | And you are — | | |
|---|---|---|---|---|
| At least | But less than | Single or Married filing separately | Married filing jointly * | Head of a household |
| | | Your tax is — | | |
| **25,000** | | | | |
| 25,000 | 25,050 | 1,432 | 1,122 | 1,255 |
| 25,050 | 25,100 | 1,436 | 1,125 | 1,258 |
| 25,100 | 25,150 | 1,440 | 1,128 | 1,262 |
| 25,150 | 25,200 | 1,443 | 1,131 | 1,265 |
| 25,200 | 25,250 | 1,447 | 1,135 | 1,269 |
| 25,250 | 25,300 | 1,451 | 1,138 | 1,272 |
| 25,300 | 25,350 | 1,455 | 1,141 | 1,275 |
| 25,350 | 25,400 | 1,459 | 1,144 | 1,279 |
| 25,400 | 25,450 | 1,462 | 1,147 | 1,282 |
| 25,450 | 25,500 | 1,466 | 1,151 | 1,286 |
| 25,500 | 25,550 | 1,470 | 1,154 | 1,289 |
| 25,550 | 25,600 | 1,474 | 1,157 | 1,292 |
| 25,600 | 25,650 | 1,478 | 1,160 | 1,296 |
| 25,650 | 25,700 | 1,481 | 1,163 | 1,299 |
| 25,700 | 25,750 | 1,485 | 1,167 | 1,303 |
| 25,750 | 25,800 | 1,489 | 1,170 | 1,306 |
| 25,800 | 25,850 | 1,493 | 1,173 | 1,309 |
| 25,850 | 25,900 | 1,497 | 1,176 | 1,313 |
| 25,900 | 25,950 | 1,500 | 1,179 | 1,316 |
| 25,950 | 26,000 | 1,504 | 1,183 | 1,320 |
| **26,000** | | | | |
| 26,000 | 26,050 | 1,508 | 1,186 | 1,323 |
| 26,050 | 26,100 | 1,512 | 1,189 | 1,326 |
| 26,100 | 26,150 | 1,516 | 1,192 | 1,330 |
| 26,150 | 26,200 | 1,519 | 1,195 | 1,333 |
| 26,200 | 26,250 | 1,523 | 1,199 | 1,337 |
| 26,250 | 26,300 | 1,527 | 1,202 | 1,340 |
| 26,300 | 26,350 | 1,531 | 1,205 | 1,343 |
| 26,350 | 26,400 | 1,535 | 1,208 | 1,347 |
| 26,400 | 26,450 | 1,538 | 1,211 | 1,350 |
| 26,450 | 26,500 | 1,542 | 1,215 | 1,354 |
| 26,500 | 26,550 | 1,546 | 1,218 | 1,357 |
| 26,550 | 26,600 | 1,550 | 1,221 | 1,360 |
| 26,600 | 26,650 | 1,554 | 1,224 | 1,364 |
| 26,650 | 26,700 | 1,557 | 1,227 | 1,367 |
| 26,700 | 26,750 | 1,561 | 1,231 | 1,371 |
| 26,750 | 26,800 | 1,565 | 1,234 | 1,374 |
| 26,800 | 26,850 | 1,569 | 1,237 | 1,377 |
| 26,850 | 26,900 | 1,573 | 1,240 | 1,381 |
| 26,900 | 26,950 | 1,576 | 1,243 | 1,384 |
| 26,950 | 27,000 | 1,580 | 1,247 | 1,388 |
| **27,000** | | | | |
| 27,000 | 27,050 | 1,584 | 1,250 | 1,391 |
| 27,050 | 27,100 | 1,588 | 1,253 | 1,394 |
| 27,100 | 27,150 | 1,592 | 1,256 | 1,398 |
| 27,150 | 27,200 | 1,595 | 1,259 | 1,401 |
| 27,200 | 27,250 | 1,599 | 1,263 | 1,405 |
| 27,250 | 27,300 | 1,603 | 1,266 | 1,408 |
| 27,300 | 27,350 | 1,607 | 1,269 | 1,411 |
| 27,350 | 27,400 | 1,611 | 1,272 | 1,415 |
| 27,400 | 27,450 | 1,614 | 1,275 | 1,418 |
| 27,450 | 27,500 | 1,618 | 1,279 | 1,422 |
| 27,500 | 27,550 | 1,622 | 1,282 | 1,425 |
| 27,550 | 27,600 | 1,626 | 1,285 | 1,428 |
| 27,600 | 27,650 | 1,630 | 1,288 | 1,432 |
| 27,650 | 27,700 | 1,633 | 1,291 | 1,435 |
| 27,700 | 27,750 | 1,637 | 1,295 | 1,439 |
| 27,750 | 27,800 | 1,641 | 1,298 | 1,442 |
| 27,800 | 27,850 | 1,645 | 1,301 | 1,445 |
| 27,850 | 27,900 | 1,649 | 1,304 | 1,449 |
| 27,900 | 27,950 | 1,652 | 1,307 | 1,452 |
| 27,950 | 28,000 | 1,656 | 1,311 | 1,456 |

| If line 26 (taxable income) is — | | And you are — | | |
|---|---|---|---|---|
| At least | But less than | Single or Married filing separately | Married filing jointly * | Head of a household |
| | | Your tax is — | | |
| **28,000** | | | | |
| 28,000 | 28,050 | 1,660 | 1,314 | 1,459 |
| 28,050 | 28,100 | 1,664 | 1,317 | 1,462 |
| 28,100 | 28,150 | 1,668 | 1,320 | 1,466 |
| 28,150 | 28,200 | 1,671 | 1,323 | 1,469 |
| 28,200 | 28,250 | 1,675 | 1,327 | 1,473 |
| 28,250 | 28,300 | 1,679 | 1,330 | 1,476 |
| 28,300 | 28,350 | 1,683 | 1,333 | 1,479 |
| 28,350 | 28,400 | 1,687 | 1,336 | 1,483 |
| 28,400 | 28,450 | 1,690 | 1,339 | 1,486 |
| 28,450 | 28,500 | 1,694 | 1,343 | 1,490 |
| 28,500 | 28,550 | 1,698 | 1,346 | 1,493 |
| 28,550 | 28,600 | 1,702 | 1,349 | 1,496 |
| 28,600 | 28,650 | 1,706 | 1,352 | 1,500 |
| 28,650 | 28,700 | 1,709 | 1,355 | 1,503 |
| 28,700 | 28,750 | 1,713 | 1,359 | 1,507 |
| 28,750 | 28,800 | 1,717 | 1,362 | 1,510 |
| 28,800 | 28,850 | 1,721 | 1,365 | 1,514 |
| 28,850 | 28,900 | 1,725 | 1,368 | 1,517 |
| 28,900 | 28,950 | 1,728 | 1,372 | 1,521 |
| 28,950 | 29,000 | 1,732 | 1,375 | 1,525 |
| **29,000** | | | | |
| 29,000 | 29,050 | 1,736 | 1,378 | 1,528 |
| 29,050 | 29,100 | 1,740 | 1,382 | 1,532 |
| 29,100 | 29,150 | 1,744 | 1,385 | 1,535 |
| 29,150 | 29,200 | 1,747 | 1,389 | 1,539 |
| 29,200 | 29,250 | 1,751 | 1,392 | 1,543 |
| 29,250 | 29,300 | 1,755 | 1,395 | 1,546 |
| 29,300 | 29,350 | 1,759 | 1,399 | 1,550 |
| 29,350 | 29,400 | 1,763 | 1,402 | 1,553 |
| 29,400 | 29,450 | 1,766 | 1,406 | 1,557 |
| 29,450 | 29,500 | 1,770 | 1,409 | 1,561 |
| 29,500 | 29,550 | 1,774 | 1,412 | 1,564 |
| 29,550 | 29,600 | 1,778 | 1,416 | 1,568 |
| 29,600 | 29,650 | 1,782 | 1,419 | 1,571 |
| 29,650 | 29,700 | 1,785 | 1,423 | 1,575 |
| 29,700 | 29,750 | 1,789 | 1,426 | 1,579 |
| 29,750 | 29,800 | 1,793 | 1,429 | 1,582 |
| 29,800 | 29,850 | 1,797 | 1,433 | 1,586 |
| 29,850 | 29,900 | 1,801 | 1,436 | 1,589 |
| 29,900 | 29,950 | 1,804 | 1,440 | 1,593 |
| 29,950 | 30,000 | 1,808 | 1,443 | 1,597 |
| **30,000** | | | | |
| 30,000 | 30,050 | 1,812 | 1,446 | 1,600 |
| 30,050 | 30,100 | 1,816 | 1,450 | 1,604 |
| 30,100 | 30,150 | 1,820 | 1,453 | 1,607 |
| 30,150 | 30,200 | 1,823 | 1,457 | 1,611 |
| 30,200 | 30,250 | 1,827 | 1,460 | 1,615 |
| 30,250 | 30,300 | 1,831 | 1,463 | 1,618 |
| 30,300 | 30,350 | 1,835 | 1,467 | 1,622 |
| 30,350 | 30,400 | 1,839 | 1,470 | 1,625 |
| 30,400 | 30,450 | 1,842 | 1,474 | 1,629 |
| 30,450 | 30,500 | 1,846 | 1,477 | 1,633 |
| 30,500 | 30,550 | 1,850 | 1,480 | 1,636 |
| 30,550 | 30,600 | 1,854 | 1,484 | 1,640 |
| 30,600 | 30,650 | 1,858 | 1,487 | 1,643 |
| 30,650 | 30,700 | 1,861 | 1,491 | 1,647 |
| 30,700 | 30,750 | 1,865 | 1,494 | 1,651 |
| 30,750 | 30,800 | 1,869 | 1,497 | 1,654 |
| 30,800 | 30,850 | 1,873 | 1,501 | 1,658 |
| 30,850 | 30,900 | 1,877 | 1,504 | 1,661 |
| 30,900 | 30,950 | 1,880 | 1,508 | 1,665 |
| 30,950 | 31,000 | 1,884 | 1,511 | 1,669 |

| If line 26 (taxable income) is — | | And you are — | | |
|---|---|---|---|---|
| At least | But less than | Single or Married filing separately | Married filing jointly * | Head of a household |
| | | Your tax is — | | |
| **31,000** | | | | |
| 31,000 | 31,050 | 1,888 | 1,514 | 1,672 |
| 31,050 | 31,100 | 1,892 | 1,518 | 1,676 |
| 31,100 | 31,150 | 1,896 | 1,521 | 1,679 |
| 31,150 | 31,200 | 1,899 | 1,525 | 1,683 |
| 31,200 | 31,250 | 1,903 | 1,528 | 1,687 |
| 31,250 | 31,300 | 1,907 | 1,531 | 1,690 |
| 31,300 | 31,350 | 1,911 | 1,535 | 1,694 |
| 31,350 | 31,400 | 1,915 | 1,538 | 1,697 |
| 31,400 | 31,450 | 1,918 | 1,542 | 1,701 |
| 31,450 | 31,500 | 1,922 | 1,545 | 1,705 |
| 31,500 | 31,550 | 1,926 | 1,548 | 1,708 |
| 31,550 | 31,600 | 1,930 | 1,552 | 1,712 |
| 31,600 | 31,650 | 1,934 | 1,555 | 1,715 |
| 31,650 | 31,700 | 1,937 | 1,559 | 1,719 |
| 31,700 | 31,750 | 1,941 | 1,562 | 1,723 |
| 31,750 | 31,800 | 1,945 | 1,565 | 1,726 |
| 31,800 | 31,850 | 1,949 | 1,569 | 1,730 |
| 31,850 | 31,900 | 1,953 | 1,572 | 1,733 |
| 31,900 | 31,950 | 1,956 | 1,576 | 1,737 |
| 31,950 | 32,000 | 1,960 | 1,579 | 1,741 |
| **32,000** | | | | |
| 32,000 | 32,050 | 1,964 | 1,582 | 1,744 |
| 32,050 | 32,100 | 1,968 | 1,586 | 1,748 |
| 32,100 | 32,150 | 1,972 | 1,589 | 1,751 |
| 32,150 | 32,200 | 1,975 | 1,593 | 1,755 |
| 32,200 | 32,250 | 1,979 | 1,596 | 1,759 |
| 32,250 | 32,300 | 1,983 | 1,599 | 1,762 |
| 32,300 | 32,350 | 1,987 | 1,603 | 1,766 |
| 32,350 | 32,400 | 1,991 | 1,606 | 1,769 |
| 32,400 | 32,450 | 1,994 | 1,610 | 1,773 |
| 32,450 | 32,500 | 1,998 | 1,613 | 1,777 |
| 32,500 | 32,550 | 2,002 | 1,616 | 1,780 |
| 32,550 | 32,600 | 2,006 | 1,620 | 1,784 |
| 32,600 | 32,650 | 2,010 | 1,623 | 1,787 |
| 32,650 | 32,700 | 2,013 | 1,627 | 1,791 |
| 32,700 | 32,750 | 2,017 | 1,630 | 1,795 |
| 32,750 | 32,800 | 2,021 | 1,633 | 1,798 |
| 32,800 | 32,850 | 2,025 | 1,637 | 1,802 |
| 32,850 | 32,900 | 2,029 | 1,640 | 1,805 |
| 32,900 | 32,950 | 2,032 | 1,644 | 1,809 |
| 32,950 | 33,000 | 2,036 | 1,647 | 1,813 |
| **33,000** | | | | |
| 33,000 | 33,050 | 2,040 | 1,650 | 1,816 |
| 33,050 | 33,100 | 2,044 | 1,654 | 1,820 |
| 33,100 | 33,150 | 2,048 | 1,657 | 1,823 |
| 33,150 | 33,200 | 2,051 | 1,661 | 1,827 |
| 33,200 | 33,250 | 2,055 | 1,664 | 1,831 |
| 33,250 | 33,300 | 2,059 | 1,667 | 1,834 |
| 33,300 | 33,350 | 2,063 | 1,671 | 1,838 |
| 33,350 | 33,400 | 2,067 | 1,674 | 1,841 |
| 33,400 | 33,450 | 2,070 | 1,678 | 1,845 |
| 33,450 | 33,500 | 2,074 | 1,681 | 1,849 |
| 33,500 | 33,550 | 2,078 | 1,684 | 1,852 |
| 33,550 | 33,600 | 2,082 | 1,688 | 1,856 |
| 33,600 | 33,650 | 2,086 | 1,691 | 1,859 |
| 33,650 | 33,700 | 2,089 | 1,695 | 1,863 |
| 33,700 | 33,750 | 2,093 | 1,698 | 1,867 |
| 33,750 | 33,800 | 2,097 | 1,701 | 1,870 |
| 33,800 | 33,850 | 2,101 | 1,705 | 1,874 |
| 33,850 | 33,900 | 2,105 | 1,708 | 1,877 |
| 33,900 | 33,950 | 2,108 | 1,712 | 1,881 |
| 33,950 | 34,000 | 2,112 | 1,715 | 1,885 |

*This column must also be used by qualifying widow(er)

Continued on next page

## 2018 Hawaii Tax Table (continued)

| If line 26 (taxable income) is — At least | But less than | And you are — Single or Married filing separately | Married filing jointly * | Head of a household |
|---|---|---|---|---|
| **34,000** | | | | |
| 34,000 | 34,050 | 2,116 | 1,718 | 1,888 |
| 34,050 | 34,100 | 2,120 | 1,722 | 1,892 |
| 34,100 | 34,150 | 2,124 | 1,725 | 1,895 |
| 34,150 | 34,200 | 2,127 | 1,729 | 1,899 |
| 34,200 | 34,250 | 2,131 | 1,732 | 1,903 |
| 34,250 | 34,300 | 2,135 | 1,735 | 1,906 |
| 34,300 | 34,350 | 2,139 | 1,739 | 1,910 |
| 34,350 | 34,400 | 2,143 | 1,742 | 1,913 |
| 34,400 | 34,450 | 2,146 | 1,746 | 1,917 |
| 34,450 | 34,500 | 2,150 | 1,749 | 1,921 |
| 34,500 | 34,550 | 2,154 | 1,752 | 1,924 |
| 34,550 | 34,600 | 2,158 | 1,756 | 1,928 |
| 34,600 | 34,650 | 2,162 | 1,759 | 1,931 |
| 34,650 | 34,700 | 2,165 | 1,763 | 1,935 |
| 34,700 | 34,750 | 2,169 | 1,766 | 1,939 |
| 34,750 | 34,800 | 2,173 | 1,769 | 1,942 |
| 34,800 | 34,850 | 2,177 | 1,773 | 1,946 |
| 34,850 | 34,900 | 2,181 | 1,776 | 1,949 |
| 34,900 | 34,950 | 2,184 | 1,780 | 1,953 |
| 34,950 | 35,000 | 2,188 | 1,783 | 1,957 |
| **35,000** | | | | |
| 35,000 | 35,050 | 2,192 | 1,786 | 1,960 |
| 35,050 | 35,100 | 2,196 | 1,790 | 1,964 |
| 35,100 | 35,150 | 2,200 | 1,793 | 1,967 |
| 35,150 | 35,200 | 2,203 | 1,797 | 1,971 |
| 35,200 | 35,250 | 2,207 | 1,800 | 1,975 |
| 35,250 | 35,300 | 2,211 | 1,803 | 1,978 |
| 35,300 | 35,350 | 2,215 | 1,807 | 1,982 |
| 35,350 | 35,400 | 2,219 | 1,810 | 1,985 |
| 35,400 | 35,450 | 2,222 | 1,814 | 1,989 |
| 35,450 | 35,500 | 2,226 | 1,817 | 1,993 |
| 35,500 | 35,550 | 2,230 | 1,820 | 1,996 |
| 35,550 | 35,600 | 2,234 | 1,824 | 2,000 |
| 35,600 | 35,650 | 2,238 | 1,827 | 2,003 |
| 35,650 | 35,700 | 2,241 | 1,831 | 2,007 |
| 35,700 | 35,750 | 2,245 | 1,834 | 2,011 |
| 35,750 | 35,800 | 2,249 | 1,837 | 2,014 |
| 35,800 | 35,850 | 2,253 | 1,841 | 2,018 |
| 35,850 | 35,900 | 2,257 | 1,844 | 2,021 |
| 35,900 | 35,950 | 2,260 | 1,848 | 2,025 |
| 35,950 | 36,000 | 2,264 | 1,851 | 2,029 |
| **36,000** | | | | |
| 36,000 | 36,050 | 2,268 | 1,854 | 2,032 |
| 36,050 | 36,100 | 2,272 | 1,858 | 2,036 |
| 36,100 | 36,150 | 2,276 | 1,861 | 2,040 |
| 36,150 | 36,200 | 2,280 | 1,865 | 2,043 |
| 36,200 | 36,250 | 2,284 | 1,868 | 2,047 |
| 36,250 | 36,300 | 2,288 | 1,871 | 2,051 |
| 36,300 | 36,350 | 2,292 | 1,875 | 2,055 |
| 36,350 | 36,400 | 2,296 | 1,878 | 2,059 |
| 36,400 | 36,450 | 2,300 | 1,882 | 2,062 |
| 36,450 | 36,500 | 2,304 | 1,885 | 2,066 |
| 36,500 | 36,550 | 2,307 | 1,888 | 2,070 |
| 36,550 | 36,600 | 2,311 | 1,892 | 2,074 |
| 36,600 | 36,650 | 2,315 | 1,895 | 2,078 |
| 36,650 | 36,700 | 2,319 | 1,899 | 2,081 |
| 36,700 | 36,750 | 2,323 | 1,902 | 2,085 |
| 36,750 | 36,800 | 2,327 | 1,905 | 2,089 |
| 36,800 | 36,850 | 2,331 | 1,909 | 2,093 |
| 36,850 | 36,900 | 2,335 | 1,912 | 2,097 |
| 36,900 | 36,950 | 2,339 | 1,916 | 2,100 |
| 36,950 | 37,000 | 2,343 | 1,919 | 2,104 |

| If line 26 (taxable income) is — At least | But less than | And you are — Single or Married filing separately | Married filing jointly * | Head of a household |
|---|---|---|---|---|
| **37,000** | | | | |
| 37,000 | 37,050 | 2,347 | 1,922 | 2,108 |
| 37,050 | 37,100 | 2,351 | 1,926 | 2,112 |
| 37,100 | 37,150 | 2,355 | 1,929 | 2,116 |
| 37,150 | 37,200 | 2,359 | 1,933 | 2,119 |
| 37,200 | 37,250 | 2,363 | 1,936 | 2,123 |
| 37,250 | 37,300 | 2,367 | 1,939 | 2,127 |
| 37,300 | 37,350 | 2,371 | 1,943 | 2,131 |
| 37,350 | 37,400 | 2,375 | 1,946 | 2,135 |
| 37,400 | 37,450 | 2,379 | 1,950 | 2,138 |
| 37,450 | 37,500 | 2,383 | 1,953 | 2,142 |
| 37,500 | 37,550 | 2,386 | 1,956 | 2,146 |
| 37,550 | 37,600 | 2,390 | 1,960 | 2,150 |
| 37,600 | 37,650 | 2,394 | 1,963 | 2,154 |
| 37,650 | 37,700 | 2,398 | 1,967 | 2,157 |
| 37,700 | 37,750 | 2,402 | 1,970 | 2,161 |
| 37,750 | 37,800 | 2,406 | 1,973 | 2,165 |
| 37,800 | 37,850 | 2,410 | 1,977 | 2,169 |
| 37,850 | 37,900 | 2,414 | 1,980 | 2,173 |
| 37,900 | 37,950 | 2,418 | 1,984 | 2,176 |
| 37,950 | 38,000 | 2,422 | 1,987 | 2,180 |
| **38,000** | | | | |
| 38,000 | 38,050 | 2,426 | 1,990 | 2,184 |
| 38,050 | 38,100 | 2,430 | 1,994 | 2,188 |
| 38,100 | 38,150 | 2,434 | 1,997 | 2,192 |
| 38,150 | 38,200 | 2,438 | 2,001 | 2,195 |
| 38,200 | 38,250 | 2,442 | 2,004 | 2,199 |
| 38,250 | 38,300 | 2,446 | 2,007 | 2,203 |
| 38,300 | 38,350 | 2,450 | 2,011 | 2,207 |
| 38,350 | 38,400 | 2,454 | 2,014 | 2,211 |
| 38,400 | 38,450 | 2,458 | 2,018 | 2,214 |
| 38,450 | 38,500 | 2,462 | 2,021 | 2,218 |
| 38,500 | 38,550 | 2,465 | 2,025 | 2,222 |
| 38,550 | 38,600 | 2,469 | 2,029 | 2,226 |
| 38,600 | 38,650 | 2,473 | 2,032 | 2,230 |
| 38,650 | 38,700 | 2,477 | 2,036 | 2,233 |
| 38,700 | 38,750 | 2,481 | 2,039 | 2,237 |
| 38,750 | 38,800 | 2,485 | 2,043 | 2,241 |
| 38,800 | 38,850 | 2,489 | 2,047 | 2,245 |
| 38,850 | 38,900 | 2,493 | 2,050 | 2,249 |
| 38,900 | 38,950 | 2,497 | 2,054 | 2,252 |
| 38,950 | 39,000 | 2,501 | 2,057 | 2,256 |
| **39,000** | | | | |
| 39,000 | 39,050 | 2,505 | 2,061 | 2,260 |
| 39,050 | 39,100 | 2,509 | 2,065 | 2,264 |
| 39,100 | 39,150 | 2,513 | 2,068 | 2,268 |
| 39,150 | 39,200 | 2,517 | 2,072 | 2,271 |
| 39,200 | 39,250 | 2,521 | 2,075 | 2,275 |
| 39,250 | 39,300 | 2,525 | 2,079 | 2,279 |
| 39,300 | 39,350 | 2,529 | 2,083 | 2,283 |
| 39,350 | 39,400 | 2,533 | 2,086 | 2,287 |
| 39,400 | 39,450 | 2,537 | 2,090 | 2,290 |
| 39,450 | 39,500 | 2,541 | 2,093 | 2,294 |
| 39,500 | 39,550 | 2,544 | 2,097 | 2,298 |
| 39,550 | 39,600 | 2,548 | 2,101 | 2,302 |
| 39,600 | 39,650 | 2,552 | 2,104 | 2,306 |
| 39,650 | 39,700 | 2,556 | 2,108 | 2,309 |
| 39,700 | 39,750 | 2,560 | 2,111 | 2,313 |
| 39,750 | 39,800 | 2,564 | 2,115 | 2,317 |
| 39,800 | 39,850 | 2,568 | 2,119 | 2,321 |
| 39,850 | 39,900 | 2,572 | 2,122 | 2,325 |
| 39,900 | 39,950 | 2,576 | 2,126 | 2,328 |
| 39,950 | 40,000 | 2,580 | 2,129 | 2,332 |

| If line 26 (taxable income) is — At least | But less than | And you are — Single or Married filing separately | Married filing jointly * | Head of a household |
|---|---|---|---|---|
| **40,000** | | | | |
| 40,000 | 40,050 | 2,584 | 2,133 | 2,336 |
| 40,050 | 40,100 | 2,588 | 2,137 | 2,340 |
| 40,100 | 40,150 | 2,592 | 2,140 | 2,344 |
| 40,150 | 40,200 | 2,596 | 2,144 | 2,347 |
| 40,200 | 40,250 | 2,600 | 2,147 | 2,351 |
| 40,250 | 40,300 | 2,604 | 2,151 | 2,355 |
| 40,300 | 40,350 | 2,608 | 2,155 | 2,359 |
| 40,350 | 40,400 | 2,612 | 2,158 | 2,363 |
| 40,400 | 40,450 | 2,616 | 2,162 | 2,366 |
| 40,450 | 40,500 | 2,620 | 2,165 | 2,370 |
| 40,500 | 40,550 | 2,623 | 2,169 | 2,374 |
| 40,550 | 40,600 | 2,627 | 2,173 | 2,378 |
| 40,600 | 40,650 | 2,631 | 2,176 | 2,382 |
| 40,650 | 40,700 | 2,635 | 2,180 | 2,385 |
| 40,700 | 40,750 | 2,639 | 2,183 | 2,389 |
| 40,750 | 40,800 | 2,643 | 2,187 | 2,393 |
| 40,800 | 40,850 | 2,647 | 2,191 | 2,397 |
| 40,850 | 40,900 | 2,651 | 2,194 | 2,401 |
| 40,900 | 40,950 | 2,655 | 2,198 | 2,404 |
| 40,950 | 41,000 | 2,659 | 2,201 | 2,408 |
| **41,000** | | | | |
| 41,000 | 41,050 | 2,663 | 2,205 | 2,412 |
| 41,050 | 41,100 | 2,667 | 2,209 | 2,416 |
| 41,100 | 41,150 | 2,671 | 2,212 | 2,420 |
| 41,150 | 41,200 | 2,675 | 2,216 | 2,423 |
| 41,200 | 41,250 | 2,679 | 2,219 | 2,427 |
| 41,250 | 41,300 | 2,683 | 2,223 | 2,431 |
| 41,300 | 41,350 | 2,687 | 2,227 | 2,435 |
| 41,350 | 41,400 | 2,691 | 2,230 | 2,439 |
| 41,400 | 41,450 | 2,695 | 2,234 | 2,442 |
| 41,450 | 41,500 | 2,699 | 2,237 | 2,446 |
| 41,500 | 41,550 | 2,702 | 2,241 | 2,450 |
| 41,550 | 41,600 | 2,706 | 2,245 | 2,454 |
| 41,600 | 41,650 | 2,710 | 2,248 | 2,458 |
| 41,650 | 41,700 | 2,714 | 2,252 | 2,461 |
| 41,700 | 41,750 | 2,718 | 2,255 | 2,465 |
| 41,750 | 41,800 | 2,722 | 2,259 | 2,469 |
| 41,800 | 41,850 | 2,726 | 2,263 | 2,473 |
| 41,850 | 41,900 | 2,730 | 2,266 | 2,477 |
| 41,900 | 41,950 | 2,734 | 2,270 | 2,480 |
| 41,950 | 42,000 | 2,738 | 2,273 | 2,484 |
| **42,000** | | | | |
| 42,000 | 42,050 | 2,742 | 2,277 | 2,488 |
| 42,050 | 42,100 | 2,746 | 2,281 | 2,492 |
| 42,100 | 42,150 | 2,750 | 2,284 | 2,496 |
| 42,150 | 42,200 | 2,754 | 2,288 | 2,499 |
| 42,200 | 42,250 | 2,758 | 2,291 | 2,503 |
| 42,250 | 42,300 | 2,762 | 2,295 | 2,507 |
| 42,300 | 42,350 | 2,766 | 2,299 | 2,511 |
| 42,350 | 42,400 | 2,770 | 2,302 | 2,515 |
| 42,400 | 42,450 | 2,774 | 2,306 | 2,518 |
| 42,450 | 42,500 | 2,778 | 2,309 | 2,522 |
| 42,500 | 42,550 | 2,781 | 2,313 | 2,526 |
| 42,550 | 42,600 | 2,785 | 2,317 | 2,530 |
| 42,600 | 42,650 | 2,789 | 2,320 | 2,534 |
| 42,650 | 42,700 | 2,793 | 2,324 | 2,537 |
| 42,700 | 42,750 | 2,797 | 2,327 | 2,541 |
| 42,750 | 42,800 | 2,801 | 2,331 | 2,545 |
| 42,800 | 42,850 | 2,805 | 2,335 | 2,549 |
| 42,850 | 42,900 | 2,809 | 2,338 | 2,553 |
| 42,900 | 42,950 | 2,813 | 2,342 | 2,556 |
| 42,950 | 43,000 | 2,817 | 2,345 | 2,560 |

*This column must also be used by qualifying widow(er)

Continued on next page

## 2018 Hawaii Tax Table (continued)

### 43,000 – 45,999

| If line 26 (taxable income) is — | | And you are — | | |
|---|---|---|---|---|
| At least | But less than | Single or Married filing separately | Married filing jointly * | Head of a household |
| | | Your tax is — | | |
| 43,000 | 43,050 | 2,821 | 2,349 | 2,564 |
| 43,050 | 43,100 | 2,825 | 2,353 | 2,568 |
| 43,100 | 43,150 | 2,829 | 2,356 | 2,572 |
| 43,150 | 43,200 | 2,833 | 2,360 | 2,575 |
| 43,200 | 43,250 | 2,837 | 2,363 | 2,579 |
| 43,250 | 43,300 | 2,841 | 2,367 | 2,583 |
| 43,300 | 43,350 | 2,845 | 2,371 | 2,587 |
| 43,350 | 43,400 | 2,849 | 2,374 | 2,591 |
| 43,400 | 43,450 | 2,853 | 2,378 | 2,594 |
| 43,450 | 43,500 | 2,857 | 2,381 | 2,598 |
| 43,500 | 43,550 | 2,860 | 2,385 | 2,602 |
| 43,550 | 43,600 | 2,864 | 2,389 | 2,606 |
| 43,600 | 43,650 | 2,868 | 2,392 | 2,610 |
| 43,650 | 43,700 | 2,872 | 2,396 | 2,613 |
| 43,700 | 43,750 | 2,876 | 2,399 | 2,617 |
| 43,750 | 43,800 | 2,880 | 2,403 | 2,621 |
| 43,800 | 43,850 | 2,884 | 2,407 | 2,625 |
| 43,850 | 43,900 | 2,888 | 2,410 | 2,629 |
| 43,900 | 43,950 | 2,892 | 2,414 | 2,632 |
| 43,950 | 44,000 | 2,896 | 2,417 | 2,636 |
| 44,000 | 44,050 | 2,900 | 2,421 | 2,640 |
| 44,050 | 44,100 | 2,904 | 2,425 | 2,644 |
| 44,100 | 44,150 | 2,908 | 2,428 | 2,648 |
| 44,150 | 44,200 | 2,912 | 2,432 | 2,651 |
| 44,200 | 44,250 | 2,916 | 2,435 | 2,655 |
| 44,250 | 44,300 | 2,920 | 2,439 | 2,659 |
| 44,300 | 44,350 | 2,924 | 2,443 | 2,663 |
| 44,350 | 44,400 | 2,928 | 2,446 | 2,667 |
| 44,400 | 44,450 | 2,932 | 2,450 | 2,670 |
| 44,450 | 44,500 | 2,936 | 2,453 | 2,674 |
| 44,500 | 44,550 | 2,939 | 2,457 | 2,678 |
| 44,550 | 44,600 | 2,943 | 2,461 | 2,682 |
| 44,600 | 44,650 | 2,947 | 2,464 | 2,686 |
| 44,650 | 44,700 | 2,951 | 2,468 | 2,689 |
| 44,700 | 44,750 | 2,955 | 2,471 | 2,693 |
| 44,750 | 44,800 | 2,959 | 2,475 | 2,697 |
| 44,800 | 44,850 | 2,963 | 2,479 | 2,701 |
| 44,850 | 44,900 | 2,967 | 2,482 | 2,705 |
| 44,900 | 44,950 | 2,971 | 2,486 | 2,708 |
| 44,950 | 45,000 | 2,975 | 2,489 | 2,712 |
| 45,000 | 45,050 | 2,979 | 2,493 | 2,716 |
| 45,050 | 45,100 | 2,983 | 2,497 | 2,720 |
| 45,100 | 45,150 | 2,987 | 2,500 | 2,724 |
| 45,150 | 45,200 | 2,991 | 2,504 | 2,727 |
| 45,200 | 45,250 | 2,995 | 2,507 | 2,731 |
| 45,250 | 45,300 | 2,999 | 2,511 | 2,735 |
| 45,300 | 45,350 | 3,003 | 2,515 | 2,739 |
| 45,350 | 45,400 | 3,007 | 2,518 | 2,743 |
| 45,400 | 45,450 | 3,011 | 2,522 | 2,746 |
| 45,450 | 45,500 | 3,015 | 2,525 | 2,750 |
| 45,500 | 45,550 | 3,018 | 2,529 | 2,754 |
| 45,550 | 45,600 | 3,022 | 2,533 | 2,758 |
| 45,600 | 45,650 | 3,026 | 2,536 | 2,762 |
| 45,650 | 45,700 | 3,030 | 2,540 | 2,765 |
| 45,700 | 45,750 | 3,034 | 2,543 | 2,769 |
| 45,750 | 45,800 | 3,038 | 2,547 | 2,773 |
| 45,800 | 45,850 | 3,042 | 2,551 | 2,777 |
| 45,850 | 45,900 | 3,046 | 2,554 | 2,781 |
| 45,900 | 45,950 | 3,050 | 2,558 | 2,784 |
| 45,950 | 46,000 | 3,054 | 2,561 | 2,788 |

### 46,000 – 48,999

| If line 26 (taxable income) is — | | And you are — | | |
|---|---|---|---|---|
| At least | But less than | Single or Married filing separately | Married filing jointly * | Head of a household |
| | | Your tax is — | | |
| 46,000 | 46,050 | 3,058 | 2,565 | 2,792 |
| 46,050 | 46,100 | 3,062 | 2,569 | 2,796 |
| 46,100 | 46,150 | 3,066 | 2,572 | 2,800 |
| 46,150 | 46,200 | 3,070 | 2,576 | 2,803 |
| 46,200 | 46,250 | 3,074 | 2,579 | 2,807 |
| 46,250 | 46,300 | 3,078 | 2,583 | 2,811 |
| 46,300 | 46,350 | 3,082 | 2,587 | 2,815 |
| 46,350 | 46,400 | 3,086 | 2,590 | 2,819 |
| 46,400 | 46,450 | 3,090 | 2,594 | 2,822 |
| 46,450 | 46,500 | 3,094 | 2,597 | 2,826 |
| 46,500 | 46,550 | 3,097 | 2,601 | 2,830 |
| 46,550 | 46,600 | 3,101 | 2,605 | 2,834 |
| 46,600 | 46,650 | 3,105 | 2,608 | 2,838 |
| 46,650 | 46,700 | 3,109 | 2,612 | 2,841 |
| 46,700 | 46,750 | 3,113 | 2,615 | 2,845 |
| 46,750 | 46,800 | 3,117 | 2,619 | 2,849 |
| 46,800 | 46,850 | 3,121 | 2,623 | 2,853 |
| 46,850 | 46,900 | 3,125 | 2,626 | 2,857 |
| 46,900 | 46,950 | 3,129 | 2,630 | 2,860 |
| 46,950 | 47,000 | 3,133 | 2,633 | 2,864 |
| 47,000 | 47,050 | 3,137 | 2,637 | 2,868 |
| 47,050 | 47,100 | 3,141 | 2,641 | 2,872 |
| 47,100 | 47,150 | 3,145 | 2,644 | 2,876 |
| 47,150 | 47,200 | 3,149 | 2,648 | 2,879 |
| 47,200 | 47,250 | 3,153 | 2,651 | 2,883 |
| 47,250 | 47,300 | 3,157 | 2,655 | 2,887 |
| 47,300 | 47,350 | 3,161 | 2,659 | 2,891 |
| 47,350 | 47,400 | 3,165 | 2,662 | 2,895 |
| 47,400 | 47,450 | 3,169 | 2,666 | 2,898 |
| 47,450 | 47,500 | 3,173 | 2,669 | 2,902 |
| 47,500 | 47,550 | 3,176 | 2,673 | 2,906 |
| 47,550 | 47,600 | 3,180 | 2,677 | 2,910 |
| 47,600 | 47,650 | 3,184 | 2,680 | 2,914 |
| 47,650 | 47,700 | 3,188 | 2,684 | 2,917 |
| 47,700 | 47,750 | 3,192 | 2,687 | 2,921 |
| 47,750 | 47,800 | 3,196 | 2,691 | 2,925 |
| 47,800 | 47,850 | 3,200 | 2,695 | 2,929 |
| 47,850 | 47,900 | 3,204 | 2,698 | 2,933 |
| 47,900 | 47,950 | 3,208 | 2,702 | 2,936 |
| 47,950 | 48,000 | 3,212 | 2,705 | 2,940 |
| 48,000 | 48,050 | 3,216 | 2,709 | 2,944 |
| 48,050 | 48,100 | 3,220 | 2,713 | 2,948 |
| 48,100 | 48,150 | 3,224 | 2,717 | 2,952 |
| 48,150 | 48,200 | 3,228 | 2,720 | 2,955 |
| 48,200 | 48,250 | 3,233 | 2,724 | 2,959 |
| 48,250 | 48,300 | 3,237 | 2,728 | 2,963 |
| 48,300 | 48,350 | 3,241 | 2,732 | 2,967 |
| 48,350 | 48,400 | 3,245 | 2,736 | 2,971 |
| 48,400 | 48,450 | 3,249 | 2,739 | 2,974 |
| 48,450 | 48,500 | 3,253 | 2,743 | 2,978 |
| 48,500 | 48,550 | 3,257 | 2,747 | 2,982 |
| 48,550 | 48,600 | 3,261 | 2,751 | 2,986 |
| 48,600 | 48,650 | 3,266 | 2,755 | 2,990 |
| 48,650 | 48,700 | 3,270 | 2,758 | 2,993 |
| 48,700 | 48,750 | 3,274 | 2,762 | 2,997 |
| 48,750 | 48,800 | 3,278 | 2,766 | 3,001 |
| 48,800 | 48,850 | 3,282 | 2,770 | 3,005 |
| 48,850 | 48,900 | 3,286 | 2,774 | 3,009 |
| 48,900 | 48,950 | 3,290 | 2,777 | 3,012 |
| 48,950 | 49,000 | 3,294 | 2,781 | 3,016 |

### 49,000 – 51,999

| If line 26 (taxable income) is — | | And you are — | | |
|---|---|---|---|---|
| At least | But less than | Single or Married filing separately | Married filing jointly * | Head of a household |
| | | Your tax is — | | |
| 49,000 | 49,050 | 3,299 | 2,785 | 3,020 |
| 49,050 | 49,100 | 3,303 | 2,789 | 3,024 |
| 49,100 | 49,150 | 3,307 | 2,793 | 3,028 |
| 49,150 | 49,200 | 3,311 | 2,796 | 3,031 |
| 49,200 | 49,250 | 3,315 | 2,800 | 3,035 |
| 49,250 | 49,300 | 3,319 | 2,804 | 3,039 |
| 49,300 | 49,350 | 3,323 | 2,808 | 3,043 |
| 49,350 | 49,400 | 3,327 | 2,812 | 3,047 |
| 49,400 | 49,450 | 3,332 | 2,815 | 3,050 |
| 49,450 | 49,500 | 3,336 | 2,819 | 3,054 |
| 49,500 | 49,550 | 3,340 | 2,823 | 3,058 |
| 49,550 | 49,600 | 3,344 | 2,827 | 3,062 |
| 49,600 | 49,650 | 3,348 | 2,831 | 3,066 |
| 49,650 | 49,700 | 3,352 | 2,834 | 3,069 |
| 49,700 | 49,750 | 3,356 | 2,838 | 3,073 |
| 49,750 | 49,800 | 3,360 | 2,842 | 3,077 |
| 49,800 | 49,850 | 3,365 | 2,846 | 3,081 |
| 49,850 | 49,900 | 3,369 | 2,850 | 3,085 |
| 49,900 | 49,950 | 3,373 | 2,853 | 3,088 |
| 49,950 | 50,000 | 3,377 | 2,857 | 3,092 |
| 50,000 | 50,050 | 3,381 | 2,861 | 3,096 |
| 50,050 | 50,100 | 3,385 | 2,865 | 3,100 |
| 50,100 | 50,150 | 3,389 | 2,869 | 3,104 |
| 50,150 | 50,200 | 3,393 | 2,872 | 3,107 |
| 50,200 | 50,250 | 3,398 | 2,876 | 3,111 |
| 50,250 | 50,300 | 3,402 | 2,880 | 3,115 |
| 50,300 | 50,350 | 3,406 | 2,884 | 3,119 |
| 50,350 | 50,400 | 3,410 | 2,888 | 3,123 |
| 50,400 | 50,450 | 3,414 | 2,891 | 3,126 |
| 50,450 | 50,500 | 3,418 | 2,895 | 3,130 |
| 50,500 | 50,550 | 3,422 | 2,899 | 3,134 |
| 50,550 | 50,600 | 3,426 | 2,903 | 3,138 |
| 50,600 | 50,650 | 3,431 | 2,907 | 3,142 |
| 50,650 | 50,700 | 3,435 | 2,910 | 3,145 |
| 50,700 | 50,750 | 3,439 | 2,914 | 3,149 |
| 50,750 | 50,800 | 3,443 | 2,918 | 3,153 |
| 50,800 | 50,850 | 3,447 | 2,922 | 3,157 |
| 50,850 | 50,900 | 3,451 | 2,926 | 3,161 |
| 50,900 | 50,950 | 3,455 | 2,929 | 3,164 |
| 50,950 | 51,000 | 3,459 | 2,933 | 3,168 |
| 51,000 | 51,050 | 3,464 | 2,937 | 3,172 |
| 51,050 | 51,100 | 3,468 | 2,941 | 3,176 |
| 51,100 | 51,150 | 3,472 | 2,945 | 3,180 |
| 51,150 | 51,200 | 3,476 | 2,948 | 3,183 |
| 51,200 | 51,250 | 3,480 | 2,952 | 3,187 |
| 51,250 | 51,300 | 3,484 | 2,956 | 3,191 |
| 51,300 | 51,350 | 3,488 | 2,960 | 3,195 |
| 51,350 | 51,400 | 3,492 | 2,964 | 3,199 |
| 51,400 | 51,450 | 3,497 | 2,967 | 3,202 |
| 51,450 | 51,500 | 3,501 | 2,971 | 3,206 |
| 51,500 | 51,550 | 3,505 | 2,975 | 3,210 |
| 51,550 | 51,600 | 3,509 | 2,979 | 3,214 |
| 51,600 | 51,650 | 3,513 | 2,983 | 3,218 |
| 51,650 | 51,700 | 3,517 | 2,986 | 3,221 |
| 51,700 | 51,750 | 3,521 | 2,990 | 3,225 |
| 51,750 | 51,800 | 3,525 | 2,994 | 3,229 |
| 51,800 | 51,850 | 3,530 | 2,998 | 3,233 |
| 51,850 | 51,900 | 3,534 | 3,002 | 3,237 |
| 51,900 | 51,950 | 3,538 | 3,005 | 3,240 |
| 51,950 | 52,000 | 3,542 | 3,009 | 3,244 |

*This column must also be used by qualifying widow(er)

Continued on next page

## 22 TAXES OF HAWAII

## 2018 Hawaii Tax Table (continued)

| If line 26 (taxable income) is — At least | But less than | Single or Married filing separately | Married filing jointly * | Head of a house-hold | If line 26 (taxable income) is — At least | But less than | Single or Married filing separately | Married filing jointly * | Head of a house-hold | If line 26 (taxable income) is — At least | But less than | Single or Married filing separately | Married filing jointly * | Head of a house-hold |
|---|---|---|---|---|---|---|---|---|---|---|---|---|---|---|
| **52,000** | | | | | **55,000** | | | | | **58,000** | | | | |
| 52,000 | 52,050 | 3,546 | 3,013 | 3,248 | 55,000 | 55,050 | 3,794 | 3,241 | 3,479 | 58,000 | 58,050 | 4,041 | 3,469 | 3,716 |
| 52,050 | 52,100 | 3,550 | 3,017 | 3,252 | 55,050 | 55,100 | 3,798 | 3,245 | 3,483 | 58,050 | 58,100 | 4,045 | 3,473 | 3,720 |
| 52,100 | 52,150 | 3,554 | 3,021 | 3,256 | 55,100 | 55,150 | 3,802 | 3,249 | 3,487 | 58,100 | 58,150 | 4,049 | 3,477 | 3,724 |
| 52,150 | 52,200 | 3,558 | 3,024 | 3,259 | 55,150 | 55,200 | 3,806 | 3,252 | 3,491 | 58,150 | 58,200 | 4,053 | 3,480 | 3,728 |
| 52,200 | 52,250 | 3,563 | 3,028 | 3,263 | 55,200 | 55,250 | 3,810 | 3,256 | 3,495 | 58,200 | 58,250 | 4,058 | 3,484 | 3,732 |
| 52,250 | 52,300 | 3,567 | 3,032 | 3,267 | 55,250 | 55,300 | 3,814 | 3,260 | 3,499 | 58,250 | 58,300 | 4,062 | 3,488 | 3,736 |
| 52,300 | 52,350 | 3,571 | 3,036 | 3,271 | 55,300 | 55,350 | 3,818 | 3,264 | 3,503 | 58,300 | 58,350 | 4,066 | 3,492 | 3,740 |
| 52,350 | 52,400 | 3,575 | 3,040 | 3,275 | 55,350 | 55,400 | 3,822 | 3,268 | 3,507 | 58,350 | 58,400 | 4,070 | 3,496 | 3,744 |
| 52,400 | 52,450 | 3,579 | 3,043 | 3,278 | 55,400 | 55,450 | 3,827 | 3,271 | 3,511 | 58,400 | 58,450 | 4,074 | 3,499 | 3,748 |
| 52,450 | 52,500 | 3,583 | 3,047 | 3,282 | 55,450 | 55,500 | 3,831 | 3,275 | 3,515 | 58,450 | 58,500 | 4,078 | 3,503 | 3,752 |
| 52,500 | 52,550 | 3,587 | 3,051 | 3,286 | 55,500 | 55,550 | 3,835 | 3,279 | 3,518 | 58,500 | 58,550 | 4,082 | 3,507 | 3,755 |
| 52,550 | 52,600 | 3,591 | 3,055 | 3,290 | 55,550 | 55,600 | 3,839 | 3,283 | 3,522 | 58,550 | 58,600 | 4,086 | 3,511 | 3,759 |
| 52,600 | 52,650 | 3,596 | 3,059 | 3,294 | 55,600 | 55,650 | 3,843 | 3,287 | 3,526 | 58,600 | 58,650 | 4,091 | 3,515 | 3,763 |
| 52,650 | 52,700 | 3,600 | 3,062 | 3,297 | 55,650 | 55,700 | 3,847 | 3,290 | 3,530 | 58,650 | 58,700 | 4,095 | 3,518 | 3,767 |
| 52,700 | 52,750 | 3,604 | 3,066 | 3,301 | 55,700 | 55,750 | 3,851 | 3,294 | 3,534 | 58,700 | 58,750 | 4,099 | 3,522 | 3,771 |
| 52,750 | 52,800 | 3,608 | 3,070 | 3,305 | 55,750 | 55,800 | 3,855 | 3,298 | 3,538 | 58,750 | 58,800 | 4,103 | 3,526 | 3,775 |
| 52,800 | 52,850 | 3,612 | 3,074 | 3,309 | 55,800 | 55,850 | 3,860 | 3,302 | 3,542 | 58,800 | 58,850 | 4,107 | 3,530 | 3,779 |
| 52,850 | 52,900 | 3,616 | 3,078 | 3,313 | 55,850 | 55,900 | 3,864 | 3,306 | 3,546 | 58,850 | 58,900 | 4,111 | 3,534 | 3,783 |
| 52,900 | 52,950 | 3,620 | 3,081 | 3,316 | 55,900 | 55,950 | 3,868 | 3,309 | 3,550 | 58,900 | 58,950 | 4,115 | 3,537 | 3,787 |
| 52,950 | 53,000 | 3,624 | 3,085 | 3,320 | 55,950 | 56,000 | 3,872 | 3,313 | 3,554 | 58,950 | 59,000 | 4,119 | 3,541 | 3,791 |
| **53,000** | | | | | **56,000** | | | | | **59,000** | | | | |
| 53,000 | 53,050 | 3,629 | 3,089 | 3,324 | 56,000 | 56,050 | 3,876 | 3,317 | 3,558 | 59,000 | 59,050 | 4,124 | 3,545 | 3,795 |
| 53,050 | 53,100 | 3,633 | 3,093 | 3,328 | 56,050 | 56,100 | 3,880 | 3,321 | 3,562 | 59,050 | 59,100 | 4,128 | 3,549 | 3,799 |
| 53,100 | 53,150 | 3,637 | 3,097 | 3,332 | 56,100 | 56,150 | 3,884 | 3,325 | 3,566 | 59,100 | 59,150 | 4,132 | 3,553 | 3,803 |
| 53,150 | 53,200 | 3,641 | 3,100 | 3,335 | 56,150 | 56,200 | 3,888 | 3,328 | 3,570 | 59,150 | 59,200 | 4,136 | 3,556 | 3,807 |
| 53,200 | 53,250 | 3,645 | 3,104 | 3,339 | 56,200 | 56,250 | 3,893 | 3,332 | 3,574 | 59,200 | 59,250 | 4,140 | 3,560 | 3,811 |
| 53,250 | 53,300 | 3,649 | 3,108 | 3,343 | 56,250 | 56,300 | 3,897 | 3,336 | 3,578 | 59,250 | 59,300 | 4,144 | 3,564 | 3,815 |
| 53,300 | 53,350 | 3,653 | 3,112 | 3,347 | 56,300 | 56,350 | 3,901 | 3,340 | 3,582 | 59,300 | 59,350 | 4,148 | 3,568 | 3,819 |
| 53,350 | 53,400 | 3,657 | 3,116 | 3,351 | 56,350 | 56,400 | 3,905 | 3,344 | 3,586 | 59,350 | 59,400 | 4,152 | 3,572 | 3,823 |
| 53,400 | 53,450 | 3,662 | 3,119 | 3,354 | 56,400 | 56,450 | 3,909 | 3,347 | 3,590 | 59,400 | 59,450 | 4,157 | 3,575 | 3,827 |
| 53,450 | 53,500 | 3,666 | 3,123 | 3,358 | 56,450 | 56,500 | 3,913 | 3,351 | 3,594 | 59,450 | 59,500 | 4,161 | 3,579 | 3,831 |
| 53,500 | 53,550 | 3,670 | 3,127 | 3,362 | 56,500 | 56,550 | 3,917 | 3,355 | 3,597 | 59,500 | 59,550 | 4,165 | 3,583 | 3,834 |
| 53,550 | 53,600 | 3,674 | 3,131 | 3,366 | 56,550 | 56,600 | 3,921 | 3,359 | 3,601 | 59,550 | 59,600 | 4,169 | 3,587 | 3,838 |
| 53,600 | 53,650 | 3,678 | 3,135 | 3,370 | 56,600 | 56,650 | 3,926 | 3,363 | 3,605 | 59,600 | 59,650 | 4,173 | 3,591 | 3,842 |
| 53,650 | 53,700 | 3,682 | 3,138 | 3,373 | 56,650 | 56,700 | 3,930 | 3,366 | 3,609 | 59,650 | 59,700 | 4,177 | 3,594 | 3,846 |
| 53,700 | 53,750 | 3,686 | 3,142 | 3,377 | 56,700 | 56,750 | 3,934 | 3,370 | 3,613 | 59,700 | 59,750 | 4,181 | 3,598 | 3,850 |
| 53,750 | 53,800 | 3,690 | 3,146 | 3,381 | 56,750 | 56,800 | 3,938 | 3,374 | 3,617 | 59,750 | 59,800 | 4,185 | 3,602 | 3,854 |
| 53,800 | 53,850 | 3,695 | 3,150 | 3,385 | 56,800 | 56,850 | 3,942 | 3,378 | 3,621 | 59,800 | 59,850 | 4,190 | 3,606 | 3,858 |
| 53,850 | 53,900 | 3,699 | 3,154 | 3,389 | 56,850 | 56,900 | 3,946 | 3,382 | 3,625 | 59,850 | 59,900 | 4,194 | 3,610 | 3,862 |
| 53,900 | 53,950 | 3,703 | 3,157 | 3,392 | 56,900 | 56,950 | 3,950 | 3,385 | 3,629 | 59,900 | 59,950 | 4,198 | 3,613 | 3,866 |
| 53,950 | 54,000 | 3,707 | 3,161 | 3,396 | 56,950 | 57,000 | 3,954 | 3,389 | 3,633 | 59,950 | 60,000 | 4,202 | 3,617 | 3,870 |
| **54,000** | | | | | **57,000** | | | | | **60,000** | | | | |
| 54,000 | 54,050 | 3,711 | 3,165 | 3,400 | 57,000 | 57,050 | 3,959 | 3,393 | 3,637 | 60,000 | 60,050 | 4,206 | 3,621 | 3,874 |
| 54,050 | 54,100 | 3,715 | 3,169 | 3,404 | 57,050 | 57,100 | 3,963 | 3,397 | 3,641 | 60,050 | 60,100 | 4,210 | 3,625 | 3,878 |
| 54,100 | 54,150 | 3,719 | 3,173 | 3,408 | 57,100 | 57,150 | 3,967 | 3,401 | 3,645 | 60,100 | 60,150 | 4,214 | 3,629 | 3,882 |
| 54,150 | 54,200 | 3,723 | 3,176 | 3,412 | 57,150 | 57,200 | 3,971 | 3,404 | 3,649 | 60,150 | 60,200 | 4,218 | 3,632 | 3,886 |
| 54,200 | 54,250 | 3,728 | 3,180 | 3,416 | 57,200 | 57,250 | 3,975 | 3,408 | 3,653 | 60,200 | 60,250 | 4,223 | 3,636 | 3,890 |
| 54,250 | 54,300 | 3,732 | 3,184 | 3,420 | 57,250 | 57,300 | 3,979 | 3,412 | 3,657 | 60,250 | 60,300 | 4,227 | 3,640 | 3,894 |
| 54,300 | 54,350 | 3,736 | 3,188 | 3,424 | 57,300 | 57,350 | 3,983 | 3,416 | 3,661 | 60,300 | 60,350 | 4,231 | 3,644 | 3,898 |
| 54,350 | 54,400 | 3,740 | 3,192 | 3,428 | 57,350 | 57,400 | 3,987 | 3,420 | 3,665 | 60,350 | 60,400 | 4,235 | 3,648 | 3,902 |
| 54,400 | 54,450 | 3,744 | 3,195 | 3,432 | 57,400 | 57,450 | 3,992 | 3,423 | 3,669 | 60,400 | 60,450 | 4,239 | 3,651 | 3,906 |
| 54,450 | 54,500 | 3,748 | 3,199 | 3,436 | 57,450 | 57,500 | 3,996 | 3,427 | 3,673 | 60,450 | 60,500 | 4,243 | 3,655 | 3,910 |
| 54,500 | 54,550 | 3,752 | 3,203 | 3,439 | 57,500 | 57,550 | 4,000 | 3,431 | 3,676 | 60,500 | 60,550 | 4,247 | 3,659 | 3,913 |
| 54,550 | 54,600 | 3,756 | 3,207 | 3,443 | 57,550 | 57,600 | 4,004 | 3,435 | 3,680 | 60,550 | 60,600 | 4,251 | 3,663 | 3,917 |
| 54,600 | 54,650 | 3,761 | 3,211 | 3,447 | 57,600 | 57,650 | 4,008 | 3,439 | 3,684 | 60,600 | 60,650 | 4,256 | 3,667 | 3,921 |
| 54,650 | 54,700 | 3,765 | 3,214 | 3,451 | 57,650 | 57,700 | 4,012 | 3,442 | 3,688 | 60,650 | 60,700 | 4,260 | 3,670 | 3,925 |
| 54,700 | 54,750 | 3,769 | 3,218 | 3,455 | 57,700 | 57,750 | 4,016 | 3,446 | 3,692 | 60,700 | 60,750 | 4,264 | 3,674 | 3,929 |
| 54,750 | 54,800 | 3,773 | 3,222 | 3,459 | 57,750 | 57,800 | 4,020 | 3,450 | 3,696 | 60,750 | 60,800 | 4,268 | 3,678 | 3,933 |
| 54,800 | 54,850 | 3,777 | 3,226 | 3,463 | 57,800 | 57,850 | 4,025 | 3,454 | 3,700 | 60,800 | 60,850 | 4,272 | 3,682 | 3,937 |
| 54,850 | 54,900 | 3,781 | 3,230 | 3,467 | 57,850 | 57,900 | 4,029 | 3,458 | 3,704 | 60,850 | 60,900 | 4,276 | 3,686 | 3,941 |
| 54,900 | 54,950 | 3,785 | 3,233 | 3,471 | 57,900 | 57,950 | 4,033 | 3,461 | 3,708 | 60,900 | 60,950 | 4,280 | 3,689 | 3,945 |
| 54,950 | 55,000 | 3,789 | 3,237 | 3,475 | 57,950 | 58,000 | 4,037 | 3,465 | 3,712 | 60,950 | 61,000 | 4,284 | 3,693 | 3,949 |

*This column must also be used by qualifying widow(er)

Continued on next page

## 2018 Hawaii Tax Table (continued)

| If line 26 (taxable income) is — At least | But less than | Single or Married filing separately | Married filing jointly * | Head of a household | If line 26 (taxable income) is — At least | But less than | Single or Married filing separately | Married filing jointly * | Head of a household | If line 26 (taxable income) is — At least | But less than | Single or Married filing separately | Married filing jointly * | Head of a household |
|---|---|---|---|---|---|---|---|---|---|---|---|---|---|---|
| **61,000** | | | | | **64,000** | | | | | **67,000** | | | | |
| 61,000 | 61,050 | 4,289 | 3,697 | 3,953 | 64,000 | 64,050 | 4,536 | 3,925 | 4,190 | 67,000 | 67,050 | 4,784 | 4,153 | 4,427 |
| 61,050 | 61,100 | 4,293 | 3,701 | 3,957 | 64,050 | 64,100 | 4,540 | 3,929 | 4,194 | 67,050 | 67,100 | 4,788 | 4,157 | 4,431 |
| 61,100 | 61,150 | 4,297 | 3,705 | 3,961 | 64,100 | 64,150 | 4,544 | 3,933 | 4,198 | 67,100 | 67,150 | 4,792 | 4,161 | 4,435 |
| 61,150 | 61,200 | 4,301 | 3,708 | 3,965 | 64,150 | 64,200 | 4,548 | 3,936 | 4,202 | 67,150 | 67,200 | 4,796 | 4,164 | 4,439 |
| 61,200 | 61,250 | 4,305 | 3,712 | 3,969 | 64,200 | 64,250 | 4,553 | 3,940 | 4,206 | 67,200 | 67,250 | 4,800 | 4,168 | 4,443 |
| 61,250 | 61,300 | 4,309 | 3,716 | 3,973 | 64,250 | 64,300 | 4,557 | 3,944 | 4,210 | 67,250 | 67,300 | 4,804 | 4,172 | 4,447 |
| 61,300 | 61,350 | 4,313 | 3,720 | 3,977 | 64,300 | 64,350 | 4,561 | 3,948 | 4,214 | 67,300 | 67,350 | 4,808 | 4,176 | 4,451 |
| 61,350 | 61,400 | 4,317 | 3,724 | 3,981 | 64,350 | 64,400 | 4,565 | 3,952 | 4,218 | 67,350 | 67,400 | 4,812 | 4,180 | 4,455 |
| 61,400 | 61,450 | 4,322 | 3,727 | 3,985 | 64,400 | 64,450 | 4,569 | 3,955 | 4,222 | 67,400 | 67,450 | 4,817 | 4,183 | 4,459 |
| 61,450 | 61,500 | 4,326 | 3,731 | 3,989 | 64,450 | 64,500 | 4,573 | 3,959 | 4,226 | 67,450 | 67,500 | 4,821 | 4,187 | 4,463 |
| 61,500 | 61,550 | 4,330 | 3,735 | 3,992 | 64,500 | 64,550 | 4,577 | 3,963 | 4,229 | 67,500 | 67,550 | 4,825 | 4,191 | 4,466 |
| 61,550 | 61,600 | 4,334 | 3,739 | 3,996 | 64,550 | 64,600 | 4,581 | 3,967 | 4,233 | 67,550 | 67,600 | 4,829 | 4,195 | 4,470 |
| 61,600 | 61,650 | 4,338 | 3,743 | 4,000 | 64,600 | 64,650 | 4,586 | 3,971 | 4,237 | 67,600 | 67,650 | 4,833 | 4,199 | 4,474 |
| 61,650 | 61,700 | 4,342 | 3,746 | 4,004 | 64,650 | 64,700 | 4,590 | 3,974 | 4,241 | 67,650 | 67,700 | 4,837 | 4,202 | 4,478 |
| 61,700 | 61,750 | 4,346 | 3,750 | 4,008 | 64,700 | 64,750 | 4,594 | 3,978 | 4,245 | 67,700 | 67,750 | 4,841 | 4,206 | 4,482 |
| 61,750 | 61,800 | 4,350 | 3,754 | 4,012 | 64,750 | 64,800 | 4,598 | 3,982 | 4,249 | 67,750 | 67,800 | 4,845 | 4,210 | 4,486 |
| 61,800 | 61,850 | 4,355 | 3,758 | 4,016 | 64,800 | 64,850 | 4,602 | 3,986 | 4,253 | 67,800 | 67,850 | 4,850 | 4,214 | 4,490 |
| 61,850 | 61,900 | 4,359 | 3,762 | 4,020 | 64,850 | 64,900 | 4,606 | 3,990 | 4,257 | 67,850 | 67,900 | 4,854 | 4,218 | 4,494 |
| 61,900 | 61,950 | 4,363 | 3,765 | 4,024 | 64,900 | 64,950 | 4,610 | 3,993 | 4,261 | 67,900 | 67,950 | 4,858 | 4,221 | 4,498 |
| 61,950 | 62,000 | 4,367 | 3,769 | 4,028 | 64,950 | 65,000 | 4,614 | 3,997 | 4,265 | 67,950 | 68,000 | 4,862 | 4,225 | 4,502 |
| **62,000** | | | | | **65,000** | | | | | **68,000** | | | | |
| 62,000 | 62,050 | 4,371 | 3,773 | 4,032 | 65,000 | 65,050 | 4,619 | 4,001 | 4,269 | 68,000 | 68,050 | 4,866 | 4,229 | 4,506 |
| 62,050 | 62,100 | 4,375 | 3,777 | 4,036 | 65,050 | 65,100 | 4,623 | 4,005 | 4,273 | 68,050 | 68,100 | 4,870 | 4,233 | 4,510 |
| 62,100 | 62,150 | 4,379 | 3,781 | 4,040 | 65,100 | 65,150 | 4,627 | 4,009 | 4,277 | 68,100 | 68,150 | 4,874 | 4,237 | 4,514 |
| 62,150 | 62,200 | 4,383 | 3,784 | 4,044 | 65,150 | 65,200 | 4,631 | 4,012 | 4,281 | 68,150 | 68,200 | 4,878 | 4,240 | 4,518 |
| 62,200 | 62,250 | 4,388 | 3,788 | 4,048 | 65,200 | 65,250 | 4,635 | 4,016 | 4,285 | 68,200 | 68,250 | 4,883 | 4,244 | 4,522 |
| 62,250 | 62,300 | 4,392 | 3,792 | 4,052 | 65,250 | 65,300 | 4,639 | 4,020 | 4,289 | 68,250 | 68,300 | 4,887 | 4,248 | 4,526 |
| 62,300 | 62,350 | 4,396 | 3,796 | 4,056 | 65,300 | 65,350 | 4,643 | 4,024 | 4,293 | 68,300 | 68,350 | 4,891 | 4,252 | 4,530 |
| 62,350 | 62,400 | 4,400 | 3,800 | 4,060 | 65,350 | 65,400 | 4,647 | 4,028 | 4,297 | 68,350 | 68,400 | 4,895 | 4,256 | 4,534 |
| 62,400 | 62,450 | 4,404 | 3,803 | 4,064 | 65,400 | 65,450 | 4,652 | 4,031 | 4,301 | 68,400 | 68,450 | 4,899 | 4,259 | 4,538 |
| 62,450 | 62,500 | 4,408 | 3,807 | 4,068 | 65,450 | 65,500 | 4,656 | 4,035 | 4,305 | 68,450 | 68,500 | 4,903 | 4,263 | 4,542 |
| 62,500 | 62,550 | 4,412 | 3,811 | 4,071 | 65,500 | 65,550 | 4,660 | 4,039 | 4,308 | 68,500 | 68,550 | 4,907 | 4,267 | 4,545 |
| 62,550 | 62,600 | 4,416 | 3,815 | 4,075 | 65,550 | 65,600 | 4,664 | 4,043 | 4,312 | 68,550 | 68,600 | 4,911 | 4,271 | 4,549 |
| 62,600 | 62,650 | 4,421 | 3,819 | 4,079 | 65,600 | 65,650 | 4,668 | 4,047 | 4,316 | 68,600 | 68,650 | 4,916 | 4,275 | 4,553 |
| 62,650 | 62,700 | 4,425 | 3,822 | 4,083 | 65,650 | 65,700 | 4,672 | 4,050 | 4,320 | 68,650 | 68,700 | 4,920 | 4,278 | 4,557 |
| 62,700 | 62,750 | 4,429 | 3,826 | 4,087 | 65,700 | 65,750 | 4,676 | 4,054 | 4,324 | 68,700 | 68,750 | 4,924 | 4,282 | 4,561 |
| 62,750 | 62,800 | 4,433 | 3,830 | 4,091 | 65,750 | 65,800 | 4,680 | 4,058 | 4,328 | 68,750 | 68,800 | 4,928 | 4,286 | 4,565 |
| 62,800 | 62,850 | 4,437 | 3,834 | 4,095 | 65,800 | 65,850 | 4,685 | 4,062 | 4,332 | 68,800 | 68,850 | 4,932 | 4,290 | 4,569 |
| 62,850 | 62,900 | 4,441 | 3,838 | 4,099 | 65,850 | 65,900 | 4,689 | 4,066 | 4,336 | 68,850 | 68,900 | 4,936 | 4,294 | 4,573 |
| 62,900 | 62,950 | 4,445 | 3,841 | 4,103 | 65,900 | 65,950 | 4,693 | 4,069 | 4,340 | 68,900 | 68,950 | 4,940 | 4,297 | 4,577 |
| 62,950 | 63,000 | 4,449 | 3,845 | 4,107 | 65,950 | 66,000 | 4,697 | 4,073 | 4,344 | 68,950 | 69,000 | 4,944 | 4,301 | 4,581 |
| **63,000** | | | | | **66,000** | | | | | **69,000** | | | | |
| 63,000 | 63,050 | 4,454 | 3,849 | 4,111 | 66,000 | 66,050 | 4,701 | 4,077 | 4,348 | 69,000 | 69,050 | 4,949 | 4,305 | 4,585 |
| 63,050 | 63,100 | 4,458 | 3,853 | 4,115 | 66,050 | 66,100 | 4,705 | 4,081 | 4,352 | 69,050 | 69,100 | 4,953 | 4,309 | 4,589 |
| 63,100 | 63,150 | 4,462 | 3,857 | 4,119 | 66,100 | 66,150 | 4,709 | 4,085 | 4,356 | 69,100 | 69,150 | 4,957 | 4,313 | 4,593 |
| 63,150 | 63,200 | 4,466 | 3,860 | 4,123 | 66,150 | 66,200 | 4,713 | 4,088 | 4,360 | 69,150 | 69,200 | 4,961 | 4,316 | 4,597 |
| 63,200 | 63,250 | 4,470 | 3,864 | 4,127 | 66,200 | 66,250 | 4,718 | 4,092 | 4,364 | 69,200 | 69,250 | 4,965 | 4,320 | 4,601 |
| 63,250 | 63,300 | 4,474 | 3,868 | 4,131 | 66,250 | 66,300 | 4,722 | 4,096 | 4,368 | 69,250 | 69,300 | 4,969 | 4,324 | 4,605 |
| 63,300 | 63,350 | 4,478 | 3,872 | 4,135 | 66,300 | 66,350 | 4,726 | 4,100 | 4,372 | 69,300 | 69,350 | 4,973 | 4,328 | 4,609 |
| 63,350 | 63,400 | 4,482 | 3,876 | 4,139 | 66,350 | 66,400 | 4,730 | 4,104 | 4,376 | 69,350 | 69,400 | 4,977 | 4,332 | 4,613 |
| 63,400 | 63,450 | 4,487 | 3,879 | 4,143 | 66,400 | 66,450 | 4,734 | 4,107 | 4,380 | 69,400 | 69,450 | 4,982 | 4,335 | 4,617 |
| 63,450 | 63,500 | 4,491 | 3,883 | 4,147 | 66,450 | 66,500 | 4,738 | 4,111 | 4,384 | 69,450 | 69,500 | 4,986 | 4,339 | 4,621 |
| 63,500 | 63,550 | 4,495 | 3,887 | 4,150 | 66,500 | 66,550 | 4,742 | 4,115 | 4,387 | 69,500 | 69,550 | 4,990 | 4,343 | 4,624 |
| 63,550 | 63,600 | 4,499 | 3,891 | 4,154 | 66,550 | 66,600 | 4,746 | 4,119 | 4,391 | 69,550 | 69,600 | 4,994 | 4,347 | 4,628 |
| 63,600 | 63,650 | 4,503 | 3,895 | 4,158 | 66,600 | 66,650 | 4,751 | 4,123 | 4,395 | 69,600 | 69,650 | 4,998 | 4,351 | 4,632 |
| 63,650 | 63,700 | 4,507 | 3,898 | 4,162 | 66,650 | 66,700 | 4,755 | 4,126 | 4,399 | 69,650 | 69,700 | 5,002 | 4,354 | 4,636 |
| 63,700 | 63,750 | 4,511 | 3,902 | 4,166 | 66,700 | 66,750 | 4,759 | 4,130 | 4,403 | 69,700 | 69,750 | 5,006 | 4,358 | 4,640 |
| 63,750 | 63,800 | 4,515 | 3,906 | 4,170 | 66,750 | 66,800 | 4,763 | 4,134 | 4,407 | 69,750 | 69,800 | 5,010 | 4,362 | 4,644 |
| 63,800 | 63,850 | 4,520 | 3,910 | 4,174 | 66,800 | 66,850 | 4,767 | 4,138 | 4,411 | 69,800 | 69,850 | 5,015 | 4,366 | 4,648 |
| 63,850 | 63,900 | 4,524 | 3,914 | 4,178 | 66,850 | 66,900 | 4,771 | 4,142 | 4,415 | 69,850 | 69,900 | 5,019 | 4,370 | 4,652 |
| 63,900 | 63,950 | 4,528 | 3,917 | 4,182 | 66,900 | 66,950 | 4,775 | 4,145 | 4,419 | 69,900 | 69,950 | 5,023 | 4,373 | 4,656 |
| 63,950 | 64,000 | 4,532 | 3,921 | 4,186 | 66,950 | 67,000 | 4,779 | 4,149 | 4,423 | 69,950 | 70,000 | 5,027 | 4,377 | 4,660 |

*This column must also be used by qualifying widow(er)

Continued on next page

## 2018 Hawaii Tax Table (continued)

| If line 26 (taxable income) is — At least | But less than | Single or Married filing separately | Married filing jointly * | Head of a household |
|---|---|---|---|---|
| **70,000** | | | | |
| 70,000 | 70,050 | 5,031 | 4,381 | 4,664 |
| 70,050 | 70,100 | 5,035 | 4,385 | 4,668 |
| 70,100 | 70,150 | 5,039 | 4,389 | 4,672 |
| 70,150 | 70,200 | 5,043 | 4,392 | 4,676 |
| 70,200 | 70,250 | 5,048 | 4,396 | 4,680 |
| 70,250 | 70,300 | 5,052 | 4,400 | 4,684 |
| 70,300 | 70,350 | 5,056 | 4,404 | 4,688 |
| 70,350 | 70,400 | 5,060 | 4,408 | 4,692 |
| 70,400 | 70,450 | 5,064 | 4,411 | 4,696 |
| 70,450 | 70,500 | 5,068 | 4,415 | 4,700 |
| 70,500 | 70,550 | 5,072 | 4,419 | 4,703 |
| 70,550 | 70,600 | 5,076 | 4,423 | 4,707 |
| 70,600 | 70,650 | 5,081 | 4,427 | 4,711 |
| 70,650 | 70,700 | 5,085 | 4,430 | 4,715 |
| 70,700 | 70,750 | 5,089 | 4,434 | 4,719 |
| 70,750 | 70,800 | 5,093 | 4,438 | 4,723 |
| 70,800 | 70,850 | 5,097 | 4,442 | 4,727 |
| 70,850 | 70,900 | 5,101 | 4,446 | 4,731 |
| 70,900 | 70,950 | 5,105 | 4,449 | 4,735 |
| 70,950 | 71,000 | 5,109 | 4,453 | 4,739 |
| **71,000** | | | | |
| 71,000 | 71,050 | 5,114 | 4,457 | 4,743 |
| 71,050 | 71,100 | 5,118 | 4,461 | 4,747 |
| 71,100 | 71,150 | 5,122 | 4,465 | 4,751 |
| 71,150 | 71,200 | 5,126 | 4,468 | 4,755 |
| 71,200 | 71,250 | 5,130 | 4,472 | 4,759 |
| 71,250 | 71,300 | 5,134 | 4,476 | 4,763 |
| 71,300 | 71,350 | 5,138 | 4,480 | 4,767 |
| 71,350 | 71,400 | 5,142 | 4,484 | 4,771 |
| 71,400 | 71,450 | 5,147 | 4,487 | 4,775 |
| 71,450 | 71,500 | 5,151 | 4,491 | 4,779 |
| 71,500 | 71,550 | 5,155 | 4,495 | 4,782 |
| 71,550 | 71,600 | 5,159 | 4,499 | 4,786 |
| 71,600 | 71,650 | 5,163 | 4,503 | 4,790 |
| 71,650 | 71,700 | 5,167 | 4,506 | 4,794 |
| 71,700 | 71,750 | 5,171 | 4,510 | 4,798 |
| 71,750 | 71,800 | 5,175 | 4,514 | 4,802 |
| 71,800 | 71,850 | 5,180 | 4,518 | 4,806 |
| 71,850 | 71,900 | 5,184 | 4,522 | 4,810 |
| 71,900 | 71,950 | 5,188 | 4,525 | 4,814 |
| 71,950 | 72,000 | 5,192 | 4,529 | 4,818 |
| **72,000** | | | | |
| 72,000 | 72,050 | 5,196 | 4,533 | 4,822 |
| 72,050 | 72,100 | 5,200 | 4,537 | 4,826 |
| 72,100 | 72,150 | 5,204 | 4,541 | 4,830 |
| 72,150 | 72,200 | 5,208 | 4,545 | 4,834 |
| 72,200 | 72,250 | 5,213 | 4,549 | 4,839 |
| 72,250 | 72,300 | 5,217 | 4,553 | 4,843 |
| 72,300 | 72,350 | 5,221 | 4,557 | 4,847 |
| 72,350 | 72,400 | 5,225 | 4,561 | 4,851 |
| 72,400 | 72,450 | 5,229 | 4,565 | 4,855 |
| 72,450 | 72,500 | 5,233 | 4,569 | 4,859 |
| 72,500 | 72,550 | 5,237 | 4,572 | 4,863 |
| 72,550 | 72,600 | 5,241 | 4,576 | 4,867 |
| 72,600 | 72,650 | 5,246 | 4,580 | 4,872 |
| 72,650 | 72,700 | 5,250 | 4,584 | 4,876 |
| 72,700 | 72,750 | 5,254 | 4,588 | 4,880 |
| 72,750 | 72,800 | 5,258 | 4,592 | 4,884 |
| 72,800 | 72,850 | 5,262 | 4,596 | 4,888 |
| 72,850 | 72,900 | 5,266 | 4,600 | 4,892 |
| 72,900 | 72,950 | 5,270 | 4,604 | 4,896 |
| 72,950 | 73,000 | 5,274 | 4,608 | 4,900 |

| If line 26 (taxable income) is — At least | But less than | Single or Married filing separately | Married filing jointly * | Head of a household |
|---|---|---|---|---|
| **73,000** | | | | |
| 73,000 | 73,050 | 5,279 | 4,612 | 4,905 |
| 73,050 | 73,100 | 5,283 | 4,616 | 4,909 |
| 73,100 | 73,150 | 5,287 | 4,620 | 4,913 |
| 73,150 | 73,200 | 5,291 | 4,624 | 4,917 |
| 73,200 | 73,250 | 5,295 | 4,628 | 4,921 |
| 73,250 | 73,300 | 5,299 | 4,632 | 4,925 |
| 73,300 | 73,350 | 5,303 | 4,636 | 4,929 |
| 73,350 | 73,400 | 5,307 | 4,640 | 4,933 |
| 73,400 | 73,450 | 5,312 | 4,644 | 4,938 |
| 73,450 | 73,500 | 5,316 | 4,648 | 4,942 |
| 73,500 | 73,550 | 5,320 | 4,651 | 4,946 |
| 73,550 | 73,600 | 5,324 | 4,655 | 4,950 |
| 73,600 | 73,650 | 5,328 | 4,659 | 4,954 |
| 73,650 | 73,700 | 5,332 | 4,663 | 4,958 |
| 73,700 | 73,750 | 5,336 | 4,667 | 4,962 |
| 73,750 | 73,800 | 5,340 | 4,671 | 4,966 |
| 73,800 | 73,850 | 5,345 | 4,675 | 4,971 |
| 73,850 | 73,900 | 5,349 | 4,679 | 4,975 |
| 73,900 | 73,950 | 5,353 | 4,683 | 4,979 |
| 73,950 | 74,000 | 5,357 | 4,687 | 4,983 |
| **74,000** | | | | |
| 74,000 | 74,050 | 5,361 | 4,691 | 4,987 |
| 74,050 | 74,100 | 5,365 | 4,695 | 4,991 |
| 74,100 | 74,150 | 5,369 | 4,699 | 4,995 |
| 74,150 | 74,200 | 5,373 | 4,703 | 4,999 |
| 74,200 | 74,250 | 5,378 | 4,707 | 5,004 |
| 74,250 | 74,300 | 5,382 | 4,711 | 5,008 |
| 74,300 | 74,350 | 5,386 | 4,715 | 5,012 |
| 74,350 | 74,400 | 5,390 | 4,719 | 5,016 |
| 74,400 | 74,450 | 5,394 | 4,723 | 5,020 |
| 74,450 | 74,500 | 5,398 | 4,727 | 5,024 |
| 74,500 | 74,550 | 5,402 | 4,730 | 5,028 |
| 74,550 | 74,600 | 5,406 | 4,734 | 5,032 |
| 74,600 | 74,650 | 5,411 | 4,738 | 5,037 |
| 74,650 | 74,700 | 5,415 | 4,742 | 5,041 |
| 74,700 | 74,750 | 5,419 | 4,746 | 5,045 |
| 74,750 | 74,800 | 5,423 | 4,750 | 5,049 |
| 74,800 | 74,850 | 5,427 | 4,754 | 5,053 |
| 74,850 | 74,900 | 5,431 | 4,758 | 5,057 |
| 74,900 | 74,950 | 5,435 | 4,762 | 5,061 |
| 74,950 | 75,000 | 5,439 | 4,766 | 5,065 |
| **75,000** | | | | |
| 75,000 | 75,050 | 5,444 | 4,770 | 5,070 |
| 75,050 | 75,100 | 5,448 | 4,774 | 5,074 |
| 75,100 | 75,150 | 5,452 | 4,778 | 5,078 |
| 75,150 | 75,200 | 5,456 | 4,782 | 5,082 |
| 75,200 | 75,250 | 5,460 | 4,786 | 5,086 |
| 75,250 | 75,300 | 5,464 | 4,790 | 5,090 |
| 75,300 | 75,350 | 5,468 | 4,794 | 5,094 |
| 75,350 | 75,400 | 5,472 | 4,798 | 5,098 |
| 75,400 | 75,450 | 5,477 | 4,802 | 5,103 |
| 75,450 | 75,500 | 5,481 | 4,806 | 5,107 |
| 75,500 | 75,550 | 5,485 | 4,809 | 5,111 |
| 75,550 | 75,600 | 5,489 | 4,813 | 5,115 |
| 75,600 | 75,650 | 5,493 | 4,817 | 5,119 |
| 75,650 | 75,700 | 5,497 | 4,821 | 5,123 |
| 75,700 | 75,750 | 5,501 | 4,825 | 5,127 |
| 75,750 | 75,800 | 5,505 | 4,829 | 5,131 |
| 75,800 | 75,850 | 5,510 | 4,833 | 5,136 |
| 75,850 | 75,900 | 5,514 | 4,837 | 5,140 |
| 75,900 | 75,950 | 5,518 | 4,841 | 5,144 |
| 75,950 | 76,000 | 5,522 | 4,845 | 5,148 |

| If line 26 (taxable income) is — At least | But less than | Single or Married filing separately | Married filing jointly * | Head of a household |
|---|---|---|---|---|
| **76,000** | | | | |
| 76,000 | 76,050 | 5,526 | 4,849 | 5,152 |
| 76,050 | 76,100 | 5,530 | 4,853 | 5,156 |
| 76,100 | 76,150 | 5,534 | 4,857 | 5,160 |
| 76,150 | 76,200 | 5,538 | 4,861 | 5,164 |
| 76,200 | 76,250 | 5,543 | 4,865 | 5,169 |
| 76,250 | 76,300 | 5,547 | 4,869 | 5,173 |
| 76,300 | 76,350 | 5,551 | 4,873 | 5,177 |
| 76,350 | 76,400 | 5,555 | 4,877 | 5,181 |
| 76,400 | 76,450 | 5,559 | 4,881 | 5,185 |
| 76,450 | 76,500 | 5,563 | 4,885 | 5,189 |
| 76,500 | 76,550 | 5,567 | 4,888 | 5,193 |
| 76,550 | 76,600 | 5,571 | 4,892 | 5,197 |
| 76,600 | 76,650 | 5,576 | 4,896 | 5,202 |
| 76,650 | 76,700 | 5,580 | 4,900 | 5,206 |
| 76,700 | 76,750 | 5,584 | 4,904 | 5,210 |
| 76,750 | 76,800 | 5,588 | 4,908 | 5,214 |
| 76,800 | 76,850 | 5,592 | 4,912 | 5,218 |
| 76,850 | 76,900 | 5,596 | 4,916 | 5,222 |
| 76,900 | 76,950 | 5,600 | 4,920 | 5,226 |
| 76,950 | 77,000 | 5,604 | 4,924 | 5,230 |
| **77,000** | | | | |
| 77,000 | 77,050 | 5,609 | 4,928 | 5,235 |
| 77,050 | 77,100 | 5,613 | 4,932 | 5,239 |
| 77,100 | 77,150 | 5,617 | 4,936 | 5,243 |
| 77,150 | 77,200 | 5,621 | 4,940 | 5,247 |
| 77,200 | 77,250 | 5,625 | 4,944 | 5,251 |
| 77,250 | 77,300 | 5,629 | 4,948 | 5,255 |
| 77,300 | 77,350 | 5,633 | 4,952 | 5,259 |
| 77,350 | 77,400 | 5,637 | 4,956 | 5,263 |
| 77,400 | 77,450 | 5,642 | 4,960 | 5,268 |
| 77,450 | 77,500 | 5,646 | 4,964 | 5,272 |
| 77,500 | 77,550 | 5,650 | 4,967 | 5,276 |
| 77,550 | 77,600 | 5,654 | 4,971 | 5,280 |
| 77,600 | 77,650 | 5,658 | 4,975 | 5,284 |
| 77,650 | 77,700 | 5,662 | 4,979 | 5,288 |
| 77,700 | 77,750 | 5,666 | 4,983 | 5,292 |
| 77,750 | 77,800 | 5,670 | 4,987 | 5,296 |
| 77,800 | 77,850 | 5,675 | 4,991 | 5,301 |
| 77,850 | 77,900 | 5,679 | 4,995 | 5,305 |
| 77,900 | 77,950 | 5,683 | 4,999 | 5,309 |
| 77,950 | 78,000 | 5,687 | 5,003 | 5,313 |
| **78,000** | | | | |
| 78,000 | 78,050 | 5,691 | 5,007 | 5,317 |
| 78,050 | 78,100 | 5,695 | 5,011 | 5,321 |
| 78,100 | 78,150 | 5,699 | 5,015 | 5,325 |
| 78,150 | 78,200 | 5,703 | 5,019 | 5,329 |
| 78,200 | 78,250 | 5,708 | 5,023 | 5,334 |
| 78,250 | 78,300 | 5,712 | 5,027 | 5,338 |
| 78,300 | 78,350 | 5,716 | 5,031 | 5,342 |
| 78,350 | 78,400 | 5,720 | 5,035 | 5,346 |
| 78,400 | 78,450 | 5,724 | 5,039 | 5,350 |
| 78,450 | 78,500 | 5,728 | 5,043 | 5,354 |
| 78,500 | 78,550 | 5,732 | 5,046 | 5,358 |
| 78,550 | 78,600 | 5,736 | 5,050 | 5,362 |
| 78,600 | 78,650 | 5,741 | 5,054 | 5,367 |
| 78,650 | 78,700 | 5,745 | 5,058 | 5,371 |
| 78,700 | 78,750 | 5,749 | 5,062 | 5,375 |
| 78,750 | 78,800 | 5,753 | 5,066 | 5,379 |
| 78,800 | 78,850 | 5,757 | 5,070 | 5,383 |
| 78,850 | 78,900 | 5,761 | 5,074 | 5,387 |
| 78,900 | 78,950 | 5,765 | 5,078 | 5,391 |
| 78,950 | 79,000 | 5,769 | 5,082 | 5,395 |

*This column must also be used by qualifying widow(er)

Continued on next page

## 2018 Hawaii Tax Table (continued)

| If line 26 (taxable income) is — | | And you are — | | |
|---|---|---|---|---|
| At least | But less than | Single or Married filing separately | Married filing jointly * | Head of a household |
| | | Your tax is — | | |
| **79,000** | | | | |
| 79,000 | 79,050 | 5,774 | 5,086 | 5,400 |
| 79,050 | 79,100 | 5,778 | 5,090 | 5,404 |
| 79,100 | 79,150 | 5,782 | 5,094 | 5,408 |
| 79,150 | 79,200 | 5,786 | 5,098 | 5,412 |
| 79,200 | 79,250 | 5,790 | 5,102 | 5,416 |
| 79,250 | 79,300 | 5,794 | 5,106 | 5,420 |
| 79,300 | 79,350 | 5,798 | 5,110 | 5,424 |
| 79,350 | 79,400 | 5,802 | 5,114 | 5,428 |
| 79,400 | 79,450 | 5,807 | 5,118 | 5,433 |
| 79,450 | 79,500 | 5,811 | 5,122 | 5,437 |
| 79,500 | 79,550 | 5,815 | 5,125 | 5,441 |
| 79,550 | 79,600 | 5,819 | 5,129 | 5,445 |
| 79,600 | 79,650 | 5,823 | 5,133 | 5,449 |
| 79,650 | 79,700 | 5,827 | 5,137 | 5,453 |
| 79,700 | 79,750 | 5,831 | 5,141 | 5,457 |
| 79,750 | 79,800 | 5,835 | 5,145 | 5,461 |
| 79,800 | 79,850 | 5,840 | 5,149 | 5,466 |
| 79,850 | 79,900 | 5,844 | 5,153 | 5,470 |
| 79,900 | 79,950 | 5,848 | 5,157 | 5,474 |
| 79,950 | 80,000 | 5,852 | 5,161 | 5,478 |
| **80,000** | | | | |
| 80,000 | 80,050 | 5,856 | 5,165 | 5,482 |
| 80,050 | 80,100 | 5,860 | 5,169 | 5,486 |
| 80,100 | 80,150 | 5,864 | 5,173 | 5,490 |
| 80,150 | 80,200 | 5,868 | 5,177 | 5,494 |
| 80,200 | 80,250 | 5,873 | 5,181 | 5,499 |
| 80,250 | 80,300 | 5,877 | 5,185 | 5,503 |
| 80,300 | 80,350 | 5,881 | 5,189 | 5,507 |
| 80,350 | 80,400 | 5,885 | 5,193 | 5,511 |
| 80,400 | 80,450 | 5,889 | 5,197 | 5,515 |
| 80,450 | 80,500 | 5,893 | 5,201 | 5,519 |
| 80,500 | 80,550 | 5,897 | 5,204 | 5,523 |
| 80,550 | 80,600 | 5,901 | 5,208 | 5,527 |
| 80,600 | 80,650 | 5,906 | 5,212 | 5,532 |
| 80,650 | 80,700 | 5,910 | 5,216 | 5,536 |
| 80,700 | 80,750 | 5,914 | 5,220 | 5,540 |
| 80,750 | 80,800 | 5,918 | 5,224 | 5,544 |
| 80,800 | 80,850 | 5,922 | 5,228 | 5,548 |
| 80,850 | 80,900 | 5,926 | 5,232 | 5,552 |
| 80,900 | 80,950 | 5,930 | 5,236 | 5,556 |
| 80,950 | 81,000 | 5,934 | 5,240 | 5,560 |
| **81,000** | | | | |
| 81,000 | 81,050 | 5,939 | 5,244 | 5,565 |
| 81,050 | 81,100 | 5,943 | 5,248 | 5,569 |
| 81,100 | 81,150 | 5,947 | 5,252 | 5,573 |
| 81,150 | 81,200 | 5,951 | 5,256 | 5,577 |
| 81,200 | 81,250 | 5,955 | 5,260 | 5,581 |
| 81,250 | 81,300 | 5,959 | 5,264 | 5,585 |
| 81,300 | 81,350 | 5,963 | 5,268 | 5,589 |
| 81,350 | 81,400 | 5,967 | 5,272 | 5,593 |
| 81,400 | 81,450 | 5,972 | 5,276 | 5,598 |
| 81,450 | 81,500 | 5,976 | 5,280 | 5,602 |
| 81,500 | 81,550 | 5,980 | 5,283 | 5,606 |
| 81,550 | 81,600 | 5,984 | 5,287 | 5,610 |
| 81,600 | 81,650 | 5,988 | 5,291 | 5,614 |
| 81,650 | 81,700 | 5,992 | 5,295 | 5,618 |
| 81,700 | 81,750 | 5,996 | 5,299 | 5,622 |
| 81,750 | 81,800 | 6,000 | 5,303 | 5,626 |
| 81,800 | 81,850 | 6,005 | 5,307 | 5,631 |
| 81,850 | 81,900 | 6,009 | 5,311 | 5,635 |
| 81,900 | 81,950 | 6,013 | 5,315 | 5,639 |
| 81,950 | 82,000 | 6,017 | 5,319 | 5,643 |

| If line 26 (taxable income) is — | | And you are — | | |
|---|---|---|---|---|
| At least | But less than | Single or Married filing separately | Married filing jointly * | Head of a household |
| | | Your tax is — | | |
| **82,000** | | | | |
| 82,000 | 82,050 | 6,021 | 5,323 | 5,647 |
| 82,050 | 82,100 | 6,025 | 5,327 | 5,651 |
| 82,100 | 82,150 | 6,029 | 5,331 | 5,655 |
| 82,150 | 82,200 | 6,033 | 5,335 | 5,659 |
| 82,200 | 82,250 | 6,038 | 5,339 | 5,664 |
| 82,250 | 82,300 | 6,042 | 5,343 | 5,668 |
| 82,300 | 82,350 | 6,046 | 5,347 | 5,672 |
| 82,350 | 82,400 | 6,050 | 5,351 | 5,676 |
| 82,400 | 82,450 | 6,054 | 5,355 | 5,680 |
| 82,450 | 82,500 | 6,058 | 5,359 | 5,684 |
| 82,500 | 82,550 | 6,062 | 5,362 | 5,688 |
| 82,550 | 82,600 | 6,066 | 5,366 | 5,692 |
| 82,600 | 82,650 | 6,071 | 5,370 | 5,697 |
| 82,650 | 82,700 | 6,075 | 5,374 | 5,701 |
| 82,700 | 82,750 | 6,079 | 5,378 | 5,705 |
| 82,750 | 82,800 | 6,083 | 5,382 | 5,709 |
| 82,800 | 82,850 | 6,087 | 5,386 | 5,713 |
| 82,850 | 82,900 | 6,091 | 5,390 | 5,717 |
| 82,900 | 82,950 | 6,095 | 5,394 | 5,721 |
| 82,950 | 83,000 | 6,099 | 5,398 | 5,725 |
| **83,000** | | | | |
| 83,000 | 83,050 | 6,104 | 5,402 | 5,730 |
| 83,050 | 83,100 | 6,108 | 5,406 | 5,734 |
| 83,100 | 83,150 | 6,112 | 5,410 | 5,738 |
| 83,150 | 83,200 | 6,116 | 5,414 | 5,742 |
| 83,200 | 83,250 | 6,120 | 5,418 | 5,746 |
| 83,250 | 83,300 | 6,124 | 5,422 | 5,750 |
| 83,300 | 83,350 | 6,128 | 5,426 | 5,754 |
| 83,350 | 83,400 | 6,132 | 5,430 | 5,758 |
| 83,400 | 83,450 | 6,137 | 5,434 | 5,763 |
| 83,450 | 83,500 | 6,141 | 5,438 | 5,767 |
| 83,500 | 83,550 | 6,145 | 5,441 | 5,771 |
| 83,550 | 83,600 | 6,149 | 5,445 | 5,775 |
| 83,600 | 83,650 | 6,153 | 5,449 | 5,779 |
| 83,650 | 83,700 | 6,157 | 5,453 | 5,783 |
| 83,700 | 83,750 | 6,161 | 5,457 | 5,787 |
| 83,750 | 83,800 | 6,165 | 5,461 | 5,791 |
| 83,800 | 83,850 | 6,170 | 5,465 | 5,796 |
| 83,850 | 83,900 | 6,174 | 5,469 | 5,800 |
| 83,900 | 83,950 | 6,178 | 5,473 | 5,804 |
| 83,950 | 84,000 | 6,182 | 5,477 | 5,808 |
| **84,000** | | | | |
| 84,000 | 84,050 | 6,186 | 5,481 | 5,812 |
| 84,050 | 84,100 | 6,190 | 5,485 | 5,816 |
| 84,100 | 84,150 | 6,194 | 5,489 | 5,820 |
| 84,150 | 84,200 | 6,198 | 5,493 | 5,824 |
| 84,200 | 84,250 | 6,203 | 5,497 | 5,829 |
| 84,250 | 84,300 | 6,207 | 5,501 | 5,833 |
| 84,300 | 84,350 | 6,211 | 5,505 | 5,837 |
| 84,350 | 84,400 | 6,215 | 5,509 | 5,841 |
| 84,400 | 84,450 | 6,219 | 5,513 | 5,845 |
| 84,450 | 84,500 | 6,223 | 5,517 | 5,849 |
| 84,500 | 84,550 | 6,227 | 5,520 | 5,853 |
| 84,550 | 84,600 | 6,231 | 5,524 | 5,857 |
| 84,600 | 84,650 | 6,236 | 5,528 | 5,862 |
| 84,650 | 84,700 | 6,240 | 5,532 | 5,866 |
| 84,700 | 84,750 | 6,244 | 5,536 | 5,870 |
| 84,750 | 84,800 | 6,248 | 5,540 | 5,874 |
| 84,800 | 84,850 | 6,252 | 5,544 | 5,878 |
| 84,850 | 84,900 | 6,256 | 5,548 | 5,882 |
| 84,900 | 84,950 | 6,260 | 5,552 | 5,886 |
| 84,950 | 85,000 | 6,264 | 5,556 | 5,890 |

| If line 26 (taxable income) is — | | And you are — | | |
|---|---|---|---|---|
| At least | But less than | Single or Married filing separately | Married filing jointly * | Head of a household |
| | | Your tax is — | | |
| **85,000** | | | | |
| 85,000 | 85,050 | 6,269 | 5,560 | 5,895 |
| 85,050 | 85,100 | 6,273 | 5,564 | 5,899 |
| 85,100 | 85,150 | 6,277 | 5,568 | 5,903 |
| 85,150 | 85,200 | 6,281 | 5,572 | 5,907 |
| 85,200 | 85,250 | 6,285 | 5,576 | 5,911 |
| 85,250 | 85,300 | 6,289 | 5,580 | 5,915 |
| 85,300 | 85,350 | 6,293 | 5,584 | 5,919 |
| 85,350 | 85,400 | 6,297 | 5,588 | 5,923 |
| 85,400 | 85,450 | 6,302 | 5,592 | 5,928 |
| 85,450 | 85,500 | 6,306 | 5,596 | 5,932 |
| 85,500 | 85,550 | 6,310 | 5,599 | 5,936 |
| 85,550 | 85,600 | 6,314 | 5,603 | 5,940 |
| 85,600 | 85,650 | 6,318 | 5,607 | 5,944 |
| 85,650 | 85,700 | 6,322 | 5,611 | 5,948 |
| 85,700 | 85,750 | 6,326 | 5,615 | 5,952 |
| 85,750 | 85,800 | 6,330 | 5,619 | 5,956 |
| 85,800 | 85,850 | 6,335 | 5,623 | 5,961 |
| 85,850 | 85,900 | 6,339 | 5,627 | 5,965 |
| 85,900 | 85,950 | 6,343 | 5,631 | 5,969 |
| 85,950 | 86,000 | 6,347 | 5,635 | 5,973 |
| **86,000** | | | | |
| 86,000 | 86,050 | 6,351 | 5,639 | 5,977 |
| 86,050 | 86,100 | 6,355 | 5,643 | 5,981 |
| 86,100 | 86,150 | 6,359 | 5,647 | 5,985 |
| 86,150 | 86,200 | 6,363 | 5,651 | 5,989 |
| 86,200 | 86,250 | 6,368 | 5,655 | 5,994 |
| 86,250 | 86,300 | 6,372 | 5,659 | 5,998 |
| 86,300 | 86,350 | 6,376 | 5,663 | 6,002 |
| 86,350 | 86,400 | 6,380 | 5,667 | 6,006 |
| 86,400 | 86,450 | 6,384 | 5,671 | 6,010 |
| 86,450 | 86,500 | 6,388 | 5,675 | 6,014 |
| 86,500 | 86,550 | 6,392 | 5,678 | 6,018 |
| 86,550 | 86,600 | 6,396 | 5,682 | 6,022 |
| 86,600 | 86,650 | 6,401 | 5,686 | 6,027 |
| 86,650 | 86,700 | 6,405 | 5,690 | 6,031 |
| 86,700 | 86,750 | 6,409 | 5,694 | 6,035 |
| 86,750 | 86,800 | 6,413 | 5,698 | 6,039 |
| 86,800 | 86,850 | 6,417 | 5,702 | 6,043 |
| 86,850 | 86,900 | 6,421 | 5,706 | 6,047 |
| 86,900 | 86,950 | 6,425 | 5,710 | 6,051 |
| 86,950 | 87,000 | 6,429 | 5,714 | 6,055 |
| **87,000** | | | | |
| 87,000 | 87,050 | 6,434 | 5,718 | 6,060 |
| 87,050 | 87,100 | 6,438 | 5,722 | 6,064 |
| 87,100 | 87,150 | 6,442 | 5,726 | 6,068 |
| 87,150 | 87,200 | 6,446 | 5,730 | 6,072 |
| 87,200 | 87,250 | 6,450 | 5,734 | 6,076 |
| 87,250 | 87,300 | 6,454 | 5,738 | 6,080 |
| 87,300 | 87,350 | 6,458 | 5,742 | 6,084 |
| 87,350 | 87,400 | 6,462 | 5,746 | 6,088 |
| 87,400 | 87,450 | 6,467 | 5,750 | 6,093 |
| 87,450 | 87,500 | 6,471 | 5,754 | 6,097 |
| 87,500 | 87,550 | 6,475 | 5,757 | 6,101 |
| 87,550 | 87,600 | 6,479 | 5,761 | 6,105 |
| 87,600 | 87,650 | 6,483 | 5,765 | 6,109 |
| 87,650 | 87,700 | 6,487 | 5,769 | 6,113 |
| 87,700 | 87,750 | 6,491 | 5,773 | 6,117 |
| 87,750 | 87,800 | 6,495 | 5,777 | 6,121 |
| 87,800 | 87,850 | 6,500 | 5,781 | 6,126 |
| 87,850 | 87,900 | 6,504 | 5,785 | 6,130 |
| 87,900 | 87,950 | 6,508 | 5,789 | 6,134 |
| 87,950 | 88,000 | 6,512 | 5,793 | 6,138 |

*This column must also be used by qualifying widow(er)

Continued on next page

## 2018 Hawaii Tax Table (continued)

| If line 26 (taxable income) is — At least | But less than | Single or Married filing separately | Married filing jointly * | Head of a household | If line 26 (taxable income) is — At least | But less than | Single or Married filing separately | Married filing jointly * | Head of a household | If line 26 (taxable income) is — At least | But less than | Single or Married filing separately | Married filing jointly * | Head of a household |
|---|---|---|---|---|---|---|---|---|---|---|---|---|---|---|
| **88,000** | | | | | **91,000** | | | | | **94,000** | | | | |
| 88,000 | 88,050 | 6,516 | 5,797 | 6,142 | 91,000 | 91,050 | 6,764 | 6,034 | 6,390 | 94,000 | 94,050 | 7,011 | 6,271 | 6,637 |
| 88,050 | 88,100 | 6,520 | 5,801 | 6,146 | 91,050 | 91,100 | 6,768 | 6,038 | 6,394 | 94,050 | 94,100 | 7,015 | 6,275 | 6,641 |
| 88,100 | 88,150 | 6,524 | 5,805 | 6,150 | 91,100 | 91,150 | 6,772 | 6,042 | 6,398 | 94,100 | 94,150 | 7,019 | 6,279 | 6,645 |
| 88,150 | 88,200 | 6,528 | 5,809 | 6,154 | 91,150 | 91,200 | 6,776 | 6,046 | 6,402 | 94,150 | 94,200 | 7,023 | 6,283 | 6,649 |
| 88,200 | 88,250 | 6,533 | 5,813 | 6,159 | 91,200 | 91,250 | 6,780 | 6,050 | 6,406 | 94,200 | 94,250 | 7,028 | 6,287 | 6,654 |
| 88,250 | 88,300 | 6,537 | 5,817 | 6,163 | 91,250 | 91,300 | 6,784 | 6,054 | 6,410 | 94,250 | 94,300 | 7,032 | 6,291 | 6,658 |
| 88,300 | 88,350 | 6,541 | 5,821 | 6,167 | 91,300 | 91,350 | 6,788 | 6,058 | 6,414 | 94,300 | 94,350 | 7,036 | 6,295 | 6,662 |
| 88,350 | 88,400 | 6,545 | 5,825 | 6,171 | 91,350 | 91,400 | 6,792 | 6,062 | 6,418 | 94,350 | 94,400 | 7,040 | 6,299 | 6,666 |
| 88,400 | 88,450 | 6,549 | 5,829 | 6,175 | 91,400 | 91,450 | 6,797 | 6,066 | 6,423 | 94,400 | 94,450 | 7,044 | 6,303 | 6,670 |
| 88,450 | 88,500 | 6,553 | 5,833 | 6,179 | 91,450 | 91,500 | 6,801 | 6,070 | 6,427 | 94,450 | 94,500 | 7,048 | 6,307 | 6,674 |
| 88,500 | 88,550 | 6,557 | 5,836 | 6,183 | 91,500 | 91,550 | 6,805 | 6,073 | 6,431 | 94,500 | 94,550 | 7,052 | 6,310 | 6,678 |
| 88,550 | 88,600 | 6,561 | 5,840 | 6,187 | 91,550 | 91,600 | 6,809 | 6,077 | 6,435 | 94,550 | 94,600 | 7,056 | 6,314 | 6,682 |
| 88,600 | 88,650 | 6,566 | 5,844 | 6,192 | 91,600 | 91,650 | 6,813 | 6,081 | 6,439 | 94,600 | 94,650 | 7,061 | 6,318 | 6,687 |
| 88,650 | 88,700 | 6,570 | 5,848 | 6,196 | 91,650 | 91,700 | 6,817 | 6,085 | 6,443 | 94,650 | 94,700 | 7,065 | 6,322 | 6,691 |
| 88,700 | 88,750 | 6,574 | 5,852 | 6,200 | 91,700 | 91,750 | 6,821 | 6,089 | 6,447 | 94,700 | 94,750 | 7,069 | 6,326 | 6,695 |
| 88,750 | 88,800 | 6,578 | 5,856 | 6,204 | 91,750 | 91,800 | 6,825 | 6,093 | 6,451 | 94,750 | 94,800 | 7,073 | 6,330 | 6,699 |
| 88,800 | 88,850 | 6,582 | 5,860 | 6,208 | 91,800 | 91,850 | 6,830 | 6,097 | 6,456 | 94,800 | 94,850 | 7,077 | 6,334 | 6,703 |
| 88,850 | 88,900 | 6,586 | 5,864 | 6,212 | 91,850 | 91,900 | 6,834 | 6,101 | 6,460 | 94,850 | 94,900 | 7,081 | 6,338 | 6,707 |
| 88,900 | 88,950 | 6,590 | 5,868 | 6,216 | 91,900 | 91,950 | 6,838 | 6,105 | 6,464 | 94,900 | 94,950 | 7,085 | 6,342 | 6,711 |
| 88,950 | 89,000 | 6,594 | 5,872 | 6,220 | 91,950 | 92,000 | 6,842 | 6,109 | 6,468 | 94,950 | 95,000 | 7,089 | 6,346 | 6,715 |
| **89,000** | | | | | **92,000** | | | | | **95,000** | | | | |
| 89,000 | 89,050 | 6,599 | 5,876 | 6,225 | 92,000 | 92,050 | 6,846 | 6,113 | 6,472 | 95,000 | 95,050 | 7,094 | 6,350 | 6,720 |
| 89,050 | 89,100 | 6,603 | 5,880 | 6,229 | 92,050 | 92,100 | 6,850 | 6,117 | 6,476 | 95,050 | 95,100 | 7,098 | 6,354 | 6,724 |
| 89,100 | 89,150 | 6,607 | 5,884 | 6,233 | 92,100 | 92,150 | 6,854 | 6,121 | 6,480 | 95,100 | 95,150 | 7,102 | 6,358 | 6,728 |
| 89,150 | 89,200 | 6,611 | 5,888 | 6,237 | 92,150 | 92,200 | 6,858 | 6,125 | 6,484 | 95,150 | 95,200 | 7,106 | 6,362 | 6,732 |
| 89,200 | 89,250 | 6,615 | 5,892 | 6,241 | 92,200 | 92,250 | 6,863 | 6,129 | 6,489 | 95,200 | 95,250 | 7,110 | 6,366 | 6,736 |
| 89,250 | 89,300 | 6,619 | 5,896 | 6,245 | 92,250 | 92,300 | 6,867 | 6,133 | 6,493 | 95,250 | 95,300 | 7,114 | 6,370 | 6,740 |
| 89,300 | 89,350 | 6,623 | 5,900 | 6,249 | 92,300 | 92,350 | 6,871 | 6,137 | 6,497 | 95,300 | 95,350 | 7,118 | 6,374 | 6,744 |
| 89,350 | 89,400 | 6,627 | 5,904 | 6,253 | 92,350 | 92,400 | 6,875 | 6,141 | 6,501 | 95,350 | 95,400 | 7,122 | 6,378 | 6,748 |
| 89,400 | 89,450 | 6,632 | 5,908 | 6,258 | 92,400 | 92,450 | 6,879 | 6,145 | 6,505 | 95,400 | 95,450 | 7,127 | 6,382 | 6,753 |
| 89,450 | 89,500 | 6,636 | 5,912 | 6,262 | 92,450 | 92,500 | 6,883 | 6,149 | 6,509 | 95,450 | 95,500 | 7,131 | 6,386 | 6,757 |
| 89,500 | 89,550 | 6,640 | 5,915 | 6,266 | 92,500 | 92,550 | 6,887 | 6,152 | 6,513 | 95,500 | 95,550 | 7,135 | 6,389 | 6,761 |
| 89,550 | 89,600 | 6,644 | 5,919 | 6,270 | 92,550 | 92,600 | 6,891 | 6,156 | 6,517 | 95,550 | 95,600 | 7,139 | 6,393 | 6,765 |
| 89,600 | 89,650 | 6,648 | 5,923 | 6,274 | 92,600 | 92,650 | 6,896 | 6,160 | 6,522 | 95,600 | 95,650 | 7,143 | 6,397 | 6,769 |
| 89,650 | 89,700 | 6,652 | 5,927 | 6,278 | 92,650 | 92,700 | 6,900 | 6,164 | 6,526 | 95,650 | 95,700 | 7,147 | 6,401 | 6,773 |
| 89,700 | 89,750 | 6,656 | 5,931 | 6,282 | 92,700 | 92,750 | 6,904 | 6,168 | 6,530 | 95,700 | 95,750 | 7,151 | 6,405 | 6,777 |
| 89,750 | 89,800 | 6,660 | 5,935 | 6,286 | 92,750 | 92,800 | 6,908 | 6,172 | 6,534 | 95,750 | 95,800 | 7,155 | 6,409 | 6,781 |
| 89,800 | 89,850 | 6,665 | 5,939 | 6,291 | 92,800 | 92,850 | 6,912 | 6,176 | 6,538 | 95,800 | 95,850 | 7,160 | 6,413 | 6,786 |
| 89,850 | 89,900 | 6,669 | 5,943 | 6,295 | 92,850 | 92,900 | 6,916 | 6,180 | 6,542 | 95,850 | 95,900 | 7,164 | 6,417 | 6,790 |
| 89,900 | 89,950 | 6,673 | 5,947 | 6,299 | 92,900 | 92,950 | 6,920 | 6,184 | 6,546 | 95,900 | 95,950 | 7,168 | 6,421 | 6,794 |
| 89,950 | 90,000 | 6,677 | 5,951 | 6,303 | 92,950 | 93,000 | 6,924 | 6,188 | 6,550 | 95,950 | 96,000 | 7,172 | 6,425 | 6,798 |
| **90,000** | | | | | **93,000** | | | | | **96,000** | | | | |
| 90,000 | 90,050 | 6,681 | 5,955 | 6,307 | 93,000 | 93,050 | 6,929 | 6,192 | 6,555 | 96,000 | 96,050 | 7,176 | 6,429 | 6,802 |
| 90,050 | 90,100 | 6,685 | 5,959 | 6,311 | 93,050 | 93,100 | 6,933 | 6,196 | 6,559 | 96,050 | 96,100 | 7,180 | 6,433 | 6,806 |
| 90,100 | 90,150 | 6,689 | 5,963 | 6,315 | 93,100 | 93,150 | 6,937 | 6,200 | 6,563 | 96,100 | 96,150 | 7,184 | 6,437 | 6,810 |
| 90,150 | 90,200 | 6,693 | 5,967 | 6,319 | 93,150 | 93,200 | 6,941 | 6,204 | 6,567 | 96,150 | 96,200 | 7,188 | 6,441 | 6,814 |
| 90,200 | 90,250 | 6,698 | 5,971 | 6,324 | 93,200 | 93,250 | 6,945 | 6,208 | 6,571 | 96,200 | 96,250 | 7,193 | 6,446 | 6,819 |
| 90,250 | 90,300 | 6,702 | 5,975 | 6,328 | 93,250 | 93,300 | 6,949 | 6,212 | 6,575 | 96,250 | 96,300 | 7,197 | 6,450 | 6,823 |
| 90,300 | 90,350 | 6,706 | 5,979 | 6,332 | 93,300 | 93,350 | 6,953 | 6,216 | 6,579 | 96,300 | 96,350 | 7,201 | 6,454 | 6,827 |
| 90,350 | 90,400 | 6,710 | 5,983 | 6,336 | 93,350 | 93,400 | 6,957 | 6,220 | 6,583 | 96,350 | 96,400 | 7,205 | 6,458 | 6,831 |
| 90,400 | 90,450 | 6,714 | 5,987 | 6,340 | 93,400 | 93,450 | 6,962 | 6,224 | 6,588 | 96,400 | 96,450 | 7,209 | 6,462 | 6,835 |
| 90,450 | 90,500 | 6,718 | 5,991 | 6,344 | 93,450 | 93,500 | 6,966 | 6,228 | 6,592 | 96,450 | 96,500 | 7,213 | 6,466 | 6,839 |
| 90,500 | 90,550 | 6,722 | 5,994 | 6,348 | 93,500 | 93,550 | 6,970 | 6,231 | 6,596 | 96,500 | 96,550 | 7,217 | 6,470 | 6,843 |
| 90,550 | 90,600 | 6,726 | 5,998 | 6,352 | 93,550 | 93,600 | 6,974 | 6,235 | 6,600 | 96,550 | 96,600 | 7,221 | 6,474 | 6,847 |
| 90,600 | 90,650 | 6,731 | 6,002 | 6,357 | 93,600 | 93,650 | 6,978 | 6,239 | 6,604 | 96,600 | 96,650 | 7,226 | 6,479 | 6,852 |
| 90,650 | 90,700 | 6,735 | 6,006 | 6,361 | 93,650 | 93,700 | 6,982 | 6,243 | 6,608 | 96,650 | 96,700 | 7,230 | 6,483 | 6,856 |
| 90,700 | 90,750 | 6,739 | 6,010 | 6,365 | 93,700 | 93,750 | 6,986 | 6,247 | 6,612 | 96,700 | 96,750 | 7,234 | 6,487 | 6,860 |
| 90,750 | 90,800 | 6,743 | 6,014 | 6,369 | 93,750 | 93,800 | 6,990 | 6,251 | 6,616 | 96,750 | 96,800 | 7,238 | 6,491 | 6,864 |
| 90,800 | 90,850 | 6,747 | 6,018 | 6,373 | 93,800 | 93,850 | 6,995 | 6,255 | 6,621 | 96,800 | 96,850 | 7,242 | 6,495 | 6,868 |
| 90,850 | 90,900 | 6,751 | 6,022 | 6,377 | 93,850 | 93,900 | 6,999 | 6,259 | 6,625 | 96,850 | 96,900 | 7,246 | 6,499 | 6,872 |
| 90,900 | 90,950 | 6,755 | 6,026 | 6,381 | 93,900 | 93,950 | 7,003 | 6,263 | 6,629 | 96,900 | 96,950 | 7,250 | 6,503 | 6,876 |
| 90,950 | 91,000 | 6,759 | 6,030 | 6,385 | 93,950 | 94,000 | 7,007 | 6,267 | 6,633 | 96,950 | 97,000 | 7,254 | 6,507 | 6,880 |

*This column must also be used by qualifying widow(er)

Continued on next page

**2018 Hawaii Tax Table (continued)**

| If line 26 (taxable income) is — | | And you are — | | | If line 26 (taxable income) is — | | And you are — | | | If line 26 (taxable income) is — | | And you are — | | |
|---|---|---|---|---|---|---|---|---|---|---|---|---|---|---|
| At least | But less than | Single or Married filing separately | Married filing jointly * | Head of a household | At least | But less than | Single or Married filing separately | Married filing jointly * | Head of a household | At least | But less than | Single or Married filing separately | Married filing jointly * | Head of a household |
| | | Your tax is — | | | | | Your tax is — | | | | | Your tax is — | | |
| **97,000** | | | | | **98,000** | | | | | **99,000** | | | | |
| 97,000 | 97,050 | 7,259 | 6,512 | 6,885 | 98,000 | 98,050 | 7,341 | 6,594 | 6,967 | 99,000 | 99,050 | 7,424 | 6,677 | 7,050 |
| 97,050 | 97,100 | 7,263 | 6,516 | 6,889 | 98,050 | 98,100 | 7,345 | 6,598 | 6,971 | 99,050 | 99,100 | 7,428 | 6,681 | 7,054 |
| 97,100 | 97,150 | 7,267 | 6,520 | 6,893 | 98,100 | 98,150 | 7,349 | 6,602 | 6,975 | 99,100 | 99,150 | 7,432 | 6,685 | 7,058 |
| 97,150 | 97,200 | 7,271 | 6,524 | 6,897 | 98,150 | 98,200 | 7,353 | 6,606 | 6,979 | 99,150 | 99,200 | 7,436 | 6,689 | 7,062 |
| 97,200 | 97,250 | 7,275 | 6,528 | 6,901 | 98,200 | 98,250 | 7,358 | 6,611 | 6,984 | 99,200 | 99,250 | 7,440 | 6,693 | 7,066 |
| 97,250 | 97,300 | 7,279 | 6,532 | 6,905 | 98,250 | 98,300 | 7,362 | 6,615 | 6,988 | 99,250 | 99,300 | 7,444 | 6,697 | 7,070 |
| 97,300 | 97,350 | 7,283 | 6,536 | 6,909 | 98,300 | 98,350 | 7,366 | 6,619 | 6,992 | 99,300 | 99,350 | 7,448 | 6,701 | 7,074 |
| 97,350 | 97,400 | 7,287 | 6,540 | 6,913 | 98,350 | 98,400 | 7,370 | 6,623 | 6,996 | 99,350 | 99,400 | 7,452 | 6,705 | 7,078 |
| 97,400 | 97,450 | 7,292 | 6,545 | 6,918 | 98,400 | 98,450 | 7,374 | 6,627 | 7,000 | 99,400 | 99,450 | 7,457 | 6,710 | 7,083 |
| 97,450 | 97,500 | 7,296 | 6,549 | 6,922 | 98,450 | 98,500 | 7,378 | 6,631 | 7,004 | 99,450 | 99,500 | 7,461 | 6,714 | 7,087 |
| 97,500 | 97,550 | 7,300 | 6,553 | 6,926 | 98,500 | 98,550 | 7,382 | 6,635 | 7,008 | 99,500 | 99,550 | 7,465 | 6,718 | 7,091 |
| 97,550 | 97,600 | 7,304 | 6,557 | 6,930 | 98,550 | 98,600 | 7,386 | 6,639 | 7,012 | 99,550 | 99,600 | 7,469 | 6,722 | 7,095 |
| 97,600 | 97,650 | 7,308 | 6,561 | 6,934 | 98,600 | 98,650 | 7,391 | 6,644 | 7,017 | 99,600 | 99,650 | 7,473 | 6,726 | 7,099 |
| 97,650 | 97,700 | 7,312 | 6,565 | 6,938 | 98,650 | 98,700 | 7,395 | 6,648 | 7,021 | 99,650 | 99,700 | 7,477 | 6,730 | 7,103 |
| 97,700 | 97,750 | 7,316 | 6,569 | 6,942 | 98,700 | 98,750 | 7,399 | 6,652 | 7,025 | 99,700 | 99,750 | 7,481 | 6,734 | 7,107 |
| 97,750 | 97,800 | 7,320 | 6,573 | 6,946 | 98,750 | 98,800 | 7,403 | 6,656 | 7,029 | 99,750 | 99,800 | 7,485 | 6,738 | 7,111 |
| 97,800 | 97,850 | 7,325 | 6,578 | 6,951 | 98,800 | 98,850 | 7,407 | 6,660 | 7,033 | 99,800 | 99,850 | 7,490 | 6,743 | 7,116 |
| 97,850 | 97,900 | 7,329 | 6,582 | 6,955 | 98,850 | 98,900 | 7,411 | 6,664 | 7,037 | 99,850 | 99,900 | 7,494 | 6,747 | 7,120 |
| 97,900 | 97,950 | 7,333 | 6,586 | 6,959 | 98,900 | 98,950 | 7,415 | 6,668 | 7,041 | 99,900 | 99,950 | 7,498 | 6,751 | 7,124 |
| 97,950 | 98,000 | 7,337 | 6,590 | 6,963 | 98,950 | 99,000 | 7,419 | 6,672 | 7,045 | 99,950 | 100,000 | 7,502 | 6,755 | 7,128 |

# 100,000 OR OVER —
# You MUST use the tax rate schedules.

*This column must also be used by qualifying widow(er)

# HAWAII INCOME TAX WITHHOLDING RATES, METHODS, AND TAX TABLES

**Effective January 1, 2013 and thereafter**

## PART 1
### ANNUALIZED INCOME TAX WITHHOLDING

## PART 2
### ALTERNATIVE METHOD OF COMPUTING TAX TO BE WITHHELD UNLESS THE ANNUALIZED METHOD OR WITHHOLDING TABLES ARE USED

## PART 3
### TAX TABLES FOR INCOME TAX WITHHOLDING

Employers using the Tax Tables in Part 3 of this appendix may disregard the formula methods shown in Part I and Part 2.

# WITHHOLDING FORMULAS EFFECTIVE
# JANUARY 1, 2013 AND THEREAFTER

## PART 1

### ANNUALIZED INCOME TAX WITHHOLDING

Annualized Income Tax Withholding: You may determine the tax to be withheld on the basis of annualized wages (using the tax computation method for annual payroll periods), then prorate the tax on the basis of the payroll period actually used. Employers with more than one payroll period (for instance, part-timers paid weekly; full-timers paid semi-monthly) may find this method helpful for conserving computer memory capacity. Only the annual rates below, wage brackets and allowance values need to be stored.

Example: An employee who is single and has only one job, is paid $375 a week. He claims three withholding allowances (one personal exemption, an allowance since he is single and has only one job, and an allowance for his estimated itemized deductions) on the Employee's Withholding Allowance and Status Certificate (Form HW-4) on file with you.

1. Multiply weekly wage of $375 x 52 weeks to determine annual wage ................................................ $ 19,500.00

2. Subtract withholding allowances ($1,144 x 3) ................................................................................... 3,432.00

3. Amount subject to withholding (line 1 minus line 2) ....................................................................... $ 16,068.00

4. Compute withholding tax on $16,068 using the WITHHOLDING TAX RATES below
   for a single person, annual payroll period:
   Tax on first $14,400 .......................................................................................................................... $ 682.00
   Tax on remaining $1,668 at 6.8% ...................................................................................................... 113.42
   Annual withholding tax ...................................................................................................................... $ 795.42

5. Compute Weekly withholding tax ($795.42 /52 weeks) ...................................................................... $ 15.30

### ANNUAL PAYROLL PERIOD

### A. SINGLE PERSONS — INCLUDING
### UNMARRIED HEADS OF HOUSEHOLD

If the amount of wages
(after subtracting withholding allowances) is:                The amount of income tax to be withheld shall be:

| Over | | But not over | | | |
|---|---|---|---|---|---|
| $ 0 | $ | 2,400 ...................................... | 1.40% of excess over | $ | 0 |
| $ 2,400 | $ | 4,800 ...................................... $ | 34.00 plus 3.20% of excess over | $ | 2,400 |
| $ 4,800 | $ | 9,600 ...................................... $ | 110.00 plus 5.50% of excess over | $ | 4,800 |
| $ 9,600 | $ | 14,400 ...................................... $ | 374.00 plus 6.40% of excess over | $ | 9,600 |
| $ 14,400 | $ | 19,200 ...................................... $ | 682.00 plus 6.80% of excess over | $ | 14,400 |
| $ 19,200 | $ | 24,000 ...................................... $ | 1,008.00 plus 7.20% of excess over | $ | 19,200 |
| $ 24,000 | $ | 36,000 ...................................... $ | 1,354.00 plus 7.60% of excess over | $ | 24,000 |
| $ 36,000 | | ...................................... $ | 2,266.00 plus 7.90% of excess over | $ | 36,000 |

### B. MARRIED PERSONS

If the amount of wages
(after subtracting withholding allowances) is:                The amount of income tax to be withheld shall be:

| Over | | But not over | | | |
|---|---|---|---|---|---|
| $ 0 | $ | 4,800 ...................................... | 1.40% of excess over | $ | 0 |
| $ 4,800 | $ | 9,600 ...................................... $ | 67.00 plus 3.20% of excess over | $ | 4,800 |
| $ 9,600 | $ | 19,200 ...................................... $ | 221.00 plus 5.50% of excess over | $ | 9,600 |
| $ 19,200 | $ | 28,800 ...................................... $ | 749.00 plus 6.40% of excess over | $ | 19,200 |
| $ 28,800 | $ | 38,400 ...................................... $ | 1,363.00 plus 6.80% of excess over | $ | 28,800 |
| $ 38,400 | $ | 48,000 ...................................... $ | 2,016.00 plus 7.20% of excess over | $ | 38,400 |
| $ 48,000 | $ | 72,000 ...................................... $ | 2,707.00 plus 7.60% of excess over | $ | 48,000 |
| $ 72,000 | | ...................................... $ | 4,531.00 plus 7.90% of excess over | $ | 72,000 |

# WITHHOLDING FORMULAS EFFECTIVE JANUARY 1, 2013

## PART 2

### ALTERNATIVE METHOD OF COMPUTING TAX TO BE WITHHELD, UNLESS THE ANNUALIZED METHOD OR WITHHOLDING TABLES ARE USED.

## WEEKLY PAYROLL PERIOD

If the period is weekly, proceed as follows:

Step 1.  Deduct from the total wage for the period an amount for the withholding allowance equal to the number of allowances claimed times $22.00.

    a.  If employee claims no allowance (zero), no deduction is made. The total wage is used in computing the amount of tax to be withheld.

    b.  If employee claims one allowance, deduct $22.00; if two, deduct $44.00; if three, deduct $66.00; and so forth.
       (If balance is negative, employee's wage is fully exempt).

Step 2.  Use the amount of wages arrived at in Step 1 to apply the rates shown in A & B below. If employee is single — unmarried head of household, A applies; if employee is married, B applies.

### A.  SINGLE PERSONS — INCLUDING UNMARRIED HEADS OF HOUSEHOLD

If the amount of wages
(after subtracting withholding allowances) is:   The amount of income tax to be withheld shall be:

| Over | But not over | | |
|---|---|---|---|
| $ 0 | $ 46 | 1.40% of excess over | $ 0 |
| $ 46 | $ 92 | .64 plus 3.20% of excess over | $ 46 |
| $ 92 | $ 185 | 2.11 plus 5.50% of excess over | $ 92 |
| $ 185 | $ 277 | 7.23 plus 6.40% of excess over | $ 185 |
| $ 277 | $ 369 | 13.12 plus 6.80% of excess over | $ 277 |
| $ 369 | $ 462 | 19.38 plus 7.20% of excess over | $ 369 |
| $ 462 | $ 692 | 26.08 plus 7.60% of excess over | $ 462 |
| $ 692 | | 43.56 plus 7.90% of excess over | $ 692 |

### B.  MARRIED PERSONS

If the amount of wages
(after subtracting withholding allowances) is:   The amount of income tax to be withheld shall be:

| Over | But not over | | |
|---|---|---|---|
| $ 0 | $ 92 | 1.40% of excess over | $ 0 |
| $ 92 | $ 185 | 1.29 plus 3.20% of excess over | $ 92 |
| $ 185 | $ 369 | 4.27 plus 5.50% of excess over | $ 185 |
| $ 369 | $ 554 | 14.39 plus 6.40% of excess over | $ 369 |
| $ 554 | $ 738 | 26.23 plus 6.80% of excess over | $ 554 |
| $ 738 | $ 923 | 38.74 plus 7.20% of excess over | $ 738 |
| $ 923 | $ 1,385 | 52.06 plus 7.60% of excess over | $ 923 |
| $ 1,385 | | 87.17 plus 7.90% of excess over | $ 1,385 |

# WITHHOLDING FORMULAS EFFECTIVE
# JANUARY 1, 2013

## BIWEEKLY PAYROLL PERIOD

If the period is biweekly, proceed as follows:

Step 1.    Deduct from the total wage for the period an amount for the withholding allowance equal to the number of
allowances claimed times $44.00.

    a.    If employee claims no allowance (zero), no deduction is made. The total wage is used in computing the
amount of tax to be withheld.

    b.    If employee claims one allowance, deduct $44.00; if two, deduct $88.00; if three, deduct $132.00; and so
forth. (If balance is negative, employee's wage is fully exempt).

Step 2.    Use the amount of wages arrived at in Step 1 to apply the rates shown in A & B below. If employee is single —
unmarried head of household, A applies; if employee is married, B applies.

## A. SINGLE PERSONS — INCLUDING UNMARRIED HEADS OF HOUSEHOLD

If the amount of wages
(after subtracting withholding allowances) is:                    The amount of income tax to be withheld shall be:

| Over | But not over | | |
|---|---|---|---|
| $ 0 | $ 92 | 1.40% of excess over | $ 0 |
| $ 92 | $ 185 | $ 1.29 plus 3.20% of excess over | $ 92 |
| $ 185 | $ 369 | $ 4.27 plus 5.50% of excess over | $ 185 |
| $ 369 | $ 554 | $ 14.39 plus 6.40% of excess over | $ 369 |
| $ 554 | $ 738 | $ 26.23 plus 6.80% of excess over | $ 554 |
| $ 738 | $ 923 | $ 38.74 plus 7.20% of excess over | $ 738 |
| $ 923 | $ 1,385 | $ 52.06 plus 7.60% of excess over | $ 923 |
| $ 1,385 | | $ 87.17 plus 7.90% of excess over | $ 1,385 |

## B. MARRIED PERSONS

If the amount of wages
(after subtracting withholding allowances) is:                    The amount of income tax to be withheld shall be:

| Over | But not over | | |
|---|---|---|---|
| $ 0 | $ 185 | 1.40% of excess over | $ 0 |
| $ 185 | $ 369 | $ 2.59 plus 3.20% of excess over | $ 185 |
| $ 369 | $ 738 | $ 8.48 plus 5.50% of excess over | $ 369 |
| $ 738 | $ 1,108 | $ 28.78 plus 6.40% of excess over | $ 738 |
| $ 1,108 | $ 1,477 | $ 52.46 plus 6.80% of excess over | $ 1,108 |
| $ 1,477 | $ 1,846 | $ 77.55 plus 7.20% of excess over | $ 1,477 |
| $ 1,846 | $ 2,769 | $ 104.12 plus 7.60% of excess over | $ 1,846 |
| $ 2,769 | | $ 174.27 plus 7.90% of excess over | $ 2,769 |

# WITHHOLDING FORMULAS EFFECTIVE
# JANUARY 1, 2013

## SEMIMONTHLY PAYROLL PERIOD

If the period is semimonthly, proceed as follows:

Step 1.    Deduct from the total wage for the period an amount for the withholding allowance equal to the number of allowances claimed times $47.65.

      a.    If employee claims no allowance (zero), no deduction is made. The total wage is used in computing the amount of tax to be withheld.

      b.    If employee claims one allowance, deduct $47.65; if two, deduct $95.30; if three, deduct $142.95; and so forth. (If balance is negative, employee's wage is fully exempt).

Step 2.    Use the amount of wages arrived at in Step 1 to apply the rates shown in A & B below. If employee is single — unmarried head of household, A applies; if employee is married, B applies.

### A. SINGLE PERSONS — INCLUDING UNMARRIED HEADS OF HOUSEHOLD

If the amount of wages
(after subtracting withholding allowances) is:

| Over | | But not over | | The amount of income tax to be withheld shall be: | | |
|---|---|---|---|---|---|---|
| $ | 0 | $ | 100 | 1.40% of excess over | $ | 0 |
| $ | 100 | $ | 200 | 1.40 plus 3.20% of excess over | $ | 100 |
| $ | 200 | $ | 400 | 4.60 plus 5.50% of excess over | $ | 200 |
| $ | 400 | $ | 600 | 15.60 plus 6.40% of excess over | $ | 400 |
| $ | 600 | $ | 800 | 28.40 plus 6.80% of excess over | $ | 600 |
| $ | 800 | $ | 1,000 | 42.00 plus 7.20% of excess over | $ | 800 |
| $ | 1,000 | $ | 1,500 | 56.40 plus 7.60% of excess over | $ | 1,000 |
| $ | 1,500 | | | 94.40 plus 7.90% of excess over | $ | 1,500 |

### B. MARRIED PERSONS

If the amount of wages
(after subtracting withholding allowances) is:

| Over | | But not over | | The amount of income tax to be withheld shall be: | | |
|---|---|---|---|---|---|---|
| $ | 0 | $ | 200 | 1.40% of excess over | $ | 0 |
| $ | 200 | $ | 400 | 2.80 plus 3.20% of excess over | $ | 200 |
| $ | 400 | $ | 800 | 9.20 plus 5.50% of excess over | $ | 400 |
| $ | 800 | $ | 1,200 | 31.20 plus 6.40% of excess over | $ | 800 |
| $ | 1,200 | $ | 1,600 | 56.80 plus 6.80% of excess over | $ | 1,200 |
| $ | 1,600 | $ | 2,000 | 84.00 plus 7.20% of excess over | $ | 1,600 |
| $ | 2,000 | $ | 3,000 | 112.80 plus 7.60% of excess over | $ | 2,000 |
| $ | 3,000 | | | 188.80 plus 7.90% of excess over | $ | 3,000 |

# WITHHOLDING FORMULAS EFFECTIVE JANUARY 1, 2013

## MONTHLY PAYROLL PERIOD

If the period is monthly, proceed as follows:

Step 1.     Deduct from the total wage for the period an amount for the withholding allowance equal to the number of allowances claimed times $95.35.

   a.   If employee claims no allowance (zero), no deduction is made. The total wage is used in computing the amount of tax to be withheld.

   b.   If employee claims one allowance, deduct $95.35; if two, deduct $190.70; if three, deduct $286.05; and so forth. (If balance is negative, employee's wage is fully exempt).

Step 2.     Use the amount of wages arrived at in Step 1 to apply the rates shown in A & B below. If employee is single — unmarried head of household, A applies; if employee is married, B applies.

## A. SINGLE PERSONS — INCLUDING UNMARRIED HEADS OF HOUSEHOLD

If the amount of wages
(after subtracting withholding allowances) is:          The amount of income tax to be withheld shall be:

| Over | But not over | | |
|---|---|---|---|
| $ 0 | $ 200 | 1.40% of excess over | $ 0 |
| $ 200 | $ 400 | $ 2.80 plus 3.20% of excess over | $ 200 |
| $ 400 | $ 800 | $ 9.20 plus 5.50% of excess over | $ 400 |
| $ 800 | $ 1,200 | $ 31.20 plus 6.40% of excess over | $ 800 |
| $ 1,200 | $ 1,600 | $ 56.80 plus 6.80% of excess over | $ 1,200 |
| $ 1,600 | $ 2,000 | $ 84.00 plus 7.20% of excess over | $ 1,600 |
| $ 2,000 | $ 3,000 | $ 112.80 plus 7.60% of excess over | $ 2,000 |
| $ 3,000 | | $ 188.80 plus 7.90% of excess over | $ 3,000 |

## B. MARRIED PERSONS

If the amount of wages
(after subtracting withholding allowances) is:          The amount of income tax to be withheld shall be:

| Over | But not over | | |
|---|---|---|---|
| $ 0 | $ 400 | 1.40% of excess over | $ 0 |
| $ 400 | $ 800 | $ 5.60 plus 3.20% of excess over | $ 400 |
| $ 800 | $ 1,600 | $ 18.40 plus 5.50% of excess over | $ 800 |
| $ 1,600 | $ 2,400 | $ 62.40 plus 6.40% of excess over | $ 1,600 |
| $ 2,400 | $ 3,200 | $ 113.60 plus 6.80% of excess over | $ 2,400 |
| $ 3,200 | $ 4,000 | $ 168.00 plus 7.20% of excess over | $ 3,200 |
| $ 4,000 | $ 6,000 | $ 225.60 plus 7.60% of excess over | $ 4,000 |
| $ 6,000 | | $ 377.60 plus 7.90% of excess over | $ 6,000 |

# WITHHOLDING FORMULAS EFFECTIVE
# JANUARY 1, 2013

## DAILY OR MISCELLANEOUS PAYROLL PERIOD

If the period is daily or miscellaneous, or if there is no payroll period (refer to section 13) using the daily wage, or the average wage per day, as instructed, proceed as follows:

Step 1.   Deduct from the total wage for the period an amount for the withholding allowance equal to the number of allowances claimed times $3.15.

    a.   If employee claims no allowance (zero), no deduction is made. The total wage is used in computing the amount of tax to be withheld.

    b.   If employee claims one allowance, deduct $3.15; if two, deduct $6.30; if three, deduct $9.45; and so forth. (If balance is negative, employee's wage is fully exempt).

Step 2.   Use the amount of wages arrived at in Step 1 to apply the rates shown in A & B below. If employee is single — unmarried head of household, A applies; if employee is married, B applies.

## A. SINGLE PERSONS — INCLUDING UNMARRIED HEADS OF HOUSEHOLD

If the amount of wages
(after subtracting withholding allowances) is:    The amount of income tax to be withheld shall be:

| Over | | But not over | | The amount of income tax to be withheld shall be: | | |
|---|---|---|---|---|---|---|
| $ | 0 | $ | 7 | 1.40% of excess over | $ | 0 |
| $ | 7 | $ | 13 | .10 plus 3.20% of excess over | $ | 7 |
| $ | 13 | $ | 26 | .29 plus 5.50% of excess over | $ | 13 |
| $ | 26 | $ | 39 | 1.01 plus 6.40% of excess over | $ | 26 |
| $ | 39 | $ | 53 | 1.84 plus 6.80% of excess over | $ | 39 |
| $ | 53 | $ | 66 | 2.79 plus 7.20% of excess over | $ | 53 |
| $ | 66 | $ | 99 | 3.73 plus 7.60% of excess over | $ | 66 |
| $ | 99 | $ | | 6.24 plus 7.90% of excess over | $ | 99 |

## B. MARRIED PERSONS

If the amount of wages
(after subtracting withholding allowances) is:    The amount of income tax to be withheld shall be:

| Over | | But not over | | The amount of income tax to be withheld shall be: | | |
|---|---|---|---|---|---|---|
| $ | 0 | $ | 13 | 1.40% of excess over | $ | 0 |
| $ | 13 | $ | 26 | .18 plus 3.20% of excess over | $ | 13 |
| $ | 26 | $ | 53 | .60 plus 5.50% of excess over | $ | 26 |
| $ | 53 | $ | 79 | 2.09 plus 6.40% of excess over | $ | 53 |
| $ | 79 | $ | 105 | 3.75 plus 6.80% of excess over | $ | 79 |
| $ | 105 | $ | 132 | 5.52 plus 7.20% of excess over | $ | 105 |
| $ | 132 | $ | 197 | 7.46 plus 7.60% of excess over | $ | 132 |
| $ | 197 | $ | | 12.40 plus 7.90% of excess over | $ | 197 |

# WITHHOLDING TABLES EFFECTIVE
# JANUARY 1, 2013

## PART 3
## TAX TABLES FOR INCOME TAX WITHHOLDING

*Weekly* PAYROLL PERIOD

For Calendar Years 2013, and thereafter

*Single* PERSONS — UNMARRIED *Heads of Household*

| WAGES ARE | | NUMBER OF WITHHOLDING ALLOWANCES CLAIMED | | | | | | | | | | |
|---|---|---|---|---|---|---|---|---|---|---|---|---|
| AT LEAST | BUT LESS THAN | 0 | 1 | 2 | 3 | 4 | 5 | 6 | 7 | 8 | 9 | 10 or more |
| | | AMOUNT OF INCOME TAX TO BE WITHHELD | | | | | | | | | | |
| 0 | 40 | 0 | 0 | 0 | 0 | 0 | 0 | 0 | 0 | 0 | 0 | 0 |
| 40 | 60 | 1 | 0 | 0 | 0 | 0 | 0 | 0 | 0 | 0 | 0 | 0 |
| 60 | 80 | 1 | 1 | 0 | 0 | 0 | 0 | 0 | 0 | 0 | 0 | 0 |
| 80 | 100 | 2 | 1 | 1 | 0 | 0 | 0 | 0 | 0 | 0 | 0 | 0 |
| 100 | 120 | 3 | 2 | 1 | 1 | 0 | 0 | 0 | 0 | 0 | 0 | 0 |
| 120 | 140 | 4 | 3 | 2 | 1 | 1 | 0 | 0 | 0 | 0 | 0 | 0 |
| 140 | 160 | 5 | 4 | 3 | 2 | 1 | 1 | 0 | 0 | 0 | 0 | 0 |
| 160 | 180 | 6 | 5 | 4 | 3 | 2 | 1 | 1 | 0 | 0 | 0 | 0 |
| 180 | 200 | 8 | 6 | 5 | 4 | 3 | 2 | 1 | 1 | 0 | 0 | 0 |
| 200 | 220 | 9 | 7 | 6 | 5 | 4 | 3 | 2 | 1 | 0 | 0 | 0 |
| 220 | 240 | 10 | 9 | 7 | 6 | 5 | 4 | 2 | 2 | 1 | 0 | 0 |
| 240 | 260 | 11 | 10 | 9 | 7 | 6 | 5 | 4 | 2 | 2 | 1 | 0 |
| 260 | 280 | 13 | 11 | 10 | 8 | 7 | 6 | 5 | 3 | 2 | 1 | 1 |
| 280 | 300 | 14 | 13 | 11 | 10 | 8 | 7 | 6 | 5 | 3 | 2 | 1 |
| 300 | 320 | 15 | 14 | 12 | 11 | 10 | 8 | 7 | 6 | 4 | 3 | 2 |
| 320 | 340 | 17 | 15 | 14 | 12 | 11 | 9 | 8 | 7 | 6 | 4 | 3 |
| 340 | 360 | 18 | 17 | 15 | 14 | 12 | 11 | 9 | 8 | 7 | 5 | 4 |
| 360 | 380 | 19 | 18 | 16 | 15 | 13 | 12 | 11 | 9 | 8 | 7 | 5 |
| 380 | 400 | 21 | 19 | 18 | 16 | 15 | 13 | 12 | 10 | 9 | 8 | 6 |
| 400 | 420 | 22 | 21 | 19 | 18 | 16 | 15 | 13 | 12 | 10 | 9 | 8 |
| 420 | 440 | 24 | 22 | 21 | 19 | 18 | 16 | 15 | 13 | 12 | 10 | 9 |
| 440 | 460 | 25 | 24 | 22 | 20 | 19 | 17 | 16 | 14 | 13 | 12 | 10 |
| 460 | 480 | 27 | 25 | 23 | 22 | 20 | 19 | 17 | 16 | 14 | 13 | 11 |
| 480 | 500 | 28 | 27 | 25 | 23 | 22 | 20 | 19 | 17 | 16 | 14 | 13 |
| 500 | 520 | 30 | 28 | 26 | 25 | 23 | 22 | 20 | 18 | 17 | 16 | 14 |

# WITHHOLDING TABLES EFFECTIVE
# JANUARY 1, 2013

### *Weekly* PAYROLL PERIOD

### For Calendar Years 2013, and thereafter

### *Single* PERSONS — UNMARRIED *Heads of Household*

| WAGES ARE | | NUMBER OF WITHHOLDING ALLOWANCES CLAIMED | | | | | | | | | | |
|---|---|---|---|---|---|---|---|---|---|---|---|---|
| AT LEAST | BUT LESS THAN | 0 | 1 | 2 | 3 | 4 | 5 | 6 | 7 | 8 | 9 | 10 or more |
| | | AMOUNT OF INCOME TAX TO BE WITHHELD | | | | | | | | | | |
| 520 | 540 | 31 | 30 | 28 | 26 | 25 | 23 | 21 | 20 | 18 | 17 | 15 |
| 540 | 560 | 33 | 31 | 29 | 28 | 26 | 24 | 23 | 21 | 20 | 18 | 17 |
| 560 | 580 | 34 | 33 | 31 | 29 | 28 | 26 | 24 | 23 | 21 | 20 | 18 |
| 580 | 600 | 36 | 34 | 32 | 31 | 29 | 27 | 26 | 24 | 23 | 21 | 19 |
| 600 | 620 | 37 | 36 | 34 | 32 | 31 | 29 | 27 | 26 | 24 | 22 | 21 |
| 620 | 640 | 39 | 37 | 36 | 34 | 32 | 30 | 29 | 27 | 26 | 24 | 22 |
| 640 | 660 | 40 | 39 | 37 | 35 | 34 | 32 | 30 | 29 | 27 | 25 | 24 |
| 660 | 680 | 42 | 40 | 39 | 37 | 35 | 34 | 32 | 30 | 29 | 27 | 25 |
| 680 | 700 | 43 | 42 | 40 | 38 | 37 | 35 | 33 | 32 | 30 | 28 | 27 |
| 700 | 720 | 45 | 43 | 42 | 40 | 38 | 37 | 35 | 33 | 32 | 30 | 28 |
| 720 | 740 | 47 | 45 | 43 | 41 | 40 | 38 | 36 | 35 | 33 | 31 | 30 |
| 740 | 760 | 48 | 46 | 45 | 43 | 41 | 40 | 38 | 36 | 35 | 33 | 31 |
| 760 | 780 | 50 | 48 | 46 | 45 | 43 | 41 | 39 | 38 | 36 | 34 | 33 |
| 780 | 800 | 51 | 50 | 48 | 46 | 44 | 43 | 41 | 39 | 38 | 36 | 34 |
| 800 | 820 | 53 | 51 | 49 | 48 | 46 | 44 | 42 | 41 | 39 | 37 | 36 |
| 820 | 840 | 54 | 53 | 51 | 49 | 48 | 46 | 44 | 42 | 41 | 39 | 37 |
| 840 | 860 | 56 | 54 | 53 | 51 | 49 | 47 | 46 | 44 | 42 | 41 | 39 |
| 860 | 880 | 58 | 56 | 54 | 52 | 51 | 49 | 47 | 45 | 44 | 42 | 40 |
| 880 | 900 | 59 | 57 | 56 | 54 | 52 | 51 | 49 | 47 | 45 | 44 | 42 |
| 900 | 920 | 61 | 59 | 57 | 56 | 54 | 52 | 50 | 49 | 47 | 45 | 43 |
| | | 7.90% of excess over $920 plus | | | | | | | | | | |
| 920 | & over | 62 | 61 | 59 | 57 | 55 | 54 | 52 | 50 | 48 | 47 | 45 |

# WITHHOLDING TABLES EFFECTIVE
# JANUARY 1, 2013

### *Weekly* PAYROLL PERIOD
### For Calendar Years 2013, and thereafter
### *Married* PERSONS

| WAGES ARE | | NUMBER OF WITHHOLDING ALLOWANCES CLAIMED | | | | | | | | | | |
| AT LEAST | BUT LESS THAN | 0 | 1 | 2 | 3 | 4 | 5 | 6 | 7 | 8 | 9 | 10 or more |
|---|---|---|---|---|---|---|---|---|---|---|---|---|
| | | AMOUNT OF INCOME TAX TO BE WITHHELD | | | | | | | | | | |
| 0 | 40 | 0 | 0 | 0 | 0 | 0 | 0 | 0 | 0 | 0 | 0 | 0 |
| 40 | 60 | 1 | 0 | 0 | 0 | 0 | 0 | 0 | 0 | 0 | 0 | 0 |
| 60 | 80 | 1 | 1 | 0 | 0 | 0 | 0 | 0 | 0 | 0 | 0 | 0 |
| 80 | 100 | 1 | 1 | 1 | 0 | 0 | 0 | 0 | 0 | 0 | 0 | 0 |
| 100 | 120 | 2 | 1 | 1 | 1 | 0 | 0 | 0 | 0 | 0 | 0 | 0 |
| 120 | 140 | 3 | 2 | 1 | 1 | 1 | 0 | 0 | 0 | 0 | 0 | 0 |
| 140 | 160 | 3 | 2 | 2 | 1 | 1 | 1 | 0 | 0 | 0 | 0 | 0 |
| 160 | 180 | 4 | 3 | 2 | 2 | 1 | 1 | 1 | 0 | 0 | 0 | 0 |
| 180 | 200 | 5 | 4 | 3 | 2 | 2 | 1 | 1 | 1 | 0 | 0 | 0 |
| 200 | 220 | 6 | 4 | 4 | 3 | 2 | 2 | 1 | 1 | 0 | 0 | 0 |
| 220 | 240 | 7 | 6 | 4 | 4 | 3 | 2 | 1 | 1 | 1 | 0 | 0 |
| 240 | 260 | 8 | 7 | 5 | 4 | 4 | 3 | 2 | 1 | 1 | 1 | 0 |
| 260 | 280 | 9 | 8 | 7 | 5 | 4 | 3 | 3 | 2 | 1 | 1 | 1 |
| 280 | 300 | 10 | 9 | 8 | 6 | 5 | 4 | 3 | 3 | 2 | 1 | 1 |
| 300 | 320 | 11 | 10 | 9 | 8 | 6 | 5 | 4 | 3 | 3 | 2 | 1 |
| 320 | 340 | 12 | 11 | 10 | 9 | 7 | 6 | 5 | 4 | 3 | 3 | 2 |
| 340 | 360 | 13 | 12 | | 10 | 9 | 7 | 6 | 5 | 4 | 3 | 3 |
| 360 | 380 | 14 | 13 | 12 | 11 | 10 | 8 | 7 | 6 | 5 | 4 | 3 |
| 380 | 400 | 16 | 14 | 13 | 12 | 11 | 9 | 8 | 7 | 6 | 5 | 4 |
| 400 | 420 | 17 | 16 | 14 | 13 | 12 | 11 | 9 | 8 | 7 | 6 | 5 |
| 420 | 440 | 18 | 17 | 15 | 14 | 13 | 12 | 10 | 9 | 8 | 7 | 6 |
| 440 | 460 | 20 | 18 | 17 | 15 | 14 | 13 | 12 | 10 | 9 | 8 | 7 |
| 460 | 480 | 21 | 19 | 18 | 17 | 15 | 14 | 13 | 11 | 10 | 9 | 8 |
| 480 | 500 | 22 | 21 | 19 | 18 | 17 | 15 | 14 | 13 | 11 | 10 | 9 |
| 500 | 520 | 23 | 22 | 21 | 19 | 18 | 16 | 15 | 14 | 12 | 11 | 10 |
| 520 | 540 | 25 | 23 | 22 | 20 | 19 | 18 | 16 | 15 | 14 | 12 | 11 |
| 540 | 560 | 26 | 25 | 23 | 22 | 20 | 19 | 18 | 16 | 15 | 13 | 12 |
| 560 | 580 | 27 | 26 | 24 | 23 | 22 | 20 | 19 | 17 | 16 | 15 | 13 |
| 580 | 600 | 29 | 27 | 26 | 24 | 23 | 21 | 20 | 19 | 17 | 16 | 14 |
| 600 | 620 | 30 | 29 | 27 | 26 | 24 | 23 | 21 | 20 | 19 | 17 | 16 |
| 620 | 640 | 31 | 30 | 28 | 27 | 25 | 24 | 23 | 21 | 20 | 18 | 17 |
| 640 | 660 | 33 | 31 | 30 | 28 | 27 | 25 | 24 | 23 | 21 | 20 | 18 |
| 660 | 680 | 34 | 33 | 31 | 30 | 28 | 27 | 25 | 24 | 22 | 21 | 20 |
| 680 | 700 | 35 | 34 | 32 | 31 | 29 | 28 | 27 | 25 | 24 | 22 | 21 |
| 700 | 720 | 37 | 35 | 34 | 32 | 31 | 29 | 28 | 26 | 25 | 24 | 22 |
| 720 | 740 | 38 | 37 | 35 | 34 | 32 | 31 | 29 | 28 | 26 | 25 | 23 |
| 740 | 760 | 40 | 38 | 37 | 35 | 34 | 32 | 31 | 29 | 28 | 26 | 25 |
| 760 | 780 | 41 | 39 | 38 | 36 | 35 | 33 | 32 | 30 | 29 | 27 | 26 |
| 780 | 800 | 42 | 41 | 39 | 38 | 36 | 35 | 33 | 32 | 30 | 29 | 27 |
| 800 | 820 | 44 | 42 | 41 | 39 | 38 | 36 | 35 | 33 | 32 | 30 | 29 |
| 820 | 840 | 45 | 44 | 42 | 41 | 39 | 38 | 36 | 35 | 33 | 32 | 30 |
| 840 | 860 | 47 | 45 | 44 | 42 | 40 | 39 | 37 | 36 | 34 | 33 | 31 |
| 860 | 880 | 48 | 47 | 45 | 43 | 42 | 40 | 39 | 37 | 36 | 34 | 33 |
| 880 | 900 | 50 | 48 | 47 | 45 | 43 | 42 | 40 | 39 | 37 | 36 | 34 |
| 900 | 920 | 51 | 50 | 48 | 46 | 45 | 43 | 42 | 40 | 38 | 37 | 35 |

# WITHHOLDING TABLES EFFECTIVE
# JANUARY 1, 2013

**Weekly** PAYROLL PERIOD

### For Calendar Years 2013, and thereafter

**Married** PERSONS

| WAGES ARE | | NUMBER OF WITHHOLDING ALLOWANCES CLAIMED | | | | | | | | | | |
|---|---|---|---|---|---|---|---|---|---|---|---|---|
| AT LEAST | BUT LESS THAN | 0 | 1 | 2 | 3 | 4 | 5 | 6 | 7 | 8 | 9 | 10 or more |
| | | AMOUNT OF INCOME TAX TO BE WITHHELD | | | | | | | | | | |
| 920 | 940 | 53 | 51 | 49 | 48 | 46 | 45 | 43 | 41 | 40 | 38 | 37 |
| 940 | 960 | 54 | 52 | 51 | 49 | 48 | 46 | 45 | 43 | 41 | 40 | 38 |
| 960 | 980 | 56 | 54 | 52 | 51 | 49 | 48 | 46 | 44 | 43 | 41 | 40 |
| 980 | 1,000 | 57 | 55 | 54 | 52 | 51 | 49 | 47 | 46 | 44 | 43 | 41 |
| 1,000 | 1,020 | 59 | 57 | 55 | 54 | 52 | 50 | 49 | 47 | 46 | 44 | 42 |
| 1,020 | 1,040 | 60 | 59 | 57 | 55 | 54 | 52 | 50 | 49 | 47 | 46 | 44 |
| 1,040 | 1,060 | 62 | 60 | 58 | 57 | 55 | 53 | 52 | 50 | 49 | 47 | 45 |
| 1,060 | 1,080 | 63 | 62 | 60 | 58 | 57 | 55 | 53 | 52 | 50 | 48 | 47 |
| 1,080 | 1,100 | 65 | 63 | 61 | 60 | 58 | 56 | 55 | 53 | 51 | 50 | 48 |
| 1,100 | 1,120 | 66 | 65 | 63 | 61 | 60 | 58 | 56 | 55 | 53 | 51 | 50 |
| 1,120 | 1,140 | 68 | 66 | 64 | 63 | 61 | 59 | 58 | 56 | 54 | 53 | 51 |
| 1,140 | 1,160 | 69 | 68 | 66 | 64 | 63 | 61 | 59 | 58 | 56 | 54 | 53 |
| 1,160 | 1,180 | 71 | 69 | 67 | 66 | 64 | 62 | 61 | 59 | 57 | 56 | 54 |
| 1,180 | 1,200 | 72 | 71 | 69 | 67 | 66 | 64 | 62 | 61 | 59 | 57 | 56 |
| 1,200 | 1,220 | 74 | 72 | 71 | 69 | 67 | 66 | 64 | 62 | 60 | 59 | 57 |
| 1,220 | 1,240 | 75 | 74 | 72 | 70 | 69 | 67 | 65 | 64 | 62 | 60 | 59 |
| 1,240 | 1,260 | 77 | 75 | 74 | 72 | 70 | 69 | 67 | 65 | 64 | 62 | 60 |
| 1,260 | 1,280 | 78 | 77 | 75 | 73 | 72 | 70 | 68 | 67 | 65 | 63 | 62 |
| 1,280 | 1,300 | 80 | 78 | 77 | 75 | 73 | 72 | 70 | 68 | 67 | 65 | 63 |
| 1,300 | 1,320 | 81 | 80 | 78 | 76 | 75 | 73 | 71 | 70 | 68 | 66 | 65 |
| 1,320 | 1,340 | 83 | 81 | 80 | 78 | 76 | 75 | 73 | 71 | 70 | 68 | 66 |
| 1,340 | 1,360 | 85 | 83 | 81 | 79 | 78 | 76 | 74 | 73 | 71 | 69 | 68 |
| 1,360 | 1,380 | 86 | 84 | 83 | 81 | 79 | 78 | 76 | 74 | 73 | 71 | 69 |
| 1,380 | 1,400 | 88 | 86 | 84 | 83 | 81 | 79 | 78 | 76 | 74 | 73 | 71 |
| 1,400 | 1,420 | 89 | 87 | 86 | 84 | 82 | 81 | 79 | 77 | 76 | 74 | 72 |
| 1,420 | 1,440 | 91 | 89 | 87 | 86 | 84 | 82 | 81 | 79 | 77 | 76 | 74 |
| 1,440 | 1,460 | 92 | 91 | 89 | 87 | 85 | 84 | 82 | 80 | 79 | 77 | 75 |
| 1,460 | 1,480 | 94 | 92 | 90 | 89 | 87 | 85 | 84 | 82 | 80 | 79 | 77 |
| 1,480 | 1,500 | 95 | 94 | 92 | 90 | 89 | 87 | 85 | 83 | 82 | 80 | 78 |
| 1,500 | 1,520 | 97 | 95 | 94 | 92 | 90 | 88 | 87 | 85 | 83 | 82 | 80 |
| 1,520 | 1,540 | 99 | 97 | 95 | 93 | 92 | 90 | 88 | 86 | 85 | 83 | 81 |
| 1,540 | 1,560 | 100 | 98 | 97 | 95 | 93 | 92 | 90 | 88 | 86 | 85 | 83 |
| 1,560 | 1,580 | 102 | 100 | 98 | 97 | 95 | 93 | 91 | 90 | 88 | 86 | 85 |
| 1,580 | 1,600 | 103 | 102 | 100 | 98 | 96 | 95 | 93 | 91 | 89 | 88 | 86 |
| | | 7.90% of excess over $1,600 plus | | | | | | | | | | |
| 1,600 & over | | 105 | 103 | 101 | 100 | 98 | 96 | 95 | 93 | 91 | 89 | 88 |

# WITHHOLDING TABLES EFFECTIVE
# JANUARY 1, 2013

### *Biweekly* PAYROLL PERIOD

### For Calendar Years 2013, and thereafter

### *Single* PERSONS — UNMARRIED *Heads of Household*

| WAGES ARE | | NUMBER OF WITHHOLDING ALLOWANCES CLAIMED | | | | | | | | | | |
|---|---|---|---|---|---|---|---|---|---|---|---|---|
| AT LEAST | BUT LESS THAN | 0 | 1 | 2 | 3 | 4 | 5 | 6 | 7 | 8 | 9 | 10 or more |
| | | AMOUNT OF INCOME TAX TO BE WITHHELD | | | | | | | | | | |
| 0 | 40 | 0 | 0 | 0 | 0 | 0 | 0 | 0 | 0 | 0 | 0 | 0 |
| 40 | 60 | 1 | 0 | 0 | 0 | 0 | 0 | 0 | 0 | 0 | 0 | 0 |
| 60 | 80 | 1 | 0 | 0 | 0 | 0 | 0 | 0 | 0 | 0 | 0 | 0 |
| 80 | 100 | 1 | 1 | 0 | 0 | 0 | 0 | 0 | 0 | 0 | 0 | 0 |
| 100 | 120 | 2 | 1 | 0 | 0 | 0 | 0 | 0 | 0 | 0 | 0 | 0 |
| 120 | 140 | 3 | 1 | 1 | 0 | 0 | 0 | 0 | 0 | 0 | 0 | 0 |
| 140 | 160 | 3 | 2 | 1 | 0 | 0 | 0 | 0 | 0 | 0 | 0 | 0 |
| 160 | 180 | 4 | 2 | 1 | 1 | 0 | 0 | 0 | 0 | 0 | 0 | 0 |
| 180 | 200 | 5 | 3 | 2 | 1 | 0 | 0 | 0 | 0 | 0 | 0 | 0 |
| 200 | 220 | 6 | 4 | 2 | 1 | 0 | 0 | 0 | 0 | 0 | 0 | 0 |
| 220 | 240 | 7 | 4 | 3 | 1 | 1 | 0 | 0 | 0 | 0 | 0 | 0 |
| 240 | 260 | 8 | 5 | 4 | 2 | 1 | 0 | 0 | 0 | 0 | 0 | 0 |
| 260 | 280 | 9 | 7 | 4 | 3 | 1 | 1 | 0 | 0 | 0 | 0 | 0 |
| 280 | 300 | 10 | 8 | 5 | 3 | 2 | 1 | 0 | 0 | 0 | 0 | 0 |
| 300 | 320 | 11 | 9 | 6 | 4 | 3 | 1 | 1 | 0 | 0 | 0 | 0 |
| 320 | 340 | 12 | 10 | 7 | 5 | 3 | 2 | 1 | 0 | 0 | 0 | 0 |
| 340 | 360 | 13 | 11 | 9 | 6 | 4 | 3 | 1 | 1 | 0 | 0 | 0 |
| 360 | 380 | 14 | 12 | 10 | 7 | 5 | 3 | 2 | 1 | 0 | 0 | 0 |
| 380 | 400 | 16 | 13 | 11 | 8 | 6 | 4 | 2 | 1 | 1 | 0 | 0 |
| 400 | 420 | 17 | 14 | 12 | 9 | 7 | 5 | 3 | 2 | 1 | 0 | 0 |
| 420 | 440 | 18 | 15 | 13 | 10 | 8 | 6 | 4 | 2 | 1 | 0 | 0 |
| 440 | 460 | 20 | 17 | 14 | 12 | 9 | 7 | 4 | 3 | 1 | 1 | 0 |
| 460 | 480 | 21 | 18 | 15 | 13 | 10 | 8 | 5 | 4 | 2 | 1 | 0 |
| 480 | 500 | 22 | 19 | 17 | 14 | 11 | 9 | 7 | 4 | 3 | 1 | 1 |
| 500 | 520 | 23 | 21 | 18 | 15 | 12 | 10 | 8 | 5 | 3 | 2 | 1 |
| 520 | 540 | 25 | 22 | 19 | 16 | 14 | 11 | 9 | 6 | 4 | 3 | 1 |
| 540 | 560 | 26 | 23 | 20 | 18 | 15 | 12 | 10 | 7 | 5 | 3 | 2 |
| 560 | 580 | 27 | 24 | 22 | 19 | 16 | 13 | 11 | 9 | 6 | 4 | 3 |
| 580 | 600 | 29 | 26 | 23 | 20 | 17 | 14 | 12 | 10 | 7 | 5 | 3 |
| 600 | 620 | 30 | 27 | 24 | 21 | 19 | 16 | 13 | 11 | 8 | 6 | 4 |
| 620 | 640 | 31 | 28 | 25 | 23 | 20 | 17 | 14 | 12 | 9 | 7 | 5 |
| 640 | 660 | 33 | 30 | 27 | 24 | 21 | 18 | 15 | 13 | 10 | 8 | 6 |
| 660 | 680 | 34 | 31 | 28 | 25 | 22 | 20 | 17 | 14 | 12 | 9 | 7 |
| 680 | 700 | 35 | 32 | 29 | 27 | 24 | 21 | 18 | 15 | 13 | 10 | 8 |
| 700 | 720 | 37 | 34 | 31 | 28 | 25 | 22 | 19 | 17 | 14 | 11 | 9 |
| 720 | 740 | 38 | 35 | 32 | 29 | 26 | 23 | 21 | 18 | 15 | 12 | 10 |
| 740 | 760 | 40 | 37 | 34 | 31 | 28 | 25 | 22 | 19 | 16 | 14 | 11 |
| 760 | 780 | 41 | 38 | 35 | 32 | 29 | 26 | 23 | 20 | 18 | 15 | 12 |
| 780 | 800 | 42 | 39 | 36 | 33 | 30 | 27 | 24 | 22 | 19 | 16 | 13 |
| 800 | 820 | 44 | 41 | 38 | 35 | 32 | 29 | 26 | 23 | 20 | 17 | 14 |
| 820 | 840 | 45 | 42 | 39 | 36 | 33 | 30 | 27 | 24 | 21 | 19 | 16 |
| 840 | 860 | 47 | 44 | 40 | 37 | 34 | 31 | 28 | 25 | 23 | 20 | 17 |
| 860 | 880 | 48 | 45 | 42 | 39 | 36 | 33 | 30 | 27 | 24 | 21 | 18 |
| 880 | 900 | 50 | 47 | 43 | 40 | 37 | 34 | 31 | 28 | 25 | 22 | 20 |
| 900 | 920 | 51 | 48 | 45 | 42 | 38 | 35 | 32 | 29 | 27 | 24 | 21 |

# WITHHOLDING TABLES EFFECTIVE
# JANUARY 1, 2013

### Biweekly PAYROLL PERIOD

### For Calendar Years 2013, and thereafter

### Single PERSONS — UNMARRIED Heads of Household

| WAGES ARE | | NUMBER OF WITHHOLDING ALLOWANCES CLAIMED | | | | | | | | | | |
| AT LEAST | BUT LESS THAN | 0 | 1 | 2 | 3 | 4 | 5 | 6 | 7 | 8 | 9 | 10 or more |
| --- | --- | --- | --- | --- | --- | --- | --- | --- | --- | --- | --- | --- |
| | | AMOUNT OF INCOME TAX TO BE WITHHELD | | | | | | | | | | |
| 920 | 940 | 53 | 49 | 46 | 43 | 40 | 37 | 34 | 31 | 28 | 25 | 22 |
| 940 | 960 | 54 | 51 | 48 | 45 | 41 | 38 | 35 | 32 | 29 | 26 | 23 |
| 960 | 980 | 56 | 52 | 49 | 46 | 43 | 40 | 37 | 34 | 31 | 28 | 25 |
| 980 | 1,000 | 57 | 54 | 51 | 47 | 44 | 41 | 38 | 35 | 32 | 29 | 26 |
| 1,000 | 1,020 | 59 | 55 | 52 | 49 | 46 | 42 | 39 | 36 | 33 | 30 | 27 |
| 1,020 | 1,040 | 60 | 57 | 54 | 50 | 47 | 44 | 41 | 38 | 35 | 32 | 29 |
| 1,040 | 1,060 | 62 | 58 | 55 | 52 | 49 | 45 | 42 | 39 | 36 | 33 | 30 |
| 1,060 | 1,080 | 63 | 60 | 57 | 53 | 50 | 47 | 44 | 40 | 37 | 34 | 31 |
| 1,080 | 1,100 | 65 | 61 | 58 | 55 | 51 | 48 | 45 | 42 | 39 | 36 | 33 |
| 1,100 | 1,120 | 66 | 63 | 60 | 56 | 53 | 50 | 47 | 43 | 40 | 37 | 34 |
| 1,120 | 1,140 | 68 | 64 | 61 | 58 | 54 | 51 | 48 | 45 | 42 | 38 | 35 |
| 1,140 | 1,160 | 69 | 66 | 63 | 59 | 56 | 53 | 49 | 46 | 43 | 40 | 37 |
| 1,160 | 1,180 | 71 | 67 | 64 | 61 | 57 | 54 | 51 | 48 | 45 | 41 | 38 |
| 1,180 | 1,200 | 72 | 69 | 66 | 62 | 59 | 56 | 52 | 49 | 46 | 43 | 40 |
| 1,200 | 1,220 | 74 | 71 | 67 | 64 | 60 | 57 | 54 | 51 | 47 | 44 | 41 |
| 1,220 | 1,240 | 75 | 72 | 69 | 65 | 62 | 59 | 55 | 52 | 49 | 46 | 42 |
| 1,240 | 1,260 | 77 | 74 | 70 | 67 | 64 | 60 | 57 | 54 | 50 | 47 | 44 |
| 1,260 | 1,280 | 78 | 75 | 72 | 68 | 65 | 62 | 58 | 55 | 52 | 49 | 45 |
| 1,280 | 1,300 | 80 | 77 | 73 | 70 | 67 | 63 | 60 | 57 | 53 | 50 | 47 |
| 1,300 | 1,320 | 81 | 78 | 75 | 71 | 68 | 65 | 61 | 58 | 55 | 51 | 48 |
| 1,320 | 1,340 | 83 | 80 | 76 | 73 | 70 | 66 | 63 | 60 | 56 | 53 | 50 |
| 1,340 | 1,360 | 85 | 81 | 78 | 74 | 71 | 68 | 64 | 61 | 58 | 54 | 51 |
| 1,360 | 1,380 | 86 | 83 | 79 | 76 | 73 | 69 | 66 | 63 | 59 | 56 | 53 |
| 1,380 | 1,400 | 88 | 84 | 81 | 78 | 74 | 71 | 67 | 64 | 61 | 57 | 54 |
| 1,400 | 1,420 | 89 | 86 | 82 | 79 | 76 | 72 | 69 | 66 | 62 | 59 | 56 |
| 1,420 | 1,440 | 91 | 87 | 84 | 81 | 77 | 74 | 71 | 67 | 64 | 60 | 57 |
| 1,440 | 1,460 | 92 | 89 | 85 | 82 | 79 | 75 | 72 | 69 | 65 | 62 | 59 |
| 1,460 | 1,480 | 94 | 90 | 87 | 84 | 80 | 77 | 74 | 70 | 67 | 64 | 60 |
| 1,480 | 1,500 | 95 | 92 | 89 | 85 | 82 | 78 | 75 | 72 | 68 | 65 | 62 |
| 1,500 | 1,520 | 97 | 94 | 90 | 87 | 83 | 80 | 77 | 73 | 70 | 67 | 63 |
| 1,520 | 1,540 | 99 | 95 | 92 | 88 | 85 | 81 | 78 | 75 | 71 | 68 | 65 |
| 1,540 | 1,560 | 100 | 97 | 93 | 90 | 86 | 83 | 80 | 76 | 73 | 70 | 66 |
| 1,560 | 1,580 | 102 | 98 | 95 | 91 | 88 | 85 | 81 | 78 | 74 | 71 | 68 |
| 1,580 | 1,600 | 103 | 100 | 96 | 93 | 89 | 86 | 83 | 79 | 76 | 73 | 69 |
| 1,600 | 1,620 | 105 | 101 | 98 | 95 | 91 | 88 | 84 | 81 | 78 | 74 | 71 |
| 1,620 | 1,640 | 107 | 103 | 100 | 96 | 93 | 89 | 86 | 82 | 79 | 76 | 72 |
| 1,640 | 1,660 | 108 | 105 | 101 | 98 | 94 | 91 | 87 | 84 | 81 | 77 | 74 |
| 1,660 | 1,680 | 110 | 106 | 103 | 99 | 96 | 92 | 89 | 85 | 82 | 79 | 75 |
| 1,680 | 1,700 | 111 | 108 | 104 | 101 | 97 | 94 | 90 | 87 | 84 | 80 | 77 |
| 1,700 | 1,720 | 113 | 109 | 106 | 102 | 99 | 95 | 92 | 89 | 85 | 82 | 78 |
| 1,720 | 1,740 | 114 | 111 | 107 | 104 | 101 | 97 | 94 | 90 | 87 | 83 | 80 |
| 1,740 | 1,760 | 116 | 113 | 109 | 106 | 102 | 99 | 95 | 92 | 88 | 85 | 81 |
| 1,760 | 1,780 | 118 | 114 | 111 | 107 | 104 | 100 | 97 | 93 | 90 | 86 | 83 |
| 1,780 | 1,800 | 119 | 116 | 112 | 109 | 105 | 102 | 98 | 95 | 91 | 88 | 85 |
| 1,800 | 1,820 | 121 | 117 | 114 | 110 | 107 | 103 | 100 | 96 | 93 | 89 | 86 |

# WITHHOLDING TABLES EFFECTIVE
# JANUARY 1, 2013

*Biweekly* PAYROLL PERIOD

For Calendar Years 2013, and thereafter

*Single* PERSONS — UNMARRIED *Heads of Households*

| WAGES ARE | | NUMBER OF WITHHOLDING ALLOWANCES CLAIMED | | | | | | | | | | |
|---|---|---|---|---|---|---|---|---|---|---|---|---|
| AT LEAST | BUT LESS THAN | 0 | 1 | 2 | 3 | 4 | 5 | 6 | 7 | 8 | 9 | 10 or more |
| | | AMOUNT OF INCOME TAX TO BE WITHHELD | | | | | | | | | | |
| | | 7.90% of excess over $1,820 plus | | | | | | | | | | |
| 1,820 | & over | 122 | 119 | 115 | 112 | 108 | 105 | 101 | 98 | 95 | 91 | 88 |

# WITHHOLDING TABLES EFFECTIVE
# JANUARY 1, 2013

*Biweekly* PAYROLL PERIOD

For Calendar Years 2013, and thereafter

*Married* PERSONS

| WAGES ARE | | NUMBER OF WITHHOLDING ALLOWANCES CLAIMED | | | | | | | | | | |
| AT LEAST | BUT LESS THAN | 0 | 1 | 2 | 3 | 4 | 5 | 6 | 7 | 8 | 9 | 10 or more |
| | | AMOUNT OF INCOME TAX TO BE WITHHELD | | | | | | | | | | |
| 0 | 40 | 0 | 0 | 0 | 0 | 0 | 0 | 0 | 0 | 0 | 0 | 0 |
| 40 | 60 | 1 | 0 | 0 | 0 | 0 | 0 | 0 | 0 | 0 | 0 | 0 |
| 60 | 80 | 1 | 0 | 0 | 0 | 0 | 0 | 0 | 0 | 0 | 0 | 0 |
| 80 | 100 | 1 | 1 | 0 | 0 | 0 | 0 | 0 | 0 | 0 | 0 | 0 |
| 100 | 120 | 2 | 1 | 0 | 0 | 0 | 0 | 0 | 0 | 0 | 0 | 0 |
| 120 | 140 | 2 | 1 | 1 | 0 | 0 | 0 | 0 | 0 | 0 | 0 | 0 |
| 140 | 160 | 2 | 1 | 1 | 0 | 0 | 0 | 0 | 0 | 0 | 0 | 0 |
| 160 | 180 | 2 | 2 | 1 | 1 | 0 | 0 | 0 | 0 | 0 | 0 | 0 |
| 180 | 200 | 3 | 2 | 1 | 1 | 0 | 0 | 0 | 0 | 0 | 0 | 0 |
| 200 | 220 | 3 | 2 | 2 | 1 | 0 | 0 | 0 | 0 | 0 | 0 | 0 |
| 220 | 240 | 4 | 3 | 2 | 1 | 1 | 0 | 0 | 0 | 0 | 0 | 0 |
| 240 | 260 | 5 | 3 | 2 | 2 | 1 | 0 | 0 | 0 | 0 | 0 | 0 |
| 260 | 280 | 5 | 4 | 3 | 2 | 1 | 1 | 0 | 0 | 0 | 0 | 0 |
| 280 | 300 | 6 | 5 | 3 | 2 | 2 | 1 | 0 | 0 | 0 | 0 | 0 |
| 300 | 320 | 7 | 5 | 4 | 2 | 2 | 1 | 1 | 0 | 0 | 0 | 0 |
| 320 | 340 | 7 | 6 | 4 | 3 | 2 | 2 | 1 | 0 | 0 | 0 | 0 |
| 340 | 360 | 8 | 6 | 5 | 4 | 2 | 2 | 1 | 1 | 0 | 0 | 0 |
| 360 | 380 | 9 | 7 | 6 | 4 | 3 | 2 | 1 | 1 | 0 | 0 | 0 |
| 380 | 400 | 10 | 8 | 6 | 5 | 4 | 2 | 2 | 1 | 1 | 0 | 0 |
| 400 | 420 | 11 | 8 | 7 | 6 | 4 | 3 | 2 | 1 | 1 | 0 | 0 |
| 420 | 440 | 12 | 9 | 8 | 6 | 5 | 3 | 2 | 2 | 1 | 0 | 0 |
| 440 | 460 | 13 | 11 | 8 | 7 | 5 | 4 | 3 | 2 | 1 | 1 | 0 |
| 460 | 480 | 14 | 12 | 9 | 7 | 6 | 5 | 3 | 2 | 2 | 1 | 0 |
| 480 | 500 | 15 | 13 | 10 | 8 | 7 | 5 | 4 | 3 | 2 | 1 | 1 |
| 500 | 520 | 16 | 14 | 11 | 9 | 7 | 6 | 5 | 3 | 2 | 2 | 1 |
| 520 | 540 | 17 | 15 | 12 | 10 | 8 | 7 | 5 | 4 | 2 | 2 | 1 |
| 540 | 560 | 18 | 16 | 14 | 11 | 9 | 7 | 6 | 4 | 3 | 2 | 2 |
| 560 | 580 | 20 | 17 | 15 | 12 | 10 | 8 | 6 | 5 | 4 | 2 | 2 |
| 580 | 600 | 21 | 18 | 16 | 13 | 11 | 9 | 7 | 6 | 4 | 3 | 2 |
| 600 | 620 | 22 | 19 | 17 | 14 | 12 | 10 | 8 | 6 | 5 | 4 | 2 |
| 620 | 640 | 23 | 20 | 18 | 16 | 13 | 11 | 8 | 7 | 6 | 4 | 3 |
| 640 | 660 | 24 | 22 | 19 | 17 | 14 | 12 | 9 | 8 | 6 | 5 | 3 |
| 660 | 680 | 25 | 23 | 20 | 18 | 15 | 13 | 11 | 8 | 7 | 5 | 4 |
| 680 | 700 | 26 | 24 | 21 | 19 | 16 | 14 | 12 | 9 | 7 | 6 | 5 |
| 700 | 720 | 27 | 25 | 22 | 20 | 18 | 15 | 13 | 10 | 8 | 7 | 5 |
| 720 | 740 | 28 | 26 | 23 | 21 | 19 | 16 | 14 | 11 | 9 | 7 | 6 |
| 740 | 760 | 30 | 27 | 25 | 22 | 20 | 17 | 15 | 12 | 10 | 8 | 7 |
| 760 | 780 | 31 | 28 | 26 | 23 | 21 | 18 | 16 | 14 | 11 | 9 | 7 |
| 780 | 800 | 32 | 29 | 27 | 24 | 22 | 20 | 17 | 15 | 12 | 10 | 8 |
| 800 | 820 | 33 | 31 | 28 | 25 | 23 | 21 | 18 | 16 | 13 | 11 | 9 |
| 820 | 840 | 35 | 32 | 29 | 27 | 24 | 22 | 19 | 17 | 14 | 12 | 10 |
| 840 | 860 | 36 | 33 | 30 | 28 | 25 | 23 | 20 | 18 | 16 | 13 | 11 |
| 860 | 880 | 37 | 34 | 32 | 29 | 26 | 24 | 22 | 19 | 17 | 14 | 12 |
| 880 | 900 | 39 | 36 | 33 | 30 | 27 | 25 | 23 | 20 | 18 | 15 | 13 |
| 900 | 920 | 40 | 37 | 34 | 31 | 29 | 26 | 24 | 21 | 19 | 16 | 14 |

# WITHHOLDING TABLES EFFECTIVE
# JANUARY 1, 2013

*Biweekly* PAYROLL PERIOD

For Calendar Years 2013, and thereafter

*Married* PERSONS

| WAGES ARE | | NUMBER OF WITHHOLDING ALLOWANCES CLAIMED | | | | | | | | | | |
|---|---|---|---|---|---|---|---|---|---|---|---|---|
| AT LEAST | BUT LESS THAN | 0 | 1 | 2 | 3 | 4 | 5 | 6 | 7 | 8 | 9 | 10 or more |
| | | AMOUNT OF INCOME TAX TO BE WITHHELD | | | | | | | | | | |
| 920 | 940 | 41 | 38 | 35 | 33 | 30 | 27 | 25 | 22 | 20 | 18 | 15 |
| 940 | 960 | 42 | 40 | 37 | 34 | 31 | 28 | 26 | 23 | 21 | 19 | 16 |
| 960 | 980 | 44 | 41 | 38 | 35 | 32 | 30 | 27 | 25 | 22 | 20 | 17 |
| 980 | 1,000 | 45 | 42 | 39 | 36 | 34 | 31 | 28 | 26 | 23 | 21 | 18 |
| 1,000 | 1,020 | 46 | 43 | 41 | 38 | 35 | 32 | 29 | 27 | 24 | 22 | 20 |
| 1,020 | 1,040 | 47 | 45 | 42 | 39 | 36 | 33 | 31 | 28 | 25 | 23 | 21 |
| 1,040 | 1,060 | 49 | 46 | 43 | 40 | 37 | 35 | 32 | 29 | 27 | 24 | 22 |
| 1,060 | 1,080 | 50 | 47 | 44 | 42 | 39 | 36 | 33 | 30 | 28 | 25 | 23 |
| 1,080 | 1,100 | 51 | 48 | 46 | 43 | 40 | 37 | 34 | 32 | 29 | 26 | 24 |
| 1,100 | 1,120 | 53 | 50 | 47 | 44 | 41 | 39 | 36 | 33 | 30 | 27 | 25 |
| 1,120 | 1,140 | 54 | 51 | 48 | 45 | 43 | 40 | 37 | 34 | 31 | 29 | 26 |
| 1,140 | 1,160 | 55 | 52 | 50 | 47 | 44 | 41 | 38 | 35 | 33 | 30 | 27 |
| 1,160 | 1,180 | 57 | 54 | 51 | 48 | 45 | 42 | 40 | 37 | 34 | 31 | 28 |
| 1,180 | 1,200 | 58 | 55 | 52 | 49 | 46 | 44 | 41 | 38 | 35 | 32 | 30 |
| 1,200 | 1,220 | 59 | 56 | 53 | 51 | 48 | 45 | 42 | 39 | 36 | 34 | 31 |
| 1,220 | 1,240 | 61 | 58 | 55 | 52 | 49 | 46 | 43 | 41 | 38 | 35 | 32 |
| 1,240 | 1,260 | 62 | 59 | 56 | 53 | 50 | 47 | 45 | 42 | 39 | 36 | 33 |
| 1,260 | 1,280 | 63 | 60 | 57 | 55 | 52 | 49 | 46 | 43 | 40 | 37 | 35 |
| 1,280 | 1,300 | 65 | 62 | 59 | 56 | 53 | 50 | 47 | 44 | 42 | 39 | 36 |
| 1,300 | 1,320 | 66 | 63 | 60 | 57 | 54 | 51 | 48 | 46 | 43 | 40 | 37 |
| 1,320 | 1,340 | 68 | 65 | 62 | 59 | 56 | 53 | 50 | 47 | 44 | 41 | 39 |
| 1,340 | 1,360 | 69 | 66 | 63 | 60 | 57 | 54 | 51 | 48 | 45 | 43 | 40 |
| 1,360 | 1,380 | 70 | 67 | 64 | 61 | 58 | 55 | 52 | 50 | 47 | 44 | 41 |
| 1,380 | 1,400 | 72 | 69 | 66 | 63 | 60 | 57 | 54 | 51 | 48 | 45 | 42 |
| 1,400 | 1,420 | 73 | 70 | 67 | 64 | 61 | 58 | 55 | 52 | 49 | 46 | 44 |
| 1,420 | 1,440 | 74 | 71 | 68 | 65 | 62 | 59 | 56 | 53 | 51 | 48 | 45 |
| 1,440 | 1,460 | 76 | 73 | 70 | 67 | 64 | 61 | 58 | 55 | 52 | 49 | 46 |
| 1,460 | 1,480 | 77 | 74 | 71 | 68 | 65 | 62 | 59 | 56 | 53 | 50 | 47 |
| 1,480 | 1,500 | 78 | 75 | 72 | 69 | 66 | 63 | 60 | 57 | 55 | 52 | 49 |
| 1,500 | 1,520 | 80 | 77 | 74 | 71 | 68 | 65 | 62 | 59 | 56 | 53 | 50 |
| 1,520 | 1,540 | 81 | 78 | 75 | 72 | 69 | 66 | 63 | 60 | 57 | 54 | 51 |
| 1,540 | 1,560 | 83 | 80 | 77 | 74 | 71 | 68 | 65 | 62 | 59 | 56 | 53 |
| 1,560 | 1,580 | 84 | 81 | 78 | 75 | 72 | 69 | 66 | 63 | 60 | 57 | 54 |
| 1,580 | 1,600 | 86 | 83 | 79 | 76 | 73 | 70 | 67 | 64 | 61 | 58 | 55 |
| 1,600 | 1,620 | 87 | 84 | 81 | 78 | 75 | 72 | 69 | 66 | 63 | 60 | 57 |
| 1,620 | 1,640 | 89 | 85 | 82 | 79 | 76 | 73 | 70 | 67 | 64 | 61 | 58 |
| 1,640 | 1,660 | 90 | 87 | 84 | 81 | 77 | 74 | 71 | 68 | 65 | 62 | 59 |
| 1,660 | 1,680 | 91 | 88 | 85 | 82 | 79 | 76 | 73 | 70 | 67 | 64 | 61 |
| 1,680 | 1,700 | 93 | 90 | 87 | 83 | 80 | 77 | 74 | 71 | 68 | 65 | 62 |
| 1,700 | 1,720 | 94 | 91 | 88 | 85 | 82 | 78 | 75 | 72 | 69 | 66 | 63 |
| 1,720 | 1,740 | 96 | 93 | 89 | 86 | 83 | 80 | 77 | 74 | 71 | 68 | 65 |
| 1,740 | 1,760 | 97 | 94 | 91 | 88 | 85 | 81 | 78 | 75 | 72 | 69 | 66 |
| 1,760 | 1,780 | 99 | 95 | 92 | 89 | 86 | 83 | 80 | 77 | 74 | 71 | 68 |
| 1,780 | 1,800 | 100 | 97 | 94 | 91 | 87 | 84 | 81 | 78 | 75 | 72 | 69 |
| 1,800 | 1,820 | 102 | 98 | 95 | 92 | 89 | 86 | 83 | 79 | 76 | 73 | 70 |

# WITHHOLDING TABLES EFFECTIVE
# JANUARY 1, 2013

### *Biweekly* PAYROLL PERIOD

### For Calendar Years 2013, and thereafter

### *Married* PERSONS

| WAGES ARE | | NUMBER OF WITHHOLDING ALLOWANCES CLAIMED | | | | | | | | | | |
|---|---|---|---|---|---|---|---|---|---|---|---|---|
| AT LEAST | BUT LESS THAN | 0 | 1 | 2 | 3 | 4 | 5 | 6 | 7 | 8 | 9 | 10 or more |
| | | AMOUNT OF INCOME TAX TO BE WITHHELD | | | | | | | | | | |
| 1,820 | 1,840 | 103 | 100 | 97 | 93 | 90 | 87 | 84 | 81 | 78 | 75 | 72 |
| 1,840 | 1,860 | 104 | 101 | 98 | 95 | 92 | 89 | 85 | 82 | 79 | 76 | 73 |
| 1,860 | 1,880 | 106 | 103 | 100 | 96 | 93 | 90 | 87 | 84 | 81 | 77 | 74 |
| 1,880 | 1,900 | 107 | 104 | 101 | 98 | 95 | 91 | 88 | 85 | 82 | 79 | 76 |
| 1,900 | 1,920 | 109 | 106 | 102 | 99 | 96 | 93 | 90 | 87 | 83 | 80 | 77 |
| 1,920 | 1,940 | 111 | 107 | 104 | 101 | 97 | 94 | 91 | 88 | 85 | 82 | 78 |
| 1,940 | 1,960 | 112 | 109 | 105 | 102 | 99 | 96 | 93 | 89 | 86 | 83 | 80 |
| 1,960 | 1,980 | 114 | 110 | 107 | 104 | 100 | 97 | 94 | 91 | 88 | 85 | 81 |
| 1,980 | 2,000 | 115 | 112 | 108 | 105 | 102 | 99 | 95 | 92 | 89 | 86 | 83 |
| 2,000 | 2,020 | 117 | 113 | 110 | 107 | 103 | 100 | 97 | 94 | 91 | 87 | 84 |
| 2,020 | 2,040 | 118 | 115 | 111 | 108 | 105 | 102 | 98 | 95 | 92 | 89 | 86 |
| 2,040 | 2,060 | 120 | 116 | 113 | 110 | 106 | 103 | 100 | 97 | 93 | 90 | 87 |
| 2,060 | 2,080 | 121 | 118 | 114 | 111 | 108 | 104 | 101 | 98 | 95 | 92 | 89 |
| 2,080 | 2,100 | 123 | 119 | 116 | 113 | 109 | 106 | 103 | 100 | 96 | 93 | 90 |
| 2,100 | 2,120 | 124 | 121 | 117 | 114 | 111 | 107 | 104 | 101 | 98 | 95 | 91 |
| 2,120 | 2,140 | 126 | 122 | 119 | 116 | 112 | 109 | 106 | 102 | 99 | 96 | 93 |
| 2,140 | 2,160 | 127 | 124 | 121 | 117 | 114 | 111 | 107 | 104 | 101 | 97 | 94 |
| 2,160 | 2,180 | 129 | 125 | 122 | 119 | 115 | 112 | 109 | 105 | 102 | 99 | 96 |
| 2,180 | 2,200 | 130 | 127 | 124 | 120 | 117 | 114 | 110 | 107 | 104 | 100 | 97 |
| 2,200 | 2,220 | 132 | 128 | 125 | 122 | 118 | 115 | 112 | 108 | 105 | 102 | 99 |
| 2,220 | 2,240 | 133 | 130 | 127 | 123 | 120 | 117 | 113 | 110 | 107 | 103 | 100 |
| 2,240 | 2,260 | 135 | 131 | 128 | 125 | 121 | 118 | 115 | 111 | 108 | 105 | 102 |
| 2,260 | 2,280 | 136 | 133 | 130 | 126 | 123 | 120 | 116 | 113 | 110 | 106 | 103 |
| 2,280 | 2,300 | 138 | 135 | 131 | 128 | 124 | 121 | 118 | 114 | 111 | 108 | 104 |
| 2,300 | 2,320 | 139 | 136 | 133 | 129 | 126 | 123 | 119 | 116 | 113 | 109 | 106 |
| 2,320 | 2,340 | 141 | 138 | 134 | 131 | 128 | 124 | 121 | 117 | 114 | 111 | 107 |
| 2,340 | 2,360 | 142 | 139 | 136 | 132 | 129 | 126 | 122 | 119 | 116 | 112 | 109 |
| 2,360 | 2,380 | 144 | 141 | 137 | 134 | 131 | 127 | 124 | 121 | 117 | 114 | 111 |
| 2,380 | 2,400 | 145 | 142 | 139 | 135 | 132 | 129 | 125 | 122 | 119 | 115 | 112 |
| 2,400 | 2,420 | 147 | 144 | 140 | 137 | 134 | 130 | 127 | 124 | 120 | 117 | 114 |
| 2,420 | 2,440 | 149 | 145 | 142 | 138 | 135 | 132 | 128 | 125 | 122 | 118 | 115 |
| 2,440 | 2,460 | 150 | 147 | 143 | 140 | 137 | 133 | 130 | 127 | 123 | 120 | 117 |
| 2,460 | 2,480 | 152 | 148 | 145 | 142 | 138 | 135 | 131 | 128 | 125 | 121 | 118 |
| 2,480 | 2,500 | 153 | 150 | 146 | 143 | 140 | 136 | 133 | 130 | 126 | 123 | 120 |
| 2,500 | 2,520 | 155 | 151 | 148 | 145 | 141 | 138 | 135 | 131 | 128 | 124 | 121 |
| 2,520 | 2,540 | 156 | 153 | 149 | 146 | 143 | 139 | 136 | 133 | 129 | 126 | 123 |
| 2,540 | 2,560 | 158 | 154 | 151 | 148 | 144 | 141 | 138 | 134 | 131 | 128 | 124 |
| 2,560 | 2,580 | 159 | 156 | 152 | 149 | 146 | 142 | 139 | 136 | 132 | 129 | 126 |
| 2,580 | 2,600 | 161 | 157 | 154 | 151 | 147 | 144 | 141 | 137 | 134 | 131 | 127 |
| 2,600 | 2,620 | 162 | 159 | 155 | 152 | 149 | 145 | 142 | 139 | 135 | 132 | 129 |
| 2,620 | 2,640 | 164 | 160 | 157 | 154 | 150 | 147 | 144 | 140 | 137 | 134 | 130 |
| 2,640 | 2,660 | 165 | 162 | 159 | 155 | 152 | 149 | 145 | 142 | 138 | 135 | 132 |
| 2,660 | 2,680 | 167 | 163 | 160 | 157 | 153 | 150 | 147 | 143 | 140 | 137 | 133 |
| 2,680 | 2,700 | 168 | 165 | 162 | 158 | 155 | 152 | 148 | 145 | 142 | 138 | 135 |
| 2,700 | 2,720 | 170 | 166 | 163 | 160 | 156 | 153 | 150 | 146 | 143 | 140 | 136 |

# WITHHOLDING TABLES EFFECTIVE
# JANUARY 1, 2013

*Biweekly* PAYROLL PERIOD

For Calendar Years 2013, and thereafter

*Married* PERSONS

| WAGES ARE | | NUMBER OF WITHHOLDING ALLOWANCES CLAIMED | | | | | | | | | | |
|---|---|---|---|---|---|---|---|---|---|---|---|---|
| AT LEAST | BUT LESS THAN | 0 | 1 | 2 | 3 | 4 | 5 | 6 | 7 | 8 | 9 | 10 or more |
| | | AMOUNT OF INCOME TAX TO BE WITHHELD | | | | | | | | | | |
| 2,720 | 2,740 | 171 | 168 | 165 | 161 | 158 | 155 | 151 | 148 | 145 | 141 | 138 |
| 2,740 | 2,760 | 173 | 169 | 166 | 163 | 159 | 156 | 153 | 149 | 146 | 143 | 139 |
| 2,760 | 2,780 | 174 | 171 | 168 | 164 | 161 | 158 | 154 | 151 | 148 | 144 | 141 |
| 2,780 | 2,800 | 176 | 173 | 169 | 166 | 162 | 159 | 156 | 152 | 149 | 146 | 142 |
| 2,800 | 2,820 | 178 | 174 | 171 | 167 | 164 | 161 | 157 | 154 | 151 | 147 | 144 |
| 2,820 | 2,840 | 179 | 176 | 172 | 169 | 166 | 162 | 159 | 155 | 152 | 149 | 145 |
| 2,840 | 2,860 | 181 | 177 | 174 | 170 | 167 | 164 | 160 | 157 | 154 | 150 | 147 |
| 2,860 | 2,880 | 182 | 179 | 175 | 172 | 169 | 165 | 162 | 159 | 155 | 152 | 149 |
| 2,880 | 2,900 | 184 | 180 | 177 | 173 | 170 | 167 | 163 | 160 | 157 | 153 | 150 |
| 2,900 | 2,920 | 185 | 182 | 178 | 175 | 172 | 168 | 165 | 162 | 158 | 155 | 152 |
| 2,920 | 2,940 | 187 | 184 | 180 | 177 | 173 | 170 | 166 | 163 | 160 | 156 | 153 |
| 2,940 | 2,960 | 189 | 185 | 182 | 178 | 175 | 171 | 168 | 165 | 161 | 158 | 155 |
| 2,960 | 2,980 | 190 | 187 | 183 | 180 | 176 | 173 | 169 | 166 | 163 | 159 | 156 |
| 2,980 | 3,000 | 192 | 188 | 185 | 181 | 178 | 174 | 171 | 168 | 164 | 161 | 158 |
| 3,000 | 3,020 | 193 | 190 | 186 | 183 | 179 | 176 | 173 | 169 | 166 | 162 | 159 |
| 3,020 | 3,040 | 195 | 191 | 188 | 184 | 181 | 178 | 174 | 171 | 167 | 164 | 161 |
| 3,040 | 3,060 | 196 | 193 | 190 | 186 | 183 | 179 | 176 | 172 | 169 | 166 | 162 |
| 3,060 | 3,080 | 198 | 195 | 191 | 188 | 184 | 181 | 177 | 174 | 170 | 167 | 164 |
| 3,080 | 3,100 | 200 | 196 | 193 | 189 | 186 | 182 | 179 | 175 | 172 | 169 | 165 |
| 3,100 | 3,120 | 201 | 198 | 194 | 191 | 187 | 184 | 180 | 177 | 173 | 170 | 167 |
| 3,120 | 3,140 | 203 | 199 | 196 | 192 | 189 | 185 | 182 | 178 | 175 | 172 | 168 |
| 3,140 | 3,160 | 204 | 201 | 197 | 194 | 190 | 187 | 184 | 180 | 177 | 173 | 170 |
| 3,160 | 3,180 | 206 | 202 | 199 | 196 | 192 | 189 | 185 | 182 | 178 | 175 | 171 |
| 3,180 | 3,200 | 208 | 204 | 201 | 197 | 194 | 190 | 187 | 183 | 180 | 176 | 173 |
| | | 7.90% of excess over $3,200 plus | | | | | | | | | | |
| 3,200 | & over | 209 | 206 | 202 | 199 | 195 | 192 | 188 | 185 | 181 | 178 | 174 |

# WITHHOLDING TABLES EFFECTIVE
# JANUARY 1, 2013

### *Semimonthly* PAYROLL PERIOD

### For Calendar Years 2013, and thereafter

### *Single* PERSONS — UNMARRIED *Heads of Household*

| WAGES ARE | | NUMBER OF WITHHOLDING ALLOWANCES CLAIMED | | | | | | | | | | |
|---|---|---|---|---|---|---|---|---|---|---|---|---|
| AT LEAST | BUT LESS THAN | 0 | 1 | 2 | 3 | 4 | 5 | 6 | 7 | 8 | 9 | 10 or more |
| | | AMOUNT OF INCOME TAX TO BE WITHHELD | | | | | | | | | | |
| 0 | 40 | 0 | 0 | 0 | 0 | 0 | 0 | 0 | 0 | 0 | 0 | 0 |
| 40 | 60 | 1 | 0 | 0 | 0 | 0 | 0 | 0 | 0 | 0 | 0 | 0 |
| 60 | 80 | 1 | 0 | 0 | 0 | 0 | 0 | 0 | 0 | 0 | 0 | 0 |
| 80 | 100 | 1 | 1 | 0 | 0 | 0 | 0 | 0 | 0 | 0 | 0 | 0 |
| 100 | 120 | 2 | 1 | 0 | 0 | 0 | 0 | 0 | 0 | 0 | 0 | 0 |
| 120 | 140 | 2 | 1 | 0 | 0 | 0 | 0 | 0 | 0 | 0 | 0 | 0 |
| 140 | 160 | 3 | 1 | 1 | 0 | 0 | 0 | 0 | 0 | 0 | 0 | 0 |
| 160 | 180 | 4 | 2 | 1 | 0 | 0 | 0 | 0 | 0 | 0 | 0 | 0 |
| 180 | 200 | 4 | 3 | 1 | 1 | 0 | 0 | 0 | 0 | 0 | 0 | 0 |
| 200 | 220 | 5 | 3 | 2 | 1 | 0 | 0 | 0 | 0 | 0 | 0 | 0 |
| 220 | 240 | 6 | 4 | 3 | 1 | 1 | 0 | 0 | 0 | 0 | 0 | 0 |
| 240 | 260 | 7 | 5 | 3 | 2 | 1 | 0 | 0 | 0 | 0 | 0 | 0 |
| 260 | 280 | 8 | 6 | 4 | 2 | 1 | 0 | 0 | 0 | 0 | 0 | 0 |
| 280 | 300 | 10 | 7 | 4 | 3 | 1 | 1 | 0 | 0 | 0 | 0 | 0 |
| 300 | 320 | 11 | 8 | 5 | 4 | 2 | 1 | 0 | 0 | 0 | 0 | 0 |
| 320 | 340 | 12 | 9 | 7 | 4 | 3 | 1 | 1 | 0 | 0 | 0 | 0 |
| 340 | 360 | 13 | 10 | 8 | 5 | 3 | 2 | 1 | 0 | 0 | 0 | 0 |
| 360 | 380 | 14 | 11 | 9 | 6 | 4 | 2 | 1 | 1 | 0 | 0 | 0 |
| 380 | 400 | 15 | 12 | 10 | 7 | 5 | 3 | 2 | 1 | 0 | 0 | 0 |
| 400 | 420 | 16 | 14 | 11 | 8 | 6 | 4 | 2 | 1 | 0 | 0 | 0 |
| 420 | 440 | 18 | 15 | 12 | 9 | 7 | 4 | 3 | 1 | 1 | 0 | 0 |
| 440 | 460 | 19 | 16 | 13 | 10 | 8 | 5 | 3 | 2 | 1 | 0 | 0 |
| 460 | 480 | 20 | 17 | 14 | 12 | 9 | 6 | 4 | 3 | 1 | 1 | 0 |
| 480 | 500 | 21 | 18 | 15 | 13 | 10 | 7 | 5 | 3 | 2 | 1 | 0 |
| 500 | 520 | 23 | 20 | 17 | 14 | 11 | 9 | 6 | 4 | 2 | 1 | 0 |
| 520 | 540 | 24 | 21 | 18 | 15 | 12 | 10 | 7 | 4 | 3 | 1 | 1 |
| 540 | 560 | 25 | 22 | 19 | 16 | 13 | 11 | 8 | 6 | 4 | 2 | 1 |
| 560 | 580 | 26 | 23 | 20 | 17 | 14 | 12 | 9 | 7 | 4 | 3 | 1 |
| 580 | 600 | 28 | 25 | 22 | 19 | 16 | 13 | 10 | 8 | 5 | 3 | 2 |
| 600 | 620 | 29 | 26 | 23 | 20 | 17 | 14 | 11 | 9 | 6 | 4 | 2 |
| 620 | 640 | 30 | 27 | 24 | 21 | 18 | 15 | 13 | 10 | 7 | 5 | 3 |
| 640 | 660 | 32 | 29 | 26 | 22 | 19 | 16 | 14 | 11 | 8 | 6 | 4 |
| 660 | 680 | 33 | 30 | 27 | 24 | 21 | 18 | 15 | 12 | 9 | 7 | 4 |
| 680 | 700 | 35 | 31 | 28 | 25 | 22 | 19 | 16 | 13 | 11 | 8 | 5 |
| 700 | 720 | 36 | 33 | 29 | 26 | 23 | 20 | 17 | 14 | 12 | 9 | 6 |
| 720 | 740 | 37 | 34 | 31 | 28 | 25 | 21 | 18 | 15 | 13 | 10 | 8 |
| 740 | 760 | 39 | 35 | 32 | 29 | 26 | 23 | 20 | 17 | 14 | 11 | 9 |
| 760 | 780 | 40 | 37 | 33 | 30 | 27 | 24 | 21 | 18 | 15 | 12 | 10 |
| 780 | 800 | 41 | 38 | 35 | 32 | 28 | 25 | 22 | 19 | 16 | 13 | 11 |
| 800 | 820 | 43 | 39 | 36 | 33 | 30 | 27 | 24 | 20 | 17 | 15 | 12 |
| 820 | 840 | 44 | 41 | 38 | 34 | 31 | 28 | 25 | 22 | 19 | 16 | 13 |
| 840 | 860 | 46 | 42 | 39 | 36 | 32 | 29 | 26 | 23 | 20 | 17 | 14 |
| 860 | 880 | 47 | 44 | 40 | 37 | 34 | 31 | 27 | 24 | 21 | 18 | 15 |
| 880 | 900 | 48 | 45 | 42 | 38 | 35 | 32 | 29 | 26 | 23 | 20 | 16 |
| 900 | 920 | 50 | 46 | 43 | 40 | 37 | 33 | 30 | 27 | 24 | 21 | 18 |

# WITHHOLDING TABLES EFFECTIVE
# JANUARY 1, 2013

*Semimonthly* PAYROLL PERIOD

For Calendar Years 2013, and thereafter

*Single* PERSONS — UNMARRIED *Heads of Household*

| WAGES ARE | | NUMBER OF WITHHOLDING ALLOWANCES CLAIMED | | | | | | | | | | |
| AT LEAST | BUT LESS THAN | 0 | 1 | 2 | 3 | 4 | 5 | 6 | 7 | 8 | 9 | 10 or more |
| --- | --- | --- | --- | --- | --- | --- | --- | --- | --- | --- | --- | --- |
| | | AMOUNT OF INCOME TAX TO BE WITHHELD | | | | | | | | | | |
| 920 | 940 | 51 | 48 | 44 | 41 | 38 | 35 | 31 | 28 | 25 | 22 | 19 |
| 940 | 960 | 53 | 49 | 46 | 43 | 39 | 36 | 33 | 30 | 26 | 23 | 20 |
| 960 | 980 | 54 | 51 | 47 | 44 | 41 | 37 | 34 | 31 | 28 | 25 | 22 |
| 980 | 1,000 | 56 | 52 | 49 | 45 | 42 | 39 | 35 | 32 | 29 | 26 | 23 |
| 1,000 | 1,020 | 57 | 54 | 50 | 47 | 43 | 40 | 37 | 34 | 30 | 27 | 24 |
| 1,020 | 1,040 | 59 | 55 | 52 | 48 | 45 | 41 | 38 | 35 | 32 | 28 | 25 |
| 1,040 | 1,060 | 60 | 57 | 53 | 50 | 46 | 43 | 40 | 36 | 33 | 30 | 27 |
| 1,060 | 1,080 | 62 | 58 | 55 | 51 | 48 | 44 | 41 | 38 | 34 | 31 | 28 |
| 1,080 | 1,100 | 63 | 60 | 56 | 53 | 49 | 46 | 42 | 39 | 36 | 33 | 29 |
| 1,100 | 1,120 | 65 | 61 | 58 | 54 | 51 | 47 | 44 | 40 | 37 | 34 | 31 |
| 1,120 | 1,140 | 66 | 63 | 59 | 55 | 52 | 49 | 45 | 42 | 39 | 35 | 32 |
| 1,140 | 1,160 | 68 | 64 | 61 | 57 | 53 | 50 | 47 | 43 | 40 | 37 | 33 |
| 1,160 | 1,180 | 69 | 66 | 62 | 58 | 55 | 51 | 48 | 45 | 41 | 38 | 35 |
| 1,180 | 1,200 | 71 | 67 | 64 | 60 | 56 | 53 | 49 | 46 | 43 | 39 | 36 |
| 1,200 | 1,220 | 72 | 69 | 65 | 61 | 58 | 54 | 51 | 48 | 44 | 41 | 37 |
| 1,220 | 1,240 | 74 | 70 | 67 | 63 | 59 | 56 | 52 | 49 | 46 | 42 | 39 |
| 1,240 | 1,260 | 75 | 72 | 68 | 65 | 61 | 57 | 54 | 50 | 47 | 44 | 40 |
| 1,260 | 1,280 | 77 | 73 | 70 | 66 | 62 | 59 | 55 | 52 | 48 | 45 | 42 |
| 1,280 | 1,300 | 78 | 75 | 71 | 68 | 64 | 60 | 57 | 53 | 50 | 46 | 43 |
| 1,300 | 1,320 | 80 | 76 | 73 | 69 | 65 | 62 | 58 | 55 | 51 | 48 | 44 |
| 1,320 | 1,340 | 81 | 78 | 74 | 71 | 67 | 63 | 60 | 56 | 53 | 49 | 46 |
| 1,340 | 1,360 | 83 | 79 | 76 | 72 | 69 | 65 | 61 | 58 | 54 | 51 | 47 |
| 1,360 | 1,380 | 85 | 81 | 77 | 74 | 70 | 66 | 63 | 59 | 56 | 52 | 49 |
| 1,380 | 1,400 | 86 | 82 | 79 | 75 | 72 | 68 | 64 | 61 | 57 | 54 | 50 |
| 1,400 | 1,420 | 88 | 84 | 80 | 77 | 73 | 69 | 66 | 62 | 59 | 55 | 52 |
| 1,420 | 1,440 | 89 | 85 | 82 | 78 | 75 | 71 | 67 | 64 | 60 | 56 | 53 |
| 1,440 | 1,460 | 91 | 87 | 83 | 80 | 76 | 72 | 69 | 65 | 62 | 58 | 54 |
| 1,460 | 1,480 | 92 | 88 | 85 | 81 | 78 | 74 | 70 | 67 | 63 | 60 | 56 |
| 1,480 | 1,500 | 94 | 90 | 86 | 83 | 79 | 76 | 72 | 68 | 65 | 61 | 57 |
| 1,500 | 1,520 | 95 | 92 | 88 | 84 | 81 | 77 | 73 | 70 | 66 | 63 | 59 |
| 1,520 | 1,540 | 97 | 93 | 89 | 86 | 82 | 79 | 75 | 71 | 68 | 64 | 60 |
| 1,540 | 1,560 | 98 | 95 | 91 | 87 | 84 | 80 | 76 | 73 | 69 | 66 | 62 |
| 1,560 | 1,580 | 100 | 96 | 92 | 89 | 85 | 82 | 78 | 74 | 71 | 67 | 64 |
| 1,580 | 1,600 | 102 | 98 | 94 | 90 | 87 | 83 | 80 | 76 | 72 | 69 | 65 |
| 1,600 | 1,620 | 103 | 99 | 96 | 92 | 88 | 85 | 81 | 77 | 74 | 70 | 67 |
| 1,620 | 1,640 | 105 | 101 | 97 | 93 | 90 | 86 | 83 | 79 | 75 | 72 | 68 |
| 1,640 | 1,660 | 106 | 102 | 99 | 95 | 91 | 88 | 84 | 80 | 77 | 73 | 70 |
| 1,660 | 1,680 | 108 | 104 | 100 | 97 | 93 | 89 | 86 | 82 | 78 | 75 | 71 |
| 1,680 | 1,700 | 109 | 106 | 102 | 98 | 94 | 91 | 87 | 83 | 80 | 76 | 73 |
| 1,700 | 1,720 | 111 | 107 | 103 | 100 | 96 | 92 | 89 | 85 | 81 | 78 | 74 |
| 1,720 | 1,740 | 113 | 109 | 105 | 101 | 98 | 94 | 90 | 87 | 83 | 79 | 76 |
| 1,740 | 1,760 | 114 | 110 | 107 | 103 | 99 | 95 | 92 | 88 | 84 | 81 | 77 |
| 1,760 | 1,780 | 116 | 112 | 108 | 104 | 101 | 97 | 93 | 90 | 86 | 82 | 79 |
| 1,780 | 1,800 | 117 | 114 | 110 | 106 | 102 | 98 | 95 | 91 | 87 | 84 | 80 |
| 1,800 | 1,820 | 119 | 115 | 111 | 108 | 104 | 100 | 96 | 93 | 89 | 85 | 82 |

# WITHHOLDING TABLES EFFECTIVE
# JANUARY 1, 2013

**Semimonthly PAYROLL PERIOD**

**For Calendar Years 2013, and thereafter**

**Single PERSONS — UNMARRIED Heads of Household**

| WAGES ARE | | NUMBER OF WITHHOLDING ALLOWANCES CLAIMED | | | | | | | | | | |
|---|---|---|---|---|---|---|---|---|---|---|---|---|
| AT LEAST | BUT LESS THAN | 0 | 1 | 2 | 3 | 4 | 5 | 6 | 7 | 8 | 9 | 10 or more |
| | | AMOUNT OF INCOME TAX TO BE WITHHELD | | | | | | | | | | |
| 1,820 | 1,840 | 120 | 117 | 113 | 109 | 105 | 102 | 98 | 94 | 91 | 87 | 83 |
| 1,840 | 1,860 | 122 | 118 | 115 | 111 | 107 | 103 | 99 | 96 | 92 | 88 | 85 |
| 1,860 | 1,880 | 124 | 120 | 116 | 112 | 109 | 105 | 101 | 97 | 94 | 90 | 86 |
| 1,880 | 1,900 | 125 | 121 | 118 | 114 | 110 | 106 | 103 | 99 | 95 | 91 | 88 |
| 1,900 | 1,920 | 127 | 123 | 119 | 115 | 112 | 108 | 104 | 100 | 97 | 93 | 89 |
| 1,920 | 1,940 | 128 | 125 | 121 | 117 | 113 | 110 | 106 | 102 | 98 | 94 | 91 |
| 1,940 | 1,960 | 130 | 126 | 122 | 119 | 115 | 111 | 107 | 104 | 100 | 96 | 92 |
| 1,960 | 1,980 | 132 | 128 | 124 | 120 | 116 | 113 | 109 | 105 | 101 | 98 | 94 |
| 7.90% of excess over $1,980 plus | | | | | | | | | | | | |
| 1,980 | & over | 133 | 129 | 126 | 122 | 118 | 114 | 111 | 107 | 103 | 99 | 95 |

# WITHHOLDING TABLES EFFECTIVE
# JANUARY 1, 2013

### *Semimonthly* PAYROLL PERIOD
### For Calendar Years 2013, and thereafter
### *Married* PERSONS

| WAGES ARE | | NUMBER OF WITHHOLDING ALLOWANCES CLAIMED | | | | | | | | | | |
|---|---|---|---|---|---|---|---|---|---|---|---|---|
| AT LEAST | BUT LESS THAN | 0 | 1 | 2 | 3 | 4 | 5 | 6 | 7 | 8 | 9 | 10 or more |
| | | AMOUNT OF INCOME TAX TO BE WITHHELD | | | | | | | | | | |
| 0 | 40 | 0 | 0 | 0 | 0 | 0 | 0 | 0 | 0 | 0 | 0 | 0 |
| 40 | 60 | 1 | 0 | 0 | 0 | 0 | 0 | 0 | 0 | 0 | 0 | 0 |
| 60 | 80 | 1 | 0 | 0 | 0 | 0 | 0 | 0 | 0 | 0 | 0 | 0 |
| 80 | 100 | 1 | 1 | 0 | 0 | 0 | 0 | 0 | 0 | 0 | 0 | 0 |
| 100 | 120 | 2 | 1 | 0 | 0 | 0 | 0 | 0 | 0 | 0 | 0 | 0 |
| 120 | 140 | 2 | 1 | 0 | 0 | 0 | 0 | 0 | 0 | 0 | 0 | 0 |
| 140 | 160 | 2 | 1 | 1 | 0 | 0 | 0 | 0 | 0 | 0 | 0 | 0 |
| 160 | 180 | 2 | 2 | 1 | 0 | 0 | 0 | 0 | 0 | 0 | 0 | 0 |
| 180 | 200 | 3 | 2 | 1 | 1 | 0 | 0 | 0 | 0 | 0 | 0 | 0 |
| 200 | 220 | 3 | 2 | 2 | 1 | 0 | 0 | 0 | 0 | 0 | 0 | 0 |
| 220 | 240 | 4 | 3 | 2 | 1 | 1 | 0 | 0 | 0 | 0 | 0 | 0 |
| 240 | 260 | 4 | 3 | 2 | 1 | 1 | 0 | 0 | 0 | 0 | 0 | 0 |
| 260 | 280 | 5 | 4 | 2 | 2 | 1 | 0 | 0 | 0 | 0 | 0 | 0 |
| 280 | 300 | 6 | 4 | 3 | 2 | 1 | 1 | 0 | 0 | 0 | 0 | 0 |
| 300 | 320 | 6 | 5 | 3 | 2 | 2 | 1 | 0 | 0 | 0 | 0 | 0 |
| 320 | 340 | 7 | 5 | 4 | 3 | 2 | 1 | 1 | 0 | 0 | 0 | 0 |
| 340 | 360 | 8 | 6 | 5 | 3 | 2 | 2 | 1 | 0 | 0 | 0 | 0 |
| 360 | 380 | 8 | 7 | 5 | 4 | 3 | 2 | 1 | 1 | 0 | 0 | 0 |
| 380 | 400 | 9 | 7 | 6 | 4 | 3 | 2 | 1 | 1 | 0 | 0 | 0 |
| 400 | 420 | 10 | 8 | 6 | 5 | 3 | 2 | 2 | 1 | 0 | 0 | 0 |
| 420 | 440 | 11 | 9 | 7 | 6 | 4 | 3 | 2 | 1 | 1 | 0 | 0 |
| 440 | 460 | 12 | 9 | 8 | 6 | 5 | 3 | 2 | 2 | 1 | 0 | 0 |
| 460 | 480 | 13 | 10 | 8 | 7 | 5 | 4 | 3 | 2 | 1 | 1 | 0 |
| 480 | 500 | 14 | 12 | 9 | 8 | 6 | 4 | 3 | 2 | 2 | 1 | 0 |
| 500 | 520 | 15 | 13 | 10 | 8 | 7 | 5 | 4 | 2 | 2 | 1 | 0 |
| 520 | 540 | 16 | 14 | 11 | 9 | 7 | 6 | 4 | 3 | 2 | 1 | 1 |
| 540 | 560 | 17 | 15 | 12 | 10 | 8 | 6 | 5 | 3 | 2 | 2 | 1 |
| 560 | 580 | 19 | 16 | 13 | 11 | 9 | 7 | 5 | 4 | 3 | 2 | 1 |
| 580 | 600 | 20 | 17 | 14 | 12 | 9 | 8 | 6 | 5 | 3 | 2 | 2 |
| 600 | 620 | 21 | 18 | 16 | 13 | 10 | 8 | 7 | 5 | 4 | 3 | 2 |
| 620 | 640 | 22 | 19 | 17 | 14 | 11 | 9 | 7 | 6 | 4 | 3 | 2 |
| 640 | 660 | 23 | 20 | 18 | 15 | 12 | 10 | 8 | 7 | 5 | 3 | 2 |
| 660 | 680 | 24 | 21 | 19 | 16 | 14 | 11 | 9 | 7 | 6 | 4 | 3 |
| 680 | 700 | 25 | 23 | 20 | 17 | 15 | 12 | 9 | 8 | 6 | 5 | 3 |
| 700 | 720 | 26 | 24 | 21 | 18 | 16 | 13 | 11 | 8 | 7 | 5 | 4 |
| 720 | 740 | 27 | 25 | 22 | 19 | 17 | 14 | 12 | 9 | 8 | 6 | 5 |
| 740 | 760 | 28 | 26 | 23 | 21 | 18 | 15 | 13 | 10 | 8 | 7 | 5 |
| 760 | 780 | 30 | 27 | 24 | 22 | 19 | 16 | 14 | 11 | 9 | 7 | 6 |
| 780 | 800 | 31 | 28 | 25 | 23 | 20 | 18 | 15 | 12 | 10 | 8 | 6 |
| 800 | 820 | 32 | 29 | 27 | 24 | 21 | 19 | 16 | 13 | 11 | 9 | 7 |
| 820 | 840 | 33 | 30 | 28 | 25 | 22 | 20 | 17 | 15 | 12 | 9 | 8 |
| 840 | 860 | 34 | 31 | 29 | 26 | 23 | 21 | 18 | 16 | 13 | 10 | 8 |
| 860 | 880 | 36 | 33 | 30 | 27 | 25 | 22 | 19 | 17 | 14 | 11 | 9 |
| 880 | 900 | 37 | 34 | 31 | 28 | 26 | 23 | 20 | 18 | 15 | 13 | 10 |
| 900 | 920 | 38 | 35 | 32 | 29 | 27 | 24 | 22 | 19 | 16 | 14 | 11 |

# WITHHOLDING TABLES EFFECTIVE
# JANUARY 1, 2013

### *Semimonthly* PAYROLL PERIOD
### For Calendar Years 2013, and thereafter
### *Married* PERSONS

| WAGES ARE | | NUMBER OF WITHHOLDING ALLOWANCES CLAIMED | | | | | | | | | | |
|---|---|---|---|---|---|---|---|---|---|---|---|---|
| AT LEAST | BUT LESS THAN | 0 | 1 | 2 | 3 | 4 | 5 | 6 | 7 | 8 | 9 | 10 or more |
| | | AMOUNT OF INCOME TAX TO BE WITHHELD | | | | | | | | | | |
| 920 | 940 | 40 | 36 | 33 | 30 | 28 | 25 | 23 | 20 | 17 | 15 | 12 |
| 940 | 960 | 41 | 38 | 35 | 32 | 29 | 26 | 24 | 21 | 18 | 16 | 13 |
| 960 | 980 | 42 | 39 | 36 | 33 | 30 | 27 | 25 | 22 | 20 | 17 | 14 |
| 980 | 1,000 | 43 | 40 | 37 | 34 | 31 | 29 | 26 | 23 | 21 | 18 | 15 |
| 1,000 | 1,020 | 45 | 42 | 39 | 35 | 32 | 30 | 27 | 24 | 22 | 19 | 17 |
| 1,020 | 1,040 | 46 | 43 | 40 | 37 | 34 | 31 | 28 | 26 | 23 | 20 | 18 |
| 1,040 | 1,060 | 47 | 44 | 41 | 38 | 35 | 32 | 29 | 27 | 24 | 21 | 19 |
| 1,060 | 1,080 | 48 | 45 | 42 | 39 | 36 | 33 | 30 | 28 | 25 | 22 | 20 |
| 1,080 | 1,100 | 50 | 47 | 44 | 41 | 38 | 35 | 31 | 29 | 26 | 24 | 21 |
| 1,100 | 1,120 | 51 | 48 | 45 | 42 | 39 | 36 | 33 | 30 | 27 | 25 | 22 |
| 1,120 | 1,140 | 52 | 49 | 46 | 43 | 40 | 37 | 34 | 31 | 28 | 26 | 23 |
| 1,140 | 1,160 | 54 | 51 | 48 | 44 | 41 | 38 | 35 | 32 | 29 | 27 | 24 |
| 1,160 | 1,180 | 55 | 52 | 49 | 46 | 43 | 40 | 37 | 34 | 31 | 28 | 25 |
| 1,180 | 1,200 | 56 | 53 | 50 | 47 | 44 | 41 | 38 | 35 | 32 | 29 | 26 |
| 1,200 | 1,220 | 57 | 54 | 51 | 48 | 45 | 42 | 39 | 36 | 33 | 30 | 28 |
| 1,220 | 1,240 | 59 | 56 | 53 | 50 | 47 | 43 | 40 | 37 | 34 | 31 | 29 |
| 1,240 | 1,260 | 60 | 57 | 54 | 51 | 48 | 45 | 42 | 39 | 36 | 33 | 30 |
| 1,260 | 1,280 | 62 | 58 | 55 | 52 | 49 | 46 | 43 | 40 | 37 | 34 | 31 |
| 1,280 | 1,300 | 63 | 60 | 56 | 53 | 50 | 47 | 44 | 41 | 38 | 35 | 32 |
| 1,300 | 1,320 | 64 | 61 | 58 | 55 | 52 | 49 | 46 | 42 | 39 | 36 | 33 |
| 1,320 | 1,340 | 66 | 62 | 59 | 56 | 53 | 50 | 47 | 44 | 41 | 38 | 35 |
| 1,340 | 1,360 | 67 | 64 | 61 | 57 | 54 | 51 | 48 | 45 | 42 | 39 | 36 |
| 1,360 | 1,380 | 68 | 65 | 62 | 59 | 55 | 52 | 49 | 46 | 43 | 40 | 37 |
| 1,380 | 1,400 | 70 | 66 | 63 | 60 | 57 | 54 | 51 | 48 | 45 | 42 | 38 |
| 1,400 | 1,420 | 71 | 68 | 65 | 61 | 58 | 55 | 52 | 49 | 46 | 43 | 40 |
| 1,420 | 1,440 | 72 | 69 | 66 | 63 | 59 | 56 | 53 | 50 | 47 | 44 | 41 |
| 1,440 | 1,460 | 74 | 71 | 67 | 64 | 61 | 58 | 55 | 51 | 48 | 45 | 42 |
| 1,460 | 1,480 | 75 | 72 | 69 | 65 | 62 | 59 | 56 | 53 | 50 | 47 | 44 |
| 1,480 | 1,500 | 77 | 73 | 70 | 67 | 64 | 60 | 57 | 54 | 51 | 48 | 45 |
| 1,500 | 1,520 | 78 | 75 | 71 | 68 | 65 | 62 | 58 | 55 | 52 | 49 | 46 |
| 1,520 | 1,540 | 79 | 76 | 73 | 70 | 66 | 63 | 60 | 57 | 54 | 50 | 47 |
| 1,540 | 1,560 | 81 | 77 | 74 | 71 | 68 | 64 | 61 | 58 | 55 | 52 | 49 |
| 1,560 | 1,580 | 82 | 79 | 75 | 72 | 69 | 66 | 63 | 59 | 56 | 53 | 50 |
| 1,580 | 1,600 | 83 | 80 | 77 | 74 | 70 | 67 | 64 | 61 | 57 | 54 | 51 |
| 1,600 | 1,620 | 85 | 81 | 78 | 75 | 72 | 68 | 65 | 62 | 59 | 56 | 53 |
| 1,620 | 1,640 | 86 | 83 | 80 | 76 | 73 | 70 | 67 | 63 | 60 | 57 | 54 |
| 1,640 | 1,660 | 88 | 84 | 81 | 78 | 74 | 71 | 68 | 65 | 61 | 58 | 55 |
| 1,660 | 1,680 | 89 | 86 | 82 | 79 | 76 | 73 | 69 | 66 | 63 | 60 | 56 |
| 1,680 | 1,700 | 90 | 87 | 84 | 80 | 77 | 74 | 71 | 67 | 64 | 61 | 58 |
| 1,700 | 1,720 | 92 | 88 | 85 | 82 | 79 | 75 | 72 | 69 | 66 | 62 | 59 |
| 1,720 | 1,740 | 93 | 90 | 86 | 83 | 80 | 77 | 73 | 70 | 67 | 64 | 60 |
| 1,740 | 1,760 | 95 | 91 | 88 | 85 | 81 | 78 | 75 | 72 | 68 | 65 | 62 |
| 1,760 | 1,780 | 96 | 93 | 89 | 86 | 83 | 79 | 76 | 73 | 70 | 66 | 63 |
| 1,780 | 1,800 | 98 | 94 | 91 | 87 | 84 | 81 | 77 | 74 | 71 | 68 | 65 |
| 1,800 | 1,820 | 99 | 96 | 92 | 89 | 85 | 82 | 79 | 76 | 72 | 69 | 66 |

# WITHHOLDING TABLES EFFECTIVE
# JANUARY 1, 2013

*Semimonthly* PAYROLL PERIOD

For Calendar Years 2013, and thereafter

*Married* PERSONS

| WAGES ARE | | NUMBER OF WITHHOLDING ALLOWANCES CLAIMED | | | | | | | | | | |
|---|---|---|---|---|---|---|---|---|---|---|---|---|
| AT LEAST | BUT LESS THAN | 0 | 1 | 2 | 3 | 4 | 5 | 6 | 7 | 8 | 9 | 10 or more |
| | | AMOUNT OF INCOME TAX TO BE WITHHELD | | | | | | | | | | |
| 1,820 | 1,840 | 101 | 97 | 94 | 90 | 87 | 83 | 80 | 77 | 74 | 70 | 67 |
| 1,840 | 1,860 | 102 | 99 | 95 | 92 | 88 | 85 | 82 | 78 | 75 | 72 | 69 |
| 1,860 | 1,880 | 103 | 100 | 97 | 93 | 90 | 86 | 83 | 80 | 76 | 73 | 70 |
| 1,880 | 1,900 | 105 | 101 | 98 | 95 | 91 | 88 | 84 | 81 | 78 | 75 | 71 |
| 1,900 | 1,920 | 106 | 103 | 99 | 96 | 93 | 89 | 86 | 82 | 79 | 76 | 73 |
| 1,920 | 1,940 | 108 | 104 | 101 | 97 | 94 | 91 | 87 | 84 | 81 | 77 | 74 |
| 1,940 | 1,960 | 109 | 106 | 102 | 99 | 95 | 92 | 89 | 85 | 82 | 79 | 75 |
| 1,960 | 1,980 | 111 | 107 | 104 | 100 | 97 | 93 | 90 | 87 | 83 | 80 | 77 |
| 1,980 | 2,000 | 112 | 109 | 105 | 102 | 98 | 95 | 91 | 88 | 85 | 81 | 78 |
| 2,000 | 2,020 | 114 | 110 | 107 | 103 | 100 | 96 | 93 | 90 | 86 | 83 | 79 |
| 2,020 | 2,040 | 115 | 112 | 108 | 105 | 101 | 98 | 94 | 91 | 88 | 84 | 81 |
| 2,040 | 2,060 | 117 | 113 | 110 | 106 | 103 | 99 | 96 | 92 | 89 | 86 | 82 |
| 2,060 | 2,080 | 118 | 114 | 111 | 108 | 104 | 101 | 97 | 94 | 90 | 87 | 84 |
| 2,080 | 2,100 | 120 | 116 | 112 | 109 | 106 | 102 | 99 | 95 | 92 | 88 | 85 |
| 2,100 | 2,120 | 121 | 118 | 114 | 110 | 107 | 104 | 100 | 97 | 93 | 90 | 86 |
| 2,120 | 2,140 | 123 | 119 | 115 | 112 | 108 | 105 | 102 | 98 | 95 | 91 | 88 |
| 2,140 | 2,160 | 124 | 121 | 117 | 113 | 110 | 106 | 103 | 100 | 96 | 93 | 89 |
| 2,160 | 2,180 | 126 | 122 | 118 | 115 | 111 | 108 | 104 | 101 | 98 | 94 | 91 |
| 2,180 | 2,200 | 127 | 124 | 120 | 116 | 113 | 109 | 106 | 102 | 99 | 96 | 92 |
| 2,200 | 2,220 | 129 | 125 | 122 | 118 | 114 | 111 | 107 | 104 | 100 | 97 | 94 |
| 2,220 | 2,240 | 130 | 127 | 123 | 119 | 116 | 112 | 109 | 105 | 102 | 98 | 95 |
| 2,240 | 2,260 | 132 | 128 | 125 | 121 | 117 | 114 | 110 | 107 | 103 | 100 | 96 |
| 2,260 | 2,280 | 133 | 130 | 126 | 122 | 119 | 115 | 112 | 108 | 105 | 101 | 98 |
| 2,280 | 2,300 | 135 | 131 | 128 | 124 | 120 | 117 | 113 | 110 | 106 | 103 | 99 |
| 2,300 | 2,320 | 136 | 133 | 129 | 125 | 122 | 118 | 115 | 111 | 108 | 104 | 101 |
| 2,320 | 2,340 | 138 | 134 | 131 | 127 | 123 | 120 | 116 | 113 | 109 | 106 | 102 |
| 2,340 | 2,360 | 139 | 136 | 132 | 129 | 125 | 121 | 118 | 114 | 111 | 107 | 104 |
| 2,360 | 2,380 | 141 | 137 | 134 | 130 | 126 | 123 | 119 | 116 | 112 | 109 | 105 |
| 2,380 | 2,400 | 142 | 139 | 135 | 132 | 128 | 124 | 121 | 117 | 113 | 110 | 107 |
| 2,400 | 2,420 | 144 | 140 | 137 | 133 | 129 | 126 | 122 | 119 | 115 | 111 | 108 |
| 2,420 | 2,440 | 145 | 142 | 138 | 135 | 131 | 127 | 124 | 120 | 117 | 113 | 109 |
| 2,440 | 2,460 | 147 | 143 | 140 | 136 | 133 | 129 | 125 | 122 | 118 | 114 | 111 |
| 2,460 | 2,480 | 149 | 145 | 141 | 138 | 134 | 130 | 127 | 123 | 120 | 116 | 112 |
| 2,480 | 2,500 | 150 | 146 | 143 | 139 | 136 | 132 | 128 | 125 | 121 | 117 | 114 |
| 2,500 | 2,520 | 152 | 148 | 144 | 141 | 137 | 133 | 130 | 126 | 123 | 119 | 115 |
| 2,520 | 2,540 | 153 | 149 | 146 | 142 | 139 | 135 | 131 | 128 | 124 | 120 | 117 |
| 2,540 | 2,560 | 155 | 151 | 147 | 144 | 140 | 136 | 133 | 129 | 126 | 122 | 118 |
| 2,560 | 2,580 | 156 | 152 | 149 | 145 | 142 | 138 | 134 | 131 | 127 | 124 | 120 |
| 2,580 | 2,600 | 158 | 154 | 150 | 147 | 143 | 140 | 136 | 132 | 129 | 125 | 121 |
| 2,600 | 2,620 | 159 | 156 | 152 | 148 | 145 | 141 | 137 | 134 | 130 | 127 | 123 |
| 2,620 | 2,640 | 161 | 157 | 153 | 150 | 146 | 143 | 139 | 135 | 132 | 128 | 124 |
| 2,640 | 2,660 | 162 | 159 | 155 | 151 | 148 | 144 | 140 | 137 | 133 | 130 | 126 |
| 2,660 | 2,680 | 164 | 160 | 156 | 153 | 149 | 146 | 142 | 138 | 135 | 131 | 128 |
| 2,680 | 2,700 | 165 | 162 | 158 | 154 | 151 | 147 | 144 | 140 | 136 | 133 | 129 |
| 2,700 | 2,720 | 167 | 163 | 160 | 156 | 152 | 149 | 145 | 141 | 138 | 134 | 131 |

# WITHHOLDING TABLES EFFECTIVE
# JANUARY 1, 2013

### *Semimonthly* PAYROLL PERIOD
### For Calendar Years 2013, and thereafter
### *Married* PERSONS

| WAGES ARE | | NUMBER OF WITHHOLDING ALLOWANCES CLAIMED | | | | | | | | | | |
|---|---|---|---|---|---|---|---|---|---|---|---|---|
| AT LEAST | BUT LESS THAN | 0 | 1 | 2 | 3 | 4 | 5 | 6 | 7 | 8 | 9 | 10 or more |
| | | AMOUNT OF INCOME TAX TO BE WITHHELD | | | | | | | | | | |
| 2,720 | 2,740 | 168 | 165 | 161 | 157 | 154 | 150 | 147 | 143 | 139 | 136 | 132 |
| 2,740 | 2,760 | 170 | 166 | 163 | 159 | 155 | 152 | 148 | 144 | 141 | 137 | 134 |
| 2,760 | 2,780 | 171 | 168 | 164 | 160 | 157 | 153 | 150 | 146 | 142 | 139 | 135 |
| 2,780 | 2,800 | 173 | 169 | 166 | 162 | 158 | 155 | 151 | 147 | 144 | 140 | 137 |
| 2,800 | 2,820 | 174 | 171 | 167 | 163 | 160 | 156 | 153 | 149 | 145 | 142 | 138 |
| 2,820 | 2,840 | 176 | 172 | 169 | 165 | 161 | 158 | 154 | 151 | 147 | 143 | 140 |
| 2,840 | 2,860 | 177 | 174 | 170 | 167 | 163 | 159 | 156 | 152 | 148 | 145 | 141 |
| 2,860 | 2,880 | 179 | 175 | 172 | 168 | 164 | 161 | 157 | 154 | 150 | 146 | 143 |
| 2,880 | 2,900 | 180 | 177 | 173 | 170 | 166 | 162 | 159 | 155 | 151 | 148 | 144 |
| 2,900 | 2,920 | 182 | 178 | 175 | 171 | 167 | 164 | 160 | 157 | 153 | 149 | 146 |
| 2,920 | 2,940 | 183 | 180 | 176 | 173 | 169 | 165 | 162 | 158 | 155 | 151 | 147 |
| 2,940 | 2,960 | 185 | 181 | 178 | 174 | 171 | 167 | 163 | 160 | 156 | 152 | 149 |
| 2,960 | 2,980 | 187 | 183 | 179 | 176 | 172 | 168 | 165 | 161 | 158 | 154 | 150 |
| 2,980 | 3,000 | 188 | 184 | 181 | 177 | 174 | 170 | 166 | 163 | 159 | 155 | 152 |
| 3,000 | 3,020 | 190 | 186 | 182 | 179 | 175 | 171 | 168 | 164 | 161 | 157 | 153 |
| 3,020 | 3,040 | 191 | 187 | 184 | 180 | 177 | 173 | 169 | 166 | 162 | 158 | 155 |
| 3,040 | 3,060 | 193 | 189 | 185 | 182 | 178 | 174 | 171 | 167 | 164 | 160 | 156 |
| 3,060 | 3,080 | 194 | 191 | 187 | 183 | 180 | 176 | 172 | 169 | 165 | 162 | 158 |
| 3,080 | 3,100 | 196 | 192 | 188 | 185 | 181 | 178 | 174 | 170 | 167 | 163 | 159 |
| 3,100 | 3,120 | 197 | 194 | 190 | 186 | 183 | 179 | 175 | 172 | 168 | 165 | 161 |
| 3,120 | 3,140 | 199 | 195 | 192 | 188 | 184 | 181 | 177 | 173 | 170 | 166 | 162 |
| 3,140 | 3,160 | 201 | 197 | 193 | 189 | 186 | 182 | 178 | 175 | 171 | 168 | 164 |
| 3,160 | 3,180 | 202 | 198 | 195 | 191 | 187 | 184 | 180 | 176 | 173 | 169 | 166 |
| 3,180 | 3,200 | 204 | 200 | 196 | 193 | 189 | 185 | 182 | 178 | 174 | 171 | 167 |
| 3,200 | 3,220 | 205 | 202 | 198 | 194 | 190 | 187 | 183 | 179 | 176 | 172 | 169 |
| 3,220 | 3,240 | 207 | 203 | 199 | 196 | 192 | 188 | 185 | 181 | 177 | 174 | 170 |
| 3,240 | 3,260 | 209 | 205 | 201 | 197 | 193 | 190 | 186 | 182 | 179 | 175 | 172 |
| 3,260 | 3,280 | 210 | 206 | 203 | 199 | 195 | 191 | 188 | 184 | 180 | 177 | 173 |
| 3,280 | 3,300 | 212 | 208 | 204 | 200 | 197 | 193 | 189 | 185 | 182 | 178 | 175 |
| 3,300 | 3,320 | 213 | 210 | 206 | 202 | 198 | 194 | 191 | 187 | 183 | 180 | 176 |
| 3,320 | 3,340 | 215 | 211 | 207 | 204 | 200 | 196 | 192 | 189 | 185 | 181 | 178 |
| 3,340 | 3,360 | 216 | 213 | 209 | 205 | 201 | 198 | 194 | 190 | 186 | 183 | 179 |
| 3,360 | 3,380 | 218 | 214 | 211 | 207 | 203 | 199 | 195 | 192 | 188 | 184 | 181 |
| 3,380 | 3,400 | 220 | 216 | 212 | 208 | 205 | 201 | 197 | 193 | 189 | 186 | 182 |
| 3,400 | 3,420 | 221 | 217 | 214 | 210 | 206 | 202 | 199 | 195 | 191 | 187 | 184 |
| 3,420 | 3,440 | 223 | 219 | 215 | 211 | 208 | 204 | 200 | 196 | 193 | 189 | 185 |
| 3,440 | 3,460 | 224 | 221 | 217 | 213 | 209 | 206 | 202 | 198 | 194 | 190 | 187 |
| 3,460 | 3,480 | 226 | 222 | 218 | 215 | 211 | 207 | 203 | 200 | 196 | 192 | 188 |
| 7.90% of excess over $3,480 plus | | | | | | | | | | | | |
| 3,480 | & over | 228 | 224 | 220 | 216 | 212 | 209 | 205 | 201 | 197 | 194 | 190 |

# WITHHOLDING TABLES EFFECTIVE
# JANUARY 1, 2013

### *Monthly* PAYROLL PERIOD
### For Calendar Years 2013, and thereafter
### *Single* PERSONS — UNMARRIED *Heads of Household*

| WAGES ARE | | NUMBER OF WITHHOLDING ALLOWANCES CLAIMED | | | | | | | | | | |
| AT LEAST | BUT LESS THAN | 0 | 1 | 2 | 3 | 4 | 5 | 6 | 7 | 8 | 9 | 10 or more |
|---|---|---|---|---|---|---|---|---|---|---|---|---|
| | | AMOUNT OF INCOME TAX TO BE WITHHELD | | | | | | | | | | |
| 0 | 40 | 0 | 0 | 0 | 0 | 0 | 0 | 0 | 0 | 0 | 0 | 0 |
| 40 | 60 | 1 | 0 | 0 | 0 | 0 | 0 | 0 | 0 | 0 | 0 | 0 |
| 60 | 80 | 1 | 0 | 0 | 0 | 0 | 0 | 0 | 0 | 0 | 0 | 0 |
| 80 | 100 | 1 | 0 | 0 | 0 | 0 | 0 | 0 | 0 | 0 | 0 | 0 |
| 100 | 120 | 2 | 0 | 0 | 0 | 0 | 0 | 0 | 0 | 0 | 0 | 0 |
| 120 | 140 | 2 | 0 | 0 | 0 | 0 | 0 | 0 | 0 | 0 | 0 | 0 |
| 140 | 160 | 2 | 1 | 0 | 0 | 0 | 0 | 0 | 0 | 0 | 0 | 0 |
| 160 | 180 | 2 | 1 | 0 | 0 | 0 | 0 | 0 | 0 | 0 | 0 | 0 |
| 180 | 200 | 3 | 1 | 0 | 0 | 0 | 0 | 0 | 0 | 0 | 0 | 0 |
| 200 | 220 | 3 | 2 | 0 | 0 | 0 | 0 | 0 | 0 | 0 | 0 | 0 |
| 220 | 240 | 4 | 2 | 1 | 0 | 0 | 0 | 0 | 0 | 0 | 0 | 0 |
| 240 | 260 | 4 | 2 | 1 | 0 | 0 | 0 | 0 | 0 | 0 | 0 | 0 |
| 260 | 280 | 5 | 2 | 1 | 0 | 0 | 0 | 0 | 0 | 0 | 0 | 0 |
| 280 | 300 | 6 | 3 | 1 | 0 | 0 | 0 | 0 | 0 | 0 | 0 | 0 |
| 300 | 320 | 6 | 3 | 2 | 0 | 0 | 0 | 0 | 0 | 0 | 0 | 0 |
| 320 | 340 | 7 | 4 | 2 | 1 | 0 | 0 | 0 | 0 | 0 | 0 | 0 |
| 340 | 360 | 8 | 5 | 2 | 1 | 0 | 0 | 0 | 0 | 0 | 0 | 0 |
| 360 | 380 | 8 | 5 | 3 | 1 | 0 | 0 | 0 | 0 | 0 | 0 | 0 |
| 380 | 400 | 9 | 6 | 3 | 1 | 0 | 0 | 0 | 0 | 0 | 0 | 0 |
| 400 | 420 | 10 | 6 | 3 | 2 | 0 | 0 | 0 | 0 | 0 | 0 | 0 |
| 420 | 440 | 11 | 7 | 4 | 2 | 1 | 0 | 0 | 0 | 0 | 0 | 0 |
| 440 | 460 | 12 | 8 | 5 | 2 | 1 | 0 | 0 | 0 | 0 | 0 | 0 |
| 460 | 480 | 13 | 8 | 5 | 3 | 1 | 0 | 0 | 0 | 0 | 0 | 0 |
| 480 | 500 | 14 | 9 | 6 | 3 | 2 | 0 | 0 | 0 | 0 | 0 | 0 |
| 500 | 520 | 15 | 10 | 7 | 4 | 2 | 0 | 0 | 0 | 0 | 0 | 0 |
| 520 | 540 | 16 | 11 | 7 | 4 | 2 | 1 | 0 | 0 | 0 | 0 | 0 |
| 540 | 560 | 17 | 12 | 8 | 5 | 2 | 1 | 0 | 0 | 0 | 0 | 0 |
| 560 | 580 | 19 | 13 | 9 | 5 | 3 | 1 | 0 | 0 | 0 | 0 | 0 |
| 580 | 600 | 20 | 14 | 9 | 6 | 3 | 2 | 0 | 0 | 0 | 0 | 0 |
| 600 | 620 | 21 | 16 | 10 | 7 | 4 | 2 | 1 | 0 | 0 | 0 | 0 |
| 620 | 640 | 22 | 17 | 11 | 7 | 4 | 2 | 1 | 0 | 0 | 0 | 0 |
| 640 | 660 | 23 | 18 | 12 | 8 | 5 | 2 | 1 | 0 | 0 | 0 | 0 |
| 660 | 680 | 24 | 19 | 14 | 9 | 6 | 3 | 1 | 0 | 0 | 0 | 0 |
| 680 | 700 | 25 | 20 | 15 | 9 | 6 | 3 | 2 | 0 | 0 | 0 | 0 |
| 700 | 720 | 26 | 21 | 16 | 11 | 7 | 4 | 2 | 1 | 0 | 0 | 0 |
| 720 | 740 | 27 | 22 | 17 | 12 | 8 | 5 | 2 | 1 | 0 | 0 | 0 |
| 740 | 760 | 28 | 23 | 18 | 13 | 8 | 5 | 2 | 1 | 0 | 0 | 0 |
| 760 | 780 | 30 | 24 | 19 | 14 | 9 | 6 | 3 | 1 | 0 | 0 | 0 |
| 780 | 800 | 31 | 25 | 20 | 15 | 10 | 6 | 3 | 2 | 0 | 0 | 0 |
| 800 | 820 | 32 | 27 | 21 | 16 | 11 | 7 | 4 | 2 | 1 | 0 | 0 |
| 820 | 840 | 33 | 28 | 22 | 17 | 12 | 8 | 5 | 2 | 1 | 0 | 0 |
| 840 | 860 | 34 | 29 | 23 | 18 | 13 | 8 | 5 | 3 | 1 | 0 | 0 |
| 860 | 880 | 36 | 30 | 25 | 19 | 14 | 9 | 6 | 3 | 2 | 0 | 0 |
| 880 | 900 | 37 | 31 | 26 | 20 | 15 | 10 | 7 | 4 | 2 | 0 | 0 |
| 900 | 920 | 38 | 32 | 27 | 22 | 16 | 11 | 7 | 4 | 2 | 1 | 0 |

# WITHHOLDING TABLES EFFECTIVE
# JANUARY 1, 2013

*Monthly* PAYROLL PERIOD

For Calendar Years 2013, and thereafter

*Single* PERSONS — UNMARRIED *Heads of Household*

| WAGES ARE | | NUMBER OF WITHHOLDING ALLOWANCES CLAIMED | | | | | | | | | | |
|---|---|---|---|---|---|---|---|---|---|---|---|---|
| AT LEAST | BUT LESS THAN | 0 | 1 | 2 | 3 | 4 | 5 | 6 | 7 | 8 | 9 | 10 or more |
| | | AMOUNT OF INCOME TAX TO BE WITHHELD | | | | | | | | | | |
| 920 | 940 | 40 | 33 | 28 | 23 | 17 | 12 | 8 | 5 | 2 | 1 | 0 |
| 940 | 960 | 41 | 35 | 29 | 24 | 18 | 13 | 8 | 5 | 3 | 1 | 0 |
| 960 | 980 | 42 | 36 | 30 | 25 | 20 | 14 | 9 | 6 | 3 | 2 | 0 |
| 980 | 1,000 | 43 | 37 | 31 | 26 | 21 | 15 | 10 | 7 | 4 | 2 | 1 |
| 1,000 | 1,020 | 45 | 39 | 32 | 27 | 22 | 17 | 11 | 7 | 4 | 2 | 1 |
| 1,020 | 1,040 | 46 | 40 | 34 | 28 | 23 | 18 | 12 | 8 | 5 | 2 | 1 |
| 1,040 | 1,060 | 47 | 41 | 35 | 29 | 24 | 19 | 13 | 9 | 6 | 3 | 1 |
| 1,060 | 1,080 | 48 | 42 | 36 | 30 | 25 | 20 | 15 | 9 | 6 | 3 | 2 |
| 1,080 | 1,100 | 50 | 44 | 38 | 31 | 26 | 21 | 16 | 10 | 7 | 4 | 2 |
| 1,100 | 1,120 | 51 | 45 | 39 | 33 | 27 | 22 | 17 | 12 | 8 | 4 | 2 |
| 1,120 | 1,140 | 52 | 46 | 40 | 34 | 28 | 23 | 18 | 13 | 8 | 5 | 2 |
| 1,140 | 1,160 | 54 | 47 | 41 | 35 | 29 | 24 | 19 | 14 | 9 | 6 | 3 |
| 1,160 | 1,180 | 55 | 49 | 43 | 37 | 31 | 25 | 20 | 15 | 10 | 6 | 3 |
| 1,180 | 1,200 | 56 | 50 | 44 | 38 | 32 | 26 | 21 | 16 | 11 | 7 | 4 |
| 1,200 | 1,220 | 57 | 51 | 45 | 39 | 33 | 28 | 22 | 17 | 12 | 8 | 5 |
| 1,220 | 1,240 | 59 | 53 | 47 | 40 | 34 | 29 | 23 | 18 | 13 | 8 | 5 |
| 1,240 | 1,260 | 60 | 54 | 48 | 42 | 36 | 30 | 24 | 19 | 14 | 9 | 6 |
| 1,260 | 1,280 | 62 | 55 | 49 | 43 | 37 | 31 | 26 | 20 | 15 | 10 | 7 |
| 1,280 | 1,300 | 63 | 56 | 50 | 44 | 38 | 32 | 27 | 21 | 16 | 11 | 7 |
| 1,300 | 1,320 | 64 | 58 | 52 | 46 | 39 | 33 | 28 | 23 | 17 | 12 | 8 |
| 1,320 | 1,340 | 66 | 59 | 53 | 47 | 41 | 35 | 29 | 24 | 18 | 13 | 8 |
| 1,340 | 1,360 | 67 | 61 | 54 | 48 | 42 | 36 | 30 | 25 | 19 | 14 | 9 |
| 1,360 | 1,380 | 68 | 62 | 55 | 49 | 43 | 37 | 31 | 26 | 21 | 15 | 10 |
| 1,380 | 1,400 | 70 | 63 | 57 | 51 | 45 | 38 | 32 | 27 | 22 | 16 | 11 |
| 1,400 | 1,420 | 71 | 65 | 58 | 52 | 46 | 40 | 34 | 28 | 23 | 18 | 12 |
| 1,420 | 1,440 | 72 | 66 | 59 | 53 | 47 | 41 | 35 | 29 | 24 | 19 | 13 |
| 1,440 | 1,460 | 74 | 67 | 61 | 54 | 48 | 42 | 36 | 30 | 25 | 20 | 15 |
| 1,460 | 1,480 | 75 | 69 | 62 | 56 | 50 | 44 | 37 | 31 | 26 | 21 | 16 |
| 1,480 | 1,500 | 77 | 70 | 64 | 57 | 51 | 45 | 39 | 33 | 27 | 22 | 17 |
| 1,500 | 1,520 | 78 | 71 | 65 | 58 | 52 | 46 | 40 | 34 | 28 | 23 | 18 |
| 1,520 | 1,540 | 79 | 73 | 66 | 60 | 54 | 47 | 41 | 35 | 29 | 24 | 19 |
| 1,540 | 1,560 | 81 | 74 | 68 | 61 | 55 | 49 | 43 | 36 | 30 | 25 | 20 |
| 1,560 | 1,580 | 82 | 75 | 69 | 63 | 56 | 50 | 44 | 38 | 32 | 26 | 21 |
| 1,580 | 1,600 | 83 | 77 | 70 | 64 | 57 | 51 | 45 | 39 | 33 | 27 | 22 |
| 1,600 | 1,620 | 85 | 78 | 72 | 65 | 59 | 53 | 46 | 40 | 34 | 29 | 23 |
| 1,620 | 1,640 | 86 | 80 | 73 | 67 | 60 | 54 | 48 | 42 | 36 | 30 | 24 |
| 1,640 | 1,660 | 88 | 81 | 74 | 68 | 61 | 55 | 49 | 43 | 37 | 31 | 26 |
| 1,660 | 1,680 | 89 | 82 | 76 | 69 | 63 | 56 | 50 | 44 | 38 | 32 | 27 |
| 1,680 | 1,700 | 90 | 84 | 77 | 71 | 64 | 58 | 52 | 45 | 39 | 33 | 28 |
| 1,700 | 1,720 | 92 | 85 | 79 | 72 | 66 | 59 | 53 | 47 | 41 | 35 | 29 |
| 1,720 | 1,740 | 93 | 86 | 80 | 73 | 67 | 60 | 54 | 48 | 42 | 36 | 30 |
| 1,740 | 1,760 | 95 | 88 | 81 | 75 | 68 | 62 | 55 | 49 | 43 | 37 | 31 |
| 1,760 | 1,780 | 96 | 89 | 83 | 76 | 70 | 63 | 57 | 51 | 44 | 38 | 32 |
| 1,780 | 1,800 | 98 | 91 | 84 | 77 | 71 | 65 | 58 | 52 | 46 | 40 | 34 |
| 1,800 | 1,820 | 99 | 92 | 85 | 79 | 72 | 66 | 59 | 53 | 47 | 41 | 35 |

# WITHHOLDING TABLES EFFECTIVE
# JANUARY 1, 2013

### Monthly PAYROLL PERIOD

### For Calendar Years 2013, and thereafter

### Single PERSONS — UNMARRIED Heads of Household

| WAGES ARE | | NUMBER OF WITHHOLDING ALLOWANCES CLAIMED | | | | | | | | | |
| AT LEAST | BUT LESS THAN | 0 | 1 | 2 | 3 | 4 | 5 | 6 | 7 | 8 | 9 | 10 or more |
|---|---|---|---|---|---|---|---|---|---|---|---|---|
| | | AMOUNT OF INCOME TAX TO BE WITHHELD | | | | | | | | | | |
| 1,820 | 1,840 | 101 | 94 | 87 | 80 | 74 | 67 | 61 | 54 | 48 | 42 | 36 |
| 1,840 | 1,860 | 102 | 95 | 88 | 82 | 75 | 69 | 62 | 56 | 50 | 43 | 37 |
| 1,860 | 1,880 | 103 | 97 | 90 | 83 | 76 | 70 | 63 | 57 | 51 | 45 | 39 |
| 1,880 | 1,900 | 105 | 98 | 91 | 84 | 78 | 71 | 65 | 58 | 52 | 46 | 40 |
| 1,900 | 1,920 | 106 | 99 | 93 | 86 | 79 | 73 | 66 | 60 | 53 | 47 | 41 |
| 1,920 | 1,940 | 108 | 101 | 94 | 87 | 81 | 74 | 68 | 61 | 55 | 49 | 42 |
| 1,940 | 1,960 | 109 | 102 | 95 | 89 | 82 | 75 | 69 | 62 | 56 | 50 | 44 |
| 1,960 | 1,980 | 111 | 104 | 97 | 90 | 83 | 77 | 70 | 64 | 57 | 51 | 45 |
| 1,980 | 2,000 | 112 | 105 | 98 | 91 | 85 | 78 | 72 | 65 | 59 | 52 | 46 |
| 2,000 | 2,020 | 114 | 107 | 100 | 93 | 86 | 79 | 73 | 66 | 60 | 54 | 48 |
| 2,020 | 2,040 | 115 | 108 | 101 | 94 | 87 | 81 | 74 | 68 | 61 | 55 | 49 |
| 2,040 | 2,060 | 117 | 110 | 103 | 96 | 89 | 82 | 76 | 69 | 63 | 56 | 50 |
| 2,060 | 2,080 | 118 | 111 | 104 | 97 | 90 | 84 | 77 | 71 | 64 | 58 | 51 |
| 2,080 | 2,100 | 120 | 112 | 106 | 99 | 92 | 85 | 78 | 72 | 65 | 59 | 53 |
| 2,100 | 2,120 | 121 | 114 | 107 | 100 | 93 | 86 | 80 | 73 | 67 | 60 | 54 |
| 2,120 | 2,140 | 123 | 115 | 108 | 102 | 95 | 88 | 81 | 75 | 68 | 62 | 55 |
| 2,140 | 2,160 | 124 | 117 | 110 | 103 | 96 | 89 | 82 | 76 | 70 | 63 | 57 |
| 2,160 | 2,180 | 126 | 118 | 111 | 104 | 98 | 91 | 84 | 77 | 71 | 64 | 58 |
| 2,180 | 2,200 | 127 | 120 | 113 | 106 | 99 | 92 | 85 | 79 | 72 | 66 | 59 |
| 2,200 | 2,220 | 129 | 122 | 114 | 107 | 100 | 94 | 87 | 80 | 74 | 67 | 61 |
| 2,220 | 2,240 | 130 | 123 | 116 | 109 | 102 | 95 | 88 | 81 | 75 | 68 | 62 |
| 2,240 | 2,260 | 132 | 125 | 117 | 110 | 103 | 96 | 90 | 83 | 76 | 70 | 63 |
| 2,260 | 2,280 | 133 | 126 | 119 | 112 | 105 | 98 | 91 | 84 | 78 | 71 | 65 |
| 2,280 | 2,300 | 135 | 128 | 120 | 113 | 106 | 99 | 92 | 86 | 79 | 73 | 66 |
| 2,300 | 2,320 | 136 | 129 | 122 | 115 | 108 | 101 | 94 | 87 | 80 | 74 | 67 |
| 2,320 | 2,340 | 138 | 131 | 123 | 116 | 109 | 102 | 95 | 89 | 82 | 75 | 69 |
| 2,340 | 2,360 | 139 | 132 | 125 | 118 | 111 | 104 | 97 | 90 | 83 | 77 | 70 |
| 2,360 | 2,380 | 141 | 134 | 126 | 119 | 112 | 105 | 98 | 91 | 85 | 78 | 72 |
| 2,380 | 2,400 | 142 | 135 | 128 | 121 | 113 | 107 | 100 | 93 | 86 | 79 | 73 |
| 2,400 | 2,420 | 144 | 137 | 129 | 122 | 115 | 108 | 101 | 94 | 87 | 81 | 74 |
| 2,420 | 2,440 | 145 | 138 | 131 | 124 | 116 | 109 | 103 | 96 | 89 | 82 | 76 |
| 2,440 | 2,460 | 147 | 140 | 133 | 125 | 118 | 111 | 104 | 97 | 90 | 83 | 77 |
| 2,460 | 2,480 | 149 | 141 | 134 | 127 | 120 | 112 | 105 | 99 | 92 | 85 | 78 |
| 2,480 | 2,500 | 150 | 143 | 136 | 128 | 121 | 114 | 107 | 100 | 93 | 86 | 80 |
| 2,500 | 2,520 | 152 | 144 | 137 | 130 | 123 | 115 | 108 | 101 | 95 | 88 | 81 |
| 2,520 | 2,540 | 153 | 146 | 139 | 131 | 124 | 117 | 110 | 103 | 96 | 89 | 82 |
| 2,540 | 2,560 | 155 | 147 | 140 | 133 | 126 | 118 | 111 | 104 | 97 | 91 | 84 |
| 2,560 | 2,580 | 156 | 149 | 142 | 134 | 127 | 120 | 113 | 106 | 99 | 92 | 85 |
| 2,580 | 2,600 | 158 | 150 | 143 | 136 | 129 | 121 | 114 | 107 | 100 | 93 | 87 |
| 2,600 | 2,620 | 159 | 152 | 145 | 137 | 130 | 123 | 116 | 109 | 102 | 95 | 88 |
| 2,620 | 2,640 | 161 | 153 | 146 | 139 | 132 | 124 | 117 | 110 | 103 | 96 | 90 |
| 2,640 | 2,660 | 162 | 155 | 148 | 140 | 133 | 126 | 119 | 112 | 105 | 98 | 91 |
| 2,660 | 2,680 | 164 | 156 | 149 | 142 | 135 | 127 | 120 | 113 | 106 | 99 | 92 |
| 2,680 | 2,700 | 165 | 158 | 151 | 144 | 136 | 129 | 122 | 115 | 108 | 101 | 94 |
| 2,700 | 2,720 | 167 | 160 | 152 | 145 | 138 | 131 | 123 | 116 | 109 | 102 | 95 |

# WITHHOLDING TABLES EFFECTIVE
# JANUARY 1, 2013

### Monthly PAYROLL PERIOD

### For Calendar Years 2013, and thereafter

### Single PERSONS — UNMARRIED Heads of Household

| WAGES ARE | | NUMBER OF WITHHOLDING ALLOWANCES CLAIMED | | | | | | | | | | |
|---|---|---|---|---|---|---|---|---|---|---|---|---|
| AT LEAST | BUT LESS THAN | 0 | 1 | 2 | 3 | 4 | 5 | 6 | 7 | 8 | 9 | 10 or more |
| | | AMOUNT OF INCOME TAX TO BE WITHHELD | | | | | | | | | | |
| 2,720 | 2,740 | 168 | 161 | 154 | 147 | 139 | 132 | 125 | 118 | 110 | 104 | 97 |
| 2,740 | 2,760 | 170 | 163 | 155 | 148 | 141 | 134 | 126 | 119 | 112 | 105 | 98 |
| 2,760 | 2,780 | 171 | 164 | 157 | 150 | 142 | 135 | 128 | 121 | 113 | 106 | 100 |
| 2,780 | 2,800 | 173 | 166 | 158 | 151 | 144 | 137 | 129 | 122 | 115 | 108 | 101 |
| 2,800 | 2,820 | 174 | 167 | 160 | 153 | 145 | 138 | 131 | 124 | 116 | 109 | 102 |
| 2,820 | 2,840 | 176 | 169 | 161 | 154 | 147 | 140 | 132 | 125 | 118 | 111 | 104 |
| 2,840 | 2,860 | 177 | 170 | 163 | 156 | 148 | 141 | 134 | 127 | 119 | 112 | 105 |
| 2,860 | 2,880 | 179 | 172 | 164 | 157 | 150 | 143 | 135 | 128 | 121 | 114 | 107 |
| 2,880 | 2,900 | 180 | 173 | 166 | 159 | 151 | 144 | 137 | 130 | 122 | 115 | 108 |
| 2,900 | 2,920 | 182 | 175 | 167 | 160 | 153 | 146 | 138 | 131 | 124 | 117 | 110 |
| 2,920 | 2,940 | 183 | 176 | 169 | 162 | 154 | 147 | 140 | 133 | 126 | 118 | 111 |
| 2,940 | 2,960 | 185 | 178 | 171 | 163 | 156 | 149 | 142 | 134 | 127 | 120 | 113 |
| 2,960 | 2,980 | 187 | 179 | 172 | 165 | 158 | 150 | 143 | 136 | 129 | 121 | 114 |
| 2,980 | 3,000 | 188 | 181 | 174 | 166 | 159 | 152 | 145 | 137 | 130 | 123 | 116 |
| 3,000 | 3,020 | 190 | 182 | 175 | 168 | 161 | 153 | 146 | 139 | 132 | 124 | 117 |
| 3,020 | 3,040 | 191 | 184 | 177 | 169 | 162 | 155 | 148 | 140 | 133 | 126 | 119 |
| 3,040 | 3,060 | 193 | 185 | 178 | 171 | 164 | 156 | 149 | 142 | 135 | 127 | 120 |
| 3,060 | 3,080 | 194 | 187 | 180 | 172 | 165 | 158 | 151 | 143 | 136 | 129 | 122 |
| 3,080 | 3,100 | 196 | 188 | 181 | 174 | 167 | 159 | 152 | 145 | 138 | 130 | 123 |
| 3,100 | 3,120 | 197 | 190 | 183 | 175 | 168 | 161 | 154 | 146 | 139 | 132 | 125 |
| 3,120 | 3,140 | 199 | 192 | 184 | 177 | 170 | 162 | 155 | 148 | 141 | 133 | 126 |
| 3,140 | 3,160 | 201 | 193 | 186 | 178 | 171 | 164 | 157 | 149 | 142 | 135 | 128 |
| 3,160 | 3,180 | 202 | 195 | 187 | 180 | 173 | 165 | 158 | 151 | 144 | 137 | 129 |
| 3,180 | 3,200 | 204 | 196 | 189 | 182 | 174 | 167 | 160 | 153 | 145 | 138 | 131 |
| 3,200 | 3,220 | 205 | 198 | 190 | 183 | 176 | 169 | 161 | 154 | 147 | 140 | 132 |
| 3,220 | 3,240 | 207 | 199 | 192 | 185 | 177 | 170 | 163 | 156 | 148 | 141 | 134 |
| 3,240 | 3,260 | 209 | 201 | 193 | 186 | 179 | 172 | 164 | 157 | 150 | 143 | 135 |
| 3,260 | 3,280 | 210 | 203 | 195 | 188 | 180 | 173 | 166 | 159 | 151 | 144 | 137 |
| 3,280 | 3,300 | 212 | 204 | 197 | 189 | 182 | 175 | 167 | 160 | 153 | 146 | 138 |
| 3,300 | 3,320 | 213 | 206 | 198 | 191 | 183 | 176 | 169 | 162 | 154 | 147 | 140 |
| 3,320 | 3,340 | 215 | 207 | 200 | 192 | 185 | 178 | 170 | 163 | 156 | 149 | 141 |
| 3,340 | 3,360 | 216 | 209 | 201 | 194 | 186 | 179 | 172 | 165 | 157 | 150 | 143 |
| 3,360 | 3,380 | 218 | 210 | 203 | 195 | 188 | 181 | 173 | 166 | 159 | 152 | 144 |
| 3,380 | 3,400 | 220 | 212 | 205 | 197 | 189 | 182 | 175 | 168 | 160 | 153 | 146 |
| 3,400 | 3,420 | 221 | 214 | 206 | 199 | 191 | 184 | 176 | 169 | 162 | 155 | 147 |
| 3,420 | 3,440 | 223 | 215 | 208 | 200 | 193 | 185 | 178 | 171 | 164 | 156 | 149 |
| 3,440 | 3,460 | 224 | 217 | 209 | 202 | 194 | 187 | 180 | 172 | 165 | 158 | 151 |
| 3,460 | 3,480 | 226 | 218 | 211 | 203 | 196 | 188 | 181 | 174 | 167 | 159 | 152 |
| 3,480 | 3,500 | 228 | 220 | 212 | 205 | 197 | 190 | 183 | 175 | 168 | 161 | 154 |
| 3,500 | 3,520 | 229 | 222 | 214 | 206 | 199 | 191 | 184 | 177 | 170 | 162 | 155 |
| 3,520 | 3,540 | 231 | 223 | 216 | 208 | 201 | 193 | 186 | 178 | 171 | 164 | 157 |
| 3,540 | 3,560 | 232 | 225 | 217 | 210 | 202 | 195 | 187 | 180 | 173 | 165 | 158 |
| 3,560 | 3,580 | 234 | 226 | 219 | 211 | 204 | 196 | 189 | 181 | 174 | 167 | 160 |
| 3,580 | 3,600 | 235 | 228 | 220 | 213 | 205 | 198 | 190 | 183 | 176 | 168 | 161 |
| 3,600 | 3,620 | 237 | 229 | 222 | 214 | 207 | 199 | 192 | 184 | 177 | 170 | 163 |

# WITHHOLDING TABLES EFFECTIVE
# JANUARY 1, 2013

### *Monthly* PAYROLL PERIOD
### For Calendar Years 2013, and thereafter
### *Single* PERSONS — UNMARRIED *Heads of Household*

| WAGES ARE | | NUMBER OF WITHHOLDING ALLOWANCES CLAIMED | | | | | | | | | | |
|---|---|---|---|---|---|---|---|---|---|---|---|---|
| AT LEAST | BUT LESS THAN | 0 | 1 | 2 | 3 | 4 | 5 | 6 | 7 | 8 | 9 | 10 or more |
| | | AMOUNT OF INCOME TAX TO BE WITHHELD | | | | | | | | | | |
| 3,620 | 3,640 | 239 | 231 | 224 | 216 | 208 | 201 | 193 | 186 | 179 | 171 | 164 |
| 3,640 | 3,660 | 240 | 233 | 225 | 218 | 210 | 202 | 195 | 187 | 180 | 173 | 166 |
| 3,660 | 3,680 | 242 | 234 | 227 | 219 | 212 | 204 | 197 | 189 | 182 | 175 | 167 |
| 3,680 | 3,700 | 243 | 236 | 228 | 221 | 213 | 206 | 198 | 191 | 183 | 176 | 169 |
| 3,700 | 3,720 | 245 | 237 | 230 | 222 | 215 | 207 | 200 | 192 | 185 | 178 | 170 |
| 3,720 | 3,740 | 246 | 239 | 231 | 224 | 216 | 209 | 201 | 194 | 186 | 179 | 172 |
| 3,740 | 3,760 | 248 | 241 | 233 | 225 | 218 | 210 | 203 | 195 | 188 | 181 | 173 |
| 3,760 | 3,780 | 250 | 242 | 235 | 227 | 219 | 212 | 204 | 197 | 189 | 182 | 175 |
| 3,780 | 3,800 | 251 | 244 | 236 | 229 | 221 | 214 | 206 | 198 | 191 | 184 | 176 |
| 3,800 | 3,820 | 253 | 245 | 238 | 230 | 223 | 215 | 208 | 200 | 193 | 185 | 178 |
| 3,820 | 3,840 | 254 | 247 | 239 | 232 | 224 | 217 | 209 | 202 | 194 | 187 | 179 |
| 3,840 | 3,860 | 256 | 248 | 241 | 233 | 226 | 218 | 211 | 203 | 196 | 188 | 181 |
| 3,860 | 3,880 | 258 | 250 | 242 | 235 | 227 | 220 | 212 | 205 | 197 | 190 | 182 |
| 3,880 | 3,900 | 259 | 252 | 244 | 237 | 229 | 221 | 214 | 206 | 199 | 191 | 184 |
| 3,900 | 3,920 | 261 | 253 | 246 | 238 | 231 | 223 | 215 | 208 | 200 | 193 | 185 |
| 3,920 | 3,940 | 262 | 255 | 247 | 240 | 232 | 225 | 217 | 210 | 202 | 194 | 187 |
| 3,940 | 3,960 | 264 | 256 | 249 | 241 | 234 | 226 | 219 | 211 | 204 | 196 | 189 |
| 7.90% of excess over $3,960 plus | | | | | | | | | | | | |
| 3,960 | & over | 265 | 258 | 250 | 243 | 235 | 228 | 220 | 213 | 205 | 198 | 190 |

# WITHHOLDING TABLES EFFECTIVE
# JANUARY 1, 2013

### *Monthly* PAYROLL PERIOD
### For Calendar Years 2013, and thereafter
### *Married* PERSONS

| WAGES ARE | | NUMBER OF WITHHOLDING ALLOWANCES CLAIMED | | | | | | | | | | |
|---|---|---|---|---|---|---|---|---|---|---|---|---|
| AT LEAST | BUT LESS THAN | 0 | 1 | 2 | 3 | 4 | 5 | 6 | 7 | 8 | 9 | 10 or more |
| | | AMOUNT OF INCOME TAX TO BE WITHHELD | | | | | | | | | | |
| 0 | 40 | 0 | 0 | 0 | 0 | 0 | 0 | 0 | 0 | 0 | 0 | 0 |
| 40 | 60 | 1 | 0 | 0 | 0 | 0 | 0 | 0 | 0 | 0 | 0 | 0 |
| 60 | 80 | 1 | 0 | 0 | 0 | 0 | 0 | 0 | 0 | 0 | 0 | 0 |
| 80 | 100 | 1 | 0 | 0 | 0 | 0 | 0 | 0 | 0 | 0 | 0 | 0 |
| 100 | 120 | 2 | 0 | 0 | 0 | 0 | 0 | 0 | 0 | 0 | 0 | 0 |
| 120 | 140 | 2 | 0 | 0 | 0 | 0 | 0 | 0 | 0 | 0 | 0 | 0 |
| 140 | 160 | 2 | 1 | 0 | 0 | 0 | 0 | 0 | 0 | 0 | 0 | 0 |
| 160 | 180 | 2 | 1 | 0 | 0 | 0 | 0 | 0 | 0 | 0 | 0 | 0 |
| 180 | 200 | 3 | 1 | 0 | 0 | 0 | 0 | 0 | 0 | 0 | 0 | 0 |
| 200 | 220 | 3 | 2 | 0 | 0 | 0 | 0 | 0 | 0 | 0 | 0 | 0 |
| 220 | 240 | 3 | 2 | 1 | 0 | 0 | 0 | 0 | 0 | 0 | 0 | 0 |
| 240 | 260 | 4 | 2 | 1 | 0 | 0 | 0 | 0 | 0 | 0 | 0 | 0 |
| 260 | 280 | 4 | 2 | 1 | 0 | 0 | 0 | 0 | 0 | 0 | 0 | 0 |
| 280 | 300 | 4 | 3 | 1 | 0 | 0 | 0 | 0 | 0 | 0 | 0 | 0 |
| 300 | 320 | 4 | 3 | 2 | 0 | 0 | 0 | 0 | 0 | 0 | 0 | 0 |
| 320 | 340 | 5 | 3 | 2 | 1 | 0 | 0 | 0 | 0 | 0 | 0 | 0 |
| 340 | 360 | 5 | 4 | 2 | 1 | 0 | 0 | 0 | 0 | 0 | 0 | 0 |
| 360 | 380 | 5 | 4 | 3 | 1 | 0 | 0 | 0 | 0 | 0 | 0 | 0 |
| 380 | 400 | 5 | 4 | 3 | 1 | 0 | 0 | 0 | 0 | 0 | 0 | 0 |
| 400 | 420 | 6 | 4 | 3 | 2 | 0 | 0 | 0 | 0 | 0 | 0 | 0 |
| 420 | 440 | 7 | 5 | 3 | 2 | 1 | 0 | 0 | 0 | 0 | 0 | 0 |
| 440 | 460 | 7 | 5 | 4 | 2 | 1 | 0 | 0 | 0 | 0 | 0 | 0 |
| 460 | 480 | 8 | 5 | 4 | 3 | 1 | 0 | 0 | 0 | 0 | 0 | 0 |
| 480 | 500 | 8 | 6 | 4 | 3 | 2 | 0 | 0 | 0 | 0 | 0 | 0 |
| 500 | 520 | 9 | 6 | 4 | 3 | 2 | 0 | 0 | 0 | 0 | 0 | 0 |
| 520 | 540 | 10 | 7 | 5 | 3 | 2 | 1 | 0 | 0 | 0 | 0 | 0 |
| 540 | 560 | 10 | 7 | 5 | 4 | 2 | 1 | 0 | 0 | 0 | 0 | 0 |
| 560 | 580 | 11 | 8 | 5 | 4 | 3 | 1 | 0 | 0 | 0 | 0 | 0 |
| 580 | 600 | 12 | 9 | 6 | 4 | 3 | 2 | 0 | 0 | 0 | 0 | 0 |
| 600 | 620 | 12 | 9 | 6 | 5 | 3 | 2 | 1 | 0 | 0 | 0 | 0 |
| 620 | 640 | 13 | 10 | 7 | 5 | 3 | 2 | 1 | 0 | 0 | 0 | 0 |
| 640 | 660 | 14 | 11 | 7 | 5 | 4 | 2 | 1 | 0 | 0 | 0 | 0 |
| 660 | 680 | 14 | 11 | 8 | 5 | 4 | 3 | 1 | 0 | 0 | 0 | 0 |
| 680 | 700 | 15 | 12 | 9 | 6 | 4 | 3 | 2 | 0 | 0 | 0 | 0 |
| 700 | 720 | 16 | 12 | 9 | 6 | 5 | 3 | 2 | 1 | 0 | 0 | 0 |
| 720 | 740 | 16 | 13 | 10 | 7 | 5 | 4 | 2 | 1 | 0 | 0 | 0 |
| 740 | 760 | 17 | 14 | 11 | 8 | 5 | 4 | 2 | 1 | 0 | 0 | 0 |
| 760 | 780 | 17 | 14 | 11 | 8 | 5 | 4 | 3 | 1 | 0 | 0 | 0 |
| 780 | 800 | 18 | 15 | 12 | 9 | 6 | 4 | 3 | 2 | 0 | 0 | 0 |
| 800 | 820 | 19 | 16 | 13 | 10 | 7 | 5 | 3 | 2 | 1 | 0 | 0 |
| 820 | 840 | 20 | 16 | 13 | 10 | 7 | 5 | 4 | 2 | 1 | 0 | 0 |
| 840 | 860 | 21 | 17 | 14 | 11 | 8 | 5 | 4 | 3 | 1 | 0 | 0 |
| 860 | 880 | 22 | 18 | 15 | 11 | 8 | 6 | 4 | 3 | 2 | 0 | 0 |
| 880 | 900 | 23 | 18 | 15 | 12 | 9 | 6 | 4 | 3 | 2 | 0 | 0 |
| 900 | 920 | 24 | 19 | 16 | 13 | 10 | 7 | 5 | 3 | 2 | 1 | 0 |

# WITHHOLDING TABLES EFFECTIVE
# JANUARY 1, 2013

### *Monthly* PAYROLL PERIOD

### For Calendar Years 2013, and thereafter

### *Married* PERSONS

| WAGES ARE | | NUMBER OF WITHHOLDING ALLOWANCES CLAIMED | | | | | | | | | | |
|---|---|---|---|---|---|---|---|---|---|---|---|---|
| AT LEAST | BUT LESS THAN | 0 | 1 | 2 | 3 | 4 | 5 | 6 | 7 | 8 | 9 | 10 or more |
| | | AMOUNT OF INCOME TAX TO BE WITHHELD | | | | | | | | | | |
| 920 | 940 | 26 | 20 | 16 | 13 | 10 | 7 | 5 | 4 | 2 | 1 | 0 |
| 940 | 960 | 27 | 21 | 17 | 14 | 11 | 8 | 5 | 4 | 3 | 1 | 0 |
| 960 | 980 | 28 | 23 | 18 | 15 | 12 | 9 | 6 | 4 | 3 | 2 | 0 |
| 980 | 1,000 | 29 | 24 | 18 | 15 | 12 | 9 | 6 | 5 | 3 | 2 | 1 |
| 1,000 | 1,020 | 30 | 25 | 19 | 16 | 13 | 10 | 7 | 5 | 3 | 2 | 1 |
| 1,020 | 1,040 | 31 | 26 | 21 | 17 | 14 | 11 | 7 | 5 | 4 | 2 | 1 |
| 1,040 | 1,060 | 32 | 27 | 22 | 17 | 14 | 11 | 8 | 5 | 4 | 3 | 1 |
| 1,060 | 1,080 | 33 | 28 | 23 | 18 | 15 | 12 | 9 | 6 | 4 | 3 | 2 |
| 1,080 | 1,100 | 34 | 29 | 24 | 19 | 15 | 12 | 9 | 6 | 5 | 3 | 2 |
| 1,100 | 1,120 | 35 | 30 | 25 | 20 | 16 | 13 | 10 | 7 | 5 | 4 | 2 |
| 1,120 | 1,140 | 37 | 31 | 26 | 21 | 17 | 14 | 11 | 8 | 5 | 4 | 2 |
| 1,140 | 1,160 | 38 | 32 | 27 | 22 | 17 | 14 | 11 | 8 | 5 | 4 | 3 |
| 1,160 | 1,180 | 39 | 34 | 28 | 23 | 18 | 15 | 12 | 9 | 6 | 4 | 3 |
| 1,180 | 1,200 | 40 | 35 | 29 | 24 | 19 | 16 | 13 | 10 | 6 | 5 | 3 |
| 1,200 | 1,220 | 41 | 36 | 30 | 25 | 20 | 16 | 13 | 10 | 7 | 5 | 4 |
| 1,220 | 1,240 | 42 | 37 | 32 | 26 | 21 | 17 | 14 | 11 | 8 | 5 | 4 |
| 1,240 | 1,260 | 43 | 38 | 33 | 27 | 22 | 18 | 14 | 11 | 8 | 5 | 4 |
| 1,260 | 1,280 | 44 | 39 | 34 | 29 | 23 | 18 | 15 | 12 | 9 | 6 | 4 |
| 1,280 | 1,300 | 45 | 40 | 35 | 30 | 24 | 19 | 16 | 13 | 10 | 7 | 5 |
| 1,300 | 1,320 | 46 | 41 | 36 | 31 | 25 | 20 | 16 | 13 | 10 | 7 | 5 |
| 1,320 | 1,340 | 48 | 42 | 37 | 32 | 27 | 21 | 17 | 14 | 11 | 8 | 5 |
| 1,340 | 1,360 | 49 | 43 | 38 | 33 | 28 | 22 | 18 | 15 | 12 | 9 | 6 |
| 1,360 | 1,380 | 50 | 45 | 39 | 34 | 29 | 24 | 18 | 15 | 12 | 9 | 6 |
| 1,380 | 1,400 | 51 | 46 | 40 | 35 | 30 | 25 | 19 | 16 | 13 | 10 | 7 |
| 1,400 | 1,420 | 52 | 47 | 41 | 36 | 31 | 26 | 20 | 17 | 14 | 10 | 7 |
| 1,420 | 1,440 | 53 | 48 | 43 | 37 | 32 | 27 | 22 | 17 | 14 | 11 | 8 |
| 1,440 | 1,460 | 54 | 49 | 44 | 38 | 33 | 28 | 23 | 18 | 15 | 12 | 9 |
| 1,460 | 1,480 | 55 | 50 | 45 | 40 | 34 | 29 | 24 | 19 | 15 | 12 | 9 |
| 1,480 | 1,500 | 56 | 51 | 46 | 41 | 35 | 30 | 25 | 20 | 16 | 13 | 10 |
| 1,500 | 1,520 | 57 | 52 | 47 | 42 | 36 | 31 | 26 | 21 | 17 | 14 | 11 |
| 1,520 | 1,540 | 59 | 53 | 48 | 43 | 38 | 32 | 27 | 22 | 17 | 14 | 11 |
| 1,540 | 1,560 | 60 | 54 | 49 | 44 | 39 | 33 | 28 | 23 | 18 | 15 | 12 |
| 1,560 | 1,580 | 61 | 56 | 50 | 45 | 40 | 35 | 29 | 24 | 19 | 16 | 13 |
| 1,580 | 1,600 | 62 | 57 | 51 | 46 | 41 | 36 | 30 | 25 | 20 | 16 | 13 |
| 1,600 | 1,620 | 63 | 58 | 52 | 47 | 42 | 37 | 31 | 26 | 21 | 17 | 14 |
| 1,620 | 1,640 | 64 | 59 | 54 | 48 | 43 | 38 | 33 | 27 | 22 | 17 | 14 |
| 1,640 | 1,660 | 66 | 60 | 55 | 49 | 44 | 39 | 34 | 28 | 23 | 18 | 15 |
| 1,660 | 1,680 | 67 | 61 | 56 | 51 | 45 | 40 | 35 | 30 | 24 | 19 | 16 |
| 1,680 | 1,700 | 68 | 62 | 57 | 52 | 46 | 41 | 36 | 31 | 25 | 20 | 16 |
| 1,700 | 1,720 | 69 | 63 | 58 | 53 | 47 | 42 | 37 | 32 | 26 | 21 | 17 |
| 1,720 | 1,740 | 71 | 65 | 59 | 54 | 49 | 43 | 38 | 33 | 28 | 22 | 18 |
| 1,740 | 1,760 | 72 | 66 | 60 | 55 | 50 | 44 | 39 | 34 | 29 | 23 | 18 |
| 1,760 | 1,780 | 73 | 67 | 61 | 56 | 51 | 46 | 40 | 35 | 30 | 25 | 19 |
| 1,780 | 1,800 | 75 | 68 | 62 | 57 | 52 | 47 | 41 | 36 | 31 | 26 | 20 |
| 1,800 | 1,820 | 76 | 70 | 64 | 58 | 53 | 48 | 42 | 37 | 32 | 27 | 22 |

# WITHHOLDING TABLES EFFECTIVE
# JANUARY 1, 2013

### *Monthly* PAYROLL PERIOD
### For Calendar Years 2013, and thereafter
### *Married* PERSONS

| WAGES ARE | | NUMBER OF WITHHOLDING ALLOWANCES CLAIMED | | | | | | | | | | |
|---|---|---|---|---|---|---|---|---|---|---|---|---|
| AT LEAST | BUT LESS THAN | 0 | 1 | 2 | 3 | 4 | 5 | 6 | 7 | 8 | 9 | 10 or more |
| | | AMOUNT OF INCOME TAX TO BE WITHHELD | | | | | | | | | | |
| 1,820 | 1,840 | 77 | 71 | 65 | 59 | 54 | 49 | 44 | 38 | 33 | 28 | 23 |
| 1,840 | 1,860 | 78 | 72 | 66 | 60 | 55 | 50 | 45 | 39 | 34 | 29 | 24 |
| 1,860 | 1,880 | 80 | 74 | 67 | 62 | 56 | 51 | 46 | 41 | 35 | 30 | 25 |
| 1,880 | 1,900 | 81 | 75 | 69 | 63 | 57 | 52 | 47 | 42 | 36 | 31 | 26 |
| 1,900 | 1,920 | 82 | 76 | 70 | 64 | 58 | 53 | 48 | 43 | 37 | 32 | 27 |
| 1,920 | 1,940 | 84 | 77 | 71 | 65 | 60 | 54 | 49 | 44 | 39 | 33 | 28 |
| 1,940 | 1,960 | 85 | 79 | 73 | 66 | 61 | 55 | 50 | 45 | 40 | 34 | 29 |
| 1,960 | 1,980 | 86 | 80 | 74 | 68 | 62 | 57 | 51 | 46 | 41 | 36 | 30 |
| 1,980 | 2,000 | 87 | 81 | 75 | 69 | 63 | 58 | 52 | 47 | 42 | 37 | 31 |
| 2,000 | 2,020 | 89 | 83 | 76 | 70 | 64 | 59 | 53 | 48 | 43 | 38 | 33 |
| 2,020 | 2,040 | 90 | 84 | 78 | 72 | 66 | 60 | 55 | 49 | 44 | 39 | 34 |
| 2,040 | 2,060 | 91 | 85 | 79 | 73 | 67 | 61 | 56 | 50 | 45 | 40 | 35 |
| 2,060 | 2,080 | 92 | 86 | 80 | 74 | 68 | 62 | 57 | 52 | 46 | 41 | 36 |
| 2,080 | 2,100 | 94 | 88 | 82 | 75 | 69 | 63 | 58 | 53 | 47 | 42 | 37 |
| 2,100 | 2,120 | 95 | 89 | 83 | 77 | 71 | 65 | 59 | 54 | 48 | 43 | 38 |
| 2,120 | 2,140 | 96 | 90 | 84 | 78 | 72 | 66 | 60 | 55 | 50 | 44 | 39 |
| 2,140 | 2,160 | 98 | 91 | 85 | 79 | 73 | 67 | 61 | 56 | 51 | 45 | 40 |
| 2,160 | 2,180 | 99 | 93 | 87 | 81 | 74 | 68 | 62 | 57 | 52 | 47 | 41 |
| 2,180 | 2,200 | 100 | 94 | 88 | 82 | 76 | 70 | 64 | 58 | 53 | 48 | 42 |
| 2,200 | 2,220 | 101 | 95 | 89 | 83 | 77 | 71 | 65 | 59 | 54 | 49 | 44 |
| 2,220 | 2,240 | 103 | 97 | 91 | 84 | 78 | 72 | 66 | 60 | 55 | 50 | 45 |
| 2,240 | 2,260 | 104 | 98 | 92 | 86 | 80 | 73 | 67 | 61 | 56 | 51 | 46 |
| 2,260 | 2,280 | 105 | 99 | 93 | 87 | 81 | 75 | 69 | 63 | 57 | 52 | 47 |
| 2,280 | 2,300 | 107 | 100 | 94 | 88 | 82 | 76 | 70 | 64 | 58 | 53 | 48 |
| 2,300 | 2,320 | 108 | 102 | 96 | 90 | 83 | 77 | 71 | 65 | 59 | 54 | 49 |
| 2,320 | 2,340 | 109 | 103 | 97 | 91 | 85 | 79 | 73 | 66 | 61 | 55 | 50 |
| 2,340 | 2,360 | 110 | 104 | 98 | 92 | 86 | 80 | 74 | 68 | 62 | 56 | 51 |
| 2,360 | 2,380 | 112 | 106 | 99 | 93 | 87 | 81 | 75 | 69 | 63 | 58 | 52 |
| 2,380 | 2,400 | 113 | 107 | 101 | 95 | 89 | 82 | 76 | 70 | 64 | 59 | 53 |
| 2,400 | 2,420 | 114 | 108 | 102 | 96 | 90 | 84 | 78 | 72 | 65 | 60 | 55 |
| 2,420 | 2,440 | 116 | 109 | 103 | 97 | 91 | 85 | 79 | 73 | 67 | 61 | 56 |
| 2,440 | 2,460 | 117 | 111 | 105 | 98 | 92 | 86 | 80 | 74 | 68 | 62 | 57 |
| 2,460 | 2,480 | 118 | 112 | 106 | 100 | 94 | 88 | 81 | 75 | 69 | 63 | 58 |
| 2,480 | 2,500 | 120 | 113 | 107 | 101 | 95 | 89 | 83 | 77 | 71 | 64 | 59 |
| 2,500 | 2,520 | 121 | 115 | 108 | 102 | 96 | 90 | 84 | 78 | 72 | 66 | 60 |
| 2,520 | 2,540 | 122 | 116 | 110 | 104 | 98 | 91 | 85 | 79 | 73 | 67 | 61 |
| 2,540 | 2,560 | 124 | 117 | 111 | 105 | 99 | 93 | 87 | 80 | 74 | 68 | 62 |
| 2,560 | 2,580 | 125 | 119 | 112 | 106 | 100 | 94 | 88 | 82 | 76 | 70 | 63 |
| 2,580 | 2,600 | 127 | 120 | 114 | 107 | 101 | 95 | 89 | 83 | 77 | 71 | 65 |
| 2,600 | 2,620 | 128 | 121 | 115 | 109 | 103 | 97 | 90 | 84 | 78 | 72 | 66 |
| 2,620 | 2,640 | 129 | 123 | 116 | 110 | 104 | 98 | 92 | 86 | 80 | 73 | 67 |
| 2,640 | 2,660 | 131 | 124 | 118 | 111 | 105 | 99 | 93 | 87 | 81 | 75 | 69 |
| 2,660 | 2,680 | 132 | 125 | 119 | 113 | 106 | 100 | 94 | 88 | 82 | 76 | 70 |
| 2,680 | 2,700 | 133 | 127 | 120 | 114 | 108 | 102 | 96 | 89 | 83 | 77 | 71 |
| 2,700 | 2,720 | 135 | 128 | 122 | 115 | 109 | 103 | 97 | 91 | 85 | 79 | 72 |

# WITHHOLDING TABLES EFFECTIVE JANUARY 1, 2013

*Monthly* PAYROLL PERIOD

For Calendar Years 2013, and thereafter

*Married* PERSONS

| AT LEAST | BUT LESS THAN | 0 | 1 | 2 | 3 | 4 | 5 | 6 | 7 | 8 | 9 | 10 or more |
|---|---|---|---|---|---|---|---|---|---|---|---|---|
| | | AMOUNT OF INCOME TAX TO BE WITHHELD | | | | | | | | | | |
| 2,720 | 2,740 | 136 | 130 | 123 | 117 | 110 | 104 | 98 | 92 | 86 | 80 | 74 |
| 2,740 | 2,760 | 137 | 131 | 124 | 118 | 112 | 105 | 99 | 93 | 87 | 81 | 75 |
| 2,760 | 2,780 | 139 | 132 | 126 | 119 | 113 | 107 | 101 | 95 | 88 | 82 | 76 |
| 2,780 | 2,800 | 140 | 134 | 127 | 121 | 114 | 108 | 102 | 96 | 90 | 84 | 78 |
| 2,800 | 2,820 | 141 | 135 | 129 | 122 | 116 | 109 | 103 | 97 | 91 | 85 | 79 |
| 2,820 | 2,840 | 143 | 136 | 130 | 123 | 117 | 111 | 105 | 98 | 92 | 86 | 80 |
| 2,840 | 2,860 | 144 | 138 | 131 | 125 | 118 | 112 | 106 | 100 | 94 | 87 | 81 |
| 2,860 | 2,880 | 146 | 139 | 133 | 126 | 120 | 113 | 107 | 101 | 95 | 89 | 83 |
| 2,880 | 2,900 | 147 | 140 | 134 | 127 | 121 | 115 | 108 | 102 | 96 | 90 | 84 |
| 2,900 | 2,920 | 148 | 142 | 135 | 129 | 122 | 116 | 110 | 104 | 97 | 91 | 85 |
| 2,920 | 2,940 | 150 | 143 | 137 | 130 | 124 | 117 | 111 | 105 | 99 | 93 | 86 |
| 2,940 | 2,960 | 151 | 145 | 138 | 132 | 125 | 119 | 112 | 106 | 100 | 94 | 88 |
| 2,960 | 2,980 | 152 | 146 | 139 | 133 | 126 | 120 | 113 | 107 | 101 | 95 | 89 |
| 2,980 | 3,000 | 154 | 147 | 141 | 134 | 128 | 121 | 115 | 109 | 103 | 96 | 90 |
| 3,000 | 3,020 | 155 | 149 | 142 | 136 | 129 | 123 | 116 | 110 | 104 | 98 | 92 |
| 3,020 | 3,040 | 156 | 150 | 143 | 137 | 131 | 124 | 118 | 111 | 105 | 99 | 93 |
| 3,040 | 3,060 | 158 | 151 | 145 | 138 | 132 | 125 | 119 | 112 | 106 | 100 | 94 |
| 3,060 | 3,080 | 159 | 153 | 146 | 140 | 133 | 127 | 120 | 114 | 108 | 102 | 95 |
| 3,080 | 3,100 | 161 | 154 | 148 | 141 | 135 | 128 | 122 | 115 | 109 | 103 | 97 |
| 3,100 | 3,120 | 162 | 155 | 149 | 142 | 136 | 129 | 123 | 116 | 110 | 104 | 98 |
| 3,120 | 3,140 | 163 | 157 | 150 | 144 | 137 | 131 | 124 | 118 | 112 | 105 | 99 |
| 3,140 | 3,160 | 165 | 158 | 152 | 145 | 139 | 132 | 126 | 119 | 113 | 107 | 101 |
| 3,160 | 3,180 | 166 | 159 | 153 | 147 | 140 | 134 | 127 | 121 | 114 | 108 | 102 |
| 3,180 | 3,200 | 167 | 161 | 154 | 148 | 141 | 135 | 128 | 122 | 115 | 109 | 103 |
| 3,200 | 3,220 | 169 | 162 | 156 | 149 | 143 | 136 | 130 | 123 | 117 | 111 | 104 |
| 3,220 | 3,240 | 170 | 164 | 157 | 151 | 144 | 138 | 131 | 125 | 118 | 112 | 106 |
| 3,240 | 3,260 | 172 | 165 | 158 | 152 | 145 | 139 | 132 | 126 | 120 | 113 | 107 |
| 3,260 | 3,280 | 173 | 166 | 160 | 153 | 147 | 140 | 134 | 127 | 121 | 114 | 108 |
| 3,280 | 3,300 | 174 | 168 | 161 | 155 | 148 | 142 | 135 | 129 | 122 | 116 | 110 |
| 3,300 | 3,320 | 176 | 169 | 163 | 156 | 150 | 143 | 137 | 130 | 124 | 117 | 111 |
| 3,320 | 3,340 | 177 | 170 | 164 | 157 | 151 | 144 | 138 | 131 | 125 | 118 | 112 |
| 3,340 | 3,360 | 179 | 172 | 165 | 159 | 152 | 146 | 139 | 133 | 126 | 120 | 113 |
| 3,360 | 3,380 | 180 | 173 | 167 | 160 | 154 | 147 | 141 | 134 | 128 | 121 | 115 |
| 3,380 | 3,400 | 182 | 175 | 168 | 161 | 155 | 149 | 142 | 136 | 129 | 123 | 116 |
| 3,400 | 3,420 | 183 | 176 | 169 | 163 | 156 | 150 | 143 | 137 | 130 | 124 | 117 |
| 3,420 | 3,440 | 185 | 178 | 171 | 164 | 158 | 151 | 145 | 138 | 132 | 125 | 119 |
| 3,440 | 3,460 | 186 | 179 | 172 | 166 | 159 | 153 | 146 | 140 | 133 | 127 | 120 |
| 3,460 | 3,480 | 187 | 181 | 174 | 167 | 160 | 154 | 147 | 141 | 134 | 128 | 122 |
| 3,480 | 3,500 | 189 | 182 | 175 | 168 | 162 | 155 | 149 | 142 | 136 | 129 | 123 |
| 3,500 | 3,520 | 190 | 183 | 177 | 170 | 163 | 157 | 150 | 144 | 137 | 131 | 124 |
| 3,520 | 3,540 | 192 | 185 | 178 | 171 | 165 | 158 | 152 | 145 | 139 | 132 | 126 |
| 3,540 | 3,560 | 193 | 186 | 179 | 173 | 166 | 159 | 153 | 146 | 140 | 133 | 127 |
| 3,560 | 3,580 | 195 | 188 | 181 | 174 | 167 | 161 | 154 | 148 | 141 | 135 | 128 |
| 3,580 | 3,600 | 196 | 189 | 182 | 175 | 169 | 162 | 156 | 149 | 143 | 136 | 130 |
| 3,600 | 3,620 | 198 | 191 | 184 | 177 | 170 | 163 | 157 | 150 | 144 | 138 | 131 |

WAGES ARE — NUMBER OF WITHHOLDING ALLOWANCES CLAIMED

# WITHHOLDING TABLES EFFECTIVE
# JANUARY 1, 2013

### *Monthly* PAYROLL PERIOD
### For Calendar Years 2013, and thereafter
### *Married* PERSONS

| WAGES ARE | | NUMBER OF WITHHOLDING ALLOWANCES CLAIMED | | | | | | | | | | |
|---|---|---|---|---|---|---|---|---|---|---|---|---|
| AT LEAST | BUT LESS THAN | 0 | 1 | 2 | 3 | 4 | 5 | 6 | 7 | 8 | 9 | 10 or more |
| | | AMOUNT OF INCOME TAX TO BE WITHHELD | | | | | | | | | | |
| 3,620 | 3,640 | 199 | 192 | 185 | 178 | 171 | 165 | 158 | 152 | 145 | 139 | 132 |
| 3,640 | 3,660 | 200 | 194 | 187 | 180 | 173 | 166 | 160 | 153 | 147 | 140 | 134 |
| 3,660 | 3,680 | 202 | 195 | 188 | 181 | 174 | 168 | 161 | 155 | 148 | 142 | 135 |
| 3,680 | 3,700 | 203 | 196 | 190 | 183 | 176 | 169 | 162 | 156 | 149 | 143 | 136 |
| 3,700 | 3,720 | 205 | 198 | 191 | 184 | 177 | 170 | 164 | 157 | 151 | 144 | 138 |
| 3,720 | 3,740 | 206 | 199 | 192 | 186 | 179 | 172 | 165 | 159 | 152 | 146 | 139 |
| 3,740 | 3,760 | 208 | 201 | 194 | 187 | 180 | 173 | 166 | 160 | 154 | 147 | 141 |
| 3,760 | 3,780 | 209 | 202 | 195 | 188 | 182 | 175 | 168 | 161 | 155 | 148 | 142 |
| 3,780 | 3,800 | 210 | 204 | 197 | 190 | 183 | 176 | 169 | 163 | 156 | 150 | 143 |
| 3,800 | 3,820 | 212 | 205 | 198 | 191 | 184 | 178 | 171 | 164 | 158 | 151 | 145 |
| 3,820 | 3,840 | 213 | 206 | 200 | 193 | 186 | 179 | 172 | 165 | 159 | 152 | 146 |
| 3,840 | 3,860 | 215 | 208 | 201 | 194 | 187 | 180 | 174 | 167 | 160 | 154 | 147 |
| 3,860 | 3,880 | 216 | 209 | 203 | 196 | 189 | 182 | 175 | 168 | 162 | 155 | 149 |
| 3,880 | 3,900 | 218 | 211 | 204 | 197 | 190 | 183 | 176 | 170 | 163 | 157 | 150 |
| 3,900 | 3,920 | 219 | 212 | 205 | 199 | 192 | 185 | 178 | 171 | 164 | 158 | 151 |
| 3,920 | 3,940 | 221 | 214 | 207 | 200 | 193 | 186 | 179 | 173 | 166 | 159 | 153 |
| 3,940 | 3,960 | 222 | 215 | 208 | 201 | 195 | 188 | 181 | 174 | 167 | 161 | 154 |
| 3,960 | 3,980 | 223 | 217 | 210 | 203 | 196 | 189 | 182 | 175 | 169 | 162 | 156 |
| 3,980 | 4,000 | 225 | 218 | 211 | 204 | 197 | 191 | 184 | 177 | 170 | 163 | 157 |
| 4,000 | 4,020 | 226 | 219 | 213 | 206 | 199 | 192 | 185 | 178 | 171 | 165 | 158 |
| 4,020 | 4,040 | 228 | 221 | 214 | 207 | 200 | 193 | 187 | 180 | 173 | 166 | 160 |
| 4,040 | 4,060 | 229 | 222 | 215 | 209 | 202 | 195 | 188 | 181 | 174 | 167 | 161 |
| 4,060 | 4,080 | 231 | 224 | 217 | 210 | 203 | 196 | 189 | 183 | 176 | 169 | 162 |
| 4,080 | 4,100 | 232 | 225 | 218 | 211 | 205 | 198 | 191 | 184 | 177 | 170 | 164 |
| 4,100 | 4,120 | 234 | 227 | 220 | 213 | 206 | 199 | 192 | 185 | 179 | 172 | 165 |
| 4,120 | 4,140 | 235 | 228 | 221 | 214 | 207 | 201 | 194 | 187 | 180 | 173 | 166 |
| 4,140 | 4,160 | 237 | 230 | 223 | 216 | 209 | 202 | 195 | 188 | 181 | 175 | 168 |
| 4,160 | 4,180 | 239 | 231 | 224 | 217 | 210 | 204 | 197 | 190 | 183 | 176 | 169 |
| 4,180 | 4,200 | 240 | 233 | 226 | 219 | 212 | 205 | 198 | 191 | 184 | 177 | 171 |
| 4,200 | 4,220 | 242 | 234 | 227 | 220 | 213 | 206 | 200 | 193 | 186 | 179 | 172 |
| 4,220 | 4,240 | 243 | 236 | 229 | 222 | 215 | 208 | 201 | 194 | 187 | 180 | 174 |
| 4,240 | 4,260 | 245 | 237 | 230 | 223 | 216 | 209 | 202 | 196 | 189 | 182 | 175 |
| 4,260 | 4,280 | 246 | 239 | 232 | 224 | 218 | 211 | 204 | 197 | 190 | 183 | 176 |
| 4,280 | 4,300 | 248 | 240 | 233 | 226 | 219 | 212 | 205 | 198 | 192 | 185 | 178 |
| 4,300 | 4,320 | 249 | 242 | 235 | 227 | 220 | 214 | 207 | 200 | 193 | 186 | 179 |
| 4,320 | 4,340 | 251 | 243 | 236 | 229 | 222 | 215 | 208 | 201 | 194 | 188 | 181 |
| 4,340 | 4,360 | 252 | 245 | 238 | 230 | 223 | 216 | 210 | 203 | 196 | 189 | 182 |
| 4,360 | 4,380 | 254 | 246 | 239 | 232 | 225 | 218 | 211 | 204 | 197 | 190 | 184 |
| 4,380 | 4,400 | 255 | 248 | 241 | 234 | 226 | 219 | 212 | 206 | 199 | 192 | 185 |
| 4,400 | 4,420 | 257 | 250 | 242 | 235 | 228 | 221 | 214 | 207 | 200 | 193 | 186 |
| 4,420 | 4,440 | 258 | 251 | 244 | 237 | 229 | 222 | 215 | 209 | 202 | 195 | 188 |
| 4,440 | 4,460 | 260 | 253 | 245 | 238 | 231 | 224 | 217 | 210 | 203 | 196 | 189 |
| 4,460 | 4,480 | 261 | 254 | 247 | 240 | 232 | 225 | 218 | 211 | 205 | 198 | 191 |
| 4,480 | 4,500 | 263 | 256 | 248 | 241 | 234 | 227 | 220 | 213 | 206 | 199 | 192 |
| 4,500 | 4,520 | 264 | 257 | 250 | 243 | 235 | 228 | 221 | 214 | 207 | 201 | 194 |

# WITHHOLDING TABLES EFFECTIVE
# JANUARY 1, 2013

*Monthly* PAYROLL PERIOD

For Calendar Years 2013, and thereafter

*Married* PERSONS

| WAGES ARE | | NUMBER OF WITHHOLDING ALLOWANCES CLAIMED | | | | | | | | | | |
|---|---|---|---|---|---|---|---|---|---|---|---|---|
| AT LEAST | BUT LESS THAN | 0 | 1 | 2 | 3 | 4 | 5 | 6 | 7 | 8 | 9 | 10 or more |
| | | AMOUNT OF INCOME TAX TO BE WITHHELD | | | | | | | | | | |
| 4,520 | 4,540 | 266 | 259 | 251 | 244 | 237 | 230 | 223 | 216 | 209 | 202 | 195 |
| 4,540 | 4,560 | 267 | 260 | 253 | 246 | 238 | 231 | 224 | 217 | 210 | 203 | 197 |
| 4,560 | 4,580 | 269 | 262 | 254 | 247 | 240 | 233 | 225 | 219 | 212 | 205 | 198 |
| 4,580 | 4,600 | 270 | 263 | 256 | 249 | 241 | 234 | 227 | 220 | 213 | 206 | 199 |
| 4,600 | 4,620 | 272 | 265 | 257 | 250 | 243 | 236 | 228 | 221 | 215 | 208 | 201 |
| 4,620 | 4,640 | 273 | 266 | 259 | 252 | 244 | 237 | 230 | 223 | 216 | 209 | 202 |
| 4,640 | 4,660 | 275 | 268 | 261 | 253 | 246 | 239 | 232 | 224 | 217 | 211 | 204 |
| 4,660 | 4,680 | 277 | 269 | 262 | 255 | 248 | 240 | 233 | 226 | 219 | 212 | 205 |
| 4,680 | 4,700 | 278 | 271 | 264 | 256 | 249 | 242 | 235 | 227 | 220 | 213 | 207 |
| 4,700 | 4,720 | 280 | 272 | 265 | 258 | 251 | 243 | 236 | 229 | 222 | 215 | 208 |
| 4,720 | 4,740 | 281 | 274 | 267 | 259 | 252 | 245 | 238 | 230 | 223 | 216 | 210 |
| 4,740 | 4,760 | 283 | 275 | 268 | 261 | 254 | 246 | 239 | 232 | 225 | 218 | 211 |
| 4,760 | 4,780 | 284 | 277 | 270 | 262 | 255 | 248 | 241 | 233 | 226 | 219 | 212 |
| 4,780 | 4,800 | 286 | 278 | 271 | 264 | 257 | 249 | 242 | 235 | 228 | 221 | 214 |
| 4,800 | 4,820 | 287 | 280 | 273 | 265 | 258 | 251 | 244 | 236 | 229 | 222 | 215 |
| 4,820 | 4,840 | 289 | 281 | 274 | 267 | 260 | 252 | 245 | 238 | 231 | 224 | 217 |
| 4,840 | 4,860 | 290 | 283 | 276 | 268 | 261 | 254 | 247 | 239 | 232 | 225 | 218 |
| 4,860 | 4,880 | 292 | 284 | 277 | 270 | 263 | 255 | 248 | 241 | 234 | 227 | 220 |
| 4,880 | 4,900 | 293 | 286 | 279 | 272 | 264 | 257 | 250 | 243 | 235 | 228 | 221 |
| 4,900 | 4,920 | 295 | 288 | 280 | 273 | 266 | 259 | 251 | 244 | 237 | 230 | 222 |
| 4,920 | 4,940 | 296 | 289 | 282 | 275 | 267 | 260 | 253 | 246 | 238 | 231 | 224 |
| 4,940 | 4,960 | 298 | 291 | 283 | 276 | 269 | 262 | 254 | 247 | 240 | 233 | 225 |
| 4,960 | 4,980 | 299 | 292 | 285 | 278 | 270 | 263 | 256 | 249 | 241 | 234 | 227 |
| 4,980 | 5,000 | 301 | 294 | 286 | 279 | 272 | 265 | 257 | 250 | 243 | 236 | 228 |
| 5,000 | 5,020 | 302 | 295 | 288 | 281 | 273 | 266 | 259 | 252 | 244 | 237 | 230 |
| 5,020 | 5,040 | 304 | 297 | 289 | 282 | 275 | 268 | 260 | 253 | 246 | 239 | 231 |
| 5,040 | 5,060 | 305 | 298 | 291 | 284 | 276 | 269 | 262 | 255 | 247 | 240 | 233 |
| 5,060 | 5,080 | 307 | 300 | 292 | 285 | 278 | 271 | 263 | 256 | 249 | 242 | 234 |
| 5,080 | 5,100 | 308 | 301 | 294 | 287 | 279 | 272 | 265 | 258 | 250 | 243 | 236 |
| 5,100 | 5,120 | 310 | 303 | 295 | 288 | 281 | 274 | 266 | 259 | 252 | 245 | 237 |
| 5,120 | 5,140 | 311 | 304 | 297 | 290 | 282 | 275 | 268 | 261 | 254 | 246 | 239 |
| 5,140 | 5,160 | 313 | 306 | 299 | 291 | 284 | 277 | 270 | 262 | 255 | 248 | 241 |
| 5,160 | 5,180 | 315 | 307 | 300 | 293 | 286 | 278 | 271 | 264 | 257 | 249 | 242 |
| 5,180 | 5,200 | 316 | 309 | 302 | 294 | 287 | 280 | 273 | 265 | 258 | 251 | 244 |
| 5,200 | 5,220 | 318 | 310 | 303 | 296 | 289 | 281 | 274 | 267 | 260 | 252 | 245 |
| 5,220 | 5,240 | 319 | 312 | 305 | 297 | 290 | 283 | 276 | 268 | 261 | 254 | 247 |
| 5,240 | 5,260 | 321 | 313 | 306 | 299 | 292 | 284 | 277 | 270 | 263 | 255 | 248 |
| 5,260 | 5,280 | 322 | 315 | 308 | 300 | 293 | 286 | 279 | 271 | 264 | 257 | 250 |
| 5,280 | 5,300 | 324 | 316 | 309 | 302 | 295 | 287 | 280 | 273 | 266 | 258 | 251 |
| 5,300 | 5,320 | 325 | 318 | 311 | 303 | 296 | 289 | 282 | 274 | 267 | 260 | 253 |
| 5,320 | 5,340 | 327 | 319 | 312 | 305 | 298 | 290 | 283 | 276 | 269 | 261 | 254 |
| 5,340 | 5,360 | 328 | 321 | 314 | 306 | 299 | 292 | 285 | 277 | 270 | 263 | 256 |
| 5,360 | 5,380 | 330 | 322 | 315 | 308 | 301 | 293 | 286 | 279 | 272 | 265 | 257 |
| 5,380 | 5,400 | 331 | 324 | 317 | 310 | 302 | 295 | 288 | 281 | 273 | 266 | 259 |
| 5,400 | 5,420 | 333 | 326 | 318 | 311 | 304 | 297 | 289 | 282 | 275 | 268 | 260 |

# WITHHOLDING TABLES EFFECTIVE
# JANUARY 1, 2013

*Monthly* PAYROLL PERIOD

For Calendar Years 2013, and thereafter

*Married* PERSONS

| WAGES ARE | | NUMBER OF WITHHOLDING ALLOWANCES CLAIMED | | | | | | | | | | |
|---|---|---|---|---|---|---|---|---|---|---|---|---|
| AT LEAST | BUT LESS THAN | 0 | 1 | 2 | 3 | 4 | 5 | 6 | 7 | 8 | 9 | 10 or more |
| | | AMOUNT OF INCOME TAX TO BE WITHHELD | | | | | | | | | | |
| 5,420 | 5,440 | 334 | 327 | 320 | 313 | 305 | 298 | 291 | 284 | 276 | 269 | 262 |
| 5,440 | 5,460 | 336 | 329 | 321 | 314 | 307 | 300 | 292 | 285 | 278 | 271 | 263 |
| 5,460 | 5,480 | 337 | 330 | 323 | 316 | 308 | 301 | 294 | 287 | 279 | 272 | 265 |
| 5,480 | 5,500 | 339 | 332 | 324 | 317 | 310 | 303 | 295 | 288 | 281 | 274 | 266 |
| 5,500 | 5,520 | 340 | 333 | 326 | 319 | 311 | 304 | 297 | 290 | 282 | 275 | 268 |
| 5,520 | 5,540 | 342 | 335 | 327 | 320 | 313 | 306 | 298 | 291 | 284 | 277 | 269 |
| 5,540 | 5,560 | 343 | 336 | 329 | 322 | 314 | 307 | 300 | 293 | 285 | 278 | 271 |
| 5,560 | 5,580 | 345 | 338 | 330 | 323 | 316 | 309 | 301 | 294 | 287 | 280 | 272 |
| 5,580 | 5,600 | 346 | 339 | 332 | 325 | 317 | 310 | 303 | 296 | 288 | 281 | 274 |
| 5,600 | 5,620 | 348 | 341 | 333 | 326 | 319 | 312 | 304 | 297 | 290 | 283 | 275 |
| 5,620 | 5,640 | 349 | 342 | 335 | 328 | 320 | 313 | 306 | 299 | 292 | 284 | 277 |
| 5,640 | 5,660 | 351 | 344 | 337 | 329 | 322 | 315 | 308 | 300 | 293 | 286 | 279 |
| 5,660 | 5,680 | 353 | 345 | 338 | 331 | 324 | 316 | 309 | 302 | 295 | 287 | 280 |
| 5,680 | 5,700 | 354 | 347 | 340 | 332 | 325 | 318 | 311 | 303 | 296 | 289 | 282 |
| 5,700 | 5,720 | 356 | 348 | 341 | 334 | 327 | 319 | 312 | 305 | 298 | 290 | 283 |
| 5,720 | 5,740 | 357 | 350 | 343 | 335 | 328 | 321 | 314 | 306 | 299 | 292 | 285 |
| 5,740 | 5,760 | 359 | 351 | 344 | 337 | 330 | 322 | 315 | 308 | 301 | 293 | 286 |
| 5,760 | 5,780 | 360 | 353 | 346 | 338 | 331 | 324 | 317 | 309 | 302 | 295 | 288 |
| 5,780 | 5,800 | 362 | 354 | 347 | 340 | 333 | 325 | 318 | 311 | 304 | 296 | 289 |
| 5,800 | 5,820 | 363 | 356 | 349 | 341 | 334 | 327 | 320 | 312 | 305 | 298 | 291 |
| 5,820 | 5,840 | 365 | 357 | 350 | 343 | 336 | 328 | 321 | 314 | 307 | 299 | 292 |
| 5,840 | 5,860 | 366 | 359 | 352 | 344 | 337 | 330 | 323 | 315 | 308 | 301 | 294 |
| 5,860 | 5,880 | 368 | 360 | 353 | 346 | 339 | 331 | 324 | 317 | 310 | 303 | 295 |
| 5,880 | 5,900 | 369 | 362 | 355 | 348 | 340 | 333 | 326 | 319 | 311 | 304 | 297 |
| 5,900 | 5,920 | 371 | 364 | 356 | 349 | 342 | 335 | 327 | 320 | 313 | 306 | 298 |
| 5,920 | 5,940 | 372 | 365 | 358 | 351 | 343 | 336 | 329 | 322 | 314 | 307 | 300 |
| 5,940 | 5,960 | 374 | 367 | 359 | 352 | 345 | 338 | 330 | 323 | 316 | 309 | 301 |
| 5,960 | 5,980 | 375 | 368 | 361 | 354 | 346 | 339 | 332 | 325 | 317 | 310 | 303 |
| 5,980 | 6,000 | 377 | 370 | 362 | 355 | 348 | 341 | 333 | 326 | 319 | 312 | 304 |
| 6,000 | 6,020 | 378 | 371 | 364 | 357 | 349 | 342 | 335 | 328 | 320 | 313 | 306 |
| 6,020 | 6,040 | 380 | 373 | 365 | 358 | 351 | 344 | 336 | 329 | 322 | 315 | 307 |
| 6,040 | 6,060 | 382 | 374 | 367 | 360 | 352 | 345 | 338 | 331 | 323 | 316 | 309 |
| 6,060 | 6,080 | 383 | 376 | 368 | 361 | 354 | 347 | 339 | 332 | 325 | 318 | 310 |
| 6,080 | 6,100 | 385 | 377 | 370 | 363 | 355 | 348 | 341 | 334 | 326 | 319 | 312 |
| 6,100 | 6,120 | 386 | 379 | 371 | 364 | 357 | 350 | 342 | 335 | 328 | 321 | 313 |
| 6,120 | 6,140 | 388 | 380 | 373 | 366 | 358 | 351 | 344 | 337 | 330 | 322 | 315 |
| 6,140 | 6,160 | 389 | 382 | 375 | 367 | 360 | 353 | 346 | 338 | 331 | 324 | 317 |
| 6,160 | 6,180 | 391 | 383 | 376 | 369 | 362 | 354 | 347 | 340 | 333 | 325 | 318 |
| 6,180 | 6,200 | 393 | 385 | 378 | 370 | 363 | 356 | 349 | 341 | 334 | 327 | 320 |
| 6,200 | 6,220 | 394 | 387 | 379 | 372 | 365 | 357 | 350 | 343 | 336 | 328 | 321 |
| 6,220 | 6,240 | 396 | 388 | 381 | 373 | 366 | 359 | 352 | 344 | 337 | 330 | 323 |
| 6,240 | 6,260 | 397 | 390 | 382 | 375 | 368 | 360 | 353 | 346 | 339 | 331 | 324 |
| 6,260 | 6,280 | 399 | 391 | 384 | 376 | 369 | 362 | 355 | 347 | 340 | 333 | 326 |
| 6,280 | 6,300 | 401 | 393 | 385 | 378 | 371 | 363 | 356 | 349 | 342 | 334 | 327 |
| 6,300 | 6,320 | 402 | 395 | 387 | 379 | 372 | 365 | 358 | 350 | 343 | 336 | 329 |

# WITHHOLDING TABLES EFFECTIVE
## JANUARY 1, 2013

*Monthly* PAYROLL PERIOD

For Calendar Years 2013, and thereafter

*Married* PERSONS

| WAGES ARE | | NUMBER OF WITHHOLDING ALLOWANCES CLAIMED | | | | | | | | | | |
|---|---|---|---|---|---|---|---|---|---|---|---|---|
| AT LEAST | BUT LESS THAN | 0 | 1 | 2 | 3 | 4 | 5 | 6 | 7 | 8 | 9 | 10 or more |
| | | AMOUNT OF INCOME TAX TO BE WITHHELD | | | | | | | | | | |
| 6,320 | 6,340 | 404 | 396 | 389 | 381 | 374 | 366 | 359 | 352 | 345 | 337 | 330 |
| 6,340 | 6,360 | 405 | 398 | 390 | 383 | 375 | 368 | 361 | 353 | 346 | 339 | 332 |
| 6,360 | 6,380 | 407 | 399 | 392 | 384 | 377 | 369 | 362 | 355 | 348 | 341 | 333 |
| 6,380 | 6,400 | 408 | 401 | 393 | 386 | 378 | 371 | 364 | 357 | 349 | 342 | 335 |
| 6,400 | 6,420 | 410 | 402 | 395 | 387 | 380 | 373 | 365 | 358 | 351 | 344 | 336 |
| 6,420 | 6,440 | 412 | 404 | 397 | 389 | 381 | 374 | 367 | 360 | 352 | 345 | 338 |
| 6,440 | 6,460 | 413 | 406 | 398 | 391 | 383 | 376 | 368 | 361 | 354 | 347 | 339 |
| 6,460 | 6,480 | 415 | 407 | 400 | 392 | 385 | 377 | 370 | 363 | 355 | 348 | 341 |
| 6,480 | 6,500 | 416 | 409 | 401 | 394 | 386 | 379 | 371 | 364 | 357 | 350 | 342 |
| 6,500 | 6,520 | 418 | 410 | 403 | 395 | 388 | 380 | 373 | 366 | 358 | 351 | 344 |
| 6,520 | 6,540 | 419 | 412 | 404 | 397 | 389 | 382 | 374 | 367 | 360 | 353 | 345 |
| 6,540 | 6,560 | 421 | 414 | 406 | 398 | 391 | 383 | 376 | 369 | 361 | 354 | 347 |
| 6,560 | 6,580 | 423 | 415 | 408 | 400 | 392 | 385 | 377 | 370 | 363 | 356 | 348 |
| 6,580 | 6,600 | 424 | 417 | 409 | 402 | 394 | 387 | 379 | 372 | 364 | 357 | 350 |
| 6,600 | 6,620 | 426 | 418 | 411 | 403 | 396 | 388 | 381 | 373 | 366 | 359 | 351 |
| 6,620 | 6,640 | 427 | 420 | 412 | 405 | 397 | 390 | 382 | 375 | 368 | 360 | 353 |
| 6,640 | 6,660 | 429 | 421 | 414 | 406 | 399 | 391 | 384 | 376 | 369 | 362 | 355 |
| 6,660 | 6,680 | 431 | 423 | 415 | 408 | 400 | 393 | 385 | 378 | 371 | 363 | 356 |
| 6,680 | 6,700 | 432 | 425 | 417 | 410 | 402 | 394 | 387 | 379 | 372 | 365 | 358 |
| 6,700 | 6,720 | 434 | 426 | 419 | 411 | 404 | 396 | 388 | 381 | 374 | 366 | 359 |
| 6,720 | 6,740 | 435 | 428 | 420 | 413 | 405 | 398 | 390 | 383 | 375 | 368 | 361 |
| 6,740 | 6,760 | 437 | 429 | 422 | 414 | 407 | 399 | 392 | 384 | 377 | 369 | 362 |
| 6,760 | 6,780 | 438 | 431 | 423 | 416 | 408 | 401 | 393 | 386 | 378 | 371 | 364 |
| 6,780 | 6,800 | 440 | 432 | 425 | 417 | 410 | 402 | 395 | 387 | 380 | 372 | 365 |
| 6,800 | 6,820 | 442 | 434 | 427 | 419 | 411 | 404 | 396 | 389 | 381 | 374 | 367 |
| 6,820 | 6,840 | 443 | 436 | 428 | 421 | 413 | 406 | 398 | 390 | 383 | 375 | 368 |
| 6,840 | 6,860 | 445 | 437 | 430 | 422 | 415 | 407 | 400 | 392 | 384 | 377 | 370 |
| 6,860 | 6,880 | 446 | 439 | 431 | 424 | 416 | 409 | 401 | 394 | 386 | 379 | 371 |
| 6,880 | 6,900 | 448 | 440 | 433 | 425 | 418 | 410 | 403 | 395 | 388 | 380 | 373 |
| 6,900 | 6,920 | 449 | 442 | 434 | 427 | 419 | 412 | 404 | 397 | 389 | 382 | 374 |
| 6,920 | 6,940 | 451 | 444 | 436 | 428 | 421 | 413 | 406 | 398 | 391 | 383 | 376 |
| 6,940 | 6,960 | 453 | 445 | 438 | 430 | 423 | 415 | 407 | 400 | 392 | 385 | 377 |
| 7.90% of excess over $6,960 plus | | | | | | | | | | | | |
| 6,960 | & over | 454 | 447 | 439 | 432 | 424 | 417 | 409 | 402 | 394 | 386 | 379 |

# WITHHOLDING TABLES EFFECTIVE
# JANUARY 1, 2013

### *Daily* PAYROLL PERIOD

### For Calendar Years 2013, and thereafter

### *Single* PERSONS — UNMARRIED *Heads of Household*

| WAGES ARE | | NUMBER OF WITHHOLDING ALLOWANCES CLAIMED | | | | | | | | | | |
|---|---|---|---|---|---|---|---|---|---|---|---|---|
| AT LEAST | BUT LESS THAN | 0 | 1 | 2 | 3 | 4 | 5 | 6 | 7 | 8 | 9 | 10 or more |
| | | AMOUNT OF INCOME TAX TO BE WITHHELD | | | | | | | | | | |
| 0 | 10 | 0 | 0 | 0 | 0 | 0 | 0 | 0 | 0 | 0 | 0 | 0 |
| 10 | 20 | 0 | 0 | 0 | 0 | 0 | 0 | 0 | 0 | 0 | 0 | 0 |
| 20 | 30 | 1 | 1 | 1 | 0 | 0 | 0 | 0 | 0 | 0 | 0 | 0 |
| 30 | 40 | 2 | 1 | 1 | 1 | 1 | 1 | 0 | 0 | 0 | 0 | 0 |
| 40 | 50 | 2 | 2 | 2 | 2 | 1 | 1 | 1 | 1 | 1 | 0 | 0 |
| 50 | 60 | 3 | 3 | 2 | 2 | 2 | 2 | 2 | 1 | 1 | 1 | 1 |
| 60 | 70 | 4 | 3 | 3 | 3 | 3 | 3 | 2 | 2 | 2 | 2 | 1 |
| 70 | 80 | 4 | 4 | 4 | 4 | 3 | 3 | 3 | 3 | 3 | 2 | 2 |
| 80 | 90 | 5 | 5 | 5 | 4 | 4 | 4 | 4 | 4 | 3 | 3 | 3 |
| 90 | 100 | 6 | 6 | 5 | 5 | 5 | 5 | 4 | 4 | 4 | 4 | 4 |
| 100 | 110 | 7 | 6 | 6 | 6 | 6 | 5 | 5 | 5 | 5 | 5 | 4 |
| 110 | 120 | 8 | 7 | 7 | 7 | 7 | 6 | 6 | 6 | 6 | 5 | 5 |
| 120 | 130 | 8 | 8 | 8 | 8 | 7 | 7 | 7 | 7 | 6 | 6 | 6 |
| 7.90% of excess over $130 plus | | | | | | | | | | | | |
| 130 | & over | 9 | 9 | 9 | 8 | 8 | 8 | 8 | 7 | 7 | 7 | 7 |

# WITHHOLDING TABLES EFFECTIVE
# JANUARY 1, 2013

*Daily* PAYROLL PERIOD

For Calendar Years 2013, and thereafter

*Married* PERSONS

| WAGES ARE | | NUMBER OF WITHHOLDING ALLOWANCES CLAIMED | | | | | | | | | | |
|---|---|---|---|---|---|---|---|---|---|---|---|---|
| AT LEAST | BUT LESS THAN | 0 | 1 | 2 | 3 | 4 | 5 | 6 | 7 | 8 | 9 | 10 or more |
| | | AMOUNT OF INCOME TAX TO BE WITHHELD | | | | | | | | | | |
| 0 | 10 | 0 | 0 | 0 | 0 | 0 | 0 | 0 | 0 | 0 | 0 | 0 |
| 10 | 20 | 0 | 0 | 0 | 0 | 0 | 0 | 0 | 0 | 0 | 0 | 0 |
| 20 | 30 | 1 | 0 | 0 | 0 | 0 | 0 | 0 | 0 | 0 | 0 | 0 |
| 30 | 40 | 1 | 1 | 1 | 1 | 0 | 0 | 0 | 0 | 0 | 0 | 0 |
| 40 | 50 | 2 | 1 | 1 | 1 | 1 | 1 | 1 | 0 | 0 | 0 | 0 |
| 50 | 60 | 2 | 2 | 2 | 2 | 2 | 1 | 1 | 1 | 1 | 1 | 1 |
| 60 | 70 | 3 | 3 | 2 | 2 | 2 | 2 | 2 | 2 | 1 | 1 | 1 |
| 70 | 80 | 3 | 3 | 3 | 3 | 3 | 2 | 2 | 2 | 2 | 2 | 2 |
| 80 | 90 | 4 | 4 | 4 | 4 | 3 | 3 | 3 | 3 | 3 | 2 | 2 |
| 90 | 100 | 5 | 5 | 4 | 4 | 4 | 4 | 4 | 3 | 3 | 3 | 3 |
| 100 | 110 | 6 | 5 | 5 | 5 | 5 | 4 | 4 | 4 | 4 | 4 | 3 |
| 110 | 120 | 6 | 6 | 6 | 6 | 5 | 5 | 5 | 5 | 4 | 4 | 4 |
| 120 | 130 | 7 | 7 | 7 | 6 | 6 | 6 | 6 | 5 | 5 | 5 | 5 |
| 130 | 140 | 8 | 7 | 7 | 7 | 7 | 7 | 6 | 6 | 6 | 6 | 5 |
| 140 | 150 | 8 | 8 | 8 | 8 | 7 | 7 | 7 | 7 | 7 | 6 | 6 |
| 150 | 160 | 9 | 9 | 9 | 8 | 8 | 8 | 8 | 8 | 7 | 7 | 7 |
| 160 | 170 | 10 | 10 | 9 | 9 | 9 | 9 | 9 | 8 | 8 | 8 | 8 |
| 170 | 180 | 11 | 10 | 10 | 10 | 10 | 10 | 9 | 9 | 9 | 9 | 8 |
| 180 | 190 | 11 | 11 | 11 | 11 | 11 | 10 | 10 | 10 | 10 | 9 | 9 |
| 190 | 200 | 12 | 12 | 12 | 12 | 11 | 11 | 11 | 11 | 10 | 10 | 10 |
| 200 | 210 | 13 | 13 | 13 | 12 | 12 | 12 | 12 | 11 | 11 | 11 | 11 |
| 210 | 220 | 14 | 14 | 13 | 13 | 13 | 13 | 12 | 12 | 12 | 12 | 11 |
| 220 | 230 | 15 | 14 | 14 | 14 | 14 | 13 | 13 | 13 | 13 | 12 | 12 |
| 7.90% of excess over $230 plus | | | | | | | | | | | | |
| 230 | & over | 15 | 15 | 15 | 15 | 14 | 14 | 14 | 14 | 13 | 13 | 13 |

# RELATED FEDERAL/HAWAII TAX FORMS

| Federal Form Number | Title or Description of Federal Form | Comparable Hawaii Form | Copy of Fed. Form May Be Submitted+ |
|---|---|---|---|
| W-2 | Wage and Tax Statement | HW-2 | Yes |
| W-4 | Employee's Withholding Allowance Certificate | HW-4 | No |
| W-10 | Dependent Care Provider's Identification and Certification | HW-16 | No |
| 1040 | U.S. Individual Income Tax Return | None | No |
| 1040 Sch A | Itemized Deductions | None | No |
| Sch B | Interest and Ordinary Dividends | None | No |
| Sch C | Profit or Loss From Business | None | Not Required |
| Sch C-EZ | Net Profit From Business | None | Not Required |
| Sch D | Capital Gains and Losses | None | No |
| Sch E | Supplemental Income and Loss | None | Not Required |
| Sch F | Profit or Loss From Farming | None | Not Required |
| Sch J | Income Averaging for Farmers and Fishermen | N-168 | No |
| Sch R | Credit for the Elderly or the Disabled | None | No |
| 1040-ES | Estimated Tax for Individuals | N-1 | No |
| 1040NR | U.S. Nonresident Alien Income Tax Return | None | No |
| 1040-V | Payment Voucher | N-200V | No |
| 1040X | Amended U.S. Individual Income Tax Return | None | No |
| 1045 | Application for Tentative Refund | N-109 | No |
| 1128 | Application To Adopt, Change, or Retain a Tax Year | None | Yes |
| 1310 | Statement of Person Claiming Refund Due a Deceased Taxpayer | N-110 | No |
| 2106 | Employee Business Expenses | None | Yes* |
| 2106-EZ | Unreimbursed Employee Business Expenses | None | Yes* |
| 2120 | Multiple Support Declaration | None | Yes |
| 2210 | Underpayment of Estimated Tax by Individuals, Estates, and Trusts | N-210 | No |
| 2441 | Child and Dependent Care Expenses | Sch X | No |
| 2848 | Power of Attorney and Declaration of Representative | N-848 | No |
| 3903 | Moving Expenses | N-139 | No |
| 4562 | Depreciation and Amortization | None | Yes |
| 4684 | Casualties and Thefts | None | Yes* |
| 4797 | Sales of Business Property | Sch D-1 | No |
| 4835 | Farm Rental Income and Expenses | None | Yes |
| 4852 | Substitute for Form W-2, Wage and Tax Statement, or Form 1099-R, Distributions From Pensions, Annuities, Retirement or Profit-Sharing Plans, IRAs, Insurance Contracts, etc. | L-15 | No |
| 4868 | Application for Automatic Extension of Time To File U.S. Individual Income Tax Return | None | No |
| 4952 | Investment Interest Expense Deduction | N-158 | No |
| 4970 | Tax on Accumulation Distribution of Trusts | N-405 | No |
| 4972 | Tax on Lump-Sum Distributions | N-152 | No |
| 5213 | Election To Postpone Determination as To Whether the Presumption Applies That an Activity Is Engaged in for Profit | None | Yes |
| 5329 | Additional Taxes on Qualified Plans (Including IRAs) and Other Tax-Favored Accounts | None | No |
| 5884 | Work Opportunity Credit | N-884 | No |
| 6198 | At-Risk Limitations | None | Yes |
| 6252 | Installment Sale Income | None | Yes |
| 6781 | Gains and Losses From Section 1256 Contracts and Straddles | None | Yes |
| 8283 | Noncash Charitable Contributions | None | Yes |
| 8332 | Release/Revocation of Release of Claim to Exemption for Child by Custodial Parent | None | Yes |
| 8582 | Passive Activity Loss Limitations | None | Yes |
| 8586 | Low-Income Housing Credit | N-586 | No |
| 8615 | Tax for Certain Children Who Have Unearned Income | N-615 | No |
| 8814 | Parents' Election To Report Child's Interest and Dividends | N-814 | No |
| 8824 | Like-Kind Exchanges | None | Yes |
| 8829 | Expenses for Business Use of Your Home | None | Yes |
| 8853 | Archer MSAs and Long-Term Care Insurance Contracts | None | No |

+If "Yes" is indicated and there is no Hawaii equivalent form, the federal form must be used.
*Use the 2017 federal form when filing the 2018 Form N-11 or Form N-15.
To request tax forms by mail, you may call 808-587-4242 or toll-free 1-800-222-3229.
You may also obtain tax forms through the Department of Taxation's website at **tax.hawaii.gov**.

# RELATED FEDERAL / HAWAII PARTNERSHIP TAX FORMS

| Federal Form Number | Title or Description of Federal Form | Use Hawaii Form | Copy of Fed. Form May Be Used |
|---|---|---|---|
| 970 | Application To Use LIFO Inventory Method | None | Yes* |
| 1065 | U.S. Return of Partnership Income | N-20 | No |
| Schedule D | Capital Gains and Losses | Sch. D (N-20) | No |
| Schedule K-1 | Partner's Share of Income, Deductions, Credits, Etc. | Sch. K-1 (N-20) | No |
| 1128 | Application to Adopt, Change, or Retain a Tax Year | None | Yes* |
| 3115 | Application for Change in Accounting Method | None | Yes* |
| 4562 | Depreciation and Amortization | None | Yes* |
| 4684 | Casualties and Thefts | None | Yes* |
| 4797 | Sales of Business Property | Sch. D-1 | No |
| 5884 | Work Opportunity Credit | N-884 | No |
| 6198 | At-Risk Limitations | None | Yes* |
| 6781 | Gains and Losses from Section 1256 Contracts and Straddles | None | Yes* |
| 7004 | Application For Automatic Extension of Time to File Certain Business Income Tax, Information, and Other Returns | N-301 | No |
| 8283 | Noncash Charitable Contributions | None | Yes* |
| 8582 | Passive Activity Loss Limitations | None | Yes* |
| 8586 | Low-Income Housing Credit | N-586 | No |
| 8693 | Low-Income Housing Credit Disposition Bond | N-587 | No |
| 8697 | Interest Computation Under the Look-Back Method for Completed Long-Term Contracts | None | Yes* |
| 8824 | Like-Kind Exchanges | None | Yes* |
| 8825 | Rental Real Estate Income and Expenses of a Partnership or an S Corporation | None | Yes* |
| 8832 | Entity Classification Election | None | Yes* |

* If there is no Hawaii equivalent form, the federal form must be used.

# RELATED FEDERAL/HAWAII CORPORATION TAX FORMS

| Federal Form Number | Title or Description of Federal Form | Use Hawaii Form | Copy of Form Ma Used* |
|---|---|---|---|
| 1120-S | U.S. Income Tax Return for an S Corporation | N-35 | No |
| Schedule D | Capital Gains and Losses and Built-In Gains | Schedule D | No |
| Schedule K-1 | Shareholder's Share of Income, Deductions, Credits, Etc. | Schedule K-1 | No |
| 970 | Application to Use LIFO Inventory Method | None | Yes |
| 1128 | Application to Adopt, Change, or Retain a Tax Year | None | Yes |
| 2220 | Underpayment of Estimated Tax by Corporations | N-220 | No |
| 2553 | Election By a Small Business Corporation | None | No |
| 3115 | Application for Change in Accounting Method | None | Yes |
| 4562 | Depreciation and Amortization | None | Yes |
| 4684 | Casualties and Theft | None | Yes |
| 6252 | Installment Sale Income | None | Yes |
| 7004 | Application for Automatic Extension of Time To File Certain Business Income Tax, Information, and Other Returns | N-301 | No |
| 8023 | Elections Under Section 338 for Corporations Making Qualified Stock Purchases | None | Yes |
| 8697 | Interest Computation Under the Look-Back Method for Completed Long-Term Contracts | None | Yes |
| 8824 | Like-Kind Exchanges | None | Yes |
| 8825 | Rental Real Estate Income and Expenses of a Partnership or an S Corporation | None | Yes |

*If there is no Hawaii equivalent form, the federal form must be used.

# RELATED FEDERAL/HAWAII S CORPORATION TAX FORMS

| Federal Form Number | Title or Description of Federal Form | Use Hawaii Form | Copy of Fed. Form May Be Used |
|---|---|---|---|
| 851 | Affiliations Schedule | N-304 | No |
| 966 | Corporate Dissolution or Liquidation | None | Yes* |
| 970 | Application to Use LIFO Inventory Method | None | Yes* |
| 990 | Return of Organization Exempt from Income Tax | None | No |
| 990T | Exempt Organization Business Income Tax Return | N-70NP | No |
| 1120 | U.S. Corporation Income Tax Return | N-30 | No |
| Schedule D | Capital Gains and Losses | Sch. D (N-30) | No |
| 1120-F | U.S. Income Tax Return of a Foreign Corporation | N-30 | No |
| 1120-H | U.S. Income Tax Return for Homeowners Associations | N-30 | No |
| 1120-IC-DISC | Interest Charge Domestic International Sales Corporation Return | N-30 | No |
| 1120-POL | U.S. Income Tax Return for Certain Political Organizations | N-30 | No |
| 1120-REIT | U.S. Income Tax Return for Real Estate Investment Trusts | N-30 | No |
| 1120-RIC | U.S. Income Tax Return for Regulated Investment Companies | N-30 | No |
| 1120-S | U.S. Income Tax Return for an S Corporation | N-35 | No |
| 1120-SF | U.S. Income Tax Return For Settlement Funds (Under Section 468B) | N-30 | No |
| 1120-W | Estimated Tax for Corporations | N-3 | No |
| 1120-X | Amended U.S. Corporation Income Tax Return | N-30 | No |
| 1122 | Authorization and Consent of Subsidiary Corporation To Be Included in a Consolidated Income Tax Return | N-303 | No |
| 1128 | Application to Adopt, Change, or Retain a Tax Year | None | Yes* |
| 1139 | Corporation Application for Tentative Refund | N-309 | No |
| 2220 | Underpayment of Estimated Tax by Corporations | N-220 | No |
| 3115 | Application for Change in Accounting Method | None | Yes* |
| 4466 | Corporation Application for Quick Refund of Overpayment of Estimated Tax | None | No |
| 4562 | Depreciation and Amortization | None | Yes* |
| 4684 | Casualties and Thefts | None | Yes* |
| 4797 | Sales of Business Property | Sch. D-1 (N-30) | No |
| 6198 | At-Risk Limitations | None | Yes* |
| 6252 | Installment Sale Income | None | Yes* |
| 6781 | Gains and Losses From Section 1256 Contracts and Straddles | None | Yes* |
| 7004 | Application For Automatic Extension of Time To File Certain Business Income Tax, Information, and Other Returns | N-301 | No |
| 8023 | Elections Under Section 338 for Corporations Making Qualified Stock Purchases | None | Yes* |
| 8283 | Noncash Charitable Contributions | None | Yes* |
| 8586 | Low-Income Housing Credit | N-586 | No |
| 8693 | Low-Income Housing Credit Disposition Bond | N-587 | No |
| 8697 | Interest Computation Under the Look-Back Method for Completed Long-Term Contracts | None | Yes* |
| 8810 | Corporate Passive Activity Loss and Credit Limitations | None | Yes* |
| 8824 | Like-Kind Exchanges | None | Yes* |
| 8842 | Election To Use Different Annualization Periods for Corporation Estimated Tax | None | Yes* |
| T(Timber) | Forest Activities Schedule | None | Yes* |

*If there is no Hawaii equivalent form, the federal form must be used.

# RELATED FEDERAL/HAWAII FIDUCIARY TAX FORMS

| Federal Form Number | Title or Description of Federal Form | Use Hawaii Form | Copy of Fed. Form May Be Used |
|---|---|---|---|
| 970 | Application To Use LIFO Inventory Method | None | Yes* |
| 1041 | U.S. Income Tax Return for Estates and Trusts | N-40 | No |
| 1041-QFT | U.S. Income Tax Return for Qualified Funeral Trusts | N-40 | No |
| Schedule D | Capital Gains and Losses | Sch. D (N-40) | No |
| Schedule J | Accumulation Distribution for Certain Complex Trusts | Sch. J (N-40) | No |
| Schedule K-1 | Beneficiary's Share of Income, Deductions, Credits, Etc. | Sch. K-1 (N-40) | No |
| 1128 | Application to Adopt, Change, or Retain a Tax Year | None | Yes* |
| 3115 | Application for Change in Accounting Method | None | Yes* |
| 4562 | Depreciation and Amortization | None | Yes* |
| 4684 | Casualties and Thefts | None | Yes* |
| 4797 | Sales of Business Property | Sch. D-1 | No |
| 4970 | Tax on Accumulation Distribution of Trusts | N-405 | No |
| 5884 | Work Opportunity Credit | N-884 | No |
| 6198 | At-Risk Limitations | None | Yes* |
| 6252 | Installment Sale | None | Yes* |
| 6781 | Gains and Losses from Section 1256 Contracts and Straddles | None | Yes* |
| 7004 | Application for Automatic Extension of Time to File Certain Business Income Tax, Information, and Other Returns | N-301 | No |
| 8582 | Passive Activity Loss Limitations | None | Yes* |
| 8586 | Low-Income Housing Credit | N-586 | No |
| 8693 | Low-Income Housing Credit Disposition Bond | N-587 | No |
| 8824 | Like-Kind Exchanges | None | Yes* |
| 8855 | Election to Treat a Qualified Revocable Trust as Part of an Estate | None | Yes* |

* If there is no Hawaii equivalent form, the federal form must be used.

## CHECK LIST OF DIFFERENCES
## BETWEEN HAWAII AND
## FEDERAL INCOME TAX LAWS

| Federal Law Section | Hawaii Law Section | Subject | Taxes of Hawaii Paragraph |
|---|---|---|---|
| 1, 2, 11 | 235-51 235-71 | Tax rates | 103 |
| 3, 4 | 235-53 | Optional tax | 104 |
| 21 | 235-110.55.6 | Child and dependent care expenses | 412b |
| 23 | | Adoption expense credit | 412 |
| 24 | | Child tax credit | 412 |
| 25 | | Hope scholarship and lifetime learning credit | 412 |
| 38 | | | 403 |
| 46-48 | | Investment credit | 412 |
| 41 | 235-110.91 | Research Activities Credit | 412s |
| 42 | 235-110.8 | Low income housing credits | 412j |
| 48 | 235-12.5 | Residential Energy Credit | 412a |
| 51, 52 | | Targeted jobs credit | 412k |
| 63 | 235-1 235-2.3 | Taxable income, standard deduction | 410 |
| 68 | | Limitation on itemized deductions | 401 |
| 72 | 235-7(a) | Pensions, etc. | 303 |
| 78 | 235-2.3 | Dividends—foreign corporations | 307 |
| 79 | | Group term insurance | 313 |
| 86 | 235-2.3 | Social security and tier 1 Railroad Retirement benefits | 317a |
| 101 | | Death benefit exclusion | 303a |
| 103 | 235-7(b) | | |
| | | Interest income | 302 |
| 104 | | Personal injury awards | 317 |
| 105 | | Medical reimbursement plans | 317 |
| 112, 134 | 235-7 | Service pay | 304 |
| 116 | 235-7 | Dividend and interest exclusion | 302 307 |
| 119 | | Meals or lodging | 303a |
| 120 | 235-7(a)(9) to (11) | Prepaid legal expenses | 317b 408a |

| Federal Law Section | Hawaii Law Section | Subject | Taxes of Hawaii Paragraph |
|---|---|---|---|
| 121 | 235-2.4 | Sale of residence | 511a |
| 122 | 235-7(a)(3) | Military personnel annuities | 303 |
| 127 | | Educational assistance | 303a |
| 132 | | Fringe Benefits | 303a |
| 136 | | Energy Conservation Subsidies | 326 |
| 141-150 | 235-2.3 | Private activity bonds | 302 |
| 151-152 | 235-54 | Personal exemptions | { 106 106a |
| 162 | | Trade or business expenses | 402 |
| 163 | 235-2.4 | Interest | 404 |
| 164 | | Taxes | 411 |
| 165 | 235-7 | Casualty losses | 409 |
| 166 | | Bad debts | 423 |
| 167 | | Deduction for depreciation | 403 |
| 168 | 235-2.4 | Accelerated cost recovery system | 403 |
| 169 | | Pollution control facilities | 424 |
| 170 | | Deductions for contributions | 405 |
| 172 | 235-7 | Operating loss carryover and carryback | 407 |
| 179 | 235-2.3, 235-2,.4 | Election to expense certain depreciable property | 403 |
| 181 | | Treatment of certain qualified film and television productions | 412m |
| 183 | | Activities not engaged in for profit | 425 |
| 190 | | Architectural barriers | 428 |
| 195 | | Amortization of start-up expenditures | 429 |
| 199A | | Qualified business income | 401 |
| 213 | | Medical expenses | 406 |
| 219 | 235-2.4 | IRA | 408 |
| 220 | 235-2.4 | Medical savings accounts | 406 |
| 221 | | Interest paid on higher education loans | 404 |
| 243-246A | 235-7(c) | Dividends received deduction | 307 |
| 245 | 235-2.3 | Distributions by foreign corporations | 307 |
| 249 | 235-7 | Bond premium deduction | 404 |
| 263A | | Inventory capitalization costs | 108 |
| 264 | | Interest to carry corporate owned life insurance | 404 |
| 265 | 235-7 | Deduction for interest | 404 |
| 267 | | Related party transactions | 113 |

| Federal Law Section | Hawaii Law Section | Subject | Taxes of Hawaii Paragraph |
|---|---|---|---|
| 291 | 235-2.3 | Corporate preference items | 421 |
| 312 | | Earnings and profits | 307 |
| 337 | | Gain or loss on certain corporate liquidations | 710 |
| 367 | 235-2.3 | Foreign corporation—exchange | 513 |
| 368 | | Corporate reorganization | 524 |
| 382 | | Net operating loss carryovers | 407 |
| 401-416 | 235-2.4 | Pension and profit-sharing plans | { 303 408 |
| 419 | | Welfare benefit plans | 408 |
| 447 | | Accounting for farms | 108 |
| 457 | | Deferred compensation plans for state and county employees | 303 |
| 460 | | Long-term contracts | 108 |
| 465 | | At risk rules | 425a |
| 471 | | Estimating inventory shrinkage | 108 |
| 475 | | Mark to market accounting method | 108 |
| 482 | 235-103 | Distortion of income | 113 |
| 483 | 235-2.3 | Interest on deferred payments | 314 |
| 501 | 235-9 | Exempt organizations | 107 |
| 501 | | Unemployment benefit trusts | 107 |
| 502 | | Feeder organizations | 107 |
| 507-509 | | Private foundations | 107 |
| 510-515 | 235-2.3, 235-2.4 | Unrelated income | 107 |
| 528 | | Exempt housing associations | 107 |
| 530 | 235-2.4 | Coverdell Savings Accounts IRA | { 303 408 |
| 582 | 241-4 | Bond losses and gains | 510 |
| 585 | 241-4 | Bad debts—financial institutions | 423 |
| 593 | 241-4 | Savings and loans—reserve for losses | 111 |
| 613 | | Depletion | 422 |
| 641-683 | 235-2.3, 235-2.45 | Trusts—"throwback" of income, taxation of spouse, charitable remainders, two-year charitable trusts, unlimited charitable deduction, foreign trusts | { 405 604 |
| 701-777 | 235-2.45 | Partnership provisions | 601 |
| 851-855 | 235.71 | Regulated investment companies | 112 |
| 856-859 | | Real estate investment trusts | 606 |
| Act 2000, Sec. 1616(b)(8) | | Savings and loans—foreclosures | 111 |
| 1400Z-1-1400Z-2 | 235-2.45 | Opportunity Zones | 525 |

| Federal Law Section | Hawaii Law Section | Subject | Taxes of Hawaii Paragraph |
|---|---|---|---|
| 902 | 235-2.3 | Dividends—foreign corporations | 307 |
| 911 | 235-2.3 | Earned income from outside U.S. | 312 |
| 912 | 235-7 | Cost-of-living allowances | 306 |
| 912 | 235-2.3 | Allowances of Peace Corps volunteers | 308 |
| 921-927 | 235-2.3 | Foreign sales corporations | 114a |
| 951-964 | 235-2.3 | Controlled foreign corporations | { 312 |
| 970-971 | 235-2.3 | | 515 |
| 991-997 | 235-2.3 | DISC | 114 |
| 1001 | | Sales and exchange | 501 |
| 1011-1023 | 235-3 | Basis—reorganizations, etc. | 502 |
| 1011 | | Basis—accounts receivable | 508 |
| 1011 | | Basis—"bargain sales" | 405 |
| 1014-1015 | | | |
| 1019 | | Basis—lessee improvements | 506 |
| 1016 | | Basis—depreciable property | 507 |
| 1031 | | Exchange of property | 503 |
| 1033 | 235-3 | Involuntary conversions, etc. | 511 |
| 1038 | | Repossession of real property | 517 |
| 1045 | | Elective rollover gain from qualified small business stock | 510 |
| 1051 | | Basis—consolidated returns | 505 |
| 1055 | 235-2.3 | Redeemable ground rents | 518 |
| 1059 | | Extraordinary dividends | 307 |
| 1091 | | Wash sales | 510 |
| 1201 | | Capital gain deduction | 510 |
| 1211 | | Capital loss deduction | 510 |
| 1212 | 235-2.45 | Capital loss carryover | 510 |
| 1222 | | Capital gains and losses | 510 |
| 1223 | | Holding period capital assets | 510 |
| 1231 | | Casualty loss offset | { 409  510 |
| 1234A | | Gains and losses from termination | 510 |
| 1245-1250 | | Sale of depreciable property | 516 |
| 1246-1247 | | Sale of foreign investment company stock | 513 |
| 1248 | | Sale of foreign corporation stock | 513 |
| 1249 | | Sale of patents to foreign corporation | 513 |
| 1252 | | Gain on sale of farm land, etc. | { 425  516a |
| 1253 | | Sale of franchise | 510 |
| 1271-1278 | | Original issue and market discount | 320a |
| 1301 | | Farm income averaging | 318 |
| 1361-1378 | 235-2.45 | Subchapter S Corporations | 602 |
| 1385 | | Special rules for cooperatives | 107 |

| Federal Law Section | Hawaii Law Section | Subject | Taxes of Hawaii Paragraph |
|---|---|---|---|
| 1504 | 235-92 | Consolidated returns | 708 |
| 3401 | { 235-61 to 235-67 | Withholding from employees | 206 |
| 4940-4948 | | Private foundations | 107 |
| 6012, 6102, 7513 | { 235-92 to 235-95 | Returns—who is required to file | 202 |
| 6013 | 235-93 | Joint returns | 105 |
| 6015, 6016 | 235-97 | Declarations of estimated tax | 205 |
| 6041-6049 | 235-96 | Information returns | 212 |
| 6048 | | Beneficiaries of foreign trusts | 607 |
| 6072 | { 231-8 235-98 235-99 | Returns—time for filing | 203 |
| 6081 | 235-98 | Extension of time for filing returns | 204 |
| 6211-6215, 6501 | { 235-107 to 235-109, 235-112 to 235-113 | Deficiencies | 208 |
| 6401-6407 | { 231-23, 231-51, 231-52, 235-55, 235-66, 235-110 | Refunds | 209 |
| 6501 | { 235-111 to 235-113 | Statute of limitations—assessments | 208 |
| 6211 to 6215 | { 232-1 to 232-24, 235-114 | Appeals | 211 |
| 6511 | 235-111 | Statute of limitation—refunds | 209 |
| 6651-6658 | { 231-34, 231-39, 235-104, 235-105 | Penalties | 210 |
| 6677 | | Beneficiaries of foreign trusts | 607 |
| 7872 | | Below-market interest loans | 302 |
| None | 53A | Enterprise Zone Credits | 412g |
| None | 235-7 | Compensation of Hansen's disease patients | 305 |
| None | 235-51 | Alternate tax for certain taxpayers doing business in more than one state | 115 |
| None | 235-55 | Tax credits—excise tax credit | 412 |
| Merchant Marine Act, Act, Sec. 607 | | Exemption for vessel acquisition | 324 |

# HAWAII REVISED STATUTES – TITLE 14

The following is a list of important Hawaii Revised Statutes chapters related to tax. Each of the chapters below can be accessed at http://www.state.hi.us/tax/a4_2hrs.htm.

| Chapter | Chapter Title |
| --- | --- |
| 231 | Administration of Taxes |
| 232 | Tax Appeals |
| 232E | Tax Review Commission |
| 233 | Tax Classification of Certain Business Relationships |
| 234 | Tax Relief for Natural Disaster Losses – Repealed |
| 235 | Income Tax Law |
| 235D | Qualified Improvement Tax Credit – Repealed |
| 236 | Inheritance and Estate Taxes Law – Repealed |
| 236A | Revised Uniform Estate Tax Apportionment Act - Repealed |
| 236D | Estate and Transfer Tax |
| 236E | Estate and Generation-Skipping Transfer Tax |
| 237 | General Excise Tax Law |
| 237D | Transient Accommodations Tax |
| 238 | Use Tax Law |
| 239 | Public Service Company Tax Law |
| 240 | Public Utilities; Franchise Tax |
| 241 | Taxation of Banks and Other Financial Corporations |
| 242 | Mortgage Loan Exemption – Repealed |
| 243 | Fuel Tax Law |
| 244 | Liquor Tax Law – Repealed |
| 244D | Liquor Tax Law |
| 245 | Cigarette Tax and Tobacco Tax Law |
| 246 | Real Property Tax Law |
| 246A | Transfer of Real Property Taxation Functions |
| 247 | Conveyance Tax |
| 248 | County Budgets; Tax Funds |
| 249 | County Vehicular Taxes |
| 251 | Rental Motor Vehicle and Tour Vehicle Surcharge Tax |
| 255 | Multistate Tax Compact |
| 255D | Hawaii Simplified Sales and Use Tax Administration Act |
| 256 | College Savings Program |
| 257 | Individual Development Accounts |

Hawaii imposes a variety of different taxes including income taxes, a gross receipts tax (called the Hawaii general excise tax), and various other taxes including estate and generation-skipping taxes.

The general excise tax currently comprises approximately half of Hawaii's general fund tax revenue. It applies to a broad spectrum of activities, taxpayers, transactions, and income producing activities. In addition to its imposition on sales of tangible personal property, the general excise tax applies to services, contracting (construction-related services), rents, royalties, and other types of income. Interest income is generally subject to the general excise tax including for businesses and certain other income producing activities. Unlike a traditional sales tax that may only apply at the retail level, the general excise tax pyramids by potentially applying at all levels of business and income producing activities including on business to business transactions and frequently at the highest tax rate at each level. Wholesale transactions are taxed and may qualify in certain circumstances for a lower tax rate, e.g., 0.5%. Unlike other states that may provide an exemption for sales to charities, certain nonprofits, and federal, state, and local governments, the general excise tax generally applies to sales, contracting, services, rents, royalties, and transactions with such charities, nonprofits, and federal, state and local governments. While there is a limited exemption for sales of tangible personal property to the federal government, such exemption does not apply to services and other types of income. Traditionally, the Hawaii Tax Department has taken the position that charities and nonprofits are subject to the general excise tax on their income except to the extent that such income producing activity primarily advances their exempt purpose. Thus, fundraisers, rents, and royalties by charities and nonprofits are generally subject to the general excise tax. As a result, the general excise tax is much broader than the federal unrelated business income tax. Finally, the general excise tax is complemented by the use tax which generally applies to property, services and construction-related services (contracting). The use tax may also apply to the importation or use in the state of property, services, and contracting (construction-related services). The use tax may apply even when the taxpayer never takes title to the personal property and merely exercises any right or power incident to ownership of the personal property under H.R.S. Section 238-1. *See also, In Re Habilitat,* 65 Haw. 199 (1982). The use and general excise taxes are discussed in detail below in Chapters 8 and 9.

# CHAPTER 1

# INCOME TAX
## IMPOSITION OF TAX, RATES, EXEMPTIONS, RESIDENCE

## ¶ 101. History and Imposition of Income Tax
### Hawaii Law: Sec. 235-2 to 235-45

Hawaii became a territory of the United States in 1900, and has had an income tax since 1901. The law has been revised frequently since that time. The present law was enacted in 1957, effective January 1, 1958; it was designed to minimize the burden of compliance by conforming as closely as possible with the federal income tax. The 1957 Hawaii law adopted the federal law as it stood at June 7, 1957, with a few exceptions and modifications. The law has been amended many times since 1957, usually for the purpose of conforming to amendments of the federal law. However, many of the federal amendments between 1957 and 1977 were not adopted by Hawaii; this resulted in numerous additional differences between Hawaii and federal laws. These differences may cause a difference between the federal and Hawaii tax basis of assets. In 1978, the Hawaii Legislature made a major revision to the law. The revision adopted the Internal Revenue Code as of December 31, 1977, with certain specified exceptions. The Hawaii law was amended in 1981 to provide that retroactive provisions in the federal law will apply for Hawaii purposes upon adoption of the federal provision. See the "Check List of Differences" for a list of the present differences between Hawaii and federal income tax laws. Hawaii became a state on August 21, 1959. This had no effect on the tax law.

Taxes are imposed upon individuals, corporations, estates, and trusts. Resident individuals, estates and trusts are taxed upon their entire income regardless of source, except for individuals who became residents before July 1, 1976, and after the age of 65; such individuals are taxed only on income from Hawaiian sources. Domestic corporations are taxed upon their entire income, except to the extent the income is allocated to another jurisdiction— see Chapter 7. Nonresidents and foreign corporations are taxed on income from sources in Hawaii, as explained in ¶ 309 and in Chapter 7.

Under a 1969 amendment to the income tax law, "corporation" is defined to include a professional corporation organized under the Professional Corporation Law that became effective July 16, 1969. This law allowed the benefits of the corporate form to certain groups, including accountants, attorneys, chiropractors, dentists, doctors of medicine, surgeons, naturopaths, opticians, optometrists, osteopaths, pharmacists, and veterinarians.

Effective for years beginning after 1987 Hawaii began treating certain publicly traded partnerships as corporations. Hawaii began following the provisions of Section 7704 of the Internal Revenue Code. The federal law was amended in 1997, effective for years beginning after December 31, 1997, to allow certain publicly traded partnerships referred to as "electing 1987 partnerships" to elect not to be treated as a corporation and in lieu thereof pay a tax of 3.5 percent of their gross income. Hawaii has not adopted this 1997 federal amendment.

The Hawaii law was amended in 1978, effective for years beginning in 1978, to allow the Department of Taxation to adopt certain Internal Revenue Code Regulations to be operable under the Hawaii law. Hawaii Administrative Rule. 18-235-2.3, formerly Reg. No. 79-1(N), was adopted on July 17, 1979, and became effective as of January 1, 1978. Hawaii Administrative Rule 18-235-2.3 adopts the federal regulations relating to Sections 1 to 1388 of the Internal Revenue Code as amended as of December 31, 1977.

In 2017, the U.S. Congress enacted the Tax Cuts and Jobs Act of 2017 that increased the standard deduction, suspended personal exemptions, and generally limited itemized deductions. In general, Hawaii did not conform to these changes.

In 2018, for all taxable years beginning after December 31, 2017, reference to the Internal Revenue Code in the Hawaii Revised Statue means Subtitle A Chapter 1 of the Federal Internal Revenue Code of 1986 as amended as of February 9, 2018. Certain sections are not operative as indicated in the following table:

¶ 101

| Subchapter | Internal Revenue Code Section |
|---|---|
| A | 1 to 59A, (except sec 1(h)(2), sec 2(a), 2(b), 2(c), sec 41, sec 42, sec 47, sec 48, and 48(d)(3)) |
| B | 78, 86, 91, 103, 114, 120, 122, 135, 139C, 141 to 150, 151, 179B, 181, 196, 199, 199A, 222, 241 to 247, 250, 267A, 280C, 291 |
| C | 367 |
| F | 501(c)(12), (15), (16), 515 |
| G | 531 to 565 |
| H | 581 to 597 (except sec 584) |
| J | 642(a) and (b), 646, 668 |
| L | 801 to 848 |
| M | 853, 853A |
| N | 861 to 999 (except sec 985 to 989) |
| O | 1042(g), 1055, 1057 |
| P | 1291 to 1298 |
| Q | 1311 to 1351 |
| R | 1352 to 1359 |
| U | 1391 to 1397F |
| W | 1400 to 1400C, 1400O, 1400P, 1400R, 1400T, 1400U-1, 1400U-2, 1400U-3, and 1400Z-1 to 1400Z-2 |

See ¶ 1403 for the complete text of Hawaii Administrative Rule 18-235-2.3. However please use caution when using the administrative rules as they are not consistently updated.

## ¶ 102. Tax Base
**Hawaii Law: Sec. 235-1**
**Federal Law: Sec. 61 to 63**

The income tax is imposed on "taxable income," which is defined as the gross income less the deductions allowed (including deductions allowed for personal exemptions). This tax base is the same, in principle, as in the federal law; however, the amount of the Hawaii "taxable income" may be different from the federal because of the differences between the two laws explained in this and subsequent chapters. Further, please note that the term "Adjusted Gross Income" (AGI) sometimes refers to federal AGI and other times refers to Hawaii AGI.

## ¶ 103. Income Tax Rates
**Hawaii Law: Sec. 235-51, 235-71**
**Federal Law: Sec. 1, 2, 11**

INDIVIDUAL, ESTATE AND TRUST RATES

For many years prior to 1987 the Hawaii tax rates remained static. Beginning in 1987 the rates and income brackets were adjusted. Reference should be made to prior editions of this book for the rates for a specific year. For the 2018 tax year, the rates graduate from a low of 1.4% to a high of 11%. See tax tables at the front of the book for the 2018 schedule of rates. For the 2017 tax year, the rates graduated from a low of 1.4% to a high of 8.25%. The tax rates for estates and trusts graduate from a low of 1.40% to an high of 8.25%. See tax tables at the beginning of the book for the 2018 estate and trust rates. Since 1967, there has been a special schedule of tax rates for "head of household"—see ¶ 105a.

## CORPORATION RATES

For years after 1986, the income tax rate on corporations is 4.4% of the first $25,000 of ordinary taxable income, 5.4% on ordinary taxable income over $25,000 and up to $100,000, and 6.4% on ordinary taxable income in excess of $100,000. Net long-term capital gains received after March 31, 1987, are taxed at 4%. References should be made to prior editions for the corporate tax rates in effect prior to 1987. The rate of franchise tax, measured by the prior year's income, imposed on banks and other financial corporations, was 11.7% for taxable years beginning on or before December 31, 1993. For taxable years beginning on or after January 1, 1994 the rate is 7.92%. For years beginning on or after January 1, 1994 there is an alternative capital gains tax of 4% on net capital gains—see ¶ 111.

"Real estate investment trusts" are taxable at the corporation rates, on undistributed income. See ¶ 606.

## CAPITAL GAINS

Hawaii adopted the pre-1987 federal rules for taxing long-term capital gains for years beginning in 1979 and has adopted the federal capital gain changes enacted in the Tax Reform Act of 1986 with the exception that Hawaii allowed a deduction of 55% of the net capital gains arising prior to April 1, 1987. Prior to 1979, Hawaii had an alternative tax of 4% for long-term capital gains of individuals. For years after 1986 the maximum rate on capital gains of individuals, estates and trusts is 7.25%. The rule for corporations remains the same as in prior years. Thus, on corporate returns the full amount of capital gains is taken into income and net long-term capital gains are taxed at the special rate of 4%.

## ¶ 103a. Non Resident and Part Year Resident Income Tax
### Hawaii Law: Sec. 235-5

Effective for tax years beginning after December 31, 1998 non residents and part year residents will be allowed the standard deduction and personal exemption only to the extent of the ratio of the adjusted gross income attributed to Hawaii to the entire adjusted gross income from all sources.

## ¶ 104. Optional Tax
### Hawaii Law: Sec. 235-53
### Federal Law: Sec. 3

An individual whose taxable income is less than $100,000 must use the tax tables for individuals shown at the beginning of the book. The $100,000 income limitation applies to a married individual filing a separate return, even though the combined income of husband and wife exceeds $100,000.

## ¶ 105. Joint Returns—Income Splitting
### Hawaii Law: Sec. 235-2.4, 235-52, 235-93
### Federal Law: Sec. 6013

The Hawaii law provides that a husband and wife may make a joint Hawaii return if they are entitled to make a joint federal return. However, taxpayers should consider the possible desirability of filing separate Hawaii returns even though they file a joint federal return. Separate returns might be advantageous because they would produce a larger medical expense deduction. Where one spouse is a nonresident (in the case of a serviceman or student, he may be a "nonresident" even though physically present in the state—see ¶ 109), separate returns might be advantageous to avoid reporting income of the nonresident spouse.

Another possible reason for filing separate Hawaii returns was that the joint liability that goes with a joint return might be greater on the Hawaii return than on the federal. The federal law was amended in January 1971 to relieve the innocent spouse in some situations from liability for tax or penalty resulting from wrongdoing by the other spouse; Hawaii adopted this federal provision in 1994 effective for deficiency notices sent to taxpayers after December 31, 1990.

The federal law was amended in 1998 to expand the relief from joint and several liability for an innocent spouse. Hawaii has adopted this amendment.

Taxpayers who file a joint Hawaii return may not change their minds and file separate returns after the due date. However, taxpayers who file separate returns may change to a joint return any time up to three years after the date the first of the separate returns was filed, with earlier limitation dates prescribed where a deficiency notice has been issued, where a refund suit has been instituted, or where there has been a closing agreement or compromise of tax liability. These rules are the same as the federal, except that federal allows three years after the original due date of the return rather than three years from date of filing. The Hawaii Regulations provide that a joint return may be filed more than three years from the date of filing the first of the separate returns, provided it is accompanied by an agreement to extend the statute of limitations and it is filed within three years of the due date of the separate returns. The law was amended, effective for tax years ending after December 31, 1997, to allow the filing of a joint return after the individual has filed a separate return without making full payment of the amount shown as tax on the joint return.

The benefits of the married filing jointly rates are available to a surviving spouse for the next two taxable years following the death of a spouse, provided the survivor was eligible to file a joint return for the year in which the spouse died. To be eligible for this benefit, the surviving spouse must maintain a home for himself (or herself) and at least one son or daughter (including stepchildren and adopted children), must not be remarried at the close of the taxable year and must qualify for a dependency deduction with respect to the child involved. The "home" must be occupied by both taxpayer and child for the entire taxable year (temporary absences due to business, vacation, illness, military service, education and child's absence of less than six months under custody agreement do not disqualify) and the taxpayer must pay more than one-half of the cost of maintaining the home.

With the minor exceptions described above, the Hawaii rules regarding joint returns and income-splitting by married couples and surviving spouses are the same as the federal.

### ¶ 105a. Head of Household
Hawaii Law: Sec. 235-1, 235-51
Federal Law: Sec. 1

The law was amended in 1967 to provide a special schedule of tax rates for a person who qualifies as "head of household." It applies to returns for the calendar year 1967 and subsequent years. See rate schedules in the front of the book.

"Head of household" means anyone who qualifies as such for federal income tax purposes. To qualify, the individual must be unmarried or a "married individual living apart," must not be a "surviving spouse" as described above in ¶ 105 and must maintain a family home. The federal law provides specific rules as to the required degree of family relationship, dependency, etc.

### ¶ 105b. Civil Unions and Same Sex Marriages
Hawaii Law: Sec. 231-21.5

Effective for taxable years starting after December 31, 2011, Hawaii law was amended to recognize civil unions. Under this amendment, partners to a civil union have the same rights and responsibilities as those afforded to married couples. With respect to this amendment civil unions are included in the definitions of spouse, family, immediate family, dependent, next of kin, and any other terms that describe a marital relationship.

For Hawaii tax purposes, civil union partners are treated the same as married couples and must file their Hawaii income tax returns as married individuals. However, for federal tax purposes, civil union partners are not treated as married and cannot file a federal income tax return as married individuals. Rev. Rul. 2013-17. To compute their Hawaii taxable income, civil union partners will need to create a federal tax return as married individuals only for the purpose of computing their Hawaii tax liability. Tax Announcement No. 2013-26.

Effective December 2, 2013, Hawaii recognizes marriages between same sex individuals under Chapter 572 of the Hawaii Revised Statutes. Hawaii also recognizes same sex marriages performed in any other jurisdiction where same sex marriage is legal. For both Hawaii and federal tax purposes, marriage between individuals of the same sex is treated the same as marriage between individuals of the opposite sex. See U.S. v. Windsor, 570 U.S. ___ (2013); Rev. Rul. 2013-17. Therefore, for both federal and Hawaii tax purposes, individuals in a same sex marriage can file both their federal and Hawaii income tax returns as married individuals. Filing status of an individual as married is determined on the last day of the individual's tax year. Tax Announcement No. 2013-26.

## ¶ 106. Deductions for Personal Exemptions
### Hawaii Law: Sec. 235-54
### Federal Law: Sec. 151 to 153, 642 (b)

Deductions for personal exemptions on individual returns for 1980 to 1984 were $1,000 for each exemption allowed under federal law, except for blind, deaf and disabled persons as explained in ¶ 106a. For years beginning after December 31, 1984, the deduction is increased to $1,040. The $1,040 allowance applies to the taxpayer, his spouse, his dependents and an extra exemption for those 65 and older. The Tax Reform Act of 1986 increased the federal deduction for personal exemptions for 1987 and 1988, repealed the additional personal exemption for taxpayers 65 or older or blind beginning in 1987 and repealed the personal exemption to be claimed on the return of a dependent child for years after 1986. Hawaii has not adopted these 1986 federal amendments except that Hawaii has adopted the provision, beginning in 1987, that denies an exemption deduction to a taxpayer that is claimed as a dependent on another taxpayer's return. The federal law was amended in 1988 to provide that beginning in 1989 a full-time student who is 24 will no longer qualify as a dependent if his or her gross income for the year exceeds the exemption amount. Hawaii has adopted this amendment. Act 97 was passed in 2011 which delays the increase in the personal exemption amounts previously approved in 2009 and make the increases permanent. As a result, the Hawaii personal exemption amount for 2011 and 2012 will remain at $1,040 and for tax year 2013 and thereafter, the personal exemption will be increased to $1,144. The Tax Cuts and Jobs Act (P.L. 115-97) has suspended the federal personal exemption, but that provision is not operative under Hawaii income tax law.

The Hawaii requirements to qualify for these exemptions are the same as the pre-1987 federal rules; in other words, if you are entitled to exemptions on your federal return, you are automatically entitled to them on your Hawaii return. Beginning in 1985, both the federal and Hawaii laws allow a dependency exemption for a disabled dependent who earns over $1,000 in a sheltered workshop if certain conditions are met. The federal law was amended in 1996 to deny an exemption deduction where the taxpayer fails to provide the dependent's current taxpayer identification number. This amendment is effective for tax returns due after September 29, 1996. Hawaii has adopted this amendment.

For tax years beginning after December 31, 2008, the personal exemption claimed by a taxpayer with adjusted gross income exceeding a threshold amount shall be reduced. For tax year 2009 only, the amount of the phase-out was 1/3 of the amount that would otherwise have been subtracted from the personal exemption amount. For taxable years beginning after December 31, 2009, there will no longer be a reduction of the phase-out amount that is subtracted from the personal exemption amount.

The Hawaii deduction for personal exemption for an estate is $400. For a trust distributing all income currently, the deduction is $200; for all other trusts, it is $80. The federal deductions are different: estate, $600; trust distributing all income, $300; other trusts, $100.

Under the federal law, effective in 1970, a foster child is treated the same as a natural or adopted child for purposes of the dependency exemption. To qualify, the foster child must have as his principal place of residence, the home of the taxpayer and must be a member of the taxpayer's household. The effect of this is to permit a dependency deduction even though the income of the foster child is more than the limitation for a dependent, provided the child is under 19 or is a student. Hawaii adopted this provision effective January 1, 1975.

Nonresidents are allowed a deduction for a personal exemption, prorated based on the ratio of Hawaii source income or income earned as a resident over total income.

## ¶ 106a. Special Exemptions for Disabled Persons
### Hawaii Law: Sec. 235-54
### Federal Law: Sec. 151

Hawaii allows special personal exemptions for persons who are blind, deaf, or otherwise disabled, as explained below. This has applied to the blind for many years and was extended in 1970 to include the deaf and disabled. Federal law allows an extra exemption for a blind person, but allows no extra exemption for deaf or disabled persons.

The Hawaii exemption for blind, deaf, and disabled persons is $7,000, effective in 1978, which is in lieu of all other personal exemptions. If both spouses qualify and a joint return is filed, the deduction for personal exemptions is $14,000. If one spouse qualifies and a joint return is filed, the deduction for personal exemptions is $7,000, plus a regular deduction ($1,144) for the other spouse and an additional regular deduction if the other spouse is 65 or older. No deductions are allowed for dependents when the $7,000 special exemption is claimed on a separate return or by either spouse on a joint return.

The Hawaii definition of blindness for purposes of the special exemption is the same as in the federal law. The definition and certification requirement for deafness, for purposes of the special exemption, is as follows:

". . . average loss in the speech frequencies (500-2,000 Hertz) in the better ear is 82 decibels, A.S.A., or worse. The impairment of deafness shall be certified to by the Department of Health or by any state, county, or city and county medical officer duly authorized by the Department of Health for this purpose, on the basis of a written report on an examination performed by a qualified otolaryngologist duly authorized by the Department of Health."

To qualify because of disabilities other than blindness or deafness, the person must be "totally disabled," as that term is defined in the law. The definition and certification requirement for such disability, for purposes of the special exemption, is as follows:

". . . a person who has:

(1) Lost or is born without both feet at or before the ankle;

(2) Lost or is born without both hands at or above the wrist;

(3) Lost or is born without one hand and one foot;

(4) An injury or defect resulting in permanent and complete paralysis of both legs or both arms or one leg and one arm;

(5) An injury or defect resulting in incurable imbecility or insanity."

The term "totally disabled" was expanded for taxable years beginning on or after January 1, 1975, to include persons totally and permanently disabled, either physically or mentally and as a result unable to engage in any substantial gainful business or occupation. The intent of the expanded definition is to allow persons afflicted with such conditions as arthritis, rheumatism, heart ailments, etc., to qualify for the special exemption. In Hawaii Tax Information Release No. 94-2 issued March 15, 1994, the Department of Taxation raised the earned income limit, before the disabled exemption is eliminated, from $10,000 to $30,000.

Prior to 1989 the law required that blindness or disability be certified by the State Department of Health, on the basis of a written report on an examination performed by a duly qualified physician duly authorized by the Department of Health. Effective January 1, 1989, the Department of Health will no longer be involved in the process. Instead, the examining physician will directly certify the taxpayer's disability on forms prescribed by the Department of Taxation. Effective as of April 17,1990 the Hawaii law was amended to allow certification by duly licensed out-of-state physicians or a commissioned medical officer in the United States military. Prior to the amendment the certifying physician had to be licensed in Hawaii. Effective for years beginning after December 31, 2001 licensed audiologists may certify for impairment for deafness.

## ¶ 107. Exempt Organizations
Hawaii Law: Sec. 207-12, 235-2.3, 235-2.4, 235-9, 235-9.5
Federal Law: Sec. 501, 502, 507 to 509, 511 to 515, 528, 1381 to 1383, 1385, 1388, 4940 to 4948

The following organizations are exempt from Hawaii income tax:

(a) Banks, building and loan associations, industrial loan companies, financial corporations, and small-business investment companies (subject to franchise tax—see ¶ 111).

(b) Trust companies, mortgage loan companies, financial holding companies, and subsidiaries of financial holding companies (subject to franchise tax - see ¶ 111) effective for years beginning after December 31, 1992.

(c) Agricultural cooperatives.

(d) Insurance companies (subject to tax on premiums—see ¶ 1308).

(e) Nonprofit religious, charitable, scientific, or educational organizations including fraternal beneficiary societies.

(f) Nonprofit cemetery organizations.

(g) Nonprofit business leagues, chambers of commerce, etc.

(h) Nonprofit civic leagues, etc.

(i) Labor organizations.

(j) Nonprofit clubs exclusively for pleasure, recreation, etc.

(k) Employees' stock bonus, pension, or profit-sharing trusts which qualify under the federal tax law.

(l) Persons or organizations that offer prepaid legal services.

(m) Fish marketing associations.

(n) Certain foreign lenders.

(o) IRC Section 501(c)(12) entities that provide potable water to residential communities that lack any access to public utility water services.

Federal law was amended in 1962, 1966, and 1969 to provide special tax rules for cooperatives. Hawaii has not adopted these rules. So far as agricultural cooperatives are concerned, the failure of Hawaii to conform to the federal law has no effect, because such organizations are exempt as shown above. So far as other cooperatives are concerned, the failure of Hawaii to conform to the federal amendments will result in different treatment under the two laws.

Hawaii adopted the provisions of the Internal Revenue Code, with a few exceptions, as of December 31, 1977. Thus for years beginning in 1978 the Hawaii exemptions are largely the same as the federal. Readers should refer to prior editions of this book for differences that existed for years prior to 1978.

The federal law was amended in 1996 to exempt from tax, certain charitable risk pools, state sponsored high-risk health insurance pools and state sponsored workmen's compensation reinsurance organizations. The federal law was amended in 1997 to provide that a state-sponsored high risk pool can provide health coverage to the spouse and children of a high risk individual. Hawaii has adopted the 1996 amendment and 1997 amendment.

The federal law was amended in 1997 to revise the unrelated business tax-

¶ 107

able income rules as they relate to "qualified sponsorship payments" and interest from related parties, to provide that cooperative hospital service organizations may purchase patient account receivables, to provide that hospitals will not lose their tax exempt status by participating in a provider-sponsored organization and to provide an exemption for certain state workmen's compensation act companies. Hawaii has adopted these 1997 federal amendments.

The Hawaii law provides tax exemption for foreign-state manufacturers that have their products warehoused in Hawaii, under certain conditions. See ¶ 709 for discussion of this exemption.

The Hawaii law was amended in 1965 to provide a permanent tax exemption on income received by insured out-of-state savings and loan associations from participation in loans with Hawaii savings and loan associations. The Hawaii law was amended, effective May 6, 1977, to provide that foreign lenders may make equity investments in Hawaii without losing their foreign lender status. However, income from the equity investments is subject to taxation under the income and general excise taxes.

The federal law was amended in 1976 to provide that certain homeowners' associations could elect to be treated as tax-exempt organizations for taxable years beginning after 1973. The exemption only applies to exempt function income such as membership dues, fees and assessments received from member-owners of residential units in the particular condominium or subdivision involved. Hawaii has adopted these provisions for years beginning after 1986.

The federal law was amended in 1997 to allow timeshare associations to be taxed similarly to homeowner associations, but at a higher rate of tax. Hawaii has adopted these amendments for years beginning after December 31, 1996.

Both Hawaii and federal laws provide for taxing "unrelated business income" of certain exempt organizations. Prior to 1970, this applied only to a limited group of organizations and the Hawaii rules were the same as the federal; that is, if "unrelated business income" was subject to federal tax, it was also subject to Hawaii tax. Beginning in 1970, however, under the Tax Reform Act of 1969, the federal law was amended to cover more income and was extended to many more types of exempt organizations. The Tax Cuts and Jobs Act also amended several provisions affecting the calculation of unrelated business income. For tax years beginning after December 31, 2018, losses from one unrelated trade or business may not be used to offset income derived from another. Certain fringe benefits that were previously deductible under pre-Tax Cuts and Jobs Act law (i.e. qualified transportation fringe benefits) must now be added to unrelated business income. Act 27, SLH 2018, provides that Hawaii law generally conforms to the federal definition of "unrelated business taxable income," except that the computation is subject to Haw. Rev. Stat. §235-3 through Haw. Rev. Stat. §235-5, and Haw. Rev. Stat. §235-7, except Haw. Rev. Stat. §235-7(c), relating to national banking dividends. A net operating loss deduction shall not take into account any amount of income or deduction that is excluded in computing unrelated business taxable income. In addition Haw. Rev. Stat. §235-2.4(ee) provides that unrelated business taxable income does not include income from a legal service plan.

The federal law was amended in 1996, effective for years beginning after December 31, 1995, to provide a new look through role for characterizing insurance income of a controlled foreign corporation. This new rule may cause Subpart F income to be treated as unrelated business income. Hawaii has not adopted this amendment, but since Hawaii does not tax Subpart F income, the amendment does not have any impact on Hawaii income.

Under the 1969 amendments, the federal tax now covers so-called "bootstrap" sale and leaseback transactions, whereby a business is sold to an exempt organization and the price is paid only from the future earnings of the business. Also, the 1969 amendments extended the federal tax on any kind of "unrelated business income" to many organizations that had not previously been subject to the tax at all, including churches, social clubs, farmers' cooperatives, etc. As stated above, these amendments are applicable to the Hawaii law for years beginning in 1979.

The Tax Reform Act of 1969 also introduced extensive new rules and restrictions for "private foundations." These provisions set up new requirements for qualifying as an exempt organization under category (d) above, prohibited certain activities of the organization, imposed a tax on investment income and provided for a variety of taxes and penalties for failure to comply with the new rules. Hawaii has not conformed to these federal provisions.

## ¶ 108. Accounting Methods and Periods
Hawaii Law: Sec. 235-2.3
Federal Law: Sec. 162, 175, 263A, 267, 278, 280, 441, 446, 447, 448, 451 to 482, 706

The Hawaii rules regarding accounting methods and periods follow the federal law. However, there are some minor differences, as explained below.

The Tax Reform Act of 1986 amended the federal law to require all partnerships, S corporations and personal service corporations to conform their tax years to the calendar year for years beginning after December 31, 1986. The amendment provides limited exceptions to this requirement. This provision was amended in 1987 to allow partnerships and S Corporations to elect a fiscal year other than a calendar year provided the partnership or corporation pays a special tax. Hawaii adopted the 1986 and 1987 amendments but did not adopt the special tax provision.

The 1986 Act also requires trusts, except for exempt trusts and wholly charitable trusts, to conform their year to the calendar year beginning after December 31, 1986. The federal law was amended in 1988 to require common trust funds to use the calendar year beginning in 1988. Beneficiaries are allowed to elect to spread the income from the short period caused by the change, over four years. Hawaii adopted both the 1986 and the 1988 amendments.

The federal law was amended, effective for years beginning after December 31, 1993, to require a security dealer to mark to market certain securities that it holds at the end of the year and recognize gain or loss on the appreciation or depreciation. The amount of gain or loss is taken into account when the securities are subsequently sold. Any adjustment required by this change was spread over a five year period. Hawaii adopted this mark to market method. The federal law was amended in 1997, effective for tax years beginning after August 5, 1997, to allow commodities dealers and traders in commodities and securities to elect the mark to market rules. The election results in a change in accounting method and any adjustment is spread over four years. Hawaii has adopted this 1997 federal amendment.

A taxpayer desiring to change an accounting method or period must obtain the consent of the Hawaii Director of Taxation as well as the Federal Commissioner of Internal Revenue. To obtain permission to change an accounting method, in general, the taxpayer must file an application by letter along with Federal Form 3115, addressed to the Director of Taxation at Honolulu, during the year in which the change is to be effective (federal law is the same). To obtain permission to change its accounting period, in general, the taxpayer must file an application (Federal Form 1128) with the Director of Taxation at Honolulu on or before the 15th day of the second month following the close of the short period resulting from the change.

If the taxpayer changes its methods of accounting, for example, from the cash basis to the accrual basis of accounting for federal tax purposes under the procedure provided in Revenue Procedure 2002-9, then the taxpayer will be permitted to make the same change for Hawaii purposes. A copy of the information submitted to the Internal Revenue Service should be submitted to the Hawaii Director of Taxation.

Under federal regulations, a corporate taxpayer may change its accounting period without specific permission if it meets certain tests and requirements as set forth in Revenue Procedure 2000-11. If the corporate taxpayer changes its accounting period under these federal rules, Hawaii will also permit the change without permission.

See ¶ 520 regarding the federal rule enacted in 1969 to permit change from installment basis to accrual basis of reporting.

See ¶ 110 for special rules of accounting for the year in which a taxpayer changes status from resident to nonresident, or vice versa. See ¶ 520 regarding reporting of installment sales made prior to period of Hawaii residence.

Hawaii follows the federal rule relating to the accrual of vacation pay. Hawaii has adopted the various federal amendments dealing with the accrual of vacation pay except that Hawaii did not adopt the pre-1959 rules during the years 1967 to 1972.

The Tax Reform Act of 1986 amended the federal rules to restrict the use of the cash method of accounting by certain corporations, partnerships with corporate partners, tax shelters and tax-exempt trusts with unrelated business income. This amendment is effective for years beginning after December 31, 1986. The Tax Reform Act of 1986 also amended the federal law to require the capitalization of inventory carrying costs in certain situations. This amendment applies to years beginning after December 31, 1986. The Technical and Miscellaneous Revenue Act of 1988 exempted qualified free lance authors, photographers and artists from the uniform capitalization rules retroactive to the effective date of the 1986 Act. The 1988 federal law also excepts cash basis farmers from the uniform capitalization rules for years beginning after December 31, 1988. Hawaii has adopted both the 1986 and 1988 amendments.

Effective for taxable years beginning after December 31, 2017, the Tax Cuts and Jobs Act, P.L. 115-97, increases the amount of gross receipts that corporations and partnerships with corporate partners can have and still use the cash method of accounting from $5,000,000 to $25,000,000. The federal law also extends the cash method of accounting to general farming entities, subject to the $25,000,000 gross receipts test that family farms are subject to. The Tax Cuts and Jobs Act extends use of the $25,000,000 gross receipts test to determining the exemption from certain inventory rules. Taxpayers with average annual gross receipts of $25,000,000 or less will be allowed to treat inventories as materials and supplies that are not incidental or to conform to their financial accounting treatment. Hawaii conforms to federal law.

The Tax Reform Act of 1984 made substantial changes to the rules governing transactions between related parties that use different accounting methods. Basically these rules provide that the party incurring the expense is not entitled to a deduction until the year in which the payee reports the income. These rules were effective for years beginning in 1984. Hawaii has adopted these new rules.

The federal law was amended in 1960 to prohibit "doubling up" of deductions for real estate taxes in a year in which the accrual date is changed by action of a local taxing jurisdiction. Hawaii adopted this provision for taxable years beginning in 1977.

The federal law was amended in 1961 to permit an accrual-basis membership organization (e.g., an automobile club) to elect to report dues income in the period earned, instead of treating it as income when received. The period of deferral may not exceed 36 months. Hawaii adopted this provision for years beginning in 1978.

Under the Revenue Act of 1964, a contested liability may be deducted by an accrual-basis taxpayer in the year the protested payment is made instead of waiting until the contest is settled. Hawaii adopted this amendment for years beginning in 1978.

Under the Tax Reform Act of 1969, federal law provides a special accounting rule for cash-basis farmers who receive insurance proceeds for destruction of or damage to crops. If the farmer can show that the income from the crops would normally have been reported in the following year, he may elect to defer reporting the income until the following year. The election applies to 1969 and subsequent years. Hawaii adopted this federal provision for taxable years beginning in 1977.

The Tax Reform Act of 1976 introduced rules to provide for special treatment for the proceeds of crop disaster payments and from the proceeds of forced sale of livestock resulting from drought conditions. Hawaii adopted these special rules for years beginning in 1977.

The federal law was amended in 1976 to provide that certain farming syndicates must capitalize amounts paid for seed, fertilizer, poultry and supplies and deduct those expenditures in the year in which the item is used except for the cost of poultry, which must be deducted ratably over the lesser of 12 months or their useful life. The cost of poultry purchased for sale must be deducted in the year of sale. These rules apply for 1976 and future years except for syndicates in existence on December 31, 1975, and for which there is no change in membership during 1976, in which case the rules apply for 1977 and future years. Farming syndicates engaged in planting, cultivating, maintaining, or developing fruit or nut groves, orchards or vineyards must capitalize development costs until the first year in which the grove, orchard or vineyard yields a commercial crop. These grove-vineyard rules apply to 1976 and future years except if the grove or vineyard was in existence on December 31, 1975. A farming syndicate includes partnerships and tax-option corporations which have been organized through a registered securities offering or where more than 35 percent of losses are allocated to limited partners. Hawaii adopted these farming syndicate rules for taxable years beginning in 1977. The Revenue Act of 1978 amended the federal rules to provide that certain farmers who are on the accrual method of accounting but not required to capitalize preproductive period costs may change to the cash method for years beginning after December 31, 1977, and before January 1, 1981. Hawaii has not adopted this amendment.

The Tax Reform Act of 1986 amended the federal law to restrict the deduction of certain prepaid expenses by taxpayers in the trade or business of farming. These amendments apply to expenditures incurred after March 1, 1986, in tax years beginning after that date. Hawaii has adopted these 1986 amendments.

The federal law was amended in 1997, effective for sales and exchanges after December 31, 1996, to allow cash basis farmers to elect to defer to the following year, gain from the forced sale of livestock due to floods or other weather conditions. This election is not available if the livestock would have normally been sold in the same tax year as the forced sale year. Hawaii has not adopted this 1997 federal amendment.

The Tax Reform Act of 1976 amended the farming rules to provide that corporations, other than family tax-option corporations and corporations with annual gross receipts of less than $1 million, must use the accrual method of accounting for years beginning after December 31, 1976. Hawaii adopted this rule for years beginning in 1977. The Revenue Act of 1978 amended the farming rules to expand the exemption of certain family or closely controlled corporations and sod farmers from the accrual accounting rules. The amendment is effective for years beginning in 1978. Hawaii adopted this change for years beginning in 1979. The federal law was amended in 1982, effective for years beginning in 1982, to provide that partnerships engaged in the business of growing sugar cane will be permitted to use the accrual method of accounting and currently deduct preproductive-period expenses. The partnership must consist of corporate partners. Hawaii has adopted this federal provision.

Under the Tax Reform Act of 1969, federal law requires capitalization of development costs of citrus groves for a period of four years after the trees are planted. This was effective in 1970, and applies to all costs of planting, cultivation, maintenance and development. This provision was extended in 1971 to almond groves, applicable to taxable years beginning after January 12, 1971. See also ¶ 424. Hawaii adopted these federal provisions for years beginning in 1977.

The federal law was amended in 1986 to limit the deduction for soil and water conservation expenses and land clearing expenses. The amendments are effective for expenditures paid or incurred after December 31, 1986. Hawaii has adopted these amendments.

The Tax Reform Act of 1976 introduced new rules for the treatment of costs incurred after December 31, 1975, of producing and distributing movies, videotapes, books, etc. These costs must be capitalized and deducted by using the income forecast method. These rules apply to all taxpayers other than corporations that are not tax-option corporations or personal holding companies. Hawaii adopted these rules for taxable years beginning in 1977.

The Tax Reform Act of 1976 provides exact rules for determining the basis of players' contracts that are acquired when a sports franchise is acquired. These rules apply to sales or exchanges made after December 31, 1975. Hawaii adopted these rules for taxable years beginning in 1977.

The Revenue Act of 1978 added a provision that allows publishers to deduct certain merchandise returned after year-end from the previous year's sales. The change is effective for years beginning after September 30, 1979. Hawaii adopted this provision for years beginning after September 30, 1979. The Revenue Act of 1978 also added a provision to allow taxpayers on the accrual method of accounting to deduct the cost of certain discount coupons issued in the year prior to the year of redemption. This change is effective for years ending after December 31, 1978. The Tax Reform Act of 1986 repealed this provision for years beginning after December 31, 1986. Hawaii adopted this provision for years beginning after December 31, 1978, and has adopted the federal repeal.

The federal rules governing the reporting of income from long-term contracts

¶ 108

were amended in 1982. Under the rules, certain costs that were previously treated as period costs will have to be included as contract costs. These rules were effective for years beginning in 1983. In addition, for years ending after 1982, rules were adopted clarifying the time at which a contract is to be considered completed. Hawaii adopted these federal amendments. The Tax Reform Act of 1986 further revised the long-term contract method to require additional costs to be capitalized and to limit the use of the long-term contract method. The Technical and Miscellaneous Revenue Act of 1988 further limited the use of the long-term contract method to contracts entered into after June 21, 1988. Hawaii adopted the 1986 and 1988 amendments. The federal law was amended in 1997 to simplify the look-back method in computing income on long-term contracts. The 1997 federal amendments apply to contracts completed in tax years ending after August 5, 1997. Hawaii has adopted these 1997 federal amendments.

The federal law was amended in 1997 to allow taxpayers to estimate inventory shrinkage if certain conditions are met. This amendment is effective for years ending after August 5, 1997. Hawaii has adopted this 1997 federal change.

The Tax Reform Act of 1984 amended the federal law to provide that rental and interest income attributable to a deferred rental agreement must be reported as if the lessor and lessee were on the accrual method of accounting. This provision applies to agreements entered into after June 8, 1984. Hawaii has adopted this 1984 amendment.

The 1984 Act also amended the federal law to provide that the "all events" test for an accrual-basis taxpayer to accrue a liability will not be satisfied until economic performance has occurred. This rule is effective for expenses accrued after July 20, 1984. Hawaii has adopted this change.

The Tax Cuts and Jobs Act, P.L. 115-97, amended the uniform rules of capitalization under IRC 263A, effective for taxable years beginning after December 31, 2017. Businesses whose average annual gross receipts from over the prior three-year period are $25 million or less may be exempt. Hawaii conforms to this treatment.

## ¶ 109. Definition of Resident
### Hawaii Law: Sec. 235-1

The Hawaii income tax law defines a "resident" to be (1) every individual *domiciled* in the state and (2) every individual who *resides* in the state whether domiciled there or not. A person is deemed to reside in the state if he is physically present in the state for other than a "temporary or transitory" purpose.

*Domicile* is defined in the regulations "as the place where an individual has his true, fixed, permanent home and principal establishment, and to which place he has the intention of returning whenever he is absent."

If an individual is physically present in the state for more than 200 days in a taxable year, he is presumed to be a resident from the time of arrival. This presumption may be overcome upon a satisfactory showing that the taxpayer maintains a permanent home outside the state and that his presence within the state is for a temporary or transitory purpose.

Individuals in the following categories are deemed not to have changed residence status because of presence in, or absence from, the state resulting from their occupation:

a. Servicemen.
b. Persons engaged in aviation or navigation.
c. Students at any institution of learning.

Under this rule, a serviceman is a Hawaii "resident" if he entered the service as a Hawaii resident and has not changed his permanent residence (domicile). On the other hand, a serviceman stationed in Hawaii who entered the service from another state is not a Hawaii "resident" unless he has adopted Hawaii as his state of permanent residence (domicile). The Department of Taxation has held that a serviceman stationed in Hawaii, who would otherwise be a nonresident under this rule, will be taxed on all income from all sources like a resident taxpayer, if he files a joint return with his wife who is a resident. Nonresident taxpayers who file jointly with a resident spouse and are unaware of this rule often seek to change their filing status to married filing separately so that the nonresident spouse is not subject to Hawaii tax on income from all sources but a trap for the unwary exists. In order to undo the joint filing, both spouses have to file married filing separately returns before the due date of the original return (April 20th). Once this date has passed, the joint filing cannot be undone. (Tax Information Release No. 90-10, Tax Information Release No. 97-1, and Tax Information Release No. 2010-01. See also ¶ 105.)

To illustrate the application of this rule to category "b" above, suppose an airline pilot who has established his permanent residence in California is assigned to Honolulu as his operating base. He flies between Hawaii and various overseas points. Even though he maintains a home in Hawaii for the entire year, he is still a California resident for tax purposes and does not become a Hawaii resident unless he adopts Hawaii as his state of permanent residence. So long as he is not a Hawaii resident for tax purposes, only his income from services performed in Hawaii (and any other income from Hawaii sources, as explained in ¶ 309) is subject to Hawaii income tax.

So far as students are concerned, this rule applies principally to Mainland or foreign residents who come to Hawaii to attend college. The nonresident status of such an individual continues so long as he is in Hawaii only because he is in school here. He may decide, while he is a student, to stay in Hawaii; in this case he becomes a resident. Such a change of residence status would ordinarily be evidenced by some action such as notification to the state of previous residence, change of club or church affiliation, etc.

Residence determinations can present very difficult problems. There are no "rules of thumb" that may be applied to all situations. Each case must be decided in light of the surrounding facts and circumstances. Generally, the state with which an individual has the closest connection during the year is the state of his residence. Among the factors to be considered are the following:

| | |
|---|---|
| Time spent | Club memberships |
| Ownership of home | Place of voting |
| Ownership of automobiles | Business interests |
| Bank accounts maintained | Place to probate will |

The administrative rules contain several examples of the application of the residence rules.

The attorney general ruled in 1965 (Opinion No. 65-5) on the residence status of a taxpayer who was living in Okinawa. The taxpayer was a native of Hawaii. He went to work for the U.S. government in Okinawa after his discharge from foreign service in the Army. The attorney general held that the taxpayer was domiciled in Hawaii and therefore was a "resident" of Hawaii even though he had lived outside the state for several years; it followed that he was subject to Hawaii tax on his entire income regardless of source.

The case of John A. Piper, decided by the Hawaii Supreme Court in November 1969, involved the residence status of an individual who worked for the U.S. government on Wake Island from 1959 to 1963. When he left Hawaii in 1959, he cut all his ties with the state. He returned to Hawaii in 1963 for reasons of health. The Department of Taxation took the position that he retained his domicile in Hawaii while he was away and that he was therefore subject to Hawaii income tax. The Supreme Court held that he had clearly abandoned his Hawaii residence in 1959 and he was not subject to Hawaii tax.

If there is any question regarding the taxpayer's residence for the year, the administrative rules suggest that a timely return be filed, accompanied by a signed statement explaining why the taxpayer believes he is not a resident. Any documentary evidence available should also be submitted with the return. Before any final determination is made that the taxpayer is a resident, he will be given an opportunity to submit additional evidence and further arguments.

See the discussion of residence status in Tax Information Release No. 97-1 at ¶ 1432.

## ¶ 110. Change of Status, Resident or Nonresident
### Hawaii Law: Sec. 235-2.3, 235-4

When the status of the taxpayer changes from resident to nonresident, or vice versa, during the year, it is necessary to determine the amount of taxable income attributable to the period of residence. The law provides that this shall be done by computing the ratio that the period of residence bears to the whole year and applying this ratio to the income for the year. However, the law permits the taxpayer the alternative of determining the actual income of the period of residence, provided the taxpayer can make this determination to the satisfaction of the Director of Taxation.

The accounting cutoff between the period of residence and nonresidence should be made on the accrual basis, even though the taxpayer reports on the cash basis of accounting. That is, an item of income earned, or an expense incurred, in a certain period should be attributed to that period even though it may be received or paid in a different period and reportable for tax purposes (by a cash-basis taxpayer) in a different period. To illustrate, suppose a California resident moves to Hawaii on January 1, 1996. On February 1, 1996, he receives a $5,000 bonus for services during the year 1994. Since the bonus "accrued" on December 31, 1995, before he became a resident of Hawaii, it is not subject to Hawaii tax. See TIR 90-3.

Where an installment sale is made before the taxpayer becomes a resident of Hawaii, installments received after he becomes a resident are not subject to Hawaii tax—see ¶ 520.

The law was amended in 1978, effective for years beginning after December 31, 1979, to provide that income earned during the period of residence is taxed regardless of source. Income earned during the period of nonresidence is taxed if it is derived or received from property owned, personal services performed, trade or business carried on and any other source in the state. Where it cannot be determined that income was received or derived during the period of residence or nonresidence, then the income shall be allocated to the state based upon a ratio of the number of days of residence to the total number of days in the year.

The law was amended in 1983, effective for years beginning after 1982, to clarify the rule that where a resident and nonresident spouse file a joint return all income of both spouses must be included regardless of the source. Nonresident taxpayers who file jointly with a resident spouse and are unaware of this rule often seek to change their filing status to married filing separately so that the nonresident spouse is not subject to Hawaii tax on income from all sources but a trap for the unwary exists. In order to undo the joint filing, both spouses have to file married filing separately returns before the due date of the original return (April 20th). Once this date has passed, the joint filing cannot be undone.

## ¶ 111. Franchise Tax
### Hawaii Law: Sec. 241-1 to 241-6
### Federal Law: Sec. 166, 593

Certain organizations are exempt from the income tax and are subject instead to a franchise tax on their net income. The following are subject to the franchise tax:

(a) Banks

(b) Building and loan associations

(c) Industrial loan companies (effective January 1, 1966)

(d) Financial corporations (Generally, a corporation is classified as "a financial corporation" if it deals in money and is in substantial competition with national banks.)

(e) Small business investment companies (effective January 1, 1976)

(f) Interbank broker, effective July 1,1990

(g) Trust companies authorized under Chapter 406 HRS (effective January 1, 1993).

(h) Mortgage loan companies licensed under Chapter 454 HRS (effective January 1, 1993)

(i) Financial holding companies (effective January 1, 1993)

(j) Subsidiaries of financial holding companies (effective January 1, 1993)

The law defines a Financial Holding Company as any corporation registered under the Federal Bank Holding Company Act of 1956 or registered as a savings and loan company under the Home Owners' Loan Act of 1933. A subsidiary of a financial holding company is defined as a corporation engaged in activities set forth in Title 12 of the Code of Federal Regulations, Sections 225.22 and 225.25 (Regulation Y) and Sections 584.2-1 and 584.2-2 (Office of Thrift Supervision).

The tax is based on net income, determined as explained below. Financial corporations are entitled to claim a credit against the franchise tax for the capital goods excise tax credit, the renewable energy technologies credit, the low-income housing tax credit, and the high technology business investment tax credit. See ¶ 412*i*, 412a, 412j, and 412q. For years beginning prior to December 31, 1993 the rate of tax was 11.7%. For years beginning after December 31, 1993 the rate of tax is 7.92%. In addition, for years beginning after December 31, 1993 there is an alternative tax which is the sum of the regular tax on income without capital gains plus 4% of the net capital gains.

The net income to which the tax rate is applied is determined in the same manner as the "taxable income" of a corporation under the income tax, with the following adjustments:

(1) So-called "tax-free" interest received on municipal bonds, etc., is included in gross income.

(2) Certain adjustments relating to the difference between Hawaii and federal treatment of transactions (reorganizations, exchanges, etc.) under prior law, as explained in ¶ 502 to ¶ 511, inclusive, are not applicable for franchise tax purposes.

(3) Special rules are provided for separate accounting in cases where the taxpayer has income from outside the state. The law was amended in 1995 to repeal the separate accounting rules and require the use of the Uniform Division of Income for Tax Purposes Act. (See discussion in Chapter 7). The change is effective for income received in the calendar year preceding January 1, 1997 or for fiscal years which include January 1, 1997.

¶ 111

(4) Where the inclusion of income is different under the franchise tax from the income tax, any deductions connected with such income shall be allowed or disallowed accordingly.

(5) Any bad debt deductions based upon Section 166 or Section 593 of the federal Internal Revenue Code are disallowed. In lieu of such deduction, a deduction is allowed for bad debts actually charged off during the year or, at the discretion of the Director of Taxation, for a reason able addition to a bad debt reserve.

(6) In the case of a life insurance company that is taxed as a financial corporation, certain specific provisions of the federal Internal Revenue Code relating to such companies do not apply for franchise tax purposes.

(7) The adjusted eligible net income of an international banking facility is allowed as a deduction from net income to the extent not deductible in determining federal taxable income.

The federal law was extensively amended in 1962 to provide new rules for taxing savings and loan associations and similar institutions. Hawaii has not adopted these amendments. The changes related particularly to deductions for loan loss reserves and to treatment of foreclosures. The changes in loss reserves did not create a new difference between federal and Hawaii, since Hawaii already had its own special rule for such deductions (see item (5) above). The changes in treatment of foreclosures did create a difference between federal and Hawaii. Prior to the 1999 Tax Act, under federal rules, a foreclosure is not treated as a taxable event; under Hawaii law, it is treated as a taxable event, as it was under current federal law.

The federal law was amended in 1993 to provide that any thrift institution which received FSLIC assistance with respect to any loss of principal, capital, or similar amount upon the disposition of any asset must take the assistance into account as compensation when it computes the deductible loss on the disposition of an asset. This amendment applies to tax years ending on or after March 4, 1991. Hawaii has not adopted this amendment.

The federal law was amended in 1996 to allow banks to transfer on a tax free basis assets from its common trust fund to a regulated investment company. This amendment is effective for transfers after December 31, 1995. Hawaii has adopted this amendment.

The tax is imposed annually, as of January 1. If the accounting period is the calendar year, the tax is measured by the income of the calendar year preceding January 1. If the accounting period is a fiscal year, the tax is measured by the income of the fiscal year in which January 1 occurs.

The law was amended, effective January 1, 1989, to provide new rules for computing the tax for the first and second year of business and for the final year

¶ 111

of business. All corporations will be required to pay an estimated tax by the 20th day of the third month following the month in which they begin business. An amended return will be filed at the end of the year to adjust for any difference in tax between the estimate and actual tax based on the taxable income for the first year. The tax due for the second year will be an estimate based upon the first year's average monthly income times 12. At the end of the second year an amended return is required, reporting the actual income for that year and any overpayment or underpayment from the estimate is adjusted. A return is also required for the final year of business. Finally, if a corporation acquires the business of another corporation through a direct acquisition or merger the acquiring corporation must include the income of the acquired corporation for the entire year in which the acquisition takes place on the acquiring corporation's return.

The law was amended in 1983, effective June 14, 1983, to allow the creation of international banking facilities. The amendment allows a bank or savings and loan association that establishes an international banking facility to deduct from its net income the eligible net income of the international banking facility. The definition of eligible net income is quite complex and reference should be made to the statute when making the computation.

The law was amended in 1986 to provide a tax credit for State enterprise zone businesses—see ¶ 412g. The law was amended in 1995 to delete the reference to corporations subject to the franchise tax since corporations subject to the franchise tax will not meet the definition of "qualifying business" for purposes of the enterprise zone credit. The law was amended in 1991 to extend the benefits of the Energy Conservation Tax Credit to financial institutions effective for years beginning after December 31, 1990. See ¶ 412a. The law was amended effective for taxable years beginning January 1, 1993, to allow corporations subject to the franchise tax to claim the low-income housing tax credit. See ¶ 412j.

The franchise tax return is due on the 20th day of the fourth month following the close of the fiscal year (same as income tax). The tax may be paid in four installments if desired: the first installment is payable on the due date of the return; subsequent installments are due on the 20th day of the second, fifth, and eighth month after the due date of the return. For years beginning after December 31, 1992 where the tax liability exceeds $100,000 then the tax must be paid in twelve equal installments on the tenth day of the month beginning with the first month following the close of the taxable year. If any installment payment is delinquent, the Department of Taxation will demand that the balance of unpaid tax be paid in full. See filled-in specimen return (Form F-l) in Part V of this book.

The rules of the income tax relating to deficiencies, refunds, appeals, etc., as explained in Chapter 2, apply generally to the franchise tax also.

## ¶ 112. Regulated Investment Companies
Hawaii Law: Sec. 235-2.3, 235-71
Federal Law: Sec. 851-855

"Regulated investment companies" (commonly known as "mutual funds") are taxed in the same way under Hawaii law as under federal law. This means that they are not allowed a deduction for dividends received, but instead are allowed a deduction for dividends paid, so that only earnings retained are taxed to the corporation. As under federal law, the shareholder is allowed a credit for the Hawaii tax paid by the corporation (at the rate of 4%) on retained capital gains that are taxable to the shareholder. The Tax Reform Act of 1976 increased the federal capital loss carryover period from five years to eight years, effective for years ending after January 1, 1970. Hawaii has adopted the eight-year federal capital loss carryover rule for years beginning in 1979.

The federal law was amended in 1984 and in 1985 to prevent certain abuses where a taxpayer purchases stock in a regulated investment company prior to the declaration of a capital gain dividend or exempt interest dividend and sells his stock at a loss 32 days after purchase. Hawaii has adopted the 1984 and 1985 amendments.

The federal law was amended in 1997, effective for tax years beginning after August 5, 1997 to repeal the rule that a regulated investment company derive less than thirty percent of its gross income from the sale of certain investments held for less than three months. Hawaii has adopted this 1997 federal amendment.

## ¶ 113. Distortion of Income Between Related Taxpayers
Hawaii Law: Sec. 235-2.3, 235-103
Federal Law: Sec. 269A, 482

The Hawaii law gives the Department of Taxation broad powers to adjust income and tax among related taxpayers, where there has been distortion or diversion of profits by arbitrary pricing or products or by other means. The Hawaii law incorporates by reference Section 482 of the federal law, which provides for allocation of income among related organizations to prevent evasion of taxes or clearly to reflect income; Hawaii also has its own specific provision (Section 235-103), which contains much broader language than the federal law.

The federal law was amended in 1982, effective for years beginning in 1983, to allow the Internal Revenue Service broader power in allocating the income and deductions of so-called personal services corporations between the corporations and their shareholders. Hawaii adopted this new federal provision for years beginning in 1983, but has repealed the Section 269A rules for taxable years beginning after December 31, 1984.

## ¶ 114. Domestic International Sales Corporation
### Hawaii Law: Sec. 235-2.3
### Federal Law: Sec. 991 to 997

Under federal law enacted in 1971, a corporation which qualified as a Domestic International Sales Corporation (DISC) was subject to special rules and federal tax benefits. Generally, only one-half of the income was taxed currently, and it was taxed directly to the shareholders. Hawaii adopted the DISC rules for years beginning in 1981, provided the corporation was incorporated in and had its principal place of business in Hawaii. In order to qualify, a Hawaii corporation had to file an election within 90 days preceding the beginning of the first taxable year for which the DISC election was to apply.

The federal law was amended in 1982, effective for years beginning in 1983, to increase the DISC deemed dividend to a corporate shareholder from 50% to 57.5%. Hawaii has adopted this federal amendment.

The Tax Reform Act of 1984 repealed the DISC rules as of December 31, 1984. The accumulated deferred income of existing DISCs will be considered previously taxed income and therefore exempt from tax. Hawaii repealed the DISC rules effective for years beginning in 1996.

## ¶ 114a. Foreign Sales Corporations
### Hawaii Law: 235-2.3
### Federal Law: Sec. 921 to 927 - Repealed

Under the Tax Reform Act of 1984, corporations which qualify as Foreign Sales Corporations (FSC) may provide favorable tax benefits to U.S. shareholders. Under the new law, the FSC's export income is exempt from U.S. income tax. Also, a U.S. corporate shareholder will receive a 100% dividend-received deduction for FSC dividends from earnings attributable to certain foreign trade income. The FSC rules are effective for transactions after 1984.

In July 1998, the European Union requested that a World Trade Organization ("WTO") dispute panel determine whether the foreign sales corporation provisions of sections 921 through 927 of the Internal Revenue Code ("the Code") comply with WTO rules, including the Agreement on Subsidies and Countervailing Measures. A WTO dispute settlement panel was established in September 1998 to address these issues. On October 8, 1999, the panel ruled that the foreign sales corporation regime was not in compliance with WTO obligations. The panel specified that "FSC subsidies must be withdrawn at the latest with effect from 1 October 2000." On February 24, 2000, the WTO Appellate Body affirmed the lower panel's ruling. The following provides a description of H.R. 4986, the "FSC Repeal and Extraterritorial Income Exclusion Act of 2000," as passed by the House of Representatives on September 13, 2000.

The bill provides that gross income for U.S. tax purposes does not include extraterritorial income. Because the exclusion of such extraterritorial income is a means of avoiding double taxation, no foreign tax credit is allowed for income taxes paid with respect to such excluded income. Extraterritorial income is eligible for the exclusion to the extent that it is "qualifying foreign trade income." Because U.S. income tax principles generally deny deductions for expenses related to exempt income, otherwise deductible expenses that are allocated to qualifying foreign trade income generally are disallowed.

EFFECTIVE DATE

The bill would be effective for transactions entered into after September 30, 2000. In addition, no corporation may elect to be a FSC after September 30, 2000. IRC sections 921 through 927 have been repealed.

### ¶ 115. Alternate Tax for Certain Individuals, Estates and Trusts Doing Business in More Than One State
#### Hawaii Law: Sec. 235-51 (e), 235-71 (e)

The Hawaii law was amended in 1974 for 1974 and future years to allow individuals, estates and trust taxpayers to report and pay an alternate income tax of 0.5% of annual gross sales if all of the following requirements are met:

(1) Taxpayer is acting as a business entity in more than one state.

(2) Taxpayer's only in-state activities consist of sales.

(3) Taxpayer does not own or rent real estate or tangible personal property in Hawaii.

(4) Taxpayer's annual gross sales in or into Hawaii during the tax year do not exceed $100,000.

(5) Special rules apply if the income consist of long term capital gains.

This provision makes the Hawaii law conform to the Multistate Tax Compact Act.

See ¶ 709 for the exemption from income tax for certain foreign-state manufacturers.

# CHAPTER 2

# INCOME TAX
## ADMINISTRATION—
## RETURNS, PAYMENT, WITHHOLDING

## ¶ 201. Administration of Tax

The tax is administered by the Department of Taxation, headed by the Director of Taxation. See the front of the book for a directory of personnel in the Department.

## ¶ 202. Returns—Who Is Required to File—Forms
### Hawaii Law: Sec. 235-92 to 235-95
### Federal Law: Sec. 6012, 6102, 7513

Individuals under 65 must file a Hawaii return for 2018 if they have Hawaii taxable gross income of $3,040 or more. An individual who has attained the age of 65 before the close of the year is required to file a Hawaii return only if his taxable gross income is $4,080 or more. Married couples under 65 filing jointly must file a return if they have a taxable gross income of $6,080. If one individual is over 65, the amount is $7,120. If both individuals are over 65, the limit is $8,160. Anyone receiving rents from

107

property in Hawaii is considered to be "doing business," and is required to file a return whether or not the person has any taxable income. These Hawaii filing requirements are quite different from the federal.

An estate or trust is required to file a return if it has $400 or more of gross income subject to tax, or, for a trust, if it has any taxable income.

A partnership is required to file a return unless it is expressly exempted. See also ¶ 601.

Every corporation having any gross income subject to tax is required to file a return.

Return forms are as follows:

Resident individuals ................................... Form N-11
(see below)
Nonresident individuals............................... Form N-15
Estates and trusts ................................... Form N-40
Partnerships....................................... Form N-20
Corporations ...................................... Form N-30
S-Corporations.................................... Form N-35
Financial Corporations ............................. Form F-1

An individual who changes residence status should file on the resident return form for the year of change. A nonresident who files a joint return with a resident spouse should also file on the resident return form. The filing of such a joint return is deemed to constitute an election by the nonresident to be taxed on income from all sources. See ¶ 109 and ¶ 110.

Taxpayers are permitted to reproduce any of these forms and to file the reproductions in lieu of the official forms if the Forms Reproduction Policy located on the Department of Taxation's website is followed. The Department of Taxation will allow the use of certain federal forms in lieu of the corresponding Hawaii form. Information as to which federal forms can be used can be obtained from the Department of Taxation or refer to the table "Related Federal/Hawaii Tax Forms" in the front of this book.

See specimen filled-in returns for the forms listed above, in Part IV of this book.

### ¶ 203. Returns—Time and Place for Filing
Hawaii Law: Sec. 231-8, 231-9.9, 235-98, 235-99
Federal Law: Sec. 6072, 7502

Calendar year returns are due on April 20 following the close of the year. Fiscal year returns are due on the 20th day of the fourth month following the close of the fiscal year. This is different from the federal law: federal individual returns are due on the 15th day of the fourth month following the close of the year; federal corporation returns are due on the 15th day of the third month.

In prior years, the return was required to be filed with the Collector for the Taxation Division in which the taxpayer's legal residence or principal place of business was located. If there was no legal residence or principal place of business in Hawaii, returns are filed with the Tax Collector in Honolulu. In 2004, the Tax Department changed its mailing address for tax forms. The Department is now receiving tax forms from all districts in Honolulu, rather than at each respective island. Please note the respective mailing addresses on the respective tax forms being filed.

When the due date falls on a Saturday, Sunday, Department of Taxation furlough day, or legal holiday, returns are considered timely if filed on the next succeeding business day. A return that is mailed to the Department of Taxation is considered timely if it is postmarked before midnight of the due date; this is covered by a specific provision in the law, enacted June 7, 1967. Except for the inclusion of furlough days, these Hawaii rules are the same as the federal.

The Hawaii law was amended, effective for taxable years ending after December 31, 1996, to include the use of certain designated delivery systems as specified in IRC Section 7502 as meeting the timely filing criteria. The designated delivery systems and type of delivery service are:

| IRS Designated PDS | Type of Delivery Services |
| --- | --- |
| Airborne Express (Airborne) | Overnight Air Express Service<br>Next Afternoon Service<br>Second Day Service |
| DHL Worlwide Expres (DHL) | DHL "Same Day" Service<br>DHL USA Overnight |
| Federal Express (FedEx) | FedEx Priority Overnight<br>FedEx Standard Overnight<br>FedEx 2Day<br>FedEx International Priority<br>FedEx International first |
| United Parcel Service (UPS) | UPS Next Day Air<br>UPS Next Day Air Saver<br>UPS 2nd Day Air<br>UPS 2nd Day Air A.M.<br>UPS Worldwide Express Plus<br>UPS Worldwide Express |

¶ 203

The Hawaii law was amended in 1997 to authorize the Department of Taxation to allow taxpayers to file tax returns through electronic, telephonic, or optical means. Electronic filing is accomplished via the Hawaii Tax Online website at hitax.hawaii.gov. Hawaii Tax Online supports Corporate Income, Franchise, General Excise, Public Service Company, Rental Motor Vehicle, Tour Vehicle, and Car-Sharing Vehicle Surcharge, Seller's Collection, Transient Accommodations, Use, and Withholding taxes. Effective November 13, 2018, Hawaii Tax Online also began to support electronic filing of individual income, partnerships, estate/transfer, and fiduciary tax types.

The Hawaii law was amended in 2009 to authorize the Director to require any person who is required to electronically file a federal return or electronically pay any federal taxes to the federal government to electronically file a state return and/or electronically pay any state taxes due. Employers who are required to pay federal withholding taxes by EFT will be required to pay state withholding taxes by EFT, effective with respect to wages paid on or after January 1, 2010.

A return must be signed to be valid. A joint return must be signed by both husband and wife.

The balance of tax shown to be due on the return should be paid in full with the return. Checks or money orders should be made payable to "Hawaii State Tax Collector."

See ¶ 205 regarding declarations of estimated tax. See ¶ 206 regarding returns of tax withheld.

## ¶ 204. Returns—Extension of Time for Filing
### Hawaii Law: Sec. 235-98
### Federal Law: Sec. 6081

The Department of Taxation may grant an extension of time for filing a return or a declaration of estimated tax, upon application by the taxpayer. In the absence of exceptional circumstances, the application must be filed on or before the due date. An extension of time for filing a return will be granted only upon condition that (1) one hundred percent of the "properly estimated tax liability" has been paid, and (2) the return is actually filed within the extended time limit, with payment of any balance of the tax. Payment of properly estimated tax liability is presumed if the tax still owing after the due date of the return is 10 percent or less of the total tax shown on the return. If these conditions are not met, penalties and interest will be assessed.

An individual taxpayer is granted an automatic 6-month extension to file an income tax return. No form is required to be filed to obtian the automatic extension. Form N-101A must be filed only if an additional tax payment must be made. Federal Form 4868, Application for Automatic Extension of

Time to File U.S. Individual Income Tax Return, may not be used as a substitute for Form N-101A.

Corporations should file for an automatic 6-month extension of time on Form N-301. This form must be filed even if a payment is not required. Federal From 7004 may not be used as a substitute for Form N-301.

Partnerships, trusts, and REMICs also use Form N-301 to request an automatic 6-month extension of time. This form must be filed even if no payment is required.

There is no automatic extension of time for servicemen or others who may be outside the state at the time a return is due. However, the law contains a provision deferring the time of payment of tax by servicemen in certain cases—see ¶ 204a and 205.

See Part IV of this book for certain specimen filled-in applications for extensions of time.

### ¶ 204a. Returns—Military Personnel
Hawaii Law: Sec. 657D-43, 235-100, 235-100.5
Federal Law: Sec. 112, 692

The law was amended in 1991, to take effect retroactively to August 2, 1990 to extend the time for filing returns and paying taxes for members of the armed services or persons serving in support of the armed services in an area designated by the President of the United States as a combat zone, or persons who are hospitalized as a result of injury received while serving in a combat zone. The extended time period includes the period of service in the zone, plus the period of continuous qualified hospitalization attributable to the injury plus the next 180 days.

The law was also to take effect retroactively to August 2, 1990, to provide an abatement of Hawaii income taxes for members of the armed services who die as a result of injuries in a combat zone. The abatement is for the year of death and any year ending on or after the first day of service in a combat zone.

The Hawaii law was amended to provide that the collection of tax be deferred for a period of not more than six months after the termination of the person's military service if such person's ability to pay such tax is materially impaired by reason of the service. Interest and penalties will not apply during this deferral period. The law was also amended to toll the statute of limitations on the collection of any tax for nine months after termination of such person's military service.

The Hawaii law was amended in 2004 to conform to the provisions in the Military Family Tax Relief Act of 2003 with respect to extending the special filing extension rules. Under these rules, the extension period that was provided to service personnel in combat zones was extended to service personnel deployed in contingency operations.

¶ 204a

## ¶ 205. Payment of Tax—Declarations of Estimated Tax
### Hawaii Law: Sec. 235-62, 235-97, 235-100
### Federal Law: Sec. 6015, 6654, 6655

Taxes are generally paid in one or more of the following three ways:

1. Withheld from employees—see ¶ 206.
2. With a declaration of estimated tax, as explained below.
3. With the return (balance of tax due).

Effective as of June 8, 1995, the Director of Taxation is authorized to require any taxpayer whose tax liability for any taxable year exceeds $100,000 to remit the taxes by electronic funds transfer. Effective June 14, 1997 the law was amended to impose a two percent penalty on those who fail to remit their taxes using electronic funds transfer method unless reasonable cause is shown for the failure. The 1997 Act also authorizes a $15 service charge for electronic funds transfer payments that are dishonored.

For years beginning after December 31, 1993, the federal requirements for payment of estimated taxes and avoidance of penalties under Internal Revenue Code Sections 6654(d), (e)(2), (e)(3), (h), (i), (j), (k) and (l), and 6655(d), (e), (g)(2), (g)(3), (g)(4), and (i) as of 1997, are applicable to Hawaii. In addition, neither individuals nor corporations are required to file estimated tax returns if their tax liability is under $500.

For years beginning before January 1, 1994, corporations are required to file declarations of estimated tax regardless of the amount of their income. However, the Director of Taxation may excuse a corporation from this requirement if the corporation is satisfied that less than 15% of the corporation's gross income for the year will be attributable to Hawaii . For taxable years beginning after December 31, 1991, S Corporations and trusts are required to file declarations of estimated tax.

Dates for filing declarations and paying estimated tax by individuals reporting on a calendar year basis are: April 20, June 20, September 20, and January 20. A declaration should be filed by April 20, if the circumstances (expected income and exemptions) on April 1 are such as to require a declaration for the year. If the circumstances occur later, then the declaration should be filed at one of the later dates. The time for filing the declaration depends upon whether the circumstances requiring it exist on the first day of the month in which the due date falls; that is, September 1 for a September 20 filing, etc.

For taxable years beginning after December 31, 2002, individual taxpayers can avoid being assessed underpayment penalties on their estimated taxes by paying in the lesser of:

• 60% of the current years's liablity or

• 100% of their current preceding year's liability.

Special rules apply to farmers. If at least 70% of total adjusted gross income is from farming, the requirement for filing may depend upon the time when the initial payment for a crop is received. The general rule in this case is that the circumstances necessitating the filing of a declaration are not deemed to occur prior to the date of the initial payment for a crop. This will not operate to defer the time for filing a declaration beyond September 20; however, if the initial payment for a crop is received after September 20 and the taxpayer can show that he is therefore unable to pay the September 20 installment, an extension of time may be obtained for filing the September declaration by a farmer.

After a declaration is filed for the year, it may be amended at any of the later quarterly filing dates. If the final return is filed by January 31, this has the effect of the filing of an amended declaration on January 20. In case of death during the year, payments of estimated tax are not required by the estate subsequent to the date of death. For years beginning before January 1, 1994, corporations were required to file a declaration and pay one-half of the estimated tax by the 20th day of the ninth month of the taxable year (September 20 for calendar year). The remaining one-half of the estimated tax is payable by the 20th of the first month following the close of the taxable year (January 20 for calendar year). For years beginning after December 31, 1993, corporations are required to file declarations of estimated tax on a quarterly basis.

Penalties are imposed for underpayment of estimated tax—see ¶ 210.

See ¶ 111 for payment dates for franchise tax.

The law provides for deferment of tax in the case of military personnel whose ability to pay is materially impaired by being in the service. The deferment may extend to a period not more than six months beyond the termination of military service. See ¶ 204a for a discussion of deferment where service is performed in a combat zone.

### ¶ 205a. Payment of Tax—Electronic Funds Transfer (EFT)
#### Hawaii Law: Sec. 231-9.9

In general, every taxpayer whose tax liability for a particular tax exceeds $100,000 in the taxable year is required to pay that tax via electronic funds transfer (EFT). In Tax Announcement No. 2018-03, the Department of Taxation announced the adoption of amended section 18-231-9.9-03, Hawaii Administrative Rules (HAR), which became effective March 17, 2018. This amended rule authorizes the Department to require enrollees in the electronic funds transfer program to pay all returns electronically, rather than merely period returns. EFT is currently required for the following types of taxes:

¶ 205

(1) General Excise and Use; (2) Withholding; (3) Transient Accomodations; and (4) Rental Motor Vehicle and Tour Vehicle Surcharge.

Effective October 1, 2011, taxpayers with liabilities in excess of $100,000 in the taxable year for the following types of taxes will need to pay the tax via EFT also: (1) Fuel; (2) Cigarette and Tobacco; (3) Liquor; (4) Franchise; and (5) Public Service Company (PSC).

Taxpayers required to file by EFT must complete and submit Form EFT-1, *Authorization Agreement for Electronic Funds Transfer*. The form is available on the website noted at the front of this book.

## ¶ 206. Withholding from Employees
### Hawaii Law: Sec. 235-61 to 235-67
### Federal Law: Sec. 3401

Employers are required to withhold tax on all payments of compensation to employees. As to Hawaii residents (see ¶ 109), withholding is required on compensation for services performed outside, as well as inside, the state. As to nonresidents, withholding is not required if it is expected that the employee will be in the state less than a total of 60 days during the calendar year.

Certain types of compensation are not subject to withholding. The exemptions are:

1. Retirement system benefits.

2. Pensions.

3. Social Security Retirement benefits. (subject to voluntary withholding)

4. Payments under employees' trusts and annuity plans.

5. Compensation of Hansen's disease patients.

6. Meals and lodging furnished for employer's convenience.

7. Compensation of deceased employees.

8. Compensation of blind persons.

9. Fees of public officials.

10. Mileage or fees of jurors, witnesses, certain public officials.

11. Remuneration of newspaper carriers under 18.

12. Remuneration for sale of newspapers and magazines.

13. Tips or gratuities.

14. Remuneration for casual services, not in trade or business.

15. Compensation of crew members of ships and airplanes in interstate travel.

16. Noncash remuneration, not in trade or business.

¶ 206

17. Expense allowances, etc.

18. Noncash remuneration of retail salesmen.

19. Other compensation that is exempt from income tax provisions.

The exemption for casual services (item 14 above) includes domestic services, among others. This exemption does not apply if the cash compensation is $50 or more per calendar quarter and the employee works on at least 24 days in a quarter. For details regarding this and other exemptions, see Booklet A, mentioned below.

The amount of withholding may be computed in each case or it may be determined from withholding tables that are supplied. See formulas and withholding tables in "income tax rate tables" section of this book. Additional amounts may be withheld, if desired, by agreement (in writing) between the employer and the employee. The Hawaii law was amended, effective June 12, 1981, to allow additional withholding exemptions to employees who have large itemized deductions, as allowed for federal income tax purposes under the Tax Adjustment Act of 1966. There are no special withholding formulas or tables for "head of household" (see ¶ 105a); such individuals use the formulas and tables for single persons, as is done for federal withholding.

Under the Tax Reform Act of 1969, an employee may avoid federal withholding by certifying to his employer that he had no income tax liability for the preceding year and anticipates none for the current year. Hawaii has not adopted this federal provision.

The employee is required to supply an exemption certificate, showing the number of personal exemptions that he claims.

The employer must obtain an identification number, which number must be shown on all returns and statements relating to withholding.

Effective June 12, 1981, a return must be filed and tax withheld paid to the Director of Taxation monthly, by the 15th day of the month following the month in which the tax was withheld; however, employers having a liability for withheld tax of $1,000 or less per year may file on a quarterly basis. The $1,000 amount was increased to $5,000 per year commencing with periods beginning on or after October 1, 2001. Effective January 1, 2018, the filing frequency for withholding tax was changed to a uniform quarterly filing frequency for all employers. However, the payment frequency of withholding taxes did not change.

For years beginning after December 31, 1992, employers whose withholding tax liability exceeds $100,000 per year will be required to file a return and pay over the withhold tax by the 10th day of the month following the month in which the tax was withheld. The Director of Taxation, for good

¶ 206

cause, may extend the time for making returns and payments, for a period up to two months. Withheld taxes are considered to be held in trust by the employer.

Effective June 10, 2004, the Governor signed into law Act 113. Under Act 113, for payroll periods beginning on or after December 31, 2004, the withholding tax liability limitation for employers will be decreased to $40,000 per year, and the withholding taxes need to be remitted to the Tax Department on a semiweekly basis. The Tax Department will not require an employer whose withholding liability exceeds $40,000 to pay by electronic funds transfer if such employer is not required to also remit their federal employment taxes electronically via the Electronic Federal Tax Payment System (EFTPS).

Effective for wages paid on or after January 1, 2010, employers who are required to deposit federal income taxes withheld using the Internal Revenue Service's semi-weekly deposit schedule shall remit state income taxes withheld to the Department of Taxation using the same schedule.

The Tax Department issued Department of Taxation Announcement No. 99-4 stating that withholding is not required on nonresident withholdings. The five criteria listed below must be met before an employee is exempt from withholdings:

1. The employee is performing services in the State for an aggregate of not more than sixty days during the calendar year;

2. The employee is a nonresident as set forth in Section 235-1, HRS, or the employer reasonably believes the employee is a nonresident;

3. The employee is paid for services performed from an office located outside the State;

4. The employee's regular place of employment (where the employee regularly performs services for the employer) is outside the State; and

5. The employer does not reasonably expect the employee to perform services in the State an aggregate of more than sixty days during the calendar year.

The employer must furnish to the employee a statement of the tax withheld. The statements must be furnished by January 31 following the close of the calendar year, or if employment is terminated during the year, the statement must be furnished within 30 days of an employee's request for same. The procedure for years prior to 1983 required that the statement be furnished on the day on which the last payment of wages is made. The form to be used for this purpose is HW-2. The employer may, if desired, supply the necessary information regarding Hawaii tax on the federal withholding form (W-2), in lieu of filing Form HW-2.

¶ 206

Copies of all Forms HW-2 for the year, together with Form HW-3, "Employers Return and Reconciliation of Hawaii Income Taxes Withheld from Wages," must be filed with the Department of Taxation by February 28. See filled-in specimen forms in Part IV of this book.

The law was amended effective May 23, 1990 to change the definition of those responsible for the collection and payment of withholding taxes to include any employee who is responsible for collecting and reporting withholdings to the state. Employees whose only function in a ministerial function are excluded from this definition. The Committee reports give as an example an employee who has authority to (1) sign the withholding return, (2) authorize payments to creditors, or (3) sign disbursements checks.

The Department of Taxation publishes Booklet A, containing complete instructions for employers on withholding. It may be obtained upon request from the Department of Taxation or at the Department's website.

It should be noted that Hawaii tax withholding is required in some cases where federal withholding is not; for example, domestic services (unless exempt as "casual services"), agricultural labor, and ministers. On the other hand, federal withholding is sometimes required where Hawaii withholding is not, such as compensation of crew members in interstate travel, tips, etc.

## ¶ 206a. Withholding on Certain Real Estate Sales
### Hawaii Law: Sec 235-68

The Hawaii law was amended in 1990 to require the purchaser or *transferee* of real property, located in Hawaii, to withhold income tax from the amount realized on the sale where the seller is a nonresident. The Hawaii law is commonly referred to as "HARPTA." Like the federal tax law that generally applies to non-U.S. persons pursuant to IRC Sections 897 and 1445 (collectively, "FIRPTA"), the Hawaii law generally applies to taxpayers who are neither Hawaii residents nor Hawaii entities subject to certain exceptions. For example, a U.S. person who is not a Hawaii resident is generally subject to HARPTA. However, the Hawaii law generally does not apply to sales or exchanges of stock like FIRPTA that can apply to sales or exchanges of stock in U.S. Real Property Holding Corporations. The withholding requirement is effective for all transfers after December 31, 1990. The initial rate of withholding was 9% of the gross proceeds. This amount was reduced to 5% effective August 1, 1991. Act 122, SLH 2018, increased the rate to 7.25%, effective September 15, 2018. The change in rate will apply to all real property dispositions that occur on or after September 15, 2018.

In sum, a transferee or buyer must withhold 7.25 percent of the amount realized by the transferor on the disposition of Hawaii real property if the transfer occurs on or after September 15, 2018, unless an exemption applies.

The purchaser is required to file a return and pay over the tax withheld to the state within 20 days of the transfer date. The seller can avoid the withholding tax by providing the buyer with an affidavit that the transfer will qualify for nonrecognition of gain under Hawaii Law, stating that the seller is a resident of Hawaii, or qualifies for certain other exemptions. The law was amended in 1991, effective August 1, 1991, to exempt transfers where the property was used by the transferor during the preceding year as a principal residence and the amount realized does not exceed $300,000. The definition of residents was amended to include a limited partnership formed or registered under Chapter 425D, and foreign partnerships that are qualified to transact business in the state pursuant to Chapters 425 and 425D. For a single member limited liability company that has not elected to be taxed as a corporation, the single member limited liability company is disregarded and the sole member shall be treated as the transferor of the real property. Also the definition of "transferee" has been clarified to include the State of Hawaii and the counties and their respective subdivisions, agencies, authorities, and boards. The 1991 amendment also provides for nonresident transferors to apply for a withholding certificate from the Department of Taxation where no gain will be realized or where there will be insufficient proceeds to pay the tax. Further, the Department of Taxation may enter into withholding agreements with taxpayers who engage in more than one real estate transaction a year.

Tax Information Release No. 2002-2, which was revised in 2017, summarizes the procedures for withholding and obtaining exemption from withholding. Tax Information Release 2002-02 (revised in 2017) also provides that the residency of a person shall be determined at the time of disposition of the property, and that the amount realized that is allocated to a non-resident owner who jointly owns property with a resident is determined by capital contributions towards the purchase of the property and if such allocation cannot be determined, fifty percent (50%) is presumed to be allocated to the nonresident owner. For spouses, each spouse is treated as realizing fifty percent (50%) unless the circumstances require otherwise. Tax Information Release 2002-2 (revised in 2017) provides guidance on withholding for agreements of sale and purchase money mortgages, waiver or adjustment of withholding, on the similarities and differences between FIRPTA and HARPTA, penalties for failing to withhold or pay the tax, and a table of the various HARPTA forms.

## ¶ 207. Reporting Federal Changes
### Hawaii Law: Sec. 235-101

If any change is made to the taxable income that has been reported on the federal return, by reason of audit of the return or otherwise, such change must be reported to the Department of Taxation within 90 days after the federal change is finally determined or an amended federal return is filed. This requirement applies also to a change in taxable income resulting from renegotiation of government contracts. The report is made by filing a Hawaii amended return. A copy of the document reporting the changes issued by the federal government must accompany the amended return. The statute of limitations is extended to one year after written notification of any federal changes to taxpayer's return upon examination by the Internal Revenue Service. The extension of the statute is one year after receipt by the Tax Department of notice of the changes from the taxpayer or Internal Revenue Service, whichever is earlier. This statutory one year period may be extended by an agreement between the taxpayer and the Department of Taxation.

## ¶ 208. Deficiencies
### Hawaii Law: Sec. 231-24, 235-107 to 235-109, 235-111 to 235-113
### Federal Law: Sec. 6211 to 6215, 6501

Additional tax may be assessed on examination of the return by the Department of Taxation. If the taxpayer receives notice that additional tax is to be assessed, he has 30 days within which he may object. After the 30 day period has elapsed and the tax is assessed, it must be paid within 20 days after the date the notice of assessment is mailed.

Under a 1969 amendment the period of limitation for assessment of additional tax generally is three years. The three-year rule does not apply where the time for assessment is extended by agreement or a fraudulent return is filed (see below). Where gain on sale or conversion of certain property is deferred, as explained in ¶ 511, the limitation period is extended to three years from the date the taxpayer notifies the Department of Taxation of the replacement of the property or his intention not to replace.

The law was amended in 1971 to conform to the federal law by extending the limitation period in cases where the return is filed before the prescribed due date. This amendment applies to taxable years beginning on or after January 1, 1971. For such years, the period runs three years from (1) the date the return was filed or (2) the prescribed due date, whichever is later. Thus, the limitation date for a 1971 return that is due on April 20, 1972, but is filed on March 1, 1972, will be April 20, 1975. For years prior to 1971, the limitation period runs from the date of filing in all cases. (The "prescribed due date" is the regular due date, without regard for any extension of time that may have been granted for filing the return.)

In the case of a fraudulent return with intent to evade tax, or failure to file a return, the tax may be assessed at any time.

The law was amended, effective April 17, 1991, to suspend the statute of limitations for assessing deficiencies where the Director is prohibited from making an assessment by reason of a bankruptcy proceeding.

The Director of Taxation may make a jeopardy assessment, which is subject to immediate collection, in any case where he determines that such action is necessary because of the removal of the taxpayer or his property from the state, or for other reasons.

The law was amended effective July 1, 2009 to adopt the federal 6-year statute of limitations if there is a substantial omission from gross income.

See ¶ 210 regarding penalties and interest on deficiencies.

## ¶ 209. Refunds
Hawaii Law: Sec. 231-23, 231-51 to 231-59, 235-55, 235-66, 235-110, 235-111
Federal Law: Sec. 6401 to 6407, 6511

Refunds (or credits) are allowed in cases where the tax has been overpaid. No special form is provided for refund claims, except in the case of a deceased taxpayer for which Form N-110, Statement of Person Claiming Refund Due a Deceased Taxpayer, is used.

The period of limitation for refund, generally, is the same as for assessments of additional tax: for years prior to 1971, three years from (1) the date the return was filed or (2) the prescribed due date for the return, whichever is later. See ¶ 208. The limitation period for filing claims for the tax credit described at ¶ 412 is one year following the close of the taxable year involved. The law was amended effective for years beginning after December 31, 1990, to allow the statute for claims due to net operating loss carrybacks to run for 3 years from the due date of the year in which the loss occurred. In the matter of the tax appeal of *Clarence O. and Lona Furuya,* the Hawaii Supreme Court decided that the statute of limitations for purposes of filing a refund claim due to a net operating loss carryback is extended where the Internal Revenue Service redetermines a taxpayer's taxable income and the Hawaii statute is extended for one year after that determination. There were special limitation periods for filing refund claims for tax paid by persons in "missing status" in Vietnam, under the exemption enacted in 1973 as explained in ¶ 304.

Effective for claims filed after December 31, 1993, the statute has been amended to provide that claims must be filed within three years from the time the return was filed or the due date of the return or within two years from the time the tax was paid, whichever is later. If the claim is filed within the three year period, the amount of refund cannot exceed the amount of tax paid within the three year period plus extensions. If the claim is filed within the two year period, the amount or refund cannot exceed the amount of tax paid within the two year period. The time limit for filing a refund claim can be extended by written agreement between the taxpayer and the Department of Taxation.

Interest is paid on overpayments of tax. The current interest rate on over-payments is 1/3 of 1% for each calendar month or faction thereof, which is equivalent to approximately 4% a year. The interest rate is also 4% per year on amounts held in the litigated claims fund. Prior to January 1, 2009, the interest rate on overpayments was 2/3 of 1% for each calendar month or fraction thereof, which is equivalent to approximately 8% a year.

Except in the special situations discussed below, interest begins with the first calendar day after the due date of the return, and ordinarily runs until the date the Director of Taxation approves the refund voucher. However, if the refund is not actually paid to the taxpayer within 90 days after the Director approves the refund, the interest continues to the date the refund is paid.

Where the original tax return shows a refund due (because withholding or payments of estimated tax exceed the tax shown on the return), no interest will be paid if (1) the Director approves the refund within 90 days of the due date (or date of filing, if later), and (2) the refund is actually paid within 90 days after the Director approves the refund. However, if either of these time limits is exceeded, interest will run from the due date of the return.

Where a tax refund results from a loss carryback to a prior year, the interest runs only from the close of the taxable year of the loss—not from the date of payment of the prior year tax. See ¶ 210 for comment regarding interest on a potential deficiency that is eliminated by a loss carryback.

The state may retain income tax refunds when the taxpayer is delinquent in the payment of child support, owes a debt to the state, has defaulted on certain student loans, owes federal income taxes, and receives a medicaid overpayment that is subject to recovery.

## ¶ 210. Penalties and Interest
Hawaii Law: Sec. 40-35.5, 231-34, 231-36.5, 231-36.6, 231-36.7, 231-36.8, 231-39, 235-97, 235-104 to 235-105
Federal Law: Sec. 6651 to 6658

Penalties are provided for failure to file a return, for failure to pay the tax when due, for a false or fraudulent return or statement, for failure to keep required records or to supply required information, and for underpayment of estimated tax. The penalty provisions of the law were extensively amended in 1967, effective January 1, 1968, to conform generally with the federal law.

The current penalty for failure to file a return is 5% for each month, or fraction thereof, up to a total of 25% of the tax due. On returns due after June 3, 1974, if a return is filed on or before the due date including extensions, and the amount shown as tax on the return is not completely paid within 90 days of the prescribed filing date, a penalty of up to 10% of the unpaid tax, as determined by the Director, was assessed. As of June 15, 1988 the penalty is increased to 20% and the time limit for paying the tax is reduced to 60 days. Prior to 1988 if any part of an underpayment was due to negligence or intentional disregard of rules and regulations, the Director could add a penalty of up to 10% of the tax. Effective June 15, 1988, the penalty rate was increased to 25%. If any part is due to fraud, the Director may impose a penalty of up to 50%; in this case the penalty for failure to file (described above) is eliminated.

Under the current law the penalty for fraudulent returns or statements is a fine of up to $100,000 for individuals and $500,000 for corporations, or imprisonment for up to five years, or both. Prior to July 1, 1975, the maximum fine was $1,000 and the maximum sentence was one year. The penalty for willfully failing to keep records as required by the law (generally to be kept for three years—prior to 1969, for five years) was $500, or imprisonment for not more than six months, or both. Effective July 1, 1995, the penalty for willfully failing to supply information required by the Department of Taxation was a fine of up to $25,000 and/or imprisonment of up to one year. The fine for corporations was up to $100,000.

Hawaii law was amended in 2009 to provide four additional penalties: (a) penalty for understatement of tax liability by a tax return preparer; (b) penalty for substantial understatement or misstatement of tax; (c) penalty for promoting abusive tax shelters; and (d) penalty for erroneous refund claims.

A tax return preparer who understates a person's tax liability based on unreasonable positions shall pay a penalty of $500 with respect to each such tax return or claim for tax refund. The penalty increases to $1,000 if the tax return preparer willfully understates a person's tax liability or recklessly disregards the tax laws or rules in understating a person's tax liability.

If there is a substantial understatement of tax in any taxable year, there shall be a penalty of 20% of the portion of any underpayment that is attributable to such substantial understatement. "Substantial understatement" means the amount of the understatement exceeds the greater of 10% of the correct tax amount or $1,500. The $1,500 is increased to $30,000 for corporations.

A person found promoting an abusive tax shelter shall pay a penalty of $1,000 for each activity specified in the statute, or, if the person establishes that the abusive tax shelter generated less than $1,000 of gross income, then 100% of the gross income derived or to be derived by the person from the activity.

The penalty for erroneous refund claims or credits shall be 20% of the excessive amount claimed. However, there shall be no penalty assessed where the penalty calculated results in an amount less than $400, or beginning after 2011 the penalty for substantial understatement has already been imposed.

¶ 210

Interest is charged on late payment of tax, at the rate of 2/3 of 1% for each month or fraction thereof (approximately 8% a year). Interest is computed beginning on the first calendar day following the date proscribed for paying the tax. This does not apply to underpayment of estimated tax, for which special penalties are provided.

There appears to be some question regarding interest on a potential deficiency that is never paid and is eliminated by a loss carryback. For example, suppose a Hawaii return shows tax of $1,000. Upon examination the tax is increased to $3,000, creating a deficiency of $2,000. Before the $2,000 deficiency is paid the next year's return is filed, showing a loss carryback that eliminates the entire $3,000 tax for the earlier year. Under Hawaii law, the taxpayer receives interest from the first day of the year following the loss year, on the refund of the first year's tax ($1,000 Hawaii tax) that was paid with the return. Under federal law the taxpayer would be charged interest on the potential deficiency from the due date of the first year's return to the end of the loss year. Under Hawaii law, Sec. 231-39 seems to say that interest would be charged as under the federal rule.

For years beginning after December 31, 1993, the determination of the amount of underpayment of estimated taxes is to be made following the provisions of Sections 6654(d), (e)(2), (e)(3), (h), (i), (j), (k), and (l); and 6655(d), (e), (g)(2), (g)(3), (g)(4) and (i) of the Internal Revenue Code. As of December 31, 1997, Hawaii has not adopted the lowering of the amounts required for safe estimates.

Effective April 7, 1995, the Department of Taxation may add any charges or fees incurred to enforce the collection of any tax due. The Department must first mail a notice demanding payment and advising the taxpayer that continued refusal to pay may result in collection efforts and additional fees. Any partial payments are to be applied to the collection fees first.

A service charge of $25 is added to any tax due when the check used to pay the tax is dishonored. No interest is charged against the $25 discharge check fee.

Effective October 15, 2008, taxpayers executing a Cash Bond—Interest Tolling Agreement may submit a deposit that will suspend the running of interest on any potential underpayment due. Under no circumstances shall the payment of a deposit be considered a payment of tax. These agreements will only be accepted prior to the issuance of a final assessment to the taxpayer.

## ¶ 211. Appeals
Hawaii Law: Sec. 40-35, 232-1 to 232-25, 235-114
Federal Law: Sec. 6211 to 6215

Taxpayers can appeal an assessment either to the board of review or to the tax appeal court. The appeal must be filed within 30 days from the date the

Final Notice of Assessment was mailed. If the appeal is filed with the board of review, the decision of the board may be appealed within 30 days to the tax appeal court. If the appeal is filed with the tax appeal court, the decision of the tax appeal court may be appealed within 30 days to the Intermediate Court of Appeals.

For the first appeal of the assessment to either the board of review or to the tax appeal court, payment of the tax assessed is not required. However, if the taxpayer loses, the assessed tax must be paid together with interest if the taxpayer appeals the decision by the board or the tax appeal court. A taxpayer who prevails before the board of review does not have to pay the assessed tax prior to an appeal by the Department of Taxation to the tax appeal court. Similarly, a taxpayer who prevails before the board of review and the tax appeal court does not have to pay the assessed tax prior to an appeal by the Department of Taxation to the Intermediate Court of Appeals.

In cases involving individual taxpayers, the tax appeal court may allow the appeal of an income tax assessment without prior payment of the tax where the total tax liability does not exceed $50,000 and the taxpayer shows that the payment of the tax would cause irreparable harm. A similar procedure may be available for general excise tax assessments.

Another option if the taxpayer misses the deadline to file an appeal with the board of review or tax appeal court is to pay the disputed tax assessment under written protest and file a refund suit in tax appeal court within 30 days from the date of payment.

A simplified appeal procedure is provided for small claims, where the tax involved is less than $1,000. Under this procedure the taxpayer waives his right to futher appeal. To invoke this procedure, the taxpayer need only file with the tax appeal court a simple one-page form showing his name and address, general excise number (if applicable), amount of disputed tax liability as determined by the Board of Review or the assessor, the nature of the tax and the periods involved.

Effective July 1, 2011, with respect to the small claims procedure of the tax appeal court, pretrial discovery is allowed only with the prior written approval of the court. Additionally, costs and fees awarded to a prevailing party are limited to the fees paid directly to the court in the course of conducting the tax appeal issue. Furthermore, the court must notify the real property assessment division of any county involved in a real property tax appeal.

Each taxation division contains a Board of Review consisting of five members appointed by the governor. The Tax Appeal Court consists of one judge appointed by the chief justice of the Hawaii Supreme Court.

¶ 211

## ¶ 212. Information Returns
### Hawaii Law: Sec. 235-96
### Federal Law: Sec. 6041 to 6049

Every individual, partner, corporation, or other organization engaged in a trade or business in Hawaii and making payments in the course of trade or business is required to file information returns with the Department of Taxation. The following must be reported:

(1) Payments of fixed or determinable income aggregating to $600 or more to one payee for the calendar year; (1) salaries, wages, commissions, fees, and other forms of compensation; (2) interest, rents, royalties, annuities, pensions, and other gains, profits, and income, except rental property expense payments of $600 of more made to corporations for taxable years beginning after December 31, 2011.

(2) Payments of dividends amounting to $10 or more to one payee for the calendar year.

(3) Foreign items (such as interest derived from the bonds of a foreign country or of a nonresident corporation) aggregating $600 or more.

Payments of the following character are not required to be reported:

(1) Payments by a broker to his customer.

(2) Payments to a corporation (except for certain distributions by cooperatives and payments made after December 31, 2011 of $600 or more to corporations not exempt from tax under Internal Revenue Code Section 501(a)).

(3) Payments of bills for merchandise, telegrams, telephone, freight, storage, etc.

(4) Rent payments to a real estate agent.

(5) Payments to a nonresident for services rendered outside Hawaii.

(6) Payments to an individual who takes up residence in Hawaii after age 65 prior to July 1, 1976, for services rendered outside Hawaii.

(7) Partnership distributions.

(8) Payments of commissions to general agents of fire insurance companies or other companies insuring property, unless the general agents are actual payers of the commission.

(9) Payments for employee business expenses, to the extent the employee accounts to the employer.

(10) Expense allowances paid to United States or State of Hawaii civil service personnel.

(11) Payments of interest coupons payable to bearer.

Banks or others who collect interest or dividends from a foreign country or corporation for the benefit of Hawaii residents (including resident individuals, estates, trusts, or partnerships) must report such items on information returns.

Payments of compensation that are subject to withholding should be reported on Form HW-2. (See ¶ 206 for reporting of wages subject to withholding.)

All other payments should be reported on federal Form 1099, with accompanying transmittal Form N-196. The use of federal forms are now required, as the Department of Taxation is no longer printing Form N-199, its version of the federal Form 1099. The forms must be filed with the Department of Taxation, and are due on February 28 in the year following payment. (See ¶ 803b for real property rental agents' reporting requirements.)

The Hiring Incentives to Restore Employment Act of 2010 requires any individual with specified foreign financial assets, including foreign bank accounts, stock or securities issued by a foreign entity, and any investment or interest in a foreign entity, to report these assets to the IRS if the aggregate value equals or exceeds $50,000. Hawaii has adopted this provision and will accept copies of the federal forms filed with the IRS.

The Energy Improvement and Extension Act of 2008 require issuers of certain securities to report activities that may affect the basis of these securities effective for taxable years starting on or after January 1, 2011. Hawaii has adopted this provision and will accept copies of the federal forms submitted to the IRS as satisfaction of this requirement.

The Housing Assistance Tax Act of 2008 requires payment settlement entities (usually the bank required to make the payment or another third party settlement organization) to issue information returns reporting the amounts of gross proceeds received by merchants from credit card transactions effective for calendar years starting after December 31, 2010. Hawaii has adopted this provision and will accept copies of the federal forms submitted to the IRS as satisfaction of this requirement.

## ¶ 213. Disclosure of Information
### Hawaii Law: Sec. 231-15.5
### Federal Law: Sec. 7216

Criminal penalties (fine or imprisonment, or both) are provided for disclosure of confidential information by a tax-return preparer. Hawaii adopted this provision in 1973, conforming to a federal provision enacted in 1971.

## ¶ 214. Confidentiality Privilege
### Hawaii Law: Sec. 231-1.5
### Federal Law: Sec. 7525

Act 174 conforms Hawaii Law to IRC Section 7525 which extends the attorney-client privilege to communications between a taxpayer and any "federally authorized tax practitioner" (which includes attorneys, certified public accountants, enrolled agents, and enrolled actuaries) with respect to "tax advice," to the extent the communication would be considered a privileged communication if it were between a taxpayer and or attorney. Effective for years beginning after December 31, 2001 privilege communications apply to all taxes administered by the Department of Taxation.

## ¶ 215. Letter Rulings
### Hawaii Law: Sec. 235-20, Sec. 235-20.5

TIR 2009-01 was issued to provide guidance on how the Department of Taxation will process requests for tax guidance. Taxpayers may request written advice on any matter relating to Hawaii tax laws within the jurisdiction of the Director of Taxation and the Department of Taxation. In general, written advice will ordinarily not be issued:

(a) if the request involves an issue under examination or consideration, or in litigation;

(b) in certain areas because of the factual nature of the problem;

(c) on which of two entities is a common law employer, whether an agency relationship has been created, or whether a partnership exists;

(d) to business associations or groups;

(e) where the request does not address the tax status, liability, or reporting obligations of the requester;

(f) on frivolous issues;

(g) on alternative plans or hypothetical situations;

A request for a ruling is made on Form A-7, and must be accompanied by appropriate documentation and materials. The requestor will generally be contacted within 21 days of receipt of the ruling request by the Department of Taxation.

In general, there are no fees or other costs associated with a request for written advice. However, the Department is authorized to assess fees associated with high technology comfort ruling requests.

## ¶ 216. Record Keeping Requirements
### Hawaii Law: Sec. 231-96

In general, all businesses are required to maintain adequate books and records and must produce on demand those books and records if requested by the special enforcement section. The Department of Taxation may impose a fine for the failure to keep adequate records of $500 for the first offense; and $1,000 for any subsequent offense, unless the taxpayer is a cash-based business, then the fine is $2,000. Only one fine can be imposed in any 30-day period. See HAR § 18-231-95-01. Prior to July 1, 2011, if a business incurs more than 10 cash transactions in a day, the business must provide a receipt or other record of these cash transactions. Failure to provide such receipts results in penalties not to exceed $1,000 per day. If the person is a cash-based business, the maximum fine per day increases to $2,000. Each day the business is in violation of this requirement is treated as a separate penalty.

Effective July, 1, 2011, the requirement to provide a receipt or other record of these cash transactions has been replaced with a requirement to offer a receipt and additionally, there is a requirement to contemporaneously record all business transactions conducted throughout the day. These record keeping requirements may be maintained either manually or by electronic cash register.

Effective July 1, 2013, the requirement to offer a receipt or other record of the transaction and maintain a contemporaneously generated record of all business transactions conducted each day applies to all business subject to the general excise tax, other than casual sales. The ten transactions per day requirement is eliminated. The Department of Taxation may impose a fine for the failure to record a transaction of $500 for the first offense; and $1,000 for any subsequent offense, unless the taxpayer is a cash-based business, then the fine is $2,000. Only one fine can be imposed in any 30-day period. The fine for a first offense may be waived at the discretion of the Department of Taxation special enforcement section employee who issued the citation, if the business has otherwise complied with its tax obligations. Fines for any subsequent offenses cannot be waived. See HAR § 18-231-96-01.

## ¶ 217. Offers-in-Compromise
### Hawaii Law: Sec. 231-9.2

A taxpayer may submit an offer-in-compromise of a tax debt on Form CM-1. See Hawaii Administrative Rules Section 18-231-3-10. An offer-in-compromise for a lump sum to be paid in five or fewer installments must be accompanied by 20% of the amount of the offer. If the offer-in-compromise is to be paid in six or more installments, then the offer-in-compromise must be accompanied by the amount of the first proposed installment. Any failure to make an installment payment while the offer is being considered by the Department of Taxation, results in the Department of Taxation treating the offer-in-compromise as withdrawn. If the offer-in-compromise is not accepted by the Department of Taxation, any payments made with the offer-in-compromise or any installment payments will be retained by the Department of Taxation and applied to the tax first assessed. The Department of Taxation may waive the payment requirements for offer-in-compromise consideration if the taxpayer meets certain low-income certification guidelines published by the Internal Revenue Service.

## ¶ 218. Voluntary Disclosures.
### Tax Information Release 2016-02

In Tax Information Release 2016-02, the Hawaii Tax Department issued a revised voluntary disclosure policy superseding the prior voluntary disclosure policy set forth in Tax Information Release 2010-07. A taxpayer who has not been contacted by the Department, and is not under any federal or state audit or criminal investigation may be eligible for a voluntary disclosure. Further, a taxpayer who has previously participated in the Department's voluntary disclosure during the prior five years is not eligible to apply for a voluntary disclosure.

As part of the voluntary disclosure, the taxpayer must disclose the following: (1) name, address, and contact information; (2) type of taxpayer (e.g., corporation); (3) full description of the real and personal property and all activities in Hawaii; (4) the date the taxpayer started activities in Hawaii; (5) a statement of all applicable Hawaii taxes and an estimate of the amounts owed; (6) the reason for noncompliance; (7) how and when the noncompliance was discovered; (8) the reason for coming forward; (9) an affidavit to fully cooperate and disclose all relevant information, and a sworn statement that all of the information is truthful, accurate and complete; and (10) whether a waiver of penalties and interest is sought and the reasons for why penalties and interest should be waived.

The taxpayer should make the voluntary disclosure through: *Tax.Voluntary. Disclosure@hawaii.gov*

## ¶ 219. Appeals Program
### Announcement No. 2016-03

Beginning February 1, 2016, the Department launched the pilot phrase of the Administrative Appeals and Dispute Resolution Program (AADR) by establishing the Administrative Appeals Office (AAO). Proceeding before the AAO is an informal process. The AAO is an independent body within the Department that reports directly to the Director of Taxation and works with Compliance Division and the taxpayer or return preparer to resolve disputes based upon the law. A taxpayer or tax preparer may petition the AADR after receiving either a notice of proposed assessment, notice of final assessment, or notice and demand for penalty. Importantly, petitioning the AADR does notsuspend the time periods including the deadlines to respond to a notice of proposed assessment or notice of final assessment. Thus, the taxpayer or tax preparer must concurrently satisfy the requirements to file a tax appeal to either the Board of Review (BOR) or the Tax Appeal Court (TAC). In its Announcement, the Department states that the taxpayer must choose either the AAO or the BOR, and must withdraw its appeal before the BOR to proceed before the AAO. For cases before the TAC, the taxpayer or tax preparer must obtain permission from the Director and TAC to proceed before the AAO. The Announcement states that the time limit to request AADR before the AAO is twenty (20) calendar days after the mailing date of the proposed assessment or thirty (30) calendar days after the mailing date of the final assessment. Interest continues to accrue on any unpaid balance unless a cash bond is posted under Tax Information Release No. 2008-03.

# CHAPTER 3

## INCOME TAX
## GROSS INCOME

## ¶ 301. Income Taxable—Tie-in with Federal Law
Hawaii Law: Sec. 235-1 to 235-2.5
Federal Law: Sec. 61 to 63

The Hawaii law provides that the terms "gross income," "adjusted gross income," and "taxable income" mean the same as those terms defined and determined under the Internal Revenue Code, except as otherwise provided. Thus, the income taxable for Hawaii tax purposes is the same as for federal tax purposes except for certain specific differences. The differences have arisen in two ways: (1) a few exceptions were spelled out when the basic Hawaii law was adopted in 1957; and (2) differences have developed since that time because federal changes either were not adopted by Hawaii or were adopted in a later year. The differences are explained in the following paragraphs.

In 2018, for all taxable years beginning after December 31, 2017, reference to the Internal Revenue Code in the Hawaii Revised Statue means Subtitle A Chapter 1 of the Federal Internal Revenue Code of 1986 as amended as of February 8, 2018.

## ¶ 302. Interest Income
Hawaii Law: Sec. 235-2.3, 235-7
Federal Law: Sec. 103, 1272, 7872

The basic Hawaii law, as enacted in 1957, provides that interest exempt from federal income tax is also exempt from Hawaii income tax. (Such interest is nevertheless subject to the franchise tax—see ¶ 111.) However, the Hawaii law was amended in 1963 to provide a difference from federal law, effective in 1964. This applies to interest derived from other states and their political subdivisions ("municipal" bond interest). Any such interest from states other than Hawaii is subject to Hawaii tax in taxable years beginning after December 31, 1963, even though the interest is not subject to federal tax.

Under the Tax Reform Act of 1969, interest on "arbitrage bonds" issued by state or local governments is subject to federal tax; the Revenue Act of 1978 made changes to the federal law that would exempt "arbitrage bond interest" in certain circumstances. Hawaii adopted the 1969 amendment effective for years beginning in 1978 and adopted the 1978 amendment for years beginning in 1979. The federal law was amended in 1982 to provide that interest on industrial development bonds issued after 1982 will not be exempt unless specific conditions relating to approval of the issue and maturity of the bond issue are satisfied. Hawaii has adopted this 1982 federal amendment. The Tax Reform Act of 1986 and the Technical and Miscellaneous Revenue Act of 1988 further restricted the interest exemption for certain municipal bonds issued after August 15, 1986. Hawaii has not adopted the 1986, 1987, or 1988 amendments. (The federal rules would have no effect on Hawaii tax so far as interest on bonds of other states is concerned, since Hawaii already taxes interest on such bonds.)

The Hawaii law was amended in 1980 to provide that interest received on special-purpose revenue bonds issued after June 13, 1980, which are issued to finance health-care facilities of nonprofit corporations, is exempt from Hawaii income tax.

Interest received on U.S. obligations is exempt from Hawaii income tax, even though almost all of such interest is now subject to federal tax. This exemption applies to agencies of the U.S. government, including Federal Land Banks, Federal Intermediate Credit Banks, Federal Home Loan Banks, and Banks for Cooperatives, as well as to direct obligations of the government. However, it does not apply to obligations of the Federal National Mortgage Association (FNMA). Also, the exemption does not apply to interest received on a refund of federal taxes.

Hawaii adopted the federal rules that provide for interest-free loans and below-market loans to be treated as if the lender made a loan at the applicable "federal rate" and the borrower paid interest in the amount of the foregone interest. These rules apply to term loans made after June 6, 1984, and demand loans outstanding on June 6, 1984, unless the demand loan is paid by September 17, 1984. The below-market loan rules were amended in 1985 to provide a limited exception for certain loans to continuing-care facilities and to change the time for testing the interest rate of loans made by employers to relocate employees.

The federal law was amended in 1997, effective for tax years beginning after August 5, 1997, to require taxpayers to accrue interest on credit card receivables during the payment grace period. Taxpayers will be required to make an estimate of the amount of receivables that will not be paid during the grace period and then estimate the interest income. Hawaii has adopted this 1997 federal amendment.

See ¶ 314 for special treatment of interest ("imputed interest") on certain deferred payment contracts.

## ¶ 303. Annuities, Pensions, Retirement Benefits
### Hawaii Law: Sec. 235-2.3, 235-7
### Federal Law: Sec. 72, 83, 122, 402, 403, 530, 1379

In general, the Hawaii taxation of income from annuities follows the federal rules. However, there is one difference, applicable to annuities that started paying before 1958. The taxation of certain annuities is based on the amount invested in the annuity contract, referred to as "investment in the contract." The amount of the investment sometimes depends upon amounts that previously were received under the contract and were excluded from gross income. Under the federal law, the excluded amount taken into account is of course the amount that was excluded for federal income tax purposes. Where an annuity started paying before 1958 (effective date of present Hawaii law), the amount excluded from income for federal income tax purposes might be different from the amount that was excluded under the Hawaii tax law in effect prior to 1958.

In such cases, the excluded amount taken into account for Hawaii tax purposes is the amount excluded from gross income under the Hawaii law, and the resulting "investment in the contract" is different from the federal.

Under a 1982 federal amendment, effective Aug. 13, 1982, partial surrenders or cash withdrawals from an annuity policy prior to the annuity starting date will be treated first as income to the extent that the cash value exceeds the investment in the contract. Hawaii has adopted this federal amendment.

The federal law was amended, effective for annuities starting after November 18, 1996, to provide a simplified method of determining the portion of an annuity that represents the non taxable return of basis. The federal law was amended in 1996 to provide that the entire investment in an annuity contract with a refund feature may be recovered tax free in the event that annuity payments cease because of the death of the annuitant. Hawaii has adopted these 1996 amendments.

The taxation of pension and retirement benefits is quite different under Hawaii law than under the federal. Under federal law, income of this type is taxable, except for amounts attributable to employee contributions, certain disability benefits and certain servicemen's annuities. Under Hawaii law, almost all income of this type is exempt.

The Hawaii law provides a specific exemption for benefits received under the state's retirement system or under any other public retirement system. It also provides a general exemption for "any compensation received in the form of a pension for past services" whether such benefits are paid from a government fund or a private fund. Benefits received under the Hawaii Temporary Disability Insurance program may be exempt—see ¶ 317.

See ¶ 317a for a discussion of the treatment of Social Security benefits.

Any increment in value attributable to an employee's contribution to a pension plan is subject to both Hawaii and federal tax. The Hawaii regulations provide detailed rules for determining the taxable amount in cases that fall under federal IRC Section 72(d), relating to recovery of employee costs in less than a three-year period.

The federal law was amended in 1982 to provide that a loan from a tax-qualified plan to an employee will be treated as a distribution from the plan to the extent that it exceeds prescribed limits. These new federal rules apply to loans made on or after Aug. 13, 1982. Hawaii has adopted this federal amendment. The federal rules further restricted loans made or extended after Dec. 31, 1986. Hawaii has adopted this amendment.

Effective January 1, 1998, the Hawaii exemption for retirement benefits does apply to benefits received by a self-employed individual under a plan set up for his own benefit. As explained in ¶ 408, contributions to such plans are now deductible for Hawaii income tax purposes, although they were not deductible under the Hawaii law prior to 1968 and deductible up to $2,500 a year between

¶ 303

1968 and 1975. Generally, benefits received under such plans were treated as annuities, with the total of nondeductible contributions to the plan being treated as the "investment in the contract." Where contributions were made to such a plan before 1976, during the period when there was a difference between Hawaii and federal deductibility, there will be a difference between Hawaii and federal amounts of the "investment in the contract"; consequently, there was a difference in prior years, at least, between the amounts reportable as income on the Hawaii and federal returns. Due to the change in 1998 those differences will continue.

The Pension Reform Act of 1974 changed the federal rules to tax lump-sum distributions after Dec. 31, 1973, from self-employed retirement plans the same as lump-sum distributions from regular corporate retirement plans. Hawaii has adopted this change for taxable years beginning in 1978. The Tax Reform Act of 1986 revised the tax treatment of lump-sum distributions from pension plans for distributions received after Dec. 31, 1986. Hawaii has adopted these 1986 amendments. The federal law was amended in 1996 to repeal the five year averaging rule for taxing lump sum distributions. The amendment is effective for years beginning after December 31, 1999. Hawaii has not adopted this amendment.

Prior to 1974, where a so-called "small business corporation," which elected to be taxed as a partnership as explained in ¶ 602, had a qualified pension or profit-sharing plan (see ¶ 408), there was a special federal rule that applied to any employee who owned more than 5% of the corporation's stock. In that case the shareholder-employee had to include in his income the excess of the corporation's contribution to the plan over what he could have deducted as a self-employed person. Any amount taxed to the shareholder-employer in those years is to be recovered later tax-free. This federal rule was enacted in the Tax Reform Act of 1969 and took effect in 1971. Hawaii adopted this rule, effective Jan. 1, 1975. Under the Pension Reform Act of 1974, the maximum contribution attributable to certain shareholder-employees was increased to the lower of 15% of compensation or $7,500. Hawaii adopted this latter change, effective Jan. 1, 1976. The federal law was amended for years beginning after 1983 to remove the contribution limitation for small business corporations. Hawaii has adopted this 1982 federal amendment.

Under the Tax Reform Act of 1969, the federal law provides special rules for taxing the beneficiary of a nonqualified employee pension or profit-sharing plan or annuity, in cases where the employee's rights are forfeitable at the time the employer's contribution is made. These rules apply to employer payments after Aug. 1, 1969. The general effect of these rules is to tax the employee in the year the employee's rights are no longer subject to a substantial risk of forfeiture. Hawaii adopted the federal rules, effective Jan. 1, 1975.

There is a difference between Hawaii and federal laws in the treatment of so-called "tax-shelter" annuity plans of certain nonprofit charitable-type organizations and public schools. Employer contributions under such plans

¶ 303

for employees of charitable-type organizations are exempt from both Hawaii and federal tax. However, the plan for employees of the Hawaii State Department of Education was not covered by the Hawaii income tax law prior to 1982, even though it was covered by the federal law; it follows that pre-1982 employer contributions to this plan were taxable to the employees even though they are exempt from federal tax. Therefore, to the extent that employees were taxed currently on these contributions they will be entitled to exclude a portion of the benefits when received.

The federal law was revised in 1986 and 1988 effective for years beginning after 1988 to limit the use of unfunded deferred compensation plans by employees of nonprofit organizations. Hawaii has adopted these amendments.

Both federal and Hawaii law provide for exclusion from income of lump sum or partial distributions from pension or profit sharing plans or from tax-sheltered annuities that are rolled over into an IRA account. There has been some confusion as to the taxability of distributions from IRAs under these circumstances since the rollover amount is exempt from tax. The Tax Department held that taxpayers may exclude from income the distributions from IRAs, to the extent that the amount contributed to the IRA would have been exempt from tax.

Tax Information Release 96-5 provides further explanation on this matter. It also states that distributions from a 401(k) plan will be taxable for Hawaii income tax purposes.

The federal law was amended in 1997, effective for tax years beginning in 1998, to provide for a new nondeductible "ROTH IRA," the distribution from which will not be taxable if certain conditions are met. The federal law was also amended in 1997, effective for tax years beginning after 1997, to eliminate the 10 percent penalty for early withdrawals used for "first-time homebuyers" and to pay qualified higher education expenses, and to create a new nondeductible education IRA, the distribution from which will be non-taxable if they are used to pay qualified higher education expenses and certain other conditions are met. Hawaii has adopted these 1997 federal amendments.

See ¶ 510 regarding treatment of lump-sum distributions from pension plans.

The Tax Increase Prevention and Reconciliation Act of 2005 allow taxpayers to convert eligible non-Roth IRAs to Roth IRAs regardless of their federal adjusted gross income for taxable years beginning after December 31, 2010. The taxable income generated by this conversion would be picked up into income over two years starting with 2011 under federal law. Hawaii has adopted the portion of this provision that allows for the conversion of the non-Roth IRA into a Roth IRA for taxable years beginning after December 31, 2009 regardless of federal adjusted gross income. However, Hawaii has not adopted the portion of this provision that allows for the income to be included over a two year period. For Hawaii purposes, the income resulting from the conversion will be included in the taxpayer's income in the taxable year of the conversion. See Tax Announcement 2010-01 for further detail.

¶ 303

## ¶ 303a. Fringe Benefits
Hawaii Law: Sec. 235-2.3
Federal Law: Sec. 101, 117, 119, 127, 132, 137

The Tax Reform Act of 1984 made extensive changes in the taxation of fringe benefits. Prior acts of Congress had prohibited the Internal Revenue Service from issuing Regulations for determining whether certain fringe benefits were taxable compensation. The new law provides statutory rules for excluding certain fringe benefits from an employee's income. The excluded fringes include: no-additional-cost services, qualified employee discounts, working condition fringes, de minimus fringes, and qualified tuition reductions. The new rules are effective Jan. 1, 1985, except for the tuition reduction exclusion, which applies to education furnished after June 30, 1985. Hawaii has adopted these new rules.

The federal law was amended in 1988 to extend the exclusion from gross income of employer-provided educational assistance through 1988. Effective for years beginning after Dec. 31, 1987, the exclusion does not apply to payments with respect to any graduate-level course of a kind normally leading to an advanced professional degree. Hawaii has adopted this amendment. Federal law was amended in 1989 to extend the exclusion for amounts paid before October 1, 1990. The federal law was amended in 1990 to extend the exclusion for amounts paid before January 1, 1992. In addition the 1990 federal amendment repealed the restriction on graduate level courses for years beginning in 1991. The federal law was amended in 1991 to extend the exclusion through June 30,1992. The federal law was amended in 1993 to retroactively extend the exclusion through December 31, 1994. The federal law was amended in 1996 to retroactively extend the exclusion through years beginning before May 31, 1997. The exclusion is not available for graduate level courses beginning after June 30, 1996. For 1997, only expenses for courses begun before July 1, 1997 are excludable. The federal law was amended in 1997 to extend the exclusion for undergraduate educational assistance to amounts paid for courses beginning before June 1, 2000. Hawaii has adopted the federal amendments. The federal law was again amended in 1999 and further extended the date to courses beginning before January 1, 2002. Hawaii adopted this amendment.

The federal law was amended to provide an exclusion from income for employer provided commuter transportation, transit passes, and parking. The exclusion for commuter transportation and transit passes was $60 a month and $155 a month for parking. These exclusions were effective for years beginning after December 31, 1992 through 1997. Effective for years beginning after 1997 the federal law was amended to provide that no amount will be included in the employee's income solely because the employee may choose between qualified parking and compensation. Hawaii adopted the 1992 federal amendment and the 1997 federal amendment for taxable years beginning after December 31, 1997. These exclusion amounts have been increased for both federal and Hawaii purposes. However, federal law was amended in 2009 to increase the exclusion for employer provided commuter transportation and

¶ 303a

transit passes to equal the exclusion amount for qualified employer provided parking. Hawaii has not adopted this increase for employer provided transit passes and vanpooling benefits to the same level as employer provided parking for 2009 and 2010.

Both federal and Hawaii law provide for the exclusion from income of meals and lodging furnished for the convenience of the employer. The Tax Reform Act of 1986 modified these rules to require the inclusion in income of campus lodging provided by a school to an employee if the amount of rent paid by the employee does not exceed a specified amount. This amendment, which Hawaii has adopted, is effective for years beginning after Dec. 31, 1985.

The federal law was amended in 1996 to allow employees of certain medical research institutions to exclude from income the value of employer provided housing provided the employee pays annual rent of at least five percent of the appraised value of the housing. This provision is effective for years beginning after December 31, 1995. Hawaii has adopted this provision.

The federal law repealed the special employer-provided death benefit exclusion for amounts up to $5,000. The repeal applies with respect to decedents dying after August 20, 1996.

The federal law was amended in 1996 to provide an exclusion from an employee's income for amounts paid or expenses incurred by an employer for the employer's qualified adoption expenses pursuant to an adoption assistance program. The exclusion of up to $5,000 for a single child is available for amounts paid or expenses incurred from January 1, 1996 to December 31, 2001. The exclusion is phased out ratably for taxpayers with adjusted gross income between $75,000 and $115,000. The exclusion and the phase-outs were increased in 2002 and are adjusted for inflation. Hawaii has adopted this amendment.

Federal law allows an exclusion from gross income for employer provided health insurance coverage provided to a taxpayer's child who has not reached the age of 27 as of the end of the taxable year. Hawaii has adopted this exclusion.

Most recently Congress passed the Tax Cuts and Jobs Act. For tax years beginning after December 31, 2017, federal law generally states that fringe benefits provided by an employer to or on behalf of an employee are taxable compensation for services unless the Internal Revenue Code specifically excludes them from an employee's income. Under current federal law, potentially excludable fringe benefits include:

Accident and health benefits;

Achievement awards (up to $1,600 for qualified plan awards; $400 for nonqualified awards);

Adoption assistance;

Athletic facilities;

De minimis (minimal) benefits;

¶ 303a

Dependent care assistance;

Educational assistance (up to $5,250 per year);

Employee discounts;

Employee stock options;

Employer-provided cell phones;

Group-term life insurance coverage;

HSAs (Health savings accounts);

Lodging on your business premises;

De minimis meals;

Meals for the employer's convenience;

No-additional-cost services;

Retirement planning services;

Transportation (commuting) benefits;

Tuition reduction;

Working condition benefits.

Hawaii generally follows federal rules relating to fringe benefits. However, Hawaii does not conform to the following suspensions of fringe benefit exclusions:

Qualified bicycle commuting reimbursement exclusion - Suspended per IRC 132(f)(8) for tax years 2018 through 2025;

Qualified moving expenses (for non-active duty U.S. military personnel) - Suspended for tax years 2018 through 2025 under IRC 132(g)(2);

United States Department of Defense Homeowners Assistance Program payments authorized by the ARRA (WHBA provision) - Suspended under IRC 132(n).

These three fringe benefits are excluded from Hawaii gross income.

## ¶ 304. Service Pay
### Hawaii Law: Sec. 235-7
### Federal Law: Sec. 112, 113, 134

Service pay, or military compensation, is subject to both Hawaii and federal tax. However, some types of service pay are exempt under both laws, and some are exempt under one law but not under the other. The exemptions under both laws are as follows:

1. Compensation for service in a "combat zone," and compensation while hospitalized as a result of such service, is exempt. This covers all such compensation of enlisted personnel and up to $500 per month of compen-

sation of commissioned officers. A "combat zone" is established by declaration of the president.

2. Allowances for subsistence and quarters are exempt.

3. Compensation of military personnel and civilian government employees who were prisoners of war or missing in action in the Vietnam conflict is exempt. For purposes of this exemption, the Vietnam conflict began on Feb. 28, 1961. Hawaii enacted this provision in 1973, to conform to the federal law; however, the federal law applies to taxable years ending on or after Feb. 28, 1961, whereas the Hawaii law applies only to taxable years beginning on or after Jan. 1, 1966.

The Tax Reform Act of 1986 prohibits any modification or adjustment to a benefit after Sept. 9, 1986, unless the adjustment is under a law or regulation in effect on Sept. 9, 1986, and is determined by a reference to a fluctuation in cost, price, currency, or similar index. Hawaii has adopted this provision.

Beginning in 1971, the first $500 of compensation received each year as a member of a military reserve unit is exempt from Hawaii tax only. This applies to reserve components of the Army, Navy, Air Force, Marine Corps, Coast Guard, and Hawaii National Guard. The amount of the exclusion is increased to $1,750 for taxable years beginning after 1989. Due to the continued massive deployment of our military service members to dangerous and unstable areas of the world, the law was further revised with Act 197 in 2004 in an attempt to provide some assistance to our National Guard and reservists. The change in law removed the exclusion amount of $1,750 and provides an exclusion of income received by members of the reserve components of the Army, Navy, Air Force, Marine Corps, or Coast Guard and the Hawaii National Guard for compensation earned with their performance of duty. The exclusion is equivalent to pay received for 48 drills and 15 days of annual duty at various pay grades and other qualifying requirements and is effective from January 1, 2005. The applicable maximum exclusion amount for the 2018 tax year is $6,410.

Only Hawaii residents are subject to Hawaii tax on service pay. As mentioned in ¶ 109, military personnel are subject to special rules as to their residence status; this affects the taxability of their service pay. A resident of Hawaii who is stationed in another state remains a Hawaii "resident" for tax purposes; his pay is taxable by Hawaii, but not by the other state. Conversely, a resident of another state who is stationed in Hawaii is not subject to Hawaii tax on his service pay, even though his income is earned in Hawaii and as a nonresident he is ordinarily subject to tax on such income. However, an out-of-state serviceman stationed in Hawaii may be considered a resident and taxed on his pay if he files a joint Hawaii return with his spouse—see comment in ¶ 105.

In 2009, the Military Spouses Residency Relief Act was passed to lessen the state tax filing requirements for spouses of service members for taxable years starting on or after January 1, 2009. In order to comply with this law,

¶ 304

Hawaii allows nonresident spouses of service members to source the income earned from services performed in Hawaii to their state of residence. In order for a nonresident spouse to qualify for this exemption, all of the following conditions must be met: (1) the service member is present in Hawaii solely in compliance with military or naval orders, (2) the spouse is in Hawaii solely to be with the service member; and (3) the spouse and service member are domiciled in the same state and the state is not Hawaii. Please note that this ability to exempt income earned in Hawaii by a nonresident spouse is only available to the spouse. If the service member earns Hawaii sourced non-military pay, it would be subject to Hawaii income tax. Additionally, in order to be exempt from Hawaii income tax, the income must be for services performed. Hawaii sourced income not earned from services performed are not exempt. Examples of income sourced to Hawaii that would not qualify for this exemption are rental income from real or tangible property located in Hawaii, capital gains from sale of real property in Hawaii, or royalty income attributable to Hawaii.

### ¶ 305. Compensation to Hansen's Disease Patients
Hawaii Law: Sec. 235-7

Compensation received from the United States or the State of Hawaii by a patient affected by Hansen's disease (leprosy) is exempt from Hawaii tax. This applies where the patient is employed in a hospital or other place for treatment of the disease. There is no comparable exemption in the federal law.

### ¶ 306. Cost-of-Living Allowances
Hawaii Law: Sec. 235-7
Federal Law: Sec. 912

The federal law provides that cost-of-living allowances received by civilian officers or employees of the U.S. government stationed outside the continental United States are exempt from tax. The Hawaii law taxes such allowances.

### ¶ 307. Dividends Received
Hawaii Law: Sec. 235-2.3, 235-4.5, 235-7
Federal Law: Sec. 78, 243 to 247, 301, 305, 312, 902, 1059

Generally, dividends from corporations are includable in gross income under both Hawaii and federal laws. However, there are several differences between the two laws, as explained below.

Under both laws, a corporate distribution may be a nontaxable return of capital if there are no "earnings and profits" out of which the distribution is made. The amount of "earnings and profits" of a corporation may be different for Hawaii tax purposes than it is for federal tax purposes; such a difference may result in a particular distribution being nontaxable under one law but a taxable dividend under the other.

Under the Tax Reform Act of 1969, federal law provided a special rule for computing "earnings and profits" where accelerated depreciation methods were used. The law provided that, for taxable years beginning after June 30, 1972, only straight-line depreciation could be used in computing "earnings and profits" for the purpose of determining taxability of dividends paid. The effect of this was to convert into a taxable dividend what would otherwise have been a return of capital. Hawaii adopted this federal provision for years beginning after Dec. 31, 1974. The Tax Reform Act of 1984 made substantial changes in the computation of earnings and profits. The 1984 changes are generally effective for distributions after March 15, 1984. Hawaii has adopted these 1984 changes.

The Tax Reform Act of 1984 added a provision limiting the dividends received deduction for dividends received by a corporate shareholder with respect to debt-financed portfolio stock. This provision was further amended in 1985. The Revenue Act of 1987 further limited the dividends received deduction for corporations that own less than 20 percent of the distributing corporation. Hawaii has not adopted the 1984, 1985, or 1987 changes since Hawaii has its own rules dealing with the dividends received deduction by corporations.

The federal law was amended in 1990 to require the inclusion of an unreasonable redemption premium on preferred stock using the economic accrual provisions of Internal Revenue Code Section 1272(a). An unreasonable redemption premium is determined under federal OID rules. Thus a redemption premium is unreasonable if it exceeds the product of one-quarter of one percent of the stated redemption price times the number of complete years to maturity. This provision is effective for preferred stock issued after October 9, 1990. Hawaii has adopted this amendment.

The federal law was amended in 1993 to provide that holders of stripped preferred stock must follow the original interest discount rules with respect to preferred stock where the dividends have been stripped by the seller. This new rule is effective for preferred stock acquired after April 30, 1993. Hawaii has adopted this rule.

Under the Tax Reform Act of 1969, federal rules were provided for taxation of stock dividends. Although the usual dividend of common stock paid on common stock is still nontaxable, all stock dividends on preferred stock and some stock dividends on common stock (disproportionate distributions, etc.) are now taxable under the federal rules. Hawaii adopted these rules effective Jan. 1, 1975.

Prior to 1981, the federal law allowed noncorporate taxpayers an exclusion of up to $100 of dividends received. Hawaii did not allow this exclusion. During 1980, the federal law was amended to allow noncorporate taxpayers an exclusion of up to $200 of dividends and/or interest received. This exclusion was to apply for 1981 and 1982. A 1981 federal amendment changed the exclusion for 1982. The 1982 federal exclusion reverts to the pre-1981 rule. Hawaii adopted the 1980 federal amendment for years beginning in 1981, and adopted

¶ 307

the 1981 federal amendment for years beginning in 1982. The Tax Reform Act of 1986 repealed the $100 dividend exclusion for years beginning in 1987. Hawaii has adopted this 1986 amendment.

A corporation is not allowed the deduction for dividends received provided in the federal law (meaning the changes made to IRC 243 by the Tax Cuts and Jobs Act are not operative for Hawaii purposes). However, a corporation is allowed certain deductions under Hawaii law, as follows:

A corporation is allowed a deduction of 100% of the dividends received on the shares of stock of a national banking association. For years beginning after December 31, 1991 the definition of dividends refers to Section 243(b) of the Internal Revenue Code and only to dividends received by members of an affiliated group.

A corporation is allowed a deduction of 70% of dividends received if the paying corporation:

(1) Is a bank or insurance company organized and doing business under the laws of Hawaii, or

(2) Is at least 95% owned by one or more corporations doing business in Hawaii at the date of payment and is subject to an income tax (other than federal) in another jurisdiction, or

(3) Attributed at least 15% of its entire gross income from all sources (without regard to taxability) to Hawaii in its taxable year preceding payment.

Department of Taxation Announcement 98-5 states that the Tax Department believes that the limitation of the dividend exclusion to payors of dividends with a Hawaii connection may be unconstitutional. Accordingly, they are allowing the 70% dividend exclusion for dividends received from foreign or domestic corporations. Tax Information Release No. 99-2 states that it will allow a dividend exclusion of 100% for affiliated groups without the requirement that the affiliated group consist of domestic corporations.

For years beginning prior to Dec. 31, 1986, the deduction was 85% and for years beginning after December 31, 1986 and before January 1, 1992, the deduction was 80%.

Prior to 1997, both Hawaii and the federal law provided for an adjustment to basis for corporate shareholders who received an extraordinary dividend. The adjustment was made at the time that the stock was sold so as to increase the gain on the sale. The federal law was amended in 1997, effective for distributions after May 1995, to require an adjustment at the beginning of the ex-dividend date and to require that gain be recognized to the extent that the non-taxable portion of the dividend exceeds the basis of the stock. The federal law was also amended in 1997, to extend the holding period for a corporation to qualify for the dividend received deduction. Hawaii has adopted this 1997 federal amendment.

The Economic Recovery Tax Act of 1981 added a new provision to the federal law relating to dividends of public utilities. Effective for years beginning after 1981, an individual who chooses under a domestic public utility's stock dividend reinvestment plan to receive a dividend in the form of common stock rather than cash may, if certain conditions are met, elect to exclude up to $750 per year of the stock dividend. The exclusion terminated after 1985. Hawaii adopted this provision.

Dividends received from regulated investment companies (mutual funds) are treated in the same manner for Hawaii income tax as for federal. This means that the portion of such dividends that constitute a capital gain distribution is taxed at capital gain rates. The federal law was amended in 1984 to provide that 100% (95% for the individual dividends received deduction) of the mutual funds income must be from dividends in order for the corporate dividends received deduction to apply. This rule is effective for years beginning after July 20, 1984. Hawaii has adopted this 1984 amendment.

Where capital gains are retained by a regulated investment company but are nevertheless taxed to shareholders as though the gains had been distributed, under a special provision of the federal law (Sec. 852 (b)(3)(D)), the gains are subject to Hawaii as well as federal tax; that is, the Hawaii shareholder must include the capital gain in his taxable income. If the corporation pays the Hawaii corporate tax of 4% on the retained capital gain, the shareholder gets a tax credit of 4% on his personal return, as explained in ¶ 412. However, the shareholder must report the income whether or not the shareholder gets a Hawaii tax credit. The retained capital gain, less the tax credit, is added to the cost basis of the shareholder's stock, to be taken into account upon ultimate disposition of the stock, as explained in ¶ 521. Thus, the stockholder is treated as though he had received a dividend and reinvested it.

The federal law was amended in 1986 to provide that certain administrative expenses of mutual funds must be reported by the shareholders as income and may be deducted as miscellaneous itemized deductions subject to the 2% of adjusted gross income limitation. This provision was to become effective in taxable years beginning after 1986. The 1987 federal amendments delayed the effective date until 1988, and 1988 federal amendments delayed the effective date until 1990. Hawaii adopted the 1986 and 1987 federal amendments and has adopted the 1988 amendment.

Hawaii adopted the special rules for "Domestic International Sales Corporations" for years beginning in 1981, but has not adopted the 1984 DISC amendments now known as a Foreign Sales Corporation. Accordingly, the special federal treatment of DISC dividends will be different for years before 1981, and for years after 1984.

The federal law was amended in 1962 to provide relief for stockholders of DuPont Corporation who received a distribution of General Motors stock as a result of an antitrust decree of the U.S. Supreme Court. Hawaii did not adopt this relief provision.

¶ 307

A distribution of property from a foreign corporation to a U.S. corporation taxed as a dividend may be treated differently under federal and Hawaii law. The federal law was amended in 1962 to provide that such distributions are to be taxed to the U.S. corporation at fair market value. Hawaii adopted this amendment for years beginning in 1978.

Under a 1962 federal amendment, a corporation receiving a dividend from a foreign subsidiary and taking a foreign tax credit must increase its dividend income by adding the amount of tax paid by the subsidiary. These federal rules have no application under Hawaii law.

The Hawaii law was amended in 1988, effective for years beginning after Dec. 31, 1987, to exclude from income of a trust or estate dividends received from a 100 percent owned foreign (non-U.S.) holding company. To be excluded, the foreign holding company cannot engage in a trade or business, and the amount excluded is limited to the amount of the income received that is paid out to a nonresident beneficiary of the trust.

For years prior to 1969, the Department of Taxation issued periodic Tax Information Releases specifying corporations whose dividends qualified for the 100% and 85% deductions described above. The last such release covered the year 1968.

## ¶ 308. Allowances of Peace Corps Volunteers
### Federal Law: Sec. 912

The federal law, enacted in 1960, provides for tax exemption of compensation paid to Peace Corps volunteers. The Hawaii law contains no such exemption.

## ¶ 309. Nonresidents—Income Taxable in Hawaii
### Hawaii Law: Sec. 235-4

Nonresidents are taxable only on income from sources within Hawaii. This means that they are taxed on:

(a) Compensation for services performed in Hawaii (except for certain nonresident spouses of service members - see ¶ 304).

(b) Income from real estate or other property located in Hawaii, including gain on disposal of such property.

(c) Income from a trade or business in Hawaii.

(d) Any other income from a Hawaii source.

Generally, the "source" of income from an intangible asset (e.g., stock of a corporation) is the owner's place of permanent residence or "domicile." (See ¶ 109 for discussion of residence rules.) This means that a nonresident is not ordinarily taxed on dividend income, even though the dividend may have been paid by a Hawaii corporation and may even have been received by the nonresident at a time when he was physically present (temporarily) in Hawaii. However, the income from an intangible asset would be deemed to be from a source in Hawaii if the asset has acquired a business situs in Hawaii.

In the case of the tax appeals of *Scott McCormac, et al.*, taxpayers were all nonresidents of the State of Hawaii. Taxpayers were beneficiaries of trust funds administered by Bishop Trust Co. Ltd. Bishop Trust distributed to taxpayers quarterly payments of trust net income consisting of interest and dividends derived from the investment of the trust corpus in United States Treasury bills, bank certificates of deposit, preferred stock, and common stock. The Hawaii Supreme Court upheld the tax director's assessment of income taxes on the theory that the assets had a business situs in Hawaii. The law was amended in 1985 to provide that nonresident beneficiaries will not be subject to Hawaii income tax on their share of intangible income earned by Hawaii trusts. This amendment is effective for years beginning after Dec. 31, 1984. The statute is ambiguous as to whether the effective date is applied to the trust's or the beneficiary's taxable year. The Department of Taxation interprets the effective date to be that of the trust. Therefore, beneficiaries of fiscal year trusts did not receive the benefit of this amendment until 1986.

In the case of *Mabel J. Van Valkenburg*, the Hawaii Tax Appeals Court held that interest payments on a purchase money mortgage paid to a nonresident were not subject to Hawaii income tax. The interest arose out of a mortgage on the sale of real estate located in Hawaii.

Prior to the Tax Cuts and Jobs Act, a nonresident who received alimony was subject to Hawaii tax on the alimony if (1) the spouse who pays it is a Hawaii resident, or (2) if the payments are attributable to property transferred to provide the alimony and the property is located in Hawaii. However, effective for divorces and separation agreements executed after December 31, 2018, alimony received is no longer included in the income of the payee under both federal and Hawaii law. See ¶ 418.

As explained in ¶ 304, nonresident military personnel are not taxed on service pay earned in Hawaii, even though they would be subject to Hawaii tax on such income under the regular rules as explained above. See ¶ 109 for treatment of income where a nonresident spouse files a joint return with his or her resident spouse.

See also Chapter 7 of this book.

## ¶ 310. Income of Minors
### Hawaii Law: Sec. 235-2.3, 235-7.5
### Federal Law: Sec. 1, 73

The income of a minor child is taxable to the child and is not included in the parent's return. The requirements for filing are the same as for any other individual. This is the same as under federal law.

If the child is supported by the parent and meets the tests to qualify as a dependent, the parent will be allowed a dependency deduction on his return even though the child is allowed an exemption on his own return, unless the child is married and files a joint return. The Tax Reform Act of 1986 amended the federal rule for years beginning in 1987. Under the change a child will not be able to claim an exemption on his own return if he is eligible to be claimed as a dependent on his parent's return. Hawaii follows the federal rule.

For years beginning in 1987, the Tax Reform Act of 1986 adopted a special tax on the unearned income of children under the age of 14. Such income is to be taxed at the parent's tax rates. The Technical and Miscellaneous Revenue Act of 1988 amended the federal law for years beginning after 1988 to eliminate this special tax if the parents include the income in their return and certain other provisions are met. Hawaii has adopted these amendments.

There was an apparent error in the Hawaii law since it adopted the federal rate of 15 percent instead of the lower Hawaii rate of 2 percent. The Department of Taxation issued Tax Information Release No. 90-7 advising taxpayers of this error and suggesting that parents who filed 1989 returns including their minor children's unearned income file amended returns revoking the election and file separate returns for the children. The election should request a waiver of penalties and interest on the child's return. This error was corrected in 1991.

## ¶ 311. Controlled Foreign Corporations
### Federal Law: Sec. 951, 964, 971, 979

The federal law was amended in 1962 to require a U.S. shareholder of certain "controlled foreign corporations" to include in his (or its) gross income his share of the foreign corporation's income. The purpose was to prevent tax avoidance by use of foreign corporations. The Tax Reform Act of 1984 amended the federal law to recharacterize certain income of "controlled foreign corporations" as U.S. source income. The federal law was amended in 1996 to repeal the rule which required shareholders of a controlled foreign corporation to include in income their share of the controlled foreign corporations' earnings invested in excess passive assets. This amendment is effective for years beginning after December 31, 1996. Hawaii has not adopted these provisions.

## ¶ 312. Earned Income from Outside U.S.
### Federal Law: Sec. 911

Under federal law a United States citizen may obtain tax relief for certain income earned outside the country. If he becomes a bona fide "resident" of a foreign country for at least a full year, or if he actually spends at least 17 months of an 18-month period outside the country (regardless of his status as a "resident"), he is entitled to a limited exclusion from federal gross income for the income earned outside the United States. This provision has been in the federal law for many years. It was amended in 1962 to provide a new definition of a "bona fide resident" and to set a new dollar ceiling on the income exclusion. This dollar ceiling was reduced by the Tax Reform Act of 1976 for years beginning in 1976. The effective date of the reduction was delayed until 1977 by a 1977 federal amendment and subsequently delayed until 1978 by a 1978 federal amendment. The Economic Recovery Tax Act of 1981 made substantial changes to the taxation of citizens working abroad. The changes are effective for years beginning in 1982. The Tax Reform Act of 1984 delayed the increases in the exclusion provided by the 1981 Act.

This relief provision was not adopted by Hawaii when the basic income tax law was enacted in 1957, nor has Hawaii adopted any of the subsequent federal amendments, so any income a Hawaii resident earns outside the United States is fully taxable.

### ¶ 313. Group-Term Life Insurance
**Hawaii Law: Sec. 235-2.3**
**Federal Law: Sec. 79**

Premiums paid by an employer on group-term life insurance, up to $50,000 coverage for each employee, are not taxable income to employees.

Prior to 1964, there was no limit on tax-free coverage under either Hawaii or federal law. The $50,000 limitation was enacted in the federal law in 1964; Hawaii conformed in 1965, applicable to insurance provided in taxable years beginning on or after Jan. 1, 1965.

The federal law was amended in 1982, effective for years beginning after 1983, to provide that if a group-term insurance plan does not meet non-discrimination rules, then key employees will be taxed on the cost of the first $50,000 of group insurance. Hawaii has adopted this 1982 federal amendment. The federal law was revised in 1986 and 1988 to provide strict non-discrimination rules for group-term life insurance programs. Hawaii has adopted these amendments.

### ¶ 313a. Life Insurance Proceeds
**Hawaii Law: Sec. 235-2.3**
**Federal Law: Sec. 101**

Both the federal and Hawaii laws provide for the exclusion of life insurance proceeds from gross income. The federal law was amended in 1982 to provide that proceeds from "flexible premium" life insurance policies will not be exempt unless they meet specific requirements. Special transitional rules apply for policies issued prior to 1983. Hawaii has adopted the "flexible premium" rules.

The federal law was amended in 1996 to provide an exclusion for accelerated death benefits received under a life insurance contract on the life of an insured, terminally or chronically ill individual. This exclusion is effective for amounts received after December 31, 1996. Hawaii has adopted this amendment.

The Tax Reform Act of 1986 repealed the surviving spouse's $1,000 annual exclusion for amounts received with respect to deaths occurring after October 1986. Hawaii has adopted this amendment.

## ¶ 314. Interest on Deferred Payment Contracts
### Hawaii Law: Sec. 235-2.3
### Federal Law: Sec. 483

Ordinarily, principal payments under a deferred payment contract for the sale of property are treated as payment of the sale price and may be taxed as capital gain. However, both Hawaii and federal law provide that under certain conditions a portion of such payments may be treated as interest income and denied capital gain treatment. This applies only where the sale exceeds $3,000 and the contract provides for no interest, or an unrealistically low rate.

The special rule explained above was enacted in the Hawaii law in 1965, applicable to payments on sales or exchanges of property occurring in taxable years beginning on or after Jan. 1, 1965. This conformed to a federal provision that was enacted in 1964 and was made applicable to payments received after 1963 on sales or exchanges made after June 30, 1963. It should be observed that there will be a continuing difference in the treatment of payments received on sales that were made between the effective dates of the respective laws; that is, on sales made during the period July 1, 1963, to Dec. 31, 1964.

The Tax Reform Act of 1984 revised the imputed interest rules on deferred payments. The new rules, generally applicable to transactions entered into after 1984, apply to transactions not covered by the original issue discount rules. See ¶ 320a. The 1984 federal rules provide for a safe harbor test equal to 110% of the applicable federal rate. The federal law dealing with deferred payments was modified in 1985 for transactions entered into after June 30, 1985. Hawaii has adopted the 1984 amendments and has adopted the 1985 modifications.

Where a deferred payment contract was consummated before the taxpayer became a resident of Hawaii, installments received after he becomes a resident are not subject to Hawaii tax—see ¶ 520. This rule applies to payments on the principal of the contract. It does not apply to interest, including imputed interest under the rule described above, to the extent the interest is applicable to the period of Hawaii residence. (See ¶ 110 regarding rules for accounting cutoff at time of change of residence status.)

## ¶ 315. Employee Stock Options and Purchase Plans
### Hawaii Law: Sec. 235-2.3, 235-9.5
### Federal Law: Sec. 83, 421 to 425

Prior to 1964, the Hawaii rules were the same as the federal. However, the Revenue Act of 1964 made extensive changes in the federal rules and created two new classes of stock options. The federal rules applied to options issued after 1963, except for certain limited cases where options were issued after 1963 under a plan in effect before 1964. The Tax Reform Act of 1976 provided that no new qualified stock plan could be adopted after May 20, 1976, and existing qualified stock options had to be exercised before May 21, 1981, to receive favorable tax treatment. Hawaii adopted these provisions for years beginning in 1978.

As a result of the Tax Reform Act of 1969, federal law provides special rules for taxing employees on "restricted stock" transactions not covered by the stock options provisions discussed above. These rules apply, with some exemptions, to stock transferred after June 30, 1969. The rules provide generally for taxing the employee in the first year that the employee's interest is freely transferable or is not subject to substantial risk of forfeiture. In that year the employee is taxed on the excess value of the stock over what he paid for it. Hawaii adopted these rules, effective Jan. 1, 1975. Prior to 1975, the pre-1969 federal rules were in effect for Hawaii tax purposes.

The Economic Recovery Tax Act of 1981 added a new type of stock option called an "incentive stock option" to the federal law. Under the new provisions, no tax consequences result from the grant of an incentive stock option or from the exercise of an incentive stock option by the employee. When the employee sells the stock, any gain will be taxed as a long-term capital gain if the employee has held the stock for at least two years from the date of the option grant and at least one year after the stock was transferred to him. The new provisions apply to options granted on or after Jan. 1, 1976, and exercised on or after Jan. 1, 1981. The Tax Reform Act of 1986 amended the incentive stock option rules. Hawaii has adopted the incentive stock option provisions, including the 1986 amendments.

For tax years beginning in 2000 and after, income recognized from stock options from a qualified high technology business is exempt from tax. This would include stock option income received by an employee, officer, director, or investor (if the investor qualifies for the high technology business investment tax credit). This income tax exemption also applies to income earned and proceeds derived from the sale of stock received through the exercise of stock options. For years after December 31, 2000 the exclusion from income applies to stock of a holding company. A holding company is defined as a business entity that process at least 80% of the value and voting power of a qualified high technology business. A qualified high technology business is defined in ¶412q.

The Tax Cuts and Jobs Act (P.L. 115-97) provided an election to defer tax on stock options received until the earlier of five years of receipt or the time the stock becomes tradeable on a securities market. If such an election is made, the option is treaded as a nonqualified stock option for FICA purposes. At least 80% of the employees must be receiving stock options in order for the company's stock options to be eligible. In addition, IRC 83(b) elections cannot be made on restricted stock units. The law is effective for options exercised or restricted stock units settled after December 31, 2017. It is operative for Hawaii law.

## ¶ 316. Iron Ore Royalties
### Hawaii Law: Sec. 235-2.3
### Federal Law: Sec. 272, 631, 1016, 1231, 1402

The Revenue Act of 1964 allows the capital gain treatment under Internal Revenue Code Section 1231 to apply to certain royalties received from iron ore deposits mined in the United States. These provisions apply to years beginning after Dec. 31, 1963. Hawaii has adopted these provisions for years beginning in 1978.

## ¶ 317. Compensation for Injury or Sickness
**Hawaii Law: Sec. 235-2.3**
**Federal Law: Sec. 104 to 106**

Amounts received under accident or health insurance, damages, workers' compensation, etc., on account of personal injuries or sickness, are tax exempt under both Hawaii and federal laws. The federal law was amended in 1978 to tax certain excess reimbursements under an employer plan that does not meet certain non-discrimination requirements. The Technical Corrections Act of 1979 made several corrections to the 1978 amendments. Hawaii has adopted the 1978 amendments, and has adopted the 1979 amendments. This exemption does not apply to amounts received as reimbursement for medical expenses allowed as deductions in prior years.

The federal law was amended in 1996 to restrict the exclusion from income of punitive damages and compensatory damages for non physical personal injury or sickness. The federal amendments are effective for amounts received after August 20, 1996. Hawaii has adopted this federal amendment.

The federal law was amended for years beginning after 1976 to limit the exclusion from income under wage continuation (sick pay) plans. Under the federal rules the exclusion only applies where the taxpayer is under age 65, is retired, and when retired was permanently and totally disabled. The maximum exclusion is $5,200 which must be reduced by any excess of adjusted gross income, including the sick pay, over $15,000. Hawaii has adopted this federal rule for years beginning in 1978. It should be noted that retirement pay is exempt from Hawaii income tax so that effectively all sick pay paid to retirees is exempt from Hawaii tax.

Benefits received by employees under the Hawaii Temporary Disability Insurance (TDI) program, described in ¶ 1207, are tax exempt to the extent the cost of the plan is paid by the employee. To the extent the cost is paid by the employer, the benefits are treated as "sick pay" under the rules discussed above.

## ¶ 317a. Social Security and Unemployment Benefits
**Hawaii Law: Sec. 235-2.3**
**Federal Law: Sec. 85 to 86**

Hawaii currently does not tax social security benefits and Tier I Railroad Retirement benefits because Hawaii does not conform to section 86 of the Internal Revenue Code. The federal law was amended, effective for 1984, to tax Social Security and Tier I Railroad Retirement benefits. The federal change requires that up to one-half of the taxpayer's Social Security and Tier I Railroad Retirement benefits be included in gross income if the taxpayer's adjusted gross income with specified modifications exceeds a base amount. The amount of taxable Social Security benefits has been increased for years beginning after December 31, 1993. Hawaii has not adopted these federal changes.

Hawaii currently taxes unemployment compensation benefits because Hawaii conforms to section 85 of the Internal Revenue Code, except for subsection (c). The federal law was amended in 1978 to tax certain recipients on the receipt of unemployment compensation benefits. The effect is to tax the benefits to taxpayers who have other income. The federal change was effective for years beginning in 1978. Hawaii adopted this rule for years beginning in 1979. The federal law was further amended in 1980 to include the definition of taxable benefit payments made under the Railroad Unemployment Insurance program. These latter payments are taxable in years beginning after 1978. Hawaii has adopted this 1980 amendment for years beginning in 1981. The federal law was amended in 1982, effective January 1, 1982, to include in income a larger portion of unemployment benefits received. Hawaii has adopted the 1982 federal amendment. The Tax Reform Act of 1986 repealed the partial exclusion for unemployment benefits received after December 31, 1986. Hawaii has adopted this 1986 amendment. Federal law was further amended in 2009 with the American Recovery and Reinvestment Act which allowed for an exclusion of up to $2,400 of unemployment compensation benefits received in 2009. Hawaii has not adopted this amendment.

### ¶ 317b. Prepaid Legal Expenses
Hawaii Law: Sec. 235-7
Federal Law: Sec. 120

Both the Hawaii and federal laws were amended in 1976 to provide an exclusion from gross income of an employee of the value of legal services received on the amounts paid by his employer to a prepaid legal service plan. The Hawaii law is effective January 1, 1976, and the federal law January 1, 1977. The federal law limits the amounts an employer may contribute to a plan for the benefit of certain shareholder employees, Hawaii law has no limit. The federal law expired on June 30, 1992. Hawaii has no expiration date in its law.

### ¶ 318. Income Averaging
Federal Law: Sec. 1301

Prior to 1987, the federal law provided for "averaging" of income over a period of years to give relief from the progressive federal tax rate schedule in certain cases of fluctuating income. There was nothing comparable in the Hawaii law.

The federal law was amended in 1997, effective for tax years beginning after December 31, 1997 and before January 1, 2001, to allow individuals engaged in farming to average their income over three years. Hawaii has adopted this 1997 federal amendment.

## ¶ 319. Recoveries of Bad Debts and Prior-Year Taxes
### Hawaii Law: Sec. 235-2.3
### Federal Law: Sec. 111

Generally, recoveries of bad debts and prior-year taxes are taxable income, since they represent an offset to expenses that were deductible in an earlier period. However, to the extent the item recovered did not result in a tax benefit when it was deducted in a prior year, the recovery is not taxable. The Hawaii rule is the same as the federal.

Refunds of Hawaii tax come under the rules set forth above, except to the extent that they are due to the credits described in ¶ 412. The Department of Taxation has ruled that these credits are, in effect, state grants and are nontaxable for Hawaii income tax purposes, although they presumably are taxable for federal purposes.

Example:

| | | |
|---|---:|---:|
| Hawaii tax withheld during 1996 (deductible in 1996) | | $100 |
| Tax on 1996 income, before credits | 90 | |
| Excise tax credit | 60 | |
| Net tax liability for 1996 | 30 | |
| Tax refund for 1996 received in 1997 | | $ 70 |
| Nontaxable portion of refund for 1997 Hawaii return | 60 | |
| Taxable portion of refund for 1997 Hawaii return | 10 | |
| Taxable refund for federal 1997 return | 70 | |

See also ¶ 411.

## ¶ 320. Income from Bond Discount
### Hawaii Law: Sec. 235-2.3
### Federal Law: Sec. 1232, 1232A, 1232B

Under the Tax Reform Act of 1969, federal law requires the holder of a bond issued at a discount to include in income each month a rateable portion of the "original issue discount." This federal rule applies to bonds issued after May 27, 1969. The income must be reported currently even though the taxpayer may use the cash basis of accounting. Hawaii adopted this provision for years beginning in 1977. The federal law was amended in 1982 to prescribe a new method for determining the inclusion of original issue discount so that it corresponds to actual accrual of interest. This new method applies to both corporate and noncorporate obligations issued after July 1, 1982. Hawaii has adopted this rule.

The federal law was also amended in 1982 to require that the purchaser of a bond stripped of coupons will be treated as having purchased an original issue discount bond. This rule applies to purchases after July 1, 1982. Hawaii has adopted this federal change. The Tax Reform Act of 1984 repealed Sections 1232, 1232A, and 1232B. See ¶ 320a for a discussion of the new federal rules for treating original issue discounts. Hawaii has adopted the 1984 amendments.

## ¶ 320a. Original Issue Discount
### Hawaii Law: Sec. 235-2.3
### Federal Law: Sec. 1258, 1271 to 1278, 1281

The Tax Reform Act of 1984 extended the original issue discount rules to obligations issued for nontraded property, issued by individuals, and not held as capital assets. The act also provides a new basis for determining the discount on these obligations to be treated as interest income. If the instrument does not satisfy a safe harbor test, then a discount rate of 120% of the applicable federal rate is imputed. These new rules are effective generally for transactions after 1984, with certain exceptions. The federal law was amended in 1985 to modify the 1984 rule for certain obligations issued after June 30, 1985. Hawaii has adopted the 1984 and 1985 amendments.

The Tax Reform Act of 1984 also treats as ordinary income the portion of any gain on the disposition of bonds issued after July 20, 1984, to the extent of any accrued market discount. The federal law was amended in 1993 to apply these provisions to all bonds, including tax exempt bonds acquired after May 1, 1993. Hawaii has adopted the 1984 amendment and has adopted the 1993 amendment. See ¶ 404 for the treatment of interest expense on debt incurred to carry market discount bonds.

The Technical Corrections Act of 1985 amended the federal law to clarify the provisions dealing with original issue discount, market discount, and stripped bonds. Hawaii has adopted the 1985 provisions.

## ¶ 321. Expense Reimbursements
### Hawaii Law: Sec. 235-2.3
### Federal Law: Sec. 82, 123, 132

Under the Tax Reform Act of 1969, federal law provides specific federal rules for certain types of expense reimbursement.

Reimbursement from an employer for moving expenses must be included in federal gross income, beginning in 1970. The moving expenses may then be deductible, to the extent explained in ¶ 420. However, to the extent the reimbursement qualifies as a non-taxable fringe benefit under Internal Revenue Code Section 132(a)(6), the reimbursement is not taxable. Hawaii adopted this provision of the Tax Reform Act of 1969, effective January 1, 1975. Prior to 1975, it was presumed that Hawaii would impose the same requirement under the authority of other provisions of Hawaii law.

Reimbursement from an insurance company for excess living expenses paid as a result of destruction (or threatened destruction) of the taxpayer's home by fire or other casualty is excluded from federal gross income. This applies to any insurance payments received after December 31, 1968. Hawaii has adopted this federal provision effective January 1, 1975.

The Tax Cuts and Jobs Act (P.L. 115-97) suspended the moving expense deduction, effective for tax years beginning after December 31, 2017. For Hawaii income tax purposes, the moving expense deduction is not suspended.

## ¶ 322. Payments to Persons Displaced
### Hawaii Law: Sec. 111-1 to 111-12, 261-31 to 261-36

Under 1970 amendments to Hawaii laws (not income tax law), payments to compensate persons displaced by any land acquisition by the state in connection with airport relocation, or to compensate persons displaced by action of any state or county governmental agency, are exempt from Hawaii income tax. There is nothing comparable in the federal law.

## ¶ 323. Income of Foreign Ships or Aircraft
### Hawaii Law: Sec. 235-7
### Federal Law: Sec. 883

Under a 1971 amendment, income of foreign ships or aircraft is exempt from Hawaii income tax if such income is exempt from federal tax under an international treaty, provided the local laws of the foreign country allow a reciprocal exemption to United States ships or aircraft. There has been a comparable exemption in the federal income tax for many years.

## ¶ 324. Merchant Marine Exemption
### Hawaii Law: Sec. 235-2.4
### Federal Law: Merchant Marine Act Sec. 607, Sec. 7518

Under the federal Merchant Marine Act, commercial fishermen and carriers can enter into an agreement with the United States Department of Commerce to deposit part of their income in a fund to acquire or construct vessels, and can reduce their federal taxable income accordingly. Detailed rules are provided for treatment of deposits, withdrawals from the fund, etc. The federal law was amended in 1986 to tax nonqualified withdrawals made after December 31, 1985. Hawaii adopted the federal law for years beginning after December 31, 1995. For Hawaii tax purposes, qualified withdrawals for the acquisition, construction or reconstruction of any asset which is attributable to deposits made before January 1, 1995 will not reduce the basis of the asset when withdrawn from the fund.

## ¶ 325. Energy Conservation Subsidies
### Federal Law: Sec. 136

The federal law was amended effective for years beginning after December 31, 1992 to provide for an exclusion from income for energy conservation subsidies provided by public utilities to residential customers. For commercial or industrial customers there is a phased-in exclusion which reaches 65 percent in 1997. Business taxpayers are not allowed deductions to the extent that subsidies are excluded from income. Hawaii has adopted this amendment.

The federal law was amended in 1996 to repeal the exclusion for non-residential customers. The repeal is effective for amounts received after December 31, 1996. Hawaii has adopted this amendment.

### ¶ 326. Student Loan Discharge
**Hawaii Law: Sec. 235-2.3**
**Federal Law: Sec. 108, 529**

For years beginning after December 31, 1982 both federal and Hawaii law provided for an exclusion from income on the discharge of student loans if the loans were made by the federal or a state government, or certain public benefit corporations, or a qualified educational institution, which had an agreement with one of the first three entities, and where the student worked in certain professions or for a certain class of employers after graduation. A qualified educational institution means an institution defined in Sec 529 of the Internal Revenue Code.

The federal law was amended in 1997 to broaden the category of student loans that are eligible for exclusion from income where the discharge occurs after August 5, 1997. The loans no longer have to come from governmental agencies if the educational institution has a program that encourages students to serve in certain occupations in certain areas. Hawaii has adopted this 1997 federal amendment.

The Tax Cuts and Jobs Act (P.L. 115-97) excludes the discharge of student loan debts from taxable income if the discharge is due to the death or total and permanent disability of the student. Hawaii has adopted this provision.

### ¶ 326a. Qualified Tuition Plans
**Hawaii Law: Sec. 256-2**
**Federal Law: Sec. 529**

Hawaii offers the "HI529 - Hawaii's College Savings Program" (formerly known as "TuitionEDGE"), a savings program created under IRC § 529 for helping families save for higher education and enable participants to obtain or maintain the federal tax benefits or treatment provided by IRC 529.

The program is open to all U.S. citizens and permanent residents. There are no income limits. Individuals that are able to set up an account include a parent, grandparent, family member, and friend. Applicable to tax years beginning after December 31, 2008, any person or entity, regardless of whether the person or entity is the account owner, can make contributions to the account after the account is opened. Prior to January 1, 2009, only the account owner could make contributions after the account was opened. Investors may open accounts for themselves. The account may be used for qualified educational costs at any accredited institution in the United States. "Qualified higher education expenses" means any qualified higher education expense defined in IRC 529.

Exemption: The law exempts from income tax amounts that are distributed from individual trust or savings accounts as long as the distributions are used to pay qualified higher education expenses of a designated beneficiary. In computing Hawaii gross income, individuals can subtract any amount of qualified educational expenses distributed from a qualified state tuition program under IRC 529 that is included in income in computing federal adjusted gross income.

Although the Tax Cuts and Jobs Act (P.L. 115-97) provides that "qualified higher education expenses" include expenses for tuition in connection with enrollment or attendance at an elementary or secondary public, private, or religious school, that provision (IRC 529(c)(7)) is not operative for Hawaii purposes.

Amounts excluded from federal adjusted gross income that were used to pay for elementary or secondary school needs to be added back when computing Hawaii adjusted gross income.

## ¶ 327. Royalty Income
### Hawaii Law: Sec 235-2.4(q), 235-7.3
### Federal Law: None

Royalties and other income derived from patents, copyrights and trade secrets by an individual or a qualified high technology business which was developed out of a qualified high technology business is exempt from tax beginning with years starting 2000 and later. See ¶ 412q for a definition of a qualified high technology business.

In general, expenses related to the generation of tax exempt income are treated as nondeductible. However, Hawaii law specifically provides that expenses for royalties and other income derived from any patents, copyrights, and trade secrets by an individual or qualified high technology business (as defined in HRS Section 235-7.3) are deductible.

TIR 2009-05 sets forth revised proposed administrative rules relating to the taxation of the motion picture and television film production industry. Taxpayers may rely on TIR 2009-5 and the revised proposed administrative rules to the extent taxpayers are authorized to rely on TIRs generally.

## ¶ 328. Federal Energy Grants

Section 1603 of the American Recovery and Reinvestment Act of 2009 created a federal energy grant that could be received in lieu of tax credits. Under federal law, these grants are excluded from gross income. Hawaii has adopted this provision. *See* Tax Information Release No. 2010-10.

## ¶ 329. Cancellation of Indebtedness Income

The American Recovery and Reinvestment Act allows income generated by a reacquisition of business debt at a discount in 2009 or 2010 to be deferred for up to 5 years and then included ratably into income over the next 5 years. Hawaii has not adopted this provision.

## ¶ 330. Cable Surcharge
### Hawaii Law: Sec 235-7(a)(12)
### Federal Law: None

The Effective July 1, 2012, amounts received in the form of a cable surcharge by an electric company acting on behalf of a certified cable company as part of the interisland electric transmission cable system are excluded from income. Any amounts retained by the electric company for collection or other costs are not exempt.

# CHAPTER 4

## INCOME TAX
## DEDUCTIONS AND CREDITS

## ¶ 401. Deductions—Tie-in with Federal Law

In general, the deductions allowable for Hawaii income tax purposes are the same as under federal law. However, there are two main differences: (1) a few that were specified when the basic Hawaii law was adopted in 1957 and (2) differences that have developed since 1957 as a result of federal changes not adopted by Hawaii. Taxpayers should be careful especially when computing depreciation and section 179 deductions and when applying the changes to itemized deductions and other deductions made by the Tax Cuts and Jobs Act (P.L. 115-97). Act 27, SLH 2018, , signed into law June 7, 2018, has specified that certain federal provisions added by the Tax Cuts and Jobs Act are not operative under Hawaii law. For example, Hawaii did not conform to the elimination of the federal deduction for entertainment expenses, and did not fully conform to the federal restriction for fines and penalties because it did not adopt any of the exceptions to the federal restriction including restitution payments, court-ordered payments in a suit to which no government is a party, and amounts paid as taxes due. HRS §235-2.4(u) and §235 2.4(i).

Hawaii law does not conform to IRC 164(b)(6)(B), which limits the federal itemized deduction for state and local taxes paid to $10,000 for tax years beginning after December 31, 2017, and before January 1, 2026.

In addition Act 27 provides that IRC 164(a)(3) (state,local, and foreign, income, war profits, and excess profits tax deduction) and IRC § 164(b)(5) (state and local sales taxes) are operative in Hawaii only for the following taxpayers:

(1) an individual taxpayer filing a single return or a married person filing separately with a federal adjusted gross income of less than $100,000;

(2) an individual taxpayer filing as a head of household with a federal adjusted gross income of less than $150,000; and

(3) an individual taxpayer filing a joint return or as a surviving spouse with a federal adjusted gross income of less than $200,000.

Hawaii law also does not conform to IRC 163(h)(3)(F), which disallows the deduction for interest paid on home equity indebtedness and limits the deduction of interest for acquisition indebtedness over a threshold amount.

Act 27 provides that IRC 67(g), which suspends miscellaneous itemized deductions, is not operative under Hawaii Law. Thus Hawaii law deviates from the Internal Revenue Code by continuing to allow miscellaneous itemized deductions under pre-Tax Cuts and Jobs Act law. In addition, miscellaneous itemized deductions remain subject to the 2% limitation under IRC 67(a), as enacted by the Tax Reform Act of 1986 and adopted by Hawaii. Certain miscellaneous itemized deductions and unreimbursed employee business expenses are deductible to the extent that they exceed 2% of adjusted gross income.

Act 27 also does not adopt the Tax Code's suspension of the limitation on itemized deductions. Previously, Hawaii had adopted the federal government's reduction of total itemized deductions (other than medical expenses, casualty and theft losses, and investment interest). The so-called "Pease limitation" reduced by an amount equal to 3% of adjusted gross income in excess of $100,000. This threshold amount was adjusted annually by inflation. In no event can the adjustment reduce itemized deductions by more than 80%. The federal law was amended in 1993 to make the limitation on itemized deductions permanent. Hawaii adopted the 1990 amendment (except the $100,000 base amount is not adjusted for inflation) and has adopted the 1993 amendment. The federal law also included a phaseout of this limitation which was ultimately repealed for tax years starting after December 31, 2009. Hawaii has adopted this law and therefore, there is no phase out of the itemized deduction limitation for tax years beginning in 2010.

The federal law was amended to extend the repeal of the itemized deduction phase-out to 2011 and 2012. Hawaii did not conform to this amendment so the itemized deduction phase-out that was operative for tax year 2009 was applicable for the tax years 2011 and 2012. Because Hawaii does not conform to the Tax Code's suspension of the limitation, currently, itemized deductions under Hawaii law are subject to phase out at the 2009 thresholds.

Accordingly, if Hawaii adjusted gross income exceeds $166,800 ($83,400 in the case of a separate return by a married individual), itemized deductions are reduced to the lesser of 3% of the amount over $168,800 or 80% of the itemized deductions for the taxable year.

For taxable years beginning after December 31, 2010 but not for taxable years beginning after December 31, 2015, Hawaii further limited itemized deductions to the lesser of the amount as determined in the previous paragraph or $25,000 for single or married filing separately if federal adjusted gross income is $100,000 or more, $37,500 for head of household if federal adjusted gross income is $150,000 or more and $50,000 for joint or surviving spouses if federal adjusted gross income is $200,000 or more. These limitations expired for tax years beginning after December 31, 2015.

Hawaii law does not recognize the qualified business income deduction provided under IRC 199A for tax years beginning after December 31, 2017. The federal deduction is meant for certain non-corporate taxpayers with business income from passthrough entities.

### ¶ 402. Business Expenses
#### Hawaii Law: Sec. 235-2.3
#### Federal Law: Sec. 162, 177, 185, 198, 274, 280G

The deductions for business expenses are the same for Hawaii as for federal, with the exceptions explained below.

The federal law was amended, effective for years beginning on or after January 1994, to limit the deduction for compensation paid by a publicly held corporation to certain employees to $1,000,000.

The federal law was amended, effective for years beginning after December 31, 1993, to deny a deduction for certain lobbying expenses. The Tax Cuts and Jobs Act (P.L. 115-97) repealed the exception that allowed certain local and Indian tribe lobbying expenses to remain deductible. Hawaii has adopted these amendments.

The federal law was amended in 1960 to permit initial purchasers of Federal National Mortgage Association stock to deduct, as a business expense, the excess of the issue price over the fair market value of the stock at the issue date. Hawaii adopted this provision for years beginning after 1978.

As explained more fully in ¶ 426, the federal law on business expense deductions was amended in 1969 and 1971 to (1) prohibit the deduction of certain types of illegal payments, etc., and (2) allow the deduction of certain expenses relating to damages received, etc. Hawaii adopted the federal rules disallowing the deduction of certain types of illegal payments effective Jan. 1, 1975.

The federal law was amended in 1986, effective for years beginning after Dec. 3, 1986, to limit deductions for business meals, entertainment, certain types of travel, use of "skyboxes" at sporting events, and deductions for tickets to entertainment events. In addition, unreimbursed employee expenses for business travel and entertainment become miscellaneous itemized deductions subject to a 2% of adjusted gross income limitation. Hawaii has adopted these 1986 federal changes. The federal law was amended in 1988, effective for years beginning after Dec. 31, 1987, to provide that the 20 percent reduction for meals would not apply to meals provided by the employer on offshore oil and gas platforms and drilling rigs and at certain related support camps for Alaskan platform and drilling rigs. Hawaii has adopted this amendment. The federal law was amended in 1993 to reduce the deductible amount of meal and entertainment expenses from 80% to 50% and to eliminate the deduction for club dues effective for years beginning after December 31, 1993. Hawaii has adopted these amendments.

The federal law was amended in 1997, effective for expenditures paid or incurred after August 5, 1997, to provide an election to deduct qualified environmental remediation expenses as a deductible expense. Hawaii has adopted this 1997 federal amendment.

The federal law was amended to provide that a taxpayer shall not be treated as being temporarily away from home during any period of employment if such period exceeds 1 year. This amendment is effective for costs paid or incurred after December 31, 1992. Hawaii has adopted this amendment. The federal law was amended in 1997 effective for amounts incurred after August 5, 1997 to eliminate the one-year rule for federal employees during any period in which the employee is certified by the Attorney General as traveling on behalf of the United States in temporary status to investigate or provide support services to the investigation of a federal crime. Hawaii has adopted the 1997 amendment.

The Tax Reform Act of 1986 repealed the 60-month amortization of trademark and trade name expenditures and the 50-year amortization of railroad grading and tunnel bore expenditures effective for expenditures incurred after Dec. 31, 1986. Hawaii has adopted these amendments.

The federal law was amended in 1986 to disallow a deduction by corporations for amounts paid or incurred in connection with stock redemptions. The amendment is effective for amounts paid or incurred after Feb. 28, 1986. Hawaii has adopted this amendment.

For taxable years beginning after December 31, 2015, Act 230 becomes applicable. Act 230 is tax-related amendments and clarification related to the States' medical marijuana dispensary program.

¶ 402

IRC section 280E denies deductions and credits to any taxpayer trafficking in a Schedule I or Schedule II substance. Prior to January 1, 2016, Hawaii conformed to this section for Hawaii income tax purposes, meaning taxpayers engaged in medical marijuana businesses could not account for Hawaii income tax the same as other legitimate businesses by deducting business expenses and claiming tax credits. Act 230 relaxes the application of this section only for medical marijuana businesses operating under Hawaii's medical marijuana dispensary program. This means that these businesses may account for Hawaii income tax the same as other legitimate businesses in Hawaii. See Hawaii Department of Taxation Announcement No. 2016-07.

The Tax Cuts and Jobs Act, P.L. 115-97, prohibits deductions for the settlement of any amount related to a sexual harassment or abuse settlement if the payment is subject to a nondisclosure agreement. The provision is effective for federal law for amounts paid or incurred after December 22, 2017. The provision is operative under Hawaii law.

The Tax Cuts and Jobs Act, P.L. 115-97, eliminated the deduction for entertainment expenses. However, under Act 27, SLH 2018, Hawaii does not conform to the federal law. Hawaii taxpayers may continue to claim a 50% deduction for entertainment expenses.

### ¶ 402a. Business Use of Home
#### Hawaii Law: Sec. 235-2.3
#### Federal Law: Sec. 280A

The federal law was amended, effective for years beginning after 1975, to restrict deductions for business use of a taxpayer's residence. Under the new federal rules, no deduction is permitted for expenses attributable to the use of taxpayer's home for business purposes except to the extent they are attributable to the portion of the home used exclusively and on a regular basis as his principal place of work or a place that is used by patients, clients, or customers in the normal course of business. In the case of an employee, the use must be for the convenience of his employer. When expenses qualify for deduction, they are limited to the amount of gross income derived from the business use of the residence. The federal law was amended in 1977 to provide a limited exception to the restrictions on deductions where a portion of the residence is used for day care of children, elderly, or handicapped persons. Hawaii adopted the 1976 federal rules for years beginning in 1977, and adopted the 1977 federal amendments for years beginning in 1978.

The Tax Reform Act of 1986 amended the federal law for years beginning after Dec. 31, 1986, to limit the deduction for business use of a taxpayer's residence to the amount of income produced from the business use of the residence. Any excess deductions are available as a carryover to offset future income from the home activities. Hawaii has adopted the 1986 federal amendments.

The federal law was amended effective for tax years beginning after December 31, 1995 to allow a deduction for expenses related to the portion of a tax-payer's home used regularly for the storage of inventory or product samples. The taxpayer must be in the business of selling products at retail or wholesale and his home must be his sole place of business. Hawaii has adopted this amendment.

The federal law was amended effective for years beginning after December 31, 1998 to expand the deductibility of home office expenses where a portion of the taxpayer's residence is used exclusively and regularly to perform administrative or management activities and the taxpayer does not conduct these activities at another fixed location. Hawaii has adopted this federal amendment.

## ¶ 403. Depreciation
### Hawaii Law: Sec. 235-2, 235-2.2, 235-2.3, 235-2.4
### Federal Law: Sec. 38, 46 to 48, 167, 168, 178, 179, 179A, 197, 274

The Hawaii rules for the deduction for depreciation generally follow the federal rules. This will be true for any federal changes made after 1980 since Hawaii has adopted these changes including the federal effective dates. However, there are a few exceptions and these are explained below.

One obvious exception relates to the basis of assets being depreciated. Where the basis is different for federal and Hawaii purposes then the depreciation deduction will be different.

As a result of the Tax Reform Act of 1969, federal law limited the use of accelerated depreciation methods on real property and by regulated public utilities. Generally, use of the 200% declining balance and sum-of-the year's-digits methods could not be used except on new residential rental property. Hawaii adopted these rules for taxable years beginning after Dec. 31, 1974.

The Tax Reform Act of 1969 provided for accelerated five-year write-off for certain expenditures made to rehabilitate old properties rented to persons of low or moderate income. This provision applied to expenditures made between July 24, 1969, and Jan. 1, 1975. The federal law has been continuously amended to allow these expenses to be amortized so that expenses incurred through January 1, 1987 are eligible for amortization. The federal law was amended in 1975, 1976, 1978, 1980 and 1984. Hawaii adopted the 1969 amendments in 1975, the 1976 amendments in 1977, the 1978 amendments in 1979, the 1980 amendments in 1981 and the 1984 amendments with the federal effective date.

The Tax Reform Act of 1969 provided for accelerated federal write-off of certain types of railroad property and of coal mine safety equipment. Hawaii adopted this federal provision for years beginning in 1978. The Revenue Act of 1971 provided for accelerated federal write-off of certain facilities for on-the-job training and for child care. The federal law was amended in 1977 to include expenditures made prior to Jan. 1, 1982. Hawaii adopted the 1971 federal amendments for years beginning in 1975 and adopted the 1977 amendment for years beginning in 1978.

The federal law was amended in 1976 to provide an election during a limited period to amortize rehabilitation expenses to certified historic structures over a 60-month period in lieu of depreciation, and further restricts depreciation to the straight-line method for new buildings built on the site of demolished historic buildings. Hawaii adopted these provisions, effective Jan. 1, 1977.

During the years 1962-1967, Hawaii allowed a special depreciation deduction on property subject to the federal "investment credit." This Hawaii deduction was for an amount equivalent to the investment credit. It was intended to match the reduction in the federal cost basis that was required when the investment credit was first introduced. The federal reduction of cost basis was repealed, but Hawaii still allowed the special reduction during the period 1962-1967. The result was a difference between Hawaii and federal cost basis; such difference in basis means a difference in depreciation and/or gain or loss upon disposition of the property in later years.

In 1997 Hawaii adopted special tax credits for the costs incurred in producing motion picture and television films and for the costs in renovating hotel properties. The credit for hotel renovation was repealed for years after December 31, 1999. It was replaced by a qualified improvement credit, which was repealed for tax years after December 31, 2008. See discussion in ¶ 412p. If the credit is claimed for these costs then the basis of any depreciable property acquired must be reduced for Hawaii income tax purposes. See discussion of the credits in ¶ 412m and ¶ 412n.

The federal law was amended in 1982 to require that the basis of property placed in service after 1982 be reduced by 50 percent of the investment tax credit claimed where the taxpayer elects to claim the full investment tax credit, energy credit, or rehabilitation investment tax credit. If the taxpayer elected to reduce the tax credit by two percentage points, then no reduction in basis was required. Hawaii did not adopt this federal change.

The federal law was amended in 1966 to suspend the use of the double declining balance and the sum-of-the-year's-digits methods of depreciation on buildings, effective Oct. 10, 1966, and was again amended in 1967, effective March 9, 1967, to restore the suspended depreciation methods. The Hawaii law was not amended to conform to either of these changes; however, the Department of Taxation ruled that the methods allowable for federal tax purposes were also allowable for Hawaii purposes. In other words, Hawaii followed the federal in not allowing accelerated depreciation methods on property acquisitions to which the suspension period was applicable.

The federal law was amended in 1993 to increase to $17,500 from $10,000 the amount of property which may be expensed in the year of purchase (IRC Sec 179). This amendment applies to property acquired after December 31, 1992. The federal law was amended in 1996 to increase the first year write-off of property. The increase is phased in from 1997 to 2003. For years beginning

¶ 403

in 1997, the write-off is $18,000. The amount of the write-off increases each year thereafter until 2003 when the maximum amount will be $25,000. Hawaii has adopted the 1993 amendment but has not adopted the 1996 amendment. The federal law was further amended in 2003 to increase the maximum deduction for certain depreciable business assets. Federal law was further amended by the Tax Cuts and Jobs Act to increase the limit to $1,000,000 for tax years beginning in 2018. Hawaii law does not conform to this increase because it was previously amended in 2004 to conform to the provisions of IRC Sec 179 with the exception of certain provisions (increase of the maximum deduction (IRC Sec 179(b)(1) and (b)(7)); increase of qualifying investment amount (IRC Sec 179(b)(2) and (b)(7)); inclusions of computer software in section 179 property (IRC Sec 179(d)(1)); inflation adjustments (IRC Sec 179(b)(5)); irrevocable election (IRC Sec 179(c)(2)); special rules for qualified disaster assistance property (IRC Sec 179(e))).

The federal law was amended in 1976 to limit the amount of additional first-year or bonus depreciation that a partnership may claim for 1976 and future years. Under the new rule the limit is applied at the partnership level as well as at the partner level. Hawaii adopted this federal rule for years beginning in 1977.

In some cases where depreciable property was acquired prior to the enactment of the present Hawaii tax law in 1957, there may be a difference in the cost basis of the property for Hawaii purposes from the basis for federal purposes. See Chapter 5 for discussion of basis of property. Such a difference in basis may result in a difference between Hawaii and federal deductions for depreciation.

In Tax Information Release No. 31-71, issued March 2, 1971, the Department of Taxation announced that Hawaii would allow depreciation under the federal Asset Depreciation Range System (ADR), effective Jan. 1, 1971. This conforms to the federal effective date, since the ADR system applies to assets placed in service after Dec. 31, 1970. Later in 1971 the federal depreciation rules were changed somewhat, in the Revenue Act of 1971, by providing for a new class-life system along the lines of the ADR system. The Department of Taxation has allowed depreciation under the revised federal system. The Hawaii Legislature adopted the class-life system for tax years beginning Jan. 1, 1975.

The federal law was amended in 1993 to provide for the amortization of purchased goodwill and certain purchased intangibles over a 15 year period beginning in the month of acquisition. The federal law is effective for intangibles purchased after August 10, 1993. Taxpayers may elect to apply this new provision to property acquired after July 25, 1991. Hawaii has adopted this federal amendment.

The federal law was amended in 1996 to provide a 15 year life for real property that qualifies as a retail motor fuels outlet. The amendment is effective for property placed in service after August 20, 1996. Hawaii has adopted this amendment.

Several changes were made to the federal law in 1997. The first change is to limit the property which qualifies for the income forecast method of depreciation so as to exclude rent-to-own tangible personal property. This amendment is effective for property placed in service after August 5, 1997. A second change is to exclude from the definition of luxury automobiles clean burning fuel vehicles. This amendment is effective for property placed in service after August 5, 1997. A third change is to classify rent to own property as MACRS 3-year property. This amendment is effective for property placed in service after August 5, 1997. Hawaii has adopted these 1997 federal amendments.

The federal law was amended in 1996 to provide a deduction to a lessor for the adjusted basis of leasehold improvements made by the lessor for the lessee at the termination of the lease. This provision is effective as of June 12,1996. Hawaii has adopted this amendment.

See ¶ 424 regarding amortization of pollution control facilities.

The Job Creation and Worker Assistance Act of 2002 (JCWAA) was signed into law on March 9, 2002. The JCWAA amended IRC section 168 to provide for a first-year "bonus" depreciation deduction. The "bonus" depreciation deduction is equal to 30% of the basis of a qualified MACRS asset for certain property acquired after September 10, 2001 and before September 11, 2004, and placed in service before January 1, 2005. The Jobs and Growth Tax Relief Reconciliation Act of 2003 increased the additional first-year depreciation deduction percentage to 50% for certain property acquired after May 5, 2003, and placed in service before January 1, 2005. The Economic Stimulus Act of 2008 reinstates the 50% bonus depreciation allowance for qualifying property acquired after December 31, 2007 and before January 1, 2009. The Economic Recovery and Reinvestment Act of 2009 extended the bonus depreciation deduction to qualifying property placed in service before January 1, 2010. The 2010 Small Business Job Act extended the 50% bonus depreciation deduction to qualifying property placed in service before January 1, 2011. The Tax Relief, Unemployment Insurance Reauthorization and Job Creation Act of 2010 increased the 50% bonus depreciation to 100% bonus depreciation for qualified investments made after September 8, 2010 and before January 1, 2012. The provision for 100% bonus depreciation expired, but the Tax Cuts and Jobs Act, P.L. 115-97, revived it. The federal law now generally provides that a 100% firstyear deduction for the adjusted basis is allowed for qualified property acquired and placed in service after September 27, 2017, and before January 1, 2023 (January 1, 2024 for certain other property). Hawaii, however, does not conform to the federal bonus depreciation provisions of IRC 168(k).

With respect to the Tax Cuts and Jobs Act's changes to depreciation method for machinery used in a farming business, however, Hawaii is in conformity with federal law. Effective for property placed in service after December 31, 2017, Federal and Hawaii tax law shorted the recovery period for machinery used in a farming business from 7 years to 5 years. The pre-TCJA requirement that the 150% declining balance method be used for 3,5, 7, and 10-year property, is repealed.

¶ 403

## ¶ 404. Interest Expense
### Hawaii Law: Sec. 235-2.3, 235-2.4, 235-2.45, 235-7
### Federal Law: Sec. 163, 189, 216, 221, 249, 263, 264, 265, 279, 291, 385, 461, 1277, 7872

Since 1981 Hawaii has generally followed the federal rules for the deduction of interest expense. There are some differences and they are discussed below. Although some of these differences no longer apply they are discussed below because the difference may affect the basis of assets. For a more detailed discussion of prior year differences reference should be made to prior editions of this book.

There may be a difference between Hawaii and federal interest deductions where interest is paid to purchase or carry tax-exempt obligations. Under both laws interest of this type is nondeductible. However, if there is a difference between Hawaii and federal tax exemption on income from the obligations purchased or carried, then there also will be a difference in the amount of interest deductible under the two laws. For example, interest paid on a loan to carry U.S. Government bonds is not deductible on the Hawaii return because the interest received on the bonds is not taxable. The same interest is deductible on the federal return because the income is taxable on that return.

The federal law was amended in 1962 to provide a limitation on deductions for interest or dividends paid to depositors by savings and loan associations and similar institutions. The amendment provided that, to the extent such payments cover a period of more than 12 months, they are not deductible in the current year but must be deducted in another year. Hawaii adopted this amendment for years beginning in 1977.

Under a 1963 federal amendment, redeemable ground rents, as defined in Internal Revenue Code Section 1055, are treated as interest on an income indebtedness secured by a mortgage. This provision was enacted primarily to cover certain property arrangements in Maryland, and was made retroactive to 1962. Hawaii has not adopted this amendment.

Under the Tax Reform Act of 1969, federal law limited the amount of investment interest that can be deducted by noncorporate taxpayers after 1971. The Tax Reform Act of 1976 further limited the amount of investment interest that can be deducted by a noncorporate taxpayer in 1976 and later years. This applies only to interest on indebtedness used to purchase or carry property held for investment. Hawaii adopted the 1976 federal provisions for years beginning in 1977. The federal law was amended in 1993, effective for years beginning after December 31, 1992, to provide that if a taxpayer wishes to treat capital gains as investment income in order to raise the allowable deduction for investment interest then the amount of capital gains eligible for the alternative tax must be reduced by the amount included as investment income. Hawaii has adopted this amendment.

Another change made to the federal law by the Tax Reform Act of 1976 was to limit the amount of interest that may be deducted during the construction of real estate. Interest that is not currently deductible is to be capitalized and amortized in accordance with a prescribed table set out in the Act. The Act differentiates between residential, nonresidential, and low income property and provides a phase-in of the new rule. Any unamortized interest at the time the property is sold is to be added to the basis of the property. Hawaii adopted this change for years beginning in 1977, with the exception that the rules relating to nonresidential real property take effect after Dec. 31, 1976; the rules relating to residential real property take effect after Dec. 31, 1977; and the rules relating to low-income housing were to take effect after Dec. 31, 1981. The federal rules relating to construction period interest were further amended in 1981, 1982, and 1984. Hawaii has adopted these amendments.

The federal tax law has been further amended to require that all construction period interest must be capitalized and added to the basis of the property. Hawaii has adopted this amendment.

The Tax Reform Act of 1969 provides for the deductibility of premium paid by a corporation to call or repurchase its own convertible bonds. Under the rule, only the normal call premium is deductible; that is, only that amount is treated as the equivalent of interest paid, and the remainder of the premium is a capital transaction. Hawaii adopted this federal provision for years beginning in 1978. The federal law was amended in 1988 to clarify the treatment of amortizable bond premium. Amortized premium is to be offset against interest income from the bond and not treated as interest expense. Hawaii has adopted the 1988 amendment.

The Tax Reform Act of 1969 provided a limit on corporate interest deductions on so-called "corporate acquisition indebtedness" effective with respect to indebtedness incurred after Oct. 9, 1969. Hawaii adopted these rules for "corporate acquisition indebtedness" incurred after Dec. 31, 1974.

The Tax Reform Act of 1969 broadened the federal rules regarding deduction of interest (and taxes) by tenant-stockholders of cooperative housing corporations, to cover situations where a portion of the corporation's income comes from a governmental entity. Hawaii adopted this provision for years beginning in 1978.

The federal law was amended in 1982, effective for years beginning in 1983, to reduce the interest expense deduction of financial institutions, which is incurred to carry tax-exempt obligations. The federal law was further amended in 1986 to deny deduction for interest incurred to carry tax-exempt obligations issued after Aug. 7, 1986. This 1986 amendment is effective for interest incurred after Dec. 31, 1986. Hawaii appears to have adopted this federal provision; however, it should not apply since financial institutions are taxed under the Franchise Tax law, and municipal interest is taxed under the Franchise Tax law.

The Tax Reform Act of 1986 amended the federal law to limit interest deductions by individuals in tax years beginning after Dec. 31, 1986. Hawaii has adopted the 1986 federal amendments. The federal law was amended

¶ 404

in 1987 to redefine the interest deduction on personal residences. Hawaii has adopted this change. The federal law was amended in 1988 to provide that interest paid on estate tax deferred under Section 6166A of the Internal Revenue Code is not personal interest. The 1988 federal amendment also clarified the residence interest rule to allow interest paid by an estate or trust on indebtedness secured by a qualified residence of a beneficiary to be classified as qualified residence interest. Hawaii has adopted these 1988 amendments.

The federal law was amended in 1997, effective for years beginning in 1998, to provide a limited deduction for interest paid on higher education loans. The federal law was also amended in 1997 to disallow an interest deduction for certain interest payable, e.g. 2.0%, on any unpaid portion of the federal estate tax for the period during which an extension of time for payment of the tax is in effect under Internal Revenue Code Section 6166. This amendment is effective for estates of decedants dying after December 31, 1997. Hawaii has adopted these 1997 federal amendments for decedants dying after 1997.

The federal law was amended in 1989 to limit the interest deduction on certain high yield original issue discount obligations issued after July 10, 1989, and to limit the interest deduction paid to related tax exempt persons on obligations issued after July 10, 1989. Hawaii has adopted these amendments.

The federal law was amended in 1996 to repeal the interest deduction on debt incurred with respect to corporate owned life insurance policies purchased after June 20, 1996. There is an exception for policies on key persons; however, there is a limit on this deduction. The federal law was amended in 1997 to further restrict the interest deduction on business owned life insurance policies. Hawaii has adopted the 1996 federal amendments. Hawaii has adopted the 1997 federal amendments for contracts issued after June 8, 1997.

The federal law was amended in 1997 to disallow the deduction for interest on certain debt instruments issued after June 8, 1997 if the interest can be paid or converted into an equity instrument of the issuer. Hawaii has adopted this 1997 federal amendment.

See ¶ 302 for a discussion of the 1984 federal amendments dealing with interest-free and below-market loans.

Hawaii Law was amended in 2004 under Act 89 to clarify its position on conforming to IRC Section 163. Hawaii Law conforms to this code section with the exception of IRC Section 163(d)(4)(B), (defining net investment income to exclude dividends), Section 163 (e)(5)(F) (suspension of applicable high yield discount obligation rules), and Section 163 (i)(1) as it applies to debt instruments issued after January 1, 2010.

The Tax Cuts and Jobs Act, P.L. 115-97, amended federal law for tax years beginning after December 31, 2017. The deduction for business interest is now limited under IRC 163(j) to the sum of the business interest income, the floor plan financing interest, and 30% of the adjusted taxable income of the taxpayer.

¶ 404

(Businesses with average annual gross receipts of $25 million or less are generally exempt from this disallowance.) Hawaii law conforms to this provision.

The law allows certain real property trades or businesses to elect out of the 163(j) limit if such a business uses the alternative depreciation system for its nonresidential, residential, and qualified improvement property. An electing farm business may also elect out of the 163(j) limitation if it uses ADS for property with a recovery period of 10 years or more. The ADS provisions are effective for property placed in service after December 31, 2017.

## ¶ 405. Contributions
Hawaii Law: Sec. 11-226, 235-2.3, 235-7
Federal Law: Sec. 41, 63, 170, 218, 642, 664, 673, 1011

Prior to 1970 the Hawaii rules for deductions of contributions to charitable-type organizations were the same as the federal (except for some differences in effective dates of prior-year amendments, as explained below). However, between 1969 and 1975 important differences between the two laws exist because of federal amendments that were not adopted by Hawaii until 1975. Hawaii adopted the Tax Reform Act of 1969 provisions affecting contributions for 1975 and future years.

The federal law has been amended to require that contributions of $250 or more must be substantiated by a receipt from the charity in order to be deductible. This new substantiation requirement applies to contributions made on or after January 1, 1994. Hawaii has adopted this federal amendment.

The federal law was amended in 1996 to allow a deduction for the fair market value of publicly traded securities to private foundations. This amendment is effective for contributions made after June 30, 1996 and before June 1, 1997. The federal law was amended in 1997 to extend the period to June 30, 1998. Hawaii has adopted the 1996, 1997 and 1998 amendments. The federal law was amended in 1998 to make permanent the allowance of a deduction for the fair market value of a publicly held stock to a private foundation. Hawaii has adopted this amendment.

Under the Tax Reform Act of 1969, effective in 1970, the federal special ceiling on charitable contributions was increased in some situations from 30% to 50% of adjusted gross income. (The basic ceiling, or limitation, is still 20% under both laws.) The Hawaii ceiling is the same as the federal for years beginning in 1975. The extra allowance over 20% applies in both laws to contributions to churches, schools, hospitals, certain government units, and some other organizations. Under the Tax Reform Act of 1969, the federal rules were broadened to make three new classes or organizations qualify for an extra allowance over 20%; these are (1) "private operating foundations," (2) certain "private nonoperating foundations," and (3) certain "community foundations." These organizations qualify for the extra allowance over 20% under Hawaii law for years beginning in 1975.

The Tax Reform Act of 1984 increased the 20% limitation to 30% for gifts made after 1984 of cash and ordinary income property to nonoperating private foundations. Hawaii has adopted this 1984 amendment.

Under the Tax Reform of Act of 1969, the so-called "unlimited" charitable deduction in the federal law was eliminated gradually over a period of years beginning in 1970, reducing the maximum deduction to 50% of adjusted gross income in 1975. The Tax Cuts and Jobs Act of 2017 increased the contribution-base percentage limit for tax years beginning after December 31, 2017, and before January 1, 2026, for deductions of cash contributions by individuals to 60% of adjusted gross incomefrom 50%.. The Hawaii rule is the same as the federal rule per Act 27, SLH 2018.

Under the Tax Reform Act of 1969, effective in 1970, the federal law restricts deductions for charitable contributions to certain types of organizations. Deductions are denied for contributions to "private foundations" and for certain transfers in trust unless the recipient organizations comply with certain conditions. Hawaii adopted these federal restrictions for 1975 and future years.

Under the Tax Reform Act of 1969, the federal law provides special rules for non-cash charitable contributions. Contributions in the form of appreciated "capital gain property" are subject to reduced limitations, and the unrealized appreciation may be subject to tax. Contributions of appreciated "ordinary income property" are deductible, generally, only to the extent of the taxpayer's cost basis of the property. The federal law was amended in 1976 to provide for a limited exception where a corporation gives appreciated inventory to certain charities for the benefit of children or the needy. The federal law was amended for years beginning after December 31, 1997 to allow a C corporation an increased deduction for gifts of computer equipment and technology to elementary and secondary schools. Hawaii has adopted this 1997 federal amendment. On "bargain sales" to charity, a portion of the appreciation in value is taxed by the device of allocating the cost basis between the portion of the property "sold" and the portion contributed to the charity. These federal rules were effective in 1970, except for contributions of letters, memoranda, etc. (effective July 26, 1969) and bargain sales (effective Dec. 20, 1969). Hawaii adopted the 1969 changes for years beginning in 1975 and the 1976 change for years beginning in 1978. The federal law was amended in 1978 to give effect to the new federal capital gain exclusion. Hawaii adopted the 1978 federal change for years beginning in 1979.

The Tax Reform Act of 1969 also introduced new federal rules for various unusual forms of charitable contributions. These rules cover gifts of partial interests (e.g., gift of right to use property), two-year charitable trusts, unlimited deductions of estates and trusts, charitable remainder trusts, transfers to pooled income funds, and contingent gifts. Generally, the rules impose limitations and restrictions on the deductibility of the contributions involved. On the other hand, the rules specifically provide for allowance of contribution deductions

¶ 405

for non-trust gifts of remainder interests in personal residences or farms. These federal rules are applicable after various effective dates in 1969. Hawaii adopted the federal changes for years beginning Jan. 1, 1975.

The Tax Reform Act of 1976 made several changes to the federal rules applicable to contributions. The first was to exclude from the definition of capital assets government publications received by the donor at little or no cost. The second was to allow corporations an additional charitable contribution deduction equal to one-half of the excess of fair market value of inventory property over its basis, up to a maximum amount of twice the basis. Only inventory donated to a charity that uses the property for the care of children, the sick, or the needy would qualify for the additional deduction. These federal changes were effective for contributions made after October 1976. A third change was to allow a deduction for the transfer of certain partial interests in property for conservation purposes between June 30, 1976, and June 14, 1977. The federal law was amended in 1977 to provide that contributions of partial interests in property for conservation purposes must be in perpetuity. Hawaii adopted the 1976 federal amendments for contributions made after Dec. 31, 1976, and adopted the 1977 amendments for years beginning in 1978.

The Revenue Act of 1964 provided for a five-year carryover of certain contributions made by individuals or corporations in excess of the yearly limitations on charitable contributions. Hawaii adopted this provision in 1967, applicable to taxable years ending after Dec. 31, 1966, but only with respect to contributions made after that date. This means that any excess contributions made in 1967 can be carried over to later years on Hawaii returns, but no Hawaii carryover is permitted for excess contributions made prior to 1967. (Prior to the 1967 amendment, Hawaii allowed individuals no carryover of contributions and allowed corporations a two-year carryover). Federal and Hawaii carryovers may be different after 1970, because of the numerous differences discussed above and also because of specific provisions regarding carryovers in the Tax Reform Act of 1969.

The federal law was amended in 1981 to increase the contribution deduction limitation of corporations from 5% to 10% for years beginning in 1982. Hawaii has adopted this increased limitation.

The federal law was amended in 1988 to allow a deduction of 80 percent of a contribution to or for the benefit of a college or university if the taxpayer receives in return a right to purchase tickets to the institution's athletic stadium. This provision was retroactive to years beginning after Dec. 31, 1983. For contributions made in tax years beginning after December 31, 2017, however, the Tax Cuts and Jobs Act provides there is no 80% deduction if the taxpayer received the right to purchase such tickets. Hawaii is in conformity with this change.

For years beginning after December 2000, a taxpayer licensed under Chapter 444, 460J or 464 of the Hawaii Revised Statutes who donates services to Hawaii public school may obtain a tax credit. See Sec. ¶ 412t for details.

¶ 405

It should be observed that the allowable Hawaii deduction may be different from the federal in cases where the percentage limitations apply. If the amount of Hawaii adjusted gross income is different from the federal, because of a difference in the amount of income taxable under the two laws, then of course the amount of the percentage limitation on deductible contributions will be different.

Under prior law, Hawaii allowed a deduction for political contributions. Prior to 1979 the law allowed a deduction for political contributions up to $100 (up to $200 on a joint return), where the contributions were made to a central or county committee of a political party whose candidates have agreed to abide by the campaign spending limits set by law. The Hawaii law was amended, effective June 21, 1979, to allow individual taxpayers to claim a deduction for political contributions up to $500, provided that the contributions are to candidates who meet the requirements of the Hawaii campaign spending law, and contributions of no more than $100 for each candidate can be deducted. The listing of political candidates who comply with the aforementioned conditions is provided by the Campaign Spending Commission. For years beginning after 1994, the limit has been raised to $250 for individual candidates and the aggregate limit has been raised to $1,000. The law also provides that candidates who fail to file the campaign spending affidavit must notify contributors immediately upon receipt of their contribution that they may not claim a tax deduction. This deduction is separate from the deduction for charitable contributions, so it is not subject to the percentage limitation and carryover provisions described above. Act 59, Session Laws of Hawaii 2010, repealed the deduction for political contributions for all tax years beginning after December 31, 2010. The Act also repealed HRS § 11-226, which provided the necessary framework a candidate had to follow in order for such deduction to qualify.

Prior to 1987 the federal law allowed a credit of $50 on a single return and $100 on a joint return for political contributions. Hawaii had no similar credit.

## ¶ 406. Medical Expenses
### Hawaii Law: Sec. 235-2.3
### Federal Law: Sec. 213, 220, 162

Prior to 1977 the federal and Hawaii rules for deducting medical expenses were different due to 1967 federal changes that Hawaii did not adopt until 1977; since 1977, the Hawaii and federal rules have been the same.

The federal law was amended in 1990, effective for years beginning in 1991, to eliminate a deduction for unnecessary cosmetic surgery and any medical insurance premiums which pay for such surgery. Hawaii has adopted this amendment.

The federal law was amended in 1986 to allow self-employed individuals a limited deduction for medical insurance payments in arriving at adjusted gross income. This limited deduction was to be effective for calendar years 1987 to 1989. Hawaii adopted this provision. The federal law was amended in 1989 to extend this deduction to amounts paid before October 1, 1990 and to enable salaried shareholders of S corporations to qualify for the deduction. The federal law was amended in 1990 to extend this deduction through December 31, 1991. Hawaii has adopted the 1989 and 1990 amendments. The federal law was amended in 1991 to extend this deduction through June 30, 1992. The federal law was amended in 1993 to retroactively extend the deduction through December 31, 1993. Hawaii has adopted the 1991 and 1993 amendments.

The federal law was amended in 1996 to retroactively reinstate the deduction for 1994 and 1995 and extends it permanently. For 1995 and 1996, the deduction is increased to 30 percent. After 1996, the deduction is increased from 30 percent to 80 percent. The increase is phased in through 2006. The federal law was further amended in 1997 to increase the deduction to 100 percent by the year 2007 and to allow self-employed persons to deduct long term care premiums even if they do not participate in an employer-provided health plan. These amendments are effective for years beginning after 1996. The law was again amended in 1998 accelerating the phase in from 2007 to 2003. Hawaii has adopted the 1996, 1997 and 1998 federal amendments.

The federal law was amended in 1996 to create a limited deduction for amounts contributed to Medical Savings Accounts. Participants and contributions are limited. The new accounts are effective for years beginning December 31, 1996. Hawaii has adopted this amendment, but only for accounts approved by the Secretary of the Treasury. The federal law was further revised in 1997 to provide that an individual can participate in a "Medicare+Choice MSA. Contributions to the account by the Secretary of Health and Human Services will not be included in the income of the account holder. Hawaii has adopted this 1997 federal amendment.

The federal law was amended in 1996 to provide a deduction for long-term care expenses, including a limited deduction for long-term care insurance premiums. This amendment is effective for tax years beginning after December 31, 1996. Hawaii has adopted this amendment for years beginning after 1998.

Federal law was amended to raise the floor on the medical expense deduction to 10% of adjusted gross income beginning in 2013 for senior citizens (age 65 or older). For tax years 2017 and 2018, the percentage is 7.5% of adjusted gross income for all taxpayers, regardless of age. Hawaii conforms to federal law.

## ¶ 407. Operating Loss Carryover
### Hawaii Law: Sec. 235-2.3, 235-7
### Federal Law: Sec. 172, 381, 382

Prior to 1967 Hawaii did not allow a net operating loss carryback and only provided for a one-year carryforward. In 1967 Hawaii conformed to the then federal provisions with the exception that no loss could be carried back to a year prior to 1967.

The federal law was amended effective for years beginning after 1975 to provide for a seven-year carryover, instead of five, for losses incurred after 1975. In addition, for losses incurred after 1975, taxpayers may elect to forgo a carryback of net operating losses. Hawaii adopted the election to forgo a carryback of net operating losses for years beginning in 1979, but did not adopt the seven-year carryover period. The Economic Recovery Tax Act of 1981 extended the federal carryover period for losses arising in tax years ending after 1975 to 15 years. Hawaii adopted this 1981 federal provision.

The federal law was amended in 1997 to limit NOL carry backs to two years and increased the carry forward to twenty years. Certain losses of small businesses and casualty or theft losses of individuals are allowed a three year carry back. The federal amendment is effective for years beginning after August 5, 1997. Carry forward of losses arising in years prior to this change are still limited to fifteen years. Hawaii adopted this 1997 federal amendment.

The federal law was amended again by the Tax Cuts and Jobs Act (P.L. 115- 97). Federal law eliminates the two-year carry back for net operating losses arising after December 31, 2017. For net operating losses incurred for years beginning after January 1, 2018, the deduction is limited to 80 percent of taxable income. The net operating loss may be carried forward indefinitely, however. Act 27, SLH 2018, provides that Hawaii law conforms to this change.

The Tax Reform Act of 1986 provides for special limitations on the use of net operating loss carryovers where there are substantial changes in corporate ownership. These new rules are effective for years beginning after Dec. 31, 1986. Hawaii has adopted the 1986 amendments. The Technical and Miscellaneous Revenue Act of 1988 further revised the loss carryover changes adopted in 1986. Hawaii has adopted the 1988 revisions. The federal law was amended in 1989 to limit the carryback of net operating losses caused by interest expense incurred in corporate equity reductions. This limitation applies to interest incurred due to transactions occurring after August 2, 1989. The federal law was amended in 1990 to limit the carryback of losses due to interest expense incurred to acquire the stock of a subsidiary. This amendment is effective for acquisitions after October 9, 1990. Hawaii has adopted the 1989 and 1990 amendments.

In computing the operating loss deduction, the Hawaii computation follows the pattern of the federal law computation set forth in Internal Revenue Code Section 172(d). In addition, there is added back to income any interest that is exempt under Hawaii law (see ¶ 302), and the loss is increased by any interest disallowed because it is related to tax-exempt interest income (see ¶ 404). As in the federal law, the Hawaii operating loss deduction is one of the deductions allowable in computing adjusted gross income.

If a corporation elects to be taxed as a "small business corporation," as explained in ¶ 602, no carryover is allowed for any year to which the election applies. This general rule has been modified by a 1991 amendment effective for the first taxable year beginning after December 31, 1989. The amendment provides that where a corporation elected S corporation status for federal but not Hawaii purposes any carryovers from pre 1990 years will be allowed in computing Hawaii S corporation taxable income for post 1989 years. The election to carryover pre 1990 losses must be made before December 31, 1992, on a timely filed S corporation income tax return for the first taxable year beginning after December 31, 1989, or an amended return filed before December 31, 1992. A copy of the election must be attached to the S corporation's return for each year to which a carryforward is carried.

### ¶ 408. Contributions to Pension and Profit-Sharing Plans
#### Hawaii Law: Sec. 235-2, 235-2.2, 235-2.3
#### Federal Law: Sec. 219, 401 to 416, 418, 419, 530

The federal law relating to pension and profit-sharing plans was amended in 1974. Extensive changes were made relating to the definition of qualified plans adopted after Sept. 2, 1974, and for 1975 and future years for plans in existence prior to Sept. 2, 1974. The federal law was amended in 1981, 1982, 1984, and 1986 to further restrict the definition of a qualified plan. Hawaii adopted the 1974 changes for years beginning in 1977 and adopted the 1981, 1982, 1984, and 1986 changes; however, the differences would not seem to matter since plans that qualify under federal law automatically qualify under Hawaii law. It is not necessary to obtain separate approval of the plan from the Hawaii Department of Taxation. One of the changes made by the 1974 federal amendments was to allow both cash and accrual taxpayers to deduct contributions to pension and profit-sharing plans made after the year-end and before the date required for filing the income tax return. Hawaii has adopted this provision for taxable years beginning in 1977.

Over the years there have been a number of differences between the federal and Hawaii deductions to retirement plans. As of Dec. 31, 1985, Hawaii has conformed to the federal rules relating to deductibility of amounts paid to retirement plans. A number of changes were made to the federal law in 1997 relating to deductions and administration of retirement plans. Hawaii has not adopted these 1997 federal amendments. Reference should be made to prior editions of this book for an analysis of the differences.

The federal law was amended in 1996 to provide for a new Savings Incentive Match Plans for Employees (SIMPLE Plans). The new rules provide for a simplified approach to deferred savings plans whereby the employee can defer up to $6,000 per year and the employer will match the employee contributions. These new plans are effective for years beginning after December 31, 1996. Hawaii has adopted this amendment.

The Tax Reform Act of 1986 amended the federal law to restrict the deduction for contributions to pension and profit-sharing plans, IRAs, 401(k) plans, and 403(b) plans. These amendments are effective for 1987 and later years. Hawaii has adopted these 1986 amendments with a provision that federal adjusted gross income will be used for purposes of computing the Hawaii deduction for contributions to an IRA.

The federal law was amended in 1996 to allow non-working spouses to make a tax deductible contribution of up to $2,000 to an IRA. This amendment is effective for tax years beginning after December 31, 1996. Hawaii has adopted this amendment.

The federal law was amended in 1997, effective for tax years beginning in 1998, to allow non-deductible contributions to a "Roth IRA," to increase the availability of IRA deductions for active pension plan participants and their spouses, and to create a new non-deductible education IRA. Hawaii has adopted these 1997 federal amendments.

Effective for years beginning in 2002 federal tax laws provided an increase in the amount that taxpayers can contribute to individual retirement accounts, Roth IRA's and 401(k) and 403(b) plans. Taxpayers 50 years and older will qualify for higher limits. Hawaii has adopted these amendments.

See ¶ 303 regarding federal rules under the Tax Reform Act of 1969, whereby certain employer payments are taxed currently to employees.

### ¶ 408a. Group Legal Services Plans
Hawaii Law: Sec. 235-7
Federal Law: Sec. 120, 501 (c) (20)

Both the federal and Hawaii laws were amended in 1976 to provide for a deduction of contributions to a group legal service plan. The Hawaii law was effective for years beginning in 1976 whereas the federal law was effective for five years beginning in 1977. The federal rule required that the plans be qualified and that they not discriminate in favor of highly paid employees. Presumably the plans will operate in the same manner as other qualified retirement plans.

### ¶ 409. Casualty Losses
Hawaii Law: Sec. 235-2.3, 235-7
Federal Law: Sec. 165, 1231

Since 1978 the Hawaii deduction for casualty losses has been the same as the federal; however, there are some differences as described below. Prior to 1978 there were differences between the federal and Hawaii laws due to timing differences in the adoption of the federal changes. Reference should be made to prior editions of this book for a more detailed discussion of the pre-1978 differences.

Hawaii law was amended in 2009 to limit individual casualty losses to amounts in excess of $100 per casualty.

See ¶ 322 regarding exclusion from income of certain insurance payments received as reimbursement for excess living expenses paid as a result of destruction (or threatened destruction) of a home by fire or other casualty.

The Tax Cuts and Jobs Act, P.L. 115-97, limited personal casualty losses for federal purposes only to losses incurred in a federally declared disaster for tax years 2018 to 2025. However, under Act 27, SLH 2018, Hawaii does not conform to the federal law. Hawaii taxpayers may continue to claim a deduction for casualty losses even if the losses were not incurred in a federally declared disaster.

### ¶ 410. Standard Deduction and Zero Bracket Amount
Hawaii Law: Sec. 235-2, 235-2.4
Federal Law: Sec. 63

Prior to 1982 the Hawaii standard deduction was 10% of adjusted gross income, with a maximum of $1,000 in the case of a return of a single person or a joint return of a married couple, and a maximum of $500 in the case of a separate return of a married person.

From 1977 to 1986 the federal law eliminated the standard deduction and instead used the "Zero Bracket Amount." Hawaii adopted the "Zero Bracket Amount" for 1982 to 1986, except that the Hawaii amounts were different from the federal amounts.

The federal law was amended in 1986 to repeal the Zero Bracket provisions for tax years beginning after 1986. The Tax Reform Act of 1986 reactivated the Standard Deduction for years beginning after 1986. Hawaii has followed the federal repeal of the Zero Bracket provisions and reinstated the Standard Deduction for 1987 and future years. Hawaii has delayed the increase in the Standard Deduction that was to go into effect for 2011 to 2013 and makes the increase permanent thereafter. The Hawaii Standard Deduction amounts, which differ from the federal amounts, are as follows:

|  | Tax Year 2009-2012 | Tax Year 2013-thereafter |
|---|---|---|
| Married persons filing jointly and surviving spouses | $4,000 | $4,400 |
| Heads of household | $2,920 | $3,212 |
| Single taxpayers | $2,000 | $2,200 |
| Married filing separate returns | $2,000 | $2,200 |

Both the federal and Hawaii laws limit the basic standard deduction for certain dependents. The federal law prior to 1998 limited the deduction to the greater of $500, indexed for inflation, or the dependent's earned income. Beginning in 1998 the federal law limits the deduction to the greater of $500, indexed for inflation, or the dependent's earned income plus $250. Hawaii limits the deduction to the greater of $500 or the dependent's earned income without any indexing for inflation.

For tax years 2008 and 2009, federal law allows the lesser of a taxpayer's real property taxes or $500 ($1,000 in the case of a joint return) to be added to the federal standard deduction. In addition, for the purchases between February 17, 2009 and December 31, 2009, sales taxes on motor vehicle purchases are also added to the federal standard deduction. Hawaii has not adopted these provisions.

## ¶ 411. Taxes Paid
Hawaii Law: Sec. 235-2.3
Federal Law: Sec. 164, 189, 216

Hawaii conforms generally with the federal law in allowing deductions for taxes paid. However, Hawaii sometimes allows a deduction for foreign income taxes, as explained below. The Tax Reform Act of 1986 repealed the federal deduction for state and local sales taxes beginning in 1987. Hawaii has adopted this 1986 federal amendment.

Beginning in 2004, Federal law allows a taxpayer to deduct either state and local sales taxes or state and local income taxes. This deduction is available through 2010. Hawaii has adopted this federal amendment. Federal income tax paid is not deductible on either the federal or Hawaii return. State and foreign income taxes, including the Hawaii tax, are deductible on both federal and Hawaii returns to the extent that foreign taxes are not taken as a credit against federal taxes.

A state or foreign tax that does not qualify for use as a credit against the Hawaii tax, because it does not meet the requirements set forth in ¶ 413, is nevertheless deductible as explained above.

The amount of Hawaii income tax deductible on the Hawaii return is the amount of the tax after applying any of the credits, except for the excise tax credit allowed to individual taxpayers. As explained in ¶ 319, the Department of Taxation has ruled that these credits are, in effect, state grants and are not taxable income. However, such credits must presumably be treated as taxable income for federal purposes; this means that the amount of Hawaii income tax deductible on the federal return is the net amount after applying any credits allowed. See also ¶ 319.

The Tax Reform Act of 1969 broadened the federal rules regarding deduction of taxes (and interest) by tenant-stockholders of cooperative housing corporations, to cover situations where a portion of the corporation's income comes from a government entity. Hawaii adopted this provision for years beginning in 1978.

Under the Tax Reform Act of 1976 the federal law was amended to limit the deduction for real property taxes paid during the construction of real property. Taxes that are not currently deducted are to be capitalized and amortized in accordance with a prescribed table set out in the Act. This federal rule differentiates between residential, nonresidential, and low income property and provided for a phase-in of the rule. Any unamortized taxes at the time the property is sold are to be added to the basis of the property. Hawaii has adopted this rule except that the rules relating to nonresidential property apply after Dec. 31, 1976; the rules relating to residential real property apply after Dec. 31, 1977; and the rules relating to low-income housing apply after Dec. 31, 1981. The federal rules were amended in

1982 to extend the construction period tax rules to corporations and again in 1984 to remove the exception for taxes incurred in the construction of residential real estate incurred by corporations. Hawaii conformed to these amendments.

For years beginning after December 31, 1986 real property taxes incurred during the construction of real property must be capitalized to the cost of the property.

Prior to 1987 the Hawaii general excise tax was deductible on both the federal and Hawaii returns as a sales tax. Reference should be made to prior editions of this book for a more detailed explanation of this deduction.

Hawaii automobile license fees are based on weight—not on value—and therefore are not classed as property taxes; this means that they are not deductible as taxes on either federal or Hawaii returns.

Federal law also provides an itemized deduction for general excise tax on sales of most new motor vehicles purchased on or after February 17, 2009 and before January 1, 2010. Hawaii has not adopted this provision.

For taxable years beginning after December 31, 2010 Hawaii eliminates the state taxes paid deduction for individual taxpayers except for single or married filing separate whose federal adjusted gross income is less than $100,000, for head of household whose federal adjusted gross income is less than $150,000 or joint or surviving spouses whose federal adjusted gross income is less than $200,000. For taxpayers who qualify to take the deduction for state taxes paid, the $10,000 limitation on the deduction under IRC 164(b)(6)—effective for tax years beginning after December 31, 2017, and before January 1, 2026—does not apply in Hawaii.

### ¶ 412. Credit Against Tax
Hawaii Law: Sec. 2
Federal Law: Sec. 33, 38, 40, 41, 42, 46 to 48, 51, 181, 852, 901 to 905

Generally, Hawaii credits must be properly claimed within twelve (12) months of year end. For example, a credit for tax year ended December 31, 20X1 must properly be claimed by December 31, 20X2. Further, even amended claims for credits may have to be filed within the twelve (12) months of year end. In *Spirent Holding Corporation and Subsidiaries v. State of Hawaii, Department of Taxation*, 216 P.3d. 1243 (7/14/09). *cert. denied*, Haw. S. Ct. 10/05/09, the Intermediate Court of Appeals held that while the taxpayer timely filed its original refund claim within twelve (12) months, it failed to timely file its amended claim for refund which increased the amount of the timely filed tax credit and which was filed beyond twelve (12) months of year end.

The Legislature adopted a special income tax credit for 1981 and future years. The credit was adopted pursuant to the 1978 Constitutional Amendment, which requires that excess state revenue be refunded to the taxpayers. The amount of the credit is multiplied by the number of qualified exemptions to which the taxpayer is entitled. In order to qualify for the credits the taxpayer need not be physically present in the state as long as the taxpayer is a resident for income tax purposes for at least nine months during the year. Additional exemptions, because of age or deficiencies in vision, hearing, or other disability, are not counted in determining qualified exemptions for the credits. Individuals who are convicted of a felony or misdemeanor and are physically confined to a prison, youth correctional facility or jail for the full taxable year are not eligible for the credit.

A taxpayer who receives dividends from a regulated investment company is allowed credit for any Hawaii tax paid by the company on undistributed capital gains that are required to be included in his return. This is the same as the federal rule, although the amount of the credit of course is different.

Hawaii has not adopted anything similar to the federal "Child Tax Credit", the "Hope Scholarship Credit", the "Lifetime Learning Credit", or the "Adoption Expense Credit."

Under a 1963 amendment, a taxpayer may receive Hawaii tax credit for his share of certain taxes paid by a corporation that is liquidating under federal Internal Revenue Code Sec. 337. This applies where the corporation is required to pay a Hawaii tax because its shareholders are not all Hawaii residents. See explanation in ¶ 710.

In *Cosmo World of Hawaii, Inc. v. Okamura,* 97 Haw. 270, 36 P.3d 814 *cert. denied,* (11/09/01), the Intermediate Court of Appeals ruled that even though the partnership of which taxpayer was a partner timely reported the capital goods tax credit allocable to the partners, the taxpayer failed to timely claim the credit within the twelve (12) month period and the court declined to adopt the informal claim doctrine and the substantial compliance doctrine.

Hawaii law was amended in 2010, subject to ratification of a constitutional amendment, to allow 5% of the year end general fund balance to be deposited into the emergency and budget reserve fund if the general fund reserves increase by 5% or more for two consecutive fiscal years. This amendment causes the general income tax credit for 2010 to be zero. Other tax credits allowed by the State of Hawaii are described in the paragraphs that follow.

Act 21 was signed into law on April 14, 2010 which provides for the express statutory ordering of income tax credit claims. As amended, Hawaii income tax law requires a taxpayer to utilize refundable income tax credits first; followed by nonrefundable income tax credits. This Act applies to tax years beginning on or after January 1, 2010.

See *Cosmo World of Hawaii, Inc. v. Okamura,* 97 Haw. 270, 36 P.3d 814 *cert. denied,* (11/09/01), the Intermediate Court of Appeals ruled that even though the partnership of which taxpayer was a partner timely reported the capital goods tax credit allocable to the partners, the taxpayer failed to timely claim the credit within the twelve (12) month period on its own tax return and thus, was not entitled to the credit.

¶ 412

## ¶ 412a.  Renewable Energy Technologies Credit
Hawaii Law: Sec. 235-12.5
Federal Law: Sec. 48

### Energy Conservation Credit

Beginning in 1976 Hawaii law provided for a tax credit for the cost of installing solar devices. The law was amended in 1981 to provide a credit for the installation of wind energy devices and heat pumps. The definition of heat pumps was amended for years beginning in 1983 to remove the requirement that the pump be used in the production of hot water in home water heaters.

The Hawaii law was amended in 1986 to extend the tax credit for solar or wind energy devices or heat pumps to ice storage systems that are installed and placed in service after Dec. 31, 1985, and before Dec. 31, 1992.

The law relating to tax credits for solar and wind energy devices, heat pumps, and ice storage systems was extensively revised for years beginning in 1990. The law now provides for a credit for each of these devices installed and placed in service after December 31, 1989.

The law was scheduled to expire on January 1, 1999, but was extended for 4 1/2 years until June 30, 2003. Most recently, the energy conservation tax credit was repealed by the Hawaii legislature in Act 18, SLH 2018, effective June 4, 2018.

### Renewable Energy Technologies Income Tax Credit

Currently, a tax credit can be claimed by individuals and corporations that file a net income tax return for every eligible renewable energy technology system that is installed and placed in service in the State during the taxable year.

For taxable years beginning after December 31, 2008, the "solar thermal energy system" and "photovoltaic energy system" classifications under prior law have been combined into a single "solar energy system" classification. The "wind-powered energy system" classification has been retained.

In general, for solar energy systems, the credit allowable is as follows:

|  | Primary Purpose of System to Heat Water for Household Use | All Others |
|---|---|---|
| Single Family Residential Property | Lesser of 35% of actual cost or $2,250 per system | Lesser of 35% of actual cost or $5,000 per system |
| Multi-Family Residential Property | Lesser of 35% of actual cost or $350 per unit per system | Lesser of 35% of actual cost or $350 per unit per system |
| Commercial Property | Lesser of 35% of actual cost or $250,000 per system | Lesser of 35% of actual cost or $500,000 per system |

In general, for wind-powered energy systems, the credit allowable is the lesser of 20% of the actual cost or $1,500 per system for single family residential property, $200 per unit per system for multi-family residential property, and $500,000 per system for commercial property.

Multiple owners of a single system shall be entitled to a single tax credit. The tax credit shall be apportioned between the owners in proportion to their contribution to the cost of the system. In the case of a partnership, S corporation, estate, or trust, the tax credit shall be determined at the entity level.

In general, if the tax credit exceeds the income tax liability of the taxpayer, the remaining unused credit can be used to offset future income tax liabilities of the taxpayer until exhausted. However, for tax years beginning after December 31, 2008, taxpayers may elect to have the excess of the credit over payments due refunded if: (a) the taxpayer reduces the eligible credit amount by 30%, and this reduced amount exceeds the amount of payments due; (b) all of the taxpayer's income is exempt from tax as income from a public retirement system or pension for past services; or (c) the taxpayer's adjusted gross income is $20,000 or less ($40,000 or less if filing a married filing joint return). The nonrefundable/refundable mechanics of this credit is further clarified in Tax Information Release 2010-10.

For tax years after January 1, 2010, Hawaii law generally requires all new single-family dwellings to include a solar water heater system. No taxpayer is allowed a credit for the portion of the renewable energy technology system required under Hawaii law that is installed and placed in service on any newly constructed single-family residential property authorized by a building permit issued on or after January 1, 2010.

Effective for tax years beginning on or after January 1, 2013, the State has adopted Administrative Rules Section 18-235-12.5-01 through 18-235-12.5-06. Please refer to Chapter 14, ¶ 1442 for a copy of these Rules.

Administrative Rule Section 18-235-12.5-01 provides definitions for the following:

1. Actual Costs

2. Commercial Property

3. Installed and Place In Service: the system is ready and available for its specific use. With respect to systems installed for residential property, all requirements will be completed and a system will be deemed to be installed and placed in service when: (1) The actual cost has been incurred; (2) all installation, including all related electrical work, has been completed; and (3) any required requests for inspection of the installation has been received by the appropriate government agency. However, if the residential installation fails to pass all the required inspections the credit is properly claimed in the taxable year in which the system passes such inspection.

4. Mixed Use Property: a property on which at least one residence is located and commercial activity takes place.

5. Multi-Family Residential Property

6. Property

7. Renewable Energy Technology System

8. Residence

9. Single-Family Residential Property

10. Standard Test Conditions

11. Total Output Capacity: the combined individual output capacities (maximum power) of all identifiable facilities, equipment, apparatus or the like that make up the renewable energy technology system installed and placed in service during a taxable year measured in kilowatts.

In Department of Taxation Announcement No. 2012-14, the definition for "installed and placed in service" was retroactively applied to single-family and multi-family residential systems which were installed and placed in service on or before December 31, 2012.

In Tax Information Release (TIR) No. 2012-01, important changes to the calculation of the renewable energy technologies income tax credit (RETITC) are highlighted. Basically, "total output capacity" is the starting point for computing the RETITC for "other solar energy systems", such as photovoltaic solar energy systems (PV systems). Since the output capacities of all installations that occur during a taxable year must be combined, the installations will not be considered separate systems simply because the installations occurred at separate times. In order to claim the RETITC for more than one system installed and placed in service on single property, each system must meet the applicable "total output capacity" requirement. For PV systems, "total output capacity" is the maximum power of the cell, module, or panel at Standard Test Conditions in kilowatts multiplied by the number of cells, modules or panels installed and placed in service during the taxable year. The maximum power of the cell, module or panel must be provided and published by the manufacturer. The "total output capacity" requirements are as follows:

1. Single-family residential property – at least 5 kilowatts per system

2. Multi-family residential property – at least 0.360 kilowatts per unit per system

3. Commercial property – at least 1,000 kilowatts per system

There are two exceptions to the "total output capacity" requirements for "other solar energy systems" provided under §18-235-12.5-03(b). The RETITC may be claimed for systems which fail to meet the applicable "total output capacity" requirement where: (1) only one system has been installed and placed in service during the taxable year on a single property, or (2) more than one system has been installed and placed in service during the taxable year and only one of the systems fails to meet the applicable "total output capacity" requirement.

Section 18-235-12.5-05 sets forth rules relating to the classification real property as "mixed-use property" for the purposes of the RETITC and allocating "actual cost" where a "renewable energy technology system" services a "mixed-use property" or multiple properties. Basically, Multiple Properties and Mixed Use Properties must allocate actual cost under any reasonable allocation method. Section 18-235-12.5-05 applies to all types of "renewable energy technology systems".

Please see TIR 2012-01 and attached Administrative Rules, copy at Chapter 14, ¶ 1442, for calculations and examples.

Claim for the credit should be filed on Form N-342 along with the income tax return.

For tax years after December 31, 2010, any individual or corporate taxpayer who is eligible to claim the Renewable Energy Credit for 10 or more systems or distributive shares of systems installed and placed in service in a single taxable year may file a composite Form N-342. Any partnership, S corporation, estate, trust, or condominium apartment association that has installed and placed in service 10 or more systems in a single taxable year may file composite Form(s) N-342A. Please see Department of Taxation Announcement No. 2012-01 at Chapter 14, ¶ 1443 for further instructions and schedules.

### ¶ 412b. Credit for Child and Dependent Care Expenses
#### Hawaii Law: Sec. 235-55.6
#### Federal Law: Sec. 21, 24

Hawaii adopted the federal rules relating to child and dependent care expenses and repealed the deduction for such expenses for taxable years beginning in 1977. The Hawaii rule follows the federal rules with two exceptions. The credit may only be claimed by resident taxpayers. Prior to 1982 the amount of the credit was 10% (5% for tax years ending before Jan. 1, 1981) of the employment related expenses. For years beginning after 1982 the applicable percentage of employment related expenses is 15% reduced (but not below 10%) by one percentage point for each $2,000 (or fraction thereof) by which the taxpayer's adjusted gross income for the taxable year exceeds $10,000. For years beginning after December 31, 1988 the adjusted gross income limitation is increased to $22,000. For years beginning after December 31, 1989 the maximum credit is increased to 25% and the minimum credit is increased to 15%. For years beginning after December 31, 2015, the credit amount that certain taxpayers may claim for expenses for household and dependent care services necessary for gainful employment has increased. The table below shows the percentages and AGI thresholds for the current credit and for the credit as amended per Hawaii Department of Taxation Announcement No. 2016-07:

| Prior Law | | As Amended | |
| --- | --- | --- | --- |
| AGI | Applicable percentage | AGI | Applicable percentage |
| $22,000 or less | 25% | $25,000 or less | 25% |
| $22,001 to $24,000 | 24% | $25,001 to $30,000 | 24% |
| $24,001 to $26,000 | 23% | $30,001 to $35,000 | 23% |
| $26,001 to $28,000 | 22% | $35,001 to $40,000 | 22% |
| $28,001 to $30,000 | 21% | $40,001 to $45,000 | 21% |
| $30,001 to $32,000 | 20% | $45,001 to $50,000 | 20% |
| $32,001 to $34,000 | 19% | over $50,000 | 15% |
| $34,001 to $36,000 | 18% | | |
| $36,001 to $38,000 | 17% | | |
| $38,001 to $40,000 | 16% | | |
| over $40,000 | 15% | | |

The federal law was amended in 1978, effective for years beginning in 1979, to allow payments to grandparents or other relatives to qualify for the credit, even though the payments are not subject to Social Security taxes. Hawaii has adopted this amendment for years beginning in 1979. The federal law was amended in 1987, effective for years beginning after 1987, to exclude expenses incurred to send a child or other dependent to an overnight camp. Hawaii has adopted this amendment.

For years beginning after December 31, 1992, the definition of household and dependent care expenses is expanded to provide that if the credit is claimed for services provided by a dependent care center located outside the state of Hawaii, the center must comply with all applicable laws, rules, and regulations of the jurisdiction in which the center is located. Prior to 1993, the credit only applied to expenses provided by a center that complied with all of the rules and regulations of Hawaii.

The Tax Reform Act of 1984 amended the rules, effective for years beginning in 1985, to allow a custodial parent to claim the credit with respect to a qualifying child even though the noncustodial parent may claim an exemption for the child. Hawaii has adopted this 1984 amendment.

Claim for the credit should be filed on Form Schedule X along with the income tax return. See Part IV for filled-in specimen forms.

## ¶ 412c. Credit for Low-Income Renters
### Hawaii Law: Sec. 235-55.7

The Hawaii law was amended in 1977 to provide a credit to low-income renters for years beginning in 1977. The credit is allowed to resident taxpayers and is equal to $20 multiplied by the number of "qualified exemptions" to which the taxpayer is entitled. The taxpayer's adjusted gross income must be less than $20,000 and he must have paid more than $1,000 in rent during the taxable year. Beginning in 1990 the adjusted gross income limitation is increased to $30,000. The law was amended, effective for tax years ending after Dec. 31, 1980, to increase the credit to $50. Where the taxpayer's adjusted gross income is reduced to zero or less than zero by deductions or losses, the taxpayer will meet the adjusted gross income requirement. The law was amended in 1990, effective for years beginning after December 31, 1989, to allow residents to claim the credit even though they have no income.

In the *Matter of the Tax Appeal of Carlynne A McCauley Musicians,* the Tax Appeal Court held that in determining the amount of rent paid the amount paid must be reduced by any rent subsidies received by the taxpayer .

"Qualified exemptions" has the same meaning as is used to determine the excise tax credit. In addition, the taxpayer must file a return to claim the credit and must not be eligible to be claimed as a dependent for federal or state income taxes by another taxpayer.

"Rent" is defined to mean the amount paid in cash by the taxpayer or his immediate family for the occupancy of the principal residence in the state. "Rent" does not include charges for utilities, parking stalls, storage of goods, yard services, furniture, etc.; rental claimed as a deduction from gross income or adjusted gross income; rental paid for use of land only; rent allowances or subsidies received; and rental of real property which is wholly or partially exempted from real property tax.

Where a rental unit is occupied by two or more individuals and more than one individual qualifies as a claimant, the claim for credit shall be based upon a pro rata share of the rent paid. If a husband and wife are entitled to file a joint return, but actually file separate returns, they may only claim the tax credits to which they would be entitled on a joint return.

The credit is deducted from the tax liability. A refund will be paid if the credit is at least $1 more than the tax. The credit is ordinarily claimed on Form Schedule X along with the income tax return. Claims must be filed within one year following the close of the taxable year involved.

## ¶ 412d. Credit for Insulation of Water Heaters
### Hawaii Law: Sec. 235-12.2

This provision expired on Dec. 31, 1984, and was formally repealed in 1988. See prior editions for a discussion of the provision.

### ¶ 412e. Credit for Fuel Taxes Paid by Commercial Fishers
Hawaii Law: Sec. 235-110.6

The law was amended in 1981 to provide a credit for Hawaii fuel taxes paid by the principal operator of a commercial fishing vessel. The credit is deducted from the principal operator's income tax liability. A refund will be made if the credit is at least $1 more than the tax. Refund claims must be filed within one year following the close of the taxable year involved. The credit is effective for years beginning in 1981. Claim for the credit should be filed on Form N-163 along with the income tax return.

A commercial fishing vessel is defined as any water vessel that is used to catch or process fish or transport fish loaded on the high seas. A principal operator means any individual or corporate resident taxpayer who derives at least 51% of the taxpayer's gross annual income from commercial fishing operations.

### ¶ 412f. Credit for Child Passenger Restraint Systems
Hawaii Law: Sec. 235-15

The law was amended in 1982 to provide a $25 tax credit for individuals who purchase one or more child passenger restraint systems. The restraint system must be in substantial conformity with specifications set forth by the federal motor vehicle safety standards in effect at the time of such purchase. A refund will be made if the credit is at least $1 more than the tax. Claims for the credit must be filed within 12 months following the year for which the credit may be claimed. A copy of the sales invoice, which states the type of child restraint system purchased, must be attached to the return. The credit is effective for years beginning after 1981.

### ¶ 412g. Enterprise Zone Credits
Hawaii Law: Sec. 209E

The Hawaii law was amended in 1986, effective April 22, 1986, to provide for tax credits to qualified businesses that do business in designated enterprise zones. A qualified business is one that begins the operation of a business within a designated enterprise zone, derives 50% or more of its gross receipts from business within the enterprise zone, and has as at least 40% of its employees individuals who meet certain low-income standards. The gross income definition was amended effective June 27, 1989, to require at least 50% of the enterprise zone establishment's gross receipts be attributable to the active conduct of a trade or business within the enterprise zone. A business that is located in an area immediately prior to the area being designated an enterprise zone may qualify if it meets the above tests and shows a 10% increase in employment of which 40% meet the low income standard. The 10% increase is reduced to 5% effective June 27, 1989.

The law was amended in 1996, effective June 18, 1996, to expand the list of service businesses eligible for the credit. The new businesses that qualify are businesses that repair ships or aircraft, provide telecommunications services, provide information technology design and production services, provide medical and health care services, but not routine medical treatment, and provide education and training services. "Telecommunications services" include terrestrial telecommunication service call centers, but not consumer services. "Call Centers" are businesses that provide services at an establishment where customers and technical support services are provided by telephone to manufacturing companies, computer hardware and software companies, credit collection services, product fulfillment services, or disaster management services. Call centers engaged in telemarketing or sales are not eligible for enterprise zone credits. The law was amended in 2000 to expand the list of qualified companies to include businesses engaged in research development, sale or production of all types of genetically-engineered medical, agricultural, or marine biotechnology products and businesses that repair assisted technology equipment. The law was further amended to allow wind farms engaged in producing electric power from wind energy for sale primarily to a public utility company for resale to the public to qualify for these benefits. The 1996 amendment repeals the requirement that 40 percent of the employees be low income employees; however, employers must now increase their full-time work force by 10 percent a year. The law was amended in 1995 to delete references to companies subject to the public services company and franchise taxes as those companies do not meet the definition of "qualified businesses." Qualified businesses must apply each year for tax credits under the Act. The law was amended, effective June 27, 1989, to require that the sale of tangible property or the rendering of services must take place within the enterprise zone in which they are sold or rendered. The tax credits that can offset the business income tax are:

| | | | | | |
|---|---|---|---|---|---|
| 1st year | 80% | 4th year | 50% | 6th year | 30% |
| 2nd year | 70% | 5th year | 40% | 7th year | 20% |
| 3rd year | 60% | | | | |

Any tax credit not usable cannot be applied to future years.

Qualified businesses are also entitled to an additional credit equal to a percentage of unemployment taxes paid. The amount of the credit follows the preceding schedule: 80 percent for the first year reduced by 10 percent each year for seven years. If a business employs persons within and without the enterprise zone, only the portion of unemployment tax paid for persons employed at qualified business establishments within enterprise zones located within the same county is used to compute the credit. There is no carryover of unused credits for credits used to offset unemployment taxes.

Partners of partnerships that qualify may claim their proportionate share of the tax credits on their personal tax returns.

¶ 412g

For qualified businesses engaged in the manufacturing of tangible personal property or the producing or processing of agricultural products, the credits described above shall continue after the seventh year at a rate of 20% for each of the subsequent three tax years.

For taxable years beginning after December 31, 2015, all EZ benefits to medical marijuana businesses are denied. See Hawaii Department of Taxation Announcement No. 2016-07.

### ¶ 412h. Food Tax Credit
#### Hawaii Law: Sec. 235-55.8

Hawaii law has for a number of years provided for consumer type tax credits. In 1974, a single credit, Excise Tax Credit, was adopted to replace several other consumer type credits. From 1987 to 1989 the Hawaii law provided for a food tax credit. The credit was equal to $45 times the number of exemptions the taxpayer claimed on his Hawaii return without regard to extra exemptions claimed for over-65 taxpayers and disabilities. In addition, every person for whom an exemption was claimed must have physically resided in the State for more than nine months during the year. Residents who were confined in jails, prisons, or correctional facilities for the entire taxable year were not eligible for the credit. Minor children receiving public support could qualify for the credit.

Beginning in 1990 Hawaii amended its law to provide for a combined food/excise tax credit. The food tax credit was increased to an amount equal to $55 times the number of qualified exemptions claimed by the taxpayer without regard to extra exemptions claimed for over-65 and disabilities. In addition to the food tax credit taxpayers were entitled to claim an excise tax credit. See prior editions of this book for an explanation of the pre-1995 application of the credit.

For years beginning after 1994, the Food/Excise tax credit has been renamed the food tax credit. The credit is equal to $27 times the number of qualified exemptions claimed by the taxpayer without the extra exemptions claimed for over 65.

"Qualified exemptions" are the regular income tax exemptions claimed for the taxpayer and his dependents, with the following special rules:

(a) Multiple exemptions are not allowed because of disability, In other words, for purposes of the tax credit, disabled taxpayers are allowed only one "qualified exemption" for themselves, even though they get extra deductions as explained in ¶ 106a. However, disabled taxpayers are allowed "qualified exemptions" for all dependents who qualify for dependency deductions for income tax purposes, even though no separate deductions for dependents are allowed to such taxpayers.

(b) The persons for whom the credit was allowed must physically reside in Hawaii for more than nine months of the year.

No credit was allowed for a dependent who dies before October 1 of the taxable year, even though a full income tax exemption is allowed for the year, since the dependent does not reside in the state more than nine months. However, the

Department of Taxation has stated that a child born after March 31 will be considered a "qualified exemption", provided the mother is a resident and physically resides in Hawaii for more than nine months of the year.

If a husband and wife were entitled to file a joint return, but actually file separate returns, they are each entitled to claim the $27 credit.

The credit needed to be claimed on a return or amended return filed within 12 months of the end of the year for which the credits are claimed. Any excess credits was not refunded to the taxpayer. The credit was treated as nontaxable income for Hawaii income tax purposes (see ¶ 319).

This credit expired on January 1, 1999 and the law was repealed in 1998.

## ¶ 412i.  Capital Goods Excise Tax Credit
### Hawaii Law: Sec. 235-110.7

For 1988 and future years, a new credit for the purchase of capital goods used in a trade or business has been added to the Hawaii law. For 1988 the amount of the credit is 3% of the cost of eligible property placed in service. For 1989 and future years, the credit is 4% of the cost of eligible property placed in service. The credit was suspended for property placed in service on or after May 1, 2009 and on or before December 31, 2009. Eligible property placed in service prior to May 1, 2009 will still be eligible for the 4% credit, as will eligible property placed in service after December 31, 2009. For periods between January 1, 1993 through December 31, 2002 any property purchased in a county in which the county general excise and use tax surcharge is in effect will be eligible for a credit of 4.5%. No credit is available for the Honolulu County Surcharge.

The determination of cost and eligibility is made with reference to the Investment Tax Credit, Recapture, and Depreciation sections of the Internal Revenue Code. Property will not qualify if it was owned or used by the taxpayer prior to 1988 or acquired from a related taxpayer. The purchase or importation of the property must have resulted in a transaction which was subject to the General Excise or Use tax provisions of the Hawaii Law. The property was deemed placed in service on the date it was acquired or available or ready for use, whichever is earlier. The law was amended, effective for years beginning after December 31, 1988, to redefine the terms placed in service and purchased. Placed in service now means the earliest of the following years; the year in which a claim for depreciation or recovery allowance with respect to the property begins or the year in which the property is put into a condition or state of readiness for a specifically assigned function. Purchase is defined to mean an acquisition of property.

The Department of Taxation issued Tax Information Release No. 88-6, which discusses the credit. See ¶ 1425 for a reprint of this release.

The credit must be claimed on a return or amended return filed within 12 months of the end of the tax year in which the credit may be claimed. Any excess credits over the taxpayer's liability will be refunded. Partners, beneficiaries of estates or trusts, and shareholders of S corporations are eligible to claim their distributive share of any credits. Landlords who reimburse tenants for purchases that otherwise qualify for the credit may claim the credit if the landlord can capitalize the purchased property, and it is not property excluded from the credit (i.e. property which is used predominantly to furnish lodging, or in connection with the furnishing of lodging). The law was amended, effective for years beginning after December 3, 1988 to provide that the determination of the credit available to partners of a partnership or shareholders of an S corporation is to be made at the partnership or corporation level.

### ¶ 412j. Low-Income Housing Tax Credit
Hawaii Law: Sec. 235-110.8
Federal Law: Sec. 42(b)

Effective for taxable years beginning after Dec. 31, 1987. Hawaii has adopted the federal low-income housing credit. The amount of the credit was equal to 30 percent of the applicable percentage of the basis of the property as determined under Internal Revenue Code Sec. 42(b) for property placed in service before July 1, 2005 (50% for property placed in service on July 1, 2005 and after). The federal law was amended in 1990 to extend the credit provision through December 31, 1991 and again amended in 1991 to extend the credit provision through June 30, 1992. The federal law was amended in 1993 to permanently extend the credit retroactive to June 30, 1992. In addition the federal law was amended to modify the various provisions of the credit law. Hawaii had not adopted the 1990, 1991, or 1993 amendments, but has subsequently adopted IRC Sec. 42.

Federal regulations require allocation of credits for income tax purposes to partners in accordance with their partnership interests. Hawaii conformed to these provisions for purposes of the Hawaii income tax law. However, for tax years beginning after December 31, 1999, these allocation provisions shall not apply to an allocation of the Hawaii low-income housing tax credit for Hawaii income tax purposes.

> **Example.** XYZ Partnership has a Hawaii partner with Hawaii income tax liabilities and two Mainland partners without Hawaii income tax liabilities. XYZ invests in a low-income housing project in Hawaii. Act 148 allows XYZ to allocate its entire State low-income housing tax credit to the Hawaii partner beginning with taxable year 2000.

For taxable years after December 31, 2016, the State tax credit is taken over five years instead of ten years, on buildings that are awarded low-income housing tax credits. This shortened period is repealed on December 31, 2021. The Hawaii Housing Finance and Development Corporation (a division of the Department of Business, Economic Development, and Tourism) continues to have primary responsibility over selection of qualified buildings and the allocation of any tax credits thereto. See Hawaii Department of Taxation Announcement No. 2016-07.

## ¶ 412k. Vocational Rehabilitation Referral Tax Credit
#### Hawaii Law: Sec. 235-55.91
#### Federal Law: Sec. 51

For years beginning after December 31, 1989 Hawaii has adopted a targeted jobs credit. The amount of the credit and the basic rules for computing the wages subject to the credit followed the provisions of Section 51 of the federal law.

In 1991 the Hawaii law was amended retroactive to October 1, 1990 and applies to vocational rehabilitation referrals. The amount of the credit is equal to 25% of the qualified first year wages paid during the tax year. The amount of the qualified first-year wages which may be taken into account with respect to any individual shall not exceed $6,000 per year. Qualified wages are defined as wages paid to an individual who is a vocational rehabilitation referral and includes only those wages paid during the first year of employment. More than one-half of the wages paid must be for services performed in a trade or business of the employer. Further wages will not include amounts paid where the employer receives federally funded payment for on the job training or where the vocational referrals substitute for striking employees.

The credit is claimed against the taxpayer's income tax liability. Any excess credits may be carried forward until they are exhausted. A claim for the credit must be filed on or before the end of the twelfth month following the close of the year for which the credits may be claimed.

Any deduction for wages paid must be reduced by the amount of the credit claimed.

## ¶ 412m. Motion Picture and Film Production Tax Credit
#### Hawaii Law: Sec. 235-17

Hawaii provides a refundable income tax credit for the "qualified production costs" incurred by a "qualified production" in the State of Hawaii. For taxable years through January 1, 2026 (as extended by Act 143, SLH 2018), the credit is 20% of the qualified production costs incurred in the City and County of Honolulu and 25% of the qualified production costs incurred in any other county in the state. If a deduction is taken for the "qualified production costs," under section 179 of the Internal Revenue Code, then no credit may be taken for those costs.

A "qualified production" includes movies, music videos, interactive games, and television programs, other than the news; public affairs programs; non-national magazine and talk shows; televised sporting events; productions that solicit funds; productions produced primarily for industrial, corporate, or institutional, or other private purposes; and pornographic productions. To qualify for the tax credit, the production must have at least $200,000 of qualified production costs; provide the state of Hawaii, at a minimum, a shared-card, end-title screen credit, where applicable; provide evidence of reasonable efforts to hire local talent and crew; and provide evidence of financial or in-kind contributions or education or workforce development efforts, in partnership with related local industry labor organizations,

¶ 412m

educational institutions, or both, toward the furtherance of the local film, television, and digital media industries. When claiming products or services acquired outside of the State, the taxpayer must show that reasonable efforts were made to secure and use comparable products or services within the State.

In general, "qualified production costs" are costs incurred by a qualified production in the state of Hawaii that are subject to Hawaii income tax or general excise tax. Examples of qualified production costs include: wages and salaries of cast, crew, and musicians; pre-production costs, such as location scouting costs; costs of set construction; purchases or rentals of props and equipment; costs of photography, sound synchronization, and lighting; airfare for flights to or from Hawaii and interisland flights; rental of vehicles and lodging for the cast and crew; and costs of editing, visual effects, music, and other post-production services. See Tax Information Release No. 2009-05 for more information regarding costs.

Beginning in the 2013 tax year, the total tax credit allowed per production was increased from $8 million per qualified production to $15 million per qualified production. Beginning in the 2019 tax year, the total film credit is limited to $35 million per year provided that if the total amount of credits applied for in any year exceeds the aggregate amount, the excess will be treated as having been applied for in the subsequent year and must be claimed in such year.

The credit must be claimed on or before the end of the twelfth month following the close of the taxable year in which the credit may be claimed. Form N-340, "Motion Picture, Digital Media and Film Production Tax Credit" must be attached to the appropriate income tax return to claim the credit. In addition, the taxpayer must pre-qualify for the tax credit and receive certification of the tax credit by the State of Hawaii Department of Business, Economic Development, and Tourism. The applicable forms are available on the website of the State of Hawaii Department of Business, Economic Development, and Tourism. The pre-qualification must be done during the development or pre-production stage of the qualified production.

Prior to the 2013 tax year, the tax credit percentages were 15% for qualified production costs in the City and County of Honolulu and 20% for qualified productions cost in the other counties of the State of Hawaii. Prior to 2006, the credit percentages were lower and different criteria were used to determine costs that qualified for the credit.

Beginning after January 1, 2018, all qualified production companies with production expenditures of $1 million or more are required to obtain an independent third-party certification of qualified production costs eligible for the film credit in the form of a tax opinion. Beginning after December 31, 2018, all qualified production companies are required to obtain a verification review by a qualified certified public accountant using procedures prescribed by the Department of Business, Economic Development, and Tourism to be submitted with the statement of qualified production costs.

The American Jobs Creation Act of 2004 added Internal Revenue Code Sec.

¶ 412m

181, which allows certain film and television productions to elect to deduct certain production expenses rather than capitalizing and depreciating such expenses. Hawaii has not adopted this rule.

## ¶ 412n. Hotel and Timeshare Remodeling Tax Credit
### Hawaii Law: Sec. 235-110.4

Hawaii provided a refundable four percent income tax credit for tax years 1999 through 2002.

The credit was applicable to the "construction or renovation costs" for a "qualified hotel facility" of a taxpayer subject to the net income tax under chapter 235, Hawaii Revised Statutes (HRS), and the transient accommodations tax under chapter 237D, HRS. A qualified hotel facility meant a hotel/condo as a defined in Section 486K-1 and included a timeshare facility or project. Taxpayers include an association of apartment owners or timeshare association.

The credit needed to be claimed on or before the end of the twelfth month following the close of the taxable year for which the credit could be claimed.A taxpayer claiming the credit could reduce the basis of property by the amount of the credit allowable and claimed under Act 195 or treat the credit as taxable income. No taxpayer that claimed this credit could claim the qualified improvement credit (see ¶ 412p).

In 2001 the law was amended to change the credit from a refundable four percent tax credit to a nonrefundable ten percent credit for cost incurred on or after November 2, 2001 though June 30, 2003. The credit will revert to the four percent refundable tax credit for costs incurred from July 1, 2003 through December 31, 2005. In 2007, this law was repealed.

## ¶ 412o. Refundable Food/Excise Tax Credit
### Hawaii Law: Sec. 253-55.85

For years beginning after December 31, 1998, Hawaii residents who were not claimed and were not eligible to be claimed by another taxpayer as a dependent are entitled to a refundable credit which was formerly called the Low Income Refundable Tax Credit. In 2007, the law was changed and the credit was renamed. In addition the adjusted gross income and credit pay out table was changed. The following is the original table:

| Adjusted Gross Income | | | Credit Per Exemption |
|---|---|---|---|
| $ 0 | under | $ 5,000 | $ 85 |
| 5,000 | under | 10,000 | 75 |
| 10,000 | under | 15,000 | 65 |
| 15,000 | under | 20,000 | 55 |
| 20,000 | under | 30,000 | 45 |
| 30,000 | under | 40,000 | 35 |
| 40,000 | under | 50,000 | 25 |
| 50,000 | and | over | 0 |

Effective July 9, 2015, and applying to taxable years beginning after December 31, 2015, the adjusted gross income and credit pay out table was changed to:

| Adjusted Gross Income for Taxpayers Filing a Single Return | | | Credit Per Exemption |
|---|---|---|---|
| $   0 | Under | $  5,000 | $ 110 |
| 5,000 | Under | 10,000 | 100 |
| 10,000 | Under | 15,000 | 85 |
| 15,000 | Under | 20,000 | 70 |
| 20,000 | Under | 30,000 | 55 |
| 30,000 | And | Over | 0 |

| Adjusted Gross Income for Heads of Household, Married Individuals Filing Separate Returns, and Married Couples Filing Joint Returns | | | Credit Per Exemption |
|---|---|---|---|
| $   0 | Under | $  5,000 | $ 110 |
| 5,000 | Under | 10,000 | 100 |
| 10,000 | Under | 15,000 | 85 |
| 15,000 | Under | 20,000 | 70 |
| 20,000 | Under | 30,000 | 55 |
| 30,000 | Under | 40,000 | 45 |
| 40,000 | Under | 50,000 | 35 |
| 50,000 | And | Over | 0 |

The resident must be physically present in the State of Hawaii for more than nine months of the year.

All claims for credit must be filed within twelve months of the end of the year for which the credits are being claimed. The law also provides that certain individuals do not qualify for the credit such as individuals confined to prison for the taxable year.

## ¶ 412p.  Qualified Improvement Tax Credit
### Hawaii Law:  Sec. 235D-2

A qualified improvement credit is allowed for capitalized cost of improvements and equipment. This law applies to costs incurred for the year beginning after December 31, 1998 and before January 1, 2006. The improvement must be of a permanent nature and be made to a qualified resort facility or a qualified general facility. A "qualified resort facility" is a facility located on property designated by zoning ordinances or the general plan as designated for resort or hotel use. A "qualified general facility" is not located on property zoned for resort or hotel use, but is property used for commercial purposes to support or service a hotel such as a golf course, golf course club house or retail complex.

The taxpayer must elect the period in which the credit will be claimed and the annual allocation of the credit which is not to exceed 10 years. The election must be made in the year the credit is claimed. Credits must be claimed within 12 months after the end of the year in which the credits were earned. Excess credits will not be refunded to the taxpayer.

If a deduction is taken for equipment, see Internal Revenue Code Section 179. No credit is allowed.

This credit may be utilized to reduce income tax, general excise tax, transients accommodation tax or the public service tax.

No credit is allowed for 1999 since this provision was enacted into law without the applicable percentage of cost being specified in the law. In 2009, this law was repealed.

### ¶ 412q. High Technology Business Investment Tax Credit for Investments in a Qualified High Technology Business (QHTB)
Hawaii Law: Sec. 235-110.9

A credit of 10% up to $500,000 of annual credit was allowed for investments in a qualified high technology business. The credit was allowed for investments made after July 1, 1999 and before January 1, 2006. The credit, to the extent unused, is allowed to be carried forward until exhausted. For this provision only, a QHTB is a business employing or owing capital or property, or maintaining an office in Hawaii where:

(1) More than

    (A) 50% of whose total business activities are Qualified Research; and

    (B) 75% of the Qualified Research must be conducted in Hawaii; or

(2) More than 75% of whose gross income is derived from qualified research; provided that this income is received from:

    (A) Products sold from, manufactured in, or produced in Hawaii; or

    (B) Services performed in Hawaii.

This law was amended in 2001 effective for taxable years 2001 through 2005. The credit is computed as follows:

In the year the investment was made, 35% of the investment up to $700,000 of tax credit per year,

    1st following year 25% of the investment up to $500,000 of tax credit,

    2nd following year 20% of the investment up to $400,000 of tax credit,

    3rd following year 10% of the investment up to $200,000 of tax credit, and

    4th following year 10% of the investment up to $200,000 of tax credit

The income tax credit is recaptured, if during the 5 year credit recognition period:

    1. The business no longer qualifies as a qualified high technology business,

    2. The business or the investment in the qualified high technology business has been sold by the taxpayer, and/or

3. The taxpayer has withdrawn his investment in whole or in part.

The amount of the recapture shall be equal to ten percent of the credit claimed in the previous two years.

The definition of qualified research has been expanded to include sensor and optic technologies, ocean sciences, astronomy, and non-fossil fuel energy related technology. Previously the definition included companies who performed research as defined in IRC Section 41(d), performing arts, biotechnology and the development and design of certain computer software.

For investments made prior to May 1, 2009, a partnership is allowed the flexibility of allocating the credits among partners without regard to their proportionate interests in the partnership. However, for investments made on or after May 1, 2009, the allocation of the credits must reflect the partners interest in the partnership.

In 2004, the law was changed to add an additional reporting requirement to assist the Department of Tax to track the credits being taken. Taxpayers must now submit Form N-318A, a statement to the Department stating the following:

• Qualified investments expended in the previous taxable year

• The amount of tax credits claimed in the previous taxable year

The Form N-318A must be submitted to the Department by March 30th of the succeeding year after the investment was made. The Department, in turn, will maintain the information submitted to them, verify the nature and amount of the qualifying investments and issue a signed certificate to the taxpayer which will include the following information:

• Verification of the information submitted,

• Qualifying investment amounts, and

• Credit amount certified for each year

Taxpayers are now required to attach the signed N-318A certification with their returns that are submitted to the Department.

Another change made in 2004 now requires economic substance and business purpose to apply to any investment made. The law outlines a presumption that a transaction will satisfy the economic substance doctrine and business purpose requirement if any special allocation of the high technology business tax credit for investments made prior to May 1, 2009 has an investment tax credit ratio of 1.5 or less of the credit for the amount invested. To the extent the ratio is between 1.5 and 2.0, the Department may review the allocation for economic substance and business purpose. To the extent the ratio is higher than 2.0, taxpayers must be prepared to substantiate the allocation ratio.

Beginning in tax year 2007, certain qualified high technology businesses are required to file an electronic annual survey (N-317) with the Department. Failure

¶ 412q

to file Form N-317 may result in a penalty of $1,000 per month, up to $6,000 for each annual survey.

For investments made on or after May 1, 2009 and on or before December 31, 2010, a claim for credits shall not exceed 80% of the taxpayer's tax liability for the taxable year in which the credit is claimed. Carryover of tax credits claimed on investments made on or after May 1, 2009 shall not be allowed in tax years 2009 and 2010. For the portion of any tax credit allowed after tax year 2010 as a result of an investment made on or after May 1, 2009, any unused credit may be carried over to a subsequent tax year in the same manner as investments made prior to May 1, 2009. In addition, investment allocation ratios greater than 1.0 of credit for every dollar invested shall not be allowed. Credits subject to the 80% limitation and prohibition against carryover shall be claimed before all other credits, including credits generated from investments made before May 1, 2009.

All claims for credit must be filed on Form N-318 within 12 months of the end of the year for which the credits are claimed. This credit is applicable for taxable years ending on or before December 31, 2010.

Form N-318 is obsolete in 2017. Refer to Form N-323, Carryover of Tax Credits, for any carryover claims of the credit.

## ¶ 412r. Renewable Fuels Production Tax Credit
### Hawaii Law: Sec. 235-110.31

Haw. Rev. Stat. §235-110.31(b) provides for a renewable fuels production tax credit against Hawaii income taxes for a taxpayer producing renewable fuels. The credit is available for a period of five consecutive years beginning with the first taxable year that a taxpayer claiming the credit begins renewable fuels production at a level of at least 2.5 billion British thermal units (BTUs) per year. (Act 143, SLH 2018, lowered the threshold from 15 billion to 2.5 billion BTUs per year for tax years before January 1, 2018.)

The credit will be applied to the taxpayer's net income tax liability for the taxable year in which the credit is properly claimed. The annual dollar amount of the credit will equal 20 cents per 76,000 British thermal units of renewable fuels using the lower heating value sold for distribution in Hawaii, provided the taxpayer's production of renewable fuels meets the threshold for renewable fuels per year. No other tax credit may be claimed for the costs related to renewable fuels production that are used to claim this credit.

The credit is capped at $3 million per taxpayer per taxable year.

In February 2018 the Department issued Tax Information Release 2018-03, which defines certain terms required to determine eligibility for and to compute the renewable fuels production tax credit. The release clarifies that:

Renewable fuels are considered "sold" when the taxpayer claiming the credit is able to substantiate that the specified quantity of the renewable fuels produced were delivered to a purchaser with no affiliation to the taxpayer and that payment for the renewable fuels was made in full to the taxpayer claiming the credit. In addition, both title and the risk of loss must be transferred to the purchaser for the sale to be complete.

"Distribution" of renewable fuels will be recognized when the renewable fuels being claimed for the credit are transferred to an external and unrelated buyer from the taxpayer producing the renewable fuels and the taxpayer can provide official transportation manifest that substantiates the delivery to this buyer.

"Renewable fuels" means fuels produced from renewable feedstocks, provided that the fuel is sold as a fuel in Hawaii and meets the relevant American Society for Testing and Materials (ASTM) International specifications or other industry specifications for the particular fuel, including but not limited to: methanol, ethanol, or other alcohols; hydrogen; biodiesel or renewable diesel; biogas; other biofuels; renewable jet fuel or renewable gasoline; or, applicable to tax years beginning after December 31, 2017, logs, wood chips, wood pellets or wood bark.

Taxpayers who seek to qualify fuels as "renewable fuels" using other industry specifications for liquid or gaseous fuels must use the industry specification that applies specifically to the type of fuel that was produced.

"Renewable feedstocks" means: (1) biomass crops and, applicable to tax years beginning after December 31, 2017, other renewable organic material, including but not limited to, logs, wood chips, wood pellets and wood bark; (2) agricultural residues; (3) oil crops, including but not limited to algae, canola, jatropha, palm, soybean, and sunflower; (4) sugar and starch crops, including but not limited to sugar cane and cassava; (5) other agricultural crops; (6) grease and waste cooking oil; (7) food wastes; (8) municipal solid wastes and industrial wastes; (9) water; and (10) animal residues and wastes that can be used to generate energy.

The Department of Business, Economic Development, and Tourism (DBEDT) will apply the aggregate cap on a first-come first-served basis. In order to administer the aggregate cap on this basis, DBEDT will allocate the credit based on the post mark date if the credit certificate is mailed; receipt date of the email transmitting the credit certificate if submitted electronically; or date stamp that DBEDT imprints upon receipt if the credit certificate is hand-delivered. To qualify for allocation, the credit certificate must be fully complete; an incomplete credit certificate will not receive a credit allocation and must be resubmitted to DBEDT. If resubmission of a credit certificate is required, the allocation priority will be based on the resubmission date, not the original submission date. If multiple taxpayers submit credit certificates with the same post mark date, email receipt date or DBEDT date stamp and the total credits requested exceeds the $3 million aggregate cap, DBEDT will apply a proportional allocation between those taxpayers who have submitted their credit certificates on the same date based on the amount of renewable fuels production.

¶ 412r

The term "year" means calendar year. The $3 million aggregate cap applies from January 1 to December 31 for each year that the credit is effective. The term "year" is not the same as the term "credit period" for the purpose of administering the credit, as DBEDT will be able to certify the credit up to one calendar year after the end of the "credit period."

If the $3 million aggregate cap is reached, DBEDT must cease certifying the credit and notify the Department of Taxation that the aggregate cap has been reached.

Applicable to taxable years beginning after December 31, 2017, every taxpayer claiming a credit must complete and file an independent, third-party certified statement, at the taxpayer's sole expense, with the Hawaii Department of Business, Economic Development, and Tourism not later than thirty days following the close of the calendar year. The statement must contain information regarding type, quantity, and value of each qualified fuel; feedstock used for each type of qualified fuel; proposed total amount of credit; cumulative amount of credit received; certain information regarding the number of employees; and number and location of all renewable fuel production facilities within and outside Hawaii. For prior taxable years, the Department is required to verify the amount of renewable fuels produced and sold, total all renewable fuels production that the Department certifies, and certify the total amount of the tax credit for each taxable year and the cumulative amount of the tax credit during the credit period.

The Department will issue a certificate to the taxpayer reporting the amount of renewable fuels produced and sold, the amount of credit that the taxpayer is entitled to claim for the previous calendar year, and the cumulative amount of the tax credit during the credit period. The taxpayer will file the certificate with the taxpayer's tax return. The amount of credits that may be certified is capped at $3 million in the aggregate.

All claims for this credit must be filed on or before the end of the 12th month following the close of the taxable year for which the credit may be claimed. Prior to production of any renewable fuels for the calendar year, taxpayers who wish to claim the credit must provide written notification to the Department of their intent to begin production of renewable fuels. Among other requirements, taxpayers are also required to file a notification 30 days prior to the start of production.

Excess credit may be carried forward until exhausted.

For partnerships, S corporations, estates, or trusts, distribution and share of the credit will be determined pursuant to IRC § 704(b)(with respect to partner's distributive share).

The renewable fuels production tax credit is effective for taxable years beginning after December, 31, 2017.

¶ 412r

## ¶ 412s. Tax Credit for Research Activities
### Hawaii Law: Sec. 235-110.91
### Federal Law: Sec. 41, 174, 280C (c)

For tax years 2013 through 2019, a refundable tax credit is available for expenses incurred in Hawaii for qualified research activities. The credit will sunset on December 31, 2019. The income tax credit is allowed to a qualified high technology business, as defined in section 235-7.3(c) of the Hawaii Revised Statutes, for qualified research activities in Hawaii equal to the credit for research activities provided by section 41 of the Internal Revenue Code. For purposes of the Hawaii credit, Internal Revenue Code section 41, as enacted on December 31, 2011, irrespective of any subsequent changes to the IRC (including those added by the Tax Cuts and Jobs Act), and section 280C(c), are operative. Therefore, unlike the prior Hawaii tax credit for research activities, the current Hawaii tax credit only applies to the increasing incremental amount of research activities. In order to claim the Hawaii credit, the taxpayer must also claim the federal credit.

To calculate the Hawaii credit, the federal tax credit amount determined under Internal Revenue Code section 41 is multiplied by a fraction, the numerator of which is the amount of eligible research expenses for research conducted in Hawaii and the denominator of which is the amount of expenses eligible for the federal section 41 tax credit. Qualified research expenses are determined under Internal Revenue Code section 41(d). See Tax Information Release No. 2013-02.

The Hawaii tax credit must be claimed on or before the end of the twelfth month following the close of the taxable year in which the qualified research expenses were incurred. The claim for the Hawaii tax credit is made by attaching to the Hawaii income tax return, Forms N-346, "Tax Credit for Research Activities" and Form N-346A, "Certified Statement of Research and Development Costs Incurred by a Qualified High Technology Business and Claim of the Tax Credit for Research Activities", including a copy of the federal Form 6765, "Credit for Increasing Research Activities", any Schedule K-1s, if applicable, and any other documents required in the instructions.

Before claiming the credit, the taxpayer must have the credit certified by the Hawaii Department of Taxation. The certification is obtained by filing the Form N-346A with the Hawaii Department of Taxation on or before March 30th of the year following the taxable year in which the qualified research activity was conducted. For fiscal year filers, the deadline is on or before the day before the last day of the third month following the close of the fiscal year. A fee applies to request certification of the credit, unless the represented credit claim is less than $25,000. The certification obtained from the Hawaii Department of Taxation on the Form N-346A must be filed with the taxpayer's income tax return to claim the tax credit.

In addition, on or before June 29th of the calendar year following the calendar year in which the credit may be claimed, the qualified high technology business that claims the credit must complete and file an electronic survey located on the website of the Hawaii Department of Business, Economic Development, and Tourism.

### ¶ 412t. Credit for Contributions to Hawaii's Public Schools
Hawaii Law: Sec. 235-110.2

For years beginning after December 31, 2001 taxpayers licensed under Chapter 444, 460J, or 464 of the Hawaii Revised Statutes may obtain a 10% tax credit on the value of in-kind services. The value of the services will be certified by the Department of Education. The amount of contribution is limited to $40,000 per taxpayer or a tax credit of $4,000. The overall amount of contribution allowed per year is limited to $2,500,000. Taxpayers who generally qualify are contractors, architects, engineers, surveyors, etc.

### ¶ 412u. Residential Construction and Remodeling Income Tax Credit
Hawaii Law: Sec. 235-110.45

A taxpayer (owner, developer, lessee) is allowed a four percent non-refundable income tax credit for residential construction and remodeling costs. The credit was applicable for years beginning after December 31, 2000 and includes costs incurred through June 30, 2002. The taxpayer may claim the credit on up to $250,000 of cost. The taxpayer may either reduce the basis of the property by the amount of credit claimed or recognize the credit as income. The credit can be claimed against the income tax liability for the taxable year when the tax credit is properly reported. To the extent the credit exceeds the income tax liability, the excess credit is carryforward to be used against future income tax liabilities until exhausted. This law was repealed in 2007.

### ¶ 412v. Drought Mitigating Facilities Tax Credit
Hawaii Law: Sec. 235-110.92

A farmer or rancher is allowed a four percent refundable tax credit on the construction cost of new drought mitigation water storage facilities or the repair or reconstruction cost of existing water storage facilities.

Construction costs are not eligible for the credit to the extent that a credit has been claimed under another provision of the law or the taxpayer received a subsidy from the federal or state government to pay for the construction cost.

The credit is available for years after December 31, 2000 through December 31, 2005. This law was repealed in 2007.

## ¶ 412w. Infrastructure Renovation Credit
### Hawaii Law: Sec. 235-110.51

A four percent non-refundable income tax credit was allowed for renovation costs incurred after December 31, 2000 through December 31, 2005. In 2004, the law was changed to extend the credit through December 31, 2010.

Renovation costs means costs incurred to plan, design, install, construct, and purchase technology enabled infrastructure equipment to provide a commercial building with technology enabled infrastructure. These costs include:

1. High speed telecommunication systems,

2. Physical security systems that identify and verify valid entry,

3. Environmental systems such as air conditioning, fire detection systems, etc., and

4. Backup and emergency electric power systems.

For renovation costs incurred on or after May 1, 2009 and on or before December 31, 2010, claims for the credit shall be limited to 80% of the taxpayer's tax liability for the taxable year in which the credit is claimed. Carryovers of tax credits claimed shall not be allowed.

## ¶ 412x. Important Agricultural Land Qualified Agricultural Cost Tax Credit
### Hawaii Law: Sec. 235-110.93

For taxable years, beginning after May 31, 2009, a taxpayer can claim a refundable tax credit for qualified agricultural costs relating to lands designated as "Important Agricultural Lands" by the Land Use Commission. No other income tax credit may be claimed for agricultural costs when this credit is claimed.

The tax credit amount equals the following:

Year 1: the lesser of: (i) 25% of qualified agricultural costs incurred after July 1, 2008, or (ii) $625,000;

Year 2: the lesser of: (i) 15% of qualified agricultural costs incurred after July 1, 2008, or (ii) $250,000;

Year 3: the lesser of: (i) 10% of qualified agricultural costs incurred after July 1, 2008, or (ii) $125,000.

Taxpayers may incur qualified agricultural costs during a tax year in anticipation of claiming the credit in a future tax year when the credit is available. The taxpayer may claim the credit in any tax year after the tax year during which the qualified agricultural costs are incurred. Form N-344, "Important Agriculatural Land Qualified Cost Tax Credit," is used to claim the credit. The credits may be claimed in consecutive or nonconsecutive tax years until exhausted. No credit shall be allowed for that portion of qualified agricultural costs for which a section 179 deduction was taken. In addition, the basis of eligible property for depreciation purposes shall be reduced by the amount of credit allowable and claimed.

The Department of Agriculture shall certify the total amount of tax credits for each tax year. The maximum amount of credits for all taxpayers that can be certified in any tax year equals $7.5 million.

Act 87 (Senate Bill 2074, S.D.1, H.D.1, C.D.1) extended the availability of this credit through the 2021 tax year.

## ¶ 412y. Capital Infrastructure Tax Credit
### Hawaii Law: Sec. 235-17.5

For taxable years beginning after December 31, 2013, a non-refundable income tax credit is provided for the capital infrastructure costs to relocate a tenant that is currently located at the former Kapalama military reservation site and will relocate to piers 24 through 28 of Honolulu harbor pursuant to the state of Hawaii's plan for the Kapalama container terminal project. The amount of the credit is 50% of the capital infrastructure costs paid or incurred by the tenant during the taxable year up to a maximum of $2.5 million in any taxable year. "Capital infrastructure costs" must be for real property and fixtures that are paid or incurred in connection with the displaced tenant's move of the tenant's current active trade or business to the tenant's new location. These costs do not include any costs for which another credit is claimed. The credit will be recaptured if within 3 years of the close of the taxable year for which the credit is claimed: (1) the displaced tenant fails to continue the line of business that it conducted on July 1, 2014; or (2) the interest in the displaced tenant, whether in whole or in part, has been sold, exchanged, withdrawn, or otherwise disposed of by the taxpayer claiming the credit. The recapture is equal to 100% of the total credit claimed in the preceding five taxable years.

Act 213, effective July 12, 2017, expands the capital infrastructure tax credit:

- Doubling the amount of credit per taxable year from $1.25 million to $2.5 million;

- Including structures, machinery, equipment, and capital assets in the definition of "capital infrastructure costs";

- Allowing any costs that cannot be used in any tax year due to the credit cap limitation to be carried over to the following year until exhausted, but in no event after December 31, 2019;

- Allowing a qualified infrastructure tenant to create Special Purpose Entity (SPE), provided that the qualified infrastructure tenant as well as all of its SPEs may claim only one credit;

- Relaxing certain IRC provisions to assist the taxpayer in obtaining financing;

- Adding as an event of recapture any qualified infrastructure tenant who fails to relocate within 90 days after executing a lease with the Department of Transportation; and

• Adding a taxpayer reporting requirement with a penalty for failure to comply

The credit is claimed on Form N-348, "Capital Infrastructure Tax Credit," which must be attached to the taxpayer's income tax return. The credit must be claimed on the appropriate tax returns with all appropriate claim forms attached on or before the end of the twelfth month following the close of the taxable year for which the credit may be claimed. The credit does not apply to taxable years beginning after December 31, 2019.

## ¶ 412z. Income Tax Credit for Converting Cesspools
### Hawaii Law: Sec. 235-16.5

For taxable years beginning after December 31, 2015, a temporary, nonrefundable income tax credit is provided for the costs incurred in converting a qualified cesspool to a septic system or to an aerobic treatment unit system, or for the cost of connecting a cesspool to a sewer system. In order to be entitled to the credit, the Department of Health must certify that the cesspool is located within 200 feet of a shoreline, perennial stream, or wetland, is located within a source water assessment program area, or is a residential large capacity cesspool. Act 182, effective July 1, 2016, applies to tax years beginning after December 31, 2015, amends the credit to allow large-capacity cesspools to qualify for a separate credit for each tax map key number associated with the large-capacity cesspool. The Department of Health must certify all credit claims, and the credit amount is 100% of qualified costs up to a maximum of $10,000 per taxpayer. The amount of tax credits certified in any given tax year cannot exceed $5 million. The credit does not apply to taxable years beginning after December 31, 2020.

Act 125, effective July 1, 2017, expands the class of cesspools for which a tax credit may be claimed on costs to upgrade them to septic systems or aerobic treatment unit systems or to connect to a sewer system. The expanded class of cesspools includes:

• A cesspool within 500 feet of a shoreline, perennial stream, or wetland

• A cesspool shown to impact drinking water supplies or recreational waters

• A cesspool certified by a county or private sewer company to be appropriate for connection to its existing sewer system

Act 133, effective July 5, 2018, eliminates the provision preventing the Department from certifying more than two residential large capacity cesspools as qualified cesspools. This change is effective for tax years beginning after December 31, 2017.

## ¶ 412aa. Organic Foods Production Tax Credit
### Hawaii Law: Sec. 235-110.94

For taxable years beginning after December 31, 2016, a nonrefundable income tax credit for qualified expenses associated with the production or handling of organic foods is created. Qualified expenses include application fees, inspection costs, fees related to arranging inspections, and costs for equipment, materials or supplies necessary for organic certification or production of organic agricultural products.

To qualify for the tax credit, a taxpayer must be a producer, handler, or handling operation as defined by federal regulations, must sell agricultural products in adherence to the federal Organic Foods Production Act, must have applied for certification in accordance with the Organic Foods Production Act, and must receive gross income from the sale of organically produced agricultural products of no more than $500,000 in the most recently reported fiscal year.

The Department of Agriculture is responsible for certifying all credit claims and may charge a fee for certification. The credit amount is 100% of qualified expenses up to a maximum of $50,000 per taxpayer. The amount of tax credits certified in any given tax year cannot exceed $2,000,000.

This is repealed on December 31, 2021. See Hawaii Department of Taxation Announcement No. 2016-07.

## ¶ 413. Credit for Taxes Paid Other States—Residents
### Hawaii Law: Sec. 235-55

Resident individuals, estates, and trusts may receive credit against their Hawaii income tax obligation for taxes paid to another state or country on income derived from sources outside Hawaii. This may apply to the tax of another state, the District of Columbia, a territory or possession of the United States, or foreign country. (In this discussion reference to "other state" should be taken to include other countries, etc.) The credit is subject to the following requirements:

(1) The tax must be a net income tax, paid on income that is also subject to Hawaii income tax.

(2) The tax must be applicable to both residents and nonresidents.

(3) The income taxed by the other state must be for the same taxable year as the year for which the Hawaii credit is being claimed.

(4) The amount of credit is limited to the amount of Hawaii income tax on income from sources without the State of Hawaii.

Net income taxes of all U.S. states and of most foreign countries are eligible for use as a credit against the Hawaii income tax liability. The Canadian withholding tax on dividends is not eligible, since it does not meet requirement 2 above; that is, it is not applicable to both residents and nonresidents.

The computation of the credit is illustrated in the following example:

|  | Worldwide Source | Hawaii Source Income |
|---|---|---|
| (a) Total gross income | $25,000 | |
| (b) Hawaii source gross income | | $10,000 |
| (c) Deductions directly attributable to income on line (b). | 1,000 | 1,000 |
| (d) Other deductions, not directly attributable to any income. | 3,000 | 1,200 |
| (e) Deduction for personal exemption | 1,040 | 1,040 |
| (f) Taxable income. | 19,960 | 6,760 |
| (g) Tax paid | 1,280 | 299 |
| (h) Limitation on credit—(1,280-299) | 981 | |

The credit for taxes paid to other states may be claimed either at the time of filing the Hawaii return, or subsequently. In either event, no credit will be allowed until the tax is actually paid to the other state. The taxpayer is required to submit a certified copy of the return of the other state and evidence of payment.

A taxpayer may obtain an extension of time for filing the Hawaii return, to enable him to pay the tax to the other state before filing his Hawaii return. If he desires to file his Hawaii return before paying the tax to the other state, he should ordinarily pay the Hawaii tax in full and claim a refund subsequently for the amount of credit. However, if he obtains the permission of the Director of Taxation, he may claim a tentative credit for the tax paid to the other state and pay his Hawaii tax accordingly.

Hawaii will allow credit for foreign income taxes only to the extent credit is not allowed against the federal tax; in other words, Hawaii will not allow as a credit the same tax allowed as a credit for the federal return. Any portion of the foreign tax not allowed as a federal credit will be allowed as a Hawaii credit, except that the credit is not allowable if the income upon which it is based is excludable or exempt for federal purposes or if the credit is allowed for federal purposes. A taxpayer claiming Hawaii credit for a foreign tax is required to submit a copy of federal Form 1116 as evidence of the amount of credit claimed on his federal return.

If the taxpayer receives a credit or refund of taxes he has paid to another state after he has claimed such taxes as a credit against Hawaii tax, he is required to report such credit or refund within 20 days to the Department of Taxation. Penalties may be imposed for failure to report within the required time and for failure to pay the resulting Hawaii tax within 10 days of notice and demand from the Department of Taxation.

¶ 413

Taxes allowed as a credit against the Hawaii tax are also allowed as a deduction in computing taxable income on the Hawaii return—see ¶ 411. Also, state and foreign income taxes that do not qualify for credit, because they do not meet the conditions set forth above, are nevertheless deductible as explained in ¶ 411.

## ¶ 414. Credit for Taxes Paid Other States—Nonresidents

Hawaii allows no credit to nonresidents for taxes paid to other states or countries. Since other states usually allow credit to their nonresidents on a reciprocal basis, Hawaii residents will usually be ineligible for such credits in other states.

## ¶ 415. Deductions Allowed Nonresidents
### Hawaii Law: Sec. 235-2.3, 235-4, 235-5

Non-residents are taxed on Hawaii sourced income. Effective for years beginning after December 31, 1998, non-residents are required to determine their Hawaii source income less directly attributable deductions. The standard deduction and personal exemptions are allowed multiplied by a ratio consisting of the Hawaii source adjusted gross income divided by their entire adjusted gross income.

## ¶ 416. Mine Exploration Expenditures
### Hawaii Law: Sec. 235-2.3
### Federal Law: Sec. 291, 615 to 617

Under both Hawaii and federal law, certain mine exploration expenditures that would ordinarily be capitalizable may be deducted or deferred at the taxpayer's election.

The federal law was amended in 1966 to provide that exploration expenditures previously deducted are to be "recaptured," taxwise, after the mine reaches the producing stage. The federal law was further amended in 1969 to revise the rules somewhat and to extend them to cover foreign and oceanographic exploration. Hawaii adopted these federal amendments for years beginning in 1978.

The federal law was amended in 1982, effective for years beginning in 1983, to provide that corporations who elect to deduct mineral exploration and developmental costs currently must reduce such expenses by 15 percent of the amount expensed. The 15% is to be amortized over a five-year period. The 15% was increased to 20% for years beginning after 1984 and increased to 30% for years ending after Dec. 31, 1986. Hawaii has not adopted these federal amendments.

## ¶ 417. Expenses of Soil Conservation, etc.
### Hawaii Law: Sec. 235-2.3
### Federal Law: Sec. 175, 180, 182

Certain expenses of soil conservation (Internal Revenue Code Sec. 175), land enrichment (Internal Revenue Code Sec. 180), and land clearing (Internal Revenue Code Sec. 182) are deductible under both Hawaii and federal law. The deduction for land enrichment expenditures was enacted in the federal law in 1960 and conformed by Hawaii in 1965. Under the Tax Reform Act of 1969, expenses of soil conservation and land clearing (but not land enrichment) may be "recaptured" when the land is sold. See ¶ 516a. Hawaii adopted this federal provision for taxable years beginning in 1977.

The federal law was amended in 1986 to limit expenses of soil and water conservation to amounts which are consistent with a plan approved by the Department of Agriculture's Soil Conservation Service or a State conservation agency. Costs that may not be expenses are costs of draining or filling wetlands or preparing land for installing and operating a pivot irrigation system. The Tax Reform Act of 1986 also repealed the deduction for land clearing expenses, except for routine brush clearance and ordinary maintenance activities. The new soil and water conservation rules are effective for amounts paid or incurred after Dec. 31, 1986, in tax years ending after that date. The new rules for land clearance expenses are effective for amounts paid or incurred after Dec. 31, 1985, in tax years ending after that date. Hawaii has adopted these federal amendments.

## ¶ 418. Alimony
### Hawaii Law: Sec. 235-2.3
### Federal Law: Sec. 215

The Hawaii law conforms to the federal law in the deduction for alimony and other periodic payments that are includable in the gross income of the spouse. For divorces and separation agreements executed before December 31, 2018, alimony is includable in the spouse's Hawaii income if (1) the spouse is a Hawaii resident, or (2) the spouse is a nonresident and the contributing spouse is a resident and the payments are attributable to Hawaii property (see ¶ 309).

The federal law was amended to make alimony payments a deduction in arriving at adjusted gross income as opposed to an itemized deduction. This federal provision applies to years beginning after 1976. Hawaii has adopted this federal rule.

The Tax Reform Act of 1984 amended the alimony rules for decrees and agreements executed after 1984. The 1984 amendments eliminate the 10-year periodic payment rule, require that alimony payments must terminate at death of the payer, and prevent so-called front loading of alimony payments. Hawaii has adopted the 1984 amendments. The Tax Reform Act of 1986 further amended the federal law to reduce the six-year front loading rule to three years. The 1986 amendments apply to agreements executed after Dec. 31, 1986, and to pre-1987 agreements modified after 1986. Hawaii has adopted this 1986 amendment.

The Tax Cuts and Jobs Act, P.L. 115-97, amended the treatment of alimony payments. For divorces and separation agreements executed after December 31, 2018, alimony is no longer deductible by the payor. Alimony received is no longer included in the income of the payee. Hawaii conforms to this amendment.

Effective for divorce or separation instruments executed or modified after 2018, the Tax Cuts and Jobs Act of 2017 (P.L. 115-97) denies the deduction for alimony and separate maintenance payments by the payor, the inclusion of such payments in the gross income of the payee and the special rules for alimony trusts. Hawaii conformed to these federal changes related to alimony.

### ¶ 419. Child and Dependent Care Expenses
Hawaii Law: Sec. 235-2
Federal Law: Sec. 44A

The deduction for child and dependent care expenses was repealed for years beginning in 1977. See prior editions of this book for an explanation of the law for years prior to 1977. See ¶ 412b for an explanation of the credit for child and dependent care expenses.

### ¶ 420. Moving Expenses
Hawaii Law: Sec. 235-2.3
Federal Law: Sec. 217

Both Hawaii and federal law allow deduction of expenses of moving to a new job. Prior to 1987 both federal and Hawaii law provide that moving expenses are deductible in computing adjusted gross income, so they can be deducted in addition to the standard deduction. The federal law was amended in 1986 to provide that for 1987 and future years moving expenses are deductible from adjusted gross income to arrive at taxable income. Hawaii has adopted this 1986 federal amendment. The federal law was amended in 1988, effective for years beginning after Dec. 31, 1986, to provide that the 80 percent limitation on meals that are deductible as moving expenses is to be applied at the employee level. Hawaii has adopted this 1988 amendment. Prior to 1970 the Hawaii rules (except for employees moving out of Hawaii—see below) were the same as the federal.

The federal deduction for moving expenses has been modified for expenses incurred after December 31, 1993. The mileage limitation has been increased to 50 miles from 35 miles. The cost of meals will not be an allowable deduction and expenses incurred in buying and selling a residence will no longer be an allowable deduction. Finally, for years beginning after December 31, 1993, moving expenses will be a deduction in arriving at gross income as opposed to being an itemized deduction. Hawaii has adopted these new rules. In Hawaii Tax Information Release No. 93-6, the Department of Taxation has stated that the full amount of the animal quarantine fee is deductible as a moving expense.

The following federal changes, effective in 1970, were adopted by Hawaii, effective in 1975:

1. The required increase in the distance between the taxpayer's former residence and his job is changed from 20 miles to 50 miles.

2. The rule that requires the employee to work at least 39 weeks in the new

location in the year following the move is modified, and is given broader application.

3. The scope of allowable expenses is extended to include house-hunting trips, temporary living expenses, expenses of selling a former residence or settling a lease obligation, and expense of purchasing or leasing a new residence. Ceiling limitations are placed on the deductibility of some categories of expense.

4. The moving expense deduction is extended to self-employed individuals.

5. Moving expense reimbursements from employers are includable in gross income (see ¶ 321), but withholding of tax on such reimbursements is not required where it is anticipated that the reimbursed expenses will be deductible.

The maximum dollar limitation on the deduction for expenses of house-hunting trips and temporary quarters, and qualified residence sale, purchase, or lease expenses has been increased to $3,000 from $2,500, of which no more than $1,500 (formerly $1,000) may be for expenses of house-hunting trips and temporary quarters. Hawaii adopted these federal rules for years beginning after 1976.

The Hawaii tax return instructions state that moving expenses will not be allowed where a taxpayer moves to a new job outside Hawaii and thereby ceases to be a "resident" of Hawaii (see ¶ 109).

Moving expenses were eliminated by the Tax Cuts and Jobs Act, P.L. 115-97, for federal purposes for tax years 2018 to 2025. However, under Act 27, SLH 2018, Hawaii does not conform to the federal law. Hawaii taxpayers may continue to claim a deduction for moving expenses.

Taxpayers claiming a deduction for moving expenses should file with their return Form N-139, Moving Expenses. See Part V for filled-in specimen form.

### ¶ 421. Mileage Expenses for Operating a Passenger Automobile
Hawaii Law: Sec. 235-2.3

Hawaii adopts the IRS optional standard mileage rates for employees, self-employed individuals, or other taxpayers to use in computing deductions for operating a passenger automobile for business, charitable, medical, or moving expense purposes. The standard mileage rates which follow the IRS rates are as follows, beginning January 1, 2018:

| | |
|---|---|
| Business | 54.5 cents per mile |
| Medical or Moving | 18 cents per mile |
| Charitable | 14 cents per mile |

These are the rates beginning January 1, 2019:

| | |
|---|---|
| Business | 54.5 cents per mile |
| Medical or Moving | 18 cents per mile |
| Charitable | 14 cents per mile |

To claim the allowable standard mileage for business purposes, use the 2017 federal Form 2106—"Employee Business Expenses" or federal Form 2106-EZ— "Unreimbursed Employee Business Expenses," as the case may be. If you do not have to file either Form 2106 or 2106-EZ, see the federal instructions form Form N-11 or N-15 to properly claim the deduction.

To claim the allowable standard mileage for charitable or medical purposes, refer to the federal instructions for Form 1040 (Schedule A—"Itemized Deductions"). The allowable standard mileage amount must be shown on Schedule A.

Hawaii Form N-139—"Moving Expenses" must be used to claim the deduction for moving expenses.

## ¶ 422. Depletion
### Hawaii Law: Sec. 235-2, 235-2.2, 235-2.3
### Federal Law: Sec. 291, 611 to 614, 636

The federal rules for cost and percentage depletion are applicable generally to Hawaii tax. The federal law was amended in 1964, 1966, 1969, and 1975. These changes were not adopted by Hawaii until 1978. The federal law was amended in 1986 to exclude lease bonuses and advance royalties from the computation of gross income for purposes of computing depletion. This 1986 amendment is effective for amounts received after Aug. 16, 1986. Hawaii has adopted this 1986 federal amendment.

The federal law was amended in 1990, effective for years beginning after December 31, 1990 to raise the net income limitation on percentage depletion from 50% to 100% of net income. In addition percentage depletion may be increased from 15% to a maximum of 25% for certain marginal production. Hawaii has adopted these 1990 amendments.

The Tax Reform Act of 1984 eliminated the distinction between primary and secondary or tertiary production after 1983. Prior to this change the percentage depletion allowance for secondary and tertiary oil production was to expire at the end of 1983. Hawaii has adopted this change.

The Revenue Act of 1964 repealed the "operating unit" rule in the computation of percentage depletion on oil and gas wells. This rule allowed certain arbitrary aggregation of operating mineral interests in different parcels of land, resulting in some cases in a larger depletion allowance under the 50% of-net-income limitation. Hawaii adopted the 1964 federal amendment for years beginning in 1977. Federal law was amended in 1966 to increase percentage depletion rates on certain shells, clay, and shale. Hawaii adopted the 1966 federal amendment for years beginning in 1978.

The Tax Reform Act of 1969 made important changes in federal depletion rates and rules. Percentage depletion on oil and gas was reduced from 27 1/2% to 22%, for taxable years beginning after Oct. 9, 1969. Rates were also revised on many other minerals. Allowance of percentage depletion was extended to brines extracted from certain salt lakes. New rules were provided for computing depletion on oil shale. Rules were provided for sale of carved-out oil production payments and so-called ABC transactions, whereby what was formerly treated as a sale is now treated as a loan (applicable generally to transactions after Aug. 6, 1969). The Tax Reduction Act of 1975 repealed the percentage depletion allowance for certain oil and gas wells, effective Jan. 1, 1975. Hawaii has conformed to these federal amendments for years beginning in 1978. The federal law was amended in 1982, effective for years beginning after 1983, to reduce the corporate percentage depletion deduction for domestic and foreign iron ore and coal. The federal law was amended in 1982, effective for years beginning after 1983, to further reduce the corporate percentage depletion deduction for domestic and foreign iron ore and coal. Hawaii has adopted these new federal rules.

It should be borne in mind that, even though Hawaii follows generally the federal depletion rules, the amount of the Hawaii depletion deduction may be different from the federal because of a difference in the cost basis of the property involved or because of a difference in the computation of net income on which the percentage depletion limitation is based.

### ¶ 423. Bad Debts
Hawaii Law: Sec. 235-2, 235-2.2, 235-2.3
Federal Law: Sec. 166, 291, 585

The Hawaii law regarding bad debts is the same as the federal law, except for the 1969 federal amendments described below.

The Tax Reform Act of 1986 amended the federal rule to eliminate the reserve method of deducting bad debts for taxpayers other than financial institutions. This amendment is effective for tax years beginning after Dec. 31, 1986. The amendment provides for any balance in the reserve account to be taken into income ratably over a four-year period. Hawaii has adopted this 1986 amendment.

The federal law was amended in 1966 to permit dealers in property to set up a bad debt reserve to cover certain debt obligations that they have sold with a guarantee of collection. This federal law provides detailed rules for setting up an initial reserve in a "suspense account," permits deductions for certain additions to the reserve and reductions in the "suspense account," and requires reporting of income under certain conditions of increase in the "suspense account." Hawaii adopted these federal provisions for years beginning in 1978. The federal rule was repealed for years beginning after 1986. Hawaii has adopted the repeal.

Under the Tax Reform Act of 1969, federal rules were provided for bad debt reserves of certain financial institutions, applicable to taxable years beginning after July 11, 1969. These rules apply to banks, small-business investment companies, business development corporations, mutual savings banks, savings and loan associations, and cooperative banks. The federal law was amended in 1982, effective for years beginning in 1983, to further reduce the bad-debt deduction of financial institutions. Hawaii has not adopted these federal provisions.

The Tax Reform Act of 1976 provides that where a noncorporate taxpayer sustains a loss arising from the guarantee of a loan he will receive the same tax treatment as that provided for a loss from a direct loan. Prior to this amendment a noncorporate taxpayer was entitled to ordinary loss if he guaranteed a business loan for a noncorporate borrower. The 1976 amendment puts the guarantor in the same position as if he were the original borrower. Hawaii adopted this new federal rule for taxable years beginning in 1977.

### ¶ 424. Amortization of Pollution Control Facilities
Hawaii Law: Sec. 235-2.3, 235-11
Federal Law: Sec. 169, 291

Hawaii adopted the federal provisions under Section 169 of the Internal Revenue Code for years beginning in 1988. Prior to 1988, Hawaii had its own provisions which paralleled the federal provisions except for the effective dates of each law.

Federal law applies to facilities completed or acquired after Dec. 31, 1968; Hawaii law applies only to those completed or acquired after Dec. 31, 1969. Federal law was effective for taxable years beginning on and after Jan. 1, 1969; Hawaii law was effective for years beginning on and after Jan. 1, 1970.

The federal law was amended in 1982, effective for years beginning in 1983, to provide that corporations who elect the rapid amortization of pollution control facilities must reduce the cost of the facility by 15%. The 15% portion of the basis is then eligible for depreciation under the ACRS rules. Hawaii has not adopted this federal rule.

### ¶ 425. Farm and Hobby Losses
Hawaii Law: Sec. 235-2.3
Federal Law: Sec. 183, 278, 280A, 1252

Since 1977, Hawaii has followed the federal rules which restrict the tax benefits of farm or hobby losses. Prior to 1977, there were differences in the two laws due to differences in the effective dates. Reference should be made to prior editions of this book for a discussion of these differences.

The Tax Reform Act of 1976 provided new federal rules to determine deductions attributable to vacation rental homes. If the home is rented for less than 15 days, then no deductions are allowed and no income derived from such rental is includable in gross income. If the property is rented for more than 14 days during a year and is used for personal purposes by the taxpayer owner, then the deductions attributable to the rental home may be limited depending on the amount of personal use by the taxpayer. These new federal rules specifically provide that deductions attributable to rental income may not exceed the gross income derived from the rental home if the home is used by the taxpayer for the greater of 15 days or more than 10% of the number of days during the year for which the home is rented. The Revenue Act of 1978 amended the federal rules to provide that the vacation rental rules do not apply to property that is the taxpayer's principal residence. This change is effective for years beginning in 1976. Hawaii adopted the 1976 federal rules effective for years beginning in 1977, and adopted the 1978 change for years beginning in 1979.

### ¶ 425a. Loss Limitations
**Hawaii Law: Sec. 235-2.2, 235-2.3**
**Federal Law: Sec. 465, 704 (d)**

The Tax Reform Act of 1976 introduced new federal rules that limit the amount of loss which a taxpayer can deduct in a given year. These rules limit the loss deduction from certain activities to the amount that the investor has at risk. These rules are effective for 1976 and later years and apply to all taxpayers except regular corporations. The rules apply to the following activities: holding, producing, or distributing motion picture films or videotapes; farming, except for tree farming; equipment leasing; and oil and gas exploration. The federal law was amended in 1978 to expand the list of activities except real estate. Hawaii adopted the 1976 changes for years beginning in 1977, and adopted the 1978 changes for years beginning in 1979. The federal law was amended in 1980 to make several technical changes to the loss limitation rules. Hawaii adopted these 1980 amendments for years beginning in 1981.

The Tax Reform Act of 1986 extended the at risk rules to real estate placed in service after Dec. 31, 1986. Hawaii has adopted this amendment.

The federal partnership rules were amended, effective in 1976, to provide that a partner's share of partnership losses is limited to the amount of the partner's investment that he actually has and will have at risk in the partnership. Real estate partnerships are excluded from this new rule. In addition the federal rules were amended in 1976 to provide that a partner may only share in the income or loss for the portion of the year that he is a member of the partnership. The Revenue Act of 1978 repealed this provision for years beginning in 1979. Hawaii adopted the 1976 loss limitation rules effective for years beginning in 1977, and adopted the 1978 amendments for years beginning in 1979.

### ¶ 425b. Passive Activities
**Hawaii Law: 235-2.3**
**Federal Law: Sec. 469**

The Tax Reform Act of 1986 created a new class of activities referred to as passive activities. The Act provides, except for a limited phase out rule, that losses from passive activities may only offset profits from other passive activities. To the extent that losses cannot be deducted in a current year, they may be carried forward to future years and used to offset profits from passive activities or can be deducted if the activity that generated the loss is sold or transferred. Hawaii has adopted the 1986 amendments, with the added provision that federal adjusted gross income is to be used to determine the limitation on rental activities.

The Technical and Miscellaneous Revenue Act of 1988 adopted technical amendments to the Passive Activity rules retroactive to years beginning after Dec. 31, 1986. These amendments deal with the treatment of gain from installment sales, the active participation rule for rental property, exemption of vacation homes from the passive activity rules, and distributions of a passive activity interest by an estate or trust. Hawaii has adopted these 1988 amendments. The federal law has been amended to eliminate from the passive activity rules losses on rental real estate where the taxpayer satisfies certain material participation rules. This amendment is effective for taxable years beginning after December 31, 1993. Hawaii has adopted this amendment.

## ¶ 426. Illegal Payments, etc.
### Hawaii Law: Sec. 235-2.3
### Federal Law: Sec. 162, 186

Under the Tax Reform Act of 1969, revised in 1971, federal law prohibits the deduction of (1) bribes or illegal kickbacks to public officials, (2) bribes or kickbacks to other than government officials, under certain conditions, (3) fines and penalties for violation of any law, and (4) two-thirds of treble damage payments under the Clayton antitrust law. Hawaii adopted these federal provisions, effective Jan. 1, 1975.

The federal law was amended in 1982 to provide that the legality of payments made after Sept. 3, 1982, to foreign government officials will be determined under the Foreign Corrupt Practices Act of 1977. Hawaii has adopted this federal change.

The Tax Reform Act of 1969 also provided a new federal rule for the recipient of damages for patent infringement, breach of contract or fiduciary duty, or Clayton Act violations. This rule permits the deduction of certain losses relating to the damages received. Hawaii adopted this federal provision for years beginning in 1978.

Hawaii does not conform to the federal exceptions for restitution payments, court-ordered payments in a suit in which no governmental entity is a party, and amounts paid as taxes due.

## ¶ 427. Corporate Losses on Worthless Stock of Subsidiary
### Hawaii Law: Sec. 235-2.3
### Federal Law: Sec. 165 (g) (3)

The Hawaii law was amended to provide that for years beginning in 1977, loss from worthlessness of stock of an 80% owned subsidiary is deductible as an ordinary loss, not subject to capital loss limitations. This is the same as the federal rule. For years prior to 1977, the Hawaii law was the same as the pre-1970 federal law, which required ownership of the subsidiary to be at least 95%.

## ¶ 428. Cost of Removing Barriers for Handicapped and Elderly Persons
Hawaii Law: Sec. 235-2.3
Federal Law: Sec. 44, 190

Under the Tax Reform Act of 1976, a special deduction was provided for the cost of removing architectural and transportational barriers to the handicapped and elderly. The maximum deduction available in any year is $25,000. This rule is effective for taxable years beginning after 1976 and ending before 1980. Hawaii adopted this federal rule for years beginning in 1977.

The Tax Reform Act of 1984 reinstated this provision for expenditures incurred in taxable years beginning after 1983 and before 1986. In addition, the maximum deduction was increased to $35,000. Hawaii has adopted the 1984 amendment. The Tax Reform Act of 1986 has extended this provision indefinitely. Hawaii has adopted this 1986 federal amendment. The federal law was amended in 1990, effective for years beginning after November 5, 1990, to reduce the deduction to $15,000. In addition the federal law provides for a credit for certain expenditures to remove barriers to handicapped individuals. To the extent the expenditures qualify for this credit then no deduction for the expenditure is allowed, Hawaii has adopted the 1990 amendment relating to the deduction but has not adopted the credit provisions.

## ¶ 429. Amortization of Start-up Expenditures
Hawaii Law: Sec. 235-2.3
Federal Law: Sec. 195

The federal law was amended in 1980 to provide an election to amortize start-up expenditures paid or incurred after July 29, 1980, in taxable years ending after that date. The expenses are to be amortized over a period of not less than 60 months. Hawaii adopted this federal provision for years beginning in 1981.

The American Jobs Creation Act of 2004 amended this provision to provide an election to deduct up to $5,000 of start-up and $5,000 of organizational expenditures in the taxable year in which the trade or business begins. However, each $5,000 amount is reduced (but not below zero) by the amount by which the cumulative cost of start-up or organizational expenditures exceeds $50,000, respectively. Start-up and organizational expenditures that are not deductible in the year in which the trade or business begins are amortized over a 15-year period. Hawaii has adopted this amendment.

The 2010 Small Business Jobs Act further amended this provision to provide an election to deduct up to $10,000 of start up expenditures for tax years beginning in 2010. The $10,000 amount is reduced (but not below zero) by the amount by which the cumulative cost of start up expenditures exceed $60,000. Start up expenditures that are not deductible for the tax year beginning in 2010 are still required to be amortized over 15 years. Hawaii has adopted this increased expensing election.

## ¶ 430. Individual Housing Accounts
### Hawaii Law: Sec. 235-5.5

The Hawaii law was amended in 1982, effective for years beginning after 1981, to provide individual taxpayers with a deduction from gross income for contributions to an individual housing account. The amount of the deduction cannot exceed $5,000 in any one taxable year, and the accumulated deductions cannot exceed $25,000. For years beginning prior to 1993, married couples are limited to the $5,000 annual and $25,000 accumulated deductions whether they file a separate return or a joint return. For years beginning after December 31, 1992, married couples may deduct up to $10,000 in any one year. However, the total accumulated deductions are still limited to $25,000.

For years beginning after December 31, 1992, if any amounts are distributed from an account within 365 days from the date a contribution was made to the account then the deduction for that contribution is disallowed.

Individual Housing Accounts are accounts trusteed by banks, savings and loans, or credit unions that are chartered or supervised under federal or state laws and whose accounts are insured by a federal or state agency. Effective April 29, 1994, depository financial services loan companies have been added to the accepted list of depository institutions. The financial institution must actively make residential real estate loans to hold trusteed accounts.

Individuals may establish an account only if they have never owned their own principal residence. To the extent that funds from an account are used to purchase the individual's first principal residence, the distribution will be exempt from tax. Any distributions from an account that are not used to purchase an individual's first principal residence will be included in gross income in the year received. In addition, a penalty tax of 10% of the distribution will have to be paid. Exemptions are provided for distributions received because of death or total disability. If the funds are used to purchase a first principal residence and the residence is later sold, the amount of the fund used to purchase the residence will be included in income in the year the residence is sold, and in addition a 10% penalty will be added to the taxpayer's tax, however if the individual has reported all of the distribution as income prior to the sale of the residence then the 10% penalty will not apply. If a taxpayer who has an individual housing account subsequently marries a person who has or has had an interest in residential property, then the account must be distributed and included in income in the year of the marriage. The 10% penalty will not apply in this circumstance.

The law was amended in 1990 to provide that beginning in 1990 distributions from an individual housing account must be reported as income over a 10 year period. If the residence, purchased with the proceeds, is sold within the 10 year period the balance of unreported income must be included in taxable income in the year the residence is sold, and the 10% penalty will apply. Individuals, who purchased a residence with proceeds from an individual housing account prior to January 1, 1990, may elect to have the new 10 year spread apply.

¶ 430

The Department has issued administrative rules relating to Individual Housing Accounts (Sec. 18-235-5.5). These rules are very detailed, and readers should refer to them for specific examples.

Individuals who have established individual housing accounts before January 1, 1990 and who have not purchased a final residence may elect to have the income reporting requirements in effect when their individual housing account were established. In addition, the ten percent penalty will be added to their gross income rather than their tax liability. This amendment is effective for years after December 31, 1996.

### ¶ 431. Exceptional Tree Deduction
#### Hawaii Law: Sec. 235-19

In 2004, a new law was enacted to allow for a tax deduction by individuals for an exceptional tree. An exceptional tree is defined to be one that has historic or cultural value or because of its age, rarity, location, size, esthetic quality or endemic status, is worth preserving. In order to take the deduction of a maximum $3,000 per tree for amounts paid during the year, the tree must be designated as exceptional by a county arborist.

### ¶ 432. Gambling Losses
#### Hawaii Law: Sec. 235-2.4(e)

Hawaii law conforms to the federal law allowing the deduction for gambling losses to the extent of gambling winnings. In 2009, the law was amended to disallow any deduction for gambling losses but this law was retroactively repealed for all years so that Hawaii has continuously conformed to the federal law.

The Tax Cuts and Jobs Act, P.L. 115-97, amended IRC 165(d) so that all otherwise deductible expenses connected to an individual's gambling activity fall within the definition of "losses from wagering transactions." Thus these deductions are limited by the amount of gambling winnings. Hawaii conforms to this amendment.

### ¶ 433. Earned Income Tax Credit
#### Hawaii Law: Sec. 235-55.75

In 2017, a new law was enacted to allow a state nonrefundable earned income tax credit (EITC) equal to 20 percent of the federal EITC allowed and properly claimed under Section 32, IRC, and reported on the taxpayer's federal income tax return. The state EITC applies to taxable years beginning after December 31, 2017.

### ¶ 434. Healthcare Preceptor Tax Credit
#### Hawaii Law: Sec. 235-110.25

Act 43, SLR 2018, establishes an income tax credit for advanced practice registered nurses, pharmacists, and physicians who supervise volunteer-based supervised clinical training rotations. The credit is equal to $1,000 per rotation supervised by the taxpayer, up to a maximum of $5,000 per taxpayer per year. Additionally, the credit is subject to an aggregate cap of $1,500,000 per year. Act 43 is effective June 13, 2018 and applies to taxable years beginning after December 31, 2018.

Act 43 also establishes the Preceptor Credit Assurance Committee. The Committee certifies all claims for the credit and issues taxpayers a certificate verifying the number of rotations supervised. The Department is authorized to require taxpayers to furnish this certificate to claim the credit. The Committee is also tasked with ceasing certifications if total claims for certification reach the aggregate cap during any year.

## ¶ 435. Home Acquisition (Mortgage) Interest
### Hawaii Law: Sec. 235-2.4

The Tax Cuts and Jobs Act, P.L. 115-97, limited the mortgage interest deduction to only the interest for acquisition debt up to $750,000. This limitation applies to acquisition debt incurred after December 14, 2018. However, under Act 27, SLH 2018, Hawaii does not conform to the federal law. Hawaii taxpayers may continue to claim a deduction for interest for mortgages up to $1 million.

# CHAPTER 5

## INCOME TAX
## SALES AND EXCHANGES

### ¶ 501. Sales and Exchanges—General Rules—Tie-in with Federal Law
Hawaii Law: Sec. 235-2.3
Federal Law: Sec. 1001

Gain or loss on disposition of property is subject to tax except where the transaction is specifically exempt. The amount of the gain or loss is the difference between the basis of the property and the amount realized. Generally,

Hawaii follows the federal rules to determine whether a transaction is taxable or exempt; however, there are some differences, as explained in this chapter. Amendments made during 1978 and 1979 to the Hawaii law provide that where the federal and Hawaii laws were different prior to 1979, the adjustments required by the pre-1979 Hawaii law should be used to determine the Hawaii basis of property.

Even where a sale or exchange is taxed under both laws, the amount taxed may be different because of a difference between the Hawaii cost basis and the federal basis for the property. Situations where such differences exist are explained in this chapter.

Under the Tax Reform Act of 1969, the federal law provides that certain term interests in property are considered to have a zero basis; the result is that the entire amount received on sale of such interests is taxed. This provision applies to: (1) life interests in property, (2) interests for a term of years, and (3) income interests in trust. Hawaii adopted this federal amendment, effective Jan. 1, 1975.

### ¶ 502. Special Rules Relating to Effect of Certain Transactions Prior to 1958
Hawaii Law: Sec. 235-3
Federal Law: Sec. 358, 362, 453, 1011 to 1019

Where a corporate organization, reorganization, or distribution took place prior to 1958, it might have been tax exempt under the federal law but taxable under Hawaii law. In such a case, the basis of the property received in the transaction, for federal tax purposes, reflects the fact that the transaction was tax-exempt. If the property is disposed of under the Hawaii law in effect after 1957, use of the federal basis in determining the taxable profit would result in double taxation in Hawaii. To avoid such double taxation, the taxpayer is permitted to increase his basis for Hawaii tax purposes by the amount of income that was recognized for Hawaii tax purposes in the prior transaction. The Hawaii regulations include detailed examples of transactions of this type.

There are also special rules regarding treatment of installment payments received on pre-1958 sales of real estate and securities. Under prior Hawaii law there was no tax on capital gains from the sale or exchange of real property held in fee simple, or stocks, bonds, and similar securities. If such a transaction is being reported on the installment basis for federal income tax purposes, the installments are of course subject to federal tax in the year received. Under the Hawaii law, however, the installments are not subject to tax, since the sale took place at a time when it was not taxable. See also ¶ 520.

### ¶ 503. Exchange of Property for Like Property
Hawaii Law: Sec. 235-2.3, 235-3
Federal Law: Sec. 1031

Under Federal Code Section 1031, there is no tax on profit realized when property held for productive use or investment is exchanged for property of a like kind. This rule applies to Hawaii tax under the current law. Under the Hawaii law prior to 1958, however, some such transactions were taxed for Hawaii purposes even though they were exempt from federal taxes.

The 1984 Tax Reform Act restricted the use of so-called "Starker" exchanges of property. The new law imposes (1) a 45-day deadline on identifying the substitute like-kind property and (2) a 180-day deadline on receipt of the exchange property. The new rules are effective for exchanges taking place after July 20, 1984. The 1984 Reform Act also prohibited tax-free exchanges of partnership interests after 1984. Hawaii has adopted these 1984 changes. The Technical Corrections Act of 1985 clarified the 45-day rule. Hawaii has adopted this clarification.

In a case where the prior exchange was taxed by Hawaii but not by the federal government, and the property received in the exchange is disposed of under the present Hawaii law, use of the federal basis to compute the Hawaii taxable income would result in double taxation. To avoid such double taxation, the taxpayer is permitted for Hawaii tax purposes to increase the basis of the property by the amount of income taxed in the prior exchange.

As a result of the Tax Reform Act of 1969, federal law contains a special provision regarding the application of the like-kind exchange rule to livestock. This provision applies retroactively, and states that livestock of different sexes is not property of like kind. Hawaii adopted this provision for tax years beginning Jan. 1, 1975.

The federal law was amended, effective for exchanges occurring after July 10, 1989, to trigger gain recognition when property is exchanged with a related party and either party disposes of the property within two years of the transfer. The 1989 federal amendment prohibits exchanges of U.S. property for foreign property. Hawaii has adopted these amendments.

The federal law was amended in 1997 to exclude the exchange of depreciable property used predominately in the U.S. for depreciable property used predominantly outside the U.S. The amendment is effective for transfers after June 8, 1997 in tax years ending after June 8, 1997. Hawaii has adopted this 1997 federal amendment for transfers after June 8, 1997.

The Tax Cuts and Jobs Act, P.L. 115-97, limits the like-kind exchange tax deferral to real property not held primarily for sale, effective for exchanges completed after December 31, 2017, unless the exchanged property is disposed of or received on or before December 31, 2017. Hawaii conforms to this provision.

### ¶ 504. Basis of Stock Where Stock Rights Involved
Hawaii Law: Sec. 235-2.3, 235-3
Federal Law: Sec. 307

Where a corporation distributes nontaxable stock rights, and the value of the rights is less than 15% of the value of the stock, the stockholder has an option as to the determination of the basis of the rights. He may elect to have the basis of the rights be zero, or he may allocate the basis of the stock between the stock and the rights received.

Where a taxpayer has made, or now makes, such an election for federal tax purposes, the election is binding for Hawaii tax purposes also. No separate election is required (or permitted) for Hawaii tax.

## ¶ 505. Basis Where Consolidated Returns Have Been Filed
### Hawaii Law: Sec. 235-2.3
### Federal Law: Sec. 1051

Under federal law the basis of property of corporations that have filed consolidated returns is sometimes determined by reference to the treatment of the property in the consolidated return. Prior to 1969 Hawaii law did not permit consolidated returns; therefore, the special provisions for determination of basis of property where consolidated returns have been filed have no application to the Hawaii tax prior to 1969.

Beginning in 1969, as explained in ¶ 708, consolidated Hawaii returns are permitted. The Hawaii law incorporates the federal law by reference and is intended to conform closely with it, so the federal basis provisions presumably will be used for Hawaii tax purposes so far as applicable. However, there will be continuing differences between Hawaii and federal basis of property that were involved in transactions prior to 1969 between corporations included in a consolidated federal return. In addition, there will be differences where some members of the federal consolidated group are not included in the Hawaii consolidated group. The Revenue Act of 1987 added a provision to the consolidated rules relating to the adjustment of basis of stock in subsidiaries where intercompany dividends are paid. This provision is effective for dispositions of stock after Dec. 15, 1987. Hawaii has adopted this provision.

## ¶ 506. Basis of Improvements by Lessee
### Hawaii Law: Sec. 235-2.3
### Federal Law: Sec. 1019

Where a lessee's improvements are received by a lessor upon termination of a lease, no taxable income is realized by the lessor under present Hawaii and federal law. In years prior to 1958, the value of such improvements was sometimes taxed for Hawaii tax purposes even though not for federal.

If property received in such a situation is now disposed of and the federal basis of the property is used to determine the taxable income, there would be double taxation of income by Hawaii. To avoid such double taxation, the Hawaii law permits the lessor to increase the federal basis by the amount of income previously taxed in Hawaii. The adjustment must of course take into account depreciation of the property.

### ¶ 507. Basis of Certain Depreciable Property
Hawaii Law: Sec. 235-2.3
Federal Law: Sec. 1016

The federal law contains special rules to give relief in certain cases where a taxpayer has deducted in loss years depreciation in excess of the amount properly "allowable." Where no tax benefit was received from the excess of "allowed" depreciation over "allowable" depreciation, the taxpayer is permitted to add the excess back to the basis of the properly. These rules also apply to the Hawaii tax.

In these exceptional cases, there may have been a difference between Hawaii and federal tax in the amount of depreciation allowed or the amount allowable. Where such a difference did exist, proper adjustment must be made to the federal basis for Hawaii tax purposes.

### ¶ 508. Basis of Certain Accounts Receivable
Hawaii Law: Sec. 235-2.3
Federal Law: Sec. 1011

An account receivable has a "basis" for tax purposes if it has been purchased or has been reported as income.

An account receivable (referred to in the tax law as an "obligation") may have a basis for federal tax purposes because it represents income reported in the federal return. It does not have a corresponding basis for Hawaii tax purposes, however, unless the income was also reported for Hawaii tax.

### ¶ 509. Basis of Property Transmitted at Death
Hawaii Law: Sec. 235-2.2, 235-2.3, 235-3
Federal Law: Sec. 1014, 1015

Prior to 1977 the basis (to the transferee) of property transmitted at death was the fair market value at date of death. This rule applied to property acquired by bequest or inheritance, and also to property acquired from a decedent in other ways such as by a transfer in trust to take effect at death.

The Tax Reform Act of 1976 made extensive revisions to the federal estate and gift tax rules. One of the changes was to provide a carryover of the decedent's basis, with certain exceptions. These rules were to apply to estates of decedents dying after Dec. 31, 1976. A special "fresh start" rule shelters pre-1977 appreciation. The Revenue Act of 1978 postponed the federal carryover basis rules until 1980. Hawaii adopted the 1976 federal rules for years beginning in 1977, and adopted the Revenue Act of 1978 postponement. Even though Hawaii adopted the federal carryover rules, it is possible for the Hawaii carryover basis to be different from the federal, if the decedent's federal basis was different from his Hawaii basis. The federal "carryover basis" rules were repealed in 1980, but with an exception that an election can be made to use the carryover basis rules for property passing from a decedent dying after 1976 and before Nov. 7, 1978. The election had to be made by July 31, 1980. Hawaii adopted this repeal provision in 1980.

The Hawaii basis may be different from the federal in some unusual cases involving other than a direct transfer at death; the Hawaii regulations provide special rules for these situations. Also, the Hawaii basis may be different where the federal estate tax was based upon the value of the property at the "optional" valuation date (now six months after death; where death occurred prior to Jan. 1, 1971, one year after death). In such cases the federal basis of the property is the value at the optional valuation date; however, since the Hawaii inheritance tax had no optional valuation date, the Hawaii basis is the value at date of death.

Hawaii repealed the inheritance tax, effective June 30, 1983. In its place an estate tax was adopted for estates of decedents dying after June 30, 1983. Under the estate tax, the basis of the property will be the same as the basis determined for federal purposes for decedents determined under section 1014 of the Internal Revenue Code.

In Hawaii Department of Taxation Announcement No. 2011-21 the law was clarified to state that Hawaii did not adopt the election mechanism in Section 1022 for persons dying during 2010 and therefore all persons dying in 2010 will receive a step-up in basis under Section 1014 of the Internal Revenue Code. Therefore, there may be a difference in the basis for Hawaii and federal income tax purposes of property acquired from persons dying in 2010 by bequest, devise or inheritance, if the decedent's estate elected to not be subject to the federal estate tax and follow the modified adjusted carryover basis rules provided in section 1022 of the Internal Revenue Code, instead of the Internal Revenue Code section 1014 step-up basis rules, for federal tax purposes.

## ¶ 510. Capital Gains and Losses
**Hawaii Law: Sec. 235-2.3**
**Federal Law: Sec. 582, 1001, 1044, 1045, 1091, 1092, 1201, 1202, 1211, 1212, 1221 to 1223, 1231, 1232, 1233, 1234, 1234A, 1243, 1253, 1256, 1259**

The Hawaii rules regarding capital gains and losses are generally the same as the federal rules, however, there have been some differences in prior years and these differences may affect capital loss carryovers. The differences are explained below.

The federal law dealing with the classification of long-term capital gains was extensively revised in 1997. The new federal law created three different holding periods: twelve months or less, more than twelve months but not more than eighteen months, and more than eighteen months. A fourth holding period begins after the year 2000 and applies to property held for more than five years. Hawaii has not adopted these new federal holding periods or the corresponding rates.

The federal law was amended in 1997 to require a taxpayer to recognize gain, but not loss, upon entering into a constructive sale of any appreciated position in stock, a partnership interest, or certain debt instruments as if the position was sold. An exception applies to transactions closed within thirty days after the close of the tax year. This provision will affect so-called short sales against the box. It is effective for transactions entered into after June 8, 1997. Hawaii has adopted this 1997 amendment.

The federal law was also amended in 1997, effective after August 5, 1997, to provide that if a taxpayer enters into a short sale of property and that property becomes substantially worthless then gain is recognized as if the transaction had been closed when the property became worthless. Hawaii has adopted this 1997 federal amendment.

Under the Tax Reform Act of 1969, certain transactions are denied capital gain treatment under federal law. This applies to (1) grant of a franchise, trade-mark, or trade name, and (2) sale of letters, memoranda, or similar property by a person whose personal efforts created them or for whom they were prepared by another, or by someone who receives them from such person by gift. These provisions became effective on various dates in 1969 and 1970. Hawaii adopted these provisions, effective Jan. 1, 1975.

Under the Tax Reform Act of 1969, federal long-term capital gain treatment does not apply (1) to the sale of cattle and horses acquired after 1969 unless they have been held for two years, and (2) to the sale of other livestock acquired after 1969 unless they have been held for one year. Hawaii adopted this federal provision, effective Jan. 1, 1975. For years prior to 1975, the pre-1970 rules apply for Hawaii tax purposes (generally, required holding periods were one year and six months, respectively).

A taxpayer may elect to forgo the preferential treatment of capital gain income and have the capital gain income treated as ordinary investment income. This will result in a higher limit for investment interest deductions. The federal provision is effective for years beginning after December 31, 1992. Hawaii has adopted this federal provision.

The federal law was amended in 1993 to allow non-corporate shareholders to exclude up to 50% of the gain realized on the disposition of qualified small business stock which was held for five years or more and which was issued after August 10, 1993. Hawaii has adopted this federal provision. The exclusion of gain has been increased to 60% for qualified stock purchased after December 21, 2000. Hawaii has not adopted these changes or any other increase in the percentage of gain excluded.

The federal law was amended in 1993 to provide for an election by individuals and C corporations to defer gain on the sale of publicly traded securities by investing the proceeds within 60 days in a Specialized Small Business Investment Company (SSBIC). There are limits on the amount of gain which can be deferred on an annual basis and a lifetime limitation. This new federal rule applies to sales on or after August 10, 1993 in tax years ending on or after August 10, 1993. Hawaii adopted this federal amendment. The Tax Cuts and Jobs Act, P.L. 115-97, however, disallows the rolloever of gain on publicly traded securities into SSBICs, effective for sales after December 31, 2017.

¶ 510

Under the Tax Reform Act of 1969, the federal rules for taxing banks on sales of bonds were revised. The new federal rules, applicable generally to years beginning after July 11, 1969, provide that gains or losses of financial institutions on sale or exchange of bonds are to be treated as ordinary income or loss. "Financial institutions" include banks, savings and loan associations, business development companies, and small-business investment companies. Hawaii adopted this federal change for years beginning on or after Jan. 1, 1975. Prior to 1975 Hawaii followed the pre-1969 federal rules.

Under the Tax Reform Act of 1969, effective in 1970, federal law permitted only 50% of excess of net long-term capital losses to be deducted from ordinary income. Under the Tax Reform Act of 1976, the maximum deduction was increased to $2,000 for years beginning in 1977 and $3,000 for years beginning after 1977. Under Hawaii law the pre- 1970 rules prevailed through Dec. 31, 1974; 100% of long-term capital loss can be deducted from ordinary income, up to a maximum of $1,000 on either a joint or a separate return. Hawaii adopted the 1969 federal rules beginning in 1975, and adopted the 1976 federal rules for years beginning in 1977.

Under both Hawaii and federal law, certain types of transactions are lumped together to determine whether they will be treated as capital gains or losses or as ordinary gains and losses (Internal Revenue Code Sec. 1231). The Hawaii rules were the same as the pre-1970 federal rules. Under the Tax Reform Act of 1969, certain casualty losses must be included with other losses and gains under Internal Revenu Code Sec. 1231 to determine whether there is a net loss or a net gain on all the transactions included in the Sec. 1231 computation. If there is a net loss, the casualty losses will be treated as ordinary losses; if there is a net gain, the casualty losses will be treated as capital losses to be offset against capital gains. See also ¶ 409. Hawaii conformed to this federal amendment, effective for tax years beginning Jan. 1, 1975.

The Revenue Act of 1978 amended the federal law to increase the net capital gains deduction from 50% to 60% on sales or exchanges after Oct. 31, 1978. Hawaii adopted this provision for years beginning in 1979. The federal law was amended in 1980 to clarify the capital gains deduction rules so that they apply to all gains received after Oct. 31, 1978, even though the sale or exchange took place before Oct. 31, 1978. Both federal and Hawaii tax forms have been designed to reflect this change. Hawaii adopted the 1980 amendment for years beginning in 1981. The Tax Reform Act of 1986 repealed the capital gain deduction, effective for years beginning after 1986. Hawaii has adopted the 1986 federal amendments with a special provision that allows a deduction of 55% of capital gains received prior to April 1, 1987. The federal law was amended in 1988 to provide that the wash sale rules will apply to options. This amendment is effective for transactions occurring after Nov. 10, 1988. Hawaii has adopted this change.

The federal law was amended in 1966 to provide special rules for capital

¶ 510

gains and losses on "straddle options" in securities trading. Hawaii adopted these special rules for years beginning in 1978.

The Hawaii tax treatment of a lump-sum distribution from a qualified employee's pension or profit-sharing plan may be different from the federal. If such a distribution constitutes a pension for past services, it is completely exempt from Hawaii tax under the pension exemption discussed at ¶ 303, although it is subject to federal tax, under the special rules applicable to such payments. To the extent it does not constitute a pension for past services, it is subject to Hawaii tax. Prior to 1975, Hawaii used the federal rules in effect before the Tax Reform Act of 1969; this meant that the amount taxable by Hawaii was treated as long-term capital gain, provided the conditions regarding timing of the distribution, etc., were met. The Tax Reform Act of 1969 substantially reduced the capital gains benefits available for distributions. These rules applied for federal purposes to distributions made between 1970 and 1973. Hawaii adopted the Tax Reform Act of 1969 rules for distributions made after Dec. 31, 1974. In 1974, the federal law was again amended for distributions made in 1974 and the future years. The federal law was amended in 1976 for distributions made in 1976 and future years to provide an election to treat the entire distribution as ordinary income. Hawaii adopted the 1974 and 1976 federal changes for years beginning in 1978.

The Pension Reform Act of 1974 provides that certain lump-sum distributions from pension and profit-sharing plans will not be includable in gross income if the distribution is transferred to an "Individual Retirement Account" or another qualified pension or profit-sharing plan. The transfer must take place on or before the 60th day after the day on which the employee received such property. The federal law was amended in 1978 to liberalize the tax-free rollover of lump-sum distributions to IRAs. Hawaii adopted the 1974 rule for years beginning after Dec. 31, 1975, and adopted the 1978 amendment for years beginning in 1979.

The federal law was amended in December 1970 to permit long-term capital gain treatment where certain property received from a decedent is sold within six months (now one year) after his death; this is accomplished by providing that in such cases the property is deemed to have been held for more than one year. Hawaii adopted this provision for years beginning in 1978.

The Economic Recovery Tax Act of 1981 extensively revised the federal rules relating to the recognition of gain or loss on commodity straddles. The Tax Reform Act of 1984 expanded these rules to stock and stock options and expanded the "mark to market" rules introduced in 1981. The federal rules were also changed in 1981 to treat part of any gain or loss on the disposition of certain U.S. government bonds issued at a discount as a short-term capital gain or loss. The new rules apply to bonds acquired or positions entered into after June 23, 1981. Hawaii adopted the 1981 and 1984 federal rules, including the federal effective dates. The federal law was amended in 1993 to include

¶ 510

all tax exempt bonds and all market discount bonds in the market discount rule regardless of when such bonds were issued. This federal amendment applies to all bonds purchased after April 30, 1993. Hawaii has adopted this rule.

Since 1981 both federal and Hawaii law have treated the cancellations, lapses, expirations, and terminations of certain capital assets as a sale or exchange. The federal law was amended in 1997 to expand the coverage of this provision to all property which is a capital asset in the hands of the taxpayer. The 1997 federal amendment is effective for terminations more than 30 days after August 5, 1997. Hawaii has adopted this 1997 federal amendment.

The Revenue Reconciliation Act of 1993 amended the federal law to treat certain transactions entered into after April 30, 1993 as "conversion transactions." A conversion transaction is an arrangement in which substantially all of the taxpayer's expected return is attributable to the time value of the taxpayer's net investment. If a transaction falls within the definition, then part of the gain will be treated as ordinary income computed by using an applicable federal interest rate. Hawaii has not adopted this amendment.

The federal law was amended in 1993 to exclude 50 percent of the gain from the sale of qualified small business stock held for more than five years. Hawaii has adopted this amendment.

The federal law was amended in 1997 to allow an election to defer the gain on the sale of qualified small business stock held for more than six months if the proceeds are rolled into the acquisition of other qualified small business stock within sixty days from the date of sale. The 1997 federal amendment is effective for sales after August 5, 1997. Hawaii has adopted this 1997 federal amendment.

See ¶ 307 for a discussion of the application of the original interest discount rules to stripped preferred stock acquired after April 30, 1993.

The federal law was amended in 1982 to require that where bonds stripped of their coupons are sold after July 1, 1982, an allocation of basis must be made between the bond and the stripped coupons. This is to prevent artificial losses from the sale of stripped bonds. Hawaii has adopted this federal provision.

Section 301 of Public Law 110-343 provides that the gain or loss from the sale or exchange of any applicable preferred stock by any applicable financial institution shall be treated as ordinary income or loss. Hawaii has not adopted this provision.

See ¶ 427 for special rule regarding corporate losses on worthless stock of subsidiary.

CAPITAL LOSS CARRYOVERS

Both Hawaii and federal law allow corporations a five-year carryover of unused capital loss. Federal law permits a 10-year carryover on certain "foreign expropriation capital losses." Hawaii has not adopted this special provision. Under the Tax Reform Act of 1969, corporations (with some exceptions) are also allowed a federal three-year capital loss carryback, starting with 1970 losses. Hawaii law provides for no capital loss carryback. Hawaii has adopted the federal restrictions enacted in 1971 regarding use of carryovers by an acquiring corporation. The Hawaii amendment is effective Jan. 1, 1975.

Both Hawaii and federal law allow taxpayers other than corporations an unlimited carryover of unused capital loss. Although the two laws are now the same, the carryover may be different because of a difference in effective dates or because of federal rules enacted in 1969. The federal law was changed from a five-year to an unlimited carryover in 1964; Hawaii law was made to conform in 1965. Federal law provides that any loss carried over to the first year beginning after 1963 is to be treated as a short-term loss; Hawaii law provides that any loss carried over to the first year beginning after 1964 is to be treated as a short-term loss.

The federal computation of capital loss carryover was revised for 1970 and subsequent years to reduce the benefit of a long-term carryover from 100% to 50%; Hawaii adopted these new federal rules for years beginning in 1975. This federal reduction was repealed for years beginning after 1986. Hawaii has adopted the federal repeal.

The Tax Reform Act of 1984 repealed the special treatment accorded pre-1970 capital loss carryovers. Beginning in 1987, such losses, instead of being short term, will be long term or short term depending upon their status when incurred. Hawaii has adopted this 1984 amendment; however, the amount of the Hawaii carryover may be different because of different effective dates as explained in the previous paragraph.

The Hawaii loss carryover may also be different from the federal because of differences in the amounts of capital gains or losses in the period during which the net loss occurred. Such differences may be due, for example, to a difference in basis of property sold, such as the possible difference on inherited property explained in ¶ 509. Also, the Hawaii carryover will be different where the federal carryover comes from a period prior to the time the taxpayer became a resident in Hawaii, since Hawaii will not permit a carryover from such prior period.

Where years prior to Jan. 1, 1958 (effective date of present Hawaii law) are involved in the carryover computation, the amount of the Hawaii loss carryover may be different from the federal. For years prior to 1958, the following items were excluded from the Hawaii capital loss carryover computation:

(1) All capital gains and losses from property owned outside the Territory.

(2) Gains and losses which were taken into account in computing taxable income under prior Territorial tax law.

(3) No deduction was made for the $1,000, or lesser amount, that was allowed under federal law as a deduction against ordinary income.

¶ 510

## ¶ 510a. Capital Loss Carryover / Qualified High Technology Business
### Hawaii Law: Sec. 235-2.45(f)

Both Federal and Hawaii law allow corporations a five-year carryover of unused capital losses. Hawaii tax law extends the five-year capital loss carryover period for qualified high technology businesses to fifteen years for Hawaii income tax purposes.

## ¶ 510b. Gain on Sale of Partnership Interests
### Hawaii Law: Sec. 235-26, 255-1
### Federal Law: None

The Hawaii law was amended in 1989, to provide that a gain or loss from the sale of a partnership interest is to be allocated to Hawaii based upon the ratio of the partnership's total original cost of tangible property located in Hawaii to the original cost of the partnership's total tangible property, determined at the time of the sale. If more than 50 percent of the partnership's assets consist of intangibles then any gain or loss on the sale of an interest in the partnership is allocated to Hawaii based upon the Hawaii sales factor for the prior taxable year. This rule is effective for sales occurring after December 31, 1988.

## ¶ 511. Involuntary Conversions, Sale and Replacement of Residence
### Hawaii Law: Sec. 235-2.1, 235-2.2, 235-2.3, 235-3
### Federal Law: Sec. 121, 1033

Prior to the 1997 federal law changes, an involuntary conversion of property and sale and replacement of a residence were treated the same under Hawaii and federal law except as noted below. This means that any gain realized was deferred and was carried over as an adjustment to the basis of the new property.

The federal law was amended in 1997 to repeal the rollover provisions of Internal Revenue Code Section 1034 on the sale or involuntary conversion of a residence. Under the new federal provisions, which are effective for sales and exchanges after May 6, 1997, the first $250,000 of gain, $500,000 for married persons filing a joint return, is excluded from income. The exclusion applies if during the five-year period ending on the date of the sale the property was owned and used by the taxpayer as the taxpayer's principal residence for periods aggregating two years of more. The exclusion does not apply if during the two-year period ending on the date of the sale there was any other sale or exchange by the taxpayer to which the exclusion applied. There are special rules for married taxpayers and taxpayers who sell their residence because of a change in employment. Hawaii has adopted this 1997 federal change for sales on or after May 7, 1997. There may be differences in the basis of the residence between federal law and Hawaii law purposes for out-of-state taxpayers who acquired their residence before May 7, 1997. See subsequent discussions for further details.

The regulations provide special rules for unusual situations where transactions of this type occurred before 1958 and proceeds of the transaction were received in 1958 or later years.

Under the Tax Reform Act of 1968, the federal law was amended to extend by one year the allowable replacement period for involuntarily converted property. This applies where disposition of the converted property occurs after Dec. 30, 1969. The federal law was amended in 1976 to provide for a three-year replacement period for real property. The three-year rule applies to condemnations begun on or after Oct. 4, 1976. Hawaii adopted the two-year rule, effective Jan. 1, 1975, and the three-year rule, effective Jan. 1, 1977. The federal law was amended in 1993 to provide special rules for taxpayers whose principal residence is involuntarily converted due to a Presidentially declared disaster. The rules provide for an extension of the replacement period to four years, no gain will result from the receipt of insurance proceeds from personal property which was part of the residence's contents and were not scheduled in the insurance policy. These new rules are effective for disasters for which a Presidential declaration is made on or after September 1, 1991. Hawaii has adopted these new rules.

The federal law was amended in 1996 to provide that businesses or investment property that is involuntarily converted as a result of a post 1994 Presidentially-declared disaster will be treated as similar or related in service or use to any tangible property of a type held for productive use in a trade or business. This provision is effective for disasters occurring after December 31, 1994. The federal law was also amended in 1996 to provide that where stock of a corporation, which owns property to replace involuntarily converted property, is acquired both the stock basis and the basis of the corporation's assets must be reduced to reflect any unrealized gain on the conversion. This provision is effective for involuntary conversions occurring after August 20, 1996. Hawaii has adopted these 1996 amendments.

The federal law was amended in 1997, effective for involuntary conversions occurring after Jun 8, 1997, to deny non recognition by individuals on purchases from related parties where there is a realized gain in excess of $100,000. Hawaii has adopted this 1997 federal amendment.

The federal law was amended in 1997, effective for sales or exchanges after December 31, 1996, to treat forced sales of livestock due to floods or other weather conditions as involuntary conversions. Hawaii has adopted this 1997 federal amendment.

Prior to 1977, there were differences between the federal and Hawaii law as to the replacement period on the sale and replacement of a residence. The Tax Reduction Act of 1975 changed the federal rule to allow an 18-month period to acquire a new residence after the sale of an old residence, or if the new residence is constructed by the taxpayer, then the replacement period is 24 months. The Revenue Act of 1978 liberalized the 18-month period to allow for more than one sale during the 18-month period if the sale is due to a business-related move by the taxpayer. This amendment is effective for sales after July 27, 1978. The Economic Recovery Tax Act of 1981 amended the federal rule to extend the replacement period to 24 months for the sale of an old residence where the sale is made after Jan. 19, 1980. Hawaii adopted the 1975 federal change for years beginning in 1977, adopted the 1978 change for years beginning in 1979, and adopted the 1981 federal amendment for sales made after Jan. 19, 1980. The federal law was amended in 1988 to allow nonrecognition of gain on the sale of a residence where one's spouse dies after the sale of the old residence and before the purchase of the replacement residence. This provision is retroactive to sales and exchanges after Dec. 31, 1984. Hawaii has adopted this amendment.

Prior to May 7, 1997 when a person purchased a home in Hawaii to replace a former home outside the state, his Hawaii basis for the new home may be different from his federal basis. In such a case the cost of the new home was reduced by the deferred gain on the old home for federal purposes; however, there was no such reduction for Hawaii purposes, because Hawaii has no jurisdiction until the person becomes a resident.

Example:

Jones sold his home in California, before he moved to Hawaii, at a profit of $20,000. After moving to Hawaii, and within a year of the sale of his old home, he bought a home in Hawaii for $150,000. His federal tax basis for the new home is $130,000 ($150,000, less $20,000 deferred gain); his Hawaii tax basis is $150,000 (cost).

For sales and exchanges of principal residences after December 31, 2008, any gain allocated to periods of nonqualified use is not excluded from gross income for federal purposes. The amount of gain allocated to periods of nonqualified use is the amount of gain multiplied by a fraction the numerator of which is the aggregate periods of nonqualified use during the period the property was owned by the taxpayer and the denominator of which is the period the taxpayer owned the property. Nonqualified use means any period after January 1, 2009 during which the property is not used by the taxpayer, the taxpayer's spouse, or the taxpayer's former spouse as a principle residence. Hawaii has adopted this provision.

Federal law was amended to exclude the discharge of qualified principal residence indebtedness from income. This exclusion applies to indebtedness discharged before January 1, 2013 and has been extended to January 1, 2018. Hawaii has conformed to this provision through the date of the annual conformity bill.

## ¶ 511a. Sale of Residence by 55-Year-Olds
### Hawaii Law: Sec. 235-2.3, 235-3
### Federal Law: Sec. 121

The Revenue Act of 1978 amended the federal law to allow any taxpayer who is at least 55 years or older a one-time exclusion of the first $100,000 of gain on the sale of taxpayer's principal residence. This federal rule applied to sales after July 26, 1978. Hawaii adopted this rule for years beginning in 1979.

The Economic Recovery Tax Act of 1981 increased the exclusion to $125,000 for sales which take place after July 20, 1981. Hawaii has adopted this 1981 federal change. The reader should refer to prior editions of this book for differences between federal and Hawaii rules for years prior to 1979.

The federal law was repealed effective for sales or exchanges made on or after May 6, 1997. See ¶ 511 for a discussion of the revised federal exclusion which applies to all sales or exchanges of a principal residence after May 6, 1997. Hawaii has adopted the 1997 federal changes.

## ¶ 512. Exchange of U.S. Bonds
### Hawaii Law: Sec. 235-2.3
### Federal Law: Sec. 1037

Under a 1959 amendment to the federal law, certain U.S. obligations issued under the Second Liberty Bond Act may be exchanged tax-free for newly issued obligations, under authorization of the Secretary of the Treasury. This applies to taxable years ending after Sept. 22, 1959. It has been applied to exchanges of certain Series E, F, and J bonds for Series H, where it has the effect of deferring interest income.

Hawaii adopted this provision for years beginning in 1978. However, to the extent the federal law operates to defer interest income, there should be no effect on Hawaii income tax, since interest on U.S. bonds is exempt from Hawaii tax (see ¶ 302).

## ¶ 513. Transactions Involving Foreign Corporations
### Hawaii Law: Sec. 235-2.3
### Federal Law: Sec. 367. 1246 to 1249

The federal law was extensively amended in 1962 to provide new rules for certain transactions involving foreign corporations in an effort to prevent tax avoidance. The transactions involved include sale or exchange of: (a) stock of a foreign investment company; (b) stock of other foreign corporations where the taxpayer owns 10% or more; and (c) patents, copyrights, etc. The general purpose of these provisions is to deny capital gain treatment. Hawaii adopted these provisions for years beginning in 1978.

Tax-free-type exchanges involving corporations created or organized in a foreign country lose their exempt status unless prior to the exchange it is established that the plan is not one having as a principal purpose the avoidance of income taxes. Prior to 1978, the Hawaii rule was the same as the federal, except for two 1971 federal amendments that have not been adopted by Hawaii. One of these federal amendments eliminates the requirement of an advance ruling where there is only a change in form of a foreign subsidiary corporation. The other federal change provides that certain contributions to capital of a foreign corporation will be treated as a taxable exchange unless an advance ruling is obtained. Hawaii repealed the Sec. 367 provision for years beginning in 1978.

¶ 511a

## ¶ 514. Special Rules for Corporate Liquidations

Please turn to ¶ 710.

## ¶ 515. Basis of Stock of Foreign Corporation, etc.
### Hawaii Law: Sec. 235-2.3
### Federal Law: Sec. 301, 961

Under 1962 amendments to the federal law, special rules are provided for determining basis of certain property relating to ownership of stock of a foreign corporation. Hawaii has not adopted these special rules, so there will be differences between Hawaii and federal basis of property in these situations.

One of these situations is that of a "controlled foreign corporation," explained in ¶ 311. Where the U.S. shareholder includes in income his share of the foreign corporation's income, the basis of his stock in the foreign corporation will be appropriately increased for federal income tax purposes but not for Hawaii.

A difference in basis will also arise where a distribution of property in kind is received prior to 1978 from a foreign corporation, as discussed in ¶ 307. If the property was valued at fair market value to determine the amount of dividend for federal purposes, and valued at adjusted basis for Hawaii purposes, there will be a difference between federal and Hawaii basis of the property in the hands of the shareholder who receives it.

## ¶ 516. Gain from Disposition of Depreciable Property
### Hawaii Law: Sec. 235-2.3
### Federal Law: Sec. 291, 1245, 1250, 1254

Both Hawaii and federal law provide for taxing as ordinary income, rather than as capital gain, the gain on disposition of certain depreciable personal property to the extent of depreciation deducted on such property after 1961. The Tax Reform Act of 1969 extended the provision to livestock for federal purposes for years beginning after Dec. 31, 1969. Hawaii has extended this provision to livestock for years beginning after Dec. 31, 1974.

Both Hawaii and federal law provide for taxing as ordinary income a portion of the gain on depreciable real estate, where accelerated depreciation methods have been used. Prior to 1970 this applied, under both laws, only to property held less than 10 years. Under the Tax Reform Act of 1969, all excess depreciation on commercial real estate and a portion of excess depreciation on residential property, held less than 200 months, for years after 1969 will be "recaptured" under these rules for federal tax purposes. Under the Tax Reform Act of 1976, all excess depreciation for years after 1975 on residential property will be recaptured. The Tax Reform Act of 1976 also provided for rules on the "recapture" of excess depreciation on the sale of certain low-income rental properties. Hawaii conformed to the 1969 federal amendment for tax years beginning Jan. 1, 1975, and the 1976 amendments for taxable years beginning on or after Jan. 1, 1977, so there may be differences in the amount of federal and Hawaii "recapture" because of the effective date of the Hawaii amendment. The federal law was amended in 1982 to treat an additional portion of the gain realized by corporations on the sale of depreciable real estate as ordinary income. This federal rule requires that 15 percent of the straight-line depreciation be added to the ordinary income to be recaptured on the sale of real estate. The rule is effective for sales after 1982. Hawaii has not adopted this federal rule.

The federal law was amended to provide a new tax rate on gains from the sale of real property which would have been treated as ordinary income if the property was classified as disposable personal property. The law was effective for gains recognized after May 6,1997. Hawaii has not adopted this amendment.

Under the Tax Reform Act of 1976, the federal law was amended to provide for the taxing as ordinary income, rather than as capital gain, the gain on disposition of oil and gas properties to the extent of intangible drilling costs deducted after Dec. 31, 1975. This federal rule applies to dispositions after Dec. 31, 1975, and only to intangible costs of producing wells. Hawaii adopted this new federal rule for taxable years beginning in 1977.

The federal law was amended in 1997 to provide that the amounts expensed as the cost of qualified clean-fuel vehicles and qualified clean-fuel refueling property and any real property whose basis was reduced by deductions under the election to expense qualified clean-fuel refueling property is to be recaptured as ordinary income. These amendments are effective for property placed in service after June 30, 1993. Hawaii has adopted these 1997 federal amendments.

### ¶ 516a. Gain from Disposition of Farm Property
Hawaii Law: Sec. 235-2.3
Federal Law: Sec. 1252

Under the Tax Reform Act of 1969, certain farm losses and expenses of soil conservation and land clearing are "recaptured" for federal purposes when the farm property is sold or otherwise disposed of. This is accomplished by treating gain on sale of the property as ordinary income instead of as capital gain. See also ¶ 417 and ¶ 425. Hawaii adopted these federal provisions for years beginning in 1977.

### ¶ 517. Repossession of Real Property
Hawaii Law: Sec. 235-2.3
Federal Law: Sec. 1038

Under a 1964 federal amendment, no gain or loss is recognized to a seller of real property upon his reacquisition of property, except to a limited extent where money or other property has been received and not previously reported as income. The prior federal law, to which Hawaii conformed, provided generally for recognition of gain or loss measured by the difference between the basis of the obligations satisfied and not previously reported as income and the value of the property repossessed. Hawaii adopted the 1964 federal amendments for years beginning in 1978.

¶ 516

This difference in the treatment of gain or loss to be recognized will also result in a difference between Hawaii and federal basis for the property repossessed.

## ¶ 518. Redeemable Ground Rents
Hawaii Law: Sec. 235-2.3
Federal Law: Sec. 1055

Under a 1963 federal amendment, redeemable ground rents are treated as the equivalent of a mortgage. This provision was enacted primarily to cover certain property transactions in Maryland, and was made retroactive to 1962. Hawaii has not adopted this amendment.

## ¶ 519. Exchange of Property for Stock
Hawaii Law: Sec. 235-2.3
Federal Law: Sec. 351

The Hawaii rules regarding exchanges of property for stock are the same as the federal, except for a 1966 federal amendment providing a June 30, 1967, deadline for tax-free exchanges of securities for shares of mutual investment funds ("swap funds"). Hawaii did not adopt this amendment until 1979; however, this difference will presumably have no practical effect, since the federal amendment stopped the organization of new "swap funds."

## ¶ 520. Installment Sales
Hawaii Law: Sec. 235-2.3, 235-4
Federal Law: Sec. 453, 453A, 453B, 1038

Since 1980 the federal and Hawaii laws relating to installment sales have been the same. There have been differences between the two laws in prior years and these differences are explained below.

The federal law was amended in 1997 to repeal the exception for sales of property by a manufacturer to a dealer. This amendment is effective for tax years beginning more than one year after August 5, 1997. Hawaii has adopted this 1997 federal change.

Under the Tax Reform Act of 1969, a dealer reporting on the installment basis was permitted to change back to the accrual basis for federal tax purposes. Hawaii adopted this federal provision for years beginning in 1977.

Under the Tax Reform Act of 1969, federal law extended the definition of "initial payments" to include certain bonds or other evidence of indebtedness of the purchaser that are designed to be readily tradable in an established securities market. This applied, generally, to sales or other dispositions after May 27, 1969, and was intended to limit use of the installment method. Hawaii adopted this provision for installment sales made on or after Jan. 1, 1975.

Profit on an installment sale made before the taxpayer becomes a resident of Hawaii is not subject to Hawaii tax. Installments received after he becomes a resident, however, are taxable on the Hawaii return. (See also ¶ 314 regarding treatment of interest element in such cases.) If the property that is sold on an installment basis is located in Hawaii, then the gain is taxable for Hawaii purposes regardless of whether the taxpayer is a resident or nonresident.

See ¶ 502 regarding installment sales made prior to 1958.

### ¶ 521. Redemption of Securities
Hawaii Law: Sec. 235-2.3
Federal Law: Sec. 249, 311

Where a corporation uses appreciated property to redeem its own stock, after Nov. 30, 1969, the corporation is subject to federal tax on the appreciation in value (with one exception). Hawaii adopted this federal provision for years beginning Jan. 1, 1975.

Where a corporation issues bonds at a discount after May 27, 1969, and redeems them before maturity, the holder's gain will ordinarily be treated as capital gain for federal tax purposes. Such federal gain will reflect the fact that a portion of the discount has been reported as income by the holder, as explained in ¶ 320. Under Hawaii law, the gain may be different since Hawaii did not adopt the amortization of discount provision until 1978.

Where a corporation redeems bonds at a premium, federal law provides a special rule for determining the deductible portion of the premium, as explained in ¶ 404. Hawaii adopted this federal provision for years beginning in 1978.

### ¶ 522. Corporate Reorganizations
Hawaii Law: Sec. 235-2.3
Federal Law: Sec. 368

Beginning in 1977, the Hawaii rules regarding tax-free reorganizations conform to the federal rules. Prior to 1977 there were some differences in the definition of "reorganization." These differences applied to various situations in which stock of a controlled or controlling corporation was used in the reorganization exchange. The federal law was amended in 1964, 1968, and 1971 to treat these situations as "reorganizations." Hawaii adopted these federal amendments for years beginning in 1977.

The Tax Reform Act of 1984 made changes in the "C" and divisive "D" reorganization rules effective for transactions under plans adopted after July 20, 1984. Hawaii has adopted these 1984 amendments.

The federal law was amended in 1997 to restrict certain tax free divisive reorganizations. The effect of these new rules is to limit the use of the "Morris Trust" transactions. The amendments are effective for distributions after April 6, 1997 and transfers after August 5, 1997. The federal law was also amended in 1997 to treat the receipt of certain preferred stock in a tax free transfer or reorganization as other property and thus taxable. This amendment is effective for transactions after June 8, 1997. Hawaii has adopted these 1997 federal amendments.

¶ 520

Both federal and Hawaii law limit the tax free status of transfers to an investment company. The federal law was amended in 1997, effective for transfers after June 8, 1997, to expand the definition of an investment company. Hawaii has adopted this 1997 federal amendment.

### ¶ 523. Real Estate Subdivided for Sale
Hawaii Law: Sec. 235-2.3
Federal Law: Sec. 1237

Profits from land subdivision activities are usually treated as ordinary income; however, at least a part of such profits may be treated as long-term capital gain under some circumstances if the taxpayer can comply fully with certain very restrictive conditions in the law.

The Hawaii law is the same as the federal for years beginning in 1978.

### ¶ 524. Tax-Free Incorporations
Hawaii Law: Sec. 235-2.3
Federal Law: Sec. 351, 357

Both federal and Hawaii law provide that no gain or loss is recognized on the transfer of assets to a corporation for stock or securities of the corporation where the transferors control at least 80% of the corporation immediately after the transfer. Prior to 1978 the assumption by the corporation of certain liabilities could cause such a transfer to be a taxable event. The Technical Corrections Act of 1979 amended the federal law, for transfers made after Nov. 6, 1978, to exclude from gain any liabilities transferred to a controlled corporation that would give rise to a deduction. Hawaii adopted the Technical Corrections Act Amendment for years beginning in 1981.

The federal law was amended in 1989 to treat the receipt of securities in a tax free transfer to a corporation as taxable income. This amendment is effective for any transfers made after October 2, 1989. Hawaii has adopted this amendment.

The federal law amended in 1997 to treat the receipt of certain preferred stock in a tax free transfer or reorganization as other property and thus taxable. This amendment is effective for transactions after June 8, 1997. Hawaii has adopted these 1997 federal amendments.

### ¶ 525. Opportunity Zones
Hawaii Law: Sec. 235-2.3
Federal Law: Sec. 1400Z-1, 1400Z-2

The Tax Cuts and Jobs Act of 2017 created a program intended to encourage long-term investments in low-income urban and rural communities. The federal program allows taxpayers to defer capital gains from the sale of property until December 31, 2026 (at the latest), by investing the gains in a "Qualified Opportunity Fund." A Qualified Opportunity Fund, is an entity organized as either a corporation, partnership, or LLC taxed as a partnership, that invests in "qualified opportunity zone business property." "Qualified opportunity zone business property" can be stock, a partnership interest, or tangible business property located in a "qualified opportunity zone."

The state of Hawaii does not conform to this temporary gain deferral on qualified investments of capital gain. It does, however, support the federal program. The Governor's office has announced that it will nominate up to 25 census tracts as being distressed areas subject to the U.S. Department of Treasury's approval for the "Opportunity Zone" designation.

Investors may realize federal tax benefits, including:

A temporary tax deferral for capital gains reinvested in an Opportunity Fund. The deferred gain must be recognized on the earlier of the date on which the Opportunity Zone investment is sold or December 31, 2026.

A step-up in basis for capital gains reinvested in an Opportunity Fund. The basis of the original investment is increased by 10% if the investment in the qualified opportunity zone fund is held by the taxpayer for at least 5 years, and by an additional 5% if held for at least 7 years, excluding up to 15% of the original gain from taxation.

A permanent exclusion from taxable income of capital gains calculated from the appreciated value of the investment in a qualified Opportunity Zone Fund less the initial investment, if the investment is held for at least 10 years.

# CHAPTER 6

# INCOME TAX
# PARTNERSHIPS, ESTATES AND TRUSTS, DECEDENTS

## ¶ 601. Partnerships
### Hawaii Law: Sec. 235-2.3, 235-2.45, 235-72
### Federal Law: Sec. 701 to 777

Partnerships are not taxed as such, but the distributive shares of partnership income are taxed to the partners in their individual returns. The Hawaii law is the same as the federal in this respect. Hawaii follows the federal rules regarding the definition of a partnership, and computation of partnership income. The federal rules were amended in 1976 to provide for the amortization of partnership organization fees over a period of 60 months. In addition, the federal rules were amended to limit the allocation of profits and losses between partners and specifically limit retroactive allocations of losses to new partners. The federal law was also amended to limit the loss deductions for limited partners except where the partnership activity was real estate. This federal rule relating to real estate was repealed in 1978 for years beginning in 1979. Hawaii adopted the 1976 rules for years beginning in 1977, and adopted the 1978 amendment for years beginning in 1979. A corporation may be a member of a partnership.

The Tax Reform Act of 1984 made substantial changes to the partnership provisions. These changes affect transfers of property to partnerships, changes in partners' interests, allocation of income and expenses to partners, and payments to partners for services. Most of these changes are effective for transactions occurring after March 31, 1984. Hawaii has adopted these 1984 changes. The Revenue Act of 1987 added provisions to the federal law that restrict disproportionate allocations where there are taxable and tax-exempt partners in the partnership. These provisions are effective for interests acquired after Oct. 13, 1987. Hawaii has adopted these 1987 amendments. The federal law was amended in 1989 to require a partner to recognize gain on property contributed to a partnership if that property is later distributed to other partners within five years of the date of contribution. This amendment is effective for property contributed to a partnership after October 3, 1989. Hawaii has adopted this amendment. The federal law was amended effective for tax distributions of property after June 25, 1992 to a partner who contributed other property to the partnership within 5 years of the distribution. The federal law was amended, effective for property contributed to a partnership after June 8, 1997, to extend the period to seven years. Hawaii has adopted the 1992 federal amendment and has adopted the 1997 federal amendment.

The federal law was also amended in 1997, effective for distributions after August 5, 1997, to provide new rules for allocating basis on distributions of property to a partner. The federal law was also amended in 1997, effective for sales or exchanges after August 5, 1997, to eliminate the requirement that inventory be substantially appreciated to trigger ordinary gain on the sale or exchange of a partnership interest. Hawaii has adopted these 1997 federal amendments.

The federal law was amended in 1993 to provide that payments made to withdrawing partners for goodwill or unrealized receivables will no longer be deductible to the partnership. There is an exception for payments made to a general partner from a partnership in which capital is not a material income-producing factor. This new federal rule is effective for partners retiring or dying on or after January 5, 1993 unless there was a binding agreement to purchase such interest in effect on January 4, 1993. Hawaii has adopted this amendment.

The federal law was amended in 1997 to allow certain large partnerships to elect to report income to their partners in a simplified manner. The partnership must have at least 100 partners and cannot be a professional service partnership. This federal amendment is effective for years beginning after December 31, 1997. Hawaii has adopted this 1997 federal amendment.

Federal law was amended in 2004 to provide an election to deduct up to $5,000 of partnership organizational expenditures in the tax year in which the partnership begins business. However, each $5,000 amount is reduced (but not below zero) by the amount by which the cumulative organizational expenditures exceeds $50,000. Expenditures that are not deductible in the year in which business begins are amortized over a 15-year period. Hawaii has adopted this amendment.

Resident partners are taxable upon their share of the entire income of the partnership, wherever derived. Nonresident partners are taxable only on their share of partnership income from sources within Hawaii.

A partnership is required to file an annual return, on Form N-20, by the 20th day of the fourth month following the close of the fiscal year. A return is required from any partnership that has income from Hawaii sources, whether or not any member of the partnership is a resident of Hawaii. See specimen return in Part V. See ¶ 510b for a discussion of the allocation of gain or loss to Hawaii on the sale of a partnership interest.

¶ 601

In general, Hawaii adopted the federal laws regarding the allocation of profits, losses and credits among the partners. However, the substantial economic effect rules do not apply to allocations of the high technology business investment tax credit for investments made before May 1, 2009, the attractions and educational facilities tax credit, and the low-income housing tax credit, and to the allocation of net operating losses of qualified high technology businesses.

For taxable years beginning after December 31, 2013, the TEFRA partnership audit procedures contained in sections 6223 through 6230, and section 6233 of the Internal Revenue Code, no longer apply for Hawaii income tax purposes. The Department of Taxation indicated that it would develop its own rules governing audits of partnerships.

Act 27, SLH 2018, conforms Hawaii to the new federal partnership audit rules that are effective on January 1, 2018.

### ¶ 602. Corporation Taxed as Partnership—'Subchapter S'
Hawaii Law: Sec. 235-2.3, 235-2.4, 235-121 to 235-130
Federal Law: Sec. 1361 to 1379

Hawaii has adopted the Model S Corporation State Income Act for years beginning after December 31, 1989. Under the Act any corporation which qualifies as an S corporation for federal purposes will be treated as such for Hawaii purposes. Non residents will be subject to Hawaii tax on their pro rata share of income earned in Hawaii by the S corporation doing business in Hawaii. Likewise Hawaii residents who are shareholders of non Hawaii S corporations will be subject to tax on their pro rata share of the S corporation's income.

Where an S corporation has nonresident shareholders the S corporation must pay to Hawaii a tax computed at the highest individual rate on each nonresident shareholder's pro rata share of income earned in Hawaii. An S corporation can avoid this payment on behalf of its nonresident shareholders by filing with the state an agreement signed by each nonresident shareholder to file a Hawaii tax return and become subject to personal jurisdiction in Hawaii for purposes of collection of unpaid tax. The law also allows an S corporation to file a composite return on behalf of its nonresident shareholders.

Where an S corporation pays tax to another state which does not allow S corporation status, then a Hawaii resident shareholder may claim a credit on his Hawaii return for this his pro rata share of the taxes paid to the other state.

Beginning in 1991 each shareholder of an S corporation is entitled to his pro rata share of the following credits, enterprise zone, energy conservation, regulated investment company capital gains tax, fuel tax for commercial fishers, capital goods excise tax, and low income housing tax credit. For non-resident shareholders the amount of credit for energy conservation is limited to property placed in service in Hawaii. For years beginning after December 31, 1991, S corporation shareholders are entitled to their pro rata share of the S corporation's credit for vocational rehabilitation referrals.

The law also provides that any tax imposed because of the recapture of a LIFO reserve may be paid in four equal annual installments.

See ¶ 407 for discussion of the special net operating and capital loss carryover rules for pre-1990 federal S corporation that did not qualify as Hawaii S corporations. This new provision is effective for taxable years beginning after December 31, 1989.

Prior to 1990, Hawaii followed the federal rules but with some differences. These differences are explained in the following paragraphs.

Prior to 1987, Hawaii requirements were the same as the 1983 federal rules, except that the federal rules refer to a nonresident alien; thus, a corporation with a California shareholder would qualify for federal purposes but not for Hawaii. For years beginning in 1987, Hawaii has repealed the rule that required all shareholders of an S Corporation to be Hawaii residents. Hawaii has adopted the 1987 federal amendment that allows S Corporations to use a fiscal year other than a calendar year, but has not adopted the special tax.

The Tax Reform Act of 1976 permitted the number of shareholders of a tax option corporation to increase from 10 to 15 after the corporation had been a tax-option corporation for five consecutive years. In addition, a grantor or a voting trust may be a shareholder. This provision was effective for years beginning after 1976. Hawaii adopted the 1976 federal provision for years beginning in 1978.

The Revenue Act of 1978 made several amendments to the Subchapter S rules. One allows the corporation to have 15 shareholders from inception. Another provides that husband and wife will be treated as one shareholder regardless of how they hold their stock. Another provides that an election can be made anytime during the year preceding the election year and within 75 days after the beginning of the election year. A final change provides that a grantor trust will have two years after the death of the grantor to dispose of the stock. These amendments are effective for years beginning in 1978. Hawaii adopted these amendments for years beginning in 1979.

The Tax Reform Act of 1984 made several technical corrections to the Subchapter S rules. These corrections deal with distribution of property on liquidation, discharge of indebtedness income, passive income, inactive subsidiaries, qualified Subchapter S trusts, short taxable years, the accumulated adjustment account, and accrual expenses paid to a cash-basis related taxpayer. These corrections are effective for years beginning in 1983. Hawaii adopted these amendments. Effective for years beginning in 1987, the Hawaii tax rate on passive income will be 6.4%.

The Tax Reform Act of 1986 amended the federal law to provide for a corporate level tax on any gain that arose before conversion from a C corporation to an S Corporation and is recognized on the sale or distribution of assets by the S

Corporation within 10 years of the date that S election took effect. This amendment is effective for elections made after Dec. 31, 1986. Hawaii adopted this amendment and taxes such gains at a rate of 6.4%. Federal law was amended for tax years beginning in 2009 and 2010 to reduce the built-in gain recognition period from 10 years to 7 years and for tax years beginning in 2011, the recognition period was temporarily reduced to 5 years. For tax years beginning after December 31, 2014, the shortened 5-year recognition period is permanently reduced. Hawaii does conform to the reduction in the built-in gain period, effective for tax years beginning after December 31, 2014. The Revenue Act of 1987 added a provision that requires corporation making an S election after Dec. 17, 1987, to recapture any LIFO reserve. Hawaii adopted this amendment.

Hawaii adopted another difference from the federal rules. For years beginning in 1979 through 1989, an S Corporation lost its status as such if more than 80 percent of its gross income was derived from sources outside the state.

The election to be taxed as an S corporation is permitted for Hawaii purposes only if it is also made for federal purposes. Hawaii rules for manner and time of making the election, termination, etc., are the same as federal rules. The federal rules with respect to termination of an election by a new shareholder were changed with respect to years ending after 1976. Under the 1979 federal change, a new shareholder must affirmatively refuse to consent to the election within 60 days after he acquires his stock. Hawaii adopted this federal provision for years beginning in 1978.

The Hawaii law was amended in 1967, effective Jan. 1, 1967, to conform to a federal provision that was enacted in 1959. This provision applies only where there is a net operating loss and a shareholder dies before the end of the corporation's taxable year; it permits deduction of a share of the loss in the shareholder's final return.

The Hawaii law was amended in 1969, effective for taxable years beginning after Dec. 31, 1968, to conform to federal amendments enacted in 1966. These amendments liberalize the "passive investment" test, prevent double taxation of certain distributions made within 2 1/2 months after the close of the year, and provide for taxing capital gain to the corporation under certain conditions.

Under the Tax Reform Act of 1969, the federal rules regarding recapture of farm losses and disallowance of hobby losses, explained in ¶ 425, are applied to "tax-option" corporations as well as to other taxpayers. Hawaii adopted the 1969 federal rules regarding hobby losses for 1975, and has adopted the farm loss rules for years beginning in 1978. Many of the tax shelter limitations enacted by the Tax Reform Act of 1976 relate to tax option corporations. Hawaii adopted these rules for years beginning in 1978.

The federal law was amended in 1971 to liberalize the "passive investment" test in certain cases where a subsidiary of an S Corporation is liquidated. Hawaii has conformed to this amendment for years beginning in 1978.

¶ 602

Following the decrease in the corporate tax rate enacted by the Tax Cuts and Jobs Act, P.L. 115-97, Congress expected many S corporations to convert to C corporations. The TCJA provides special rules for taking into account adjustments under Code Sec. 481 that are attributable to the revocation of S corporation elections during the two-year post-termination transition period beginning on December 22, 2017. The corporation must have had the same owners on the revocation date as it did on December 22, 2017 to be eligible for the extended period. Under these rules, the adjustments are taken into account ratably over a sixtax year period beginning with the year of change. Hawaii law conforms to this change.

See filled-in specimen return (Form N-35) in Part IV of this book.

### ¶ 603. Limited Liability Companies
**Hawaii Law: Sec. 428-101 to 428-1302, The Hawaii Uniform Limited Liability Company Act**

Hawaii authorizes the creation of limited liability companies (LLCs), as more fully described below.

Generally, LLCs are companies with limited liability that may be treated as either corporations, partnerships, or disregarded entities for tax purposes.

LLC characteristics.—An LLC is a business entity that shares characteristics of both partnerships and corporations. Like a partnership, an LLC is a pass through entity (in those states such as Hawaii in which LLCs are not specifically subjected to the corporate income tax) in which the profits and losses are passed through to its members. However, unlike a limited partnership in which the individual partners are personally liable for amounts up to and including the amount of their contributions to the partnership, or a general partnership in which all members are liable for the partnership obligations, members of an LLC incur no personal liability. The characteristics of an LLC are similar to those of an S corporation, but LLCs are not subject to the many restrictions currently placed on S corporations, such as the limitations on the number and types of shareholders, the allowable classes of stock, and the flowthrough of losses.

Hawaii treatment of LLCs.—The Hawaii Uniform Limited Liability Company Act (the Act) is derived from the model provisions recommended by the National Conference of Commissioners on Uniform State Laws. Under the Act, one or more persons may organize an LLC, consisting of one or more members, by delivering articles of organization to the office of the director for filing. A foreign LLC may apply for a certificate of authority to transact business in Hawaii by delivering an application to the Director of Commerce and Consumer Affairs for filing.

While the Act does not provide for the taxation of LLCs, the Department of Taxation has indicated that Hawaii will follow federal criteria for determining whether an LLC is to be treated as a partnership or a corporation. Thus if a federal employer identification number is required for federal purposes, the

Department of Taxation will also require a taxpayer to obtain a GET license. (Tax Information Release No. 97-4). See ¶ 601 for exceptions to the general rule for the allocation of losses and tax credit.

Overview of LLC Act.—The following is a brief and general overview of the provisions relating to LLCs in Hawaii. State law provisions relating to LLCs:

**Name of Act:** Hawaii Uniform Limited Liability Company Act.

**Federal Tax Classification:** The LLC statute is flexible. Note that although single member LLCs can be ignored for income tax purposes, such disregarded entities would still be subject to the General Excise Tax.

**State Tax Treatment:** State tax classification follows federal classification.

**Recordkeeping:** The Hawaii statute is silent as to records and information required to be kept by LLCs. However, it might be prudent for the LLC to compile and maintain:

(1) a current list of the name and address of each member and manager;

(2) copies of federal, state and local income tax returns and company information;

(3) copies of the articles of organization, including any amendments;

(4) copies of any effective written operating agreement;

(5) financial statements;

(6) information regarding members' capital contributions, agreements to contribute capital and the date each became a member; and

(7) any other information regarding LLC affairs that is just and reasonable to maintain.

## ¶ 604. Estates and Trusts
### Hawaii Law: Sec. 235-2.3, 235-4, 235-54
### Federal Law: Sec. 641 to 685

The Hawaii tax applies to estates and trusts, as well as to individuals and corporations. The Hawaii rules for estates and trusts are the same as the federal, except as explained below.

An estate is allowed a deduction of $400 for "personal exemption" (comparable federal: $600). A trust that, under its governing instrument, is required to distribute all of its current income is allowed a deduction of $200 (comparable federal: $300). All other trusts are allowed a deduction of $80 (comparable federal: $100).

Under the Tax Reform Act of 1969, revised in 1971, federal law provided a number of new rules designed to restrict the tax benefits from the use of trusts. The new rules include: (1) an unlimited "throwback" rule for taxing accumulated income to trust beneficiaries; (2) taxing to a spouse the income from a trust created for the benefit of the other spouse; (3) limitations on benefits from charitable remainder trusts; and (4) elimination of the two year charitable trust. Hawaii adopted these federal provisions, effective in 1975, except for the rule relating to taxing a spouse on income from a trust created for the benefit of the other spouse; this rule was adopted for years beginning in 1978.

The Tax Reform Act of 1976 eliminated the capital gain throwback rule for years beginning in 1976. The 1976 Act also restored the pre-1969 rule that distributions of income accumulated by a trust prior to a beneficiary's 21st birthday are not subject to the accumulation distribution rules. Hawaii adopted these provisions for taxable years beginning in 1977. This federal provision was repealed effective for distributions made in tax years beginning after August 5, 1997. Hawaii has adopted this 1977 amendment.

The Tax Reform Act of 1976 introduced a new special tax where property is sold at a gain within two years from the date of its transfer to a trust. The tax imposed on the trust is the same as the tax that would have been paid by the transferor as if he had sold the property. This federal rule applies to transfers after May 21, 1976. Hawaii adopted this rule for taxable years beginning in 1977. This federal provision was repealed effective for sales or exchanges after August 5, 1997. Hawaii has adopted this 1977 amendment.

The Tax Reform Act of 1984 amended the federal law to provide that a distribution of property to a beneficiary carries out distributable net income only to the extent of the lesser of the property's basis or fair market value, unless the trustee elects to treat the distribution as a taxable event. This rule is effective for distributions after June 1, 1984. The 1984 Act also provided that for years beginning after March 1, 1984, multiple trusts that meet certain requirements will be treated as one trust. Hawaii has adopted these 1984 amendments.

Several changes in the federal law affecting the taxation of estates and trusts were made in 1997. One change allows the executor of an estate and the trustee of a qualified revocable trust to elect to have the trust treated as part of the estate. This amendment is effective for estates of decedents dying after August 5, 1997. Another change, effective for tax years beginning after August 5, 1997, allows an estate to elect to treat distributions within 65 days after the close of the estate's tax year as having been made on the last day of that tax year. A third change extends the separate shares rule to estates. This change is effective for estates of decedents dying after August 5, 1997. Hawaii has adopted these 1997 federal changes.

The Tax Reform Act of 1986 made extensive revisions to the "Clifford Trust" and "Spousal Remainder Trust" rules. Under the revisions "Clifford" and "Spousal Remainder" trusts created after March 1, 1986, will be treated as "Grantor" trusts with the income being taxed to the grantor. Hawaii has adopted these revisions.

The Tax Reform Act of 1986 amended the federal law to provide that all trusts, except for tax-exempt and charitable trusts, must use the calendar year as their tax year. This provision is effective for tax years beginning after Dec. 31, 1986. Hawaii has adopted this federal amendment.

Under federal law an estate or trust is allowed an unlimited deduction for income used under the terms of the will or trust instrument for certain charitable-type purposes. This has the effect of providing tax exemption to the income of a charitable trust, so long as the income is used for approved purposes. The unlimited deduction rule also applies under the Hawaii tax, but only where the contributions are to be used exclusively in the State of Hawaii. If they are not to be used exclusively in Hawaii, the Hawaii deduction for contributions is limited to the amount that would be allowed to an individual. Under the Tax Reform Act of 1969, the federal unlimited charitable deduction of a trust is restricted to income actually paid out and does not include income that is only "set aside"; Hawaii adopted this federal amendment, effective in 1975.

The federal law was amended in 1997 to restrict the ability to create a charitable remainder trust where the pay out to the beneficiary exceeds 50 percent and the charitable remainder is less than 10 percent. This federal provision with regard to the 50 percent rule is effective for transfers in trust after June 8, 1997. The 10 percent rule is effective for transfers in trust after July 28, 1997. Hawaii has adopted this 1997 federal amendment.

As explained in ¶ 107, the Tax Reform Act of 1969 introduced extensive new federal rules and restrictions on "private foundations." These provisions apply to certain trusts, including trusts that benefit from the unlimited charitable deduction explained above, as well as to other types of organizations. Hawaii has not adopted any of these federal provisions.

The federal law was amended in 1997 to allow trustees of qualified funeral trusts to have the trust be taxable on its income as opposed to treating the trust as a grantor trust. The federal amendment is effective for years ending after August 5, 1997. Hawaii has adopted this federal amendment.

A resident estate or trust is taxed upon all of its income, regardless of the source. A nonresident estate or trust is taxed only upon income from Hawaii sources (see ¶ 309). An estate or trust is deemed to be a "resident" if its administration is carried on entirely in Hawaii. It is also deemed to be "resident" if the fiduciary (or all fiduciaries, if there is more than one) is a resident of Hawaii, regardless of the place where the administration is carried on.

If the administration of a trust is partly within Hawaii and partly outside the state, it is deemed to be a "resident" if half or more of the fiduciaries reside (or if the sole fiduciary resides) in Hawaii.

See ¶ 309 for a discussion of the treatment of nonresident beneficiaries of a resident trust.

There may be a difference between Hawaii and federal returns in the deduction of casualty or theft losses by an estate. Under federal law such losses are not allowed on the income tax return of the estate if they have been allowed for estate tax purposes in computing the taxable estate. Under Hawaii law such losses are always deductible for income tax purposes (subject to the limitation mentioned in ¶ 409), since losses of this type are not allowed for Hawaii inheritance tax purposes and there is therefore no possibility of a double deduction.

In 2010 Hawaii adopted the Permitted Transfer In Trust Act under Act 182 and it was subsequently amended in 2011 by Act 161 which expanded, clarified or removed certain limitations that existed under Act 182. These so called "Asset Protection Trusts" will be treated as a grantor trust for Hawaii purposes which conforms to the federal tax treatment.

### ¶ 605. Income of Decedents
Hawaii Law: Sec. 235-2.3, 235-59
Federal Law: Sec. 691, 692

Where a decedent was entitled to, or had a right to, income that was not included in taxable income during his life, the income is taxed when received by his estate or heirs. The Hawaii rules are the same as the federal. However, there is ordinarily a difference in the amounts taxed, because under federal law the federal estate tax is taken into account in computing the amount taxable, whereas under Hawaii law the Hawaii Estate tax is used. (See Chapter 10 regarding new Estate and Transfer tax.)

In determining the amount of income of a decedent to be taxed after his death, an offset is allowed for the amount of death tax paid on the right to receive the income. The amount of death tax allowed as an offset is an allocated portion of the total death tax on the estate. As stated above, the tax used in this computation for federal income tax purposes is the federal estate tax; the tax used in the Hawaii income tax is the Hawaii Estate tax.

Example:

Smith died late in 1987. In 1988 his widow received a $10,000 bonus he had earned in 1987. The federal estate tax attributable to the inclusion in Smith's estate of the right to receive the bonus is $1,000. The Hawaii Estate tax attributable to the same item is $100. The amount taxable in the widow's federal income tax return is $9,000 ($10,000 less $1,000). The amount taxable in her Hawaii income tax return is $9,900 ($10,000 less $100).

### ¶ 606. Real Estate Investment Trusts
Hawaii Law: Sec 235-2.3, 235-71
Federal Law: Sec 856 to 858

The federal law was amended in 1961 to provide special rules for taxing real estate investment trusts that distribute their income currently. The general plan is to tax income to the beneficiaries and to relieve the trust of tax, in the manner of taxing regulated investment companies as explained in ¶ 112. Hawaii adopted these special provisions in 1965, effective June 28, 1965.

The Tax Reform Act of 1986 eased some of the qualification requirements for REITs. The new rules are effective for taxable years beginning after Dec. 31, 1986. Hawaii has adopted these 1986 amendments.

The Taxpayer Relief Act of 1997 made a number of amendments to the REIT provisions which further ease some of the qualification requirements, allow a REIT to retain capital gains and pay the tax on those gains, and allow shareholders to make 100 percent basis adjustments for deemed distributed capital gains. These federal amendments are effective for tax years beginning after August 5, 1997. Hawaii has adopted these 1997 federal amendments.

### ¶ 606a. Real Estate Mortgage Investment Conduits
Hawaii Law: 235-2.3
Federal Law: Sec 860A to 860G

The Tax Reform Act of 1986 created a new tax vehicle, Real Estate Mortgage Investment Conduits (REMICs). For years beginning after Dec. 31, 1986, REMICs are intended to be the exclusive vehicle for issuing multiple-class mortgage-backed securities. Any entity that meets the qualification requirements will be taxed under the REMIC provisions. Similarly, holders of interests in a REMIC will be taxed in accordance with the REMIC provisions. Hawaii has adopted the REMIC provisions.

### ¶ 607. Beneficiaries of Foreign Trusts
Federal Law: Sec 643, 669, 6048, 6677

The federal law was amended in 1962 and 1976 to provide rules for taxing beneficiaries of foreign trusts, in an effort to prevent tax avoidance by the use of such trusts. Hawaii adopted these provisions for years beginning in 1978.

# CHAPTER 7

## INCOME TAX
## ALLOCATION OF INCOME

## ¶ 701. Allocation of Income—General
### Hawaii Law: Sec. 235-5, 235-21 to 235-39

Special rules are provided to determine the allocable portion of income subject to Hawaii tax, in cases where the entire income is not taxed because part of it was from sources outside Hawaii.

The following classes of taxpayers are taxed only on income from Hawaii sources:

a. Nonresident individuals (see ¶ 309).

b. Nonresident estates (see ¶ 604).

c. Nonresident trusts (see ¶ 604).

d. Foreign corporations (incorporated in jurisdictions other than Hawaii).

e. Domestic corporations (incorporated in Hawaii) that have income that is derived from sources outside the state and are subject to the possibility of being taxed by another state or foreign country, as explained below.

This chapter discusses the problem of determining the income of these taxpayers that is allocable to Hawaii. It applies not only to situations involving one taxpayer, but also to some situations involving affiliated taxpayers (corporations) as discussed at ¶ 708.

During 1967 Hawaii enacted the Uniform Division of Income for Tax Purposes Act, which has also been adopted by many other states. It applies to taxable years beginning after Dec. 31, 1967. It provides a uniform set of rules for allocation and apportionment of income of multistate businesses. We shall refer to this law as the Uniform Act.

During 1968 Hawaii enacted the Multistate Tax Compact, developed by the Council of State Governments. It is designed to promote uniformity among the states and to avoid duplicate taxation. The compact includes the allocation and apportionment rules of the Uniform Act, discussed above, almost word for word.

When the Uniform Act and the Multistate Tax Compact were enacted, the prior Hawaii law was left in force. In 1989 the law was amended, effective for years beginning after December 31, 1988, to require the use of the apportionment methods specified in the Uniform Act to business activities. From 1968 to 1988 the law provided two methods for allocation and apportionment of multistate income: (1) the old rules prescribed under the pre-1968 law; and (2) the new rules prescribed by the Uniform Act, which are the same as the rules under the Multistate Tax Compact. According to the official instructions (revised in 1969) for Form N-30 Schedules O and P, the taxpayer could elect for 1968 to 1988 to use either of these methods. This means that from 1968 to 1988 the taxpayer could choose whichever method was more advantageous to him.

In the case of *Charles Pankow Associates*, the Hawaii Tax Appeals Court held that for multistate corporations, apportionment is the rule and the Director has the burden of proving another method is more proper. In the *Pankow* case all of the taxpayer's construction activities were in the State of Hawaii, and the Director's requirement of separate accounting was upheld. The Hawaii Supreme Court upheld the Tax Appeals Court decision in the *Pankow* case, citing Section 235-38 HRS as the Director's authority for requiring separate accounting where the allocation and apportionment provisions do not fairly represent taxpayer's business activities in Hawaii.

In 1984 the Hawaii Legislature amended the income tax law to prohibit the use of the worldwide unitary apportionment method that was approved by the U.S. Supreme Court in *Container Corporation of America v. Franchise Tax Board*. Prior to 1984 the Director had the authority to require this method for allocating income to Hawaii; however, it was never used.

Reference to prior editions of this book should be made for a discussion of the pre-1968 law. The following discussion relates to the Uniform Act.

## ¶ 701a. Allocation and Apportionment Under Uniform Act
### Hawaii Law: Sec. 235-21 to 235-23

The law provides that allocation and apportionment of income is required where business activities are *taxable* within and without Hawaii. For this purpose, a taxpayer is deemed to be taxable without Hawaii if one of two specific qualifications is met:

(a) The taxpayer is subject to a net income tax, a franchise tax measured by net income, a franchise tax for the privilege of doing business, or a corporate stock tax in another state, or

(b) Another state has jurisdiction to levy a net income tax on the taxpayer, *whether or not* the other state actually subjects the taxpayer to the tax.

It should be observed that under (b) above, a Hawaii corporation is entitled to allocate income outside Hawaii where its outside activities are sufficient to give taxing jurisdiction to another state or country, even though the corporation may actually pay no tax outside Hawaii.

As used in these qualification tests, "another state" also means the District of Columbia, Puerto Rico, U.S. territories and possessions, or any foreign country or political subdivision.

### ¶ 702. Treatment of Nonbusiness Income Under Uniform Act
#### Hawaii Law: Sec. 235-24 to 235-28

Under the Uniform Act, all income that is not classified as "business income" is defined as "nonbusiness income." Specific rules are provided for allocation of nonbusiness income, as follows:

1.  Net rents and royalties from real property, and gains and losses from the sale thereof, are allocable to the state in which the property is located.

2.  Net rents and royalties from tangible personal property are allocable to the state in which the property is utilized. However, if the taxpayer was not organized in, or is not taxable in, the state in which the property is utilized, such income is taxable in the state of the owner's commercial domicile. If tangible personal property is utilized in more than one state, the income is allocated on the basis of the number of days of physical location within and without Hawaii during the rental or royalty period of the income year. If the physical location during the period is unknown or unascertainable by the taxpayer, the property is deemed utilized in the state in which the property is located at the time the payer of the rent or royalty obtained possession.

3.  Gains and losses from sale of tangible personal property are allocable to the state where the property is located at the time of sale. However, if the taxpayer is not taxable in the state in which the property is located at the time of sale, the gain or loss is allocable to the state of the taxpayer's commercial domicile.

4.  Interest and dividends, as well as gains and losses from sale of intangible personal property, are allocable entirely to the state of the taxpayer's

commercial domicile. In Department of Taxation Announcement No. 99-5, the department clarified that multistate taxpayers must include dividends, interest, royalties and gains from foreign corporations in business income subject to apportionment.

5. Patent and copyright royalties are allocable to the state in which the patent or copyright is utilized by the payer of the royalties. However, if the taxpayer is not taxable in the state in which the property is utilized, the royalty income is allocable to the state of commercial domicile. If a patent is utilized in more than one state in production, fabrication, manufacturing, etc., or if a patented product is produced in more than one state, the royalty income is allocable to the states of utilization on the basis of gross royalty receipts. However, if the taxpayer fails to maintain accounting records to reflect the states of utilization, the entire amount is allocable to the state of the taxpayer's commercial domicile. A copyright is deemed to be utilized in the state in which printing or other publication originates.

The law defines "commercial domicile" as "the principal place from which the trade or business of the taxpayer is directed or managed." This is generally similar to the pre-1968 law.

## ¶ 703. Apportionment of Business Income Under Uniform Act
### Hawaii Law: Sec. 235-29 to 235-38

The Uniform Act defines "business income" as "income arising from transactions and activity in the regular course of the taxpayer's trade or business and includes income from tangible and intangible property if the acquisition, management, and disposition of the property constitute integral parts of the taxpayer's regular trade or business operations." The law provides detailed rules for apportionment of business income by formula, indicating that use of the formula will be required in most cases and that separate accounting will be the exception. However, the law permits the use of separate accounting where apportionment by formula does not fairly represent the extent of the taxpayer's business activity in the state, and provides that the taxpayer may petition for use of separate accounting.

The apportionment formula provided in the Uniform Act is the average of the following three factors:

(a) Ratio of Hawaii property to total property.
(b) Ratio of Hawaii payroll to total payroll.
(c) Ratio of Hawaii sales to total sales.

As to each factor, the amount within Hawaii and the total within and without Hawaii are computed. From these figures, the percentage of each factor within the state is determined, and the average of the three percentages computed. The resulting average percentage is then applied to the total "business" income to determine the portion taxable in Hawaii.

Example:

|  | Total | Within Hawaii | Hawaii Ratio |
|---|---|---|---|
| Property | $ 500,000 | $ 400,000 | 80% |
| Payroll | $ 300,000 | $ 210,000 | 70% |
| Sales | $ 1,000,000 | $ 300,000 | 30% |
| Total of 3 ratios |  |  | 180% |
| Average ratio |  |  | 60% |
| Total "business" income |  | $100,000 |  |
| Portion subject to Hawaii tax |  | $ 60,000 |  |

It should be kept in mind that the amounts attributed to Hawaii in computing the various factors in the formula are not taxed directly, but are only used in the computation of the percentage to be applied to the business income. That is, the factors are used only to determine a measure of the taxpayer's activity within and without Hawaii.

The law permits deviation from the standard formula, by excluding one or more factors or by including one or more additional factors, where the regular provisions "do not fairly represent the extent of the taxpayer's business activity in this state." The Director of Taxation presumably will permit some industries (e.g., some service businesses) to deviate from the three-factor formula where such deviation is necessary to produce a reasonable result.

### ¶ 704. Property Factor Under Uniform Act
#### Hawaii Law: Sec. 235-30 to 235-32

The Uniform Act provides specific rules for computation of the property factor. The property factor includes land, buildings, machinery, inventories, and any other tangible property used to produce "business" income. It includes rented, as well as owned, property. Property used to produce "nonbusiness" income should be excluded, but property used to produce both "nonbusiness" and "business" income should be included to the extent it is used to produce "business" income.

Property owned and used in the business is included in the property factor at its original cost. This would include fully depreciated property that is still in use. The law does not define "original cost"; presumably it is the unadjusted first tax cost basis, and may be a predecessor's basis where a tax-free transfer has occurred. Depreciation is ignored. Inventories should be included in accordance with the method of valuation used for income tax purposes.

Rented property is included in the factor at eight times the net annual rental rate. The law provides that "the net annual rental rate is the annual rental rate paid by the taxpayer less any annual rental rate received by the taxpayer from subrentals." Inter-company rentals should be eliminated, where both corporations involved are included in a combined return.

The amount to be included in the property factor is the average value for the year. This is usually determined by averaging the values at the beginning and end of the year. However, the Department of Taxation may require or allow averaging by monthly values, where substantial fluctuations occur during the year or large amounts of property are acquired or disposed of during the year.

It is presumed that the rules that have been developed under the pre-1968 law for determining the property factor in specialized industries, such as transportation, will be applied under the Uniform Act. See ¶ 707 for special rules for ocean carriers and airlines.

## ¶ 705. Payroll Factor Under Uniform Act
### Hawaii Law: Sec. 235-33 and 235-34

Under the Uniform Act, the computation of the payroll factor conforms generally to the reporting for state payroll tax purposes. Compensation is attributable to Hawaii where:

(a) the employee performs services entirely within Hawaii; or

(b) the employee performs services both within and without the state, but the services performed outside the state are merely incidental to those performed within the state; or

(c) the employee performs some services within and without the state, and the base of operations is in the state, or if there is no base of operations, the place from which services are directed or controlled is in Hawaii; or

(d) the employee performs some services within the state and the base of operations, or the place from which services are directed or controlled, is not in any state in which some part of the services are performed, but the employee's residence is in Hawaii.

If a person is not considered to be an employee for payroll tax purposes, his compensation should not be included in the factor. Any compensation attributable to "nonbusiness" income should be excluded from the factor.

See ¶ 707 for special rules for ocean carriers and airlines.

## ¶ 706. Sales Factor Under Uniform Act
### Hawaii Law: Sec. 235-35 to 235-37

The Uniform Act provides specific rules for the sales factor, generally similar to the pre-1968 Hawaii law. Sales are ordinarily allocated on the basis of destination. Special rules are provided for sales to the U.S. Government.

For purposes of the sales factor, the term "sales" means generally the gross receipts from operations that produce "business" income, less returns and allowances.

Sales of tangible personal property are deemed to be Hawaii sales if the property is delivered or shipped to a purchaser, other than the United States Government, located in Hawaii. The f.o.b. point, or other conditions of the sale, are not material in making this determination. Such sales are also attributed to Hawaii if shipped from an office, warehouse, store, factory, or other storage facility in Hawaii, where the purchaser is the U.S. Government or where the seller is not taxable in the state where the purchaser is located. The law does not define a sale to the U.S. Government; presumably this would be any sale for which direct payment is made by the government.

The reference above to cases "where the seller is not taxable in the state where the purchase is located" refers principally to situations covered by federal Public Law 86-272. If Public Law 86-272 would preclude taxing of the seller by the other state, sales shipped from Hawaii are attributable to Hawaii. "Other state" would include U.S. territories and foreign countries, in such cases the question is whether the territory or country could tax the seller if Public Law 86-272 were in force there. If the other state, territory, or country could tax the seller but does not actually do so, the seller is nevertheless deemed to be "taxable" there and sales shipped there from Hawaii are not attributable to Hawaii.

Sales of other than tangible personal property are deemed to be Hawaii sales if the activity which produced the sale is performed in Hawaii. If the income-producing activity is performed both within and without the state, then the sale is attributed to Hawaii only if a greater portion of the income producing activity is performed in Hawaii than in any other state, based on costs of performance.

Regulation 18-235-38-03 was amended in 1998 to include section (f). This amendment provides that gains and losses on the sale of liquid assets which would normally be held in connection with the taxpayers treasury function will be included in the sales factor. Exceptions are provided in the regulations.

See ¶ 707 for special rules for ocean carriers and airlines.

## ¶ 707. Special Rules for Ocean Carriers and Airlines
### Hawaii Law: Sec. 235-5
### Regulations: Sec. 18-235-5(e)

Regulations issued before the enactment in 1967 of the Uniform Division of Income for Tax Purposes Act provide special apportionment formulas for ocean carriers and airlines. These formulas are based upon "revenue tons handled," "originating revenue," "voyage days," and "flight operating hours."

See ¶ 324 regarding exemption for income of foreign ships or aircraft.

## ¶ 708. Affiliated Corporations
### Hawaii Law: Sec. 235-92
### Federal Law: Sec. 1501 to 1505

The Hawaii Law was amended in 1968 to permit consolidated returns of affiliated corporations, effective for taxable years beginning after Dec. 31, 1968. The Hawaii law incorporates the federal law by reference, and is intended to conform closely with it. Generally, 80% intercompany ownership is required for inclusion in a consolidated return.

The Tax Reform Act of 1984 changed the ownership requirement to require that the common parent own 80% or more of the value of the outstanding stock of at least one of the other corporations in addition to owning 80% or more of the voting control. This change is effective for years beginning after 1984 except that it will not apply until 1988 to any consolidated return group in existence on June 22, 1984. Hawaii has adopted this 1984 change.

The federal regulations provide detailed rules for consolidated returns. Subjects covered, among many others, include making and changing an election to file consolidated, intercompany transactions, methods of accounting, and inventory adjustments. Under the federal law, to which Hawaii has conformed, the making of a consolidated return constitutes consent of all the included corporations to all regulations prescribed prior to the due date for filing the return.

Only "domestic" affiliated corporations may be included in the Hawaii return. For this reason, an affiliated group for federal tax purposes may be different from the affiliated group for Hawaii tax purposes. If any of the corporations included in the Hawaii consolidated return have taxable activities outside Hawaii, as explained in ¶ 701, the allocation rules described in this chapter should be applied to the entire Hawaii consolidated group.

Prior to 1969 the Hawaii law did not permit consolidated returns of affiliated corporations. See the 1962 decision of the Tax Appeal Court of the State of Hawaii, in the case of *E.G. Elliott, Ltd., and Elliott's Coffee Shop, Ltd.*

Even though there were no consolidated returns, as such, under the Hawaii law prior to 1969, the Director of Taxation could require the filing of returns on a consolidated (better described as a "combined") basis in certain cases. He could require such returns where it was deemed necessary in order to prevent evasion of taxes and to clearly reflect the income from sources within Hawaii. The director still has the right to require a combined return for 1969 or later years under such circumstances, where the corporations involved cannot or do not choose to file a consolidated return.

## ¶ 709. Exemption for Foreign-State Manufacturers Using Hawaii Warehouses
### Hawaii Law: Sec. 235-6

The Hawaii law was amended in 1963, effective for years beginning after Dec. 31, 1962, to provide tax exemption for some out-of-state manufacturers who have their products warehoused in Hawaii. The law provides that a foreign corporation engaged in manufacturing outside Hawaii shall not be deemed to be engaged in trade or business in Hawaii if these conditions are met:

(a) The corporation's products are warehoused in Hawaii by someone who is subject to the excise (gross income) tax or public utilities tax.

(b) All deliveries are made on orders obtained from someone who is licensed under the general excise tax and who is purchasing for resale.

(c) All orders are accepted outside Hawaii.

(d) All collections on sales are made outside Hawaii.

(e) The corporation is not doing business otherwise under the income tax law.

A corporation receiving the benefit of this income tax exemption is nevertheless subject to tax as a wholesaler under the general excise tax law.

## ¶ 710. Special Rules for Corporate Liquidations
### Hawaii Law: Sec. 235-2.3
### Federal Law: Sec. 332, 333, 336, 337, 338, 545

Under federal law prior to 1987, relief from "double taxation" was provided for certain situations where a corporation sells appreciated property and then liquidates. This was accomplished by relieving the corporation of tax on sales of property if the corporation completed its liquidation within a 12-month period. Hawaii conformed to this federal law in the enactment of the basic Hawaii law in 1957.

The Hawaii law was amended in 1963, effective for taxable years beginning after Dec. 31, 1963, to limit this relief to corporations whose shareholders are all residents of Hawaii. In case the corporation is denied relief because of this rule, then Hawaii shareholders are granted relief by giving them credit for their share of the tax paid by the corporation. In other words, the Hawaii shareholder treats his share of the corporation's tax as though he had paid the tax directly. In determining his gain or loss upon the liquidation, the shareholder must add to the amount he receives on liquidation his share of the corporation's tax. This special residency requirement was repealed for tax years beginning after 1986.

The Technical Corrections Act of 1985 made changes to the provisions of Internal Revenue Code Sections 332 and 337 to conform to changes made in 1984 in the definition of affiliate corporations under Internal Revenue Code Section 1504 and to require the liquidation of a distributee corporation in a Section 332 liquidation. Hawaii has adopted these 1985 amendments.

The federal law was amended in 1988 to provide that if a corporate distributee receives property in a complete liquidation under Section 332 and the liquidating corporation recognizes gain or loss with respect to the property distributed, then the distributee will take a fair market value for its basis in the distributed property. Hawaii has adopted this 1988 amendment.

The Tax Reform Act of 1986 repealed the provisions of Internal Revenue Code Sections 336 and 337, which provided that a corporation will not recognize gain on the distribution of assets in a complete or partial liquidation with a few exceptions. The new rules apply to liquidating distributions after Dec. 31, 1986. Hawaii has adopted these 1986 amendments.

The Revenue Act of 1964 introduced new rules for "personal holding companies" into the federal law, and provided a special relief provision for the liquidation of certain corporations affected by the new rules. Hawaii has not adopted this provision.

Both Hawaii and federal law provide special rules for determining the basis of property received by a corporation upon liquidation of a subsidiary, where the stock of the subsidiary was acquired as part of a plan to purchase its assets and the liquidation is merely a step in that plan. However, there may be some differences because of 1966 federal amendments that were not adopted by Hawaii until 1977 and 1978. One of these federal amendments removes a restriction formerly imposed on a corporation that acquires stock from another controlled corporation for the purpose of meeting the 80% ownership requirement under the special rules. The other federal amendment provides for realization of gain on distribution of installment notes in liquidations effected under these rules. Hawaii has adopted this latter rule for taxable years beginning in 1977, and adopted the earlier rule for years beginning in 1978. The federal rules were extensively amended in 1982. Hawaii has adopted the 1982 federal amendments.

The federal law was amended in 1982 to limit the nonrecognition of gain on distribution of corporate property. For distributions made after Aug. 31, 1982, nonrecognition will apply only to complete liquidations and certain partial liquidations. Hawaii has adopted this federal rule. The federal law was amended in 1986 to require a corporation to recognize gain on the distribution of appreciated property that is not distributed pursuant to a plan of reorganization. Hawaii has adopted this federal amendment which is effective for years beginning after December 31, 1986.

### ¶ 711. Special Rules for the Sale of Partnership Interests
#### Hawaii Law: Sec. 235-5

See ¶ 510b for a discussion of the allocation of gain or loss to Hawaii on the sale of a partnership interest.

### ¶ 712. Special Rules for Radio, Television Broadcast Stations, and Publishing Related Businesses

In 1998, the Tax Department modified Regulation 18-235-38-06-04. This amendment provides new rules for the radio and television broadcast industry in determining the sales, property and payroll factors for the purposes of apportioning income among taxing jurisdictions.

Regulation 18-235-38-06-05 modified the rules with regard to taxpayers who are engaged in the business of publishing, selling, licensing, or distributing newspapers, magazines, periodicals, trade journals or other printed materials. The rules were amended to provide new definition for determining sales and property for the industry.

# PART II

## Other Taxes

# CHAPTER 8

## GENERAL EXCISE (GROSS INCOME) TAX

## ¶ 801. History and Imposition of General Excise (Gross Income) Tax
### Hawaii Law: Sec. 237-1, 237-8

The general excise tax, based upon gross income, has been in effect in Hawaii since 1935. The present law was originally enacted in 1955 and has been amended frequently. The tax is administered by the Director of Taxation.

The tax is imposed upon gross income from business and other economic activity related to Hawaii. §237-2 broadly defines business as "all activities (personal, professional, or corporate), engaged in or caused to be engaged in with the object of gain or economic benefit either direct or indirect, but does not include casual sales." For example, for profit and nonprofit taxpayers receiving rental income are generally subject to the general excise tax. It is an excise tax on the privilege of doing business in the state. The tax is levied on the person receiving the income, and is collected from that person; it is not a sales tax on the buyer or consumer. As a practical matter, however, the tax on retail sales is commonly passed on to the consumer and becomes part of the sales price as explained in ¶ 803.

The use tax law, explained in Chapter 9, was enacted in 1965, effective January 1, 1966, to complement and prevent avoidance of the general excise tax. Prior to 1966 there were two types of use tax, the compensating tax and the consumption tax.

## ¶ 802. Rates of Tax
### Hawaii Law: Sec. 182-16, 237-8.6, 237-13, 237-13.3, 237-13.5, 237-13.8, 237-17

The general excise tax rates are as follows:

| | |
|---|---|
| Manufacturers | 0.5% |
| Retailers of tangible personal property | 4.0% |
| Wholesalers of tangible personal property | 0.5% |
| Contractors | 4.0% |
| Theaters, amusements, radio broadcasting stations, etc. | 4.0% |
| Sales representatives | 4.0% |
| Service businesses | 4.0% |
| Services to an intermediary | 0.5% |
| Insurance producers | 0.15% |
| Professions | 4.0% |
| Sugar benefit payment received | 0.5% |
| Sales of geothermal resources, or electrical energy produced from geothermal resources | 0.5% |
| Sales of electric power to public utilities for resale to the public | 0.5% |
| Sales and other taxable gross receipts of the blind, deaf, and disabled or their corporations, partnerships, limited liability partnerships, limited liability companies | 0.5% |
| Sales of prepaid telephone calling service | 4.0% |
| All other business | 4.0% |

Effective January 1, 2007, a county surcharge tax was added to the general excise tax to pay for Oahu's mass transit system. The tax rate is 1/2% added to the 4% GE tax resulting in a total tax of 4.5% on Oahu related transactions subject to 4%. See Hawaii Administrative Rules (HAR) Sections 18-237-8.6-01 to 18-237-8.6-10 for definitions and rules of Oahu related transactions, which were revised in 2018. See Announcement No. 2018 04.

Effective January 1, 2019, through December 31, 2030, Ordinance No. 1021 authorized a Kauai county surcharge of .5% on GE tax. See Tax Announcement No. 2018-14.

Hawaii County also passed Ordinance 1874 authorizing imposition of a .25% county surcharge on GE tax beginning on January 1, 2019, and ending on December 31. 2020. See Tax Announcement No. 2018-15. Thus, for profit and nonprofit taxpayers should refer to the aforementioned rules, and if such taxpayers have gross income sourced in more than one island, they should segregate their transactions by taxing districts. The county surcharge tax does not apply to gross income taxable at the 0.5% or 0.15% rates, or exempt transactions. HRS Section 237-8.6(d).

See ¶ 803p for discussions of the transactions that can now be treated as wholesale sales and that are subject to the phased in rates. See ¶ 804 for discussion on the classification of sales, and on changes in classifications in recent years.

The general excise tax applies to the total gross receipts including the tax, i.e., there is a tax upon the tax. Whether the general excise tax is passed is a contractual matter between the parties. If the general excise tax is passed on, the maximum effective tax rate is 4.166% for the 4.0% rate and 4.712% for the 4.5% rate. See Announcement 2006-15 and Tax Facts 96-1.

## ¶ 803. What Is Subject to Tax
**Hawaii Law: Sec. 237-1, 237-2, 237-3, 237-7, 237-13, 237-18, 237-20, 237-21**

The general excise tax is imposed against persons on account of their business and other activities in the State. The tax is applied to the values of products, gross proceeds from sales, or gross income, based on the type of transaction. Anyone subject to the tax must apply to the Department of Taxation for a license, see ¶ 808.

The law defines "person" to include "every individual, partnership, society, unincorporated association, joint venture, group, hui, joint stock company, corporation, trustee, personal representative, trust estate, decedent's estate, trust, trustee in bankruptcy, or other entity, whether such persons are doing business for themselves or in a fiduciary capacity, and whether the individuals are residents or nonresidents of the State, and whether the corporation or other association is created or organized under the laws of the State or of another jurisdiction".

"Business activity" is defined to include "all activities (personal, professional, or corporate), engaged in or caused to be engaged in with the objective of gain or economic benefit either direct or indirect, but does not include casual sales".

HRS Section 237-1 defines "casual sale" as an occasional or isolated sale or transaction involving (1) tangible personal property by a person who is not required to be licensed under the general excise tax law, or (2) tangible personal property which is not ordinarily sold in the business of a person who is regularly engaged in business.

¶ 802

The Department of Taxation administrative rule Section 18-237-1 defines the term "casual sale". The administrative rule implies that one must look to the size, number, and/or frequency of the transaction. In addition, certain transfers under Sections 332 to 337, 351, 354, 361, 368, and 721 of the Internal Revenue Code will also be treated as casual sales.

The following are some specific examples included in the regulations that illustrate, the Department's interpretation of the term "casual sale":

Example 1:

ABC Corp. is engaged in the retail chain-grocery business and needs new display equipment. Experience has indicated that new display equipment has a useful life of seven years. Accordingly, the taxpayer purchases the new equipment and sells the old equipment. The foregoing sale of the old equipment is not subject to the general excise tax in as much as the sale is considered a "casual sale."

Example 2:

Hawaii Typewriter Co. is a dealer in typewriters, adding machines, and other related office machines. It accepts trade-ins of used office machines, which are reconditioned by the company and eventually sold as "used office machines." The company also withdraws new typewriters and adding machines from its inventory for use in its own business office. The company capitalizes the cost of the machines and claims deductions under IRC Section 168 for income tax purposes. In the ordinary course of business these office machines, which were used in its own business office, are also reconditioned and sold by the company as "used office machines." The sale of these machines, which are used in the trade or business and are assets of like nature as those carried in the merchandise inventory of the taxpayer, therefore is subject to the general excise tax.

Example 3:

Rentals Inc. is engaged in the automobile rental and leasing activity. Every three years or thereabouts, taxpayer makes way for new rental by selling the old rental automobiles. The sale of the old rental automobiles is subject to the general excise tax. Although the taxpayer is not engaged primarily in the business of selling rental automobiles, there are a sufficient number of recurring sales as to constitute engaging in the business of selling automobiles. Thus, such sales are not considered "casual sales."

Example 4:

Subsequent to losing its lease, ABC Drug Store decides to terminate its business. Accordingly, the entire merchandise inventory is sold in bulk to another drug store. The foregoing sale of merchandise inventory is subject to the general excise tax.

In 2003 the definition of "retailing" or "sales at retail" was added to the law.

¶ 803

The law now states that retailers are those taxpayers who sell tangible personal property for consumption or use by a purchaser and which is not for resale, the renting of tangible personal property and the rendering of services by one engaged in a service business or calling to a person who is not purchasing the service for resale.

"Service business or calling" includes all activities engaged in for other persons for a consideration that involves the rendering of a service as distinguished from the sale of tangible property or the production and sale of tangible property. However, "Service business or calling" does not include services rendered by an employee to the employee's employer.

Any rental activity is considered to be a "business" and is subject to tax—see ¶ 803b.

In the Third Special Session, the legislature changed the law to provide relief to transportation service providers, due to the impact of the terrorist attacks on September 11. Previously, transportation service providers were required to pay a 4% tax under the public service company rules, which was computed based on the provider's prior year income. However, the anticipated declining travel market, caused by the terrorist attacks, would result in the providers paying more tax than its current income could possibly support. Therefore the law was amended to include "transportation service" in the definition of service business or calling. This now allows the transportation service providers to pay the same 4% tax, however the tax is now computed on the providers current year income under the general excise tax rules.

The case of *C. Dudley Pratt*, decided by the Hawaii Supreme Court in April 1972, involved the taxability of fees received by an attorney for services as corporate director, as trustee for private trusts, and as an executor of estates. The taxpayer received fees in each of these capacities. The court held that these activities constituted a "business" for purposes of the general excise tax and therefore the fees were taxable. (See also ¶ 803j regarding status of directors' fees.)

In the case of *Vincent Guntzer*, decided by the Hawaii Supreme Court in May 1970, a trustee in bankruptcy contended that he was exempt from tax because he was not "doing business" and for other reasons. The Supreme Court held that he was subject to tax, affirming a decision of the tax appeal court to that effect.

Out-of-state vendors who are not doing business in the state are not subject to tax on interstate sales to purchasers within the state. However, in order to equalize competition, a 1971 amendment to the law regarding purchases by state and county governments provides that, for the sole purpose of determining who is the lowest bidder, the bid price of such out-of-state vendors is to be increased by the applicable retail rate of general excise tax. See ¶ 903 concerning the addition of the 0.5% use tax to out-of-state bids.

In the case of *E-Z Serve, Inc.*, the taxpayer purchased gasoline from Hawaiian Independent Refinery. Title was to pass by agreement within the Foreign-

¶ 803

Trade Zone. The gasoline was delivered by pipeline to *E-Z's* nominee, Aloha Petroleum, for sale to retailers. The Hawaii Tax Appeals Court held that *E-Z* was doing business in Hawaii and subject to the general excise tax on the transfer to Aloha Petroleum. The decision was affirmed by the Hawaii Supreme Court in 1982.

In the case of *Heftel Broadcasting Honolulu, Inc.,* decided Aug. 3, 1976, the Hawaii Supreme Court ruled that rentals of TV films by a Hawaii TV station from a Mainland supplier are subject to the general excise tax. The court found that the renting of the films was sufficient business activity within the state even though all negotiations were consummated outside of Hawaii.

In the tax appeal of *United Parcel Service, Inc.* and *Lynden Air Freight, Inc.,* the issue of whether the preemption of state taxation of air commerce and air transportation under federal law extends to revenue from ground transportation that is related to air transportation. The Tax Appeal Court ruled that federal law preempts the imposition of the general excise tax and the public service company tax upon these revenues. The Department of Taxation appealed the Tax Appeal Court's decision to the Hawaii Supreme Court in both cases. The Hawaii Supreme Court held that the Tax Appeal Court erroneously interpreted the preemption and remanded both cases with instructions to the Tax Appeal Court to enter a summary judgment in favor of the department.

"Gross income" generally includes "the gross receipts, cash or accrued, of the taxpayer, received as compensation for personal services and the gross receipts of the taxpayer derived from trade, business, commerce, or sales and the value proceeding or accruing from the sale of tangible personal property, or service, or both, and all receipts, fees, or other emoluments however designated and without any deductions on account of the cost of property sold, the cost of materials used, labor costs, taxes, royalties, interest, or discount paid or any other expenses whatsoever". Generally, the taxpayer is required to use the same accounting method (cash or accrual) for general excise tax purposes as is used for income tax purposes.

Note there are various exclusions, deductions, exemptions and special rules relating to what constitutes gross income. These are discussed in subsequent paragraphs of this chapter.

The tax is charged on the full sales price, including in the price any tax that is passed on to the purchaser as an addition to the price.

Example:

Stated sales price of merchandise sold at retail ........................... $100.00
General excise tax added ............................................................. $4.00

Total amount charged to buyer (actual amount of sale) .............. $104.00
General excise tax on seller (4% of $104.00)............................... $ 4.16

The general excise tax can also apply to transactions among associated parties. The law provides that a person or company having shareholders or members

¶ 803

(corporation, association, group, trust, partnership, joint venture, or other person) is taxable upon its business with them, and they are taxable upon their business with it. A person or company, whether or not called a cooperative, through which shareholders or members are pursuing a common objective (for example obtaining property or services for their individual businesses or use, or the marketing of their individual products) is a taxable person, and such facts do not give rise to any tax exemption or tax benefit except as otherwise provided in the law (see subsequent paragraphs of this chapter). Even though a business has some of the aspects of agency it shall not be regarded as such unless it is a true agency. See ¶ 803d for a related discussion concerning expense reimbursements.

The above statement means, for example, that partnerships and joint ventures are taxable entities for purposes of the general excise tax.

In the case of *Leonard L. Ray, Jr. and Patricia Ray*, the taxpayers operated a hotel and received as compensation 25% of the income from room rentals. The Hawaii Tax Appeal Court held in 1972 that the compensation to the operators was subject to general excise tax, even though the full amount of the rentals had been taxed when received by the hotel.

In the case of *Hawaiian Holiday, Inc.,* the taxpayer was a general partner and manager of the limited partnerships engaged in the macadamia nut business. The taxpayer received a guaranteed salary for its services as general manager, even though the partnerships suffered losses. The Hawaii Tax Appeal Court held in 1972 that the salary payments were not subject to general excise tax, since there was a true partnership and the payments constituted, in effect, a reallocation of the capital contributions of the partners.

In the matter of the tax appeal of *Island Holidays, Ltd.* (July 12, 1978), the taxpayer entered into a joint venture agreement to manage a hotel. Under the terms of the agreement, the taxpayer was to receive a guaranteed payment of 3% of the gross revenues received by the hotel. The taxpayer was to receive no other payments for its services and the agreement could be terminated at any time. The Hawaii Supreme Court held that the guaranteed payments were in the nature of compensation for services and therefore subject to the general excise tax under HRS Section 237-20. In the lower court, the Tax Appeals Court had reached the same conclusion but on the basis that the agreement in question was not a true partnership. Since the Supreme Court's decision in the *Island Holidays, Ltd.,* case does not rest on the question of whether the agreement was a true partnership, there is some question whether the holding in the *Hawaiian Holiday, Inc.,* case is still valid.

In the matter of the tax appeal of *Bishop Square Associates,* (December 27, 1991) the taxpayer was a partnership composed of an insurance company and a California employee retirement system, both of which are exempt from the general excise tax under HRS Sections 237-23(a)(4) and 237-24(21) [now 237-24.3(4)]. The partnership owned and managed commercial property. The business of the partnership was neither insurance nor an employee benefit plan. The

Tax Appeal Court concluded that under HRS Section 237-1, "person" includes every partnership and that the taxpayer is therefore a person subject to the general excise tax as a separate entity. The court also confirmed that general excise tax exemptions of individuals or entities do not extend to taxable persons of which such individuals or entities are members. In addition, the court decision stated that under the general excise tax law, exemptions of individual partners do not extend and do not apply to the partnership of which the individual partners are members.

*In the Matter of the Tax Appeal of Wasson-Bendon Partners v. Kamikawa,* No. 22403 (4/28/00), *cert. denied* at (6/02/00), the Intermediate Court of Appeals held that the payments to a partner were for equipment leases and not distributions of profits and thus, were subject to general excise tax.

In Announcement 2016-06 summarizing *Travelocity v. Director, 135 Hawaii 88 (2015)*, the Department stated that "physical presence" is not required to satisfy "in the state" requirement of Section 237-13, i.e., conducting business or other activity in the state.

On June 21, 2018, the United States Supreme Court ruled in *South Dakota v. Wayfair, No. 17-494, 2018 WL 3058015, at *17 (U.S. Jun. 21, 2018)*, that South Dakota's law taxing out of state sellers without a physical presence in state was not unconstitutional because physical presence was not required to meet the substantial nexus standard under the Commerce Clause. Even prior to the Wayfair decision, Act 41, SLH 2018 was signed into law." See also Annoucement 2018-10 (as amended July 10, 2018).

Act 41 provides that a taxpayer must maintain a GET license, file GET returns and remit GET to the state if any of the following tests apply:

(1) Taxpayer has a physical presence in Hawaii;

(2) In the current or preceding calendar year, taxpayer has gross income or gross proceeds of $100,000 or more from any of the following, or combination of the following, activities:

    a. Tangible property delivered in Hawaii;

    b. Services used or consumed in Hawaii; or

    c. Intangible property used in Hawaii; or

(3) In the current or preceding calendar year, taxpayer has entered into 200 or more separate transactions involving any of the following, or combination of the following, activities:

    a. Tangible property delivered in Hawaii;

    b. Services used or consumed in Hawaii; or

    c. Intangible property used in Hawaii.

While Act 41 provides that the Act takes effect on July 1, 2018, and shall apply to taxable years beginning after December 31, 2017, the Department

¶ 803

announced that it will not retroactively administer Act 41. Taxpayers who lacked physical presence in Hawaii prior to July 1, 2018, but who met the $100,000 or 200-transaction threshold in 2017 or 2018, will not be required to remit GET for the period from January 1, 2018, to June 30, 2018. The taxpayer would be subject to GET beginning on July 1, 2018. Fiscal year taxpayers would be subject to GET beginning on July 1, 2018, or the first day of the tax year beginning after December 31, 2017, whichever is later. The taxpayer will receive a grace period of one period to file the first periodic return.

The following chart provides the first filing deadlines for calendar year taxpayers who will be filing on a monthly basis:

(1) A taxpayer who meets the threshold test and qualifies for the grace period may need to report income that it recognized prior to and during the period being reported. This "catchup income" may be reported, without penalty or interest, in one of two ways: In full on the first periodic return; or

(2) Prorated equally throughout the remaining periods in the current tax year.

The Department has issued answers to anticipated frequently asked questions in Announcement No. 2018-10.

### ¶ 803a. Interest
#### Hawaii Law: Sec. 237-3, 237-23.5, 237-24.8

Interest income is subject to tax if it is received in connection with a trade or business. In Tax Information Release No. 42-74 (April 19, 1974), the Department of Taxation issued guidelines to determine when interest is taxable. The department's position, in summary, is that wherever funds have been derived from a business and are invested or where funds that have been invested are to be used in a business, the interest is taxable. In addition, where property that was used in a business is sold on an installment basis, interest on the payments received is taxable. Thus, where rental property is sold on an agreement of sale, the interest received on the agreement of sale is subject to tax. Where interest is received by a taxpayer from an investment that is not part of his business and is not from the sale of business property, the interest is not taxable. Tax Information Release No. 42-74, included in Part III of this book, contains many examples that are too numerous to be included here but should be referred to for clarification of this question in situations that are not clear cut.

The Department of Taxation issued Tax Information Release No. 94-1 to clarify the taxation of interest earned by trusts. Such release provides that because trusts are generally organized to protect and conserve property, rather than to engage in business, the interest income earned by a trust is generally not subject to the general excise tax unless the trust is engaged in a business activity.

The law specifically exempts interest received by "financial institutions" from the general excise tax. See ¶ 803m for the definition of "financial institution". Also, as of June 6, 1987, interest on mortgage securities issued by the Housing Finance and Development Corporation to raise funds for housing loan programs, is exempt from the general excise tax.

The general excise tax also does not apply to imputed or stated interest attributable to loans, advances, or use of capital between related entities (see ¶ 807).

In *Hawaiian Beaches, Inc., et al.,* the Hawaii Supreme Court held, in August 1970, that interest received on a contract for sale of land in fee simple is taxable. Such interest does not come within the exemption (see ¶ 807) for sales of such land.

In the tax appeal of *Grayco Land Escrow, Ltd. and Hawaiian Ranchos, Inc.,* decided on Jan. 14, 1977, the Hawaii Supreme Court held that interest from deferred land contracts were subject to the Hawaii general excise tax even though the taxpayer was not domiciled in Hawaii.

## ¶ 803b. Rentals
### Hawaii Law: Sec. 237-3, 237-30.5

Rental of property is considered to be a trade or business for purposes of the general excise tax. This also applies to the rental of residential real estate (Tax Information Release No. 90-13). A general excise tax license must be obtained from, and the tax return filed in, the taxation district office where the taxpayer resides or in the taxation district where the rental property is situated. For out-of-state residents or persons having gross income from more than one taxation district, the tax return must be filed with the Oahu district office. The general excise tax is imposed on rental income at 4% on the gross rental income received. In addition, H.R.S. Section 237-8.6 counties to impose a surcharge of up to .5% on the state general excise tax. The taxpayer's accounting method governs when gross rental income will be subject to the general excise tax. For example, advance rental payments may be taxable to the cash method taxpayer when received, but for the accrual method taxpayer when payments are due or earned.

"Gross rental income received" is is computed without any deductions on account of expenses such as commissions paid to rental agents or general excise taxes passed on to renters. The Department of Taxation issued Tax Information Release No. 92-5 on November 20, 1992, to remind taxpayers that the general excise tax applies to the total payments, including real property taxes received from a lessee or sublessee as consideration or rental for use or occupancy of real property. The release also states that the payment of real property taxes directly to a county taxing authority by a lessee or sublessee on an owner/lessor/sublessor's real property does not affect the inclusion of the real property taxes in the owner/lessor/sublessor's income subject to the general excise tax where both the rent and the requirement to pay taxes are in consideration for the use of the property. Even if these payments are separately referred to as rent and taxes, both constitute rental income for use of the property and are subject to the general excise tax.

Property managers are subject to certain reporting requirements. Every written rent collection agreement must have the name, address, Social Security number, and, if available, the general excise tax number of the real property owner. In addition, rental agreements must have the following statement on the first page, set forth in bold print and 10-point type size:

"Hawaii general excise taxes must be paid on the gross rents collected by renting property in the State of Hawaii. A copy of the first page of this agreement, or of federal Internal Revenue Form 1099 stating the amount of rents collected, shall be filed with the Hawaii Department of Taxation."

Agents must file a copy of the first page of the written agreement or federal Form 1099 with the Department of Taxation within 30 days after entering into the agreement. For oral agreements, rent collectors must furnish the Department of Taxation with the same information stated above and also give a copy of the statement to the property owner.

Sale of property for rental use (e.g., machinery) may be subject to tax as a retail sale at the 4% rate, even though the income from the rental of the property will also be taxed at 4%. Property imported for rental use may be subject to the use tax at time of delivery, as explained in ¶ 903, even though the subsequent rentals of the property to be received will be subject to the general excise tax at the same rate. See ¶ 804 for special rule on sales of capital goods to licensed leasing companies.

Effective October 1, 1998 sublessors are allowed to deduct from gross rents, a portion of the lease rent paid by the sublessor in determining gross rents subject to the Hawaii general excise tax. The amount of the lease rent allowed as a deduction is the lease rent allocable to the portion of the real property being subleased. The allocation of the lease rent paid is to take into consideration factors such as the square footage and quality of space being leased. The Hawaii Administrative Rules section 18-237-16.5- provides guidance regarding the application of the sublease deduction. The allowable deduction is to be phased in over seven years and will be limited to a maximum of 87.5 percent of lease rent paid. The allowable deduction percentage for 1998 was 12.5 percent. This amount increased by 12.5 percent each year until the calendar year 2004 when the percentage became 87.5 percent. The concept can be illustrated by the example below:

Assume taxpayer A leases a building to taxpayer B for $1,000 per month and taxpayer B leases one-half of the building for $900 a month to taxpayer C. Further, assume that the lease rent of the building is proportionate based on area. Taxpayer B will be allowed in the year 2004 to deduct from the $900 lease rent income, 87.5 percent of the one-half of the $1,000 taxpayer B pays to taxpayer A. Taxpayer B will be obligated to pay Hawaii general excise tax of 4% on $642.50 ($900-(87.5% x $500)).

In *Subway Real Estate Corp. v. Director of Taxation, State of Hawaii*, 110 Haw. 25 (2006), the Hawaii Supreme Court held that the taxpayer subleased properties to the franchisees of an affiliate franchisor, the substance over form doctrine was inapplicable, and the taxpayer did not qualify for the reimbursement exemption under H.R.S. Section 237-20, and thus, the taxpayer was subject to the general excise tax on its deemed sublease rent even though the franchisee/sublessee directly paid the landlord.

Hawaii law was amended in 2011 and Act 105 was passed to temporarily suspend the sublease deduction from July 1, 2011 thru June 30, 2013. Act 105 provides that for binding written contracts entered into prior to July 1, 2011 which do not permit the passing on of increased rates of taxes, the sublease deduction will still be available. However, upon the expiration of the contract, the sublease deduction will not be available to the sublessor and the sublessor will be liable to pay 4% general excise tax on the gross rents received from the sublessee. See ¶ 807a for a discussion of the exemptions and deductions previously suspended by Act 105.

## ¶ 803c. Construction Contractors
### Hawaii Law: Sec. 237-6, 237-13

In general, the law imposes a general excise tax at the rate of 4% upon the gross income of a contractor in a contracting business. However to cure the potential for double taxation where subcontractors are involved, the prime contractor is allowed a deduction (called the subcontract deduction) from gross income for payments made to: (1) another contractor, (2) a specialty contractor duly licensed by the Department of Commerce and Consumer Affairs in respect of the specialty contractor's business or, (3) a specialty contractor who is not licensed by the Department of Commerce and Consumer Affairs but who performs contracting activities on federal military installations and nowhere else in the State. For the prime contractor to obtain this deduction, both the prime contractor and subcontractor (or specialty contractor) must be licensed under the general excise tax law (have a GET license). Refer to Part III of this book for Rules Section 18-237-13-03, relating to tax upon contractors, for definitions and examples concerning the subcontract deduction.

The subcontractor deduction was suspended from July 1, 2011 – June 20, 2013. Refer to the end of this section for further information

Contractors and others who, as a business enterprise, construct improvements on land they own or lease, may be taxable on the proceeds of sale of the property, to the extent the proceeds are applicable to construction of the improvements. There is no tax if the improvements were constructed with the intention of holding the property for at least one year. The measure of tax is the lesser of (1) proceeds of the sale attributable to improvements or (2) the amount that would have been taxable to a contractor if the construction of the improvements had been contracted out.

Example:

A, who is a contractor, owns a piece of property. To sell it he builds a house on it. Had he contracted this job out, it would have cost him $250,000. The property, including the house, is sold for $400,000, allocable $100,000 to the land and $300,000 to the house. At the time of the sale A is liable for general excise tax of 4% on $250,000, or $10,000.

Sales to the federal government by cost-plus contractors are not exempt from tax, despite the general exemption for sales of tangible property to the federal government. However, such a contractor may exclude from his gross income amounts received as reimbursement of costs incurred for materials, plant, or equipment purchased from a taxpayer who is licensed under the general excise tax law if the taxpayer agrees to pay tax on such amounts computed the same as upon a sale to the state government. This exemption for reimbursements received by federal cost-plus contractors for the costs of purchased materials, plant, and equipment was temporarily suspended by Act 105 from July 1, 2011 – June 30, 2013. See ¶ 807a for a discussion of the exemptions and deductions previously suspended by Act 105.

See ¶ 803h for a discussion of the taxability of out-of-state construction contracts.

See ¶ 807 for exemption of certain scientific contracts with the United States and exemption for construction of an aircraft service and maintenance facility.

In prior years, a general contractor could claim the subcontractor deduction only if the subcontractor's name and amount of the deduction was listed on the general contractor's general excise tax return and the 4% general excise tax was paid on the gross income received by the subcontractor. If, however, the subcontractor did not pay the general excise tax, then the State would deny the deduction taken by the general contractor who would then be liable for the tax on the amount paid to the contractor. In 1998, the law was amended with the intention of relieving the general contractor of the liability for the general excise taxes on the contract amounts paid to the subcontractor. The new law now states that the general contractor can claim the deduction from its gross contracting income equal to the amount that was paid to the subcontractor as long as the subcontractor's name, general excise number and the amount of the deduction are listed on the general contractor's excise tax return. If these items are not listed on the return, the deduction will be disallowed. Hence, the information that is now being required allows the State to pursue the subcontractor instead of holding the general contractor liable for the unpaid taxes.

Hawaii law was amended in 2011 and Act 105 was passed to temporarily suspend the subcontractor deduction from July 1, 2011 thru June 30, 2013. Act 105 provides that for binding, written contracts entered into prior to July 1, 2011 which do not permit the passing on of increased rates of taxes, the subcontractor deduction will still be available. If there is no binding contract prior to July 1, 2011, both the contractor and subcontractor will be subject to tax at the rate of 4%. There will be no 0.5% wholesale rate for this transaction.

¶ 803c

## ¶ 803d. Expense Reimbursements
### Hawaii Law: Sec. 237-20

Prior to 1967, payments from one person to another, as reimbursement of costs or advances made for the person making the payment, were considered income subject to the general excise tax. In 1967, the law was amended to provide that payment of such reimbursements does not constitute income of the recipient unless the recipient "also receives additional monetary consideration for making such costs or advances."

The Department of Taxation issued regulations interpreting this change as Hawaii Administrative Rules section 18-237-20. The reimbursement exemption applies when:

(1) Taxpayer pays a cost or advance to Third Party;

(2) For or on behalf of Reimbursing Party; and

(3) Taxpayer is repaid the cost or advance and receives no additional monetary consideration for making the cost or advance.

HAR § 18-237-20-02.

The following are interpretations included in the administrative rules, exactly as stated therein, with highly condensed versions of some of the examples used:

1. "Additional monetary consideration" means any amount, which Taxpayer receives that is in excess of the cost or advance to Third Party. For there to be no additional monetary consideration, the amount received by Taxpayer must be no more than the cost or advance.

   Example 1: On behalf of Reimbursing Party, Consultant pays Third Party for tickets on behalf of Reimbursing Party. Consultant receives a fee and the amount covering the tickets' price. Consultant received additional monetary consideration.

   Example 2: Equipment Seller and Equipment Manufacturer have a cost-splitting agreement to share advertising expenses and expect to equally benefit from the advertising. Seller will initially pay the advertising agency for all costs and Manufacturer will pay Seller 50 percent of the advertising costs, with no additional amounts for Seller's overhead or profit. No additional monetary consideration.

2. "Additional monetary consideration" includes money, property, services, or any-in-kind payment or value, which Taxpayer receives that is, related to the cost or advance.

   Example 4: Real Estate Broker and Real Estate Agents, independent contractors, enter into a cost-splitting agreement relating to the use of Broker's telephones for long-distance calls. Broker pays the telephone company for all charges and collects from each agent the exact amount of charges attributable to that agent. Broker receives a "rebate" from the telephone company based on the volume of long-distance calls, which it does not share with Agents. Broker receives additional monetary consideration unless the rebate is passed-on to each agent in proportion to calls made by each agent.

3. "Additional monetary consideration" does not include amounts received by the Taxpayer that are unrelated to the cost or advance to Third Party.

Example 5: Supermarket advances money to Third Party on behalf of Fish Market for the purchase of a truck. Supermarket receives the amount advanced as well as a refund from returned products from Fish Market. No additional monetary consideration because the refund is unrelated to the cost or advance.

4. "Cost or advance", defined. (a) "Cost or advance" means the actual invoice amount that a Taxpayer pays to a Third Party.

Example 7: Manufacturer directs Repairer to perform warranty work. Repairer has Third Party perform the work. Repairer pays the $100 invoice amount to Third Party and Manufacturer pays $100 to Repairer. The $100 is a cost or advance.

5. "Cost or advance" does not include an amount that a Taxpayer pays for costs or expenses consumed by the Taxpayer, such as an amount that the Taxpayer pays to its own employees; or an amount representing usage of the Taxpayer's supplies or equipment.

Example 8: Repairer bills Manufacturer a fee of $1,250 plus $1,000 representing the wages paid to Repairer's employees for services and replaced parts. The $1,000 is not a cost or advance.

Example 10: Law Firm bills Client $1,000 for professional services plus $100 for copying costs at 10 cents a page. The copies were made on Law Firm's equipment by Law Firm's employees. The $100 is not a cost or advance.

6. "For or on behalf of Reimbursing Party", defined. (a) A payment of a cost or advance is "for or on behalf of Reimbursing Party" when done at the request or direction of Reimbursing Party.

(b) A cost or advance is done at the request or direction of Reimbursing Party if:

(1) (A) The payment is made pursuant to a preexisting contract between Reimbursing Party and Third Party that creates a direct obligation for Reimbursing Party to pay Third Party for property or services;

(B) The payment is made pursuant to a preexisting contract between Reimbursing Party and Taxpayer whereby Taxpayer pays Third Party for property or services to satisfy an obligation of Reimbursing Party; or

(C) The payment is made pursuant to a preexisting cost-splitting contract whereby Taxpayer pays Third Party for property or services provided to both Taxpayer and Reimbursing Party, and Taxpayer receives from Reimbursing Party a payment proportionate to Reimbursing Party's share of the cost of the property or services based upon an actually calculable factor that has an economic basis (e.g., quantity of property, square footage, time spent, lines of advertising);

(2) A Taxpayer does not use, consume, or alter the property or services provided by Third Party. Third Party's property or services are used, consumed, or altered by Taxpayer if the property or services are incorporated into or combined with the Taxpayer's property or services or are amounts paid for the Taxpayer's overhead.

(c) "The payment is made pursuant to a preexisting contract between Reimbursing Party and Third Party that creates a direct obligation for Reimbursing Party to pay Third Party for property or services" is illustrated as follows:

Example 12: Manager manages Owner's apartment and the management agreement states that Owner is ultimately responsible for paying all major expenditures. Manager contracts with Contractor to replace the carpet (a major expenditure) and Owner approves. The contract with Contractor is entered into in Manager's name and Manager pays Contractor. Owner repays Manager for Contractor's fee with no additional consideration. The payment is made pursuant to a preexisting contract whereby Manager pays Contractor for property or services to satisfy an obligation of Owner.

Example 13: Owner leases a potion of an office building to Tenant and agrees to provide janitorial services. Owner contracts with Janitor to clean the building and pays Janitor. Tenant pays Owner rent and its share of cleaning expenses. Neither the lease nor the janitorial services contract is a preexisting contract that creates an obligation, direct or otherwise, for Tenant to pay Janitor for the janitorial services.

Example 15: Renter leases real property from Landlord and subleases the property to Franchisee. Renter discharges its rental obligation in its sublease agreement by requiring Franchisee to directly pay Landlord. Franchisee's sublease rent payment is not considered a payment by Renter made for or on behalf of Franchisee because the sublease obligates Franchisee to Renter and not to Landlord. Because the payment also discharges Renter's underlying obligation to Landlord, the payment is not a reimbursement of a cost or advance for or on behalf of Franchisee to Landlord. The sublease merely requires that Franchisee's sublease rent payment be directed to Landlord to satisfy Renter's lease rent obligation. Franchisee's sublease rent payment directly to Landlord is a payment for or on behalf of Renter and not for or on behalf of Franchisee. The sublease is not a preexisting contract that creates a direct obligation for Franchisee to pay Landlord the sublease rent. However, Renter may be eligible for the sublease deduction under section 237-16.5, HRS.

¶ 803d

7. "The payment is made pursuant to a preexisting contract between Reimbursing Party and Taxpayer whereby Taxpayer pays Third Party for property or services to satisfy an obligation of Reimbursing Party" is illustrated as follows:

Example 16: Manufacturer directs Repairer to perform warranty work. Repairer has Third Party perform the work. These warranty work expenses are paid pursuant to a preexisting contract between Repairer and Manufacturer whereby Repairer pays Third Party for property or services to satisfy an obligation of Manufacturer.

Example 18: Attorney enters into an agency agreement to represent Client. Attorney passes on to Client the costs paid for traveling expenses, longdistance telephone calls, and the cost of reproduction to Third Parties. These costs are not the obligation of Client. These costs are the obligation of Attorney because they are necessarily incurred by Attorney to allow Attorney to perform legal services for Client. Attorney uses, consumes, or alters Third Parties' services to perform legal services. *See* section 18-237-20-6(f).

8. "The payment is made pursuant to a preexisting cost-splitting contract whereby Taxpayer pays Third Party for property or services provided to both Taxpayer and Reimbursing Party, and Taxpayer receives from Reimbursing Party a payment proportionate to Reimbursing Party's share of the cost of the property or services based upon an actually calculable factor that has an economic basis (e.g., quantity of property, square footage, time spent, lines of advertising)" is illustrated as follows:

Example 22: Real Estate Broker and Real Estate Sales Agents, independent contractors, have a preexisting cost splitting contract relating to advertising property listings in Third Party's newspaper. All listings are in a single advertisement in the paper. Broker initially pays Third Party for all advertising costs and each agent repays Broker a portion of the advertising costs attributable to each agent's listings. The payment to Third Party is made pursuant to a preexisting cost-splitting contract whereby Broker pays Third Party for property or services provided to both Broker and each agent, and Broker receives from each agent a payment proportionate to the agent's share of the cost of the property or services based upon an actually calculable factor that has an economic basis.

Example 29: Architect enters into a contract with Client whereby Architect will receive its fee for professional services and incidental costs (travel, long-distance telephone calls, copying, etc.) paid to third parties. Architect pays third parties and breaks down the billing into its professional services and payments to third parties. The payments to third parties are not made pursuant to a preexisting cost-splitting contract whereby Architect pays third parties for property or services provided to both Architect and Client, and Architect receives from Client a payment proportionate to Client's share of the cost of the property or services based upon an actually calculable factor that has an economic basis. These services are provided to Architect to allow Architect to fulfill its contract with Client; the services are not provided to both Architect and Client.

Example 31: Owner leases an office building to tenants and agrees to provide janitorial services. Owner contracts with a property management company to rent and maintain the building and the property management company contracts with a janitorial services company to clean the building. The reimbursement exemption is not applicable to either Owner or the property management company. (1) Owner is subject to the general excise tax on the rent received from tenants, including the amounts received for janitorial services. The reimbursement exemption is not applicable because the payment to the janitorial service company is not made pursuant to a preexisting cost-splitting contract. (2) The property management company is subject to the general excise tax on the income received for managing the building, but not for Owner's income, including the amounts received by Owner for janitorial services.

Example 32: Renter leases real property from Landlord and subleases the property for Franchisee. The sublease agreement specifies that Franchisee's sublease rent is equal to or less than the amount of lease rent that Renter is required to pay Landlord. Franchisee pays its rent to Renter; Renter pays its rent to Landlord. The sublease is not a preexisting contract that creates a direct obligation between Franchisee and Landlord. Franchisee's sublease rent payment is made pursuant to a sublease between Renter and Franchisee, not pursuant to a preexisting cost-splitting contract. Unlike a preexisting cost-splitting contract involving three parties where Taxpayer (Renter) and Reimbursing Party (Franchisee) agree to proportionately share the cost of property or services provided by Third Party to both Taxpayer (Renter) and Reimbursing Party (Franchisee), a sublease is a contract between only two parties where one party (Franchisee/Reimbursing Party) agrees to pay rent to another (Renter/Taxpayer) in return for the use and possession of property. In this lease-sublease arrangement, Landlord (Third Party) provides the use and possession of property to Renter in exchange for rent. Subsequently, Renter provides the use and possession of the property to franchisee/Reimbursing Party in exchange for rent. The property is not provided to Renter and franchisee at the same time, and the cost of using real property is not shared by Renter and Franchisee.

9. "Taxpayer does not use, consume, or alter the property or services provided by Third Party" is illustrated as follows:

Example 33: Manufacturer directs Repairer to perform warranty work. Repairer has Third Party perform the work. Repairer does not use, consume,

¶ 803d

or alter Third Party's services because the warranty work is not incorporated into or combined with Repairer's property or services. Third Party's warranty work is provided to Manufacturer's customer.

Example 34: Architect enters into a contract with Client whereby Architect will receive its fee for professional services and incidental costs (travel, long-distance telephone calls, copying, etc.) paid to third parties. Architect pays third parties and breaks down the billing into its professional services and payments to third parties. The traveling expenses, long-distance telephone calls, the reproduced items, and postage are used, consumed, or altered because these incidental services are incorporated into or combined with Architect's architecture services.

Example 36: Customer hires Accounting Firm to audit its financial records. Accounting Firm contracts with Third Party to perform part of the audit and combines Third Party's work with the work of Accounting Firm's employees. Accounting Firm pays Third Party. Even if Accounting Firm separately bills Customer for the exact amount paid to Third Party, Accounting Firm uses, consumes, or alters Third Party's services because the services are incorporated into or combined with Accounting Firm's services.

10. A cost or advance cannot be made for or on behalf of Reimbursing Party if Taxpayer makes the cost or advance before a request by Reimbursing Party.

Example 37: Manufacturer directs Repairer to perform warranty work. Repairer has Third Party perform the work. The payment for warranty work is a cost or advance because Repairer makes the cost or advance (payment of expenses) after a request by Manufacturer.

Example 38: Taxpayer signs a contract with Third Party that provides Taxpayer unlimited access to a research database. Taxpayer subsequently allows Reimbursing Party to access the database using Taxpayer's account and charges Reimbursing Party one-half of the access fee. The access fee is not a cost or advance for or on behalf of Reimbursing Party because Taxpayer makes the cost or advance (purchase of access to the data base) prior to any request by Reimbursing Party.

The appeal of *Foodland Super Market, Ltd.,* decided by the Hawaii Supreme Court in 1969 involved the taxability of amounts received by a food market from manufacturers under various cooperative advertising agreements. None of the agreements provided for exact reimbursement of advertising expenses incurred by the market. The taxpayer contended that the payments were, in effect, discounts on the taxpayer's purchases from the manufacturers. The court held that the payments represented taxable income from advertising and promotional services. Since the Foodland case was decided on the basis of its own peculiar facts, it will not necessarily be controlling in other cases involving cooperative advertising and marketing agreements.

¶ 803d

The appeal of *Pacific Machinery, Inc.,* decided by the Hawaii Supreme Court in 1982, involved the taxability of amounts received by a dealer from a manufacturer for amounts paid to third parties for advertising of the manufacturer's products. Under a cooperative advertising agreement, the dealer invoiced the manufacturer for 50% of the amounts billed to the dealer by third parties for pre-approved advertising of the manufacturer's products. The invoicing to the manufacturer did not include any costs for overhead, salaries, or other internal expenses or profit incurred by the dealer in connection with advertising the manufacturer's products. The court held that the amounts paid by the manufacturer were expense reimbursements and not taxable.

The law as amended in 1967, was involved in a 1972 decision of the Tax Appeal Court in the case of *711 Motors, Inc.* The court held that an automobile dealer was not taxable on reimbursements received from a manufacturer for the dealer's costs incurred in making good the manufacturer's warranty on cars sold. However, this ruling was reversed in 1973, in the *Aloha Motors* case discussed below.

In the tax appeal of *Aloha Motors, Inc. and Edward R. Bacon Company of Hawaii, Limited,* the Hawaii Supreme Court held in 1975 that payments received by automobile dealers from manufacturers for warranty service to customers are taxable sales. However, the court held that where the dealer farms out the work to others and is reimbursed by the manufacturer for the exact amount paid out, the reimbursement is not taxable. Further, the court held that payments received for repair work on equipment damaged in transit are exempt from tax as compensatory damages (see ¶ 807).

In the matter of the appeal of *C. Brewer and Company, Ltd.,* TA 1793 (Dec. 19, 1978) the taxpayer performed administrative services for both its wholly owned and less than wholly owned subsidiaries. In its dealings with the less than wholly owned subsidiaries, the taxpayer was reimbursed for its expenses. But for similar services performed for wholly owned subsidiaries, the taxpayer chose to record the allocated expense as a contribution by the taxpayer to the capital of the subsidiaries. For federal and state income tax purposes, the taxpayer reported the amount of services performed for its wholly owned subsidiaries as other income. The Tax Appeals Court upheld the Tax Director's assessment of additional general excise tax on these items of expense as gross receipts to the taxpayer. The decision was affirmed by the Hawaii Supreme Court in 1982.

Citing Brewer, the Hawaii Intermediate Court of Appeals in *In the Matter of the Tax Appeal of Trade Wind Tours of Hawaii, Inc., 6 Haw App 260 (April 22, 1986),* upheld imposition of the general excise tax on a corporation that had provided management and administrative services to its wholly owned subsidiary corporations. The taxpayer had incurred certain overhead and administrative expenses, which it alternately reported as "Unrecorded Management Fees" under gross income and, in subsequent years, "Overhead Expenses Allocated"

¶ 803d

under expenses. The court found that for purposes of the general excise tax statute "it matters not whether the business is conducted between related or unrelated persons or entities."

Effective June 6, 1988, a favorable change in the law was made that exempts from general excise tax amounts received, charged, or attributable to services furnished by one related entity to another related entity. This exemption is outlined in Hawaii Revised Statutes section 237-23.5. The exemption also applies to interest income and amounts received by common paymasters where related entities are involved. See ¶ 807.

In the matter of the appeal of *Waikiki Development Co., Inc.,* the taxpayer subleased 21 parcels of land in Waikiki. The subleases required the sublessees to construct substantial improvements on the property and also required the sublessees to pay all taxes assessed against the property. The Tax Director determined that the payments of real property taxes by the sublessees were rental income to the taxpayer and therefore taxable under the general excise tax law. Taxpayer admitted that the payment of real property taxes paid by the sublessees on the lease of land is ordinarily considered rental income to the sublessor. However, the taxpayer argued that where the sublessee built and paid for the improvements, then payment of taxes on the improvements is not income to the sublessor. The Tax Appeals Court upheld the Tax Director's determination.

In the matter of the appeal of *Island Tobacco Company, Ltd.,* the taxpayer, a wholesaler, sold its products to retailers and the military exchange. The taxpayer had entered into an agreement with one of its suppliers, wherein the taxpayer agreed to perform certain distributive and promotional services to promote the sales of the supplier's products. Payments were made upon satisfactory proof submitted by the taxpayer in monthly report forms to its supplier. In addition, a bonus incentive based upon the taxpayer's increase in sales volume of the supplier's products over the prior year's sales volume was paid after the end of the year. The taxpayer also received a service fee and price rebates from manufacturer for sales to the military. The service fee was a specified amount per case or percentage of sale price for services rendered in supplying military retail outlets with the manufacturer's products. The price rebate was based on the difference between the taxpayer's cost and the military's cost where the manufacturer increased its price and the taxpayer was unable to increase its price to the military because of its contract with the military exchange. The Tax Appeals Court held that the promotional and sales fees were commissions for services performed and were not exempt from the general excise tax. The court found that the price rebates were a price protection measure and therefore a reduction of purchase price.

Maintenance payments received from the owner of a cooperative apartment by a cooperative housing corporation are not considered taxable income, provided:

(1) the corporation has only one class of stock;

¶ 803d

(2) each stockholder is entitled by reason of his ownership to occupy a unit in the corporation's property;

(3) no stockholder is entitled to receive any distribution out of earnings except in a complete or partial liquidation.

There is also an exemption for amounts received by the manager or board of directors of an association of apartment owners (established in accordance with Chapter 514A of the HRS) or a nonprofit homeowner or community association (incorporated in accordance with Chapter 415B of the HRS), in reimbursement of sums paid for common expense.

The Department of Taxation, in Tax Information Release No. 65-79, has held that amounts received by homeowners' associations from rentals of parking stalls, interest, commissions, vending machines, coin-operated laundry facilities, and other similar amounts are taxable for general excise purposes.

## ¶ 803e. Shows, etc.
### Hawaii Law: Sec. 237-18, 237-44

Special rules are provided for taxing receipts from shows, etc.

Where gate receipts or other admissions are divided between a local producer of a show and a promoter, the entire tax on the proceeds is imposed on the promoter, who in turn may withhold the appropriate portion of the tax from the producer.

Example:

A promoter engages M Co. to produce a show with an agreement that M Co. is to receive 60% of total gate receipts. The gate receipts amount to $15,000. The promoter is liable for a tax of 4% on the entire $15,000, or $600. He is, however, permitted to recover $360 by deducting that amount from the $9,000 he pays to M Co.

Where a transient taxpayer is putting on a show, anyone receiving admissions is required to set aside and hold in trust a portion of the amount collected, to assure payment of tax by the transient taxpayer. The amount to be set aside is 5% of the admissions, or a smaller amount if approved by the Director of Taxation. Furthermore, if a person engages a transient taxpayer to put on a show, the person engaging the transient taxpayer shall collect from such taxpayer, by withholding or otherwise, the general excise tax levied on the income from the show.

## ¶ 803f. Savings Stamps

Persons who give to their customers stamps, coupons, tickets, certificates, cards, or other similar devices that are redeemable in goods or merchandise are taxed upon the full amount of their sales, without deduction for the cost of the stamps or other devices. The person who furnishes the stamps or other devices to the store and redeems the stamps for the store's customers is taxed upon his gross income from sale of the stamps (at 4%). There is no tax to anyone at the time the stamps are redeemed.

## ¶ 803g. Bulk Sales
### Hawaii Law: Sec. 237-43

Effective July 1, 1995, the bulk sale rules were expanded to apply to the sale or certain transfers of fixtures, merchandise, or other assets or property of a business, not in the ordinary course of business. The term transfer means the sale, conveyance, or distribution by any mode, direct or indirect, absolute or conditional, voluntary or involuntary, title to or beneficial ownership or interest in property. The term property means anything that may be the subject of ownership, including every kind of asset, whether real or personal, tangible or intangible, but does not include certain interests in residential real property.

A bulk sale or transfer of merchandise, fixtures, or other assets of property of a business, not in the ordinary course of business, must be reported by the seller within 10 days after the possession, control, or title to property or any part thereof, has passed. The purchaser must withhold payment until he receives a bulk sales certificate showing a brief description of the property sold or transferred, the date of sale or transfer, and other information required by the Director of Taxation. If the purchaser does not secure a bulk sales certificate, he may be personally liable for all of the seller's taxes, penalties, and interest administered by the Department or constituting a lien upon the property to the extent of the purchase price, which is defined as the total fair market value of all property transferred. While a bulk sales certificate or report can be a complete defense to any liability of the purchaser, the Form G-8A expressly provides that such bulk sales certificate or report shall be voidable if any material misrepresentation has been made in this report. Criminal penalties and a fine may be imposed on the failure to make the bulk sales certificate or report. Certain taxes including the general excise tax upon the sale of inventory and a covenant not to compete may be due and payable as part of the Department's issuance of the bulk sales certificate or report. The purchaser may make the bulk sales certificate or report for the seller.

## ¶ 803h. Out-of-State Sales
### Hawaii Law: Sec. 237-13, 237-21, 237-22, 237-29.5, 237-29.6

Generally, tangible personal property sold outside the state is not subject to the general excise tax. Also, the tax does not apply to services or contracting performed outside the state. However, manufacturers are subject to the 0.5% tax for out-of-state sales unless the export exemption (effective January 1, 1988) applies. See Tax Information Release 88-1 for guidance in claiming such an exemption which applies to proceeds arising from the manufacture, production, or sale of tangible personal property shipped to out-of-state purchasers for resale or use out of the state. The seller and purchaser are required to complete an exemption certificate at the time of the sale.

Similarly, producers (persons in the business of raising or producing agricultural products, fishing, or aqua culture, for sale) are subject to tax at the 0.5% producer's rate for sales outside the state except that such tax does not apply to producers who sell their products to a purchaser who will process the products outside the state.

Liability for taxes on out-of-state shipments is determined by the place at which the buyer accepts the goods and assumes the risk of loss. Where goods are not accepted prior to shipment out of state (as in the case of goods ordered by sample or mail, or when the agreement stipulates delivery outside the state at the seller's risk), the sale is not taxable.

Example:

A foreign buyer arranges to purchase used cars from a dealer in Hawaii. The sale is made directly through correspondence, and the shipping arrangement is made by the seller. There is no tax liability on this transaction since the sale is considered to be made outside the state.

When the buyer accepts the goods and assumes the risk of loss prior to their shipment out of state, a local delivery occurs and the sale is subject to the excise tax. Where the sale is secured through an agent or representative of the purchaser located in Hawaii and the transportation arrangement is made by such agent or representative, the sale is considered to be made in Hawaii and is taxable.

In December 1995, the Department of Taxation issued Tax Information Release 95-5 (See Appendix) to clarify the application of the general excise tax on sales of tangible personal property by an out-of-state seller, including drop shipments. This Tax Information Release has been reprinted in Part IV of this book. See ¶ 1404. Tax Information Releases 88-1 and 88-2, which refer to title passage are superseded to the extent that they are inconsistent with Tax Information Release 95-5. The 95-5 Release states that Hawaii does not impose the general excise tax on sales of tangible personal property which originate outside of Hawaii unless the place of delivery is in Hawaii and the seller has nexus.

Where delivery of goods is made by the taxpayer to affiliated companies or persons, or where the relation is such that the consideration paid does not reflect the true value of the product, the amount taxable is the true value. If the product is such that there is no price for determination of the true value, the Director of Taxation will prescribe rules for determining the value.

Where the site of a construction job is outside the state, the contractor is not taxable on income from the work done outside the state.

### ¶ 803i. Sales of Capital Assets Used in Business
#### Hawaii Law: Sec. 237-1

As explained in ¶ 803, casual sales are excluded from the definition of "business" for general excise tax purposes. Sales of capital assets used in a business, not directly related to the business activity, are treated as "casual sales" and therefore are not subject to the tax. This may apply, for example, to certain sales of an automobile by a person who uses the automobile in his or her business.

As mentioned in ¶ 803, "casual sale" is defined as an occasional or isolated transaction involving (a) a person not required to be licensed under the general excise tax law, or (b) tangible personal property not ordinarily sold in the business in which a person is regularly engaged. This clearly seems to cover certain automobile sales discussed above. It also seems to provide tax exemption on occasional private sales of automobiles, boats, etc., between individuals. See ¶ 803 for a more detailed discussion of casual sales.

## ¶ 803j. Directors' Fees
### Hawaii Law: Admin Rules Sec. 18-237-13-06.05

The taxability of directors fees is addressed in the Department of Taxation regulation Section 18-237-13-06.05. These regulations attempt to summarize several court decisions. Under the regulations, a person will be subject to tax on directors' fees if he (1) serves as a fiduciary in four or more of each or combination of any of the following capacities during the taxable year:

(a) director of corporation

(b) trustee of a trust

(c) executor of an estate

(d) any other fiduciary

or (2) receives fees or commissions in an aggregate amount of more than $1,200 in a taxable year for the performance of his duties as a fiduciary.

The regulations give several examples to illustrate their application. Simply stated, an individual will be subject to tax on the fees he receives if he serves, for a fee as a director or trustee of four or more entities regardless of the total fees received or, in the alternative, he will be subject to tax if he receives more than $1,200 during any one year regardless of the number of entities on which he serves.

## ¶ 803k. Travel Agencies and Motor Carriers
### Hawaii Law: Sec. 237-18

Under a 1965 attorney general's opinion, travel agencies were taxed on their income from commissions, fees, or net return for services rendered. Where a travel agent sold a package tour and pays for hotel accommodations, transportation, or other costs of the tour, only the net amount after payment of such costs was subject to tax. If a Hawaii travel agent sells tours outside Hawaii and/or serves as a tour conductor outside Hawaii, his income from such activities is subject to tax unless he maintains an office outside Hawaii. If a travel agent outside Hawaii comes to Hawaii as a tour conductor, he is not subject to tax unless he (or a related entity) maintains an office in Hawaii.

The law was amended in 1986, retroactive to July 1, 1985, to allow a division of gross income between a travel agency or tour packager and the provider of tourism-related services. Each person is to be taxed on his respective portion of gross income. For this purpose, "tourism-related services" means catamaran cruises, canoe rides, dinner cruises, and sightseeing tours not subject to the public service company tax. This definition of "tourism-related services" was amended in 1991 to include (effective July, 1991) lei greeters, transportation included in a tour package and admissions to luaus, dinner shows, extravaganzas, cultural and educational facilities, and other services rendered directly to the customer or tourist, but only if the providers of the services other than air transportation are subject to a 4% tax either under the general excise tax law or the public service company tax law. The law was also amended in 1988, effective June 6, 1988, to provide that where transient accommodations are furnished by a travel agency or tour packager at noncommissioned negotiated contract rates and the gross income is divided between the operator of the accommodations and the travel agency or tour packager, then each party will be responsible for general excise tax on his respective portion of the gross income.

In *Ramsey Travel, Inc., et al., (1972),* the Hawaii Supreme Court reversed a lower court decision and held that commissions received by Hawaii travel agents for travel outside Hawaii are subject to the general excise tax. The court's opinion suggested possible action to force the Director of Taxation to collect comparable tax from airlines and steamship lines, which have been considered exempt from tax on such income. Appeal of this case to the U.S. Supreme Court was denied in 1973.

*Travelocity et al. v. Director,* 346 P.3d 157 (2014), the Hawaii Supreme Court affirmed in part and reversed in part the tax appeal court, and held that online travel companies were acting as travel agencies doing business in Hawaii. The court rejected the imposition of the transient accommodations tax because the online travel companies were not "operators" for purposes of the transient accommodations tax. However, the court upheld the imposition of the general excise tax on the online travel companies' mark-up, charges, and other fees. It rejected the Department's imposition of the general excise tax on the portion paid to such hotels and other transient accommodations lodging, which was already subject to general excise tax. The court also upheld the failure to file and failure to pay penalties, the latter of which requires negligence or intentional disregard of the rules.

*In Priceline.com v. Director, the Director,* SCAP No. 17-0000367, pending before the Hawaii Supreme Court, the Department assessed general excise tax, penalties and interest against various online travel companies for their stand-alone car rentals as well as car rentals included as part of travel or tour packages.

With respect to the income from transportation of passengers or property furnished through arrangements between motor carriers, in 2002, the law was changed to allow a division of gross income between motor carriers. HRS 237-18(h) provides that each motor carrier is to be taxed on its respective share of its gross income. Since 2002 there has been increased usage of transportation network companies (TNCs), which provide a website, mobile application, or both (the App) where persons seeking transportation to certain destinations (Riders) may request motor vehicle transportation to such destinations.

Thus in 2018, the Department issued Tax Information Release 2018-01 clarifying the GET liability of certain transportation network companies (TNCs) and drivers who transport riders to destinations via use of the TNC's website or mobile application. The TNC is generally subject to the general excise tax on the gross proceeds of the transaction (the total amount collected from a rider) where it controls the manner in which the service is provided, the price charged, payment processing, or provides insurance coverage for the transaction. However, the person who ultimately receives a discretionary tip is subject to tax on the amount that is received at the retail rate. See ¶1443 for the full text of Tax Information Release 2018-01.

## ¶ 8031. Telecommunication Services
### Hawaii Law: Sec. 237-13

The general excise tax law provides for the taxing of interstate and foreign common carrier telecommunication services other than as a home service provider. The general excise tax at a rate of 4% is imposed on the portion of gross income received for service that is originated or terminated in Hawaii and is charged to a telephone number, customer, or account in Hawaii, except for gross income subject to the public service company tax. This general excise tax on telecommunication services became effective on Dec. 1, 1988, upon the development of an apportionment formula by the Department of Taxation. The apportionment formula is set forth in Section 18. 237-13-06.16(f) of the Hawaii Administrative Rules.

For those businesses that are engaged as home service providers, a tax is imposed on the gross income received from providing interstate or foreign mobile telecommunications services to a customer with a place of primary use in this state. The services must originate in one state and terminate in another state, territory or foreign country, provided that all charges for the mobile telecommunications services that are billed for the home service provider are deemed to be provided by the home service provider at the customer's place of primary use, regardless of where the telecommunications originates or terminates or passes through. The law defines "home service provider" as the facility based carrier or reseller with which the customer contracts for the provision of mobile telecommunication services. "Place of primary use" is defined as the street address representative of where the customer's use of the telecommunications service primarily occurs. This is usually the residential or business' street address of the customer and must be within the licensed service area of the provider. Gross income for these rules do not include the following:

- Receipts from services provided to a customer with a place of primary use outside this state;
- Receipts subject to tax under Chapter 239;

- Receipts taxed for prepaid telephone calling services; and

- Receipts of a home service provider acting as a serving carrier providing telecommunications services to another home service provider's customer. Act 105 temporarily suspended this exemption from July 1, 2011 – June 30, 2013. See ¶ 807a for a discussion of the exemptions and deductions suspended by Act 105. However, the Department of Taxation in Tax Information Release No. 2011-03 found that the general excise taxation of the income from a Hawaii home service provider acting as a serving carrier providing telecommunications services to a non-Hawaii home service provider's customer was pre-empted under federal law, notwithstanding the suspension of the exemption from general excise taxation under Act 105.

## ¶ 803m. Financial Institutions
### Hawaii Law: Sec. 237-24.8

Act 106 of the 1992 Legislative Session revised the manner in which financial institutions are taxed in Hawaii. The Act became effective January 1, 1993. Prior to Act 106, banks and other financial institutions were subject to the franchise tax instead of the general excise and corporate income tax. The revised law limits the exemption from the general excise tax to specific banking activities and reduces the franchise tax from 11.7% to 7.92%. See ¶ 112 for an additional explanation of the franchise tax.

Effective January 1, 1993, the following amounts received by financial institutions are exempt from the general excise tax:

(1) Interest, discounts, points, commitment fees, loan fees, loan origination charges and finance charges which are part of the computed annual percentage rate of interest and which are contracted and received for the use of money.

(2) Leasing of personal property.

(3) Fees relating to the administration of deposits.

(4) Gains resulting from changes in foreign currency exchange rates.

(5) Amounts received from the servicing and sales of loans.

(6) Interest received from the investment of deposits received by the financial institution from financial or debt instruments.

Also, effective January 1, 1993, trust companies or trust departments of financial institutions are not subject to general excise on amounts received from trust agreements and retirement plans where the trust company or department is acting as fiduciary; nor does the tax apply to amounts received from custodial agreements; nor does the tax apply to amounts received from activities relating to the general servicing of fiduciary and custodial accounts held by the trust company or department. In addition, amounts received from brokerage services by financial corporations acting as interbank brokers are not subject to the general excise tax.

The 1992 Act defines "financial institution" to mean banks, building and loan associations, development companies, financial corporations, financial services loan companies, small business investment companies, financial holding companies, mortgage loan companies and trust companies.

Prior to January 1, 1993, the general excise tax law treated certain types of financial institutions differently. Prior to the 1992 Act there was no definition of financial institution for general excise tax purposes. Instead, banks and building and loan associations were totally exempt from the general excise tax (entity exemption). In contrast, financial services loan companies and development companies only received the exemption in connection with gross income derived from engaging in the business of a financial services loan company or development company (transaction exemption).

## ¶ 803n. Revocable Trusts
### Hawaii Law: Sec. 237-9.5

Act 12 of the 1994 Legislative Session clarified the general excise tax law to conform with the state and federal income tax laws on the issue of the registration and filing requirements for certain revocable trusts. Effective July 1, 1994, certain revocable trusts (described below) are not subject to licensing or filing requirements or tax liability under the general excise tax law. In such case, the individual grantor(s), and not the trust, is required to file the general excise tax returns and pay any general excise tax due if the trust income is from engaging in business.

These rules apply to any trust that, for state and federal income tax reporting purposes: (1) has no registration or filing requirements separate and apart from its grantor or grantors; (2) is subject to the requirement that all items of income, deduction, and credit are to be reported by the individual grantor or grantors; and (3) is revocable by the grantor or grantors.

Prior to July 1, 1994, these trusts were taxed, for general excise tax purposes, as a separate entity from its grantor.

## ¶ 803o. Covenant Not To Compete

In regards to *Ronald G. Keehn*, TA 3045 (January 10, 1994) the Tax Appeal Court held that income received by a taxpayer under a covenant not to compete was gross income subject to the general excise tax. Based on this decision, the Department issued TIR 95-1 on June 1, 1995, which states that although the seller of the covenant is receiving payment to refrain from acting, instead of being paid to act, the seller is still considered to be engaging in business. Accordingly, the gross receipts from a covenant not to compete are subject to the general excise tax at the rate of four percent.

## ¶ 803p. Wholesale Sales of Goods and Services

In 1999, the law was changed to provide relief from the pyramiding of the general excise tax by expanding the application of the wholesale treatment of certain transactions for general excise tax purposes. The new wholesale treatment applies to mixed goods and services transactions.

| Transaction | Type | Qualifying/ Non-qualifying |
|---|---|---|
| In-room amenities (shampoo, soap, etc.) and toiletries (tissues, toilet paper); guests may take home. | Goods to TA | Qualifying |
| Furniture (subject to depreciation) in hotel guest rooms | Overhead | Non-qualifying |
| Newspapers provided for free to guests | Goods to TA | Qualifying |
| Floral arrangements and other perishable decorations in guest rooms | Goods to TA | Qualifying |
| Keys and electronic locks for guest rooms | Overhead | Non-qualifying |
| Floral, ice carvings and other decorations provided to customers renting banquet hall | Goods to Svcs | Qualifying |
| Paint sold to an auto body shop for a customer's car | Goods to Svcs | Qualifying |
| Area rug sold to an interior designer for customer's lobby | Goods to Svcs | Qualifying |

GOODS FOR SERVICES OR TRANSIENT ACCOMMODATIONS

One type of transaction that qualifies for the wholesale rate is where goods are sold to licensed sellers for purposes of rendering services or furnishing transient accommodations. The goods must be identifiable elements of the services being rendered and do not include purchases of overhead. "Overhead" is defined as general costs incurred in the normal course of business. The following are a few examples provided by the Department of Taxation clarifying the transaction applicable. Although the following examples have been withdrawn by the Department of Taxation by TIR 2008-1, they are still illuminating:

SERVICES PURCHASED FOR RESALE

Another type of transaction that qualifies for the wholesale rate is where services are purchased by a licensed seller rendering another service or a licensed

| Transaction | Type | Qualifying/ Non-qualifying |
|---|---|---|
| Laundry service of sheets and towels for hotel guest rooms | Svcs to TA | Qualifying |
| Maid services purchased by hotel for executive offices | Overhead | Non-qualifying |
| Maid services purchased by hotel to clean guest rooms | Svcs to TA | Qualifying |
| Site or building clean up service for final acceptance | Svc to Contracting | Qualifying |
| Environmental impact study done for an architect for a specific project | Svcs to Contracting | Qualifying |
| Rental of trailer or equipment for contractor's office on job site | Rental | Non-qualifying |
| Auto body shop subs only the sandblasting of car to another body shop | Svcs to Svcs | Qualifying |
| Graphic artist designs a graphic image to be applied to a coffee mug | Svcs to Goods | Qualifying |
| Engraver inscribes wedding rings for a jeweler's customer | Svcs to Goods | Qualifying |
| CPA performs services for an attorney preparing a legal opinion for a client | Svcs to Svcs | Qualifying |

seller who is manufacturing, producing, preparing or acquiring goods or a licensed contractor needing assistance with a contracting project or a taxpayer subject to the transient accommodations tax who needs services for the taxpayer's transient accommodations. The services being purchased must pass on to the customer of the purchaser of the services and the service must be an identifiable element of the service, goods, contracting or transient accommodations being ultimately passed on to the customer of the purchaser. As with the transactions involving goods for services or transient accommodations discussed above, the services can not be for overhead. To further clarify the transactions applicable to this new law, the Department of Taxation has provided the following examples:

However, these examples have been withdrawn by the Department of Taxation by TIR 2008-1.

¶ 803p

In order to qualify for treatment under these laws, the activities being performed must be qualified activities as described above. Examples of some of the activities that do not qualify include leasing transactions, public service company transactions, activities generating commission income, activities from theaters, amusements and radio broadcasting and activities provided by insurance agents.

## PHASE IN RATES

The Department of Taxation implemented this reduction in tax by using a deduction against the gross income reported on the taxpayer's returns. Therefore, to compute the deduction against the gross income reported, a taxpayer was required to use the worksheet provided by the Department (discussed below). The phase in rates applied to the qualifying transactions are as follows:

Phase In Rates for Qualifying Transactions:

| Year | New Rate | Deduction |
|---|---|---|
| 2000 | 3.5% | 12.5% |
| 2001 | 3.0% | 25% |
| 2002 | 2.5% | 37.5% |
| 2003 | 2.0% | 50% |
| 2004 | 1.5% | 62.5% |
| 2005 | 1.0% | 75% |
| 2006 and thereafter | .5% | 87.5% |

The formula for calculating the deduction is:
**Gross Receipts × Deduction Factor = Allowable Deduction**

then, subtract the allowable deduction from the gross receipts reported on the return:
**Gross Receipts – Allowable Deduction = Taxable Amount × 4% = Tax Liability**

The Department of Taxation has issued several forms which are to be used for the transactions qualifying for the wholesale rates. Form G-17, Resale Certificate General Form 1, is used to certify that the goods being purchased are being resold and should be retained by the seller who is treating this transaction as a wholesale transaction. Forms G-18, Resale Certificate General Form 2, and G-19, Resale Certificate Special Form, are also used for wholesale treatment of goods sales but they apply in relation to construction projects. Form G-82, Certificate for Sales and Amusements Which Qualify as Wholesale Transactions, is used to certify that the amusements or services being purchased are being resold and should be retained by the seller who is treating this transaction as a wholesale transaction.

¶ 803p

## ¶ 804. Classification of Sales — General
### Hawaii Law: Sec. 237-4, 237-5, 237-13, 237-14

Since sales by manufacturers, producers and wholesalers are taxed at a rate of only 0.5%, there have been many questions about what can properly be included in these categories.

The law's definition of "manufacturing" which was last amended in 1977 includes compounding, canning, preserving, packing, printing, publishing, milling, processing, refining or preparing for sale, profit, or commercial use, either directly or through the activity of others, in whole or in part, any articles, substance or substances, commodity or commodities.

A "producer" means any person engaged in the business of raising and producing agricultural products in their natural state, or in producing natural resource products, or engaged in the business of fishing or aquaculture, for sale, or for shipment or transportation out of the State, of the agricultural or aquaculture products in their natural or processed state, or butchered and dressed, or the natural resource products, or fish. The term "agricultural products" includes floricultural, horticultural, viticultural, forestry, nut, coffee, dairy, livestock, poultry, bee, animal, and any other farm, agronomic, or plantation product.

The law defines "wholesaler" (or "jobber") by stating that such term(s) apply only to a person making sales at wholesale. A sale will be considered made at wholesale only if it falls into one of the 13 categories listed in HRS Sec. 237-4, which are as follows:

(1) Sales to a licensed seller for resale.

(2) Sales to a licensed manufacturer of material or commodities which are to be incorporated into a finished or saleable product (including the container or package in which the product is contained) which will remain in such finished or saleable product in such form as to be perceptible to the senses and which will be sold and not otherwise used by the manufacturer.

(3) Sales to a licensed producer or cooperative association of materials or commodities which are are to be incorporated into a finished or saleable product which is to be sold.

(4) Sales to a licensed contractor, of material or commodities which are to be incorporated by the contractor into the finished work or project and which will remain in such finished work or project in such form as to be perceptible to the senses.

(5) Sales to a licensed producer (or certain cooperative associations) for sales to such producer, or to a licensed person operating a feed lot, poultry or animal feed, hatching eggs, semen, replacement stock, breeding services for the purpose of raising or producing animals or poultry products for sale, for shipment or transportation out of the State or to be incorporated in a manufactured product or for the purpose of breeding, hatching, milk-

ing, or egg laying other than for the customer's own consumption. The sale of feed for poultry or animals to be used for hauling, transportation, or sports purposes are not wholesale sales. Also, any amount derived from the furnishing of feed lot services, other than the segregated cost of feed, shall be deemed taxable at the service business rate.

(6) Sales to a licensed producer (or certain cooperative associations) for sale to the producer, of seed for producing agricultural products or bait for catching fish (including the catching of bait for catching fish), which agricultural products or fish are to be sold, shipped out of the State or incorporated in a manufactured product.

(7) Sales to a licensed producer (or certain cooperative associations) for sales to such producer, of polypropylene shade cloth; of polyfilm; of polyethylene film; of cartons and such other containers, wrappers, sacks, and binders to be used for packaging eggs, vegetables, fruits, and other agricultural products; of seedlings and cuttings for producing nursery plants; or of chick containers; which are sold, shipped out of the State or incorporated in a manufactured product.

(8) Sales of tangible personal property to a licensed person engaged in the service business or calling; provided that i) the property is not consumed or incidental to the performance of the services; ii) there is a resale of the article at the retail rate; iii) the resale of the article is separately charged or billed by the person rendering the service. Further, the tangible personal property must be sold upon the order or request of a licensed seller for the purpose of rendering a service, the property must continue to be an identifiable element of the service and the cost of the property does not constitute overhead to the seller.

(9) Sales to a licensed leasing company of capital goods which are thereafter leased as a service to others. "Capital goods" means goods which have a depreciable life and which are purchased by the leasing company for lease to its customers.

(10) Sales of services to a licensed seller engaging in a business or calling whenever: (1) a service is rendered upon the request of a licensed seller for the purpose of rendering another service in the course of the seller's service business or calling; in 2009 this has been expanded to include the furnishing of goods and services to the purchaser of tangible personal property to fulfill a warranty obligation of the manufacturer of the property; (2) in the context of a service-to-tangible personal property transaction, a service is rendered upon the request of a licensed seller for the purpose of manufacturing, producing, or preparing tangible personal property to be sold; (3) in the context of a services-to-contracting transaction, a service is rendered upon the order or request of a licensed contractor as defined in section 237-6 for the purpose of assisting that licensed contractor; or (4) in the context

of a services-to-transient accommodations rental transaction, a service is rendered upon the order or request of a person subject to tax under section 237D-2 for the purpose of furnishing transient accommodations. The benefit of the service must also pass to the customer as an identifiable element of the other service or property to be sold; the cost of the service does not constitute overhead; the gross income of the licensed seller is not divided between the licensed seller and another licensed seller; the gross income of the licensed seller is not subject to a deduction under this chapter or chapter 237D; and the resale is subject to the tax imposed under this chapter at the highest tax rate.

(11) Sales subject to a licensed retail merchant, jobber or other licensed seller of bulk condiments or prepackaged single serving packets of condiments that are provided to customers by the licensed sellers.

(12) Sales to a licensed retail merchant, jobber or other licensed seller of tangible personal property that will be incorporated or processed into a finished or saleable product during the course of its preparation for market where the finished product is to be sold and not consumed.

(13) Sales of amusements subject to taxation to a licensed seller engaging in a business or calling whenever the benefit of the amusement passes to the customer of the licensed seller as an identifiable element of the other service or property to be sold, the cost of the amusement does not constitute overhead, the gross income is not divided between the licensed seller and another licensed seller, the gross income is not subject to a deduction under the GET rules, and the resale of the service, property or amusement is subject to GET at the highest rate.

(14) Sales by a printer to a publisher of magazines or similar printed materials containing advertisements, where the publisher is under contract with the advertisers to distribute a minimum number of magazines or similar printed materials to the public, where or not there is a charge to the person who actually received the printed materials.

The Director of Taxation has issued HRS rules Section 18-237-4 concerning the definition of "wholesaler" and "jobber" which have been reprinted in Part III of this book ¶ 1402.

The law was clarified in 2001 to ensure that wholesale transactions of aquaculture production are taxed at the wholesale rate of 0.5% by including them in the definition of sales at wholesale. The definitions under HRS section 237-4 now include the sale of seedstock and aquacultural products and is effective July 1, 2001.

Sales are taxed according to their nature, regardless of the regular business of the seller. Thus a manufacturer, producer or a wholesaler may make some sales at retail; if so, such sales will be taxed at the retail rate. Conversely, a retailer may make a sale at wholesale, for resale by the purchaser; in this case such sale is taxed at the wholesale rate. To obtain the benefit of the wholesale rate, a taxpayer must obtain a resale certificate from the purchaser. Form G-17, "Resale Certificate for Goods General Form 1," Form G-18, "Resale Certificate General Form 2," (For use when the Purchaser is to give Certificate in Special Form when making purchases for projects where a building permit is required.), and Form G-19, "Resale Certificate Special Form," which can also be used by contractors purchasing materials for a project, are provided by the Department of Taxation for use as resale certificates. Also, in November 1993, the Department of Taxation issued Tax Information Release No. 93-5 announcing that the Uniform Sales and Use Tax Certificate issued by the Multistate Tax Commission may be used as a resale certificate in Hawaii. However, taxpayers are cautioned that such certificate is not an exemption certificate in Hawaii.

In the matter of the appeal of *Photo Management, Inc.,* the taxpayer took color prints of arriving passengers at Honolulu International Airport. The pictures were taken at the request of various retail photo companies. The taxpayer sold the finished prints to these retail photo companies at a set price per print. The retail photo company then tried to sell these prints to the tourists. Taxpayer reported its income under the category of intermediary services. The Tax Director assessed additional general excise taxes on the theory that taxpayer's income was from services subject to the rate of 4%. On appeal of the director's assessment, the taxpayer argued that its sales were wholesale sales. The Hawaii Supreme Court upheld the Tax Appeals Court decision, which held that the appropriate classification of the taxpayer's income was wholesale sales.

Every taxpayer is required to keep a record of his revenue. Where a taxpayer has more than one type of income, subject to different tax rates, the records must clearly show the segregation of the different types of income. If the taxpayer fails to segregate the transactions subject to different tax rates, he will be taxed at the 4% rate on all his income.

As stated above, classification of sales subject to different tax rates is often very difficult. The Department of Taxation has issued rulings dealing with this question for several types of business, some of which are discussed below in ¶ 804a. The department will advise any taxpayer on specific questions of this type, upon request.

In the case of the *Honolulu Star Bulletin, Ltd. vs. Burns,* the Hawaii Supreme Court decided in 1968 that advertising revenue of a newspaper does not qualify for the manufacturer's rate (1/2%) but is subject to the rate (4%) applicable to service and other businesses. The law was amended in 1977 to treat publishers as manufacturers so that wholesale sales of their products are taxed at 1/2%. However, this change did not affect the treatment of advertising revenue.

In the appeal of the case of *Hawaii Hochi, Ltd.,* the taxpayer printed a tourist publication for Visitor Publications, Inc. Visitor Publications solicited advertising for the publication and distributed the publication free of charge. The Hawaii Supreme Court upheld the decision of the Tax Appeals Court that the

¶ 804

printing of the publication was a sale at retail since Visitor Publications did not resell the publication.

Tax Information Release 96-4 discusses whether a sale of pesticides to a pest control operator are to be taxed as a wholesale transaction. The Tax Information Release states that three elements must exist to qualify the transaction as a wholesale sale. These elements are: (1) the pesticide must be sold to a licensed pest control operator, (2) the pesticide must be incorporated into the treated structure and soil and (3) it must be perceptible to the senses (emphasis added).

### ¶ 804a. Classification of Sales—Special Rules
#### Hawaii Law: Sec. 237-14, 237-15, 237-18

Sale of merchandise to a savings stamp company by a supplier, to be used for redemption of stamps, is considered to be a wholesale transaction and the rate of 1/2 of 1% applies, even though the redemption transaction is not taxed (see ¶ 803f).

Example:

Stamp Co. purchases three dozen blankets from Supply Co. for $216. The tax to Supply Co. on this sale is 1/2 of 1% on $216, or $1.08.

Technicians who supply dentists or physicians with dentures, orthodontic devices, etc., in accordance with specifications furnished by the dentist or physician, to be used by the dentist or physician as part of his professional services, are classified as manufacturers and are subject to the 1/2% rate.

The law was amended, effective July 1, 1977, to provide that real estate salesmen, who are treated as independent contractors, shall only be subject to the general excise tax on their share of commissions.

The law contains a special rule for situations where two service businesses are involved and one acts as an "intermediary" between the one rendering the service and the ultimate consumer. The rule provides that the person rendering the service is taxed at the 1/2% rate and the intermediary is taxed at 4%.

Example:

Midtown Service arranges for Tire Recapping Co. to recap a tire belonging to a customer. It costs Midtown Service $8 for the recapping. The customer is charged $12 for it. Tire Recapping Co. is taxable on $8 at 1/2% and Midtown Service is taxable on $12 at 4%.

When services are rendered upon the request or recommendation of a person who does not act as an "intermediary," the person rendering the service is taxed at the 4% rate.

Example:

Upon recommendation of his service station, Mr. A takes his automobile to Auto Paint Shop to have it painted. It costs him $95. Since he is not an "intermediary," Auto Paint Shop is taxable on the $95 at 4%.

¶ 804

**Please note that the cases below may not be valid under current law. See ¶ 803(p).**

In the case of *Busk Enterprises, Inc., et al.,* the Hawaii Supreme Court held in 1972 that persons preparing new automobiles for delivery to purchasers, at the request of automobile dealers, are not performing services for intermediaries and are therefore taxable at 4%. Since the dealers had to prepare the cars as a part of the total sales costs, the auto dealers themselves, not the auto buyers, were the recipients of the preparer's services.

In the matter of the tax appeal of *McDonald's Restaurants of Hawaii, Inc.,* decided May 15, 1986, the Hawaii Supreme Court affirmed the decision of the Tax Appeal Court that the taxpayer was not entitled to the special 1/2% rate for intermediary service providers. The taxpayer's parent company, McDonald's Corp., is not a "taxpayer engaged in a service business," and therefore cannot qualify as an intermediary.

The appeal of *Pacific Laundry Co., Ltd.,* decided by the Hawaii Supreme Court in 1982, involved the rate of general excise tax imposed on an independent laundry providing services to hotel guests. The hotel guests requesting personal laundry service would fill out a laundry slip bearing the name of the hotel and the independent laundry. The hotels acted as agents in handling the laundry and billing the guests. The hotels remitted amounts collected from the guests to the independent laundry, retaining a portion of the amount collected as a commission. The hotels were taxed at 4% on the amount received as a commission. The Supreme Court affirmed the Tax Appeal Court's decision that the independent laundry was subject to the 4% rate of tax on the gross amount received from the hotels, and that the hotels' commissions could not be deducted from the gross receipts.

Where a product is milled, processed, or manufactured by order of another taxpayer who is a manufacturer, the person rendering the service is taxed at the 1/2% rate. The value of the entire product must be included in taxable income by the manufacturer when sold by him, at the rate of 1/2 of 1% if sold at wholesale and 4% if sold at retail.

Example:

Company A manufactures furniture. It farms out the sawing of lumber to Carpenter Shop for which the charge is $55. The completed furniture, which includes the lumber milled at the Carpenter Shop, is sold to a furniture store for $500. Carpenter Shop is taxable on $55 at 1/2%. Company A is taxable on $500 at 1/2%.

There has been controversy and uncertainty over a period of time regarding the proper classification of sales of parts to service businesses that incorporate the parts, in one form or another, in the final product sold to the consumer. The problem appears to have been resolved by the 1970 amendment which added category (8) to wholesale sales and provides that such sales are to be treated as wholesale sales under certain conditions. Also, the 1972 decision by the Hawaii Supreme Court in

*Alexander & Baldwin, Inc.*, held that sales of appliance parts to licensed repairmen are wholesale sales taxable at 1/2%, where the repairmen sells the parts and bill them separately to their customers.

The Department of Taxation clarified its position regarding the classification of sales of packaging products to fast-food retailers in Tax Information Release No. 88-5, dated Aug. 26, 1988. Sales of packaging products such as food containers, napkins, and prepackaged condiments are retail sales unless the retailer can demonstrate that there has been a resale. Release No. 88-5 provides that sales are "resales" only when the retailer sells the container or packaging materials for a separately stated price and therefore qualifies the original purchase of the container or packaging materials by the retailer as a sale at wholesale. The law was changed in 1999 to now specifically include the sale of bulk condiments or prepackaged single-serving packets of condiments that are provided to customers by a licensed retail merchant as a wholesale sale.

## ¶ 805. Deductions Allowed
### Hawaii Law: Sec. 237-3

The following may be deducted from gross receipts in computing the amount subject to tax:

(a) Cash discounts allowed and taken.

(b) Sales returns.

> The amount deductible is the total of returns during the period covered by the return, whether or not the items returned are attributable to sales of the same period.

(c) Bad debts charged off for income tax purposes.

This applies to amounts actually written off during the period.

Example:

Sales of Company A for one month were $7,000. During the same month the company charged off as bad debts $230 of uncollectible accounts resulting from sales of prior months, and collected $50 on an account that had been written off three months earlier. Assuming no adjustments for cash discounts or returns, the tax liability is computed as follows:

| | |
|---|---:|
| Sales for the month | $7,000 |
| Less: bad debt written off | 230 |
| | 6,770 |
| Add: bad debt recovered | 50 |
| Taxable amount for month | $6,820 |
| Retail tax at 4% is | $272.80 |

In years where the amount of bad debt expense exceeds interest income, the bad debt deduction may be carried back to the prior year to offset income. The taxpayer would amend the G-49.

(d) Sales represented by "trade-ins," provided the full sale price of article is included in gross income.

Example:

B operates a business machine company. During the month he sells $1,500 worth of typewriters. He allows $300 on old typewriters as trade-ins. B must report $1,500 as his gross income, but he can deduct the $300 trade-ins and compute his tax on the net amount of $1,200.

In Tax Information Release No. 82-5, the Tax Department dealt with rebates offered by automobile manufacturers. The release sets out seven types of transactions and the tax treatment to the automobile dealer as follows:

| Transaction | Amount Taxable |
|---|---|
| 1. Manufacturer's cash bonus paid directly to purchaser. | Gross sale. No deduction for the bonus. |
| 2. Dealer's cash bonus paid to purchaser. | Net sale, resulting from gross sale minus bonus, which is treated as a discount. |
| 3. Manufacturer's and dealer's cash bonuses (based upon agreed percentage) paid to purchaser. | Net sale, resulting from the gross sale minus the dealer's share of the bonus payment, which is treated as a discount. |
| 4 Manufacturer's cash bonus received by the purchaser and applied as a down payment by the purchaser. | Gross sale. No deduction for the bonus. |
| 5. Manufacturer's and dealer's cash bonuses (based upon agreed percentage) received by the purchaser and applied as a down payment by the purchaser. | Net sale, resulting from the gross sale minus the dealer's share of the bonus payment, which is treated as a discount. |
| 6. Manufacturer's cash bonus received by dealer/lessor who leases automobiles usually held for sale. | Bonus taxable as "Other Income." |
| 7. Local distributor makes rebate payments to local dealer for specific automobiles sold to bona-fide daily rental and U-drive operators. Under this arrangement, the rebate is based upon quantity or volume sales and is payable subsequent to the transaction. | Local dealer: Entire rebate taxable as "Other Income," if not passed on to purchaser. Same as in No. 2, if all or a portion of the rebate is passed on to the purchaser. |

¶ 805

## ¶ 806. Exempt Organizations
### Hawaii Law: Sec. 237-23, 237-29.7. 237-29.8

The following persons or organizations are exempt from the general excise tax:

(a) Public service companies subject to the public service company tax and public utilities owned and operated by the State or any county or other political subdivision thereof.

(b) Insurance companies authorized to do business under HRS chapter 431; however see below for change in law effective January 1, 1992.

(c) Certain fraternal benefit organizations.

(d) Religious, charitable, scientific, or educational organizations, including those operating certain senior citizens' housing facilities or homeless facilities.

(e) Business leagues, chambers of commerce, agricultural & horticultural organizations, etc.

(f) Hospitals, infirmaries, and sanitaria.

(g) Internal Revenue Code Section 501(c)(12) tax exempt companies that provide potable water to residential communities that lack any access to public utility water services.

(h) Cooperative associations.

(i) Hansen's disease sufferers.

(j) Nonprofit cemetery organizations.

(k) Nonprofit shippers associations operating under Civil Aeronautics Board regulations.

(l) Persons or organizations that provide or operate a prepaid legal services plan.

(m) Qualified persons or organizations authorized to do business in State enterprise zones.

(n) Qualifying activities within a foreign trade zone.

(o) Call centers.

(p) Public Internet Data Centers (see below for further discussion).

Anyone desiring the benefits of the exemptions listed in (c) through (g) must file an application for exemption and must register annually.

The law was amended in 2001 to streamline the exemption application process for certain nonprofit organizations. The law was changed for the taxpayers listed in (c) through (g) in the list above who received or have applied for tax exempt status under the Internal Revenue Code section 501 (c)(3), (4), (6), (8) or (12). These taxpayers need to register with the Department of Taxation by filing a statement with the necessary information required and attaching a copy of the exemption or application. The changes in the law also now allow the Department of Tax to extend the time for filing the exemption application if the taxpayer can provide good cause for longer than the previously allowed 2 months. This change was put in effect July 1, 2001.

Effective July 1, 2001, the gross income, received by a Public Internet Data Center are now exempt from the general excise tax. This exemption is for gross income received after June 30, 2001 and but not after December 31, 2005. The Public Internet Data Center is defined in the law to be a facility that is available for compensated use by the public and designed to do the following activities:

- house data servers;
- operate on a 24 hour, 7 day a week basis;
- have redundant systems for electricity, air conditioning, fire suppression and security, and
- provide services such as bandwidth, co-location, data backup, complex web hosting, and aggregation for application service providers.

Prior to January 1, 1993, banks and building and loan associations were totally exempt from the general excise tax as they were subject to the Hawaii franchise tax. See the discussion at ¶ 803m regarding the change in law effective January 1, 1993, which subjects these entities to the general excise tax but provides exemption for certain specific banking transactions. See transaction exemptions at ¶ 807.

The law was amended in 1991 regarding the exemption (b) relating to insurance companies. Effective January 1, 1992, the general excise tax exemption for insurance companies does not apply to gross income received as rents from investments in real property in this State. However such income will continue to be exempt where the related contracts were entered into prior to January 1, 1992 and they do not provide the passing on of taxes or tax increases, until the contracts are renegotiated, renewed or extended.

State enterprise zone businesses (exemption (m)) require annual certification of their exemption by the Department of Business Economic Development and Tourism. The exemption period generally cannot exceed seven years.

Under a 1963 amendment to the income tax law, certain out-of-state manufacturing corporations that have their products warehoused in Hawaii are deemed not to be engaged in a trade or business in Hawaii and are therefore exempt from the income tax. (Explained in ¶ 709.) However, for general excise tax purposes, such corporations are deemed to be wholesalers and are subject to the general excise tax on Hawaii sales disqualifying them from being exempt.

In the matter of the tax appeal of *Hawaiian Telephone Co.*, decided Feb. 17, 1980, the Hawaii Supreme Court held that directory advertising revenue and revenue from the sale of old directories is not subject to the public service company tax but is subject to the lower general excise tax.

The Department of Taxation has consistently treated fundraising activities of nonprofit organizations that have the primary purpose of producing income as being subject to the general excise tax. In the matter of the tax appeal of *Habilitat,*

¶ 806

*Inc.,* decided Aug. 18, 1982, the Hawaii Supreme Court held that the exemption of nonprofit organizations from general excise tax "...does not extend to the proceeds of any activity designed to produce income, even if such receipts are thereafter employed to further the organization's altruistic goals. It applies only where the primary purpose of the activity is not to produce income and the activity is also a primary reason for the organization's existence." The court further held that an activity, the primary purpose of which is to produce income, is not exempt from tax despite the fact that the activity is integrated with the organization's exempt function. In Tax Information Release No. 91-2, the Department of Taxation, relying on *Habilitat, Inc.,* restated its position that the gross proceeds received by a nonprofit organization from the sales of donated tangible personal property for fundraising purposes are subject to the general excise tax.

In June of 1989, the Department of Taxation issued Tax Information Release No. 89-6 to clarify the application of the general excise tax on fund-raising activities of public school sponsored groups. Effective July 1, 1989, proceeds from fundraisers by school sponsored groups (e.g. yearbook, student clubs, student government, class organization, etc.) must be paid into, processed and disbursed from the respective school's nonappropriated fund account. Therefore, since public schools are exempt from the general excise tax, income from such fundraising activities will be exempt. This treatment does not extend to certain support groups organized to benefit or assist the public schools (PTAs, PTSAs, PTOs, class alumni associations, etc.).

In the matter of the tax appeal of the *Queen's Medical Center,* decided April 11, 1983, the Hawaii Supreme Court held that the exemption of hospitals from general excise tax does not include rental of space in the Physicians Office Building and the operation of the adjacent parking facility. The court took a literal interpretation of the statute exempting "...the activities of such hospitals, infirmaries, and sanitaria as such," and concluded that the activities did not constitute hospital activities.

In the matter of the tax appeal of *Central Union Church—Arcadia Retirement Residence,* decided March 4, 1981, the Hawaii Supreme Court held that the entrance and monthly service fees charged to residents of a church-owned retirement and health-care home were exempt from general excise taxes. The court held that the primary purpose of charging the fees was to further the charitable purpose of providing housing for the elderly.

In *Director of Taxation, State of Hawaii v. Medical Underwriters,* 115 Haw. 80, 166 P.3d. 353 (8/30/07), a taxpayer that acted as an attorney-in-fact and managed a foreign insurer, a reciprocal insurance exchange authorized to do business in Hawaii, did not qualify as an insurance company exempt from the general excise tax and was not eligible for the 0.15% tax rate under H.R.S. Section 237-13(7), because it had a separate corporate identity including not sharing in the liabilities of the foreign insurer, filing its own corporate income tax returns, and was statutorily mandated to sue or be sued in its own name.

¶ 806

## ¶ 807. Exempt Transactions
Hawaii Law: Sec. 237-3, 237-13, 237-22, 237-23.5 to 237-29.8

The following classes of gross income are exempt from tax:

(1)  Death proceeds from life insurance contracts.

(2)  Proceeds from endowment, annuity and life insurance contracts.

(3)  Accident or health insurance proceeds.

(4)  Gifts and bequests.

(5)  Damages for personal injuries or other compensatory damages for damage to property.

(6)  Compensation received for services as an employee.

(7)  Alimony and similar payments.

(8)  Amounts collected as fuel tax by distributors.

(9)  Taxes on liquor.

(10) Taxes on cigarettes and tobacco.

(11) Federal retail excise taxes.

(12) Up to $2,000 of annual business income of a blind, deaf, or disabled person, a corporation, general partnership, limited liability partnership and limited liability company, all of whose outstanding stock, partners or members are owned by individuals who are blind, deaf or totally disabled.

(13) Federal excise taxes on manufactured sugar.

(14) Certain amounts received by independent sugar cane farmers. Act 105 suspended this exemption from July 1, 2011 – June 30, 2013. See ¶ 807a for a discussion of the exemptions and deductions suspended by Act 105.

(15) Sales of tangible property to the federal government (sales of services to the federal government are not exempt). The Red Cross is considered a federal instrumentality for this purpose. Also, see comment below. Act 105 suspended this exemption from July 1, 2011 – June 30, 2013. See ¶ 807a for a discussion of the exemptions and deductions suspended by Act 105.

(16) Certain petroleum products of qualifying refiners. Act 105 suspended this exemption from July 1, 2011 – June 30, 2013. See ¶ 807a for a discussion of the exemptions and deductions suspended by Act 105.

(17) Sale of securities.

(18) Sale of land in fee simple.

(19) Dividends, as defined in the income tax law.

(20) Amounts received from the state or an eleemosynary organization for the care of children in foster homes.

¶ 807

(21) Amounts received as reimbursement for lease rent, real property taxes, and other maintenance expenses by a cooperative housing corporation.

(22) Certain scientific contracts with the United States (see below).

(23) Charges for certain inter-island shipping of agricultural commodities (see below). Act 105 suspended this exemption from July 1, 2011 – June 30, 2013. See ¶ 807a for a discussion of the exemptions and deductions suspended by Act 105.

(24) Sale of liquor and certain tobacco and food products to transportation companies for out-of-state use. This exemption was repealed for tax years beginning after December 31, 2013. Act 105 suspended this exemption from July 1, 2011 – June 30, 2013. See ¶ 807a for a discussion of the exemptions and deductions suspended by Act 105.

(25) Gross income received for planning, design, financing, construction, sale, or lease of certain low and moderate income housing projects regulated by law, including certain rehabilitated projects and rents received from tenants in such projects as long as there is the proper certification from the Hawaii Housing Finance and Development Corporation showing that the project is an affordable housing project. Contractors also receive an exemption from general excise tax and use tax for the contracting costs in building such a project, up to a maximum aggregate tax exemption of $30 million per year for all such projects approved by the Hawaii Housing Finance and Development Corporation. Act 39, SLH 2018, prohibits discrimination against tenants based solely on receipt of assistance under section 8 of the United States Housing Act of 1937.

(26) Amounts received by an association of apartment owners or a nonprofit homeowners or community association in reimbursement of sums paid for common expenses. (Effective July 1, 1992).

(27) Sale of certain new air pollution control facilities and of tangible personal property used in the construction, use, or maintenance of such facilities (see below). Act 105 suspended this exemption from July 1, 2011 – June 30, 2013. See ¶ 807a for a discussion of the exemptions and deductions suspended by Act 105.

(28) Proceeds from shipbuilding and ship repairs rendered to surface vessels federally owned or engaged in interstate or international trade. Act 105 has suspended this exemption from July 1, 2011 – June 30, 2013. See ¶ 807a for a discussion of the exemptions and deductions suspended by Act 105.

(29) Gross income from the sale or transfer of materials and supplies, interest on loans, engineering, construction, maintenance, or managerial services by one member of an affiliated public service company group to another member of the same group.

(30) Amounts received from loading or unloading of ships, aircraft, etc.; tug boat services including pilotage fees and towage of ships, barges, or vessels in and out of harbors or from one pier to another; and the transportation of pilots or governmental officials to ships, barges, or vessels offshore, rigging gear, for checking freight and similar services, standby charges, and use of moorings and running mooring lines. Act 105 suspended this exemption from July 1, 2011 – June 30, 2013. See ¶ 807a for a discussion of the exemptions and deductions suspended by Act 105.

(31) Sale of "alcohol fuels" at retail.

(32) Amounts received by an employee benefit plan by way of contributions, dividends, interest, and other income (except rental income—see below).

(33) Transient accommodations taxes passed on and collected by operators holding certificates of registration.

(34) Amounts received as dues by an unincorporated merchant's association from its membership for advertising or promotion, providing the costs for advertising and promotion must be for the benefit of the association members as a whole and not the benefit of an individual member or group of members less than the entire membership.

(35) Sale of prescription drugs and prosthetic devices by a hospital, infirmary, medical clinic, health care facility, pharmacy, or practitioner licensed to administer the drug or prosthetic device (see below).

(36) Amounts received for purchases made with United States Department of Agriculture food coupons (food stamps or WIC food vouchers).

(37) Amounts received by a labor organization for real property leased to a labor organization or trust fund established by a labor organization for certain benefits of its members and their families. Act 105 suspended this exemption from July 1, 2011 – June 30, 2013. See ¶ 807a for a discussion of the exemptions and deductions suspended by Act 105.

(38) Sale by producers to purchasers who will process the products outside of the state. (Effective July 1, 1993).

(39) The value or gross proceeds arising from the manufacture, production or sale of tangible personal property shipped to out-of-state purchasers for resale or use out-of-state (see below).

(40) Interest from mortgage securities issued by the Housing Finance and Development Corporation (formerly issued by the Hawaii Housing Authority) to raise funds for housing loan programs.

(41) Certain amounts arising from a sale or leaseback of a solid waste processing, disposal, and electric generating facility by a county.

(42) Certain amounts for services and interest costs between related entities (see below).

¶ 807

(43) Amounts received by common paymasters (see below).

(44) Certain amounts received by a stock exchange and its members.

(45) Amounts received by the operator of a hotel from the owner of the hotel equal to and disbursed for employee wages, salaries and benefits. Expanded in 2007 to include timeshare associations and amounts received by a suboperator of a hotel from the owner, timeshare association or hotel operator.

(46) Amounts received by the operator of a county transportation system. (Effective January 1, 1991).

(47) Rental motor vehicle and tour vehicle surcharge taxes.

(48) Amounts received by the operator of an orchard property from the owner of such property in amounts equal to and which are disbursed by the operator for employee wages, salaries, payroll taxes, insurance premiums, and benefits, including retirement, vacation, sick pay, and health benefits. (Effective July 1, 1992).

(49) Amounts received under property and casualty insurance policies for damage or loss of business inventory located within the state and in an area that is declared a natural disaster area by the governor.

(50) Taxes on nursing facility by HRS Chapter 346E and passed on and collected by operators of nursing facilities.

(51) Amounts received by financial institutions for interest, loan fees, fees relating to customer deposits, gains from currency exchanges and leasing of personal property (see ¶ 803m).

(52) Amounts received by trust companies (or trust departments of financial institutions) for trust agreements, retirement plans, custodial accounts and for activities relating to the general servicing of such accounts where the trust company (or department) is acting as a fiduciary or custodian (see ¶ 803m).

(53) Amounts received from the sale of tangible personal property to a credit union. (Effective July 1, 1994). Act 105 suspended this exemption from July 1, 2011 – June 30, 2013. See ¶ 807a for a discussion of the exemptions and deductions suspended by Act 105.

(54) Interest received by a person domiciled outside the State from a trust company (as defined in Section 412:8-101) acting as payment agent or trustee on behalf of the issuer or payees of an interest bearing instrument or obligation, if the interest would not have been subject to the general excise tax if paid directly to the person domiciled outside the State. (Effective January 1, 1995).

(55) Amounts received as compensation by community organizations, school booster clubs, and nonprofit organizations under a contract with the chief election officer for the provision and compensation of precinct

officials and other election related personnel, services, and activities. (Effective May 25 1995).

(56) Effective July 1, 1997, proceeds received for construction of an aircraft service and maintenance facility shall be exempt. Aircraft service and maintenance facility means a facility for aircraft service and maintenance that is not less than 80,000 square feet in area. In 1998, the law allowing this exemption was amended to revise various definitions of the terms used in this exemption. One of the terms that were redefined was the definition of an "aircraft service maintenance facility". This term is now defined as a facility for aircraft service and maintenance that is not less than 30,000 square feet in area. The revisions to this section of the law are effective for taxable periods beginning after June 30, 1997. Act 105 suspended this exemption from July 1, 2011 – June 30, 2013. See ¶ 807a for a discussion of the exemptions and deductions suspended by Act 105.

(57) Amounts received by a management company from related entities engaged in the business of selling interstate or foreign common carrier telecommunications services in amounts equal to and which are disbursed by the management company for employee wages, salaries, payroll taxes, insurance premiums and benefits including retirement, vacation, sick pay and health benefits. Act 105 suspended this exemption from July 1, 2011 – June 30, 2013. See ¶ 807a for a discussion of the exemptions and deductions suspended by Act 105.

(58) Amounts received as grants under Section 206M-15. Act 105 suspended this exemption from July 1, 2011 – June 30, 2013. See ¶ 807a for a discussion of the exemptions and deductions suspended by Act 105.

(59) An exemption is allowed for all of the gross proceeds or gross income arising from the sale of tangible personal property imported to Hawaii from a foreign or domestic source to a licensed taxpayer for subsequent resale for the purpose of wholesale.

(60) Amounts paid for services or contracting performed in Hawaii that are exported outside of Hawaii for resale, consumption or use (see below).

(61) Amounts received from foreign diplomats and consular officials holding cards issued from the U.S. Department of State granting them an exemption from state taxes, including both General Excise Tax (GET) and Transient Accommodations Tax (TAT). Tax Facts No. 2016-01, Tax Exemptions for Foreign Diplomats and Consular Officials, provides a detailed discussion regarding the following tax exemptions. Refer to Announcement 2011-25 for additional information regarding the Asia-Pacific Economic Cooperation (APEC) Summit which was held in Honolulu in November 2011. Procedures to obtain a general excise tax exemption for the purchase and lease of motor vehicles by foreign diplomats and consular officials are provided in Tax Announcement 2013-03.

¶ 807

(62) Amounts received as rent for the leasing of aircraft or aircraft engines used by the lessee for interstate air transportation of passengers and goods. Effective July 1, 2001. Act 105 suspended this exemption from July 1, 2011 – June 30, 2013. See ¶ 807a for a discussion of the exemptions and deductions suspended by Act 105.

(63) The value or gross income derived from the sale of a net operating loss by a qualified high technology business. Determined by the Department of Tax as being a casual sale. Effective January 1, 2001 through December 31, 2005. (Repealed in 2007)

(64) Amounts received as a beverage container deposit collected under chapter 342G.

(65) Fraternal benefit, religious, charitable, scientific, educational, and other nonprofit organizations are exempt from paying general excise tax on fees for conventions, conferences or trade show exhibits or display spaces, effective July 1, 2004. (Announcement 2004-10). *See* Tax Information Release No. 2011-01. Act 105 suspended this exemption effective July 1, 2011 – June 30, 2013. See ¶ 807a for a discussion of the exemptions and deductions suspended by Act 105.

(66) Proceeds from the retail sale of alcohol fuel which is defined as neat biomass-derived alcohol liquid fuel or a petroleum derived fuel and alcohol liquid fuel mixture consisting of at least 10 volume per cent denatured biomass-derived alcohol. This alcohol fuel is fuel that is commercially used to power aircraft, sea craft, motor vehicles or other motorized vehicles. Effective July 1, 2007 and is repealed June 30, 2009. (Announcement 2007-12)

(67) Amounts received by the operator of the Hawaii Convention Center for reimbursement of costs made based on a contract with the Hawaii Tourism Authority. Effective June 13, 2007. (Announcement 2007-09)

(68) Amounts received by a Professional Employment Organization (PEO) from a client company for disbursements for wages, salaries, payroll taxes, insurance premiums and benefits. Effective July 1, 2007. (Announcement 2007-15). The PEO must be properly registered in order to maintain the exemption. The PEO must be in compliance with the Department of Labor. *See* Tax Announcement 2013-21.

(69) Amounts received for the use of intangible property outside the State. See Tax Announcement 2018-13, citing Act 183, effective July 1, 2018.

(70) Amounts received by a managed care support contractor of the TRICARE program that is established under Title 10 United States Code Chapter 55, as amended, for the actual cost or advancement to third party health care providers pursuant to a contract with the United States. (This exemption is currently slated to be repealed on December 31, 2018. See Tax Information Release 2018-02.)

¶ 807

In addition to the specific exemptions listed above, the law provides for exemption of any income, the state is precluded from taxing under the Constitution and laws of the United States. See ¶ 803h for discussion of out-of-state sales.

Exemption (15) for sale of tangible property to the federal government does not apply to amounts received through vending machine sales, even though the vending machines are on federal property.

Exemption (22) for scientific contracts covers prime contracts or subcontracts with the United States for certain "scientific work" and includes a limited exemption on sales of tangible personal property to contractors or subcontractors. The exemption relates generally to design, construction and operation of aerospace, agricultural, astronomical, biomedical, electronic, geophysical, oceanographic, test range, or other scientific facilities, and may apply to "housekeeping" functions. In Tax Information Release No. 35-71 (July 1971), the Department of Taxation illustrated the application of this exemption, including certain 1970 amendments effective in 1971, with a series of questions and answers.

Exemption (23) excludes agricultural, meat, or fish products grown, raised, or caught in Hawaii, when such sales are made to any person or common carrier in interstate or foreign commerce for consumption out-of-state by such person, crew, or passengers on such shipper's vessels or airplanes. In the matter of the tax appeal of *Hawaiian Flour Mills, Inc.,* decided March 31, 1993, the Tax Appeal Court determined that the general excise tax exclusion for locally grown raised, or caught agricultural, meat, or fish products is unconstitutional under Article I, Section 8, clause 3 of the United States Constitution. Act 141 of the 1994 Legislative Session corrected this exemption by removing references in the law that may be interpreted as discriminating against manufacturers and producers selling their products in interstate commerce.

Act 135, in 2003 further repealed a portion of this exemption that made reference to "grown, raised, or caught in Hawaii..." as this was deemed to be unconstitutional in the matter of the tax appeal of *Hawaiian Flour Mills, Inc.*

Under exemption (25), in order to obtain certification from the Hawaii Housing Finance and Development Corporation, the housing project must be affordable for a minimum number of years as noted in the table below:

| Type of Project | Term |
| --- | --- |
| Moderate Rehabilitation | 5 years from date specified in regulatory agreement |
| Substantial Rehabilitation | 10 years from date specified in regulatory agreement |
| Newly Constructed | 30 years from date of issuance of certificate of occupancy |

This is effective July 1, 2015 and applies to projects with an initial certification date after June 30, 2015.

¶ 807

Exemption (27) for air pollution control facilities was enacted in 1970, applicable to taxable years beginning after Dec. 31, 1970. The exemption applies to new facilities, as specifically defined in the law, that are used to abate or control atmospheric pollution. It does not apply to air conditioners, fans, or other similar facilities for the comfort of persons at a place of business. This general excise tax exemption applies only after a claim for property tax exemption has been filed with and approved by the Hawaii Director of Health, as explained in ¶ 1102.

Exemption (32) for employee benefit plans is effective May 10, 1985. This exemption also applies to amounts received by a nonprofit organization or office for costs and expenses incurred for the administration of an employee benefit plan. This exemption was amended, effective July 1, 1994, to repeal its application to amounts received by an employee benefit plan from rental income of real estate investments. The exemption will not apply to rental income received after June 30, 1994, unless the rental income is received as a result of written contracts executed prior to July 1, 1994, in which case it will not be taxed until the contracts are renegotiated, renewed, or extended, or until after December 31, 1998, whichever is earlier.

Exemption (35) for prescription of drugs and prosthetic devices does not apply to any amounts received for services provided in selling the prescription drugs or prosthetic devices. The Department of Taxation has issued Tax Information Release No. 86-4, dated Oct. 16, 1986, to clarify the exemption. The law was amended effective July 1, 1987, to include in the definition of prescription drugs sales of drugs by licensed practitioners and to include in the definition of prosthetic device sales by dealers of prosthetic devices and any replacement parts subsequently purchased for the device.

Furthermore, for taxable years beginning after December 31, 2015, the general excise tax exemption for prescription drugs does not apply to sales of medical marijuana. See Hawaii Department of Taxation Announcement No. 2016-07.

Under exemptions (39) the seller must receive a certificate from the purchaser, who will be liable to the seller for any additional tax imposed as a result of the purchaser's failure to use the goods in accordance with the exemption. Millers and processors of sugar, and canners of pineapple and pineapple juice are covered by this out-of-state sales exemption.

Exemption (42) for related entities is effective June 6, 1988. Services applicable to this exemption are defined as legal and accounting services and those managerial and administrative services performed by an employee, officer, partner, trustee, or sole proprietor, and includes overhead costs attributable to those services. Related entities mean affiliated or controlled group of corporations within the meaning of Internal Revenue Code Sections 1504 and 1563, respectively, or those entities connected through ownership of at least 80 percent of the total value of each such entity. In 1999, the law was changed to include in the definition of "related entities" an additional requirement for the ownership of affiliated or controlled groups. The addition to the law now requires that the entities be connected through ownership of at least 80 percent of the total value and at least 80 percent of the total voting power of each such entity. Further, the law now also includes in this same definition, limited liability partnerships or limited liability companies. Finally, the definition of "related entities" now also includes any group or combination of entities that constitute a unitary business for income tax purposes.

Exemption (42) was further expanded in 2001 to expand the exemption for certain services furnished by one related entity to another for services that includes the use of computer software and hardware, information technology services and for database management services. This expanded definition applies to gross income that was received after June 3 0, 2001.

Exemption (43) for common paymasters is effective June 6, 1988, and applies to amounts received by common paymasters that are disbursed as remuneration on behalf of such corporations. Receipts for payroll taxes and employee benefits are also exempted. Reference is made to Treasury Department regulations Section 31.3121(s)-1(b) for the definition of related corporations, common paymasters, multiple common paymasters, and concurrent employment. In general, corporations are related for purposes of the common paymaster exemption if there exists more than 50 percent ownership or management control or 30 percent or more of one corporation's employees are concurrently employees of the other corporation.

In 1999, the law was changed to exempt exported services and contracting (architectural and engineering) that was performed in Hawaii which was then exported outside of Hawaii for resale, consumption, or use. This change is reflected as Hawaii Revised Statutes Section 237-29.53. The exemption may be taken if the customer provides a certificate which states that the services or contracting being provided is to be resold, consumed, or used outside of Hawaii. If it is determined that the services or contracting was not, in fact, resold, consumed, or used outside of Hawaii, the customer is obligated to pay the seller the additional tax owed ("used or consumed" test). This exemption also applies to service or contracting transactions which are bundled and exported.

Upon the promulgation of the rules on the exemption for exported services and contracting, the Department rendered TIR 2009 02 obsolete. The Department adopted rules effective March 17, 2018. See Announcement No. 2018-05. The adopted rules clarify how to determine whether gross income derived from services or contracting is exempt from the general excise tax as exported services or contracting. Specifically, the rules add definitions, categorize different types of service or contract transactions, and provide examples. Example 7 of the adopted rules Hawaii Administrative Rules section 18-237-29.53, reproduced below, illustrate an application of the exported services exemption.

Example 7: SP LLC, a software programmer located in Hawaii, is hired by MedServ, Inc., a medical service provider doing business in several states, including Hawaii, to create a customized and integrated patient file and billing program for use at all of its medical offices for a fee of $70,000. MedServ, Inc. has two of its seven medical offices in Hawaii. SP LLC's services are used or consumed where MedServ, Inc.'s business activities relating to SP LLC's services occurred, pursuant to section 18-237-29.53-11(a)(1). Because SP LLC's service is used or consumed both in and outside of the State, SP LLC shall apportion its income pursuant to section 18-237-29.53-02(b). In this case, it is reasonable for SP LLC to apportion two-sevenths of its gross income to Hawaii. SP LLC shall report $70,000 in gross income on its general excise tax return and may claim $50,000 as exempt under section 237-29.53, HRS.

In 2018, the Department issued Tax Information Release 2018-06, which further clarifies where contracting or services are used or consumed for purposes of applying the exemption. The TIR covers the following types of contracting or services:

- Contracting, as defined in section 237-6, HRS, is used or consumed where the real property to which the contracting activity pertains is located. HAR § 18-237-29.53-03.

- Services related to real property, including property management, real estate sales, real estate inspections, and real estate appraisals, are used or consumed where the real property is located. HAR § 18-237-29.53-04.

- Services Related to Tangible Personal Property (TPP) including inspection, appraisal, testing, and repair, are used or consumed where the TPP is delivered after the services are performed. HAR § 18-237-29.53-05. Services performed by a commissioned agent, however, have different sourcing rules. A taxpayer is a commissioned agent, with respect to TPP, if the taxpayer sells, buys, leases, or procures TPP on behalf of a principal with the principal's assent for a predetermined fee and the total price of the sale is controlled by the principal. HAR § 18-237-29.53-01.

- Income from the sale, booking, or arrangement of transient accommodations or travel-related bookings (including tours, excursions, transportation, rental vehicles, shows, dining, spa services, and other reservations or bookings) by a travel agency or tour packager is sourced based on whether the transaction was booked on a commissioned or noncommissioned basis and whether the booking was made online.

- A booking is made on a commissioned basis if the travel agency or tour packager books the transient accommodation or travel-related booking on behalf of a principal with the principal's assent for a predetermined fee and the total price of the booking is controlled by the principal. HAR §18-237- 29.53-01.

See ¶1450 for the full text of Tax Information Release 2018-06.

## ¶ 807a. Exemptions Temporarily Suspended

In June of 2011, Act 105 was signed into law. This Act temporarily suspended the exemptions for certain persons and certain amounts of gross income from general excise and use tax and required the payment of both taxes at four percent. The suspension of the exemptions was effective from July 1, 2011 – June 30, 2013. Refer to Announcement 2011-09 at ¶ 1441 for a complete listing of suspended exemptions.

The suspended exemptions were taxed at four percent assuming the grandfathering rules did not apply – see below. Although these exemptions were suspended for general excise tax purposes, these exemptions continued to apply for the 0.5% Oahu county surcharge.

Grandfathering rules applied to certain contracts in place prior to July 1, 2011. With respect to the suspended exemptions, if there were any binding written contracts in place prior to July 1, 2011 which did not allow the increase in tax to be passed on to the consumer, those amounts which would be otherwise exempt prior to Act 105, continued to be exempt from general excise tax. The three main components of the grandfathering clause were (1) the contract must be binding and in place prior to July 1, 2011; (2) the contract must not allow for the increase in tax to be passed on to the consumer; and (3) the contract must be written. See Announcement 2011-10 for further information regarding the grandfathering rules.

## ¶ 808. Returns and Payment
### Hawaii Law: Sec. 237-9 to 237-12, 237-30, 237-31, 237-33 to 237-35, 237-41

Anyone subject to the general excise tax is required to obtain a license from the Department of Taxation upon the payment of a one-time fee of $20.

Form BB-1 is used to register and obtain a general excise tax license, employer's withholding and transient accommodations numbers.

The law was amended in 1998 to allow a company engaged in a network or multi-level marketing arrangement to obtain a single general excise tax license for all of its direct sellers doing business in the State. The company would then become a tax collection agent responsible for reporting, collecting and remitting the general excise and use taxes due from the business activities of its direct sellers. In turn, the direct sellers would be exempt from the licensing and reporting requirement of the general excise law but only with respect to the business conducted directly through the marketing arrangement.

The general excise tax is ordinarily due each month, on or before the 20th day of the month, for the previous month and is payable with Form G-45, Monthly Gross Excise/Use Tax Return. Such form and tax can be filed and paid on a quarterly basis if the taxpayer's liability for the calendar or fiscal year will not exceed $4,000 or on a semi-annual basis where the total annual liability is $2,000 or less.

In addition to the Form G-45, an annual return for each year must be filed on Form G-49, Annual Return and Reconciliation of General/Use Tax. The G-49 is due by the 20th day of the fourth month following the close of the fiscal year. The Director of Tax may grant extensions for filing Form G-49 for a period up to six months. The extensions are for filing only (not payment of the tax) and must be requested via Form G-39. All copies of the returns filed and related records and documents that support the amounts shown on the returns need to be preserved for 3 years and available for examination by the request of the Department of Taxation. Further, the records must be in English.

¶ 808

When the due date falls on a Saturday or Sunday, or legal holiday, returns are considered timely if filed on the following day which is not a Saturday, Sunday, or holiday. A return that is mailed to the Department of Taxation is considered timely if it is postmarked before midnight of the due date.

Prior to July 1, 1993, the law required the reporting of the general excise tax by taxation districts. Schedule C, Form G-45 and Schedule C, Form G-49 were used for this purpose. The Department of Taxation issued Rules under Section 18-237-34 to provide guidance relating to the assignment of the general excise/use tax to taxation district. The law was amended effective July 1, 1993, to eliminate this reporting requirement (by district) and now requires that all monthly and annual returns be transmitted to the office of the taxation district in which the privilege upon which the tax accrued is exercised. Where the privilege is exercised in more than one taxation district the returns shall be transmitted to the office of the First District.

If there is a change of ownership or complete transfer of business, or if a taxpayer goes out of business or otherwise ceases to conduct business activity, the taxpayer must notify the director of the change, transfer, or cessation of business not more than ten days after such occurrence. The taxpayer shall also prepare and submit an annual tax return summarizing the months of the year engaged in the business activity on or before the twentieth day of the fourth month following the month in which the change of ownership, complete transfer of business, or cessation of business took place.

In 2010, Act 155 was enacted which penalizes taxpayers for (1) failing to obtain a general excise tax license and (2) failing to file their annual general excise tax returns within 12 months of the due date. If the annual general excise tax return is not timely filed then the Department of Taxation has the authority to deny the benefits of exemptions and lower rates to the taxpayers. For example if a taxpayer does not timely file a return the taxpayer may not be entitled to the benefit of a lower tax rate such as the lower rate for wholesalers. The law does provide safe harbor provisions from the denial of benefits for certain transactions such as selected tax exempt organizations as well as for reasonable cause but not for willful neglect. This law does not prohibit any taxpayer who has timely filed their annual general excise tax return to file an amended return to claim an exemption or the benefits of a lower rate if such a return is filed within the statue of limitations.

On July 5, 2012, Act 219 was enacted which mandates that "nonprofit organizations" be given written notice of noncompliance with HRS 237-9.3 (described as Act 155 above). The "nonprofit organization" has 90 days from the receipt of the notice to become compliant before the denial of the general excise tax benefits. Act 219 is effective July 1, 2012.

See Part IV of this book for filled-in specimen returns for reporting general excise tax.

Act 105 temporarily suspended certain general excise and use tax exemptions for the period July 1, 2011 – June 30, 2013. In order to provide information regarding the impact of Act 105, additional reporting requirements have been created. Effective for tax year 2010, 2011, and 2012, any taxpayer claiming general excise and use tax deductions will be required to file Form GE-1. This form details the exemptions and deductions claimed each year by the taxpayer. Nonprofit organizations that have applied for and received an exemption from the general excise tax will not be required to file Form GE-1. This form may only be filed electronically at www.ehawaii.gov/efile. See Announcement 2011-26 for further information regarding the filing of Form GE-1.

## ¶ 809. Deficiencies, Refunds, Appeals
### Hawaii Law: Sec. 237-36, 237-40, 237-42, 235-114

Additional tax may be assessed upon examination of the return. The taxpayer may appeal the assessment of additional tax, in the same manner as allowed for income tax purposes as explained in Chapter 2. Prior to 2004, taxpayers had to pay the additional tax assessed when appealing.

The limitation period for additional assessments is three years from (1) the date the annual return is filed, or (2) the prescribed due date for the return, whichever is later. In the case of a false or fraudulent return, there is no time limit on assessment of additional tax.

Claims for refund or overpayment of tax generally must be filed within three years after the later of the due date of the return or the date the return was filed. However, if the return was not filed or was filed more than three years after the due date, a claim for a refund or credit must be filed within three years after the tax was paid, or three years after the date the return was due, whichever is later.

The law was amended effective January 1, 1994, to require taxpayers who have changed, corrected, adjusted or recomputed their federal income tax in any year to also report these changes, as they affect gross receipts and gross proceeds subject to the general excise tax, to the Department of Taxation. Such report is made in the form of an amended general excise/use tax return and is due within 90 days after the change is finally determined or an amended return is filed with the Internal Revenue Service. In addition, the statutory period for assessment of any deficiency or the determination of any refund attributable to such report does not expire before the expiration of 1 year from the date the Department is notified by the taxpayer or by the Internal Revenue Service, whichever is earlier.

## ¶ 810. Penalties and Interest
### Hawaii Law: Sec. 237-32, 237-39, 237-49, 231-39

Penalties are provided for failure to file a return, to pay the tax after filing timely returns, for a false or fraudulent return or statement, and for failure to keep required records or to supply required information.

The penalty for failure to file a return is 5% for each month, or fraction thereof, up to a total of 25% on the tax due. If a return is filed on or before the due date including extensions, and the amount shown as tax on the return is not completely paid within 60 days of the prescribed filing date, a penalty of up to 20% of the unpaid tax, as determined by the Director of Taxation, will be assessed. If any part of an underpayment is due to negligence or intentional disregard of rules and regulations, the director may add a penalty of up to 25% of the tax. If any part is due to fraud, the director may impose a penalty of up to 50%; in this case, the penalty for failure to file (described above) is eliminated. Failure to obey summons issued by the department or refusing to provide requested information can result in a fine of $50 for the first offense and $100 for each succeeding offense.

Interest is charged on late payment of tax, at the rate of 2/3 of 1% for each month or fraction thereof (approximately 8% a year).

Interest paid on refunds when applicable is 1/3 of 1% per month or 4% per year. This interst rate became effective on or after January 1, 2009. Prior to January 1, 2009, the interest rate on overpayments and underpayments was the same (approximately 8% a year).

The law prohibits representations by a taxpayer to the public to the effect that he is not passing on the tax in the price to the purchaser. The penalty for violation is not more than $50 for each offense.

## ¶ 811. Personal Liability for Unpaid Taxes
### Hawaii Law: Sec. 237-9, 237-33, 237-41.5

Effective on July 1, 2010, for liabilities incurred on or after this date a taxpayer can be held personally liable for unpaid general excise taxes and related penalties and interest. The general excise tax is viewed as being collected in a trust fund on behalf of the State of Hawaii regardless if the tax is stated or unstated on the customer's receipt. The individual that may be liable for the unpaid taxes includes any officer, member, manager or any other person who has the responsibility for the payment of the general excise tax. The personal liability applies if the individual willfully does not pay the tax as interpreted by the judicial doctrines. The tax director also has the authority to exempt the payment if good cause can be demonstrated.

Act 219 amended HRS 237-41.5 to remove the application of personal liability to "nonprofit organizations" as defined in HRS 237-41.5. Personal liability shall not apply to any officer, manager, or other person having control or supervision over amounts of gross proceeds or gross income collected to pay the general excise tax and held in trust, or who is charged with the responsibility for the filing of returns or the payment of general excise tax on gross income or gross proceeds collected and held in trust for a nonprofit organization.

# CHAPTER 9

## USE TAX

## ¶ 901. History and Imposition of Use Tax
### Hawaii Law: Sec. 238-1, 238-2, 238-6

The use tax was enacted in 1965, effective Jan. 1, 1966, replacing the consumption tax and, to some extent, the compensating tax.

The use tax is designed to complement the general excise (gross income) tax and is imposed on the use (in the State of Hawaii) of tangible personal property which is imported or purchased from an unlicensed seller. For this purpose an "unlicensed seller" is defined as a seller who, with respect to a particular sale, is not subject to the general excise tax under Chapter 237 of the Hawaii Revised Statutes (whether or not the seller holds a license under that chapter). However, the definition of seller does not include any seller with respect to any sale which is expressly exempted from the tax imposed by Chapter 237. Thus the use tax is intended to apply where: (1) a person acquires tangible personal property from an out-of-state seller for use in Hawaii or (2) where a person acquires tangible personal property within the state from persons not taxable on the transaction under the gross income tax.

In 1999, the law was changed to add a new section to the Use Tax Law. For taxes accruing from January 1, 2000, there is now imposed a tax on the value of services that are performed by an unlicensed seller at a point outside of Hawaii. The services need to be imported or purchased for use in Hawaii. A "service business" is defined as activities engaged in for other persons, for a consideration that involves the rendering of a service. This includes professional services but not services performed by an employee for an employer.

In 2000, under Act 198, the law was changed to impose the use tax on the importation of contracting work that is for resale or use in Hawaii. This change was implemented to complement the GET exemption for exported contracting and because for GET purposes there is a distinction between the definition of services (which became taxable in 1999) and contracting.

In 2004, Act 114 was enacted to make changes to the use tax law as a result of the 2004 Hawaii Supreme Court case *Baker & Taylor, Inc v. Kawafuchi*. The changes made to the law were to clarify when a seller is subject to use tax and to provide clarification on when use tax applies to sellers who acquire goods outside the State and import the products for sale or resale in the State. See ¶ 903 for specific changes made to the law.

In 2011, the Hawaii Supreme Court in *CompUSA Stores LP v. Department of Taxation, State of Hawaii,* 128 Hawaii 116 , 284 P.3d. 209 (2011) held that tangible personal property (TPP) which a retail store chain purchased on mainland and shipped to Hawai'i for distribution to and sale in the chain's Hawaii stores were subject to the use tax, where the chain held a general excise license, was a retailer, used the goods in Hawai'i by keeping the property for sale, and imported the goods into Hawai'i for the purposes of resale, and such goods were purchased from an unlicensed seller not subject to the state's general excise tax. (2003); §238-2 (1998). CompUSA clarified the use tax portion of Hawaii Supreme Court's decision in *Baker & Taylor v. Kawafuchi,* 82 P.3d. 804 (1/14/04).

Normally the use tax will be paid by the importer or purchaser. However, the law requires the seller of the property to collect the tax in situations where the seller has a "presence" in the state and the sale is at the retail (4%) level. Traditionally, a "presence" means having a place of business, property or a representative in Hawaii, whether or not the seller is qualified to do business in Hawaii.

In 2018, Act 183 (HB2416 HD1 SD1 CD1), expanded the use tax to apply to intangible property acquired from an unlicensed seller or imported into the state, and exempted intangible property used outside of Hawaii effective after 2018.

## ¶ 902. Rate of Tax
### Hawaii Law: Sec. 238-2, 238-4

The rate of tax varies according to the nature of the transaction. There are two basic rates, (1) the 0.5% (1/2 of 1.0%) rate where the imported/purchased property, service or contracting is sold at the retail level or (2) the 4.0% rate where the property or service imported/purchased is consumed by the importer/purchaser. The 4% rate will be increased by 1/2% if the transaction is on Oahu see ¶ 802 for further details. However, since a particular property or service can only be subject to the use tax once, certain uses will incur no use tax as explained in the table below and in ¶ 903.

The use tax rates are as follows for purchases/imports:

By a wholesaler for resale in a wholesale transaction ..............................N/A

By a manufacturer for incorporation into a finished product
    to be sold to another manufacturer in a wholesale transaction ..............N/A

By a producer for resale in a wholesale transaction .................................N/A

By a retailer for resale .........................................................................0.5%

By a manufacturer for incorporation into a finished product
to be sold at retail.............................................................................0.5%

By a contractor for incorporation into finished work ............................0.5%

By a producer for resale at retail.........................................................0.5%

By persons engaged in service businesses, calling or furnishing
of transient accommodations where the import or purchase of
tangible personal property qualifies as a wholesale sale ....................0.5%

By a publisher of magazines containing ads when publisher
is under contract to distribute a minimum number of magazines
to the public .................................................................................0.5%

By persons engaged in service or contracting businesses that are
performed outside the State and imported for use in the state.............0.5%

All other imports/purchases subject to the use tax ................................4.0%

The tangible personal property that is imported or purchased and which is incorporated into a finished product by a manufacturer or contractor must remain perceptible to the senses. For services that are imported or purchased, the services must remain identifiable elements in the final product.

## ¶ 903. What is Subject to Tax
### Hawaii Law: Sec. 238-1, 238-2, TIR 93-3, 95-5

The tax applies to the importation of property, services contracting, or intangible property from outside of Hawaii and to the purchase of property, services or contracting from an unlicensed seller for use in the State. New for tax years beginning after December 31, 2018, the use tax applies to the importation of intangible property into the state. See Act 183, SLH 2018.

Example:

Oahu Paper Co., a licensed retailer, imports paper from a Mainland manufacturer, who is not licensed to do business in Hawaii, at a cost of $6,000 delivered in Hawaii. Oahu Paper resells all of the imported merchandise at retail. The purchase is subject to tax of 1/2 of 1% on the $6,000 cost.

Example:

James Smith, a resident of Hawaii, goes on a vacation to the Mainland and brings home an automobile that he purchased in Detroit. The cost of the automobile was $15,000, and the ocean freight amounted to $500. Smith is liable for use tax equivalent to 4% of $15,500, or $620.

The tax does not apply where (1) the importer or purchaser is licensed under the general excise tax law (see Chapter 8), and (2) the property or service will become subject to the general excise tax later at the manufacturer or wholesale level.

Example:

Mattress Co., a manufacturer of mattresses, imports bedsprings. The springs are used in the manufacture of mattresses, which are sold at wholesale to furniture stores. There is no tax liability on the purchase of the bedsprings.

A wholesaler or manufacturer who also sells at retail is subject to the use tax, but is entitled to a deduction, refund, or credit to the extent he can show that his business is exempt as described above. The Department of Taxation has provided for alternative methods of determining the amount subject to tax in such cases.

The use tax rate is applied to the purchase price of the property, service or contracting, if the purchase and sale are consummated in Hawaii. If the purchase and sale are consummated outside Hawaii or if there is no purchase price applicable to the transaction, the tax rate is applied to the value of the property. The value of the property, in general, is the landed cost of such property in Hawaii, including any applicable freight.

In addition to including freight in the landed value, other items also need to be both included and excluded in order to determine the proper taxable base. For example, customs duty is includable in the base for the tax. Cash discounts may be deducted. Charges for installation of parts or services to equipment performed outside the State are included in the base for the tax. Costs for similar items performed within the State are not subject to use tax but would be reported by the person performing the services under the general excise tax. If imported property is damaged after unloading, a reasonable amount may be deducted for the damages if they can be substantiated. If imported equipment on which use tax was originally paid is returned unused within a reasonable time and the full purchase price is refunded, a refund or credit will be allowed. However, the law makes no provision for refund or credit due to repossessions.

Where the tax is imposed on a purchase from a licensed dealer (e.g., purchase of an automobile, as discussed below), any trade-in allowance is deducted from the purchase price in determining the amount subject to tax. In such a case, the resale of the trade-in by the dealer is subject to tax. On the other hand, where the tax is imposed on a purchase from an unlicensed seller, no deduction is allowed for a trade-in.

In Tax Information Release 93-3 (August, 1993), the Department of Taxation (superseded Tax Information Release 91-6) ruled on how to calculate the use tax base of motor vehicles imported into Hawaii for use in Hawaii. The landed value of the motor vehicle is the cost of the motor vehicle (usually the invoice price paid by the purchaser), plus freight, insurance, custom duty and other charges incident to landing the motor vehicle in Hawaii less any trade-in allowance received for the old motor vehicle if the trade-in vehicle is turned over to a local automobile dealer and less any charges paid for license plates outside Hawaii and any retail tax paid to another state or local government, if the sales tax is included in the landed value. The landed value may be further reduced for a depreciation allowance in cases where the taxpayer has used the motor vehicle prior to bringing it into Hawaii. The amount of the depreciation allowed depends upon the mileage and condition of the motor vehicle. There is a depreciation chart printed on the back of the Use Tax Return (Form G-26) for use in calculating the depreciation allowance.

The Department of Taxation issued Tax Information Release 95-5 to clarify the application of the use tax to sales of tangible personal property (TPP) by an out-of-state seller, including drop shipments. A copy of this Tax Information Release is reprinted in Part III of this book. The determination of who pays the use tax when a Hawaii customer purchases TPP from an out-of-state seller depends upon whether or not the out-of-state seller has nexus in Hawaii. The following example from Tax Information Release 95-5 illustrates this concept.

Example:

S, an out-of-state seller of TPP, receives an order over the telephone or through the mail, from H, a Hawaii customer who is the ultimate customer. H requests that the TPP be delivered to H in Hawaii. S ships the TPP for delivery to and acceptance by H in Hawaii.

There are two possible outcomes, depending on whether S has nexus with Hawaii:

(1) If S has nexus with Hawaii, S's sale of TPP constitutes business in Hawaii for purposes of the general excise tax law. As a result, S must obtain a GE/Use tax license. S is considered the importer for resale at retail and is subject to the use tax at one-half of one percent. S is also subject to the general excise tax at four percent on the sale.

(2) If S does not have nexus with Hawaii, pursuant to Section 237-22, HRS, the general excise tax is not imposed upon S. Because S is not a licensed seller and the import is for consumption by H, H is subject to the use tax at four percent.

The use tax is levied on the importer of tangible personal property based upon the landed value of the tangible personal property imported. The tax rate is one-half of one percent if the tangible personal property is intended for resale at retail, four percent if it is intended for consumption or use by the importer or purchaser, or no tax if it is intended for resale to a reseller licensed under the general excise tax law.

The appeal of *Kaiser Cement Corporation,* decided by the Hawaii Supreme Court in 1982, involved the importation and use of coal as a fuel that is burned in the course of the manufacture of cement. The manufacturer claimed an exemption under Sec. 238-2(1)(B) of the HRS because the burning of coal leaves an ash residue, which is incorporated into the finished product and can be detected by chemical analysis. The Supreme Court affirmed the Tax Appeals Court's decision that the imported coal is subject to the use tax because anyone examining cement cannot perceive the existence of coal ash therein by sight, taste, touch, or smell.

¶ 903

In the matter of the tax appeal of *James Lowe, Inc.,* decided April 29, 1975, the Tax Appeals Court held that a scale modeler was subject to the use tax at the 4% rate on items imported for use in making displays. The court reasoned that the taxpayer was in a service business and not in the business of selling tangible products. In a subsequent case, in the matter of the tax appeals of *Otis Elevator Company,* decided Aug. 15, 1977, the Hawaii Supreme Court held that parts imported for the company's service business were subject to the use tax at the rate of 4%, while parts imported for the company's contracting business were subject to the use tax at the rate of 0.5%. In the matter of the tax appeal of *American Express Travel Related Services Company, Inc.,* decided January 23, 1997, the Hawaii Supreme Court decided that the distribution of promotional materials and merchandise catalogs qualified as use of materials by the taxpayer in Hawaii and therefore was subject to use tax. The Court stated that the use tax could be imposed even though the taxpayer never took possession of the materials in Hawaii. The taxpayer was only required to use the materials in Hawaii which occurred upon distribution of the materials in Hawaii.

Prior to the 1976 Hawaii Supreme Court decision in *711 Motors, Inc.,* the Tax Department took the position that if property is imported for rental purposes, it is subject to use tax at the time of delivery even though the rental receipts will be subject to the general excise tax. (This does not apply to aircraft and vessels which are specifically exempt—see item (18) in ¶ 904.) In light of the Hawaii Supreme Court decision in the *711 Motors* case, the Tax Department has reversed its position. The case states that if such property is sold, either before or after it is rented, the sale is subject to the general excise tax. If the sale is made before the property is rented and the sale is to someone for resale, the wholesale rate of the general excise tax applies and the importer-seller can file a claim for refund and recover the use tax paid on the importation of the property. The law was amended in 1982, effective for taxable years beginning in 1983, to eliminate the requirement that capital goods must have three-year depreciable lives to qualify for the 0.5% rate for capital goods purchased by a leasing company. The amendment redefines capital goods that are purchased by a leasing company for lease to its customers to mean goods that have a depreciable life.

For purposes of determining the lowest bid price on all state contracts, the 0.5% use tax is applied to all out-of-state bids. See ¶ 803 concerning the addition of the 4% excise tax on out-of-state bids.

The value for services, in general, is the fair and reasonable cash value at the time of accrual of the tax. It does not include costs for overhead. Overhead is defined as a continuous cost in the normal course of a business. Examples of such costs that are considered part of overhead costs would be items like labor, rent, taxes, royalties, interest, discounts paid, insurance, lighting, heating, cooling, accounting, legal fees, equipment and facilities, telephone systems, depreciation and amortization costs. Further, services that are imported for resale to a foreign customer who is located outside of Hawaii and of which the service is

¶ 903

resold, consumed or used by the foreign customer outside of Hawaii, this service is not subject to the use tax.

The appeal of *Baker & Taylor, Inc. v. Kawafuchi*, decided by the Hawaii Supreme Court in 2004, involved both the general excise tax and the use tax. The Supreme Court decided against the Department of Taxation with respect to the assessment of the use tax against Baker & Taylor. In this case, the corporation argued that title had passed to the purchaser on the mainland and that it hadn't imported tangible personal property into Hawaii for resale as the Department had claimed. The Department also claimed that the company used the goods when it directed the delivery of the goods to its Hawaii customers. The Court ruled that the language in the statue is clear in that with the definitions of "import" and "purchase" as defined in the law, the company did not import from itself or purchase from itself. Therefore, based on the facts of the case, the company was not subject to the use tax. To counter the results of this case, the law was amended by Act 114 in 2004 to change the definition of "Import", "Purchaser" and "Use". *See also, CompUSA Stores LP v. Department of Taxation, State of Hawaii*, 128 Hawaii 116 , 284 P.3d. 209 (2011) where Hawaii Supreme Court clarified the imposition of the use tax and held that the retailer's importation into and use in Hawaii of the goods for sale were subject to the use tax.

## ¶ 904. Exemptions
### Hawaii Law: Sec. 238-1 to 238-4

The following are exempt from or excluded from the use tax:

(1)    Property purchased/imported by a wholesaler, manufacturer or producer to be resold in a wholesale transaction (see ¶ 903).

(2)    Property (not perishable) imported for temporary use in the state. This would include contractor's equipment, moving picture films for exhibition, and autos or other belongings of transient visitors. (If a transient visitor sells property that he brought into the state for temporary use, the purchaser is liable for use tax on the transaction.)

(3)    Gifts.

(4)    Property received on loan or temporary trial basis.

(5)    Ship's stores for use in interstate or foreign commerce.

(6)    Household goods, personal effects, and private automobiles imported for use in the state, provided they were acquired outside the state while a bona fide nonresident of Hawaii, were acquired for use outside the state, and were actually used substantially outside the state. It is presumed (unless clearly proved to the contrary) that any article purchased within three months prior to its importation into the state does not qualify for this exemption.

(7)    Aircraft leased or rented for use in interstate air transportation of passengers and goods.

(8)   Newspapers and magazines purchased on a subscription plan.

(9)   Property or use that is constitutionally exempt from tax.

(10)  Property taxed under the general excise tax.

(11)  Property previously subject to use tax.

(12)  Purchase of materials for performance of certain scientific contracts and subcontracts with the United States. (See ¶ 807 for general excise tax exemption.)

(13)  Purchase of certain property (feed, hatching eggs, seed, bait, etc.) by cooperatives and feed lot operators. (To conform with treatment of sales of such items under the gross income tax—see ¶ 804.)

(14)  Importation of liquor, cigarettes or tobacco products to be sold to a common carrier for consumption outside the state. Act 105 suspended this exemption from July 1, 2011 – June 30, 2013. See ¶ 807a for a discussion of the exemptions and deductions suspended by Act 105.

(15)  Purchase of certain property (cartons for agricultural products; seedlings and cuttings for nursery plants; chick containers) by licensed producers and cooperative associations. (To conform with treatment under gross income tax—see ¶ 804.)

(16)  Vessels constructed prior to July 1, 1969, under the Fisheries New Vessel Construction Loan Program.

(17)  Certain air pollution control facilities exempt from general excise tax— see ¶ 807. Act 105 suspended this exemption from July 1, 2011 – June 30, 2013. See ¶ 807a for a discussion of the exemptions and deductions suspended by Act 105.

(18)  Aircraft and vessels imported for use in a lease or rental business, provided the income is subject to general excise tax. Act 105 suspended this exemption from July 1, 2011 – June 30, 2013. See ¶807a for a discussion of the exemptions and deductions suspended by Act 105.

(19)  Oceangoing vehicles used for passenger or passenger and goods transportation from one point to another within the state as a public utility. Act 105 suspended this exemption from July 1, 2011 – June 30, 2013. See ¶ 807a for a discussion of the exemptions and deductions suspended by Act 105.

(20)  Purchases of surplus equipment from the U.S. Department of the Army.

(21)  Goods imported into the Hawaii Foreign-Trade Zone either for use within the zone or incorporation into a finished product to be exported.

(22)  Use of property in connection with the planning, design, financing, construction, sale, or lease of certain low and moderate income housing projects where the gross income from such activities is exempt from the general excise tax law (see ¶ 807 for general excise tax exemption).

¶ 904

(23) Ocean-going vessels, barges, or other capital equipment imported into the State or sold to any nonprofit entity that is tax-exempt pursuant to Section 501(c)(4) of the Internal Revenue Code, which assists in the implementation of the national contingency plan or area contingency plan created in response to the Oil Pollution Act of 1990 (effective July 1, 1992 and to be repealed on June 30, 1994).

(24) The use of material, parts, or tools imported or purchased by a person licensed under chapter 237 which are used for aircraft service and main-tenance, or the construction of an aircraft service and maintenance facility. Act 105 suspended this exemption from July 1, 2011 – June 30, 2013. See ¶ 807a for a discussion of the exemptions and deductions suspended by Act 105.

(25) Service costs that are overhead costs.

(26) Services that are imported and resold to foreign customer for resale, consumption or use outside of Hawaii.

(27) Use of property, services or contracting imported by foreign diplomats and consular officials who are holding cards issued or authorized by the United States Department of State granting them an exemption from state taxes.

(28) Contracting imported or purchased by a contractor that become iden-tifiable elements, excluding overhead, of the finished work or project required under the contract; provided that (1) the gross proceeds derived by the contractor are subject to tax under section 237-13(3) as a contractor; and (2) the contractor could have deducted amounts paid to the subcontractor under section 237-13(3)(B) if the subcontractor was subject to general excise tax.

(29) Services or contracting purchased/imported by a wholesaler or manufac-turer to be resold in a wholesale transaction.

## ¶ 905. Returns and Payment
### Hawaii Law: Sec. 238-5, 237-30

Persons licensed under the general excise tax law and subject to the use tax must generally file a return each month, on or before the 20th day of the month, for the previous month's activity that is payable on Form G-45, General Excise/ Use Tax Return. Such form and tax can be filed and paid on a quarterly basis if the taxpayer's total excise and use liability for the calendar year or fiscal year does not exceed $4,000, or on a semi-annual basis if the total annual liability is $2,000 or less. A taxpayer who is not licensed under the general excise tax law should report any transactions subject to the use tax by the end of the month fol-lowing the date of the transaction. Form G-26 is used for this purpose.

In addition to the Form G-45, an annual return for each year must be filed on Form G-49, Annual Return and Reconciliation of General/Use Tax. The Form G-49 is due by the 20th day of the fourth month following the close of the year. The Director of Tax may grant extensions for filing Form G-49 for a period not to exceed six months. The extensions are for filing purposes only (not for payment of the tax) and must be requested with Form G-39, Application For Extension of Time to File The Annual Return and Reconciliation General Excise/Use Tax.

When the due date falls on a Saturday, Sunday, or legal holiday, returns are considered timely if filed on the following day which is not a Saturday, Sunday, or holiday. A return that is mailed to the Department of Taxation is considered timely if it is postmarked before midnight of the due date.

All records supporting the information provided on the returns should be kept for 3 years.

## ¶ 906. Deficiencies, Refunds, Appeals
### Hawaii Law: Sec. 238-7, 238-8, 238-11, 235-114

Additional tax may be assessed upon examination of the return. The taxpayer may appeal against an assessment of additional tax in the same manner as allowed for income tax purposes as explained in Chapter 2. The law was changed in 2004 eliminating the requirement that the use tax be paid before an appeal, in the case where the taxpayer is appealing to the Board of Review or Tax Appeal court for the first appeal.

The limitation period for additional assessments is the same as for the general excise tax, as explained in ¶ 809, except that the period is based on the monthly use tax return in cases where an annual return is not required.

Claims for refunds for overpayment of tax must be filed within three years after payment of tax or within three years after the due date of the annual return, whichever is later.

Tax Information Release No. 94-3, issued on May 24, 1994 discusses the rules and procedures relating to the audit of returns, appeal rights, claims for refund and payments to State under protest.

## ¶ 907. Credit for Tax Paid to Another State
### Hawaii Law: Sec. 238-3

The law provides a credit for sales or use tax paid to another state on the same transaction for property subject to the Hawaii use tax. The credit may not exceed the amount of the Hawaii use tax imposed on the same property. The taxpayer claiming the credit may be required to substantiate the claim with receipts or other evidence of payment to the other state.

Example:

Smith is a resident of Hawaii. He buys an automobile in California and pays $900 California sales tax on the purchase. He ships the car to Hawaii, where the use tax amounts to $600. The credit for California sales tax offsets and completely eliminates the Hawaii use tax.

## ¶ 908. Penalties and Interest
### Hawaii Law: Sec. 238-10, 231-39

Penalties are provided for failure to file a return, to pay the tax when due, for a false or fraudulent return or statement and for failure to keep required records or to supply required information.

The penalty for failure to file a return is 5% for each month, or fraction thereof, up to a total of 25% of the tax due. If a return is filed on or before the due date including extensions, and the amount shown as tax on the return is not completely paid within 60 days of the prescribed filing date, a penalty of up to 20% of the unpaid tax, as determined by the Director of the Department of Taxation will be assessed. If any part of an underpayment is due to negligence or intentional disregard of rules, the director may add a penalty of up to 25% of the underpayment. If any part of an underpayment is due to fraud, the director may impose a penalty of up to 50%; in this case, the penalty for failure to file (described above) is eliminated.

Interest is charged on the late payment of tax, at the rate of 2/3 of 1% for each month or fraction thereof (approximately 8% a year). The interest rate on overpayments of tax is 1/3 of 1% a month for each month or fraction thereof (approximately 4% a year). Prior to January 1, 2009, the interest rate on overpayments and underpayments was the same (approximately 8% a year).

# CHAPTER 10

# ESTATE AND GENERATION-SKIPPING TRANSFER TAX

## ¶ 1001. History of Estate, Generation-Skipping Transfer and Inheritance Taxes
### Hawaii Law: Chapter 236D and Chapter 236E

From 1892 to 1983, Hawaii imposed an inheritance tax. Upon its repeal in 1983, the inheritance tax law was replaced by an Estate and Transfer tax law that was adopted for all estates of decedents dying after June 30, 1983. For an explanation of the repealed inheritance tax, refer to prior editions of this book.

From 1983 until 2005, the Hawaii death tax was equal to the amount allowable as a credit for state death taxes on the federal estate tax return. If an estate had no federal estate tax and therefore no state death tax credit against its federal estate tax, then the estate was not liable for any Hawaii death taxes.

The Economic Growth and Tax Relief Reconciliation Act of 2001 phased out the amount of state death tax credit allowable on the federal return starting from 2002 through 2005. As the credit phased out over the years, (reduced by 25% each respective year) the state death tax for Hawaii gradually reduced to zero in 2005, when the state death tax credit was repealed. Simply put, for those dying after January 1, 2005 and before May 1, 2010, the Hawaii estate tax was "0".

Hawaii's Estate and Transfer Tax was reenacted in 2010 under Act 74 for persons dying between May 1, 2010 and January 25, 2012. The Hawaii estate tax again equalled the maximum federal credit for death taxes imposed under IRC §2011. The applicable exclusion amount for purposes of Act 74 was $3,500,000 per decedent. Therefore, decedents dying between May 1, 2010 and January 25, 2012 with a taxable estate of $3,500,000 or less were not subject to the estate tax.

Act 74 also imposed estate tax on the transfer of a taxable estate located in Hawaii of every nonresident who was not a citizen of the United States at the time of their death. The estate tax is calculated in the same manner as it applies to nonresidents, except for the applicable exclusion amount. Since Hawaii does not have a gift tax, the basic exclusion amount was not reduced by the amount of taxable gifts made.

In 2018, Act 44, SLH 2018, conformed Chapter 236E, Hawaii's estate and generation-skipping tax chapter, to the Internal Revenue Code as it existed on December 21, 2017. (Like the income tax, an annual conformity bill needs to be introduced to update the estate and generation-skipping tax to the Internal Revenue Code.) The December 21 date means that the estate tax and generation skipping tax exemption will remain the same as under federal law prior to enactment of the Tax

Cuts and Jobs Act (P.L. 115-97). The federal increase from $5.49 million to $11.18 million, in other words, will not apply for Hawaii estate tax or GST purposes.

Act 27 still requires that the applicable exclusion amount be reduced by the amount of taxable gifts made by the decedent that reduces the federal applicable exclu- sion amount, even though Hawaii does not have a gift tax. In effect, Hawaii is imposing a tax on gifts made during the decedent's lifetime at the time of the decedent's death. Act 27 applies to decedents dying and taxable transfers occurring after December 31, 2017.

The Economic Growth and Tax Relief Reconciliation Act of 2001 also repealed the federal generation-skipping transfer tax for transfers made after December 31, 2009. Along with the Estate and Transfer tax, this tax also phased out the amount of generation skipping transfer tax starting with transfers from 2002 through 2005 when the tax was completely repealed.

Similar to the estate tax, SLH 2010, Act 74 also reenacted Hawaii's generation-skipping transfer tax by adopting the federal generation-skipping tax at certain fixed points in time. Under Act 74, decedents were entitled to utilize the exemption amount of $3,500,000 to determine whether a transfer was subject to tax.

### ¶ 1002. Imposition of Estate and Generation-Skipping Transfer Tax
Hawaii Law: Sec. 236E-1 to 236E-26
Federal Law: Sec. 2001 to 2108
Sec. 2601 to 2663

ESTATE TAX

The estate tax is a tax imposed on the transfer of property at death. The decedent's gross estate in general will include all property the decedent owns at the time of the decedent's death. The value of the property included in the gross estate will be its fair market value. Some of the types of assets included in the decedent's estate could be assets like real estate, tangible personal prop- erty, life insurance, pension plans or other retirement plans and other assets. Property owned by a decedent through a single-member limited liability company that is disregarded for income tax purposes will be treated as owned directly by the decedent for Hawaii estate and generation-skipping tax purposes.

On July 5, 2012, the Governor signed Act 220 which added a revised Hawaii Estate and Generation-Skipping Transfer Tax as new chapter 236E within the Hawaii Revised Statutes applicable to all decedents dying after January 25, 2012. The intent of the new law was to conform the estate and generation-skipping transfer tax law of Hawaii as closely as possible to the Internal Revenue Code in order to simplify the filing of returns and minimize compliance burdens.

In 2018, however, the Hawaii legislature passed Act 27, SLH 2018, which does not conform strictly to federal estate tax law.

For Hawaii resident decedents, the applicable exclusion amount will be the same as the 2017 federal exclusion amount; for nonresidents, the applicable exclusion amount will be an amount computed by multiplying the applicable exclusion amount by a fraction, the numerator of which is the value of the property in Hawaii subject to tax and the denominator of which is the federal gross estate; and for nonresidents who are not citizens, the applicable exclusion amount will be an amount computed by multiplying the exemption equivalent of the unified credit by a fraction, the numerator of which is the value of the property in Hawaii subject to tax and the denominator of which is the federal gross estate.

For residents, the "Hawaii taxable estate" will be the same as the federal taxable estate but without the deduction for state death taxes paid. For nonresidents, the "Hawaii taxable estate" will be the same as the federal taxable estate without the deduction for state death taxes paid multiplied by the fraction of real property and personal property with a situs in Hawaii over the entire federal gross estate. For nonresidents not citizens, the "Hawaii taxable estate" will be the federal taxable estate without the deduction for state death taxes paid multiplied by the fraction of real and personal property with a situs in Hawaii over the entire federal gross estate.

For purposes of the Hawaii estate tax, civil union partners and individuals in a same sex marriage will be treated as married and included within the definition of "spouse."

A Hawaii estate tax return must be filed in the case of every decedent whose estate is required to file a federal estate tax return is required to file a federal estate tax return or owes taxes under Chapter 236, i.e., Hawaii estate tax or generation-skipping tax. The tax applies to a decedent who, at the time of death, was a resident of Hawaii or a nonresident whose gross estate includes any real property situated in Hawaii or tangible personal property having a situs in Hawaii. Section 236E-8 provides that the tax based on the Hawaii net taxable estate is as follows:

- 10% of the Hawaii net taxable estate if the Hawaii net taxable estate is $1 million or less.

- $100,000 plus 11% of the amount by which the Hawaii net taxable estate exceeds $1 million if the Hawaii net taxable estate is over $1 million but not greater than $2 million.

- $210,000 plus 12% of the amount by which the Hawaii net taxable estate exceeds $2 million if the Hawaii net taxable estate is over $2 million but not greater than $3 million.

- $330,000 plus 13% of the amount by which the Hawaii net taxable estate exceeds $3 million if the Hawaii net taxable estate is over $3 million but not greater than $4 million.

- $460,000 plus 14% of the amount by which the Hawaii net taxable estate exceeds $4 million if the Hawaii net taxable estate is over $4 million but not greater than $5 million.

- $600,000 plus 15.7% of the amount by which the Hawaii net taxable estate exceeds $5 million if the Hawaii net taxable estate is over $5 million.

A resident who is subject to estate tax in another state, and the tax imposed by the other state is not qualified by a reciprocal provision allowing the property to be taxed in the state of the decedent's domicile, is entitled to a credit against the Hawaii estate tax of the lesser of (1) the amount of death tax actually paid to the other state; and (2) an amount computed by multiplying the Hawaii estate tax by a fraction, the numerator of which is the value of the property subject to the death tax imposed by the other state and the denominator of which is the total value of the decedent's gross estate.

Act 27, SLR 2018, updates section 236E-3, HRS, to ensure that it conforms generally to Subtitle B of the Internal Revenue Code as amended December 31, 2017. See Hawaii Department of Taxation Announcement No. 2018-13.

## GENERATION-SKIPPING TRANSFER

In addition to the estate tax, Hawaii also imposes a tax on gifts that skip a generation called the generation-skipping transfer tax. An example of this type of transfer would be when a grandparent gifts an asset to a grandchild and skips the generation in between.

Similar to the Hawaii estate tax, Act 220 conformed the generation-skipping transfer tax law of Hawaii as closely as possible to the Internal Revenue Code in order to simplify the filing of returns and minimize compliance burdens for all decedents dying after January 25, 2012. In 2018, however, the Hawaii legislature passed Act 27, SLH 2018, which does not conform strictly to generation-skipping transfer tax law. As with the Hawaii estate tax, the applicable GST exclusion amount will be the same as the 2017 federal exclusion amount.

The generation-skipping transfer tax applies to transferred property located in Hawaii and transferred property from a resident trust. The generation-skipping transfer tax is equal to 2.25% multiplied by the federal generation-skipping taxable amount multiplied by the fraction, the numerator of which is the Hawaii taxable transfer and the denominator is the total amount of all federal taxable transfers. A credit is allowed a resident taxpayer if the transfer is also subject to generation-skipping transfer tax in another state.

For purposes of the Hawaii generation-skipping transfer tax, civil union partners and individuals in a same sex marriage will be treated as married and included within the definition of "spouse."

## ¶ 1003. Administration of Estate and Generation-Skipping Transfer Tax
### Hawaii Law: Sec. 236E-8, 236E-16 to 236E-25

## FILING REQUIREMENTS

Any personal representative who is required to file a federal estate tax return must file a report with the Department of Taxation on Form M-6, "Hawaii

Estate Tax Report." The report must be filed with the Department on or before the due date that the federal estate tax return is required to be filed, which is within 9 months after the date of the decedent's death. Any extensions of time that may have been allowed for filing the federal return also apply to the Hawaii report. An automatic six-month extension to file Form M-6 will be granted if (1) a copy of the IRS approved extension to file the federal estate tax return (federal Form 4768, "Application for Extension of Time To File a Return and/or Pay U.S. Estate (and Generation-Skipping Transfer) Taxes" ) is attached to the Form M-6; and Form M-6 is filed by the due date specified by the IRS for filing the federal estate tax return.

A person who has control, custody, or possession of any of the decedent's property and delivers that property to the personal representative outside Hawaii can be liable for the estate tax unless he first secures payment of the tax or security for payment of the tax.

Any personal representative who distributes any property without first paying or securing payment of the estate taxes due is personally liable for the taxes due to the extent of the value of the property that may have come into the personal representative's possession.

If the IRS adjusts the federal estate tax return or an amended federal estate tax return is filed, an amended Form M-6 must be filed with the Department of Taxation within 90 days of the final adjustment or change.

If an amended federal estate return is filed, an amended Hawaii report must also be filed. The personal representative must give written notice to the Department of the final determination of the federal estate tax within 60 days of such final determination. Any additional tax due by reason of the final determination must be paid at the time the notice is given including interest at the rate of approximately 8% per year. Refund claims may be filed up to two years from the date the federal tax has been finally determined.

Any person who is required to file the Hawaii Generation-Skipping Transfer Tax Report must file Form M-6GS with the Department of Taxation on or after January 1 but no later than April 15 of the year following the years distributions were made. An automatic six-month extension will be granted if an extension has been granted by the IRS and Form M-6GS will be due on the date that the federal generation-skipping transfer tax return is due. An IRS approved copy of the federal Form 7004, "Application for Automatic Extension of Time To File Certain Business Income Tax, Information, and Other Returns," must be submitted with the Form M-6GS.

TAX PAYMENTS

The amount of tax due with the report must be paid on or before the due date of the report. If the tax is not paid timely, interest is added at the rate of 2/3 of 1% for each month or fraction thereof (approximately 8% per year) from the due date of the report until the tax is paid. The penalty for failure to file a required estate tax return or generation-skipping transfer tax return is 5% of the tax due for each month the return is not filed, up to a maximum of 25%. The penalty for failure to pay any estate tax or generation skipping transfer tax due is 20% of the tax unpaid within 60 days of the due date.

A lien on the property of the gross estate arises upon the death of the decedent for a period of ten years. Any part of the gross estate that is transferred to a bona fide purchaser is divested of the lien and the lien is transferred to the proceeds arising from the transfer.

## RELEASE

Upon payment of any tax and the presentation of a sworn statement by the personal representative that the taxes have been paid, the Department will issue a release and thereby authorize the personal representative to distribute the assets of the estate.

If the estate is not subject to estate tax, then no Hawaii report needs to be filed. In order to protect the personal representative and the estate, a sworn statement stating that no estate taxes are due, needs to be sent to the Department of Taxation when requesting a release. When issued, the release will indicate that the Department has determined that the estate is not subject to estate taxes. Form M-6A is to be used for this purpose.

Due to the changes enacted by the Economic Growth and Tax Relief Reconciliation Act of 2001, the Department issued guidance in Announcement 2005-20 relating to the filing of the Estate tax reports. The Announcement states that for decedents dying after December 31, 2004 through December 31, 2010, the Department would not require the representative of the estate to file the "Hawaii Estate Tax Report" (Form M-6) or the "Request for Release to be Filed for Decedents Dying After June 30, 1983" (Form M-6A) reports.

## STATUTE OF LIMITATIONS

Act 27, SLH 2018, enacted a new three-year statute of limitations on proceedings to assess underpayments of tax under Section 263E. The provision under Section 235E-21 states that if a federal transfer tax return is due, then the Department shall commence a

proceeding to assess the underpayment amount within the longer of the following periods:

(A) Three years from the date the federal transfer tax return was filed; or

(B) One year after the date of final determination of the related federal transfer tax.

If a federal transfer tax return was not due, then the periods are:

(A) Three years from the date the Hawaii transfer tax return was filed; or

(B) One year after the date of final determination of the related Hawaii transfer tax.

# CHAPTER 11

# PROPERTY TAXES

## ¶ 1101. History and Imposition of Property Taxes
### Hawaii Law: Sec. 246

Prior to July 1, 1981, the State was responsible for all real property tax functions. However, effective for the tax year beginning July 1, 1981, all real property functions were transferred to the respective counties.

A tax on real property has been in effect since the early days of the Territory. All real property in the State is subject to tax unless specifically exempt (see ¶ 1102 for a list of exemptions). Prior to 1948 there was also a tax on personal property, but there has been none since that time.

The law defines "real property" to mean and include all land and appurtenances and the buildings, structures, fences and improvements erected on or affixed to the property. The definition includes any fixture which is erected on or affixed to the land, buildings, structures, fences and improvements, including all machinery and other mechanical or other allied equipment and the foundations, whose use is necessary for the utility of such land, buildings, structures, fences and improvements. Further, if the removal of the above items cannot be accomplished without substantial damage to the land, buildings, structures, fences and improvements, excluding, however, any growing crops, then those items are also considered part of the real property.

In general, real property tax is assessed against the owner of the property. However, in certain instances the tax is assessed against a lessee or a person holding property under an agreement to purchase. Under a 1965 amendment to the law, the assessing of property tax against the lessee is limited to improved residential land (single-family dwelling) under lease for a term of 15 years or more. Another 1965 amendment prohibits the shifting of an increase in property tax from the owner to the lessee in specified circumstances where the increase is due to a change in the classification of the property. A tenant of government property is also treated as the owner where the tenant's occupancy runs for a year or longer; however, this does not apply where the tenant occupies the property solely for residential purposes on a month-to-month tenancy.

In the matter of the tax appeal of *David P. Ainoa,* taxpayer, a lessee of Hawaiian Homeland on Molokai appealed his property tax assessment for the year 1975–1976 on the basis that the tax on the land was on his leasehold interest which had a value of $0. The Hawaii Supreme Court upheld the Board of Review and held that the tax is based on the fee-simple value of the land and not on the leasehold interest.

For purposes of accountability there is a minimum tax assessed against each parcel of real property, including property which is completely exempt from taxation.

Act 52 repeals obsolete State law, which imposed a real property tax, by repealing chapters 246 and 246A, HRS, in their entirety.

The Department reviewed the proposed repeal of chapters 246 and 246A, HRS, and the conforming amendments to ensure the changes had no substantive effect and were merely a cleanup of the statute. The power to tax real property was transferred to the counties by the Hawaii Constitution, therefore chapters 246 and 246A, HRS, have no effect and their repeal has no substantive effect. See Hawaii Department of Taxation Announcement No. 2016-07.

## ¶ 1102. Property Exempt

Certain types of property qualify for exemptions from real property tax. However, each county has adopted different exemptions. The following are examples of types of property which may qualify for real property tax exemptions:

(a) Total or partial exemptions are granted to property owned and occupied as a home, including cooperative apartments, condominiums and property under long-term lease. See ¶ 1103.

(b) Homes of totally disabled veterans.

(c) Urban lands dedicated for certain uses and approved by the county Director of Finance.

(d) Property up to a taxable value of $25,000 owned by a person affected with Hansen's disease (leprosy).

(e) Property with a taxable value of up to $25,000 owned by persons with impaired sight or hearing and persons totally disabled.

(f) Certain property used for school purposes.

(g) Hospitals and nursing homes that serve the public.

(h) Churches, including property used for incidental activities.

(i) Cemeteries, except property used for cremation purposes.

(j) Property dedicated to public use, under certain conditions.

(k) Property of certain labor organizations or trusts, government employees' organizations, or an association of federal credit unions.

(l) Property of non-profit organizations of a community, character building, social service or educational nature including museums, libraries and art academies.

(m) Property used in manufacture of pulp and paper (five-year period only).

(n) Property belonging to the United States, to the state, or to a county.

(o) All fixtures which are categorized as machinery and equipment used in the production of tangible personal products.

(p) Certain low- and moderate-income housing developed by a nonprofit organization and regulated by law.

(q) Crop shelters of specified types, provided they are maintained in good condition (10 year period).

(r) Certain new air pollution facilities, as defined in the general excise tax law (see ¶ 807), completed or acquired after June 30, 1969, and placed in service before July 1, 1975.

(s) Alternate energy improvements placed in service after June 30, 1976, but before December 31, 1981.

(t) Historic residential real property dedicated for preservation.

(u) Property owned or leased by a credit union.

(v) Property used as slaughterhouses.

(w) Certain qualifying construction work commencing on or after January 1, 1999 and completed on or before June 30, 2003 (7year period).

The exemption for dedicated lands in urban districts (item (c) above) is for landscaping, open spaces, public recreation and other similar uses. The exemption is obtained by filing a petition for exemption with the county Director of Finance. Once approved, the owner forfeits any right to change the use of the land for a minimum period of ten years, automatically renewable indefinitely, subject to cancellation by either the owner or the director upon a five years' notice at any time after the end of the fifth year.

For pollution control facilities (item (r) above), claim for exemption must be filed with the Hawaii State Director of Health. If satisfied, the Director of Health certifies the facility to the Director of Finance for property tax exemption. A new certificate must be obtained from the Director of Health every two years.

In December 1995, an ordinance was passed which repealed the exemption provided to privately owned properties that are leased to the State or County. No exemption is allowed unless a claim for exemption is filed by the appropriate deadline.

Except for pollution control facilities, as explained above, a claim for exemption must be filed with the assessor. The deadline for filing a claim in all counties except Honolulu and the Big Island is December 31 of the preceding tax year for which the claim is filed (for low income housing projects, deadline is 60 days from date property is "qualified"). The deadline for filing a claim for Honolulu is September 30 of the preceding tax year. The deadline for filing a claim for the Big Island is June 30th and December 31st of the previous year. A claim, once filed, has continuing effect as a claim for subsequent years, provided the claimant notifies the county assessor of any changes in his eligibility.

## ¶ 1103. Homeowner's Exemption

Individuals are entitled to an exemption on real property owned and occupied as their home. In effect, the assessed value of the homeowner's real property is reduced by the exemption amount and is not subject to the real property tax.

In order to qualify for the exemption, (1) the home must be owned and occupied as the "principal" home as of the date of assessment (October 1 for Oahu, January 1 for other counties), (2) ownership must be recorded by the Bureau of Conveyances, State Department of Land and Natural Resources, in Honolulu on or before September 30 for Oahu, December 31 for other counties preceding the tax year for which the exemption is claimed and (3) a claim for home exemption, must be filed with the Real Property Assessment Division on or before September 30 for Oahu, December 31 for other counties preceding the tax year for which the exemption is claimed. In the case of a lease, the document must indicate that the lessee has a lease for residential purposes for a term of five years or more and will pay all property taxes.

Where property is jointly owned by husband and wife, the multiple exemption is allowed where either spouse qualifies. In cases where the husband and wife are living apart, they must apportion one exemption amount between them.

Each county now has special rules in determining the amount of exemption for property located in their county. The rules, by county, are as follows.

HONOLULU

Beginning July 1, 2010, the assesment for the basic home exemption for homeowners under 65 is now $80,000. For those homeowners who are 65 years and older, the home exemption amount is now at $120,000. To qualify for the exemption, the homeowner must be 65 years and older on June 30th of the preceding tax year.

For those homeowners who are 75 years and older and whose household qualifies as low income, higher exemption amounts are as follows:

| Age of Homeowner | Exemption Amount |
| --- | --- |
| 75 to 79 years | $140,000 |
| 80 to 84 years | $160,000 |
| 85 to 89 years | $180,000 |
| 90 years and older | $200,000 |

The age limits must be met on June 30th of the preceding tax year. Further, taxpayers must re-file for the exemption as they reach the age range for the next higher level of exemption.

For exemptions prior to July 1, 2010, please refer to prior editions of this book.

## HAWAII AND KAUAI

The basic homeowners' exemption for properties located in Hawaii county is $40,000 plus an additional 20% exemption of the assessed property value not to exceed $80,000. Kauai county is $160,000 of the assessed values. Home exemptions are allowed to senior citizens (Hawaii county—$80,000 if 60–69 years of age; $100,000 for those 70 and older and Kauai county—$180,000 if 60–70 years of age; $200,000 if 71 and older). To obtain the homeowners exemption, the senior citizen must be 60 years of age or older on or before December 31 for Hawaii county and September 30 for Kauai county preceding the tax year for which the exemption is claimed.

## MAUI

The basic homeowner's exemption for property located in Maui county has been adjusted and is $200,000. Maui county also provides relief from property taxes under the Circuit Breaker Tax Credit Program for certain property owners whose property taxes exceed two percent of their household federal adjusted gross income. Applications are required annually and must be submitted during the period beginning August 1 and ending December 31 immediately preceeding the tax year for which the credit is claimed.

## ¶ 1104. Basis and Rate of Tax

Since January 1, 1983, the assessed valuation has been based on 100% of the property's fair market value.

Assessed values are subject to some special rules. The assessed value of a building may not be increased for a period of years as a result of maintenance or repairs made by an owner-occupant under an urban redevelopment project or to comply with certain government code requirements. Under certain conditions, land may be dedicated to agricultural use and assessed at its value in such use. Under certain conditions, land may be classified wasteland development property and assessed at its value as wasteland. Under a 1969 amendment, land may be dedicated to use as a golf course and assessed at its value in such use. Under a 1971 amendment, land may be dedicated for a 10-year period to residential use and assessed at its value in such use.

In the case of losses due to damage of real property resulting from a natural disaster and certified by the natural disaster claims commission, the taxpayer may receive a limited refund or forgiveness of a portion of real property taxes. The claims must be filed on or before June 30th of the year the disaster occurred or within 60 days after the declaration by the Mayor of the natural disaster. "Natural Disaster" means any unfortunate, severe, and extraordinary damage caused by seismic wave, tsunami, hurricane, volcanic eruption, typhoon, earthquake, or prolonged drought declared by the governor to have caused losses and suffering of such character and magnitude to require and justify rehabilitative assistance from the State.

For the fiscal years beginning July 1, 1981 and July 1, 1982, the same tax rate was applied to both land and buildings. For the fiscal year beginning July 1, 1983, different rates were applied to land and buildings and to different classes of property, similar to the method in effect for fiscal years prior to 1980. See prior editions of this book for the rates in effect for prior years. The following are the rates, per $1,000 of assessed value, for the fiscal year July 1, 2018 to June 30, 2019:

| Honolulu County | Tax Rate per $1,000 Net Taxable Property |
|---|---|
| Residential | $ 3.50 |
| Commercial | 12.40 |
| Industrial | 12.40 |
| Agricultural | 5.70 |
| Preservation | 5.70 |
| Hotel and Resort | 12.90 |
| Public Service | 0.00 |
| Vacant Agricultural | 8.50 |
| Residental A: Tier 1 | 4.50 |
| Residental A: Tier 2 | 9.00 |

| Maui County | Tax Rate Per $1,000 Net Taxable Building | Tax Rate Per $1,000 Net Taxable Land |
|---|---|---|
| Residential | $ 5.54 | $ 5.54 |
| Apartment | 6.32 | 6.32 |
| Commercial | 7.28 | 7.28 |
| Industrial | 7.49 | 7.49 |
| Agricultural | 6.01 | 6.01 |
| Conservation | 6.37 | 6.37 |
| Hotel and Resort | 9.37 | 9.37 |
| Homeowner | 2.86 | 2.86 |
| Time Share | 15.43 | 15.43 |
| Commercialized Residential | 4.56 | 4.56 |

| Hawaii County | | |
|---|---|---|
| Residential | $ 11.10 | $ 11.10 |
| Apartment | 11.70 | 11.70 |
| Commercial | 10.70 | 10.70 |

¶ 1104

| | | |
|---|---|---|
| Industrial | 10.70 | 10.70 |
| Agricultural or Native Forests | 9.35 | 9.35 |
| Conservation | 11.55 | 11.55 |
| Hotel and Resort | 11.55 | 11.55 |
| Homeowner | 6.15 | 6.15 |
| Affordable Rental Housing | 6.15 | 6.15 |

| Kauai County | Tax Rate Per $1,000 Net |
|---|---|
| Residential | $ 6.05 |
| Vacation Rental | 9.85 |
| Commercial | 8.10 |
| Industrial | 8.10 |
| Agricultural | 6.75 |
| Conservation | 6.75 |
| Hotel and Resort | 10.85 |
| Homestead | 3.05 |
| Residential Investor | 8.05 |
| Commericalized Home Use | 5.05 |

Property tax rates are set by the individual counties prior to the start of each new fiscal year on July 1. Tax rates after this date need to be confirmed.

## ¶ 1105. Administration—Assessment, Payment, Penalties

Prior to July 1, 1981, property tax was administered by the Director of Taxation. Effective July 1, 1981, the administration of the real property tax was transferred to the counties. The administrative rules for assessments, appeals, and payment of tax remained substantially the same as they were at the State level.

In 1996, the County of Honolulu changed various assessment dates to allow more time for the City and County Council to review the operating budget and consider any changes in the real property tax rates. The dates for the County of Honolulu were previously the same as the dates indicated for other counties however they now differ:

| | County of Honolulu | County of Hawaii | County of Maui | County of Kauai |
|---|---|---|---|---|
| Deadline for filing exemptions | Sept. 30 | Dec. 31, Jun. 30 | Dec. 31 | Sept. 30 |
| Valuation date | Oct. 1 | Jan. 1 | Jan. 1 | Oct. 1 |
| Assessment notices mailed | Dec. 15 | Mar. 15 | Mar. 15 | Dec. 1 |
| Deadline for assessment appeals | Jan. 15 | Apr. 9 | Apr. 9 | Dec. 31 |

The appeal deadline occurs the 9th day of the month following the mailing of the assessment notices, with the exception of the County of Honolulu which occurs on the 15th day of the month and the county of Kauai which occurs on the 31st day of the month. There are four bases for appeal: (1) the property is assessed by more than 20 percent (10 percent for Honolulu County and 15 percent for Kauai County) of the market value of the property; (2) there is an inequality or lack of uniformity resulting from the use of illegal assessment methods or an error in the application of methods; (3) the assessment denies an exemption to which the property owner is entitled or (4) the assessment methods are unconstitutional or in violation of state laws or county ordinances.

The appeal may be filed with the Board of Review in the taxation district where the property is located, or to the Tax Appeal Court. Appeals filed with the Tax Appeal Court require a non-refundable payment of $100 for each case. The deposits for appeals filed with the Board of Review are: Honolulu, $25; Maui, $75; Hawaii, $50; and Kauai, $25 for owner occupants, and $75 for all other property owners, which is refundable if the appeal is successful.

Billing and payment dates for real property taxes have remained the same for Oahu and the other counties and are as follows:

| | |
|---|---|
| First Billing Date | July 20 |
| First Installment Due Date | Aug. 20 |
| Second Billing Date | Jan. 20 |
| Second Installment Due Date | Feb. 20 |

Penalty for late payment is up to 10% of the delinquent tax. In addition, delinquent taxes and penalties bear interest at the rate of 1% a month until paid. Interest and penalties are computed beginning with the first calendar month following the month payment was due. Also, the law was amended in 1978 to provide that the tax due becomes a lien on the property as of July 1, in each year until paid.

# CHAPTER 12

## UNEMPLOYMENT TAX AND TEMPORARY DISABILITY INSURANCE

### ¶ 1201. Scope of Chapter

This chapter explains briefly the Hawaii unemployment insurance tax and the Temporary Disability Insurance Law.

The Hawaii Employment Security and Temporary Disability Insurance Laws are administered by the Department of Labor and Industrial Relations through its Director and the Unemployment Insurance and Employment Service Divisions. The Hawaii Employment Security Law is tied in with the federal unemployment tax, as are similar taxes in other states.

### ¶ 1202. Employers Subject to Tax

The tax applies to employers who employ one or more individuals for some portion of a day within the current calendar year. However, there are exemptions for some classes of employment, as explained in ¶ 1203.

Any individual or organization which has one or more workers performing services for it, must register with the Unemployment Insurance Division within twenty days after the employment services begin. Taxpayers will then be assigned an employer account identification number known as the Department of Labor (DOL) number. Upon the issuance of the DOL number, each employer is sent a registration packet which includes a Handbook for Employers and various forms which the employer needs to complete. New businesses are required to complete Form BB-1 to register to do business in Hawaii (see specimen form in Part IV of this book).

Taxpayers should be aware the requirement for reporting new hires to the Child Support Enforcement Agency. Beginning from October 1, 1998, the Hawaii Child Support Enforcement Agency (CSEA) took over the responsibility of maintaining the new hire reporting directory which was mandated by the Personal Responsibility and Work Opportunity Reconciliation Act of 1996.

Employers are required to send new hire reports directly to the CSEA. The agency requires that information on newly hired employees should be submitted by mailing or faxing a copy of the employee's Form W-4, tax withholding form to the agency within twenty days after the date the employee starts work. Alternatively, the agency will also accept a list of the employees, as long as the employee's name, address, social security number and date of hire are also submitted. Further, the worksheet must also include the employers name, address and FEIN. A penalty for failure to file the reports timely and accurately can be assessed against taxpayers who do not comply with these procedures. New hire reports can be faxed to (808) 692-7001 or mailed to:

> Child Support Enforcement Agency New Hire Reporting
> Kakuhihewa Building
> 601 Kamokila Blvd., Suite 251
> Kapolei, Hawaii 96707

### ¶ 1203. Exemptions

Certain employers have been exempted from the Hawaii Employment Security law if they pay wages for the following:

(a) Agricultural labor if the employer has no more than nine agricultural employees for no more than 19 weeks in the current or preceding calendar year and who had a total cash payroll of less than $20,000 for agricultural employment in any quarter of the current or preceding calendar year.

(b) Casual labor not in the course of a trade or business earning less than $50 per quarter and working less than 24 days per quarter in the current or preceding calendar quarters.

(c) Domestic service, if the employer's total cash payroll for such service for any quarter in the current and preceding calendar year is less than $1,000.

(d) Certain fishing labor if worked for less than 20 weeks in the current or preceding calendar year on a fishing vessel weighing 10 net tons or less.

(e) Governmental employees, including service performed in the employment of a foreign government, except that this exemption does not apply to employees of the State of Hawaii or its political subdivisions.

(f) Insurance agents on a commission basis.

(g) Certain student nurses and hospital interns.

(h) Ministers and members of religious orders in organizations exempt from the income tax.

(i) Newspaper carriers under 18 years of age.

(j) Employees of certain tax-exempt organizations, provided quarterly compensation is less than $50.

(k) Certain family employment.

(l) Service by two family members who each own at least 50% of the shares of a family owned corporation.

(m) Students employed by schools in which they are enrolled.

(n) A registered sales representative for a registered travel agency where such individual is compensated by way of commissions.

(o) A vacuum-cleaner salesman where such individual is compensated by way of commission.

(p) Real estate salesperson where such individual is compensated solely by way of commission.

(q) Service performed by direct sellers.

The list of excluded wages above is not all inclusive but provides the most common type of wages that are exempt. If employers who are not subject to the Hawaii Employment Security laws however, wish to obtain coverage, they may do so voluntarily by filing a written request with the Employer Services Section. If this election is made and is approved, then the election is valid for at least two calendar years and the coverage maybe terminated by written notice filed at least 30 days prior to the end of the second year.

One further note on excluded wages, regarding entities that are non-profit organizations qualifying for income tax exemption under the Internal Revenue Code. This type of entity is not specifically exempted from the Hawaii Employment Security law, however, it may apply for exemption from paying contributions by requesting to be placed on a self-financing basis.

### ¶ 1204. Tax Base and Rates

Since 1974, the wage base subject to unemployment tax has been 100 percent of the state's average annual wage, rounded to the nearest $100, except for 1988 in which it was at 50 percent and for 1990 when the wage base was set at $7,000 by law. Prior to 1974, the applicable rate was 90 percent. The wage base set for the year 2018 is $45,900 as long as the balance of the unemployment trust fund does not fall below a reserve amount as defined.

Wage base for prior years:

| | | | |
|---|---|---|---|
| 2017 | $44,000 | 2007 | $35,300 |
| 2016 | $42,200 | 2006 | $34,000 |
| 2015 | $40,900 | 2005 | $32,300 |
| 2014 | $40,400 | 2004 | $31,000 |
| 2013 | $39,600 | 2003 | $30,200 |
| 2012 | $38,800 | 2002 | $29,300 |
| 2011 | $38,200 | 2001 | $28,400 |
| 2010 | $34,900 | 2000 | $27,500 |
| 2009 | $13,000 | 1999 | $27,000 |
| 2008 | $13,000 | 1998 | $26,400 |

For purposes of the unemployment tax, "wages" is defined by the law to mean all remuneration for services from whatever source, including commissions, bonuses, tips or gratuities paid directly to an individual by a customer of the employer and reported to the employer and the cash value of all renumeration in any medium other than cash. However, the following items are not included in determining wages subject to tax:

(a) Payments under a plan for retirement, sickness, disability pay or death.

(b) Certain other retirement payments.

(c) Payments for sickness or accident disability made over six months after termination of employment.

(d) Payments in connection with a trust or annuity plan exempt from federal income tax.

(e) Noncash compensation for service not in the course of a trade or business.

(f) Payments (other than vacation or sick pay) to an employee 65 years of age or over if the individual did not perform services for the period in which such payment is made.

(g) Payments (not required under any contract of hire) to former employees in armed forces.

(h) Payments under a written agreement to supplement benefits.

This list is not all inclusive and employers should refer to the rules for other exempt wages.

## CONTRIBUTION/EXPERIENCE RATES

A separate account for each employer is required to be maintained by the Director. Contributions are credited to an employer's account while payments to former employees are charged against the account.

An employer may be eligible for reduced rates under "experience rating" as measured by the employer's reserve ratio. The employer's reserve ratio is based upon its reserve account. The "reserve ratio" is computed by dividing the most recent balance of the employer's reserve account by his most recent average annual payroll (generally a three-year average).

From 1979 through 1991, an employer's contribution rate for a particular year was the sum of the employer's "basic contribution rate" and the "fund solvency contribution rate" determined for that year. The basic contribution rate reflected each employer's own experience with unemployment, while the fund solvency rate reflected the trust fund's financial condition and the experience of all contributing employers.

¶ 1204

Effective with calendar year 1992, there are eight contribution rate schedules (schedules A through H). The contribution rate schedule for a particular year is determined on the basis of the relationship between the most recent current reserve fund and the most recent adequate reserve fund. Thus, beginning in 1992, the employer's contribution rate is based on a single table amount which considers both the employer's reserve ratio and the financial condition of the trust fund. For 2015, contribution rate schedule "C" is in effect and is as follows:

### CONTRIBUTION RATE SCHEDULE
#### For Calendar Year 2015
#### (Rates are percentages)

| Employer Reserve Ratio | Contribution Rate |
|---|---|
| .1500 and over | 0.0 |
| .1400 to    .1499 | 0.1 |
| .1300 to    .1399 | 0.2 |
| .1200 to    .1299 | 0.4 |
| .1100 to    .1199 | 0.6 |
| .1000 to    .1099 | 0.8 |
| .0900 to    .0999 | 1.0 |
| .0800 to    .0899 | 1.2 |
| .0700 to    .0799 | 1.4 |
| .0600 to    .0699 | 1.6 |
| .0500 to    .0599 | 1.8 |
| .0300 to    .0499 | 2.0 |
| .0000 to    .0299 | 2.4 |
| -.0000 to   -.0499 | 2.8 |
| -.0500 to   -.0999 | 3.2 |
| -.1000 to   -.4999 | 3.6 |
| -.5000 to   -.9999 | 4.2 |
| -1.0000 to -1.4999 | 4.8 |
| -1.5000 to -1.9999 | 5.4 |
| -2.0000 and less | 5.6 |

Until January 1, 1992 new employers paid 3.6% plus any applicable solvency rate, except that the combined rate could not be greater than 5.4% and no new employer with a negative reserve ratio may have the basic 3.6% rate

¶ 1204

reduced. Beginning January 1, 1992, new employers pay the contribution rate assigned to any employer with a zero reserve ratio based on the rate schedule in effect for the year (2.4% for 2018).

## EMPLOYMENT AND TRAINING ASSESSMENT

Employers are also being subjected to a state employment and training assessment. The rate for 2018 is 0.01% of the taxable wages. No portion of this assessment will be credited against the employer's reserve account. To determine the amount of E&T due, the total taxable wages is multiplied by the 0.01% E&T assessment and entered on Form UC-B6. This is a State of Hawaii assessment and this amount cannot be taken as a credit against the federal unemployment tax.

## TRANSFER OF EXPERIENCE-RATING RECORD

An employing unit that acquires a trade or business, substantially all the assets of a trade or business, or the business organization itself may be able to succeed to the experience rate of the predecessor employing unit. The predecessor employment unit must execute and file with the Department a waiver (Form UC-86, Waiver of Employer's Experience Record) relinquishing all rights to its prior experience record and request a transfer to the successor employment unit. The Form UC-86 must be signed by both the predecessor and the successor employers. Further, the successor employer must continue to employ all or most of the predecessor's employees and all outstanding contributions must be paid. Finally, the predecessor employer must submit all information and reports required by the UI Division. The waiver must be filed within 60 days after the date of acquisition.

## NO EMPLOYEES BUT ACTIVER EMPLOYER

Active employers with no payroll must continue to submit Form UC-B6 with "no payroll" until such time that there are no longer employees and/or the business has terminated.

## ¶ 1205. Benefits

The weekly benefit amount is 1/21 (1/25 prior to 1992) of the claimant's total wages for insured work paid during the high quarter of his base period, but not less than $5 or more than 70% (2/3 prior to 1992) of an annually determined state average weekly wage. The maximum weekly benefit for 2018 is $619. Benefits are ordinarily paid for a maximum period of 26 weeks. However, under certain conditions of disaster or heavy unemployment, additional benefits may be paid.

### ¶ 1206. Administration—Returns, Payments, Deficiencies

Employers are required to file a completed Form UC-B6, Quarterly Wage, Contribution and Employment and Training Assessment Report with required payments by the last day of the month following the close of each calendar quarter.

If the employer fails to file the quarterly return, then a notice will be sent to the employer notifying it of its non-compliance. If the employer continues to be in non-compliance, then a tax will be assessed based on the information available to the DOL along with penalties and interest. The employer then has 20 days to either provide the Department with the correct information or the assessment will become final. If the delinquency is still not cleared, then a lien would be placed on any real or personal property of the employer.

If an employer has not submitted its Form UC-B6 for any of the quarters for the year, then at the time the employer's experience rate is being determined by the Department (usually at the beginning of each year) the employer will be assigned the maximum rate.

### ¶ 1207. Insurance Coverage Requirements

Employers with one or more employees working part time or full time in Hawaii must comply with the requirement under the regulations, to obtain the following insurance. Workers' Compensation (WC), which provides for wage replacement benefits, medical and hospital care for work related illness or injury incurred by their employees. For non-work related illness or injury, the wage replacement is provided by the Temporary Disability Insurance (TDI) and medical and hospital care by Prepaid Health Care Coverage (PHC).

### ¶ 1208. Temporary Disability Insurance

The Hawaii Temporary Disability Insurance law provides a system of cash benefits for unemployment due to non-occupational disease or injury. The benefits are paid under private plans maintained by individual employers, except for benefits for those who are unemployed when they become disabled. The following is a brief summary of the principal features of the program.

The insurance premium contribution applies to employers of one or more employees.

The exempt classes of employment are substantially the same as for the unemployment tax, as shown in ¶ 1203, except that there is no exemption for agricultural labor in the Temporary Disability Insurance Law. The items to be excluded in determining wages covered by disability insurance are the same as the exclusions for the unemployment tax, as shown in ¶ 1204.

The employer may provide disability insurance to its employees by (1) purchasing insurance from an insurance company or (2) maintaining its own self-insured plan. If it chooses to be self-insured, it must deposit security or a surety bond with the Director of Finance, unless it can satisfy the Director of Labor and Industrial Relations that it should not be required to post security or bond.

Employees may be required to contribute up to one-half the cost of the plan not to exceed 0.5% of their wages or to exceed the maximum permissible employee contribution computed each year based on the state-wide average weekly wage for the preceding calendar year.

In addition to paying the cost of maintaining the plan for its own employees, the employer or its insurance carrier may be required to contribute to a state fund to provide benefits for employees who become disabled while unemployed and for employees whose employer's plan becomes insolvent. If the Special Fund for Disability Benefits is below $500,000 on any December 31, a levy will be assessed against each insurer or employer.

Benefits are payable after seven-consecutive days of disability, at the basic rate of 58% of the average weekly wages the employee would have received if not disabled. Certain minimum employment in the prior year is required to be eligible for benefits. The maximum weekly benefit in 2018 is $620. Benefits are payable for a maximum of 26 weeks in one year. There is no duplication of unemployment insurance benefits.

# CHAPTER 13

# OTHER HAWAII TAXES

## ¶ 1301. Scope of Chapter

This chapter outlines briefly other Hawaii taxes that have not been covered elsewhere in the book. The purpose is to provide a picture of the nature and impact of these taxes.

## ¶ 1302. Transient Accommodations Tax
### Hawaii Law: Sec. 237D

The transient accommodations tax law was enacted on January 1, 1987 to impose a tax on the rental proceeds from the furnishing of transient accommodations.

**Imposition of the Tax**—This tax, which is commonly referred to as the "hotel room tax", is imposed on persons who receive revenue from the furnishing of transient accommodations and who are required to pay general excise tax on such revenue. The tax is also imposed upon every occupant of a resort time share vacation unit on the fair market rental value of the time share unit." Department of Taxation Announcement 2017-10. For tax years beginning after December 31, 2018, Act 211, SLH 2018, imposes the TAT on transient accommodations brokers, travel agencies, and tour packagers who arrange transient accommodations at noncommissioned negotiated contract rates on their share of the proceeds. See ¶1451 for the full text of Tax Information Release 2018-07, which discusses how travel agencies should calculate their gross rental proceeds subject to the TAT. In order to compute the transient accommodations tax, a general understanding of the terms is necessary.

A "transient accommodation" is defined as a room, apartment, suite or the like which is customarily occupied by a transient for less than 180 consecutive days for each renting by a hotel, apartment, motel, time share, condominium property regime or apartment, cooperative apartment, rooming house that provides living quarters, sleeping or housekeeping accommodations or other place in which lodgings are regularly furnished to transients for consideration. In addition, the definition was expanded to also include resort time share vacation units.

The Department has also clarified in Tax Information Release 2018-05 when hotel rooms rented by airlines are not considered transient accommodations for purposes of applying the TAT. (An agreement entered into between an airline and a hotel under which the airline is obligated to pay for hotel reooms for a period of at least 180 consecutive days, regardless of whether its airline crew memebers physically occupy the rooms, is a long-term rental agreement. Gross proceeds paid to the hotel for those rooms are not subject to the TAT.) See ¶1449 for the full text of Tax Information Release 2018-05.

A "transient" is a person who does not have the intention of making the accommodation a permanent place of residence. In general, the accommodation should be occupied for a period of less than 180 consecutive days.

The "gross rental" or "gross rental proceeds" that is received from the rental of the accommodations is defined as the gross receipts, received or accrued, as compensation for the rental of the transient accommodation. This amount, however, does not include any deductions for the cost of the property, services or materials used, labor costs, royalties, interest, discounts or any other expense.

In Temporary Rule §18-237D-1-08, the Department provided examples of a transient accommodations broker to include an online business pursuant to HRS Section 237D-1. In Temporary Rule §18-237D-4-01, the Department provided a definition and examples of who is an operator and set forth the responsibilities of operators and plan managers including the filing of the certificate of registration including its name, address, business name, type of entity and place of business subject to the transient accommodations tax by the end of the taxable year or within 30 days of acquisition or giveaway, whichever is later.

**Excluded Items and Exemptions**—In addition to the definition of gross rental proceeds above, the amount of gross receipts used for computing the transient accommodations tax does not include any of the following:

1. General excise taxes visibly passed on and collected;

2. Transient accommodations tax visibly passed on and collected;

3. Charges for guest amenities, including meals, beverages, telephone calls, and laundry; and

4. Service charges.

It should be noted that for items 1 and 2 above, in order to exclude the general excise and transient accommodations taxes collected from the room revenues, when computing the transient accommodations tax, the taxes must be visibly passed on and collected. If the taxes are not visibly passed on to the tenant, then the entire rental proceeds would be subject to the tax. See Tax Information Release No. 90-9 for examples showing how to compute the transient accommodations tax by excluding these items.

Further, in addition to the items excluded above, the law specifically identifies certain exemptions from being taxable for the transient accommodations tax. Those exemptions are as follows:

1. Health care facilities as described in Section 321-11(10), HRS.

2. School dormitories of a public or private educational institution, which provide education to grades kindergarten through 12 or any institution of higher education.

3. Lodging provided by nonprofit corporations or associations for religious, charitable or educational purposes. However, the exemption only applies to the activities of such organization and not to any rental or gross rental of which the primary purpose is to produce income even if the income is used to further the activities of the organization.

4. Living accommodations for persons in the military on permanent duty assignment in Hawaii, including the furnishing of transient accommodations to those military personnel who receive temporary lodging allowances while seeking accommodations in Hawaii or while awaiting reassignment to new duty stations outside Hawaii.

5. Low-income renters receiving state or federal rental subsistence and whose rental periods are for less than 60 days.

6. Operators of transient accommodations who furnish accommodations to full-time students enrolled in an institution offering post-secondary education. This exemption shall also apply to operators who furnish transient accommodations to students during summer employment.

7. Accommodations furnished without charge such as, but not limited to, complimentary accommodations, accommodations furnished to contract personnel such as physicians, golf or tennis professionals, swimming and dancing instructors and other personnel to whom no salary is paid or to employees who receive room and board as part of their salary or compensation.

8. Accommodations furnished to foreign diplomats and consular officials who are holding cards issued or authorized by the United States State Department granting them an exemption from state taxes.

**Resort Time Share Vacation Units**—In 1998, the law was amended to impose the transient accommodations tax on the occupants of resort time share vacation units. Timeshare plan managers are now liable for the payment of the transient accommodations tax and a plan manager is required for each resort time share vacation plan. To compute the tax on the resort time share unit, the tax rate (discussed below) is multiplied by the fair market rental value of the unit. The unit's fair market rental value is defined in the law as an amount equal to one half of the gross daily maintenance fees that are paid by the owner and are attributable to the time share unit. This value also includes maintenance costs, operational costs, insurance, repair costs, administrative costs, taxes (other than transient accommodations tax) and other costs including payments required for reserves or sinking funds.

In the case where the timeshare unit is rented, the operator of the time share unit is liable for the transient accommodations tax on the gross rental proceeds. In this situation, the plan manager will then be released from liability for the transient accommodations tax, for that unit.

**Tax Rates**—The tax rates imposed on the gross rental proceeds on transient accommodations, since its inception, are as follows:

- For the period January 1, 1987 to June 30, 1994      5%
- For the period July 1, 1994 to December 31, 1998      6%
- For the period January 1, 1999 to June 30, 2009      7.25%
- For the period July 1, 2009 to June 30, 2010      8.25%
- For the period July 1, 2010 to December 31, 2017      9.25%
- For the period January 1, 2018 to December 30, 2030      10.25%

The increase from 6% to 7.25% was made to dedicate a source of funds to support the Hawaii Tourism Authority and was recommended by the Economic Revitalization Task Force. The Hawaii Tourism Authority was established to develop and implement a strategic marketing plan which promotes and markets Hawaii as a visitor destination.

The tax rate on time share occupancy by the owner of the unit is lower than the tax rate on other transient accommodations. However, a different tax base is used to compute the tax on time share units. The tax rate imposed on the occupant of a time share unit is as follows:

| Percentage of the Fair Market Rental Value | Timeframe |
|---|---|
| 7.25% | until December 31, 2015 |
| 8.25% | between January 1, 2016 and December 31, 2016 |
| 9.25% | between January 1, 2017 and December 31, 2017 |
| 10.25% | between January 1, 2018 and December 31, 2030 |

If a time share owner rents the unit to a third person, rather than occupying the unit, then the time share owner will be subject to the transient accommodations tax on the rent received at the higher transient accommodations tax rate of

9.25%. The plan manager will not be liable for the transient accommodations tax for the nights the unit is rented by the owner to a third party. See Tax Facts 98-4.

**License and Permits**—Every operator or plan manager of a transient accommodation unit or resort time share vacation plan must register with the Department of Taxation, the name and address of each unit. Upon receipt of the certificate of registration, the certificate will remain effective until canceled. The fee to register is a one time fee, based on the number of units being registered. The current fees imposed are as follows:

Transient Accommodation units:
- For each registration of 1 to 5 units           $ 5
- For each registration of 6 or more units      $15

Resort Time Share Vacation Plans:
- For each resort time share vacation plan      $15

If additional units are purchased after the one time fee is paid, additional fees are not assessed. However, the additional units need to be registered with the Department of Taxation.

**Tax Payment and Filing Requirements**—The tax on the transient accommodations revenue is payable on or before the twentieth day of each month. Payment should be attached to the return which must by filed reporting the revenue earned from the previous month. If the taxes owed for the tax year are not expected to exceed $4,000, then the taxpayer may file quarterly returns in lieu of the monthly returns. If the taxes owed for the tax year are not expected to exceed $2,000, then in lieu of the monthly returns, the taxpayer may file semiannual returns.

At the end of the tax year, an annual return must be filed on or before the 20th day of the fourth month following the close of the taxable year. For calendar year taxpayers, the due date of the annual return would be April 20th. This annual return is a reconciliation of the monthly returns filed, which includes a summary of the years rental income activity and the taxes paid on this income. If it is determined that additional taxes are owed at the time of filing the annual return, then payment for the taxes should be made with the return.

For the provisions on any deficiencies, refunds, appeals, penalties and interest please refer to the general excise tax laws as explained in ¶809 and ¶810 as they are the same.

**Local Contact Requirements**—Effective July 1, 2012, Act 326 requires all operators of transient accommodations to designate a local contact on the same island as the transient accommodation, provide the local contact's information to any entity with covenants, bylaws or administrative provisions operational with respect to the property on which the transient accommodation exists, include the local contact's information (name, phone number and email address) in any contract or written rental agreement, and provide on a website or by online link and display in all advertisements and solicitations on websites the TAT registration number and local contact information. Any persons that fail to do so may be cited and fined by the Department of Taxation.

Act 326 also requires all nongovernmental entities with covenants, bylaws, and administrative provisions to provide to the Department of Taxation relevant information related to operators leasing transient accommodations on its property.

Effective January 1, 2016, Act 204 requires that the TAT registration number and local contact information (name, phone number, and email address) must be displayed in all transient accommodation units and in all advertisements (including online) of such unit or to the guest upon check-in. In lieu of displaying the registration, a notice may also be posted stating where the registration may be inspected and examined. Operators or plan managers that fail to do so may be cited and fined by the Department of Taxation.

Tax Announcement No. 2014-03, issued on April 3, 2014, superseded and updated prior announcements issued with respect to the implementation of Act 326, SLH 2012, which imposed reporting requirements on transient accommodation operators, condominium associations and planned community associations. After delaying the requirements for operators to report to the associations and for the associations to report to the Department of Taxation, the reporting requirements were implemented in 2014. Operators were required to report to the associations by March 31, 2014, for units operated any time on or after January 1, 2013 through January 15, 2014. Operators must report any changes to the associations within 60 days of the change. Associations were required to report to the Department of Taxation on any units that were operated as transient accommodations by June 30, 2014, for units that were operated as transient accommodations between January 1, 2013 and January 1, 2014. The information must be reported to the Department of Taxation by logging into the Department of Taxation's website. In the future, the associations must report any changes to the Department of Taxation within 60 days of the change or by December 31st of the year of the change, whichever is later. Associations should log into the website at least once a year to check the accuracy of the information reported.

## ¶ 1303. Alcoholic Beverage Taxes
### Hawaii Law: Sec. 244D

Hawaii imposes a tax on the sale or use of alcoholic beverages.

**Tax Rates**—Prior to July 1, 1986, the tax was at a rate of 20% of the wholesale price. Effective July 1, 1986, the law was amended and changed the imposition of the tax from an excise to a gallonage basis. The tax rates for the period July 1, 1998 and thereafter are as follows:

| Liquor Categories | Tax Rate Per Wine Gallon |
|---|---|
| (1) Distilled spirits | $5.98 |
| (2) Sparkling wine | $2.12 |

| (3) Still wine | $1.38 |
| (4) Cooler beverages | $ .85 |
| (5) Beer, other than draft beer | $ .93 |
| (6) Draft beer | $ .54 |

**Exemption**—The law allows an exemption from this tax if the manufacturer, producer or seller ships the liquor outside of the State where the liquor is resold, consumed or used outside of the State. In order to exempt the gross proceeds received from this type of sale from being taxed, the seller must receive from the purchaser a certificate that certifies that the liquor purchased is to be resold, consumed or used outside of the State.

**Permit**—Manufacturers and wholesalers of alcoholic beverages must apply for a permit before commencing any sales of liquor. The process involved in obtaining a permit first requires the dealer to obtain, from the liquor commission, a license. The commission will then notify the Department of Taxation which licenses were approved. The Department then issues its permit to the dealer for the period covered by the license upon the receipt of payment for its fee of $2.50. This annual fee which expires on June 30 of the succeeding year and needs to be renewed before July 1. If a permit is lost, defaced or destroyed then the Department may replace the permit for a fee of 50 cents.

**Tax Payment and Filing Requirements**—On or before the twentieth day of each month, dealers are required to complete Form M-18, Combined Monthly Return of Liquor Tax and Report of Wine Gallons and Dollar Volume of Taxable Sales or Uses. This form reports the total sales of liquor by gallonage and dollar volume in each liquor category sold in the previous month and computes the taxes due on the sales. Form M-18, once properly completed, should then be submitted to the tax department for filing along with payment for the taxes computed on the return. All records supporting the information reported on the returns need to be kept on hand for 5 years.

## ¶ 1304. Fuel Taxes
### Hawaii Law: Sec. 243

The fuel tax is a license tax imposed, in general, on the distributors of fuel. In addition to the license tax, distributors are also liable for an environmental response tax. The fuel tax is a combined State and county tax that is imposed on diesel fuel, gasoline and all other liquid motor fuels with the exception of certain specifically identified fuels. The tax rates set by the State are all imposed at a single rate according to the type of fuel. However, the tax rates set by the respective counties all vary depending on the type of fuel and the county. This tax is administered by the Department of Taxation.

During the 2001 legislative session, the legislature discussed the economic and environmental benefits to Hawaii, of using and producing alternative transportation fuels. Up to then, these alternative fuels were being taxed at the same rate as the motor fuels (other than liquid petroleum) and are at a disadvantage on a cost per mile basis. Therefore, to remove this disincentive and to encourage use of alternative fuels the legislature adjusted the transportation fuel tax rates to reflect the energy content of alternative fuels and reduced the tax rates for the next several years.

Effective January 1, 2002, the law was changed to include the definition of "Alternative fuel". This fuel includes methanol, denatured ethanol and other alcohols; mixtures containing 85% or more by volume of methanol, denatured ethanol, and other alcohols with gasoline or other fuels; natural gas; liquefied petroleum gas; hydrogen; coal-derived liquid fuels; biodiesel; mixtures containing 20% or more by volume of biodiesel with diesel or other fuels; fuels (other than alcohol) derived from biological materials; and any other fuel that is substantially not a petroleum product and that the governor determines would yield substantial energy security benefits or substantial environmental benefits. (HRS §243-1)

Effective July 1, 2015, the law was changed to include "fossil fuel" sold by a distributor, subject to the Environmental Response, Energy, and Food Security Tax at the rate of 19 cents per one million British thermal units of fossil fuel sold by a distributor. The law also included the definition of "fossil fuel", which includes a hydrocarbon deposit, such as coal, natural gas, or liquefied natural gas, derived from the accumulated remains of ancient plans or animals and used for fuel; provided that the term specifically does not include petroleum product. (HRS §243-3.5(h))

Also effective July 1, 2015, coal used to fulfill a power purchase agreement that is in effect as of June 30, 2015 between an independent power producer and an electric utility is exempt from the Environmental Response, Energy, and Food Security Tax. In addition, the law allows independent power producers to pass the cost of the tax on to an electric utility. An electric utility is allowed to recover the cost of the tax through an appropriate surcharge to the end user. A gas utility is allowed to recover the cost of the tax as part of its fuel cost in its fuel adjustment charge.

Effective June 20, 2016 and applies retroactively beginning January 1, 2016, a special rate of 2 cents per gallon of naphtha fuel sold to a power-generating facility is added. It also adds a definition of "power-generating facility" and amends section 206M-15.5, HRS, pertaining to the high technology special fund. See Hawaii Department of Taxation Announcement No. 2016-07.

Fuel tax rates reinstated for diesel, gasoline and naphtha, effective January 1, 2016 per Hawaii Department of Taxation Announcement No. 2016-07. Naphtha will be taxed at the liquid fuel tax rate and the term "Power-generating facility" will be removed. Naphtha will continue to be reported separately from the liquid fuel due to federal reporting requirements.

## SCHEDULE OF FUEL TAX RATES
(Effective July 1, 2018)
(Fuel Tax rates in cents per gallon)

| TYPE OF FUEL | STATE TAX | COUNTY TAX | TOTAL TAX |
|---|---|---|---|
| **AVIATION FUEL** | | | |
| All Counties | 1.0 | 0 | 1.0 |
| **NAPHTHA (Power Generating Facility)** | | | |
| City & County of Honolulu | 2.0 | 0 | 2.0 |
| County of Maui | 2.0 | 0 | 2.0 |
| County of Hawaii | 2.0 | 0 | 2.0 |
| County of Kauai | 2.0 | 0 | 2.0 |
| **DIESEL OIL (On Highway)** | | | |
| City & County of Honolulu | 16.0 | 16.5 | 32.5 |
| County of Maui | 16.0 | 23.0 | 39.0 |
| County of Hawaii | 16.0 | 19.0 | 35.0 |
| County of Kauai | 16.0 | 17.0 | 33.0 |
| **GASOLINE & ALL OTHER LIQUID FUEL** | | | |
| City & County of Honolulu | 16.0 | 16.5 | 32.5 |
| County of Maui | 16.0 | 23.0 | 39.0 |
| County of Hawaii | 16.0 | 19.0 | 35.0 |
| County of Kauai | 16.0 | 17.0 | 33.0 |
| **BIODIESEL (On Highway)** | | | |
| City & County of Honolulu | 4.0 | 8.3 | 12.3 |
| County of Maui | 4.0 | 0.0 | 4.0 |
| County of Hawaii | 4.0 | 0.0 | 4.0 |
| County of Kauai | 4.0 | 0.0 | 4.0 |
| **COMPRESSED NATURAL GAS** | | | |
| City & County of Honolulu | 4.0 | 8.2 | 12.2 |
| County of Maui | 4.0 | 11.4 | 15.4 |
| County of Hawaii | 4.0 | 9.4 | 13.4 |
| County of Kauai | 4.0 | 8.4 | 12.4 |
| **ETHANOL** | | | |
| City & County of Honolulu | 2.4 | 2.4 | 4.8 |
| County of Maui | 2.4 | 11.5 | 13.9 |
| County of Hawaii | 2.4 | 2.8 | 5.2 |
| County of Kauai | 2.4 | 2.5 | 4.9 |

¶ 1304

| TYPE OF FUEL | STATE TAX | COUNTY TAX | TOTAL TAX |
|---|---|---|---|
| **LIQUEFIED NATURAL GAS** | | | |
| City & County of Honolulu | 4.0 | 8.2 | 12.2 |
| County of Maui | 4.0 | 11.4 | 15.4 |
| County of Hawaii | 4.0 | 9.4 | 13.4 |
| County of Kauai | 4.0 | 8.4 | 12.4 |
| **LIQUID PETROLEUM GAS** | | | |
| City & County of Honolulu | 5.2 | 5.4 | 10.6 |
| County of Maui | 5.2 | 11.5 | 16.7 |
| County of Hawaii | 5.2 | 6.3 | 11.5 |
| County of Kauai | 5.2 | 5.6 | 10.8 |
| **METHANOL** | | | |
| City & County of Honolulu | 1.9 | 1.8 | 3.7 |
| County of Maui | 1.9 | 11.5 | 13.4 |
| County of Hawaii | 1.9 | 2.1 | 4.0 |
| County of Kauai | 1.9 | 1.9 | 3.8 |

### Schedule of Environmental Response, Energy, and Food Security Tax
(Effective July 1, 2015)
(Tax rates in dollars)

| TYPE OF FUEL | STATE TAX | COUNTY TAX | TOTAL TAX |
|---|---|---|---|
| **PETROLEUM PRODUCTS (per barrel)** | | | |
| City & County of Honolulu | 1.05 | 0 | 1.05 |
| County of Maui | 1.05 | 0 | 1.05 |
| County of Hawaii | 1.05 | 0 | 1.05 |
| County of Kauai | 1.05 | 0 | 1.05 |
| **FOSSIL FUEL (per 1 million BTU)** | | | |
| City & County of Honolulu | 0.19 | 0 | 0.19 |
| County of Maui | 0.19 | 0 | 0.19 |
| County of Hawaii | 0.19 | 0 | 0.19 |
| County of Kauai | 0.19 | 0 | 0.19 |

Distributors of alternative fuels for the operation of an internal combustion engine must pay one-quarter of one cent for each gallon of the alternative fuel sold or consumed (prior to July 1, 2004, rate was one cent for each gallon). In addition to this tax, the distributors are required to pay a fuel tax for each

¶ 1304

gallon of alternative fuel tax sold or consumed for use of operating a motor vehicle on public highways a tax at a rate that is proportional to the rate of tax paid for diesel oil as follows: (effective July 1, 2004 and applicable to taxable years beginning after December 31, 2003).

| | |
|---|---|
| Ethanol | – 0.145 times the rate for diesel |
| Methanol | – 0.11 times the rate for diesel |
| Biodiesel | – 0.25 times the rate for diesel |
| Liquefied petroleum | – 0.33 times the rate for diesel |

For other alternative fuels, the rate will be based on the energy content of the fuels as compared to diesel fuel. On an energy content basis, the tax rate for these other alternative fuels will be equal to one quarter of the rate for diesel fuel, using a lower heating value of 130,000 BTU's per gallon for diesel fuel.

**Environmental Response Tax**—In 1993, the law was amended to impose an environmental response tax of 5¢ per barrel on distributors of petroleum products for products sold to any retail dealer or end user, other than a refiner. The tax, as shown on the schedule above is imposed on each barrel (or partial barrel) of petroleum product sold. "Petroleum product" is defined as any liquid hydrocarbon at standard temperature and pressure that is the product of the fractionalization, distillation or other refining or processing of crude oil. The taxes collected by the State are to be set aside and used to address concerns relating to the impact on the environment and drinking water. Hawaii law was amended in 2010 to rename the Environmental Response Tax to the Environmental Response, Energy, and Food Security Tax. It also increased the tax from 5 cents per barrel to $1.05 per barrel of petroleum product that is not aviation fuel, effective on or after July 1, 2010. This additional tax will be distributed amongst the various special funds and general fund.

**License and Permits**—Every distributor must obtain a license from the Department of Taxation which will remain valid until revoked by the Department. Retail dealers also need to apply for a permit from the Department of Taxation. This permit is issued annually and expires at the end of the calendar year. A fee of $5 is charged for each permit and renewal.

The purpose of the permit for retail dealers is to validate the certificate which is prepared by the retail dealers for the distributors. This certificate, which reports the number of gallons of the various types of fuel sold, is sent to the distributor and is attached to the distributor's monthly return. This in turn, allows the distributor to obtain an evaporation allowance which entitles the distributor to subtract one gallon for each 99 gallons of fuel sold by the retail dealer when computing the tax liability of the distributor. This savings can then be passed on to the retail dealer.

**Exemptions from the Tax**—The following are situations where the fuel tax is exempt:

¶ 1304

- Sales to another licensed distributor;
- Sales of liquid fuel to the federal government for official use;
- Sales of liquid fuel that is exported;
- No tax is imposed on imports as long as the fuel is beyond the taxing powers of the State (i.e., foreign trade zone or sales of bonded aviation fuel to air carriers coming from or going to foreign ports);
- Diesel oil and aviation fuel used for agricultural equipment in non-highway use - a refund of the tax in excess of 1 cent per gallon may be obtained;
- Diesel oil used to operate motor vehicles in areas other than on public highways - (certificate required);
- Use of alternative fuel is for use in operating a motor vehicle in areas other than on public highways of the State. (Certificate required.); and
- Use of alternative fuel for heating in homes.

**Tax Payment and Filing Requirements**—On or before the twentieth day of each month, distributors are required to complete a monthly return. The return must by filed reporting the required information from the previous month, including a breakdown of fuel sold or used, by county and for the Islands of Lanai and Molokai and the Environmental Response Tax to the Department of Taxation along with the taxes owed. In an attempt to reduce the filing burden of taxpayers, the law regarding information that is to be reported on the returns was changed in 2000. Fuel distributors now do not have to submit information about the total number of gallons of fuel imported and information about the fuel distributors' inventory. Distributors liable for the tax may pass the tax on to its customers. All records supporting the information reported on the returns need to be kept on hand for 5 years in case of audit by the tax department.

## ¶ 1305. Motor Vehicle Taxes
### Hawaii Law: Sec. 249

The county imposes an annual tax on vehicles and motor vehicles. The rates for the different type of vehicles vary but are based, generally, on the vehicle's net weight.

**Exemptions** - The law provides the following as exemptions from this tax:

1. All new vehicles in stock which are held for purposes of being sold;

2. Motor vehicles that are owned or leased for 12 months or longer by the State or any county;

3. All motor vehicles and motorcycles owned or leased for 12 months or longer by police officers of the State or any county that are used by them in their travel on official business.

4. If you are the owner of an antique motor vehicle, then in lieu of this tax, the owner is subject to an annual tax of $10 for the entire period of nonuse pro-

vided that the owner submits a signed and sworn certificate to the Director of Finance. The certificate must attest to the period of the vehicle's nonuse.

5. If the motor vehicle is stored so that it is not used for transportation purposes, then an exemption from this tax is allowed. However, the owner must provide the Director of Finance a signed statement stating that the vehicle is stored and other facts required by the Department along with the vehicle's last issued certificate of registration, license plates and emblem for the vehicle.

6. Passenger cars that are owned by persons who are disabled veterans that have been furnished cars by the government and have been certified by the veterans administration, are exempt from the tax. This exemption does not apply if the vehicle is used for commercial use or to other vehicles owned by the disabled veteran.

7. A resident disabled veteran is exempt from the payment of annual vehicle registration fees for one vehicle per year. A disabled veteran is one that:

   a. Has been other than dishonorably discharged from the United States uniformed armed forces;

   b. Is determined by the United States Department of Veterans Affairs or its predecessor to have a service-connected disability rating of one hundred percent; and

   c. Is in receipt of disability retirement pay from any branch of the uniformed armed services.

This applies to motor vehicle registrations issued or renewed after January 1, 2016. This exemption does not apply if the vehicle is used for commercial purposes.

**State Registration Fee and Weight Tax**—In addition to the annual county tax, the State imposes an annual registration fee of $45 (prior to July 1, 2011 amount was $25) on all vehicles and motor vehicles. This fee is also imposed on the owners of antique motor vehicles but is not imposed on those vehicles that qualify as exempted, as described in the paragraph above. The State also imposes a vehicle weight tax at varying rates based on the weight of the vehicle. Members of the armed forces in good standing are exempt from tax on one noncommercial vehicle. The rates are:

| Vehicle net weights | Per Pound priod to July 1, 2011 | Per Pound effective July 1, 2011 |
| --- | --- | --- |
| • Up to 4,000 pounds | 0.75¢ | 1.75¢ |
| • Over 4,000 pounds to 7,000 pounds | 1.00¢ | 2.00¢ |
| • Over 7,000 pounds to 10,000 pounds | 1.25¢ | 2.25¢ |
| • Over 10,000 pounds | $150 flat rate | $300 flat rate |

¶ 1305

**Tax Payment**—The annual tax for the county and State registration fee and weight tax are due on a staggered basis as determined by the county. These taxes should be paid in the county in which the vehicle is located with the annual registration of the vehicle.

## ¶ 1306. Cigarette and Tobacco Taxes
### Hawaii Law: Sec. 245

Every wholesaler and dealer involved in the sale or use of cigarette and tobacco products has imposed on them a tax for these activities. Cigarette and tobacco products not only include cigarettes but also products like cigars, snuff, chewing tobacco and smoking tobacco. The tax does not apply, however, to retail or wholesale sales of electronic smoking devices. See Tax Announcement 2018-13.

**Stamping of Cigarettes**—In an effort to reduce the abuse of selling untaxed cigarettes and to eliminate the sale of cigarettes through the black market, cigarette and tobacco wholesalers and dealers are required to affix stamps to individual cigarette packages as proof of payment of the cigarette tax. This law was effective as of January 1, 2001.

**License**—In order to engage in the business as a wholesaler or dealer of cigarette and tobacco products, a license must be obtained. This license is requested from the Department of Taxation and requires a fee of $2.50. The license, which is renewable annually on July 1, expires on June 30th of each year.

In 2005, the law was changed to include provisions that allow the Department to suspend, revoke or decline to renew licenses on the grounds that the Department finds that the licensee failed to comply with the law. The Department is required to have good cause which the law defines as submission of false or fraudulent applications, providing false statements or possession or displaying false licenses. Good cause however is not limited to the definitions provided in the code. If the Department suspends, revokes or declines to renew a license the taxpayer has the ability to resolve the matter with a hearing.

In addition, retailers of cigarette and tobacco products must obtain a permit. Every retailer engaged in the retail sale of cigarettes and other tobacco products which is taxable within the State, must obtain a retail tobacco permit. The permit, which is issued by the Department of Tax, requires the retailer to apply for the permit and pay a fee of $20. The permits will be valid for 1 year from December 1 to November 30th and must be renewed annually. If the permit needs to be replaced due to it being destroyed, lost or due to a relocations of a business location, the Department can issue a duplicate for a fee of $5. In addition, for retailers with multiple establishments, the law requires a separate permit for each retail location owned, operated or controlled by the retailer. The permit must be displayed at the retailer's location. The retailer must retain complete and accurate records of its cigarette and tobacco inventory. The records need to be retained by the retailer for 3 years. For additional information on record keeping requirements and administrative and criminal sanctions, please refer to Announcement 2005-06 issued by the Department of Taxation on July 29, 2005.

**Exemptions**—The law provides two basic exemptions. The first is that no tax is imposed if the tobacco products are not taxable under U.S. laws. The second exemption excludes from taxation all sales to the U.S. government or any of its instrumentalities.

**Tax Payment and Filing Requirements**—The tax rate imposed on the cigarette and tobacco products has been continuously increased. From July 1, 1993 to August 31, 1997 the excise tax on cigarettes was 3 cents per cigarette. From September 1, 1997 to June 30, 1998 the excise tax on cigarettes was 4 cents per cigarette. From July 1, 1998, the excise tax on cigarettes increased to 5 cents for each cigarette sold. Effective from October 1, 2002, the excise tax on cigarettes increased to 6 cents per cigarette. From July 1, 2003 to June 30, 2004, the excise tax on cigarettes was increased to 6.5 cents per cigarette. Effective from July 1, 2004, the excise tax on cigarettes increased to 7 cents for each cigarette sold. In 2006, ACT 316 increased the excise tax by 1 cent increments over the next 6 years per cigarette sold. In 2009, Act 56 increased the excise tax for years after July 1, 2009. In 2010, Act 59 increased the excise tax for years on or after July 1, 2010. The law now includes the following:

| | |
|---|---|
| On or after September 30, 2006 | 8 cents |
| On or after September 30, 2007 | 9 cents |
| On or after September 30, 2008 | 10 cents |
| On or after July 1, 2009 | 13 cents |
| On or after July 1, 2010 | 15 cents |
| On or after July 1, 2011 | 16 cents |

In 2009, Act 58 increased the tax on other tobacco products from 40% of their wholesale price to 70% of their wholesale price. Act 58 also added a definition of "little cigar" to HRS 245-1. Hawaii law was amended in 2010 with Act 90 to change the definition of "little cigar" to "any roll for smoking wrapped in a tobacco substance other than natural leaf tobacco and which weighs not more than four pounds per thousand rolls." Act 90 also added a definition of "large cigar." "Large cigar" is defined as "any roll for smoking made wholly or in part of tobacco if such product is wrapped in any substance containing tobacco and weighs more than four pounds per thousand." Act 90 also amends the taxation of tobacco products by expressly taxing "large cigars" at the rate of 50% of wholesale price.

In an attempt to help cover the costs of affixing the stamps to each package of cigarettes prior to distribution, the law was amended to include a discount for the licensed cigarette wholesalers and dealers. Effective September 1, 2001, licensed cigarette wholesalers and dealers can now purchase the cigarette tax stamp at a reduction of 0.4% of the denominated value of each stamp purchased.

The tax is applied to cigarettes through the use of stamps. The stamps need to be purchased from the Department of Taxation at a rate of 1.7% of the demonstrated value and have been available since December 15, 2000. Further, the Department of Taxation has permitted the sale of stamps by designated financial institutions located in the state. A list of financial institutions is available at the Department. Payment for the stamps should be made at the time of purchase. However, the law allows the deferral of payment for one month upon the licensee's application.

All licensees are required to file with the Department of Taxation on or before the twentieth day of the month, a monthly return. The return should indicate the number of tobacco products sold, possessed or used by the licensee during the previous month and the amount of stamps purchased and used. In addition, the licensee is required to attach a statement to the return which provides the number and wholesale price of the cigarettes sold and the wholesale price of the tobacco products sold, possessed or used.

All records supporting the information reported on the returns need to be kept for 5 years in case of audit by the Department. Records that are required to be kept include, but are not limited to the following:

- Every sale or use of cigarettes and tobacco products;
- The number and wholesale price of the cigarettes;
- The wholesale price of tobacco products that were sold, used or that are currently held by the taxpayer;
- The taxes payable on the tobacco products sold, used or that are currently held that haven't been paid to the Department; and
- The amount of stamps purchased and used.

This information must be readily available for inspection and examination at any time if the Department requests an inspection. Failure to have the above information available allows the Department to determine and assess the amount of taxes it believes the taxpayer owes based on the best information available by the Department.

## ¶ 1307. Public Service Company
### Hawaii Law: Sec. 239, 240-1

A Public Service Company is a public utility, motor carrier or a contract carrier but does not include transportation service providers. A special tax is levied on public service companies which are generally telephone, power, gas, electric, etc. The tax is in lieu of other state taxes with the exception of the income taxes, motor vehicle taxes, public service commission fees, employment taxes, taxes imposed on the consumption or use of tangible personal property and any tax imposed by the terms of its franchise.

**Income Subject to the Tax**—This tax is based on the public utility's gross income from its public utility business. The rate of tax is based on the ratio of net income of the company to its gross income. The net income is defined as the total operating revenues less operating expenses and tax accruals. The term gross income is all of the utility's income but does not include items like the following:

- dividends paid by one member of an affiliated public service company to another member of the same group,
- between one member of an affiliated public service company group to another member of the same group for
  – income from the sale or transfer of materials or supplies,
  – interest on loans,
  – provision for engineering, construction, maintenance or managerial services,
- gross income for the transportation of passengers or property that is divided among motor carriers, the portion paid to the other motor carrier is not included in gross income,
- gross income for tourism related services that are furnished through arrangements made by other travel agencies or tour packagers and the income is divided among the parties providing the package, the portion paid to the other parties is not included in gross income, and
- worthless accounts charged off for net income tax purposes.

In 2001, an agreement was entered into by the State of Hawaii and the city and counties of Honolulu, Maui, Kauai and Hawaii. It was agreed that the public service company tax revenues would be shared with those counties that established by ordinance, an exemption from real property tax for public service companies. Therefore, in situations where the public utility is involved in other lines of business, to the extent the real property is being used for the other lines of business, that portion of the property will be taxed in accordance with the applicable county tax ordinance.

## EXCLUDED ITEMS, CREDITS AND EXEMPTIONS

In situations where a public utility suffers damages due to a State declared emergency and incurs costs for the repair of its facilities, then the State may allow the public utility to charge a monthly surcharge assessment to its customers. This surcharge, charged to its customers utilizing the facility that was damaged, will not be included in the gross income for purposes of computing the public service company tax. However, any amounts that are retained by the utility for collection or other costs are not included in this exemption.

**Lifeline Telephone Service**—Telephone public utilities which are subject to this tax are also allotted a tax credit against the utility's tax in certain circumstances, in connection with the gross income earned from the Lifeline Telephone Service. This service is authorized by the Public Utilities Commission to establish lifeline telephone service rates for limited income elderly or handicapped persons. A tax credit, equal to the lifeline telephone service costs incurred can be applied against the public service company tax imposed. The amount of the credit is determined and must be certified annually by the Public Utilities Commission.

**Enterprise Zone Credit**—Certain taxpayers carrying on a trade of business in a designated enterprise zone may qualify for a credit against taxes due to the State, if they meet the requirements outlined in the law for the enterprise zone. The qualifying business will be entitled to a credit of 80% of the tax due in the first year. The credit percentage drops by 10% each year ending in the 7th year at 10% of the tax due. Any unused credit cannot be carried forward to future years or refunded.

Further, if a public service company is engaged in other lines of business other than its public service company business, the income received from the other lines of business are not taxable when computing the company's public service company tax. However, the income earned from the other lines of business will be taxable under the other sections in the law.

EXEMPTIONS

In 2001, the law was changed to add an exemption relating to call centers which impacts the tax liability of the public service company tax. This exemption allows taxpayers who receive income from businesses operating call centers to exempt this gross income from being subject to this tax. The taxpayers must be in the business of selling telecommunications as a common carrier for interstate or foreign telecommunication services, including toll free telecommunications, telecommunication capabilities for electronic mail, voice and data telecommunications, computerized telephone support, facsimile, wide area telecommunications services or computer to computer communications. The law allows the Department of Taxation, if they choose to do so, to provide to taxpayers a certificate that can be completed by the businesses operating the call centers. This certificate will be used to certify that the amounts paid for telecommunication services are for operating a call center. Taxpayers should be aware that absent this certificate, the Department will make the assumption that the amounts received from the sale of the telecommunication services are not for operating a call center. This exemption is effective through June 30, 2010.

Effective July 1, 2012, the law was amended to exclude income received by an electric utility company in the form of a "cable surcharge" from the calculation of gross income for the purpose of the Public Utility Tax and the Franchise Tax.

Effective July 2, 2015, the amounts collected by electric utilities for the repayment of 'on-bill' obligations are exempt from state and county taxes, including the general excise tax, the public service company tax, the public utility fee, and the public utility franchise tax. For the on-bill financing program, electric utilities serve as billing and collection agents in a "pass-through" capacity. Only the amounts collected under the on-bill financing

¶ 1307

program are exempt; it does not impact other fees or taxes imposed on other amounts received in the normal course of operations by the electric utilities.

**Tax Rates**—The rate of tax on the gross income of the public utility will be 4%. In addition to this tax, there will also be assessed a tax in excess of the 4% on the gross income allocable to the respective counties, provided the county provides a real property tax exemption to the public utility. The tax in excess of the 4% would then need to be paid by the public utility to the respective county. The tax rates in excess of the 4% imposed are based on the ratio of net income to gross income as discussed above. The tax rates are:

- If the ratio is 15% or less, the tax rate in excess of the 4% tax is 1.885%.

- If the ratio is more than 15%, the base tax rate of 1.885% is increased on a graduated scale up to a maximum rate of 4.2%. For each 1% increase in the ratio the tax rate increase .2675%.

- Gross income of a carrier of passengers by land on scheduled routes, is taxed at a rate of 5.35%.

- For income of a public utility which consists of sales of products or services to another public utility which will then be resold and taxed, the tax rate is 0.5%.

- For public utility companies that are engaged to sell telecommunication services to companies that are engaged in the selling of interstate and foreign common carrier telecommunication services for resale in and outside of the State, the tax on the gross income will be as follows:

| | |
|---|---|
| Calendar year 2000 | 5.5% |
| Calendar year 2001 | 5.0% |
| Calendar year 2002 | 4.5% |
| Calendar year 2003 | 4.0% |
| Calendar year 2004 | 3.5% |
| Calendar year 2005 | 3.0% |
| Calendar year 2006 | 2.5% |
| Calendar year 2007, and thereafter | 0.5% |

The resale of the products, services or telecommunication services under the two bullet points above must be subject to tax under the Public Service Company tax rules or the highest rate of tax for general excise tax purposes to use the rates as described above.

- Airlines, motor carriers, contract carriers other than a motor carrier and common carrier by water are subject to a tax rate of 4%. In the case of airlines, the rate is reduced to 3% if the airline provides reduced rates for school groups. The tax under this chapter for airlines was challenged in the cases of Aloha Airlines, Inc. and Hawaiian Airlines, Inc. and deemed to be invalid. See Reference to Judical Decisions below. Beginning October 1, 2002, gross income received by airlines, motor carriers, common carriers by water and contract carriers other than motor carriers will be subject to general excise tax.

- For motor carriers receiving gross income from the sale of its products or services to a contractor, lower tax rates are being implemented. The rules identify specific requirements that the motor carriers must qualify for before using these lower tax rates. Please consult your tax advisor to identify what the requirements are and to see if your company qualifies for using the lower rates. The tax on the gross income received by motor carriers by contractors will be as follows:

| Calendar year 2000 | 3.5% |
| Calendar year 2001 | 3.0% |
| Calendar year 2002 | 2.5% |
| Calendar year 2003 | 2.0% |
| Calendar year 2004 | 1.5% |
| Calendar year 2005 | 1.0% |
| Calendar year 2006, and thereafter | 0.5% |

- If the amount of public service company tax of an electric-light or power company is less than 2.5% of the gross receipts from all electric light or power furnished to its consumers during the calendar year, then the utility must pay the difference between its actual tax and the tax of 2.5% on the gross receipts.

**Tax Payment and Filing Requirements**—Payment for the public service company tax is due on the 20th day of the fourth month following the close of the taxable year. The company may however, elect to pay the tax in 4 equal installments. If this election is made, the payments will then be due on the 20th day of the fourth month (following the close of the taxable year), sixth month, ninth month and the final payment will be due on the 20th day of the twelfth month.

In the case where the total liability exceeds $100,000, then the tax due is payable in 12 equal installments. Each installment is due on the 10th day of each month. Payments of the tax for the Department of Taxation should be made with Form FP-1. An annual return is then required to be filed by the 20th day of the fourth month following the close of the taxable year.

Where there is a tax levied and assessed in excess of the 4% tax that needs to be paid to a county, the public utility will need to file with the Director of Finance of the respective county, a statement showing all the gross income from the public utility business on which the tax was calculated. If more than one county is paid, then the allocation of the gross income to all the counties will need to be included in the statement.

This tax is administered by both the Department of Taxation and the county Director of Finance. On October 1, 2010, the Department of Taxation issued

Announcement 2010-12 which indicated that the Department is exercising its election to accelerate the balance due of all installment payments of PSC and Franchise Taxes if an installment is not paid by its due date. Beginning January 1, 2011, any late installment payment will cause the balance of the tax to be due and payable on demand by the Department within 10 days of the notice.

OTHER MATTERS

To conform to the federal Mobile Telecommunications Sourcing Act (effective August 1, 2002), the legislature enacted provisions that state all wireless calls will be sourced to the state the subscriber's plan is purchased. The rules will be come effective on July 1, 2002 and apply to gross income received after August 1, 2002. These provisions also exempt wholesale sales of mobile telecommunication services made between home service providers from general excise tax and public service company tax.

**Judicial Decisions**—Several judicial decisions impacting the airlines and telephone companies have been included below.

In the appeal of *Aloha Airlines, Inc., and Hawaiian Airlines, Inc.,* decided June 23, 1982, by the Hawaii Supreme Court, the Hawaii-based airlines challenged the constitutionality of the public service company tax on the basis that it violated the interstate commerce clause of the United States Constitution and that the Hawaii tax was preempted by federal statutes. The court denied the taxpayers' argument and upheld the constitutionality of the public service company tax. On November 1, 1983, the U.S. Supreme Court reversed the Hawaii Supreme Court decision and held that the federal statutes preempt the Hawaii statute.

In a similar case, *Air Polynesia, Inc. d/b/a/ DHL Cargo,* decided May 24, 1985, stated the Hawaii Tax Appeal Court in its decision, followed the U.S. Supreme Court and held that the federal statute preempts the Hawaii tax.

In the matter of the tax appeal of *Hawaiian Telephone Company,* decided January 22, 1977, stated the Hawaii Supreme Court, in its decision, held that gross income did not include a credit given for the use of U.S. government property where the telephone company rendered service to the U.S. government.

In another case involving *Hawaiian Telephone Company,* decided February 27, 1980, the Hawaii Supreme Court held that directory advertising revenue and revenue from the sale of old directories are not subject to the public service company tax but are subject to the lower general excise tax.

In the appeal of *United Parcel Service, Inc.,* decided October 29, 1998 by the Hawaii Supreme Court, it was held that gross receipts from the ground transportation portion of a common carrier's interisland delivers and deliveries between Hawaii and the mainland are subject to tax under the public service company tax law. The court stated that the Federal Aviation Act preempts the state taxation on the air transportation and does not extend to the activities of the common carrier.

¶ 1307

In the tax appeal of *Laie Treatment Works, Inc.*, decided on August 19, 2004, the Hawaii Tax Appeal Court held in favor of the taxpayer that the definition of gross income within the law did not include income from sewer and/or wastewater treatment services. Therefore, the taxpayer in this case was not subject to the public service company tax for this income. Due to the conclusion of this case, taxpayers should be aware that the law has subsequently been changed to now include in the definition of gross income within this Chapter "operations of a private sewer company or private sewer facility".

## ¶ 1308. Insurance Companies
### Hawaii Law: Sec. 431, 431:7, 431:19

Insurance companies are subject to special taxes based on its gross premiums of gross underwriting profits. In addition to the taxes, they are required to also pay annual filing fees to the Department of Commerce and Consumer Affairs for services.

**Tax Rates**—The insurance premium tax is determined by applying the applicable rate to the gross premiums from all risks or property resident, less return premiums and any reinsurance accepted. In addition to these reductions, Life insurers and Ocean marine insurers may be able to reduce its gross premiums by other items. The applicable tax rates are:

- Insurers other than life, ocean marine, and annuities          4.2650%
- Life insurers                                                  2.7500%
- Ocean marine insurers                                          0.8775%
- Surplus line brokers                                           4.6800%

**Tax Credits**—Various tax credits are allowed in the law, which can be taken against the taxes owed in this section. The credits include the following:

- A credit is allowed for Hawaii insurers for taxes paid to other states under the condition that the taxes are greater than the taxes required of insurers organized and domiciled in the other state.

- A credit is allowed where the insurer conducts its business in a certain manner designed to encourage insurers to maintain in Hawaii, the records and personnel necessary to provide less costly, more effective and timely state regulation for the entire year. The credit allowed is equal to 1% of premiums subject to the gross premium tax.

- The low income housing credit, equal to 50% of the federal low income housing credit, can be offset against the insurance tax liability.

- The expired high technology business investment tax credit could be offset against the insurance tax. This credit, which was allowed against a taxpayer's net income tax liability for the taxable year in which the investment is made. The credit was allowed over a 5 year period and is capped in each respective year. See Chapter 3 for more information on the high technology business.

**Tax Payment and Filing Requirements**—Authorized insurers including captive insurers are required to file an annual return to the commissioner no later than March 1. For Surplus Lines brokers, the annual statement is due on March 15th. This return should include the total business transacted and the amount of gross premiums received by the insurer during the year. Further, effective July 1, 2010, each authorized insurer is also required to file monthly reports with the commissioner along with their respective tax payments. The monthly return is due on or before the twentieth day of each month. Prior to July 1, 2010, periodic returns were due on a quarterly basis.

If an insurer fails to pay the required taxes when due, a fine, the greater of $500 or 10% of the tax due could be assessed. In addition, interest at a rate of 12% per annum on the delinquent taxes will also be added to the amount owed. If any insurer fails to file its monthly or annual tax statements by the required due date, a fine of not less than $100 but no more than $500 per day could be assessed. For Surplus Lines brokers the penalty is $25 per day.

The tax and fees imposed on insurers under the provisions in HRS section 431:7-201 and 431:7-204 are in lieu of all other taxes except real property, use, unemployment and general excise taxes.

This tax is administered by the Department of Commerce and Consumer Affairs.

OTHER MATTERS

Captive insurance companies licensed to do business in the state of Hawaii must pay taxes on gross premiums as follows:
.25% on $0 to $25,000,000 of gross premiums
.15% on $25,000,001 to $50,000,000 of gross premiums
.05% on $50,000,001 to $250,000,000 of gross premiums
.00% on $250,000,001 or more of gross premiums

The annual maximum aggregate tax on gross premiums to be paid by the captive insurance company should not exceed $200,000. Captive insurance companies are exempt from all taxes, except for the above tax, unemployment tax, property tax and use tax.

## ¶ 1309. Realty Conveyance Tax
### Hawaii Law: Sec. 247

The conveyance tax is imposed on transfers of realty or any interest, by way of deeds, long-term leases (unexpired term of five years or more), agreements of sale or any other documents where an interest in land is conveyed and the consideration is over $100.

**Tax Rates and Payments**—The tax rate has been 10 cents per $100 of consideration with a minimum tax of $1 per transaction.

Effective July 1, 2005, the tax is based on the actual and full consideration paid or to be paid for all transfers or conveyance of realty or any interest there-

¶ 1308

in, that shall include any liens or encumbrances thereon at the time of sale, lease, sublease, assignment, transfer, or conveyance. In 2009, Act 59 increased conveyance tax rates for higher value properties effective on any transfer or conveyance or realty or any interest therein (unless exempt) that occurs on or after July 1, 2009. The conveyance tax is imposed at the following rates:

(A.) Sale of properties other than as described in (B.) below:

| Property Value | Tax Rate |
| --- | --- |
| Less than $600,000 | 10 cents per $100 |
| $600,000 or more but less than $1,000,000 | 20 cents per $100 |
| $1,000,000 or more but less than $2,000,000 | 30 cents per $100 |
| $2,000,000 or more but less than $4,000,000 | 50 cents per $100 |
| $4,000,000 or more but less than $6,000,000 | 70 cents per $100 |
| $6,000,000 or more but less than $10,000,000 | 90 cents per $100 |
| $10,000,000 or more | $1.00 per $100 |

(B.) Sale of a condominium or single family residence for which the purchaser is ineligible for a county homeowner's exemption on property tax:

| Property Value | Tax Rate |
| --- | --- |
| Less than $600,000 | 15 cents per $100 |
| $600,000 or more but less than $1,000,000 | 25 cents per $100 |
| $1,000,000 or more but less than $2,000,000 | 40 cents per $100 |
| $2,000,000 or more but less than $4,000,000 | 60 cents per $100 |
| $4,000,000 or more but less than $6,000,000 | 85 cents per $100 |
| $6,000,000 or more but less than $10,000,000 | $1.10 per $100 |
| $10,000,000 or more | $1.25 per $100 |

This tax is paid by the transferor or seller no later than 90 days after the transaction. If not paid, then penalties and interest will be added to the amount due.

**Excluded Items**—The following conveyances are exempted from the conveyance tax:

1. Conveyances that confirm or correct a document previously recorded or filed.

2. Conveyances between a husband and wife, reciprocal beneficiaries, or parent and child, in which only a nominal consideration is paid.

3. Conveyances in which a nominal consideration of $100 or less is paid or to be paid.

4. Conveyances in fulfillment of an agreement of sale and, where applicable, an assignment of agreement of sale, if the conveyance tax on the agreement of sale was previously paid when the agreement of sale was recorded.

5. Conveyances involving a tax sale for delinquent taxes or assessments.

6. Conveyances involving partition deeds among co-owners, provided each

¶ 1309

exemption claimed declares each owner's undivided interest in the real property and the value of that interest before partition, and each owner's proportionate interest and the value of that interest after partition.

7. Conveyances between marital partners or reciprocal beneficiaries who are parties to a divorce action or termination of reciprocal beneficiary relationship which are executed pursuant to an order of the court in the divorce action or termination of reciprocal beneficiary relationship.

8. Conveyances from a testamentary trust to a trust beneficiary.

9. Conveyance from the grantor to a grantor's revocable living trust or from a grantor's revocable living trust to the grantor.

To obtain these exemptions, a Form P-64B, "Exemption from Conveyance Tax," must be filed with the Department of Taxation or the Bureau of Conveyances, depending on the type of conveyance.

**Judicial Decisions**—As stated above, the conveyancy tax is generally imposed on all conveyances of interest in real property from one person to another. This, for example, includes transfers of real property from a partner to his or her partnership as clarified in the matter of the tax appeal of *Gentry-Pacific, Ltd.,* (decided May 10, 1990).

### ¶ 1310. Rental Motor Vehicle and Tour Vehicle Surcharge Tax
#### Hawaii Law: Sec. 251

Effective January 1, 1993, Hawaii imposes a surcharge tax on rental motor vehicles and tour vehicles. The rental motor vehicle tax is imposed on the lessor, for any day or portion of the day that a rental motor vehicle is rented or leased. The law defines "rental motor vehicle" as every vehicle which is self propelled and/or which is propelled by electric power. It does not include, however, vehicles operated on rails. The vehicles must be rented, leased or offered for rent or lease in Hawaii for a period of 6 months or less. The rental can be for personal or commercial use and covers vehicles designed to carry 17 or fewer passengers. It also does not include rentals to a lessee to replace a vehicle which is being repaired.

The types of vehicles not included in the definition are mopeds, trucks, truck-tractors, tractor-semi-trailer combinations and truck trailer combinations with a nominal carrying capacity of 1,000 pounds or more. The trucks with barriers or separations between the operator's compartment and the cargo area or cargo vans with no more than two seats, including the driver's seat are also not included.

The tour vehicle tax is levied on the tour vehicle operators. The definition of a "tour vehicle" includes any vehicle including vans, minibuses and buses used for the purpose of transporting persons for pleasure or sightseeing trips. Not included in this definition are vehicles used to transport individuals to and from work, schools or transporting individuals with disabilities.

**License**—All persons in the business of providing rental motor vehicles or engaged in the tour vehicle operations, are required to register with Department of Taxation and pay a one time fee of $20.

**Tax Rates**—The tax rate imposed for the surcharge tax on rental motor vehicles was $2 per day (or any portion of the day) through August 31, 1999. The tax rate was increased to $3 a day (or any portion of the day) from the period of September 1, 1999 to August 31, 2007. The law was amended and the end date for the $3 surcharge was extended to June 30, 2011. July 1, 2011 through June 30, 2012, the surcharge increased to $7.50. Beginning July 1, 2012 the surcharge reverted back to $3 per day. Effective January 1, 2019, the surcharge increases to $5 a day for any rental for which the lessee does not have a valid Hawaii driver's license. The surcharge remains at $3 per day if the lessee has a valid Hawaii driver's license.

The tour vehicle surcharge tax is based on the passenger capacity of the vehicle. For vehicles with over a 25 passenger seat category, a charge of $65 for each vehicle used or partially used during the month is imposed. Effective January 1, 2019, the surcharge increases to $66 per month. For vehicles with 8 to 25 passenger seats, the surcharge is $15 for each vehicle used or partially used during the month. Effective January 1, 2019, the surcharge increases to $16 per month.

**Tax Payment and Filing Requirements**—The payment for the tax is to be paid monthly. Taxpayers subject to the tax must file a return with the Department of Taxation together with a remittance for the amount of the tax. The return is due on or before the twentieth day of the month. If the total surcharge tax liability does not exceed $4,000 for the year, then returns and payments can be made on a quarterly basis. If the total surcharge tax liability does not exceed $2,000 for the year, then returns and payments can be made on a semi-annual basis. The law also requires every taxpayer subject to the tax to file an annual return summarizing its tax liability for the year by the 20th day of the fourth month following the close of the taxable year. If good cause is shown, the annual return can be extended.

**Car-sharing Vehicle Surcharge Tax** – In 2014, Hawaii Revised Statutes section 251-2.5 was enacted and imposes a car-sharing vehicle surcharge tax on "car-sharing organizations" in lieu of the rental motor vehicle surcharge tax imposed by HRS § 251-2. A "car-sharing organization" is defined as a rental car lessor that operates a membership program in which:

1. Self-service access to a fleet of vehicles is provided, with or without reservation, exclusively to members of the organization who have paid a membership fee;

2. Members are charged a usage rate, either hourly or by the minute, for each use of a vehicle;

3. Members are not required to enter into a separate written agreement with

¶ 1310

the organization each time the member reserves and uses a vehicle; and

4. The average paid use period for all vehicles provided by the organization during any taxable period is six hours or less.

The car-sharing vehicle surcharge tax rate is 25 cents per half-hour, or any portion of a half-hour, that the vehicle is rented or leased by a car-sharing organization; provided that for each rental of six hours or more the rental motor vehicle surcharge tax imposed by HRS § 251-2 applies. The rental motor vehicle surcharge tax is $3.00 per day. The car-sharing vehicle surcharge tax will be reported on Form RV-2, "Periodic Rental Motor Vehicle and Tour Vehicle Surcharge Tax," and Form RV-3, "Rental Motor Vehicle and Tour Vehicle Surcharge Tax Annual Return and Reconciliation."

Beginning August 2017, the Department will begin the process of mandating monthly filing. Quarterly filers will be changed to monthly if a return for the month ending July 31, 2017 (return due August 20, 2017), or any month thereafter, is filed. Semi-annual filers will be changed to monthly if a return for the month ending July 31, 2017 (return due August 20, 2017), or any month thereafter, is filed, or quarter ending September 30, 2017 (return due October 20, 2017), or any quarter thereafter, is filed.

Filing frequency changes will be effective for the month following the filing of the return that triggered the filing and payment frequency change. This means that quarterly and semiannual filers who file a return for month ending July 31, 2017 must begin to file monthly returns starting with the month ending August 31, 2017. Monthly returns must be filed and the tax due must be paid on or before the twentieth day of the calendar month following the month being reported. Failure to comply with the requirements will result in the assessment of penalties and interest. The filing frequency of quarterly and semi-annual taxpayers who file properly according to their tax liability thresholds will not be changed. A taxpayer whose filing frequency has been changed may request that the filing frequency be changed to quarterly or semiannual pursuant to sections 237-30, 237D-6, or 251-4, HRS. However, taxpayers who request this change must file with the filing frequency requested on an ongoing basis unless the filing frequency is subsequently changed by the Department.

### ¶ 1311. Corporate Organization and Qualification Fees
Hawaii Law: Sec. 414, 414D, 425, 425D, 428

Domestic corporations are subject to a fee of $50 for initial incorporation and $25 for any amendments. Nonprofit domestic corporations are subject to a fee of $25 for initial incorporation and $10 for any amendments.

Foreign corporations must file for a certificate of authority with the Department of Commerce and Consumer Affairs in order to transact business in Hawaii. When filing for the certificate, the foreign corporation must pay a minimum fee of $50. Nonprofit foreign corporations pay a fee of $25.

Other business registration filing fees are:

| General Partnership: | | Limited Liability Partnership: | |
|---|---|---|---|
| Domestic | $ 15 | Domestic | $ 25 |
| Foreign | $ 15 | Foreign | $ 50 |
| Limited Partnership | $ 25 | Trade Name | $ 25 |
| Limited Liability Company | $ 50 | | |

## BUSINESS LICENSE FEES

License fees are imposed on a long list of businesses and professions. Information regarding these fees may be obtained from the Department of Taxation.

Each corporation doing business in the state must file an annual corporate exhibit with a $15 filing fee ($5 for nonprofit organizations, general partnerships and limited partnerships).

For years prior to 2003, annual corporate exhibits for all domestic and foreign corporations were filed between January 1 and April 1 of the following calendar year. The exhibit reflected information relating to the corporation as of December 31 of the year preceding the year of filing. No extensions were granted for filing the exhibits.

Effective January 1, 2003, annual corporate exhibits for all domestic and foreign corporations must be filed based on the date of incorporation or registration within the state of Hawaii. (See table on next page for dates.)

**ANNUAL REPORTS**

| Date of Incorporation or Registration | Due Date of Annual Exhibits | Reflect the Corporation's Affairs as of the Year of Filing |
|---|---|---|
| January 1 and March 31 | On or Before March 31 | January 1 |
| April 1 and June 30 | On or Before June 30 | April 1 |
| July 1 and September 30 | On or Before September 30 | July 1 |
| October 1 and December 31 | On or Before December 31 | October 1 |

## ¶ 1312. Streamlined Sales Tax Project
### Hawaii Law: Sec. 255D

In 2003 under Act 173, a new chapter was added to the Hawaii Revised Statutes. This new chapter authorizes Hawaii to participate in the multistate discussions on the Streamlined Sales Tax Project ("SSTP").

The vision of SSTP was for all states to agree on a simplified and uniform manner of imposing sales and use tax so that out-of-state vendors could easily collect a state's sales tax thereby eliminating the undue burden prohibited in Quill

Corporation v. North Dakota, 504 U.S. 298 (1992). On November 12, 2002, the Streamlined Sales Tax implementing states, a group of states that had agreed with the rationale of SSTP, adopted the Streamlined Sales and Use Tax Agreement ("SSUTA"). The SSUTA become effective on October 1, 2005, when at least 10 states comprising at least twenty percent of the total population, as determined by the 2000 federal census became participating member states.

The SSUTA provides simplified and uniform rules that each state must meet to ameliorate the Constitutional Commerce Clause concerns of Quill in the following areas.

1. Tax Base Simplification and Uniformity

2. Tax Rate Simplification

3. Uniform Sourcing Rules

4. Administrative Simplification and Uniformity

To become a participating member state, a state must petition the Streamlined Sales Tax Governing Board for membership and certify that its laws comply with the SSUTA. As of October 1, 2012, twenty-one states had been approved as full member states. Hawaii has not amended its laws to comply with the SSUTA. Therefore, Hawaii is not a full member state.

# PART III

## Administrative Rules, Tax Memoranda, Tax Announcements and Tax Information Releases

# CHAPTER 14

## SELECTED ADMINISTRATIVE RULES, TAX MEMORANDA, TAX ANNOUNCEMENTS AND TAX INFORMATION RELEASES

## ¶ 1401. General Discussion

Reprinted in this chapter are selected Administrative Rules, Tax Memoranda, Tax Announcements, and Tax Information Releases. We have endeavored to reprint those administrative releases that we feel will be of greatest interest to the majority of our readers. If a particular release is not included in this chapter, a copy may be obtained directly from the Department of Taxation.

## ¶ 1402. Rules

In this chapter we have also included for your reference sections from the Administrative Rules that explain and help implement the tax laws. However, caution is advised when reading and relying on the Administrative Rules as the Department has not updated all the rules to reflect the changes in the tax laws and therefore, some inconsistencies may exist. Please consult a tax advisor when dealing with the rules.

## ¶ 1403. Rules Section 18-235-2.3 Conformance to The Federal Internal Revenue Code

(a) In general.

(1) In order to permit a proper administration of the Hawaii net income tax law which by Act 62, S.L.H. 1979, adopted by reference various provisions of the federal Internal Revenue Code, as amended as of December 31, 1979, the director of taxation finds it desirable to establish and publish income tax rules and regulations, conforming to the requirements of chapter 91, HRS. When

promulgated as required by law, these rules and regulations have the force and effect of law under chapter 235, HRS, and any other chapters which contain provisions relating to chapter 235. The law and regulations must be read together, because the regulations relating to a particular section of the law do not necessarily cover every point in the section.

(2) Scope. These rules and regulations are promulgated to:

(A) Adopt the Federal Tax Regulations relating to subtitle A, Chapters 1 and 6 of the Internal Revenue Code of 1954 as amended as of December 31, 1978, set forth in this regulation.

(B) List the inoperative sections of the Internal Revenue Code. The related federal regulations to these Internal Revenue Code sections shall also be inoperative.

(C) As provided by section 235-2.3 (c) to (m), HRS, certain Internal Revenue Code sections, subsections, parts of subsections, and federal Public Law that do not apply or that are otherwise limited in application also shall apply to the related federal regulations as contained in this regulation.

(3) Adoption of federal tax regulations. The regulations relating to those sections of subtitle A, Chapters 1 and 6, Internal Revenue Code of 1954, as amended as of December 31, 1978, adopted by section 235-2.3, HRS, which are contained in the Federal Tax Regulations 1979 (Title 26, Internal Revenue, 1954 Code of Federal Regulations), with amendments and adoptions to January 1, 1979, and which are not in conflict with provisions contained in chapters 235, 231, or 232, Hawaii Revised Statutes, are hereby adopted by reference and made a part of the rules and regulations of the department of taxation, as they apply to the determination of gross income, adjusted gross income, ordinary income and loss, and taxable income, except insofar as the regulations pertain to provisions of the Internal Revenue Code and federal Public Law, which pursuant to chapter 235, HRS, and this regulation, do not apply or are otherwise limited in application. Provisions in this regulation in conflict with those sections of the Internal Revenue Code, the Federal Regulations or the federal Public Law shall be limited as provided under section 235-2.3(n), HRS.

(b) Inoperative federal tax regulations. The federal regulations relating to the following Internal Revenue Code subchapters, parts of subchapters, sections, subsections, and parts of subsections shall not be operative for the purposes of HRS chapter or this regulation unless otherwise provided. (See section 235-2.3(b), HRS.)

| Subchapter | Section of I.R.C. |
| --- | --- |
| A | 1 to 58 |
| B | 78, 103, 116, 120, 122, 151, 169, 241 to 250 (except 248 and 249), 280C |
| C | 367 |
| E | 457 |
| F | 501 to 528 (except 512 to 515) |
| G | 531 to 565 |
| H | 581 to 596 |
| J | 642(a), (b), (d), 668 |
| L | 801 to 844 |
| M | 853 |
| N | 861 to 999 |
| O | 1055, 1057 |
| P | 1201 |
| Q | 1301 to 1351 |
| T | 1381 to 1388 |

(c) Zero bracketing. The federal regulations relating to the determinations, provisions, and requirements to zero-bracket amounts in the amendments to the Internal Revenue Code by Public Law

¶ 1403

95-30, sections 101 and 102 (with respect to change in tax rates and tax tables to reflect permanent increase in standard deduction and change in definition of taxable income to reflect change in tax rates and tables) shall not be operative. (See section 235-2.3(c), HRS.)

(d) Standard deduction; individuals not eligible for standard deduction and election of standard deduction. (I.R.C. Sections 141, 142, 144). As provided by section 235-2.3(d), HRS, Internal Revenue Code Sections 141, 142, and 144 shall be operative as of June 7, 1957, as amended as of that date. The federal regulations relating to these Internal Revenue Code sections shall be inoperative for this State. The standard deduction as adopted by the State allows individuals to itemize or to elect to take a 10 per cent standard deduction, but not both.

(1) Standard deduction. IRC Section 141, as amended, as of June 7, 1957, provides as follows: "Sec. 141. Standard deduction. The standard deduction referred to in section 63 (b) (defining taxable income in case of individual electing standard deduction) shall be an amount equal to 10 per cent of the adjusted gross income or $1,000, whichever is the lesser, except that in the case of a separate return by a married individual the standard deduction shall not exceed $500." In the case of a joint return, there is only one adjusted gross income and only one standard deduction. The standard deduction is $1,000 or 10 per cent of the combined adjusted gross income, whichever is the lesser.

*Example:* If a husband has an income of $15,000 and his spouse has an income of $12,000 for the taxable year for which they file a joint return, and they have no deductions allowable for the purpose of computing adjusted gross income, the adjusted gross income shown by the joint return is the combined income of $27,000, and the standard deduction is $1,000 and not $2,000.

(2) Eligibility.

(A) IRC Section 142, as amended, as of June 7, 1957, provides as follows:

"Sec. 142. Individuals not eligible for standard deduction.

(a) Husband and wife.—The standard deduction shall not be allowed to a husband or wife if the tax of the other spouse is determined under section 1 on the basis of the taxable income computed without regard to the standard deduction.

(b) Certain other taxpayers ineligible.—The standard deduction shall not be allowed in computing the taxable income of—

(1) a nonresident alien individual;

(2) a citizen of the United States entitled to the benefits of section 931 (relating to income from sources within possessions of the United States);

(3) an individual making a return under section 443(a)(1) for a period of less than 12 months on account of a change in his annual accounting method; or

(4) an estate or trust, common trust fund, or partnership."

(B) For the purpose of section 235-2.3(d), HRS, the reference in IRC Section 142(a) to section 1 shall be deemed a reference to section 235-51, HRS. In the case of husband and wife, if the tax of one spouse is determined under section 235-51, HRS, on the basis of the taxable income computed without regard to the standard deduction and, the other spouse may not elect to take the standard deduction. If each spouse files a separate Form N-12 or N-15, both must elect to take the standard deduction or both spouses are denied the standard deduction. If one spouse files Form N-12 or N-15 and does not elect to take the standard deduction, the other spouse may not elect to take the standard deduction and, accordingly, may not compute his tax under the provisions of section 235-53, HRS, or file Form N-13 as his separate return for the taxable year.

*Example:* If A and his wife B, both residents of Hawaii, have gross income of $16,000 and $3,500, respectively, from wages subject to withholding and A files Form N-12 (long form) and does not elect thereon to take the standard deduction, B may not file Form N-13 (short form) but must file Form N-12, taking thereon only her actual allowable deductions and not the standard deduction. In such case, however, if both elect to take the standard deduction, A must file Form N-12 (since his gross income exceeds the amount provided by section 235-53, HRS) but B may file Form N-13, or in the alternative, she may file Form N-12 and compute the tax by using the optional tax table. Under either alternative, effect is given to the standard deduction.

(3) Election.

(A) IRC Section 144, as amended, as of June 7, 1957, provides as follows:

"Sec. 144. Election of standard deduction.

(a) Method and effect of election.—

(1) If the adjusted gross income shown on the return is $5,000 or more, the standard deduction shall be allowed if the taxpayer so elects in his return, and the Secretary or his delegate shall by regulations prescribe the manner of signifying such election in the return. If the adjusted gross income shown on the return is $5,000 or more, but the correct adjusted gross income is less than $5,000, then an election by the taxpayer under the preceding sentence to take the standard deduction shall be considered as his election to pay the tax imposed by section 3 (relating to tax based on tax table); and his failure to make under the preceding sentence an election to take the standard deduction shall be considered his election not to pay the tax imposed by section 3.

(2) If the adjusted gross income shown on the return is less than $5,000, the standard deduction shall be allowed only if the taxpayer elects in the manner provided in section 4, to pay the tax imposed by section 3. If the adjusted gross income shown on the return is less than $5,000, but the correct adjusted gross income is $5,000 or more, then an election by the taxpayer to pay the tax imposed by section 3 shall be considered as his election to take the standard deduction; and his failure to elect to pay the tax imposed by section 3 shall be considered his election not to take the standard deduction.

(3) If the taxpayer on making his return fails to signify in the manner provided by paragraph (1) or (2), his election to take the standard deduction or to pay the tax imposed by section 3, as the case may be, such failure shall be considered his election not to take the standard deduction.

(b) Change of election. Under regulations prescribed by the Secretary or his delegate, a change of an election for any taxable year to take or not to take, the standard deduction, or to pay, or not to pay, the tax under section 3, may be made after the filing of the return for such year. If the spouse of the taxpayer filed a separate return for any taxable year corresponding, for purposes of section 142(a), to the taxable year of the taxpayer, the change shall not be allowed unless, in accordance with such regulations:

(1) The spouse makes a change of election with respect to the standard deduction for the taxable year covered in such separate return, consistent with the change of election sought by the taxpayer; and

(2) The taxpayer and his spouse consent in writing to the assessment, within such period as may be agreed on with the Secretary or his delegate, of any deficiency, to the extent attributable to such change of election, even though at the time of the filing of such consent the assessment of such deficiency would otherwise be prevented by the operation of any law or rule of law. This subsection shall not apply if the tax liability of the taxpayer's spouse, for the taxable year corresponding (for purposes of section 142(a)) to the taxable year of the taxpayer, has been compromised under section 7122."

(B) For the purpose of section 235-2.3(d), HRS, the reference in IRC section 144, to sections 3, 4, and 7122 shall be deemed references to sections 235-53, 52, and 231-3(10), HRS, respectively.

(C) A taxpayer whose adjusted gross income as shown by his return equals to or exceeds the amount provided under section 235-53, HRS, or who otherwise is ineligible to use the optional tax tables but is eligible for the standard deduction (such as a person entitled to the special exemption under section 235-54(c), HRS, shall be allowed the standard deduction if he elects on such return to take such deduction. Such taxpayer shall so signify by claiming on his return the ten per cent standard deduction instead of itemizing the non-business deductions allowed in computing taxable income.

(D) A change of election must be made within the period of three years after filing of the return for the taxable year involved, or within three years of the due date prescribed for the filing of said return, whichever is later.

(E) The director cannot allow an overpayment credit after expiration for the period of time prescribed in section 235-111, HRS, which limits both credits and assessments of additional taxes.

This period of time is not extended by the making of a change of election.

(e) Employee annuity. (I.R.C. Section 403). Taxation of employee annuity shall be the same except for the amount of premium withheld from the salary of an employee by the Department of Education and the University of Hawaii for the purchase of an annuity contract under Act 40, S.L.H. 1967. This amount is includible as taxable gross income and subject to the withholding tax provisions of this State. Amendments to I.R.C. Section 403 by Public Law 87-370, section 3 were not adopted by this State. (See section 235-2.3(e), HRS.)

(f) Administering pensions, profit sharing, etc. (I.R.C. Section 401 to 415).

(1) The Department of Taxation shall follow the applicable provisions set forth in the federal tax regulations in respect to related provisions of I.R.C. Sections 410 to 415.

(2) Records substantiating (i) all data and information on returns (as defined in I.R.C. Section 6103(b) required on all forms and reports, (ii) authenticated copies of the federal returns filed relating to pensions, profit sharing, stock bonus and other retirement plans, (iii) assessments made by the Internal Revenue Service, including tax on premature distributions (I.R.C. Section 72(m)(5)) and excise taxes imposed by I.R.C. Sections 4971 to 4975, shall be kept and made available for inspection at the principal place of business of the self-employed individual or the employer maintaining the plan or the plan administrator (defined in I.R.C. Section 414(g)) at all times. (See section 235-2.3(f), HRS.)

(g) Unrelated business taxable income. (I.R.C. Sections 512 to 515).

(1) In general. The federal regulations relating to the taxation of unrelated business taxable income shall apply to the State except that in the computation thereof sections 235-3 to 235-5, and 235-7 (except subsection (c)), HRS, shall also apply, and any amount of income or deduction which is excluded in computing the unrelated business taxable income shall not be allowed in determining the net operating loss deduction under section 235-7(d), HRS. Any income from a prepaid legal service plan shall not be considered. (See section 235-2.3(g), HRS).

(2) Returns. Every person and organization, described in section 235-9, HRS, which is otherwise exempt from income tax and which is subject to income tax imposed on unrelated business taxable income under section 235-2.3(g), HRS, shall file a return for each taxable year if it has gross income of $1,000 or more included in computing unrelated business taxable income for such taxable year. The filing of a return of unrelated business income does not relieve the person or organization of other filing requirements.

(h) With respect to estates and trusts, the following rules apply.

(1) With regard to section 641(a) (with respect to tax on estates and trusts), IRC, as operative under chapter 235, HRS, the applicable tax rates are as set forth in section 235-51(d), HRS.

(A) If an estate or trust has a net capital gain, the estate or trust may elect the alternative tax set forth in section 235-51(f), HRS.

(B) Estates and trusts are not allowed the standard deduction, except that the estate of an individual in bankruptcy shall be allowed the standard deduction in section 235-2.4(a)(4), HRS, pursuant to section 1398(c)(3) (with respect to basic standard deduction in an individual's title 11 case), IRC, if the estate does not itemize deductions.

(C) Estates and trusts shall not use the tax tables to compute tax.

(2) Section 642(a) (with respect to foreign tax credit), IRC, is not operative in Hawaii. A resident trust shall be allowed a credit for taxes paid to another jurisdiction to the extent permitted by section 235-55, HRS, and the rules thereunder, but only in respect of so much of those taxes paid to another jurisdiction that is not properly allocable to any beneficiary. A nonresident trust shall not be allowed the credit in section 235-55, HRS.

(3) Section 642(b) (with respect to deduction for personal exemption), IRC, is not operative in Hawaii. An estate or trust shall be allowed the deduction for personal exemption set forth in section 235-54(b), HRS. A trust shall be eligible for the personal exemption of $200 under section 235-54(b)(2), HRS, if it is required by the terms of its governing instrument to distribute all of its income currently, whether or not the trust is described in section 651 (with respect to simple trusts), IRC.

¶ 1403

*Example 1:* A trust's governing instrument provides that all of its income is to be distributed to charity every year. Although the trust is not a simple trust under section 651, IRC, it is eligible for the $200 personal exemption.

*Example 2:* A trust's governing instrument provides that $1000 is to be distributed to its sole beneficiary every year. The trust is eligible for the $200 personal exemption in any year in which the trust's income is not more than $1000.

(4) With regard to section 642(d) (with respect to unlimited deduction for amounts paid or permanently set aside for a charitable purpose), IRC, as operative under chapter 235, HRS, an estate or trust shall be allowed a deduction equal to the smaller of the following two amounts:

(A) The amount allowable under section 681 (with respect to limitation on charitable deduction), IRC; or

(B) The greater of the amounts in clause (i) and (ii):

(i) The amount qualifying under section 642(c), IRC, that is paid, or permanently set aside, to be used exclusively in Hawaii for charitable purposes; or

(ii) The amount qualifying under section 642(c), IRC, that is actually paid for charitable purposes, subject to the percentage limitations in section 170(b)(1) (with respect to percentage limitations applicable to contributions by an individual), IRC. In computing the percentage limitations, the contribution base of the estate or trust shall be adjusted gross income as defined in section 235-1, HRS, computed without regard to any net operating loss carryback to the taxable year.

(5) Section 642(d) (with respect to net operating loss deduction), IRC, is not operative in Hawaii. An estate or trust shall be allowed the net operating loss deduction to the extent permitted by section 235-7(d), HRS, and the rules thereunder.

(6) With respect to section 644 (with respect to gain on property transferred to trust at less than fair market value), IRC, as operative under chapter 235, HRS:

(A) In section 644(a)(2)(A), IRC, the tax shall be computed under chapter 235, HRS; and

(B) In section 644(a)(2)(B), IRC, the interest rate shall be that specified in section 231-39(b)(4), HRS.

(7) With respect to section 667 (with respect to treatment of amounts deemed distributed by a complex trust in preceding years), IRC, as operative under chapter 235, HRS:

(A) In section 667(a)(1) and (2), IRC, the tax shall be computed under chapter 235, HRS; and

(B) Interest income exempt from Hawaii tax under section 235-7, HRS, in the hands of a trust, retains its character when distributed to a beneficiary pursuant to section 662(b) (with respect to character of amounts distributed), IRC. Other interest income that is not exempt from Hawaii tax in the hands of a trust pursuant to section 235-7(b), HRS, is considered a taxable amount for purposes of computing the tax under section 667, IRC, when that income is distributed.

(8) Section 668 (with respect to interest charge on accumulation distributions from foreign trusts), IRC, is not operative in Hawaii.

(i) to (k) (Reserved)

(l) Capital loss carrybacks and carryovers. (I.R.C. section 1212).

(1) In general. The federal regulations relating to capital loss carrybacks and carryovers in the Internal Revenue Code shall be operative except that the provisions relating to capital loss carryback shall not be operative and the capital loss carryover allowed by I.R.C. section 1212(a) shall be limited to five years. Individual taxpayers shall be allowed capital loss carryovers until exhausted. (See section 235-2.3(l), HRS.)

(m) Subchapter S. (I.R.C. sections 1371 to 1379).

(1) In general. The federal regulations relating to the Internal Revenue Code on election of small business corporation shall be operative subject to certain other requirements and modifications for this State. (See section 235-2.3(l), HRS.)

(A) A small business corporation shall not have (A) A nonresident as a shareholder; or (B) A resident individual who has taken up residence in the State after age 65 and before 7/1/76 and who is taxed under chapter 235 only on the income from within this State, unless such individual shall have waived the benefit of section 3, Act 60, L. 1976, and shall have included all income from sources within and without this State in the same manner as if the individual had taken up residence in the State after 6/30/76.

(2) Election. Effective 1/1/79, an election under I.R.C. Section 1372(a) not to be subject to income taxes shall terminate for the taxable year in which such corporation derives more than 80 per cent of its gross income from sources outside the State. Termination shall remain in effect for all succeeding taxable years.

(A) An election under I.R.C. section 1372 shall not be valid unless there is also in effect for such taxable year, an election for federal tax purposes.

(B) The tax imposed by I.R.C. section 1378(a) is hereby imposed by this chapter and shall be at a rate of 3.08 per cent on the amount by which the net capital gain exceeds $25,000.00. For purposes of I.R.C. section 1378(c)(3), the amount of tax to be determined shall not exceed 3.08 per cent of the net capital gain attributable to property described under that section.

(3) Returns. Every small business corporation as described in I.R.C. section 1371 and this article shall file an income tax return for each taxable year on Form N-35, stating specifically items of its gross income and deductions and such other information as required by the form or in the instruction issued thereto provided under section 235-80, HRS. [Eff 2/16/82; am 9/3/94] (Auth: HRS §§231-3(9), 235-118) (Imp: HRS §§235-2.3, 235-2.4)

Act 53, effective July 1, 2016, repeals sections 235-2, 235-2.1, and 235-2.2, HRS, and amends section 235-2.3, HRS. These sections conformed Hawaii income tax law to the IRC prior to 1978. The repealed sections are no longer necessary for conformity. Act 53 also amends section 235-2.3, HRS, to ensure that years prior to 1978 are still governed by prior law.

## ¶ 1404. Rules Section 18-235-4-01 Income Taxes by the State; Residents, Nonresidents, Corporations, Estates and Trusts

As used in sections 18-235-4-02 to 18-235-4-08, and sections 18-235-5-01 to 18-235-5-04:

"Adjusted gross income" or "adjusted gross income from all sources" means the same as in section 62 (with respect to adjusted gross income defined), IRC.

"From whatever source derived" means the same as in section 61(a) (with respect to gross income defined), IRC.

"Hawaii adjusted gross income" means Hawaii source income minus the deductions that are allowed as adjustments to gross income under chapter 235, HRS.

"Hawaii source income" means income received or derived from property owned, services performed, trade or business carried on, and any and every other source in the State.

"IRC" means the Internal Revenue Code of 1986, as operative under chapter 235, HRS.

"Jurisdiction" means any state of the United States, the District of Columbia, the Commonwealth of Puerto Rico, any territory or possession of the United States, and any foreign country or political subdivision of a foreign country.

"Out-of-state income" means income from whatever source derived, other than Hawaii source income.

"Part-year resident" means an individual who becomes a resident, or ceases to be a resident, during the taxable year.

"State", when not referring specifically to Hawaii, means any state of the United States, the District of Columbia, the Commonwealth of Puerto Rico, or any territory or possession of the United States.

"Taxable in" another jurisdiction means the same as in section 235-23, HRS.

"Territory or possession of the United States" means the same as in section 927(d)(5) (with respect to definition of "possessions"), IRC.

"Without regard to source" means the same as "from whatever source derived". [Eff 2/16/82; am and ren §18-235-4-01 9/3/94] (Auth: HRS §§231-3(9), 235-118) (Imp: HRS §§235-4, 235-5, 235-7, 235-55, 235-97)

## ¶ 1405. Rules Section 18-235-4-02 Residents Taxable On Entire Income

(a) A resident, as defined in section 235-1, HRS, is taxable on income from whatever source derived. For a resident, it is immaterial whether the source of the income is Hawaii or another jurisdiction, except that if out-of-state income is taxable in another jurisdiction, a tax credit may be allowed under section 235-55, HRS, and section 18-235-55.

(b) A resident shall not exclude or deduct any income allocated or apportioned to another jurisdiction under the Uniform Division of Income for Tax Purposes Act, sections 235-21 to 235-39, HRS, or section 18-235-5-02.

(c) For rules relating to change of residence during the taxable year, see section 18-235-4-04. [Eff 2/16/82; am and ren §18-235-4-02 9/3/94] (Auth: HRS §§231-3(9), 235-96, 235-118) (Imp: HRS §§235-4, 235-5, 235-7, 235-55, 235-97)

Historical note: §18-235-4-02 is based substantially upon §18-235-4(a). [Eff 2/16/82; amand ren §18-235-4-02 9/3/94]

## ¶ 1406. Rules Section 18-235-4-03 Nonresidents Taxable On Hawaii Income

(a) A nonresident, as defined in section 235-1, HRS, is taxable on Hawaii source income and is not taxable on out-of-state income. A nonresident is not allowed a credit for taxes paid to another state under section 235-55, HRS.

(b) A nonresident shall determine Hawaii source income by allocation and apportionment under the Uniform Division of Income for Tax Purposes Act, sections 235-21 to 235-39, HRS, if:

(1) The nonresident derives income from business activity both within and without the State,

(2) The nonresident's business activity is taxable in both this State and another jurisdiction, and

(3) The income is not derived from the rendering of purely personal services. Otherwise, a nonresident shall determine Hawaii source income by allocation and separate accounting pursuant to section 235-5, HRS, and section 18-235-5-02.

(c) A nonresident, foreign corporation, or other nonresident taxpayer:

(1) Which acts as a business entity in more than one state;

(2) Whose only activities within the State, either alone or as part of a unitary group, consist of sales and do not include:

(A) Owning or renting real estate or tangible personal property, or

(B) Personal services; and

(3) Whose annual gross sales in or into this State during the tax year are not in excess of $100,000, may elect to report and pay a tax of 0.5 per cent of such gross sales in lieu of the tax otherwise imposed by chapter 235, HRS. An election under this subsection shall constitute the election described in article III, paragraph 2 of the Multistate Tax Compact, chapter 255, HRS, and provided in section 235-51(e) or 235-71(e), HRS. The election may be made by timely filing the form prescribed by the department for this purpose. The election shall be made not later than the last day prescribed by law (including extensions of time) for filing the net income tax return that otherwise would be filed for the tax year.

(d) If a nonresident files a joint return with a spouse who is a resident for the full taxable year, the tax is imposed on aggregate income for the full taxable year without regard to source. A nonresident spouse filing a joint return does not thereby become a resident for purposes of chapter 235, HRS.

(e) This section shall apply to individuals described in section 3 of Act 60, SLH 1976, namely those who have taken up residence in the State: (1) after attaining the age of sixty-five years, and (2) before July 1, 1976. For those individuals, subsection (c) shall not apply, and no credit for tax paid to another state under section 235-55, HRS, shall be allowed. Any individual may waive the benefits of section 3 of Act 60, SLH 1976, by filing a written election with the department. This subsection shall not apply to any individual who has made such a waiver.

(f) For rules relating to change of residence during the taxable year, see section 18-235-4-04.

(g) For rules used to determine the source of income, see section 18-235-4-08.

(h) For deductions of a nonresident, and rules regarding income from alimony or separate maintenance payments, see section 18-235-5-03. [Eff 2/16/82; am and ren §18-235-4-03 9/3/94] (Auth: HRS §§231-3(9), 235-96, 235-118) (Imp: HRS §§235-4, 235-5, 235-7, 235-22, 235-51(e), 235-52, 235-71(e), 235-93, 235-97, 255-1)

Historical note: §18-235-4-03 is based on §18-235-4(b). [Eff 2/16/82; am and ren §18-235-4-03 9/3/94]

## ¶ 1407. Rules Section 18-235-4-04 Change of Residence During Taxable Year

(a) The following rules are applied if during the taxable year the status of a taxpayer changes from resident to nonresident, or from nonresident to resident.

(1) For the period of residence, the tax is imposed on income from whatever source derived, as provided in section 18-235-4-02.

(2) For the period of nonresidence, the tax is imposed on Hawaii source income, as provided in section 18-235-4-03. Part-year residents shall not be eligible for the election in section 18-235-4-03(c).

(3) If it cannot be determined whether all or part of a taxpayer's income was generated during the period of residence, that amount of income shall be multiplied by the ratio that the period of residence bears to the entire taxable year. The product shall be the portion attributable to Hawaii, unless the taxpayer demonstrates to the satisfaction of the department that the result attributes to Hawaii out-of-state income that was received or derived during the period of nonresidence.

(4) The credit for tax paid to another state under section 235-55, HRS, shall be allowed only for tax paid on out-of-state income allocable to the period of residence.

*Example:* T, an unmarried cash basis calendar year taxpayer, was a resident of Arizona on January 1, 1993. T moved to Hawaii on April 1, 1993, and continued to work as an insurance agent. T is a Hawaii resident for the remainder of 1993. T received $20,000 as gain from the sale on March 20, 1993, of Arizona real property held for investment. T earned commissions of $25,000 for policies sold after April 1, 1993. T earned initial and renewal commissions of $12,000 for policies sold before that date, $4,000 of which T earned before April 1, 1993. In addition, T had signed a business consulting contract with one Arizona client, for which T was paid an additional $1,200 for services rendered throughout the year. T's Hawaii income is computed as follows:

(1) The $20,000 gain is out-of-state income earned when T was a nonresident. None of it is attributable to Hawaii.

(2) The commissions of $25,000 are from a trade or business carried on in Hawaii, and are Hawaii source income. The commissions were earned when T was a Hawaii resident. All of these commissions are attributable to Hawaii.

(3) The $12,000 in commissions earned before April 1993 is from a trade or business carried on in Arizona, and is thus out-of-state income. However, only $4,000 was earned when T was a nonresident. The remaining $8,000 is attributable to Hawaii.

(4) It cannot be determined whether the remaining $1,200 in commission income was generated while T was a Hawaii resident. Thus, because T was a resident for nine months in 1993, 9/12 x $1,200, or $900, shall be attributable to Hawaii unless T demonstrates otherwise to the satisfaction of the department.

(b) The following rules are applied for joint returns.

(1) If a nonresident or a part-year resident files a joint return with a spouse who is a resident for the full taxable year, the tax is imposed on aggregate income for the full taxable year without regard

to source and without regard to either spouse's period of residence.

(2) If a joint return is filed by two individuals neither of whom is a resident for the full taxable year, the tax is imposed on aggregate income without regard to source for the period in which either spouse was a resident.

(3) By filing a joint return, a nonresident spouse does not become a resident, and a part-year resident spouse does not thereby become a resident for any other part of the year, for purposes of chapter 235, HRS.

(c) For deductions of a part-year resident, and rules regarding income from alimony or separate maintenance payments, see section 18-235-5-03. [Eff 2/16/82; am and ren §18-235-4-04 9/3/94] (Auth: HRS §§231-3(9), 235-5(d), 235-96, 235-118) (Imp: HRS §§235-4, 235-5, 235-7, 235-22, 235-52, 235-55, 235-97, 255-1)

Historical note: §18-235-4-04 is based on §18-235-4(f). [Eff 2/16/82; am and ren §18-235-4-04 9/3/94]

## ¶ 1408. Rules Section 18-235-4-05 Corporations; Domestic and Foreign

(a) Domestic corporations, including professional and nonprofit corporations, are subject to tax on Hawaii source income. Domestic corporations also are subject to tax on out-of-state income that is not taxable in another jurisdiction.

(b) Income from business activity within and without Hawaii that is taxable in another jurisdiction shall be apportioned under the Uniform Division of Income for Tax Purposes Act, sections 235-21 to 235-39, HRS. A domestic corporation is subject to tax in Hawaii on income that is allocated or apportioned to any jurisdiction in which that corporation is not taxable.

*Example 1:* Corporation X, a Hawaii corporation, is actively engaged in selling farm equipment in Hawaii and State A. Both Hawaii and State A impose a net income tax but State A exempts corporations engaged in selling farm equipment. Corporation X is taxable in both Hawaii and State A. Corporation X is not subject to tax in Hawaii on income that is allocated or apportioned to State A.

*Example 2:* The facts are the same as in Example 1, except that State A may not impose a net income tax on Corporation X because of Public Law No. 86-272, 15 U.S.C. sections 381-384. Corporation X is taxable in Hawaii and is not taxable in State A. Corporation X is subject to tax in Hawaii on income that is allocated or apportioned to State A.

(c) Foreign corporations are subject to tax on Hawaii source income and are not subject to tax on out-of-state income.

(d) For rules relating to corporations for which an election under section 1362 (with respect to S corporations), IRC, is in effect, see section 18-235-122.

(e) For the election available under the Multistate Tax Compact to a foreign corporation whose only activities within the State consist of sales, see section 18-235-4-03(c).

(f) For rules used to determine the source of income, see section 18-235-4-08. [Eff 2/16/82; am and ren §18-235-4-05 9/3/94] (Auth: HRS §§231-3(9), 235-118) (Imp: HRS §§235-4, 235-5, 235-7, 235-22, 255-1)

Historical note: §18-235-4-05 is based upon §18-235-5(a)(2)-(3). [Eff 2/16/82; am 9/3/94]

## ¶ 1409. Rules Section 18-235-4-06 Residents and Nonresident Estates, Trusts, and Beneficiaries

(a) As used in this section:

"Beneficiary" includes an heir, legatee, devisee, and any person to whom income of a trust is attributed under section 671 (with respect to trust income, deductions, and credits attributable to grantors and others as substantial owners), IRC.

"Beneficiary's share of income" means that portion of the income of an estate or trust: (1) that the beneficiary is required to include in income under subchapter J (with respect to estates, trusts, beneficiaries, and decedents), IRC; or (2) that is attributed to the beneficiary under section 671, IRC.

"Resident beneficiary" means a beneficiary who is a "resident person" within the meaning of section 235-68(a), HRS.

(b) An estate or trust shall report its gross income from whatever source derived, each beneficiary's share of income, and each beneficiary's share of Hawaii source income if:

(1) It is a resident estate or trust, as defined in section 235-1, HRS;

(2) Any of its beneficiaries is a resident beneficiary; or

(3) Any part of its income is attributed to a resident beneficiary under section 671, IRC.

(c) An estate or trust not described in subsection (b) shall report all Hawaii source income, and also shall report each beneficiary's share of Hawaii source income.

(d) An estate or trust shall determine Hawaii source income by allocation and apportionment under the Uniform Division of Income for Tax Purposes Act, sections 235-21 to 235-39, HRS, if:

(1) The estate or trust derives income from business activity both within and without the State,

(2) The estate's or trust's business activity is taxable in both this State and another jurisdiction, and

(3) The income is not derived from the rendering of purely personal services.

Otherwise, an estate or trust shall determine Hawaii source income by allocation and separate accounting pursuant to section 235-5, HRS, and section 18-235-5-02.

(e) A resident estate or trust is taxable on income from whatever source derived, whether or not the administration of the estate or trust is principal, ancillary, or carried on in this State. A resident estate or trust shall not exclude or deduct any income allocated or apportioned to another jurisdiction under the Uniform Division of Income for Tax Purposes Act, sections 235-21 to 235-39, HRS. If a resident estate or trust has out-of-state income that is taxable in another jurisdiction, a tax credit may be allowed under section 235-55, HRS, and section 18-235-55.

(f) A nonresident estate or trust is taxable on Hawaii source income and is not taxable on out-of-state income.

(g) A beneficiary is subject to tax on that beneficiary's share of income as if the beneficiary had received that income directly, and had directly incurred any deductions allowable under subsection (h), whether or not the estate or trust is a resident, and whether or not the estate or trust is required to file a return.

(1) A resident beneficiary is subject to tax upon that beneficiary's share of income from whatever source derived.

(2) A nonresident beneficiary (or a beneficiary taking up residence in the State after attaining the age of sixty-five years but before July 1, 1976) is subject to tax upon that beneficiary's share of Hawaii source income. If a nonresident beneficiary of a resident trust derives income from intangibles, see section 235-4.5, HRS.

(h) In computing an estate's or trust's Hawaii adjusted gross income or taxable income, or any beneficiary's share of Hawaii source income, deductions shall be allowed only to the extent permitted by section 235-5(c), HRS, and section 18-235-5-03.

(i) The recipient of income in respect of a decedent is subject to tax as if the decedent had received that income directly, and had directly incurred any deductions, losses, or credits allowable to the recipient under section 691 (with respect to recipients of income in respect of decedents), IRC. In computing a recipient's allowable deductions, see section 235-5(c), HRS, and section 18-235-5-03. Thus, if the decedent were a resident at the time of death, the recipient, whether or not a resident, is subject to tax upon the income whether or not it is Hawaii source income. [Eff 2/16/82; am and ren §18-235-4-06 9/3/94] (Auth: HRS §§231-3(9), 235-96, 235-118) (Imp: HRS §§235-4, 235-5, 235-7, 235-22, 235-94(d))

¶ 1409

Historical note: §18-235-4-06 is based on §§18-235-2.3(h)(8)(E), (h)(9), (h)(10) [Eff 2/16/82; am 9/3/94], and 18-235-4(c), (d), and (g)(4). [Eff 2/16/82; am and ren §18-235-4-06 9/3/94]

## ¶ 1410. Rules Section 18-235-4-07 Residents and Nonresident Partners of a Partnership

(a) A resident partner is subject to tax on the partner's distributive share of the partnership income from whatever source derived.

(b) A nonresident partner is subject to tax on the partner's distributive share of Hawaii source income.

(c) Partners of a partnership shall be subject to tax on their distributive shares of partnership income whether or not the partnership is required to file a return.

(d) A partnership shall determine Hawaii source income by allocation and apportionment under the Uniform Division of Income for Tax Purposes Act, sections 235-21 to 235-39, HRS, if:

(1) The partnership derives income from business activity both within and without the State,

(2) The partnership's business activity is taxable in both this State and another jurisdiction, and

(3) The income is not derived from the rendering of purely personal services. Otherwise, a partnership shall determine Hawaii source income by allocation and separate accounting pursuant to section 235-5, HRS, and section 18-235-5-02.

(e) A partnership return made pursuant to section 235-95, HRS, shall report the gross income, gains, losses, deductions, and credits from whatever source derived, and each partner's distributive share of those items. The partnership also shall report each partner's distributive share of income, gains, losses, deductions, and credits from sources within the State.

(f) For corporations that are partners of a partnership, see section 18-235-4-05. [Eff 2/16/82; am and ren §18-235-4-07 9/3/94] (Auth: HRS §§231-3(9), 235-96, 235-118) (Imp: HRS §§235-4, 235-5, 235-7, 235-95)

Historical note: §18-235-4-07 is based substantially on §18-235-4(e). [Eff 2/16/82; amand ren §18-235-4-07 9/3/94]

## ¶ 1411. Rules Section 18-235-4-08 Source Of Income

(a) Income derived from real or tangible personal property is sourced at the place where the property is owned, namely the place where the property has its situs. If tangible personal property is owned and used in different locations, income from the property shall be allocated as provided in section 235-25, HRS.

(b) Income from intangible property, such as interest and dividends, is sourced at the place of the owner's domicile unless the property has acquired a business situs at another place, in which event the income is sourced at that place. Intangible property has a business situs in this State if it is employed as capital in this State or the possession and control of the property has been localized in this State.

*Example 1:* A corporation owns stocks, bonds, and other intangible personal property. It pledges the property in Hawaii as security for the payment of indebtedness, taxes, and other expenses incurred in connection with a business in this State. The pledged property has a business situs in Hawaii.

*Example 2:* A corporation maintains a branch office here and opens a bank account on which the agent in charge of the branch office may draw for the payment of expenses in connection with the activities in this State. The bank account has a business situs in Hawaii.

*Example 3:* The corpus of a trust contains United States Treasury bills, bank certificates of deposit, and shares of preferred and common stock. The trustee of the trust, a Hawaii corporation, exclusively holds, controls, and administers the corpus of the trust. The trustee is permitted broad discretion to invest trust income and accumulations and is responsible for the collection and disbursement of any income generated by the trust assets. The property forming the corpus of the trust has a business situs in Hawaii.

Thus, the trust's income is Hawaii source income; however, the exclusion in section 235-4.5, HRS, may apply in some cases.

(c) Income from an interest in real property, such as a leasehold, has its situs where the real property is located. The situs of the purchaser's interest under a contract for the sale of real property is where the real property is located.

(d) Income from a trade or business is sourced at the place where the trade or business is carried on.

(e) Income from the performance of personal services has its source at the place where the services are performed.

(f) A gain or loss on the sale or other disposition of property has its source at the place where the property was owned, that is, where it had its situs, at the time of the sale or other disposition. This rule applies whenever gain or loss is considered as resulting from the sale or other disposition of the underlying property, irrespective of where the contract for the sale or other disposition of the property was made. Thus, if property is disposed of on the installment method, the portion of any installment payment that represents gross profit is income that has its source at the place where the underlying property had its situs at the time of disposition.

*Example:* Y is the vendor on an agreement of sale for real property on Kauai. In 1994, Y sells Y's interest to S and realizes a gain of $5,000 under section 453B (with respect to gain or loss on disposition of installment obligations), IRC. Under section 453B, IRC, the gain is considered to be from the sale or exchange of the property in respect of which the installment obligation was received. Thus, because the underlying property is located in Hawaii, the $5,000 is Hawaii source income. [Eff 2/16/82; am and ren9/3/94] (Auth: HRS §§231-3(9), 235-118) (Imp: HRS §§235-4, 235-5, 235-7)

Historical note: §18-235-4-08 is based substantially upon §18-235-4(g)(1)-(7). [Eff 2/16/82; am and ren §18-235-4-08 9/3/94]

## ¶ 1412. Rules Section 18-235-5-01 Allocation of Income of Persons Not Taxable Upon Their Entire Income

(a) The definitions contained in section 18-235-4-01 apply to sections 18-235-5-01 to 18-235-5-04.

(b) The rules contained in sections 18-235-5-01 to 18-235-5-04 apply to taxpayers having only nonbusiness income, individual taxpayers having income from the rendering of purely personal services, and public utilities taxable under chapter 239, HRS, whether determining Hawaii source income or out-of-state income.

(c) In computing the unrelated business taxable income of a tax exempt organization under sections 512 to 514 (with respect to unrelated business taxable income, unrelated trade or business, and unrelated debt-financed income), IRC, that is subject to tax in Hawaii, sections 235-21 to 235-39, HRS, shall apply.

(d) Taxpayers described in subsection (b) shall use these rules for determining estimated tax, determining the amount of credit permitted under section 235-55, HRS, and other purposes that require allocation or apportionment of income between jurisdictions. Other taxpayers shall use sections 235-21 to 235-39, HRS, for those purposes.

(e) Section 235-5(c), HRS, and section 18-235-5-03 apply to all taxpayers. [Eff 2/16/82; am and ren §18-235-5-01 9/3/94] (Auth: HRS §§231-3(9), 235-118) (Imp: HRS §§235-4, 235-5, 235-7)

Historical note: §18-235-5-01 is based upon §18-235-4(g)(8). [Eff 2/16/82; am and ren 9/3/94]

## ¶ 1413. Rules Section 18-235-5-02 Allocation and Separate Accounting

(a) Taxpayers described in section 18-235-5-01(b) who are required to determine Hawaii source income shall determine Hawaii source income by allocation and separate accounting.

(1) If the nature of the taxpayer's activity renders direct allocation impracticable, or the taxpayer's books of account and records do not clearly reflect income properly taxable by Hawaii, income shall be allocated or apportioned under sections 235-21 to 235-39, HRS.

(2) Income also shall be allocated or apportioned under sections 235-21 to 235-39, HRS, when the activity within the State is an integral part of a unitary business carried on within and without the State.

(b) When the separate accounting method is used, separate records shall be maintained for sales, cost of sales, and expenses which are attributable to activity within Hawaii. Overhead expenses not directly allocable to activity within or without Hawaii shall be allocated according to the facts and circumstances, and in conformity with generally accepted accounting principles.

(c) If the director of taxation determines that the method set forth in this section does not fairly determine income derived from or attributable to Hawaii, the director may direct or permit the use of an allocation method or apportionment formula based on other factors that would more clearly reflect income attributable to Hawaii. A taxpayer may petition the director of taxation to use an apportionment formula other than that specified in section 235-29, HRS, by written request pursuant to section 235-38, HRS.

(d) A change in the taxpayer's allocation method or apportionment formula is a change in the taxpayer's method of accounting within the meaning of sections 446 (with respect to methods of accounting) and 481 (with respect to adjustments required by changes in method of accounting), IRC. [Eff 2/16/82; am and ren §18-235-5-02 9/3/94] (Auth: HRS §§231-3(9), 235-118) (Imp: HRS §235-5)

Historical note: §18-235-5-02 is based upon §18-235-5(a)(1) and (b)(1), (3). [Eff 2/16/82; am and ren §18-235-5-02 9/3/94]

## ¶ 1414. Rules Section 18-235-5-03 Deductions Connected With Gross Income From Hawaii Sources

(a) This section applies to all taxpayers, pursuant to section 235-5(c), HRS, and section 265 (with respect to expenses and interest connected with tax-exempt income), IRC.

(b) In computing the taxable income of a taxpayer subject to tax on Hawaii source income only:

(1) Deductions connected with Hawaii source income shall be allowed.

(2) Deductions connected with out-of-state income shall not be allowed.

(3) Pursuant to section 235-7(e), HRS, no deduction is allowed for interest paid or accrued on debt incurred or continued:

(A) To purchase or carry bonds if interest paid by the bond issuer is out-of-state income or is exempt from taxation under section 235-7(a), HRS;

(B) To purchase or carry property owned outside of the State; or

(C) To carry on a trade or business outside of the State.

(4) Deductions from Hawaii adjusted gross income that are not connected with particular property or income, such as medical expenses, shall be allowed only to the extent of the ratio of Hawaii adjusted gross income to adjusted gross income from all sources.

(5) Adjustments to income that are not connected with particular property or income shall be allowed only in the proportion determined under the following formula.

(A) Determine the aggregate amount of the adjustments not connected with particular property or income.

(B) Determine Hawaii source income and subtract all adjustments to income other than those included in (A).

(C) Add the amount in (A) to adjusted gross income from all sources.

(D) The ratio of (B) to (C) is the proportion of the adjustments that are allowable.

(6) Deductions are connected with a particular kind of income if the deductions would be allocable to that income under the principles of section 265 (with respect to expenses and interest connected with tax-exempt income), IRC, and section 1.265-1(c) (with respect to allocation of expenses to a class or classes of exempt income), Treasury Regulations.

*Example:* T, a single person aged 60, is a nonresident owning rental property in the State from which T derives $3,500 of gross income during the taxable year and incurs $500 of associated expenses, such as general excise and real property taxes. T also has paid $1,500 in interest on a mortgage on T's personal residence in Iowa. T's adjusted gross income from all sources is $12,000. During the taxable year, T's expenses of medical care, qualifying as such under section 213 (with respect to medical, dental, and similar expenses), IRC, are $1,000.

(1) Because the $500 in expenses is attributable to the rental property in Hawaii, the entire amount is allowed as a deduction. T therefore has $3,500 - $500, or $3,000, in Hawaii adjusted gross income.

(2) Because the $1,500 in interest is connected with real property outside Hawaii, no part of that amount is allowed as a deduction against Hawaii income.

(3) The $1,000 of medical expenses, wherever incurred, is not connected with any particular property or income. Thus, it shall be prorated by applying the ratio of Hawaii adjusted gross income to adjusted gross income from all sources. In this case the result is ($3,000/$12,000 x $1,000), or $250. If T does not take the standard deduction, T may deduct medical expenses in excess of 7.5 per cent of T's Hawaii adjusted gross income. Because 7.5 per cent of $3,000 is $225, T's medical expense deduction for Hawaii purposes is limited to $250 - $225, or $25.

(c) If a taxpayer is taxable only upon Hawaii source income and the taxpayer's deductions connected with out-of-state income exceed the amount of out-of-state income, the excess shall not be deductible against Hawaii source income and shall not be carried over or carried back to offset Hawaii source income in any other taxable year.

(d) If a taxpayer is a part-year resident, the following procedure shall be followed.

(1) Income shall be allocated between the period of residence and the period of nonresidence, under section 18-235-4-04.

(2) Deductions shall be allocated between those connected with income allocable to the period of residence, and those connected with income allocable to the period of nonresidence. Deductions shall be allocated in the same ratio as the connected income, unless the taxpayer demonstrates to the satisfaction of the department of taxation that the result materially distorts Hawaii income.

(3) Deductions connected with income allocable to the period of residence shall be allowed.

(4) Other deductions shall be allowed or disallowed under the principles in subsections (b) and (c), but in applying those subsections to a part-year resident, Hawaii adjusted gross income shall include all income and adjustments allocable to the period of residence.

(5) If a joint return is filed by two taxpayers neither of whom was a resident for the full taxable year, the period of residence shall be the period in which either spouse was a resident, and the period of nonresidence shall be the period in which neither spouse was a resident.

*Example:* T, an unmarried cash basis calendar year taxpayer, was a resident of Arizona on January 1, 1993. T moved to Hawaii on April 1, 1993, and continued to work as an insurance agent. T is a Hawaii resident for the remainder of 1993. T received $20,000 as gain from the sale on March 20, 1993, of Arizona real property held for investment. T earned commissions of $25,000 for policies sold after April 1, 1993. T earned initial and renewal commissions of $12,000 for policies sold before that date, $4,000 of which T earned before April 1, 1993. In addition, T had signed a business consulting contract with one Arizona client, for which T was paid an additional $1,200 for services rendered throughout the year. (For analysis of T's income, see section 18-235-4-04(a), Example.)

(1) On January 15, 1993, T paid $100 to renew T's Arizona insurance agent's license. None of the $100 is deductible against Hawaii income because the license only relates to out-of-state income received when T was a nonresident.

(2) T incurs $3,600 in business expenses connected with T's business as an insurance agent, but the expenses cannot be connected to specific sales of policies. As explained in section 18-235-4-04(a), Example, $33,900 of the $38,200 of commission income is allocable to T's period of residence. Thus, ($33,900 / $38,200) x $3,600, or $3,195, of the expenses are allocable to the period of residence and are deductible as trade and business deductions. Because the remaining commission income is out-of-state income allocable to a period of nonresidence, the remaining $405 of expenses is not deductible unless T demonstrates to the satisfaction of the department that the result materially distorts income.

¶ 1414

(3) T pays $2,000 to an accountant to prepare T's tax return. T's adjusted gross income from all sources is $20,000 - $1,500 + $38,200 - $3,600, or $53,100, and T 's Hawaii adjusted gross income, which includes T's out-of-state income earned while T was a Hawaii resident, is $33,900 - $3,195, or $30,705. Because T's tax return preparation expenses are not connected with particular property or income, the amount allowable in Hawaii is ($30,705 / $53,100) x $2,000, or $1,156. The tax return preparation expense is a miscellaneous itemized deduction subject to the 2 per cent floor of section 67, IRC. If T does not take the standard deduction and has no other miscellaneous itemized deductions, T may deduct the amount in excess of 2 per cent of Hawaii adjusted gross income, so the deductible amount is $1,156 - (0.02 x $30,705) = $542.

(e) This subsection applies to payments of alimony or separate maintenance.

(1) As used in this subsection:

"Alimony" means the same as "alimony or separate maintenance payment" in sections 71(b) (with respect to alimony and separate maintenance payments) and 215 (with respect to deduction for alimony and similar payments), IRC.

"Contributing spouse" means the spouse, or former spouse, who pays alimony.

"Recipient spouse" means the spouse, or former spouse, who receives alimony.

(2) Alimony is included in the gross income of the recipient spouse where:

(A) The recipient spouse is a resident;

(B) The recipient spouse became a resident after attaining the age of sixty-five and before July 1, 1976, and either the contributing spouse is a resident or the payments are attributable to property owned in the State that is transferred (in trust or otherwise) in discharge of a legal obligation to make alimony payments; or

(C) The recipient spouse is a nonresident, the contributing spouse is a resident, and the payments are attributable to property owned in the State that is transferred (in trust or otherwise) in discharge of a legal obligation to make alimony payments.

(3) Alimony is deductible from the income of the contributing spouse as follows:

(A) If the contributing spouse is a resident for the full taxable year, the payment of alimony is deductible in full; or

(B) If the contributing spouse is not a resident for the full taxable year, the payment of alimony shall be prorated under subsection (b)(4) to yield the deductible amount.

(f) This subsection applies to deductions by individual taxpayers for contributions to pension, profit sharing, stock bonus, and similar plans.

(1) An individual's deduction for contributions to a retirement plan, such as that under sections 219 (with respect to retirement savings), 404(a)(8) (with respect to deduction for contributions of self-employed individuals), or 408 (with respect to individual retirement accounts), IRC, shall be allowed only to the extent that the deduction is attributed to compensation earned:

(A) In this State, or

(B) While the individual was a resident.

(2) As used in this subsection, "compensation" means the same as in section 219(f)(1), IRC.

(3) An individual's deduction for contribution to an individual retirement account shall be presumed to be made pro rata from all compensation earned during the taxable year in which the contribution is deductible.

(4) A rollover contribution, as described in section 219(d)(2), IRC, shall not be reduced or disallowed under this subsection.

(5) For rules to determine where compensation is earned, see section 235-34, HRS.

*Example:* In 1994, T earned $30,000 in California while residing there and working for BMI Co. On May 13, 1994, T moved to Hawaii to work for Exrox Co. and earned $20,000 during 1994. After the move, T rolled over the entire BMI Co. retirement plan balance to an individual retirement account (IRA). T established another IRA in Hawaii and contributed $2,000 on April 1,

1995, that is deductible for federal purposes in 1994. T is a part-year resident. Under paragraph (4), T's establishment of the rollover IRA is not subject to tax. Under paragraph (3), the $2,000 IRA contribution is prorated between all compensation sources. Hawaii compensation is $20,000 and total compensation is $50,000. Thus, $2,000 x ($20,000 / $50,000), or $800, is considered to be from Hawaii compensation and is thus deductible in Hawaii. [Eff 2/16/82; am and ren §18-235-5-03 9/3/94] (Auth: HRS §§231-3(9), 235-5(d), 235-118) (Imp: HRS §§235-4, 235-5, 235-7)

Historical note: §18-235-5-03 is based upon §18-235-5(c). [Eff 2/16/82; am and ren §18-235-5-03 9/3/94]

## ¶ 1415. Rules Section 18-235-5-04 Allocation of Income and Deductions Among Taxpayers

(a) If two or more organizations, trades, or businesses, whether or not incorporated or organized in Hawaii, are owned or controlled directly or indirectly by the same interests, the director may distribute, apportion, or allocate gross income, deductions, credits, or allowances between or among the organizations, trades, or businesses, if the director determines that the distribution, apportionment, or allocation is necessary in order to clearly reflect the income attributable to any taxpayer's activity in this State.

(b) This section shall not be construed to permit the filing of consolidated returns by two or more affiliated corporations except as provided by section 235-92, HRS.

(c) The director shall not allocate or apportion income to Hawaii in excess of what is considered just and reasonable under the circumstances. [Eff 2/16/82; am and ren §18-235-5-04 9/3/94] (Auth: HRS §§231-3(9), 235-5(d), 235-118) (Imp: HRS §235-5)

Historical note: §18-235-5-04 is based substantially upon §18-235-5(b)(4). [Eff 2/16/82; am and ren §18-235-5-04 9/3/94]

## ¶ 1416. Rules Section 18-237-1 Definitions

(a) As used in this chapter:

"Asset used in a trade or business" means tangible personal property, used in the trade or business, of a character which is or has been subject to the allowance for depreciation provided in section 167 of the Internal Revenue Code of 1954, as amended, and which is not property of a kind which is ordinarily included in the merchandise inventory of the taxpayer if on hand at the close of the taxable year, or property held by the taxpayer primarily for sale to customers in the ordinary course of a trade or business. The term shall include, but is not limited to, machinery and equipment or furniture and fixtures used in a trade or business.

"Business," "engaging in business" includes all activities (personal, professional or corporate), engaged in or caused to be engaged in with the object of gain or economic benefit either direct or indirect, but does not include casual sales.

"Casual sale" means an occasional, isolated, irregular, infrequent or incidental sale or transaction involving tangible personal property which is not ordinarily sold in the usual course of trade or business.

(1) Application. Section 237-13, HRS, subjects virtually every economic activity to the general excise tax. The sale of tangible personal property may be taxed either by subsection (1), (2), (10) or by section 237-16, HRS. Subsection (1) imposes a tax upon manufacturers. Subsection (2) specifically imposes a tax upon the sale of tangible personal property. Subsection (10) imposes a tax upon any person engaging in any trade, business, activity, occupation or calling not otherwise included in section 237-13, HRS. Section 237-16, HRS, imposes a tax upon all retailers. Casual sales of tangible personal property, however, are not deemed to constitute doing business or engaging in business.

(A) When a person engaged in trade or business sells tangible personal property which is not usually carried in his merchandise inventory and the sales thereof do not show a pattern of conduct that he sells tangible personal property other than inventory merchandise, the transaction will be deemed casual and the gross receipts derived therefrom shall not be deemed to constitute gross income.

(B) When a person engaged in trade or business either sells capital assets (furniture, fixtures, equipment) used in his trade or business because of (1) obsolence; (2) replacement; (3) damage or (4) such capital assets are used as trade-ins, the transaction will be deemed casual and the proceeds derived from the sale, or the trade-in value will not be deemed to constitute taxable gross receipts.

*Example 1:* ABC Corporation is engaged in the retail chain-grocery business and needs new display equipment. Experience has indicated that new display equipment has a useful life of seven years. Accordingly, the taxpayer purchases the new equipment and sells the old equipment. The foregoing sale of the old equipment is not subject to the general excise tax inasmuch as the sale is considered a "casual sale."

*Example 2:* Rapid Service Laundry, in an overall plan for modernizing and renovating its existing facilities, sells most of its laundry and dry cleaning equipment and purchases new equipment as replacements. The foregoing sale of laundry and dry cleaning equipment is not subject to the general excise tax.

*Example 3:* Oahu Pineapple Company, engaged in the pineapple canning business, decides to discontinue its operations due to competition and major setback suffered as a result of numerous labor disputes. As a consequence, most of its pineapple processing and canning equipment are sold to other pineapple canneries. The foregoing sale of equipment is not subject to the general excise tax.

(C) When a person engaged in a trade or business exchanges (or transfers) but does not sell, merchandise or assets used in his trade or business pursuant to a plan of partnership, incorporation, reorganization (including statutory merger or consolidation), liquidation, etc., where no gain or loss is recognized under the Internal Revenue Code, the transaction will be deemed a casual transaction such as may occur in the following situations:

(i) Sole proprietorship to partnership. (owner becomes a partner);

(ii) Sole proprietorship to corporation. (IRC section 351, eighty per cent or more controlled by the individual transferor);

(iii) Partnership to corporation. (IRC section 351, eighty per cent or more controlled by the transferor partners);

(iv) Statutory mergers, consolidations, acquisitions in exchange for stock, recapitalization, and the like. (IRC sections 354, 361, and 368);

(v) Corporate liquidations. (IRC sections 332 to 337); or

(vi) Distribution or liquidations of assets of an estate or trust to beneficiaries.

(D) When a person engaged in a trade or business sells assets which are of like nature as those carried in his merchandise inventory, the transaction will be deemed to have occurred in the usual course of business and will not be deemed a casual transaction.

*Example 4:* Hawaii Typewriter Company is a dealer in typewriters, adding machines and other related office machines. It accepts trade-ins of used office machines which are reconditioned by the Company and eventually sold as "used office machines." The Company also withdraws new typewriters and adding machines from its inventory for use in its own business office. The Company capitalizes the cost of the machines and claims deductions under IRC section 167 for income tax purposes. In the ordinary course of business these office machines, which were used in its business office, are also reconditioned and sold by the Company as "used office machines." The sale of these machines, used in the trade or business, are assets which are of like nature as that carried in the merchandise inventory of the taxpayer, and therefore is subject to the general excise tax.

*Example 5:* XYZ Motors, an automobile dealer, in the ordinary course of business withdraws a number of new automobiles from its inventory for use as "company cars." XYZ Motors capitalizes the cost of these automobiles and claims depreciation thereon for income tax purposes. The "company cars" are eventually sold by XYZ Motors as used cars. The foregoing sale of "company cars" is subject to the general excise tax.

*Example 6:* Range Dairy Company operates a dairy farm having approximately 500 milking cows. The Company capitalizes the cost of the milking cows and claims deductions under IRC section 167 for income tax purposes. In addition to its regular sales, the Company sells the milking cows whenever they have served their useful purpose. The sale of the milking cows is subject to the general excise tax.

(E) Where a person engaged in a trade or business sells tangible property which is not usually carried in his merchandise inventory, but by reason of the frequency, number and size, the sales thereof show a pattern of conduct that he sells tangible property other than inventory merchandise, the transaction will be deemed to be in the usual course of business and not a casual transaction.

*Example 7:* Rentals Incorporated is engaged in the automobile rental and leasing activity. Every three years or thereabouts, taxpayer makes way for new rental automobiles by selling the old rental automobiles. The sale of the old rental automobiles is subject to the general excise tax. Although the taxpayer is not engaged primarily in the business of selling rental automobiles, there are a sufficient number of recurring sales as to constitute engaging in the business of selling automobiles. Thus, such sales are not considered "casual sales."

*Example 8:* Playtime Company derives part of its income from various amusement and vending machines — pinball, cigarette, candy and related machines — located in stores and amusement parlors. Playtime Company has agreements with the foregoing stores and amusement parlors to the effect that receipts from the machines would be divided on a certain percentage. To attract new customers and remain in the market competitively, Playtime acquires new pinball machines every six months and sells the used pinball machines. The sale of those pinball machines is subject to the general excise tax.

(F) Where a person engaged in trade or business sells his merchandise inventory in bulk, other than in the ordinary course of his trade or business, or where the sale in bulk occurs upon the termination of a business activity which is one of several activities conducted by the business, the transaction will be deemed to have occurred in the usual course of the taxpayer's business and will not be deemed to constitute a casual sale.

*Example 9:* Subsequent to losing its lease, ABC Drug Store decides to terminate its business. Accordingly, the entire merchandise inventory is sold in bulk to another drug store. The foregoing sale of merchandise inventory is subject to the general excise tax.

*Example 10:* S & S Bicycle Shop is engaged in the business of selling and servicing bicycles. Due to lack of store space and decline in sales, the taxpayer decides to terminate the "sales" and concentrate on the service activity of the business. The inventory of bicycles is sold in bulk to a large department store. The foregoing sale of merchandise inventory is subject to the general excise tax. [Eff 2/16/82] (Auth: HRS §§231-3(9), 237-8) (Imp: HRS §237-1)

## ¶ 1417. Rules Section 18-237-4 "Wholesaler," "jobber" defined

(a) Sales at wholesale defined. Pursuant to section 237-4, HRS, and taking into consideration sections 237-13(3)(C) and 237-13(3)(D), HRS, only the following are sales at wholesale:

(1) Sales to a licensed retail merchant, jobber or other licensed seller for purposes of resale;

(2) Sales to a licensed manufacturer of materials or commodities which are to be incorporated by such manufacturer into a finished or saleable product (including the container or package in which the product is contained) during the course of its preservation, manufacture or processing, including preparation for market, and which will remain in such finished or saleable product in such form as to be perceptible to the senses, which finished or saleable product is to be sold and not otherwise used by such manufacturer;

(3) Sales to a licensed agricultural or aquacultural producer or agricultural or aquacultural cooperative association of materials or commodities which are to be incorporated, used, or applied by the producer or by the cooperative association for the purpose of producing or raising a finished or saleable product or crop which is to be sold and not otherwise used by the producer or cooperative association, including specifically materials or commodities incorporated, used, or applied as essential to the planting, growth, nurturing, and production of agricultural or aquacultural products or crops which are sold by the producer or by the cooperative association;

(4) Sales to a licensed contractor of materials or commodities which are to be incorporated by the contractor into the finished work or project required by the contract and which will remain in the

finished work or project in a form which is perceptible to the senses, unless governed by the election provided for by section 237-13(3)(C), HRS; and sales to a purchaser holding a license under the general excise tax law, of materials or commodities which are to be incorporated by the purchaser into a building, structure or other improvements on land held by the purchaser and which will remain in such improvement in a form which is perceptible to the senses, provided that the improvements are made with the intention of selling or otherwise disposing of them and that the property is afterward sold or otherwise disposed of in such manner as to render the purchaser of the materials or commodities, so incorporated, liable to the same tax as if engaged in the business of contracting;

(5) Sales to a licensed producer, or to a cooperative association described in section 237-23(9), HRS, for sale to such producer, or to a licensed person operating a feed lot, of:

(A) Poultry or animal feed, hatching eggs, semen, replacement stock, breeding services for the purpose of raising or producing animal or poultry products for disposition as described in section 237-5, HRS, or to be incorporated in a manufactured product as described in paragraph (2), or for the purpose of breeding, hatching, milking, or egg laying other than for the customer's own consumption of the meat, poultry, eggs, or milk so produced;

(B) In the case of a feed lot operator:

(i) Only the segregated cost of the feed furnished by the feed lot operator as part of his services to a licensed producer of poultry or animals to be butchered, or to a cooperative association described in section 237-23(1), HRS, of such licensed producers shall be deemed to be a sale at wholesale; and

(ii) Any amount derived from the furnishing of feed lot services, other than the segregated cost of feed, shall be deemed taxable at the service business rate.

(C) This paragraph shall not apply to the sale of feed for poultry or animals to be used for hauling, transportation, or sports purposes;

(6) Sales to a licensed producer, or to a cooperative association described in section 237-23(9), HRS, for sale to such producer, of:

(A) Seed for producing agricultural products to be sold or otherwise disposed of as described in section 237-5, HRS, or to be incorporated in a manufactured product as described in paragraph (2); or

(B) Bait for catching fish (including the catching of bait for catching fish) which are to be sold or otherwise disposed of as described in section 237-5, HRS, or to be incorporated in a manufactured product as described in paragraph (2);

(7) Sales to a licensed producer or to a cooperative association described in section 237-23(9), HRS, for sale to the producer, of:

(A) Cartons and other containers, wrappers and sacks, and binders to be used for packaging eggs, vegetables, fruits and other agricultural products; or

(B) Seedlings and cuttings for producing nursery plants; or

(C) Chick containers; which are to be used as described in section 237-5, HRS, or to be incorporated in a manufactured product as described in paragraph (2);

(8) Sales of tangible personal property to a licensed person engaged in the service business, provided that:

(A) The property is not consumed or incidental to the performance of service; and

(B) There is a sale of the article at the retail rate of four per cent; and

(C) The resale of the article is separately charged or billed by the person rendering the service; and

(9) Sales to a licensed leasing company which leases capital goods as a service to others. For this purpose, capital goods are goods which in the hands of a licensed leasing company has a depreciable life and which are to be used by the licensed leasing company for leasing to others for a consideration.

The words "cooperative association" as used in paragraphs (5) to (7) mean a cooperative association incorporated under chapter 421 or under chapter 422, HRS, and which fully meet the requirements for tax exemption as specified in section 237-23(9), HRS.

The words "agricultural producer" as used in paragraph (3) and section 237-5, HRS, mean a producer of plant crops, including floriculture, horticulture, viticulture (vineyards), timber, nut, coffee, sugar cane, pineapple, or other similar agricultural activity where the products or crops are sold, but shall not include any animal or poultry products or a person operating a golf course, a cemetery, a property management activity, or an agricultural research organization.

The words "aquaculture producer" as used in paragraph (3) and section 237-5, HRS, mean a producer of aquatic plant and animal life for food or fiber within a controlled salt, brackish, or freshwater environment.

(b) Subsection (c) and (d) relate to the tax rates applicable under the general excise tax law with respect to containers and packaging materials sold in the State.

(c) Nonreturnable containers, packaging materials.

(1) Sale to manufacturer for incorporation during preparation for market.

(A) This paragraph applies to nonreturnable containers and packaging materials which are sold to a licensed manufacturer who incorporates the container or packaging material into a finished or saleable product during the course of its preservation, manufacturing, processing, or preparation for market, and which will remain in a form which is perceptible to the senses, which is to be sold and not otherwise used by the manufacturer.

(B) When containers and packaging materials to which this subparagraph applies are sold to a person and for the purpose above stated, they take the rate of:

(i) One-half of one per cent if sold by the manufacturer of the container or packaging material; or

(ii) One-half of one per cent if sold by a wholesaler.

*Example 1:* Taxpayer manufacturers cracker boxes, which taxpayer supplies to a cracker manufacturer. The boxes are used for packaging crackers, which are displayed and sold in packaged form. The rate applicable to the manufacture and sale of the boxes by the box manufacturer is one-half of one per cent.

*Example 2:* Taxpayer imports from the mainland cardboard cartons which are sold to a brewery. The brewery takes the cartons to a printer who imprints the brewery's name and trade mark together with information as to the contents. The cartons are used by the brewery in putting cans of beer in case lots. This is done at the time of manufacture, and the beer is offered for sale by the case. The rate applicable to the taxpayer upon the sale of the cartons to the brewery is one-half of one per cent.

(2) Special charge for container. Nonreturnable containers and packaging materials take a rate of one-half of one per cent when sold to a licensed retailer or other licensed seller, who adds a special charge on account of the type of container or packaging materials used for his merchandise, for example, a special charge for a gift box.

(3) Four per cent rate, when applicable. All sales to unlicensed persons, and all other sales of containers and packaging materials that are not shown to be covered by the one-half of one per cent rate as set forth in subparagraphs (A) or (B) shall be deemed to be sales taking the four per cent rate. The fact that the purchaser is engaged in making sales and uses the purchased containers or packaging materials for the purpose of delivering the goods sold or otherwise completing sales transactions shall not cause a lesser rate to apply.

*Example 3:* Taxpayer imports from the mainland boxes and wrapping paper, which are used by retail stores at the time of sale of their merchandise to box or wrap purchases made by customers. The four per cent rate applies to the sale of the boxes and wrapping paper to the retail stores.

(d) Returnable containers.

(1) Sales of containers to licensed persons whose customers receive title to the containers shall take the one-half of one per cent rate when the instance would be covered by subsection (c)(1) or (2), except for the fact that the containers are returnable by these customers. The circumstance that the

customers may return the containers and receive a credit or refund for doing so does not necessarily show that title does not pass to the customers.

(2) However, in some instances involving returnable containers title to the containers does not pass to the customers of the purchaser and accordingly the containers are not "resold" by the purchaser; in such cases the sale of the containers to the purchaser so using them takes the four per cent rate. For example, the name of the purchaser may appear on the containers in such a way as to show that there is no intention on his part to pass title to the containers, and accordingly the containers are not "resold" by the purchaser and the sale of the containers to this purchaser takes the four per cent rate.

Whether paragraph (1) or (2) applies depends upon all the facts, which shall be submitted for ruling.

(e) Agricultural or aquacultural materials or commodities sold in the State. This subsection relates to the tax rates applicable under the general excise tax law with respect to agricultural and aquacultural materials or commodities sold in the State.

(1) This paragraph applies to the sale of materials or commodities incorporated, used, or applied as essential to the planting, growth, nurturing, and production of agricultural or aquacultural commodities to a licensed agricultural or aquacultural producer or cooperative association for use by the person in the production, processing, and preparation of agricultural or aquacultural products or crops for sale.

(A) Some examples of sales of materials or commodities representing qualifying uses include, but are not limited to: antibiotics (for aquaculture and not for cattle and animals), expendable drip irrigation tubings, fertilizers, fumigants, fungicides, growth regulators, herbicides, packaging supplies, polyethylene mulch films, pesticides, processing materials, roofing papers (used in field furrows), soil amendments, surfactants (wetting agents), water purchased for irrigation (from nonpublic utility companies). Pesticides shall be defined by section 149A-2(26), HRS.

(B) Some examples of sales of materials or commodities representing nonqualifying uses include, but are not limited to: construction materials and supplies, equipment and repair parts, filtering devices, harvesting equipment, irrigation systems, janitorial supplies, office supplies, odor control devices and materials, PVC pipes, all rendition of services.

(C) When materials or commodities to which this paragraph applies are sold to a person and for the purposes above stated, such sale takes the rate of:

(i) One-half of one percent, if sold for qualifying purposes, or

(ii) Four per cent, if sold for nonqualifying purposes.

(2) In the event materials or commodities are both qualifying and nonqualifying uses, an allocation shall be made in order that only the sales made for qualifying uses will be reported at the rate of one-half of one per cent as provided in paragraph (1)(C)(i). The materials or commodities sold for nonqualifying uses shall be reported at the rate of four per cent as provided in paragraph (1)(C)(ii).

*Example 1:* Taxpayer sells materials and commodities to a licensed aquacultural producer engaged in research activities in addition to taxpayer's usual business of producing aquacultural products for market. The materials or commodities used in the research activities represent nonqualifying uses; therefore, the applicable rate imposed upon the sale of such materials and commodities is four per cent.

*Example 2:* Taxpayer sells certain materials and commodities to a licensed agricultural producer, including a soil amendment in order to obtain optimum crop production. It is found, however, that the soil amendment releases certain offensive odors creating a serious pollution problem for the nearby community. To combat this situation, the agricultural producer adds odor controlling materials to the soil amendment which do not adversely affect crop production. Insamuch as the soil amendment is deemed essential to the production of agricultural commodities, the applicable rate of such sale is one-half of one per cent. The applicable rate to the sale of the odor controlling materials is four per cent since they are not considered essential to the production of agricultural commodities.

*Example 3:* After harvesting, a sugar plantation treats the soil with a substance which controls odors and which also acts as a fungicide. Without this fungicide treatment, subsequent yields would be adversely affected. In this situation, the applicable tax rate on the sale of the odor controlling fungicide to the plantation is one-half of one per cent because of its dual use as a fungicide.

¶ 1417

*Example 4:* A landscape contractor maintains its own nursery. The plants grown in the nursery are used in contracting activities or may be sold apart from any landscaping contract. The contractor also provides grounds maintenance services for various clients. The applicable tax rate on sales to this contractor of fertilizers and pesticides for nursery use is one-half of one per cent. However, the applicable tax rate on sales of these same products for use in maintenance services is four per cent.

(3) A seller may obtain a resale certificate from the buyer. For purposes of resale certificates, section 18-237-13(b)(4) applies. [Eff 2/16/82; am 4/25/83] (Auth: HRS §§231-3(9), 237-8) (Imp: HRS §§237-4, 237-5)

## ¶ 1418. Rules Section 18-237-13-02.01 Tax on business of selling tangible personal property by an out-of-state seller, including drop shipments

(a) For the purposes of this section:

"Accept or Acceptance" means the purchaser or its agent inspecting the tangible personal property and taking physical possession of the tangible personal property or having dominion and control over the tangible personal property.

"Agent" means a person authorized by the purchaser to act on behalf of the purchaser and includes the power to inspect and accept or reject the tangible personal property.

"Delivery" means the act of transferring possession of tangible personal property. It includes, the transfer of goods from consignor to freight forwarder or for-hire carrier, from freight forwarder to for-hire carrier, one for-hire carrier to another, or for-hire carrier to consignee.

"Drop Shipment", sometimes known as direct delivery, means the delivery and acceptance of tangible personal property by a customer in Hawaii from a manufacturer or wholesaler who is someone other than the seller with whom the customer placed the order.

"Landed value" means the value of imported tangible personal property which is the fair and reasonable cash value of the tangible personal property when it arrives in Hawaii. It includes the sales price, shipping and handling fees, insurance costs, and customs duty. It does not include sales tax paid to another state.

"Nexus" means the activity carried on by a seller in Hawaii which is sufficiently connected with the seller's ability to establish or maintain a market for its products in Hawaii. It includes issues of taxability addressed under the Due Process and Commerce Clauses of the United States Constitution to support the application of the general excise tax and the use tax under chapters 237 and 238, HRS, respectively.

"Place of delivery" means the state or place where the purchaser or its agent accepts a delivery of tangible personal property.

(b) Imposition of general excise tax on sales of tangible personal property to customers in Hawaii. Section 237-13, HRS, imposes "privilege taxes against persons on account of their business and other activities in the State . . . ." Section 237-2, HRS, states that "business" includes "all activities (personal, professional, or corporate), engaged in or caused to be engaged in with the object of gain or economic benefit either direct or indirect . . . ."

(1) The act or place of passing of title is not the determinative factor for purposes of imposing the general excise tax. In states imposing a retail sales tax where a sale is defined as the transfer of title or ownership, the place where title passes may be relevant. The general excise tax, however, is not a sales tax imposed when title passes. Rather, the general excise tax is a gross receipts tax imposed when business is transacted in Hawaii.

(2) The general excise tax law looks to the place of delivery of tangible personal property to determine whether the sale of tangible personal property is business transacted in Hawaii.

(3) Hawaii does not impose the general excise tax on sales of tangible personal property which originate outside of this State unless the place of delivery of the tangible personal property is in Hawaii and the seller has nexus. There must be both: (1) a place of delivery within Hawaii by the purchaser, or its agent; and (2) the seller must have nexus for the general excise tax to apply to a

particular sale. The general excise tax will not be imposed if one of these elements is missing.

(4) Delivery of tangible personal property to a freight consolidator, freight forwarder, or for-hire carrier utilized only to arrange for and/or transport the tangible personal property does not constitute acceptance of the tangible personal property by the purchaser or its agent unless the freight consolidator, freight forwarder, or for-hire carrier has expressed written authority to accept the tangible personal property as an agent for the purchaser. Simply signing the bill of lading without this expressed written authority is not sufficient.

(5) When the place of delivery of the tangible personal property is to a customer in Hawaii and the seller has nexus, the sale of that tangible personal property constitutes business subject to the general excise tax. Section 237-22, HRS, states that gross income or gross proceeds of sale will be exempt if the State is prohibited from taxing the gross income under federal law or constitutional principles. If an out-of-state seller has no nexus with Hawaii, its gross income or gross proceeds of sale would be exempt under section 237-22, HRS.

(c) Imposition of the use tax on the sale of tangible personal property to a customer in Hawaii. Section 238-2, HRS, imposes use tax "on the use in this State of tangible personal property which is imported . . . for use in the State" if it is purchased from a seller that does not have a general excise tax license. All tangible personal property used or consumed in the State is subject to a uniform tax burden irrespective of whether it is acquired within or without the State.

(1) The use tax is levied on the importer of tangible personal property based upon the landed value of the tangible personal property imported.

(2) The tax rate is one-half of one per cent if the tangible personal property is intended for resale at retail, four per cent if the tangible personal property is intended for consumption or use by the importer or purchaser, or no tax if the tangible personal property is intended for resale to a reseller licensed under the general excise tax law.

(d) The liability for paying the general excise tax or the use tax is dependent on all the factual circumstances.

(e) The following is an example involving two parties and is treated as a single transaction.

*Example:* S, an out-of-state seller of tangible personal property, receives an order over the telephone or through the mail, from H, a Hawaii customer who is the ultimate consumer. H requests that the tangible personal property be delivered to H in Hawaii. S ships the tangible personal property for delivery to and acceptance by H in Hawaii.

The additional fact as to whether or not S has nexus with Hawaii determines the result in this example:

(1) If S has nexus with Hawaii, S's sale of tangible personal property constitutes business in Hawaii for purposes of the general excise tax law. As a result, S must obtain a general excise/use tax license. S is considered the importer for resale at retail and is subject to the use tax at one-half of one per cent. S is also subject to the general excise tax at four per cent on the sale.

(2) If S does not have nexus with Hawaii, pursuant to section 237-22, HRS, the general excise tax is not imposed upon S. Because S is not a licensed seller and the import is for consumption by H, H is subject to the use tax at four per cent.

(f) The following is an example of a drop shipment that involves three parties and is treated as two separate transactions.

*Example:* S, an out-of-state seller of tangible personal property, receives an order over the telephone or through the mail, from H, a Hawaii customer who is the ultimate consumer. W is an out-of-state wholesaler of tangible personal property. S notifies W of the order and requests that W ship the tangible personal property directly to H in Hawaii. W then ships the tangible personal property for delivery to and acceptance by H in Hawaii.

The following are the results when differing additional facts as to whether S and W have nexus with Hawaii and are properly licensed under the general excise tax law are incorporated into the example:

¶ 1418

(1) If neither S nor W has nexus with Hawaii and both are unlicensed, the importation of the tangible personal property by H is from an unlicensed seller for consumption. H is subject to the use tax at four per cent.

(2) If S has nexus with Hawaii and is licensed but W is unlicensed and has no nexus, S is considered to have imported the tangible personal property for resale at retail and is subject to the use tax at one-half of one per cent. The sale from S to H is a retail sale. S's gross income from the sale is subject to the general excise tax at the rate of four per cent.

(3) If both S and W have nexus with Hawaii and are licensed, both sales would be subject to the general excise tax. The sale from W to S is a wholesale sale. W's gross income is taxable at one-half of one per cent. The sale from S to H is a retail sale. S's gross income is taxable at four per cent. There is no use tax because W imported the tangible personal property for resale to a licensed reseller.

(4) If W has nexus with Hawaii and is licensed but S is unlicensed and has no nexus, the sale from W to S does not qualify as a wholesale sale under section 237-4(1), HRS, because S is not a licensed seller for general excise purposes, therefore, W is subject to the general excise tax at the rate of four per cent. W is considered to have imported the tangible personal property for resale at retail and is subject to the use tax at one-half of one per cent. The general excise tax is not imposed on the sale from S to H because S does not have sufficient nexus with Hawaii. Since W is the importer of the tangible personal property and H is not, H would not be subject to the use tax. [Eff 5/26/98 ] (Auth: HRS §§231-3(9), 237-8) (Imp: HRS §§237-4(1), 237-13(2), 237-21, 237-22, 238-2, 238-3(c))

## ¶ 1419. Rules Section 18-237-13-03 Tax upon contractors

(a) For the purposes of this section:

"Contractor" includes every person engaging in the business of contracting to erect, construct, repair, or improve buildings or structures, of any kind or description, including any portion thereof, or to make any installation therein, or to make, construct, repair, or improve any highway, road, street, sidewalk, ditch, excavation, fill, bridge, shaft, well, culvert, sewer, water system, drainage system, dredging or harbor improvement project, electric or steam rail, lighting or power system, transmission line, tower, dock, wharf, or other improvements; every person engaging in the practice of architecture, professional engineering, land surveying, and landscape architecture, as defined in section 464-1, HRS; and every person engaged in the practice of pest control or fumigation as a pest control operator as defined in section 460J-1, HRS.

"Licensed specialty contractor" means the same as the term is defined in section 444-7, HRS, in chapter 16-77 and in Exhibit A entitled, Specialty Contractors Classifications, located at the end, and made a part, of this chapter, and who is licensed under chapter 444, HRS.

"Owner-contractor" means an owner or lessee of property who builds or improves residential, farm, industrial, or commercial buildings or structures on such property for the owner-contractor's own use, or for use by the owner-contractor's grandparents, parents, siblings, or children and does not offer such building or structure for sale or lease, as distinguished from the business of contracting which is taxed under section 237-13(3)(D), HRS. The sale or lease, or offering for sale or lease, of such structure within one year after completion is prima facie evidence that the construction or improvement of such structure was undertaken for the purpose of sale or lease; provided that this shall not apply to residential properties sold or leased to employees of the owner or lessee; provided further that the owner or lessee registers for an exemption from the contractors licensing law, under section 444-9.1, HRS.

"Person" means the same as the term is defined in section 237-1, HRS.

"Prime contractor" means a person who: (1) contracts directly with the owner, lessor, lessee, developer, mortgagor, mortgagee, or any other person, including another contractor or licensed specialty contractor, to engage in the activities listed in the definition of a contractor in chapter 237, HRS; or (2) performs the activities listed in the definition of a contractor in chapter 237, HRS, except that this does not include an owner-contractor.

"Subcontractor" means a person who contracts with the prime contractor to engage in the activities listed in the definition of a contractor in chapter 237, HRS, and this rule.

(b) Subcontract deduction. Section 237-16, HRS, imposes the general excise tax at the rate of four per cent upon the gross income received or derived from the business of a contractor. That section, however, does not apply to gross income received from contracting with the state, county, or federal government, those persons exempted under section 237-23, HRS, and those persons licensed under chapter 237, HRS.

The gross income of a contractor which is not subject to taxation under section 237-16, HRS, however, shall be subject to taxation under section 237-13(3), HRS. Section 237-13(3)(A), HRS, imposes the general excise tax at the rate of four per cent on the gross income of the contracting business. A prime contractor is allowed a deduction from gross income for payments made to a subcontractor or licensed specialty contractor; provided the requirements of section 237-13(3)(B), HRS, and this section are satisfied.

These requirements are as follows:

(1) The prime contractor is licensed under chapter 237, HRS;

(2) The subcontractor or specialty contractor is licensed under chapter 237, HRS;

(3) The subcontractor is a contractor as defined in section 237-6, HRS, or the subcontractor is a specialty contractor licensed by the department of commerce and consumer affairs, pursuant to chapter 444, HRS, except that where a prime contractor and subcontractor or specialty contractor perform work exclusively on federal property the specialty contractor must be licensed under chapter 237, HRS, but need not be licensed pursuant to chapter 444, HRS;

(4) The general excise taxes due on the amount claimed as a deduction by the prime contractor must be paid by the subcontractor or the licensed specialty contractor or by the prime contractor on behalf of the subcontractor or the licensed specialty contractor. The prime contractor may attempt to secure the payment of the excise tax by the subcontractor or licensed specialty contractor by issuing a check payable jointly to the subcontractor or licensed specialty contractor and the department of taxation for the amount of the general excise tax due for the work done by the subcontractor or licensed specialty contractor. Subsequently, the subcontractor or licensed specialty contractor may sign the check and deposit it with the department of taxation. If the subcontractor or licensed specialty contractor fails to deposit the check with the department of taxation, however, the prime contractor shall not be entitled to the subcontract deduction. Rather than relying upon the subcontractor or licensed specialty contractor to pay the tax to the department of taxation, the prime contractor may withhold the general excise tax from the gross income paid to the subcontractor or licensed specialty contractor and remit those taxes to the department of taxation together with a separate general excise tax return with the name and general excise number of the subcontractor or licensed specialty contractor. There must exist, however, some indicia that the subcontractor or licensed specialty contractor has authorized the prime contractor to withhold the tax due and remit the tax to the department of taxation. The prime contractor shall provide the subcontractor with a copy of the general excise tax return filed by the prime contractor on behalf of the subcontractor or licensed specialty contractor. A copy of the general excise tax return may serve as the receipt required by section 231-13(3)(B), HRS. The department of taxation may audit the prime contractor and disallow the prime contractor's subcontract deduction if the tax is not paid by the subcontractor or licensed specialty contractor or by the prime contractor on behalf of the subcontractor or licensed specialty contractor. If the subcontract deduction is disallowed, the prime contractor shall pay to the department of taxation the amount of the additional tax due, including any applicable interest from the date of the filing of the return in which the prime contractor claimed the subcontract deduction. The statute of limitations for collecting the tax and interest from the prime contractor shall run from the date of the filing of the return in which the prime contractor claimed the subcontract deduction. If the department of taxation collects the tax and interest relating to a disallowed subcontract deduction from the prime contractor, the department will not subsequently attempt to collect a tax which is attributable to the disallowed subcontract deduction from the subcontractor or licensed specialty contractor who initially failed to pay the tax; and

(5) The prime contractor shall provide the department of taxation with the name and general excise number of each subcontractor or licensed specialty contractor for which the deduction is claimed and the total amount of gross proceeds paid to each subcontractor or licensed specialty contractor. The prime contractor shall report this information on either the back side of the prime contractor's general excise tax monthly, quarterly, or semi-annual return and summarized on the annual return or on a separate schedule attached to the respective returns. A prime contractor may claim the subcontract deduction only when the prime contractor correctly reports its gross income as contracting income on the prime contractor's general excise tax returns. Thus, a taxpayer who reports gross income as professional services, rather than as contractor income, is erroneously reporting the income and will be questioned by the department of taxation about the subcontract deduction.

(c) Whether a prime contractor qualifies for the subcontract deduction shall be determined on the basis of all the facts of each particular case. The application of this deduction is illustrated in the following examples:

*Example 1:* ABC Construction Company, a contractor licensed under chapter 237, HRS, is the prime contractor in the construction of a commercial building for $100,000. ABC then subcontracts various aspects of the job to architect W for $10,000, engineer X for $10,000, land surveyor Y for $10,000, and landscape architect Z for $10,000, all of whom are licensed pursuant to chapters 237 and 444, HRS, and are included in the definition of a contractor in section 237-6, HRS. Section 237-13(3)(B), HRS, allows a prime contractor a deduction for payments to subcontractors and licensed specialty contractors. Accordingly, ABC, the prime contractor, is subject to the general excise tax at the rate of four per cent on $60,000, which is the $100,000 contract less the $10,000 taxable to each of the four subcontractors, W, X, Y, and Z. W, X, Y, and Z are subject to the general excise tax at the rate of four per cent on the payments received from ABC.

*Example 2:* Assume the same facts as in Example 1, except that W fails to pay the general excise tax due on the payment that W receives from ABC and ABC claims the subcontract deduction for the payment to W. ABC shall pay to the director, upon demand, $400, which is the amount of the additional tax due on the amount W received.

*Example 3:* X, an engineer, contracts for $100,000 to perform engineering work on a building. X is acting as a prime contractor and subcontracts $10,000 of the engineering work to Y, another engineer who specializes in designing fire sprinkler systems. X reports the gross income for the contract as professional services and deducts $10,000 from gross income for the subcontract for Y. This deduction will be questioned because X incorrectly reported the gross income received as professional services. Providers of professional services are not allowed to take subcontract deductions. If X had correctly reported the gross income as contracting income, the subcontract deduction would not be questioned.

*Example 4:* ABC Construction Company, a contractor licensed under chapter 237, HRS, is the prime contractor in the renovation of a residential building for $50,000. While renovating the building, ABC discovers termites and subcontracts with DEF Pest Control Operator, a pest control operator licensed pursuant to chapters 237 and 460J, HRS, to fumigate the building for $5,000. Additionally, ABC subcontracts a portion of the job for $5,000 to GHI Acoustical and Installation Contractor, a specialty contractor licensed pursuant to chapters 237 and 444, HRS. Section 237-13(3)(B), HRS, allows a prime contractor a deduction for payments to subcontractors and licensed specialty contractors. Accordingly, ABC, the prime contractor, is subject to the general excise tax at the rate of four per cent on $40,000, which is the $50,000 contract less the $5,000 taxable to DEF, the subcontractor, and the $5,000 taxable to GHI, the licensed specialty contractor. DEF and GHI are subject to the general excise tax at the rate of four per cent on the payments received from ABC.

*Example 5:* ABC Land Planning Company works with architects and engineers to plan construction projects by providing financial and market analysis and feasibility studies. ABC contracts with X Landscape Surveyor and Y Landscape Architect, who are both licensed under chapter 237, HRS, and are included in the definition of a contractor in section 237-6, HRS, to do various aspects of the projects. Section 237-13(3)(B), HRS, allows a prime contractor a deduction for payments to subcontractors and licensed specialty contractors. ABC is not a prime contractor since it is not engaged in the business of contracting. See, section 237-6, HRS. Accordingly, ABC is not entitled to

¶ 1419

a deduction for the payments to X and Y.

*Example 6:* ABC Construction Company, a contractor licensed under chapter 237, HRS, is the prime contractor in the construction of a residential building. ABC purchases cabinets manufactured by D Supply House from D and ABC installs the cabinets. ABC also rents equipment from E Rental Company and subcontracts with F Solar Energy Systems Contractor, a specialty contractor licensed under chapters 237 and 444, HRS, to assemble and install a solar hot water system. Section 237-13(3)(B), HRS, allows a prime contractor a deduction for payments to contractors and licensed specialty contractors. Neither D nor E are subcontractors or licensed specialty contractors. F, however, is a licensed specialty contractor. Accordingly, ABC, the prime contractor, is entitled to a deduction for the payment to F but is not entitled to a deduction for the payments to D and E. F is subject to the general excise tax at the rate of four per cent on the payment received from ABC.

*Example 7:* ABC Supply House sells customized cabinets to its customers, including DEF Construction Company. DEF installs the cabinets for its customers. Additionally, ABC, which has a specialty contractor's license, sells and installs cabinets for GHI Construction Company. GHI is entitled to a subcontract deduction for the payment to ABC. DEF, however, is not entitled to a deduction for the payment to ABC as ABC is not engaged in the contracting business, as such, when ABC sells the cabinets to DEF.

*Example 8:* ABC Construction Company, a contractor licensed under chapter 237, HRS, is the prime contractor in the construction of a residential building. ABC contracts with Edifice Wrecks, a licensed specialty contractor, to demolish the existing structure and remove the debris. ABC purchases lumber from E Supply House to be used in the construction of the building. ABC subsequently contracts with F Hauling Company, who is licensed by the Public Utilities Commission as a carrier of general commodities and household goods, to haul the lumber to the job site. F is subject to chapter 239, HRS, and is not licensed under chapter 237, HRS. Section 237-13(3)(B), HRS, allows a prime contractor a deduction for payments to contractors and licensed specialty contractors. ABC is entitled to a deduction for the payments to Edifice Wrecks, a licensed specialty contractor. ABC, however, is not entitled to a deduction for the payments to E and F.

*Example 9:* ABC Construction Company, DEF Construction Company, and XYZ Bank form a joint venture to develop a shopping center. The joint venture will sell or otherwise dispose of the shopping center within one year of the completion. The joint venture contracts with G Landscape Surveyor and H Landscape Architect, who are both licensed under chapter 237, HRS, and are included in the definition of a contractor in section 237-6, HRS, to do various aspects of the project. Section 237-13(3)(B), HRS, allows a prime contractor a deduction for payments to subcontractors and licensed specialty contractors. The definition of a person under section 237-1, HRS, includes a joint venture. Accordingly, the joint venture is a prime contractor and taxable as a contractor on the disposition of the property. The joint venture, however, is entitled to a deduction for the payments to G and H. G and H are subject to the general excise tax at the rate of four percent on the payments received from the joint venture.

*Example 10:* Individual A, who is not engaged in the construction business, purchases land and decides to build a residence. A, an owner-contractor under sections 444-2 and 444-9.1, HRS, and this section, contracts with Contractor X, who is licensed under chapter 237, HRS, and is included in the definition of a contractor in section 237-6, HRS, to do various aspects of the job. The definition of a prime contractor does not include an owner-contractor, such as A. Thus, A is not entitled to a subcontract deduction for the payments to X, and X is subject to the general excise tax at the rate of four per cent on the payments received from A. If, however, X fails to pay the general excise tax due on the payment that X receives from A, A is not liable for the nonpayment of the tax.

*Example 11:* Assume the same facts as Example 10, except that X contracts with Contractors Y and Z, who are both licensed under chapter 237, HRS, and are included in the definition of a contractor in section 237-6, HRS, to do various aspects of the project. X is entitled to a deduction for the payments to Y and Z. Y and Z are subject to the general excise tax at the rate of four per cent on the payments received from X.

*Example 12:* ABC Construction Company, a contractor licensed under chapter 237, HRS, is the prime contractor for the construction of a commercial building. ABC then subcontracts with DEF

Company, a specialty contractor licensed under chapter 237, HRS, but not licensed under chapter 444, HRS, to do part of the job. Section 237-13(3)(B), HRS, allows a prime contractor a deduction for payments to subcontractors and specialty contractors licensed under chapter 444, HRS. DEF, however, is an unlicensed specialty contractor. Accordingly, ABC is not entitled to a deduction for the payments to DEF.

*Example 13:* Assume the same facts as in Example 12 above, except that the renovation will be done on a commercial building which is exclusively on federal property. The specialty contractor, DEF, is not required to be licensed under chapter 444, HRS, because its contracting activities on the federal property are not within the regulatory jurisdiction of the State. Accordingly, ABC is entitled to a deduction for the payments to DEF if DEF pays the general excise tax at the rate of four per cent on the payments received from ABC. DEF is required to be licensed as a taxpayer under chapter 237, HRS.

*Example 14:* ABC Construction Company, a contractor licensed under chapter 237, HRS, but unlicensed under chapter 444, HRS, is the prime contractor for the renovation of a commercial building. ABC then contracts with DEF Acoustical and Installation Construction Company, a specialty contractor licensed under chapters 237 and 444, HRS, to do part of the job. Section 237-13(3)(B), HRS, allows a prime contractor a deduction for payments to subcontractors and licensed specialty contractors. There is no requirement that the prime contractor be licensed under chapter 444, HRS. Accordingly, ABC is entitled to a deduction for the payments to DEF. DEF is subject to the general excise tax at the rate of four per cent on the payments received from ABC.

*Example 15:* Customer X purchases tile from ABC Retailer, a company licensed under chapter 237, HRS, but unlicensed under chapter 444, HRS. ABC then contracts with DEF Tile Contractor, a specialty contractor licensed under chapters 237 and 444, HRS, to prepare the base and install the tile. Section 237-13(3)(B), HRS, allows a prime contractor a deduction for payments to subcontractors and licensed specialty contractors. ABC, however, is not a contractor under section 237-6, HRS. Accordingly, ABC is not entitled to a deduction for the payments to DEF. DEF is subject to the general excise tax at the rate of four per cent on the payments received from ABC.

(d) Exemption from the general excise tax of all rents and proceeds received from housing projects, including all gross proceeds received by contractors for the construction of housing projects developed pursuant to chapters 201E and 356, HRS.

(1) Scope. This subsection sets forth the general excise tax exemption provisions of section 201E-205, HRS.

(2) Definitions. For the purposes of this subsection:

"Corporation" means the housing finance and development corporation established under chapter 201E, HRS.

"Housing" or "housing project" means dwelling units developed and constructed pursuant to contracts or partnership agreements executed between the corporation and eligible bidders (as defined in section 201E-213, HRS).

(3) Application of exemption from the general excise tax.

(A) Qualifying process. The following are exempted from the general excise tax under chapter 237, HRS:

(i) All rents received on account of the lease or rental of dwelling units developed and constructed pursuant to sections 201E-211 and 201E-213, HRS, and

(ii) All gross proceeds received by a contractor for the development and construction of dwelling units pursuant to sections 201E-211 and 201E-213, HRS.

(B) Non-qualifying proceeds. Gross proceeds shall not be exempt from the general excise tax where they are received by any person who furnishes tangible personal property or renders service to:

(i) Another person who receives rental payments which are exempted from the general excise tax under this section; or

¶ 1419

(ii) A contractor for the development and construction of housing or housing projects pursuant to sections 201E-211 and 201E-213, HRS.

(4) Filing of claim; time and place. An exemption claim (FORM G-37) shall be prepared by the claimant and submitted to the corporation for certification after final execution of the partnership agreement or contract or both between such claimant and the corporation. The original copy of the certified exemption claim shall be filed with the tax assessor for the taxation district in which the claimant files the claimant's general excise tax return (FORM G-HW-1).

(5) Failure to file claim. The exemption shall not be allowed unless the original copy of the certified exemption claim is filed with the tax assessor.

(6) Records. A claimant shall keep at the claimant's principal place of business such records as will enable the director to verify the accuracy of the amount of exemption claimed. [Eff 2/16/82; am 12/1/88; am 2/1/89; am 7/1/90; am and ren §18-237-13-03 12/27/90] (Auth: HRS §§231-3(9), 237-8) (Imp: HRS §237-13)

## ¶ 1420. General Excise Tax Memorandum No. 3 Imposition of General Excise Tax

Hawaii Dept. of Taxation Memorandum No. 3, 08/02/1957

Date Issued: 08/02/1957

Tax Type(s): Sales and Use Tax

TO: ALL CONTRACTORS AND OTHER PERSONS WHO, AS A BUSINESS OR AS A PART OF A BUSINESS IN WHICH THEY ARE ENGAGED, CONSTRUCT BUILDINGS OR MAKE OTHER IMPROVEMENTS ON LAND HELD BY THEMSELVES IN FEE SIMPLE;

and

TO: ALL PERSONS WHO ENGAGE IN BUSINESS WHICH INVOLVES THE MAKING OR SALE OF LEASEHOLDS.

Subject: Imposition of General Excise Tax

I. *GENERAL*

Scope of this memorandum; provisions of law involved. This memorandum relates to the provisions of sections 3(a) and 3(n) of Act 1, Special Session Laws of 1957. Section 3(n) reads as follows: (now 237-13, paragraph D)

"(n) Section 117-14 is amended by adding to subsection (c) a new paragraph to read as follows:

"'(4) A person who, as a business or as a part of a business in which he is engaged, erects, constructs, or improves any building or structure, of any kind or description, or makes, constructs or improves any road, street, sidewalk, sewer or water system, or other improvements on land held by him (whether held as a leasehold, fee simple, or otherwise), shall upon the sale or other disposition of the land or improvements, even if the work was not done pursuant to a contract, be liable to the same tax as if engaged in the business of contracting, unless he shall show that at the time he was engaged in making such improvements it was, and for the period of at least one year after completion of the building, structure or other improvements it continued to be, his purpose to hold and not to sell or otherwise dispose of the land or improvements. The tax in respect of such improvements shall be measured by the amount of the proceeds of such sale or other disposition that is attributable to the erection, construction or improvement of such building or structure, or the making, constructing or improving of such road, street, sidewalk, sewer or water system, or other improvements. The measure of tax in respect of the improvements shall not exceed the amount which would have been taxable had such work been performed by another, subject as in other cases to the deductions allowed by paragraph (2) of this subsection. Upon the election of the taxpayer this paragraph may be applied notwithstanding the improvements were not made by the taxpayer, or were not made as or as a part of a business, or were made with the intention of holding the same. However, this paragraph shall not apply in respect of any proceeds that constitute or are in the nature of rent; all such gross income shall be taxable under subsection (h).'"

Section 20(d) of Act 1 provides that this provision: "shall not, except upon the election of the taxpayer, apply to any work done under a building permit issued prior to May 1, 1957, or to any gross income derived from a sale or other disposition actually and finally agreed upon prior to May 1, 1957, but the burden shall be upon the person claiming the benefit of this subsection to show his compliance therewith."

Section 3(a) amends the exemption (section 117-3), which formerly read: "gross receipts from the sale of ***** stocks or from the sale of real property", to read:

"gross receipts from the sale of ***** stocks or, except as otherwise provided, from the sale of land in fee simple, improved or unimproved *****".

What persons are affected. The persons affected by the quoted law are both those who sell fee simple land and those who make or sell leaseholds.

As to sales of fee simple land the persons affected are, in general, those who make improvements on their own land, without hiring a licensed contractor, or who hire a licensed contractor for only part of the work. A typical case is that of a landowner who himself is a contractor. If all the work is contracted out to another who is a licensed contractor and pays the tax on the contracting business so done by him, when the property afterward is sold there is no tax on the sales proceeds. However, if the work is parceled out among a number of contractors in such a manner that the project owner occupies a position equivalent to that of a general contractor, there generally will be a tax to be paid on the proceeds attributable to the improvements. The taxable amount will be reduced by deductions allowed for the amounts on which the contractors who occupy the position of sub-contractors are taxed, as stated in Part II.

As to the making and selling of leaseholds, if the land has been developed or improved it may well be that some portion of the proceeds is deductible by reason of the quoted law. Any person who considers the possibility of claiming such a deduction should acquaint himself with the principles involved. Leaseholds also are affected by reason of the fact that, under certain circumstances, the making of improvements is taxable upon the disposition of the improvements, thus eliminating, in such circumstances, the question whether the sale of the leasehold in itself is "business". See Part III.

The following persons are not affected by the quoted law, if the property is fee simple property or is a leasehold the sale of which does not constitute "business":

Those whose construction activities are not in the course of a business.

Those whose build for rental purposes or with the intention of holding the property (unless there is a change of purpose within the year).

Those who sell property on which the improvements are just the same as those on the property when it was acquired.

It should be noted that the furnishing of equipment which is not installed as a part of the structure is, and always has been, a sale of tangible personal property by the supplier, contractor or project owner, as the case may be. The quoted law does not change this.

When the tax is due. No tax is due prior to sale or other disposition of the property. The tax applies as the price is received if the taxpayer is on the cash basis, or at the time of sale if the taxpayer is on the accrual basis.

II. *FEE SIMPLE PROPERTY*

Upon the sale of fee simple land by one who has made improvements in such a way as to be affected by the quoted law (see Part I), the measure of the tax is the lower of these two amounts:

(a) The amount of sales proceeds attributable to the improvements,

or

(b) The amount which would have been taxable as contracting business of a licensed contractor if the work had been contracted out in the usual manner.

As to any work contracted out, the amount on which tax was paid by that contractor may be deducted from the tax base in determining the tax, the same as is done by a general contractor having subcontractors.

III . *LEASEHOLDS*

In some instances the sale of a leasehold does not constitute "business" (for example, an isolated sale of a home situated on leasehold property), and in such instances the sales proceeds may be accounted for simply on the ground that the improvements, if any, made by the seller while he held the property were not made in the course of a business, or were made by a licensed contractor, or were made with the intention of holding the property which purpose continued for at least one year.

When a leasehold is made, or when the sale of a leasehold constitutes "business", all of the proceeds are taxable with the possible exception of those attributable to the sale or other disposition of the improvements. For example, the tax always applies to a premium attributable to a rise in land values, which represents the difference between the ground rent stipulated in the lease and that which would be commanded at the time of sale.

As used herein the expression "sales proceeds attributable to the improvements" does not signify any proceeds that constitute or are in the nature of rent.

The amount of sales proceeds attributable to the improvements is subject to reduction, as to the taxable amount, in the following manner: By showing, if lower than the amount of sales proceeds attributable to the improvements, the amount which would have been taxable as contracting business of a licensed contractor if the work had been contracted out in the usual manner, and by deducting from this amount any amounts as to which it is claimed that licensed contractors have paid the tax, or that persons taxable as contractors (for example, land developers) have paid the tax. The balance constitutes the tax base so far as the amount of sales proceeds attributable to the improvements is concerned.

If all of the improvements were made by a licensed contractor in the usual manner the entire amount of sales proceeds attributable to the improvements may be deducted on that ground.

The deduction always are subject to the required tax having in fact been paid by others.

IV. *METHOD OF REPORTING AND MAKING RETURNS*

Every licensee making a sale of fee simple land, and every licensee making or selling a leasehold who claims that any amount of the proceeds is deductible or non-taxable, must attach to the first return relating to the particular project answers to a questionnaire, the form of which will be supplied by the Tax Office. This questionnaire is to furnish the information set out below under the heading: "Questionnaire A." In addition, if there are any "yes" answers to this questionnaire, unless the filing of further data is excused by the Director on the basis of the answers furnished, the taxpayer is to attach to the first return of payments from or sales of a given project a schedule showing the amount of tax returned and to be returned as computed by him for that project, and just how the amount has been computed for the project as a whole and also, how the amount presently returnable has been determined. On subsequent returns relating to the same project reference should be made to the questionnaire and this schedule and to the time of filing them, unless other copies are attached, and the amount returned on the subsequent returns should be tied in to the initial schedule and questionnaire.

The information called for by Questionnaire B must be available in the records of the person filing the return, and upon demand of the Director answers to this questionnaire, or portions of it as designated by the Director, must be furnished as a supplementary return and special statement under section 121-36, made applicable to the general excise tax law by section 117-9.

Questionnaire A

(To be answered by persons selling fee simple land, and by persons making or selling a leasehold who claim that any amount of the proceeds is deductible or non-taxable.)

1. Location and area of the project; date of the sale or other disposition of the property; whether the sale was of the fee simple; if a leasehold, date of the lease, name of lessor, ground rent provided for by the lease.

2. Did the person making the return, as a business or as a part of a business in which he was

engaged, make improvements on the property without hiring a licensed contractor for the job, or by hiring a licensed contractor for only part of the job, or by parceling out the job among a number of contractors?

3. If the answer to No. 2 is "yes", when were these improvements made?

4. If the answer to No. 2 is "yes", what was the purpose in making the improvements?

5. If it is stated in answer to No. 4 that the purpose was to hold the property, when did a change of purpose occur?

6. If the making or sale of a leasehold is involved, does the person making the return claim that any amount of the proceeds is deductible or non-taxable? Why?

7. If the making or sale of a leasehold is involved, does the person making the return elect to have paragraph (4) of section 117-14(c) of the General Excise Tax Law apply? (now paragraph (D) of section 237-13 (3) )

Questionnaire B

(To be filled out, upon demand of the Director, in whole or in part as designated by the Director.)

(a) Roads or streets, sidewalks, sewers or water system, driveways, and other improvements to land, except buildings, made or constructed as a part of the project. (In the case of leasehold property, designate also improvements of this type made by a previous developer.)

(b) To what extent, if any, were the improvements listed in (a) contracted out and performed by a licensed contractor who, it is claimed, paid the general excise tax on this contracting business. (In the case of leasehold property designate also improvements of this type on which it is claimed a previous developer paid the same tax as a licensed contractor.)

(c) As to any improvements listed in (a), that were not contracted out or made as explained in (b), a description of them giving square feet or cubic feet, type of materials and construction, and cost of each.

(d) Number of buildings constructed and for what purpose (e.g. number of houses, garages etc.); for each type of building, statement as to class of construction, type of materials, and floor area, with attached blue print.

(e) For each unit constituting a sales unit a description stating land area and buildings; floor area and number of floors of each class of construction and type; fixtures and equipment included; additional facilities included in the sales price, such as parking space, use of lobby, elevators, hallways etc.; also total number of sales units.

(f) Cost of construction for each type of building, segregated between material and labor; sources of supply for materials (named companies); cost of fixtures and equipment.

(g) Sales proceeds, per unit, and opinion of taxpayer as to proper division of this amount of sales proceeds between (1) raw land; (2) improvements listed in (a); (3) buildings, fixtures and equipment.

(h) Dates of commencement and completion of the project.

(i) If sale is on agreement of sale, outline of sales plan, as to down payments, installments, rate of interest, etc.

(j) Name of financial institution handling loans, if any.

(k) Names of contractors on the project and, for each, the subject matter of his contract and the amount on which it is claimed that tax has been paid by him.

## ¶ 1421. General Excise Tax Memorandum No. 3A Questions Concerning General Excise Tax Memorandum No. 3

This concerns questions raised by persons attending the meetings on June 24 and 28, 1957. These meetings were held for discussion of a preliminary draft of memorandum "To all contractors and other persons who, as a business or as a part of a business in which they are engaged, construct buildings or make other improvements on land held by themselves (leasehold or fee simple property).

Q. 1. What is meant by the reference on page 2 [6766] to the "furnishing of equipment which is not installed as part of the structure"?

Comment. This refers to items such as stoves or refrigerators, furnished by the supplier to the person erecting the project.

If the person erecting the project is a licensed contractor who has included the stoves and refrigerators in the contract price, and title passes from the supplier to the contractor and then again from the contractor to the property owner, this is a sale at wholesale on the part of the supplier. Even though the stoves and refrigerators remain "tangible personal property" throughout, and are not deemed part of the structure or an installation therein, this is a sale by the supplier to a licensed seller, namely the contractor.

In the case of a sale by the supplier to a person erecting the project who himself is the property owner, holding the site either as a fee simple property or as a leasehold, it is necessary for the supplier to ascertain whether the project owner buying this equipment is going to sell the property, including the equipment, or is going to hold it.

If the project owner is going to sell the property, there will be a 3 1/2% tax on the project owner when he does so, upon his sale to tangible personal property, that is the stoves and refrigerators. This liability on the part of the project owner exists and has existed right along; such liability is not dependent upon the application of the new Section 117-14(c)(4). In this case the supplier's sale is "at wholesale."

If the project owner is not going to sell the property, this is a 3 1/2% sale upon the part of the supplier. Should the project owner, after renting the property or putting it to some other use thereafter sells it, this would not change the rate of tax upon the supplier.

Q. 2. In the case of a supplier selling building materials to a project owner who intends to continue to hold the property, for example, for rental purposes, at what point can the project owner make the election referred to at the end of Section 117-14(c)(4)? How is the supplier to determine the rate of tax on the sale of the building materials?

Comment. The election referred to at the end of Section 117-14(c)(4) is not made until the sale of the property by the project owner. (In the case of a project on leasehold property, such election may be advantageous to the project owner as noted below in the comment on the next question.) So far as the supplier is concerned he determines the rate of tax according to whether the purchase does or does not intend to sell the property to dispose of the improvements at the time of purchase of the building materials.

Should the purchase of the building materials say that he intends to sell the property but not sell it, the supplier of the building materials might be assessed an additional tax to bring the tax on the sale of the building materials to the 3 1/2% rate. The supplier of the building materials then would have recourse against the purchase of the materials if the supplier had taken a resale certificate.

Q. 3. When would it be advantageous for a property owner to make the election permitted by Section 117-(3), as amended, does not exempt gross receipts from the sale of leaseholds. The mended law is the same in this respect as the law before the 1957 amendment, that is, the sale of leasehold in itself is taxable if constituting "business." However, by making the election above referred to, the leaseholder making the sale can reduce the amount of tax in most cases. This comes about as follows:

Under section 117-14(c)(4), if applicable under the circumstances or by reason of an election, the amount of the sales proceeds attributable to the improvements is not necessarily altogether taxed. If the amount of the sales proceeds attributable to the improvements exceeds the amount which would have been taxed to a licensed contractor erecting or making the improvements, the excess is not taxed. Or if the leaseholder making the sale can show that in fact a licensed contractor already has paid the tax upon the performance of the work on the improvements, there is no tax on the amount of sales proceeds attributable to the improvements. Thus, if the work was performed in the first place by a licensed contractor who paid the tax on the work, it would be advantageous to the leaseholder selling the improvements to make the election even though the improvements had depreciated and the amount of sales proceeds attributable to the improvements was less than the amount representing the contract job in the first place.

The foregoing are examples. The property owner making the sale will determine for himself from the combination of circumstances in the particular case what is to his advantage.

Q. 4. How does the tax apply to the premium in the following three instances?

A. An estate, owning a fee simple, makes a contract in order to have put in the streets, water connections, etc., and then offers leaseholds, setting the ground rent on the basis of the improved land. A few of the lots do not sell for a considerable period, or perhaps having been sold are turned back and new leases issued by the fee simple owner. During this lapse of time there has been an upward trend in land values, and if the fee simple owner were setting the ground rents at this later time they would be higher. Accordingly the fee simple owner requires the payment of a premium by persons taking leases at this later time.

Comment. The proceeds derived from the making of a lease are, in general, taxable except as the taxable amount is reduced by application of the election permitted by Section 117-14(c)(4) specifically says that the paragraph does not apply "in respect of any proceeds that constitute or are in the nature of rent." The tax applies to this premium.

A-1. In the situation already stated, the person taking the lease is a contractor builder who has a number of lots on which he builds and later sells by assigning the lease. The question arises as to whether the portion of the sales proceeds charged in order to recover the premium paid for the lease may be deducted by this contractor builder from his sales proceeds.

Comment. There is no deduction for this premium. This resembles the case of a monthly rent received from a sublessee, all of which is taxable without any deduction for the rent which the sublessor pays under the master lease.

B. An estate, the owner of the fee simple, sets the ground rent on the basis of the raw land. A developer puts in the streets, water connections, etc. He contracts to do this but without any obligation on the part of the fee simple owner to pay him for the work. A lease is made to a lessee who intends to himself have a home built by a contractor in the usual manner. In order to obtain the lot, this person enters into a lease in which the ground rent represents the raw land, as above stated, and he also pays the developer the sum of $2,500.00, which represents a proportionate part of the improvements made by the developer, with a profit for the developer.

Comment. The developer is viewed as a "licensed contractor" putting in the street improvements and the like under a contract with the estate which owns the fee simple. The developer is taxable on the entire proceeds even though paid to him by the lot purchaser.

B-1. The facts are as stated in B except that the lessee is a contractor builder who buys this lease, together with other leases, in order to put houses on the lots and sell the same by assigning the leases. He receives $16,500.00, $2,500.00 being recovery of the payment to the developer and $14,000.00 being for the house. May he deduct the $2,500.00 from his sales proceeds?

Comment. Yes, in this case the deduction may be taken because the $2,500.00 represents a portion of the sales proceeds attributable to improvements upon which the tax already has been paid. That is, it was paid by the original developer. This is not a premium that is in the nature of rent.

C. An estate is the owner of the fee simple. The estate fixes the ground rent on the basis of the improved land, contracting in the usual manner for the street improvements and the other improvements to the land. The lessee taking the original lease is a contractor builder who has a number of such lots on which he builds himself, and afterwards sells them by assigning the leases. During the interval of time between his obtaining of the lease and the sale, the land values in the area have increased, and if a lease were made at this time it would command a higher ground rent. In making the sale this is considered. A part of the sales proceeds represents a premium, which is the amount of the difference, for the remainder of the term of the lease, between the ground rent fixed in the lease and what would be commanded at the present time, discounted to the present time and computed in a lump sum. Can the contractor builder deduct this portion of the sales proceeds in computing his tax?

Comment. No, he may not deduct this for the reasons stated in the comment on A, and A-1.

Q. 5. In the case of a fee simple owner who claims that the entire amount of the sales proceeds is exempt, for example on the ground that the improvements, though made by himself, were made with the intention of holding the property, which intention continued for a period of at least one year after the completion of the improvements, what proof is required?

Comment. A form of questionnaire will be prepared so as to set out questions having to do with claims of exemption by fee simple owners upon the sale of the property. The answers to this questionnaire will constitute part of the taxpayer's return, and the penalties provided by law concerning information supplied on a return (Section 115-38) will apply. It will not be necessary to make an affidavit.

Q. 6. Will there be instances in which it is of advantage for a person selling leasehold to compute "(a) the amount of sales proceeds attributable to the improvements," or "(b) the amount which would have been taxable as contracting business of a licensed contractor if the work had been contracted out in the usual manner." Will not the seller of leasehold simply deduct the amount on which the tax has been paid by the contractor that he employs?

Comment. Even if the seller of the leasehold only seeks to deduct the amount on which the contractor has paid the tax, that deduction cannot exceed "the amount of sales proceeds attributable to the improvements," so in every case it will be necessary for a person selling a leasehold to determine that amount if he claims any deduction at all. Then, if that amount is in excess of "the amount which would have been taxable as contracting business of a licensed contractor if the work had been contracted out in the usual manner," it will be advantageous to the seller of the leasehold to show the latter figure.

Q. 7. What is the significance of information to be furnished by the taxpayer as to the sales plan, down payments and installments, rate of interest, etc.?

Comment. This is significant only in the case of a sale made under an agreement of sale. It is necessary to determine what part of the total payments constitutes interest. Interest always is taxable.

Q. 8. Assume a contractor builder who is erecting houses on his own property plans to sell each house and lot for $15,000.00. He arranges financing. Under these arrangements a $10,000.00 mortgage loan is made to the buyer at a discount payable by the builder in the amount of 3%. The buyer makes a down payment of $5,000.00. Of the remaining $10,000.00 the builder receives from the mortgage company $9,700.00, the balance of $300.00 being the 3% discount which is paid by the builder in order to obtain financing. Is this $300.00 deductible from the sales proceeds?

Comment. The $300.00 is part of the sales proceeds attributable to the improvements, but of that amount the taxable amount cannot exceed "the amount which would have been taxable as contracting business if a licensed contractor if the work had been contracted out in the usual manner." The computation of this last amount will exclude the $300.00 and in that sense the $300.00 is deductible.

## ¶ 1422. Rules Section 18-238-1 Definitions

For purposes of this chapter:

"Consummated" is the place of delivery meaning the state or place where the purchaser or its agent accepts a delivery of tangible personal property.

"Landed value" means the value of imported tangible personal property which is the fair and reasonable cash value of the tangible personal property when it arrives in Hawaii. It includes the purchase price, shipping and handling fees, insurance costs, and customs duty. It does not include sales tax paid to another state.

"Place of delivery" means the state or place where the purchaser or its agent accepts a delivery of tangible personal property.

"Price" means the total amount for which tangible personal property is purchased, valued in money, whether paid in money or otherwise, and wheresoever paid, provided that cash discounts, trade and quantity discounts allowed and taken on sales shall not be included. [Eff 5/26/98] (Auth: HRS §§231-3(9), 238-16) (Imp: HRS §238-1)

## ¶ 1423. Tax Information Release No. 42-74
## Application of the General Excise Tax to Interest Income

Advice has been requested as to the application of the general excise tax to interest income received by taxpayers from various sources and activities.

Section 237-13, HRS, provides that there is levied and shall be assessed and collected "privilege taxes against persons on account of their business and other activities in the State."

Section 237-2, HRS, defines "business" or "engaging in business" to include *all activities* (personal, professional, or corporate) engaged in or caused to be engaged in *with the object of gain or economic benefit either direct or indirect,* but does not include casual sales.

Section 237-3, HRS, defines "gross income" to mean the gross receipts, cash or accrued, of the taxpayer received as compensation for personal services and the gross receipts of the taxpayer derived from trade, business, commerce, or sales and the value proceeding or accruing from the sale of tangible personal property, or service, or both, and all receipts, actual or accrued as hereinafter provided, by reason of the investment of the capital of the business engaged in including interest discount, rentals, royalties, fees, and the like.

In general, all gross income from "engaging in business" or "business income" are subject to the general excise tax. "Business income" means income arising from transactions and activities in the ordinary course of the taxpayer's trade or business and includes income from tangible and intangible property if the acquisition, management, and disposition of the property constitute integral parts of the taxpayer's ordinary trade or business operations.

Similarly, interest income is business income subject to the general excise tax where it arises out of or was derived in the ordinary course of the taxpayer's trade or business or where the purpose for acquiring and holding the intangible is related to or incidental to such trade or business operations.

Business entities, such as corporations, partnerships, joint ventures, sole proprietorships, are generally created for the purpose of making profits, and practically all interest income earned by such business entities are considered business income subject to the general excise tax. It is only when interest income is earned by an individual on his personal savings account, if such individual is not engaged in any trade or business, that the income is considered exempt; the theory being that the individual is not engaged in business when he merely makes deposits in his personal savings account for safekeeping purposes.

Some specific situations with corresponding conclusions are presented below to exemplify the circumstances under which interest may or may not be subject to the general excise tax.

TAXABLE SITUATIONS

*Example 1:* "A," an individual, receives rental income from a 20-unit apartment situated on a fee simple property and upon which income the general excise tax was reported and paid. In 1972, due to his failing health, "A" sold the entire 20-unit apartment on an agreement of sale.

The interest received under the agreement of sale is subject to tax as the interest thus received is deemed to be earned by reason of the investment of the capital of the business in which engaged (rental of the apartments) as provided in Section 237-3.

*Example 2:* "B" operates a soda fountain as a sole proprietor. In addition to this business income, he derives other income from actively trading stocks which are purchased by the use of the funds from his business. The profits from his business, together with the proceeds from the sales of stocks, are deposited in a savings account at a bank. In 1972, "B" remodeled his business premises and dipped into this savings account for the necessary payment. Furthermore, he consistently relies on this savings account as a source of funds to supplement the financial needs of his business.

Since "B" is engaged in business, as defined in Section 237-2, the interest earned on the deposits of the profits from his business is subject to tax by reason of his investing the capital of the business. As to the interest earned on the deposits of the proceeds from the sales of stocks, it too is subject to tax because such proceeds are used in the business.

Notwithstanding the foregoing the general excise tax shall not be imposed on the interest earned on the deposits of the proceeds from the sales of stocks if "B" can prove to the satisfaction of the Director of Taxation that such sales proceeds are clearly segregated from the profits of his business and are deposited in a personal savings account and are not used to supplement the financial needs of his business.

*Example 3:* A group of individuals formed an investment club for the purpose of purchasing common stocks. Initially, each member was required to invest $1,000; thereafter, each member paid in an additional $10 each month. In the interim, the amounts thus pooled were deposited in a savings and loan institution which paid 5 percent interest. As sufficient cash was accumulated, withdrawals were made to purchase the common stocks. Any dividends from the stocks as well as the gross proceeds from the sale of the stocks were also deposited in this savings account. At the end of the year, interest in the amount of $250 was credited to the club's savings account.

As defined in Section 237-2, the club is deemed to be engaged in business since it was formed with "the object of gain or economic benefit either direct or indirect—"; consequently, the interest is subject to the general excise tax.

*Example 4:* "C" Corporation operates a department store. For the convenience of its many charge customers, "C" Corporation has a 30-day charge plan as well as a revolving charge plan. If the amount due on the 30-day charge plan is delinquent, a service charge in the form of interest at the rate of one-half of 1 percent on the previous month's balance is added to the account. A similar procedure is followed with respect to the revolving charge plan.

The interest received from the foregoing source is subject to tax since such interest is earned in the regular course of the business.

*Example 5:* "D" Corporation is engaged in the business of acquiring, holding, and selling real property in Hawaii. During 1972, it sold to purchasers on the mainland fee-simple Hawaii land on agreements of sales in the ordinary course of its business.

The interest earned on the agreements of sale is deemed gross income of the business as defined in Section 237-2 because the sales originate from real property situated in Hawaii. The foregoing principle is applicable notwithstanding the agreements of sale are executed outside of Hawaii and the transactions involve persons who are not residents of Hawaii.

Although Section 237-3 excludes gross income derived from the sale of land in fee, "D" Corporation cannot contend that the interest arising from such agreements of sale is also excludable. The interest arises not from the sale of the land, but rather as a charge for the use of money. "D" Corporation is investing its money (business income), getting back the sum lent plus a return in the form of interest.

*Example 6:* Realty Associates, a registered partnership, was formed solely for the purpose of purchasing certain real property in Hawaii as an investment. No other properties were sold in Hawaii and no improvements were made on said property purchased by this partnership. Subsequently, the real property was sold on installment.

The interest received by the partnership under the installment sale constitutes gross income within the meaning of Section 237-3; it is a return on investment of the partnership's business; therefore, the interest is subject to tax. As was held in the previous example, the interest received on an agreement of sale arises not from the sale but as a charge for the use of the unpaid portion of the sale price.

*Example 7:* XYZ Memorial Park Ltd., a profit cemetery company, is engaged in the business of selling cemetery plots, crypts, and niches. A percentage of the selling price of the cemetery plots, crypts, and niches is set aside for a perpetual care fund, the income from which is applied to the perpetual care and maintenance of the cemetery plots, crypts, and niches. The fund is turned over to XYZ Memorial Park Association, a nonprofit organization composed of purchasers of the cemetery plots, crypts, and niches in the memorial park. XYZ Memorial Park Association invests the perpetual care fund in corporate and governmental bonds receiving interest thereon.

The interest income received by XYZ Memorial Park Association is subject to the general excise tax, notwithstanding the fact that it is a nonprofit organization, on the premise that the perpetual care fund provides an essential part of the function of the cemetery company itself. Where the company actually operating the cemetery is itself a profit-making enterprise, the perpetual care fund operated in connection with it would also partake of this character, and the interest income thus received is subject to tax. Furthermore, as the service and facilities furnished by a perpetual care fund to a cemetery operated for profit constitutes substantial assistance in its business by affecting the salability and selling price of lots, and relieving The company itself of a legal or contractual obligation, net earnings of such funds inure to the benefit of the profit company or its stockholders.

NONTAXABLE SITUATIONS

*Example 1:* "E," an individual, sells his automobile for $1,000. He uses his automobile primarily for commuting to and from work and for other personal purposes. He deposits the proceeds from this sale in his savings account, which is maintained for depositing a part of his monthly salary .

Notwithstanding the fact that "E" has made a sale of property and deposited some or all of the money so received, the interest earned thereon is not subject to tax because he is not deemed to be in "business" or "engaging" in business as provided in Section 237-2.

*Example 2:* "F," an employee of Alpha Corporation, sold his residence situated on Kauai because he was to be relocated to a new job site in Honolulu. He executed an agreement of sale for a term of five years with interest at the rate of 8 percent per annum.

The interest received on the agreement of sale does not constitute "gross income" as defined in Section 237-3, nor does the transaction involve "engaging" in business as provided under Section 237-2. Consequently, the interest received in this situation is not subject to the tax.

*Example 3:* Peter, Paul, and Mary Singers inherited from their father a large parcel of unimproved land situated in Hawaii. The property was held jointly for several years, without producing any income therefrom, after which it was sold on an agreement of sale.

The interest received under the agreement of sale is not subject to tax since the acquisition and subsequent joint ownership of the property were for purposes other than of acquiring, using, holding, and leasing real property for the production of income.

However, if the Singers leased the real property prior to the sale whereby income attributable to the lease was earned, the interest received on the agreement of sale is subject to tax as provided under Section 237-2 on the premise that the Singers were engaged in business.

*Example 4:* "G" Corporation, a local development company qualifying for loans under Section 502 of the Small Business Investment Act of 1958, as amended, applies for and obtains a loan of $100,000 through the Small Business Administration at an interest rate of 5 percent. It lends $25,000 of the funds so obtained through the SBA to Fred Carpenter at the same interest rate of 5 percent. Mr. Carpenter will use the loan for purposes of establishing himself in a retail drug business.

"G" Corporation is exempted from the general excise tax relative to the interest earned on this type of loan as provided in Section 237-23(15), since the interest on its loan to be repaid to the SBA and the interest to be received from Mr. Carpenter are at the same rate; otherwise, the exemption as provided in Section 237-23(15) will not be applicable.

*Example 5:* ABC Lodge (an exempt organization as provided in Section 237-23(a)(5) deposits in a savings account monies it receives from contributions, donations, and dues as well as from the sale of the lodge's real property. Interest in the amount of $1,500 was credited to this savings account at the end of the year. This organization does not receive income other than from the foregoing sources.

The contributions, donations, and dues received by the organization as well as the proceeds from the sale of the property which are deposited in the bank do not constitute "investment of the capital of the business in which engaged." The interest received is deemed incidental to the primary purpose of depositing the monies in the bank—that of safekeeping such funds; consequently, the interest is not subject to tax.

¶ 1423

*Example 6:* ABC Cemetery Park Inc., a nonprofit cemetery company, is engaged in the cemetery business, which qualifies for the general excise tax exemption as provided under Section 237-23(a)(12). Included in the selling price of the cemetery plots, crypts, and niches is an amount for a perpetual care fund, the income from which the company applies to the perpetual care and maintenance of the cemetery plots, crypts, and niches. ABC Cemetery Park Inc. invests the funds in corporate and governmental bonds receiving interest income thereon.

The interest income received by ABC Cemetery Park Inc. is not subject to the general excise tax inasmuch as the overall activity of ABC Cemetery Park Inc. is deemed to be in the establishment and conduct of a cemetery, no part of the net earnings of which inures to the financial benefit of any private stockholder or individual.

In conclusion, the determination as whether interest income is subject to the general excise tax must be based upon an independent review of the facts in each situation. If the interest income is business income as described in this memorandum, such interest income is subject to the general excise tax.

## ¶ 1424. Tax Information Release No. 88-6 Capital Goods Excise Tax Credit

Throughout this Tax Information Release ("TIR"), reference is made to the "Code." Unless otherwise stated, a reference to the Code means the Internal Revenue Code of 1954, as amended, which includes the Internal Revenue Code of 1986 and the Internal Revenue Code of 1986, as amended.

Although certain investment tax credit ("ITC") definitions are adopted, for purposes of the capital goods excise tax credit ("credit"), ITC principles do not dictate the availability of the credit.

I. *CAPITAL GOODS EXCISE TAX CREDIT LAW GENERALLY*

Effective January 1, 1988, there shall be allowed to each taxpayer subject to the tax imposed by Chapter 235, Hawaii Revised Statutes ("HRS"), a credit if:

(1) The taxpayer purchases or imports Section 38 property, new Section 38 property, or used Section 38 property. The terms Section 38 property, new Section 38 property, and used Section 38 property are defined in section V of this TIR. Hereinafter, unless otherwise stated, the terms Section 38 property, new Section 38 property, or used Section 38 property are referred to as eligible property;

(2) The purchase or import of eligible property results in a transaction which is subject to the imposition and payment of tax at the rate of four percent under Chapter 237 or 238, HRS;

(3) The eligible property is used by the taxpayer in a trade or business;

(4) The eligible property is purchased and placed in service within Hawaii after December 31, 1987; and

(5) The taxpayer files a claim for the credit on or before the end of the 12th month following the close of the taxable year for which the credit may be claimed.

The credit is deductible from the taxpayer's net income tax liability for the year in which it qualifies. If the credit exceeds the taxpayer's net income tax liability, the excess of credit over liability shall be refunded to the taxpayer; however, no refund on account of the credit shall be made for an amount less than $1. There shall be no carryback or carryover of excess credit over liability.

A claim for the credit, including an amended claim, must be filed on or before the end of the 12th month following the close of the taxable year for which the credit may be claimed. An extension of time for filing a return does not extend the time for claiming the credit. The claim for the credit shall be made on Form N-312 which is provided by the Department of Taxation of the State of Hawaii ("Department"). Failure to comply with these filing requirements shall constitute a waiver of the right to claim the credit.

II. *PURCHASED AND PLACED IN SERVICE WITHIN HAWAII AFTER DECEMBER 31, 1987*

A. *In General*

The credit may be claimed with respect to eligible property only in the first taxable year in which the property is purchased and placed in service within Hawaii.

The phrase "purchased and placed in service" means the date the property is acquired, available, or ready for use, whichever is earlier.

B. *Purchase*

A purchase means an acquisition of property, provided it is not acquired in a related-party transaction (as defined in Code Section 179(d)(2)(A) or (B)).

C. *Placed In Service*

The term "placed in service" is the earlier of the following taxable years:

(1) The taxable year in which the period for depreciation with respect to the property begins or the taxable year in which under the Accelerated Cost Recovery System ("ACRS") a claim for recovery allowances with respect to the property begins; or

(2) The taxable year in which the property is placed in a condition or state of readiness and available for a specifically assigned function by the taxpayer.

Equipment acquired for a specifically assigned function for the taxpayer and which is operational is considered to be placed in service even though it may be undergoing testing to eliminate defects.

D. *Examples*

Example 1. In 1988, a taxpayer pays the entire purchase price for eligible property which is to be delivered in 1989. The taxpayer takes possession of the property in 1989. The property shall be considered to have been purchased and placed in service in 1988. Assuming that the property is used 100 percent for business purposes and otherwise qualifies for the credit, the entire basis shall be considered in 1988 to determine the amount of credit allowable.

Example 2. In 1988, a taxpayer pays one-half of the entire purchase price for eligible property which is to be delivered in 1989. The taxpayer pays the remaining purchase price and takes possession of the property in 1989. The property shall be considered to have been purchased and placed in service in 1988. Assuming that the property is used 100 percent for business purposes and otherwise qualifies for the credit, the entire basis shall be considered in 1988 to determine the amount of credit allowable.

Example 3. In 1988, a taxpayer takes possession of and uses eligible property for which the taxpayer makes no payment in 1988, but for which the taxpayer will make full payment in 1989. The taxpayer does in fact pay the entire purchase price for the property in 1989. The property shall be considered to have been purchased and placed in service in 1988. Assuming that the property is used 100 percent for business purposes and otherwise qualifies for the credit, the entire basis shall be considered in 1988 to determine the amount of credit allowable.

Example 4. In 1988, a taxpayer enters into an installment sales contract to purchase eligible property and takes possession of the property. The property shall be considered to have been purchased and placed in service in 1988. Assuming that the property is used 100 percent for business purposes and otherwise qualifies for the credit, the entire basis shall be considered in 1988 to determine the amount of credit allowable.

Example 5. In 1988, a taxpayer enters into an installment sales contract to purchase eligible property. The taxpayer takes possession of the property in 1989. The property shall be considered to have been purchased and placed in service in 1988. Assuming that the property is used 100 percent for business purposes and otherwise qualifies for the credit, the entire basis shall be considered in 1988 to determine the amount of credit allowable.

Example 6. In 1987, a taxpayer pays the entire purchase price for eligible property which is to be delivered in 1988. The taxpayer takes possession of the property in 1988. The property shall be considered to have been purchased and placed in service in 1987 and thereby is not eligible for the credit.

Example 7. In 1987, a taxpayer takes possession of and uses eligible property for which the taxpayer makes no payment in 1987, but for which the taxpayer will make full payment in 1988. The taxpayer does in fact pay the entire purchase price for the property in 1988. The property shall be considered to have been purchased and placed in service in 1987 and thereby is not eligible for the credit.

¶ 1424

### E. *Sale-Leaseback*

A special rule applies to determine when property is purchased and placed in service in a sale-leaseback situation. A sale-leaseback situation is a transaction in which Section 38 property is originally purchased and placed in service by a taxpayer, and is sold and leased back by that same taxpayer, or is leased to that same taxpayer, within three months after the date the property was originally purchased and placed in service. In the case of a sale-leaseback, the property shall be considered to be purchased and placed in service on the date the property was first purchased and placed in service by the seller-lessee.

## III. *BASIS*

### A. *In General*

The basis of eligible property means the cost of property. Cost means the lesser of either:

(1) The actual invoice price of eligible property; or

(2) The basis from which a deduction is taken under Code Section 167 (with respect to depreciation) or under Code Section 168 (with respect to ACRS).

### B. *Partners, S Corporation Shareholders, And Beneficiaries Of Estates Or Trusts*

#### 1. *In General*

Each partner of a partnership, shareholder of a S corporation, or beneficiary of an estate or trust shall separately take into account for the partner's, shareholder's, or beneficiary's taxable year with or within which the partnership, S corporation, or the estate or trust's taxable year ends, the partner's, shareholder's, or beneficiary's share of the basis and resulting credit for eligible property. The basis of eligible property is determined at the partnership, S corporation, or estate or trust level. The credit is for eligible property which is purchased and placed in service by the partnership, S corporation, or estate or trust during its respective taxable year. Each partner, shareholder, or beneficiary shall be treated as the taxpayer with respect to the partner's, shareholder's, or beneficiary's share of the basis of partnership, S corporation, or estate or trust eligible property. Partnership, S corporation, or estate or trust eligible property, by reason of each partner's. shareholder's, or beneficiary's taking its respective share of the basis into account, shall not lose its character as eligible property.

#### 2. *Partnership*

Each partner's share of the basis of eligible property shall be determined in accordance with the ratio in which the partners divide the general profits of the partnership. This is the rule regardless of whether the partnership has a profit or loss for the taxable year during which the eligible property is purchased and placed in service; however, if the ratio in which the partners divide the general profits of the partnership changes during the taxable year of the partnership, the ratio which is in effect on the date on which the property is purchased and placed in service shall be applied.

The basis of partnership eligible property which is subject to a special allocation that is recognized under Code Section 704(a) and (b) shall be recognized for purposes of the credit.

#### 3. *S Corporation*

Each shareholder's basis of eligible property is the shareholder's allocated share of the corporation's basis in the eligible property.

#### 4. *Estate Or Trust*

In the case of an estate or trust, the basis of eligible property for any taxable year is apportioned between the estate or trust and the beneficiaries on the basis of the income of the estate or trust allocable to each. If during the taxable year of an estate or trust, a beneficiary's interest in the income of the estate or trust terminates, the basis of the eligible property which is purchased and placed in service by the estate or trust after the termination is not to be apportioned to the beneficiary.

The term "beneficiary" includes an heir, legatee, or devisee.

#### 5. *Examples*

Example 1. Partnership ABCD purchases and places in service on January 1, 1988, and September 1, 1988, items of eligible property. Partnership ABCD and each of its partners report income on the calendar year basis. Partners A, B, C, and D share partnership profits equally. Each partner's share of the basis of each eligible property which was purchased and placed in service by partnership ABCD is 25 percent, and each partner's credit is 25 percent of the total credit allowable for the eligible property.

Example 2. Assume the same facts as in example 1 above, and the following additional facts. Partner A dies on June 30, 1988, and partner B purchases partner A's interest as of that date. Each partner's share of the profits from January 1, to June 30, is 25 percent. From July 1, to December 31, B's share of the profits is 50 percent, and partners C and D's share of the profits is 25 percent each. For partner A's last taxable year (i.e., January 1, to June 30, 1988), partner A's share of the basis and resulting credit for eligible property which was purchased and placed in service on January 1, is 25 percent. Partner B shall take into account 25 percent of the basis and resulting credit for eligible property which was purchased and placed in service on January 1 and 50 percent of the basis of the eligible property which was purchased and placed in service on September 1. Partners C and D shall each take into account 25 percent of the basis and resulting credit for each eligible property which was purchased and placed in service by the partnership in 1988.

### C. *Basis Limitation If A Deduction Is Taken Under Code Section 179*

If a deduction is taken under Code Section 179 (regarding an election to expense certain depreciable business assets), the portion of the basis of property for which the deduction is taken is not considered in determining the amount of credit allowable.

Example 1. A taxpayer purchases Section 179 property (as defined in Code Section 179(d)) for $5,000. The taxpayer elects to treat $2,000 of the cost of the property as an expense which is not chargeable to capital account. In this case, the taxpayer shall only be allowed to compute the credit on a basis of $3,000 ($5,000 less $2,000).

### D. *Basis Limitation For Automobiles*

For purposes of determining the amount of credit available, the basis for passenger automobiles used predominantly (over 50 percent) for business purposes is limited to $11,250. The $11,250 basis limitation figure is derived from Code Section 280F(a)(l) which is adopted by Section 235-110.7(d), HRS ($11,250 multiplied by 6 percent applicable federal rate equals the $675 investment tax credit limitation figure for passenger automobiles). The limit applies to 4-wheeled vehicles rated at 6,000 pounds or less which are manufactured principally for use on public roads. The limit does not apply to an ambulance, hearse, truck, van, or other vehicle used directly in the trade or business of transporting persons or property for compensation or hire .

Example 1. Taxpayer purchases and places in service a $20,000 passenger automobile for business use in calendar year 1989. The maximum credit allowable in this case is $450 ($11,250 multiplied by 4 percent).

This limitation applies prior to any percentage reduction for personal use (as discussed in Section III(E) of this TIR). Thus, if the taxpayer in Example 1 above uses the automobile for personal purposes 25 percent of the time in the year the automobile is purchased and placed in service, the maximum credit is $337.50 ($450 multiplied by 75 percent).

If more than one taxpayer have an interest in a passenger automobile, they are treated as one taxpayer for purposes of the basis limitation. The limitation is to be apportioned among the taxpayers according to their interests in the automobile.

### E. *Basis Limitation For Listed Property Which Does Not Satisfy The More-Than-50 Percent Business Use Test*

Listed property will not be treated as eligible property, and the credit is denied if the property does not satisfy the more-than-50 percent business use test. Listed property is generally defined as passenger automobiles and other property used as a means of transportation; property generally used for purposes of entertainment, recreation, or amusement; computers and related peripheral equipment; and other property as determined by the Department.

The more-than-50 percent business use test requires that certain business use of property (referred to as qualified business use) exceeds 50 percent.

**¶ 1424**

If the business use exceeds the more-than-50 percent business use test, but is not used 100 percent for business, the amount of credit is limited to the percentage of business use.

Example 1. A listed property is used 60 percent for business and otherwise qualifies for the credit. In this case, the taxpayer is allowed to determine the amount of credit available based on only 60 percent of the basis.

For purposes of determining the more-than-50 percent business use test, use in a trade or business does not include use in an investment or other activity conducted for the production of income. However, if the more-than-50 percent business use test has been met, the percentage of investment use may be added in when figuring the total business use for purposes of calculating the amount of credit available.

Example 2. A taxpayer uses listed property in a business in the taxable year in which it is purchased and placed in service. The business use percentage for the listed property is not greater than 50 percent. In this case, since the taxpayer does not satisfy the more-than-50 percent business use test, no credit is allowed for the listed property.

Example 3. A calendar year taxpayer purchases and places in service in 1989, listed property with a cost of $5,000. The property is used 55 percent for qualified business use, 35 percent for investment activities, and 10 percent for personal purposes. In this case, the credit is determined and allowed on 90 percent (55 percent plus 35 percent) of the basis, which is the combined business use. The credit allowable is $180 (90 percent of $5,000 multiplied by the 4 percent applicable credit rate in 1989).

Example 4. The taxpayer purchases and places in service in 1989, listed property that is used 45 percent for qualified business use and 55 percent for investment purposes. In this case, no credit is allowable because the taxpayer does not satisfy the more-than-50 percent business use test .

The amount of credit allowable in the taxable year in which the property is purchased and placed in service is unaffected by any increase in the business use percentage in a subsequent year. However, if there is a reduction in the business use of property, then the credit taken with respect to the property may be subject to recapture.

IV. *AMOUNT OF CREDIT*

A. *In General*

The amount of credit available is determined by applying the following rates against the basis of eligible property:

(1) For calendar years prior to 1988, there is no tax credit;

(2) For calendar year 1988, the rate is 3 percent;

(3) For calendar years beginning after December 31, 1988, the rate is 4 percent; and

(4) For taxpayers with fiscal taxable years, the rate is the rate for the calendar year in which the eligible property is purchased and placed in service within Hawaii.

B. *Limitation On Credit For Eligible Property For Which A Credit For Sales Or Use Taxes Paid To Another State Is Allowable Under Section 238-3(i) HRS*

In the case of eligible property for which a credit for sales or use taxes paid to another state is allowable under Section 238-3(i), HRS, the amount of the capital goods excise tax credit allowable shall not exceed the amount of use tax actually paid under Chapter 238, HRS, with regard to the eligible property.

V. *PROPERTY ELIGIBLE FOR THE CREDIT*

The determination of whether property is eligible for the credit must be made with respect to the first taxable year in which the property is purchased and placed in service by the taxpayer. Generally, property which is eligible for the credit is (A) Section 38 property, (B) new Section 38 property, and (C) used Section 38 property.

A. *Section 38 Property*

Section 38 property is generally defined as:

(1) Property which is (A) tangible personal property, or (B) other tangible property;

(2) Recovery property (within the meaning of Code Section 168, without regard to useful life), or any other property with respect to which depreciation (or amortization in lieu of depreciation) is allowable to the taxpayer; and

(3) Property which has an estimated useful life or recovery period (determined as of the time the property is purchased and placed in service) of three years or more. A property shall have the same estimated useful life or recovery period as that which is used for depreciation or ACRS purposes.

### 1. Tangible Personal Property

Tangible personal property may qualify as Section 38 property:

(1) If the property is not an air conditioning or heating unit;

(2) Regardless of whether it is used as an integral part of manufacturing, production, extraction, or furnishing transportation, communications, electrical energy, gas, water, or sewage disposal services;

(3) Regardless of whether it is a research or storage facility used in connection with any of the activities referred to in paragraph (2) above; and

(4) Regardless of whether it is used in connection with any of the activities referred to in paragraph (2) above for the bulk storage of fungible commodities (including commodities in a liquid or gaseous state).

### 2. Other Tangible Property

In addition to tangible personal property, other tangible property may qualify as Section 38 property if one of the following conditions is met:

(1) The property is used as an integral part of manufacturing, production, extraction, or furnishing transportation, communications, electrical energy, gas, water, or sewage disposal services;

(2) The property is a research or storage facility used in connection with any of the activities referred to in paragraph (1) above; or

(3) The property is a facility used in connection with any of the activities referred to in paragraph (1) above for the bulk storage of fungible commodities (including commodities in a liquid or gaseous state).

### 3. Definitions For Terms Used In Connection With Tangible Personal Property And Other Tangible Property

See the Treasury Regulations in connection with Code Section 48, as amended as of December 31, 1984, for definitions of the following terms: (1) manufacturing, production, and extraction; (2) transportation businesses; (3) communication businesses; (4) integral part of one of the specified activities; (S) research or storage facility; and (6) bulk storage.

### 4. Recovery Property / Depreciable Property

Section 38 property must be either recovery property (within the meaning of Code Section 168, without regard to useful life), or any other property with respect to which depreciation (or amortization in lieu of depreciation) is allowable to the taxpayer.

If only part of a property is depreciable, only a pro rata portion of the property may qualify as Section 38 property.

Example 1. A property is used 90 percent of the time in a trade or business and 10 percent of the time for personal purposes. In this case, only 90 percent of the basis of the property may qualify as Section 38 property which is eligible for the credit.

Property does not qualify as Section 38 property to the extent that a deduction for depreciation thereon is disallowed under Code Section 274 (regarding the disallowance of certain entertainment, etc., expenses).

5. *Property Which Generally Does Not Qualify As Section 38 Property*

Certain classes of property which generally do not qualify as Section 38 property and thereby are not eligible for the credit include:

1. A building or its structural components;
2. Property purchased for use in a foreign trade zone (as defined under Chapter 212, HRS);
3. Property used by an organization which is exempt from the tax imposed by Chapter 235, HRS. Exceptions to this general rule are stated in Code Section 48(a)(4), as amended as of December 31, 1984;
4. Intangible property (e.g., patent, copyright, subscription list); and
5. Property used for lodging.

a. *Building and Structural Components*

In the case of both tangible personal property and other tangible property, a building and its structural components do not qualify as Section 38 property.

(i) *Building*

Generally, a building is any structure or edifice which encloses a space within its walls, and is usually covered by a roof. The purpose of the structure or edifice is, for example, to provide shelter or housing, or to provide working, office, parking, display, or sales space. The term includes, among other structures, apartments, factory and office buildings, warehouses, barns, garages, bus stations, and stores. The term also includes any such structure which is constructed by or for a lessee even if the structure must be removed, or ownership of the structure reverts to the lessor at the termination of the lease.

A building does not include (a) a structure which is essentially an item of machinery or equipment, or (b) a structure which houses property used as an integral part of manufacturing, producing, extracting, or furnishing transportation, communications, electrical energy, gas, water, or sewage disposal services if the use of the structure is so closely related to the use of the property that the structure can be expected to be replaced when the property it initially houses is replaced.

Factors which indicate that a structure is closely related to the use of a particular property it houses include the following: (1) the structure is specifically designed to provide for the stress and other demands of the property; and (2) the structure could not be economically used for other purposes. Examples of such structures include oil and gas storage tanks, feed storage bins, silos, and crop shelters.

(ii) *Structural Component*

Whether property is classified as a structural component is largely determined by the manner of attachment to the land or the structure, and how permanently the property is designed to remain in place.

The following are among the factors which the Department may consider in making this determination:

(1) The manner of affixation (permanent or detachable) of the property to the land;
(2) Whether the property is capable of being moved, and whether it has in fact been moved;
(3) Whether the property is designed or constructed to remain permanently in place;
(4) Circumstances which tend to show the expected or intended length of affixation;
(5) Whether the removal of the property is substantial and time consuming;
(6) Whether the property is readily removable; and
(7) The extent of damage that the property will sustain if it is removed.

A structural component includes parts of a building such as walls, partitions, floors, ceilings, and permanent coverings therefor such as paneling or tiling; windows and doors; all components (whether in, on, or adjacent to the building) of a central air conditioning or heating system, including motors, compressors, pipes, and ducts; plumbing and plumbing fixtures (e.g., sinks and bathtubs); electric wiring and lighting fixtures; chimneys, stairs, escalators, and elevators, including all components relating to the operation or maintenance of a building.

The term structural component does not include machinery, the sole justification for the installation of which is to meet temperature or humidity requirements which are essential for the operation of other machinery or the processing of materials or foodstuffs. Machinery may meet this sole justification test even though it incidentally provides for the comfort of employees, or serves, to an insubstantial degree, areas where the temperature or humidity requirements are not essential.

b. *Property Used For Lodging*

The term "Section 38 property" generally does not include property which is used predominantly (1) to furnish lodging, or (2) in connection with the furnishing of lodging (as defined in the Treasury Regulations regarding Code Section 48(a)(3), as amended as of December 31, 1984).

There are three exceptions to this special rule. First, a nonlodging commercial facility which is available to persons not using the lodging facility on the same basis as it is available to tenants of the lodging facility may qualify as Section 38 property. Examples include restaurants, drug stores, grocery stores, and vending machines located in the lodging facility.

Second, property used by a hotel or motel in connection with the trade or business of furnishing lodging where the predominant portion (i.e., more than one-half) of the accommodation in the hotel, motel, etc. is used by transients may qualify as Section 38 property. An accommodation shall be considered to accommodate transients if the rental period is normally less than 30 days. Thus, if greater than one-half of the living quarters of a hotel, motel, etc., is used during the taxable year to accommodate transients, the property used by the hotel, motel, etc. may qualify as Section 38 property which is eligible for the credit. On the other hand, if one-half or less of the living quarters of a hotel, motel, etc. is used during the taxable year to accommodate transients, the property used by the hotel, motel, etc. would not qualify as Section 38 property.

Third, coin-operated vending machines and coin-operated washing machines and dryers may qualify as Section 38 property.

B. New Section 38 Property

New Section 38 property qualifies for the credit. New Section 38 property is:

(1) Section 38 property, the original use of which commences with the taxpayer; or

(2) Section 38 property which is originally purchased and placed in service by a taxpayer, and is sold and leased back by that same taxpayer, or is leased to that same taxpayer, within three months after the date the property was originally purchased and placed in service.

The term "original use" means the first use to which the property is put, whether or not it is the taxpayer's first use of the property. In a sale-leaseback situation, however, the original use begins not earlier than the date the property is used under the lease.

Example 1. A taxpayer (1) buys property from a manufacturer, (2) purchases and places it in service, and (3) sells and leases the property back within three months of the date that it was originally purchased and placed in service. In this case, the original use begins not earlier than the date the property is used under the lease.

C. *Used Section 38 Property*

Used Section 38 property is:

(1) Section 38 property;

(2) Not new Section 38 property, as defined in Section V(B) of this TIR; and

(3) Property which is not used by the same person (i.e., taxpayer or a related person as defined in Code Section 179(d)(2)(A) or (B)) both before and after the purchase.

1. *Use By Prior User*

Property shall not be treated as used Section 38 property if the property is used by the same person (i.e., taxpayer or a related person) both before and after its purchase.

While used Section 38 property must not be used by the same person both before and after its purchase, only substantial use before a purchase disqualifies used property for purposes of the credit. Casual use before a purchase would not disqualify used property from eligibility for the credit.

Example 1. A person rents equipment (1) for a period of 25 days and for a different 2-day period

**¶ 1424**

within eleven months of the first rental, and (2) then purchases the equipment. In this case, the prior use of the property will not disqualify it as used Section 38 property because the prior use will be considered to have been only on a casual basis.

Property sold under a sale-leaseback arrangement in the hands of the purchaser-lessor does not qualify as used Section 38 property because the seller-lessee continues to use the property. The same result follows where a taxpayer who has been leasing property subsequently purchases the property it had leased.

## ¶ 1425. Tax Information Release No. 88-8 Capital Goods Excise Tax Credit Recapture

This Tax Information Release ("TIR") is limited to the issue of the recapture of the capital goods excise tax credit ("credit"), except where otherwise stated. Refer to TIR No. 88-6 for a discussion of other credit-related issues.

Although Code Section 47, as amended as of December 31, 1984, which is adopted by Section 235-110.7(d), HRS, sets forth different methods for investment tax credit ("TIC") recapture, the method of recapture for purposes of the credit does not track all ITC principles. The Department has used only those ITC principles of recapture that apply due to the fact that the availability of the credit is based on limited ITC grounds. Those ITC principles of recapture used in this TIR were also chosen for ease of administration for both the taxpayer and the Department.

I. *GENERAL DEFINITIONS FOR PURPOSES OF TIR NO. 88-8*

"Code" means the Internal Revenue Code of 1954, as amended, which includes the Internal Revenue Code of 1986 and the Internal Revenue Code of 1986, as amended, unless otherwise stated.

"Eligible property" means Section 38 property, new Section 38 property, or used Section 38 property (as defined in section V of TIR No. 88-6).

"Recapture period" means the period beginning on the first day of the month the eligible property is purchased or placed in service (as defined in section 11 of TIR No. 88-6), whichever is earlier, and extending for a full three years.

II. *RECAPTURE OF CREDIT: CERTAIN DISPOSITIONS ETC. OF ELIGIBLE PROPERTY*

A . *IN GENERAL*

Subject to exceptions which are discussed in Section III of this TIR, the recapture rule applies to recompute previously taken credit if eligible property is disposed of or otherwise ceases to be eligible property within the recapture period. See Section II(C) of this TIR for a discussion of when property ceases to be eligible property.

Pursuant to Section 241-4.5, HRS, the credit as provided under Section 235-110.7, HRS, TIR No. 88-6, and this TIR shall apply to banks and other financial corporations.

B. *RECOMPUTATION*

The credit is recomputed by multiplying the previously taken credit by a recapture percentage, and there should be taken into account any prior recapture determination in connection with the same property.

The following table determines the recapture percentage.

Recapture period: If the recovery property. The recapture percentage is: or depreciable property ceases to be eligible property within:

| | |
|---|---|
| (i)   One full year after purchase and placed in service | 100% |
| (ii)  One full year after the close of the period described in clause (i) | 66% |
| (iii) One full year after the close of the period described in clause (ii) | 33% |
| (iv)  One full year after the close of the period described in clause (iii), and thereafter | -0- |

Example 1. On June 15, 1989, Taxpayer A purchases and places in service eligible property with a basis of $10,000. The asset is used entirely for business purposes. The amount of credit allowable and taken for taxable year 1989 is $400 ($10,000 x 4%). On June 16, 1991, A sells the asset. In taxable year 1991, A must recapture $132 ($400 x 33%) of the previously taken credit.

An increase in income tax due to recapture is limited to the total credit claimed.

A recomputation of the credit shall be made on Part 11 of Form N-312 which is provided by the Department.

In the case of a taxpayer who is involved in a pass-through entity (i.e., partnership, S corporation, estate, or trust) and who claims a credit for the entity's eligible property, the taxpayer shall attach to Form N-312, a copy of the Schedule K-1 and any other statement (relating to the credit) which is provided by the pass-through entity. A copy of the Schedule K-1 and other statement shall be attached to Form N-312 both when the credit is claimed, and when the credit is subject to recapture.

C. *RECAPTURE EVENT (I.E. PROPERTY CEASES TO BE ELIGIBLE PROPERTY)*

1. *In General*

Property ceases to be eligible property with respect to a taxpayer:

(1) As a result of the occurrence of an event on a specific date (e.g., a sale, transfer, retirement, gift, distribution, or other disposition). The cessation shall be treated as having occurred on the actual date of the event); or

(2) For any reason other than the occurrence of an event on a specific date (e.g., the property is used predominantly in connection with the furnishing of lodging during the taxable year and does not fall within one of the exceptions; decrease in business use of listed property). The cessation shall be treated as having occurred on the first day of the taxable year.

2. *Decrease In The Business Use Of Listed Properly To Less Than 50 Percent*

During the recapture period, all or a portion of the credit taken in an earlier year for listed property may be subject to recapture if: (1) the percentage of business use falls below the percentage of business use for the year the listed property was purchased and placed in service; or (2) the listed property is converted from business use to personal use and does not satisfy the more-than-50 percent business use test. The terms "listed property" and "the more-than-50 percent business use test" are defined in section III(E) of TIR No. 88-6.

Example 1. A, a calendar-year taxpayer, purchased and placed in service on January 15, 1988, an automobile for $7,000. In 1988, A uses the automobile 75 percent for business, 15 percent for the production of income, and 10 percent for personal use. For taxable year 1988, A claims a credit in the amount of $189 ($7,000 x 90% x 3%). In 1989, A uses the automobile 60 percent for business, 15 percent for the production of income, and 25 percent for personal use. The increased personal use triggers partial recapture of the credit of $20.79 [[($7.000 x 90% x 3%) – ($7,000 x 75% x 3%)] x 66%]. In 1990, A uses the automobile 50 percent for business, 25 percent for the production of income, and 25 percent for personal use. Although recapture is not required on the basis that the percentage of personal use remained the same in taxable years 1989 and 1990, Code Section 280F, which is adopted by Section 235-110.7(d), HRS, requires recapture because the automobile ceases to be eligible property for failure to satisfy the more-than-50 percent business use test. Accordingly, A must recapture a further $51.98 [[($7.000 x 75% x 3%) - ($7,000 x 0% x 3%)] x 33%].

3. *Decrease In Basis Of Eligible Property*

During the recapture period, all or a portion of previously taken credit may be subject to recapture as a result of a cessation such as a decrease in the basis of eligible property (either through a refund in purchase price or usage of the property for personal purposes).

Example 1. A, a calendar-year taxpayer, purchased and placed in service on January 1, 1988, property, which is not listed property, with a basis of $20,000. In taxable year 1988, A uses the asset 80 percent for business, and 20 percent for personal purposes. Thus, for taxable year 1988, only 80 percent, or $16,000 ($20,000 x 80%) of the basis of the asset qualifies as eligible property. The credit allowable in 1988 is $480 ($16,000 x 3%). In taxable year 1989, A uses the asset 60 percent for business, and 40 percent for personal purposes. The increased personal use triggers partial recapture of the credit in taxable year 1989 of $79.20 [[($20,000 x 80% x 3%) - ($20,000 x 60% x 3%)] x 66%].

4. *Partnership, S Corporation, Estate Or Trust.*

a. *In General*

In the case of a partnership, S corporation, estate, or trust, the recapture rule applies to a partner, shareholder, or beneficiary who originally received the benefit of a credit if within the recapture period: (1) the S corporation, partnership, estate, or trust disposes of eligible property (or if eligible property otherwise ceases to be eligible property in the hands of the entity); or (2) the partner's, shareholder's, or beneficiary's interest in the entity is reduced (for example, by a sale of the partner's, shareholder's, or beneficiary's interest in the entity) below a specified percentage.

The term "specified percentage" means that if a partner's, shareholder's, or beneficiary's interest in the entity is reduced below 66-2/3 percent of its interest at the time the credit was taken, a pro rata share of the partner's, shareholder's, or beneficiary's interest in the entity's eligible property will cease to be eligible property with respect to the partner, shareholder, or beneficiary ("66-2/3 percent rule"), and credit recapture will be required.

Once there has been a recapture by reason of the 66-2/3 percent rule, there is no further recapture until the partner's, shareholder's, or beneficiary's interest is reduced to less than 33-1/3 percent of its interest at the time the credit was taken ("33-1/3 percent rule"). Thereafter, any reduction in interest, however small, will again subject the partner, shareholder, or beneficiary to the recapture provisions.

In making a recapture determination, there should be taken into account any prior recapture determination made with respect to the partner, shareholder, or beneficiary in connection with the same property.

Example 1. *General Facts.* Corporation S, a calendar year S corporation, purchased and placed in service on June 1, 1988, the following three items of eligible property:

| Asset number | Basis |
| --- | --- |
| 1 | $30,000 |
| 2 | $30,000 |
| 3 | $30,000 |

On December 31, 1988, Corporation S had 200 shares of stock outstanding which were owned equally by shareholders A and B, calendar year taxpayers. The total bases of the three eligible properties were apportioned to shareholders A and B as follows:

| | |
| --- | --- |
| Total bases | $90,000 |
| Shareholder A (100/200) | $40,000 |
| Shareholder B ( 100/200) | $40,000 |

In taxable year 1988, each shareholder took a credit of $450 ($15,000 x 3%) for each of the three eligible properties, or a total credit of $1,350 ($15,000 x 3% x 3).

Example 2. Assume the facts as in Example 1 above, and the following fact. On December 21, 1989, Corporation S sells asset No. 3 to Corporation X. For taxable year 1989, shareholders A and B must each recapture $297 ($450 x 66%) of their previously taken credit. Corporation X would not be subject to recapture because it never benefitted from the credit.

Example 3. Assume the facts as in Example 1 above, and the following fact. On November 11, 1990, shareholder A sells 50 of A's 100 shares to C. As a result, 50 percent of A's share of the basis of each of the three eligible properties cease to be eligible properties with respect to A since immediately after the sale, A's proportionate interest in Corporation S is reduced to 50 percent of A's interest at the time the credit was taken. For taxable year 1990, A must recapture $222.75 ($1,350 x 50% x 33%).

Example 4. Assume the facts as in Examples 1 and 3 above, and the following fact. On September 1, 1991, shareholder A disposes of 10 more shares to E, leaving A with 40 of A's original 100 shares. The sale in 1991 does not trigger recapture for A because of the 33-1/3 percent rule—since A was subject to recapture by reason of a reduction in interest below 66-2/3 percent (i.e., 50 percent) in 1990, A experiences no further recapture until A's interest is reduced to less than 33-1/3 percent of A's original interest. The sale in 1991 reduces A's interest to only 40 percent. E would not be subject to recapture.

Example 5. Assume the facts as in Example I above, and the following fact. On November 11, 1990, shareholder A sells 15 of A's 100 shares to D. The sale does not trigger recapture for A because of the 66-2/3 percent rule—A's interest in Corporation S has not been reduced below 66-2/3 percent of A's interest at the time the credit was taken. This result occurs despite the fact that A now owns only 85 percent of A's original stock interest. D would not be subject to recapture.

### b. S Corporation Election

Generally, if a corporation makes a valid election under Section 235-2.4, HRS, to be an S corporation, then on the last day of the taxable year immediately preceding the first taxable year for which the election is effective, any eligible property the basis of which was taken into account to compute the corporation's credit allowable in taxable years prior to the first taxable year for which the election is effective (and which has not been disposed of or otherwise ceased to be eligible property with respect to the corporation prior to such last day) shall be considered as having ceased to be eligible property with respect to the corporation and the recapture rule shall apply. However, the recapture rule shall not apply if the corporation and each of its shareholders on the first day of the first taxable year for which the election under Section 235-2.4, IRS, is to be effective, or on the date of the election, whichever is later, execute an agreement as is described below.

The agreement shall: (1) be signed (a) by the shareholders, and (b) on behalf of the corporation by a person who is duly authorized; (2) state that if eligible property for which the credit was taken is later disposed of by, or ceases to be eligible property with respect to the corporation during the recapture period and during a taxable year of the corporation for which the S election is effective, each signer agrees (a) to notify the director of a disposition or cessation, and (b) to be jointly and severally liable to pay the director an amount equal to the increase in tax provided by the recapture rule; (3) state the name, address, and taxpayer account number (e.g., social security number) of each party to the agreement; (4) be filed with the Department for the taxable year immediately preceding the first taxable year for which the S election is effective; and (5) be filed with the Department on or before the due date (including extensions of time) of the return, unless the director permits, upon a showing of good cause, that the agreement may be filed on a later date.

A shareholder's share of the amount of credit recapture shall be determined as if the property had ceased to be eligible property as of the last day of the taxable year immediately preceding the first taxable year for which the S election is effective; however, the recapture percentage shall be determined as if the property ceased to be eligible property on the date the property actually ceased to be eligible property.

## III. EXCEPTIONS TO THE RECAPTURE RULE

### A . TRANSFER BY REASON OF DEATH

A transfer by reason of death is not considered to be a disposition of eligible property, subject to the recapture rule.

Example 1. A, a calendar-year taxpayer, purchased and placed in service in 1988, eligible property with a basis of $5,000. In taxable year 1988, A takes a credit in the amount of $150 ($5,000 x 3%). A dies in 1989, and the property is transferred to A's heir. In 1989, no credit is required to be recaptured. Further, the heir can immediately dispose of the property without the possibility of credit recapture.

### B.TRANSACTION TO WHICH CODE SECTION 381(a) APPLIES

A disposition of eligible property in a transaction to which Code Section 381(a) (regarding carryovers in certain corporate acquisitions) applies is not considered to be a disposition of eligible property, subject to the recapture rule. However, if the acquiring corporation disposes of the eligible property before the close of the recapture period, there will be an early disposition and the recapture rule will be triggered.

### C. MERE CHANGE IN FORM OF CONDUCTING A TRADE OR BUSINESS

#### 1. In General

Recapture is not required as a result of a mere change in the form of conducting a trade or business

**¶ 1425**

if: (1) the property is retained as eligible property in the same trade or business; (2) the transferor (or in a case where the transferor is a partnership, estate or trust, or S corporation, the partner, beneficiary, or shareholder) of eligible property retains a substantial interest in the trade or business; (3) substantially all the property (whether or not eligible property) necessary to operate the trade or business is transferred in the change of form; and (4) the basis of eligible property in the hands of the transferee is determined in whole or in part by reference to the basis of eligible property in the hands of the transferor (i.e., carryover basis).

This subparagraph shall not apply to the transfer of eligible property if Code Section 381 (regarding carryovers in certain corporate acquisitions) applies to the transfer.

### 2. *Substantial Interest*

For purposes of this exception, a transferor (or in a case where the transferor is a partnership, estate or trust, or S corporation, the partner, beneficiary, or shareholder) is considered to have retained a substantial interest in the trade or business if, after the change in form, the transferor's interest in the trade or business is: (1) substantial in relation to the total interest of all the owners; or (2) equal to or greater than the transferor's interest prior to the change in form.

Example 1. A taxpayer owns a five percent interest in a partnership. After an incorporation of the partnership, the taxpayer retains at least a five percent interest in the corporation. In this case, the taxpayer will be considered to have retained a substantial interest in the business as of the date of the change in form.

A taxpayer will not be considered to have retained a substantial interest where the only basis for claiming substantial interest is that the values of the interests exchanged are equal.

Example 2. A taxpayer exchanges a 48 percent partnership interest for a seven percent interest in a corporation (seven percent of the outstanding stock), contending that the values of the interests exchanged are equal. In this case, the taxpayer will not be considered to have retained a substantial interest.

The determination of whether a taxpayer has retained a substantial interest in the trade or business is to be made immediately after the change in the form of conducting the trade or business, and after each time the taxpayer disposes of a portion of the taxpayer's interest in the new enterprise.

### 3. *S Corporation*

Neither an election to be treated as an S corporation, nor a termination or loss of S corporate status automatically triggers recapture. However, recapture may result if either of the two recapture events discussed in Section II(C)(4) of this TIR occurs. In determining whether a reduction in a shareholder's interest (for example, by a sale of stock) will result in recapture, the 66-2/3 percent and 33-1/3 percent rules (as discussed in Section II(C)(S) of this TIR) apply even if the corporation is no longer an S corporation.

### 4. *Disposition Or Cessation*

Property ceases to be eligible property with respect to a transferor (or in a case where the transferor is a partnership, estate or trust, or S corporation, the partner, beneficiary, or shareholder), and the transferor must make a recapture determination if during the recapture period: (1) eligible property is disposed of by the transferee (or otherwise ceases to be eligible property with respect to the transferee); or (2) the transferor (or in a case where the transferor is a partnership, estate or trust, or S corporation, the partner, beneficiary, or shareholder) does not retain a substantial interest in the trade or business directly or indirectly (through ownership in other entities provided that the other entities' bases in the interests are determined in whole or in part by reference to the basis of the interests in the hands of the transferor).

A taxpayer who seeks to establish the taxpayer's interest in a trade or business under this exception (i.e., mere change in form of conducting a trade or business) must maintain adequate records to demonstrate the taxpayer's direct or indirect interest, or both, in the trade or business after any transfer.

### D. *SALE-LEASEBACK TRANSACTION*

Recapture is not required when eligible property is disposed of and as part of the same transaction, is leased back to the seller within three months after the date the property was originally purchased and placed in service. This result occurs regardless of whether the seller-lessee recognizes a gain or loss, or that the seller-lessee is no longer entitled to take depreciation on the property. If, during the recapture period, the seller-lessee later terminates or assigns the lease, or otherwise disposes of the property, the seller-lessee may be subject to recapture. For recapture purposes, the recapture period will be measured from the earlier of the date the property was purchased or placed in service by the seller-lessee.

The law regarding recapture in a sale-leaseback transaction is directed to the seller-lessee because in a typical sale-leaseback transaction involving the acquisition of eligible property by the buyer-lessor from the seller-lessee, the buyer-lessor is not eligible for the credit. The buyer-lessor is not eligible for the credit because the seller-lessee is treated as the owner of the property for credit purposes.

### E . TRANSFER BETWEEN SPOUSES OR INCIDENT TO DIVORCE

A transfer between spouses or incident to divorce is not considered to be a disposition, subject to the recapture rule. However, a later disposition by the transferee during the recapture period may result in recapture to the same extent as if the disposition had been made by the transferor at that later date.

This rule applies to transfers made after December 31, 1987, in taxable years ending after December 31, 1987. It does not apply to transfers under an instrument in effect before January 1, 1988.

### IV. IDENTIFICATION OF PROPERTY

#### A. IN GENERAL

A taxpayer must maintain records from which the taxpayer can establish, with respect to each item of eligible property, the following facts:

(1) The date the property is disposed of or otherwise ceases to be eligible property;

(2) The estimated useful life or recovery period that was assigned to the property to determine eligibility for the credit;

(3) The month and the taxable year in which the property was purchased or placed in service, whichever is earlier; and

(4) The basis, actually or reasonably determined, of the property.

The above stated facts will be analyzed to determine both the eligibility for the credit, and the necessity for any recapture of credit.

If the taxpayer's records are insufficient to establish the above stated facts, it will generally be assumed that the most recently acquired eligible property was disposed of first.

#### B. MASS ASSETS

Where the maintenance of records of details on mass assets is impractical, the taxpayer may adopt reasonable recordkeeping practices, consonant with good accounting and engineering practices, and consistent with the taxpayer's prior recordkeeping practices.

Mass assets means a mass or group of individual items of property (1) not necessarily homogeneous, (2) each of which is minor in value relative to the total value of the mass or group, (3) numerous in quantity, (4) usually accounted for only on a total dollar or quantity basis, and (5) with respect to which separate identification is impracticable. Examples include portable air and electric tools, jigs, and hardware.

#### C. TAXPAYER USES AN AVERAGING CONVENTION TO COMPUTE DEPRECIATION FOR ELIGIBLE PROPERTY

A taxpayer's use of an averaging convention to compute depreciation for eligible property will be recognized to determine if recapture is required for a particular property. The averaging convention provides for assumed dates that property is purchased and placed in service, or ceases to be eligible property. For example, it might be assumed that all additions and retirements made during the first half of a given year were made on the first day of that year, and that all additions and retirements during the second half of that year were made on the first day of the following year. The taxpayer must consistently use the assumed dates to compute the taxpayer's recapture credit on all eligible property depreciated under the taxpayer's averaging convention. In any event, however, the Director may disregard the taxpayer's use of the averaging convention dates if the use results in a substantial distortion of eligibility for the credit.

## V. *INCREASE IN INCOME TAX*

An increase in income tax under this section shall be treated as income tax imposed on the taxpayer by Chapter 235, HRS, for the recapture year. This is the rule despite the fact that absent the increase, the taxpayer has no income tax liability, has a net operating loss, or no income tax return is otherwise required for the taxable year.

## ¶ 1426. Tax Information Release No. 89-4 The Taxpayer Who Is Entitled To The Capital Goods Excise Tax Credit When The Parties Characterize A Transaction As A Lease Or Sale-Leaseback

This Tax Information Release ("TIR") is limited to the issue of who is entitled to the capital goods excise tax credit ("credit") when the parties characterize a transaction as a lease or sale-leaseback (as defined in Section 1).

Note that the analysis in this TIR should be made only if:

(1) The acquired property is eligible for the credit (i.e., new or used Section 38 property as defined in Section I); and

(2) The transaction is subject to the imposition and payment of tax at the rate of four percent under Chapter 237 or 238, HRS;

### I. *GENERAL DEFINITIONS FOR PURPOSES OF TIR NO. 89-4*

"Acquired" means purchased and placed in service (as defined in TIR No. 88-6) for transactions occurring during calendar year 1988, and placed in service (as defined in TIR No. 88-6) for transactions occurring after December 31, 1988. The terms "purchased and placed in service" and "placed in service" focus on when a claim for the credit may be filed. The timing difference between transactions occurring during calendar year 1988, and transactions occurring after December 31, 1988, is a result of recent legislation (i.e., Act 7, SLH 1989 ("Act 7")).

"Lease" and "sale-leaseback" are defined as they are for federal income tax purposes. The Department adopts the federal income tax characterization of an acquisition. For example, if a transaction is characterized as a lease for federal income tax purposes, the transaction will likewise be characterized as a lease for credit purposes.

"New Section 38 property" is defined as stated in TIR No. 88-6 for property acquired both during calendar year 1988, and after December 31, 1988.

"Property acquired after December 31, 1988" includes fiscal year taxpayer acquisitions occurring after December 31, 1988.

"Property acquired during calendar year 1988" includes fiscal year taxpayer acquisitions occurring during the period beginning January 1, 1988, to December 31, 1988.

"Used Section 38 property" is defined differently for property acquired during calendar year 1988, and for property acquired after December 31, 1988. For property acquired during calendar year 1988, the term "used Section 38 property" is defined as stated in TIR No. 88-6.

In contrast, for property acquired after December 31, 1988, the term "used Section 38 property" requires that the property be:

(1) Section 38 property (as defined in TIR No. 88-6); and

(2) Not new Section 38 property (as defined in TIR No. 88-6).

Note that unlike the case of property acquired during calendar year 1988, property acquired after December 31, 1988, may qualify as used Section 38 property even if the property is used by the same person both before and after the acquisition.

The reason for the change in the definition of the term "used Section 38 property" is Act 7. Act 7, effective for taxable years after December 31, 1988, amends, among other provisions, Section 235-110.7(e), Hawaii Revised Statutes, by deleting the following language:

"Purchased and placed in service" means the date the property was acquired, or available or ready for use, whichever is earlier. *Property purchased and placed in service does not include property which was owned or used at any time during 1987 by the taxpayer or related person, or property acquired in a transaction in which the user of such property does not change.* [Emphasis added.]

As a result of the above stated statutory amendment, the requirement (as stated in TIR No. 88-6) that used Section 38 property not be property which is used by the same person both before and after the acquisition is inapplicable for property acquired after December 31, 1988.

II. *IN GENERAL*

The determination of the taxpayer who is entitled to the credit when the parties characterize a transaction as a lease or sale-leaseback requires an analysis of:

Whether the transaction is, in fact, a lease or sale-leaseback for federal income tax purposes.

The characterization of a transaction as a lease or sale-leaseback determines who is the economic owner ("owner") of the property and thereby entitled to the tax benefits (e.g., credit) associated with the property. Only one party, the owner of the property, is entitled to claim any available credit.

III. *LEASE*

If a transaction is a lease for federal income tax purposes, the lessor, entering into a lease agreement with respect to property which is eligible for the credit (i.e., new or used Section 38 property), is treated as the owner of the property. The lessor may thereby claim any available credit .

IV. *SALE-LEASEBACK*

If a transaction is a sale-leaseback for federal income tax purposes, the buyer/lessor, entering into a sale-leaseback arrangement with respect to property which is eligible for the credit (i.e., new Section 38 property for transactions occurring during calendar year 1988, and new or used Section 38 property for transactions occurring after December 31, 1988) is treated as the owner of the property. The buyer/lessor may thereby claim any available credit.

V. *SALE*

(Note: For purposes of this paragraph, the term "lessee" is used for convenience, without intending to suggest the propriety of the parties' characterization of the transaction as a lease.) If the parties characterize the transaction as a lease, but it is in reality a sale for federal income tax purposes, the lessee is the owner of the property. Assuming that the property is eligible for the credit, the lessee may thereby claim any available credit.

## ¶ 1427. Tax Information Release No. 97-2 RE: Filing Of A Combined Hawaii Income Tax Return By A Unitary Business As Part Of A Unitary Group (Revised)

Tax Information Release (TIR) No. 97-2, issued May 7, 1997 is re-issued to clarify the first sentence in the third paragraph of the original TIR. The sentence reads: "A combined income tax return means a single tax return that is filed to reflect the income of the unitary business, i.e., all entities in the unitary group with sufficient nexus requiring the filing of a return, but does not mean a consolidated tax return." This sentence may be misinterpreted to mean that only unitary corporations with nexus with Hawaii will be included in a Hawaii combined income tax return. This TIR as revised clarifies that if any corporation in the unitary group has sufficient nexus with Hawaii, the combined income tax return must include the income and apportionment factors of all corporations of the unitary group.

The text of the TIR as issued May 7, 1997 follows without revision except in the citation format to the Hawaii Revised Statutes and Hawaii Administrative Rules.

This Tax Information Release (TIR) reiterates the requirement that a corporate taxpayer engaged in a unitary business as part of a unitary group must file a combined Hawaii income tax return. This requirement is effective for tax years beginning after December 31, 1994.

For each taxable year, an income tax return shall be made by every corporate taxpayer having gross income subject to tax under Chapter 235, Hawaii Revised Statutes (HRS). Haw. Rev. Stat.

Section 235-92(2) (1993). A corporate taxpayer that is engaged in a unitary business as part of a unitary group doing business in Hawaii is required to file a combined income tax return for tax years beginning after December 31, 1994. The combined unitary income shall be apportioned to Hawaii based upon factors of property, payroll, and sales. The taxpayer must file Hawaii Form N-30, Corporation Income Tax Return, Form N-30, Schedule O, Allocation and Apportionment of Income, and Form N-30, Schedule P, Apportionment Formula. For further information, refer to sections 235-21 to 235-39, HRS, and sections 18-235-21 to 18-235-38.5, Hawaii Administrative Rules (HAR).

A combined income tax return means a single tax return that is filed to reflect the income of the unitary business, i.e., all entities in the unitary group with sufficient nexus requiring the filing of a return, but does not mean a consolidated tax return. A consolidated Hawaii income tax return only can be filed by a group of corporations in which all affiliated members are corporations organized under the laws of Hawaii. Haw. Rev. Stat. section 235-92(2) (1993).

A unitary business means a business carried on by a group of entities that includes the taxpayer and where there are flows of value among the entities resulting from: (1) functional integration, (2) centralization of management, and (3) economies of scale. Generally, if the operation of a business within Hawaii is integrated with, dependent on, or contributes to the operation of the business outside Hawaii, the entire business is unitary in character. Haw. Admin. Rules section 18-235-22-01 (1994).

A unitary group means a group of entities carrying on a unitary business but does not include: (1) a foreign affiliate of a taxpayer in which no part of the foreign affiliate's business income is subject to federal income tax under the Internal Revenue Code (IRC) of 1986, as amended, whether or not the foreign affiliate is owned or controlled directly or indirectly by the same interests or (2) any entity that is not related to the taxpayer within the meaning of IRC section 267(b) and (c), with respect to the disallowance of deductions for transactions between related taxpayers. Haw. Admin. Rules section 18-235-22-01 (1994).

## ¶ 1428. Tax Information Release No. 98-5 RE: General Excise Tax Exemption for Tangible Personal Property, Including Souvenirs and Gift Items, Shipped out of the State

This Tax Information Release (TIR) provides guidance regarding the application of the general excise tax exemption under Section 237-29.5, Hawaii Revised Statutes (HRS), for tangible personal property shipped outside the State where such property is resold, consumed, or used outside the State; the interplay between Section 237-29.5, HRS, and Section 237-13(2)(C), HRS, which exempts a manufacturer or producer from the general excise tax when the property is sold for delivery outside the State; and an exemption for certain products manufactured, produced, or sold to any person or common carrier in interstate or foreign commerce for consumption outside the State on the shipper's vessels or airplanes.

Tangible personal property includes souvenirs and gift items, such as macadamia nut candies, fruits, t-shirts, liquor, and other sundry items.

The place of delivery of tangible personal property determines whether a sale is subject to the general excise tax. See Haw. Admin. Rules Section 18-237-13-02.01(b)(2) (1998), Att. Gen. Op. Nos. 57-49 and 59-15. The general excise tax, therefore, is applicable to the gross income received from the sale of tangible personal property only where the place of delivery is in the State. Haw. Rev. Stat. Sections 237-29.5 (Supp. 1997), 237-13(2)(C) (1993). The "place of delivery" is defined as "the state or place where the purchaser or the purchaser's agent accepts delivery of the property."

I. *APPLICABLE LAW*

The value or gross proceeds arising from the manufacture, production or sale of tangible personal property (property) which is shipped by the manufacturer, producer, or seller (Taxpayer) to a place outside the State, where such property is resold, consumed, or used outside the State is not subject to the general excise tax. Haw. Rev. Stat. Section 237-29.5(a)(1) (Supp. 1997).

The Taxpayer must obtain from the purchaser either a certificate prescribed by the Department of

Taxation (Department) or alternative documentation which establishes that the Taxpayer has shipped the property to a point outside the State where the property will be resold, consumed, or used outside the State. Haw. Rev. Stat. Section 237-29.5(b) (Supp. 1997). See Part V of this TIR.

## II. *APPLICATION OF THE LAW TO MANUFACTURERS AND PRODUCERS*

Manufacturers and producers engaged in multiple activities, including sales of property that is manufactured or produced, are exempt from the general excise tax on the value or gross proceeds derived from sales of property shipped outside the State where the property is resold, consumed, or used outside the State. Haw. Rev. Stat. Section 237-29.5(a)(1). The principle embodied in Section 237-29.5(a)(1), HRS, is also found in Section 237-13(2)(C), HRS, which exempts from the general excise tax the gross income received from manufacturing or producing products that are sold for delivery outside of the State. Manufacturers and producers, therefore, are exempt from the general excise tax on the gross income derived from both the manufacture and production of property and the sale of property where the place of delivery is outside the State.

A manufacturer is a person engaged in compounding, canning, preserving, packing, printing, publishing, milling, processing, refining, or preparing for sale, profit, or commercial use, either directly or through the activity of others, in whole or in part, any article or articles, substance or substances, commodity or commodities. Haw. Rev. Stat. Section 237-13(1)(A) (1993).

A producer means a person who raises and produces agricultural products in their natural state, a person who produces natural resource products, a person engaged in the business of fishing or aquaculture, for sale, or for shipment or transportation out of the State under certain conditions. Haw. Rev. Stat. Section 237-5 (1993).

## III. *WHEN IS A TAXPAYER NOT LIABLE FOR THE PAYMENT OF THE GENERAL EXCISE TAX?*

The gross income received by a Taxpayer from the sale of tangible personal property is not subject to the general excise tax under Sections 237-13(2)(C) and 237-29.5(a)(1), HRS, if the property is shipped outside the State where the property is resold, consumed, or used outside the State. Stated another way, the general excise tax is not applicable where the place of delivery is outside the State. "Place of delivery" is defined as "the state or place where the purchaser or the purchaser's agent *accepts delivery* of the property." (Emphasis added)

"Accept or Acceptance" is defined as the "purchaser or the purchaser's agent inspecting the property and taking physical possession of the property or having dominion and control over the property."

"Delivery" is defined as "the act of transferring possession of the property, and incudes the transfer of goods from consignor to freight forwarder or for-hire carrier, from freight forwarder to for-hire carrier, one-for-hire carrier to another, or for-hire carrier to consignee."

The responsibility for shipping charges or passage of title does not determine the place of delivery.

*Example 1:* TP manufactures macadamia nut candy. Customers may tour TP's factory and view the candy-making process and purchase candy at the factory's gift shop. TP will ship the candy directly to the customers' out-of-state residences. However, customers are also free to purchase the candy at the factory and arrange for their own shipping of the candy. Customer Z requests that TP send the two dozen boxes of candy Z has purchased to Z's home in Bangor, Maine. Z receives a receipt for payment of the candy and the candy is loaded onto a truck for transport to a freight forwarder. TP is not subject to the general excise tax on the income received from Z (manufacture and sale) under Section 237-13(2)(C), HRS, and Section 237-29.5(a)(1), HRS. The place of delivery is outside the State because Z did not accept delivery of the candy in the State. Z did not accept the candy in the State because Z did not take physical possession of the candy or have dominion and control over the candy. The candy is delivered outside the State to Z's residence in Maine.

*Example 2:* A, a protea farmer in Kula, and D, an anthurium grower in Hilo, take orders for cut flowers to be shipped to mainland florists. Both A and D are not subject to the general excise tax on the income received from the mainland florists (production and sale). The place of delivery is outside the State because the mainland florists did not accept delivery of the flowers in the State. The mainland florists did not accept delivery of the flowers in the State because the florists did not take physical possession of the flowers or have dominion and control over the flowers. The property is delivered outside the State.

*Example 3:* TP grows coffee beans for sale both in the State and outside the State. TP agrees to sell coffee beans to a coffee seller in Washington. TP ships the coffee beans to Washington where the coffee seller's agent accepts delivery of the beans at the Seattle dock.

TP is not subject to the general excise tax on the income received from the coffee bean shipment to the coffee seller (production and sale). The place of delivery is outside the State because the coffee seller did not accept delivery of the coffee beans in the State. The coffee seller did not accept delivery of the coffee beans in the State because neither the coffee seller nor its agent took physical possession of the coffee beans or had dominion or control over the coffee beans in the State. The coffee beans are delivered outside the State to Washington.

*Example 4:* B company advertises the sale of tropical flower arrangements. B company does not actually send the flower arrangements itself but contracts with C company, a grower of tropical flowers, to provide the flower arrangements to out-of-state purchasers. C company will ship the flower arrangements directly to purchasers and charge B company for the deliveries.

B company is not subject to the general excise tax on the income received from these transactions. The place of delivery is outside the State because the purchasers did not accept delivery of the flowers in the State. C company also is exempt from the general excise tax (production and sale). The purchasers did not accept delivery of the flowers in the State because they did not take physical possession of the flowers or have dominion or control over the flowers in the State, despite the fact that both B company and C company are located in Hawaii. The flowers are delivered outside the State as the place of contracting or receipt of purchase price alone is not determinative of the location of the sale. In re Tax Appeal of Heftel Broadcasting, Inc., 57 Haw. 175, 554 P.2d 242 (1976).

IV. *WHEN IS A TAXPAYER LIABLE FOR PAYMENT OF THE GENERAL EXCISE TAX?*

The following examples are situations where the place of delivery is in the State and therefore, do not qualify for the general excise tax exemption for tangible personal property shipped outside the State. The place of delivery is in the State because the purchaser accepts delivery in the State.

*Example 5:* Assume the same facts as Example 1, except that TP sells candy to customer Z at TP's factory and Z takes the candy when Z leaves the factory. TP is subject to the general excise tax on the income received from Z. The place of delivery is in the State because Z accepts delivery of the candy in the State. The candy is delivered to Z in the State. Z accepts the candy in the State by taking physical possession of the candy.

*Example 6:* X, a tourist from Japan, orders a box of macadamia nut candy, a box of pineapple candy, and a package of beef jerky from the souvenir and gift items brochure of X's tour operator. At the airport, on the day of X's departure back to Japan, the tour operator's personnel give X a bag containing X's candies and beef jerky. The tour operator's personnel request that X check the contents of the bag against X's order slip to ensure that all the items are there in the quantity that X ordered, are the correct items, and are not damaged. X is instructed to take the bag to the airline check-in counter with X's luggage to be checked in if the order matches X's order slip. X finds all of the items are in order and checks in the bag of candies and beef jerkey with the rest of X's luggage.

The tour operator is subject to the general excise tax on the value of the candies and beef jerky sold to X. The place of delivery is in the State because X accepts delivery of the candies and beef jerky in the State. The candies and beef jerky are delivered to X at the local airport. X accepted the candies and beef jerky in the State by taking physical possession of the items at the local airport. The baggage check for the bag of candies and beef jerkey is indicative of X's ownership of the candies and beef jerky and authorizes X to make a claim against the airline if the candies and beef jerky are damaged or lost.

V. *EXPORT EXEMPTION CERTIFICATE (FORM G-61)*

To claim the exemption, Section 237-29.5(b), HRS, requires the Taxpayer to take from the purchaser the Department's Export Exemption Certificate (Form G-61), certifying that the purchased property will be shipped to a point outside the State where the property is resold or consumed or used outside the State. The law requires the purchaser to pay to the Taxpayer upon demand the amount of the additional tax imposed upon the Taxpayer if the property purchased is not resold, consumed, or used outside the State. Refer to the <u>attached Form G-61</u> for further information and instructions concerning the completion, execution, and other requirements.

An alternative form or document may be used to provide the information requested in <u>Form G-61</u>.

All records relating to the manufacture, production, and sale of the property, including <u>Form G-61</u> or an alternative form or document shall be kept in the English language and maintained in the State for a minimum of three years. Hawaii Administrative Rules Section 18-231-3-14.25 (1994).

*Example 7:* Assume the same facts as in Example 1 and that Customer Z receives a receipt for payment of the candy which has Z's name and out-of-state address where the candy will be shipped, a description of the candy, and the purchase price or value of the candy. TP is not required to take the Form G-61 from Z under these circumstances.

## VI. *EXEMPTION FOR SALE OF CERTAIN PRODUCTS DELIVERED IN THE STATE*

While Parts I through V of this TIR discuss the general excise tax exemption under Section 237-29.5(a)(1), HRS, that is applicable where the place of delivery is outside the State, this part of the TIR explains the application of Section 237-29.5(a)(2), HRS, which exempts from the general excise tax the value or gross proceeds arising from the manufacture, production or sale of certain products exempt under Section 237-24.3(2), HRS, even if the place of delivery is in the State. Section 237-24.3(2)(A), HRS, exempts manufacturers and producers from the general excise tax on both the manufacture and production <u>and</u> sale of liquor as defined in Chapter 244D, HRS, to any person or common carrier in interstate or foreign commerce for consumption outside the State on the shipper's vessels or airplanes. Section 237-24.3(2)(B), HRS, exempts manufacturers and producers from the general excise tax on both the manufacture and production and sale of cigarettes and tobacco products as defined in Chapter 245, HRS, to any person or common carrier in interstate or foreign commerce for consumption outside the State on the shipper's vessels or airplanes.

The exemption in Section 237-24.3(2)(C), HRS, for sales of agricultural, meat, or fish products grown, raised or caught in the State to any person or common carrier in interstate or foreign commerce for consumption outside the State on the shipper's vessels or airplanes was held to be unconstitutional by the Hawaii Supreme Court in <u>In re Hawaiian Flour Mills, Inc.</u>, 76 Haw. 1 (1994). A bill was introduced during the 1998 legislative session to repeal this exemption but the bill was not passed by the legislature. Notwithstanding the lack of legislative clarification of this issue, the Department will administer Section 237-23.3(2)(C), HRS, without regard to the requirement that the products be grown, raised or caught in the State.

## VII. *SUPERSEDING TIR NO. 88-1*

This TIR supersedes TIR No. 88-1, relating to the general excise tax exemption for sales of tangible personal property shipped out of the State. To the extent not consistent with this TIR, the prior determination letters by the Department which refer to title passage are superseded as of the date of this TIR.

## ¶ 1429. Tax Information Release No. 95-5
### RE: Application of the General Excise ("GE") and Use Taxes on Sales of Tangible Personal Property ("TPP") by an Out-Of-State Seller, Including Drop Shipments

The purpose of this Tax Information Release ("TIR") is to provide guidance as to (1) when a sale of TPP by an out-of-state seller is subject to the GE tax or the use tax, and (2) when a sale of TPP by an out-of-state seller is subject to the GE or the use tax when the TPP is delivered to a buyer by someone other than the seller. This TIR is effective for all tax years that are open under the applicable statute of limitations.

*DEFINITIONS*

The following terms and definitions are applicable with respect to the administration of this TIR.

"Accept or Acceptance" means the purchaser or its agent inspecting the TPP and taking physical possession of the TPP or having dominion and control over the TPP.

"Agent" means a person authorized by the purchaser to act on behalf of the purchaser and includes the power to inspect and accept or reject the TPP.

"Delivery" means the act of transferring possession of TPP. It includes, the transfer of goods from consignor to freight forwarder or for-hire carrier, from freight forwarder to for-hire carrier, one for-hire carrier to another, or for-hire carrier to consignee. "Drop Shipment", sometimes known as direct delivery, means the delivery and acceptance of TPP by a customer in Hawaii from a manufacturer or wholesaler who is someone other than the seller with whom the customer placed the order.

"Landed value" means the value of imported TPP which is the fair and reasonable cash value of the TPP when it arrives in Hawaii. It includes the sale price, shipping and handling fees, insurance costs, and customs duty. It does not include sales tax paid to another state.

"Nexus" means the activity carried on by a seller in Hawaii which is sufficiently connected with the seller's ability to establish or maintain a market for its products in Hawaii. It includes issues of taxability addressed under the Due Process and Commerce Clauses of the United States Constitution to support the application of the GE tax and the use tax under Chapters 237 and 238, Hawaii Revised Statutes ("HRS"), respectively.

"Place of delivery" means the state or place where the purchaser or its agent accepts a delivery of TPP.

*WHEN IS THE GE TAX IMPOSED ON A SALE OF TPP TO A CUSTOMER IN HAWAII?*

Section 237-13, HRS, of our GE Tax Law imposes "privilege taxes against persons on account of their business and other activities in the State". Section 237-2, HRS, states that "business" includes "all activities (personal, professional, or corporate), engaged in or caused to be engaged in with the object of gain or economic benefit either direct or indirect".

The act or place of passing of title is not the determinative factor for purposes of imposing the GE tax. In states imposing a retail sales tax where a sale is defined as the transfer of title or ownership, the place where title passes may be relevant. The GE tax, however, is not a sales tax imposed when title passes. Rather, the GE tax is a gross receipts tax imposed when business is transacted in Hawaii.

Section 237-13(2)(C), HRS, provides that the place of delivery determines whether goods manufactured in Hawaii are exempt from the GE tax on the business of selling such goods. Section 237-21, HRS, provides in part that the delivery of goods outside the State triggers the inquiry of whether there is a need for apportionment of the tax. These provisions evidence that the GE Tax Law looks to the place of delivery of TPP to determine whether the sale of TPP is business transacted in Hawaii.

Hawaii does not impose the GE tax on sales of TPP which originate outside of this State unless the TPP's place of delivery is in Hawaii and the seller has nexus. We emphasize that there must be both (1) a place of delivery within Hawaii by the purchaser, or its agent, and (2) the seller must have nexus for the GE tax to apply to a particular sale. The GE tax will not be imposed if one of these elements is missing.

Delivery of TPP to a freight consolidator, freight forwarder, or for-hire carrier utilized only to arrange for and/or transport the TPP does not constitute acceptance of the TPP by the purchaser or its agent unless the freight consolidator, freight forwarder, or for-hire carrier has expressed written authority to accept the TPP as an agent for the purchaser. Simply signing the bill of lading without this expressed written authority is not sufficient.

When the TPP's place of delivery is to a customer in Hawaii and the seller has nexus, the sale of that TPP constitutes business subject to the GE tax. Hawaii's tax treatment of TPP with a place of delivery to a customer in Hawaii is comparable to the State of Washington's business and occupations tax which is imposed on sales of goods delivered to customers in Washington from out-of-state sellers, and which was upheld in *Standard Pressed Steel Co. v. Department of Revenue*, 419 U.S. 560 (1975).

In *Standard Pressed Steel*, the Court held that Washington's business and occupations tax, as applied to out-of-state sellers of TPP delivered within the State, (a) did not violate due process because the measure of the tax bore a relationship to the benefits conferred on appellant by the state, and (b) was not repugnant to the Commerce Clause, because all of the activities taxed occurred within the state.

Section 237-22, HRS, states that gross income or gross proceeds of sale will be exempt if the State is prohibited from taxing the gross income under federal law or constitutional principles. If an out-of-state seller has no nexus with Hawaii, its gross income or gross proceeds of sale would be exempt under Section 237-22, HRS.

### WHEN IS THE USE TAX IMPOSED ON THE SALE OF TPP TO A CUSTOMER IN HAWAII?

Section 238-2, HRS, imposes use tax "on the use in this State of tangible personal property which is imported... for use in the State" if it is purchased from a seller that does not have a GE tax license. The general theory behind the tax is to make all TPP used or consumed in the State subject to a uniform tax burden irrespective of whether it is acquired within or without the State. *In re Hawaiian Flour Mills, Inc.*, 76 Haw. 1, 13 (1994) (quoting *Halliburton Oil Well Cementing Co. v. Reily*, 373 U.S. 64 (1963)).

The use tax is levied on the importer of TPP based upon the landed value of the TPP imported. The tax rate is one-half of one percent if the TPP is intended for resale at retail, four percent if the TPP is intended for consumption or use by the importer or purchaser, or no tax if the TPP is intended for resale to a reseller licensed under the GE Tax Law.

### WHO IS LIABLE FOR PAYING THE GE OR USE TAX?

The following is an example involving two parties and is treated as a single transaction.

S, an out-of-state seller of TPP, receives an order over the telephone or through the mail, from H, a Hawaii customer who is the ultimate customer. H requests that the TPP be delivered to H in Hawaii. S ships the TPP for delivery to and acceptance by H in Hawaii.

There are two possible outcomes, depending on whether S has nexus with Hawaii:

(1) If S has nexus with Hawaii, S's sale of TPP constitutes business in Hawaii for purposes of the GE Tax Law. As a result, S must obtain a GE/Use tax license. S is considered the importer for resale at retail and is subject to the use tax at one-half of one percent. S is also subject to the GE tax at four percent on the sale.

(2) If S *does not* have nexus with Hawaii, pursuant to Section 237-22, HRS, the GE tax is not imposed upon S. Because S is not a licensed seller and the import is for consumption by H, H is subject to the use tax at four percent.

### WHO IS LIABLE FOR PAYING THE GE OR USE TAX ON A DROP SHIPMENT?

The following is an example involving three parties and is treated as two separate transactions.

S, an out-of-state seller of TPP, receives an order over the telephone or through the mail, from H, a Hawaii customer who is the ultimate consumer. W is an out-of-state wholesaler of TPP. S notifies W of the order and requests that W ship the TPP directly to H in Hawaii. W then ships the TPP for delivery to and acceptance by H in Hawaii.

There are four possible outcomes, depending on whether S and W have nexus with Hawaii and are properly licensed under the GE Tax Law:

(1) If neither S nor W has nexus with Hawaii and both are unlicensed, the importation of the TPP by H is from an unlicensed seller for consumption. H is subject to the use tax at four percent.

(2) If S has nexus with Hawaii and is licensed but W is unlicensed and has no nexus, S is considered to have imported the TPP for resale at retail and is subject to the use tax at one-half of one percent. The sale from S to H is a retail sale. S's gross income from the sale is subject to the GE tax at the rate of four percent.

(3) If both S and W have nexus with Hawaii and are licensed, both sales would be subject to the GE tax. The sale from W to S is a wholesale sale. W's gross income is taxable at one-half of one percent. The sale from S to H is a retail sale. S's gross income is taxable at four percent. There is no use tax because W imported the TPP for resale to a licensed reseller.

¶ 1429

(4) If W has nexus with Hawaii and is licensed but S is unlicensed and has no nexus, the sale from W to S does not qualify as a wholesale sale under Section 237-4(1), HRS, because S is not a licensed seller for GE purposes, therefore, W is subject to the GE tax at the rate of four percent. W is considered to have imported the TPP for resale at retail and is subject to the use tax at one-half of one percent. The GE tax is not imposed on the sale from S to H because S does not have sufficient nexus with Hawaii. Since W is the importer of the TPP and H is not, H would not be subject to the use tax.

*WHAT EFFECT DOES THIS TIR HAVE ON OTHER TIRs ISSUED BY THE DEPARTMENT?*

TIR Nos. 88-1 and 88-2, which refer to title passage, are superseded to the extent that they are inconsistent with this TIR.

## ¶ 1430. Tax Information Release No. 98-8
### RE: Application of Act 247, Session Laws of Hawaii 1998 (Act 247), Relating to the General Excise Tax Exemption for Tangible Personal Property Imported into the State for Resale at Wholesale

Under Act 247, Chapter 237 of the Hawaii Revised Statutes (HRS), relating to the general excise tax, has been amended to provide a general excise tax exemption for the sale of tangible personal property that is imported into the State from a foreign or domestic source to a licensed taxpayer for subsequent resale at wholesale as defined in Section 237-4, HRS. This exemption applies only to the initial sale of imported tangible personal property to a licensed taxpayer for subsequent resale at wholesale, and does not apply to subsequent wholesale sales, if any. Act 247 is effective July 1, 1998, and applies to gross receipts received after June 30, 1998.

### A. *IN GENERAL*

To claim the exemption, the seller must take from the purchaser of imported tangible personal property Form G-17, a Resale Certificate (see attached) certifying that the purchaser shall resell the imported tangible personal property at wholesale as defined under Section 237-4, HRS. If the sale is in fact not a sale for resale at wholesale, the purchaser who furnished the certificate shall be obligated to pay to the seller, upon demand, the amount of the additional tax which is imposed upon the seller. In addition, the absence of a certificate raises the presumption that the sale is not a sale for resale at wholesale, unless the purchaser's business is exclusively sales for resale at wholesale. The Department will allow the seller and purchaser to modify the Resale Certificate as necessary in accordance with their particular business operations, i.e., to accommodate purchasers who resell goods both at retail and wholesale.

Prior to Act 247, the gross proceeds from the sale of imported tangible personal property by a wholesaler to a distributor for resale at wholesale was subject to the 1/2% general excise tax rate. Act 247 reduces the pyramiding of the general excise tax for smaller businesses by exempting the wholesaler from the 1/2% general excise tax on the sale of goods to a distributor for resale at wholesale. Accordingly, in the majority of cases the 1/2% general excise tax is imposed only once on the subsequent sale from the distributor to the retailer. Act 247 allows smaller businesses to compete more effectively with larger businesses which generally can take advantage of economies of scale and structure their distribution system to avoid a transaction from a wholesaler to a distributor, such that the larger businesses are taxed at 1/2% only once on the sale from the distributor to the retailer. Act 247 not only reduces the cost of doing business in Hawaii, but also ultimately reduces costs for Hawaii's consumers.

### B. *APPLICATION OF ACT 247 TO DROP SHIPMENTS*

Act 247 may also apply to drop shipments. A "drop shipment," which is sometimes known as direct delivery, means the delivery and acceptance of tangible personal property by a retailer or customer in Hawaii from a manufacturer or wholesaler who is someone other than the seller with whom the retailer or customer placed the order.

The application of Act 247 to drop shipments is best illustrated by examples. The following is an example of a typical drop shipment arrangement that would be impacted by Act 247: D, an out-of-state distributor receives an order for goods over the telephone from a Hawaii retailer. D places the order for goods with an out-of-state manufacturer, M. M ships the goods directly to the Hawaii retailer. The Hawaii retailer sells the goods to a Hawaii consumer. There are four possible tax outcomes depending upon whether M and D have nexus with Hawaii.

1. If M and D do not have nexus:

    (a) The retailer is considered to have imported the goods for resale at retail and is subject to .5% use tax on the purchase price of the goods (Act 247 does not apply because it is limited to imports for resale at wholesale); and

    (b) The retailer is also subject to the 4% general excise tax on the gross income from the retail sale of goods to the consumer.

2. If M does not have nexus and D has nexus:

    (a) Sale of goods from M to D is not taxable because M does not have nexus;

    (b) D is not subject to the use tax because D is importing goods for resale at wholesale;

    (c) D is subject to .5% general excise tax on the gross income from the wholesale sale of goods to the retailer; and

    (d) Retailer is subject to 4% general excise tax on the gross income from the retail sale of goods to the consumer.

3. If M and D both have nexus:

    (a) Sale of goods from M to D falls within the Act 247 general excise tax exemption;

    (b) D is subject to .5% general excise tax on the gross income from the wholesale sale of goods to the retailer;

    (c) Retailer is subject to 4% general excise tax on the gross income from the retail sale of goods to the consumer; and

    (d) M is not subject to the use tax because M has imported goods for resale at wholesale.

4. If M has nexus and D does not have nexus:

    (a) Sale of goods from M to D does not qualify for the Act 247 general excise tax exemption because M is selling goods to D, an unlicensed taxpayer;

    (b) Sale of goods from M to D does not qualify as a wholesale sale because D is an unlicensed taxpayer, thus, the sale from M to D is treated as a retail sale and the gross income from the retail sale is subject to 4% general excise tax;

    (c) M is subject to use tax at .5% on the purchase price of the goods because M is considered to have imported the goods for resale at retail (sale of goods from M to D treated as a retail sale because D is unlicensed);

    (d) D is not subject to the general excise tax on the gross income from the sale of goods to the retailer because D does not have nexus; and

    (e) Retailer is subject to 4% general excise tax on the gross income from the retail sale of goods to the consumer.

Tax Information Release (TIR) No. 95-5 and Hawaii Administrative Rules (HAR) Section 18-237-13-02.01 provide guidance as to the application of the general excise and use taxes to a three-party drop shipment involving an out-of-state seller, out-of-state wholesaler, and Hawaii customer. Act 247 does not apply to a three-party drop shipment situation because a three-party drop shipment does not involve a sale of goods to a licensed taxpayer for subsequent resale at wholesale. Taxpayers should reference this TIR for guidance as to the application of Act 247 to a four-party drop shipment involving a sale of goods to a licensed taxpayer for subsequent resale at wholesale. The Department intends to amend HAR Section 18-237-13-02.01 to include a discussion of the application of Act 247.

If you have any questions regarding this Tax Information Release, please call Administrative Rules Specialist Iris Kitamura at 808-587-1570. Forms and other tax information may be downloaded from the Department's website at http://www.state.hi.us/tax/tax.html. On Oahu, forms may be ordered by calling the Department's Forms Request Line at 808-587-7572. Persons who are not calling from Oahu may call 1-800-222-7572 to receive forms by mail or 808-678-0522 from a fax machine to receive forms by fax.

## ¶ 1431. Tax Information Release No. 97-1 Determination of Residence Status

This Tax Information Release (TIR) is intended to provide taxpayers with further guidance in determining their residency status, and is based on Section 235-1, Hawaii Revised Statutes (HRS) and Section 18-235-1, Hawaii Administrative Rules (HAR) (1982).

I. *IN GENERAL*

For Hawaii State income tax purposes, a resident is defined as:
1. Every individual domiciled in Hawaii, and
2. Every other individual whether domiciled in Hawaii or not, who resides in Hawaii for other than a temporary or transitory purpose.

A nonresident is defined as every individual other than a resident.

The status of an individual as a resident or nonresident is determined by all of the factual circumstances.

II. *ESTABLISHING RESIDENCE BY DOMICILE*

An individual who is domiciled in Hawaii is considered a resident. Domicile is the place of the individual's true, fixed, permanent home and principal establishment, and to which place the individual has the intention of returning whenever the individual is absent. An individual can have several residences or dwelling places, but an individual can only have one domicile at a time. An individual's domicile may change where there is a concurrence of: (1) an abandonment of the old domicile with a specific intent to abandon the old domicile, (2) an intent to acquire a specific new domicile, and (3) an actual physical presence in the new domicile.

An individual can acquire a domicile by birth, choice, or operation of law.

*A. DOMICILE BY BIRTH*

"Domicile by birth" is acquired by every individual at birth and continues until replaced by the acquisition of another domicile. A child is given the domicile of the child's parents at the time of the child's birth. A domicile by birth, however, may not be the same place where the child is born. If the domicile of the parents is other than where the child is born, the parents' domicile is the domicile of the child.

If a child is born to parents who have different places of domicile, the child's domicile will generally be the same as the domicile of the parent who is able to claim the child as a dependent.

*Example 1:* A, a domiciliary resident of Hawaii, married a domiciliary resident of Oregon. Their first child was born in Hawaii and their second child was born in Texas. A files a separate Hawaii resident income tax return. A is able to claim both children as dependents.

*Conclusion:* Both children are deemed to be domiciliary residents of Hawaii since A, a domiciliary resident of Hawaii, is able to claim both children as dependents.

*B. DOMICILE BY CHOICE*

"Domicile by choice" is a domicile chosen by an individual to replace the individual's former domicile. An individual can acquire a domicile by choice when (1) the individual is no longer eligible to be claimed as a dependent on another person's federal or Hawaii income tax return, and (2) the individual has reached the legal age of majority in Hawaii. The individual may then voluntarily establish the place of the individual's domicile wherever he or she may be. In doing so, however, the individual must meet all the requirements of law for the purpose of establishing a new domicile.

*Example 2:* B was born in Honolulu to domiciliary residents of Hawaii, attended grade school and high school here, then lived on the mainland while attending college for 4 years. During this period, B did not own any property in Hawaii, did not vote in Hawaii, had no bank or savings accounts in Hawaii, and did not belong to any church, social or business groups or associations. Upon B's graduation from college, B decided to make his home in California and B did, in fact, establish permanent domicile there. B bought a home, voted in California elections, became active in community affairs, and joined various school and business clubs. After working for several years in California, B departed for the Trust Territory on a 2-year contract where B is presently working for a mainland contractor.

*Conclusion:* B is deemed to be a domiciliary resident of Hawaii at birth. During the 4-year period that B lived on the mainland while attending college, B remained a resident of Hawaii. A Hawaii domiciliary resident who attends school outside of Hawaii remains a Hawaii domiciliary resident unless the individual establishes a domicile outside of Hawaii. B abandoned B's domicile in Hawaii when a permanent domicile was established in California upon B's graduation from college. B is now deemed to be a nonresident of Hawaii.

*Example 3:* C, a resident of Hawaii, attended college on the mainland. While there, C traveled to a foreign country to perform mission work. Upon returning to the mainland, C completed college. C then returned to Hawaii and got married. C secured employment with an agency of the United States government and moved to Japan to work. In C's applications for employment, transportation agreement, passport, and other formal documents and papers pertaining to employment in Japan, C stated that C's legal residence was in Honolulu, Hawaii. C continued to make deposits in C's bank and savings and loan company in Hawaii. C also opened a bank account in Japan and made some investments through Japan companies. It was not C's intention to make Japan C's permanent and indefinite home. Accordingly, C made no effort to establish a new domicile in Japan nor to abandon the old domicile in Hawaii.

*Conclusion:* C is deemed to be a resident of Hawaii during the period that C attended college on the mainland, traveled to a foreign country to perform mission work, and worked in Japan. A Hawaii domiciliary resident who attends school outside of Hawaii remains a Hawaii domiciliary resident unless the individual establishes domicile outside of Hawaii. It is apparent that C did not establish the foreign country or Japan as a permanent home. C was in the foreign country only for the purpose of performing mission work and is in Japan only for the purpose of employment and has not acquired a new domicile. Nor has C abandoned the domicile in Hawaii. Under the facts presented, the same answer would apply if C was working in Korea, Germany, on the mainland United States, or elsewhere.

*Example 4:* D, a resident of Hawaii, contracts to work for a company in Japan. The contract is a renewable 3-year contract. D is married and D's spouse and children accompany D to Japan. D rents a home and opens bank accounts in Japan. D's children attend local schools in Japan. D does not own any property in Hawaii and has not voted in Hawaii since moving to Japan. At the end of the 3-year contract, D renews D's contract with the company in Japan for another 3 years. At the renewal period, D's applications for employment, transportation agreement, passport, and other formal documents and papers pertaining to employment in Japan stated that D's legal residence was in Honolulu, Hawaii. It was not D's intention to make Japan D's permanent and indefinite home. Accordingly, D made no effort to establish a new domicile in Japan nor to abandon the old domicile in Hawaii.

*Conclusion:* D is deemed to be a resident of Hawaii during the period that D worked in Japan. It is apparent that D did not establish Japan as a permanent home. D is there only for the purpose of employment and has not acquired a new domicile. Nor has D abandoned the domicile in Hawaii. Under the facts presented, the same answer would apply if D was working in Korea, Germany, on the mainland United States, or elsewhere.

### C. DOMICILE BY OPERATION OF LAW

"Domicile by operation of law" is one which is assigned or attributed to an individual by law independently of the individual's residence or intention. In the usual case, domicile by operation of law is applied to those individuals, who, because of certain disabilities, are unable to acquire a domicile by choice. These would include such individuals as minor children and incompetents.

If a child becomes a dependent, for tax purposes, of someone with a different domicile, the child's domicile will generally be the same as the domicile of the individual who is able to claim the child as a dependent.

¶ 1431

*Example 5:* E, a Hawaii domiciliary resident, has one child from an earlier marriage to another Hawaii domiciliary resident. E subsequently marries F, a domiciliary resident of Utah. F provides all of the support for both E and E's child (F's stepchild). F is able to claim the child as a dependent.

*Conclusion:* The child is deemed to be a nonresident of Hawaii since F, a domiciliary resident of Utah, claims the child as a dependent.

The question of domicile is one of law and fact. A change of domicile will depend upon the acts and declarations of the individual concerned in order to ascertain whether or not the individual possessed the required intention which the law says the individual must have to effect a change of domicile. The status of an individual as a resident or nonresident is determined by all the factual circumstances. No single factor, such as an individual's oral declarations of intention or the marriage of a resident and a nonresident, is controlling. Some of the relevant factors include the length of time spent in Hawaii; leasing, buying, negotiating for or building a home; ownership of a motor vehicle; place of issuance of license to drive a motor vehicle; place where the motor vehicle is registered; place of marriage; where the residence of one spouse is in issue, the place of residence of the other spouse; residence of the family of the individual; place of schools attended by the individual's children; the presence of bank accounts; club memberships; place of voting; place of business interests, profession, or employment; contributions to local charities; declarations regarding residence made to public authorities, friends, relatives or employers, or in documents such as deeds, leases, mortgages, contracts, and insurance policies; proposed place of burial or acquisition of burial place for the individual or members of the individual's family; and the place to probate a will. See TIR No. 90-3 which discusses these factors in the context of the income taxation and eligibility for credits of an individual taxpayer whose status changes from resident to nonresident or from nonresident to resident.

III. *ESTABLISHING RESIDENCY BY RESIDING IN HAWAII*

An individual who is not domiciled in Hawaii may acquire the status of a resident by virtue of being physically present in Hawaii for other than temporary or transitory purposes. See Section 235-1, HRS (Definition of "Resident").

Whether or not the purpose for which an individual is in Hawaii will be considered temporary or transitory in character will depend upon the facts and circumstances of each particular case.

If an individual is simply passing through Hawaii to another state or country, or is here for a brief rest or vacation, the individual is in Hawaii for temporary or transitory purposes. Also, if an individual's presence in Hawaii is required for a short period to complete a particular transaction or perform a particular contract, the individual will be deemed to be in Hawaii for a temporary or transitory purpose and will not be deemed a resident.

If, however, an individual is in Hawaii to improve the individual's health and the individual's illness is of such a character as to require a long or indefinite period to recuperate, or the individual is here for business purposes which will require a long or indefinite period to accomplish, or is employed in a position that may last permanently or indefinitely, or has retired from business and moved to Hawaii with no definite intention of leaving shortly thereafter, the individual is in Hawaii for other than a temporary or transitory purpose and will be deemed a resident.

If an individual has been in Hawaii more than 200 days of the taxable year in the aggregate (not consecutive), the individual is presumed to have been a resident of Hawaii from the time of the individual's arrival. The presumption may be overcome if the individual rebuts the presumption with evidence satisfactory to the Department of Taxation that the individual maintains a permanent place of abode outside of Hawaii and is in Hawaii for a temporary or transitory purpose.

*Example 6:* G, a civil engineer, is domiciled in New York where G owns a house in which G's family lives. G votes in New York, maintains a bank account there and returns to his home in New York whenever possible. G is employed by a company as supervising engineer of its projects. In 1995, the company enters into a contract for construction work in Hawaii which will require G to spend 18 months in Hawaii. G comes to Hawaii and spends nearly the whole of 1995 here, living in a rented apartment. G's spouse and family remain in New York except for a summer visit to Hawaii. Upon completion of the project, G will return to New York to await another assignment.

*Conclusion:* Since G has been in Hawaii more than 200 days of the taxable year in the aggregate, G is presumed to have been a resident of Hawaii from the time of G's arrival. G, however, rebuts the presumption under the above circumstances showing that G maintains a permanent place of abode outside Hawaii and is in Hawaii for a temporary or transitory purpose. Accordingly, G is deemed to be a nonresident of Hawaii.

*Example 7:* H, a civil engineer, is domiciled in California. H is employed by a company in California. In 1991, H was transferred to Hawaii with the same company. H did not request the transfer to Hawaii. The transfer was made for the convenience of H's employer and H was required to work indefinitely in Hawaii or lose H's position with the company. H's spouse and children accompanied H to Hawaii. H has always considered California to be H's permanent home and always intended to return to California. No affirmative steps were taken either to abandon the domicile in California or to establish a permanent domicile in Hawaii.

*Conclusion:* H is deemed to be a resident of Hawaii. Although H is domiciled in California, H is in Hawaii for other than a temporary or transitory purpose since H's employment in Hawaii is for an indefinite period.

Since each state's definition of "resident" may be different, it is possible for an individual to be considered a resident of more than one state.

IV. *INDIVIDUAL'S PRESENCE OR ABSENCE IN COMPLIANCE WITH MILITARY OR NAVAL ORDERS, WHILE ENGAGED IN AVIATION OR NAVIGATION, OR WHILE A STUDENT*

An individual's status as a resident or nonresident shall not change solely because of the individual's presence or absence in compliance with military or naval orders of the United States, while engaged in aviation or navigation, or while a student at any institution of learning. See Section 235-1, HRS.

A nonresident individual who is in Hawaii (1) on military duty, (2) while engaged in aviation or navigation, or (3) while attending school is not a Hawaii resident unless the individual establishes domicile in Hawaii. Similarly, a Hawaii domiciliary resident who (1) enters the military and is stationed outside of Hawaii, (2) is outside of Hawaii while engaged in aviation or navigation, or (3) attends school outside of Hawaii remains a Hawaii domiciliary resident unless the individual establishes domicile in the other state or foreign country.

Spouses of nonresident service members, crew members, or students who came to Hawaii will remain nonresidents of Hawaii if their principal reason for moving to Hawaii was to accompany their spouse, and if it is their intention to leave Hawaii when their spouse is transferred, discharged, or, in the case of the student spouse, graduates.

*Example 8:* J is employed by an interstate airline as a crew member. J has no family, J votes in Pennsylvania, where J was born and raised, and which J regards as J's domicile. J lays over in Hawaii between flights and for rest periods, using hotel accommodations. In 1994, J is physically present in Hawaii for more than 200 days during the calendar year.

*Conclusion:* J is deemed to be a nonresident of Hawaii. This example falls under the provision of the statute which provides that a person shall not be deemed to have gained a residence in Hawaii simply because of the presence in Hawaii while engaged in aviation.

*Example 9:* Mr. and Mrs. K are residents of Michigan. Their daughter, L, also is a Michigan resident. L came to Hawaii to attend college and took action to become a permanent resident of Hawaii. L closed her bank account in Michigan and opened a bank account in Hawaii. L also became a member of a local church in Hawaii. Although L works part-time, more than half her support comes from her parents. Her parents are able to claim her as a dependent.

*Conclusion:* L is deemed to be a nonresident of Hawaii. Although L took action to become a permanent resident of Hawaii, her principal reason for being in Hawaii is to attend college. This example falls under the provision of the statute which provides that a person shall not be deemed to have gained a residence in Hawaii simply because of the presence here while attending school. A nonresident individual who is in Hawaii while attending school will not be deemed to be a resident of Hawaii unless the individual establishes domicile in Hawaii. L cannot establish a new domicile in Hawaii since L is still eligible to be claimed as a dependent on L's parents' federal income tax return.

¶ 1431

*Example 10:* M, who was born and educated in Hawaii, enlisted in the military and was stationed outside of Hawaii. M has the intention of returning to Hawaii after discharge from the military. Accordingly, M made no effort to establish a new domicile outside of Hawaii nor to abandon M's old domicile in Hawaii.

*Conclusion:* M is deemed to be a resident of Hawaii regardless of the length of M's absence from Hawaii while stationed at bases outside of Hawaii.

See TIR No. 90-10 for a discussion on the taxation and the eligibility for personal exemptions and credits of residents and nonresidents in the military and spouses and dependents of persons in the military.

## V. *ALIENS*

In the past, the Department of Taxation has treated an alien (an individual who is not a U.S. citizen) as a nonresident of Hawaii if the alien did not have permanent resident alien status (green card) in Hawaii. After consideration of this issue, it is concluded that although an alien who does not have a green card cannot be domiciled in Hawaii, the alien may nevertheless be residenced in Hawaii. The Department, therefore, will consider an alien a resident of Hawaii if the alien (1) has permanent resident alien status (green card), or (2) resides in Hawaii for other than a temporary or transitory purpose. Thus, like all other individuals, the status of an alien as a resident or nonresident for Hawaii income tax purposes is determined by all of the factual circumstances.

Hawaii has not adopted the federal provisions of Internal Revenue Code (IRC) Section 7701(b) (with respect to the definition of resident alien and nonresident alien). In addition, income tax treaties between the United States and a foreign country do not apply to sub-nation states' taxing authority and therefore do not control for Hawaii income tax purposes.

In certain situations, a taxpayer may be considered a nonresident alien for federal income tax purposes and a resident for Hawaii income tax purposes. In these situations, the special rules applicable to individuals who are considered nonresident aliens for federal income tax purposes will apply when the individual files a Hawaii resident income tax return. See TIR No. 92-3 for a discussion of certain income tax issues affecting nonresident aliens.

*Example 11:* N, a Hawaii resident, married O, a citizen of Australia, while both were attending college in Hawaii. Upon their graduation from college, they both found employment in Hawaii. After their marriage, O filed the required documents and became a permanent resident alien.

*Conclusion:* O is deemed to be a resident of Hawaii. O acquired a new domicile in Hawaii when O became a permanent resident alien.

*Example 12:* P is a Japanese national who is domiciled in Japan. In 1995, P came to Hawaii to work. P was admitted by the U.S. Immigration and Naturalization Service as a nonimmigrant alien. P's authorized stay can be extended periodically. During 1995, P was physically present in Hawaii for more than 200 days during the taxable year.

*Conclusion:* P is deemed to be a resident of Hawaii. Although P is a nonimmigrant alien who is domiciled in Japan, P is in Hawaii for other than temporary or transitory purposes.

*Example 13:* Q accepted a tenure track position at the University of Hawaii, and arrived to begin employment on August 1, 1996. Q is in the U.S. on an H visa for now, but Q eventually wants to get tenure at the U.H. and remain in the U.S. as a permanent resident alien.

*Conclusion:* Although Q was not in Hawaii for more than 200 days in 1996, Q is in Hawaii for other than a temporary or transitory purpose. Therefore, Q should file as a part-year resident even though the 200 day test of the presumption of residency is not met.

*Example 14:* Mr. and Mrs. R and their son are citizens of Brazil and are in Hawaii on J visas. Mr. R is a teacher and does not meet the substantial presence test under IRC Section 7701(b)(3) and is, therefore, a nonresident alien for federal income tax purposes. Mr. R files a federal Form 1040NR on which his filing status is required to be married filing a separate return. IRC Section 6013(a)(1) does not allow the filing of a joint return if either spouse was a nonresident alien at any time during the taxable year. Mrs. R also works part-time in Hawaii. Mr. and Mrs. R and their son were in Hawaii for more than 200 days in 1996 and will be filing as Hawaii residents. Can Mr. and Mrs. R file a joint Hawaii resident tax return?

*Conclusion:* Section 235-93, HRS, provides that a husband and wife, having that status for purposes of the IRC and entitled to make a joint federal return for the taxable year, may make a single return jointly of taxes under this chapter for the taxable year. Hawaii has adopted the provisions of IRC Section 6013(a)(1) through Section 18-235-93(a)(2), HAR. IRC Section 6013(a)(1) provides that no joint return shall be made if either the husband or the wife at any time during the taxable year is a nonresident alien. Accordingly, Mr. and Mrs. R cannot file a joint Hawaii tax return Mr. and Mrs. R must each file separate Hawaii resident tax return.

*Example 15:* The facts are the same as stated in Example 14. Can Mr. R claim his son as his dependent on his Hawaii resident tax return?

*Conclusion:* Section 235-54, HRS, provides that the number of personal exemptions an individual may claim is in part determined by ascertaining the number of personal exemptions that the individual may lawfully claim under IRC Section 151. IRC Section 873(b)(3), limits a nonresident alien individual to claim, under IRC Section 151, a single deduction for personal exemption unless the taxpayer is a resident of a contiguous country or a national of the United States. IRC Section 152(b)(3) further states that the term "dependent," for purposes of determining personal exemptions under IRC Section 151, does not include any individual who is not a citizen or national of the United States unless such individual is a resident of the United States of country contiguous to the United States. For federal income tax purposes, Mr. R cannot claim his son as a dependent since his son is not a U.S. citizen, U.S. national, resident alien or resident of a country contiguous to the United States. Accordingly, Mr. R cannot claim his son as a dependent on his Hawaii resident tax return.

*Example 16:* The facts are the same as stated in Example 14. Can Mr. R claim the standard deduction on his Hawaii resident tax return?

*Conclusion:* IRC Section 63(c)(6), which Hawaii adopts through Section 235-2.4(a), HRS, provides that a nonresident alien individual cannot claim the standard deduction. Accordingly, Mr. R cannot claim the standard deduction on his Hawaii resident tax return. Mr. R must itemize any allowable deductions.

*Example 17:* Mr. and Mrs. S are in Hawaii on H visas. Mr. S is a college professor. Mr. S meets the federal substantial presence test but files a federal Form 1040NR to claim the treaty benefits which exclude his wages as a professor from federal taxation for two years. Mr. and Mrs. S were in Hawaii for more than 200 days in 1996 and will be filing as Hawaii residents. Will the treaty also exclude Mr. S's wages from Hawaii taxation?

*Conclusion:* The provisions of income tax treaties are between the United States and the foreign country. Income tax treaties are designed to protect taxpayers from double and discriminating taxation by either treaty country, and normally do not preempt state tax laws. Accordingly, the treaty has no effect on Hawaii Income Tax Law and Mr. S's wages as a professor are subject to Hawaii income tax.

VI. *AMENDMENT PURSUANT TO ACT 187, SLH 1996*

Section 235-55, HRS, allows a resident individual taxpayer to claim a credit for income tax paid to another state or to a foreign country when the taxpayer is taxed by Hawaii on worldwide income and is also subject to income tax in such other jurisdiction. Section 235-93, HRS, provides that a husband and wife who are entitled to file a joint federal return may file a joint Hawaii resident return whether or not both husband and wife are Hawaii resident, however, they will be taxed on worldwide income.

Act 187, SLH 196, amended Section 235-55, HRS, to clarify that the credit for income tax paid to another state or to a foreign country is allowed to a husband and wife filing a joint Hawaii resident return (whether or not both are Hawaii residents) since Section 235-93, HRS, provides that they are taxed by Hawaii on worldwide income. The discussion in TIR Nos. 90-3 and 90-10 relating to the credit under Section 235-55, HRS, not being allowed for the nonresident spouse even if a joint Hawaii resident return is filed is superseded by Act 187, SLH 1996.

## ¶ 1432. TAX INFORMATION RELEASE NO. 2008-03
### RE: Deposits in the Nature of Cash Bond Made to Suspend the Running of Interest on Potential Underpayments

The purpose of this Tax Information Release (TIR) is to provide guidance to taxpayers and practitioners on the Department of Taxation's (Department) procedures allowing deposits in the nature of a cash bond to be made to suspend the running of interest on potential underpayments.

### I. *DEPOSITS ALLOWED TO SUSPEND THE RUNNING OF INTEREST ON UNDERPAYMENTS*

Effective immediately, taxpayers may submit a deposit to the Department that will suspend the running of interest on any potential underpayment later determined due to the State. Under current law, a taxpayer is obligated to pay interest to the State on underpayments at a rate of approximately 8% per year. By submitting a deposit as described in this TIR pursuant to the attached agreement, a taxpayer can effectively suspend the interest on an underpayment.

### II. *PROCEDURES FOR MAKING A DEPOSIT*

Any taxpayer seeking to suspend the running of interest on any matter that could result in a potential underpayment of tax should first contact the Department of Taxation Rules Office in writing, and advise the Rules Officer of the taxpayer's intent to submit a cash bond pursuant to this TIR. Once the Rules Office is notified of the taxpayer's intent to submit a cash bond, a staff attorney will contact the taxpayer and arrange for the drafting of the Cash Bond—Interest Tolling Agreement, as well as other internal procedural matters that must be commenced prior to the deposit being tendered to the Department.

### III. *TERMS*

No cash bond with the effect of suspending the interest on potential underpayments will be accepted by the Department unless it is accompanied by an executed copy of the standard Cash Bond—Interest Tolling Agreement. A sample copy of this agreement is included with this TIR to apprise taxpayers and practitioners of the terms.

#### *Power of Attorney*

Any tax practitioner advising a taxpayer with regard to this TIR should be prepared to submit a Power of Attorney on Form N-848 with the initial notice to the Rules Office.

#### *Disclosures Pursuant to Internal Revenue Code § 6603*

Taxpayers should be prepared to make disclosures to the Department similar to those disclosures required under IRC § 6603 and Rev. Proc. 2005-18, 2005-1 CB 798.

#### *Description of Circumstances Surrounding Deposit*

Taxpayers should be prepared with a narrative describing the circumstances surrounding the cash bond deposit. For example, the Department will be requesting information regarding the tax type, whether the taxpayer is under federal examination, and the tax periods under which the deposit will be made.

#### *Identification of Funds*

All deposits must include a notation on the face of the check and include a phrase substantially similar to: "DEPOSIT IN THE NATURE OF A CASH BOND—TAX YEARS 200X, 200Y, 200Z."

#### *Beginning of Interest Suspension*

Immediately upon receipt of the cash bond deposit, the Department will credit the taxpayer's account by placing the deposit into a trust account in favor of the taxpayer. The Department will use internal Form A-63 to make this deposit. Form A-63 is not available to the public or the taxpayer executing the Cash Bond—Interest Tolling Agreement.

*Not Entitled to Interest*

Taxpayers will not be entitled to earn interest on the deposit while the deposit is under the custody and control of the Department. However, where the deposit is moved into a fund mandated by law or court rule in order to perfect an appeal, taxpayer will be entitled to earn any interest provided by law.

*Return of Deposit on Demand*

Taxpayers will be entitled to demand return of the cash bond. Immediately upon receipt of demand for return of the cash bond, the Department has five (5) days to initiate return of the deposit. The deposit will not be returned where the Department determines the assessment or collection would be in jeopardy.

*Application of the Cash Bond*

Where the taxpayer agrees to the ultimate assessment, the cash bond will be credited to the underpayment. Taxpayers can also direct that any remaining deposit be directed to the payment of any other tax liability.

*Extension of the Statute of Limitations on Assessment*

Lastly, the taxpayer will be required to include a provision extending the statute of limitations on assessment for 12 months following the Department's receipt of notice of the taxpayer's final tax liability determination where the deposit is being made due to a concurrent federal examination. Extensions of the statute of limitations for an audit conducted by the Department will be arranged through existing means, such as ordinary extension agreements.

IV. *RULES OFFICE CONTACT*

The initial notice of intent to submit a cash bond deposit and all subsequent correspondence regarding this TIR should be directed to the following—

Rules Office
C/O CASH BOND DEPOSIT CORRESPONDENCE
Hawaii Department of Taxation
PO Box 259
Honolulu, Hawaii 96809-0259
Phone: (808) 587-1569
Fax: (808) 587-1584

## ¶ 1433. TAX INFORMATION RELEASE NO. 2009-02
### RE: Exemption for Contracting or Services Exported out of State, HRS Section 237-39.53; Imposition of tax on imported services or contracting, HRS section 238-2.3

This Tax Information Release (TIR) provides guidance as to the application of the general excise tax exemption for contracting or services exported out-of-state, and the application of the use tax to contracting or services imported into Hawaii, pursuant to sections 237-29.53 and 238-2.3, Hawaii Revised Statutes (HRS), respectively. This TIR supersedes TIR No. 98-9 and TIR No. 2001-2.

I. *HISTORICAL BACKGROUND*

Section 237-21, HRS, the apportionment statute, requires the following:

If any person . . . is engaged in business both within and without the State . . ., and if under the Constitution or laws of the United States . . . the entire gross income of such person cannot be included in the measure of this tax, there shall be apportioned to the State and included in the measure of the tax that portion of the gross income which is derived from activities within the State, to the extent that the apportionment is required by the Constitution or laws of the United States."

HAW. REV. STAT. § 237-21 (emphasis added). Prior to the enactment of Act 98, 2002 Session Laws of Hawaii ("Act 98"), Chapter 237, HRS, did not expressly provide a credit for sales or use taxes paid to another state for a transaction as an offset against any general excise taxes that may be owing with respect to the same transaction. To comply with the provisions of section 237-21, HRS, and avoid any constitutional concerns caused by the lack of an offset for taxes paid to other states, for purposes of Chapters 237 and 238, HRS, the Department sourced and apportioned gross receipts from (or payments for) transactions based on "place of performance," as explained in TIR Nos. 98-9 and 2001-2 (see below). As stated therein, only that portion of services actually performed in Hawaii was subjected to general excise and use taxes.[1]

Act 98 amended section 237-22, HRS, "Conformity to Constitution, etc.," by providing an offset for taxes paid to other states as follows:

(b) To the extent that any deduction, allocation, or other method to determine tax liability is necessary to comply with subsection (a), each taxpayer liable for the tax imposed by this chapter shall be entitled to full offset for the amount of legally imposed sales, gross receipts, or use taxes paid by the taxpayer with respect to the imported property, service, or contracting to another state and any subdivision thereof; provided that such offset shall not exceed the amount of general excise tax imposed under this chapter upon the gross proceeds of sales or gross income from the sale and subsequent sale of the imported property, service, or contracting. The amount of legally imposed sales, gross receipts, or use taxes paid by the taxpayer with respect to the import shall be first applied against any use tax, as permitted under section 238-3(i), and any remaining amount may be applied under this section for the same imported property, service, or contracting.

The director of taxation shall have the authority to implement this offset by prescribing tax forms and instructions that require tax reporting and payment by deduction, allocation, or any other method to determine tax liability to the extent necessary to comply with the foregoing.

The director of taxation may require the taxpayer to produce the necessary receipts or vouchers indicating the payment of the sales, gross receipts, or use taxes to another state or subdivision as a condition for the allowance of this offset.

HAW. REV. STAT. §237-22(b).

In summary, without a statutory provision allowing a credit or offset for taxes paid to another state, there was a risk that gross receipts would be double taxed unless gross receipts were sourced and apportioned based on "place of performance." Generally, the enactment of section 237-22(b), HRS, eliminated the prerequisite to apportion gross receipts to satisfy constitutional concerns of double taxation. Accordingly, the enactment of the above provision eliminated the need to impose a sourcing and apportionment scheme based on "place of performance" and effectively repealed the "place of performance" test. Further, upon enactment, section 237-22(b), HRS, was retroactive and expressly effective "for all open tax years and for tax years that are pending appeal at the time of approval." See Act 98, 2002 SESSION LAWS OF HAWAII at 291.

II. *SOURCING RULE – "PLACE USED OR CONSUMED"*

In TIR No. 98-9, the Department adopted a "place of performance" test to determine whether the sale of a service was sourced to Hawaii and thus subject to general excise tax. "Place of performance" was "defined as the state or place where services are performed." TIR No. 98-9. "Performance" meant "the discharge, fulfillment, or accomplishment of a promise, contract, or other obligation according to its terms, relieving the taxpayer of all further obligation or liability thereunder." Accordingly, the examples provided in TIR No. 98-9 focused on where the taxpayer-service provider was physically located to determine whether services were provided in the State of Hawaii and subject to general excise

---

[1]  Even before Act 98 was passed, Chapter 238, HRS, which governs use taxes, already allowed a taxpayer a credit for sales or use taxes paid to another state with respect to imported property. In 1999 and 2000, the credit provision contained in Chapter 238, HRS, was expanded to provide an offset for taxes paid to another state for imported services and contracting, respectively, in addition to the credit relating to imported property. See HAW. REV. STAT. 238-3(i). The Department applied the "place of performance" sourcing and apportionment rules to Chapter 238, HRS, despite the offset provision contained in section 238-3(i), HRS, to provide internal and external consistency.

tax. With the enactment of section 237-29.53,[2] HRS, the "place of performance" test as discussed in TIR No. 98-9 became obsolete.[3] See, e.g., TIR No. 98-9 ("The general excise tax applies to the gross income where the place of performance is wholly within the State. It does not matter that the services are performed wholly within the State but consumed outside the State ('exported services')."). The exemption provided by section 237-29.53, HRS, expressly requires that the contracting or service purchased is for "resale, consumption, or use outside the State," effectively superseding the "place of performance" test. HAW. REV. STAT. § 237-29.53.

The "used or consumed" test sources gross receipts to the place "in which the services are intended to be used or consumed." See HAW. ADMIN. RULES §18-237-8.6-03. The sourcing focus, then, shifts from where the taxpayer-service provider is physically located (as under the "place of performance" test) to the place where the customer uses or receives a benefit from the services. The Department's administrative rules regarding the county surcharge imposed by section 237-8.6, HRS, reflects the "used or consumed" test.

With respect to contracting, the purchaser uses or consumes the contracting services in the locale where the real property to which the contracting relates is situated.

In certain circumstances, where services are used or consumed both within and outside of Hawaii (i.e., the purchaser receives substantial and direct benefits traceable and identifiable to business activities both within and outside of Hawaii), only that portion of gross income from services used or consumed in Hawaii is subject to general excise tax, in accordance with section 237-21, HRS. See PROPOSED HAW. ADMIN. RULES §18-237-29.53(e), (f), and (g) Examples 7 and 10; and §18-238-2.3(e), (f) and (g) Example 5 for further guidance on the application of apportionment principles set forth in section 237-21, HRS.

2 Act 70, which enacted sections 237-29.53 and 238-2.3, HRS, was effective for taxable years beginning on or after January 1, 2000. Act 70, 1999 SESSION LAWS OF HAWAII at 106.

3 Given the effective dates of Act 98, which enacted the constitutional credit provisions, and Act 70, it is the Department's position that TIR Nos. 98-9 and 2001-2 were superseded retroactively to taxable years beginning on or after January 1, 2000.

III. *SOURCING RULE FOR PURPOSES OF CHAPTER 238*

Section 238-2.3, HRS, requires a Hawaii importer to pay use tax on imported contracting or services, subject to the exemptions enumerated therein and elsewhere in chapter 238, HRS. Generally, whether the use tax must be paid on imported contracting or services is determined by where the services are used or consumed.

As the "place of performance test" pronounced in TIR No. 98-9 has been superseded, the application of the "used or consumed" test to section 238-2.3, HRS, renders examples provided in TIR No. 2001-2 that relied upon TIR No. 98-9 obsolete. For instance, the following examples that were provided in TIR No. 2001-2 are no longer correct for the reasons cited herein:

*EXAMPLE 4. A Washington based computer software company designs and programs customized software for business clients, one of whom is located in Hawaii. The software company sends employees to Hawaii to audit the Hawaii client's business to determine the needs of the client. The employees then travel back to Washington where they complete the actual programming of the software. The software company is subject to the GET on the services it performs in Hawaii, and*

---

2   Act 70, which enacted sections 237-29.53 and 238-2.3, HRS, was effective for taxable years beginning on or after January 1, 2000. Act 70, 1999 SESSION LAWS OF HAWAII at 106.

3   Given the effective dates of Act 98, which enacted the constitutional credit provisions, and Act 70, it is the Department's position that TIR Nos. 98-9 and 2001-2 were superseded retroactively to taxable years beginning on or after January 1, 2000.

*it may apportion the gross receipts it receives by using a separate accounting method such as the number of hours billed while in Hawaii over the number of total hours billed. The Hawaii client is also allowed to apportion the value of the services for use tax purposes, and pay the use tax at the rate of 4% on the value attributable to services performed outside of Hawaii.*

Applying the "used or consumed" test and the general framework discussed below, assuming the Washington-based computer software company has nexus to Hawaii, the Washington company must pay general excise tax on all of its gross receipts from the Hawaii client for the services provided, and the Hawaii client is not subject to use tax. If the Washington-based computer software company is required to pay a Washington gross receipts tax on the services performed, such company may claim a credit against its Hawaii general excise taxes under section 237-22, HRS. It is improper to apportion gross receipts based on time spent by the company performing services in Hawaii and in Washington as the Hawaii client uses and consumes the customized software program in Hawaii.

*EXAMPLE 7. Assume the same facts as Example 6, except that the Oregon archeologist performs some of its services in Hawaii (e.g., views and inspects the site). Of the 200 hours billed to the job, 60 hours are billed for services performed within Hawaii, and the balance (140 hours) is billed for services performed in Oregon. The local contractor may apportion the value of the services and pay the use tax only upon the value of the services attributable to the services performed in Oregon (140 hours). This amount will be subject to the use tax rate of one-half of one percent (1/2%). The archeologist will be liable for the GET on the services performed in Hawaii (60 hours).*

As in Example 4, assuming the archaeologist has nexus to Hawaii, the archeologist must pay general excise tax on all of his or her gross receipts from the Hawaii contractor for the services provided, and the local contractor is not subject to use tax. The archaeologist's services are used and consumed by the local contractor in Hawaii.

IV. *"CONTRACTING" AND "SERVICE BUSINESS OR CALLING" DEFINED*

Section 237-29.53, HRS, provides a general excise tax exemption for gross income derived from contracting or from a service business or calling that is exported out-of-state. "'Contracting' is defined as the business activities of a contractor." HAW. REV. STAT. § 237-6. A contractor is defined as:

(1) Every person engaging in the business of contracting to erect, construct, repair, or improve buildings or structures, of any kind or description, including any portion thereof, or to make any installation therein, or to make, construct, repair, or improve any highway, road, street, sidewalk, ditch, excavation, fill, bridge, shaft, well, culvert, sewer, water system, drainage system, dredging or harbor improvement project, electric or steam rail, lighting or power system, transmission line, tower, dock, wharf, or other improvements;

(2) Every person engaging in the practice of architecture, professional engineering, land surveying, and landscape architecture, as defined in section 464-1; and

(3) Every person engaged in the practice of pest control or fumigation as a pest control operator as defined in section 460J-1.

HAW. REV. STAT. § 237-6.

"'Service business or calling' includes all activities engaged in for other persons for a consideration which involve the rendering of a service, including professional and transportation services, as distinguished from the sale of tangible property or the production and sale of tangible property." HAW. REV. STAT. § 237-7. It "does not include the services rendered by an employee to the employee's employer." HAW. REV. STAT. § 237-7.

The same taxpayer may be engaged in both contracting and in a service business or calling, depending on the work performed. For instance, an architect or engineer is engaged in contracting when managing a construction project; and is engaged in a service business or calling when performing a feasibility study or other consultation that is unrelated to a specific construction job. See Hawaii Tax Facts 99-3.

## V. *CREDIT FOR TAXES PAID TO ANOTHER STATE OR SUBDIVISION THEREOF*

Sections 237-22(b) and 238-3(i),[4] HRS, provide a credit for sales, gross receipts, or use taxes paid to another state with respect to the same transaction that is being subjected to Hawaii's general excise or use tax.[5] The credit cannot exceed the tax amounts previously paid upon the transaction to the other state or subdivision thereof, nor may it exceed the applicable rate of the Hawaii general excise or use tax. Therefore, the maximum credit that may be claimed is the lesser of the sales/use tax paid to the other state or the general excise or use tax due to the Department with respect to the same transaction. The Department of Taxation requires proof of payment of the tax, such as a sales invoice showing the taxes paid.[6]

The following examples illustrate the application of the credit against general excise and use taxes:

*Example 1*: Taxpayer, a New Mexico-based consulting company, is hired by a Hawaii retailer for a contract price of $1,000. Taxpayer performs its services in New Mexico, which imposes a gross receipts tax at the rate of 5% upon consulting services. Taxpayer's accounting records substantiate the 5% gross receipts tax paid to New Mexico for its contract with the Hawaii retailer. Taxpayer regularly travels to Hawaii to meet with and provide support to its Hawaii customers, including the Hawaii retailer, establishing nexus to Hawaii. Taxpayer is subject to Hawaii's general excise tax at the rate of 4%.[7] Because the credit is limited to the general excise tax imposed by Hawaii, the credit is equal to $40 (or 4% of the value of the services), rather than the $50 that Taxpayer actually paid for New Mexico taxes.[8] Although Taxpayer's net Hawaii general excise tax liability with respect to the transaction with the Hawaii retailer is zero as a result of the credit, Taxpayer must still file a general excise tax return and claim the credit on such return.

*Example 2*: Assume the same facts as in Example 1, except that Taxpayer is subject to a gross receipts tax at the rate of 3% (or $30), as evidenced by Taxpayer's accounting records. Because the credit is limited to the gross receipts tax imposed by New Mexico, the credit is equal to $30 (or 3% of the value of services) and Taxpayer is liable for $10 in Hawaii general excise taxes ($40 Hawaii general excise tax less $30 credit for New Mexico gross receipts tax).

*Example 3*: Assume the same facts as in Example 1, except that Taxpayer is hired to produce printed brochures and New Mexico imposes a manufacturing tax (which is not comparable to a sales tax) at the rate of 3% on the transaction. Taxpayer paid the tax as evidenced by Taxpayer's accounting records.

---

4   Section 238-3(i), HRS, provides as follows:
    (i) Each taxpayer liable for the tax imposed by this chapter on tangible personal property, services, or contracting shall be entitled to full credit for the combined amount or amounts of legally imposed sales or use taxes paid by the taxpayer with respect to the same transaction and property, services, or contracting to another state and any subdivision thereof, but such credit shall not exceed the amount of the use tax imposed under this chapter on account of the transaction and property, services, or contracting. The director of taxation may require the taxpayer to produce the necessary receipts or vouchers indicating the payment of the sales or use tax to another state or subdivision as a condition for the allowance of the credit.

    HAW. REV. STAT. §238-3(i).

5   A tax paid for manufacturing, extraction, or other taxes that are not sales or use taxes may not be used as a credit against the Hawaii general excise or use tax.

6   The required documents proving that taxes were paid to another state should be maintained and furnished upon the Department's request.

7   The Oahu county surcharge of .5% will apply, where applicable. See HAW. REV. STAT. § 237-8.6 and HAW.

    ADMIN. RULES §§ 18-237-8.6-01, et seq.

8   If the Oahu county surcharge tax is applicable, the credit is $45 (or 4.5% of the value of the services).

¶ 1433

Taxpayer is subject to general excise tax at the rate of 4% upon the value of the printing and provision of the brochures ($40). Taxpayer is not allowed to claim a credit for the manufacturing taxes it has paid to New Mexico because a manufacturing tax is not a sales, gross receipts, or use tax.

*Example 4*: Taxpayer, a Hawaii business, engages a marketing consultant for a contract price of $1,000. The consultant performs its services in New Mexico, which imposes a gross receipts tax at the rate of 5% upon consulting services. The consultant's sales invoice shows the sales price of the services and the 5% tax upon the services rendered ($1,000 plus $50). Assuming the consultant has no nexus to Hawaii, the Taxpayer is subject to the 4% use tax upon the value of the imported services, but may claim a credit for the New Mexico taxes paid with respect to that transaction. Because the credit is limited to the use tax imposed upon the importation of the services, the credit is equal to $40 (or 4% of the value of the services), rather than the $50 that Taxpayer actually paid for New Mexico taxes.

*Example 5*: Assume the same facts as in Example 4, except that the consultant is subject to a gross receipts tax at the rate of 3% (or $30), which Taxpayer paid as evidenced by a sales invoice. Assuming the consultant has no nexus to Hawaii, the Taxpayer is subject to the use tax at the rate of 4% upon the value of the imported services, but may claim a credit for the New Mexico taxes paid with respect to that transaction (i.e., $30). Taxpayer is liable for $10 ($40 Hawaii use tax less $30 credit for New Mexico gross receipts tax) in Hawaii use taxes.

*Example 6*: Assume the same facts as in Example 4, except that the consultant is hired to produce printed brochures and is subject to a manufacturing tax (which is not comparable to a sales tax) at the rate of 3%. Taxpayer paid the tax as evidenced by a sales invoice. Taxpayer is subject to the use tax at the rate of 4% upon the value of the printed brochures ($40), which it has imported for its own consumption. Taxpayer is not allowed to claim a credit for the manufacturing taxes it has paid because a manufacturing tax is not a sales, gross receipts, or use tax.

## VI. *FRAMEWORK FOR PROPOSED ADMINISTRATIVE RULES*

The following analysis should be used to determine whether the exported services exemption applies or whether the use tax on imported services must be paid:

1) Are the contracting or services "used or consumed" in Hawaii?

a. If "YES," the transaction is subject to either the general excise tax or the use tax. Go to (2).

b. If "NO," the transaction is not subject to either the general excise tax or the use tax.[9]

c. If "BOTH" (i.e., services used or consumed both within and outside of Hawaii), then, under certain circumstances as described above, that portion of the gross receipts from the transaction for which the contracting or services are "used or consumed" in Hawaii is subject to either the general excise tax or the use tax. See HAW. REV. STAT. § 237-21. Go to (2).

(2) Does the contractor or service provider have nexus to Hawaii?

a. If "YES," then the contractor or service provider must pay general excise tax on its gross receipts with respect to contracting and services used or consumed in Hawaii, unless a specific exemption applies (e.g., section 23726, HRS, "Exemption of certain scientific contracts with the United States").

b. If "NO," then the Hawaii importer must pay use tax with respect to contracting and services imported into Hawaii, unless a specific exemption applies (e.g., exemption for contracting services imported by a contractor provided in section 238-1, HRS, paragraph (10) of definition of "use").

See Exhibit A for a diagram illustrating the above analysis.

---

9  As required by section 237-29.53, HRS, the seller claiming the GET exemption for exported contracting or services must obtain an "Export Exemption Certificate," Form G-61 (or an equivalent certification), from its customer.

EXHIBIT "A"

DIAGRAM OF EXPORTED/IMPORTED CONTRACTING AND SERVICES
GENERAL EXCISE AND USE TAX ANALYSIS

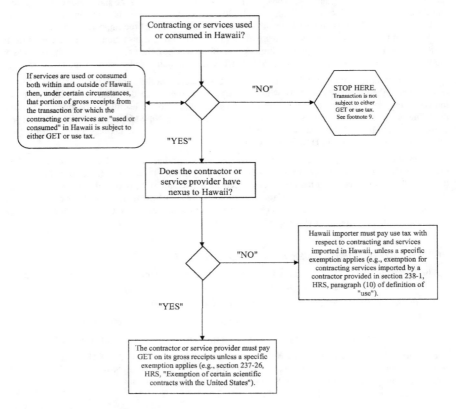

## VII. *NOTICE OF PROPOSED RULES*

Effective immediately, the Department will be pursuing the promulgation of administrative rules that provide additions and amendments to Chapter 237 (general excise tax law) and Chapter 238 (use tax law), HRS, as herein described.

In order to ensure optimal compliance with the revenue laws, as well as to provide guidance to the tax community, the Department is issuing this TIR, which is comprised in substantial part of the proposed administrative rules the Department will be promulgating, upon which taxpayers may rely as discussed herein.

## VIII. *INVITATION FOR PUBLIC COMMENT*

The Department invites the public to comment on the proposed rules accompanying this TIR by August 1, 2009.

¶ 1433

Public comments may be sent to the following address:

> Jodene K. Arakaki
> Administrative Rules Specialist
> Rules Office
> Department of Taxation
> P.O. Box 259
> Honolulu, Hawaii 96813
> Telephone: (808) 587-1481
> Fax: (808) 587-1584
> Email: Jodene.K.Arakaki@hawaii.gov

## IX. *ADMINISTRATIVE POSITION OF THE DEPARTMENT; RELIANCE*

This TIR and the accompanying proposed administrative rules serve as the Department's position on the administration of sections 237-29.53 and 238-2.3, HRS. Taxpayers may rely upon this TIR and the accompanying proposed administrative rules to the extent taxpayers are authorized to rely upon TIRs generally as the Department's administrative interpretation. The Department will be enforcing its position as described in this TIR and the accompanying proposed administrative rules accordingly.

## X. *EFFECTIVE DATE*

TIR Nos. 98-9 and 2001-2 are retroactively revoked and this TIR is retroactively effective pursuant to the enactment of Act 98, Session Laws of Hawaii. The accompanying proposed administrative rules are effective immediately. The portion of this TIR comprised of the proposed administrative rules will be obsolete upon the formal adoption of such rules.

> Kurt Kawafuchi
> Director of Taxation

HRS Sections Explained: 237-29.53 and 238-2.3.
TIR Nos. 98-9 and 2001-2 are superseded.

*PROPOSED ADMINISTRATIVE RULE APPLYING HRS §238-29.53*

§18-238-29.53 Exemption for Contracting or Services Exported Out-of-state

§18-237-29.53 Exemption for contracting or services exported out of state (a) Gross receipts from contracting (as defined under section 237-6, Hawaii Revised Statutes (HRS)) or services performed by a person engaged in a service business or calling in the State is exempt from general excise tax if the contracting or services are intended to be used or consumed outside of the State.

(b) Contracting or services are intended to be used or consumed outside of the State if the purchaser ultimately uses or receives the primary benefit of the acquired contracting or services outside of the State.

(c) The purchaser ultimately uses or receives the primary benefit of the acquired contracting outside of the State if the real property to which the contracting activity relates is situated outside of the State.

(d) The following factors will be considered in determining whether the purchaser ultimately uses or receives the primary benefit of the acquired services outside of the State:

(1) Whether the purchaser's residence (if the purchaser is an individual) or commercial domicile (if the purchaser is a business entity) is located outside of the State. As defined by section 23521, HRS, a purchaser's commercial domicile is the principal place from which the trade or business of the taxpayer is directed or managed.

(2) Whether the services were acquired primarily for the benefit of the purchaser's overall business activities or specific business activities (if the purchaser conducts business activities in more than one state), and to what extent, if any, a purchaser's Hawaii business activities directly and substantially

¶ 1433

benefit from the services provided.

No single factor is determinative and all facts and circumstances will be considered in determining whether the purchaser ultimately uses or receives the primary benefit of the acquired services outside of the State.

(e) If the purchaser is engaged in business activities in the State and outside of the State and the services are provided for the benefit of the purchaser's out-of-state business activities, any insubstantial, indirect benefit received by a purchaser's Hawaii business activities will be disregarded in applying this exemption, pursuant to section 237-21, HRS. Conversely, gross receipts from services will be subject to general excise tax based upon the direct and substantial benefit realized by a purchaser's Hawaii business activities from the services provided.

(1) Any reasonable method of apportioning gross receipts based on direct and substantial benefits realized by a purchaser's Hawaii activities may be used, provided that such method is supported by verifiable data that reasonably quantifies the proportionate benefit realized by a purchaser's Hawaii activities.

(2) All facts and circumstances will be considered in determining whether the Hawaii activities of a multi-state business directly and substantially benefits from the services provided, including, but not limited to, the nature and purpose of the service provided in relation to Hawaii business activities and whether the service provided represents overhead for the purchaser's commercial domicile.

(f) If a purchaser receives multiple substantial and direct benefits that are traceable and identifiable to business activities both within and outside of the State, gross receipts from the services provided will be subject to general excise tax in proportion to the direct and substantial benefit realized by the purchaser in Hawaii from the services provided.

(g) Application of the principles cited in this section is illustrated by the following examples:

*Example 1:* TP, a Hawaii attorney, is hired by Emma Entrepreneur, a Colorado resident who owns stock and partnership interests in various enterprises, as well as Hawaii real estate, to prepare her estate plan. TP and Emma have meetings at TP's offices in Hawaii and correspond via the email and over the phone to discuss Emma's estate plan. The legal fees that TP receives from Emma are exempt from general excise tax pursuant to section 237-29.53, HRS, as the services are used or consumed in Colorado, Emma's domicile.

*Example 2:* TP, a Hawaii attorney, is hired by Personal Representative to file and oversee an ancillary probate of Emma Entrepreneur's Hawaii estate (for additional real property purchased after Emma's estate plan was prepared, and for which title was taken individually and not in trust). Emma was domiciled in Colorado at her date of death. Personal Representative never travels to Hawaii with respect to the affairs of Emma's estate. All communications with Personal Representative are conducted via the phone or through mail. The legal fees that TP receives from Personal Representative are subject to general excise tax, and are not exempt from general excise tax pursuant to section 237-29.53, HRS, as the services are used or consumed in Hawaii, by the Hawaii ancillary probate.

*Example 3:* TP, a Hawaii market researcher, is hired by CHO Enterprises, a hotelier whose commercial domicile is in Nevada and who currently operates a Hawaii resort, to investigate expanding its resort operations in Hawaii. TP prepares a report and presents its finding to representatives of CHO Enterprises at CHO Enterprises' Nevada office. CHO Enterprises' existing Hawaii resort is expected to substantially benefit from the planned expansion. All of the fees that TP receives from CHO Enterprises are subject to general excise tax, and are not exempt from general excise tax pursuant to section 237-29.53, HRS, as the services are used or consumed in Hawaii.

*Example 4:* TP, a Hawaii employee benefits consultant, is hired by the corporate headquarters of a Washington-based retailer, KSB Inc., to draft an employee handbook to be used by all of its corporate offices and retail stores, including a retail store located in Hawaii. The Hawaii retail store is a small percentage of KSB Inc.'s total number of retail stores and represents a small percentage of KSB Inc.'s overall revenues and profits. All of the fees that TP receives from KSB Inc. are exempt from general excise tax pursuant to section 237-29.53, HRS, because the Hawaii retail store indirectly and insubstantially benefits from the employee handbook.

¶ 1433

*Example 5:* TP, a Hawaii real property management company, is hired by ACD Corporation, a Hawaii corporation, to manage a California property owned by ACD Corporation. All of the management fees that TP receives from ACD Corporation are exempt from general excise tax pursuant to section 237-29.53, HRS, because the management services are used and consumed in California, where the real property is situated.

*Example 6:* Hawaii Hotels Inc. ("HHI"), a Hawaii corporation that owns a hotel located on Oahu, hires Management Company ("MgmtCo"), a New York-based hotel management company, to manage and operate its Oahu hotel. As provided by the Agreement, HHI's hotel is operated under MgmtCo's brand name, 5 Star Resorts. Hotel personnel remain the employees of HHI, but represent to the public that they are employees of "5 Star Resorts On Waikiki Beach." MgmtCo reviews hotel operations, and provides on-going advice (in the areas of, e.g., human resources, marketing, grounds maintenance) on operating and maintaining a luxury hotel. HHI pays MgmtCo a fee for its services. MgmtCo infrequently visits Hawaii and provides advice to HHI from its corporate offices in New York. MgmtCo does not maintain an office in Hawaii; however, it has nexus with Hawaii through its agents and management contracts with HHI and other Hawaii-based hotels. All of the management fees received by MgmtCo from HHI are subject to general excise tax as the services are used and consumed on Oahu.

*Example 7:* TP, Hawaii-based software programmer, is hired by MSP, INC., a medical service provider that has activities in several states, including Hawaii, to write a customized and integrated patient file and billing program for use at all of its medical offices, including the office located in Hawaii, for a fee of $70,000. MSP's commercial domicile is located in California. TP installs the customized software at 7 of MSP's medical offices, of which 2 are located in Hawaii. There is no significant difference in the time or resources spent by TP on the installation at each location. MSP's Hawaii medical offices directly and substantially benefit from the creation and installation of the customized software. TP apportions 2/7 of its gross receipts received from MSP to Hawaii. The method of apportionment is reasonable. TP must report the full fee received from MSP, or $70,000, in column (a) of Form G-45 and claim a $50,000 deduction pursuant to section 237-29.53, HRS, for that portion of the fee apportioned out-of-state (or 5/7 of $70,000).

*Example 8:* GSA Contractor, a general contractor that is a Hawaii corporation, is hired to perform general contracting services for a construction project located in Guam. Developer, the owner of the project, is a Hawaii corporation. Employees of GSA Contractor meet with Developer at Developer's Hawaii office on a weekly basis throughout the project's construction period to discuss project plans, progress, and other matters related to the project. All of the contracting revenues that GSA Contractor receives from Developer are exempt from general excise tax pursuant to section 237-29.53, HRS, because the contracting services are used or consumed in Guam, where the construction project is situated.

*Example 9:* ABC Insurance Co., a mainland corporation ("InsCo"), issues long-term disability insurance policies to individuals in Hawaii, as well as in other states. Its management company, XYZ Management Co., a mainland corporation ("MgmtCo"), services the policies, assisting policyholders in completing applications, filing claims, etc. InsCo's principal office is located in California. MgmtCo, whose principal office is located in California, has a Hawaii office staffed by employees who reside in Hawaii. MgmtCo's Hawaii office performs the initial work in reviewing applications and investigates claims before sending the documents to MgmtCo's principal office for final processing. InsCo pays MgmtCo a management fee for the services performed on InsCo's behalf. MgmtCo has nexus with Hawaii. The services performed by MgmtCo (in Hawaii and on the mainland) with respect to Hawaii policyholders are used or consumed in Hawaii as InsCo's Hawaii business activities receive the primary benefit of MgmtCo's services. Thus, MgmtCo must pay general excise tax on 100% of the management fees it receives from InsCo with respect to servicing and managing policies held by Hawaii residents.

*Example 10:* Same facts as Example 9. MgmtCo also maintains a Colorado office to service InsCo's long-term disability insurance policies for Colorado residents. MgmtCo receives a lump sum monthly fee of $50,000 from InsCo for the services it provides to both Hawaii and Colorado residents. MgmtCo allocates the fees received from InsCo to Hawaii based upon the number of insurance policies held by Hawaii residents (1,000, figured annually) in proportion to the total number of insurance policies held by Hawaii and Colorado residents (collectively, 1,500). The method of apportionment is reasonable. MgmtCo must report 2/3 (1,000/1,500) of the monthly fee or $33,333 in column (a) of Form G-45. It should not report the gross monthly fee of $50,000 and a deduction of 1/3 of the monthly fee (for the portion attributable to Colorado) on Form G-45.

*PROPOSED ADMINISTRATIVE RULE APPLYING HRS §238-2.3*

§18-238-2.3 Imposition of Tax on Imported Services or Contracting; Exemptions

§18-238-2.3 Imposition of tax on imported services or contracting; exemptions (a) The excise tax enumerated in section 238-2.3, HRS, is applied to the value of services or contracting as defined in section 237-6, Hawaii Revised Statutes (HRS), that are performed by an unlicensed seller at a point outside the State and imported or purchased for use or consumption in this State.

(b) Imported services or contracting are used or consumed in this State if the importer or purchaser ultimately uses or receives the primary benefit of the acquired contracting or services in the State.

(c) The importer or purchaser ultimately uses or receives the primary benefit of the acquired contracting in the State if the real property to which the contracting activity relates is situated in the State.

(d) The following factors will be considered in determining whether the purchaser ultimately uses or receives the primary benefit of the acquired services in the State:

(1) Whether the purchaser's residence (if the purchaser is an individual) or commercial domicile (if the purchaser is a business entity) is located in the State. As defined by §235-21, Hawaii Revised Statutes, a purchaser's commercial domicile is the principal place from which the trade or business of the taxpayer is directed or managed.

(2) Whether the services were acquired primarily for the benefit of the purchaser's overall business activities or specific business activities (if the purchaser conducts business activities in more than one state), and to what extent, if any, a purchaser's non-Hawaii business activities directly and substantially benefit from the services provided. No single factor is determinative and all facts and circumstances will be considered in determining whether the purchaser ultimately uses or receives the primary benefit of the acquired services in the State.

(e) If the purchaser is engaged in business activities in the State and outside of the State and the services are provided for the benefit of the purchaser's out-of-state business activities, any insubstantial, indirect benefit received by a purchaser's Hawaii business activities will be disregarded in applying this tax. Conversely, a purchaser will be subject to use tax based upon the direct and substantial benefit realized by a purchaser's Hawaii business activities from the services provided.

(1) Any reasonable method of apportioning the value of the services based on direct and substantial benefits realized by a purchaser's Hawaii activities may be used, provided that such method is supported by verifiable data that reasonably quantifies the proportionate benefit realized by a purchaser's Hawaii activities.

(2) All facts and circumstances will be considered in determining whether the Hawaii activities of a multi-state business directly and substantially benefits from the services provided, including, but not limited to, the nature and purpose of the service provided in relation to Hawaii business activities and whether the service provided represents overhead for the purchaser's commercial domicile.

(f) If a purchaser receives multiple substantial and direct benefits that are traceable and identifiable to business activities both within and outside of the State of Hawaii, the value of services acquired will be subject to use tax in proportion to the direct and substantial benefit realized by a purchaser in Hawaii from the services provided.

(g) Application of the principles cited in this section is illustrated by the following examples, all of which assume the out-of-state service provider does not have nexus with Hawaii:

*Example 1:* TP, a Hawaii bank, contracts with a California-based storage and data back-up service to back-up and secure its data files. The California service provider performs its services via the internet. TP must pay the use tax on the value of the services provided because it receives the primary benefit of the back-up services at its office in Hawaii.

*Example 2:* TP, a Hawaii retailer with stores in Hawaii and California, retains a California employee benefits consultant to draft an employee handbook to be used by its corporate headquarters (located in Hawaii) and all of its retail stores. TP must pay use tax on all of the value of the services rendered by the California employee benefits consultant because it receives the primary benefit of the employee handbook at its corporate headquarters, which oversees personnel matters.

*Example 3:* TP, a Hawaii corporation with no out-ofstate operations, hires a New York broker to manage its investment portfolio. TP pays investment advisory fees to the New York broker. TP must pay use tax on the value of the investment advisory services as it receives the primary benefit of the investment advice in Hawaii, where TP controls the brokerage account from its Hawaii office.

*Example 4:* TP, a Hawaii contractor, hires a California architect to design a building for a construction project located in Hawaii. The design services provided by the California architect are used or consumed in Hawaii. However, section 238-1(10), HRS, excludes from the definition of "use," contracting imported or purchased by a contractor, as defined in section 237-6, HRS, who is (1) licensed under chapter 237, HRS, (2) engaged in business as a contractor, and (3) otherwise subject to the tax imposed under section 238-2.3, HRS. Accordingly, TP does not have to pay use tax on the imported contracting services provided by the California architect. However, TP may not claim a subcontractor deduction, pursuant to section 237-13(3), HRS, for payments to the California architect. Thus, if TP receives $100,000 from the Owner of which TP pays $10,000 to the California architect for the design services, TP must pay general excise tax on $100,000 and is not entitled to a subcontract deduction of $10,000.

*Example 5:* TP, a medical service provider that is commercially domiciled in Hawaii and has activities in Hawaii and California, hires a software programmer commercially domiciled in Washington to write a customized and integrated patient file and billing program for use at all of its medical offices, including the office located in Hawaii, for a fee of $70,000. The customized software is used at 7 of TP's medical offices, of which 2 are located in Hawaii. There is no significant difference in the time or resources spent by the software programmer to install the program at each office via the internet. TP's Hawaii medical offices directly and substantially benefit from the creation and installation of the customized software. TP apportions 2/7 of the cost of the customized software to Hawaii and pays use tax only on such portion. Although TP's overall operations benefit from the customized software, the direct and substantial benefit is realized by each medical office. The method of apportionment is reasonable. TP must report and pay use tax on $20,000 (or 2/7 of $70,000) with respect to the services used and consumed in Hawaii.

*Example 6:* TP, Delaware corporation that is a nationwide retailer, hires a New York attorney to draft leases for its retail spaces in Hawaii and California. TP pays the New York attorney $20,000 in legal fees with respect to the Hawaii leases. TP must report and pay use tax on $20,000 with respect to the legal services used and consumed in Hawaii.

Refer to HAR § 18-237-29.53 and the examples contained in subsection (g) for application of the general excise tax to out-of-state businesses that import services into Hawaii and establish nexus with Hawaii.

## ¶ 1434. TAX INFORMATION RELEASE NO. 2010-05
### RE: Act 155, Session Laws of Hawaii 2010, Relating to General Excise Tax; The General Excise Tax Protection Act

On June 1, 2010, Governor Linda Lingle signed into law House Bill 2595 HD 1 SD 2 CD 1, which became law as Act 155, Session Laws of Hawaii 2010 (also referred to as the "GET Protection Act").

Act 155 amends Chapter 237, Hawaii Revised Statutes (HRS), by adding two new sections. The first new section statutorily denies certain general excise tax benefits to taxpayers that fail to comply with administrative procedures. The second new section creates trust fund liability, or personal liability, for certain amounts where a responsible person willfully fails to pay over those amounts to the government.

The purpose of this Tax Information Release is to provide guidance on the Department's interpretation of Act 155, in addition to providing examples and safe harbors for certain of its provisions.

*DENIAL OF GENERAL EXCISE TAX BENEFITS*

Section 2 of Act 155 creates a new obligation for all persons doing business in Hawaii with gross income or gross receipts as defined by HRS § 237-3, to comply with two administrative requirements. Failure to comply with the administrative requirements will result in the taxpayer's loss of any benefit available under the general excise tax law, including exemption from the law.

A. Administrative Requirements

In order to maintain entitlement to any general excise tax benefit, the person claiming the benefit must:

1) File for and obtain a general excise tax license, available on Form BB-1, State of Hawaii Basic Business Application; and

2) File an annual general excise tax reconciliation tax return on Form G-49, Annual Return & Reconciliation of General Excise/Use Tax Return, within 12 months from the due date for the return.

Taxpayers with gross income or gross receipts who are engaging in business within the meaning of Chapter 237, HRS, were always required to comply with both of these requirements. See HRS §§ 237-9, 237-33.

The GET Protection Act simply requires taxpayers to obtain a general excise tax license and file the annual reconciliation return. Failure to claim the general excise tax benefit on the annual return will not automatically preclude the taxpayer from claiming the general excise tax benefit on an amended return filed within the statute of limitations for assessment or refund, or from receiving the general excise tax benefit by adjustment upon audit.

B. General Excise Tax Benefits

A general excise tax benefit that could be jeopardized for failure to comply with the statutory administrative requirements of the GET Protection Act includes any of the following:

1) Exemption amount, including exemption from application of Chapter 237;

2) Exempt taxpayer or entity, including exemption from application of Chapter 237;

3) Any exclusion, including the exclusion for exporting tangible personal property, contracting, or services;

4) Reduction from the measure of general excise tax;

5) Deduction, including the subcontractor's deduction;

6) Tax credit, including an offsetting credit for taxes paid to another state;

7) Lower rate of tax, including the 0.15% rate for insurance producers or the 0.5% rate for certain manufacturing or wholesaling; or

8) Segregation or splitting of a gross income or gross receipts, including commission splitting or segregation involving agency relationships, reimbursements, or tourism activities.

Please note that the foregoing list is not exhaustive.

C. Reasonable Cause; Safe Harbor Protection

The GET Protection Act authorizes the Director of Taxation to waive the denial of general excise tax benefits in certain situations where the failure to obtain a general excise tax license or file an annual reconciliation return is due to reasonable cause and not willful neglect.

The following circumstances are deemed to have reasonable cause within the meaning of Act 155 and the Department will not utilize Act 155 to deny a general excise tax benefit in the following situations:

1) The provisions of the United States Constitution or laws of the United States prohibit the Department from imposing the tax;

2) The person is not "engaging" in "business" within the meaning of HRS § 237-2;

**¶ 1434**

3) The amounts involved are not "gross income" or "gross proceeds of sale" as defined in HRS § 237-3(b);

4) The person is a Public Service Company and the gross income or gross proceeds are included in the measure of the tax imposed by Chapter 239, HRS;

5) Amounts received by persons exempt under HRS § 237-23(a)(3) through (6); provided that such person is exempt from filing federal Form 990, Return of Organization Exempt from Income Tax, or Form 990-EZ, Short Form—Return of Organization Exempt from Income Tax;

6) Amounts received that are exempt under HRS §§ 237-24(1) through (7) (with respect to certain insurance proceeds, gifts, bequests, compensatory tort damages, salaries or wages, and alimony);

7) Amounts received that are exempt under HRS § 237-24.8(a) (with respect to certain amounts not taxable for financial institutions);

8) Amounts received that are exempt under HRS § 237-29.7 (with respect to certain amounts not taxable for insurance companies);

9) Credit unions chartered under Chapter 412, HRS, and exempt from tax as provided in HRS § 412:10-122;

10) Any other amounts, persons, or transactions as determined by the Director to be made by subsequent Announcement or Tax Information Release.

The safe harbors set forth above are illustrated by the following examples:

*EXAMPLE 1*—ABC Corp. is headquartered and conducts primarily all of its business outside Hawaii. ABC Corp.'s business activity is the wholesaling of tangible personal property for resale at retail. ABC Corp. sells a small amount of tangible personal property in Hawaii and takes the position that it has no nexus with Hawaii. ABC Corp. therefore has not obtained a general excise tax license nor filed any general excise tax annual returns. The Department opens an audit of ABC Corp.'s nexus to determine whether ABC Corp. should have been filing Hawaii general excise tax returns. The Department determines that, because ABC Corp. was found to have a sales agent in Hawaii, ABC Corp. is responsible for the Hawaii general excise tax and should have obtained a general excise tax license and further should have filed general excise tax returns. ABC Corp. appeals the Department's assessment, exhausting its appeals. Ultimately, it is determined that ABC Corp. has nexus with Hawaii for general excise tax purposes. Under Act 155, ABC Corp. will lose its general excise tax benefit of the lower 0.5% wholesale rate because it failed to obtain a general excise tax license and file a general excise tax annual return. ABC Corp. is not entitled to the safe harbor protection because Hawaii was not without the authority to assert the general excise tax against ABC Corp. based upon the United States Constitution's Commerce Clause. See Safe Harbor 1, above. [ABC Corp. would have maintained its general excise tax benefit (i.e., the lower 0.5% general excise tax rate for wholesaling, assuming ABC Corp. does in fact qualify for the lower 0.5% rate) if, prior to being audited, ABC Corp. would have obtained a general excise tax license and filed an annual general excise tax return claiming it had no nexus with Hawaii, even if the position was ultimately found to be in error.]

*EXAMPLE 2*—Assume the same facts as in Example 1, except that ABC Corp. is successful upon final appeal and is found not to have nexus with Hawaii and that Hawaii is without the power to tax ABC Corp. under the Commerce Clause. ABC Corp. falls within the safe harbor protection because Hawaii is without the power under the US Constitution to tax ABC Corp. See Safe Harbor 1, above.

*EXAMPLE 3*—Larry Landowner sold land that he owned in fee simple. Amounts received from the sale of land in fee simple are not considered "gross income" under the general excise tax. Larry Landowner will not lose his exemption from the sale of land in fee simple if he does not obtain a general excise tax license or file an annual general excise tax return because amounts received from the sale of land in fee simple is within the safe harbor protection for amounts not considered "gross income" under HRS § 237-3(b). See Safe Harbor 3, above.

*EXAMPLE 4*—John Doe is a salaried employee for Bonanza Corp. Salary and wages are exempt from general excise tax. John Doe will not lose his exemption for his salary if he does not obtain a general excise tax license or file an annual general excise tax return because employees who receive salary or wages are within the safe harbor protection for amounts received under HRS § 237-24(6).

See Safe Harbor 6, above.

*EXAMPLE 5*—XYZ Organization, a nonprofit organization that provides social services to the low-income, holds a general excise tax exemption certificate from the Department. XYZ Organization's gross receipts are less than $15,000 per year, which are comprised of both donations and small fees charged for services that would be exempt under HRS § 237•23(a)(4). XYZ Organization is exempt from filing federal Forms 990 and 990-EZ because its gross receipts are less than the federal threshold amount (i.e., normally $25,000 or less in gross receipts per year). The Department will not utilize Act 155 to deny XYZ Organization its general excise tax exemption because XYZ Organization is within the safe harbor protection for certain organizations exempt from filing federal Forms 990 and 990-EZ. See Safe Harbor 5, above.

*EXAMPLE 6*—Assume the same facts as in Example 5, except that XYZ Organization's $15,000 in gross receipts per year is comprised of fees charged in furtherance of its exempt purpose that are exempt from general excise tax under HRS § 237-23(a)(4) and fundraising activities taxable under the general excise tax. Under this scenario, the Department will not utilize Act 155 to deny XYZ Organization its general excise tax exemption because XYZ Organization falls within the safe harbor protection for certain organizations exempt from filing federal Forms 990 and 990-EZ; however, upon audit, XYZ Organization will be required to obtain a general excise tax license and file general excise tax returns for the taxable receipts from fundraising activity. XYZ Organization's tax exemption for the fees under HRS § 237-23(a)(4) will be preserved under the safe harbor protection. See Safe Harbor 5, above. The safe harbor protection from Act 155 in this TIR does not relieve a taxpayer from general excise tax responsibility for taxable activities.

*EXAMPLE 7*—Assume the same facts as in Example 5, except that XYZ Organization has gross receipts of $100,000 per year and is required by federal law to file a federal 990 series form. Assume further that $50,000 of XYZ Organization's receipts constitute gifts and donations, $30,000 of the receipts constitute fees charged in furtherance of its exempt purpose that are exempt from general excise tax under HRS § 237-23(a)(4), and $20,000 is from taxable fundraising. Assume further that XYZ Organization has obtained a general excise tax license; however has failed to file an annual general excise tax return within the time required by Act 155. When audited, XYZ Organization will have the following adjustments due to the application of Act 155: (1) All of the $50,000 constituting gifts or donations will continue to be exempt from general excise tax and will not have Act 155 utilized to deny the exemption for these amounts because gifts and donations are protected under a separate safe harbor. See Safe Harbor 6 for amounts received as gifts. (2) XYZ Organization is not entitled to the safe harbor protection for certain tax-exempt organizations under HRS § 237-23(a)(4) because its gross receipts require filing a federal 990 series form.

XYZ Organization will lose the general excise tax exemption for the fees charged in furtherance of its tax exempt purpose that were otherwise tax exempt under HRS § 237•23(a)(4) by operation of Act 155. (3) XYZ Organization will owe any unpaid general excise tax for the fundraising because there is no general excise tax benefit for this amount. The conclusions in this example assume that XYZ Organization had no reasonable cause outside the safe harbors in this TIR.

*EXAMPLE 8*—Assume the same facts as in Example 7; however XYZ Organization demonstrated to the Director of Taxation that it had reasonable cause for failing to file its annual general excise tax return. Under these facts, XYZ Organization will be entitled to maintain the exempt character of its fees charged in furtherance of its tax exempt purpose that are exempt under HRS § 237-23(a)(4). The gifts always remained protected. XYZ Organization will owe any unpaid general excise tax for the fundraising.

*TRUST FUND LIABILITY*

Section 2 of Act 155 also creates liability for certain key individuals involved in the financial management of taxpayers.

A. Amounts Held in Trust

Under the new amendment, certain key individuals will be personally liable for unpaid general excise tax involving the following amounts:

1) Any amount separately stated as a tax. This amount includes any separately stated amount on a receipt, invoice, contract or other evidence of the business activity where the amount is designated as a tax; or

2) An imputed tax liability equal to the general excise tax owed on a transaction where the amount of tax is not separately stated. The imputed liability amount is the gross income multiplied by the proper tax rate. For example, assume ABC Corp. sold an automobile for $20,000 cash with no tax separately stated. Under Act 155, the amount of imputed tax subject to trust fund liability is $800 of the $20,000 received (i.e., $20,000 x 4% GET (assuming no county surcharge)).

The foregoing amounts are statutorily held in trust for the benefit of the State and for payment to the State as general excise tax liability. A key individual will be held personally liable for these amounts. Liability under Act 155 remains notwithstanding dissolution of the taxpayer's business.

B. Key Individuals

Persons subject to personal liability under Act 155 are the following persons typically involved in the financial management of taxpayers: any officer, member, manager, or other person having control or supervision over amounts of gross proceeds or gross income to be held in trust; as well as any person who is charged with the responsibility of filing or paying general excise taxes.

The liability of these key individuals is limited to the extent the person was in control or in a capacity of supervision, responsibility, or duty to act for the taxpayer.

C. Willful Failure

A person is personally liable under the GET Protection Act only where the Department proves that the person acted willfully. To prove that a person acted willfully, the Department must show that the person voluntarily and intentionally violated a known legal duty.

Act 155 authorizes the interpretation of trust fund liability to be construed in accordance with case law and regulations interpreting similar provisions of the Internal Revenue Code. The Department will utilize case law and regulations interpreting Sections 6672 and 7202 of the Internal Revenue Code (with respect to civil and criminal penalties for willful failure to pay over taxes held in trust) in construing the willful standard contained in Act 155.

D. Good Cause

The Director is authorized to relieve key individuals from liability for good cause. The burden of proof and persuasion to demonstrate good cause is upon the person seeking relief from liability.

E. Personal Liability is Prospective Only

Act 155 is effective on July 1, 2010. Personal liability under Act 155 for certain key individuals only applies to gross income or gross proceeds received by a taxpayer on or after that date. Personal liability is prospective only and does not extend to gross income or gross proceeds received prior to July 1, 2010.

*EFFECTIVE DATE*

Act 155 is effective on July 1, 2010, and applies to gross income or gross proceeds received on or after its effective date.

# ¶ 1435. Tax Information Release No. 2010-06
## Re: Act 74, Session Laws of Hawaii 2010; Estate & Transfer Tax

On April 29, 2010, the Legislature overrode Governor Linda Lingle's veto of House Bill 2866 HD 1 SD 1 CD 1, which became law as Act 74, Session Laws of Hawaii 2010.

Act 74 reenacts Hawaii's Estate & Transfer Tax under Chapter 236D, Hawaii Revised Statutes (HRS), in a form that adopts conforming provisions to the Internal Revenue Code (IRC), Title 26, Subtitle B, Estate & Gift Tax, involving two separate points in time. The mechanics of the conforming provisions is discussed in more detail below. Act 74 applies to decedents dying on or after May 1, 2010.

The purpose of this Tax Information Release (TIR) is to set forth the Department's interpretation of Act 74 and to provide guidance on its application.

### HISTORY OF HAWAII'S ESTATE & TRANSFER TAX

Prior to Act 74, Chapter 236D, HRS, included two estate and transfer taxes. The first tax was the estate tax assessed against the taxable estate of persons dying as residents of Hawaii or as nonresidents with property interests in Hawaii. The second tax was the generation-skipping transfer tax, which was a tax on certain transfers at death of residents and nonresidents to persons more than one generation from the decedent.

Prior law assessed an estate tax and a generation-skipping transfer tax in amounts equal to the federal credits for state taxes paid under Sections 2011 and 2604, IRC, respectively. For example, prior to Act 74, Section 2011, IRC, allowed a federal credit for state death taxes paid up to certain amounts based upon graduated rates. Whatever the state death tax credit allowable based upon the Section 2011 graduated rate table; Hawaii would "pick-up" as the Hawaii estate tax.

Beginning after the year 2000, the credits under Sections 2011 and 2604, IRC, which comprised the bases for Hawaii's Estate & Transfer Tax, began to phase out by operation of the Economic Growth & Tax Relief Reconciliation Act of 2001 (EGTRRA). As a matter of federal tax policy, EGTRRA was the means of slowly eliminating the federal estate and generation-skipping transfer taxes. As part of EGTRRA's phase out of the federal transfer taxes, the credits for state taxes paid likewise were slowly eliminated. Because Hawaii's Estate and Transfer Tax bases were the amounts equal to the federal credits available, once the credits began to phase out, so did Hawaii's tax under Chapter 236D, HRS. Ultimately, Hawaii's Estate & Transfer Tax became "dormant" beginning in 2005 when the federal credits for state taxes paid were effectively repealed. Hawaii would continue without an Estate & Transfer Tax so long as the tax base remained tied to the federal credit for state taxes paid.

As part of EGTRRA, the federal estate and generation-skipping taxes terminated for persons dying in 2010. Under law existing as of the date of this TIR, the federal estate and generation- skipping taxes will be reenacted beginning on January 1, 2011 in a form similar to the law prior to EGTRRA; however with differing rates and exclusion amounts. The federal credits for state death taxes paid also reenact beginning on January 1, 2011.

### ACT 74 APPLICABLE TO DECEDENTS ON OR AFTER MAY 1, 2010

Act 74 and the Estate and Transfer Tax liability under Chapter 236D, HRS, applies to individuals dying on or after May 1, 2010.

### UNIFIED CREDIT; APPLICABLE EXCLUSION AMOUNT

Act 74 explicitly and independently provides for the entitlement of all applicable exclusion or exemption amounts available under the IRC as of December 31, 2009.

For example, before being subject to the Hawaii Estate Tax, the decedent will be entitled to the "applicable exclusion amount" under Section 2010, IRC. Under federal estate tax law, decedents are entitled to a "lifetime" unified credit with which the amount will be utilized to offset any estate and/or gift tax owed in their lifetime. The unified credit amount, when calculated and adjusted under federal law, results in an exclusion at death of a certain amount. This exclusion amount is referred to as the "applicable exclusion amount."

The applicable exclusion amount is the threshold amount before a decedent's taxable estate is subject to the federal estate tax, by computation of the applicable credit amount against the estate tax rates as provided in Section 2010, IRC. The applicable exclusion amount for purposes of Act 74, which is the applicable exclusion amount as of December 31, 2009, is $3,500,000 per decedent. Therefore, decedents dying on or after May 1, 2010 with a taxable estate of $3,500,000 or less are not subject to Chapter 236D, HRS.

The applicable exclusion amount will include any additional adjustments made under Section 2010, IRC, including any reduction in the applicable exclusion amount due to taxable gifts made during a person's lifetime.

As stated above, all exclusion or exemption amounts available in Subtitle B, IRC, are available to decedents subject to Chapter 236D, HRS. Additional exemptions include the exemption for generation-skipping transfer taxes available under Section 2631, IRC, in the amount of $3,500,000 per decedent. Further, nonresident decedents not citizens of the United States are entitled to the unified credit available under Section 2102, IRC, which results in an exemption equivalent amount of $60,000.

### CONFORMITY TO FEDERAL ESTATE TAX—US CITIZENS

Act 74 amends Chapter 236D, HRS, by "reenacting" Hawaii's previously-dormant estate tax. Act 74 adds a new definition of "Internal Revenue Code," which makes the IRC operative for purposes of the Estate and Transfer Tax as of December 31, 2009. However, Section 2011, IRC, which provides for the federal estate tax credit for state death taxes paid, is made operative as of December 31, 2000.

The effect of this new definition of "Internal Revenue Code" is that decedents are entitled to utilize the higher applicable exclusion amount to determine whether an estate is subject to Chapter 236D as of December 31, 2009 (i.e., $3,500,000 per decedent). However, to maintain the prior tax base for Hawaii estate tax purposes, which was the prior federal estate tax credit for state death taxes paid that phased out in 2005, Act 74 picks up the prior version of the state death tax credit prior to its phase out as it applied on December 31, 2000.

The Hawaii Estate and Transfer Tax is intended to operate similar to how the tax was determined prior to becoming dormant in 2005—the primary substantive adjustment being the threshold where estates become subject to the tax. The legislature determined that the $3,500,000 per decedent exclusion amount was in the best interest of the State—rather than the $675,000 exclusion that was available for deaths occurring in 2000.

One additional substantive amendment made by Act 74 that impacts the calculation of Hawaii estate tax is that the deduction for state death taxes paid is not made operative. As part of EGTRRA, the federal estate tax credit for state death taxes paid was phased out in favor of a deduction for state death taxes paid. Chapter 236D, HRS, does not conform to the deduction for state death taxes paid when calculating Hawaii estate tax liability.

Except for the Section 2011, IRC, credit for state death taxes and the Section 2058, IRC, deduction for state death taxes, the determination of gross estate, taxable estate, and adjusted taxable estate will be determined in all other respects under the IRC as Subtitle B existed on December 31, 2009.

Nonresident decedents with property interests taxable in Hawaii under Chapter 236D will continue to apportion the credit based upon property interests with a situs in Hawaii as provided in HRS § 236D-4.

### CONFORMITY TO FEDERAL ESTATE TAX—NONRESIDENTS NOT US CITIZENS

Act 74 adds a new provision to Chapter 236D, HRS, which provides for the assessment of the estate tax on transfers made by nonresidents who are not United States citizens. Patterned after the estate tax on transfers made by residents and nonresidents under prior law, Act 74 imposes an estate transfer tax on transfers of property interests located in Hawaii made by the estates of nonresident decedents not citizens of the United States.

The amount of the tax is arrived at by apportioning the amount of the federal credit based upon property interests with a situs in Hawaii over the value of the decedent's gross estate. Specifically, noncitizen transfers subject to the tax are transfers of real property with a situs in Hawaii, whether or not held in trust; a beneficial interest in a land trust that owns Hawaii property; and tangible and intangible personal property having a situs in Hawaii.

Act 74 defines "noncitizen transfer" as a transfer defined under Section 2101, IRC. "Nonresident not a citizen" means a nonresident who is not of United States citizenship.

Act 74 defines "situs" as meaning the location of a decedent's property within the meaning of Section 2104, IRC. However, in implementing the definition of situs for Hawaii estate tax purposes, the term "Hawaii" is substituted for the phrase "the United States."

As amended, Section 2104, IRC, for purposes of the Hawaii estate tax will be implemented as follows:

§ 2104 Property within Hawaii

(a) Stock in corporation. For purposes of this subchapter shares of stock owned and held by a nonresident not a citizen of the United States shall be deemed property within Hawaii only if issued by a Hawaii corporation.

(b) Revocable transfers and transfers within 3 years of death. For purposes of this subchapter, any property of which the decedent has made a transfer, by trust or otherwise, within the meaning of sections 2035 to 2038 , inclusive, shall be deemed to be situated in Hawaii, if so situated either at the time of the transfer or at the time of the decedent's death.

(c) Debt obligations.

For purposes of this subchapter, debt obligations of—

(1) a Hawaii person, or

(2) Hawaii or any political subdivision thereof,

owned and held by a nonresident not a citizen of the United States shall be deemed property within Hawaii. With respect to estates of decedents dying after December 31, 1969, deposits with a Hawaii branch of a foreign corporation, if such branch is engaged in the commercial banking business, shall, for purposes of this subchapter, be deemed property within Hawaii. This subsection shall not apply to a debt obligation to which section 2105(b) applies or to a debt obligation of a domestic corporation if any interest on such obligation, were such interest received by the decedent at the time of his death, would be treated by reason of section 861(a)(1)(A) as income from sources without Hawaii.

*CONFORMITY TO FEDERAL GENERATION-SKIPPING TRANSFER TAX*

Act 74 also amends Chapter 236D, HRS, by reenacting Hawaii's previously dormant generation-skipping transfer tax. Act 74 makes the definition of Section 2604, IRC, operative as of December 31, 2000, which provides for the federal credit for state generation-skipping transfer taxes paid.

The effect of this new definition of "Internal Revenue Code" is that decedents are entitled to utilize the higher exemption amount of $3,500,000 available under Section 2631, IRC, to determine whether a transfer is subject to Chapter 236D (versus the prior $1,000,000 exemption indexed for inflation). However, to maintain the prior tax base for Hawaii generation skipping transfer tax purposes, which was the prior federal credit for state generation skipping transfer taxes paid that phased out in 2005, Act 74 picks up the prior version of the state tax credit prior to phase out as it applied on December 31, 2000.

The application of the Hawaii Estate and Transfer Tax is intended to operate similar to how the tax was determined prior to becoming dormant in 2005, with the only substantive adjustment being the threshold where generation-skipping transfers become subject to the tax.

*HAWAII ESTATE AND GENERATION-SKIPPING TRANSFER TAXES STAND ALONE*

Prior to Act 74, Hawaii's Estate and Transfer Tax was directly tied to federal law as it was amended from time-to-time. This direct relation to federal law resulted in the Hawaii tax becoming dormant when the federal credits for state taxes paid were suspended. Without the credit, there was no tax base for Hawaii.

Under current federal law, for example, the estate tax does not apply to decedents dying in 2010. However, the federal estate tax is set to resurrect on January 1, 2011. Presently, there have been several formal and informal proposals in Congress that are intended to amend the federal estate tax in varying ways. Some of the policies propose to retroactively tax decedents dying as early as January 1, 2010. Other proposals eliminate the federal credit for state death taxes paid on a going-forward basis. Still, other proposals seek to offer a choice between paying federal estate tax in 2010 and enjoying the stepped-up basis for beneficiaries; or opting to forego federal estate tax for 2010 with the current carryover basis for beneficiaries. In sum, as of the date of this TIR, it is unclear how Congress intends to pursue federal estate tax policy in the near future.

Due to the uncertainty of what form the federal estate tax and generation-skipping tax will take, Act 74 avoids this issue by adopting the federal estate tax and generation-skipping tax at certain fixed times where the tax law was certain. Generally, Act 74 adopts the IRC as of December 31, 2009; except for the federal credits for state death or transfer taxes paid, which are adopted for Hawaii tax purposes as written on December 31, 2000. Because specific provisions were adopted at fixed points in time, the projected uncertainty regarding federal estate tax law has no impact on Hawaii Estate and Transfer Tax under Chapter 236D, HRS. Whatever policies become law federally will no longer have any impact on Hawaii law. As the federal estate and generation-skipping transfer tax laws exist today, the taxes will resurrect on January 1, 2011 with a provision for a federal tax credit for state death taxes paid. This credit will no longer have a direct impact on Hawaii law. Administration of the Hawaii Estate and Transfer Tax will be dictated as the law provides on December 31, 2009, with the credits for taxes provided on December 31, 2000.

### DECEMBER 31, 2000 FEDERAL CREDITS FOR STATE TAXES PAID

Due to potential issues with sourcing federal law as it existed in the year 2000, set forth at the end of this TIR are the December 31, 2000 versions of the federal credits for transfer taxes paid, which are made operative under Act 74. The most recent December 31, 2009 federal estate and generation-skipping transfer tax laws are widely available and remain in usable form from many sources.

### FORMS & ADDITIONAL GUIDANCE

The Department is presently working on updating the Hawaii Estate and Transfer Tax forms and instructions.

The Department projects that it may be some months before the forms are finalized. Tax returns under Chapter 236D, HRS, are generally due nine months from the decedent's date of death. A six month extension is available and is routinely granted.

The Department welcomes calls or questions from executors or tax practitioners who, in the interim before forms are completed, may be dealing with issues related to Hawaii's Estate and Transfer Tax. The Department will use its best efforts to assist with tax-related matters while the forms are being developed so as not to materially impact the administration, distribution, and/or probate of taxable estates.

### SECTION 2011, IRC, AS OF DECEMBER 31, 2000—

§ 2011 Credit for State death taxes.

(a) In general.

The tax imposed by section 2001 shall be credited with the amount of any estate, inheritance, legacy, or succession taxes actually paid to any State or the District of Columbia, in respect of any property included in the gross estate (not including any such taxes paid with respect to the estate of a person other than the decedent).

(b) Amount of credit.

(1) In general.

Except as provided in paragraph (2), the credit allowed by this section shall not exceed the appropriate amount stated in the following table:

| If the adjusted taxable estate is: | The maximum tax credit shall be: |
| --- | --- |
| Not over $90,000 | 8/10ths of 1% of the amount by which the adjusted taxable estate exceeds $40,000. |
| Over $90,000 but not over $140,000. | $400 plus 1.6% of the excess over $90,000. |
| Over $140,000 but not over $240,000. | $1,200 plus 2.4% of the excess over $140,000. |
| Over $240,000 but not over $440,000. | $3,600 plus 3.2% of the excess over $240,000. |
| Over $440,000 but not over $640,000. | $10,000 plus 4% of the excess over $440,000. |
| Over $640,000 but not over $840,000. | $18,000 plus 4.8% of the excess over $640,000. |
| Over $840,000 but not over $1,040,000. | $27,600 plus 5.6% of the excess over $840,000. |
| Over $1,040,000 but not over $1,540,000. | $38,800 plus 6.4% of the excess over $1,040,000. |
| Over $1,540,000 but not over $2,040,000. | $70,800 plus 7.2% of the excess over $1,540,000. |

| | |
|---|---|
| Over $2,040,000 but not over $2,540,000. | $106,800 plus 8% of the excess over $2,040,000. |
| Over $2,540,000 but not over $3,040,000. | $146,800 plus 8.8% of the excess over $2,540,000. |
| Over $3,040,000 but not over $3,540,000. | $190,800 plus 9.6% of the excess over $3,040,000. |
| Over $3,540,000 but not over $4,040,000. | $238,800 plus 10.4% of the excess over $3,540,000. |
| Over $4,040,000 but not over $5,040,000. | $290,800 plus 11.2% of the excess over $4,040,000. |
| Over $5,040,000 but not over $6,040,000. | $402,800 plus 12% of the excess over $5,040,000. |
| Over $6,040,000 but not over $7,040,000. | $522,800 plus 12.8% of the excess over $6,040,000. |
| Over $7,040,000 but not over $8,040,000. | $650,800 plus 13.6% of the excess over $7,040,000. |
| Over $8,040,000 but not over $9,040,000. | $786,800 plus 14.4% of the excess over $8,040,000. |
| Over $9,040,000 but not over $10,040,000. | $930,800 plus 15.2% of the excess over $9,040,000. |
| Over $10,040,000 | $1,082,800 plus 16% of the excess over $10,040,000. |

For purposes of this section, the term "adjusted taxable estate" means the taxable estate reduced by $60,000.

(c) Period of limitations on credit.

The credit allowed by this section shall include only such taxes as were actually paid and credit therefor claimed within 4 years after the filing of the return required by section 6018, except that—

(1) If a petition for redetermination of a deficiency has been filed with the Tax Court within the time prescribed in section 6213(a), then within such 4-year period or before the expiration of 60 days after the decision of the Tax Court becomes final.

(2) If, under section 6161 or 6166, an extension of time has been granted for payment of the tax shown on the return, or of a deficiency, then within such 4-year period or before the date of the expiration of the period of the extension.

(3) If a claim for refund or credit of an overpayment of tax imposed by this chapter has been filed within the time prescribed in section 6511, then within such 4-year period or before the expiration of 60 days from the date of mailing by certified mail or registered mail by the Secretary to the taxpayer of a notice of the disallowance of any part of such claim, or before the expiration of 60 days after a decision by any court of competent jurisdiction becomes final with respect to a timely suit instituted upon such claim, whichever is later.

Refund based on the credit may (despite the provisions of sections 6511 and 6512) be made if claim therefor is filed within the period above provided. Any such refund shall be made without interest.

(d) Basic estate tax.

The basic estate tax and the estate tax imposed by the Revenue Act of 1926 shall be 125 percent of the amount determined to be the maximum credit provided by subsection (b). The additional estate tax shall be the difference between the tax imposed by section 2001 or 2101 and the basic estate tax.

(e) Limitation in cases involving deduction under section 2053(d).

In any case where a deduction is allowed under section 2053(d) for an estate, succession, legacy, or inheritance tax imposed by a State or the District of Columbia upon a transfer for public, charitable, or religious uses described in section 2055 or 2106(a)(2), the allowance of the credit under this section shall be subject to the following conditions and limitations:

(1) The taxes described in subsection (a) shall not include any estate, succession, legacy, or inheritance tax for which such deduction is allowed under section 2053(d).

(2) The credit shall not exceed the lesser of—

(A) the amount stated in subsection (b) on an adjusted taxable estate determined by allowing such deduction authorized by section 2053(d), or

¶ 1435

(B) that proportion of the amount stated in subsection (b) on an adjusted taxable estate determined without regard to such deduction authorized by section 2053(d) as (i) the amount of the taxes described in subsection (a) as limited by the provisions of paragraph (1) of this subsection, bears to (ii) the amount of the taxes described in subsection (a) before applying the limitation contained in paragraph (1) of this subsection.

(3) If the amount determined under subparagraph (B) of paragraph (2) is less than the amount determined under subparagraph (A) of that paragraph , then for purposes of subsection (d) such lesser amount shall be the maximum credit provided by subsection (b).

(f) Limitation based on amount of tax.

The credit provided by this section shall not exceed the amount of the tax imposed by section 2001, reduced by the amount of the unified credit provided by section 2010.

*SECTION 2102, IRC, AS OF DECEMBER 31, 2000—*

§ 2102 Credits against tax.

(a) In general.

The tax imposed by section 2101 shall be credited with the amounts determined in accordance with sections 2011 to 2013, inclusive (relating to State death taxes, gift tax, and tax on prior transfers), subject to the special limitation provided in subsection (b).

(b) Special Limitation.

The maximum credit allowed under section 2011 against the tax imposed by section 2101 for State death taxes paid shall be an amount which bears the same ratio to the credit computed as provided in section 2011(b) as the value of the property, as determined for purposes of this chapter, upon which State death taxes were paid and which is included in the gross estate under section 2103 bears to the value of the total gross estate under section 2103. For purposes of this subsection, the term 'State death taxes' means the taxes described in section 2011(a).

(c) Unified credit.

(1) In general.

A credit of $13,000 shall be allowed against the tax imposed by section 2101.

(2) Residents of possessions of the United States.

In the case of a decedent who is considered to be a "nonresident not a citizen of the United States" under section 2209, the credit under this subsection shall be the greater of—

(A) $13,000, or

(B) that proportion of $46,800 which the value of that part of the decedent's gross estate which at the time of his death is situated in the United States bears to the value of his entire gross estate wherever situated.

(3) Special rules.

(A) Coordination with treaties. To the extent required under any treaty obligation of the United States, the credit allowed under this subsection shall be equal to the amount which bears the same ratio to the applicable credit amount in effect under section 2010(c) for the calendar year which includes the date of death as the value of the part of the decedent's gross estate which at the time of his death is situated in the United States bears to the value of his entire gross estate wherever situated. For purposes of the preceding sentence, property shall not be treated as situated in the United States if such property is exempt from the tax imposed by this subchapter under any treaty obligation of the United States.

(B) Coordination with gift tax unified credit. If a credit has been allowed under section 2505 with respect to any gift made by the decedent, each dollar amount contained in paragraph (1) or (2) or subparagraph (A) of this paragraph (whichever applies) shall be reduced by the amount so allowed.

(4) Limitation based on amount of tax.

The credit allowed under this subsection shall not exceed the amount of the tax imposed by section 2101.

(5) Application of other credits.

For purposes of subsection (a), sections 2012 and 2013 shall be applied as if the credit allowed under this subsection were allowed under section 2010.

*SECTION 2604, IRC, AS OF DECEMBER 31, 2000— § 2604 Credit for certain State taxes.*

(a) General rule.

If a generation-skipping transfer (other than a direct skip) occurs at the same time as and as a result of the death of an individual, a credit against the tax imposed by section 2601 shall be allowed in an amount equal to the generation-skipping transfer tax actually paid to any State in respect to any property included in the generation-skipping transfer.

(b) Limitation.

The aggregate amount allowed as a credit under this section with respect to any transfer shall not exceed 5 percent of the amount of the tax imposed by section 2601 on such transfer.

## ¶ 1436. Department of Taxation Announcement No. 2012-01
### RE: Composite Filing of Forms N-342 and/or N-342A for Taxpayers Claiming the Renewable Energy Technologies Income Tax Credit, § HRS 235-12.5 for 10 or More Systems

The Renewable Energy Technologies Income Tax Credit ("Renewable Energy Credit") provided by § 235-12.5, Hawaii Revised Statutes ("HRS"), is claimed by filing a separate Form N-342 for each eligible system for which the taxpayer is claiming the Renewable Energy Credit. In the case of a partnership, S corporation, estate, trust, or condominium apartment association, the entity is required to prepare a separate Form N-342A for each partner, member, shareholder, or beneficiary to indicate the partner's, member's, shareholder's, or beneficiary's prorated share of the credit. Generally, the entity must use a separate form for each eligible system.

In order to ease the administrative burden on taxpayers, the Department of Taxation (the "Department"), will allow taxpayers to file composite Form(s) N-342 and composite Form(s) N-342A in certain situations. However, the composite filing of Form(s) N-342 and Form(s) N-342A shall not change the calculation and application of the Renewable Energy Credit as provided for by § 235-12.5, HRS. This Tax Announcement outlines the procedures by which qualifying taxpayers may file composite Form(s) N-342 and N-342A.

*I. WHO MAY FILE A COMPOSITE FORM N-342 OR FORM N-342A*

  A. Composite Form N-342. Any individual or corporate taxpayer who is eligible to claim the Renewable Energy Credit for 10 or more systems or distributive shares of systems installed and placed in service in a single taxable year may file a composite Form N-342.

  B. Composite Form N-342A. Any partnership, S corporation, estate, trust, or condominium apartment association that has installed and placed in service 10 or more systems in a single taxable year may file composite Form(s) N-342A.

*II. FOR WHICH TAXABLE YEARS MAY A COMPOSITE FORM N-342 OR N-342A BE FILED*

A taxpayer who qualifies to file a composite Form N-342 and/or Form N-342A may do so for taxable years that begin on or after January 1, 2011.

*III. WHEN MUST A COMPOSITE FORM N-342 BE FILED*

All claims for the credit, including amended claims, must be filed on or before the end of the twelfth month following the close of the taxable year for which the credit may be claimed.

*IV. WHERE TO FILE*

Attach the composite Form N-342 to the taxpayer's Hawaii income tax return ("income tax return") along with all other required forms, schedules, and attachments and submit the complete income tax return to the Department in the manner prescribed in the applicable Hawaii income tax return instructions. A composite Form N-342 cannot be electronically filed at this time.

In addition, the taxpayer must also submit a "soft" or electronic copy of the composite Form(s) N-342 and the Composite Schedule(s) for Form N-342 to the Department in one of the following ways:

- Email to: Tax.Directors.Office@hawaii.gov
- Mail or hand-delivery to:
  - o Department of Taxation
    Attn: Director's Office
    830 Punchbowl Street
    Honolulu, HI 96813
  - o Composite Form(s) N-342 and Composite Schedule(s) for N-342 (Form N-342C for tax years 2012 and later) must be written/stored on a digital media storage source such as a CD-R or DVD-R
    - Note: Digital media storage sources will not be returned by the Department.

*V. HOW TO FILE A COMPOSITE FORM(S) N-342 TO CLAIM MULTIPLE RENEWABLE ENERGY CREDITS*

A taxpayer that elects to file a composite Form(s) N-342 must attach to the taxpayer's Hawaii income tax return the following forms and schedules in the order listed:

(1) Composite Form(s) N-342,

(2) Composite Schedule(s) for Form N-342 (Form N-342C for tax years 2012 and later)

(3) Form(s) N-342A (if required, see below),

(4) Composite Schedule(s) for Form N-342A, (Form N-342B for tax years 2012 and later), (if required, see below), and

(5) Any other form(s) or schedule(s) required to claim to the Renewable Energy Credit Failing to properly file and/or comply with the terms and conditions for composite filing may result in the disallowance of all or part the credits and the revocation of the election to composite file.

*VI. WHAT INFORMATION MUST BE REPORTED*

A. *Composite Form N-342*

Print the word "COMPOSITE" in capital letters at the top of each composite Form N-342, Renewable Energy Technologies Income Tax Credit.

B. *Credit Election*

A separate election may be made for each separate system that generates a renewable energy tax credit. Once an election is made, it is irrevocable. Taxpayers filing a composite Form N-342 may elect to claim all the credits as refundable, all the credits as nonrefundable, or a combination of both. For example, a taxpayer who has installed and placed in service 11 systems during a taxable year may claim 11 refundable credits, or 11 nonrefundable credits, or a combination of refundable and nonrefundable credits (e.g., 5 non-refundable credits and 6 refundable credits). The taxpayer may not make separate elections to apportion the credit for a single system. Thus, the taxpayer may not elect refundable credits for 5.5 systems and nonrefundable credits for 5.5 systems.

1. *Single Election*

A taxpayer filing a composite Form N-342 who elects all refundable credits (or all non-refundable), must file a single composite Form N-342 which reflects the aggregate amounts for each required line item. Therefore, taxpayers making a single election shall file one Form N-342 (representing all systems).

2. *Dual Elections*

Taxpayers electing a combination of both refundable and non-refundable credits shall file two composite Forms N-342. Each composite Form N-342 shall reflect the aggregate amounts for each required line item according to the proportion of the election. Therefore, taxpayers making separate elections shall file two separate Forms N-342 (one for refundable and one for nonrefundable credits) together with two separate Composite Schedules for Form N-342 (Form N-342C for tax years 2012 and later).

C. Composite Schedule for Form N-342 (Form N-342C for tax years 2012 and later)

The taxpayer must also prepare and submit a Composite Schedule(s) for Form N-342.[1] All information required on the Composite Schedule for Form N-342 must be provided in the required format. A taxpayer making separate system elections regarding refundable and non-refundable credit must prepare two separate Composite Schedules for Form N-342. As noted above, the filing of composite Form(s) N-342 and Composite Schedule(s) for Form N-342 does not change the calculation and application of the Renewable Energy Credit as provided for by § 235-12.5, HRS.

A taxpayer who receives Form(s) N-342A from an entity through which the taxpayer is claiming the Renewable Energy Credit should report its distributive share for each system in a separate column of the Composite Schedule for Form N-342. A taxpayer who receives a composite Form N-342A and Composite Schedule for Form N-342A from an entity shall report each line from the Composite Schedule for Form N-342A on a separate column of the Composite Schedule for Form N-342.

*Composite Schedule for Form N-342 Header (Form N-342C for tax years 2012 and later)*

- Composite Schedule for Form N-342 for Tax Year __ __ __ __ or Fiscal Year beginning _____ and ending _____

- Taxpayer's Name

- Taxpayer's SSN or FEIN

- Hawaii Tax ID No. (if any)

- "Total Number of Properties" on which systems were installed that are listed on Part II. of the Composite Schedule for Form N-342.

    o  If more than one Composite Schedule for Form N-342 is required, the total number of properties for all Composite Schedules for Form N-342 should be reported on the first Composite Schedule for Form N-342.

- "Property Number" must correspond to the order in which the real property addresses are listed on Part II. of the Composite Schedule for Form N-342.

    o  For example, if three systems were installed on the first property listed on Part II. of the Composite Schedule for Form N-342, the property number "1" would be placed in the row titles "property No." in the first 3 columns.

- Type of System (Solar Water, Other Solar, or Wind)

- "Date Installed & Placed in Service" of each system

*Part I. Corresponding Form N-342 Line Number*

Part I. of the Composite Schedule for Form N-342 contains 53 rows, each of which represents a corresponding line on Form N-342. Rows should only be completed if the corresponding line on the Form N-342 would have been completed. Each column represents a separate system that was installed and placed in service. Each column must contain the same information as a single Form N-342. Use additional Composite Schedules for Form N-342 if more than 10 systems are being reported.

*Part II. Physical Property Addresses*

Where Each System was Installed and Placed in Service The physical addresses of the real property on which the renewable energy systems were installed and placed in service should be listed in Part II. List the addresses only once, even if more than one system was installed on that property. If multiple Composite Schedules for Form N-342 are being submitted, the addresses must be listed in a continuous numerical order starting with property number "1" on Part II. of the first Composite Schedules for Form N-342. If there are more than 29 addresses to be reported, property number

"30" should be the first property listed on Part II. of the second Composite Schedules for Form N-342, and so on.

## VII. COMPOSITE FILING GUIDELINES FOR HAWAII S CORPORATIONS, PARTNERSHIPS, ESTATES, TRUSTS, OR CONDOMINIUM ASSOCIATIONS

Every Hawaii S corporation, partnership, estate, trust, or condominium apartment association is required to prepare a Form N-342A for each individual or corporate shareholder, member, or beneficiary, respectively, in order that the prorated amount of such entity's tax credit may be claimed by the individual or corporate taxpayer. Generally, the entity must use a separate form for each eligible system.

A copy of composite Form N-342A and Composite Schedule for Form N-342A (Form N-342B for tax years 2012 and later) reflecting the member's distributive share of the tax credit shall be issued to that member as required by the Form N-342A Instructions. The entity must also attach a copy of each Form N-342A and Composite Schedule for Form N-342A (Form N-342B for tax years 2012 and later) issued to its members to the entity's tax return.

An entity that elects to file a composite Form(s) N-342 must attach to the entity's income tax return the following forms and schedules specifically in the order listed:

(1) Composite Form(s) N-342,

(2) Composite Schedule(s) for Form N-342 (Form N-342C for tax years 2012 and later),

(3) Composite Form(s) N-342A,

(4) Composite Schedule(s) for Form N-342A (Form N-342B for tax years 2012 and later), and

(5) Any other form(s) or schedule(s) required to claim to the Renewable Energy Credit

Failing to properly file may result in the disallowance of all or part the credits and the composite filing election may be revoked by the Department upon failure to comply with the terms and conditions of this election.

### 1. Composite Form N-342A

The entity shall prepare a composite Form(s) N-342A for each shareholder, member, or beneficiary reflecting an aggregate total of the credits being claimed and the shareholder's, member's, or beneficiary's distributive share as generally required. The word "COMPOSITE" in capital letters must be written at the top of each composite Form N-342A.

### 2. Composite Schedule for Form N-342A (Form N-342B for tax years 2012 and later)

Each entity shall also prepare a Composite Schedule for Form N-342A (that corresponds to the composite Form N-342A) for each shareholder, member, or beneficiary of the entity.[2] All information required on Composite Schedule(s) for Form N-342A and Form(s) N-342A must be provided and submitted in the required format.

*Composite Schedule for Form N-342A Header*

- Composite Schedule for Form N-342A for Tax Year __ __ __ __ or Fiscal Year beginning _____ and ending _____

- Name of Issuing Entity (S Corporation, Partnership, Estate, or Trust, or Condominium Apartment Association)

- Issuing Entity's SSN or FEIN

- Hawaii Tax ID No. (if any)

- Name of the recipient for whom the statement is being prepared

- Recipient's SSN or FEIN

- "Property Number" must correspond to the order in which the real property addresses are listed on Part II. of the Composite Schedule for Form N-342A.

    o For example, if three systems were installed on the first property listed on Part II. of the Composite Schedule for Form N-342A, the property number "1" would be placed in the row titles "property No." in the first 3 columns.

¶ 1436

- Type of System (Solar Water, Other Solar, or Wind)
- "Date Installed & Placed in Service" of each system

*Part I. Corresponding Form N-342A Line Number*

Part I. of the Composite Schedule for Form N-342A contains 42 rows, each representing a corresponding line on Form N-342A. Each column must contain the same information as a single Form N-342A. Rows should only be completed if the corresponding line on the Form N-342A would have been completed. Each column represents a separate system that was installed and placed in service. Use additional Composite Schedules for Form N-342A if more than 10 systems are being reported.

*Part II. Physical Property Addresses Where Each System was Installed and Placed in Service*

Each physical addresses of the real property on which the renewable energy systems were installed and placed in service should be listed in Part II. List the addresses only once, even if more than one system was installed on that property.

If more than one Composite Schedule for Form N-342A is being submitted, the addresses must be listed in continuous numerical order starting with property number "1" on Part II. of the first Composite Schedule for Form N-342A. If there are more than 28 addresses to be reported, property number "29" should be the first property listed on Part II. of the second Composite Schedule for Form N-342A, and so on.

*3. Instructions for the Individual, Corporate Shareholder, Member, or Beneficiary who Receives a Composite Form(s) N-342A or 10 or More Forms N-342A*

Each individual or corporate shareholder, member, or beneficiary of an entity through which the Renewable Energy Credit is being claimed must attach to the taxpayer's income tax return the following documents specifically in the order listed:

(1) Composite Form(s) N-342,

(2) Composite Schedule for Form N-342 (Form N-342C for tax years 2012 and later),

(3) Composite Form(s) N-342A (or separate Form(s) N-342A), and

(4) Composite Schedule for Form N-342A (Form N-342B for tax years 2012 and later), and

(5) Any other form(s) or schedule(s) required to claim to the Renewable Energy Credit

Entity members making separate refundabililty elections must follow the election requirements as set forth above. Specifically, a member making separate elections must prepare two separate composite Forms N-342 and two separate Composite Schedules for Form N-342.

*Multiple Level Pass-Through Entities*

For situations in which there are multiple levels of investors in a renewable energy technology system, each level of investor must prepare and submit the required forms, schedules, and attachments as the "first level" of investors. Since the Renewable Energy Credit is determined at the entity level, entities that receive Form(s) N-342A which are then required to issue Form(s) N- 342A to its members must attach to the entity's tax return specifically in the order listed:

(1) Composite Form N-342

(2) Composite Schedule for Form N-342 (Form N-342C for tax years 2012 and later)

(3) Composite Forms N-342A (one for each member of the entity)

(4) Composite Schedules for Form N-342A (one for each member of the entity) (Form N-342B for tax years 2012 and later), and

(5) Any other form(s) or schedule(s) required to claim to the Renewable Energy Credit

For more information on this issue, please contact the Technical Section at 808-587-1577 or by e-mail at Tax.Technical.Section@hawaii.gov.

# DEPARTMENT OF TAXATION ANNOUNCEMENT NO. 2012-01

## ATTACHMENT A

## COMPOSITE SCHEDULE FOR FORM N-342

## COMPOSITE SCHEDULE FOR FORM N-342

for calendar tax year 2011 or fiscal year beginning _____, 2011, and ending _____, 20 ___

(ATTACH THIS FORM TO YOUR FORM N-342)

Name ___

SSN or FEIN ___

Hawaii Tax ID No. (if any)
W

| Property No. | | | | | | | | | | | | | | |
|---|---|---|---|---|---|---|---|---|---|---|---|---|---|---|
| Type of System | | | | | | | | | | | | | | |
| Date Installed & Placed in Service | | | | | | | | | | | | | | |

**PART I. CORRESPONDING FORM N-342 LINE NUMBER**

| 1 | | | | | | | | | | | | | | |
|---|---|---|---|---|---|---|---|---|---|---|---|---|---|---|
| 2 | | | | | | | | | | | | | | |
| 3 | | | | | | | | | | | | | | |
| 4 | | | | | | | | | | | | | | |
| 5 | | | | | | | | | | | | | | |
| 6 | | | | | | | | | | | | | | |
| 7 | | | | | | | | | | | | | | |
| 8 | | | | | | | | | | | | | | |
| 9 | | | | | | | | | | | | | | |
| 10 | | | | | | | | | | | | | | |
| 11 | | | | | | | | | | | | | | |
| 12 | | | | | | | | | | | | | | |
| 13 | | | | | | | | | | | | | | |
| 14 | | | | | | | | | | | | | | |
| 15 | | | | | | | | | | | | | | |
| 16 | | | | | | | | | | | | | | |
| 17 | | | | | | | | | | | | | | |
| 18 | | | | | | | | | | | | | | |
| 19 | | | | | | | | | | | | | | |
| 20 | | | | | | | | | | | | | | |
| 21 | | | | | | | | | | | | | | |
| 22 | | | | | | | | | | | | | | |
| 23 | | | | | | | | | | | | | | |

Name

SSN or FEIN

**PART I. CORRESPONDING FORM N-342 LINE NUMBER (CONTINUED)**

PAGE 2

| Property No. | | | | | | | | | | | |
|---|---|---|---|---|---|---|---|---|---|---|---|
| 24 | | | | | | | | | | | |
| 25 | | | | | | | | | | | |
| 26 | | | | | | | | | | | |
| 27 | | | | | | | | | | | |
| 28 | | | | | | | | | | | |
| 29 | | | | | | | | | | | |
| 30 | | | | | | | | | | | |
| 31 | | | | | | | | | | | |
| 32 | | | | | | | | | | | |
| 33 | | | | | | | | | | | |
| 34 | | | | | | | | | | | |
| 35 | | | | | | | | | | | |
| 36 | | | | | | | | | | | |
| 37 | | | | | | | | | | | |
| 38 | | | | | | | | | | | |
| 39 | | | | | | | | | | | |
| 40 | | | | | | | | | | | |
| 41 | | | | | | | | | | | |
| 42 | | | | | | | | | | | |
| 43 | | | | | | | | | | | |
| 44 | | | | | | | | | | | |
| 45 | | | | | | | | | | | |
| 46 | | | | | | | | | | | |
| 47 | | | | | | | | | | | |
| 48 | | | | | | | | | | | |
| 49 | | | | | | | | | | | |
| 50 | | | | | | | | | | | |
| 51 | | | | | | | | | | | |
| 52 | | | | | | | | | | | |
| 53 | | | | | | | | | | | |

Name

SSN or FEIN

PAGE 3

**PART II. PHYSICAL PROPERTY ADDRESSES WHERE EACH SYSTEM WAS INSTALLED AND PLACED IN SERVICE**

| Property No. | Address (Number and Street) | City or Town | Postal/ZIP Code |
|---|---|---|---|
| | | | |

**DEPARTMENT OF TAXATION ANNOUNCEMENT NO. 2012-01**

**ATTACHMENT B**

**COMPOSITE SCHEDULE FOR FORM N-342A**

## COMPOSITE SCHEDULE FOR FORM N-342A

for calendar tax year 2011 or fiscal year beginning _____, 2012, and ending _____, 20____
(ATTACH THIS SCHEDULE TO FORM N-342)

Name of issuing entity (S Corporation, Partnership, Estate, or Trust, or Condominium Apartment Association) | Issuing entity's SSN or FEIN | Hawaii Tax ID No. (if any)
W

Name of recipient for whom this statement is being prepared: | Recipient's SSN or FEIN:

**PART I. CORRESPONDING FORM N-342A LINE NUMBER**

| Property No. | | | | | | | | | | | | |
| --- | --- | --- | --- | --- | --- | --- | --- | --- | --- | --- | --- | --- |
| Type of System | | | | | | | | | | | | |
| Date Installed & Placed in Service | | | | | | | | | | | | |
| 1 | | | | | | | | | | | | |
| 2 | | | | | | | | | | | | |
| 3 | | | | | | | | | | | | |
| 4 | | | | | | | | | | | | |
| 5 | | | | | | | | | | | | |
| 6 | | | | | | | | | | | | |
| 7 | | | | | | | | | | | | |
| 8 | | | | | | | | | | | | |
| 9 | | | | | | | | | | | | |
| 10 | | | | | | | | | | | | |
| 11 | | | | | | | | | | | | |
| 12 | | | | | | | | | | | | |
| 13 | | | | | | | | | | | | |
| 14 | | | | | | | | | | | | |
| 15 | | | | | | | | | | | | |
| 16 | | | | | | | | | | | | |
| 17 | | | | | | | | | | | | |
| 18 | | | | | | | | | | | | |

Name of issuing entity

Name of recipient for whom this statement is being prepared:

Issuing entity's SSN or FEIN

Recipient's SSN or FEIN

PAGE 2

**PART I. CORRESPONDING FORM N-342A LINE NUMBER (CONTINUED)**

| Property No. | | | | | | | | | | | | |
|---|---|---|---|---|---|---|---|---|---|---|---|---|
| 19 | | | | | | | | | | | | |
| 20 | | | | | | | | | | | | |
| 21 | | | | | | | | | | | | |
| 22 | | | | | | | | | | | | |
| 23 | | | | | | | | | | | | |
| 24 | | | | | | | | | | | | |
| 25 | | | | | | | | | | | | |
| 26 | | | | | | | | | | | | |
| 27 | | | | | | | | | | | | |
| 28 | | | | | | | | | | | | |
| 29 | | | | | | | | | | | | |
| 30 | | | | | | | | | | | | |
| 31 | | | | | | | | | | | | |
| 32 | | | | | | | | | | | | |
| 33 | | | | | | | | | | | | |
| 34 | | | | | | | | | | | | |
| 35 | | | | | | | | | | | | |
| 36 | | | | | | | | | | | | |
| 37 | | | | | | | | | | | | |
| 38 | | | | | | | | | | | | |
| 39 | | | | | | | | | | | | |
| 40 | | | | | | | | | | | | |
| 41 | | | | | | | | | | | | |
| 42 | | | | | | | | | | | | |

¶ 1436

Name of issuing entity

Issuing entity's SSN or FEIN

Name of the recipient for whom this statement is being prepared:

Recipient's SSN or FEIN

**PART II. PHYSICAL PROPERTY ADDRESSES WHERE EACH SYSTEM WAS INSTALLED AND PLACED IN SERVICE**

| Property No. | Address (Number and Street) | City or Town | Postal/ZIP Code |
|---|---|---|---|
| | | | |

## ¶ 1437. Department of Taxation Announcement No. 2016-03
### Re: New Appeals Program to Resolve Tax Disputes Quicker

The Department of Taxation (DOTAX) is launching the pilot phase of the Administrative Appeals and Dispute Resolution Program (AADR). AADR is a streamlined method to quickly and fairly resolve tax disputes involving audit assessments without litigation.

I. *WHAT IS THE ADMINISTRATIVE APPEALS AND DISPUTE RESOLUTION PROGRAM?*

AADR is an informal appeals process that uses a neutral intermediary, the Administrative Appeals Office, to resolve tax disputes between DOTAX and a taxpayer or return preparer that involve a proposed, final, or return preparer penalty assessment.

The Administrative Appeals Office (AAO) is an independent body within DOTAX headed by the Administrative Appeals Officer who reports directly to the Director of Taxation. AAO works with the Compliance Division and the taxpayer or return preparer by phone, mail, or in person to understand and resolve tax disputes based on the law. When the solution to a dispute is not clear, the Administrative Appeals Officer is authorized to settle the dispute based on the hazards of litigation, equally considering the positions of the Compliance Division and the taxpayer or return preparer.

**Program Benefits:**

- Simple application process.
- Fair and neutral evaluation of tax disputes.
- Timely resolution. Complete the process within 6-12 months upon acceptance.
- Save time, money, and resources. AADR is a quicker and less costly alternative to litigation.
- Free. There are no fees to apply to AADR.

II. *ELIGIBILITY AND CRITERIA*

Before seeking help from AAO, taxpayers and return preparers must try to resolve all issues with the Compliance Division. This includes, but is not limited to:

- Providing the auditor or examiner with all the requested information;
- Providing the auditor or examiner a written explanation of the disputed items; and
- Providing the auditor or examiner with evidence to support your position.

The goal of AADR is to resolve tax disputes fairly, quickly, and without litigation. Since piecemeal resolutions do not provide these benefits, any settlement reached must resolve the entire case. Generally, AAO will not raise new issues or examine issues where the parties are in agreement. AAO will only accept cases where:

- The issues and facts are fully developed and documented;
- There are a limited number of issues in dispute; and
- The parties are willing to resolve all of the disputed issues and act in good faith to find a resolution.

AAO may at its discretion determine that AADR is not appropriate for certain cases. AADR is not available for:

- Issues designated for litigation by the Attorney General;
- Issues for which there are no legal precedent;
- Industry specialization issues;
- Disputing an adjustment letter or billing notice that is unrelated to an audit;
- Collection issues; and
- Jeopardy assessments.

III. *WHO MAY APPLY*

If you were audited by DOTAX and issued a Proposed Notice of Assessment, Final Notice of

Assessment, or a Notice and Demand of Penalty that you believe is incorrect, you may apply. A taxpayer can apply to AADR for either a proposed assessment or final assessment, but not both.

## IV. *HOW TO APPLY*

Submit Form AA-1, Appeal Application, with a copy of each DOTAX assessment that you dispute to AAO and provide a copy of the application to the auditor or examiner assigned to your case. Please see the instructions for Form AA-1 for more information. AAO will inform you and the assigned auditor or examiner in writing whether your case is accepted. The decision to not accept a case into AADR is not appealable.

## V. *DEADLINE TO APPLY*

If you are appealing a proposed assessment, the deadline to apply is 20 calendar days after the mailing date of the proposed assessment. If you are appealing a final assessment or preparer penalty assessment, the deadline to apply is 30 calendar days after the mailing date of the final assessment. There are no extensions of time to apply.

## VI. *INTEREST*

Interest on any unpaid balance will continue to accrue while your case with AAO is pending. To stop the interest from accruing while your case is with AAO, you may pay the assessment in full or submit a cash bond deposit. For information on cash bond deposits, see Tax Information Release No. 2008-03.

## VII. *REPRESENTATION*

You may represent yourself or choose someone to represent you. Usually, a representative is a certified public accountant (CPA), attorney, or other tax professional.

## VIII. *TYPES OF APPEALS*

This section provides general information about three jurisdictions (Administrative Appeals Office (AAO), Board of Review (BOR), and Tax Appeal Court (TAC)) where tax appeals may be filed. If you are thinking about filing an appeal, discuss your case with a trusted tax advisor and the auditor or examiner to see which option works best for you.

(A) Pre-Assessment Appeals

A taxpayer that disagrees with a Proposed Notice of Assessment issued as a result of a DOTAX audit may appeal to AAO, but not to the BOR or TAC. If the case is unresolved or not accepted by AAO, DOTAX will issue a final assessment. A taxpayer may appeal a final assessment to either the BOR or TAC (section 235-114, Hawaii Revised Statutes (HRS)).

(B) Post-Assessment Appeals

1. *Single appeal.* A taxpayer that disagrees with a Final Notice of Assessment issued as a result of a DOTAX audit may appeal to the AAO, BOR, or TAC. Alternatively, a taxpayer may file multiple appeals as discussed below.

2. *AAO and BOR.* A taxpayer may appeal to both AAO and BOR. However, if AAO accepts the case, the taxpayer must choose either AAO or BOR to hear its case. If the taxpayer chooses AAO, the taxpayer must withdraw its appeal from the BOR and vice versa.

3. *AAO and TAC.* A taxpayer may appeal to both AAO and TAC. If AAO accepts the case, the taxpayer must obtain permission from the Director of Taxation and TAC to participate in AADR. A taxpayer does not have to withdraw its appeal from TAC to participate in AADR.

4. *Post-AADR appeal options.* If AAO does not resolve the case, then the taxpayer may proceed with an existing TAC appeal as described in section VIII.B.3 or if no TAC appeal exists, the taxpayer may pay the disputed portion of the final assessment under written protest and seek to recover the taxes by filing an action in TAC within 30 calendar days from date of payment (section 40-35, HRS).

(C) Other Types of Appeals

A return preparer that disagrees with a Notice and Demand of Penalty (return preparer penalty assessment) may appeal to AAO and/or TAC, but not the BOR. If the return preparer appeals to both AAO and TAC and AAO accept the case, then the return preparer must obtain permission from the Director of Taxation and TAC to participate in AADR. A return preparer does not have to withdraw its appeal from TAC to participate in AADR. If AAO does not resolve the case, then the return preparer may proceed with its appeal before TAC. Department of Taxation Announcement No. 2016-03 February 1, 2016 Page 4

(D) BOR and TAC Filing Deadlines Are Not Affected by AADR

Applying or participating in AADR does not toll the statute of limitations for filing an appeal with the BOR or TAC. The deadline to appeal a final assessment to the BOR or TAC is 30 calendar days after the final assessment mailing date (section 235-114, HRS). Alternatively, if an appeal is not filed with the BOR or the TAC by the deadline, a taxpayer may pay the disputed portion of the final assessment under written protest and seek to recover the taxes by filing an action in TAC within 30 calendar days from date of payment (section 40-35, HRS).

(E) Withdrawal or Termination from AADR

AADR is optional for taxpayers and return preparers. A taxpayer or return preparer may withdraw its case from AADR by submitting written notification to the Administrative Appeals Officer. If AAO determines that meaningful progress towards resolution has stopped, it may terminate a case with AADR by notifying the auditor or examiner and the taxpayer or return preparer in writing. Taxpayers and return preparers retain all applicable appeal rights as provided for under the law, provided that the time to file an appeal has not expired. For more information, see:

- Tax Information Release No. 2002-01, Audit of Net Income, General Excise, and Use Tax Returns; Appeal Rights, Claims for Refund; and Payment to State Under Protest.

- Hawaii Taxpayer Bill of Rights

IX. *DECISIONS*

The Administrative Appeals Officer will provide a written decision to the parties in the case. The decision applies only to the taxpayer or return preparer in the case and cannot be used or cited as precedent or as the basis for new or alternative applications of the law. Decisions do not change or modify DOTAX policies and practices and the Administrative Appeals Officer's decisions cannot be appealed.

X. *EFFECTIVE DATE*

The Administrative Appeals Office will accept applications for the pilot phase of AADR beginning February 1, 2016.

XI. *QUESTIONS AND COMMENTS*

The purpose of the pilot phase is to test and evaluate the program's effectiveness and efficiency in resolving tax disputes. Your comments are an important part of evaluating AADR and will help us consider ways to improve the program. If you have any comments or questions about AADR, please email us at tax.appeals@hawaii.gov. For more information, visit our website at tax.hawaii. gov/appeals.

HRS section explained: 231-7.5

## ¶ 1438. Department of Taxation Announcement No. 2016-06
### Re: Summary and Digest of the Hawaii Supreme Court decision in *Travelocity.com L.P. v. Director of Taxation*, 13 Hawaii 88 (2015).

*SUMMARY*

On March 17, 2015, the Supreme Court of Hawaii issued its decision in *Travelocity.com, L.P. v. Director of Taxation*, 135 Hawaii 88 (2015), holding that online travel companies (OTCs), including Travelocity.com, LLP, Expedia, Inc., Orbitz, LLC, Hotwire, Inc., and Priceline.com, are subject to Hawaii's general excise tax (GET), but not subject to Hawaii's transient accommodations tax (TAT).

The Hawaii Supreme Court states that the OTCs operate websites where transients can research destinations and make reservations for airfare, car rentals, and hotels. The Department of Taxation (Department) assessed the OTCs in connection with income derived from the sales of room accommodations in Hawaii under a business model whereby hotels granted the OTCs the right to sell occupancy for a hotel room and the OTCs then sold the right to occupy the room to a transient.

The court held that the OTCs were engaged in business in the state and therefore subject to the GET. The court further held that the OTCs' services were used or consumed in Hawaii. Accordingly, the OTCs' income was sourced to Hawaii and application of the exported services exemption was disallowed. The court also held that the OTCs were only subject to GET on their share of the gross income because the income-splitting provision in section 237-18(g), Hawaii Revised Statutes (HRS), applied. With respect to the TAT, the court held that the OTCs were not operators and therefore not subject to the TAT.

As discussed in detail below, the following are key points from the court's decision:

- Physical presence in Hawaii is not required to satisfy the statutory "in the State" requirement in section 237-13, HRS, and be subject to the GET's "wide and tight net"
- For purposes of the income-splitting provision in section 237-18(g), HRS, the term "travel agency" means an "enterprise engaged in arranging and selling travel services" and does not exclude an entity in direct contractual privity with the transient
- The TAT is imposed once on a single operator of a transient accommodation
- The Department's assessment of penalties for failure to pay taxes is presumed correct, thereby imposing the burden on the taxpayer to prove that the failure to pay was not due to negligence or intentional disregard of the rules

*GENERAL EXCISE TAX*

(A) Physical Presence is Not Required

The GET is a privilege tax imposed on all business and other activities "in the State."[1] The OTCs asserted that the statutory phrase "in the State" means that a taxpayer must have a physical presence in Hawaii (i.e. a taxpayer's business activities must be performed in Hawaii) in order to be subject to the GET.[2] The OTCs claimed that their services, performed outside Hawaii, were not subject to the GET despite the fact that the travel occurred within Hawaii.[3] The court rejected the OTCs' argument, explaining that the GET, a tax designed to reach "virtually every economic activity imaginable," does not have any physical geographical limitation.[4]

The court held that the OTCs had sufficient business and other activities in the state to subject them to the GET.[5] Specifically, the court explained that the taxable event—the receipt of income from transients for providing accommodations in hotel rooms in Hawaii—provided the OTCs with an economic gain arising from property located in Hawaii.[6] Additionally, although the agreements between the OTCs

---

[1]  Haw. Rev. Stat. § 237-13.

[2]  *Travelocity*, 135 Hawaii at 103.

[3]  *Id.* at 100.

[4]  *Id.* at 103-105.

[5]  *Id.* at 105.

[6]  *Id.* at 104-105 (discussing similarities with *In re Tax Appeal of Subway Real Estate Corp. v. Director of Taxation*, 110 Hawaii 25 (2006)).

¶ 1438

and transients took place outside of Hawaii, the intent was that "performance would occur entirely in Hawaii," where the occupancy rights were "wholly consumable and only consumable in Hawaii."[7] The court also noted that the OTCs were not passive sellers of services to Hawaii consumers, as they actively solicited customers for Hawaii hotel rooms and actively solicited hotels to allow them to sell occupancy rights.[8] Further, the court explained, the OTCs constructively benefited through the transients' use and benefit of state services, such as the use of roads and access to police, fire, and lifeguard protection services.[9] Accordingly, the OTCs were engaged in business "in the State."[10]

(B) Sourcing and Exported Services Exemption

The court next rejected the OTCs' argument that the GET did not apply because the OTCs' services were used or consumed outside of the State.[11] The OTCs, relying on the exported services exemption in section 237-29.53, HRS, and the offset for taxes paid to other states provided for in section 237-22, HRS, asserted that their services were not used or consumed in Hawaii, but rather, in "whatever out-of-state location the transient is located at the time of purchase."[12] The court rejected the OTCs' argument, holding that it was "clear that the Assessed Transactions are business transactions that continue in the state," where the hotel rooms are used or consumed.[13]

(C) Division of Income Under Section 237-18(g), HRS

The GET is imposed on a business' gross proceeds or gross income, which is defined as all gross receipts "without any deduction on account of the cost of the property sold, the cost of materials used, labor cost, taxes, royalties, interest, or discount paid or any other expenses whatsoever."[14] In limited circumstances, however, and only as provided by statute, a business will be subject to the GET only for its share of gross income.

Section 237-18(g), HRS, provides such an exception: "Where transient accommodations are furnished through arrangements made by a travel agency or tour packager at noncommissioned negotiated contract rates and the gross income is divided between the operator of transient accommodations on the one hand and the travel agency or tour packager on the other hand, the tax imposed by this chapter shall apply to each such person with respect to such person's respective portion of the proceeds, and no more."

The court held that section 237-18(g), HRS, applied to the assessed transactions, clarifying that the OTCs fell within the ordinary definition of "travel agency"—an "enterprise engaged in arranging and selling travel services."[15] The court explained that the fact that the OTCs were in direct contractual privity with the transients (as opposed to merely being an intermediary between the hotels and the transients) did not preclude them from qualifying as travel agents.[16] The court also clarified that a noncommissioned rate is an amount of money paid to an entity or person other than an agent or employee.[17] The court explained that unlike a commissioned transaction, in which a fee is usually paid as a percentage of the income received, in a noncommissioned transaction, a hotel has no

---

[7]   *Travelocity*, 135 Hawaii at 105 (discussing similarities with *In re Tax Appeal of Heftel Broadcasting Honolulu, Inc.*, 57 Haw. 175 (1976)).

[8]   *Travelocity*, 135 Hawaii at 105 (discussing similarities with *In re Tax Appeal of Baker & Taylor, Inc.*, 103 359 (2004)).

[9]   *Travelocity* Hawaii, 135 Hawaii at 105 (discussing similarities with *In re Tax Appeal of Grayco Land Escrow, Ltd.*, 57 Haw. 436 (1977)).

[10]  *Travelocity*, 135 Hawaii at 105.

[11]  *Id.* at 100, 105 n.20.

[12]  *Id.*

[13]  *Id.* at 105 n.20.

[14]  Haw. Rev. Stat. § 237-3.

[15]  *Id.* at 106-108.

[16]  *Id.* at 108.

[17]  *Id.* at 111.

means of knowing what the travel agent's mark-up will be.[18] Because the court found the OTCs operated as travel agents, divided income with the hotels, and furnished transient accommodations at noncommissioned negotiated contract rates in the assessed transactions, the court held that the OTCs were subject to the GET for their share of the gross income.[19]

### TRANSIENT ACCOMMODATIONS TAX

The TAT is imposed on the gross proceeds derived from furnishing transient accommodations.[20] The TAT is payable by operators, defined in section 237D-1, HRS, as "any person operating a transient accommodation, whether as owner or proprietor or as lessee, sublessee, mortgagee in possession, licensee, or otherwise, or engaging or continuing in any service business which involves the actual furnishing of transient accommodation."[21] The court held that the OTCs were not operators, as defined by statute, because there can only be a single operator that furnishes transient accommodations.[22] Because it was undisputed that the hotels were operators, the OTCs could not also be operators.[23] Accordingly, the court held that the OTCs were not subject to the TAT.[24]

### PENALTIES

The Supreme Court, having determined that the OTCs were subject to the GET, affirmed the Tax Appeal Court's ruling that the OTCs were subject to penalties under section 231-39(b)(1), HRS, for failing to timely file a tax return.[25] The court held that the OTCs failed to demonstrate an honest belief that they were not responsible for filing a GET return and were therefore subject to the failure to file penalty.[26]

The Supreme Court also affirmed the Tax Appeal Court's ruling that the OTCs were subject to penalties under section 231-39(b)(2)(A), HRS, for underpayment of tax due to negligence or intentional disregard.[27] The court explained that because the Department's assessments are prima facie correct, the burden is on the taxpayer to prove that the failure to pay was not due to negligence or intentional disregard of the rules.[28] Because the OTCs failed to present any evidence to rebut the presumed validity of the penalty, the Tax Appeal Court's ruling was affirmed.[29]

This Tax Announcement is a summary and digest of the Hawaii Supreme Court decision in *Travelocity.com, L.P. v. Director of Taxation*, 135 Hawaii 88 (2015) and should not be relied upon as a statement of law or fact. For more information please refer to the decision or call the Administrative Rules Office at 808-587-1530.

### ¶ 1439. Department of Taxation Announcement No. 2018-01
#### Re: Adoption of Amended Hawaii Administrative Rules Section 18-231-3-14.17, Relating to Revocation of Tax Licenses Due to Abandonment

The Department of Taxation has adopted a rule amending Hawaii Administrative Rules Section 18-231-3-14.17 that authorizes the Department to revoke a tax license that has been deemed

---

18  *Id.* at 111-13.

19  *Id.* at 113.

20  Haw. Rev. Stat. § 237D-2(a).

21  Haw. Rev. Stat. §§ 237D-1, 237D-2(a).

22  *Travelocity*, 135 Hawaii at 127.

23  Id.

24  Id.

25  *Id.* at 113-14.

26  Id.

27  *Id.* at 114-15.

28  *Id.* (citing Haw. Rev. Stat. § 231-20).

29  *Travelocity*, 135 Hawaii at 114-15.

abandoned by publishing notice of intent to revoke on the Department's website. The rule provides that the notice of intent will be published for a period of at least 45 days.

The adoption replaces the temporary rule announced in the Department Announcement 2016-04, which expired October 4, 2017.

## ¶ 1440. Department of Taxation Announcement No. 2018-02
### Re: Adoption of New Administrative Rules Section 18-231-3-14.26, Relating to Registration of Representatives

The Department of Taxation (Department) announces the adoption of temporary administrative rules, as described below, which will take effect on April 4, 2016 and expire on October 4, 2017. Pursuant to section 231-10.7, Hawaii Revised Statutes (HRS), temporary rules have the same force and effect as any other administrative rules.

(1) Attorneys;

(2) Accountants;

(3) Enrolled Agents;

(4) Enrolled Actuaries

(5) Enrolled Retirement Plan Agents; and

(6) All other persons who represent taxpayers and receive compensation for their services.

The new rule makes permanent and supersedes temporary rules previously announced through Department of Taxation Announcement No. 2017-03.

## ¶ 1441. Department of Taxation Announcement No. 2018-10
### Re: Implementation of Act 41, Session Laws of Hawaii 2018, Relating to When a Taxpayer is Engaging in Business in the State for Purposes of Hawaii's General Excise Tax

This Announcement amends and supersedes Announcement No. 2018-10, previously issued on June 27, 2018. Taxpayers are advised that the Department will not retroactively administer Act 41, which is effective July 1, 2018.

*BACKGROUND*

The general excise tax (GET) is a privilege tax imposed on all business and other activities "in the State." Haw. Rev. Stat § 237-13. Although it is clear that a business with a physical presence in Hawaii satisfies the statutory "in the State" requirement and is therefore subject to GET, the law was previously unclear as to the circumstances under which a business that lacks a physical presence in Hawaii would satisfy the "in the State" requirement. SeeTravelocity.com, L.P. v. Director of Taxation, 135 Hawaii 88, 103 (2015) (rejecting argument that taxpayers must have physical presence in the State to satisfy the statutory "in the State" requirement).

Act 41, Session Laws of Hawaii 2018 (Act 41) clarifies the "in the State" requirement by creating a bright-line rule for businesses that lack a physical presence in Hawaii. Specifically, Act 41 provides that a person is engaging in business in the State, regardless of whether the person is physically present in the State, if in the current or preceding calendar year:

(1) The person has gross income of $100,000 or more from the sale of tangible personal property delivered in the State, services used or consumed in the State, or intangible property used in the State; or

(2) The person has entered into 200 or more separate transactions involving tangible personal property delivered in the State, services used or consumed in the State, or intangible property used in the State.

Somewhat overlapping with the statutory "in the State" requirement is the requirement imposed by the U.S. Commerce Clause that a taxpayer's activity must have a substantial nexus with the taxing jurisdiction. SeeBaker & Taylor, Inc. v. Kawafuchi, 103 Hawaii 359, 365-71 (2004) (analyzing whether taxpayer was engaged in business "in the State" and whether taxpayer's activity had a substantial nexus with the State); see also Complete Auto Transit v. Brady, 430 U.S. 274, 279 (1977) (articulating substantial nexus requirement).

In South Dakota v. Wayfair, Inc., No. 17-494, 2018 WL 3058015, at *17 (U.S. Jun. 21, 2018), the U.S. Supreme Court held that South Dakota's law, Senate Bill 106, which has a similar $100,000 or 200-transaction threshold, satisfies the substantial nexus requirement imposed by the U.S. Commerce Clause, as "[t]his quantity of business could not have occurred unless the seller availed itself of the substantial privilege of carrying on business in [the state]."

In sum, the imposition of the GET on a taxpayer who lacks physical presence in Hawaii, but who has gross income of $100,000 or more or who has entered into 200 or more transactions attributable to Hawaii, comports with the statutory "in the State" requirement as well as the U.S. Commerce Clause's substantial nexus requirement.

A taxpayer will therefore be required to maintain a GET license, file GET returns, and remit GET to the State if any of the following applies:

(1) Taxpayer has a physical presence1 in Hawaii;

(2) In the current or preceding calendar year, taxpayer has gross income or gross proceeds of $100,000 or more from any of the following, or combination of the following, activities:

    a. Tangible property delivered in Hawaii;

    b. Services used or consumed in Hawaii; or

    c. Intangible property used in Hawaii; or

(3) In the current or preceding calendar year, taxpayer has entered into 200 or more separate transactions involving any of the following, or combination of the following, activities:

    a. Tangible property delivered in Hawaii;

    b. Services used or consumed in Hawaii; or

    c. Intangible property used in Hawaii.

Implementation of Act 41 in 2018

*RETROACTIVITY*

Although the U.S. Supreme Court, in South Dakota v. Wayfair, Inc., held that Senate Bill 106 satisfied the substantial nexus requirement, the Court did not rule on whether Senate Bill 106 violated other principles of the U.S. Commerce Clause. Wayfair, 2018 WL 3058015, at *17 . The Court noted, however, that South Dakota's law contains "several features that appear designed to prevent discrimination against or undue burdens upon interstate commerce," including a prohibition on retroactive application of Senate Bill 106. Id.

To avoid any constitutional concerns, the Department will not retroactively administer Act 41. Accordingly, taxpayers who lacked physical presence in Hawaii prior to July 1, 2018, but who met the $100,000 or 200-transaction threshold in 2017 or 2018, will not be required to remit GET for the period from January 1, 2018 to June 30, 2018.

*DEADLINE TO FILE FIRST RETURN*

Periodic returns are due on the 20th day following the close of the filing period. A taxpayer's filing period is monthly if more than $4,000 in GET will be paid for the year; quarterly if more than $2,000, but $4,000 or less in GET will be paid for the year; or semiannually if $2,000 or less in GET will be paid for the year. Annual returns are due on the 20th day of the fourth month following the close of the tax year.

If, prior to July 1, 2018, a taxpayer lacks physical presence in Hawaii and meets the $100,000 or 200-transaction threshold for 2017 or 2018, the taxpayer will be subject to GET beginning on July 1, 2018 (or on the first day of the tax year beginning on or after July 1, 2018 if the taxpayer is a fiscal year taxpayer) and must file its first periodic return by the deadline for that period.

If a taxpayer who lacks physical presence in Hawaii meets the $100,000 or 200-transaction threshold between July 1, 2018 and December 31, 2018, the taxpayer will be subject to GET beginning on July 1, 2018 (or on the first day of the tax year beginning on or after July 1, 2018 if the taxpayer is a fiscal

**¶ 1441**

year taxpayer). The taxpayer will be given a grace period of one period for the filing of the first periodic return. Accordingly, the taxpayer must file its first periodic return by the deadline for the periodic return following the period in which the taxpayer met the $100,000 or 200-transaction threshold.

If the taxpayer meets the threshold during the last period of the tax year, the taxpayer will not be required to file a periodic return for that period. Instead, the taxpayer's first return will be the annual return for that tax year.

The following chart provides the first filing deadlines for calendar year taxpayers who will be filing on a monthly basis:

| When Threshold Was First Met | First Filing Deadline |
|---|---|
| 1/1/17 – 12/31/17 | 8/20/18 |
| 1/1/18 – 6/30/18 | 8/20/18 |
| 7/1/18 – 7/31/18 | 9/20/18 |
| 8/1/18 – 8/31/18 | 10/22/18 |
| 9/1/18 – 9/30/18 | 11/20/18 |
| 10/1/18 – 10/31/18 | 12/20/18 |
| 11/1/18 – 11/30/18 | 1/21/19 |
| 12/1/18 – 12/31/18 | 4/22/19 (annual return) |

## CATCHUP INCOME

Because taxpayers who meet the $100,000 or 200-transaction threshold after July 1, 2018 are given a grace period for the filing of their first return, said taxpayers will need to report "catchup income" (income recognized prior to and during the period in which the taxpayer meets the threshold) and pay GET on said income. The Department will allow taxpayers to report and pay GET on catchup income, without penalty and interest, as follows:

(1) The taxpayer may report and pay GET on all catchup income in full on the first periodic return; or

(2) The taxpayer may report and pay GET on catchup income by spreading the liability equally over the remaining periods in the current tax year.

If, however, the taxpayer meets the threshold during the last period of the tax year, the taxpayer must report and pay GET on all catchup income in full on the annual return.

Implementation of Act 41 in Subsequent Years

In 2019 and later years, if a taxpayer lacks physical presence in Hawaii and did not meet the $100,000 or 200-transaction threshold in the preceding calendar year, the taxpayer will be given a grace period of one period for the filing of the first periodic return. Accordingly, the taxpayer must file its first periodic return by the deadline for the periodic return following the period in which the taxpayer met the $100,000 or 200-transaction threshold. Additionally, the Department will allow taxpayers to report and pay GET on catchup income, without penalty and interest, in the same manner described above.

## FAQS

### Engaging in Business in the State

1. I have a physical presence in Hawaii, but I have less than $100,000 in gross income and have entered into less than 200 transactions in 2017 and 2018. Will I be subject to GET for the tax year beginning in 2018?

Yes, because you have a physical presence in Hawaii, you are engaging in business in the State and are subject to GET even if you do not meet the $100,000 or 200-transaction threshold.

¶ 1441

2. I do not have a physical presence in Hawaii, but I have $100,000 in gross income attributable to Hawaii in 2018. Will I be subject to GET for the tax year beginning in 2018?

Yes, you are engaging in business in the State because you met the $100,000 threshold in the current calendar year.

3. I do not have a physical presence in Hawaii. My gross income attributable to Hawaii was $100,000 in 2017 and $50,000 in 2018. Will I be subject to GET for the tax year beginning in 2018?

Yes, you are engaging in business in the State because you met the $100,000 threshold in the preceding calendar year.

4. I do not have a physical presence in Hawaii, but in 2017, I entered into 100 transactions for tangible property delivered in Hawaii and 100 transactions for intangible property used in Hawaii. Will I be subject to GET for the tax year beginning in 2018?

Yes, you are engaging in business in the State because you have entered into 200 transactions attributable to Hawaii in the preceding calendar year. The 200-transaction threshold may be met by any combination of tangible property delivered in the State, services used or consumed in the State, or intangible property used in the State.

5. I do not have a physical presence in Hawaii. If I entered into 200 transactions attributable to Hawaii in 2018, but have less than $100,000 in gross income, will I be subject to GET for the tax year beginning in 2018?

Yes, you are engaging in business in the State because you have entered into 200 transactions attributable to Hawaii in the current calendar year. You will be subject to GET if you meet the $100,000 or the 200-transaction threshold; you do not need to meet both. Filing and Payment Deadlines

6. I do not have a physical presence in Hawaii, but, I have $100,000 in gross income attributable to Hawaii between January 1, 2018 and June 30, 2018. Will I be subject to GET for the $100,000?

You will be subject to GET for the tax year beginning in 2018, but will not be subject to GET for any periods between January 1, 2018 and June 30, 2018.

7. I do not have a physical presence in Hawaii, but, I have $100,000 in gross income attributable to Hawaii between January 1, 2018 and June 30, 2018. When is the deadline to file my first GET return?

If you are a calendar year taxpayer and will be filing on a monthly basis, your first return is due on August 20, 2018; if you are a calendar year taxpayer and will be filing on a quarterly basis, your first return is due on October 22, 2018; if you are a calendar year taxpayer and will be filing on a semiannual basis, your first return is due on January 21, 2019.

8. I do not have a physical presence in Hawaii, but I have $100,000 in gross income attributable to Hawaii between January 1, 2018 and June 30, 2018. I have $20,000 in gross income for July 2018. How much income should I report on my next periodic return?

Assuming you are a calendar year taxpayer who will be filing on a monthly basis, you should report $20,000 in gross income on the return due on August 20, 2018.

9. I do not have a physical presence in Hawaii and do not have any gross income or transactions attributable to Hawaii in 2017. I have $80,000 in gross income attributable to Hawaii between January 1, 2018 and June 30, 2018; $10,000 in gross income for July 2018; $14,000 in gross income for August 2018; and $16,000 in gross income for September 2018. When is the deadline to file my first GET return? How much income should I report?

Assuming you are a calendar year taxpayer who will be filing on a monthly basis, you are required to file your first return by October 22, 2018. Because you met the threshold in August 2018, you are given a grace period of one month, to October 22, 2018, to file your first periodic return. On the October 22, 2018 return, you may either: (1) report $40,000 in gross income (catchup income of $24,000 plus $16,000 in income for September); or (2) report $22,000 in gross income (catchup income of $24,000 divided over four monthly periods, or $6,000, plus $16,000 in income for September).

10. I do not have a physical presence in Hawaii and do not have any gross income or transactions attributable to Hawaii in 2017. I met the $100,000 threshold in December 2018. My gross income between July 1, 2018 and December 31, 2018 is $50,000. When is the deadline to file my first GET return? How much income should I report?

Assuming you are a calendar year taxpayer, you are required to file an annual return by April 22, 2019 and report $50,000 in gross income on that return. You are not required to file a periodic return for the 2018 tax year because you met the threshold during the last period of the tax year. Additionally, you may not pay the catchup income in installments because there are no remaining periods in the tax year.

11. I do not have a physical presence in Hawaii and do not have any gross income or transactions attributable to Hawaii in 2017 or 2018. I have $90,000 in gross income attributable to Hawaii in January 2019; $80,000 in gross income in February 2019; and $50,000 in gross income in March 2019. When is the deadline to file my first GET return? How much income should I report?

Assuming you are a calendar year taxpayer who will be filing on a monthly basis, you are required to file your first return by April 22, 2019. Because you met the threshold in February 2019, you are given a grace period of one month, to April 22, 2019, to file your first periodic return. On the April 22, 2019 return, you may either: (1) report $220,000 in gross income (catchup income of $170,000 plus $50,000 in income for March); or (2) report $67,000 in gross income (catchup income of $170,000 divided over 10 monthly periods, or $17,000, plus $50,000 in income for March).

For additional information regarding Act 41, contact the Rules Office at (808) 587-1530 or by email at Tax.Rules.Office@hawaii.gov. For general information regarding Hawaii's GET, and to obtain tax forms, instructions, and publications, visit the Department's website at tax.hawaii.gov.

LINDA CHU TAKAYAMA
Director of Taxation

1. Physical presence includes, but is not limited to, having an office, employees or representatives, inventory, or other property in Hawaii, or providing services in Hawaii, such as installation, training, maintenance, or repair services.

2 See sections 18-237-29.53-01 through 18-237-29.53-13, Hawaii Administrative Rules, and Tax Information Release No. 2018-06 for more information regarding the sourcing of income from services.

# ¶ 1442. Department of Taxation Tax Information Release 2018-01
## Re: General Excise Tax Obligations of Transportation Network Companies and Drivers

This Tax Information Release discusses the General Excise Tax (GET) obligations of transportation network companies (TNCs) and drivers who transport riders to destinations via use of the TNC's website or mobile application, including different treatment for amounts paid as a fare versus amounts paid as discretionary tips for drivers.

TNCs provide a website, mobile application, or both (the App) where persons seeking transportation to certain destinations (Riders) may request motor vehicle transportation to such destinations. The TNC provides a Rider requesting a ride through the App with an individual able to drive to that destination (Driver). After the ride is completed, the TNC charges the Rider a fare, possibly with an opportunity to add a discretionary tip for the Driver.

The GET is imposed on the gross income or gross proceeds of all business activities in the State unless an exemption applies. Hawaii Revised Statutes (HRS) § 237-13. Because TNC transactions involve three parties, it may not be immediately clear which party is in contract with the Rider and therefore liable for GET on the gross proceeds of the transaction.

### GET Liability of TNCs

The TNC will be subject to GET on the gross proceeds of the transaction (i.e., the total amount collected from a Rider), except for discretionary tips, at the retail rate (four percent plus any applicable county surcharge) if any of the following are true:

1. The TNC controls the manner in which the service is provided;

2. The TNC controls the price charged to the Rider for transportation;

3. The TNC processes payments for the transaction, whether directly or by using third party payment processors, as opposed to merely providing a Rider's payment information to a Driver to bill the Rider his or herself; or

4. The TNC provides insurance coverage for the transaction.

### GET Liability of Drivers

The Driver owes GET on his or her gross income (i.e., the total amount the TNC and/or the Rider remits to the Driver). The Driver may be eligible to pay GET at the reduced wholesale rate of 0.5 percent on the nontip portion of the income he or she receives if the elements in section 237-4, HRS, are met.[1]

### GET on Tip Income

With respect to discretionary tips, the person who ultimately receives the tip is subject to tax on the amount received at the retail rate. If the tip is divided between the TNC and the Driver, the tax applies to both the TNC and the Driver on each person's respective portion.

Discretionary tip income is:

1. An amount the Rider pays that is not part of the negotiated price of the transportation service;

2. Given voluntarily by the Rider; and

3. Given by the Rider in a situation where the payment is clearly a discretionary tip such as a labeled, separate line to add a tip on a paper credit card receipt, a labeled, separate field in an electronic payment application, or the opportunity to hand cash in addition to the negotiated price directly to a Driver.

Mandatory tips, such as an automatic gratuity added to large parties or rides requiring special automobiles or other special accommodations, or other mandatory payments, are taxable to the TNC at the retail rate with no deductions or income splitting.

### Example

Rider uses TNC to request transportation in Honolulu. Driver's agreement with TNC entitles her to the amount of the "TNC Fare" minus a 25 percent commission plus any amounts paid as tips, which is discretionary. After Driver takes Rider to her destination, TNC charges Rider as follows:

| | |
|---|---|
| Base Fare | $2.00 |
| Distance ($1.50 x 5.25 miles) | $7.88 |
| Time ($0.22 x 20 minutes) | $4.40 |
| TNC Fare | $14.28 |
| Service Fee | $1.75 |
| Tip | $3.00 |
| Total | $19.03 |

---

[1] If the Driver is an employee of the TNC, amounts received as a salary or wage are exempt from GET under section 237-24(6), HRS.

¶ 1442

TNC will be liable for GET at the retail rate on $16.03, the entire amount charged minus the tip. Driver's GET base is 75% of $14.28, or $10.71, plus the $3.00 tip, for a total amount of $13.71. However, Driver may be eligible to pay GET at the reduced wholesale rate on the $10.71 of nontip income it receives from the TNC. Driver must pay GET at the retail rate on its tip income of $3.00.

LINDA CHU TAKAYAMA
Director of Taxation

## ¶ 1443. Department of Taxation Tax Information Release 2018-02
### Re: General Excise Tax Exemption for TRICARE

This Tax Information Release discusses the General Excise Tax (GET) exemption for amounts received by a TRICARE managed care support contractor under Hawaii Revised Statutes (HRS) section 237-24(17). TRICARE (which was formerly known as "CHAMPUS") is a federal government program established in the 1990's to supplement the existing military health care system by allowing active duty and retired military service members, as well as certain dependents, to utilize civilian health care providers.

*GET Exemption for TRICARE Managed Care Support Contractors*

TRICARE is funded as part of the annual defense appropriations budget, and is administered by the TRICARE Management Activity, a unit of the United States Department of Defense. Under the applicable federal laws and regulations, TRICARE procures the services of what they denominate as a "managed care support contractor", which is in effect a third party administrator and disbursing agent for the federal government. The managed care support contractor's job is to effectuate a network of private health care providers which the military personnel may utilize, to receive claims and invoices from these health care providers, and then pay those claims according to the amounts and guidelines as set by the federal government. The federal government then reimburses the contractor for the amounts so paid, as well as an administrative fee for its services.

Hawaii Revised Statutes section 237-24(17) was enacted by Act 70, Session Laws of follows Hawaii 2009 (Act 70), and provides as follows[2]:

Amounts received by a managed care support contractor of the TRICARE program that is established under Title 10 United States Code Chapter 55, as amended, for the actual cost or advancement to third party health care providers pursuant to a contract with the United States[.]

The TRICARE exemption was enacted to clarify that amounts received by a managed care support contractor of TRICARE are exempt from the GET. As noted in Section 1 of Act 70:

The legislature understands that some uncertainty may exist about whether the amounts received by a managed care support contractor of the TRICARE program for the actual cost or advancement to third party health care providers, on behalf of the federal government, are subject to the state general excise tax. The legislature finds that, to avoid increasing the costs of health care services delivered through the TRICARE program and any adverse consequences to members of our uniformed services and their families from the increased costs, it is desirable to clarify that the amounts received by a managed care support contractor of the TRICARE program are not subject to the state general excise tax.

The purpose of this Act is to clarify that the amounts received by a managed care support contractor of the TRICARE program for the actual cost or advancement to third party health care providers, pursuant to a contract with the United States for the administration of the TRICARE program, are excluded from the state general excise tax.

Section 1 of Act 70 also makes clear that "managed care support contractors" are third party administrators used "to establish and maintain networks of TRICARE-authorized civilian health care providers in various regions of the United States. On behalf of the United States Department of Defense, managed care support contractors make advances to health care providers, including doctors, hospitals, and other providers, for costs of health care services provided to TRICARE beneficiaries."

---

[2]  Act 70 originally provided that the exemption would be repealed on December 31, 2013. Act 164, Session Laws of Hawaii 2014, extended the exemption such that it is now scheduled to be repealed on December 31, 2018.

Act 70 and HRS section 237-24(17) are very clear in that the exemption applies only to the amounts received by the managed care support contractor and only for such amounts it received as repayment for the actual cost or advancement it had made to third party health care providers. This exemption does not apply to the third party health care providers, as well as to the amounts received by the managed care support contractor as fees for its services. It is also important to note that a general excise tax exemption for medical services does not exist.

For more information on this issue, please contact the Technical Section at 808-587-1577 or by e-mail at Tax.Technical.Section@hawaii.gov.

## ¶ 1444. Department of Taxation Tax Information Release 2018-03
### Re: Renewable Fuels Production Tax Credit, Hawaii Revised Statutes Section 235-110.31

The purpose of this Tax Information Release (TIR) is to define certain terms related to the Renewable Fuels Production Tax Credit (RFPTC) that are not defined in section 235-110.31, Hawaii Revised Statutes (HRS), and as applicable, Act 142, Session Laws of Hawaii 2017, and to provide the Department of Business, Economic Development, and Tourism (DBEDT) with guidance in regard to its verification and certification duties and administration of the $3 million aggregate cap. This TIR, like the RFPTC, is effective for taxable years beginning after December 31, 2016.

1. For which tax years is the RFPTC available?

The RFPTC is effective for the "credit period," which is defined in section 235-110.31(a), HRS, as a period of five consecutive years beginning with the first taxable year that a taxpayer claiming the RFPTC begins renewable fuels (RF) production at a level of at least 15 billion British thermal units (BTUs) per year. For example, if a taxpayer properly qualifies for the RFPTC for tax year 2017 for the first time, the RFPTC will be available for tax years 2017 through 2021.

2. What is the definition of the term "sold" for the purpose of the RFPTC?

Renewable Fuels are considered "sold" when the taxpayer claiming the RFPTC is able to substantiate that the specified quantity of the RFs produced were delivered to a purchaser with no affiliation to the taxpayer and that payment for the renewable fuels was made in full to the taxpayer claiming the RFPTC. In addition, both title and the risk of loss must be transferred to the purchaser for the sale to be complete.

For the purpose of verification and certification by DBEDT under section 235-110.31(c), HRS, DBEDT has the authority to determine whether the taxpayer has provided adequate substantiation to support RFPTC certification at its discretion. The Department of Taxation retains the authority to examine and adjust a RFPTC Credit Certificate (CC) after DBEDT certification.

3. What is the definition of "distribution" for the purpose of the RFPTC?

"Distribution" of RF under section 235-110.31, HRS, will be recognized when the RF being claimed for the RFPTC is transferred to an external and unrelated buyer from the taxpayer producing the RF and the taxpayer can provide official transportation manifest that substantiates the delivery of this RF to this buyer.

4. How should the $3 million RFPTC aggregate cap be administered and applied?

The RFPTC has a $3 million dollar cap to be administered by DBEDT, however, section 235-110.31(c), HRS, does not provide any instruction or guidance as to how it should be applied. Because there is no statutory guidance, DBEDT shall apply the aggregate cap on a first-come first-served basis.

In order to administer the aggregate cap on a first-come first-served basis, DBEDT will allocate the RFPTC based on the:

- Post mark date if the CC is mailed;

- Receipt date of the email transmitting the CC if submitted electronically; or

- Date stamp that DBEDT imprints upon receipt if the CC is hand-delivered.

To qualify for allocation, the CC must be fully complete; an incomplete CC will not receive an

RFPTC allocation and must be resubmitted to DBEDT. If resubmission of a CC is required, the allocation priority will be based on the resubmission date, not the original submission date. In the event that multiple taxpayers submit CCs with the same post mark date, email receipt date or DBEDT date stamp and the total RFPTC requested exceeds the $3 million aggregate cap, DBEDT shall apply a proportional allocation between those taxpayers who have submitted their CCs on the same date based on the amount of RF production. The following examples illustrate this allocation:

*Example 1*: Taxpayers A, B and C, each submit CCs for RFPTC. Taxpayer A submits its CC one day before Taxpayers B and C, who both submitted on the same day. Taxpayer A submits a CC for $1 million, Taxpayer B submits a CC for $950,000, and Taxpayer C submits a CC for $950,000, for a total of $2.9 million for all three CCs. It is assumed that all calculations to derive the total RFPTC earned by each taxpayer in dollars is correct and adheres to the RFPTC requirements. Although Taxpayers B and C submit on the same day, no proration is required because after Taxpayer A is allocated $1 million, $2 million is left to allocate. Taxpayer B and C will each be allocated $950,000 as requested. $100,000 is left to allocate.

*Example 2*: Assume the same facts as in Example 1 except that Taxpayer B submits a CC for $1,000,000, and Taxpayer C submits a CC for $3 million. Since Taxpayer A has submitted first, it will be allocated the full $1 million. After the allocation to Taxpayer A, only $2 million of the aggregate cap is available for allocation between Taxpayers B and C. The allocation will be done proportionally to their respective total RF production amounts. Based on Taxpayer B's CC for $1 million, Taxpayer B produced 380 billion BTUs and based on Taxpayer C's CC for $3 million, Taxpayer C produced 1.14 trillion BTUs. Taxpayer B will be allocated $500,000 or 25% of $2 million (380 billion BTUs/(380 billion BTUs + 1.14 trillion BTUs)) and Taxpayer C will be allocated $1.5 million in RFPTC or 75% of $2 million (1.14 trillion BTUs/(380 billion BTUs + 1.14 trillion BTUs)).

5. What is the definition of "year" for the purpose of administering the $3 million aggregate cap?

The term "year," as used in section 235-110.31(c), HRS, means calendar year. The $3 million aggregate cap applies from January 1 to December 31 for each year that the RFPTC is effective. It should be noted that the term "year" is not the same as the term "credit period" for the purpose of administering the RFPTC, as DBEDT will be able to certify the RFPTC up to one calendar year after the end of the "credit period."

For example, if a taxpayer first qualifies for the RFPTC for tax year 2017, the RFPTC will be available through tax year 2021. This means that the "credit period" ends with tax year 2021. In this case, DBEDT may continue to certify the RFPTC until the aggregate cap of $3 million for the January 1 to December 31, 2022 period is reached or December 31, 2022, whichever is later.

DBEDT shall apply and administer the aggregate cap accordingly. If the $3 million aggregate cap is reached, DBEDT is to cease certifying the RFPTC and notify the Department of Taxation that the aggregate cap has been reached.

6. What is the applicable fuel specification for a fuel to qualify as a "renewable fuel" for the purpose of the RFPTC?

In pertinent part, the definition of "renewable fuels" in section 235-110.31(a) provides, "[t]he fuels meet the relevant ASTM International specifications for the particular fuel or other industry specifications for liquid or gaseous fuels." Taxpayers may therefore qualify the fuels produced as a "renewable fuel" under either specification.

Taxpayers who seek to qualify the fuels as "renewable fuels" using the "other industry specifications for liquid or gaseous fuels" must use the industry specification that applies specifically to the type of fuel that was produced. For example, if biogas is produced, the "other industry specification" that can be applied must apply specifically to biogas.

DBEDT shall perform its verification and certification under section 235-110.31(c), HRS, in accordance with this TIR. For more information on this issue, please contact the Rules Office at 808-587-1530 or by e-mail at Tax.Rules.Office@hawaii.gov.

LINDA CHU TAKAYAMA
Director of Taxation

¶ 1444

## ¶ 1445. Department of Taxation Tax Information Release 2018-04
### Re: Guidance Regarding the Motion Picture, Digital Media, and Film Production Income Tax Credit; Temporary Hawaii Administrative Rules §§ 18-235-17-01 to 18-235-17-20; Act 143, Session Laws of Hawaii 2017

The Department of Taxation (Department) promulgated temporary administrative rules sections 18-235-17-01 to 18-235-17-20, relating to the motion picture, digital media, and film production income tax credit (film credit) under section 235-17, Hawaii Revised Statutes. These temporary administrative rules were effective on October 20, 2016 and expire on April 20, 2018. As discussed below, taxpayers may continue to rely on these temporary administrative rules until December 31, 2018.

On July 10, 2017, Governor David Y. Ige signed Act 143, Session Laws of Hawaii 2017 (Act 143) into law, which amends the film credit. Act 143 is effective on December 31, 2018 and generally applies to taxable years beginning after December 31, 2018. The following is a summary of changes that Act 143 makes to the film credit:

- Requires productions that are claiming products or services acquired outside of the State as part of the film credit to provide evidence that reasonable efforts were made to secure and use comparable products or services within the State;

- Deletes the provision that failure to prequalify by registering with the Department of Business, Economic Development, and Tourism (DBEDT) during the development or preproduction stage may constitute a waiver to claim the film credit;

- Requires all qualified production companies to obtain a verification review by a qualified certified public accountant using procedures prescribed by DBEDT to be submitted with the statement of qualified production costs;

- Limits the aggregate amount of the film credit to $35 million per year, provided that if the total amount of credits applied for in any year exceeds the aggregate limit, the excess will be treated as having been applied for in the subsequent year and must be claimed in such year;

- Extends the sunset date from January 1, 2019 to January 1, 2026;

- Prohibits the adoption of rules pursuant to chapter 91, HRS, that expand the scope of the film credit if the rules conflict with the legislative intent of the film credit;

- Requires each qualified production company with production expenditures of $1 million or more to obtain an independent third-party certification of qualified production costs eligible for the film credit in the form of a tax opinion by January 1 of each year; and

- Requires DBEDT, in collaboration with the Department, to submit to the Governor and Legislature an annual report on the number of jobs created in the State by the film productions receiving the film credit.

The Department is currently working with DBEDT on developing administrative rules for the film credit that are consistent with Act 143. To eliminate any uncertainty between April 20, 2018, when the temporary rules expire, and December 31, 2018, when Act 143 takes effect, the Department will continue to administer the film credit based on temporary administrative rules sections 18-235-17-01 to 18-235-17-20 until December 31, 2018, when Act 143 takes effect. Taxpayers may therefore continue to rely on these temporary rules until December 31, 2018.

The temporary administrative rules discussed in this Tax Information Release are attached for reference. For more information, please contact the Rules Office at 808-587-1530 or by e-mail at Tax.Rules.Office@hawaii.gov.

## ¶ 1446. Department of Taxation Tax Information Release 2018-05
### Re: Transient Accommodations Tax Obligations for Rooms Rented to Airline Crew Members

The purpose of this Tax Information Release (TIR) is to remind taxpayers that Transient Accommodations Tax (TAT) is owed on gross income received in exchange for furnishing rooms to airlines for use by crew members unless the airline is obligated to pay for the room for a period of

180 consecutive days or more, regardless of whether airline crew is actually physically present in the room for the entire period. Contracts that provide the airline with the option of renting a room for a period of 180 days or longer, but which obligate the airline to pay only for rooms the airline actually elects to rent for use by its crew are not long-term rental agreements, and gross rental proceeds from such contracts are subject to TAT regardless of the rental period contained in the contract. Taxpayers who fail to report and pay the TAT owed are subject to applicable penalties and interest.

*Relevant Law*

Section 237D-2, Hawaii Revised Statutes (HRS), levies the TAT on every operator for the gross rental or gross rental proceeds derived from furnishing transient accommodations.

"Transient accommodations" is defined in section 237D-1, HRS, as: "the furnishing of a room, apartment, suite, single family dwelling, or the like to a transient for less than one hundred eighty consecutive days."

The term "transient" is defined in section 18-237D-1-06, Hawaii Administrative Rules (HAR), as "any person who stays for only a short and temporary period, such as a person who comes and goes with only a brief stop."

*Section 18-237D-1-07(h), HAR, further provides:*

The transient accommodations tax does not apply to transient accommodations that are occupied by a party pursuant to a long-term rental agreement (e.g., over 180 consecutive days) and used by its employees as an integral part of conducting its business operations. A party entering into a long-term rental agreement with an operator is not a "transient" ... because the contracting party is not occupying the premises for a "short and temporary period", but has agreed to rent the accommodations for an extended period. The fact that a contracting party allows its employees to occupy the hotel rooms or apartments for a shorter period of time is irrelevant because the contracting party is considered the occupant of the accommodations under the long-term rental agreement.

*Section 18-237D-1-07(h) also adds the following example:*

An airline enters into a one-year contract with a hotel operator to rent several rooms for use by its crew members who regularly lay over in Hawaii. The transient accommodations tax does not apply to the gross income received by the hotel operator because the hotel rooms are occupied by the airline for an extended period of time and used by the airline's employees as an integral part of the airline's flight operations.

*Analysis*

In the transient accommodations industry, it is common for hotels to enter into contracts with airlines whereby the hotel agrees to make available a minimum number of rooms long term for the airline's crew every night. Under some of these agreements, the airline is only required to pay the hotel for rooms actually physically occupied by airline crew despite a larger number of rooms, or a "pool" of rooms, being made available to the airline on a regular basis. An operator will not be subject to the TAT for rooms furnished pursuant to a contract entered into with an airline if the agreement provides for the rental of rooms for at least 180 consecutive days.

If an airline is obligated by its agreement to pay for rooms for a period of at least 180 consecutive days, regardless of whether any of its crew is actually physically present in the rooms every night for the entire period, the TAT will not apply. By contrast, if the airline is not obligated to pay for the rooms for at least 180 consecutive days, such as when an agreement allows the airline to determine the number of rooms it needs for its crew on a night-by-night or short-term (less than 180 consecutive days) basis, the TAT will apply to all gross rental proceeds received under the agreement.

The Department notes that the number of rooms the hotel agrees to set aside under the contract is irrelevant. What is relevant instead is the number of rooms let for a period of 180 consecutive days or longer, for which the airline is required to pay regardless of whether its crew in fact physically occupies the rooms. Such rooms are not subject to TAT.

¶ 1446

*Example 1:*

Harry's Hotel (Hotel) and Kapua Airlines (Airline) enter into a contract for hotel accommodations for Airline's crew members to use during layovers. The contract states in relevant part that Hotel shall reserve 10 rooms for Airline crew members every night for a period of one year, running from January 1 until December 31. The contract provides that Airline shall pay Hotel a $100 rate per night per room actually occupied. If Airline requires more than 10 rooms for a given night, it may rent the additional rooms from Hotel at the agreed upon $100 rate, if they are available.

Hotel and Airline have not entered into a long-term rental agreement for 180 consecutive days because the contract only requires Airline to pay Hotel for the rooms that are physically occupied. Accordingly, all gross rental proceeds Airline pays Hotel under this rental agreement are subject to TAT. Even if Airline elects to rent all 10 reserved rooms for 180 consecutive days for use by its crew, Hotel still owes TAT on the gross rental proceeds.

*Example 1:*

Assume the same facts as in Example 1, except that Airline is not allowed to pay Hotel for only the rooms that are physically occupied. Airline is obligated to pay $365,000 (10 rooms x $100 a night x 365 days) regardless of whether its crew members physically occupy all of the rooms for all of the nights.

Hotel and Airline have entered into a long-term rental agreement for at least 180 consecutive days. Accordingly, the gross proceeds Airline pays Hotel for these 10 rooms are not subject to TAT.

*Example 3:*

Assume the same facts as in Example 2, except that in addition to obligating Airline to pay for 10 rooms under a long-term contract, the agreement also contains language giving Airline the options to rent additional rooms at a rate of $100 per night on a night-by-night basis.

Airline elects to rent three rooms at $100 per night for 30 days pursuant to the agreement. The $9,000 (3 rooms x $100 a night x 30 days) Hotel receives for the three rooms is subject to TAT because Hotel and Airline do not have a long term rental agreement for 180 consecutive days for the three additional rooms.

The Department encourages all taxpayers furnishing rooms to the crews of airlines to review their accounting and tax filings to ensure they are reporting the correct gross rental subject to TAT in accordance with the Tax Law and this TIR. Taxpayers who fail to report and pay the TAT owed are subject to assessment for underreporting, including applicable penalties and interest.

For more information on this issue, please contact the Rules Office at (808) 587-1530 or by email at Tax.Rules.Office@hawaii.gov.

> LINDA CHU TAKAYAMA
> Director of Taxation

## ¶ 1447. Department of Taxation Tax Information Release 2018-06
### Re: General Excise Tax Exemption for Contracting and Services Exported Outside the State; Sourcing of Income from Contracting and Services

This Tax Information Release (TIR) discusses the sourcing and apportionment of income from contracting or services for purposes of the general excise tax (GET) and the exemption for contracting or services exported outside the State pursuant to section 237-29.53, Hawaii Revised Statutes (HRS), and sections 18-237-29.53-01 to 18-237-29.53-13, Hawaii Administrative Rules (HAR). These administrative rules were adopted and made effective on March 29, 2018.

This TIR provides general information and is not intended to replace the law or change its meaning. If any conflict exists between this TIR and the HRS and/or HAR, the HRS and/or HAR shall be controlling.

*HISTORICAL BACKGROUND*

Prior to the enactment of the exported services exemption, section 237-29.53, HRS, the Department sourced and apportioned gross income from services based on a "place of performance" test. Under the place of performance test, a taxpayer was subject to GET if the taxpayer was physically in the State at the time the service was performed.

The sourcing of income was necessary pursuant to section 237-21, HRS, which provides:

If any person . . . is engaged in business both within and without the State . . . and if under the Constitution or laws of the United States . . . the entire gross income of such person cannot be included in the measure of this tax, there shall be apportioned to the State and included in the measure of the tax that portion of the gross income which is derived from activities within the State, to the extent that the apportionment is required by the Constitution or laws of the United States.

Because the State did not offer a credit or offset for taxes paid to another state, there was a risk that gross income would be subject to double taxation in violation of the U.S. Commerce Clause.[3] See Complete Auto Transit, Inc. v. Brady, 430 U.S. 274, 279 (1977) (tax must be "fairly apportioned" to comport with U.S. Commerce Clause); see also Tyler Pipe Industries, Inc. v. Washington State Dep't of Revenue, 483 U.S. 232, 248 (1987) (credit provision for tax paid to another state would cure discrimination in violation of U.S. Commerce Clause).

Act 70, Session Laws of Hawaii 1999, which became effective on January 1, 2000, created section 237-29.53, HRS, which provides a GET exemption for contracting or services used or consumed outside the State. Act 70 therefore superseded the "place of performance" test and replaced it with a "used or consumed" test. Under the used or consumed test, a taxpayer is subject to GET if the service is used or consumed in the State, and conversely, is exempt from GET if the service is used or consumed outside the State.

*EXPORTED SERVICES EXEMPTION*

To determine where contracting or services are used or consumed for purposes of section 237-29.53, HRS, taxpayers will need to determine which one of the nine categories listed in sections 18-237-29.53-03 through 18-237-29.53-11, HAR, the contracting or services fall under and follow the corresponding sourcing rule. If contracting or services are used or consumed both in and outside of the State, the taxpayer must apportion gross income using any reasonable method, provided that it is consistently used by the taxpayer and supported by verifiable data.

*1. Contracting*

Contracting, as defined in section 237-6, HRS, is used or consumed where the real property to which the contracting activity pertains is located. HAR § 18-237-29.53-03.

*2. Services Related to Real Property*

Services related to real property, including property management, real estate sales, real estate inspections, and real estate appraisals, are used or consumed where the real property is located. HAR § 18-237-29.53-04.

*3. Services Related to Tangible Personal Property (TPP)*

Services related to TPP, including inspection, appraisal, testing, and repair, are used or consumed where the TPP is delivered after the services are performed. HAR § 18-237-29.53-05.

Services performed by a commissioned agent, however, have different sourcing rules. A taxpayer is a commissioned agent, with respect to TPP, if the taxpayer sells, buys, leases, or procures TPP on behalf of a principal with the principal's assent for a predetermined fee and the total price of the sale is controlled by the principal. HAR § 18-237-29.53-01. If the commissioned agent sells, purchases, leases, or procures TPP online (exclusively through a website or app without

---

3  Act 98, Session Laws of Hawaii 2002, amended section 237-22, HRS, by providing an offset for taxes paid to another state.

any in-person contact), the commissioned agent's service is used or consumed where the TPP is delivered. HAR §18-237-29.53-10(a)(1). If the TPP is not sold, purchased, leased, or procured online, the commissioned agent's service is used or consumed where the agent is located at the time the service is performed. HAR §18-237-29.53-10(a).

The sourcing rules for services relating to TPP are illustrated in the following diagram:

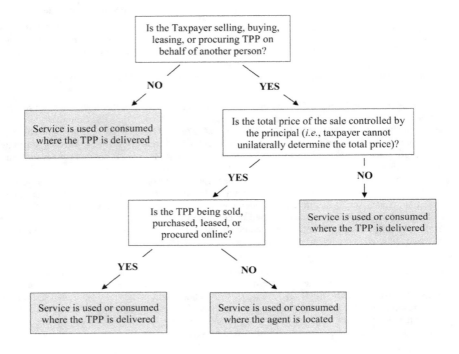

### 4. Booking Services by a Travel Agency or Tour Packager

Income from the sale, booking, or arrangement of transient accommodations or travel-related bookings (including tours, excursions, transportation, rental vehicles, shows, dining, spa services, and other reservations or bookings) by a travel agency or tour packager is sourced based on whether the transaction was booked on a commissioned or noncommissioned basis and whether the booking was made online.

A booking is made on a commissioned basis if the travel agency or tour packager books the transient accommodation or travel-related booking on behalf of a principal with the principal's assent for a predetermined fee and the total price of the booking is controlled by the principal. HAR § 18-237-29.53-01. A booking is made on a noncommissioned basis if the travel agency or tour packager has a contract with an operator of a transient accommodation or operator of a travel-related booking that specifies the rate the operator will receive for a booking and the travel agency or tour packager may unilaterally determine the mark-up and the total price charged to the customer. Id.

Income from bookings made on a noncommissioned basis is sourced to where the transient accommodation or travel-related booking is located. HAR § 18-237-29.53-06. Similarly, income from bookings made online (exclusively through a website or app without any in-person contact) on a commissioned basis is sourced to where the transient accommodation or travel-related booking is located. HAR § 18-237-29.53-10(a)(3). Income from bookings made on a commissioned basis that are not completed online is sourced to where the travel agency or tour packager is located at the time the booking is made. HAR § 18-237-29.53-10(a).

The sourcing rules for travel agencies and tour packagers are illustrated in the following diagram:

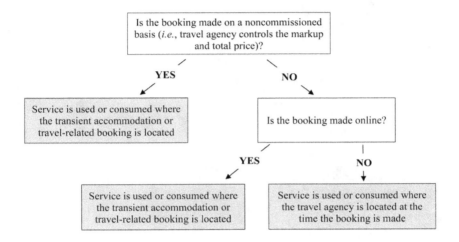

### 5. Legal Services

Legal services provided to a party in a judicial or administrative action or proceeding, arbitration, mediation, or other method of dispute resolution are used or consumed where the case or matter is filed. HAR § 18-237-29.53-07.

If an action or proceeding is not pending, or if the customer is not a party to the action or proceeding, income from legal services is sourced based on whether the client is an individual, business, or military or government. HAR § 18-237-29.53-11. Legal services provided to an individual are used or consumed where the individual resides. HAR § 18-237-29.53-11(a)(3). Legal services provided to the military or government are used or consumed where the benefit of the services is received. HAR § 18-237-29.53-11(a)(4). If legal services are provided to a business and the legal services relate to the client's business activities, the legal services are used or consumed where the client's related business activities occur. HAR § 18-237-29.53-11(a)(1). If legal services are provided to a business and the legal services are unrelated to the client's business activities, the legal services are used or consumed where the client's principal place of business is located. HAR § 18-237-29.53-11(a)(2).

The sourcing rules for legal services are illustrated in the following diagram:

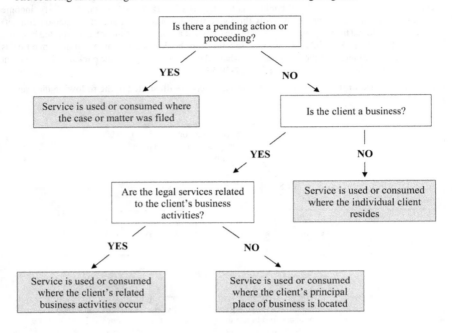

### 6. Debt Collection

Debt collection services are used or consumed where the collection actions take place. HAR § 18-237-29.53-08.

### 7. Services Requiring the Customer to be Physically Present

Services that require the customer to be physically present at the time the services are performed are used or consumed where the services are performed. HAR § 18-237-29.53-09. This rule does not apply to contracting, services related to real property, services related to TPP, services provided by a travel agency or tour packager, legal services, and debt collection services. Id.

### 8. Sale, Purchase, or Procurement of Services by a Commissioned Agent

Income of a commissioned agent who sells, buys, or procures services online (exclusively through a website or app without any in-person contact) is sourced to where the transacted services are performed. HAR § 18-237-29.53-10(a)(2). If the transacted services are not sold, purchased, or procured online, the commissioned agent's services are used or consumed where the agent is located at the time the agent's services are performed. HAR § 18-237-29.53-10(a).

### 9. Other Services Not Covered Above

All other services that are not covered in the rules above are sourced as follows:

• Services provided to individuals are used or consumed where the individual resides;

• Services provided to the military or federal, state, or local government are used or consumed where the benefit of the services are received;

• Services provided to a business that relate to the customer's business activities are used or consumed where the customer's related business activities occur;

- Services provided to a business that are unrelated to the customer's business activities are used or consumed where the customer's principal place of business is located.

HAR § 18-237-29.53-11.

A summary of the sourcing rules discussed above may be found in the attached table. For more information, please contact the Rules Office at (808) 587-1530 or by email at Tax.Rules.Office@ hawaii.gov.

LINDA CHU TAKAYAMA
Director of Taxation

### Summary of GET Sourcing Rules Under Section 237-29.53, HRS

| ACTIVITY | WHERE USED OR CONSUMED |
|---|---|
| **1. Contracting** | |
| All contracting, as defined in section 237-6, HRS | Location of real property |
| **2. Services relating to real property** | |
| All services that relate to real property | Location of real property |
| **3. Services relating to TPP** | |
| If taxpayer is a commissioned agent (*i.e.*, selling, buying, leasing, or procuring TPP on behalf of a principal and the total price of the sale is controlled by the principal) and | |
| The transaction is made online | Place of delivery of TPP |
| The transaction is not made online | Location of agent |
| All other services that relate to TPP | Place of delivery of TPP |
| **4. Booking services by travel agency or tour packager** | |
| If the booking is made on a noncommissioned basis (*i.e.*, travel agency controls markup and total price) | Location of transient accommodation or travel-related booking |
| If the booking is made on a commissioned basis (*i.e.*, travel agency does not control markup and total price) and | |
| The booking is made online | Location of transient accommodation or travel-related booking |
| The booking is not made online | Location of travel agent at the time the booking is made |
| **5. Legal services** | |
| If there is a pending action or proceeding | Where the case was filed |
| If there is no pending action or proceeding and | |
| The client is an individual | Client's residence |
| The client is the military or government | Where the benefit of the service is received |
| The client is a business and | |
| The legal services are related to the client's business activities | Where the related business activities occur/occurred |
| The legal services are unrelated to the client's business activities | The business' principal place of business |

| 6. Debt collection | |
|---|---|
| If the service involves enforcement of a money judgment or collection of a debt | Location of collection action |
| **7. Services requiring customer to be physically present** | |
| Services that require the customer to be physically present | Where service is performed |
| **8. Sales of services by commissioned agent** | |
| If taxpayer is selling, purchasing, or procuring services, the total price of the sale is controlled by the principal, and | |
| The sale is completed online | Where the transacted service is performed |
| The sale is not completed online | Location of agent |
| **9. Other services not covered above** | |
| If the customer is an individual | Customer's residence |
| If the customer is the military or government entity | Where the benefit of the service was received |
| If the customer is a business and | |
| The service relates to the customer's business activities | Where the customer's related business activities occur |
| The service does not relate to the customer's business activities | Customer's principal place of business |

## ¶ 1448. Department of Taxation Tax Information Release 2018-07
### Re: Act 211, Session Laws of Hawaii 2018 - Transient Accommodations Tax and Allocation of Gross Rental Proceeds to Transient Accommodations Brokers, Travel Agencies, and Tour Packagers

This Tax Information Release discusses the amount of transient accommodations tax (TAT)imposed on a transient accommodations broker, travel agency, or tour packager (hereinaftercollectively referred to as "travel agency") who sells transient accommodations at noncommissioned negotiated contract rates.

Pursuant to Act 211, Session Laws of Hawaii 2018, when transient accommodations are furnished through arrangements made by a travel agency at noncommissioned negotiated contract rates[4] and the gross income is divided by the operator and the travel agency, the TAT applies to both the operator and travel agency with respect to each person's respective portion of the proceeds.

*Standalone Transactions*

In standalone transactions, where a travel agency books or sells transient accommodations at noncommissioned negotiated contract rates that are not part of a travel package, gross rental proceeds of the travel agency are determined by subtracting the amount paid to the operator from the total sales price.

*Example 1*: Travel Agency sells a hotel room for $100. Pursuant to a noncommissioned negotiated contract with the hotel, Travel Agency remits $75 to the hotel and keeps $25. Travel Agency's gross rental proceeds are $25.

---

4   A booking is made on a noncommissioned basis if the travel agency has a contract with an operator of a transient accommodation that specifies the rate the operator will receive for the booking and the travel agency may unilaterally determine the mark-up and the total price charged to the customer. See Hawaii Administrative Rules §18-237-29.53-01.

¶ 1448

*Travel Packages*

In packaged transactions, where a travel agency books or sells transient accommodations at non-commissioned negotiated contract rates as part of a travel package, gross rental proceeds of the travel agency shall be determined by an allocation based upon the fair market value (FMV) of the transient accommodation or by a reasonable allocation that falls within the safe harbor or is approved by the Director. Regardless of which allocation method is used, the method must be consistently used by the travel agency and must be supported by verifiable data.

*Allocation Based on the FMV of the Transient Accommodation*

The method of calculating the gross rental proceeds of a travel agency based on the FMV of the transient accommodation shall be as follows: FMV of the transient accommodation divided by the FMV of all components in the travel package (including the transient accommodation), multiplied by the difference of the sales price of the package minus the total amount paid to vendors for the components in the travel package. Vendors include operators, airlines, and sellers of other travel related bookings. This is represented by the following formula:

$$\frac{\textit{FMV of transient accommodation}}{\textit{FMV of all Components}} \times \textit{(Sales Prices} - \textit{Total Paid to Vendors)} = \textit{Gross Rental Proceeds}$$

In determining the FMV of the components in the travel package, the following principles shall apply:

(1) If the vendor of a component sells the component individually, the FMV of the component shall be the fair market price of the component when sold individually.

(2) If the vendor does not sell a component individually, the FMV of the component shall be determined by the comparable sales price of similar components sold by other vendors as determined by the Department.

(3) If the travel agency provides a component, the FMV of the component shall be determined by either the fair market price of the component if sold individually or, if the component is not sold individually, the comparable sales prices of similar components sold by other vendors as determined by the Department.

Note that the FMV formula may only be used to determine gross rental proceeds where transient accommodations are sold as part of a travel package; the formula shall not be used for standalone transactions.

*Example 2*: Travel Agency sells a package consisting of hotel accommodations, a rental car, and admissions to a luau for $750. Travel Agency has an agreement with the hotel to sell rooms at noncommissioned negotiated contract rates. The FMV of the room is $500, the FMV of the rental car is $200 and the FMV of the luau tickets are $100. Travel Agency paid a total of $650 to the vendors (hotel, rental car company, and luau promoter). The gross rental proceeds of Travel Agency based on the FMV of the transient accommodation are calculated as follows:

$$\textit{Gross Rental Proceeds} = \frac{\$500}{\$800} \times (\$750 - \$650) = \$62.50$$

A. Safe Harbor

Notwithstanding the foregoing, the Department will not challenge a formula used by a travel agency to determine gross rental proceeds for its package sales if the travel agency's margin for the tax year is 20% or more. The margin is calculated by dividing the gross rental proceeds of the travel agency for its package sales by the sum of the gross rental proceeds of the travel agency for its package sales and the amount paid to the operators for its package sales.

$$\textit{Margin} = \frac{\textit{Gross Rental Proceeds of Travel Agency}}{\textit{Gross Rental Proceeds of Travel Agency} + \textit{Amount Paid to Operators}}$$

¶ 1448

Note that the safe harbor only applies where transient accommodations are sold as part of a travel package; it does not apply to standalone transactions. Further, even if the criteria for the safe harbor is met, the travel agency must still consistently use the same formula and must be able to provide verifiable data in support of the formula.

*Example 3*: Travel Agency sells packages that include transient accommodations at noncommissioned negotiated contract rates, among other components. Travel Agency does not use the allocation method based on the fair market value of the transient accommodation, as described above, and has not obtained approval from the Director to use its own allocation method.

Nevertheless, Travel Agency has consistently used the same formula and has verifiable data to support its formula. In tax year 2019, Travel Agency paid $750,000 to operators for transient accommodations sold at noncommissioned negotiated contract rates as part of travel packages. Further, the formula Travel Agency uses results in gross rental proceeds of $250,000. The Department will not challenge Travel Agency's formula because Travel Agency's margin for transient accommodations for 2019 is 25% ($250,000 divided by ($250,000 + $750,000)).

B. Other Reasonable Allocation Approved by the Director

In lieu of allocating gross rental proceeds based on the FMV of the transient accommodation, a travel agency may use any reasonable allocation method approved by the Director to determine the gross rental proceeds of transient accommodations sold as part of a travel package. The allocation method must consistently be used by the travel agency, be supported by verifiable data, and reasonably reflect the gross rental proceeds attributable to the travel agency.

To obtain approval, please submit a written request to the Rules Office with the following information:

(1) Description of the proposed formula;

(2) List of all components available in the travel packages you sell (e.g., airfare, bus transportation, luau tickets, hotel room, etc.);

(3) Calculation of gross rental proceeds based on the proposed formula using actual data from the last quarter;

(4) Calculation of gross rental proceeds based on the FMV of the transient accommodation, as described in section A, using actual data from the last quarter;

(5) Calculation of your margin for transient accommodations, as described in section B, based on the proposed formula and using actual data from the last quarter;

(6) Explanation of why the formula based on the FMV of the transient accommodation is inappropriate or unreasonable;

(7) Explanation of why the proposed formula better reflects the gross rental proceeds or why the proposed formula is reasonable;

(8) A declaration signed and dated by the taxpayer (not a representative) in the following form:

I declare, under the penalties set forth in section 231-36, HRS, that I have personal knowledge of the facts involved in this request and that I have examined this request, including accompanying documents, and, to the best of my knowledge and belief, the facts presented in support of this request are true, correct and complete.

I understand that if any of the facts presented are later found to be in error, any approval received will be void.

Please mail your completed request to the following address:

State of HawaiiDepartment of Taxation
Rules Office
P.O. Box 259
Honolulu, HI 96809-0259

For more information, please contact the Rules Office at (808) 587-1530 or by email at Tax.Rules.Office@hawaii.gov.

¶ 1448

# PART IV

## Specimen
## Tax Forms

In this section, we have included samples of completed forms that we believe either are commonly used or are different and therefore warrant an example in this section.

## Where To Find Forms

In this age of computer technology, most of us either have computers or have access to one. So, if you are looking for forms to download and print, the tax forms, instructions and information for these forms are available on the Department of Taxation's website at tax.hawaii.gov.

In addition, a Tax Information CD-ROM can be ordered for a nominal charge. The Tax Information CD includes the Tax Statutes and Administrative Tax Rules (unofficial) and is updated through the end of the previous calendar year. Order forms may be obtained at the Department's website, at any district tax office or by calling the Taxpayer Services Branch.

The Tax Information CD contains tax forms with writable fields for the current year, unofficial compilations of the Hawaii Tax Statutes and Administrative Tax Rules, selected unpublished court decisions, and attorney general tax opinions, informational brochures, publications, releases, reports, and more.

For those who don't have access to a computer, the forms can be obtained by calling the Taxpayer Services Branch and speaking directly to the Call Center representatives — 808-587-4242 or 1-800-222-3229 (toll free from the neighbor islands and Continental US).

This service is available 24 hours a day, 7 days a week. Call the number and ask for the forms to be mailed to you. The call center representative will ask you to provide the following information:

- Form number or publication name
- Tax year, and
- Your mailing address

The Department of Taxation offers electronic filing of various income, general excise tax, transient accommodations tax, and various other forms on its website. In addition, bulk filing is available for certain filers, such as tax professionals, payroll providers, and property management companies. The Department of Taxation's permission to participate in the bulk filing of returns is required. For more information on electronic filing, contract the Electronic Processing Section of the Department of Taxation by phone at (808) 587-1740, or by e-mail at Tax.Efile@hawaii.gov.

Of course, you can always go down to the district tax office to obtain the forms.

**Form No.** **Page**

FORM
**F-1**
(REV. 2018)

STATE OF HAWAII — DEPARTMENT OF TAXATION

THIS SPACE FOR DATE RECEIVED STAMP

# FRANCHISE TAX RETURN

**BANKS, OTHER FINANCIAL CORPORATIONS, AND SMALL BUSINESS INVESTMENT COMPANIES**

**CALENDAR YEAR 2019 OR FISCAL YEAR BEGINNING IN 2019**

(Based on income for calendar year 2018 or fiscal year beginning on _____ , 2018 and ending _____ , 20 _____ ) (First year, Second year, & Final return filers, see Instructions)

☐ **AMENDED Return** (Attach Sch. AMD)

☐ **IRS** Adjustment
☐ **NOL** Carryback

Hawaii Tax I.D. Number
GE-234-567-8901-23

Federal Employer I.D. No.
12-3456789

**PRINT OR TYPE**

Name
HONOLULU NATIONAL BANK

Main Business Activity

DBA (if any)

Date Business Began in Hawaii
08-07-1953

Mailing Address (number and street)
960 WALL ST

Date of Incorporation
08-07-1953

City, State, and Postal/ZIP Code
HONOLULU, HI 96000

State or Foreign Country of Incorporation
HAWAII

CHECK BOX, IF APPLICABLE:

☐ First year return     ☐ Second year return     ☐ Change of Address

☐ Final return (Business end date _____ , 20 _____ )     ☐ Election to pay via the installment payment method

**A COPY OF ALL PAGES OF YOUR FEDERAL RETURN MUST ACCOMPANY THIS RETURN.**

**If this is a consolidated return, attach copy of Hawaii Forms N-304 and N-303 for each subsidiary.**

**GROSS INCOME**

| | | Gross Amount of Interest | Less: Amortizable Bond Premium | | |
|---|---|---|---|---|---|
| 1. | Gross Receipts _____ 0.00 Less: Returns and allowances _____ 0.00 | | | 1 | 0.00 |
| 2. | Less: Cost of goods sold and/or operations (Attach schedule) | | | 2 | 0.00 |
| 3. | Gross Profit (line 1 minus line 2) | | | 3 | 0.00 |
| 4. | Dividends (Schedule C) | | | 4 | 15300.00 |
| 5. | Interest on government obligations | 178000.00 | 300.00 | 5 | 177700.00 |
| 6. | Other interest | 1045000.00 | | 6 | 1045000.00 |
| 7. | (a) Rents 22900.00 Plus 7(b) Royalties 0.00 , Sum ➤ | | | 7(c) | 22900.00 |
| 8. | (a) Net capital gains (from federal Schedule D) (See Instructions) | | | 8(a) | 86000.00 |
| | (b) Ordinary gain or loss (from federal Schedule 4797) | | | 8(b) | 0.00 |
| 9. | Other income (Attach schedule) | | | 9 | 540500.00 |
| 10. | TOTAL INCOME — Add lines 3 through 9. Enter here and on page 2, line 10(a) | | | 10● | 1888000.00 |

**TAX**

| | | | | | |
|---|---|---|---|---|---|
| 69. | TOTAL TAX from page 3, line 68 | | | 69● | 25956.00 |
| 70. | Total Refundable Credits. Enter the result from page 4, Schedule I, line 3 | | | 70● | 0.00 |
| 71. | Line 69 minus line 70. If line 71 is zero or less, see Instruction XV | | | 71 | 25956.00 |
| 72. | Total Nonrefundable Credits from Schedule H, line 6 | | | 72● | 0.00 |
| 73. | Capital Infrastructure Tax Credit (Attach Form N-348) | | | 73● | 0.00 |
| 74. | Line 71 minus the sum of lines 72 and 73 (See Instruction XVI) | | | 74 | 25956.00 |
| 75. | Payment with extension (Attach Form N-755) | 75● | 26000.00 | | |
| 76. | Tax installment payments (See Instruction XIV) | 76● | | | |
| 77. | Add lines 75 and 76 and enter result | | | 77 | 26000.00 |
| 78. | TAX DUE (Line 74 minus line 77. If line 77 is greater than line 74, skip line 79 and go to line 80) | | | 78● | 0.00 |
| 79. | Tax amount paid with this return | | | 79● | |
| 80. | OVERPAYMENT (If line 77 is larger than line 74) (See Instruction XVIII) . . enter AMOUNT OVERPAID ➤ | | | 80● | 44.00 |
| 81. | Enter amount of line 80 you want **Credited to 2020 installment payments** ➤ | 81● | 0.00 | | |
| 82. | Amount to be **REFUNDED TO YOU** (line 80 minus line 81) . . . . . . . . . . . . . . . . . . . . . REFUND ➤ | | | 82 | 44.00 |

**Amended Return**

| | | | |
|---|---|---|---|
| 83. | Amount paid (overpaid) on original return — **AMENDED RETURN ONLY** (See Instructions. Attach Sch. AMD) | 83 | |
| 84. | **BALANCE DUE (REFUND)** with amended return (See Instructions. Attach Sch. AMD) | 84 | |

**Please Sign Here**

I declare, under the penalties set forth in section 231-36, HRS, that this return (including any accompanying schedules or statements) has been examined by me and, to the best of my knowledge and belief, is a true, correct, and complete return, made in good faith, for the taxable year stated, pursuant to the Hawaii Income Taxation of Banks and Other Financial Corporations, Chapter 241, HRS.

➤ _____
Signature of officer          Date

➤ _____
Title

**Paid Preparer's Information**

Preparer's Signature, and Print Preparer's Name ➤ HOMER JONES

Date

Check if self-employed ☐

Preparer's identification number
P00000000

Firm's name (or yours if self-employed), address, and Postal/ZIP Code
KMH LLP, 1003 BISHOP ST, #2400, HONOLULU, HI 96813

Federal E.I. No. ➤ 42-1539623

Phone No. ➤ (808) 526-2255

F1_I 2018A 01 VID01

ID NO 01

FORM F-1

**FORM F-1 (REV. 2018)**                        **Page 2**

| Name as shown on return | Federal Employer Identification Number |
|---|---|
| HONOLULU NATIONAL BANK | 12-3456789 |

| | | | |
|---|---|---|---:|
| 10. | **(a)** TOTAL INCOME — from page 1, line 10 | 10(a) | 1888000.00 |

**DEDUCTIONS**

| | | | |
|---|---|---|---:|
| 11. | Compensation of officers (Schedule E) | 11 | 210900.00 |
| 12. | Salaries and wages (not deducted elsewhere) | 12 | 377500.00 |
| 13. | Repairs (Do not include cost of improvements or capital expenditures) | 13 | 24100.00 |
| 14. | **(a)** Bad debts (Schedule F) 179200.00    Plus **14(b)** Rents 9000.00 , Sum ➤ | 14(c) | 188200.00 |
| 15. | **(a)** Taxes (Attach schedule) 64700.00    Plus **15(b)** Interest 303500.00 , Sum ➤ | 15(c) | 368200.00 |
| 16. | Contributions or gifts paid (Attach schedule) | 16 | 3000.00 |
| 17. | Amortization (Attach schedule) | 17 | |
| 18. | Depletion | 18 | |
| 19. | Depreciation (from federal Form 4562) | 19 | 28700.00 |
| 20. | Advertising | 20 | 90800.00 |
| 21. | Amounts contributed under:   **(a)** Pension, profit-sharing, stock bonus, annuity plans (Attach schedule) | 21(a) | |
| | **(b)** Other employee benefit plans (Attach schedule) | 21(b) | |
| 22. | Other deductions (Attach schedule) | 22 | 233600.00 |
| 23. | TOTAL DEDUCTIONS — Add lines 11 through 22 | 23● | 1525000.00 |
| 24. | Net income before Hawaii adjustments (line 10(a) minus line 23) | 24 | 363000.00 |

**STATE ADJUSTMENTS**

**ADD:**

| | | | |
|---|---|---|---:|
| 25. | Taxable dividends from Schedule C, line 10 | 25 | 2150.00 |
| 26. | **(a)** Interest on obligations of the United States or its possessions or on securities issued under an Act of Congress. (See instruction VI(a)(1)) | 26(a) | |
| | **(b)** Interest on state, territorial, municipal, county, or other bonds or securities, including Hawaiian issues, not included on line 6. (See instruction VI(a)(2)) | 26(b) | 38000.00 |
| 27. | Amount of deduction for bad debts taken on line 14(a). (See Instructions IV(b) and VII) | 27 | 179200.00 |
| 28. | Other additions required by law — submit schedule. (See Instruction IV(b)) | 28 | |
| 29. | Total of lines 24 through 28 | 29 | 582350.00 |

**DEDUCT:**

| | | | | |
|---|---|---|---|---:|
| 30. | Entire dividends as reported on page 1, line 4 | 30 | 15300.00 | |
| 31. | Bad debt deduction allowed by section 241-4(b)(3), HRS. (See Instruction VII(c)) | 31 | 179200.00 | |
| 32. | Other deductions authorized by law — submit schedule. (See Instructions VI(b) and X(b)) | 32 | 17265.00 | |
| 33. | Total of lines 30 through 32 | 33 | | 211765.00 |
| 34. | Net income after Hawaii adjustments (line 29 minus line 33) | 34 | | 370585.00 |

**Note: If you do not need to apportion your income, skip lines 35 through 56, enter the amount on line 34 on line 57, and continue with line 58. Otherwise, continue with line 35.**

**ADJUSTMENTS TO ARRIVE AT APPORTIONABLE BUSINESS INCOME SUBJECT TO TAX**

**DEDUCT:**

| | | | | |
|---|---|---|---|---:|
| 35. | Nonbusiness dividends included on page 1, line 4, and included on line 24 above | 35 | | |
| 36. | Nonbusiness interest (Attach schedule) | 36 | | |
| 37. | Royalties from nonbusiness assets (Attach schedule) | 37 | | |
| 38. | Net profit from nonbusiness rental property | 38 | | |
| 39. | Net gain from nonbusiness assets (Attach schedule) | 39 | | |
| 40. | Other adjustments (Attach schedule) | 40 | | |
| 41. | Total (lines 35 to 40, inclusive) | 41 | | 0.00 |
| 42. | Balance (line 34 minus line 41) | 42 | | 370585.00 |

**ADD:**

| | | | | |
|---|---|---|---|---:|
| 43. | Net loss from nonbusiness rental property | 43 | | |
| 44. | Net loss from nonbusiness assets (Attach schedule) | 44 | | |
| 45. | Total of lines 43 and 44 | 45 | | 0.00 |
| 46. | Business income from sources within and without Hawaii (line 42 plus line 45) | 46 | | 370585.00 |
| 47. | Allocate_____% (from Schedule P, line 8), as apportionable income attributable to Hawaii and subject to tax. (Multiply line 46 by the %) | 47 | | 370585.00 |

FORM F-1 (REV. 2018)      Page 3

| Name as shown on return | Federal Employer Identification Number |
|---|---|
| HONOLULU NATIONAL BANK | 12-3456789 |

**CLASSIFICATION OF APPORTIONABLE BUSINESS INCOME SUBJECT TO TAX**

| | | | |
|---|---|---|---|
| 48. | Enter the portion of the amount on line 47 that is ordinary income. | 48 | |
| 49. | Enter the portion of the amount on line 47 that is net capital gain. Also, enter on line 60 | 49 | |
| 50. | Total (lines 48 and 49). This total must be equal to the amount on line 47. | 50 | 0.00 |

**INCOME WHOLLY ATTRIBUTABLE TO HAWAII SUBJECT TO TAX**

| | | | |
|---|---|---|---|
| 51. | Gain (or loss) from sale of real estate and other tangible assets located in Hawaii | 51 | |
| 52. | Royalties from property located in Hawaii | 52 | |
| 53. | Net profit (or loss) from nonbusiness rental property within Hawaii | 53 | |
| 54. | Net gain from sale of nonbusiness assets located in or having tax situs in Hawaii: | | |
| | (a) Net short-term capital gain | 54(a) | |
| | (b) Net capital gain attributable to Hawaii. (This amount, if any, also should be entered on line 60) | 54(b) | |
| | (c) Net gain (or loss) from sale or exchange of property other than capital assets | 54(c) | |
| 55. | Income from intangible personal property. Include entire income (or loss) of intangibles which, because of domicile of the corporation or business situs of intangibles, are located in Hawaii. Add back Hawaii allocated, nonbusiness income and dividends. | | |
| | (a) Dividends included on line 35 above (Attach schedule). | 55(a) | |
| | (b) Interest | 55(b) | |
| | (c) All other income from intangibles (Attach schedule) | 55(c) | |
| 56. | Total income wholly attributable to Hawaii (lines 51 to 55(c)). | 56 | 0.00 |
| 57. | Total of lines 47 and 56 (or the amount from line 34 if you did not need to apportion your income) | 57 | 370585.00 |
| 58. | Net operating loss deduction—submit schedule. (See instruction XI) | 58● | |
| 59. | Net income (or loss) for Hawaii tax purposes (line 57 minus line 58). | 59 | 370585.00 |

**TAX COMPUTATION**

| | | | |
|---|---|---|---|
| 60. | Enter the amount of net capital gains as shown on page 1, line 8(a). (If you apportioned your income, enter the amounts from lines 49 and 54(b), if any, instead) | 60 | 86600.00 |
| 61. | Line 59 minus line 60 (If less than zero, enter zero) ► | 61 | 283985.00 |
| 62. | (a) Tax on capital gain — 4% of amount on line 60. | 62(a) | 3464.00 |
| | (b) Tax on net income — 7.92% of amount on line 61 | 62(b) | 22492.00 |
| | (c) Total of lines 62(a) and 62(b) | 62(c) | 25956.00 |
| | (d) Using the 7.92% rate, compute tax on all taxable income using amount from line 59 | 62(d) | 29350.00 |
| 63. | Total tax (enter lesser of line 62(c) or 62(d)) | 63 | 25956.00 |
| 64. | Recapture of Capital Goods Excise Tax Credit from Form N-312, Part II | 64 | 0.00 |
| 65. | Recapture of Low-Income Housing Tax Credit from Form N-586, Part III | 65 | 0.00 |
| 66. | Recapture of Capital Infrastructure Tax Credit from Form N-348, Part IV | 66 | 0.00 |
| 67. | Total recapture of tax credits (Add lines 64, 65, and 66) | 67 | 0.00 |
| 68. | Total tax (Add lines 63 and 67). Enter here and on page 1, line 69 ► | 68 | |

**Schedule C    INCOME FROM DIVIDENDS (Classified for Hawaii Purposes)**

| 1. Name of declaring corporation | 2. National Banking Associations | 3. Received from an affiliate (including foreign) as IRC section 243(b) qualifying dividend | 4. Received by a small business investment co. operating under Small Business Investment Act | 5. All other dividends |
|---|---|---|---|---|
| HAWAIIAN ELECTRIC CORP | | | | 7166.00 |
| XYZ CORP | | 8134.00 | | |

| | | |
|---|---|---|
| 6. | Total dividends (Add amounts in columns 2, 3, 4, and 5). Enter here and on page 1, line 4 | 15300.00 |
| 7. | Dividends qualifying for the 70% dividends received deduction (Total of amounts in column 5) | 7166.00 |
| 8. | Multiply line 7 by .30 (30%). | 2150.00 |
| 9. | Taxable mutual funds dividends | |
| 10. | Total taxable dividends (Add lines 8 and 9). Enter here and on page 2, line 25 | 2150.00 |

F1_I 2018A 03 VID01      ID NO 01

FORM F-1 (REV. 2018)                                                                    Page 4

| Name as shown on return | Federal Employer Identification Number |
|---|---|
| HONOLULU NATIONAL BANK | 12-3456789 |

## Schedule E    COMPENSATION OF OFFICERS

| 1. Name and address of officer | 2. Official title | 3. Time devoted to business | Percent of corporation stock owned 4. Common | 5. Preferred | 6. Amount of compensation |
|---|---|---|---|---|---|
| JACK BLACK | PRESIDENT | 100 | 0 | 0 | 80000.00 |
| ORVILLE OIDE | VICE PRESIDENT | 100 | 0 | 0 | 60000.00 |
| JUDD BROWN | SECRETARY | 100 | 0 | 0 | 40000.00 |
| GEORGE JONES | TREASURER | 100 | 0 | 0 | 30900.00 |

Total compensation of officers (Enter here and on page 2, line 11) . . . . . . . . . . . . . . . . . . . . . . . . .    210900.00

## Schedule F    BAD DEBTS

| 1. Last 3 Prior and Current Taxable Years | 2. Amount of Notes and Accounts Receivable Outstanding at End of Year | 3. Taxable (or Net) Income Reported | 4. Sales on Account | 5. Bad Debts of Corporation If No Allowance Is Carried on Books | If Corporation Carries An Allowance 6. Gross Amount Added to Allowance | 7. Amount Charged Against Allowance | 8. Balance of Allowance |
|---|---|---|---|---|---|---|---|
| 20 18 | 6000000.00 | 370585.00 | | | 500000.00 | 179200.00 | 600000.00 |
| 20 17 | 5400000.00 | 175000.00 | | | 367200.00 | 179200.00 | 350000.00 |
| 20 16 | 9950000.00 | 88300.00 | | | 395000.00 | 171000.00 | 161000.00 |
| 20 15 | 6200000.00 | 15000.00 | | | 160000.00 | 172000.00 | 38000.00 |

## Schedule H    NONREFUNDABLE CREDITS

| | | | |
|---|---|---|---|
| 1. | Carryover of the Credit for Energy Conservation (Attach Form N-323) . . . . . . . . . . . . . . . . . . | 1● | 0.00 |
| 2. | Low-income Housing Tax Credit (Attach Form N-586) . . . . . . . . . . . . . . . . . . . . . . . . . . . | 2● | 0.00 |
| 3. | Carryover of the High Technology Business Investment Tax Credit (Attach Form N-323) . . . . . . . . . | 3● | 0.00 |
| 4. | Carryover of the Renewable Energy Technologies Income Tax Credit (for systems installed and placed in service before July 1, 2009) (Attach Form N-323) . . . . . . . . . . . . . . . . . . . . . . . . . . . . . . | 4● | 0.00 |
| 5. | Renewable Energy Technologies Income Tax Credit for Systems Placed in Service on or after July 1, 2009 (Attach Form N-342) Check the type of energy system: ☐ Solar  ☐ Wind . . . . . . . . . . . . . . | 5● | 0.00 |
| 6. | Total Nonrefundable Credits. Add lines 1 through 5. (Enter here and on page 1, line 72). . . . . . . . ➤ | 6 | 0.00 |

## Schedule I    REFUNDABLE CREDITS

| | | | |
|---|---|---|---|
| 1. | Capital Goods Excise Tax Credit (Attach Form N-312) . . . . . . . . . . . . . . . . . . . . . . . . . . | 1● | 0.00 |
| 2. | Renewable Energy Technologies Income Tax Credit for Systems Placed in Service on or after July 1, 2009 (Attach Form N-342) (Note: The refundable credit applies only to solar energy systems and not to wind powered energy systems) | 2● | 0.00 |
| 3. | Total Refundable Credits. Add lines 1 and 2. (Enter here and on page 1, line 70) . . . . . . . . . . . ➤ | 3 | 0.00 |

## Schedule P    COMPUTATION OF APPORTIONMENT FACTORS

| Property — (use original cost) | In Hawaii Beginning of taxable year | End of taxable year | Total Everywhere Beginning of taxable year | End of taxable year |
|---|---|---|---|---|
| Land | | | | |
| Buildings | | | | |
| Loans | | | | |
| Credit card receivables | | | | |
| Leasehold interests* | | | | |
| Rented Property* | | | | |
| Other Property | | | | |
| Total | | | | |

* Enter net annual rent X 8.

| | | A. In Hawaii | B. Everywhere | Percent in Hawaii** |
|---|---|---|---|---|
| 1 | Property values (average value of property above) | | | |
| 2 | Property factor (line 1, col. A divided by line 1, col. B) . . . . . . . . . . . . . . . . . . . . . . . . . | | | % |
| 3 | Total compensation | | | |
| 4 | Payroll factor (line 3, col. A divided by line 3, col. B) . . . . . . . . . . . . . . . . . . . . . . . . . | | | % |
| 5 | Total receipts | | | |
| 6 | Receipts factor (line 5, col. A divided by line 5, col. B) . . . . . . . . . . . . . . . . . . . . . . . . . | | | % |
| 7 | Total of factors (add lines 2, 4, and 6) . . . . . . . . . . . . . . . . . . . . . . . . . . . . . . . . . | | | % |
| 8 | Average of factors (divide line 7 by 3). Enter here and on page 2, line 47. . . . . . . . . . . . . . . . | | | % |

** Compute all percentages to 5 decimal places (.00000%).

F1_I 2018A 04 VID01                       ID NO 01

## FRANCHISE TAX RETURN SCHEDULES

### HONOLULU NATIONAL BANK

OTHER INCOME

| | | |
|---|---|---|
| Investment securities | $ | 200,000 |
| Income from partnerships | | 250,500 |
| Miscellaneous income | | 90,000 |
| Total Other Income | $ | 540,500 |

TAXES

| | | |
|---|---|---|
| States tax | $ | 35,000 |
| General excise tax | | 10,000 |
| Payroll tax | | 19,700 |
| Total Taxes Paid | $ | 64,700 |

CONTRIBUTIONS

| | | |
|---|---|---|
| Honolulu Community Theatre | $ | 3,000 |
| Total Contributions | $ | 3,000 |

OTHER DEDUCTIONS

| | | |
|---|---|---|
| Legal and professional fees | $ | 35,100 |
| Stationery and office supplies | | 84,300 |
| Publications | | 5,200 |
| Credit reports and appraisals | | 12,700 |
| Dues | | 5,100 |
| Telephone and telegraph | | 23,000 |
| Postage and mail insurance | | 15,700 |
| Travel and automobile | | 6,400 |
| Utilities | | 7,800 |
| Insurance | | 14,500 |
| Recruitment and development | | 5,900 |
| Sundry | | 17,900 |
| Total Other Deductions | | $ 233,600 |

Statement 1

## FRANCHISE TAX RETURN SCHEDULES

### HONOLULU NATIONAL BANK

STATE ADJUSTMENT

| | | |
|---|---|---:|
| Other deductions — line 32 | | |
| Income from sources without Hawaii: | | |
| Rents | $ | 23,400 |
| Less related rental expenses | | 8,335 |
| | $ | 15,065 |
| Amortization of premium on bonds exempt for federal purposes | | 2,200 |
| Total Other Deductions - State Adjustments | $ | 17,265 |

Statement 2

**FORM G-45**
(Rev. 2018)

STATE OF HAWAII — DEPARTMENT OF TAXATION     **DO NOT WRITE IN THIS AREA**     **10**

### GENERAL EXCISE/USE
### TAX RETURN

**Place an X in this box ONLY if this is an AMENDED return**

PERIOD ENDING     01-19          HAWAII TAX I.D. NO.     GE-012-345-6789-01

Last 4 digits of your FEIN or SSN     1234

NAME: _KAIMUKI GOLF SHOP_                                          ID NO 88

| BUSINESS ACTIVITIES | Column a VALUES, GROSS PROCEEDS OR GROSS INCOME | Column b EXEMPTIONS/DEDUCTIONS (Attach Schedule GE) | Column c TAXABLE INCOME (Column a minus Column b) | |
|---|---|---|---|---|
| **PART I - GENERAL EXCISE and USE TAXES @ ½ OF 1% (.005)** | | | | |
| 1. Wholesaling | 4324 | 0 | 4324 | 1 |
| 2. Manufacturing | 0 | 0 | 0 | 2 |
| 3. Producing | 0 | 0 | 0 | 3 |
| 4. Wholesale Services | 0 | 0 | 0 | 4 |
| 5. Landed Value of Imports for Resale | 4200 | 0 | 4200 | 5 |
| 6. Business Activities of Disabled Persons | 0 | 0 | 0 | 6 |
| 7. Sum of Part I, Column c (Taxable Income) — Enter the result here and on page 2, line 24, Column c | | | 8524 | 7 |
| **PART II - GENERAL EXCISE and USE TAXES @ 4% (.04)** | | | | |
| 8. Retailing | 13421 | 0 | 13421 | 8 |
| 9. Services Including Professional | 0 | 0 | 0 | 9 |
| 10. Contracting | 0 | 0 | 0 | 10 |
| 11. Theater, Amusement and Broadcasting | 0 | 0 | 0 | 11 |
| 12. Commissions | 0 | 0 | 0 | 12 |
| 13. Transient Accommodations Rentals | 0 | 0 | 0 | 13 |
| 14. Other Rentals | | 0 | 0 | 14 |
| 15. Interest and All Others | 0 | 0 | 0 | 15 |
| 16. Landed Value of Imports for Consumption | 0 | 0 | 0 | 16 |
| 17. Sum of Part II, Column c (Taxable Income) — Enter the result here and on page 2, line 25, Column c | | | 13421 | 17 |

• ATTACH CHECK OR MONEY ORDER HERE •

**DECLARATION** - I declare, under the penalties set forth in section 231-36, HRS, that this return (including any accompanying schedules or statements) has been examined by me and, to the best of my knowledge and belief, is a true, correct, and complete return, made in good faith for the tax period stated, pursuant to the General Excise and Use Tax Laws, and the rules issued thereunder.

IN THE CASE OF A CORPORATION OR PARTNERSHIP, THIS RETURN MUST BE SIGNED BY AN OFFICER, PARTNER OR MEMBER, OR DULY AUTHORIZED AGENT.

| SIGNATURE | TITLE | DATE | DAYTIME PHONE NUMBER |
|---|---|---|---|
| | | 02/01/19 | |

G45_T 2018A 01 VID88     **Continued on page 2 — Parts V & VI MUST be completed**     Form G-45 (Rev. 2018) **10**

**Form G-45**
(Rev. 2018)
Page 2 of 2

Name: KAIMUKI GOLF SHOP

ID NO 88

Hawaii Tax I.D. No.    GE-012-345-6789-01

Last 4 digits of your FEIN or SSN  1234

PERIOD ENDING  01-19

| BUSINESS ACTIVITIES | Column a VALUES, GROSS PROCEEDS OR GROSS INCOME | Column b EXEMPTIONS/DEDUCTIONS (Attach Schedule GE) | Column c TAXABLE INCOME (Column a minus Column b) | |
|---|---|---|---|---|
| **PART III - INSURANCE COMMISSIONS @ .15% (.0015)** | | | Enter this amount on line 26, Column c | |
| 18. Insurance Commissions | 0 | 0 | 0 | 18 |

**PART IV - COUNTY SURCHARGE –** Enter the amounts from Part II, line 17, Column c attributable to each county. Multiply Column c by the applicable county rate(s) and enter the total of the result(s) on Part VI, line 27, Column e.

| | Column a | Column b | Column c | |
|---|---|---|---|---|
| 19. Oahu (rate = .005) | 13421 | 0 | 13421 | 19 |
| 20. Maui | 0 | | | 20 |
| 21. Hawaii (rate = .0025) | 0 | 0 | 0 | 21 |
| 22. Kauai (rate = .005) | 0 | 0 | 0 | 22 |

**PART V — SCHEDULE OF ASSIGNMENT OF TAXES BY DISTRICT** (ALL taxpayers MUST complete this Part and may be subject to a 10% penalty for noncompliance.)
Place an X in the box of the taxation district in which you have conducted business. IF you did business in MORE THAN ONE district, place an X in the box for "MULTI" and attach Form G-75.

| 23. | X  Oahu | Maui | Hawaii | Kauai | MULTI | 23 |
|---|---|---|---|---|---|---|

| **PART VI - TOTAL PERIODIC RETURN** | TAXABLE INCOME Column c | TAX RATE Column d | | TOTAL TAX Column e = Column c X Column d | |
|---|---|---|---|---|---|
| 24. Enter the amount from Part I, line 7 ............... | 8524 | x .005 | 24. | 42.62 | |
| 25. Enter the amount from Part II, line 17 ............. | 13421 | x .04 | 25. | 536.84 | |
| 26. Enter the amount from Part III line 18, Column c ........... | 0 | x .0015 | 26. | 0.00 | |
| 27. COUNTY SURCHARGE TAX. See Instructions for Part IV. Multi district complete Form G-75 ... 27. | | | | 67.11 | |
| 28. TOTAL TAXES DUE. Add column e of lines 24 through 27 and enter result here (but not less than zero). If you did not have any activity for the period, enter "0.00" here ............................................. 28. | | | | 646.57 | |
| 29. Amounts Assessed During the Period .................... PENALTY  $_____ (For Amended Return ONLY) INTEREST  $_____ | | | 29. | | |
| 30. TOTAL AMOUNT. Add lines 28 and 29 ............................................................. 30. | | | | 646.57 | |
| 31. TOTAL PAYMENTS MADE FOR THE PERIOD (For Amended Return ONLY) ............................... 31. | | | | | |
| 32. CREDIT TO BE REFUNDED. Line 31 minus line 30 (For Amended Return ONLY) ....................... 32. | | | | | |
| 33. ADDITIONAL TAXES DUE. Line 30 minus line 31 (For Amended Return ONLY) ........................ 33. | | | | | |
| 34. **FOR LATE FILING ONLY ➔** PENALTY  $   0.00 INTEREST  $   0.00  34. | | | | 0.00 | |
| 35. TOTAL AMOUNT DUE AND PAYABLE (Original Returns, add lines 30 and 34; Amended Returns, add lines 33 and 34) .......................................................... 35. | | | | 646.57 | |
| 36. PLEASE ENTER THE AMOUNT OF YOUR PAYMENT. Attach a check or money order payable to "HAWAII STATE TAX COLLECTOR" in U.S. dollars to Form G-45. Write the filing period and your Hawaii Tax I.D. No. on your check or money order. Mail to: HAWAII DEPARTMENT OF TAXATION, P. O. BOX 1425, HONOLULU, HI 96806-1425 or file and pay electronically at hitax.hawaii.gov. If you are NOT submitting a payment with this return, please enter "0.00" here. .................. 36. | | | | 646.57 | |
| 37. GRAND TOTAL OF EXEMPTIONS/DEDUCTIONS CLAIMED. (Attach Schedule GE) If Schedule GE is not attached, exemptions/deductions claimed will be disallowed ................ 37. | | | | 0 | |

G45_T 2018A 02 VID88

Form G-45 **10**
(Rev. 2018)

**FORM G-49**
(Rev. 2018)

STATE OF HAWAII — DEPARTMENT OF TAXATION

DO NOT WRITE IN THIS AREA

**16**

### GENERAL EXCISE/USE ANNUAL RETURN & RECONCILIATION

**Place an X in this box ONLY if this is an AMENDED return**

TAX YEAR ENDING    12-31-18    HAWAII TAX I.D. NO.    GE-012-345-6789-01

Last 4 digits of your FEIN or SSN    1234

ID NO 88

NAME:  ALOHA GOLF SUPPLY CO.

| BUSINESS ACTIVITIES | Column a VALUES, GROSS PROCEEDS OR GROSS INCOME | Column b EXEMPTIONS/DEDUCTIONS (Attach Schedule GE) | Column c TAXABLE INCOME (Column a minus Column b) | |
|---|---|---|---|---|
| **PART I - GENERAL EXCISE and USE TAXES @ ½ OF 1% (.005)** | | | | |
| 1. Wholesaling | 16000 | 0 | 16000 | 1 |
| 2. Manufacturing | 0 | | 0 | 2 |
| 3. Producing | 0 | | 0 | 3 |
| 4. Wholesale Services | 0 | 0 | 0 | 4 |
| 5. Landed Value of Imports for Resale | 0 | 0 | 0 | 5 |
| 6. Business Activities of Disabled Persons | 0 | 0 | 0 | 6 |
| 7. Sum of Part I, Column c (Taxable Income) — Enter the result here and on page 2, line 24, Column c | | | 16000 | 7 |
| **PART II - GENERAL EXCISE and USE TAXES @ 4% (.04)** | | | | |
| 8. Retailing | 101000 | 0 | 101000 | 8 |
| 9. Services Including Professional | 0 | 0 | 0 | 9 |
| 10. Contracting | 0 | 0 | 0 | 10 |
| 11. Theater, Amusement and Broadcasting | 0 | 0 | 0 | 11 |
| 12. Commissions | 0 | 0 | 0 | 12 |
| 13. Transient Accommodations Rentals | 0 | 0 | 0 | 13 |
| 14. Other Rentals | 0 | 0 | 0 | 14 |
| 15. Interest and All Others | 0 | 0 | 0 | 15 |
| 16. Landed Value of Imports for Consumption | 0 | 0 | 0 | 16 |
| 17. Sum of Part II, Column c (Taxable Income) — Enter the result here and on page 2, line 25, Column c | | | 101000 | 17 |

•ATTACH CHECK OR MONEY ORDER HERE•

**DECLARATION** - I declare, under the penalties set forth in section 231-36, HRS, that this return (including any accompanying schedules or statements) has been examined by me and, to the best of my knowledge and belief, is a true, correct, and complete return, made in good faith for the tax period stated, pursuant to the General Excise and Use Tax Laws, and the rules issued thereunder.

IN THE CASE OF A CORPORATION OR PARTNERSHIP, THIS RETURN MUST BE SIGNED BY AN OFFICER, PARTNER OR MEMBER, OR DULY AUTHORIZED AGENT.

| SIGNATURE | TITLE | DATE | DAYTIME PHONE NUMBER |
|---|---|---|---|
| | | 04/01/19 | |

G49_T 2018A 01 VID66    **Continued on page 2 — Parts V & VI *MUST* be completed**    Form G-49 (Rev. 2018) **16**

**FORM G-49**
(Rev. 2018)
Page 2 of 2

Name: ALOHA GOLF SUPPLY CO.

ID NO 88

Hawaii Tax I.D. No.   GE-012-345-6789-01

(mm/dd/yy)

Last 4 digits of your FEIN or SSN   1234      TAX YEAR ENDING   12-31-18

| BUSINESS ACTIVITIES | Column a<br>VALUES, GROSS PROCEEDS OR GROSS INCOME | Column b<br>EXEMPTIONS/DEDUCTIONS<br>(Attach Schedule GE) | Column c<br>TAXABLE INCOME<br>(Column a minus Column b) | |
|---|---|---|---|---|
| **PART III - INSURANCE COMMISSIONS @ .15% (.0015)** | | | Enter this amount on line 26, Column c | |
| 18. Insurance Commissions | 0 | 0 | 0 | 18 |

**PART IV - COUNTY SURCHARGE –** Enter the amounts from Part II, line 17, Column c attributable to each county. Multiply Column c by the applicable county rate(s) and enter the total of the result(s) on Part VI, line 27, Column e.

| | | | | |
|---|---|---|---|---|
| 19. Oahu (rate = .005) | 101000 | 0 | 101000 | 19 |
| 20. Maui | 0 | | | 20 |
| 21. Hawaii (rate = .0025) | 0 | 0 | 0 | 21 |
| 22. Kauai (rate = .005) | 0 | | 0 | 22 |

**PART V — SCHEDULE OF ASSIGNMENT OF TAXES BY DISTRICT** (ALL taxpayers MUST complete this Part and may be subject to a 10% penalty for noncompliance.)
Place an X in the box of the taxation district in which you have conducted business. IF you did business in MORE THAN ONE district, place an X in the box for "MULTI" and attach Form G-75.

23.    **X** Oahu      Maui      Hawaii      Kauai      MULTI      23

**PART VI - TOTAL RETURN AND RECONCILIATIO**

| | | TAXABLE INCOME<br>Column c | TAX RATE<br>Column d | | TOTAL TAX<br>Column e = Column c X Column d | |
|---|---|---|---|---|---|---|
| 24. | Enter the amount from Part I, line 7 .......... | 16000 | x .005 | 24. | 80.00 | |
| 25. | Enter the amount from Part II, line 17 ........ | 101000 | x .04 | 25. | 4040.00 | |
| 26. | Enter the amount from Part III, line 18, Column c | 0 | x .0015 | 26. | 0.00 | |
| 27. | COUNTY SURCHARGE TAX. See Instructions for Part IV. Multi district complete Form G-75 . | | | 27. | 505.00 | |
| 28. | TOTAL TAXES DUE. Add column e of lines 24 through 27 and enter result here (but not less than zero).<br>If you did not have any activity for the period, enter "0.00" here ........... | | | 28. | 4625.00 | |
| 29. | Amounts Assessed During the Period | PENALTY $ 0.00<br>INTEREST $ 0.00 | | 29. | 0.00 | |
| | (For Amended Return ONLY) | | | | | |
| 30. | TOTAL AMOUNT. Add lines 28 and 29 ........ | | | 30. | 4625.00 | |
| 31. | TOTAL PAYMENTS MADE LESS ANY REFUNDS RECEIVED FOR THE TAX YEAR. ........ | | | 31. | 4000.00 | |
| 32. | CREDIT CLAIMED ON ORIGINAL ANNUAL RETURN. (For Amended Return ONLY) ........ | | | 32. | | |
| 33. | NET PAYMENTS MADE. Line 31 minus line 32 ........ | | | 33. | 4000.00 | |
| 34. | CREDIT TO BE REFUNDED. Line 33 minus line 30 ........ | | | 34. | 0.00 | |
| 35. | ADDITIONAL TAXES DUE. Line 30 minus line 33 ........ | | | 35. | 625.00 | |
| 36. | **FOR LATE FILING ONLY➔** | PENALTY $ 0.00<br>INTEREST $ 0.00 | | 36. | 0.00 | |
| 37. | TOTAL AMOUNT DUE AND PAYABLE (Add lines 35 and 36) ........ | | | 37. | 625.00 | |
| 38. | PLEASE ENTER THE AMOUNT OF YOUR PAYMENT. If you are NOT submitting a payment with this return, please enter "0.00" here. ........ | | | 38. | 625.00 | |
| 39. | GRAND TOTAL OF EXEMPTIONS/DEDUCTIONS CLAIMED. (Attach Schedule GE) If Schedule GE is not attached, exemptions/deductions claimed will be disallowed. ........ | | | 39. | 0 | |

G49_T 2018A 02 VID88

Form G-49
(Rev. 2018)   **16**

*Not Approved for Paper Filing*

**FORM HW-14**
(Rev. 2018)

STATE OF HAWAII
DEPARTMENT OF TAXATION
**WITHHOLDING TAX RETURN**

DO NOT WRITE IN THIS AREA

**30**

Place an X in this box ONLY if this is an AMENDED return

M M     Y Y

Quarter Ending                                            03-19

HAWAII TAX I.D. NO.                      WH-001-234-5678-01

Last 4 digits of your FEIN or SSN                     1234

NAME: INNOVATORS, INC.

This return must be filed on or before the **15th** day of the month following the close of the calendar quarter.

1. TOTAL WAGES PAID (include COLA, 3rd party sick leave, and other benefits) Enter "0" if no wage
   were paid or no tax withheld .................................................................................1         13246.83

2. TOTAL HAWAII INCOME TAX WITHHELD .................................................................2          1647.11

   2a. PENALTIES PREVIOUSLY ASSESSED .........

   2b. INTEREST PREVIOUSLY ASSESSED .........

2c. TOTAL AMOUNT DUE for this quarter (Add lines 2, 2a, and 2b) ...................... 2c        1647.11
3. TOTAL PAYMENTS MADE for the quarter (including any penalty or interest
   paid during the period) ..................................................................................... 3         0.00
4. AMOUNT OF CREDIT TO BE REFUNDED (If line 2c is greater than line 3, skip to line 5. Otherwise,
   line 3 minus line 2c and enter "0.00" on lines 5, 7 and 8.) .................................... 4         0.00

5. UNPAID TAXES due for this quarter (line 2c minus line 3) ................................. 5         1647.11

   6a. PENALTY ......................         0.00
6. **FOR LATE**
   **FILING ONLY**     6b. INTEREST ......................         0.00

*REMINDER:* All EFT payments
must be transmitted by the payment
due date or a 2% EFT penalty will
be applied.

7. TOTAL AMOUNT now due and PAYABLE (Add lines 5, 6a, and 6b) .................................... 7         1647.11
8. **Enter AMOUNT of payment.** Attach your check or money order payable to
   "*Hawaii State Tax Collector*" in U.S. dollars drawn on any U.S. bank to Form HW-14.
   Write the filing period and your Hawaii Tax I.D. No. on your check or money order.        AMOUNT OF PAYMENT
   **IF NO PAYMENT ATTACHED, ENTER "0.00."** You may also e-pay at: **hitax.hawaii.gov** .................8         1647.11

• ATTACH CHECK OR MONEY ORDER •

I declare under the penalties set forth in section 231-36, HRS, that this is a
true and correct return, prepared in accordance with the withholding
provisions of the Hawaii Income Tax Law and the rules issued thereunder.

| SIGNATURE | DATE 04-07-19 |
|---|---|
| TITLE | DAYTIME PHONE NUMBER |

— MAILING ADDRESS —
HAWAII DEPARTMENT OF TAXATION
P.O. BOX 3827
HONOLULU, HI 96812-3827

ID NO 88            Form HW-14 **30**

HW14_T 2018A 01 VID88

**FORM**
## VP-1
(REV. 2018)

**STATE OF HAWAII — DEPARTMENT OF TAXATION**
**GENERAL EXCISE/USE, TRANSIENT**
**ACCOMMODATIONS AND RENTAL MOTOR VEHICLE,**
**TOUR VEHICLE & CAR-SHARING VEHICLE SURCHARGE**

## TAX PAYMENT VOUCHER
### GENERAL INSTRUCTIONS

### CHANGES YOU SHOULD NOTE

If payment is submitted with a return (general excise/use, transient accommodations, withholding and rental motor vehicle, tour vehicle & car-sharing vehicle surcharge), DO NOT attach Form VP-1 to the tax return.

### INTERNET FILING

Form VP-1 can be filed and paid electronically through the State's Internet portal. For more information, go to **tax.hawaii.gov/eservices/.**

### PURPOSE OF FORM

Use this form if submitting Form BB-1 or submitting a payment without a tax return.

### HOW TO COMPLETE FORM

1) Print the name in the space provided.
2) Check the appropriate "Tax Type" box.
3) Check the appropriate "Filing Type" box and fill in the period or year in the space provided.
   If filing Form BB-1, check the box "License Fee."
   Add lines 22b through 22f on Form BB-1 and enter the amount of payment in the space provided.
   Enter the last day of the first filing period. (e.g., a calendar year quarterly filer, began business on January 21, 2019, the first filing period end date is 03/31/19.
4) In the space provided, print the Hawaii Tax I.D. No. starting with the tax type (i.e. GE, TA, WH or RV), the 10 digit account number with the 2 digit extension; and the amount of payment.

5) Make the check or money order payable in U.S. dollars to the **"Hawaii State Tax Collector."** Make sure the name, tax type, filing period, and Hawaii Tax I.D. No. appear on the check or money order. Do not postdate the check. **Do not send cash.**

### WHERE TO FILE

Detach Form VP-1 along the dotted line. If filing Form BB-1, attach the payment and Form VP-1 to the front of the form and send it to the Form BB-1 mailing address below. If submitting only a tax payment (without a return), send Form VP-1 and the payment to the mailing address noted below for the type of tax. The mailing addresses are as follows:

**General Excise/Use Tax**
Hawaii Department of Taxation
P.O. Box 1425
Honolulu, HI 96806-1730

**Transient Accommodations Tax And**
**Rental Motor Vehicle, Tour Vehicle & Car-Sharing**
**Vehicle Surcharge Tax**
Hawaii Department of Taxation
P.O. Box 2430
Honolulu, HI 96804-2430

**Hawaii Withholding**
Hawaii Department of Taxation
P.O. Box 3827
Honolulu, HI 96812-3827

**Form BB-1**
Hawaii Department of Taxation
P.O. Box 1425
Honolulu, HI 96806-1425

---

✂ - - - - - - - - - - - - - - - - - - - - - - - -  DETACH HERE  · - - - - - - - - - - - - - - - - - - - - - - - - - ✂

Form (Rev. 2018)
**VP-1**

**STATE OF HAWAII — DEPARTMENT OF TAXATION**
**TAX PAYMENT VOUCHER**

DO NOT WRITE OR STAPLE IN THIS SPACE

**DO NOT SUBMIT A PHOTOCOPY OF THIS FORM**

Name (Please print): **INNOVATORS, INC.**

Print the amount of your payment in the space provided. ATTACH THIS VOUCHER WITH CHECK OR MONEY ORDER PAYABLE TO "HAWAII STATE TAX COLLECTOR" Write the tax and filing types, and your Hawaii Tax I.D. Number on your check or money order.

| Tax Type (check only 1) | Filing Type (check only 1) Enter Date as MM DD YY | |
|---|---|---|
| General Excise (GE) | License Fee | |
| | 1st Period End | |
| Transient Accommodations (TA) | | |
| **X** Hawaii Withholding (WH) | **X** Periodic Return | |
| | Period End | 03-31-19 |
| Rental Motor, Tour & Car-Sharing | Annual Return | |
| Vehicles (RV) | Tax Year End | |

Hawaii Tax I.D. Number

WH-001-234-5678-01

Amount of Payment

1647.11

VP1_T 2018A 01 VID88                    ID NO 88

## PROBLEM FOR SPECIMEN RETURN
## RESIDENT INDIVIDUAL FILING FEDERAL INCOME TAX RETURN

### Form N-11

Jack and Jill Hill are residents of Hawaii. They live at 1250 Bishop Street in Honolulu. They have two children who lived with them the entire year; Molly is 6 and Bill is 5.

The Hills' adjusted federal gross income was $30,500. Jack's Hawaii wages were $3,000 higher than his federal wages due to his federal cost-of-living adjustment. The Hills had a state tax refund of $1,000 which was reported as income on their federal income tax return.

The Hills also had interest income of $4,000 comprised of the following:

| | |
|---|---|
| Federal obligations | $ 3,000 |
| Other state bonds | $  250 |
| Savings account | $  750 |

The Hills incurred $3,565 of medical expenses for surgery on Mrs. Hill's knee during 2006. Mortgage interest on their home for 2006 amounted to $12,000. The Hills' state withholding was $2,500 and they paid real estate taxes of $1,300. In addition, they made cash contributions of $400 to Aloha United Way. The Hills also paid $2,000 to a qualified day care center for Bill while Jack and Jill were working.

| FORM | STATE OF HAWAII — DEPARTMENT OF TAXATION | DO NOT WRITE IN THIS AREA |
|---|---|---|
| **N-11** (Rev. 2018) | **Individual Income Tax Return** **RESIDENT** | |

Calendar Year **2018**
OR

Fiscal Year
Beginning _____ and Ending _____

AMENDED Return          FOR OFFICE USE ONLY
NOL Carryback
IRS Adjustment          _____

**Do NOT Submit a Photocopy!!**

Place an X in applicable box, if appropriate

First Time Filer          Address or Name Change

• ATTACH COPY 2 OF FORM W-2 HERE •    ↓ Place Label Here ↓

◆ **IMPORTANT — Complete this Section** ◆

| | | | | |
|---|---|---|---|---|
| Your First Name **JACK** | M.I. | Your Last Name **HILL** | Suffix | Enter the first four letters of your last name. Use **ALL CAPITAL** letters **HILL** |
| Spouse's First Name **JILL** | M.I. | Spouse's Last Name **HILL** | Suffix | Your Social Security Number **234 – 56 – 7890** |

Care Of (See Instructions, page 7.)

Deceased ___ Date of Death ___

Present mailing or home address (Number and street, including Rural Route)
**1250 BISHOP STREET**

Enter the first four letters of your Spouse's last name. Use **ALL CAPITAL** letters **HILL**

| City, town or post office **HONOLULU** | State | Postal/ZIP code **96000** |
|---|---|---|

Spouse's Social Security Number **345 – 67 – 8901**

If Foreign address, enter Province and/or State ___ Country ___

Deceased ___ Date of Death ___

**(Place an X in only ONE box)**

| 1 | | Single |
|---|---|---|
| 2 | **X** | Married filing joint return (even if only one had income). |
| 3 | | Married filing separate return. Enter spouse's SSN and the first four letters of last name above. Enter spouse's full name here. _____ |

4 ___ Head of household (with qualifying person). If the qualifying person is a child but not your dependent, enter the child's full name. ▶ _____

5 ___ Qualifying widow(er) (see page 9 of the Instructions)

Enter the year your spouse died ___

• ATTACH CHECK OR MONEY ORDER HERE •

CAUTION: If you can be claimed as a dependent on another person's tax return (such as your parents'), DO NOT place an X on line 6a, but be sure to place an X above line 21.

| 6a | **X** | Yourself...................................... | Age 65 or over........................................ | } Enter the number of Xs on 6a and 6b........... ◆ **2** |
|---|---|---|---|---|
| 6b | **X** | Spouse......................................... | Age 65 or over........................................ | |

If you placed an X on lines 3 and 6b above, see the Instructions on page 9 and if your spouse meets the qualifications, place an X here ___

| 6c and 6d | Dependents: 1. First and last name | If more than 4 dependents use attachment | 2. Dependent's social security number | 3. Relationship | Enter the number of your children listed .. **6c** ◆ **2** |
|---|---|---|---|---|---|
| | BILL HILL | | 456–78–9012 | SON | |
| | MOLLY HILL | | 575–99–1357 | DAUGHTER | Enter number of other dependents .... **6d** ◆ **0** |
| | | | | | |
| | | | | | |

6e   Total number of exemptions claimed. Add numbers entered in boxes **6a** thru **6d** above .......................................... 6e ◆ **4**

ID NO 88

N11_T 2018A 01 VID88                                                                                    **FORM N-11**

**Form N-11 (Rev. 2018)**

Page 2 of 4

Your Social Security Number | Your Spouse's SSN

234 - 56 - 7890 | 345 - 67 - 8901

JACK HILL
Name(s) as shown on return JILL HILL

**ROUND TO THE NEAREST DOLLAR**

| | | | |
|---|---|---|---|
| 7 | Federal adjusted gross income (AGI) (see page 11 of the Instructions) ........ | **7** | 30500 |
| 8 | Difference in state/federal wages due to COLA, ERS, etc. (see page 12 of the Instructions) .................. **8** | 3000 | |
| 9 | Interest on out-of-state bonds (including municipal bonds) ............... **9** | 250 | |
| 10 | Other Hawaii additions to federal AGI (see page 12 of the Instructions) .......... **10** | 0 | |
| 11 | Add lines 8 through 10 ......... **Total Hawaii additions to federal AGI** **11** | | 3250 |
| 12 | Add lines 7 and 11 ................................... | **12** | 33750 |
| 13 | Pensions taxed federally but not taxed by Hawaii (see page 14 of the Instructions)................. **13** | 0 | |
| 14 | Social security benefits taxed on federal return ......... **14** | 0 | |
| 15 | First $6,564 of military reserve or Hawaii national guard duty pay .............. **15** | | |
| 16 | Payments to an individual housing account ......... **16** | | |
| 17 | Exceptional trees deduction (attach affidavit) (see page 15 of the Instructions) .......... **17** | | |
| 18 | Other Hawaii subtractions from federal AGI (see page 15 of the Instructions) .......... **18** | 3000 | |
| 19 | Add lines 13 through 18 ................. **Total Hawaii subtractions from federal AGI** **19** | | 3000 |
| 20 | Line 12 minus line 19 ......................... Hawaii AGI ➤ **20** | | 30750 |

*CAUTION:* *If you can be claimed as a dependent on another person's return, see the Instructions on page 16, and place an X here.*

21 If you do not itemize your deductions, go to line 23 below. Otherwise go to page 17 of the Instructions and enter your itemized deductions here.

| | | |
|---|---|---|
| 21a | Medical and dental expenses (from Worksheet A-1) ................... **21a** | 1260 |
| 21b | Taxes (from Worksheet A-2) .................... **21b** | 3800 |
| 21c | Interest expense (from Worksheet A-3) ............. **21c** | 12000 |
| 21d | Contributions (from Worksheet A-4) .............. **21d** | 400 |
| 21e | Casualty and theft losses (from Worksheet A-5) ......... **21e** | 0 |
| 21f | Miscellaneous deductions (from Worksheet A-6) ......... **21f** | 0 |

**TOTAL ITEMIZED DEDUCTIONS**

**22** Add lines 21a through 21f. If your Hawaii adjusted gross income is above a certain amount, you may not be able to deduct all of your itemized deductions. See the Instructions on page 22. Enter total here and go to line 24.

17460

| | | |
|---|---|---|
| 23 | If you checked filing status box: 1 or 3 enter $2,200; 2 or 5 enter $4,400; 4 enter $3,212 ............. Standard Deduction ➤ **23** | 4400 |
| 24 | Line 20 minus line 22 or 23, whichever applies. (This line MUST be filled in) ......... **24** | 13290 |

ID NO 88

**FORM N-11**

Form N-11 (Rev. 2018)                                                          Page 3 of 4

Your Social Security Number          Your Spouse's SSN

234 − 56 − 7890          345 − 67 − 8901
JACK HILL
Name(s) as shown on return  JILL HILL

25 Multiply $1,144 by the total number of exemptions claimed on line 6e.
   If you and/or your spouse are blind, deaf, or disabled, place an X in the applicable box(es),
   and see page 22 of the Instructions.
   Yourself        Spouse ...............................................................  25          4576

26 **Taxable Income.** Line 24 minus line 25 (but not less than zero) ............. **Taxable Income ➤** 26    8714
27 Tax. Place an X if from   **X** Tax Table;    Tax Rate Schedule; or    Capital Gains Tax
   Worksheet on page 39 of the Instructions.
   (      Place an X if tax from Forms N-2, N-103, N-152, N-168, N-312, N-338,
   N-344, N-348, N-405, N-586, N-615, or N-814 is included.) ..................... **Tax ➤** 27          193
27a If tax is from the Capital Gains Tax Worksheet, enter
   the net capital gain from line 14 of that worksheet ............ **27a**              0

28 Refundable Food/Excise Tax Credit
   (attach Form N-311) **DHS, etc.** exemptions    0   ..... **28**        140
29 Credit for Low-Income Household
   Renters (attach Schedule X) .............................................. 29          0
30 Credit for Child and Dependent
   Care Expenses (attach Schedule X) .................................. 30        400
31 Credit for Child Passenger Restraint
   System(s) (attach a copy of the invoice) ........................... 31
32 Total refundable tax credits from
   Schedule CR (attach Schedule CR) .................................. 32          0

33 Add lines 28 through 32 ............................................. **Total Refundable Credits ➤** 33          540

34 Line 27 minus line 33. If line 34 is zero or less, see Instructions ................................... 34  **X**    347

35 Total nonrefundable tax credits (attach Schedule CR) .............................................. 35              0

36 Line 34 minus line 35 .............................................. **Balance ➤** 36  **X**    347
37 Hawaii State Income tax withheld (attach W-2s)
   (see page 28 of the Instructions for other attachments) ................... 37        2500

38 2018 estimated tax payments ........................................... 38          0

39 Amount of estimated tax applied from 2017 return ........... 39          0

40 Amount paid with extension ................................. 40          0

41 Add lines 37 through 40 ............................................. **Total Payments ➤** 41        2500

42 If line 41 is larger than line 36, enter the amount **OVERPAID** (line 41 minus line 36) (see Instructions)  42    2847
43 **Contributions to** (see page 29 of the Instructions): ......................   Yourself   Spouse
   **43a** Hawaii Schools Repairs and Maintenance Fund ....................   $2     $2
   **43b** Hawaii Public Libraries Fund ..................................................  $5     $5
   **43c** Domestic and Sexual Violence / Child Abuse and Neglect Funds ...........  $5     $5
44 Add the amounts of the Xs on lines 43a through 43c and enter the total here ............................. 44      0

   45  Line 42 minus line 44 ............................................................................... 45     2847

   ID NO 88

N11_T 2018A 03 VID88                                                         FORM N-11

Form N-11 (Rev. 2018)

Page 4 of 4

Your Social Security Number 234 - 56 - 7890

Your Spouse's SSN 345 - 67 - 8901

JACK HILL
Name(s) as shown on return JILL HILL

**46** Amount of line 45 to be **applied** to your
**2019 ESTIMATED TAX** .................................. **46**      0

**47a** Amount to be **REFUNDED TO YOU** (line 45 minus line 46) If filing late,
see page 29 of Instructions ................................................................ **47a**      2847

    Place an X in this box if this refund will ultimately be deposited to a foreign (non-U.S.) bank. Do not complete lines 47b, 47c, or 47d.

**47b** Routing number            **47c** Type:    Checking    Savings

**47d** Account number

**48** **AMOUNT YOU OWE** (line 36 minus line 41) ............................................. **48**      0

**49** **PAYMENT AMOUNT** Submit payment online at hitax.hawaii.gov or attach check or
money order payable to "Hawaii State Tax Collector." .................................. **49**      0

**50** **Estimated tax penalty.** (See page 30 of
Instructions.) Do not include on line 42 or 48. Place an X in
this box if Form N-210 is attached ➤    .................**50**      0

**51** **AMENDED RETURN ONLY** – Amount paid (overpaid) on original return. (See Instructions) (attach Sch. AMD).......... **51**      0

**52** **AMENDED RETURN ONLY** – Balance due (refund) with amended return. (See Instructions) (attach Sch. AMD)......... **52**      0

**53** Did you file a federal Schedule C?    Yes **X** No    If yes, enter **Hawaii** gross receipts      0
your main business activity: _____ ,
your main business product: _____ , **AND** your HI Tax I.D. No. for this activity **GE**

**54** Did you file a federal Schedule E
for any rental activity?    Yes **X** No    If yes, enter **Hawaii** gross rents received      0
**AND** your HI Tax I.D. No. for this activity **GE**

**55** Did you file a federal Schedule F?    Yes **X** No    If yes, enter **Hawaii** gross receipts      0
your main business activity: _____
your main business product: _____ , **AND** your HI Tax I.D. No. for this activity **GE**

**DESIGNEE** If designating another person to discuss this return with the Hawaii Department of Taxation, complete the following. This is not a full power of attorney. See page 31 of the Instructions.

Designee's name ➤      Phone no. ➤      Identification number ➤

**HAWAII ELECTION CAMPAIGN FUND** ➤ Do you want $3 to go to the Hawaii Election Campaign Fund? **X** Yes No    Note: Placing an X in the "Yes" box will not increase your tax or reduce your refund.
If joint return, does your spouse want $3 to go to the fund? **X** Yes No

DECLARATION — I declare, under the penalties set forth in section 231-36, HRS, that this return (including accompanying schedules or statements) has been examined by me and, to the best of my knowledge and belief, is a true, correct, and complete return, made in good faith, for the taxable year stated, pursuant to the Hawaii Income Tax Law, Chapter 235, HRS.

**PLEASE SIGN HERE**

Your signature      Date      Spouse's signature (if filing jointly, BOTH must sign)      Date

Your Occupation      Daytime Phone Number      Your Spouse's Occupation      Daytime Phone Number

**Paid Preparer's Information**

Preparer's ➤ Signature      Date      Check if self-employed ➤      Preparer's identification number

Print Preparer's Name ➤ HOMER JONES      Federal E.I. No. ➤ 42-1539623

Firm's name (or yours if self-employed), Address, and ZIP Code ➤ KMH LLP, 1003 BISHOP ST #2400 HONOLULU, HI 96813      Phone No. ➤ (808) 526-2255

ID NO 88

N11_T 2018A 04 VID88      **FORM N-11**

**SCHEDULE X**
(FORM N-11/N-15)
(REV. 2018)

STATE OF HAWAII—DEPARTMENT OF TAXATION

# TAX CREDITS FOR HAWAII RESIDENTS

Both pages of Schedule X **must** be attached
to Form N-11 or N-15

**2018**

**Caution:** Before completing Schedule X, please read the **Instructions on pages 33 - 36** of the Form N-11 booklet, or **pages 37 - 40** of the Form N-15 booklet.

| Name(s) as shown on Form N-11 or N-15 | Your social security number |
|---|---|
| JACK AND JILL HILL | 234-56-7890 |

## PART I: CREDIT FOR LOW-INCOME HOUSEHOLD RENTERS

1   Is your adjusted gross income (Form N-11, line 20; or Form N-15, line 35, Column A) less than $30,000?
    If "No," **STOP**. You cannot claim this credit. If "Yes," go to Question 2.

2   Are you a resident who was present in Hawaii more than nine months of the taxable year? If "No," **STOP**. You cannot claim this credit. If "Yes," go to Question 3.

3   Can you be claimed as a dependent by another taxpayer? If "Yes," **STOP**. You cannot claim this credit. If "No," go to line 4.

4   Enter required information for each rental unit that was fully subject to real property tax. Do not list rental units that were wholly or partially exempt from real property tax. If you occupied
    more than one qualified unit, submit the required information for each additional unit on a separate sheet. If you shared the unit with others, enter only your share of the rent.

Address (give Apt. No., if any)

Occupied From _____ , 2018, To _____ , 2018. Total rent paid for this period.     0
                 month                       month

Owned by (or agent for owner) _____                                    GE _____
                                  name                      address              (Hawaii Tax I.D. No.)

| | | |
|---|---|---|
| 5   Add up your share of rent paid during the taxable year for all the units you have listed ............... | **5** | 0 . 00 |
| 6   Enter the amount of your exclusions (e.g., utilities, parking stalls, ground rent, rental subsidies such as public assistance) ......... | **6** | 0 . 00 |
| 7   Line 5 minus line 6. If this amount is $1,000, or less, **STOP**. You cannot claim this credit ...................... | **7** | 0 . 00 |

8   List YOURSELF, YOUR SPOUSE, AND YOUR DEPENDENTS that meet all of the following: a) Resident of Hawaii, b) Present
    in Hawaii for more than nine months in 2018, and c) Cannot be claimed as a dependent by another taxpayer.
    Include minor children receiving more than half of their support from public agencies which you can claim as dependents.

| 8 | Name | Relationship | Name | Relationship |
|---|---|---|---|---|
| | | Self | | |
| | | Spouse | | |

| | | |
|---|---|---|
| Enter the number of qualified persons listed above ...................................... | **8** | 0 |
| 9   If you are a qualified exemption and you are age 65 or over, enter 1. Otherwise, enter -0- ............... | **9** | 0 |
| 10  If you are married filing jointly or married filing separately where your spouse is not filing a Hawaii return, had no income, and was not the dependent of someone else; and your spouse is a qualified exemption; and your spouse is age 65 or over; enter 1. Otherwise, enter -0- ........... | **10** | 0 |
| 11  Add lines 8 through 10 ...................................... | **11** | 0 |
| 12  Multiply the number of exemptions on line 11 by $50 and enter the result here and on Form N-11, line 29; or Form N-15, line 46. This is your credit for low-income household renters. (Whole dollars only) ............ | **12** | 0 00 |

## PART II: CREDIT FOR CHILD AND DEPENDENT CARE EXPENSES

### Section A: Care Provider Information

Complete line 1 columns (a) through (e) for each person or organization that provided the care. If you do not give the information asked for in each colum
or if the information you give is not correct, your credit and, if applicable, the exclusion of employer-provided dependent care benefits may be disallowed.

| 1 | (a) Care provider's name | (b) Address (number, street, city, state, and Postal/ZIP code) | (c) Identification number (SSN or FEIN) | (d) Hawaii Tax I.D. No. | (e) Amount paid |
|---|---|---|---|---|---|
| | DAYCARE LTD | 1001 PALOLO AVENUE HONOLULU HI 96813 | 12-3456789 | GE 123456789001 | 2000 .00 |
| | | | | GE | 0 .00 |

### Section B:  Dependent Care Benefits — (If you did not receive dependent care benefits, skip to line 21)

| | | |
|---|---|---|
| 2   Enter the total amount of dependent care benefits you received in 2018. Amounts you received as an employee should be shown in Box 10 of your federal Form(s) W-2. If you were self-employed or a partner, include amounts you received under a dependent care assistance program from your sole proprietorship or partnership. ............... | **2** | 0 .00 |
| 3   Enter the amount, if any, you carried over from 2017 and used in 2018 during the grace period ............... | **3** | 0 .00 |
| 4   Enter the amount, if any, you forfeited or carried forward to 2019. (See the Instructions) ............... | **4** | ( 0 .00) |
| 5   Combine lines 2 through 4 ...................................... | **5** | 0 .00 |

SCHX_T 2018A 01 VID88

ID NO 88

**SCHEDULE X**

SCHEDULE X (FORM N-11/N-15) (REV. 2018)                                                          PAGE 2

| Name(s) as shown on Form N-11 or N-15 | Your social security number |
|---|---|
| JACK AND JILL HILL | 234-56-7890 |

| | | | |
|---|---|---|---|
| 6 | Enter the total amount of qualified expenses incurred in 2018 for the care of the qualifying person(s) .... | 6 | 0.00 |
| 7 | Enter the smaller of line 5 or 6 ..................................................................... | 7 | 0.00 |
| 8 | Enter your earned income. (See the Instructions) ......................................... | 8 | 0.00 |
| 9 | If married filing jointly, enter your spouse's earned income (if you or your spouse was a student or disabled, see the Instructions); if married filing separately, see the Instructions; all others, enter the amount from line 8. ..................................... | 9 | 0.00 |
| 10 | Enter the smallest of line 7, 8, or 9. ................................................................ | 10 | 0.00 |
| 11 | Enter $5,000 ($2,500 if married filing separately and you were required to enter your spouse's earned income on line 9). .......................................................... | 11 | 5000.00 |
| 12 | Is any amount on line 2 from your sole proprietorship or partnership? **No.** Enter -0-. **Yes.** Enter the amount here .............................................................. | 12 | 0.00 |
| 13 | Line 5 minus line 12 ........................................................................... | 13 | 0.00 |
| 14 | **Deductible benefits.** Enter the smallest of line 10, 11, or 12. Also, include this amount on the appropriate line(s) of your return ...................................................................................... | 14 | 0.00 |
| 15 | **Excluded benefits.** If line 12 is zero, enter the smaller of line 10 or 11. Otherwise, subtract line 14 from the smaller of line 10 or 11. If zero or less, enter -0-. ........................................... | 15 | 0.00 |
| 16 | **Taxable benefits.** Line 13 minus line 15. If zero or less, enter -0-. Also, include this amount on Form N-15, line 7. On the dotted line next to line 7, write "DCB." (Form N-11 filers, see the Instructions) .................. | 16 | 0.00 |
| 17 | Enter $2,400 ($4,800 if two or more qualifying persons) ............................... | 17 | 0.00 |
| 18 | Add lines 14 and 15. ........................................................................... | 18 | 0.00 |
| 19 | Line 17 minus line 18. If zero or less, **STOP.** You cannot take the credit. **Exception.** If you paid 2017 expenses in 2018, see the Instructions for line 28 ....................................................... | 19 | 0.00 |
| 20 | Complete line 21. Do not include in column (d) any benefits shown on line 18. Then, add the amounts in column (d) and enter the total here. ........................................................................... | 20 | 0.00 |

**Section C: Credit for Child and Dependent Care Expenses** — (If you are married, you must file a joint return to claim the tax credit.)

| 21 | (a) Qualifying person's name | (b) Relationship | (c) Qualifying person's social security number | (d) Qualified expenses you incurred and paid in 2018 for the person listed in column (a) |
|---|---|---|---|---|
| | BILL HILL | SON | 456-78-9012 | 2000.00 |
| | | | | 0.00 |

| | | | |
|---|---|---|---|
| 22 | Add the amounts in column (d) of line 21. Do not enter more than $2,400 for one qualifying person or $4,800 for two or more persons. If you completed Section B, enter the smaller of line 19 or 20. ......................... | 22 | 2000.00 |
| 23 | Enter your earned income. (See the Instructions) ...................................................................... | 23 | 24500.00 |
| 24 | If married filing jointly, enter your spouse's earned income (if you or your spouse was a student or disabled, see the Instructions); all others, enter the amount from line 23 ........................................... | 24 | 24500.00 |
| 25 | Enter the smallest of line 22, 23, or 24. .............................................................................. | 25 | 2000.00 |
| 26 | Enter your adjusted gross income from Form N-11, line 20; or Form N-15, line 35, Column A ........................................................... | 26 | 30750.00 |

27 Enter on line 27 the decimal amount shown below that applies to the amount on line 26.

| If line 26 is: | Decimal amount is: | If line 26 is: | Decimal amount is: |
|---|---|---|---|
| Under $25,001 | .25 | $40,001 – 45,000 | .21 |
| $25,001 – 30,000 | .24 | $45,001 – 50,000 | .20 |
| $30,001 – 35,000 | .23 | $50,001 and over | .15 |
| $35,001 – 40,000 | .22 | | |

| | | | |
|---|---|---|---|
| | | 27 | X .23 |
| 28 | Multiply line 25 by the decimal amount on line 27. If you paid 2017 expenses in 2018, see the Instructions. Enter the result here and on Form N-11, line 30; or Form N-15, line 47. This is your credit for child and dependent care expenses. (Whole dollars only) ................................................................. | 28 | 460 00 |

SCHX_T 2018A 02 VID88                              ID NO 88

FORM
**N-615**
(REV.2018)

STATE OF HAWAII — DEPARTMENT OF TAXATION
**Computation of Tax for Children Under Age 14 Who
Have Unearned Income of More than $1,000**

**2018**

➤ **See Separate Instructions**
➤ **Attach only to the child's Form N-11 or Form N-15**
(NOTE: References to "married" and "spouse" are also references to
"in a civil union" and "civil union partner," respectively.)

| Child's name shown on return | Child's social security number |
|---|---|
| LINDA ALOHA | 987-56-4322 |

| **A** Parent's name (first, initial, last) **(Caution:** See Instructions before completing) | **B** Parent's social security number |
|---|---|
| JOHN ALOHA | 123-45-6789 |

**C** Parent's filing status (check one):

☐ Single   ☒ Married filing jointly   ☐ Married filing separately   ☐ Head of household   ☐ Qualifying widow(er)

### Part I   Child's Net Unearned Income

| | | |
|---|---|---|
| 1 Enter the child's unearned income. (See Instructions. If this amount is $1,000 or less, stop here; do not file this form.) | 1 | 1200 |
| 2 If the child **did not** itemize deductions on Form N-11 or Form N-15, enter $1,000. If the child itemized deductions, see Instructions. | 2 | 1000 |
| 3 Line 1 minus line 2. (If zero or less, stop here; do not complete the rest of this form but **do** attach it to the child's return.) | 3 | 200 |
| 4 Enter the child's **taxable income** (from Form N-11, line 26 or Form N-15, line 43) | 4 | 200 |
| 5 Enter the **smaller** of line 3 or line 4. (If zero, stop here; do not complete the rest of this form but **do** attach it to the child's return.) ➤ | 5 | 200 |

### Part II   Tentative Tax Based on the Tax Rate of the Parent

| | | |
|---|---|---|
| 6 Enter the parent's **taxable income** (from Form N-11, line 26 or Form N-15, line 43). If zero or less, enter zero | 6 | 10379 |
| 7 Enter the total, if any, from Forms N-615, line 5, of **all other** children of the parent named above. (**Do not** include the amount from line 5 above.) | 7 | |
| 8 Add lines 5, 6, and 7. | 8 | 10579 |
| 9 Enter the tax on the amount on line 8 based on the **parent's** filing status above. See Instructions. Check if from ☒ Tax Table, ☐ Tax Rate Schedule, ☐ Capital Gains Tax Worksheet in the Instructions for Form N-11 or Form N-15, ☐ Form N-168 | 9 | 275 |
| 10 Enter the parent's tax (from Form N-11, line 27 or Form N-15, line 44). **Do not** include any tax from Form N-152 or Form N-814. Check if from ☒ Tax Table, ☐ Tax Rate Schedule, ☐ Capital Gains Tax Worksheet in the Instructions for Form N-11 or Form N-15, ☐ Form N-168 | 10 | 264 |
| 11 Line 9 minus line 10. Enter the result. (If line 7 is blank, also enter this amount on line 13 and go to **Part III**.) | 11 | 11 |
| 12a Add lines 5 and 7. | 12a | 0 |
| b Divide line 5 by line 12a. Enter the result as a decimal (rounded to at least three places) ➤ | 12b | 0.0000 |
| 13 Multiply line 11 by line 12b. | 13 | 11 |

### Part III   Child's Tax — If lines 4 and 5 above are the same, enter -0- on line 15 and go to line 16.

| | | |
|---|---|---|
| 14 Line 4 minus line 5 | 14 | 0 |
| 15 Enter the tax on the amount on line 14 based on the **child's** filing status. See Instructions. Check if from ☐ Tax Table, ☐ Tax Rate Schedule, ☐ Capital Gains Tax Worksheet in the Instructions for Form N-11 or Form N-15, ☐ Form N-168 | 15 | 0 |
| 16 Add lines 13 and 15. | 16 | 11 |
| 17 Enter the tax on the amount on line 4 based on the **child's** filing status. See Instructions. Check if from ☒ Tax Table, ☐ Tax Rate Schedule, ☐ Capital Gains Tax Worksheet in the Instructions for Form N-11 or Form N-15, ☐ Form N-168 | 17 | 3 |
| 18 Enter the **larger** of line 16 or line 17 here and on the **child's** Form N-11, line 27 or Form N-15, line 44. (Whole dollars only) Be sure to indicate that tax from Form N-615 is included ➤ | 18 | 11  00 |

## How to Use the Payment Voucher

(1) Enter your name, address, and social security number in the space provided. If you are filing a joint payment voucher, enter your spouse's name and social security number in the space provided.

(2) If you have a foreign address, enter the complete country name in the space provided.

(3) If you are an alien and were issued an individual taxpayer identification number (ITIN) by the IRS, enter your ITIN in the space provided for the social security number. If you applied for an ITIN but the IRS has not yet issued the ITIN, write "ITIN Applied For" in the space above the box where you enter your name.

(4) If you are making a tax payment for a composite Form N-15, check the box for Composite Taxpayer. Enter "Partners" or "Shareholders" in the space provided for the first name. Enter the partnership's or the S corporation's name in the space provided for the last name. Enter the partnership's or S corporation's federal employer identification number in the space provided for the social security number in social security number format (i.e., 123-45-6789).

(5) Enter the amount of your payment in the space provided (Whole dollars only).

(6) Make your check or money order payable in U.S. dollars to "Hawaii State Tax Collector" and attach it to the front of the payment voucher. Make sure your name and address appear on your check or money order. Please write your social security number (federal employer identification number if you are a composite taxpayer), daytime phone number, and "2019 Form N-1" on your check or money order. Do not send cash.

(7) The payment voucher should be filed with the: **Hawaii Department of Taxation**
P.O. Box 1530
Honolulu, Hawaii 96806-1530

---

✂ — — — — — — — — — — CUT HERE — — — — — — — — — — — ✂

| Form (Rev. 2018) | Tax Year | STATE OF HAWAII — DEPARTMENT OF TAXATION | DO NOT WRITE OR STAPLE IN THIS SPACE |
|---|---|---|---|
| **N-1** | **2019** | **INDIVIDUAL ESTIMATED INCOME TAX** | |

### Voucher No. 1

**Calendar Year — Due April 20, 2019**

DO NOT SUBMIT A PHOTOCOPY OF THIS FORM

Composite Taxpayer

| Your first name | M.I. | Last name | Suffix | |
|---|---|---|---|---|
| JOHN | | ALOHA | | |

| If joint return, spouse's first name | M.I. | Last name | Suffix | Your Social Security Number |
|---|---|---|---|---|
| MARY | | ALOHA | | 123 - 45 - 6789 |

Present mailing or home address (Number and street, including rural route) — Apartment Number

1234 OAHU STREET

Spouse's Social Security Number

| City, town, or post office | State | Postal/ZIP Code | Country | For office use only | |
|---|---|---|---|---|---|
| HONOLULU | HI | 96800 | | | 987 - 65 - 4321 |

Amount of Payment

MAIL THIS VOUCHER WITH CHECK OR MONEY ORDER PAYABLE TO "HAWAII STATE TAX COLLECTOR." Write your social security number, daytime phone number, and "2019 Form N-1" on your check or money order.

ID NO 01

200

N1_F 2018A 01 VID01

| PART III. Amended Computation | | PART IV. Record of Estimated Tax Payments | | | | |
|---|---|---|---|---|---|---|
| (Used if your estimated tax substantially changes after you file your first payment voucher.) | | Voucher Number | Date | Amount Paid | Prior year overpayment credit applied to installment | Total amount paid and credited from the 1st day of the taxable year through the installment date shown. Add (b) and (c) |
| | | | (a) | (b) | (c) | (d) |
| 1. Amended estimated tax .................................. | | | | | | |
| 2. Less: | | 1 | | | | |
|   (a) Amount of last year's overpayment elected for credit to current year's estimated tax and applied to date ..................... | | | | | | |
| | | 2 | | | | |
|   (b) Estimated tax payments to date.................. | | | | | | |
|   (c) Total of lines 2(a) and 2(b) ........................ | | 3 | | | | |
| 3. Unpaid balance (line 1 minus line 2(c)).............. | | | | | | |
| | | 4 | | | | |
| 4. Amount to be paid (line 3 divided by number of remaining installments). Enter here and on payment voucher ..................... | | Total.................. ➤ | | | | |

## MAILING ADDRESS

**Hawaii Department of Taxation**
P.O. Box 1530
Honolulu, Hawaii 96806-1530
(830 Punchbowl Street)

✂ — — — — — — — — — — — CUT HERE — — — — — — — — — — — — ✂

Form (Rev. 2018)

**N-3**

**STATE OF HAWAII — DEPARTMENT OF TAXATION**
**CORPORATION ESTIMATED INCOME TAX**

### Voucher No. 1

**THIS VOUCHER IS DUE ON OR BEFORE THE 20th DAY OF THE 4th MONTH OF THE TAXABLE YEAR.**

**DO NOT SUBMIT A PHOTOCOPY OF THIS FORM**

DO NOT WRITE OR STAPLE IN THIS SPACE

Name

**STARGATE CORPORATION**
Dba or C/O

Federal Employer Identification Number (FEIN)

**12 – 3456789**

Mailing Address                          Suite Number

**101 KEANU BLVD**
City, town, or post office    State    Postal/ZIP Code    Country    For office use only

Calendar or Fiscal Year Ending (MM DD YY)

**HONOLULU       HI    96000**

**12 – 31 – 19**

Amount of Payment

MAIL THIS VOUCHER WITH CHECK OR MONEY ORDER PAYABLE TO "HAWAII STATE TAX COLLECTOR." Write your FEIN, the year for which payment is made, and "Form N-3" on your check or money order.

**5000.00**

N3_F 2018A 01 VID01                          ID NO 01

## PROBLEM FOR SPECIMEN RETURN
## NONRESIDENT INDIVIDUAL INCOME TAX RETURN

### Form N-15

John Reed is an executive employed by California Canners Co. and he received a salary of $90,000 during the year. John spent 40% of his time on company business in Hawaii during the year.

John, his wife Barbara, and their two daughters, Lynn and Diane, are residents of California. John also supports his father, Henry, age 72, who lives with them at 217 Palm Drive, Encino. Their daughters are college students.

The following dividends were received during the year:

| | |
|---|---:|
| California Canners Co. | $ 500 |
| Honolulu Electric Company | 100 |
| Los Angeles Manufacturing Co., Inc. | 50 |
| Hawaii Fund, Inc. (Mr. Reed has been notified that 25% is taxable as long-term capital gain for federal income tax purposes) | 200 |
| Interest received on City of Los Angeles, California municipal bonds. | 200 |
| Interest on savings account at Encino National Bank | 250 |

On November 15, John sold for $4,150 (net proceeds) 100 shares of Honolulu Electric stock he had purchased on June 15, 1983 for $2,350. On the same date he sold for $3,150 (net proceeds) 100 shares of Los Angeles Manufacturing Co. stock he had purchased February 1, 1981 for $3,850.

John is also a partner in the ROK Pineapple Ranch located in Napoopoo, Hawaii. (See specimen partnership return—Form N-20 for additional income and expense items that need to be included in John's income tax return).

Barbara received the following income during the year as beneficiary of a trust established by her parents with the Honolulu National Bank as trustee:

| | |
|---|---:|
| Long term capital gains | $ 2,000 |
| Other income | 3,180 |

The following contributions were paid during the year:

| | |
|---|---:|
| Los Angeles Community Chest | $ 100 |
| Los Angeles County Heart Association | 100 |
| Honolulu Foster Home | 200 |
| Southern California Symphony Association. | 100 |

## PROBLEM FOR SPECIMEN RETURN
## NONRESIDENT INDIVIDUAL INCOME TAX RETURN

### Form N-15

Interest:
   On loan incurred to purchase home in California............................... $ 2,100

Taxes:
   Property tax on home in California.................................................... $   650
   California income tax.................................................................... 760
   Hawaii income tax ...................................................................... 250
   Sales tax .................................................................................. 500

Medical:
   Drugs...................................................................................... $   580
   John Doe, M.D........................................................................... 750
   J. Smith, M.D. ........................................................................... 200
   A. Brown, D.D.S. ........................................................................ 250
   Encino Community Hospital (Other Deductions: expenses of
      John's father—excluding drugs)........................................................ 2,186

Other Deductions:
   Westates University—professional seminars required by employer . $ 1,000
   Accounting fees for preparation of tax returns ....................................... 700
   Safe deposit box rental—Encino National Savings Bank—
      where all securities are kept....................................................... 15

## EXPLANATION OF ITEMS ON SPECIMEN RETURN
## NONRESIDENT INDIVIDUAL INCOME TAX RETURN

### Form N-15

Page 1 — dividends

Situs of the stock on which dividends were received is California, the state in which the taxpayer is a resident, even though some of the companies paying the dividends derive income from Hawaii.

Page 1 — capital gains

Total capital gain is computed as follows:

Share from—

| | |
|---|---|
| ROK Partnership | $1,000 |
| Trust | 2,000 |
| Hawaii Fund, Inc. | 50 |
| Sale of stock— | |
| Honolulu Electric | 1,800 |
| Los Angeles Manufacturing Co., Inc. | (700) |
| | $4,150 |

(The stock transactions are not reportable on the Hawaii return because they are attributable to the taxpayers state of residence.)

Contributions:

Allocated in proportion to adjusted gross income.

Interest:

Interest paid on California mortgage is not deductible in Hawaii.

Taxes:

California property tax and income tax are not deductible in Hawaii. Hawaii income tax is fully deductible. The sales tax is allocated in proportion to adjusted gross income.

Medical expenses:

Allocated in proportion to adjusted gross income.

Other deductions:

Safe deposit box rental is not deductible in Hawaii. Other expenses are allocated in proportion to adjusted gross income.

FORM **N-15** (Rev. 2018)

STATE OF HAWAII — DEPARTMENT OF TAXATION

# Individual Income Tax Return
## NONRESIDENT and PART-YEAR RESIDENT

ID NO 88

Calendar Year **2018**

**OR**

Tax Year thru

Part-Year Resident (Enter period of Hawaii residency above) | Nonresident | Nonresident Alien or Dual-Status Alien | MSRRA | Composite

AMENDED Return
NOL Carryback
IRS Adjustment

FOR OFFICE USE ONLY

**Do NOT Submit a Photocopy!!**

Place an X in applicable box, if appropriate

First Time Filer | Address or Name Change

**ATTACH A COPY OF YOUR 2018 FEDERAL INCOME TAX RETURN**

• ATTACH COPY 2 OF FORM W-2 HERE •

Place Label Here

| Your First Name | M.I. | Your Last Name | Suffix |
|---|---|---|---|
| JOHN | | REED | |
| Spouse's First Name | M.I. | Spouse's Last Name | Suffix |
| BARBARA | | REED | |

Care Of *(See Instructions, page 8.)*

Present mailing or home address (Number and street, including Rural Route): 217 PALM DR

City, town or post office: ENCINO | State: CA | Postal/ZIP code: 90120

If Foreign address, enter Province and/or State | Country

◆ IMPORTANT — Complete this Section ◆

Enter the first four letters of your last name. Use **ALL CAPITAL** letters: REED

Your Social Security Number: 111 - 23 - 4567

Deceased | Date of Death

Enter the first four letters of your Spouse's last name. Use **ALL CAPITAL** letters: REED

Spouse's Social Security Number: 111 - 98 - 7654

Deceased | Date of Death

*(Place an X in only ONE box)*

1 Single
2 X Married filing joint return (even if only one had income).
3 Married filing separate return. Enter spouse's SSN and the first four letters of last name above. Enter spouse's full name here. ______
4 Head of household (with qualifying person). If the qualifying person is a child but not your dependent, enter the child's full name. ➤ ______
5 Qualifying widow(er) (see page 9 of the Instructions)
Enter the year your spouse died

. ATTACH CHECK OR MONEY ORDER HERE .

***CAUTION:*** If you can be claimed as a dependent on another person's tax return (such as your parents'), DO NOT place an X on line 6a, but be sure to place an X below line 37.

6a X Yourself ........ Age 65 or over ........
6b X Spouse ........ Age 65 or over ........
} Enter the number of Xs on **6a** and **6b** ........ 2

If you placed an X on lines 3 and 6b above, see the Instructions on page 9 and if your spouse meets the qualifications, place an X here

6c and 6d

| Dependents: 1. First and last name (If more than 6 dependents use attachment) | 2. Dependent's social security number | 3. Relationship |
|---|---|---|
| LYNN REED | 222-12-3456 | DAUGHTER |
| DIANE REED | 222-98-7654 | DAUGHTER |
| HENRY REED | 333-12-3456 | FATHER |
| | | |
| | | |
| | | |

Enter number of your children listed ... **6c** 2
Enter number of other dependents...... **6d** 1

**6e** Total number of exemptions claimed. Add numbers entered in boxes **6a thru 6d** above........ **6e** 5

N15_T 2018A 01 VID88

**FORM N-15**

**Form N-15 (Rev. 2018)**

 ID NO 88

**Page 2 of 4**

Your Social Security Number      Your Spouse's SSN

111 – 23 – 4567        111 – 98 – 7654

JOHN REED

Name(s) as shown on return BARBARA REED

| | | Col. A - Total Income | | Col. B - Hawaii Income |
|---|---|---|---|---|
| 7 | Wages, salaries, tips, etc. (attach Form(s) W-2) .......... | 89094 | 7 | 31934 |
| 8 | Interest income from the worksheet on page 41 of the Instructions ........................................................... | 250 | 8 | 0 |
| 9 | Ordinary dividends ...................................................... | 800 | 9 | |
| 10 | State income tax refund from the worksheet on page 41 of the Instructions ......................................... | 0 | 10 | 0 |
| 11 | Alimony received ......................................................... | 0 | 11 | |
| 12 | Business or farm income or (loss) .............................. | 0 | 12 | 0 |
| 13 | Capital gain or (loss) from the worksheet on page 41 of the Instructions ......................................... | 4150 | 13 | 0 |
| 14 | Supplemental gains or (losses) (attach Schedule D-1) ................................ **X** | 453 | 14 **X** | 453 |
| 15 | IRA distributions ......................................................... | 0 | 15 | |
| 16 | Pensions and annuities (see Instructions and attach Schedule J, Form N-11/N-15/N-40) ................. | 0 | 16 | 0 |
| 17 | Rents, royalties, partnerships, estates, trusts, etc. ..... | 1600 | 17 **X** | 1580 |
| 18 | Unemployment compensation (insurance)................... | 0 | 18 | |
| 19 | Other income (state nature and source) _____ ................ | 0 | 19 | 0 |
| 20 | Add lines 7 through 19 .................. **Total Income** ➤ | 96347 | 20 | 33967 |
| 21 | Certain business expenses of reservists, performing artists, and fee-basis government officials .................. | 0 | 21 | |
| 22 | IRA deduction ............................................................. | 0 | 22 | 0 |
| 23 | Student loan interest deduction from the worksheet on page 46 of the Instructions ..................................... | 0 | 23 | 0 |
| 24 | Health savings account deduction .............................. | 0 | 24 | 0 |
| 25 | Moving expenses (attach Form N-139) ...................... | 0 | 25 | 0 |
| 26 | Deductible part of self-employment tax ...................... | 0 | 26 | 0 |
| 27 | Self-employed health insurance deduction ................. | 0 | 27 | |
| 28 | Self-employed SEP, SIMPLE, and qualified plans ...... | 0 | 28 | 0 |
| 29 | Penalty on early withdrawal of savings ...................... | 0 | 29 | 0 |
| 30 | Alimony paid (Enter name and SS No. of recipient) _____ ................ | 0 | 30 | 0 |
| | 31 Payments to an individual housing account | | 31 | |
| | 32 First $6,564 of military reserve or Hawaii national guard duty pay ............................. | | 32 | |

**Form N-15 (Rev. 2018)**　　　　　　　　　　　　　　　　　　　**Page 3 of 4**

ID NO 88

Your Social Security Number　　　　Your Spouse's SSN

111 - 23 - 4567　　　　111 - 98 - 7654

JOHN REED

Name(s) as shown on return　BARBARA REED

| | | | | |
|---|---|---|---|---|
| 33 | Exceptional trees deduction (attach affidavit) ............ (see page 21 of the Instructions) ............................... | | **33** | |
| 34 | Add lines 21 through 33 ....... **Total Adjustments ➤** | 0 | **34** | 0 |
| 35 | Line 20 minus line 34 . **Adjusted Gross Income ➤** | 96347 | **35** | 33967 |
| 36 | **Federal** adjusted gross income (see page 21 of the Instructions) ........ **36** | | 96347 | |

37　Ratio of Hawaii AGI to Total AGI. Divide line 35, Column B, by line 35, Column A (Compute to 3 decimal places and round to 2 decimal places) ........................ **37**　0.35

**CAUTION:** If you can be claimed as a dependent on another person's return, see the Instructions on page 21, and place an X here.

38　If you do not itemize deductions, enter zero on line 39 and go to line 40a. Otherwise go to page 22 of the Instructions and enter your Hawaii itemized deductions here.

**38a**　Medical and dental expenses (from Worksheet NR-1 or PY-1) ............................ **38a**　250

**38b**　Taxes (from Worksheet NR-2 or PY-2) ................. **38b**　0

**38c**　Interest expense (from Worksheet NR-3 or PY-3) ....... **38c**　0

**38d**　Contributions (from Worksheet NR-4 or PY-4) ...... **38d**　184

Casualty and theft losses

**38e**　(from Worksheet NR-5 or PY-5) ............................ **38e**　0

**38f**　Miscellaneous deductions (from Worksheet NR-6 or PY-6) ............................ **38f**　0

**TOTAL ITEMIZED DEDUCTIONS**

**39**　If your Hawaii adjusted gross income is above a certain amount, you may not be able to deduct all of your itemized deductions. See the Instructions on page 27. Enter total here and go to line 41.　434

| | | | | |
|---|---|---|---|---|
| **40a** | If you checked filing status box: 1 or 3 enter $2,200; 2 or 5 enter $4,400; 4 enter $3,212 ............................... **40a** | 4400 | | |
| **40b** | Multiply line 40a by the ratio on line 37 ............................ **Prorated Standard Deduction ➤ 40b** | | | 1540 |
| 41 | Line 35, Column B minus line 39 or 40b, whichever applies. (This line MUST be filled in) ........... **41** | | | 32427 |
| **42a** | Multiply $1,144 by the total number of exemptions claimed on line 6e. If you and/or your spouse are blind, deaf, or disabled, place an X in the applicable box(es), and see the Instructions.　Yourself　Spouse ...................................... **42a** | 5720 | | |
| **42b** | Multiply line 42a by the ratio on line 37 ......................................... **Prorated Exemption(s) ➤ 42b** | | | 2002 |
| 43 | **Taxable Income.** Line 41 minus line 42b (but not less than zero) ............ **Taxable Income ➤ 43** | | | 30425 |

44　**Tax.** Place an X if from: **X** Tax Table;　Tax Rate Schedule; or　Capital Gains Tax Worksheet on page 44 of the Instructions.

(　Place an X if tax from Forms N-2, N-103, N-152, N-168, N-312, N-338, N-344, N-348, N-405, N-586, N-615, or N-814 is included.)　**Tax ➤ 44**　1474

| | | | |
|---|---|---|---|
| **44a** | If tax is from the Capital Gains Tax Worksheet, enter the net capital gain from line 8 of that worksheet ......................................... **44a** | 0 | |
| 45 | Refundable Food/Excise Tax Credit (attach Form N-311) **DHS, etc.** exemptions 0 ...... **45** | 0 | |
| 46 | Credit for Low-Income Household Renters (attach Schedule X) ............................................... **46** | 0 | |
| 47 | Credit for Child and Dependent Care Expenses (attach Schedule X) ............................ **47** | 0 | |
| 48 | Credit for Child Passenger Restraint System(s) (attach a copy of the invoice) ........................... **48** | | |
| 49 | Total refundable tax credits from Schedule CR (attach Schedule CR) .................. **49** | 0 | |
| 50 | Add lines 45 through 49 ................................................ **Total Refundable Credits ➤ 50** | | 0 |
| 51 | Line 44 minus line 50. If line 51 is zero or less, see Instructions ...................................... **51** | | 1474 |

N15_T 2018A 03 VID88　　　　　　　　　　　　　　　　　　**FORM N-15**

**Form N-15 (Rev. 2018)**

Page 4 of 4

ID NO 88

Your Social Security Number

111 - 23 - 4567

Your Spouse's SSN

111 - 98 - 7654

JOHN REED

Name(s) as shown on return BARBARA REED

| No. | Description | | Amount |
|---|---|---|---|
| 52 | Total nonrefundable tax credits (attach Schedule CR) | **52** | 130 |
| 53 | Line 51 minus line 52 **Balance ▶** | **53** | 1344 |
| 54 | Hawaii State Income tax withheld (attach W-2s) (see page 33 of the Instructions for other attachments) **54** | | 250 |
| 55 | 2018 estimated tax payments on Forms N-1 _____ 0 ; N-288A _____ **55** | | 0 |
| 56 | Amount of estimated tax applied from 2017 return **56** | | 0 |
| 57 | Amount paid with extension **57** | | 0 |

**TOTAL PAYMENTS**

58 Add lines 54 through 57.

| | | | |
|---|---|---|---|
| 58 | | | 250 |
| 59 | If line 58 is larger than line 53, enter the amount **OVERPAID** (line 58 minus line 53) (see Instructions) **59** | | 0 |

60 **Contributions to** (see page 33 of the Instructions):................ **Yourself Spouse**

| | | Yourself | Spouse |
|---|---|---|---|
| 60a | Hawaii Schools Repairs and Maintenance Fund | $2 | $2 |
| 60b | Hawaii Public Libraries Fund | $2 | $2 |
| 60c | Domestic and Sexual Violence / Child Abuse and Neglect Funds | $5 | $5 |

| | | | |
|---|---|---|---|
| 61 | Add the amounts of the Xs on lines 60a through 60c and enter the total here **61** | | 0 |
| 62 | Line 59 minus line 61 **62** | | 0 |
| 63 | Amount of line 62 to be **applied** to your **2019 ESTIMATED TAX** **63** | | 0 |
| 64a | Amount to be **REFUNDED TO YOU** (line 62 minus line 63) If filing late, see page 34 of Instructions. Place an X here ultimately be deposited to a foreign (non-U.S.) bank. Do not complete lines 64b, 64c, or 64d. | | if this refund will |
| 64b | Routing number    **c** Type:   Checking   Savings | | |
| 64d | Account number ................ **64a** | | 0 |
| 65 | **AMOUNT YOU OWE** (line 53 minus line 58) **65** | | 1094 |
| 66 | **PAYMENT AMOUNT** Submit payment online at hitax.hawaii.gov or attach check or money order payable to "Hawaii State Tax Collector." **66** | | |
| 67 | **Estimated tax penalty.** (See page 35 of Instr.) Do not include this amount in line 59 or 65. Check this box if Form N-210 is attached **▶ X**   **67** | | 37 |
| 68 | **AMENDED RETURN ONLY -** Amount paid (overpaid) on original return. (See Instructions) (attach Sch. AMD) **68** | | 0 |
| 69 | **AMENDED RETURN ONLY -** Balance due (refund) with amended return. (See Instructions) (attach Sch. AMD) **69** | | 0 |

**DESIGNEE** If designating another person to discuss this return with the Hawaii Department of Taxation, complete the following. This is not a full power of attorney. See page 35 of the Instructions.

Designee's name ▶    Phone no. ▶    Identification number ▶

**HAWAII ELECTION CAMPAIGN FUND** (See page 35 of the Instructions)

| | Yes | No | |
|---|---|---|---|
| Do you want $3 to go to the Hawaii Election Campaign Fund? | Yes | X No | Note: Placing an X in the "Yes" box will not increase your tax or reduce your refund. |
| If joint return, does your spouse want $3 to go to the fund? | Yes | X No | |

**DECLARATION — I** declare, under the penalties set forth in section 231-36, HRS, that this return (including accompanying schedules or statements) has been examined by me and, to the best of my knowledge and belief, is a true, correct, and complete return, made in good faith, for the taxable year stated, pursuant to the Hawaii Income Tax Law, Chapter 235, HRS.

**PLEASE SIGN HERE**

Your signature   Date   Spouse's signature (if filing jointly, BOTH must sign)   Date

Your Occupation   Daytime Phone Number   Your Spouse's Occupation   Daytime Phone Number

**Paid Preparer's Information**

Preparer's Signature ▶   Date   Check if self-employed ▶ ☐   Preparer's identification number P000000000

Print Preparer's Name ▶ HOMER JONES   Federal E.I. No. ▶ 42-1539623

Firm's name (or yours if self-employed), Address, and ZIP Code ▶ KMH LLP, 1003 BISHOP ST #2400 HONOLULU, HI 96813   Phone No. ▶ (808)526-2255

N15_T 2018A 04 VID88

**FORM N-15**

STATE OF HAWAII — DEPARTMENT OF TAXATION

# Sales of Business Property

**Schedule D-1**
(Rev. 2018)

(Also Involuntary Conversions and Recapture Amounts Under IRC Sections 179 and 280F(b)(2))

**2018**

➤ To be filed with Form N-15, N-20, N-30, N-35, N-40, etc. – See separate instructions, including those for N-11 or N-15

**CAUTION: Do not confuse this schedule with the federal Schedule D-1.**

| Name(s) as shown on tax return | Social Security Number or Federal Employer I.D. No. |
|---|---|
| JOHN AND BARBARA REED | 111-23-4567 |

**Part I**  **Sales or Exchanges of Property Used in a Trade or Business and Involuntary Conversions From Other Than Casualty and Theft — Most Property Held More Than 1 Year**

Notes:
- Use federal Form 4684 to report involuntary conversions from casualty and theft.
- File federal Form 6198 if you are reporting a loss and have amounts invested in the activity for which you are not at risk. (See Instructions under "At-Risk Rules")
- Complete federal Form 8582 before you complete Schedule D-1 if you are reporting a loss from a passive activity. (See Instructions under "Passive Loss Limitations")

1  Enter the gross proceeds from sales or exchanges reported to you for 2018 on federal Form(s) 1099-B or 1099-S (or a substitute statement) that you will be including on line 2 (Column d), line 11 (Column d), or line 21 . . | **1** |

| 2  (a) Description of property | (b) Date acquired (mo., day, yr.) | (c) Date sold (mo., day, yr.) | (d) Gross sales price | (e) Depreciation allowed (or allowable) since acquisition | (f) Cost or other basis, plus improvements and expense of sale | (g) LOSS (f) minus the sum of (d) and (e) | (h) GAIN (d) plus (e) minus (f) |
|---|---|---|---|---|---|---|---|
| DISTRIB. | | | | | | 453.00 | |
| SHARE FROM | | | | | | | |
| P/S ROK | | | | | | | |
| PINEAPPLE | | | | | | | |
| NAPOOPOO, HI | | | | | | | |

| | | |
|---|---|---|
| 3  Gain, if any, from federal Form 4684, line 39 . . . . . . . . . . . . . . . . . . . . . . . . . . . . . . . . . . . . . . . . . . . . | **3** | |
| 4  IRC section 1231 gain from installment sales from federal Form 6252, line 26 or 37 . . . . . . . . . . . . . . . . . . | **4** | |
| 5  IRC section 1231 gain or (loss) from like-kind exchanges from federal Form 8824 . . . . . . . . . . . . . . . . | **5** | |
| 6  Gain, if any, from Part III, line 33, from other than casualty or theft . . . . . . . . . . . . . . . . . . . . . . . . . . . | **6** | |
| 7  Add lines 2 through 6 in columns (g) and (h) . . . . . . . . . . . . . . . . . . . . . . . . . . . . . . . . . . . . . . . . . . . . | **7** ( 453.00 ) | |

8  Combine columns (g) and (h) of line 7. Enter gain or (loss) here, and on the appropriate line as follows: *Partnerships on N-20, Sch. K, line 10; S corps on N-35, Sch. K, line 9. Skip lines 9, 10, 12 & 13.* . . . . . . . . . . . . . . . . . . | **8** | −453.00 |

If line 8 is zero or a loss, enter the amount on line 12 below and skip lines 9 and 10. If line 8 is a gain and you did not have any prior year IRC section 1231 losses, or they were recaptured in an earlier year, enter the gain as a long-term capital gain on Schedule D for your return or on the Capital Gain/Loss Worksheet in the Form N-15 Instructions and skip lines 9, 10, 12, and 13, below.

| | | |
|---|---|---|
| 9  Nonrecaptured net IRC section 1231 losses from prior years (see Instructions) . . . . . . . . . . . . . . . . . . . . . | **9** | |
| 10  Line 8 minus line 9. If zero or less, enter zero . . . . . . . . . . . . . . . . . . . . . . . . . . . . . . . . . . . . . . . . . . | **10** | 0.00 |

If line 10 is zero, enter the amount from line 8 on line 13 below. If line 10 is more than zero, enter the amount from line 9 on line 13 below, and enter the amount from line 10 as a long-term capital gain on Schedule D for your return or on the Capital Gain/Loss Worksheet in the Form N-15 Instructions. (See specific Instructions for line 10.)

**Part II**  **Ordinary Gains and Losses**

11  Ordinary gains and losses not included on lines 12 through 17 (include property held 1 year or less)

| | | |
|---|---|---|
| 12  Loss, if any, from line 8 . . . . . . . . . . . . . . . . . . . . . . . . . . . . . . . . . . . . . . . . . . . . . . . . . . . . . . . . . . . | **12** | −453.00 |
| 13  Gain, if any, from line 8, or amount from line 9 if applicable . . . . . . . . . . . . . . . . . . . . . . . . . . . . . . . . | **13** | |
| 14  Gain, if any, from Part III, line 32 . . . . . . . . . . . . . . . . . . . . . . . . . . . . . . . . . . . . . . . . . . . . . . . . . . . | **14** | |
| 15  Net gain or (loss) from federal Form 4684, lines 31 and 38a . . . . . . . . . . . . . . . . . . . . . . . . . . . . . . . . | **15** | |
| 16  Ordinary gain from installment sales from federal Form 6252, line 25 or 36 . . . . . . . . . . . . . . . . . . . . . . | **16** | |
| 17  Ordinary gain or (loss) from like-kind exchanges from federal Form 8824 . . . . . . . . . . . . . . . . . . . . . . . | **17** | |
| 18  Add lines 11 through 17 in columns (g) and (h) . . . . . . . . . . . . . . . . . . . . . . . . . . . . . . . . . . . . . . . . . | **18** ( −453.00 ) | |

19  Combine columns (g) and (h) of line 18. Enter gain or (loss) here, and on the appropriate line as follows: . . . . . . . . . . . . . . . . . | **19** | −453.00 |

a  For all except individual returns: Enter the gain or (loss) from line 19, on the return being filed. (Form N-30, etc.)

b  For individual return, Form N-15, see below. See instructions for Form N-11.

(1) If the loss on line 12 includes a loss from federal Form 4684, line 35, column (b) (ii), enter that part of the loss here. Enter the part of the loss from income-producing property on Worksheet A-6, line 30, in the Form N-11 Instructions or on Worksheet NR-6, line 31 or 32, or on Worksheet PY-6, line 57 or 58 in the Form N-15 Instructions; and the part of the loss from property used as an employee on Worksheet A-6, line 25, on Worksheet NR-6, line 25 or 26, or on Worksheet PY-6, line 48 or 49. Identify as from "Schedule D-1, line 19b(1)." | **19b(1)** |

(2) Redetermine the gain or (loss) on line 19, excluding the loss (if any) on line 19b(1). Enter here and on Form N-15, line 14 . . . . . . . . . . . . . . . . . . . . . . . . . . . . . . . . . . . . . . . . . . . . . . . . . | **19b(2)** |

**Schedule D-1**

SCHD1_I 2018A 01 VID01                                    ID NO 01

Schedule D-1 (Rev. 2018) PAGE 2

| Part III | Gain from Disposition of Property Under IRC Sections 1245, 1250, 1252, 1254, and 1255 | | |
|---|---|---|---|

| | | (b) Date acquired (mo., day, yr.) | (c) Date sold (mo., day, yr.) |
|---|---|---|---|
| 20 | (a) Description of IRC sections 1245, 1250, 1252, 1254, or 1255 property: | | |
| A | | | |
| B | | | |
| C | | | |
| D | | | |

| Relate lines 20A through 20D to these columns ➤ ➤ ➤ | | Property A | Property B | Property C | Property D |
|---|---|---|---|---|---|
| 21 Gross sales price (**Note:** *See line 1 before completing.*) | 21 | | | | |
| 22 Cost or other basis plus expense of sale | 22 | | | | |
| 23 Depreciation (or depletion) allowed or allowable | 23 | | | | |
| 24 Adjusted basis. Line 22 minus line 23 | 24 | | | | |
| 25 Total gain. Line 21 minus line 24 | 25 | | | | |
| 26 **If IRC section 1245 property:** | | | | | |
| a Depreciation allowed or allowable after applicable date (see Instructions) | 26a | | | | |
| b Enter **smaller** of line 25 or 26a | 26b | | | | |
| 27 **If IRC section 1250 property:** (If straight line depreciation was used, enter zero on line 27i) | | | | | |
| a Additional depreciation after 12/31/76 (see Instructions) | 27a | | | | |
| b Applicable percentage times the **smaller** of line 25 or line 27a (see Instructions) | 27b | | | | |
| c Line 25 minus line 27a. If residential rental property **or** line 25 is not more than line 27a, skip lines 27d through 27h | 27c | | | | |
| d Additional depreciation after 12/31/74 and before 1/1/77 | 27d | | | | |
| e Applicable percentage times the **smaller** of line 27c or 27d (see Instructions) | 27e | | | | |
| f Line 27c minus line 27d. If line 27c is not more than line 27d, skip lines 27g and 27h | 27f | | | | |
| g Additional depreciation after 12/31/64 and before 1/1/75 | 27g | | | | |
| h Applicable percentage times the **smaller** of line 27f or 27g (see Instructions) | 27h | | | | |
| i Add line 27b, 27e, and 27h | 27i | | | | |
| 28 **If IRC section 1252 property:** Skip this section if you did not dispose of farmland or if this form is being completed for a partnership. | | | | | |
| a Soil, water and land clearing expenses made after 12/31/76 | 28a | | | | |
| b Line 28a times applicable percentage (see Instructions) | 28b | | | | |
| c Enter **smaller** of line 25 or 28b | 28c | | | | |
| 29 **If IRC section 1254 property:** | | | | | |
| a Intangible drilling and development costs deducted after 12/31/76 (see Instructions) | 29a | | | | |
| b Enter **smaller** of line 25 or 29a | 29b | | | | |
| 30 **If IRC section 1255 property:** | | | | | |
| a Applicable percentage of payments excluded from income under IRC section 126 (see Instructions) | 30a | | | | |
| b Enter **smaller** of line 25 or 30a | 30b | | | | |

**Summary of Part III Gains (Complete Property columns A through D through line 30b before going on to line 31.)**

| | | | |
|---|---|---|---|
| 31 Total gains for all properties. Add columns A through D, line 25 | | 31 | |
| 32 Add property columns A through D, lines 26b, 27i, 28c, 29b, and 30b. Enter here and on Part II, line 14 | | 32 | |
| 33 Line 31 minus line 32. Enter the portion from casualty or theft on federal Form 4684, line 33. Enter the portion from other than casualty or theft on Schedule D-1, Part I, line 6 | | 33 | |

| Part IV | Recapture Amounts Under IRC Sections 179 and 280F(b)(2) When Business Use Drops to 50% or Less (See Instructions for Part IV.) |
|---|---|

| | | | (a) Section 179 | (b) Section 280F(b)(2) |
|---|---|---|---|---|
| 34 IRC section 179 expense deduction or depreciation allowable in prior years | | 34 | | |
| 35 Recomputed depreciation (see Instructions) | | 35 | | |
| 36 Recapture amount. (line 34 minus line 35) (see Instructions for where to report) | | 36 | | |

FORM
**N-210**
(REV. 2018)

STATE OF HAWAII — DEPARTMENT OF TAXATION
**Underpayment of Estimated Tax by**
**Individuals, Estates, and Trusts**
➤ **See Separate Instructions**
➤ **Attach to Form N-11, N-15, or N-40**
(NOTE: References to "married" and "spouse" are also references to "in a civil union" and "civil union partner," respectively.)

**2018**

| Name(s) as shown on tax return | Social Security Number or FEIN |
|---|---|
| JOHN AND BARBARA REED | 111-23-4567 |

**Part I**  **Reasons For Filing** — If a, b, or c below applies to you, you may be able to lower or eliminate your penalty. But you MUST check the boxes that apply and file Form N-210 with your tax return. If d below applies to you, check that box and file Form N-210 with your tax return.

Check whichever boxes apply:

a ☐ You request a **waiver**. In certain circumstances, the Department of Taxation will waive all or part of the penalty. See the Instructions for **Waiver of Penalty.**

b ☐ You use the **annualized income installment method.** If your income varied during the year, this method may reduce the amount of one or more required installments. See the **Instructions for Schedule A.**

c ☐ You had Hawaii income tax withheld from wages and you treat it as paid for estimated tax purposes when it was **actually** withheld instead of in equal amounts on the payment due dates. See the Instructions for line 10.

d ☐ One or more of your required installments (line 9) are based upon your 2017 tax and you filed or are filing a joint return for either 2017 or 2018 but not for both years.

**Part II**  **All Filers Must Complete This Part**

| | | |
|---|---|---:|
| 1 | 2018 tax liability. (See Instructions) | 1,474 |
| 2 | Total credits.  (See Instructions) | 130 |
| 3 | Balance. Line 1 minus line 2. | 1,344 |
| 4 | Hawaii income taxes withheld. (See Instructions) | 250 |
| 5 | Balance. Line 3 minus line 4. If this amount is less than $500, stop here; **do not** complete or file this form. You do not owe the penalty. | 1,094 |
| 6 | Multiply the amount on line 3 by 60% (.60) | 806 |
| 7 | Enter the tax amount from your 2017 income tax return. (**Caution:** See Instructions.) | 1,003 |
| 8 | Enter the **smaller** of line 6 or line 7. (See Instructions) | 806 |

**Part III**  **Figure Your Underpayment**

| | | | PAYMENT DUE DATES | | | | | | |
|---|---|---|---|---|---|---|---|---|---|
| | | | (a) 4/20/2018 | (b) 6/20/2018 | (c) 9/20/2018 | (d) 1/20/2019 | | | |
| 9 | **Required installments.** If you are using the Annualized Income Installment Method, enter the amounts from Schedule A, line 24. Farmers and fishermen, enter the amount from line 8 in column (d). All others, enter ¼ of line 8 in each column. ... | 9 | 202 | 201 | 202 | 201 |
| 10 | Estimated and other tax payments made. (See Instructions) For column (a) only, also enter the amount from line 10 on line 14. If line 10 is equal to or more than line 9 for all payment periods, stop here; you do not owe a penalty ........... | 10 | 63 | 62 | 63 | 62 |
| | *Complete lines 11 through 17 of one column before going to line 11 of the next column.* | | | | | |
| 11 | Enter the amount, if any, from line 17 of previous column ....... | 11 | | 0 | 0 | 0 |
| 12 | Add lines 10 and 11................. | 12 | | 62 | 63 | 62 |
| 13 | Add the amounts on lines 15 and 16 of previous column ........ | 13 | | 139 | 278 | 417 |
| 14 | Line 12 minus line 13.  If zero or less, enter -0-. For column (a) only, enter the amount from line 10........ | 14 | 63 | 0 | 0 | 0 |
| 15 | If line 14 is zero, line 13 minus line 12. Otherwise, enter -0-. ......... | 15 | | 77 | 215 | |
| 16 | **Underpayment.** If line 9 is equal to or more than line 14, subtract line 14 from line 9. Then go to line 11 of next column. Otherwise, go to line 17. ................. | 16 | 139 | 201 | 202 | 201 |
| 17 | **Overpayment.** If line 14 is more than line 9, subtract line 9 from line 14. Then go to line 11 of next column. ...................... | 17 | 0 | 0 | 0 | |

*Complete Part IV on page 2 to figure the penalty. If there are no entries on line 16, no penalty is owed.*

N210_T 2018A 01 VID88        ID NO 88                                    Form N-210

**Form N-210**
(Rev. 2018)

JOHN AND BARBARA REED

111-23-4567

Page 2

| Part IV | Figuring the Penalty (See Instructions) | | (a) 4/20/2018 | (b) 6/20/2018 | (c) 9/20/2018 | (d) 1/20/2019 |
|---|---|---|---|---|---|---|
| 18 | Enter the date the amount on line 16 was paid or April 20, 2019, whichever is earlier. | 18 | 4/20/2019 | 4/20/2019 | 4/20/2019 | 4/20/2019 |
| 19 | Enter the number of months from the payment due date through the date of payment on line 18. If April 20, 2019, is the date entered on line 18, enter 12, 10, 7, and 3, respectively, here. | 19 | 12 | 10 | 7 | 3 |
| 20 | Multiply the following: Number of months on line 19 x .00667 x underpayment on line 16 for columns (a) through (d) | 20 | 11 | 13 | 9 | 4 |
| 21 | Penalty — Add the amounts on line 20 in all columns. Enter the total here and on Form N-11, line 50; Form N-15, line 67; or Form N-40, Schedule G, line 8. | | | | 21 | 37 |

**Schedule A** Required Installments Using the Annualized Income Installment Method

**Annualized Income Installment Method**

| Estates and trusts, **do not** use the period ending dates shown to the right. Instead, use the following: 2/28/18, 4/30/18, 7/31/18, and 11/30/18. | | (a) 1/1/18-3/31/18 | (b) 1/1/18-5/31/18 | (c) 1/1/18-8/31/18 | (d) 1/1/18-12/31/18 |
|---|---|---|---|---|---|
| 1 Enter your adjusted gross income for each period (See Instructions). (Estates and trusts, enter your taxable income without your exemption for each period.) | 1 | 0 | 0 | 0 | 0 |
| 2 Annualization amounts (Estates and trusts, see Instructions) | 2 | 4 | 2.4 | 1.5 | 1 |
| 3 Annualized income. Multiply line 1 by line 2 | 3 | 0 | 0 | 0 | 0 |
| 4 If you itemize, enter itemized deductions for the period shown in each column. All others, enter -0-, and skip to line 7. (Estates and trusts, enter -0-, skip to line 9, and enter the amount from line 3 on line 9.). | 4 | | | | |
| 5 Annualization amounts | 5 | 4 | 2.4 | 1.5 | 1 |
| 6 Multiply line 4 by line 5 (See Instructions. Your itemized deductions may be limited.) | 6 | 0 | 0 | 0 | 0 |
| 7 In each column, enter the full amount of your standard deduction. If you itemized deductions, enter -0- (See Instructions) | 7 | 0 | 0 | 0 | 0 |
| 8 Enter the **larger** of line 6 or line 7 | 8 | 0 | 0 | 0 | 0 |
| 9 Line 3 minus line 8 | 9 | 0 | 0 | 0 | 0 |
| 10 In each column, multiply $1,144 by the total number of exemptions claimed. If you use the personal exemption for disabled persons instead, enter the appropriate amount for 2018 (Estates and trusts, enter the exemption amount shown on your return.) (See Instructions) | 10 | 0 | 0 | 0 | 0 |
| 11 Line 9 minus line 10. If zero or less, enter -0 | 11 | 0 | 0 | 0 | 0 |
| 12 Figure your tax on the amount on line 11 (See Instructions) | 12 | 0 | 0 | 0 | 0 |
| 13 Enter any other taxes for each period (See Instructions) | 13 | | | | |
| 14 Total tax. Add lines 12 and 13 | 14 | 0 | 0 | 0 | 0 |
| 15 For each period, enter the same type of credits as allowed on Form N-210, Part II, line 2 (See Instructions) | 15 | 0 | 0 | 0 | 0 |
| 16 Total tax after credits. Line 14 minus line 15. If zero or less, enter -0 | 16 | 0 | 0 | 0 | 0 |
| 17 Applicable percentage. | 17 | 15% | 30% | 45% | 60% |
| 18 Multiply line 16 by line 17 | 18 | 0 | 0 | 0 | 0 |
| **Complete lines 19 through 24 of one column before going to line 19 of the next column.** | | | | | |
| 19 Add the amounts in all previous columns of line 24 | 19 | | 0 | 0 | 0 |
| 20 Line 18 minus line 19. If zero or less, enter -0 | 20 | 0 | 0 | 0 | 0 |
| 21 Enter ¼ of Form N-210, Part II, line 8, in each column | 21 | 0 | 0 | 0 | 0 |
| 22 Subtract line 24 of the previous column from line 23 of that column | 22 | | 0 | 0 | 0 |
| 23 Add lines 21 and 22 | 23 | 0 | 0 | 0 | 0 |
| 24 Enter the **smaller** of line 20 or line 23 here and on Form N-210, Part III, line 9 | 24 | 0 | 0 | 0 | 0 |

ID NO 88

## TAX RETURN SCHEDULES

### JOHN AND BARBARA REED

111-23-4567 and 111-98-7654

Medical Expenses

    Drugs                                                        $  580

    Other Medical:

| | |
|---|---:|
| John Doe, M.D. | $  750 |
| J. Smith, M.D. | 200 |
| A. Brown, D.D.S. | 250 |
| Encino Community Hospital | 2,186 |
| | $3,966 |

Contributions

| | |
|---|---:|
| Distributive share from partnership | $   25 |
| Honolulu Foster Home | 200 |
| Los Angeles Community Chest | 100 |
| Los Angeles County Heart Association | 100 |
| Southern California Symphony Association | 100 |
| | $  525 |

Other Deductions

| | |
|---|---:|
| Accounting fees | $  700 |
| Educational expense | 1,000 |
| | $1,700 |

## PROBLEM FOR SPECIMEN RETURN
## PARTNERSHIP RETURN OF INCOME

### Form N-20

On January 1, 1999, John Reed, Takeo Ono, and Shigeru Kishi formed the partnership, ROK Pineapple Ranch for the purpose of acquiring a pineapple orchard.

John Reed and Shigeru Kishi contributed $30,000 and $10,000, respectively, into the partnership to remain as permanent capital. Over a period, not to exceed five years, Takeo Ono was to leave $5,000 out of his share of partnership income in the partnership as additional permanent capital. All partners were to receive interest on the amount of capital invested.

Takeo Ono acts as general manager of the operations on a full-time basis. He is assisted by Shigeru Kishi, who spends 15% of his time on the partnership business.

Ono and Kishi receive salaries measured by the amount of time they devote to the affairs of the partnership. Ordinary income or loss after partners' salaries, interest, and any special income credits or deductions are shared equally by the partners.

During the year, the ROK Pineapple Ranch acquired solar energy equipment costing $1,115. The solar energy equipment is primarily being used to generate electricity for general usage (i.e. powering the lights, computers, appliances, etc.) on their Ranch. The partners have not elected to treat the credit as refundable.

FORM
**N-20**
(REV. 2018)

STATE OF HAWAII—DEPARTMENT OF TAXATION

THIS SPACE FOR DATE RECEIVED STAMP

# PARTNERSHIP RETURN OF INCOME
For calendar year **2018**

or other tax year beginning ● _____ , 2018

and ending ● _____ , 20 ____

| | |
|---|---|
| Partnership Name **ROK PINEAPPLE RANCH** | **A** Federal Employer I.D. No. ● 98-7654321 |
| Dba or C/O | **B** Business Code No. (from federal Form 1065) ● 400000 |
| Mailing Address (number and street) **15 MOUNTAIN RD** | **C** Principal business activity **FARMING** |
| City or town, State, and Postal/ZIP Code. If foreign address, see Instructions. **NAPOOPOO, HI 96000** | **D** Hawaii Tax I.D. No. ● W12345678-01 |

**E** Check applicable boxes: **(1)** ☐ Initial Return **(2)** ☐ Final Return **(3)** ☐ Change of Address **(4)** ☐ Amended Return (Attach Sch AMD) **(5)** ☐ IRS Adjustment

## FOR LINES 1 - 9, ENTER AMOUNTS FROM COMPARABLE LINES ON FEDERAL FORM 1065

| | | | |
|---|---|---:|---:|
| **1 a** Gross receipts or sales | **1a●** | 50800 | |
| **b** Returns and allowances | **1b●** | | |
| **c** Line 1a minus line 1b | | **1c●** | 50800 |
| **2** Cost of goods sold | | **2●** | |
| **3** Gross profit (line 1c minus line 2) | | **3●** | 50800 |
| **4** Ordinary income (loss) from other partnerships, estates, and trusts | | **4** | |
| **5** Net farm profit (loss) (attach federal Schedule F (Form 1040)) | | **5** | |
| **6** Net gain (loss) from federal Form 4797, Part II, line 17 | | **6** | |
| **7** Other income (loss) | | **7●** | |
| **8** TOTAL income (loss) | | **8●** | 50800 |
| **9** TOTAL deductions | | **9●** | 55540 |
| **10** Ordinary income (loss) from trade or business activities before Hawaii adjustments (line 8 minus line 9) | | **10●** | −4740 |
| **ADD:** | | | |
| **11 a** Deductions allowable for federal tax purposes but not allowable or allowable only in part for Hawaii tax purposes (attach schedule) | **11a** | | |
| **b** Net gain or (loss) from Schedule D-1, Part II, line 19 | **11b●** | | |
| **c** The portion of the Hawaii jobs credit claimed applicable to current year new employees | **11c** | | |
| **d** Other additions (attach schedule) | **11d** | | |
| **12** Total of lines 11a, 11b, 11c, and 11d | | **12** | |
| **13** Total of lines 10 and 12 | | **13** | −4740 |
| **DEDUCT:** | | | |
| **14 a** Net gain or (loss) from federal Form 4797, Part II, line 17 (line 6 above) | **14a** | | |
| **b** Federal employment credits | **14b** | | |
| **c** Other deductions (attach schedule) | **14c** | | |
| **15** Total of lines 14a, 14b, and 14c | | **15** | |
| **16** Ordinary income (loss) from trade or business activities for Hawaii tax purposes (line 13 minus line 15) | | **16** | −4740 |
| **17** **PAYMENT DUE** (see instructions) | | **17●** | 0 |

**DECLARATION** I declare, under the penalties set forth in section 231-36, HRS, that this return (including any accompanying schedules or statements) has been examined by me and, to the best of my knowledge and belief, is a true, correct, and complete return, made in good faith, for the taxable year stated, pursuant to the Hawaii Income Tax Law, Chapter 235, HRS. Declaration of preparer (other than general partner or limited liability company member manager) is based on all information of which preparer has any knowledge.

➤● _____                                 ➤ _____

Signature of general partner or limited liability company member                              Date

★ May the Hawaii Department of Taxation discuss this return with the preparer shown below? . . . . . . . . . . . . . ☐ Yes    ☐ No
(See page 2 of the Instructions)    **This designation does not replace Form N-848, Power of Attorney**

| Paid Preparer's Information | Preparer's Signature Print Preparer's Name **HOMER JONES** | Date | Check if self-employed ☐ | Preparer's Tax I. D. Number ● P00000000 |
|---|---|---|---|---|
| | Firm's name (or yours if self-employed) ➤ **KMH LLP, 1003 BISHOP ST. #2400** | | Federal E.I. No. ➤ 42-1539623 | |
| | Address and Postal/ZIP Code **HONOLULU, HI 96813** | | Phone no. ➤ (808) 526-2255 | |

FORM N-20

N20_I 2018A 01 VID01                                  ID NO 01

FORM N-20 (REV. 2018) **Page 2**

| Partnership Name | Federal Employer I.D. No. |
|---|---|
| ROK PINEAPPLE RANCH | 98-7654321 |

| Schedule K | PARTNERS' Pro Rata Share Items | b. Attributable to Hawaii | | c. Attributable Everywhere |
|---|---|---|---|---|
| **Income (Losses)** | 1 Ordinary income (loss) from trade or business activities (page 1, line 16) . . . . . | -4740 | 1 | -4740 |
| | 2 Net income (loss) from rental real estate activities (attach federal Form 8825) . . | | 2 | |
| | 3 a Gross income (loss) from other rental activities . . . . . . . . . . . . . . . . . | | 3a | |
| | b Expenses from other rental activities (attach schedule) . . . . . . . . . . . . . | | 3b | |
| | c Net income (loss) from other rental activities (line 3a minus line 3b) . . . . . . | | 3c | |
| | 4 Guaranteed Payments to Partners . . . . . . . . . . . . . . . . . . . . . | 18500 | 4 | 18500 |
| | 5 Interest income . . . . . . . . . . . . . . . . . . . . . . . . . . . . . . | | 5 | |
| | 6 Ordinary dividends . . . . . . . . . . . . . . . . . . . . . . . . . . . . | | 6 | |
| | 7 Royalty income . . . . . . . . . . . . . . . . . . . . . . . . . . . . . . | | 7 | |
| | 8 Net short-term capital gain (loss) (Schedule D (Form N-20)) . . . . . . . . . . | | 8 | |
| | 9 Net long-term capital gain (loss) (Schedule D (Form N-20)) . . . . . . . . . . | 3000 | 9 | 3000 |
| | 10 Net gain (loss) under IRC section 1231 (attach Schedule D-1) . . . . . . . . . | -1359 | 10 | -1359 |
| | 11 Other income (loss) (attach schedule) . . . . . . . . . . . . . . . . . . . . | | 11 | |
| **Deductions** | 12 Charitable contributions (attach schedule) . . . . . . . . . . . . . . . . . . | 75 | 12 | 75 |
| | 13 IRC section 179 expense deduction (attach federal Form 4562) . . . . . . . . . | | 13 | |
| | 14 Deductions related to portfolio income (loss) (attach schedule) . . . . . . . . . | | 14 | |
| | 15 Other deductions (attach schedule) . . . . . . . . . . . . . . . . . . . . . | | 15 | |
| **Credits** | 16 Total cost of qualifying property for the Capital Goods Excise Tax Credit (attach Form N-312) . . . | | 16 | |
| | 17 Fuel Tax Credit for Commercial Fishers (attach Form N-163) . . . . . . . . . . | | 17 | |
| | 18 Amounts needed to claim the Enterprise Zone Tax Credit (attach Form N-756) . . | See Instructions | 18 | |
| | 19 Hawaii Low-Income Housing Tax Credit (attach Form N-586) . . . . . . . . . . | | 19 | |
| | 20 Credit for Employment of Vocational Rehabilitation Referrals (attach Form N-884) . . | | 20 | |
| | 21 Motion Picture, Digital Media, and Film Production Income Tax Credit (attach Form N-340) . . . . | | 21 | |
| | 22 Credit for School Repair and Maintenance (attach Form N-330) . . . . . . . . . | | 22 | |
| | 23 Renewable Energy Technologies Income Tax Credit (attach Form N-342) . . . . | 390 | 23 | |
| | 24 Important Agricultural Land Qualified Agricultural Cost Tax Credit (attach Form N-344) . . . . . . | | 24 | |
| | 25 Tax Credit for Research Activities (attach Form N-346) . . . . . . . . . . . . | | 25 | |
| | 26 Capital Infrastructure Tax Credit (attach Form N-348) . . . . . . . . . . . . | | 26● | |
| | 27 Cesspool Upgrade, Conversion or Connection Income Tax Credit (attach Form N-350) . | | 27 | |
| | 28 Renewable Fuels Production Tax Credit (attach Form N-352) . . . . . . . . . . | | 28 | |
| | 29 Organic Foods Production Tax Credit (attach Form N-354) . . . . . . . . . . . | | 29 | |
| | 30 Credit for income tax withheld on Form N-288 (net of refunds) . . . . . . . . . | | 30 | |
| **Investment Interest** | 31 a Interest expense on investment debts . . . . . . . . . . . . . . . . . . . . | | 31a | |
| | b (1) Investment income included on lines 5, 6, and 7, Schedule K . . . . . . . | | 31b(1) | |
| | (2) Investment expenses included on line 14, Schedule K . . . . . . . . . . . | | 31b(2) | |
| **Other Items** | 32 Attach schedule for other items and amounts not reported above (e.g., credit recapture amounts) See Instructions. Check box if schedules attached ☐ . . . . . . . . . . . . | | 32 | |
| **Analysis** | 33 a Income (loss). Combine lines 1 through 11 in column c. From the result, minus the sum of lines 12 through 15 and 31a in column c . . . . . . . . . . . | | 33a | 15326 |
| | b Analysis by type of partner: | | | |

| | (a) Corporate | (b) Individual | | (c) Partnership | (d) Exempt organization | (e) Nominee/Other |
|---|---|---|---|---|---|---|
| | | i. Active | ii. Passive | | | |
| 1. General Partners | | 15326 | | | | |
| 2. Limited Partners | | | | | | |

**FORM N-20**

| FORM **N-342** (REV. 2018) | STATE OF HAWAII – DEPARTMENT OF TAXATION **RENEWABLE ENERGY TECHNOLOGIES INCOME TAX CREDIT** (FOR SYSTEMS INSTALLED AND PLACED IN SERVICE ON OR AFTER JULY 1, 2009) Note: Use a separate form for each eligible system and for carryover credit(s). Or fiscal year beginning _____ , 2018, and ending _____ , 20 ___ | TAX YEAR **2018** |

**ATTACH THIS SCHEDULE TO YOUR FORM F-1, N-11, N-15, N-20, N-30, N-35, N-40, OR N-70NP**

| Name | SSN or FEIN |
|---|---|
| ROK PINEAPPLE RANCH | 98-7654321 |

PHYSICAL PROPERTY ADDRESS WHERE THE SYSTEM WAS INSTALLED AND PLACED IN SERVICE: (Enter "CARRYOVER" if claiming carryover credit(s).)

| Address (Number and Street) | City or Town | Postal/ZIP Code |
|---|---|---|
| 15 MOUNTAIN RD | NAPOOPOO | 96000 |

**COMPUTATION OF TAX CREDIT**

**Note:** If you are only claiming your distributive share of a tax credit distributed from an S corporation, partnership, estate, or trust (Form N-342A), skip lines 1 through 39 and begin on line 40.

**Note:** If you are claiming carryover credit(s), skip lines 1 through 47 and begin on line 48. **Note:** Form N-20 and Form N-35 filers complete only lines 1 thru 41.

**SOLAR ENERGY SYSTEM**    Enter date system was installed and placed in service ➤ 11/11/2018 (Leave blank if claiming carryover credit(s).)

Enter **Total Output Capacity** if credit is for an "other solar energy system" (See instructions) ➤ _____ (Leave blank if claiming carryover credit(s).)

| | | | | | |
|---|---|---|---:|---|---:|
| 1. | Enter your total cost of the qualified solar energy system installed and placed in service in Hawaii (See instructions if there are multiple owners of the system.) | **1** | 1,115 | | |
| 2. | Enter the amount of consumer incentive premiums, costs used for other credits, and utility rebate, if any, received for the qualifying solar energy system | **2** | 0 | | |
| 3. | Actual cost of the solar energy system. (Subtract line 2 from line 1 and enter result.) | **3** | 1,115 | | |
| 4. | Is this solar energy system primarily used to heat water for household use? | | | | |
| | ☐ Yes. Go to line 5. **SYSTEM PRIMARILY USED TO HEAT WATER FOR HOUSEHOLD USE (lines 5 - 14)** | | | | |
| | ☐ No. Go to line 15. | | | | |
| 5. | Enter the amount from line 3 that is installed and placed in service in Hawaii on **single-family residential** property. | **5** | | | |
| 6. | Enter 35% of line 5 or $2,250, whichever is less | | | **6** | 0 |
| 7. | Enter the amount from line 3 that is installed and placed in service in Hawaii on **multi-family residential** property. | **7** | | | |
| 8. | Divide the total square feet of your unit by the total square feet of all units in the multi-family residential property. Enter the decimal (rounded to 2 decimal places). (See instructions.) | **8** | | | |
| 9. | Actual per unit cost of the solar energy system. (Multiply line 7 by line 8 and enter result.) | **9** | 0 | | |
| 10. | Enter 35% of line 9 or $350, whichever is less | **10** | 0 | | |
| 11. | Multiply line 10 by the number of units you own to which the allocated unit cost on line 9 is applicable. (Number of units you own _____ ) | | | **11** | 0 |
| 12. | Enter the amount from line 3 that is installed and placed in service in Hawaii on **commercial** property. | **12** | | | |
| 13. | Enter 35% of line 12 or $250,000, whichever is less | | | **13** | 0 |
| 14. | Add lines 6, 11, and 13, and enter result (but not less than zero) | | | **14** | 0 |
| | **SYSTEM NOT PRIMARILY USED TO HEAT WATER FOR HOUSEHOLD USE (lines 15 - 26)** | | | | |
| 15. | Enter the amount from line 3 that is installed and placed in service in Hawaii on **single-family residential** property. | **15** | | | |
| 16. | Enter 35% of line 15 or $5,000, whichever is less | **16** | 0 | | |
| 17. | Was this system used as a substitute for a solar water heating system that is required for new single-family residential property constructed on or after January 1, 2010? | | | | |
| | ☐ Yes. Enter 35% of line 15 or $2,250, whichever is less. | | | | |
| | ☐ No. Enter zero. | **17** | 0 | | |
| 18. | Line 16 minus line 17. | | | **18** | 0 |
| 19. | Enter the amount from line 3 that is installed and placed in service in Hawaii on **multi-family residential** property. | **19** | | | |
| 20. | Divide the total square feet of your unit by the total square feet of all units in the multi-family residential property. Enter the decimal (rounded to 2 decimal places). (See instructions.) | **20** | | | |
| 21. | Actual per unit cost of the solar energy system. (Multiply line 19 by line 20 and enter result.) | **21** | 0 | | |
| 22. | Enter 35% of line 21 or $350, whichever is less | **22** | 0 | | |
| 23. | Multiply line 22 by the number of units you own to which the allocated unit cost on line 21 is applicable. (Number of units you own _____ ) | | | **23** | 0 |
| 24. | Enter the amount from line 3 that is installed and placed in service in Hawaii on **commercial** property | **24** | 1,115 | | |
| 25. | Enter 35% of line 24 or $500,000, whichever is less | | | **25** | 390 |
| 26. | Add lines 18, 23, and 25, and enter result (but not less than zero) | | | **26** | 390 |

(Continued on back)

ROK PINEAPPLE RANCH            98-7654321
**Form N-342**
**(REV. 2018)**           **Page 2**

| **WIND-POWERED ENERGY SYSTEM** Enter date system was installed and placed in service ➤ | | (Leave blank if claiming carryover credit(s).) |
|---|---|---|
| 27. Enter your total cost of the qualified wind-powered energy system installed and placed in service in Hawaii (See instructions if there are multiple owners of the system.) | **27** | |
| 28. Enter the amount of consumer incentive premiums, costs used for other credits, and utility rebate, if any, received for the qualifying wind-powered energy system. | **28** | |
| 29. Actual cost of the wind-powered energy system (Subtract line 28 from line 27 and enter result.). | **29**   0 | |
| 30. Enter the amount from line 29 that is installed and placed in service in Hawaii on **single-family residential** property. | **30** | |
| 31. Enter 20% of line 30 or $1,500, whichever is less | | **31**   0 |
| 32. Enter the amount from line 29 that is installed and placed in service in Hawaii on **multi-family residential** property. | **32** | |
| 33. Divide the total square feet of your unit by the total square feet of all units in the multi-family residential property. Enter the decimal (rounded to 2 decimal places). (See instructions.) | **33** | |
| 34. Actual per unit cost of the wind-powered energy system. (Multiply line 32 by line 33 and enter result.) | **34**   0 | |
| 35. Enter 20% of line 34 or $200, whichever is less | **35**   0 | |
| 36. Multiply line 35 by the number of units you own to which the allocated unit cost on line 34 is applicable. (Number of units you own _____ ) | | **36**   0 |
| 37. Enter the amount from line 29 that is installed and placed in service in Hawaii on **commercial** property. | **37** | |
| 38. Enter 20% of line 37 or $500,000, whichever is less | | **38**   0 |
| 39. Add lines 31, 36, and 38, and enter result (but not less than zero) | | **39**   0 |
| **DISTRIBUTIVE SHARE OF TAX CREDIT** | | |
| 40. Distributive share of solar energy tax credit from attached Form N-342A. | | **40** |
| 41. Distributive share of wind-powered energy tax credit from attached Form N-342A. | | **41** |

**STOP HERE IF YOU ARE FILING FORM N-20 OR FORM N-35**

| **REFUNDABLE TAX CREDIT**   To elect to claim the tax credit as a refundable tax credit, complete this section. Otherwise, skip to line 47. | | |
|---|---|---|
| **Note:** *Refundable election cannot be revoked or amended.* | | |
| 42. Check the appropriate box: | | |
|     ☐ **a.** I elect to treat the tax credit for a solar energy system as refundable. The amount of the tax credit will be **reduced** by **30%**. | | |
|     ☐ **b.** I elect to treat the tax credit for a solar energy system or a wind-powered energy system as refundable. **ALL** of my income is exempt from Hawaii taxation under a public retirement system or received in the form of a pension for past services **or** my Hawaii adjusted gross income is $20,000 or less ($40,000 or less if filing jointly). | | |
| 43. If you checked the box on line 42(a), enter the amount from line 14, 26, or 40. (If you checked the box on line 42(b), go to line 46.) | **43**   0 | |
| 44. Multiply line 43 by 30% (0.30). | **44**   0 | |
| 45. Line 43 minus line 44. This is your refundable renewable energy technologies income tax credit. Enter this amount, rounded to the nearest dollar, on the appropriate line on Schedule CR; Form N-40, Schedule F; or Form F-1, Schedule I; whichever is applicable. (Stop here. Do not complete the rest of the form.) | **45**   0 | |
| 46. If you checked the box on line 42(b), enter the amount from line 14, 26, 39, 40, or 41. This is your refundable renewable energy technologies income tax credit. Enter this amount, rounded to the nearest dollar, on the appropriate line on Schedule CR (Stop here. Do not complete the rest of the form.) | **46**   0 | |
| **NONREFUNDABLE TAX CREDIT** | | |
| 47. Carryover of unused renewable energy technologies income tax credit (for systems installed and placed in service on or after July 1, 2009) from prior years. (See instructions). | **47**   0 | |
| 48. Enter the amount from line 14, 26, 39, 40, or 41 | **48**   390 | |
| 49. Add lines 47 and 48 and enter result | | **49**   390 |
| **Adjusted tax liability** | | |
| 50.   **a.** Individuals — Enter the amount from Form N-11, line 34; or Form N-15, line 51. | | |
|      **b.** Corporations — Enter the amount from Form N-30, line 13. | | |
|      **c.** Other filers — Enter the amount from Form F-1, line 71; Form N-40, Schedule G, line 3; or Form N-70NP, line 18. | **50**   0 | |
| 51. If you are claiming other credits, including the nonrefundable renewable energy technologies income tax credit for another system, complete the credit worksheet in the instructions and enter the total here | | **51**   0 |
| 52. Line 50 minus line 51. This represents your tax liability, as adjusted. If the result is zero or less than zero, enter zero | | **52**   0 |
| 53. **Total credit allowed** — Enter the smaller of line 49 or line 52. This is your nonrefundable renewable energy technologies income tax credit allowable for the year. Enter this amount, rounded to the nearest dollar, on the appropriate line on Schedule CR; Form N-40, Schedule E; or Form F-1, Schedule H; whichever is applicable | | **53**   390 |
| 54. Line 49 minus line 53. This represents your carryover of unused credit. The amount of any unused tax credit may be carried over and used as a credit against your tax liability in subsequent years until exhausted | | **54**   0 |

         **FORM N-342**

| FORM **N-342A** (REV. 2018) | STATE OF HAWAII–DEPARTMENT OF TAXATION **INFORMATION STATEMENT** CONCERNING RENEWABLE ENERGY TECHNOLOGIES INCOME TAX CREDIT FOR SYSTEMS INSTALLED AND PLACED IN SERVICE ON OR AFTER JULY 1, 2009 (TO BE CLAIMED BY INDIVIDUAL OR CORPORATE SHAREHOLDERS OF S CORPORATIONS, MEMBERS OF PARTNERSHIPS, BENEFICIARIES OF ESTATES OR TRUSTS, OR CONDOMINIUM APARTMENT ASSOCIATIONS) Or fiscal year beginning _____ , 2018, and ending _____ , 20 ____ . | **TAX YEAR** **2018** |

**ATTACH THIS STATEMENT TO FORM N-342**

Name (S Corporation, Partnership, Estate, or Trust, or Condominium Apartment Association)

ROK PINEAPPLE RANCH

Social Security Number or Fed. Employer I.D. Number

98-7654321

Number and Street

15 MOUNTAIN RD

City or Town, State and Postal/ZIP Code

NAPOOPOO                                                  HI          96000

Name of individual or corporation for whom this statement is being prepared

JOHN REED

- ☐ S Corporation
- ☒ Partnership
- ☐ Estate or Trust
- ☐ Condominium Apartment Association

**NOTE:** *Every Hawaii S corporation, partnership, estate, trust, or condominium apartment association is required to prepare this statement for each individual or corporate shareholder, member, or beneficiary, respectively, in order that the prorated amount of such entity's tax credit may be claimed by the individual or corporate taxpayer. Use a separate form for each eligible system. Also attach a copy of this form as issued to each member to the return of the S corporation, partnership, estate, trust, or condominium apartment association.*

**MEMBERS: USE THE INFORMATION PROVIDED ON THIS STATEMENT TO COMPLETE THE FORM N-342 USED TO CLAIM YOUR SHARE OF THIS TAX CREDIT. ATTACH BOTH THE FORM N-342 AND A COPY OF THIS FORM TO THE RETURN YOU FILE.**

**PHYSICAL PROPERTY ADDRESS WHERE THE SYSTEM WAS INSTALLED AND PLACED IN SERVICE:**

| Address (Number and Street) | City or Town | Postal/ZIP Code |
|---|---|---|
| 15 MOUNTAIN ROAD | NAPOOPOO | 96000 |

**COMPUTATION OF TAX CREDIT**

| SOLAR ENERGY SYSTEM | Enter date system was installed and placed in service ▶  11/11/2018 |
|---|---|
| | Enter **Total Output Capacity**, if credit is for an "other solar energy system" ▶ |

| | | | |
|---|---|---|---|
| 1. Enter your total cost of the qualified solar energy system installed and placed in service in Hawaii . | **1** | 1,115 | |
| 2. Enter the amount of consumer incentive premiums, costs used for other credits, and utility rebate, if any, received for the qualifying solar energy system | **2** | 0 | |
| 3. Actual cost of the solar energy system. (Subtract line 2 from line 1 and enter result.) .......... | **3** | 1,115 | |
| 4. Is this solar energy system primarily used to heat water for household use? | | | |
| ☐ Yes. Go to line 5. | | | |
| ☐ No. Go to line 15. | | | |
| **SYSTEM PRIMARILY USED TO HEAT WATER FOR HOUSEHOLD USE (lines 5 - 14)** | | | |
| 5. Enter the amount from line 3 that is installed and placed in service in Hawaii on **single-family residential** property .............. | **5** | | |
| 6. Enter 35% of line 5 or $2,250, whichever is less ............................................................ | | **6** | 0 |
| 7. Enter the amount from line 3 that is installed and placed in service in Hawaii on **multi-family residential** property .............. | **7** | | |
| 8. Divide the total square feet of your unit by the total square feet of all units in the multi-family residential property. Enter the decimal (rounded to 2 decimal places). (See instructions.) .... | **8** | | |
| 9. Actual per unit cost of the solar energy system. (Multiply line 7 by line 8 and enter result.). | **9** | 0 | |
| 10. Enter 35% of line 9 or $350, whichever is less ................................................................ | **10** | 0 | |
| 11. Multiply line 10 by the number of units you own to which the allocated unit cost on line 9 is applicable. (Number of units you own _____ ) ........................................ | | **11** | 0 |
| 12. Enter the amount from line 3 that is installed and placed in service in Hawaii on **commercial** property .......... | **12** | | |
| 13. Enter 35% of line 12 or $250,000, whichever is less ....................................................... | | **13** | 0 |
| 14. Add lines 6, 11, and 13, and enter result (but not less than zero) ..................................... | | **14** | 0 |
| **SYSTEM NOT PRIMARILY USED TO HEAT WATER FOR HOUSEHOLD USE (lines 15 - 26)** | | | |
| 15. Enter the amount from line 3 that is installed and placed in service in Hawaii on **single-family residential** property .............. | **15** | | |
| 16. Enter 35% of line 15 or $5,000, whichever is less ........................................................... | | **16** | 0 |
| 17. Was this system used as a substitute for a solar water heating system that is required for new single-family residential property constructed on or after January 1, 2010? | | | |
| ☐ Yes. Enter 35% of line 15 or $2,250, whichever is less. | | | |
| ☒ No. Enter zero ................................................................................................. | **17** | 0 | |
| 18. Line 16 minus line 17. ........................................................................................... | | **18** | 0 |
| 19. Enter the amount from line 3 that is installed and placed in service in Hawaii on **multi-family residential** property ................ | **19** | | |
| 20. Divide the total square feet of your unit by the total square feet of all units in the multi-family residential property. Enter the decimal (rounded to 2 decimal places). (See instructions.) .... | **20** | | |

(Continued on back)

N342A_T 2018A 01 VID88                    ID NO 88                              **FORM N-342A**

ROK PINEAPPLE RANCH                                 98-7654321

**Form N-342A**
**(REV. 2018)**                                             **Page 2**

| | | | |
|---|---|---|---|
| 21. Actual per unit cost of the solar energy system. (Multiply line 19 by line 20 and enter result.) | 21 | 0 | |
| 22. Enter 35% of line 21 or $350, whichever is less | 22 | 0 | |
| 23. Multiply line 22 by the number of units you own to which the allocated unit cost on line 21 is applicable. (Number of units you own _____ ) | | 23 | 0 |
| 24. Enter the amount from line 3 that is installed and placed in service in Hawaii on **commercial** property | 24 | 1,115 | |
| 25. Enter 35% of line 24 or $500,000, whichever is less | | 25 | 390 |
| 26. Add lines 18, 23, and 25, and enter result (but not less than zero) | | 26 | 390 |

**WIND-POWERED ENERGY SYSTEM**    Enter date system was installed and placed in service ➤

| | | | |
|---|---|---|---|
| 27. Enter your total cost of the qualified wind-powered energy system installed and placed in service in Hawaii. | 27 | | |
| 28. Enter the amount of consumer incentive premiums, costs used for other credits, and utility rebate, if any, received for the qualifying wind-powered energy system. | 28 | | |
| 29. Actual cost of the wind-powered energy system (Subtract line 28 from line 27 and enter result.). | 29 | 0 | |
| 30. Enter the amount from line 29 that is installed and placed in service in Hawaii on **single-family residential** property. | 30 | | |
| 31. Enter 20% of line 30 or $1,500, whichever is less | | 31 | 0 |
| 32. Enter the amount from line 29 that is installed and placed in service in Hawaii on **multi-family residential** property | 32 | | |
| 33. Divide the total square feet of your unit by the total square feet of all units in the multi-family residential property. Enter the decimal (rounded to 2 decimal places). (See instructions.) | 33 | | |
| 34. Actual per unit cost of the wind-powered energy system. (Multiply line 32 by line 33 and enter result.). | 34 | 0 | |
| 35. Enter 20% of line 34 or $200, whichever is less | 35 | 0 | |
| 36. Multiply line 35 by the number of units you own to which the allocated unit cost on line 34 is applicable. (Number of units you own _____ ) | | 36 | 0 |
| 37. Enter the amount from line 29 that is installed and placed in service in Hawaii on **commercial** property. | 37 | | |
| 38. Enter 20% of line 37 or $500,000, whichever is less | | 38 | 0 |
| 39. Add lines 31, 36, and 38, and enter result (but not less than zero) | | 39 | 0 |

**DISTRIBUTIVE SHARE OF TAX CREDIT**

| | | |
|---|---|---|
| 40. Distributive share of solar energy tax credit from another Form N-342A. | 40 | |
| 41. Distributive share of wind-powered energy tax credit from another Form N-342A. | 41 | |

**TOTAL AND DISTRIBUTIVE SHARE OF RENEWABLE ENERGY TECHNOLOGIES INCOME TAX CREDIT**

| | | |
|---|---|---|
| 42. Total tax credit claimed. Enter the amount from lines 14, 26, or 39, and 40 and 41. | 42 | 390 |
| 43. **Distributive share of solar energy tax credit.** Each shareholder, partner, member, or beneficiary shall enter this amount on Form N-342, line 40. | 43 | 130 |
| 44. **Distributive share of wind-powered energy tax credit.** Each shareholder, partner, member, or beneficiary shall enter this amount on Form N-342, line 41 | 44 | 0 |

## GENERAL INSTRUCTIONS

For requirements for claiming the renewable energy technologies income tax credit and definitions, see the Instructions for Form N-342.

## SPECIFIC INSTRUCTIONS

Complete one Form N-342A for each individual and corporate shareholder, partner, member, or beneficiary receiving a distributive share of the renewable energy technologies income tax credit. Use a separate form for each eligible system. Attach a copy of the Forms N-342A as issued to each partner, member, beneficiary, or shareholder to the return of the S corporation, partnership, estate, trust, or condominium apartment association.

Be sure to enter in the appropriate space (1) the physical property address where the system was installed and placed in service, (2) the date the system was installed and placed in service, and (3) the Total Output Capacity, if the credit being claimed is for an "other solar energy system".

**Lines 1 through 42** — Fill in the lines as they apply to your claim.

**Lines 1 or 27** — Enter the qualifying cost of the eligible renewable technology system installed and placed in service in Hawaii.

**Lines 2 or 28** — Enter the dollar amount of any consumer incentive premiums unrelated to the operation of the system or offered with the sale of the system (such as "free solar powered products," "free gifts," offers to pay electricity bills, or rebates), costs for which another credit is claimed, and any utility rebate received for the qualifying renewable energy technology system.

These dollar amounts are to be deducted from the cost of the qualifying system before determining the credit.

**Lines 8, 20, and 33** — The per unit cost of a solar or wind-powered energy system installed and placed in service in Hawaii in a multi-family residential property may be determined as follows:

$$\frac{\text{Total square feet of your unit}}{\text{Total square feet of all units in the multi-family residential property}} \times \frac{\text{The actual cost}}{\text{of the system}}$$

If the above per unit cost calculation does not fairly represent the owners' contribution to the cost of the system, provide an alternative calculation.

**Line 43 — Distributive share of solar energy tax credit.** Each individual and corporate shareholder, partner, member, or beneficiary of an S corporation, partnership, estate, trust, or condominium apartment association receiving a Form N-342A must enter this amount on Form N-342, line 40. Both the Form N-342 and a copy of the Form N-342A must be attached to the individual or corporate income tax return on which the credit is claimed.

**Line 44 — Distributive share of wind-powered energy tax credit.** Each individual and corporate shareholder, partner, member, or beneficiary of an S corporation, partnership, estate, trust, or condominium apartment association receiving a Form N-342A must enter this amount on Form N-342, line 41. Both the Form N-342 and a copy of the Form N-342A must be attached to the individual or corporate income tax return on which the credit is claimed.

## COMPOSITE FILING OF FORM N-342A

For taxable years that begin on or after January 1, 2011, any S corporation, partnership, estate, trust, or condominium apartment association that has installed and placed in service **10 or more** systems in a single taxable year may file **composite Form(s) N-342A**. A composite Form N-342A, which is designated with the word "COMPOSITE" printed in capital letters at the top of the form, is used to report the total amounts from Form N-342B, Composite Information Statement for Form N-342A. For more information and instructions on filing a composite Form N-342A, see Department of Taxation Announcement No. 2012-01 and the Instructions for Form N-342B.

ID NO 88                                                **FORM N-342A**

| FORM | STATE OF HAWAII–DEPARTMENT OF TAXATION | TAX |
|---|---|---|
| **N-342A** | **INFORMATION STATEMENT** | YEAR |
| (REV. 2018) | CONCERNING RENEWABLE ENERGY TECHNOLOGIES INCOME TAX CREDIT | **2018** |

FOR SYSTEMS INSTALLED AND PLACED IN SERVICE ON OR AFTER JULY 1, 2009
(TO BE CLAIMED BY INDIVIDUAL OR CORPORATE SHAREHOLDERS OF S CORPORATIONS, MEMBERS OF PARTNERSHIPS, BENEFICIARIES OF ESTATES OR TRUSTS, OR CONDOMINIUM APARTMENT ASSOCIATIONS)

Or fiscal year beginning _____, 2018, and ending _____, 20 ____.

**ATTACH THIS STATEMENT TO FORM N-342**

| Name (S Corporation, Partnership, Estate, or Trust, or Condominium Apartment Association) | Social Security Number or Fed. Employer I.D. Number |
|---|---|
| ROK PINEAPPLE RANCH | 98-7654321 |

| Number and Street | |
|---|---|
| 15 MOUNTAIN RD | ☐ S Corporation |
| City or Town, State and Postal/ZIP Code | ☒ Partnership |
| NAPOOPOO                          HI        96000 | ☐ Estate or Trust |
| Name of individual or corporation for whom this statement is being prepared | ☐ Condominium Apartment Association |
| TAKEO ONO | |

**NOTE:** Every Hawaii S corporation, partnership, estate, trust, or condominium apartment association is required to prepare this statement for each individual or corporate shareholder, member, or beneficiary, respectively, in order that the prorated amount of such entity's tax credit may be claimed by the individual or corporate taxpayer. Use a separate form for each eligible system. **Also attach a copy of this form as issued to each member to the return of the S corporation, partnership, estate, trust, or condominium apartment association.**

**MEMBERS: USE THE INFORMATION PROVIDED ON THIS STATEMENT TO COMPLETE THE FORM N-342 USED TO CLAIM YOUR SHARE OF THIS TAX CREDIT. ATTACH BOTH THE FORM N-342 AND A COPY OF THIS FORM TO THE RETURN YOU FILE.**

**PHYSICAL PROPERTY ADDRESS WHERE THE SYSTEM WAS INSTALLED AND PLACED IN SERVICE:**

| Address (Number and Street) | City or Town | Postal/ZIP Code |
|---|---|---|
| 15 MOUNTAIN ROAD | NAPOOPOO | 96000 |

**COMPUTATION OF TAX CREDIT**

| SOLAR ENERGY SYSTEM | Enter date system was installed and placed in service ▶ | 11/11/2018 |
|---|---|---|
| | Enter **Total Output Capacity**, if credit is for an "other solar energy system" ▶ | |

| | | | | |
|---|---|---|---|---|
| 1. | Enter your total cost of the qualified solar energy system installed and placed in service in Hawaii . | 1 | 1,115 | |
| 2. | Enter the amount of consumer incentive premiums, costs used for other credits, and utility rebate, if any, received for the qualifying solar energy system ............................................. | 2 | 0 | |
| 3. | Actual cost of the solar energy system. (Subtract line 2 from line 1 and enter result.) .......... | 3 | 1,115 | |
| 4. | Is this solar energy system primarily used to heat water for household use? | | | |
| | ☐ Yes. Go to line 5. | | | |
| | ☐ No. Go to line 15. | | | |

**SYSTEM PRIMARILY USED TO HEAT WATER FOR HOUSEHOLD USE (lines 5 - 14)**

| | | | | |
|---|---|---|---|---|
| 5. | Enter the amount from line 3 that is installed and placed in service in Hawaii on **single-family residential** property ............... | 5 | | |
| 6. | Enter 35% of line 5 or $2,250, whichever is less ................................................................. | | 6 | 0 |
| 7. | Enter the amount from line 3 that is installed and placed in service in Hawaii on **multi-family residential** property .............. | 7 | | |
| 8. | Divide the total square feet of your unit by the total square feet of all units in the multi-family residential property. Enter the decimal (rounded to 2 decimal places). (See instructions.) .... | 8 | | |
| 9. | Actual per unit cost of the solar energy system. (Multiply line 7 by line 8 and enter result.). | 9 | 0 | |
| 10. | Enter 35% of line 9 or $350, whichever is less .................................................................. | 10 | 0 | |
| 11. | Multiply line 10 by the number of units you own to which the allocated unit cost on line 9 is applicable. (Number of units you own _____ ) .................................................. | | 11 | 0 |
| 12. | Enter the amount from line 3 that is installed and placed in service in Hawaii on **commercial** property ........... | 12 | | |
| 13. | Enter 35% of line 12 or $250,000, whichever is less ............................................................ | | 13 | 0 |
| 14. | Add lines 6, 11, and 13, and enter result (but not less than zero) ........................................ | | 14 | 0 |

**SYSTEM NOT PRIMARILY USED TO HEAT WATER FOR HOUSEHOLD USE (lines 15 - 26)**

| | | | | |
|---|---|---|---|---|
| 15. | Enter the amount from line 3 that is installed and placed in service in Hawaii on **single-family residential** property ............... | 15 | | |
| 16. | Enter 35% of line 15 or $5,000, whichever is less ................................................................. | | 16 | 0 |
| 17. | Was this system used as a substitute for a solar water heating system that is required for new single-family residential property constructed on or after January 1, 2010? | | | |
| | ☐ Yes. Enter 35% of line 15 or $2,250, whichever is less. | | | |
| | ☒ No. Enter zero. | 17 | 0 | |
| 18. | Line 16 minus line 17. .............................................................................................. | | 18 | 0 |
| 19. | Enter the amount from line 3 that is installed and placed in service in Hawaii on **multi-family residential** property ................ | 19 | | |
| 20. | Divide the total square feet of your unit by the total square feet of all units in the multi-family residential property. Enter the decimal (rounded to 2 decimal places). (See instructions.) .... | 20 | | |

(Continued on back)

N342A_T 2018A 01 VID88                     ID NO 88                              **FORM N-342A**

ROK PINEAPPLE RANCH                                              98-7654321

**Form N-342A**
**(REV. 2018)**                                                  **Page 2**

| | | |
|---|---|---|
| 21. Actual per unit cost of the solar energy system. (Multiply line 19 by line 20 and enter result.) | **21** 0 | |
| 22. Enter 35% of line 21 or $350, whichever is less ................................................ | **22** 0 | |
| 23. Multiply line 22 by the number of units you own to which the allocated unit cost on line 21 is applicable. (Number of units you own _____ ) ................................................ | | **23** 0 |
| 24. Enter the amount from line 3 that is installed and placed in service in Hawaii on **commercial** property ........... | **24** 1,115 | |
| 25. Enter 35% of line 24 or $500,000, whichever is less ................................................ | | **25** 390 |
| 26. Add lines 18, 23, and 25, and enter result (but not less than zero) ................................................ | | **26** 390 |

**WIND-POWERED ENERGY SYSTEM**    Enter date system was installed and placed in service ➤ _____

| | | |
|---|---|---|
| 27. Enter your total cost of the qualified wind-powered energy system installed and placed in service in Hawaii. ................................................ | **27** | |
| 28. Enter the amount of consumer incentive premiums, costs used for other credits, and utility rebate, if any, received for the qualifying wind-powered energy system. ................................. | **28** | |
| 29. Actual cost of the wind-powered energy system (Subtract line 28 from line 27 and enter result.). .................... | **29** 0 | |
| 30. Enter the amount from line 29 that is installed and placed in service in Hawaii on **single-family residential** property. ................................................ | **30** | |
| 31. Enter 20% of line 30 or $1,500, whichever is less ................................................ | | **31** 0 |
| 32. Enter the amount from line 29 that is installed and placed in service in Hawaii on **multi-family residential** property .............. | **32** | |
| 33. Divide the total square feet of your unit by the total square feet of all units in the multi-family residential property. Enter the decimal (rounded to 2 decimal places). (See instructions.) .... | **33** | |
| 34. Actual per unit cost of the wind-powered energy system. (Multiply line 32 by line 33 and enter result.). ................................................ | **34** 0 | |
| 35. Enter 20% of line 34 or $200, whichever is less ................................................ | **35** 0 | |
| 36. Multiply line 35 by the number of units you own to which the allocated unit cost on line 34 is applicable. (Number of units you own _____ ) | | **36** 0 |
| 37. Enter the amount from line 29 that is installed and placed in service in Hawaii on **commercial** property. ........... | **37** | |
| 38. Enter 20% of line 37 or $500,000, whichever is less ................................................ | | **38** 0 |
| 39. Add lines 31, 36, and 38, and enter result (but not less than zero) ................................................ | | **39** 0 |

**DISTRIBUTIVE SHARE OF TAX CREDIT**

| | | |
|---|---|---|
| 40. Distributive share of solar energy tax credit from another Form N-342A. ................................ | | **40** |
| 41. Distributive share of wind-powered energy tax credit from another Form N-342A ................................ | | **41** |

**TOTAL AND DISTRIBUTIVE SHARE OF RENEWABLE ENERGY TECHNOLOGIES INCOME TAX CREDIT**

| | | |
|---|---|---|
| 42. Total tax credit claimed. Enter the amount from lines 14, 26, or 39, and 40 and 41. ................................ | | **42** 390 |
| 43. **Distributive share of solar energy tax credit.** Each shareholder, partner, member, or beneficiary shall enter this amount on Form N-342, line 40. ................................................ | | **43** 130 |
| 44. **Distributive share of wind-powered energy tax credit.** Each shareholder, partner, member, or beneficiary shall enter this amount on Form N-342, line 41. ................................................ | | **44** 0 |

## GENERAL INSTRUCTIONS

For requirements for claiming the renewable energy technologies income tax credit and definitions, see the Instructions for Form N-342.

## SPECIFIC INSTRUCTIONS

Complete one Form N-342A for each individual and corporate shareholder, partner, member, or beneficiary receiving a distributive share of the renewable energy technologies income tax credit. Use a separate form for each eligible system. Attach a copy of the Forms N-342A as issued to each partner, member, beneficiary, or shareholder to the return of the S corporation, partnership, estate, trust, or condominium apartment association.

Be sure to enter in the appropriate space (1) the physical property address where the system was installed and placed in service, (2) the date the system was installed and placed in service, and (3) the Total Output Capacity, if the credit being claimed is for an "other solar energy system".

**Lines 1 through 42** — Fill in the lines as they apply to your claim.

**Lines 1 or 27** — Enter the qualifying cost of the eligible renewable technology system installed and placed in service in Hawaii.

**Lines 2 or 28** — Enter the dollar amount of any consumer incentive premiums unrelated to the operation of the system or offered with the sale of the system (such as "free solar powered products," "free gifts," offers to pay electricity bills, or rebates), costs for which another credit is claimed, and any utility rebate received for the qualifying renewable energy technology system.

These dollar amounts are to be deducted from the cost of the qualifying system before determining the credit.

**Lines 8, 20, and 33** — The per unit cost of a solar or wind-powered energy system installed and placed in service in Hawaii in a multi-family residential property may be determined as follows:

$$\frac{\text{Total square feet of your unit}}{\text{Total square feet of all units in the multi-family residential property}} \times \text{The actual cost of the system}$$

If the above per unit cost calculation does not fairly represent the owners' contribution to the cost of the system, provide an alternative calculation.

**Line 43 — Distributive share of solar energy tax credit.** Each individual and corporate shareholder, partner, member, or beneficiary of an S corporation, partnership, estate, trust, or condominium apartment association receiving a Form N-342A must enter this amount on Form N-342, line 40. Both the Form N-342 and a copy of the Form N-342A must be attached to the individual or corporate income tax return on which the credit is claimed.

**Line 44 — Distributive share of wind-powered energy tax credit.** Each individual and corporate shareholder, partner, member, or beneficiary of an S corporation, partnership, estate, trust, or condominium apartment association receiving a Form N-342A must enter this amount on Form N-342, line 41. Both the Form N-342 and a copy of the Form N-342A must be attached to the individual or corporate income tax return on which the credit is claimed.

## COMPOSITE FILING OF FORM N-342A

For taxable years that begin on or after January 1, 2011, any S corporation, partnership, estate, trust, or condominium apartment association that has installed and placed in service **10 or more** systems in a single taxable year may file **composite Form(s) N-342A.** A composite Form N-342A, which is designated with the word "COMPOSITE" printed in capital letters at the top of the form, is used to report the total amounts from Form N-342B, Composite Information Statement for Form N-342A. For more information and instructions on filing a composite Form N-342A, see Department of Taxation Announcement No. 2012-01 and the Instructions for Form N-342B.

ID NO 88                                                    **FORM N-342A**

| FORM<br>**N-342A**<br>(REV. 2018) | STATE OF HAWAII–DEPARTMENT OF TAXATION<br>**INFORMATION STATEMENT**<br>CONCERNING RENEWABLE ENERGY TECHNOLOGIES INCOME TAX CREDIT<br>FOR SYSTEMS INSTALLED AND PLACED IN SERVICE ON OR AFTER JULY 1, 2009<br>(TO BE CLAIMED BY INDIVIDUAL OR CORPORATE SHAREHOLDERS OF S CORPORATIONS, MEMBERS OF PARTNERSHIPS,<br>BENEFICIARIES OF ESTATES OR TRUSTS, OR CONDOMINIUM APARTMENT ASSOCIATIONS)<br>Or fiscal year beginning _____ , 2018, and ending _____ , 20 ___ . | TAX<br>YEAR<br>**2018** |

**ATTACH THIS STATEMENT TO FORM N-342**

| Name (S Corporation, Partnership, Estate, or Trust, or Condominium Apartment Association) | Social Security Number or Fed. Employer I.D. Number |
|---|---|
| ROK PINEAPPLE RANCH | 98-7654321 |

Number and Street
15 MOUNTAIN RD

City or Town, State and Postal/ZIP Code
NAPOOPOO          HI       96000

☐ S Corporation
☒ Partnership
☐ Estate or Trust
☐ Condominium Apartment Association

Name of individual or corporation for whom this statement is being prepared
SHIGERU KISHI

NOTE: *Every Hawaii S corporation, partnership, estate, trust, or condominium apartment association is required to prepare this statement for each individual or corporate shareholder, member, or beneficiary, respectively, in order that the prorated amount of such entity's tax credit may be claimed by the individual or corporate taxpayer. Use a separate form for each eligible system. **Also attach a copy of this form as issued to each member to the return of the S corporation, partnership, estate, trust, or condominium apartment association.***

**MEMBERS: USE THE INFORMATION PROVIDED ON THIS STATEMENT TO COMPLETE THE FORM N-342 USED TO CLAIM YOUR SHARE OF THIS TAX CREDIT. ATTACH BOTH THE FORM N-342 AND A COPY OF THIS FORM TO THE RETURN YOU FILE.**

PHYSICAL PROPERTY ADDRESS WHERE THE SYSTEM WAS INSTALLED AND PLACED IN SERVICE:

| Address (Number and Street) | City or Town | Postal/ZIP Code |
|---|---|---|
| 15 MOUNTAIN ROAD | NAPOOPOO | 96000 |

**COMPUTATION OF TAX CREDIT**

| SOLAR ENERGY SYSTEM | Enter date system was installed and placed in service ➤ | 11/11/2018 |
|---|---|---|
| | Enter **Total Output Capacity**, if credit is for an "other solar energy system" ➤ | |

| | | | | | |
|---|---|---|---|---|---|
| 1. | Enter your total cost of the qualified solar energy system installed and placed in service in Hawaii . | **1** | 1,115 | | |
| 2. | Enter the amount of consumer incentive premiums, costs used for other credits, and utility rebate, if any, received for the qualifying solar energy system | **2** | 0 | | |
| 3. | Actual cost of the solar energy system. (Subtract line 2 from line 1 and enter result.) | **3** | 1,115 | | |
| 4. | Is this solar energy system primarily used to heat water for household use?<br>☐ **Yes.** Go to line 5.<br>☐ **No.** Go to line 15. | | | | |

**SYSTEM PRIMARILY USED TO HEAT WATER FOR HOUSEHOLD USE (lines 5 - 14)**

| | | | | | |
|---|---|---|---|---|---|
| 5. | Enter the amount from line 3 that is installed and placed in service in Hawaii on **single-family residential** property | **5** | | | |
| 6. | Enter 35% of line 5 or $2,250, whichever is less | | | **6** | 0 |
| 7. | Enter the amount from line 3 that is installed and placed in service in Hawaii on **multi-family residential** property | **7** | | | |
| 8. | Divide the total square feet of your unit by the total square feet of all units in the multi-family residential property. Enter the decimal (rounded to 2 decimal places). (See instructions.) | **8** | | | |
| 9. | Actual per unit cost of the solar energy system. (Multiply line 7 by line 8 and enter result.) | **9** | 0 | | |
| 10. | Enter 35% of line 9 or $350, whichever is less | **10** | 0 | | |
| 11. | Multiply line 10 by the number of units you own to which the allocated unit cost on line 9 is applicable. (Number of units you own _____ ) | | | **11** | 0 |
| 12. | Enter the amount from line 3 that is installed and placed in service in Hawaii on **commercial** property | **12** | | | |
| 13. | Enter 35% of line 12 or $250,000, whichever is less | | | **13** | 0 |
| 14. | Add lines 6, 11, and 13, and enter result (but not less than zero) | | | **14** | 0 |

**SYSTEM NOT PRIMARILY USED TO HEAT WATER FOR HOUSEHOLD USE (lines 15 - 26)**

| | | | | | |
|---|---|---|---|---|---|
| 15. | Enter the amount from line 3 that is installed and placed in service in Hawaii on **single-family residential** property | **15** | | | |
| 16. | Enter 35% of line 15 or $5,000, whichever is less | **16** | 0 | | |
| 17. | Was this system used as a substitute for a solar water heating system that is required for new single-family residential property constructed on or after January 1, 2010?<br>☐ **Yes.** Enter 35% of line 15 or $2,250, whichever is less.<br>☒ **No.** Enter zero | **17** | 0 | | |
| 18. | Line 16 minus line 17. | | | **18** | 0 |
| 19. | Enter the amount from line 3 that is installed and placed in service in Hawaii on **multi-family residential** property | **19** | | | |
| 20. | Divide the total square feet of your unit by the total square feet of all units in the multi-family residential property. Enter the decimal (rounded to 2 decimal places). (See instructions.) | **20** | | | |

(Continued on back)

N342A_T 2018A 01 VID88                              ID NO 88                              **FORM N-342A**

ROK PINEAPPLE RANCH                                                               98-7654321

**Form N-342A**
**(REV. 2018)** Page 2

| | | | |
|---|---|---|---|
| 21. Actual per unit cost of the solar energy system. (Multiply line 19 by line 20 and enter result.) | 21 | 0 | |
| 22. Enter 35% of line 21 or $350, whichever is less ................................ | 22 | 0 | |
| 23. Multiply line 22 by the number of units you own to which the allocated unit cost on line 21 is applicable. (Number of units you own _____ ) ....................................... | | 23 | 0 |
| 24. Enter the amount from line 3 that is installed and placed in service in Hawaii on **commercial** property ........... | 24 | 1,115 | |
| 25. Enter 35% of line 24 or $500,000, whichever is less .................................... | | 25 | 390 |
| 26. Add lines 18, 23, and 25, and enter result (but not less than zero) ...................................... | | 26 | 390 |

**WIND-POWERED ENERGY SYSTEM** Enter date system was installed and placed in service ➤ _____

| | | | |
|---|---|---|---|
| 27. Enter your total cost of the qualified wind-powered energy system installed and placed in service in Hawaii. ..................................... | 27 | | |
| 28. Enter the amount of consumer incentive premiums, costs used for other credits, and utility rebate, if any, received for the qualifying wind-powered energy system. .......................... | 28 | | |
| 29. Actual cost of the wind-powered energy system (Subtract line 28 from line 27 and enter result.). ................... | 29 | 0 | |
| 30. Enter the amount from line 29 that is installed and placed in service in Hawaii on **single-family residential** property. ..................................... | 30 | | |
| 31. Enter 20% of line 30 or $1,500, whichever is less ...................................... | | 31 | 0 |
| 32. Enter the amount from line 29 that is installed and placed in service in Hawaii on **multi-family residential** property ............... | 32 | | |
| 33. Divide the total square feet of your unit by the total square feet of all units in the multi-family residential property. Enter the decimal (rounded to 2 decimal places). (See instructions.) ..... | 33 | | |
| 34. Actual per unit cost of the wind-powered energy system. (Multiply line 32 by line 33 and enter result.). ..................................... | 34 | 0 | |
| 35. Enter 20% of line 34 or $200, whichever is less ...................................... | 35 | 0 | |
| 36. Multiply line 35 by the number of units you own to which the allocated unit cost on line 34 is applicable. (Number of units you own _____ ) ....................................... | | 36 | 0 |
| 37. Enter the amount from line 29 that is installed and placed in service in Hawaii on **commercial** property. .......... | 37 | | |
| 38. Enter 20% of line 37 or $500,000, whichever is less ...................................... | | 38 | 0 |
| 39. Add lines 31, 36, and 38, and enter result (but not less than zero) ...................................... | | 39 | 0 |

**DISTRIBUTIVE SHARE OF TAX CREDIT**

| | | | |
|---|---|---|---|
| 40. Distributive share of solar energy tax credit from another Form N-342A. ...................................... | | 40 | |
| 41. Distributive share of wind-powered energy tax credit from another Form N-342A ...................................... | | 41 | |

**TOTAL AND DISTRIBUTIVE SHARE OF RENEWABLE ENERGY TECHNOLOGIES INCOME TAX CREDIT**

| | | | |
|---|---|---|---|
| 42. Total tax credit claimed. Enter the amount from lines 14, 26, or 39, and 40 and 41. ...................................... | | 42 | 390 |
| 43. **Distributive share of solar energy tax credit.** Each shareholder, partner, member, or beneficiary shall enter this amount on Form N-342, line 40. ...................................... | | 43 | 130 |
| 44. **Distributive share of wind-powered energy tax credit.** Each shareholder, partner, member, or beneficiary shall enter this amount on Form N-342, line 41 ...................................... | | 44 | 0 |

## GENERAL INSTRUCTIONS

For requirements for claiming the renewable energy technologies income tax credit and definitions, see the Instructions for Form N-342.

## SPECIFIC INSTRUCTIONS

Complete one Form N-342A for each individual and corporate shareholder, partner, member, or beneficiary receiving a distributive share of the renewable energy technologies income tax credit. Use a separate form for each eligible system. Attach a copy of the Forms N-342A as issued to each partner, member, beneficiary, or shareholder to the return of the S corporation, partnership, estate, trust, or condominium apartment association.

Be sure to enter in the appropriate space (1) the physical property address where the system was installed and placed in service, (2) the date the system was installed and placed in service, and (3) the Total Output Capacity, if the credit being claimed is for an "other solar energy system".

**Lines 1 through 42** — Fill in the lines as they apply to your claim.

**Lines 1 or 27** — Enter the qualifying cost of the eligible renewable technology system installed and placed in service in Hawaii.

**Lines 2 or 28** — Enter the dollar amount of any consumer incentive premiums unrelated to the operation of the system or offered with the sale of the system (such as "free solar powered products," "free gifts," offers to pay electricity bills, or rebates), costs for which another credit is claimed, and any utility rebate received for the qualifying renewable energy technology system.

These dollar amounts are to be deducted from the cost of the qualifying system before determining the credit.

**Lines 8, 20, and 33** — The per unit cost of a solar or wind-powered energy system installed and placed in service in Hawaii in a multi-family residential property may be determined as follows:

$$\frac{\text{Total square feet of your unit}}{\text{Total square feet of all units in the multi-family residential property}} \quad x \quad \frac{\text{The actual cost of the system}}{}$$

If the above per unit cost calculation does not fairly represent the owners' contribution to the cost of the system, provide an alternative calculation.

**Line 43 — Distributive share of solar energy tax credit.** Each individual and corporate shareholder, partner, member, or beneficiary of an S corporation, partnership, estate, trust, or condominium apartment association receiving a Form N-342A must enter this amount on Form N-342, line 40. Both the Form N-342 and a copy of the Form N-342A must be attached to the individual or corporate income tax return on which the credit is claimed.

**Line 44 — Distributive share of wind-powered energy tax credit.** Each individual and corporate shareholder, partner, member, or beneficiary of an S corporation, partnership, estate, trust, or condominium apartment association receiving a Form N-342A must enter this amount on Form N-342, line 41. Both the Form N-342 and a copy of the Form N-342A must be attached to the individual or corporate income tax return on which the credit is claimed.

## COMPOSITE FILING OF FORM N-342A

For taxable years that begin on or after January 1, 2011, any S corporation, partnership, estate, trust, or condominium apartment association that has installed and placed in service **10 or more** systems in a single taxable year may file **composite Form(s) N-342A**. A composite Form N-342A, which is designated with the word "COMPOSITE" printed in capital letters at the top of the form, is used to report the total amounts from Form N-342B, Composite Information Statement for Form N-342A. For more information and instructions on filing a composite Form N-342A, see Department of Taxation Announcement No. 2012-01 and the Instructions for Form N-342B.

**SCHEDULE K-1**
**FORM N-20**
**(REV. 2018)**

STATE OF HAWAII — DEPARTMENT OF TAXATION
# PARTNER'S SHARE OF INCOME, CREDITS, DEDUCTIONS, ETC.— 2018
For calendar year 2018 or other tax year
beginning_____, 2018 and ending _____, 20_____

PREPARE IN TRIPLICATE

1  File with N-20
2  For partnership
3  For partner

| Partner's Social Security No. or Federal Employer I.D. No. ➤ 111-23-4567 | Partnership's Federal Employer Identification No. ➤ 98-7654321 |
|---|---|
| Partner's name, address, and Postal/ZIP Code<br><br>JOHN REED<br>217 PALM DR<br>ENCINO, CA 90120 | Partnership's name, address, and Postal/ZIP Code<br><br>ROK PINEAPPLE RANCH<br>15 MOUNTAIN RD<br>NAPOOPOO, HI 96000 |

**A**  This partner is a  ☑ general partner  ☐ limited partner
☐ LLC member-manager  ☐ other LLC member

**B**  What type of entity is this partner? ➤ INDIVIDUAL

**C**  Enter partner's percentage of:

|  | (i) Before change or termination | (ii) End of year |
|---|---|---|
| Profit sharing | _____% | 33.000% |
| Loss sharing | _____% | 33.000% |
| Ownership of capital | _____% | 33.000% |

**D**  Partner's share of liabilities:
Nonrecourse ...................................................... $_____
Qualified nonrecourse financing ........................... $_____
Other............................................................. $  8,576.00

**E**  Check here if this partnership is a publicly traded partnership as defined in IRC section 469(k)(2) ........ ☐

**F**  Check applicable boxes:  (1) ☐ Final K-1  (2) ☐ Amended K-1

**G**  Reconciliation of partner's capital account:

| (a) Capital account at beginning of year | (b) Capital contributed during year | (c) Income included in column (c) below, plus nontaxable income | (d) Deductions included in col. (c) below, plus unallowable deductions | (e) Withdrawals and distributions | (f) Capital account at end of year (combine columns (a) through (e)) |
|---|---|---|---|---|---|
| 16,745.00 | | −580.00 ( | 478.00 )( | 666.00) | 15,021.00 |

*Caution: Refer to Partner's Instructions for Schedule K-1 (Form N-20) before entering information from this schedule on your tax return.*

| | (a) Distributive share items | (b) Attributable to Hawaii | (c) Attributable Everywhere | (d) Form N-11 & N-15 filers enter the amount in column (b) and /or column (c) on: |
|---|---|---|---|---|
| **Income (Loss)** | 1  Ordinary income (loss) from trade or business activities............. | −1,580.00 | −1,580.00 | See Partner's Instructions for Schedule K-1 (Form N-20) |
| | 2  Net income (loss) from rental real estate activities................... | | | |
| | 3  Net income (loss) from other rental activities......................... | | | |
| | 4  Guaranteed payments to partner.......................................... | | | |
| | 5  Interest................................................................................ | | | Interest Worksheet |
| | 6  Ordinary Dividends.............................................................. | | | See Partner's Instructions for Schedule K-1 (Form N-20). |
| | 7  Royalties............................................................................. | | | |
| | 8  Net short-term capital gain (loss)......................................... | | | Capital Gain/Loss Worksheet |
| | 9  Net long-term capital gain (loss).......................................... | 1,000.00 | 1,000.00 | Capital Gain/Loss Worksheet |
| | 10  Net IRC section 1231 gain (loss) (attach Schedule D-1)....... | −453.00 | −453.00 | See Partner's Instr. for Sch. K-1 (Form N-20). |
| | 11  Other income (loss) (attach schedule)................................ | | | Enter on applicable line of your return. |
| **Deductions** | 12  Charitable contributions (attach schedule)............................ | 25.00 | 25.00 | See Partner's Instructions for Schedule K-1 (Form N-20). |
| | 13  Expense deduction for recovery property (IRC section 179) (attach schedule) | | | |
| | 14  Deductions related to portfolio income (attach schedule)...... | | | |
| | 15  Other deductions (attach schedule).................................... | | | Enter on applicable line of your return. |
| **Credits** | 16  Total cost of qualifying property for the Capital Goods Excise Tax Credit.... | | | Form N-312 |
| | 17  Fuel Tax Credit for Commercial Fishers............................... | | | Form N-163 |
| | 18  Amounts needed to claim the Enterprise Zone Tax Credit ...... | See attached Form N-756A | | Form N-756 |
| | 19  Hawaii Low-Income Housing Tax Credit............................... | | | Form N-586 |
| | 20  Credit for Employment of Vocational Rehabilitation Referrals... | | | Form N-884 |
| | 21  Total qualified production costs for the Motion Picture, Digital Media, and Film Production Income Tax Credit............ | | | Form N-340 |

Schedule K-1 (Form N-20) (REV. 2018)                                                                                          Page 2

| | (a) Distributive share items | (b) Attributable to Hawaii | (c) Attributable Everywhere | (d) Form N-11 & N-15 filers enter the amount in column (b) and /or column (c) on: |
|---|---|---|---|---|
| **Credits (cont.)** | 22  Credit for School Repair and Maintenance.......................................... | | | Form N-330 |
| | 23  Renewable Energy Technologies Income Tax Credit........................ | See attached Form N-342A | | Form N-342 |
| | 24  Important Agricultural Land Qualified Agricultural Cost Tax Credit............. | | | Form N-344 |
| | 25  Tax Credit for Research Activities.................................................... | | | Form N-346 |
| | 26  Capital Infrastructure Tax Credit..................................................... | | | Form N-348 |
| | 27  Cesspool Upgrade, Conversion or Connection Income Tax Credit........... | | | Form N-350 |
| | 28  Renewable Fuels Production Tax Credit........................................... | | | Form N-352 |
| | 29  Organic Foods Production Tax Credit............................................... | | | Form N-354 |
| | 30  Credit for income tax withheld on Form N-288 (net of refunds)................. | | | Sch. CR, line 26a |
| **Investment Interest** | 31  a  Interest expense on investment debts ............................................ | | | Form N-158, line 1 |
| |     b  (1)  Investment income included on Schedule K-1, lines 5 through 7..... | | | See Partner's Instructions for |
| |        (2)  Investment expenses included in Schedule K-1, line 14 ................. | | | Schedule K-1 (Form N-20) |
| **Recapture of Tax Credits** | 32  Recapture of Hawaii Low-Income Housing Tax Credit | | | |
| |     a  From IRC section 42(j)(5) partnerships ............................................ | | | Form N-586, Part III |
| |     b  Other than on line 32a ................................................................ | | | |
| | 33  Capital Goods Excise Tax Credit Properties........................................ | See attached Form N-312, Part II | | Form N-312, Part II |
| | 34  Recapture of Tax Credit for Flood Victims........................................ | | | Form N-338 |
| | 35  Recapture of Important Agricultural Land Qualified Agricultural Cost Tax Credit...... | | | Form N-344 |
| | 36  Recapture of Capital Infrastructure Tax Credit.................................... | | | Form N-348 |
| **Other** | 37  List below other items and amounts not included on lines 1 through 36 that are required to be reported separately to each partner | | | See Partner's Instructions for Schedule K-1 (Form N-20). |

**Other Information Provided by Partnership:**

_____

_____

_____

_____

_____

_____

_____

_____

_____

_____

_____

_____

_____

_____

_____

_____

_____

## PROBLEM FOR SPECIMEN RETURN
## CORPORATION INCOME TAX RETURN

### Form N-30

The Maui Manufacturing Corp. was incorporated under the laws of the State of Hawaii on September 1, 1961 and is currently engaged in the manufacture of a specialized line of household furniture which it sells as a retailer in Hawaii and as a wholesaler in California. The company maintains sales offices and warehouses in both states. Main offices are located at 333 Beach Avenue, Honolulu, Hawaii.

The Hawaii income tax return (Form N-30) for the company's current year is shown below.

A further analysis of certain items on the federal return discloses the following information:

Rents are received from a ground lease with Hawaiian Telephone
   Co., Inc. Under the terms of the lease, the tenant pays all property
   taxes and insurance ........................................................................ $ 2,400

Payments on declaration of estimated tax ............................................. 2,500

Net operating loss carry over from preceding year ............................... 2,075

FORM
**N-30**
(REV. 2017)

STATE OF HAWAII — DEPARTMENT OF TAXATION

# CORPORATION INCOME TAX RETURN

**CALENDAR YEAR** 2017

THIS SPACE FOR DATE RECEIVED STAMP

or other tax year beginning ● _____ , 2017
and ending ● _____ , 20 ____

☐ **Change of Address**  ☐ **AMENDED Return (Attach Sch AMD)**

☐ **IRS Adjustment**
☐ **NOL Carryback**

| | | |
|---|---|---|
| Name | ● Federal Employer I.D. No. | |
| MAUI MANUFACTURING CORP. | 99-1234567 | |
| Dba or C/O | ● Business Activity Code No. (Use code shown on federal form 1120 or 1120A) | |
| Mailing Address (number and street) | Date business began in Hawaii | |
| 333 BEACH AVENUE | 09-01-1961 | |
| City or town, State, and Postal/ZIP Code. If foreign address, see Instructions. | Hawaii Business Activity | |
| HONOLULU, HI 96000 | MANUFACTURING | |

● PRINT OR TYPE ●

**THIS RETURN IS (CHECK BOX, IF APPLICABLE):**

☐● For a multi-state corporation using separate accounting.  ☐● For a real estate investment trust (REIT).
☐● A combined return of a unitary group of corporations. (See instructions)  ☐ A consolidated return. (Domestic (Hawaii) corporations only.)
☐● A separate return of a member corporation of a unitary group. (See instructions)  (Attach a copy of Hawaii Forms N-303 and N-304 for each subsidiary)

● Hawaii Tax I.D. No.
GE-001-234-5678-01

## FOR LINES 1 - 5 and 7 - 10, ENTER AMOUNTS FROM COMPARABLE LINES ON FEDERAL RETURN.

| | | | | |
|---|---|---|---|---|
| 1 | (a) Gross receipts or sales | 1(a)● | 1,245,000 | |
| | (b) Returns and allowances | 1(b)● | 25,000 | |
| | (c) Line 1(a) minus line 1(b) | 1(c)● | | 1,220,000 |
| 2 | Cost of goods sold | 2● | | 890,000 |
| 3 | Interest | 3● | | 525 |
| 4 | Gross rents | 4● | | 2,400 |
| 5 | Gross royalties | 5● | | |
| 6 | (a) Capital gain net income (attach Hawaii Schedule D) | 6(a)● | | 9,500 |
| | (b) Net gain (loss) from Hawaii Schedule D-1, Part II, line 19 (attach Schedule D-1). | 6(b) | | -1,000 |
| 7 | Other income | 7● | | 1,100 |
| 8 | TOTAL INCOME — **TOTAL INCOME ➤** | 8● | | 342,525 |
| 9 | TOTAL DEDUCTIONS — **TOTAL DEDUCTIONS ➤** | 9● | | 252,500 |
| 10 | Taxable income before Hawaii adjustments — Line 8 minus line 9. Enter here and on Schedule J, line 1 | 10 | | 90,025 |
| 11 | TOTAL TAX (Schedule J, line 24) — **TOTAL TAX ➤** | 11● | | 3,032 |
| 12 | Total refundable credits from Schedule CR, line 26 | 12● | | |
| 13 | Line 11 minus line 12. If line 13 is zero or less, see Instructions. | 13● | | 3,032 |
| 14 | Total nonrefundable credits from Schedule CR, line 18 | 14● | | |
| 15 | Line 13 minus line 14 | 15● | | 3,032 |
| 16 | (a) 2016 overpayment allowed as a credit | 16(a)● | | |
| | (b) 2017 estimated tax payments (including any Form N-288A withholdings. See Instructions) | 16(b)● | 2,500 | |
| | (c) Payments with extension (attach Form N-301) | 16(c)● | | |
| | (d) Total (Add lines 16(a), 16(b), and 16(c)) — **TOTAL ➤** | 16(d) | | 2,500 |
| 17 | Estimated tax penalty (see Instructions). Check if Form N-220 is attached — ➤ ●☐ | 17● | | |
| 18 | TAX DUE (If the total of lines 15 and 17 are larger than line 16(d)), enter AMOUNT OWED | 18● | | 532 |
| 19 | If line 16(d) is larger than the total of lines 15 and 17, enter AMOUNT OVERPAID. See Instructions. | 19● | | |
| 20 | Enter amount of line 19 you want **Credited to 2018 estimated tax** ➤ 20(a) $● | | **Refunded ➤** | 20(b)● |
| 21 | Amount paid (overpaid) on original return — **AMENDED RETURN ONLY** (See Instructions. Attach Sch AMD) | 21 | | |
| 22 | **BALANCE DUE (REFUND) with amended return** (See Instructions. Attach Sch AMD) | 22 | | |

*Left margin vertical text:* ● ATTACH CHECK OR MONEY ORDER AND FORM N-201V HERE ●
*Section labels:* TAXABLE INCOME / TAX AND TAX PAYMENTS / Amended Return

I declare, under the penalties set forth in section 231-36, HRS, that this return (including any accompanying schedules or statements) has been examined by me and, to the best of my knowledge and belief, is true, correct, and complete. Declaration of preparer (other than taxpayer) is based on all information of which preparer has any knowledge.

**Please Sign Here**

➤ ●

Signature of officer    Print or type name and title of officer    Date

★ May the Hawaii Department of Taxation discuss this return with the preparer shown below? (See page 2 of the Instructions) This designation does not replace Form N-848  ☑ Yes  ☐ No

| **Paid Preparer's Information** | Preparer's signature and date | | Preparer's identification no. | Check if self-employed ➤ ☐ |
|---|---|---|---|---|
| | Print Preparer's Name ➤ HOMER JONES | | ● P00000000 | |
| | Firm's name (or yours, if self-employed) ➤ KMH LLP, 1003 BISHOP STREET, #2400 | | Federal E.I. No. ➤ 42-1539623 | |
| | Address and ZIP Code ➤ HONOLULU, HI 96813 | | Phone no. ➤ (808) 526-2255 | |

**FORM N-30**

N30_F 2017A 01

**FORM N-30 (REV. 2017)**                                                                                     **Page 2**

| Name as shown on return | Federal Employer Identification Number |
|---|---|
| MAUI MANUFACTURING CORP. | 99-1234567 |

## Schedule C — Income From Dividends (Classified for Hawaii Purposes)

| 1 Name of declaring corporation (Attach a separate sheet if more space is needed.) | 2 National Bank Associations or certain high technology businesses | 3 Received from an affiliate (including foreign) as IRC section 243(b) qualifying dividend | 4 Received by a Small Business Investment Co. operating under Small Business Investment Act | 5 Columns 2 through 4 and all other dividends |
|---|---|---|---|---|
| HAWAII OFFSHORE DRILLING | 900 | | | 900 |
| ROAD TRANSIT | | | | 200 |
| 6 Total dividends. (Subtotal of column 5) . . . . . . . . . . . . . . . . . . . . . . 6 | | | | 1,100 |
| 7 Sum of columns 2 through 4 . . . . . . . . . . . . . . . . . . . . . . . . . . . 7 | | | | 900 |
| 8 Subtotal. Line 6 minus line 7 . . . . . . . . . . . . . . . . . . . . . . . . . . 8 | | | | 200 |
| 9 Multiply line 8 by .30 (30%) . . . . . . . . . . . . . . . . . . . . . . . . . . . 9 | | | | 60 |
| 10 Taxable mutual funds dividends | | | | |
| 11 Total taxable dividends. Line 9 plus line 10 . . . . . . . . . . . . . . . . . . ▶ 11 | | | | 60 |

## Schedule J — Adjustments to Income for Hawaii Purposes and Tax Computation

| | | | |
|---|---|---|---|
| 1 | Taxable income (loss) before Hawaii adjustments from page 1, line 10 (Unitary business taxpayers, see Instructions) . . . | 1 | |
| 2 | (a) Taxable dividends from Schedule C, Line 11 . . . . . . . . . . . . . . 2(a) | | |
| | (b) Deductions allowable for federal tax purposes but not allowable or allowable only in part for Hawaii tax purposes (attach schedule) . . . 2(b) | | |
| | (c) The portion of the Hawaii jobs credit claimed applicable to current year new employees from Schedule CR, line 5 (see Instructions) . . . . . . . 2(c) | | |
| | (d) Other adjustments (attach schedule) . . . . . . . . . . . . . . . . . . 2(d) | | |
| 3 | Total additions (Add lines 2(a), 2(b), 2(c) and 2(d)). . . . . . . . . . . . . . . . . . . . | 3 | |
| 4 | Total of lines 1 and 3 . . . . . . . . . . . . . . . . . . . . . . . . . . . . . . . . . . . . | 4 | |
| 5 | Entire dividends as reported on federal return and included on page 1, line 8 . . . 5 | | |
| 6 | Interest on obligations of the United States included on page 1, line 8 . . . . . 6 | | |
| 7 | Net income from sources outside Hawaii received by a foreign or domestic corporation, except for unitary business taxpayers using Form N-30, Schedules O & P. . . . . . 7 | | |
| 8 | Amortization of casualty losses where election is made to amortize for Hawaii tax purposes under section 235-7(f), HRS (attach explanation) . . . . . . . . . . . 8 | | |
| 9 | Net operating loss deduction (under section 235-7(d), HRS) (attach schedule) . . . 9● | | |
| 10 | Other deductions or adjustments (attach schedule) . . . . . . . . . . . . . . 10 | | |
| 11 | Total subtractions (Add lines 5, 6, 7, 8, 9, and 10) . . . . . . . . . . . . . . . . . . ▶ | 11 | |
| 12 | Taxable income (loss) for Hawaii tax purposes (line 4 minus line 11) . . . . . . . . . . . . . . . . . . | 12● | 61,300 |
| 13 | Enter the amount of net capital gains as shown on Schedule D, line 18 (Schedules O & P taxpayers, see Instructions) . . . | 13● | 2,000 |
| 14 | Line 12 minus line 13 (if less than zero, enter zero) . . . . . . . . . . . . . . . . . . ▶ | 14 | 59,300 |
| 15 | (a) Tax on capital gain, line 13 — Enter 4% of amount on line 13 . . . . . . . . . . . . . | 15(a) | 80 |
| | (b) Tax on all other taxable income, line 14 — If the amount on line 14 is: | | |
| | (i) Not over $25,000 — Enter 4.4% of line 14 . . . . . . . . . . . . | 15(b)(i) | 0 |
| | (ii) Over $25,000 but not over $100,000 — Enter 5.4% of line 14 $ 3,202 | | |
| | Subtract $250.00 and enter difference. . . . . . . . . . . . . . . . . . . . . . . . | 15(b)(ii) | 2,952 |
| | (iii) Over $100,000 — Enter 6.4% of line 14 $_____ | | |
| | Subtract $1,250.00 and enter difference. . . . . . . . . . . . . . . . . . . . . . | 15(b)(iii) | 0 |
| | (c) Total of lines 15(a) and 15(b) . . . . . . . . . . . . . . . . . . . . . . . . . . . . . . | 15(c) | 3,032 |
| | (d) Using the rates listed on line 15(b), compute tax on all taxable income using amount from line 12 . . . . . | 15(d) | 3,060 |
| 16 | Total tax (enter the lesser of line 15(c) or 15(d)) (Combined unitary group filers, see Instructions) . . . . . . . | 16● | 3,032 |
| 17 | Recapture of Capital Goods Excise Tax Credit from Form N-312, Part II. . . . 17 | | |
| 18 | Recapture of Low-Income Housing Tax Credit from Form N-586, Part III . . . 18 | | |
| 19 | Recapture of Tax Credit for Flood Victims from Form N-338 . . . . . . . 19 | | |
| 20 | Recapture of Important Agricultural Land Qualified Agricultural Cost Tax Credit from Form N-344 . . 20 | | |
| 21 | Recapture of Capital Infrastructure Tax Credit from Form N-348, Part IV . . . 21 | | |
| 22 | Total recapture of tax credits (Add lines 17, 18, 19, 20, and 21) . . . . . . . . . | 22● | |
| 23 | Interest due under the look-back method — completed long-term contracts (See Instructions. Attach federal Form 8697) . . . | 23● | |
| 24 | Total tax (Add lines 16, 22, and 23). Enter here and on page 1, line 11 . . . . . . . . . . . . . . . . . . ▶ | 24 | 3,032 |

**FORM N-30**

N30_F 2017A 02

SCHEDULE O
FORM N-30
(REV. 2018)

STATE OF HAWAII — DEPARTMENT OF TAXATION

# ALLOCATION AND APPORTIONMENT OF INCOME

See separate instructions before completing this Schedule O.
**ATTACHMENT TO FORM N-30**

This schedule must be completed and filed with Hawaii Corporation Income Tax Return (Form N-30), by every corporation engaged in a business within and without Hawaii.

(a) Exact corporate title MAUI MANUFACTURING CORPORATION _____ Income year ended 12/31/18

(b) Federal Employer Identification Number (FEIN)  99-1234567 _____

(b) Business activities engaged in within and without Hawaii  MANUFACTURING AND SALE OF FURNITURE _____

(c) Business activities engaged in within Hawaii only  MANUFACTURING AND SALE OF FURNITURE _____

(d) Indicate location of business activities  SAN JOSE, CALIFORNIA, HAWAII _____

(e) Are the amounts shown on Schedule O, lines 12 through 17, 20, and 21 the same as those reported in returns or reports to other states under the Uniform Division of Income for Tax Purposes Act? ☐ YES ☐ NO If "NO," attach explanation. See Instructions.

**Item No.**

| | | | |
|---|---|---|---|
| 1. | Taxable income (or loss) before Hawaii adjustments as shown on Form N-30, Schedule J, line 1 | 1 | 90025 |

**State Adjustments**

**ADD:**

| | | | |
|---|---|---|---|
| 2. | Dividends from N-30, Schedule C, line 11 | 2 | 60 |
| 3. | Deductions allowable for federal tax purposes but not allowable or allowable only in part for Hawaii tax purposes (Attach schedule) | 3 | 0 |
| 4. | Deduction for charitable contributions included in line 1 | 4 | 0 |
| 5. | Other adjustments (Attach schedule) | 5 | 0 |
| 6. | Total (lines 2 to 5 inclusive) | 6 | 60 |

**DEDUCT:**

| | | | | | |
|---|---|---|---|---|---|
| 7. | Dividends received included on Form N-30, page 1, line 8 | 7 | 1100 | | |
| 8. | Interest on obligations of United States included on Form N-30, page 1, line 8 | 8 | 115 | | |
| 9. | Other deductions or adjustments (Attach schedule) | 9 | 0 | | |
| 10. | Total (lines 7 to 9, inclusive) | | | 10 ● | 1215 |
| 11. | Taxable income after Hawaii adjustments (line 1 plus line 6, minus line 10) | | | 11 | 88870 |

## Adjustments to Arrive at Unitary Business Income Subject to Tax

**DEDUCT:**

| | | | | | |
|---|---|---|---|---|---|
| 12. | Non-business or nonunitary dividends | 12 | 470 | | |
| 13. | Interest from nonunitary business (Attach schedule) | 13 | | | |
| 14. | Royalties from nonunitary business assets (Attach schedule) | 14 | | | |
| 15. | Net profit from nonunitary business (including rental property) operated on a separate accounting basis. | 15 | 2400 | | |
| 16. | Net gain from nonunitary business assets (Attach schedule). | 16 | 9500 | | |
| 17. | Other adjustments (Attach schedule). | 17 | 0 | | |
| 18. | Total (lines 12 to 17, inclusive) | | | 18 | 12370 |
| 19. | Balance (line 11 minus line 18). | | | 19 | 76500 |

**ADD:**

| | | | | | |
|---|---|---|---|---|---|
| 20. | Net loss from nonunitary business (including rental property) operated on a separate accounting basis. | 20 | | | |
| 21. | Net loss from nonunitary business assets (Attach schedule). | 21 | 0 | | |
| 22. | Total of lines 20 and 21. | | | 22 | 0 |
| 23. | Unitary business income from sources within and without Hawaii (line 19 plus line 22) | | | 23 ● | 76500 |
| 24. | Allocate  76.47710 % (from Schedule P, line 5), as income from unitary business attributable to Hawaii and subject to tax. (Multiply line 23 by the %) | | | 24 | 58505 |

**SCHEDULE O — FORM N-30 (REV. 2018)**                                                        **Page 2**

| Name | FEIN |
|---|---|
| MAUI MANUFACTURING CORPORATION | 99-1234567 |

### Classification of Unitary Business Income Subject to Tax

| | | | |
|---|---|---|---|
| 25. | Enter the portion of the amount on line 24 that is ordinary income. | 25 | 56505 |
| 26. | Enter the portion of the amount on line 24 that is net capital gain. Also, enter on Form N-30, Schedule J, line 13 ... | 26 | 2000 |
| 27. | Total (lines 25 and 26). This total must be equal to the amount on line 24. | 27 | 58505 |

### Income Wholly Attributable to Hawaii Subject to Tax

| | | | |
|---|---|---|---|
| 28. | Gain (or loss) from sale of real estate and other tangible assets not connected with the unitary business | 28 | |
| 29. | Royalties from property not used in the unitary business. | 29 | |
| 30. | Net profit (or loss) from business other than unitary (including rental property) within Hawaii | 30 | 2400 |
| 31. | Net gain from sale of assets not connected with unitary business, located in or having tax situs in Hawaii: | | |
| | (a) Net short-term capital gain — from Form N-30, Schedule D, line 17 | 31(a) | |
| | (b) Net capital gain attributable to Hawaii, from Form N-30, Schedule D, line 18, if any. (This amount, if any, also should be entered on Form N-30, Schedule J, line 13) | 31(b) | 2000 |
| | (c) Net gain (or loss) from sale or exchange of property other than capital assets — from Schedule D-1, line 19 | 31(c) | |
| 32. | Income from intangible personal property. Include entire income (or loss) of intangibles which, because of domicile of the corporation or business situs of intangibles, are located in Hawaii. Add back Hawaii allocated, non-business or nonunitary income and dividends. | | |
| | (a) Dividends included on line 12 (Attach schedule) | 32(a) | 470 |
| | (b) Interest | 32(b) | |
| | (c) All other income from intangibles (Attach schedule). | 32(c) | |
| 33. | Total income wholly attributable to Hawaii (lines 28 to 32c) | 33 | 4870 |
| 34. | Total of lines 27 and 33 | 34 | 63375 |
| 35. | Hawaii contribution deduction (total contributions included in line 1 multiplied by Hawaii allocation %, subject to 10% limitation. See Instructions.) | 35 | 0 |
| 36. | Net operating loss deduction (Attach schedule). | 36 ● | 2075 |
| 37. | Total of lines 35 and 36. | 37 | 2075 |
| 38. | Taxable income (or loss) for Hawaii tax purposes (line 34 minus line 37). Enter here and on Form N-30, Schedule J (page 2, line 12) | 38 | 61300 |

N30SCHO_T 2018A 02 VID88        ID NO 88

SCHEDULE P
FORM N-30
(REV. 2018)

STATE OF HAWAII — DEPARTMENT OF TAXATION

# APPORTIONMENT FORMULA

See separate instructions before completing this Schedule P.
ATTACHMENT TO FORM N-30

This schedule must be completed and filed with Hawaii Corporation Income Tax Return (Form N-30), by every corporation engaged in a business within and without Hawaii. Attach a worksheet showing the requested information for each member of a combined unitary group.

Exact corporate title MAUI MANUFACTURING CORPORATION                Income year ended 12/31/18

| | TOTAL WITHIN AND WITHOUT HAWAII (a) | | TOTAL WITHIN HAWAII (b) | | PERCENT WITHIN HAWAII* (b) ÷ (a) |
|---|---|---|---|---|---|
| | Beginning of taxable year | End of taxable year | Beginning of taxable year | End of taxable year | |
| **1. PROPERTY FACTOR: (use original cost)** | | | | | |
| Inventory | 184,000 | 184,000 | 83,000 | 83,000 | |
| Buildings | 66,180 | 66,180 | 66,180 | 66,180 | |
| Machinery and equipment | 30,830 | 30,830 | 29,000 | 29,000 | |
| Furniture and equipment | 19,690 | 19,690 | 11,000 | 11,000 | |
| Delivery equipment | 29,100 | 29,100 | 25,000 | 25,000 | |
| Land | 30,000 | 30,000 | 30,000 | 30,000 | |
| Leasehold interests (Net Annual Rent x 8) | | | | | |
| Rented properties (Net Annual Rent x 8) | | 0 | | 0 | |
| Leasehold improvements | 0 | 0 | 0 | 0 | |
| Other tangible assets (Attach schedule) | 0 | 0 | 0 | 0 | |
| **TOTAL PROPERTY VALUES (average value of property)** | 1(a) ● | 359,800 | 1(b) ● | 244,180 | 67.86548% |
| **2. PAYROLL FACTOR:** | | | | | |
| Wages, salaries, commissions and other compensation of employees included in: | | | | | |
| Cost of goods sold (Compensation only) | | 611,000 | | 611,000 | |
| Cost of operations (Compensation only) | | 0 | | 0 | |
| Compensations of officers | | 55,000 | | 55,000 | |
| Salesmen's salaries | | 35,000 | | | |
| Salesmen's commissions | | | | | |
| Other salaries and wages | | 0 | | 0 | |
| Repairs (Compensation only) | | | | | |
| Other deductions (Compensation only) | | | | | |
| **TOTAL PAYROLL VALUES** | 2(a) ● | 701,000 | 2(b) ● | 666,000 | 95.00713% |
| **3. SALES FACTOR:** | | | | | |
| Sales delivered or shipped to purchasers in Hawaii a. From outside Hawaii | | | | 812,016 | |
| b. From within Hawaii | | | | 0 | |
| Sales shipped from Hawaii to the U.S. Gov't | | | | 0 | |
| Sales delivered or shipped to purchasers outside Hawaii | | | | 0 | |
| **GROSS SALES, LESS RETURNS AND ALLOWANCES** | 3(a) ● | 1,220,000 | 3(b) ● | 812,016 | 66.55869% |

4. Total percent (sum of the percentages above) ..................................................... 229.43130%

5. Average percent (see Instructions). Enter here and on Schedule O, line 24 ....................................... 76.47710%

*Compute all percentages to 5 decimal places (.00000%)

SCHEDULE P

N30SCHP_T 2018A 01 VID88                ID NO 88

STATE OF HAWAII - DEPARTMENT OF TAXATION

**FORM**
**N-220**
(REV. 2018)

## Underpayment of Estimated Tax by Corporations
## and S Corporations

➤ Attach this form to your tax return   ➤ See separate Instructions

**2018**

| Name as shown on tax return | Federal Employer I.D. Number |
|---|---|
| MAUI MANUFACTURING CORPORATION | 99-1234567 |

**Part I** — Reasons For Filing—Check whichever box(es) applies. If none of the boxes apply to the corporation or S corporation, go on to Part II. File Form N-220 with Form N-30, Form N-35, or Form N-70NP.

a ☐ The corporation or S corporation is using the annualized income installment method.
b ☐ The corporation or S corporation is using the adjusted seasonal installment method.
c ☐ The corporation is a "large corporation" computing its first installment based on the prior year's tax.

**Part II    Figuring Your Underpayment**

| | | | | |
|---|---|---|---|---|
| 1 Total tax (see Instructions) | | | **1** | 3,032.00 |
| 2a Total credits. (see Instructions) (S Corporations, enter -0-) | **2a** | 0.00 | | |
| b Look-back interest included on line 1 for completed long-term contracts | **2b** | 0.00 | | |
| c Total. Add lines 2a and 2b | | | **2c** | 0.00 |
| 3 Line 1 minus line 2c. If the result is less than $500, **do not** complete or file this form. The corporation does not owe the penalty. | | | **3** | 3,032.00 |
| 4 Enter the tax shown on the corporation's 2017 income tax return. (**CAUTION:** *See Instructions before completing this line.*) | | | **4** | 2,122.00 |
| 5 Enter the **smaller** of line 3 or line 4. If the corporation must skip line 4, enter the amount from line 3 on line 5 | | | **5** | 2,122.00 |

| | | (a) | (b) | (c) | (d) |
|---|---|---|---|---|---|
| 6 **Installment due dates.** Enter in columns (a) through (d) the 20th day of the 4th, 6th, and 9th months of the corporation's tax year and the 20th day of the 1st month following the close of the tax year ➤ | **6** | 04/20/18 | 06/20/18 | 09/20/18 | 01/20/19 |
| 7 **Required installments.** If box a and/or b above is checked, enter the amounts from Schedule A, line 38. If box c (but not a or b) is checked, see page 2 of the instructions for the amounts to enter. If none of these boxes are checked, enter 25% of line 5 above in each column | **7** | 531.00 | 531.00 | 531.00 | 529.00 |
| 8 Estimated tax paid or credited for each period (see Instructions). For column (a) only, enter the amount from line 8 on line 12. | **8** | 625.00 | 625.00 | 625.00 | 625.00 |
| *Complete lines 9 through 15 of one column before going to the next column.* | | | | | |
| 9 Enter amount, if any, from line 15 of the preceding column | **9** | | 94.00 | 188.00 | 282.00 |
| 10 Add lines 8 and 9 | **10** | | 719.00 | 813.00 | 907.00 |
| 11 Add amounts on lines 13 and 14 of the preceding column | **11** | | 0.00 | 0.00 | 0.00 |
| 12 Line 10 minus line 11. If zero or less, enter -0-. For column (a) only, enter the amount from line 8 | **12** | 625.00 | 719.00 | 813.00 | 907.00 |
| 13 If the amount on line 12 is zero, subtract line 10 from line 11. Otherwise, enter -0-. | **13** | | 0.00 | 0.00 | |
| 14 **Underpayment.** If line 7 is equal to or more than line 12, subtract line 12 from line 7, then go to line 9 of the next column. Otherwise go to line 15. (see Instructions) | **14** | 0.00 | 0.00 | 0.00 | 0.00 |
| 15 **Overpayment.** If line 12 is more than line 7, subtract line 7 from line 12, then go to line 9 of the next column | **15** | 94.00 | 188.00 | 282.00 | 378.00 |

*Complete Part III on page 2 to figure the penalty. If there are no entries on line 14, no penalty is owed.*

Form N-220

N220_I 2018A 01 VID01                          ID NO 01

FORM N-220
(REV. 2018)
PAGE 2

| **Part III**  **Figuring the Penalty** | | (a) | (b) | (c) | (d) |
|---|---|---|---|---|---|
| 16 | Enter the amount of underpayment(s) from Part II, line 14 in the respective columns (a) through (d) .......................... **16** | 0.00 | 0.00 | 0.00 | 0.00 |
| 17 | Enter the estimated tax installment due dates used in Part II, line 6 in the respective columns (a) through (d) ........... **17** | 04/20/18 | 06/20/18 | 09/20/18 | 01/20/19 |
| 18 | Enter the date each estimated tax installment was paid or the 20th day of the fourth month following the close of the tax year, whichever is earlier for columns (a) through (d).. **18** | 04/20/19 | 04/20/19 | 04/20/19 | 04/20/19 |
| 19 | Enter the number of months from the date shown on line 17 to the date on line 18 for columns (a) through (d) (See instructions) ...................................................................... **19** | 12 | 10 | 7 | 3 |
| 20 | Multiply the following: Number of months on line 19  x  .00667 x underpayment on line 16 for columns (a) through (d)........... **20** | 0.00 | 0.00 | 0.00 | 0.00 |

21 **Underpayment penalty** — Add line 20, columns (a) through (d).  Enter the total here and on Form N-30, line 17; Form
N-35, line 24; or Form N-70NP, line 22........................................................................................................................  **21**   0.00

---

**Schedule A**  **Required Installments Using the Annualized Income Installment Method and/or the Adjusted Seasonal Installment Method Under IRC Section 6655(e)**

Form N-35 filers: *For lines 2, 12, 13, and 14 below, "taxable income" refers to excess net passive income or the amount on which tax is imposed under IRC section 1374(a) (or the corresponding provisions of prior law), whichever applies.*

| **Part I — Annualized Income Installment Method** | | (a) First _____ months | (b) First _____ months | (c) First _____ months | (d) First _____ months |
|---|---|---|---|---|---|
| 1 | Annualization period (see Instructions). **1** | | | | |
| 2 | Enter taxable income for each annualization period. **2** | | | | |
| 3 | Annualization amount (see Instructions). **3** | 4.00 | 2.40 | 1.50 | 1.09 |
| 4 | Annualized taxable income. Multiply line 2 by line 3. **4** | 0.00 | 0.00 | 0.00 | 0.00 |
| 5 | Figure the tax on the net capital gains and ordinary income in each column on line 4 by following the instructions for Form N-30, Schedule J, lines 13 thru 16; Form N-35, lines 22a and 22b; or Form N-70NP, Part I or Part II. **5** | | | | |
| 6 | Enter other taxes for each payment period (see Instructions). **6** | | | | |
| 7 | Total tax. Add lines 5 and 6. **7** | 0.00 | 0.00 | 0.00 | 0.00 |
| 8 | For each period, enter the same type of credits as allowed for Form N-220, line 2a (see Instructions). **8** | 0.00 | 0.00 | 0.00 | 0.00 |
| 9 | Total tax after credits. Line 7 minus line 8. If zero or less, enter -0-. **9** | 0.00 | 0.00 | 0.00 | 0.00 |
| 10 | Applicable percentage. **10** | 25% | 50% | 75% | 100% |
| 11 | Multiply line 9 by line 10. **11** | 0.00 | 0.00 | 0.00 | 0.00 |

Form N-220

FORM N-220
(REV. 2018)
PAGE 3

**Schedule A**

**Part II — Adjusted Seasonal Installment Method (Caution:** *Use this method only if the base period percentage for any 6 consecutive months is at least 70%. See the Instructions for more information.***)**

| | | (a) First 3 months | (b) First 5 months | (c) First 8 months | (d) First 11 months |
|---|---|---|---|---|---|
| **12** Enter the taxable income for the following periods: | | | | | |
| **a** Tax year beginning in 2015 | **12a** | | | | |
| **b** Tax year beginning in 2016 | **12b** | | | | |
| **c** Tax year beginning in 2017 | **12c** | | | | |
| **13** Enter taxable income for each period for the tax year beginning in 2018. | **13** | | | | |

| | | (a) First 4 months | (b) First 6 months | (c) First 9 months | (d) Entire year |
|---|---|---|---|---|---|
| **14** Enter the taxable income for the following periods: | | | | | |
| **a** Tax year beginning in 2015 | **14a** | | | | |
| **b** Tax year beginning in 2016 | **14b** | | | | |
| **c** Tax year beginning in 2017 | **14c** | | | | |
| **15** Divide the amount in each column on line 12a by the amount in column (d) on line 14a. | **15** | | | | |
| **16** Divide the amount in each column on line 12b by the amount in column (d) on line 14b. | **16** | | | | |
| **17** Divide the amount in each column on line 12c by the amount in column (d) on line 14c. | **17** | | | | |
| **18** Add lines 15 through 17. | **18** | | | | |
| **19** Divide line 18 by 3. | **19** | | | | |
| **20** Divide line 13 by line 19. | **20** | | | | |
| **21** Figure the tax on line 20 following the instructions for Form N-30, Schedule J, lines 13 thru 16; Form N-35, lines 22a and 22b; or Form N-70NP, Part I or Part II. | **21** | | | | |
| **22** Divide the amount in columns (a) through (c) on line 14a by the amount in column (d) on line 14a. | **22** | | | | |
| **23** Divide the amount in columns (a) through (c) on line 14b by the amount in column (d) on line 14b. | **23** | | | | |
| **24** Divide the amount in columns (a) through (c) on line 14c by the amount in column (d) on line 14c. | **24** | | | | |
| **25** Add lines 22 through 24. | **25** | | | | |
| **26** Divide line 25 by 3. | **26** | | | | |
| **27** Multiply the amount in columns (a) through (c) of line 21 by the amount in the corresponding column of line 26. In column (d), enter the amount from line 21, column (d). | **27** | | | | |

*(Continued on page 4)*

Form N-220

**FORM N-220**
**(REV. 2018)**
**PAGE 4**

| Schedule A |
|---|

**Part II — Continued**

| | | (a) | (b) | (c) | (d) |
|---|---|---|---|---|---|
| | | First 4 months | First 6 months | First 9 months | Entire year |
| 28 | Enter other taxes for each payment period (see Instructions). | 28 | | | | |
| 29 | Total tax. Add lines 27 and 28. | 29 | | | | |
| 30 | For each period, enter the same type of credits as allowed for Form N-220, line 2a (see Instructions). | 30 | | | | |
| 31 | Total tax after credits. Line 29 minus line 30. If zero or less, enter -0-. | 31 | | | | |

**Part III — Required Installments**

| | Note: *Complete lines 32 through 38 of one column before completing the next column.* | | 1st installment | 2nd installment | 3rd installment | 4th installment |
|---|---|---|---|---|---|---|
| 32 | If only one of the above parts is completed, enter the amount in each column from line 11 or line 31. If both parts are completed, enter the **smaller** of the amounts in each column from line 11 or line 31. | 32 | 0.00 | 0.00 | 0.00 | 0.00 |
| 33 | Add the amounts in all preceding columns of line 38 (see instructions) | 33 | | 0.00 | 0.00 | 0.00 |
| 34 | Line 32 minus line 33. If zero or less, enter -0-. | 34 | 0.00 | 0.00 | 0.00 | 0.00 |
| 35 | Divide line 5, page 1 of Form N-220, by 4 and enter the result in each column. (**Note:** *"Large corporations" see the instructions for line 7 for the amount to enter.*) | 35 | 531.00 | 531.00 | 531.00 | 529.00 |
| 36 | Subtract line 38 of the preceding column from line 37 of the preceding column. | 36 | | 531.00 | 1,062.00 | 1,593.00 |
| 37 | Add lines 35 and 36. | 37 | 531.00 | 1,062.00 | 1,593.00 | 2,122.00 |
| 38 | **Required installments.** Enter the smaller of line 34 or line 37 here and on page 1 of Form N-220, line 7. | 38 | 0.00 | 0.00 | 0.00 | 0.00 |

Form N-220

## PROBLEM FOR SPECIMEN RETURN
## SMALL BUSINESS CORPORATION RETURN OF INCOME

### Form N-35

George Onishi, Bruce Kosaka and Jack Armstrong have been operating a supermarket in Honolulu since January 1. Each owns one-third of the outstanding stock of Surfers Supermarket, Ltd. On January 15, the three stockholders filed an election to be taxed as a Small Business Corporation for the year ending December 31, for both federal and Hawaii purposes.

In addition to salaries of $9,000 apiece, each shareholder received a distribution of $1,000 during the year. Insurance premiums of $250 each were paid on the life of each officer by the corporation. The corporation is the beneficiary of these policies. The information for the various schedules on the return was taken directly from the corporation's books.

**FORM**
**N-35**
(REV. 2018)

STATE OF HAWAII—DEPARTMENT OF TAXATION

## S CORPORATION INCOME TAX RETURN

For calendar year 2018

or other tax year beginning ● _____ , 2018

and ending ● _____ , 20 _____

THIS SPACE FOR DATE RECEIVED STAMP

☐ AMENDED Return (Attach Sch AMD)

| | | | |
|---|---|---|---|

**PRINT OR TYPE**

Name
**SURFER'S SUPERMARKET, LTD.**

Dba or C/O

Mailing Address (number and street)
**4990 BEACH BOULEVARD**

City or town, State, and Postal/ZIP Code. If foreign address, see Instructions.
**HONOLULU, HI 96000**

● Federal Employer I.D. No.
**12-3456789**

● Business Activity Code (Use code shown on federal Form 1120S)

● Hawaii Tax I.D. No.
**GE-001-234-5678-01**

Enter the number of Schedules NS
attached to this return ●

Is the corporation electing to be an S corporation beginning with this tax year? . . . . . . . . . . . . . . . . . . . . . . . . . . . . . . . ☐ Yes ☒ No

Check if: (1) ☐ Initial Return (2) ☐ Final Return (3) ☐ S Election Termination or Revocation (4) ☐ Name Change (5) ☐ Change of Address (6) ☐ IRS Adjustment

How many months in 2018 was this corporation in operation? _____ Was this corporation in operation at the end of 2018? . ☒ Yes ☐ No

CAUTION: Include only trade or business income and expenses on lines 1a through 20. See Instructions for more information.

**INCOME**

| | | | | |
|---|---|---|---|---|
| 1 | a Gross receipts or sales (see Instructions) . . . . . . . . . . . . . . | 1a● | 2240000 | |
| | b Returns and allowances . . . . . . . . . . . . . . . . . . | 1b● | 0 | |
| | c Line 1a minus line 1b . . . . . . . . . . . . . . . . . . . . . . . | 1c● | | 2240000 |
| 2 | Cost of goods sold (Schedule A, line 8) . . . . . . . . . . . . . . . . . . . | 2● | | 1765000 |
| 3 | Gross profit (line 1c minus line 2) . . . . . . . . . . . . . . . . . . . . . . | 3● | | 475000 |
| 4 | Net gain or (loss) from Schedule D-1, Part II, line 19 (attach Schedule D-1) . . | 4● | | 0 |
| 5 | Other income (see Instructions) (attach schedule) . . . . . . . . . . . | 5● | | 31000 |
| 6 | TOTAL income (loss) — Add lines 3 through 5 and enter here . . . . . . ▶ | 6● | | 506000 |

**DEDUCTIONS**

| | | | |
|---|---|---|---|
| 7 | Compensation of officers . . . . . . . . . . . . . . . . . . . . . . . . . | 7 | 27000 |
| 8 | Salaries and wages (less employment credit) . . . . . . . . . . . . . . . . | 8 | 253000 |
| 9 | Repairs and maintenance . . . . . . . . . . . . . . . . . . . . . . . . . | 9 | 3200 |
| 10 | Bad debts (see Instructions) . . . . . . . . . . . . . . . . . . . . . . . . | 10 | 0 |
| 11 | Rents . . . . . . . . . . . . . . . . . . . . . . . . . . . . . . . . . . . | 11 | 26600 |
| 12 | Taxes and licenses (attach schedule) . . . . . . . . . . . . . . . . . . . . | 12 | 25300 |
| 13 | Interest . . . . . . . . . . . . . . . . . . . . . . . . . . . . . . . . . . | 13 | 9800 |
| 14 | Depreciation from federal Form 4562 not claimed elsewhere on return (see Instructions) . . . . . . . . . . . | 14 | 32540 |
| 15 | Depletion (Do not deduct oil and gas depletion. See Instructions) . . . . . | 15 | 0 |
| 16 | Advertising . . . . . . . . . . . . . . . . . . . . . . . . . . . . . . . . | 16 | 20900 |
| 17 | Pension, profit-sharing, etc. plans . . . . . . . . . . . . . . . . . . . . . | 17 | |
| 18 | Employee benefit programs . . . . . . . . . . . . . . . . . . . . . . . . | 18 | 16100 |
| 19 | Other deductions (attach schedule) . . . . . . . . . . . . . . . . . . . . | 19 | 77700 |
| 20 | TOTAL deductions — Add lines 7 through 19 and enter here . . . . . . ▶ | 20● | 492140 |
| 21 | Ordinary income (loss) from trade or business activities — line 6 minus line 20 (To Sch. K, line 1) . . . . . . | 21● | 13860 |

**DECLARATION:** I declare, under the penalties set forth in section 231-36, HRS, that this return (including any accompanying schedules or statements) has been examined by me and, to the best of my knowledge and belief, is true, correct, and complete, made in good faith, for the taxable year stated, pursuant to the Hawaii Income Tax Law, Chapter 235, HRS. Declaration of preparer (other than taxpayer) is based on all information of which preparer has any knowledge.

**Please Sign Here**

▶ ● _____ _____ _____
Signature of officer / Date / Type or print name and title of officer

* May the Hawaii Department of Taxation discuss this return with the preparer shown below? . . . . . . . . . . . ☒ Yes ☐ No
(See page 3 of the Instructions) This designation does not replace Form N-848, Power of Attorney.

**Paid Preparer's Information**

| | | | |
|---|---|---|---|
| Preparer's Signature ▶ | | Date | Check if self-employed ☐ | Preparer's identification no. ● P00000000 |
| Print Preparer's Name **HOMER JONES** | | | |
| Firm's name (or yours if self-employed) ▶ **KMH LLP, 1003 BISHOP ST #2400** | Federal E.I. No. ▶ **42-1539623** | |
| Address and Postal/ZIP Code **HONOLULU, HI 96813** | Phone no. ▶ **(808)526-2255** | |

**FORM N-35**

N35_T 2018A 01 VID88

ID NO 88

*Not Approved for Paper Filing* (watermark)

FORM N-35 (REV. 2018)                                                                          **Page 2**

| Name as shown on return | Federal Employer Identification Number |
|---|---|
| SURFER'S SUPERMARKET, LTD. | 12-3456789 |

**TAX & PAYMENTS**

| | | | |
|---|---|---|---|
| 22 | **a** Excess net passive income tax (attach schedule(s)) . . . . . . . . . . . . | 22a● | 0 |
| | **b** Tax from Schedule D (Form N-35), line 21 . . . . . . . . . . . . . . | 22b● | 0 |
| | **c** Number of N-4's attached ● _____ Taxes withheld on attached N-4's | 22c● | |
| | **d** LIFO recapture tax . . . . . . . . . . . . . . . . . . . . . | 22d● | |
| | **e** Interest due under look-back method . . . . . . . . . . . . . . . | 22e● | |
| | **f** Add lines 22a, 22b, 22c, 22d, and 22e . . . . . . . . . . . . . . | 22f ● | 0 |
| 23 | **a** 2017 overpayment allowed as a credit . . . . . . . . . . . . . . | 23a● | 0 |
| | **b** 2018 estimated tax payments from N-3s _____ 0 and N-288s _____ | 23b● | 0 |
| | **c** Payments with extension . . . . . . . . . . . . . . . . . . . . | 23c● | 0 |
| | **d** Add lines 23a, 23b, and 23c . . . . . . . . . . . . . . . . . . | 23d● | 0 |
| 24 | Underpayment of estimated tax penalty. (see Instructions) Check if Form N-220 is attached . . . ➤ ☐ | 24 ● | 0 |
| 25 | OVERPAYMENT (If line 23d is larger than the total of lines 22f and 24), enter AMOUNT OVERPAID . . . | 25 ● | 0 |
| 26 | Enter amount of line 25 you want **Credited to 2019 estimated tax** ➤ 26a $● 0 Refunded ➤ | 26b● | 0 |
| 27 | TAX DUE (If the total of lines 22f and 24 is larger than line 23d) enter the amount due . . . | 27 ● | 0 |
| 28 | **AMOUNT OF PAYMENT** (see Instructions) . . . . . . . . . . . . . . . . | 28 ● | 0 |

**AMENDED RETURN**

| | | | |
|---|---|---|---|
| 29 | Amount paid (overpaid) on original return — **AMENDED RETURN ONLY** . . . . . . . . . | 29 | |
| 30 | **BALANCE DUE (REFUND)** with amended return (See Instructions) . . . . . . . . . . . . | 30 | |

**Schedule A    Cost of Goods Sold (See Instructions for Schedule A)**

| | | | |
|---|---|---|---|
| 1 | Inventory at beginning of year . . . . . . . . . . . . . . . . . . . . . . | 1 | 1815000 |
| 2 | Purchases . . . . . . . . . . . . . . . . . . . . . . . . . . . . | 2 | 0 |
| 3 | Cost of labor . . . . . . . . . . . . . . . . . . . . . . . . . . | 3 | 0 |
| 4 | Additional IRC section 263A costs (see federal Instructions and attach a schedule) . . . . . . | 4 | 0 |
| 5 | Other costs (attach schedule) . . . . . . . . . . . . . . . . . . . . . | 5 | 0 |
| 6 | Total—Add lines 1 through 5 . . . . . . . . . . . . . . . . . . . . ➤ | 6 | 1815000 |
| 7 | Inventory at end of year . . . . . . . . . . . . . . . . . . . . . . | 7 | 50000 |
| 8 | Cost of goods sold—Line 6 minus line 7. (Enter here and on page 1, line 2) . . . . . . . ➤ | 8 | 1765000 |

9 **a** Check all methods used for valuing closing inventory:

    **(i)** ☐ Cost as described in Treasury Regulations section 1.471-3.

    **(ii)** ☐ Lower of cost or market as described in Treasury Regulations section 1.471-4 (see Instructions)

    **(iii)** ☐ Other (specify method used and attach explanation) ➤

  **b** Check if there was a writedown of subnormal goods as described in Treasury Regulations section 1.471-2(c) . . . . . . . . . . . ☐

  **c** Check if the LIFO inventory method was adopted this tax year for any goods (if checked, attach federal Form 970) . . . . . . . . ☐

  **d** If the LIFO inventory method was used for this tax year, enter percentage (or amounts) of

    closing inventory computed under LIFO . . . . . . . . . . . . . . . . . . **9d** | 0

  **e** Do the rules of section 263A (with respect to property produced or acquired for resale) apply to the corporation? . . . . . ☐ Yes ☒ No

  **f** Was there any change in determining quantities, cost or valuations between opening and closing inventory? . . . . . . . ☐ Yes ☒ No

    If "Yes," attach explanation.

**Schedule B    Other Information**

1 Check method of accounting: **a** ☐ Cash  **b** ☒ Accrual  **c** ☐ Other (specify) ➤

2 **a** Date of incorporation _1/1/1995_  **b** Date business began in Hawaii _1/1/1995_

  **c** Under laws of _HAWAII_  **d** Date of federal election as an S corporation _1/15/1995_

3 Refer to the listing of Business Activity Codes at the end of the federal Instructions for Form 1120S and state your principal:
Business Activity ➤ _____ ; Product or service ➤ _____

4 Did the corporation at the end of the tax year own, directly or indirectly, 50% or more of the voting stock of a domestic
corporation? (For rules of attribution, see IRC section 267(c).) If "Yes" attach a schedule showing: (a) name, address
and employer identification number (b) percentage owned, and (c) if 100% owned, was QSSS election made? . . . . . . . ☐ Yes ☒ No

5 Enter the number of shareholders in the corporation at the end of the tax year who are:
residents of Hawaii _____ nonresidents of Hawaii _____

6 Did the corporation derive income from sources outside Hawaii which is not includable in the Hawaii return? . . . . . . . ☐ Yes ☒ No

7 If the corporation: (1) was a C corporation before it elected to be an S corporation or the corporation acquired an asset with a basis
determined by reference to its basis (or the basis of any other property) in the hands of a C corporation, and (2) has net unrealized built-in
gain (defined by IRC section 1374(d)(1)) in excess of the net recognized built-in gain from prior years, enter the net unrealized built-in
gain reduced by net recognized built-in gain from prior years . . . . . . . . $ _____

N35_T 2018A 02 VID88                              ID NO 88                                    **FORM N-35**

**FORM N-35 (REV. 2018)**                                                                 **Page 3**

| Name as shown on return | Federal Employer Identification Number |
|---|---|
| SURFER'S SUPERMARKET, LTD. | 12-3456789 |

| Schedule K | Shareholders' Pro Rata Share Items | b. Attributable to Hawaii | | | c. Attributable Elsewhere |
|---|---|---|---|---|---|
| **Income (Losses)** | 1 Ordinary income (loss) from trade or business activities (page 1, line 21) | 13860 | 1 | | 0 |
| | 2 Net income (loss) from rental real estate activities (attach federal Form 8825) | 0 | 2 | | 0 |
| | 3 a Gross income from other rental activities | 0 | 3a | | 0 |
| | b Expenses from other rental activities (attach schedule) | 0 | 3b | | 0 |
| | c Net income (loss) from other rental activities. Line 3a minus line 3b | 0 | 3c | | 0 |
| | 4 Interest income | 300 | 4 | | 0 |
| | 5 Ordinary dividends | 0 | 5 | | 0 |
| | 6 Royalty income | 0 | 6 | | 0 |
| | 7 Net short-term capital gain (loss) (Schedule D (Form N-35)) | 0 | 7 | | 0 |
| | 8 Net long-term capital gain (loss) (Schedule D (Form N-35)) | 0 | 8 | | 0 |
| | 9 Net gain (loss) under IRC section 1231 (attach Schedule D-1) | 0 | 9 | | 0 |
| | 10 Other income (loss) (attach schedule) | 0 | 10 | | |
| **Deductions** | 11 Charitable contributions (attach schedule) | 1200 | 11 | | |
| | 12 IRC section 179 expense deduction (attach federal Form 4562) | 10000 | 12 | | |
| | 13 Deductions related to portfolio income (loss) (attach schedule) | 0 | 13 | | 0 |
| | 14 Other deductions (attach schedule) | 0 | 14 | | 0 |
| **Investment Interest** | 15 a Interest expense on investment debts paid or accrued in 2018 | 0 | 15a | | 0 |
| | b (1) Investment income included on lines 4, 5, and 6, above | 300 | 15b(1) | | |
| | (2) Investment expenses included on line 13, above | 0 | 15b(2) | | 0 |
| **Credits** | 16 a Fuel Tax Credit for Commercial Fishers (attach Form N-163) | 0 | 16a | | |
| | b Total cost of property qualifying for the Capital Goods Excise Tax Credit (See Instructions) | 122500 | 16b | | |
| | c Amounts needed to claim the Enterprise Zone Tax Credit (attach Form N-756) | See Instructions | 16c | | |
| | d Hawaii Low-Income Housing Tax Credit (attach Form N-586) | | 16d | | |
| | e Credit for Employment of Vocational Rehabilitation Referrals (attach Form N-884) | 0 | 16e | | |
| | f Motion Picture, Digital Media, and Film Production Income Tax Credit (attach Form N-340) | | 16f | | |
| | g Credit for School Repair and Maintenance (attach Form N-330) | | 16g | | |
| | h Renewable Energy Technologies Income Tax Credit (attach Form N-342) | 0 | 16h | | |
| | i Important Agricultural Land Qualified Agricultural Cost Tax Credit (attach Form N-344) | | 16i | | |
| | j Tax Credit for Research Activities (attach Form N-346) | 0 | 16j | | |
| | k Capital Infrastructure Tax Credit (attach Form N-348) | | 16k● | | |
| | l Cesspool Upgrade, Conversion or Connection Income Tax Credit (attach Form N-350) | | 16l | | |
| | m Renewable Fuels Production Tax Credit (attach Form N-352) | | 16m | | |
| | n Organic Foods Production Tax Credit (attach Form N-354) | | 16n | | |
| | o Hawaii income tax withheld on Forms N-288 (See Instructions) | 0 | 16o | | |
| | p Total Hawaii income tax withheld on Forms N-4 | | 16p | | |
| | q Net income tax paid by the S corporation to states which do not recognize the corporation's "S" status. Identify state(s) | | 16q | | |
| **Other Items** | (Attach a separate schedule if more space is needed for any item.) | | | | |
| | 17 Total property distributions (including cash) other than dividend distributions reported on line 22, below. Date of Distribution _____6/1/2018_____ | 3000 | 17 | | |
| | 18 Tax exempt interest income | 0 | 18 | | 0 |
| | 19 Other tax exempt income | 0 | 19 | | 0 |
| | 20 Non-deductible expenses | 750 | 20 | | |
| | 21 Other items and amounts not included on lines 1 through 20, above, that are required to be reported separately to shareholders (attach schedule) | | 21 | | |
| | 22 Total dividend distributions paid from accumulated earnings and profits | 0 | 22 | | 0 |
| | 23 Income (loss) — Combine lines 1 through 10. From the result, subtract the sum of lines 11 through 15a | 2960 | 23 | | 0 |
| | 24 Corporate adjustments to income attributable to Hawaii (attach schedule) | | 24 | | |
| | 25 Interest penalty on early withdrawal of savings | | 25 | | |

**FORM N-35**

N35_T 2018A 03 VID88                          ID NO 88

**FORM N-35 (REV. 2018)**          **Page 4**

| Name as shown on return | Federal Employer Identification Number |
|---|---|
| SURFER'S SUPERMARKET, LTD. | 12-3456789 |

**Schedules L, M-1, and M-2**    Attach a copy of page 4 of federal Form 1120S to this return. Attach Sch. M-3, if applicable.

**Schedule N**    List of Shareholders (Attach a separate sheet if more space is needed)

| | Name and Address | SSN or FEIN | No. of shares owned at all times during the year | State of Residence | Year Sch. NS filed, if any (Indicate if revoked) | Amount of Payment on Form N-4 attached |
|---|---|---|---|---|---|---|
| 1 | GEORGE ONISHI<br>333 FLORAL DRIVE<br>HONOLULU, HI 96100 | 575123456 | 330 | HI | | |
| 2 | BRUCE KOSAKA<br>4343 DESMOND ROAD<br>HONOLULU, HI 96000 | 575987654 | 330 | HI | | |
| 3 | JACK ARMSTRONG<br>98-423 HURLEY PLACE<br>HONOLULU, HI 96000 | 576454545 | 330 | HI | | |

**Schedule O**    Apportionment of Income (See Attributable to Hawaii in the Instructions.)

| | | |
|---|---|---|
| 1 | Ordinary income (loss) from trade or business activities (From page 1, line 21) . . . . . . . . . . . . . | 13860 |
| 2 | Apportionment factor (from Schedule P, line 8) . . . . . . . . . . . . . . . . . . . . . . . | % |
| 3 | Business income apportioned to Hawaii (line 1 multiplied by line 2) (To Schedule K, line 1, col. b) . . . . . . | |
| 4 | Business income apportioned elsewhere (line 1 minus line 3). (To Schedule K, line 1, col. c) . . . . . . . . | 13860 |
| 5 | Are the totals of columns b and c, Schedule K, lines 2 through 6, and the amounts shown on Schedule P, column B, the same as those reported in returns or reports to other states under the Uniform Division of Income for Tax Purposes Act? . . . . . . . ☐ Yes ☐ No<br>If "No", please explain | |

**Schedule P**    Computation of Apportionment Factors (See Attributable to Hawaii in the Instructions.)

| Property — (use original cost) | In Hawaii | | Total Everywhere | |
|---|---|---|---|---|
| | Beginning of taxable year | End of taxable year | Beginning of taxable year | End of taxable year |
| Land | 0 | 0 | 0 | 0 |
| Buildings | 0 | 0 | 0 | 0 |
| Inventories | 0 | 0 | 0 | 0 |
| Leasehold interests* | | | | |
| Rented Property* | | 0 | | 0 |
| Other Property | 0 | 0 | 0 | 0 |
| Total | 0 | 0 | 0 | 0 |

* Enter net annual rent X 8.

Compute all percentages to 5 decimal places (0.00000%)

| | | A. In Hawaii | B. Everywhere | |
|---|---|---|---|---|
| 1 | Property values (average value of property above) . . . . . . . . . . . . . . | 0 | 0 | |
| 2 | Property factor (line 1, col. A divided by line 1, col. B) . . . . . . . . . . . | | | % |
| 3 | Total compensation . . . . . . . . . . . . . . . . . . . . . | 0 | 0 | |
| 4 | Payroll factor (line 3, col. A divided by line 3, col. B) . . . . . . . . . . . | | | % |
| 5 | Total sales . . . . . . . . . . . . . . . . . . . . . . . . | 0 | 0 | |
| 6 | Sales factor (line 5, col. A divided by line 5, col. B) . . . . . . . . . . . . | | | % |
| 7 | Total of factors (add lines 2, 4, and 6) . . . . . . . . . . . . . . . . . . | | | % |
| 8 | Average of factors (see instructions) (To Schedule O, line 2) . . . . . . . . . . . . . . . . | | | % |

**Designation of Tax Matters Person (See Instructions.)**

Enter below the shareholder designated as the tax matters person (TMP) for the tax year of this return, if one has been designated:

| Name of designated TMP | ▸ GEORGE ONISHI | Identifying number of TMP | ▸ 575-12-3456 |
|---|---|---|---|
| Address of designated TMP | ▸ 333 FLORAL DRIVE<br>HONOLULU, HI 96000 | | |

**FORM N-35**

STATE OF HAWAII—DEPARTMENT OF TAXATION

**FORM**
**N-312**
(REV. 2018)

# CAPITAL GOODS
# EXCISE TAX CREDIT
### SEE SEPARATE INSTRUCTIONS BEFORE COMPLETING THIS FORM.

**2018**

Or fiscal year beginning _____ , 2018, and ending _____ , 20 _____

| | |
|---|---|
| ATTACH THIS SCHEDULE TO FORM F-1, N-11, N-15, N-20, N-30, N-35, N-40, OR N-70NP | SSN OR FEIN  12-3456789 |
| Name  SURFER'S SUPERMARKET, LTD. | Hawaii Tax Identification Number  001234567801 |

**CAUTION:** The deadline to claim the credit, including amended claims, is 12 months after the close of your taxable year. An extension of time for filing a return does not extend the time for claiming the credit. The taxpayer shall treat the amount of the credit allowable and claimed as a taxable income item for the taxable year in which it is properly recognized under the method of accounting used to compute taxable income. Alternatively, the basis of eligible property for depreciation purposes for State income taxes shall be reduced by the amount of the credit allowable and claimed. **No credit may be claimed for property for which the Motion Picture, Digital Media, and Film Production Income Tax Credit is claimed. In addition, no credit may be claimed for any cost that is used to claim the Renewable Energy Technologies Income Tax Credit.**

**PART I    COMPUTATION OF TAX CREDIT**

| (a) Description of Property — Attach a separate sheet if more space is needed | (b) Date property was placed in service | (c) Cost of qualifying property |
|---|---|---|
| **1.** Hawaii purchases | | |
| EQUIPMENT | 4/1/2018 | 6,000 |
| VARIOUS OFFICE EQUIPMENT | 1/1/2018 | 50,000 |
| STORE EQUIPMENT | 1/15/2018 | 66,500 |
| | | |
| | | |
| | | |
| **2a.** Purchases from out-of-state sellers | | |
| | | |
| | | |
| | | |

**2b.** Was 4% Use Tax paid on these purchases?     Yes ☐     No ☐     Some ☐

| | | |
|---|---|---|
| **3.** Total qualifying cost of eligible property. Add amounts in column (c), lines 1 and 2. (Estates, trusts, and cooperatives, see Instructions) ............................................................................ | **3** | 122,500 |
| **4.** Tax credit percentage. ................................................................................................................ | **4** | 4% |
| **5.** Multiply line 3 by line 4 and enter result here ........................................................................ | **5** | 4,900 |
| **6.** Amount of sales or use taxes paid to another state or jurisdiction for which a credit was claimed under section 238-3(i), Hawaii Revised Statutes. (see Instructions) ............................................ | **6** | |
| **7.** Capital Goods Excise Tax Credit — Line 5 minus line 6. Enter difference (> zero) rounded to the nearest dollar for individual taxpayers and enter on Form F-1, Schedule I, line 1 or Schedule CR, line 20 .................... | **7** | 4,900 |

| | Yes | No |
|---|---|---|
| A. Was a deduction taken under Internal Revenue Code Section 179 (regarding an election to expense certain depreciable business assets) on any property listed on lines 1 or 2a? | | X |
| B. Was any property listed on lines 1 or 2a acquired from a related company or person? | | X |
| C. Is any property listed on lines 1 or 2a subject to the limitation on capital goods excise tax credit and the depreciation deduction under Internal Revenue Code Section 280F? | | X |
| D. Is any property listed on lines 1 or 2a an integral part of a building or structure? | | X |
| E. Does any of the property listed on lines 1 or 2a have a useful life of less than 3 years? | | X |

If you answered "Yes" to any question above, please attach an explanation as to how the qualifying basis was determined and identify the property involved on lines 1 or 2a, Part I using the applicable letter(s) for the description above.

N312_T 2018A 01 VID88

ID NO 88

**FORM N-312**

FORM N-312     SURFER'S SUPERMARKET, LTD.                                    12-3456789
(REV. 2018)                                                                          PAGE 2

## PART II — RECAPTURE OF CAPITAL GOODS EXCISE TAX CREDIT

| Name(s) as shown on return or of individual or entity for whom this statement is being prepared. | FEIN or SSN |
|---|---|

| Name of pass-through entity. | FEIN or SSN |
|---|---|

| Properties | Description of property. (Attach a separate sheet if more space is needed.) |
|---|---|
| A | |
| B | |
| C | |
| D | |
| E | |

### RECAPTURE COMPUTATION:
(See Specific Instructions)

| | | A | B | C | D | E |
|---|---|---|---|---|---|---|
| 1. Original rate of credit (4%). | 1 | 4% | 4% | 4% | 4% | 4% |
| 2. Date recapture period begins (see Instructions). | 2 | | | | | |
| 3. Date property ceased to be eligible capital goods excise tax credit property. (see Instructions) | 3 | | | | | |
| 4. Number of full years between the date on line 2 and the date on line 3. | 4 | 0 | 0 | 0 | 0 | 0 |
| 5. Original apportioned cost of qualifying property. Use this amount on line a of the worksheet in the Instructions for Part II, line 9 of Form N-312. | 5 | | | | | |
| 6. Original apportioned amount of the deduction allowed under IRC section 179. Use this amount on line d of the worksheet for Part II, line 9 of Form N-312. | 6 | | | | | |
| 7. Original apportioned sales or use tax credit claimed under section 238-3(i), HRS. Use this amount on line h of the worksheet for Part II, line 9 of Form N-312 | 7 | | | | | |
| 8. Original or previously recomputed credit claimed. (see Instructions) | 8 | | | | | |
| 9. Recomputed credit. (see Instructions) | 9 | 0 | 0 | 0 | 0 | 0 |
| 10. Decrease in credit due to disposition. (Line 8 minus line 9.) | 10 | 0 | 0 | 0 | 0 | 0 |
| 11. Recapture percentage. (from Instructions) | 11 | 100% | 100% | 100% | 100% | 100% |
| 12. Recapture tax. (Line 10 multiplied by line 11.) | 12 | 0 | 0 | 0 | 0 | 0 |
| 13. Total increase in tax. (Add line 12 columns A through E.) Round this amount to the nearest dollar and enter on the appropriate form listed below. | 13 | | | | | 0 |

Enter or include the amount on line 13 above on Form F-1, line 64; Form N-11, line 27; Form N-15, line 44; Form N-30, Schedule J, line 17; Form N-40, Schedule G, line 1; or Form N-70NP, line 11.

ID NO 88

SCHEDULE K-1 | STATE OF HAWAII — DEPARTMENT OF TAXATION
FORM N-35
(REV. 2018)

# SHAREHOLDER'S SHARE OF INCOME, CREDITS, DEDUCTIONS, ETC. **2018**

For calendar year 2018 or tax year
beginning _____, 2018 and ending _____, 20 _____

(NOTE: Prepare in triplicate. (1) File with N-35. (2) For S corp. (3) For shareholder.)

| Shareholder's identifying number ➤ 575-12-3456 | Corporation's Federal identifying number (FEIN) ➤ 12-3456789 |
|---|---|
| Shareholder's name, mailing address, and Postal/ZIP code | Corporation's name, mailing address, and Postal/ZIP code |
| GEORGE ONISHI | SURFER'S SUPERMARKET |
| 333 FLORAL DRIVE | 4990 BEACH BOULEVARD |
| HONOLULU, HI 96000 | HONOLULU, HI 96000 |

**A** (1) Shareholder's percentage of stock ownership for tax year ➤ 33.33 % and (2) Number of shares owned by shareholder at
tax year end ➤ 330 (See Instructions for Schedule K-1)

**B** Check applicable boxes: (1) ☐ Final K-1 (2) ☐ Amended K-1

**Caution:** Refer to Shareholder's Instructions for Schedule K-1 before entering information from Schedule K-1 on your tax return.

| (a) Pro rata share items | (b) Attributable to Hawaii | (c) Attributable Elsewhere | (d) Form N-11*/ N-15** filers enter the amounts in col. (b) and col. (c) on: |
|---|---|---|---|
| **Income (Losses)** | | | |
| 1 Ordinary income (loss) from trade or business activities | 4,620 | | } See Shareholder's Instructions for Schedule K-1 (N-35). |
| 2 Net income (loss) from rental real estate activities | | | |
| 3 Net income (loss) from other rental activities | | | |
| 4 Interest | 100 | | Interest Worksheet |
| 5 Ordinary Dividends | | | Line 9 |
| 6 Royalties | | | See Shareholder's Instructions. |
| 7 Net short-term capital gain (loss) | | | Capital Gain/Loss Worksheet |
| 8 Net long-term capital gain (loss) | | | Capital Gain/Loss Worksheet |
| 9 Net section 1231 gain (loss) | | | Schedule D-1, line 2 |
| 10 Other income (loss) (attach schedule) | | | (Enter on applicable line of your return) |
| **Deductions** | | | |
| 11 Charitable contributions | 400 | | Worksheet A-4, PY-4, or NR-4 |
| 12 IRC section 179 expense deduction (attach schedule) | 3,333 | | See Shareholder's Instructions. |
| 13 Deductions related to portfolio income (loss) (attach schedule) | | | Worksheet A-6, PY-6, or NR-6 |
| 14 Other deductions (attach schedule) | | | (Enter on applicable line of your return) |
| **Investment Interest** | | | |
| 15 a Interest expense on investment debts | | | Form N-158, line 1 |
| b (1) Investment income included on lines 4, 5, and 6 above | 100 | | } See Shareholder's Instructions for Schedule K-1 (N-35). |
| (2) Investment expense included on line 13 above | | | |

**\* For Form N-11 filers, if your federal Schedule K-1 (Form 1120S) and Hawaii Schedule K-1 (Form N-35) amounts are different, the necessary adjustments are to be made in the Hawaii Additions Worksheet and/or Hawaii Subtractions Worksheet in the Form N-11 Instructions.
\*\*For Form N-15 filers, the referenced worksheets are located in the Form N-15 Instructions.**

**Purpose of Schedule K-1** — The S corporation uses Schedule K-1 (Form N-35) to report to you your share of the corporation's income (reduced by any tax the corporation paid on the income), credits, deductions, etc. Please keep it for your records.

Although the corporation is subject to a built-in gains tax, an excess net passive income tax, and a LIFO recapture tax, you are liable for the income tax on your share of the corporation's income, whether or not distributed, and you must include your share on your tax return.

Use these instructions to help you report the items shown on Schedule K-1 on your Hawaii income tax return. Where "(attach schedule)" appears on lines 10, 12, 13, 14, and 22a, it means the information for these lines (if applicable) will be shown on line 29, or if additional space was needed, the corporation will have attached a statement to your Schedule K-1 to show the information. The notation "(See

Instructions for Schedule K-1)" in item A is directed only to the corporation.

Schedule K-1 does not show the amount of actual dividend distributions the corporation paid to you. The corporation must report to you such amounts on Form 1099-DIV. Resident shareholders' actual dividend distributions are already included in federal adjusted gross income (federal AGI) for Form N-11 filers.

Schedule K-1 now provides you with information relating to the source of your share of the income of the S corporation. This is required under provisions of section 235-128, Hawaii Revised Statutes. How this income is reported by you to the State of Hawaii depends on your residency status. Shareholders who are Hawaii residents are to report the total sum of the income, deductions, and credits attributable to Hawaii and the income, deductions, and credits attributable elsewhere. Shareholders who are

not residents of Hawaii or who are part-year residents of Hawaii are to use amounts attributable to Hawaii and the total sum of amounts attributable to Hawaii and amounts attributable elsewhere in preparing their Hawaii income tax returns. Income attributable to Hawaii is reported by all shareholders net of adjustments allowed to corporations. The total of your share of these adjustments is shown on line 22a and are explained on line 29. Items of income or deductions should be reported on your return net of these adjustments. Resident shareholders may make an adjustment to income reported on their net income tax return for interest penalty on early withdrawal of savings, if a penalty was imposed on the early withdrawal of savings by the S corporation and the interest income is not attributable to Hawaii. The amount of this deduction appears on line 23.

FORM N-35
SCHEDULE K-1

N35SCHK1_I 2018A 01 VID01      ID NO 01

**SCHEDULE K-1**
**(FORM N-35)**
**(REV. 2018)**                                                                                                    PAGE 2

| (a) Pro rata share items | (b) Attributable to Hawaii | (c) Attributable Elsewhere | (d) Form N-11/N-15 filers enter on: |
|---|---|---|---|
| **Credits** | | | |
| 16 a  Fuel Tax Credit for Commercial Fishers | | | Form N-163 |
| b  Total cost of qualifying property for the Capital Goods Excise Tax Credit | 40,833 | | Form N-312, Part I |
| c  Amounts needed to claim the Enterprise Zone Tax Credit | See attached Form N-756A. | | Form N-756 |
| d  Hawaii Low-Income Housing Tax Credit | | | Form N-586 |
| e  Credit for Employment of Vocational Rehabilitation Referrals | | | Form N-884 |
| f  Qualified production costs for the Motion Picture, Digital Media, and Film Production Income Tax Credit | | | Form N-340 |
| g  Credit for School Repair and Maintenance | | | Form N-330 |
| h  Renewable Energy Technologies Income Tax Credit | See attached Form N-342A. | | Form N-342 |
| i  Important Agricultural Land Qualified Agricultural Cost Tax Credit | | | Form N-344 |
| j  Tax Credit for Research Activities | | | Form N-346 |
| k  Capital Infrastructure Tax Credit | | | Form N-348 |
| l  Cesspool Upgrade, Conversion or Connection Income Tax Credit | | | Form N-350 |
| m  Renewable Fuels Production Tax Credit | | | Form N-352 |
| n  Organic Foods Production Tax Credit | | | Form N-354 |
| o  Credit for Hawaii income tax withheld on Form N-288 | | | |
| p  Credit for Hawaii income tax withheld on Form N-4 (Nonresident shareholders only) | | | See Shareholder's Instructions for Schedule K-1 (Form N-35) |
| q  Pro rata share of net income tax paid by the S corporation to states which do not recognize the corporation's "S" status. (Resident and part-year resident shareholders only) | | | |
| **Other Items** | | | |
| 17  Property distributions (including cash) other than dividend distributions reported to you on federal Form 1099-DIV | 1,000 | | |
| 18  Tax exempt interest income | | | |
| 19  Other tax exempt income | | | |
| 20  Nondeductible expenses | 250 | | See Shareholder's Instructions for Schedule K-1 (Form N-35) |
| 21  Amount of loan repayments for "Loans from Shareholders." | | | |
| 22 a  Corporate adjustments to income attributable to Hawaii (attach schedule) | | | |
| b  Personal adjustments to income attributable elsewhere | | | |
| 23  Interest penalty on early withdrawal of savings | | | |
| **Recapture of Tax Credits** | | | |
| 24  Recapture of Hawaii Low-Income Housing Tax Credit: | | | |
| a  From IRC section 42(j)(5) partnerships | | | Form N-586, Part III |
| b  Other than on line 24a | | | |
| 25  Capital Goods Excise Tax Credit Properties | See attached  N-312, Part II. | | Form N-312, Part II |
| 26  Recapture of Tax Credit for Flood Victims | | | Form N-338 |
| 27  Recapture of Important Agricultural Land Qualified Agricultural Cost Tax Credit | | | Form N-344 |
| 28  Recapture of Capital Infrastructure Tax Credit | | | Form N-348 |

29  Supplemental information for lines 10, 12, 13, 14, 22a, or other items and amounts not included in lines 1 through 28 that are required to be reported separately to each shareholder (attach additional schedules if more space is needed):

## S CORPORATION INCOME TAX RETURN

## SURFERS SUPERMARKET, INC.

## Form N-35

### OTHER INCOME

| | |
|---|---:|
| Income from partnerships | $ 30,000 |
| Miscellaneous income | 1,000 |
| Total Other Income | $ 31,000 |

### TAXES AND LICENSES

| | |
|---|---:|
| States tax | $ 5,000 |
| General excise tax | 9,300 |
| Payroll tax | 11,000 |
| Total Taxes and Licenses | $ 25,300 |

### OTHER DEDUCTIONS

| | |
|---|---:|
| Amortization | $ 400 |
| Supplies | 19,400 |
| Trading stamps expense | 30,900 |
| Automobile and truck expense | 2,000 |
| Utilities and telephone | 12,000 |
| Insurance | 1,600 |
| Loss on bad checks | 6,400 |
| Professional fees | 2,500 |
| Sundry | 1,800 |
| Office supplies | 700 |
| Total Other Deductions | $ 77,700 |

### CHARITABLE CONTRIBUTIONS

| | |
|---|---:|
| Aloha United Way | $ 1,000 |
| UH Foundation | 200 |
| Total Contributions | $ 1,200 |

Statement 1

## PROBLEM FOR SPECIMEN RETURN
## FIDUCIARY INCOME TAX RETURN

### Form N-40

During the taxable year ended December 31, the Honolulu Trust Co., as trustee for the Nancy R. Nakagawa Trust, received the following items of income:

| | |
|---|---|
| Dividends.......................................................... | $ 18,700 |
| Interest on savings account ......................................... | 2,300 |
| Rents on office building in Honolulu ............................... | 6,000 |
| Interest on Honolulu Water District municipal bonds................. | 3,600 |
| Gain from sale of 500 shares of Honolulu Electric Company held over one year and sold April 16............................ | 5,400 |

Made the following expenditures:

| | |
|---|---|
| Friendly Mortgage Co.—payment on mortgage on rental property (interest $2,600; principal $2,600).............. | $ 5,200 |
| Honolulu County real estate taxes................................ | 1,200 |
| Hawaii income tax on trust income................................ | 2,600 |
| Accounting fees.................................................. | 500 |
| Island Insurance Company—fire and extended coverage on office building............................................. | 351 |
| Administrative and investment fees............................... | 650 |
| Safe deposit box rental .......................................... | 15 |

Under the provisions of the trust instrument, Nancy is to receive $5,000 yearly from the trust's income, with the balance remaining as corpus. At age 25 Nancy may elect to have the entire trust income distributed to her each year. At age 30 all assets of the trust are to be distributed to her. In the event of death before age 30, by will, Nancy has the power to dispose of all assets of the trust.

Nancy is now 23 years of age and is a resident of Hawaii.

## EXPLANATION OF ITEMS ON SPECIMEN RETURN
## FIDUCIARY INCOME TAX RETURNS

### Form N-40

## COMPUTATION OF BENEFICIARY'S SHARE OF INCOME

| | Income | % of total | Expense Allocated | Distributable Net Income | % of Total |
|---|---|---|---|---|---|
| Gross rents | $ 6,000 | | | | |
| Less expenses allocable: | | | | | |
| Interest. . . . . . . . . . $ 2,600 | | | | | |
| Taxes . . . . . . . . . . . . . 1,200 | | | | | |
| Insurance . . . . . . . . . . . 351 | | | | | |
| Depreciation . . . . . . . . 1,000 | | | | | |
| Total expenses | 5,151 | | | | |
| | | | | | |
| Net rents | $   849 | 3.11 | $   33 | $   816 | 2.75 |
| Dividends | 18,700 | 68.63 | 720 | 17,980 | 60.57 |
| Taxable interest | 2,300 | 8.44 | 88 | 2,212 | 7.45 |
| Net capital gains | 5,400 | 19.82 | 208 | 5,192 | 17.49 |
| | $ 27,249 | 100.00% | 1,049 | | |
| | | | | | |
| Municipal bond interest | $ 3,600 | | 116 | 3,484 | 11.74 |
| | | | $ 1,165 | $29,684 | 100.00% |

| | | | |
|---|---|---|---|
| Distribution to beneficiary: | | | |
| Rents | 2.75 x 5,000 | | $ 137.50 |
| Depreciation–distributed as separate item | | | |
| (137.50/816.00 x 1,000) | | | 168.50 |
| | | | |
| Gross rental income | | | $ 306.00 |
| Dividends | 60.57 x 5,000 | | 3,028.50 |
| Interest | 7.45 x 5,000 | | 372.50 |
| | | | |
| Taxable as ordinary income | | | $ 3,707.00 |
| Net long-term capital gain | 17.49 x 5,000 | | 874.50 |
| Tax-exempt interest | 11.74 x 5,000 | | 587.00 |
| | | | $ 5,168.50 |
| | | | |
| Less depreciation expense– | | | |
| distributed as separate item | | | 168.50 |
| | | | |
| | 100.00% | | $5,000.00 |

Allocation of deductions, other than direct charges, to tax-exempt income is based on the ratio of tax-exempt income to total gross income ($3,600/36,000 = 10%).

Required $5,000 distribution to the beneficiary is allocated according to the ratio of each individual type of trust net income to the total trust net income.

**FORM N-40** (REV. 2018)

STATE OF HAWAII—DEPARTMENT OF TAXATION

# FIDUCIARY INCOME TAX RETURN

For calendar year **2018**

THIS SPACE FOR DATE RECEIVED STAMP

or other tax year beginning ● _____ , 2018

and ending ● _____ , 20 _____

● ☐ Composite Qualified Funeral Trusts

| A | Type of entity (see instr.): | Name of estate or trust (Grantor type trust, see Instructions) | C | ☒ FEIN ☐ SSN ☐ ITIN |
|---|---|---|---|---|
| | ☐ Decedent's estate | | | ● 23-4567891 |
| | ☐ Simple trust | NANCY R. NAKAGAWA TRUST | D | Date entity created |
| | ☒ Complex trust | Name and title of fiduciary | | 05-15-1985 |
| | ☐ Qualified disability trust | | E | Nonexempt charitable and split-interest trusts, check applicable boxes: |
| | ☐ ESBT (S portion only) | HONOLULU TRUST COMPANY | | |
| | ☐ Grantor type trust | Mailing Address of fiduciary (number and street) | | |
| | ☐ Bankruptcy estate – Ch. 7 | | | ☐ Described in IRC section 4947(a)(1) |
| | ☐ Bankruptcy estate – Ch. 11 | 123 BEACH BOULEVARD | | ☐ Not a private foundation |
| | ☐ Pooled income fund | City, State and Postal/ZIP Code. If foreign address, see Instructions. | | ☐ Described in IRC section 4947(a)(2) |
| B | Number of Schedules K-1 Attached ➤ 1 | HONOLULU, HI 96813 | | |

| F | Check applicable boxes: | ☐ Initial return ☐ Final Return ☐ Amended Return (Attach Sch AMD) ☐ NOL Carryback (Attach Sch AMD) ☐ IRS Adjustment |
|---|---|---|
| | | ☐ Change in fiduciary ☐ Change in fiduciary's name ☐ Change in fiduciary's address ☐ Trust Name Change |

G   Check here if the estate or filing trust made an IRC section 645(a) election and attach a copy of the federal form 8855. ➤ ☐

**INCOME**

| | | | |
|---|---|---|---|
| 1. | Interest Income | 1● | 2300 |
| 2. | Ordinary Dividends | 2 | 18700 |
| 3. | Income or (losses) from partnerships, other estates or other trusts (Attach federal Schedule E) (See Instructions) | 3 | |
| 4. | Net rent and royalty income or (loss) (Attach federal Schedule E) | 4● | 849 |
| 5. | Net business and farm income or (loss) (Attach federal Schedules C and F) | 5● | |
| 6. | Capital gain or (loss) (Attach Schedule D (Form N-40)) | 6 | 5400 |
| 7. | Ordinary gains or (losses) (From Schedule D-1, line 19) | 7 | |
| 8. | Other income (State nature of income) | 8● | |
| 9. | **Total** income (Add lines 1 through 8) | 9 | 27249 |

**DEDUCTIONS**

| | | | |
|---|---|---|---|
| 10. | Interest (Explain in Schedule C) | 10 | |
| 11. | Taxes (Explain in Schedule C) | 11 | 2600 |
| 12. | Fiduciary fees (Explain in Schedule C) | 12 | 585 |
| 13. | Charitable deduction (From Schedule A, line 6 or 7(c)) | 13 | |
| 14. | Attorney, accountant and return preparer fees (Explain in Schedule C) | 14 | 450 |
| 15. | Other deductions NOT subject to the 2% floor (Explain in Schedule C) | 15 | 14 |
| 16. | Allowable miscellaneous itemized deductions subject to the 2% floor (Explain in Schedule C) | 16 | |
| 17. | **Total** (Add lines 10 through 16) | 17 | 3649 |
| 18. | Line 9 minus line 17 (Complex trusts and estates also enter this amount on Schedule B, line 1) | 18 | 23600 |
| 19. | Income distribution deduction (From Schedule B, line 17) (See Instructions) (attach Schedules K-1 (Form N-40)) | 19 | 4413 |
| 20. | Exemption ($400 for an estate; trusts see Instructions) | 20 | 80 |
| 21. | **Total** (Add lines 19 and 20) | 21 | 4493 |
| 22. | Taxable income of fiduciary (Line 18 minus line 21) | 22● | 19107 |

**DECLARATION:** I declare, under the penalties set forth in section 231-36, HRS, that this return (including any accompanying schedules or statements) has been examined by me and, to the best of my knowledge and belief, is a true, correct, and complete return, made in good faith, for the taxable year stated, pursuant to the Hawaii Income Tax Law, Chapter 235, HRS. Declaration of preparer (other than taxpayer) is based on all information of which preparer has any knowledge.

**Please Sign Here**

➤ ● _____
Signature of fiduciary or officer representing fiduciary    Date

➤ _____
Print or type name of fiduciary or officer representing fiduciary    Title

★ May the Hawaii Department of Taxation discuss this return with the preparer shown below? (See page 1 of the Instructions) ☒ Yes ☐ No
This designation does not replace Form N-848, Power of Attorney.

| Paid Preparer's Information | Preparer's signature | | Date | Check if self-employed ➤ ☐ | Preparer's identification no. |
|---|---|---|---|---|---|
| | Print Preparer's Name | HOMER JONES | | | ● P00000000 |
| | Firm's name (or yours, if self-employed) | KMH LLP, 1003 BISHOP ST., #2400 | | Federal E.I. No. ➤ 42-1539623 | |
| | Address and ZIP Code | HONOLULU, HI 96813 | | Phone no. ➤ (808) 526-2255 | |

FORM N-40

N40_I 2018A 01 VID01      ID NO 01

*Text in left margin: ATTACH CHECK OR MONEY ORDER AND FORM N-4 HERE*

FORM N-40 (REV. 2018)                                                      **Page 2**

| Name as shown on return | Federal Employer Identification Number |
|---|---|
| NANCY R. NAKAGAWA TRUST | 23-4567891 |

## Schedule A — COMPUTATION OF CHARITABLE DEDUCTION (See Instructions for Schedule A)
### (Submit statement giving name and address of charitable organizations)

| | | | |
|---|---|---|---|
| 1. | Amounts paid or permanently set aside for charitable purposes from current year's gross income . . . . . . . | **1** | |
| 2. | (a) Tax exempt interest and other income nontaxable irrespective of source, allocable to charitable distribution. . . . . . . . . . . . . . . . . . . . . **2(a)** | | |
| | (b) Income of a nonresident estate or trust nontaxable because it is derived from property owned outside Hawaii or other source outside Hawaii, allocable to charitable distribution. . . . . . . . . . . . . . . . . . . . . . . . . . **2(b)** | | |
| | (c) Total (Add lines 2(a) and 2(b)) . . . . . . . . . . . . . . . . . . | **2(c)** | |
| 3. | Balance (Line 1 minus line 2(c)) . . . . . . . . . . . . . . . . . . . . . . . | **3** | |
| 4. | Enter the net short-term capital gain and the net long-term capital gain of the current tax year allocable to corpus paid or permanently set aside for charitable purposes . . . . . . . . . . . . . . . . . . . . | **4** | |
| 5. | Amounts paid or permanently set aside for charitable purposes from gross income of a prior year (See Instructions). . . . . . . . . . . . . . . . . . . . . . . . . . . . . . . . . . . . . . | **5** | |
| 6. | Total (Add lines 3, 4, and 5). Enter here and on page 1, line 13, IF TOTAL OF CHARITABLE DISTRIBUTIONS ARE TO BE USED EXCLUSIVELY IN HAWAII. In other cases, complete line 7. . . . . . . . . . . | **6** | |
| 7. | (a) Portion of line 6 amount which is to be used exclusively in Hawaii . . . . . . **7(a)** | | |
| | (b) Portion of excess of line 6 amount over amount on line 7(a) which is within percentage limitations (See Instructions) . . . . . . . . . . . . **7(b)** | | |
| | (c) Enter here and on page 1, line 13, the sum of lines 7(a) and (b). . . . . . . . . . . . . . . . | **7(c)** | |

## Schedule B — COMPUTATION OF INCOME DISTRIBUTION DEDUCTION (See Instructions for Schedule B)

| | | | |
|---|---|---|---|
| 1. | Enter amount from page 1, line 18, computed by using Schedule A, line 6 for page 1, line 13 (If loss, see Instructions). . . . . . . . . . . . . . . . . . . . . . . . . . | **1** | 23600 |
| 2. | (a) Tax-exempt interest and other income nontaxable irrespective of source (as adjusted) . . . . . . . . . . . . . . . . . . . . . . . **2(a)** 3484 | | |
| | (b) Nontaxable income of nonresident estate or trust from property owned outside Hawaii or other source outside Hawaii (as adjusted) . . . . . . . **2(b)** | | |
| | (c) Add lines 2(a) and 2(b). . . . . . . . . . . . . . . . . . . . . . . . . | **2(c)** | 3484 |
| 3. | Net gain shown on Schedule D (Form N-40), line 19, column (a) (If net loss, enter zero) . . . . . . . . . . | **3** | 875 |
| 4. | Schedule A, line 4 plus line 5. . . . . . . . . . . . . . . . . . . . . . . . . . | **4** | |
| 5. | Long-term capital gain, included on Schedule A, line 1 (See Instructions) . . . . . . . . . . . . . | **5** | |
| 6. | Short-term capital gain, included on Schedule A, line 1 (See Instructions) . . . . . . . . . . . . . | **6** | |
| 7. | If the amount on page 1, line 6, is a capital loss, enter here as a positive figure. . . . . . . . . . . . . | **7** | |
| 8. | If the amount on page 1, line 6, is a capital gain, enter here as a negative figure . . . . . . . . . . . . | **8** | -5400 |
| 9. | Distributable net income (Combine lines 1 and 2c through 8) . . . . . . . . . . . . . . . . . | **9** | 22259 |
| 10. | Amount of income for the tax year determined under the governing instrument (accounting income) . . . . . . . . . . . . . . . . . . . . **10** 29684 | | |
| 11. | Amount of income required to be distributed currently (See Instructions) . . . . . . . . . . . . . . | **11** | 5000 |
| 12. | Other amounts paid, credited, or otherwise required to be distributed (See Instructions) . . . . . . . . . | **12** | |
| 13. | Total distributions (Add lines 11 and 12). (If greater than line 10, see Instructions) . . . . . . . . . . . . | **13** | 5000 |
| 14. | Enter the total amount of tax-exempt income included on line 13 . . . . . . . . . . . . . . . . . | **14** | 587 |
| 15. | Tentative income distribution deduction (Line 13 minus line 14) . . . . . . . . . . . . . . . . . | **15** | 4413 |
| 16. | Tentative income distribution (Line 9 minus line 2(c)). . . . . . . . . . . . . . . . . . . . | **16** | 19075 |
| 17. | Income distribution deduction. Enter the smaller of line 15 or line 16 here and on page 1, line 19 . . . . . . | **17** | 4413 |

### Schedule C is on the bottom of page 4.

N40_I 2018A 02 VID01                    ID NO 01                              **FORM N-40**

**FORM N-40 (REV. 2018)**                                                              Page 3

| Name as shown on return | Federal Employer Identification Number |
|---|---|
| NANCY R. NAKAGAWA TRUST | 23-4567891 |

## Schedule E - Nonrefundable Credits (Enter fiduciary's share only.)

| | | |
|---|---|---|
| 1. | Income tax paid to another state or foreign country by a resident estate or trust . . . . . . . . . . . . . . . . . | 1● |
| 2. | Carryover of the Energy Conservation Tax Credit. (Attach Form N-323) . . . . . . . . . . . . . . . . . . . | 2● |
| 3. | Enterprise Zone Tax Credit. (Attach Form N-756) . . . . . . . . . . . . . . . . . . . . . . . . . . . . . . | 3● |
| 4. | Low-Income Housing Tax Credit. (Attach Form N-586) . . . . . . . . . . . . . . . . . . . . . . . . | 4● |
| 5. | Credit for Employment of Vocational Rehabilitation Referrals. (Attach Form N-884) . . . . . . . . . . . . | 5● |
| 6. | Carryover of the High Technology Business Investment Tax Credit. (Attach Form N-323) . . . . . . . . . . | 6● |
| 7. | Carryover of the Individual Development Account Contribution Tax Credit. (Attach Form N-323). . . . . . . . . | 7● |
| 8. | Carryover of the Technology Infrastructure Renovation Tax Credit. (Attach Form N-323) . . . . . . . . . . | 8● |
| 9. | Credit for School Repair and Maintenance. (Attach Form N-330) . . . . . . . . . . . . . . . . . . . . . | 9● |
| 10. | Carryover of the Hotel Construction and Remodeling Tax Credit. (Attach Form N-323). . . . . . . . . . . | 10● |
| 11. | Carryover of the Residential Construction and Remodeling Tax Credit. (Attach Form N-323) . . . . . . . . | 11● |
| 12. | Carryover of the Renewable Energy Technologies Income Tax Credit. (Before July 1, 2009) (Attach Form N-323). | 12● |
| 13a. | RETITC (Attach Form N-342) . . . . . . . .Check type of energy system: ● ☐ Solar ● ☐ Wind Powered | 13a● |
| 13b. | RETITC amount claimed on line 13a attributed to a credit carryforward from previous years . . . . . . . . | 13b● |
| 14. | Capital Infrastructure Tax Credit. (Attach Form N-348) . . . . . . . . . . . . . . . . . . . . . . . . . | 14● |
| 15. | Cesspool Upgrade, Conversion or Connection Income Tax Credit. (Attach Form N-350) . . . . . . . . . . | 15● |
| 16. | Renewable Fuels Production Tax Credit. (Attach Form N-352). . . . . . . . . . . . . . . . . . . . . . | 16● |
| 17 | Organic Foods Production Tax Credit. (Attach Form N-354) . . . . . . . . . . . . . . . . . . . . . . . | 17● |
| 18. | Total nonrefundable credits. (Add lines 1 through 13a and 14 through 17) Also, enter amount on Schedule G, line 4 | 18● |

## Schedule F - Refundable Credits (Enter fiduciary's share only.)

| | | |
|---|---|---|
| 1. | Fuel Tax Credit for Commercial Fishers. (Attach Form N-163) . . . . . . . . . . . . . . . . . . . . . | 1● |
| 2. | Motion Picture, Digital Media and Film Production Income Tax Credit. (Attach Form N-340) . . . . . . . . . . | 2● |
| 3. | Credit from a regulated investment company . . . . . . . . . . . . . . . . . . . . . . . . . . . . . . | 3● |
| 4. | Capital Goods Excise Tax Credit. (Attach Form N-312) . . . . . . . . . . . . . . . . . . . . . . . . . | 4● |
| 5. | Tax Withheld on Form N-4. (Attach Form N-4 to front of this return.) . . . . . . . . . . . . . . . . . . | 5● |
| 6. | Renewable Energy Technologies Income Tax Credit. (Attach Form N-342) | |
| | (Note: The refundable credit applies only to solar energy systems and not to wind powered energy systems) . . . | 6● |
| 7. | Important Agricultural Land Qualified Agricultural Cost Tax Credit. (Attach Form N-344) . . . . . . . . . . . . | 7● |
| 8. | Tax Credit for Research Activities. (Attach Form N-346) . . . . . . . . . . . . . . . . . . . . . . . . | 8● |
| 9. | Total refundable credits. (Add lines 1 through 8.) Also, enter this amount on Schedule G, line 2. . . . . . . . . | 9● |

## Schedule G - Tax Computation

| | | | |
|---|---|---|---|
| 1. | **Tax** on amount on page 1, line 22 (Use tax rate schedule or ● ☐ Schedule D (Form N-40) . . . . . . . . . . | 1● | 1064 |
| | (● ☐ Includes tax from Forms N-152, N-312, N-338, N-344, N-348, N-586, and section 641(c) tax. Attach appropriate Forms) | | |
| | (a) Enter amount from Schedule D (Form N-40), line 43. . . . . . . . . . . . . . | 1(a)● | | |
| 2. | Total refundable credits from Schedule F, line 9 . . . . . . . . . . . . . . . . . . . . . . . . . . . ➤ | 2● | 1064 |
| 3. | Difference — Line 1 minus line 2. If line 3 is zero or less, see Instructions. . . . . . . . . . . . . . . . . | 3● | |
| 4. | Total nonrefundable credits from Schedule E, line 18 . . . . . . . . . . . . . . . . . . . . . . . . . . | 4● | |
| 5. | Difference — Line 3 minus line 4. . . . . . . . . . . . . . . . . . . . . . . . . . . . . . . . . . . . | 5● | |
| 6. | **OTHER** (a)  2018 Estimated tax payments: | | |
| | N-5 _____  N-288A _____ | 6(a)● | 1300 |
| | **CREDITS:** (b)  Estimated tax payments allocated to beneficiaries (from N-40T) . . . . . . . | 6(b)● | |
| | (c)  Line 6(a) minus line 6(b) . . . . . . . . . . . . . . . . . . . . . . . . | 6(c)● | 1300 |
| | (d)  Amount applied from 2017 return . . . . . . . . . . . . . . . . . . . . | 6(d)● | |
| | (e)  Payments with extension . . . . . . . . . . . . . . . . . . . . . . . | 6(e)● | |
| 7. | Total (Add lines 6(c) through 6(e)) . . . . . . . . . . . . . . . . . . . . . . . . . . . . . . . . . ➤ | 7● | 1300 |
| 8. | Penalty for underpayment of estimated tax. (See Instructions.) If Form N-210 is attached, check this box. ☐ ● . | 8● | |
| 9. | TAX DUE — If the total of lines 5 and 8 is larger than line 7, enter AMOUNT OWED . . . . . . . . . . . . . | 9● | |
| 10. | PAYMENT AMOUNT  Send a check or money order payable to the "Hawaii State Tax Collector". . . . . . . . . | 10● | |
| 11. | OVERPAYMENT — If line 7 is larger than the total of lines 5 and 8, enter AMOUNT OVERPAID . . . . . . . . | 11● | 236 |
| 12. | Enter the amount of line 11 to be CREDITED to 2019 estimated tax . . . . . . . . . . . . . . . . . . . . | 12● | 236 |
| 13. | Enter the amount of line 11 to be REFUNDED. . . . . . . . . . . . . . . . . . . . . . . . . . . . . . . | 13● | |
| 14. | Amount paid (overpaid) on original return — AMENDED RETURN ONLY (See Instructions). . . . . . . . . . . | 14 | |
| 15. | BALANCE DUE (REFUND) with amended return (See Instructions) . . . . . . . . . . . . . . . . . . . . . | 15 | |

N40_I 2018A 03 VID01                          ID NO 01                                    FORM N-40

FORM N-40 (REV. 2018)                                                                                         Page 4

| Name as shown on return | Federal Employer Identification Number |
|---|---|
| NANCY R. NAKAGAWA TRUST | 23-4567891 |

## ADDITIONAL INFORMATION REQUIRED

| | | YES | NO |
|---|---|---|---|
| 1. | Was an income tax return filed for the preceding year? . . . . . . . . . . . . . . . . . . . . . . . . . . . . . . . | X | |
| 2. | Was a final Hawaii individual income tax return filed for the decedent? . . . . . . . . . . . . . . . . . . . . . . . . . | | X |
| 3. | (a) If a complex trust, is the trust making the election under IRC section 663(b)? . . . . . . . . . . . . . . . . . . . . | | X |
| | If "Yes," state amount _____ | | |
| | (b) If a complex trust, was there undistributed net income at the beginning of the year? . . . . . . . . . . . . . . . | X | |
| 4. | Is an election under IRC section 643(e)(3) being made? (Attach Schedule D (Form N-40)) . . . . . . . . . . . . | | X |
| 5. | If a trust, was there an accumulation distribution? . . . . . . . . . . . . . . . . . . . . . . . . . . . . . . . . . | | X |
| | If "Yes," attach Schedule J (Form N-40) | | |
| 6. | Did the estate or trust receive tax-exempt income? (If "Yes," enter amount $ _____ ). . . . . . . . . . | X | |
| | If "Yes," did you deduct any expense allocable to it? (Attach a computation of the allocation of expenses) . . . . . . . . . | X | |
| 7. | Did the estate or trust receive all or any part of the earnings (salary, wages, and other compensation) of any individual by | | |
| | reason of a contract assignment or similar arrangement? . . . . . . . . . . . . . . . . . . . . . . . . . . . . . . . | | X |
| 8. | If return is for a trust, enter name and address of grantor: | | |
| | Name _____ | | |
| | Address _____ | | |
| | City/State and Postal/Zip Code _____ | | |
| 9. | Is this the final return? . . . . . . . . . . . . . . . . . . . . . . . . . . . . . . . . . . . . . . . . . . . . . . . | | X |
| 10. | Is this return for a short taxable year? . . . . . . . . . . . . . . . . . . . . . . . . . . . . . . . . . . . . . . | | X |
| 11. | Did the estate or trust have any passive activity loss(es)? (If "Yes," enter the amount of any such loss(es) on federal | | |
| | Form 8582, Passive Activity Loss Limitations, to figure the allowable loss) . . . . . . . . . . . . . . . . . . . . . . | | X |

### Schedule C — EXPLANATION OF DEDUCTIONS CLAIMED ON PAGE 1, LINES 10, 11, 12, 14, 15, and 16
(See Instructions. Attach a separate schedule if more space is needed.)

| Line No. | Explanation | Amount |
|---|---|---|
| 11 | HAWAII INCOME TAX | 2600 |
| 12 | SEE SCHEDULE | 585 |
| 13 | SEE SCHEDULE | 450 |
| 14 | SEE SCHEDULE | 14 |
| | | |
| | | |
| | | |
| | | |
| | | |
| | | |
| | | |
| | | |
| | | |
| | | |
| | | |
| | | |

FORM N-40

SCHEDULE D
FORM N-40
(REV. 2018)

STATE OF HAWAII—DEPARTMENT OF TAXATION

# Capital Gains and Losses

Attach this Schedule to Fiduciary Income Tax Return (Form N-40)

**2018**

| Name of Estate or Trust | Federal Employer Identification Number |
|---|---|
| NANCY R. NAKAGAWA TRUST | 23-4567891 |

## PART I — Short-term Capital Gains and Losses — Assets Held One Year or Less

| (a) Description of property (Example, 100 shares 7% preferred of "Z" Co.) | (b) Date acquired (Mo., day, yr.) | (c) Date sold (Mo., day, yr.) | (d) Gross sales price | (e) Cost or other basis, as adjusted, plus expense of sale (see instructions) | (f) Gain or (loss) (Col. (d), minus col. (e)) |
|---|---|---|---|---|---|
| 1 | | | | | |
| | | | | | |
| | | | | | |
| | | | | | |
| | | | | | |
| | | | | | |
| | | | | | |
| | | | | | |
| | | | | | |
| | | | | | |

| | | | |
|---|---|---|---|
| 2 Short-term capital gain or (loss) from federal Forms 4684, 6252, 6781, and 8824 | 2 | | 0 |
| 3 Net short-term gain or (loss) from partnerships, S Corporations, and other estates or trusts | 3 | | 0 |
| 4 Short-term gain from stock acquired through stock options from qualified high technology businesses | 4 | ( | ) |
| 5 Short-term capital loss carryover from 2017 Schedule D, line 30 | 5 | ( | ) |
| 6 **Net short-term gain or (loss)**, (combine lines 1 through 5). Enter here and on line 15 below ➤ | 6 | | 0 |

## PART II — Long-term Capital Gains and Losses — Assets Held More Than One Year

| 7 | | | | | |
|---|---|---|---|---|---|
| 500 SHARES OF HONOLULU ELECTRIC | 05/28/86 | 04/16/18 | 11,650 | 6,250 | 5,400 |
| | | | | | |
| | | | | | |
| | | | | | |
| | | | | | |
| | | | | | |
| | | | | | |
| | | | | | |

| | | | |
|---|---|---|---|
| 8 Long-term capital gain or (loss) from federal Forms 2439, 4684, 6252, 6781, and 8824 | 8 | | 0 |
| 9 Net long-term gain or (loss) from partnerships, S Corporations, and other estates or trusts | 9 | | 0 |
| 10 Capital gain distributions | 10 | | 0 |
| 11 Enter the gain, if applicable, from Schedule D-1, Part I, line 8 or 10 | 11 | | 0 |
| 12 Long-term gain from stock acquired through stock options from qualified high technology businesses | 12 | ( | ) |
| 13 Long-term capital loss carryover from 2017 Schedule D, line 37 | 13 | ( | ) |
| 14 **Net long-term gain or (loss)**, (combine lines 7 through 13). Enter here and on line 16 below ➤ | 14 | | 5,400 |

## PART III — Summary of Parts I and II

| | | (a) Beneficiaries | (b) Fiduciary | (c) Total |
|---|---|---|---|---|
| 15 Net short-term gain or (loss) from line 6, above | 15 | 0 | 0 | 0 |
| 16 Net long-term gain or (loss) from line 14, above | 16 | 875 | 4,525 | 5,400 |
| 17 Total net gain or (loss), (combine lines 15 and 16) ➤ | 17 | 875 | 4,525 | 5,400 |

If line 17, column (c), is a net gain, enter the gain on Form N-40, line 6. If lines 16 and 17, column (b), are net gains, go to Part VI, and DO NOT complete Parts IV and V.
If line 17, column (c), is a net (loss), complete Parts IV and V, as necessary.

N40SCHD_I 2018A 01 VID01                ID NO 01                SCHEDULE D (FORM N-40)

SCHEDULE D (FORM N-40) (REV. 2018)                                                                    PAGE 2

**PART IV**   **Computation of Capital Loss Limitation**

**18** Enter here and enter as a (loss) on Form N-40, line 6, the **smaller** of:

    *(i)*   The net loss on line 17, column (c); **or**

    *(ii)*  $3,000 ................................................................................................................ | **18** |(            )

    *If the net loss on line 17, column (c) is more than $3,000, OR if the taxable income on line 22, page 1, of Form N-40 is zero or less, complete Part V to determine your capital loss carryover.*

**PART V**   **Computation of Capital Loss Carryovers From 2018 to 2019**

### Section A. — Computation of Carryover Limit

| | | |
|---|---|---|
| **19** Enter the taxable income or (loss) for 2018 from Form N-40, line 22....................... | **19** | 0 |
| **20** Enter the loss from line 18 as a positive amount.................................................. | **20** | 0 |
| **21** Enter the amount from Form N-40, line 20 ........................................................... | **21** | 0 |
| **22** Adjusted taxable income (combine lines 19, 20, and 21, but not less than zero)............ | **22** | 0 |
| **23** Enter the lesser of line 20 or line 22 .................................................................. | **23** | 0 |

### Section B. — Short-Term Capital Loss Carryover
*(Complete this section only if there is a loss shown on line 6 and line 17, column (c).)*

| | | |
|---|---|---|
| **24** Enter the loss shown on line 6 as a positive amount............................................. | **24** | 0 |
| **25** Enter the gain, if any, shown on line 14. (If that line is blank or shows a loss, enter zero) ....... | **25** | 0 |
| **26** Enter the amount from line 23 ........................................................................... | **26** | 0 |
| **27** Add lines 25 and 26............................................................................................ | **27** | 0 |
| **28** Line 24 minus line 27. If zero or less, enter zero. This is your short-term capital loss carryover from 2018 to 2019. If this is the final return of the trust or decedent's estate, also enter on line 8b, Schedule K-1 (Form N-40)................ | **28** | 0 |

### Section C. — Long-Term Capital Loss Carryover
*(Complete this section only if there is a loss shown on line 14 and line 17, column (c).)*

| | | |
|---|---|---|
| **29** Enter the loss shown on line 14 as a positive amount............................................. | **29** | 0 |
| **30** Enter the gain, if any, shown on line 6 (If that line is blank or shows a loss, enter zero) ........... | **30** | 0 |
| **31** Enter the amount from line 23 ........................................................................... | **31** | 0 |
| **32** Enter the amount from line 24 ........................................................................... | **32** | 0 |
| **33** Line 31 minus line 32. If zero or less, enter zero ................................................... | **33** | 0 |
| **34** Add lines 30 and 33............................................................................................ | **34** | 0 |
| **35** Line 29 minus line 34. If zero or less, enter zero. This is your long-term capital loss carryover from 2018 to 2019. If this is the final return of the trust or decedent's estate, also enter on line 8c, Schedule K-1 (Form N-40)................ | **35** | 0 |

**PART VI**   **Tax Computation Using Maximum Capital Gains Rate** *(Complete this part only if lines 16 and 17, column (b) are net capital gains.)*

| | | |
|---|---|---|
| **36** Enter your taxable income from Form N-40, line 22................................................. | **36** | 19,107 |
| **37a** Net capital gain taxable to the estate or trust. Enter the **smaller** of line 16 or 17, column (b) .................. | **37a** | 4,525 |
|   **b** If you completed Form N-158, enter the amount from Form N-158, line 4e........................ | **37b** | 0 |
|   **c** Line 37a minus line 37b. If zero or less, enter zero ................................................ | **37c** | 4,525 |
| **38** Line 36 minus line 37c. If zero or less, enter zero .................................................. | **38** | 14,582 |
| **39** Enter the **greater** of line 38 or $20,000............................................................... | **39** | 20,000 |
| **40** Tax on amount on line 39. If line 39 is $20,000, enter $1,128.00 ................................ | **40** | 1,128 |
| **41** Line 36 minus line 39. If zero or less, enter zero and on line 42. Also, enter this amount on Form N-40, Schedule G, line 1(a)................................. | **41** | 0 |
| **42** Multiply the amount on line 41 by 7.25% (.0725) .................................................... | **42** | 0 |
| **43** Maximum capital gains tax. Add lines 40 and 42..................................................... | **43** | 1,128 |
| **44** Regular tax on amount on line 36 above (see Form N-40, Schedule G, line 1, instructions)............ | **44** | 1,064 |
| **45** Enter the **smaller** of line 43 or line 44 here and also on Form N-40, Schedule G, line 1 and check the "Schedule D (Form N-40)" box. .................................................... | **45** | 1,064 |

**SCHEDULE K-1**
**(FORM N-40)**
**(REV. 2018)**

STATE OF HAWAII — DEPARTMENT OF TAXATION

# Beneficiary's Share of Income, Deductions, Credits, etc.

for Calendar Year 2018, or fiscal year

beginning _____, 2018 and ending _____, 20_____

COMPLETE A SEPARATE SCHEDULE K-1 FOR EACH BENEFICIARY

**2018**

☐ Amended K-1
☐ Final K-1

Name of trust or decedent's estate ➤
NANCY R. NAKAGAWA TRUST

| Beneficiary's identifying number ➤ 575-12-3456 | Estate's or trust's EIN➤ 23-4567891 |
|---|---|
| Beneficiary's name, mailing address and Postal/ZIP Code | Fiduciary's name, mailing address, and Postal/ZIP Code |
| NANCY R. NAKAGAWA | HONOLULU TRUST COMPANY |
| 123 BEACH BOULEVARD | 123 BEACH BOULEVARD |
| HONOLULU, HI 96000 | HONOLULU, HI 96000 |

| | (a) Allocable share item | (b) Amount | (c) Calendar year 2018 Form N-11*/N-15** filers enter the amounts in column (b) on: |
|---|---|---|---|
| 1 | Interest . . . . . . . . . . . . . . . . . . . . | 372 | Interest Worksheet (N-15) |
| 2 | Ordinary Dividends. . . . . . . . . . . . . . . . . | 3,028 | Form N-15, line 9 |
| 3 a | Net short-term capital gain . . . . . . . . . . . | | Capital Gain/Loss Worksheet, line 3 (N-15) |
| b | Net long-term capital gain . . . . . . . . . . . . . | 875 | Capital Gain/Loss Worksheet, line 10 (N-15) |
| 4 a | Annuities, royalties, and other nonpassive income before directly apportioned deductions . . . . . . . . . . | | Form N-15, line 17 |
| b | Depreciation . . . . . . . . . . . . . . . | | |
| c | Depletion . . . . . . . . . . . . . . . | | Include on applicable line of |
| d | Amortization . . . . . . . . . . . . . . . | | appropriate tax form |
| 5 a | Trade or business, rental real estate, and other rental income before directly apportioned deductions. (see Instructions). . . . | 306 | Form N-15, line 17 |
| b | Depreciation . . . . . . . . . . . . . . . | 168 | |
| c | Depletion . . . . . . . . . . . . . . . | | Include on applicable line of |
| d | Amortization . . . . . . . . . . . . . . . | | appropriate tax form |
| 6 | Net income taxes paid to another state or foreign country (list on a separate sheet) . . . . . . . . . . . . . . . . . | | See Instructions for Form N-11, lines 21b and 35 or Form N-15, lines 38b and 52 |
| 7 a | Total cost of qualifying property for the Capital Goods Excise Tax Credit . . . . . . . . . . . . . . . . . | | Form N-312 |
| b | Low-Income Housing Tax Credit . . . . . . . . . . . . . . | | Form N-586 |
| c | Tax Credit for Research Activities. . . . . . . . . . . . . | | Form N-346 |
| 8 | Deductions in the final year of trust or decedent's estate: | | |
| a | Excess deductions on termination (see Instructions) . . . . . . . . . . . . . . | | Worksheet A-6, line 25 (N-11); Worksheet NR-6, line 26 (N-15); or Worksheet PY-6, line 49 (N-15) |
| b | Short-term capital loss carryover . . . . . . . . . . . . . . | | Capital Gain/Loss Worksheet, line 6 (N-15) |
| c | Long-term capital loss carryover . . . . . . . . . . . . . . | | Capital Gain/Loss Worksheet, line 14 (N-15) |
| d | Net operating loss (NOL) carryover. . . . . . . . . . . . . | | Form N-15, line 19 |
| e | . . . . . . . . . . . . . . . . . . . . . . . | | } Include on applicable line of |
| f | . . . . . . . . . . . . . . . . . . . . . . . | | appropriate tax form |
| 9 | Other (itemize): | | |
| a | Payments of estimated tax credited to you . . . . . . . . . . . | | Form N-11, line 38; Form N-15, line 55 |
| b | Tax-exempt interest . . . . . . . . . . . . . . . | 587 | See Instructions for Form N-11, lines 10 and 18 or Form N-15, line 8 |
| | . . . . . . . . . . . . . . . . . . . . . . . | | Include on applicable line of appropriate tax form |
| c | | | |

DISTRIBUTION OF INCOME NOT SUBJECT TO TAX IN HAWAII TO NONRESIDENT BENEFICIARIES — See Instructions

| | | | |
|---|---|---|---|
| 10 | Interest . . . . . . . . . . . . . . . . . . . . . | | |
| 11 | Dividends. . . . . . . . . . . . . . . . . . . . | | Include on applicable line on |
| 12 | Other intangible income (state nature of income) . . . . . . . . . | | Form N-15, Column A |
| 13 | Capital gain (loss) on intangibles. . . . . . . . . . . . . . . | | |

\* For Form N-11 filers, if your federal Schedule K-1 (Form 1041) and Hawaii Schedule K-1 (Form N-40) amounts are different, the necessary adjustments are to be made on the Hawaii Additions Worksheet and/or the Hawaii Subtractions Worksheet in the Form N-11 Instructions.

\*\* All referenced worksheets are located in the Form N-15 Instructions.

**SCHEDULE K-1**
**FORM N-40**

N40SCHK1_I 2018A 01 VID01    ID NO 01

## FIDUCIARY INCOME TAX RETURN

### NANCY R. NAKAGAWA TRUST

Explanation of Deductions:

Line 12 – fiduciary fees:

| | | |
|---|---|---|
| Administrative and investment fees | $ 650 | |
| Less amount attributable to tax-exempt income (10%) | 65 | $  585 |

Line 14 – attorney, accountant
and return preparer fees:

| | | |
|---|---|---|
| Accounting fees | $  500 | |
| Less amount attributable to tax-exempt income (10%) | 50 | $  450 |

Line 15a – other deductions:

| | | |
|---|---|---|
| Safe deposit box rental | $    15 | |
| Less amount attributable to tax-exempt income (10%) | 1 | $    14 |

Line 4 – net rental income:

| | | |
|---|---|---|
| Gross rents | | $6,000 |
| | | |
| Rental expenses: | | |
| Friendly Mortgage interest | $2,600 | |
| Real property taxes | 1,200 | |
| Insurance | 351 | |
| Depreciation | 1,000 | 5,151 |
| Net rental income | | $  849 |

## PROBLEM FOR SPECIMEN RETURN
## EXEMPT ORGANIZATION BUSINESS INCOME TAX RETURN

### Form N-70NP

Charitable, Inc. is a nonprofit corporation organized under the laws of the State of Hawaii. Charitable, Inc. provides certain nonexempt services which account for its unrelated business income. The deductions as shown on page 1, line 7 of Form N-70NP are those which are directly connected with the unrelated business income. This activity is a very small portion of the total activities of Charitable, Inc.

FORM
**N-70NP**
(REV. 2018)

STATE OF HAWAII—DEPARTMENT OF TAXATION

# EXEMPT ORGANIZATION BUSINESS
# INCOME TAX RETURN

For calendar year **2018**

or other taxable year beginning ● _____ , 2018
and ending ● _____ , 20____

THIS SPACE FOR DATE RECEIVED STAMP

☐ **Change of Address**  ☐ **Amended Return (Attach Sch AMD)**  ☐ **IRS Adjustment**  ☐ **NOL Carryback**

| | |
|---|---|
| Name of organization | ●A  Federal Employer I.D. No. |
| CHARITABLE, INC. | 34-5678912 |
| Dba or C/O | ●B  Unrelated business activity code(s) |
| Mailing Address (number and street) | ●C  Hawaii Tax I.D. No. |
| 15 MOUNTAIN RD | GE-000-345-6789-01 |
| City or town, State and Postal/ZIP code. If this is a foreign address, see Instructions. | ●D  This organization is a (check one): |
| NAPOOPOO, HI 96000 | ☒ Corporation  ☐ Charitable Trust |

ENTER APPROPRIATE AMOUNTS FROM FEDERAL FORM 990-T. **Note: The sum of lines 1 - 5 DO NOT equal line 6.**

| | | | |
|---|---|---|---:|
| 1 | Gross receipts or sales | 1● | 66278 |
| 2 | Returns and allowances | 2● | |
| 3 | Cost of goods sold and/or operations | 3● | |
| 4 | Capital gain net income (see Instructions) | 4● | |
| 5 | Other income | 5● | |
| 6 | Total unrelated trade or business income | 6● | 66278 |
| 7 | Total deductions | 7● | 60738 |
| 8 | Unrelated business taxable income | 8 | 5540 |
| 9 | Tax — From TAX COMPUTATION SCHEDULE on page 2, Part I, line 9. ➤ | 9● | 244 |
| 10 | Tax — From TAX COMPUTATION SCHEDULE on page 2, Part II, line 14. ➤ | 10● | |
| 11 | Recapture of Capital Goods Excise Tax Credit from Form N-312, Part II (attach Form N-312) | 11 | |
| 12 | Recapture of Low-Income Housing Tax Credit from Form N-586, Part III (attach Form N-586) | 12 | |
| 13 | Recapture of Tax Credit for Flood Victims from Form N-338 (attach Form N-338) | 13 | |
| 14 | Recapture of Important Agricultural Land Qualified Agricultural Cost Tax Credit (attach Form N-344) | 14 | |
| 15 | Recapture of Capital Infrastructure Tax Credit (attach Form N-348) | 15 | |
| 16 | Total tax (add lines 9 or 10 and 11, 12, 13, 14, and 15) | 16● | 244 |
| 17 | Total refundable tax credits from Schedule CR, line 27 | 17● | |
| 18 | Line 16 minus line 17.  If line 18 is zero or less, see Instructions. | 18● | 244 |
| 19 | Total nonrefundable credits from Schedule CR, line 19 | 19● | 0 |
| 20 | Line 18 minus line 19 | 20● | 244 |
| 21 | Credits and payments: | | |
| | (a) 2017 overpayment credited to 2018.  21(a)● | | |
| | (b) Estimated tax payments.  21(b)● | | |
| | (c) Tax paid with automatic extension of time to file  21(c)●  300 | | |
| | (d) Total credits and payments (add lines 21(a) through 21(c)). | 21(d)● | 300 |
| 22 | Estimated tax penalty (see Instructions). Check if Form N-220 is attached  ➤ ●☐ | 22● | 0 |
| 23 | **TAX DUE** — If line 21(d) is smaller than the total of lines 20 and 22, enter amount owed (see Instructions) | 23● | 0 |
| 24 | **OVERPAYMENT** — If line 21(d) is larger than the total of lines 20 and 22, enter amount overpaid (see Instructions) ➤ | 24● | 56 |
| 25 | (a) Enter the amount of line 24 you want **Credited to 2019 estimated tax** | 25(a)● | 0 |
| | (b) Enter the amount of line 24 you want **Refunded to you** (line 24 minus line 25(a)). ➤ | 25(b)● | 56 |
| 26 | Enter **AMOUNT PAID** with this return | 26 ● | |
| 27 | Amount paid (overpaid) on original return — AMENDED RETURN ONLY (see Instructions) | 27 | |
| 28 | BALANCE DUE (REFUND) with amended return (see Instructions) | 28 | |

**ATTACH COPY OF
FEDERAL FORM
990-T**

I declare, under the penalties set forth in section 231-36, HRS, that this return (including any accompanying schedules or statements) has been examined by me and, to the best of my knowledge and belief, is true, correct, and complete. Declaration of preparer (other than taxpayer) is based on all information of which preparer has any knowledge.

➤● _____    ➤ _____
Signature of officer                    Date                    Name and title of officer

★ May the Hawaii Department of Taxation discuss this return with the preparer shown below? (See page 5 of the Instructions)  ☒ Yes  ☐ No
This designation does not replace Form N-848, Power of Attorney.

**Please Sign Here**

| | | | |
|---|---|---|---|
| **Paid Preparer's Information** | Preparer's signature Print Preparer's Name ➤  HOMER JONES | Date | Check if self-employed ☐ ● | Preparer's identification no.  P00000000 |
| | Firm's name (or yours, if self-employed) ➤  KMH LLP, 1003 BISHOP ST, #2400 | Federal E.I. No. ➤ 42-1539623 | |
| | Address and ZIP Code ➤  HONOLULU, HI 96813 | Phone no. ➤ (808) 526-2255 | |

N70NP_I 2018A 01 VID01              ID NO 01                              **FORM N-70NP**

*Vertical left margin text:* • ATTACH CHECK OR MONEY ORDER HERE •

*Vertical section labels:* PRINT OR TYPE  •  Taxable Income  •  Tax Computation  •  Total Income Tax  •  Amended Return

FORM N-70NP (REV. 2018)                                                                          **Page 2**

| Name as shown on return | Federal Employer Identification Number |
|---|---|
| CHARITABLE, INC. | 34-5678912 |

## TAX COMPUTATION SCHEDULE

**PART I — Organizations Taxable as CORPORATIONS (See Instructions for Tax Computation)**

| | | | |
|---|---|---|---|
| 1 | Enter the amount of unrelated business taxable income as shown on page 1, line 8 . . . . . . . . . . . . | 1 | 5540 |
| 2 | Enter the total of other deductions (see Instructions, attach schedule). . . . . . . . . . . . . . . . . . . | 2● | |
| 3 | Difference — line 1 minus line 2 . . . . . . . . . . . . . . . . . . . . . . . . . . . . . . . . . . . . . . . | 3 | 5540 |
| 4 | Hawaii additions to income (see Instructions, attach schedule) . . . . . . . . . . . . . . . . . . . . . . . | 4 | |
| 5 | Sum of lines 3 and 4 . . . . . . . . . . . . . . . . . . . . . . . . . . . . . . . . . . . . . . . . . . . . . | 5 | 5540 |
| 6 | Enter the amount of taxable net capital gain from line 18, Schedule D (Form N-30/N-70NP) . . . . . . . . . | 6 | 0 |
| 7 | Difference — line 5 minus line 6 (if zero or less, enter zero) . . . . . . . . . . . . . . . . . . . . . . . . | 7 | 5540 |
| 8 | **(a)** Tax on net capital gain — 4% of the amount on line 6 . . . . . . . . . . . . . . . . . . . . . . . . | 8(a) | 0 |
| | **(b)** Tax on all other taxable income — If the amount on line 7 is: | | |
| |    (i)   Not over $25,000 — Enter 4.4% of line 7 . . . . . . . . . . . . . . . . . . . . . . . . . . . | 8(b)(i) | 244 |
| |    (ii)  Over $25,000 but not over $100,000 — Enter 5.4% | | |
| |        of line 7 $_____. Subtract $250 and enter the difference . . . . . . . . . . | 8(b)(ii) | |
| |    (iii) Over $100,000 — Enter 6.4% | | |
| |        of line 7 $_____. Subtract $1,250 and enter the difference . . . . . . . . | 8(b)(iii) | |
| | **(c)** Total of lines 8(a) and 8(b). . . . . . . . . . . . . . . . . . . . . . . . . . . . . . . . . . . . . . | 8(c) | 244 |
| | **(d)** Using the rates listed on line 8(b), compute the tax on the amount on line 5 above . . . . . . . . . . . | 8(d) | 244 |
| 9 | Total tax (enter the smaller of line 8(c) or line 8(d)). **Also, enter this amount on page 1, line 9** . . . . . . . | 9 | 244 |

**PART II — TRUSTS Taxable at Trust Rates (See Instructions for Tax Computation)**

| | | | |
|---|---|---|---|
| 1 | Enter the amount of unrelated business taxable income as shown on page 1, line 8 . . . . . . . . . . . . | 1 | |
| 2 | Enter the total of other deductions (see Instructions, attach schedule). . . . . . . . . . . . . . . . . . . | 2 | |
| 3 | Difference — line 1 minus line 2 . . . . . . . . . . . . . . . . . . . . . . . . . . . . . . . . . . . . . . . | 3 | |
| 4 | Hawaii additions to income (see Instructions, attach schedule) . . . . . . . . . . . . . . . . . . . . . . . | 4 | |
| 5 | Sum of lines 3 and 4 . . . . . . . . . . . . . . . . . . . . . . . . . . . . . . . . . . . . . . . . . . . . . | 5 | |
| 6 | Net capital gain taxable to the trust. Enter the smaller of line 18 or 19, col. (b), Schedule D (Form N-40) . . . | 6 | |
| 7 | Difference — line 5 minus line 6 (if zero or less, enter zero) . . . . . . . . . . . . . . . . . . . . . . . . | 7 | |
| 8 | Enter the greater of line 7 or $20,000. . . . . . . . . . . . . . . . . . . . . . . . . . . . . . . . . . . . | 8 | |
| 9 | Using the Trust Tax Rates below, compute the tax on the amount on line 8. If line 8 is $20,000, enter $1,128 . | 9 | |
| 10 | Difference — line 5 minus line 8 (if zero or less, enter zero) . . . . . . . . . . . . . . . . . . . . . . . . | 10 | |
| 11 | Multiply the amount on line 10 by 7.25% . . . . . . . . . . . . . . . . . . . . . . . . . . . . . . . . . . . | 11 | |
| 12 | Total of lines 9 and 11 . . . . . . . . . . . . . . . . . . . . . . . . . . . . . . . . . . . . . . . . . . . . | 12 | |
| 13 | Using the Trust Tax Rates below, compute the tax on the amount on line 5 above. . . . . . . . . . . . . . . | 13 | |
| 14 | Total tax (enter the smaller of line 12 or line 13). **Also, enter this amount on page 1, line 10** . . . . . . . . | 14 | |

### TRUST TAX RATES FOR PERIODS AFTER 12/31/01

| If the taxable income is: | The tax shall be: |
|---|---|
| Not over $2,000 . . . . . . . . . . . . . . . . . . . . . . . . | 1.4% of taxable income |
| Over $2,000 but not over $4,000. . . . . . . . . . . . . . . . | $28.00 plus 3.20% of excess over $2,000 |
| Over $4,000 but not over $8,000. . . . . . . . . . . . . . . . | $92.00 plus 5.50% of excess over $4,000 |
| Over $8,000 but not over $12,000 . . . . . . . . . . . . . . . | $312.00 plus 6.40% of excess over $8,000 |
| Over $12,000 but not over $16,000 . . . . . . . . . . . . . . | $568.00 plus 6.80% of excess over $12,000 |
| Over $16,000 but not over $20,000 . . . . . . . . . . . . . . | $840.00 plus 7.20% of excess over $16,000 |
| Over $20,000 but not over $30,000 . . . . . . . . . . . . . . | $1,128.00 plus 7.60% of excess over $20,000 |
| Over $30,000 but not over $40,000 . . . . . . . . . . . . . . | $1,888.00 plus 7.90% of excess over $30,000 |
| Over $40,000. . . . . . . . . . . . . . . . . . . . . . . . . . | $2,678.00 plus 8.25% of excess over $40,000 |

## EXEMPT ORGANIZATION BUSINESS
## INCOME TAX RETURN

### CHARITABLE, INC.
HAWAII I.D. NO. 00000000

### Form N-70NP

Total Deductions

|  | Attributable To Gross Income |
|---|---|
| Salaries and wages | $ 22,355 |
| Repairs | 512 |
| Interest | 47 |
| Taxes | 4,677 |
| Depreciation | 608 |
| Employee benefit programs | 3,182 |
| Utilities | 1,729 |
| Telephone and telegraph | 159 |
| Miscellaneous | 573 |
| Travel and entertainment | 211 |
| Office supplies | 56 |
| Auto expense | 91 |
| Insurance | 94 |
| Dues and subscriptions | 40 |
| Professional services | 92 |
| Postage | 145 |
| Other technical expenses | 361 |
| Advertising | 65 |
| Engineering expense | 61 |
| Rent | 128 |
| Commissions | 506 |
| Net operating loss carryover | 24,046 |
| Specific deduction | 1,000 |
| Total Deductions | $ 60,738 |

FORM
**N-4**
(REV. 2018)

STATE OF HAWAII—DEPARTMENT OF TAXATION
**STATEMENT OF WITHHOLDING**
**FOR A NONRESIDENT SHAREHOLDER**
**OF AN S CORPORATION**

THIS SPACE FOR DATE RECEIVED STAMP

**20** 18

S Corporation's Tax Year Ending ___DECEMBER___ , ● 20 18

**Copy A - Attach to Form N-35**

| 1.  S Corporation's Name and Mailing Address | ● 2. Shareholder's SSN or FEIN |
|---|---|
| LETHAL WEAPON GUN DEALERS<br>99 REMINGTON ROAD<br>COLT CITY, HI 96855 | 456-45-4564 |
|  | ● 3. Amount of Hawaii Tax Withheld<br>10,000.00 |
| 4.  S Corporation's FEIN<br>99-1237890 | ● 5. Shareholder's Name and Mailing Address<br>MEL GIBSON<br>763 RIFLE ROAD<br>LOS ANGELES, CA 92000 |
| 6.  Shareholder's Share of S Corporation's Hawaii Income<br>100,000.00 |  |

ID NO 01        **ATTACH TO THE FRONT OF FORM N-35 WHERE INDICATED**

N4_I 2018A 01 VID01                                                          **FORM N-4**

✂ — — — — — — — — — — — DETACH HERE — — — — — — — — — — ✂

FORM
**N-4**
(REV. 2018)

STATE OF HAWAII—DEPARTMENT OF TAXATION
**STATEMENT OF WITHHOLDING**
**FOR A NONRESIDENT SHAREHOLDER**
**OF AN S CORPORATION**

THIS SPACE FOR DATE RECEIVED STAMP

**20** 18

S Corporation's Tax Year Ending ___DECEMBER___ , ● 20 18

**Copy A - Attach to Form N-35**

| 1.   S Corporation's Name and Mailing Address | ● 2. Shareholder's SSN or FEIN |
|---|---|
| LETHAL WEAPON GUN DEALERS<br>99 REMINGTON ROAD<br>COLT CITY, HI 96855 | 456-45-4564 |
|  | ● 3. Amount of Hawaii Tax Withheld<br>10,000.00 |
| 4.  S Corporation's FEIN<br>99-1237890 | ● 5. Shareholder's Name and Mailing Address<br>MEL GIBSON<br>763 RIFLE ROAD<br>LOS ANGELES, CA 92000 |
| 6.   Shareholder's Share of S Corporation's Hawaii Income<br>100,000.00 |  |

ID NO 01        **ATTACH TO THE FRONT OF FORM N-35 WHERE INDICATED**

N4_I 2018A 01 VID01                                                          **FORM N-4**

# MAILING ADDRESS

## Hawaii Department of Taxation
P.O. Box 1530
Honolulu, Hawaii 96806-1530
(830 Punchbowl Street)

# IMPORTANT NOTE

Form N-5 is designed for electronic scanning that permits faster processing with fewer errors. To avoid delays:

1. Print amounts only on those lines that are applicable.
2. Use only a black or dark blue ink pen. Do not use red ink, pencils, felt tip pens, or erasable pens.
3. Because this form is read by a machine, please print your numbers inside the boxes like this:

$$123,456,789.00$$

4. Do NOT print outside the boxes.
5. Do NOT use dollar signs, commas, slashes, dashes or parentheses in the boxes.
6. **DO NOT SUBMIT A PHOTOCOPY OF THIS FORM.** Photocopying of this form could cause delays in processing your payment.

✂ — — — — — — — — — — CUT HERE — — — — — — — — — — ✂

Form (Rev. 2018)

**N-5**

STATE OF HAWAII — DEPARTMENT OF TAXATION

DO NOT WRITE OR STAPLE IN THIS SPACE

ESTIMATED INCOME TAX FOR ESTATES AND TRUSTS

## Voucher No. 1

THIS VOUCHER IS DUE ON OR BEFORE THE 20th DAY
OF THE 4th MONTH OF THE TAXABLE YEAR.

DO NOT SUBMIT A PHOTOCOPY OF THIS FORM

Composite Qualified Funeral Trusts

Name

INDIANA JONES GRANTOR TRUST

Dba or C/O

Federal Employer Identification Number (FEIN)

Mailing Address                          Suite Number

9876 HOLLYWOOD DRIVE

88 - 1234567

City, town, or post office    State    Postal/ZIP Code    Country    For office use only

Calendar or Fiscal Year Ending (MM DD YY)

TOUCHSTONE    HI    96899

12 - 31 - 19

MAIL THIS VOUCHER WITH CHECK OR MONEY ORDER PAYABLE
TO "HAWAII STATE TAX COLLECTOR." Write your FEIN, the year for
which payment is made, and Form N-5 (e.g., "2019 Form N-5") on your
check or money order.

Amount of Payment

10000.00

N5_F 2018A 01 VID01

ID NO 01

FORM
## N-101A
(REV. 2018)

STATE OF HAWAII — DEPARTMENT OF TAXATION

# INDIVIDUAL INCOME TAX EXTENSION PAYMENT VOUCHER

(NOTE: References to "married" and "spouse" are also references to
"in a civil union" and "civil union partner," respectively.)

## About this Form

Form N-101A is designed for electronic scanning that permits faster processing with fewer errors. To avoid delays:

1. Print amounts only on those lines that are applicable.
2. Use only a black or dark blue ink pen. Do not use red ink, pencils, felt tip pens, or erasable pens.
3. Because this form is read by a machine, please print your numbers inside the boxes like this:

**1 2 3 , 4 5 6 , 7 8 9 . 00**

4. Do NOT print outside the boxes.
5. Do NOT use dollar signs, commas, slashes, dashes or parentheses in the boxes.
6. Do not photocopy this form.

## General Instructions

You are granted an automatic 6-month extension of time to file Form N-11 or N-15. You don't need to file an application to request the extension. The automatic 6-month extension is granted if the following requirements are met:

- On or before the prescribed due date of your return, 100% of the properly estimated tax liability is paid;
- The tax return is filed on or before the expiration of the 6-month extension period;
- The tax return is accompanied by full payment of any tax not already paid; and
- A court has not ordered you to file the tax return on or before the prescribed due date.

Properly estimated tax liability means you made a bona fide and reasonable attempt to locate and gather all of the necessary information to make a proper estimate of tax liability for the taxable year.

If you must make a tax payment to meet the requirement that 100% of the properly estimated tax liability is paid on or before the prescribed due date of your return, you must file Form N-101A with your payment.

**Internet Filing**—Form N-101A can be filed and payment made electronically through the State's Internet portal. For more information, go to **tax.hawaii.gov/eservices/**.

**1. Purpose of Form N-101A.**— Use this form to make a tax payment if you will have a balance due when you file Form N-11 or N-15.

Federal Form 4868, Application for Automatic Extension of Time To File U.S. Individual Income Tax Return, may **not** be used in lieu of Form N-101A to make a tax payment.

**2. How to Obtain Tax Forms.**— Tax forms are available on the Department of Taxation's website at **tax.hawaii.gov**.

To request tax forms and publications by mail, you may call 808-587-4242 or toll-free 1-800-222-3229.

**3. When to File.**— File Form N-101A with your payment by the prescribed due date of your return. If the due date falls on a Saturday, Sunday or legal holiday, file by the next regular workday.

**4. Where to File.**— This form must be submitted to:

**Hawaii Department of Taxation**
P.O. Box 1530
Honolulu, Hawaii 96806-1530

**5. Where to Call for Information.**— You may get information by calling the following:

Telephone
808-587-4242
or 1-800-222-3229
Telephone for the hearing impaired
808-587-1418
or 1-800-887-8974

**6. Filing Your Tax Return.**— You may file your tax return any time before the extension expires. But remember, the extension does not extend the time to pay taxes. If you do not pay the amount due by the prescribed due date, you will owe interest. You may also be charged penalties.

**7. Penalties.**— Late Filing of Return – The penalty for failure to file a return on time is assessed on the tax due at a rate of 5% per month, or part of a month, up to a maximum of 25%.

Failure to Pay Tax After Filing Timely Return – The penalty for failure to pay the tax after filing a timely return is 20% of the tax unpaid within 60 days of the prescribed due date.

**8. Interest.**— Interest at the rate of 2/3 of 1% per month or part of a month shall be assessed on unpaid taxes and penalties

✂ — — — — — — — — — — CUT HERE — — — — — — — — — — — ✂

Form (Rev. 2018)

STATE OF HAWAII — DEPARTMENT OF TAXATION     DO NOT WRITE OR STAPLE IN THIS SPACE

## N-101A

### INDIVIDUAL INCOME TAX EXTENSION PAYMENT VOUCHER

**DO NOT SUBMIT A PHOTOCOPY OF THIS FORM**

| Composite Taxpayer | | | | Your Social Security Number |
|---|---|---|---|---|
| Your first name | M.I. | Last name | Suffix | |
| JOHN | F | LARSON | | 123 - 45 - 6789 |
| If joint return, spouse's first name | M.I. | Last name | Suffix | Spouse's Social Security Number |
| EDNA | L | LARSON | | 987 - 65 - 4321 |
| Present mailing or home address (Number and street, including rural route) | | | Apartment Number | Tax Year Ending (MM DD YY) |
| 1037 CORAL DRIVE | | | | |
| City, town, or post office | State | Postal/ZIP Code | Country | For office use only | |
| HONOLULU | HI | 96000 | | | 12 - 31 - 18 |

Amount of Payment

MAIL THIS VOUCHER WITH CHECK OR MONEY ORDER PAYABLE TO "HAWAII STATE TAX COLLECTOR." Write your social security number, daytime phone number, the year for which payment is made, and "Form N-101A" on your check or money order.

ID NO 01

200.00

N101A_F 2018A 01 VID01

STATE OF HAWAII — DEPARTMENT OF TAXATION

| FORM<br>N-103<br>(REV. 2018) |  | **SALE OF YOUR HOME**<br>SEE SEPARATE INSTRUCTIONS.<br>ATTACH TO FORM N-11 OR N-15. | **2018** |
|---|---|---|---|

(NOTE: References to "married" and "spouse" are also references to "in a civil union" and "civil union partner," respectively.)

**PRINT OR TYPE**

| Your first name and initial | Last name | Your social security number |
|---|---|---|
| JOHN F. | LARSON | 123-45-6789 |
| If a joint return, spouse's first name and initial | Last name | Spouse's social security number |
| EDNA L. | LARSON | 987-65-4321 |

Fill in your address if you are filing this form by itself and not with your tax return

Present mailing or home address (Number and street, including apartment number or rural route)
1037 CORAL DRIVE

City, town or post office, State, and Postal/ZIP code
HONOLULU, HI 96000

### PART I    General Information

| | | | | |
|---|---|---|---|---|
| 1 | Date your former main home was sold (month, day, year) ................................................ ➤ | 06/07/2018 | | |
| 2 | Was any part of your former main home rented out or used for business? (If "Yes," see Instructions.) ...................................... | ☐ Yes | ☑ No | |
| 3 | Was your former main home purchased with funds from an Individual Housing Account? .................................... | ☐ Yes | ☑ No | |
| | (If "Yes," go to line 4; if "No," go to line 8.) | | | |
| 4 | When was your former main home purchased? (month, day, year) .................................... ➤ | 01/21/1996 | | |
| 5 | Amount of distribution from your Individual Housing Account used to purchase your former main home.......... | **5** | | |
| 6 | Amount of line 5 not previously reported. (See Instructions.) If line 6 is zero, go to line 8. If line 6 is more than zero, include this amount on Form N-11, line 10, or Form N-15, line 19, and go to line 7. | **6** | | |
| 7 | Enter 10% (.10) of line 5. (See Instructions for where to include this amount on Form N-11 or N-15) ................. | **7** | 0 | .00 |

### PART II    Gain or (Loss), Exclusion, and Taxable Gain

| | | | | |
|---|---|---|---|---|
| 8 | Sale price of home. (Do not include payment received for personal property that you sold with your home.)....... | **8** | 134,000 | .00 |
| 9 | Selling expenses (including commissions, advertising and legal fees, and seller-paid loan charges) ................. | **9** | 7,000 | .00 |
| 10 | Amount realized. Line 8 minus line 9. .................................................................. | **10** | 127,000 | .00 |
| 11 | Adjusted basis of home sold. (See Instructions)......................................................... | **11** | 23,000 | .00 |
| 12 | **Gain or (loss)** on the sale. Line 10 minus line 11. If this amount is zero or less, stop here................. | **12** | 104,000 | .00 |
| | If you used any part of your home for business or rental purposes between May 6, 1997, and the date of sale, continue to line 13. Otherwise, skip to line 14, and enter the amount from line 12 on line 14. | | | |
| 13 | Enter the total of all depreciation deductions that you took or could have taken for the use of your home for business or rental purposes between May 6, 1997, and the date of sale.......................................... | **13** | 0 | .00 |
| 14 | Line 12 minus line 13. This is your net gain. ............................................................ | **14** | 104,000 | .00 |
| | If there was a period, after the year 2008, when neither you nor your spouse (or your former spouse) used the property as a main home, and that period of non-use occurred during the 5-year period prior to the date of sale and before the time when you or your spouse (or your former spouse) used that property as a main home, continue to line 15. Otherwise, skip to line 19, and enter the amount from line 14 on line 19. | | | |
| | **Note:** If the period of non-use was for (1) 2 years or less and due to a change in employment, a health condition, or other unforeseen circumstance, or (2) 10 years or less and due to a "stop the clock" exception for certain military, intelligence, and Peace Corps personnel, skip to line 19, and enter the amount from line 14 on line 19. | | | |
| 15 | Enter the total number of days after 2008 when neither you nor your spouse (or former spouse) used the home as a main residence. This number is your non-use days. .................................................. | **15** | | |
| 16 | Enter the total number of days you owned your home (counting all days, not just days after 2008). This number is your number of days owned. ............................................................ | **16** | | |
| 17 | Divide the amount on line 15 by the amount on line 16. This number is your non-residence factor. ............. | **17** | | |
| 18 | Line 14 multiplied by line 17. This number is your non-qualified use gain. ................................... | **18** | | |
| 19 | Gain eligible for exclusion. Line 14 minus line 18........................................................ | **19** | 104,000 | .00 |
| 20 | If you qualify to exclude gain on the sale, enter your maximum exclusion. (See Instructions) If you qualify for a partial exclusion, enter the amount from the Find Your Exclusion Limit Worksheet in federal Publication 523. If you do not qualify to exclude gain, enter -0-. | **20** | 500,000 | .00 |
| 21 | **Exclusion.** Enter the smaller of line 19 or line 20. .................................................... | **21** | 104,000 | .00 |
| 22 | **Taxable gain.** Line 12 minus line 21. (See Instructions for where to report your taxable gain.).............. | **22** | 0 | .00 |

**Sign here if you are filing this form by itself and not with your tax return**

I declare, under the penalties set forth in section 231-36, HRS, that I have examined this form, including attachments, and to the best of my knowledge and belief, it is true, correct, and complete.

➤ _____     _____
Your signature          Date

_____     _____
Spouse's signature          Date
(If joint return, both must sign)

**FORM N-103**

N103_I 2018A 01 VID01          ID NO 01

FORM HW-3
(REV. 2018)

DO NOT WRITE IN THIS AREA **36**

STATE OF HAWAII—DEPARTMENT OF TAXATION
**EMPLOYER'S ANNUAL RETURN
AND RECONCILIATION OF HAWAII
INCOME TAX WITHHELD FROM WAGES**

FOR CALENDAR YEAR 2018

SPEED INCORPORATED

**AMENDED Return**

**HAWAII TAX I.D. NO.**    WH-001-234-5678-01      **FEIN**   00-0001234

FOR AMENDED RETURNS, ATTACH ANY CORRECTED FORMS HW-2 (OR FEDERAL FORMS W-2C)

| | | |
|---|---|---|
| 1. | Number of HW-2 forms, COPY A, or federal Form W-2, COPY 1 ......................1 | 57 |
| 2. | TOTAL WAGES shown on these forms (include COLA, 3rd party sick leave, and other benefits) ......................2 | 681000.00 |
| 3. | TOTAL HAWAII INCOME TAX WITHHELD from wages shown on these forms ......................3 | 34010.00 |
| 3a. | PENALTIES ASSESSED ON PERIODIC RETURNS ............... | |
| 3b. | INTEREST ASSESSED ON PERIODIC RETURNS ............... | |
| 3c. | TOTAL AMOUNT DUE (Add lines 3, 3a, and 3b) ......................3c | 34010.00 |
| 4. | TOTAL PAYMENTS OF TAXES WITHHELD (including any penalty or interest paid with the periodic returns; Amended Returns, also include amount paid with original HW-3) ......................4 | 34010.00 |
| 5. | AMOUNT OF CREDIT TO BE REFUNDED (line 4 minus line 3c) ......................5 | 0.00 |
| 6. | AMOUNT OF TAXES now due and PAYABLE (line 3c minus line 4) ......................6 | 0.00 |

**• ATTACH CHECK OR MONEY ORDER •**

| | | |
|---|---|---|
| 7. | **FOR LATE FILING ONLY.** 7a. PENALTY......................... | 0.00 |
| | 7b. INTEREST......................... | 0.00 |

**REMINDER:** *All EFT payments must be transmitted by the payment due date or a 2% EFT penalty will be applied.*

| | | |
|---|---|---|
| 8. | TOTAL AMOUNT now due and PAYABLE (Add lines 6, 7a, and 7b) ......................8 | 0.00 |
| 9. | **Enter AMOUNT of payment.** Attach your check or money order payable to **"Hawaii State Tax Collector"** in U.S. dollars drawn on any U.S. bank to Form HW-3. Write the filing period and your Hawaii Tax I.D. No. on your check or money order. **IF NO PAYMENT, ENTER "0.00."** You may also e-pay at: **hitax.hawaii.gov** ............9 | |

AMOUNT OF PAYMENT

0.00

**Please file two copies of this form
together with the Statements of Hawaii
Income Tax Withheld and Wages Paid
(copy A of Form HW-2 or copy 1 of federal
Form W-2).**

THE SPACE BELOW RESERVED FOR DEPARTMENTAL USE

I declare under the penalties set forth in section 231-36, HRS, that this is a true and correct return, prepared in accordance with the withholding provisions of the Hawaii Income Tax Law and the rules issued thereunder.

| SIGNATURE | DATE |
|---|---|
| | 01-28-19 |
| TITLE | DAYTIME PHONE NUMBER |

SIGN THE RETURN AND MAIL TO:

Hawaii Department of Taxation
P.O. Box 3827
Honolulu, HI 96812-3827

Form HW-3 **36**

ID NO 88

HW3_T 2018A 01 VID88

FORM
**N-139**
(REV. 2018)

STATE OF HAWAII — DEPARTMENT OF TAXATION

# MOVING EXPENSES

**2018**

or other taxable year beginning _____ and ending _____
(NOTE: References to "married" and "spouse" are also references to "in a civil union" and "civil union partner," respectively.)

**CAUTION:** If a resident taxpayer leaves the State of Hawaii for other than temporary or transitory purposes and is not domiciled in Hawaii, he or she ceases to be a resident; in such a case, as with a nonresident taxpayer, expenses incurred in moving to a new place of employment outside the State of Hawaii shall not be allowed.

| Name(s) as shown on Form N-11 or N-15 | Your Social Security Number |
|---|---|
| STANLEY AND KAREN WALKER | 702-72-7002 |

**Caution:** *See the Distance Test and Time Test in the Instructions to find out if you can deduct your moving expenses.*
*If you are a member of the armed forces, see the Instructions to find out how to complete this form.*

**A** You are deducting moving expenses for (check only one box):
- [X] Moving within or to Hawaii. Date of move _____ 10/18/2018 _____
- [ ] Moving outside of Hawaii. Date of move _____

**B** Enter the address of your:
- Old home  123 LARCUS AVENUE, BAKERSFIELD, CA 93300
- New workplace  456 MAKA DRIVE, HONOLULU, HI 96000
- Old workplace  111 CHESTER STREET, BAKERSFIELD, CA 93300

**C** Enter the number of weeks you worked at your new workplace  _____

| | | | |
|---|---|---|---|
| **1** Enter the number of miles from your **old home** to your **new workplace** . . . . . . . | **1** | 2,600 miles | |
| **2** Enter the number of miles from your **old home** to your **old workplace** . . . . . . . | **2** | 10 miles | |
| **3** Line 1 minus line 2. If zero or less, enter -0- . . . . . . . . . . . . . . . . . . . | **3** | 2,590 miles | |

**Is line 3 at least 50 miles?**

- [X] **Yes.** You meet the distance test. Go to line 4. Also, see **Time Test** in the Instructions.

- [ ] **No.** You do not meet the distance test. You **cannot** deduct your moving expenses. **Do not** complete Form N-139.

| | | |
|---|---|---|
| **4** Enter the amount you paid for transportation and storage of household goods and personal effects . . . . . . . . . | **4** | 1,000 |
| **5** Enter the amount you paid for travel (including lodging) from your old home to your new home. **Do not** include the cost of meals . . . . . . . . . . . . . . . . . . . | **5** | 650 |
| **6** Add lines 4 and 5 . . . . . . . . . . . . . . . . . . . . . . . . . . . . . . . . | **6** | 1,650 |
| **7** Enter the total amount your employer paid you for the expenses listed on lines 4 and 5 that is **not** included in the wages box of your Form HW-2 or federal Form W-2. This amount should be shown in box 12 of your federal Form W-2 with code **P** . . . . . . . . . . . . . . . . . . . . . . . | **7** | 1,000 |

**8** Is line 6 **more than** line 7?

- [ ] **No.** You **cannot** deduct your moving expenses. If line 6 is less than line 7, subtract line 6 from line 7 and include the result on Form N-11, line 10 (if not already included on Form N-11, line 7), or on Form N-15, line 7.

- [X] **Yes.** Line 6 minus line 7. Enter the result here and on Form N-11, line 18 (if not already included on Form N-11, line 7), or on Form N-15, line 25.
  (Whole dollars only) This is your **moving expense deduction.**

| | | |
|---|---|---|
| | **8** | 650 00 |

**FORM N-139**

FORM
**N-301**
(REV. 2018)

STATE OF HAWAII — DEPARTMENT OF TAXATION

# CORPORATION, PARTNERSHIP, TRUST, OR REMIC
# INCOME TAX EXTENSION PAYMENT VOUCHER

(Includes Filers of Forms N-20, N-30, N-35, N-40, N-66, N-70NP and N-310)

## About this Form

Form N-301 is designed for electronic scanning that permits faster processing with fewer errors. To avoid delays:

1. Print amounts only on those lines that are applicable.
2. Use only a black or dark blue ink pen. Do not use red ink, pencils, felt tip pens, or erasable pens.
3. Because this form is read by a machine, please print your numbers inside the boxes like this:

1 2 3 , 4 5 6 , 7 8 9 . 00

4. Do NOT print outside the boxes.
5. Do NOT use dollar signs, slashes, dashes, or parentheses in the boxes.
6. Do NOT submit a photocopy of this form.

## INTERNET FILING

Form N-301 can be filed and payment made electronically through the State's Internet portal. For more information, go to: **tax.hawaii.gov/eservices/**.

## GENERAL INSTRUCTIONS

**Note:** The use of federal Form 7004 or other forms is not allowed as a substitute for Form N-301.

**1. Purpose of Form N-301.** — Use this form to make a tax payment if you will have a balance due when you file Form N-20, N-30, N-35, N-40, N-66, N-70NP, or N-310.

An extension of time to file your income tax return will not extend the time to pay your income tax. Therefore, pay your income tax balance due (i.e., total income tax liability reduced by payments and credits) in full with this form. Use the Income Tax Balance Due Worksheet below to determine the amount of your income tax balance due.

You are granted an automatic six-month extension of time to file Form N-20, N-30, N-35, N-40, N-66, N-70NP, or N-310. You do not need to file an application to request the extension. The automatic six-month extension is granted if the following requirements are met:

---

### INCOME TAX BALANCE DUE WORKSHEET

1  Total properly estimated income tax liability for the taxable year. .......................................1 _____

   **Note:** You **must** enter an amount on line 1. If you do not expect to owe tax, enter zero (0).

2  Current year's estimated tax payments (include prior year's overpayment

   allowed as credit)..................................................................................................2 _____

3  Other payments and credits ....................................................................................3 _____

4  Total (add lines 2 and 3) .........................................................................................4 _____

5  Income tax balance due (line 1 minus line 4). Pay in full with this form...............................5 _____

Pay amount on line 5 in full. Detach the voucher from this form. Attach check or money order to the voucher for full amount payable to "**Hawaii State Tax Collector.**" Write your **Federal Employer Identification Number, the year for which payment is made,** and "**Form N-301**" on the check or money order. Pay in U.S. dollars drawn on U.S. bank. Do not send cash. File with the Hawaii Department of Taxation, P.O. Box 1530, Honolulu, HI 96806-1530, or file electronically through: **tax.hawaii.gov/eservices/**.

---

✂ — — — — — — — — — — — — — — — CUT HERE — — — — — — — — — — — — — — — ✂

Form (Rev. 2018)
**N-301**

STATE OF HAWAII — DEPARTMENT OF TAXATION
**CORPORATION, PARTNERSHIP,
TRUST OR REMIC
INCOME TAX EXTENSION PAYMENT VOUCHER**

DO NOT SUBMIT A PHOTOCOPY OF THIS FORM

DO NOT WRITE OR STAPLE IN THIS SPACE

**X** CORPORATION      PARTNERSHIP      FIDUCIARY      REMIC

Name

HAWAII CLEARING INC. & SUBSIDIARY

Dba or C/O

Mailing Address                          Suite Number

872 HILO AVE
City, town, or post office    State    Postal/ZIP Code    Country    For office use only

HILO                  HI  96000

Federal Employer Identification Number (FEIN)

12 - 3456789

Calendar or Fiscal Year Ending (MM DD YY)

12 - 31 - 18

Amount of Payment

2600.00

MAIL THIS VOUCHER WITH CHECK OR MONEY ORDER
PAYABLE TO "HAWAII STATE TAX COLLECTOR." Write your
FEIN, the year for which payment is made, and "Form N-301"
on your check or money order.

N301_F 2018A 01 VID01

ID NO 01

## HAWAII CLEARING, INC. & SUBSIDIARY
HAWAII I.D. NO. W23456789-01

## Form N-301

| Name and Address of Each Member of the Affiliated Group of Domestic Entities | Federal Identification Number |
|---|---|
| Hawaii Equipment Sales & Services<br>872 Hilo Avenue<br>Hilo, Hawaii 96000 | 22-2222222 |

DO NOT WRITE IN THIS SPACE

**FORM**
**N-755**
(REV. 2018)

STATE OF HAWAII — DEPARTMENT OF TAXATION

## APPLICATION FOR AUTOMATIC EXTENSION OF TIME
## TO FILE HAWAII FRANCHISE TAX RETURN (FORM F-1)
## OR PUBLIC SERVICE COMPANY TAX RETURN (FORM U-6)

☐ Change of address

| | | |
|---|---|---|
| Name<br>HONOLULU INTERNATIONAL BANK | ☐ Extension REJECTED. (See below for reasons.) | |
| DBA (if any) | Federal Employer Identification Number<br>98-1234597 | |
| Mailing Address (number and street)<br>900 WALL STREET | Hawaii Tax I.D. No.<br>FR 123-456-7890-12 | |
| City, State, and Postal/ZIP Code<br>HONOLULU, HI 96000 | | |

*(left margin: Type or Print)*

**Check type of return to be filed:**   ☑ Form F-1   ☐ Form U-6

(Check here ➤ ☐ if you do not have an office or place of business in Hawaii)

1   (a)   I request an automatic 6-month extension of time to file the franchise or public service company tax return of the entity named above for:

**calendar year 20** 18          **, or tax year ending** _____ **, 20** _____

   (b)   If this tax year is for less than 12 months, check reason:
   ☐ Initial return          ☐ Final return          ☐ Change in accounting period approved          ☐ Consolidated return to be filed
   ☐ Amended Return       ☐ First Year         ☐ Second Year          ☐ Third Year

2   Does this application also cover subsidiaries to be included in a consolidated return? .......................................... ☐ Yes   ☑ No
    If "Yes," attach a list showing the name, address, and Federal Employer Identification Number of each member of the affiliated group of domestic entities.

| | | |
|---|---|---|
| 3   Total tax liability for the taxable year (You may estimate this amount)........................................... | **3** | 100,000 00 |

   **NOTE:** *You must enter an amount on line 3. If you do not expect to owe tax,* enter zero (0) and skip lines 4a, 4b, and 4c.

4   Are you paying the tax in:
   **4a.**  4 equal installments?................................... ☐ Yes   ☑ No
   **4b.**  12 equal installments (required for those whose total tax liability
          exceeds $100,000)?...................................... ☑ Yes   ☐ No
   **4c.**  If line 4a is checked "Yes" — enter 1/4 of line 3 on line 4c.
          If line 4b is checked "Yes" — enter 1/3 of line 3 on line 4c.

| | | |
|---|---|---|
| If "No" is checked for line 4a and 4b — enter the amount of line 3 on line 4c...................... | **4c** | 8,333 00 |

Pay amount on line 4c in full. Attach check or money order for full amount payable to **"Hawaii State Tax Collector."** Write your **Federal Employer Identification Number, the taxable year, and Form N-755** on it. Pay in U.S. dollars. Do not send cash.

Installment Payments. — If you are making installment payments instead of paying the tax in full, use the "Franchise Tax or Public Service Company Tax Installment Payment Voucher" (Form FP-1) to report and pay the remaining amount(s) due.

---

### REASONS FOR REJECTION OF EXTENSION

   ☐ 1.  The request was not in this office or mailed on or before the date prescribed by law for filing this return.
   ☐ 2.  Separate requests are required for each type of tax and for each taxpayer involved.
   ☐ 3.  The tax return was not filed within the time specified by the automatic extension.

---

**FORM BB-1**
**(Rev. 2017)**

## STATE OF HAWAII
## BASIC BUSINESS APPLICATION
### (or Amended Application)

This Space For Office Use Only

For faster service apply online at **tax.hawaii.gov/eservices**
Online applications are processed in 2-4 business days.

**TYPE OR PRINT LEGIBLY**

**1. Purpose of Application** — Check only one. For **1b, 1c** and **1d**, Complete lines 1 through 5 and ONLY the information you are adding, deleting or changing.
  **a.** X New **b.** Add **c.** Delete **d.** Change (Use Form GEWTARV-1 to CANCEL any tax licenses, registrations or permits)

**2.** X FEIN    TIN    SSN    | **3.** Hawaii Tax I.D. No.

77-1234567

**4. Taxpayer's/Employer's/Plan Manager's Legal Name** | **5. Trade name or doing business as (DBA) name, if any**

LEI, INC

**6. Mailing Care of:** | **7. Physical location street address of business in Hawaii (If different from mailing)**

SAME AS MAILING

Mailing Street address or P.O. Box | Physical location City    State    Postal/Zip Code

300 FLOWER STREET | If none, provide name, phone number and address of the person performing services in HI.
Mailing City    State    Postal/Zip Code

HONOLULU, HI 96000

**8. Type of legal organization**
  X Corporation    S Corporation    General Partnership    Limited Partnership    Nonprofit
  Sole Proprietorship    Single-Member LLC    LLC    Government    Other (Please specify)

**9.** Does all or part of this business qualify for a disability exemption? (See Instructions) | **10. Date Business Began in Hawaii** | **11. Date of Organization** | **12. State of Organization**
  Yes    X No | 01/05/2019 | 01/01/2019 | HI

**13. Accounting period** (check only one) | **14. Accounting method** (check only one) | **15. NAICS and business activity** (See Instructions)
  X Calendar Year | X Cash    Accrual |
  Fiscal Year ending |  |
Effective | Effective |

**16. Business Phone** | Alternate Phone | Fax Number | E-mail address

808-531-2000 | 808-555-0000 | 808-531-2002 | JOHN.ALOHA@GMAIL.COM

**17. Parent Corporation's FEIN** | **18. Name of Parent Corporation** | **19. Parent Corporation's Mailing Address**

**20.** List all sole proprietors, partners, members, or corporate officers (See Instructions) *Attach a separate sheet of paper if more space is required.*

| FEIN/TIN/SSN | Name (Individuals - Last, First, M.I.) | Title | Residential Address | Contact Phone No. |
|---|---|---|---|---|
| FEIN TIN X SSN | | | | |
| 123-12-1231 | ALOHA, JOHN | PRESIDENT | 400 HIBISCUS STREET | 808-531-2002 |
| FEIN TIN SSN | | | | |

**21. TOTAL REGISTRATION FEE DUE.** Add the amounts from lines 22b through 22i. See Instructions for Forms VP-1 and VP-2. Attach a check or money order made payable to "HAWAII STATE TAX COLLECTOR" in U.S. dollars drawn on any U.S. Bank along with the appropriate Forms VP-1 and/or VP-2 . . . . . . . . . . . . . . . . . . . . . . . . . . . . . . . . . . . . . . . . 20.00

**CERTIFICATION:** The above statements are hereby certified to be correct to the best of the knowledge and belief of the undersigned who is duly authorized to sign this application.

Mail the completed application to:
HAWAII DEPARTMENT OF TAXATION
P.O. Box 1425
Honolulu, HI 96806-1425

Signature of Owner, Partner or Member, Officer, or Agent

Print Name    Title    Date    **02**

*• ATTACH CHECK OR MONEY ORDER AND FORMS VP-1 AND VP-2 HERE •*

LEI, INC                                              77-1234567

### Form BB-1, Page 2

| 22. Select Tax Type(s): | Date Activity Began in Hawaii -OR- Effective Date If Changing Filing Period* (mm/dd/yyyy) | Filing Period Mo. Qtr. Semi | Fee | Fee Due |
|---|---|---|---|---|
| **22a.** X Withholding | | (See also http://labor.hawaii.gov/ui/) | no fee | |
| **22b.** General Excise/Use — Select ONLY one type of GE/Use license: | | | | |
| X GET/Use Tax | | X | $20.00 | 20.00 |
| GE One-Time Event | | | $20.00 | |
| Please enter the name of the One-time Event *(See Instructions)* | | | | |
| Use Tax Only | | | no fee | |
| Seller's collection | | | no fee | |
| **22c.** Transient Accommodations [24] | | | 1-5 units - $5.00 / 6 or more units - $15.00 | 0.00 |
| **22d.** Timeshare Occupancy [25] | | Number of Timeshare Plans represented | x $15.00 | 0.00 |
| **22e.** Rental Motor Vehicle, Tour Vehicle, and Car-Sharing Vehicle [24] | | | $20.00 | 0.00 |
| **22f.** Liquid Fuel Distributor | | | no fee | |
| Produce    Refine    Manufacture    Compound | | | | |
| **22g.** Liquid Fuel Retail Dealer [24] | | | $5.00 | 0.00 |
| **22h.** Liquor [23]   Enter your county liquor license no. | | | | 0.00 |
| Manufacturer | | | $2.50 | |
| Wholesaler | | | $2.50 | |
| **22i.** Cigarette & Tobacco [23] | | | | |
| Non-Retail:    Dealer    Wholesaler | | | $2.50 | 0.00 |
| Retail Tobacco Permit [24] | | Number of retail locations | x $20.00 | 0.00 |

**23.** Have you ever been cited for either a tobacco and/or liquor violation?     Yes     No

**24.** Check the appropriate tax type and list the address(es) of your transient accommodations (TA) rental real property; rental motor vehicle, tour vehicle, and/or car-sharing vehicle (RV); Liquid Fuel Retail Dealer's Permit (Fuel); and/or Retail Tobacco Permit (RTP) business locations. For Retail Tobacco locations, if location is a vehicle, include the Vehicle Identification Number (VIN), otherwise include the name of the retail location. *Attach a list if more space is needed.*

TA   RV   Fuel   RTP                          **Address**                          **Name or VIN**

**25.** Resort Time Share Vacation Plan Information. List each resort time share vacation plan represented by you. *Attach a list if more space is needed.*

New    Add    Cancel        DCCA Plan No.        Plan Name        Plan Address

BB1_T 2017A 02

* NOTE: The requested change will take effect after the current filing period is over. The filing frequency cannot be changed retroactively.        **Form BB-1 (Rev. 2017)**

FORM
## VP-1
(REV. 2018)

STATE OF HAWAII — DEPARTMENT OF TAXATION
GENERAL EXCISE/USE, TRANSIENT
ACCOMMODATIONS AND RENTAL MOTOR VEHICLE,
TOUR VEHICLE & CAR-SHARING VEHICLE SURCHARGE

# TAX PAYMENT VOUCHER
## GENERAL INSTRUCTIONS

## CHANGES YOU SHOULD NOTE

If payment is submitted with a return (general excise/use, transient accommodations, withholding and rental motor vehicle, tour vehicle & car-sharing vehicle surcharge), DO NOT attach Form VP-1 to the tax return.

## INTERNET FILING

Form VP-1 can be filed and paid electronically through the State's Internet portal. For more information, go to tax.hawaii.gov/eservices/.

## PURPOSE OF FORM

Use this form if submitting Form BB-1 or submitting a payment without a tax return.

## HOW TO COMPLETE FORM

1) Print the name in the space provided.
2) Check the appropriate "Tax Type" box.
3) Check the appropriate "Filing Type" box and fill in the period or year in the space provided.
   If filing Form BB-1, check the box "License Fee."
   Add lines 22b through 22f on Form BB-1 and enter the amount of payment in the space provided.
   Enter the last day of the first filing period. (e.g., a calendar year quarterly filer, began business on January 21, 2019, the first filing period end date is 03/31/19.
4) In the space provided, print the Hawaii Tax I.D. No. starting with the tax type (i.e. GE, TA, WH or RV), the 10 digit account number with the 2 digit extension; and the amount of payment.

5) Make the check or money order payable in U.S. dollars to the **"Hawaii State Tax Collector."** Make sure the name, tax type, filing period, and Hawaii Tax I.D. No. appear on the check or money order. Do not postdate the check. **Do not send cash.**

## WHERE TO FILE

Detach Form VP-1 along the dotted line. If filing Form BB-1, attach the payment and Form VP-1 to the front of the form and send it to the Form BB-1 mailing address below. If submitting only a tax payment (without a return), send Form VP-1 and the payment to the mailing address noted below for the type of tax. The mailing addresses are as follows:

**General Excise/Use Tax**
Hawaii Department of Taxation
P.O. Box 1425
Honolulu, HI 96806-1730

**Transient Accommodations Tax And
Rental Motor Vehicle, Tour Vehicle & Car-Sharing
Vehicle Surcharge Tax**
Hawaii Department of Taxation
P.O. Box 2430
Honolulu, HI 96804-2430

**Hawaii Withholding**
Hawaii Department of Taxation
P.O. Box 3827
Honolulu, HI 96812-3827

**Form BB-1**
Hawaii Department of Taxation
P.O. Box 1425
Honolulu, HI 96806-1425

✂ - - - - - - - - - - - - - - - - - - - - - DETACH HERE - - - - - - - - - - - - - - - - - - - - - - ✂

Form (Rev. 2018)
## VP-1

STATE OF HAWAII — DEPARTMENT OF TAXATION
TAX PAYMENT VOUCHER

DO NOT WRITE OR STAPLE IN THIS SPACE

DO NOT SUBMIT A PHOTOCOPY OF THIS FORM

Name (Please print): LEI, INC

Tax Type (check only 1)

Filing Type (check only 1) Enter Date as MM DD YY

Print the amount of your payment in the space provided. ATTACH THIS VOUCHER WITH CHECK OR MONEY ORDER PAYABLE TO "HAWAII STATE TAX COLLECTOR" Write the tax and filing types, and your Hawaii Tax I.D. Number on your check or money order.

General Excise (GE)

X License Fee
1st Period End          03-31-19

Transient Accommodations (TA)

Periodic Return
Period End

Hawaii Tax I.D. Number

Hawaii Withholding (WH)

Rental Motor, Tour & Car-Sharing
Vehicles (RV)

Annual Return
Tax Year End

Amount of Payment

20.00

FORM   STATE OF HAWAII — DEPARTMENT OF TAXATION

THIS SPACE FOR DATE RECEIVED STAMP

# U-6 PUBLIC SERVICE COMPANY TAX RETURN
(REV. 2018)                            CALENDAR YEAR **2019**

(Based on income for calendar year 2018 or fiscal year beginning on
_____ , 2018 and ending _____ , 20 ___ )
(First year, Second year, and Final year return filers, see Instructions)

**(NOTE: Do NOT use Form U-6 to calculate and/or remit the counties' share of the public service company tax.)**

| | |
|---|---|
| Name<br>TRANSPORTATION, INC. | Date Business Began in Hawaii<br>01-01-1997 |
| DBA (if any) | Hawaii Tax I.D. No.<br>GE-001-234-5678-01 |
| Mailing Address (number and street)<br>201 POI STREET | Federal Employer I.D. No.<br>77-7121234 |
| City, State, and Postal/ZIP Code<br>HONOLULU, HI 96000 | Amount paid with this return<br>●$                              5816.00 |

PRINT OR TYPE

CHECK BOX IF APPLICABLE:
☐ First year  ☐ Second year  ☐ Final year  ☐ Amended return  ☐ Paying tax in installments
☐ Change of Address

TOTAL TAX (from page 2; Do Not enter
TAX DUE amount)
$                              25816.00

## SECTION I - COMPUTATION OF ADJUSTED GROSS INCOME

**GROSS INCOME FROM PRECEDING TAXABLE YEAR BEGINNING IN 2018**

| | | | |
|---|---|---|---|
| 1 Gross Income from Public Utility Business (describe fully from what sources received) | | | |
| a (1) Passenger Fares for Transportation Between Points on a<br>Scheduled Route By Land | 1a(1) | 482545.00 | |
| (2) Worthless Accounts Charged Off for Net Income Tax<br>Purposes (see Instructions) | 1a(2) | | |
| (3) Adjusted Gross Income (line 1a(1) minus line 1a(2)) | | 1a(3) | 482545.00 |
| b (1) Sales of Products or Services to Another Public Utility for<br>Resale to the Consumer | 1b(1) | | |
| (2) Worthless Accounts Charged Off for Net Income Tax<br>Purposes (see Instructions) | 1b(2) | | |
| (3) Adjusted Gross Income (line 1b(1) minus line 1b(2)) | | 1b(3) | |
| c (1) Sales of Telecommunication Services to a Person Defined in<br>Section 237-13(6)(D), HRS, for Resale to the Consumer | 1c(1) | | |
| (2) Worthless Accounts Charged Off for Net Income Tax<br>Purposes (see Instructions) | 1c(2) | | |
| (3) Adjusted Gross Income (line 1c(1) minus line 1c(2)) | | 1c(3) | |
| d (1) | 1d(1) | | |
| (2) Worthless Accounts Charged Off for Net Income Tax<br>Purposes (see Instructions) | 1d(2) | | |
| (3) Adjusted Gross Income (line 1d(1) minus line 1d(2)) | | 1d(3) | |
| 2 Equipment Rentals Received (attach schedule and describe fully) | | 2 | |
| 3 Joint Facility Rentals Received | | 3 | |
| 4 Non-Operating Income from Public Utility Business (attach schedule and describe fully) | | 4 | |
| 5 TOTAL ADJUSTED GROSS INCOME (add lines 1 through 4) | | 5 | 482545.00 |

Please Sign Here

**DECLARATION** — I declare, under the penalties set forth in section 231-36, HRS, that this return (including any accompanying schedules or statements) has been examined by me and, to the best of my knowledge and belief is a true, correct, and complete return, made in good faith, for the taxable year stated, pursuant to the Public Service Company Tax Law, Chapter 239, HRS.

► _____    ► _____
Signature of officer        Date        Title

| Paid Preparer's Information | Preparer's Signature and Print Preparer's Name ► HOMER JONES | Date | Check if self-employed ☐ | Preparer's identification number<br>● P00000000 |
|---|---|---|---|---|
| | Firm's name (or yours if self-employed), Address, and Postal/Zip Code ► KMH LLP, 1003 BISHOP STREET, #2400<br>HONOLULU, HI 96813 | | Federal E.I. No ► 42-1539623 | |
| | | | Phone No. ► (808) 526-2255 | |

U6_I 2018A 01 VID01                    ID NO 01                    FORM U-6

**FORM U-6 (REV. 2018)** PAGE 2

| Name as shown on return | Federal Employer Identification Number |
|---|---|
| TRANSPORTATION, INC. | 77-7121234 |

**SECTION II — COMPUTATION OF TAX** (Line references are to lines on page 1.) **Note:** Enter **TOTAL TAX** amount on **page 1.**

**PART I. — FOR PUBLIC UTILITIES TAXED UNDER SECTION 239-5 (a), (b) and (c), HRS.**

**Note: A Public Utility taxed under section 239-5(a), HRS, must also attach to this return year-end balance sheets, income statements, and an analysis of retained earnings for the utility and non-utility portions of the business.**

| | | | | | | |
|---|---|---|---|---|---|---|
| A | Line 5 less lines 1a(3), 1b(3), and 1c(3) . . . . . . . . . . . | | x 4.0% (fixed rate) . . . . . .TAX AMOUNT | A | | |
| B | Line 1a(3) . . . . . . . . . . | 482545.00 | x 5.35% (fixed rate) . . . . . .TAX AMOUNT | B | 25816.00 | |
| C | Line 1b(3) . . . . . . . . . | | x .5 % (fixed rate) . . . . .TAX AMOUNT | C | | |
| D | Line 1c(3) . . . . . . . . . | | x .5 % . . . . . . . . . .TAX AMOUNT | D | | |
| E | **TOTAL TAX** (add lines A, B, C, and D). . . . . . . . . . . . . . . . . . . . . . ► | | | E● | 25816.00 | |
| F | Nonrefundable Tax Credit - Credit for Lifeline Telephone Service Subsidy (see Instructions) . . . . . . . . . . . . . . . . . . | | | F● | | |
| G | Balance (line E minus line F, but not less than zero). . . . . . . . . . . . | | | G | | |
| H | Payment with Extension (attach Form N-755) (see Instructions) . . . . . . . . | H | | | | |
| I | Tax Installment Payments (see Instructions). . . . . . . . . . . . . . . . . . | I | 20000.00 | | | |
| J | Total Payments (add lines H and I). . . . . . . . . . . . . . . . . . . . . . . | | | J● | 20000.00 | |
| K | TAX DUE (if line G is larger than J), enter AMOUNT OWED. (if line G exceeds $100,000, see Instructions, When Is the Tax Payable) . . . . . . . . . . . | | | K● | 5816.00 | |
| L | OVERPAYMENT (if line J is larger than line G), enter AMOUNT OVERPAID . . . . . . . . . . | | | L● | | |

**PART II. — FOR PUBLIC UTILITIES TAXED ONLY UNDER SECTION 239-5(b), HRS.**

| | | | | | |
|---|---|---|---|---|---|
| A | **TOTAL TAX** (line 1a(3) . . . . . . | | x 5.35% (fixed rate)) . . . . . . . . . . . ► | A● | |
| B | Payment with Extension (attach Form N-755) (see Instructions) . . . . . . . . | B | | | |
| C | Tax Installment Payments (see Instructions). . . . . . . . . . . . . . . . . . | C | | | |
| D | Total Payments (add lines B and C) . . . . . . . . . . . . . . . . . . . . . | | | D● | |
| E | TAX DUE (if line A is larger than line D), enter AMOUNT OWED. (if line A exceeds $100,000, see Instructions, When Is the Tax Payable) . . . . . | | | E● | |
| F | OVERPAYMENT (if line D is larger than line A), enter AMOUNT OVERPAID . . . . . . . . . . | | | F● | |

**PART III. — FOR PUBLIC UTILITIES TAXED ONLY UNDER SECTION 239-5(c), HRS.**

| | | | | | |
|---|---|---|---|---|---|
| A | Line 1b(3) . . . . . . . . . . | | x .5 % (fixed rate) . . . . . .TAX AMOUNT | A | |
| B | Line 1c(3) . . . . . . . . . . | | x .5 % . . . . . . . . . .TAX AMOUNT | B | |
| C | **TOTAL TAX** (add lines A and B) . . . . . . . . . . . . . . . . . . . . . . . ► | | | C● | |
| D | Payment with Extension (attach Form N-755) (see Instructions) . . . . . . . . | D | | | |
| E | Tax Installment Payments (see Instructions). . . . . . . . . . . . . . . . . . | E | | | |
| F | Total Payments (add lines D and E) . . . . . . . . . . . . . . . . . . . . . . | | | F● | |
| G | TAX DUE (if line C is larger than line F), enter AMOUNT OWED. (if line C exceeds $100,000, see Instructions, When Is the Tax Payable) . . . . . . . . . . . . . . . . . . . | | | G● | |
| H | OVERPAYMENT (if line F is larger than line C), enter AMOUNT OVERPAID . . . . . . . . . . . . . . | | | H● | |

**FORM TA-1**
(Rev. 2018)

ID NO 88

STATE OF HAWAII — DEPARTMENT OF TAXATION   DO NOT WRITE IN THIS AREA   **20**

**TRANSIENT ACCOMMODATIONS**
**TAX RETURN**
For periods beginning AFTER December 31, 2017

**Place an "X" in this box ONLY if this is an AMENDED return**

**PERIOD ENDING**   01-19      **HAWAII TAX I.D. NO.**   TA-123-456-7890-01

NAME:   JOHN ALOHA                          Last 4 digits of your FEIN or SSN   1231

| | DISTRICT | Column a GROSS RENTAL OR GROSS RENTAL PROCEEDS | Column b EXEMPTIONS/DEDUCTIONS (Explain on Reverse Side) | Column c TAXABLE PROCEEDS (Column a minus Column b) | |
|---|---|---|---|---|---|
| **PART I - TRANSIENT ACCOMMODATIONS TAX** | 1. OAHU | 1200.00 | 0.00 | 1200.00 | 1 |
| | 2. MAUI, MOLOKAI, LANAI | | 0.00 | 0.00 | 2 |
| | 3. HAWAII | | 0.00 | 0.00 | 3 |
| | 4. KAUAI | | 0.00 | 0.00 | 4 |

|   |   | TOTAL FAIR MARKET RENTAL VALUE |
|---|---|---|
| **PART II - TIMESHARE OCCUPANCY TAX** | 5. OAHU DISTRICT ............................................................ 5. | |
| | 6. MAUI, MOLOKAI, LANAI DISTRICT ........................................ 6. | |
| | 7. HAWAII DISTRICT ......................................................... 7. | |
| | 8. KAUAI DISTRICT .......................................................... 8. | |

| **PART III - TAX COMPUTATION** | 9. **TOTAL AMOUNT TAXABLE.** Add Column c of lines 1 through 4 and lines 5 through 8. Enter result here (but not less than zero). ............... 9. | 1200.00 |
|---|---|---|
| | 10. **Tax Rate** 10. | x 0.1025 |
| | 11. **TOTAL TAXES DUE.** Multiply line 9 by line 10 and enter the result here. **If you did not have any activity for the period, enter "0.00" here** ............... 11. | 123.00 |

| **PART IV - ADJUSTMENTS** | 12. Amounts Assessed During the Period ...... PENALTY ——————— | |
|---|---|---|
| | *(For Amended Return ONLY)*   INTEREST_____ 12. | 0.00 |
| | 13. **TOTAL AMOUNT.** Add lines 11 and 12. *(For Amended Return ONLY)* ............... 13. | 123.00 |
| | 14. TOTAL PAYMENTS MADE FOR THE PERIOD *(For Amended Return ONLY)* ...... 14. | |
| | 15. **CREDIT TO BE REFUNDED.** Line 14 minus line 13 *(For Amended Return ONLY)* ...... 15. | 0.00 |
| | 16. **ADDITIONAL TAXES DUE.** Line 13 minus line 14 *(For Amended Return ONLY)* ...... 16. | 0.00 |

• ATTACH CHECK OR MONEY ORDER HERE •

**DECLARATION** - I declare, under the penalties set forth in section 231-36, HRS, that this return (including any accompanying schedules or statements) has been examined by me and, to the best of my knowledge and belief, is a true, correct, and complete return, made in good faith for the tax period stated, pursuant to the Transient Accommodations Tax Laws, and the rules issued thereunder.

IN THE CASE OF A CORPORATION OR PARTNERSHIP, THIS RETURN MUST BE SIGNED BY AN OFFICER, PARTNER OR MEMBER, OR DULY AUTHORIZED AGENT.

| SIGNATURE | TITLE OWNER | DATE 02/15/19 | DAYTIME PHONE NUMBER (808) 531-2000 |
|---|---|---|---|

TA1_T 2018A 01 VID88   **Continued on page 2 — Parts V & VI MUST be completed**   Form TA-1 (Rev. 2018) **20**

**FORM TA-1**
(Rev. 2018)

Name: JOHN ALOHA

Hawaii Tax I.D. No.    TA-123-456-7890-01

Last 4 digits of your FEIN or SSN    1231          PERIOD ENDING (MM/YY) 01-19

**PART V - TOTAL AMOUNT DUE**

17. **FOR LATE FILING ONLY** →   PENALTY _____ 0.00
                                 INTEREST _____ 0.00        17. _____ 0.00

18. **TOTAL AMOUNT DUE AND PAYABLE**(Original Returns, add lines 11 and 17;
    Amended Returns, add lines 16 and 17) .................................... 18. _____ 123.00

19. **PLEASE ENTER THE AMOUNT OF YOUR PAYMENT.**Attach a check or money order
    payable to "HAWAII STATE TAX COLLECTOR" in U.S. dollars drawn on any U.S. bank to
    Form TA-1. Write "TA," the filing period, and your Hawaii Tax I.D. No. on your check or money order.
    Mail to: HAWAII DEPARTMENT OF TAXATION, P. O. Box 2430, HONOLULU, HI 96804-2430
    or file and pay electronically at tax.hawaii.gov/eservices/. If you are NOT submitting a
    payment with this return, please enter "0.00" here ...................... 19. _____ 123.00

## PART VI — SCHEDULE OF EXEMPTIONS/DEDUCTIONS

**Note:** Most ordinary business expenses are NOT DEDUCTIBLE (e.g., materials, supplies, etc.) on your transient accommodations tax return. For more information, see the Form TA-1 Instructions.

You must explain your exemptions and deductions, otherwise they will be disallowed and you will owe more taxes.

| DISTRICT / ED CODE | AMOUNT | DISTRICT / ED CODE | AMOUNT | DISTRICT / ED CODE | AMOUNT |
|---|---|---|---|---|---|
| | | | | | |
| | | | | | |
| | | | | | |
| | | | | | |

**Grand Total of Exemptions and Deductions** — Add the amounts above in Part VI and enter here. If more space is needed, attach a schedule. Include the total deductions claimed from any attachments in this total. (See Instructions) .................... 0.00

**Additional Instructions for Exemptions/Deductions (ED)**

For each exemptions/deductions you have claimed, enter:

1. For the "DISTRICT" column, enter the number that represents the Tax District from which the income was earned.
   1 = Oahu; 2 = Maui; 3 = Hawaii; and 4 = Kauai
2. For the ED Code please see the list of codes below and enter the corresponding Exemption/Deduction code.
3. Enter your total amount of the exemption/deduction claimed for that District and ED Code.

*Example:* Taxpayer A received gross rental proceeds of $2,000.00 from the Consul General of the Philippines for lodging on Maui. Taxpayer A enters the following to justify the deduction entered in Part I, Line 2, Column b of the Transient Accommodations Tax Return:

DISTRICT / ED CODE    **AMOUNT**
2 / 1 1 0      , 2, 0 0 0 . 0 0

| Description (HRS) | ED Code | Description (HRS) | ED Code | Description (HRS) | ED Code |
|---|---|---|---|---|---|
| Complimentary Accommodations (§237D-3(7)) | 100 | Nonprofit Organization, Lodging provided by a (§237D-3(3)) | 140 | Temporary Lodging Allowance for military (§237D-3(4)) | 180 |
| Diplomats and Consular Officials (§237D-3(8)) | 110 | School Dormitories (§237D-3(2)) | 150 | Working Fringe Benefit (§237D-3(7)) | 190 |
| Federal or state subsidized lodging (§237D-3(5)) | 120 | Students — | | | |
| Health care facilities defined in HRS§321-11(10) (§237D-3(1)) | 130 | Full-time Post-secondary (§237D-3(6)) | 160 | | |
| | | Summer Employment (§237D-3(6)) | 170 | | |

FORM TA-2
(Rev. 2018)

STATE OF HAWAII — DEPARTMENT OF TAXATION          DO NOT WRITE IN THIS AREA    26

**TRANSIENT ACCOMMODATIONS TAX
ANNUAL RETURN & RECONCILIATION**
For Tax Years Ending After December 31, 2017

ID NO 01

**Place an "X" in this box ONLY if this is an AMENDED return**

**TAX YEAR ENDING** 12-31-18   **HAWAII TAX I.D. NO.**   TA-123-456-7890-01

NAME: JOHN ALOHA                    Last 4 digits of your FEIN or SSN    1231

| | DISTRICT | Column a<br>GROSS RENTAL OR<br>GROSS RENTAL PROCEEDS | Column b<br>EXEMPTIONS/DEDUCTIONS<br>(Explain on Reverse Side) | Column c<br>TAXABLE PROCEEDS<br>(Column a minus Column b) | |
|---|---|---|---|---|---|
| PART I — TRANSIENT ACCOMMODATIONS TAX | 1. OAHU | 7200.00 | 0.00 | 7200.00 | 1 |
| | 2. MAUI, MOLOKAI, LANAI | | 0.00 | 0.00 | 2 |
| | 3. HAWAII | | 0.00 | 0.00 | 3 |
| | 4. KAUAI | | 0.00 | 0.00 | 4 |

TOTAL FAIR MARKET RENTAL VALUE

| PART II — TIMESHARE OCCUPANCY TAX | | | |
|---|---|---|---|
| 5. OAHU DISTRICT ................................................................. | 5. | |
| 6. MAUI, MOLOKAI LANAI DISTRICT ........................................ | 6. | |
| 7. HAWAII DISTRICT ............................................................. | 7. | |
| 8. KAUAI DISTRICT ............................................................. | 8. | |

**PART III — TAX COMPUTATION**

9. **TOTAL AMOUNT TAXABLE.** Add Column c of lines 1 thru 4 and lines 5 thru 8.
   Enter result here (but not less than zero). ...................... 9.            7200.00
10. **Tax Rate** ....................................................... 10.              x0.1025
11. **TOTAL TAXES DUE.** Multiply Line 9 by Line 10 and enter the result here. **If you did
    not have any activity for the year, enter "0.00" here** ............ 11.           738.00

**PART IV — ADJUSTMENTS & RECONCILIATION**

12. Amounts assessed during the year...   PENALTY       0.00
                                          INTEREST       0.00    12.                 0.00
13. **TOTAL AMOUNT.** Add lines 11 and 12. ................................ 13.        738.00
14. TOTAL PAYMENTS MADE LESS ANY REFUNDS RECEIVED FOR THE TAX YEAR. ......... 14.    1200.00
15. CREDIT CLAIMED ON ORIGINAL ANNUAL RETURN (For Amended Return ONLY) ......... 15.
16. **NET PAYMENTS MADE.** Line 14 minus line 15 ................................ 16.  1200.00
17. **CREDIT TO BE REFUNDED.** Line 16 minus line 13 ........................... 17.   462.00
18. **ADDITIONAL TAXES DUE.** Line 13 minus line 16 ........................... 18.    0.00

**DECLARATION** - I declare, under the penalties set forth in section 231-36, HRS, that this return (including any accompanying schedules or statements) has been examined by me and, to the best of my knowledge and belief, is a true, correct, and complete return, made in good faith for the tax period stated, pursuant to the Transient Accommodations Tax Laws, and the rules issued thereunder.

IN THE CASE OF A CORPORATION OR PARTNERSHIP, THIS RETURN MUST BE SIGNED BY AN OFFICER, PARTNER OR MEMBER, OR DULY AUTHORIZED AGENT.

| SIGNATURE | TITLE | DATE | DAYTIME PHONE NUMBER |
|---|---|---|---|
| | OWNER | 04/20/19 | (808) 531-2000 |

TA2_F 2018A 01 VID01

Continued on page 2 — Parts V, VI & VII *MUST* be completed

Form TA-2
(Rev. 2018) **26**

• ATTACH CHECK OR MONEY ORDER HERE •

**FORM TA-2**
(Rev. 2018)

Name: JOHN ALOHA

Hawaii Tax I.D. No.   TA-123-456-7890-01

Last 4 digits of your FEIN or SSN   1231          TAX YEAR ENDING   12-31-18

**PART V — TOTAL AMOUNT DUE**

19. **FOR LATE FILING ONLY** →    PENALTY      0.00
                                  INTEREST     0.00    19.         0.00

20. **TOTAL AMOUNT DUE AND PAYABLE.** Add lines 18 and 19.......................20.    0.00

21. **PLEASE ENTER THE AMOUNT OF YOUR PAYMENT.** Attach a check or money order payable to "HAWAII STATE TAX COLLECTOR" in U.S. dollars drawn on any U.S. bank to Form TA-2. Write "TA," the filing period, your Hawaii Tax I.D. No., and your daytime phone number on your check or money order. Mail to: HAWAII DEPARTMENT OF TAXATION, P.O. BOX 2430, HONOLULU, HI 96804-2430 or file and pay electronically at **tax.hawaii.gov/eservices/. If you are NOT submitting a payment with this return, please enter "0.00" here**..........................21.    0.00

## PART VI — SCHEDULE OF EXEMPTIONS/DEDUCTIONS

**Note:** Most ordinary business expenses are NOT DEDUCTIBLE (e.g., materials, supplies, etc.) on your transient accommodations tax return. For more information, see the Form TA-2 Instructions.

You must explain your exemptions and deductions, otherwise they will be disallowed and you will owe more taxes.

| DISTRICT / ED CODE | AMOUNT | DISTRICT / ED CODE | AMOUNT | DISTRICT / ED CODE | AMOUNT |
|---|---|---|---|---|---|
| | | | | | |

**Grand Total of Exemptions and Deductions** — Add the amounts above in Part VI and enter here. If more space is needed, attach a schedule. Include the total deductions claimed from any attachments in this total. (See Instructions).........................    0.00

**Additional Instructions for Exemptions/Deductions (ED)**

For each exemptions/deductions you have claimed, enter:
1. For the "DISTRICT" column, enter the number that represents the Tax District from which the income was earned.
   1 = Oahu; 2 = Maui; 3 = Hawaii; and 4 = Kauai
2. For the ED Code please see the list of codes below and enter the corresponding Exemption/Deduction code.
3. Enter your total amount of the exemption/deduction claimed for that District and ED Code.

*Example:*  Taxpayer A received gross rental proceeds of $2,000.00 from the Consul General of the Philippines for lodging on Maui. Taxpayer A enters the following to justify the deduction entered in Part I, Line 2, Column b of the Transient Accommodations Tax Return:

DISTRICT / ED CODE    AMOUNT
2 / 1 1 0          2,000.00

| Description (HRS) | ED Code | Description (HRS) | ED Code | Description (HRS) | ED Code |
|---|---|---|---|---|---|
| Complimentary Accommodations (§237D-3(7)).....100 | | Nonprofit Organization, Lodging provided by a | | Temporary Lodging Allowance for military | |
| Diplomats and Consular Officials (§237D-3(8))......110 | | (§237D-3(3))..............................140 | | (§237D-3(4))................................180 | |
| Federal or state subsidized lodging | | School Dormitories (§237D-3(2)).....................150 | | Working Fringe Benefit (§237D-3(7))..............190 | |
| (§237D-3(5)).................................120 | | Students — | | | |
| Health care facilities defined in HRS§321-11(10) | | Full-time Post-secondary (§237D-3(6))........160 | | | |
| (§237D-3(1)).................................130 | | Summer Employment (§237D-3(6))............170 | | | |

## PART VII — RECONCILIATION OF GROSS RENTAL OR GROSS RENTAL PROCEEDS

**AMOUNT**

7200.00  1. Gross rental or gross rental proceeds — Total of Part I, column (a), lines 1 through 4. (Note: Does NOT include general excise taxes visibly passed on or transient accommodations taxes visibly passed on.)

500.00  2. Total general excise taxes visibly passed on.

7700.00  3. Add lines 1 and 2. This amount is your gross proceeds from furnishing transient accommodations that are reportable on line 13, column c of your General Excise/Use Tax Annual Return & Reconciliation (Form G-49).

ID NO 01

Form TA-2
Page 2 of 2   **26**

TA2_F 2018A 02 VID01

FORM
## N-288
(REV. 2018)

STATE OF HAWAII—DEPARTMENT OF TAXATION
## HAWAII WITHHOLDING TAX RETURN FOR
## DISPOSITIONS BY NONRESIDENT PERSONS
## OF HAWAII REAL PROPERTY INTERESTS

## 2019

### Complete Lines 1 - 6.

(NOTE: References to "married" and "spouse" are also references to "in a civil union" and "civil union partner," respectively.)

**(Copy A of Form(s) N-288A and your check or money order MUST be attached.)**

### To Be Completed by the Transferee/Buyer Required to Withhold

ATTACH YOUR CHECK OR MONEY ORDER HERE

| 1 Name of transferee/buyer | Transferee/Buyer's SSN or FEIN |
|---|---|
| JOHN ALOHA | 123-45-1231 |

Address (number and street)
1200 KALAKAUA AVENUE

City, State, and Postal/ZIP Code (province, postal code, and country)
HONOLULU, HI 96000

2  Description and location of property acquired (Include tax map key number)
APARTMENT BUILDING          TAX MAP KEY: 8-45-7
1130 HOOHOO STREET
HONOLULU, HI 96000

| 3 Date of transfer | 4 Number of Forms N-288A attached | 5 Total Amount realized on the transfer | 6 Total Amount withheld |
|---|---|---|---|
| 01-20-2019 | | 1,000,000.00 | 50,000.00 |

**Please Sign Here**

I hereby declare under penalties provided by section 231-36, HRS, that I have examined this return and accompanying attachments, and, to the best of my knowledge and belief, they are true, correct, and complete. Declaration of preparer (other than individual, partner or member, fiduciary, or corporate officer) is based on all information of which preparer has any knowledge.

▶ _____
Signature of transferee/buyer (individual, partner or member, fiduciary, or corporate officer)      Title (if applicable)      Date

**Paid Preparer's Use Only**

| Preparer's signature Print preparer's name ▶ HOMER JONES | Date | Check if self-employed ▶ ☐ | Preparer's identification number P00000000 |
|---|---|---|---|
| Firm's name (or yours if self-employed), address, and Postal/ZIP Code | KMH LLP, 1003 BISHOP STREET #2400 HONOLULU, HI 96813 | Federal E.I. No. ▶ 42-1539623 Phone No. ▶ (808) 526-2255 | |

## General Instructions

### Purpose of Form

A 7.25% withholding obligation is generally imposed on the transferee/buyer when a Hawaii real property interest is acquired from a nonresident person. This withholding serves to collect Hawaii income tax that may be owed by the nonresident person. Use this form to report and transmit the amount withheld.

**Note:** *You are not required to withhold if any of the exceptions listed on page 2 apply.*

See Tax Facts 2010-1, *Understanding HARPTA*, and Tax Information Release No. 2017-01, *Withholding of State Income Taxes on the Disposition of Hawaii Real Property*, for more information.

### Amount to Withhold

Generally, you must withhold 7.25% of the amount realized on the disposition by the transferor. See *Amount realized* under *Definitions*, later.

**Joint Transferors/Sellers.**—If one or more nonresident persons and one or more resident persons jointly transfer a Hawaii real property interest,

first, determine the amount subject to withholding by allocating the amount realized from the transfer among the transferors/sellers based on their capital contribution to the property. For this purpose, a taxpayer and spouse are treated as having contributed 50% each. Second, withhold on the total amount allocated to nonresident transferors/sellers. Third, credit the amount withheld among the nonresident transferors/sellers as they mutually agree. The transferors/sellers must request that the withholding be credited as agreed upon by the 10th day after the date of transfer. If no agreement is reached, credit the withholding by evenly dividing it among the nonresident transferors/sellers.

### Who Must File

A transferee/buyer of a Hawaii real property interest, including an individual, corporation, partnership, or fiduciary, must file Form N-288 to report and transmit the amount withheld. If two or more persons are joint transferees/buyers, each of them is obligated to withhold. However, the obligation of each will be met if one of the joint transferees/buyers withholds and transmits the required amount to

the State of Hawaii, Department of Taxation (Department).

### When to File

A transferee/buyer must report and transmit to the Department the tax withheld by the 20th day after the date of transfer. Timely mailing of Forms N-288 and N-288A by U.S. mail will be treated as timely filing.

Hawaii has adopted the Internal Revenue Code (IRC) provision to allow documents and payments delivered by a designated private delivery service to qualify for the "timely mailing treated as timely filing/paying rule." The Department will conform to the Internal Revenue Service (IRS) listing of designated private delivery service and type of delivery services qualifying under this provision. Timely filing of mail which does not bear the U.S. Post Office cancellation mark or the date recorded or marked by the designated delivery service will be determined by reference to other competent evidence. The private delivery service can tell you how to get written proof of the mailing date.

STATE OF HAWAII — DEPARTMENT OF TAXATION   Copy A - For State of Hawaii, Department of Taxation

**FORM**
**N-288B**
(REV. 2016)

## Application for Withholding Certificate for Dispositions by Nonresident Persons of Hawaii Real Property Interest

- File Copies A and B of this form with the Department of Taxation.
- DO NOT file Form N-288B if the transfer of property has already taken place. The Department of Taxation will not approve Form N-288B after the date of transfer reported on line 4a has passed.
- Please be sure to complete ALL lines and attach ALL supporting documentation OR your application will be rejected.
- See Instructions on the back of Copy B.

| 1 Name of applicant (Transferor/seller) | Identification number (SSN or FEIN) |
|---|---|
| MEL GIBSON | 444-55-4444 |

| Mailing address where you want withholding certificate sent | Daytime phone no. of applicant |
|---|---|
| 2300 PACIFIC AVENUE | (213) 123-4567 |

City, State, and ZIP code (province, postal code, and country)
NEW YORK, NY 19000

| 2 Names of all transferors/sellers (Attach additional sheets if more than one transferor/seller.) | Identification number (SSN or FEIN) |
|---|---|

Address (number and street)

City, State, and ZIP code (province, postal code, and country)

| 3 Names of all transferees/buyers (Attach additional sheets if more than one transferee/buyer.) | I.D. no. (Last 4 numbers of the SSN or FEIN) |
|---|---|
| HARRISON FORD | 1234 |

Address (number and street)
6663 MARINES RIDGE

City, State, and ZIP code (province, postal code, and country)
HONOLULU, HI 96000

4  Description of Hawaii real property transaction:

**a** Date of transfer (month, day, year).     6/9/2019     DO NOT file Form N-288B if the transfer of property has already taken place. The Department of Taxation will not approve Form N-288B after the date of transfer has passed.

**b** Location and general description of property (Include tax map key number)   KAMAAINA RESORTS, 12 KALAKAUA AVENUE
WAIKIKI, HI 96000 TAX MAP KEY: 1-1-001-112

5  Check the box to indicate the reason a withholding certificate should be issued.
**NOTE:** *The transferor/seller is required under section 235-92, HRS, to file an income tax return whether or not the person derives a taxable gain.*

[X] **a**   The transferor/seller will not realize any gain with respect to the transfer. (Complete **5a** on the back of Copy A.)

[ ] **b**   There will be insufficient proceeds to pay the withholding required under section 235-68(b), Hawaii Revised Statutes, after payment of all costs, including selling expenses and the amount of any mortgage or lien secured by the property. (Complete **5b** on the back of Copy A.)

| 6  Was the property used at anytime as a rental? ................................Yes [X]  No [ ] | Hawaii Tax I.D. Number |
|---|---|
| If yes, enter your Hawaii Tax I.D. Number. | GE  123-456-7890-01 |

**Please Sign Here**

I hereby declare under penalties provided by section 231-36, HRS, that I have examined this application and accompanying attachments, and, to the best of my knowledge and belief, they are true, correct, and complete.

➤ _____   _____   6/6/2019
   Signature                  Title (If applicable)      Date

➤ _____   _____   _____
   Spouse's signature (If applicable)   Title (If applicable)   Date

## FOR OFFICIAL USE ONLY:

Approved: _____     Disapproved: _____
         Month      Day      Year                        Month      Day      Year

Amount required to be withheld   $ _____

Signature _____

88

FORM N-288B

MEL GIBSON                                                                    444-55-4444
**Form N-288B**
(REV. 2016)

**5a.** Calculation and written justification showing that the transferor/seller will not realize any gain with respect to the transfer. Attach a copy of a tentative statement from your escrow company for this transaction showing the gross sales price. Also attach a copy of your closing escrow statement from your purchase or acquisition of this property. (Note: You must provide documentation for all items in the calculation.)

   1. Sales Price                                                                  $       12,000,000

   2. Cost or other basis (including selling expenses). *Attach a schedule or list below to indicate the breakdown of your calculations.* (If you checked "Yes" on line 6, page 1, or used the property for business purposes, provide your adjusted basis for the property, i.e., cost less depreciation. Also, attach a copy of your depreciation schedule, regardless of whether or not you have taken any depreciation.) Do not include any carryforward losses or net operating losses.       12,000,000

   3. Line 1 minus line 2. (If greater than zero, was the property used as your main home and do you qualify to exclude the **entire** gain? If yes, use Form N-103 as a worksheet and attach to Form N-288B. Otherwise, you **DO NOT** qualify for a waiver of the withholding. Do not file this form with the State of Hawaii, Department of Taxation.)                               $       0

ORIGINAL COST $14,000,000      DEPRECIATION <$3,000,000>
SELLING EXPENSE $1,000,000
BASIS $12,000,000

**5b.** Calculation and written justification showing that there will be insufficient proceeds to pay the withholding required under section 235-68(b), Hawaii Revised Statutes, after payment of all costs, including selling expenses and the amount of any mortgage or lien secured by the property. Attach a copy of a tentative statement from your escrow company for this transaction showing the distribution of funds received.

   1a. Sales price                                                     $

   1b. Sales proceeds to be received in forms other than cash (describe) _____

   1c. Sales proceeds to be received in cash (Line 1a minus line 1b)       0

   2a. Selling expenses. *Attach a schedule or list below to indicate the breakdown of your calculations.*       $

   2b. Mortgage(s) secured by the property sold to be paid off with cash proceeds.

   2c. Other (list):

   3. Add lines 2a through 2c                        0

   4. Amount to be withheld. Line 1c minus line 3 (If less than zero, enter zero.)       $       0

FORM

**N-288C**
(REV. 2018)

STATE OF HAWAII—DEPARTMENT OF TAXATION

**APPLICATION FOR TENTATIVE REFUND OF WITHHOLDING
ON DISPOSITIONS BY NONRESIDENT PERSONS OF HAWAII
REAL PROPERTY INTERESTS**

THIS SPACE FOR DATE RECEIVED STAMP

For calendar year **2019**

or other tax year beginning ● _____, 2019
and ending ● _____, 20_____

(NOTE: References to "married" and "spouse" are also references to "in a civil union" and "civil union partner," respectively.)

NOTE: DO NOT file this form unless you have received notification from the Department of Taxation that we have received your withholding payment. ☐ **Address Change**

| Name ● TOM | Last Name HARDY | Suffix | ● Your Social Security Number 111-22-3333 |
|---|---|---|---|
| Spouse's Name ● | Spouse's Last Name | Suffix | ● Spouse's Social Security Number |
| Name (Corporation, Partnership, Trust, or Estate) ● | | | ● Federal Employer I.D. No. |
| Trade Name/Doing Business As (DBA) Name or C/O ● | | | Daytime Phone No. ( ) |
| Mailing Address (number and street) ● 1234 CHERRY AVENUE | | | |
| City or Province ● TORONTO | State | Postal/ZIP Code | Country CANADA |

Description of Hawaii real property transaction:          01/20/19

**a.** Date of transfer (mm/dd/yyyy)

**b.** Location and general description of property

APARTMENT BUILDING
1130 HOOHOO STREET, HONOLULU HI 96000

**c.** Tax map key number     8-45-7

Check only ONE box:

☒ Individual   ☐ Corporation   ☐ Trust
☐ Partnership   ☐ Estate

Was the property used at anytime as a rental? **Yes** ☒ **No** ☐ If yes, enter your Hawaii Tax I.D. Number: **GE** 123 - 456 - 7898 - 76
and indicate the start date and end date of the rental activity: (month, day, year) 01-01-18 to (month, day, year) 01-01-19

| | | | |
|---|---|---|---|
| 1. Enter the amount withheld on Form N-288A. (Attach a copy of Form N-288A) ............................ | **1 ●** | | 50,000.00 |
| 2. Sales price ......................................................................... | **2** | 1,000,000.00 | |
| 3. Cost or other basis (see Instructions) ................................... | **3** | 673,000.00 | |
| 4. Gain. Line 2 minus line 3 (see Instructions for installment sales) .................. | **4** | 327,000.00 | |
| 5. Enter the tentative tax on the gain (see Instructions)................................ | **5 ●** | | 23,322.00 |
| 6. **REFUND** of amount withheld. Line 1 minus line 5. (**This line MUST be filled in.**) ...................... | **6 ●** | | 26,678.00 |

**Please Sign Here**

I hereby declare under penalties provided by section 231-36, HRS, that I examined this application and accompanying attachments, and, to the best of my knowledge and belief, they are true, correct, and complete.

● _____    _____    _____
  Signature                 Title (If applicable)        Date

● _____    _____    _____
  Signature                 Title (If applicable)        Date

**MAILING ADDRESS**
HAWAII DEPARTMENT OF TAXATION
P. O. BOX 1530
HONOLULU, HAWAII 96806-1530

**FORM N-288C**

N288C_J 2018A 01 VID01                    ID NO 01

| FORM **N-288A** (Rev. 2018) | STATE OF HAWAII—DEPARTMENT OF TAXATION<br>**Statement of Withholding on Dispositions By Nonresident Persons of Hawaii Real Property Interests** | Calendar Year **2019** | THIS SPACE FOR DATE RECEIVED STAMP |
|---|---|---|---|

**Copy A — Submit to the State of Hawaii - Department of Taxation.** *See Copy C for Instructions*

| 1. Description and Location of Property Transferred *(Include tax map key number)*<br>APARTMENT BUILDING TAX MAP KEY: 8-45-7<br>1130 HOOHOO STREET, HONOLULU, HI 96000 | 2. Transferor/Seller's Share of Amount Realized<br>1,000,000.00 | 3. Date of Transfer OR<br>☐ Installment Payment Date<br>01-20-2019 |
|---|---|---|

| 4. Transferor/Seller is an: ☒ Individual or RLT ☐ Partnership<br>☐ Corporation ☐ S corporation ☐ Trust or Estate | 5. Transferor/Seller's Hawaii Income Tax Withheld<br>50,000.00 |
|---|---|

| 6. Transferor/Seller's Business Name | 6a. Transferor/Seller's FEIN |
|---|---|

| 7. Transferor/Seller's First Name<br>TOM | M.I. | Last Name<br>HARDY | Suffix | 7a. Transferor/Seller's SSN<br>111-22-3333 |
|---|---|---|---|---|
| 8. Transferor Spouse's First Name | M.I. | Last Name | Suffix | 8a. Transferor/Seller's Spouse SSN |

| 9. Transferor/Seller's Street Address<br>1234 CHERRY AVENUE | |
|---|---|

| 10. City or Province<br>TORONTO | State | Postal/ZIP code | Non U.S.A. Country<br>CANADA |
|---|---|---|---|

| 11. Transferee/Buyer's name<br>JOHN ALOHA | 12. Transferee/Buyer's FEIN |
|---|---|

| 13. Street Address<br>1200 KALAKAUA AVENUE | 14. Transferee/Buyer's SSN<br>123-45-0000 |
|---|---|

| 15. City or Province<br>HONOLULU | State<br>HI | Postal/ZIP code<br>96000 | Non U.S.A. Country |
|---|---|---|---|

**THIS FORM IS TO BE USED FOR TRANSFERS OR PAYMENTS MADE IN 2019 ONLY.**
ATTACH THIS COPY OF FORM(S) N-288A AND YOUR CHECK OR MONEY ORDER TO FORM N-288 (Payable to "Hawaii State Tax Collector")

N288A_I 2018A 01 VID01                    ID NO 01                    FORM N-288A

**Form FP-1**
(REV. 2018)

**2019**

STATE OF HAWAII — DEPARTMENT OF TAXATION
**FRANCHISE TAX OR
PUBLIC SERVICE COMPANY TAX**
INSTALLMENT PAYMENT VOUCHER

DO NOT WRITE OR STAPLE IN THIS SPACE

Based on income for calendar tax year 2018, or fiscal tax year 2018
beginning on _____, 2018 and ending on _____, 20 _____

Check one: ☑ Franchise Tax ☐ Public Service Company Tax

**Payment Number 2**

| PRINT OR TYPE | | |
|---|---|---|
| Hawaii Tax I.D. No.<br>FR-123-456-7890-12 | Federal Employer I.D. No.<br>98-1234567 | 1. Estimated tax liability for the year............➤ $ 144,000 |
| Name<br>HONOLULU INTERNATIONAL BANK | | 2. Amount of this installment.......................➤ $ 12,000 |
| DBA (if any) | | 3. Amount of any unused overpayment<br>credit to be applied....................................➤ $ |
| Mailing Address (number and street)<br>900 WALL STREET | | 4. Amount of this payment.<br>(Line 2 minus line 3.).................................➤ $ 12,000 |
| City, State, and Postal/ZIP Code<br>HONOLULU, HI 96000 | | |

**MAIL THIS VOUCHER WITH CHECK OR MONEY ORDER PAYABLE
TO "HAWAII STATE TAX COLLECTOR."**
Write your Federal Employer I.D. Number on your check or money order.
**DUE DATES FOR MONTHLY PAYMENTS:**

Payment due on or before February 10, 2019, for calendar year taxpayers
and on or before the 10th day of the second month after the close of the
fiscal year for fiscal year taxpayers.

☐ **Change of Address**

**-MAILING ADDRESS-**
**HAWAII DEPARTMENT OF TAXATION**
P. O. BOX 1530
HONOLULU, HI 96806-1530

FP1_I 2018A 02 VID01    ID NO 01    *See Instructions on the reverse side.*

**Form FP-1**

✂ — — — — — — — — — — — CUT HERE — — — — — — — — — — — ✂

**Form FP-1**
(REV. 2018)

**2019**

STATE OF HAWAII — DEPARTMENT OF TAXATION
**FRANCHISE TAX OR
PUBLIC SERVICE COMPANY TAX**
INSTALLMENT PAYMENT VOUCHER

DO NOT WRITE OR STAPLE IN THIS SPACE

Based on income for calendar tax year 2018, or fiscal tax year 2018
beginning on _____, 2018 and ending on _____, 20 _____

Check one: ☑ Franchise Tax ☐ Public Service Company Tax

**Payment Number 1**

| PRINT OR TYPE | | |
|---|---|---|
| Hawaii Tax I.D. No.<br>FR-123-456-7890-12 | Federal Employer I.D. No.<br>98-1234567 | 1. Estimated tax liability for the year............➤ $ 144,000 |
| Name<br>HONOLULU INTERNATIONAL BANK | | 2. Amount of this installment.......................➤ $ 12,000 |
| DBA (if any) | | 3. Amount of any unused overpayment<br>credit to be applied....................................➤ $ |
| Mailing Address (number and street)<br>900 WALL STREET | | 4. Amount of this payment.<br>(Line 2 minus line 3.).................................➤ $ 12,000 |
| City, State, and Postal/ZIP Code<br>HONOLULU, HI 96000 | | |

**MAIL THIS VOUCHER WITH CHECK OR MONEY ORDER PAYABLE
TO "HAWAII STATE TAX COLLECTOR."**
Write your Federal Employer I.D. Number on your check or money order.
**DUE DATES FOR MONTHLY PAYMENTS:**

Payment due on or before January 10, 2019, for calendar year taxpayers
and on or before the 10th day of the first month after the close of the fiscal
year for fiscal year taxpayers.

☐ **Change of Address**

**-MAILING ADDRESS-**
**HAWAII DEPARTMENT OF TAXATION**
P. O. BOX 1530
HONOLULU, HI 96806-1530

FP1_I 2018A 01 VID01    ID NO 01    *See Instructions on the reverse side.*

**Form FP-1**

**FORM N-289**
(REV. 2013)

STATE OF HAWAII — DEPARTMENT OF TAXATION

## CERTIFICATION FOR EXEMPTION FROM THE WITHHOLDING OF TAX ON THE DISPOSITION OF HAWAII REAL PROPERTY

(To be completed by transferor/seller and given to transferee/buyer. The transferor/seller should NOT file Form N-289 with the Department of Taxation for approval.)

Section 235-68, Hawaii Revised Statutes (HRS), provides that a transferee/buyer of Hawaii real property must withhold tax if the transferor/seller is a nonresident person. To inform the transferee/buyer that withholding of tax is not required upon the disposition of Hawaii real property by BRADY, THOMAS _____ (name of transferor/seller), the undersigned hereby certifies the following:

Transferor/seller's identification number (Last 4 numbers of the SSN or FEIN) _____ 333-22-4444

Transferor/seller's address (home address for individuals, office address for corporations, partnerships, trusts, or estates)

1234 ALOHA ROAD

HONOLULU, HI 96000

The withholding of tax is not required upon the disposition of Hawaii real property because (check whichever box is applicable):

[X]  1   The transferor/seller is a resident person as defined in section 235-68, HRS. **Resident person** means any: (1) Individual included in the definition of "resident" in section 235-1, HRS; (2) Corporation incorporated or granted a certificate of authority under Chapter 414, 414D, or 415A, HRS; (3) Partnership formed or registered under Chapter 425 or 425E*, HRS; (4) Foreign partnership qualified to transact business pursuant to Chapter 425 or 425E*, HRS; (5) Limited liability company formed under Chapter 428, HRS, or any foreign limited liability company registered under Chapter 428, HRS; provided that if a single member limited liability company has not elected to be taxed as a corporation, the single member limited liability company shall be disregarded for purposes of section 235-68, HRS, and section 235-68, HRS, shall be applied as if the sole member is the transferor; (6) Limited liability partnership formed under Chapter 425, HRS; (7) Foreign limited liability partnership qualified to transact business under Chapter 425, HRS; (8) Trust included in the definition of "resident trust" in section 235-1, HRS; or (9) Estate included in the definition of "resident estate" in section 235-1, HRS.
         *Note: Chapter 425E, HRS, replaced chapter 425D, HRS, effective July 1, 2004.

[ ]  2   That by reason of a nonrecognition provision of the Internal Revenue Code as operative under chapter 235, HRS, or the provisions of any United States treaty, the transferor/seller is not required to recognize any gain or loss with respect to the transfer. (See Instructions) (Complete A and B below.)

         A.  Brief description of the transfer:

         B.  Brief summary of the law and facts supporting the claim that recognition of gain or loss is not required with respect to the transfer:

[ ]  3   For the year preceding the date of the transfer the property has been used by the transferor/seller as a principal residence, and that the amount realized for the property does not exceed $300,000. (See Instructions)

BRADY, THOMAS _____ (name of transferor/seller) understands that this certification may be disclosed to the State of Hawaii, Department of Taxation by the transferee/buyer and that any false statement contained herein could be punished by fine, imprisonment, or both.

I declare, under the penalties set forth in section 231-36, HRS, that this certification has been examined by me, and to the best of my knowledge and belief, it is true, correct, and complete. In the case of corporations, partnerships, trusts, or estates, I further declare that I have authority to sign this document on behalf of BRADY, THOMAS _____ (name of transferor/seller).

Signed: _____          Print Name:  BRADY, THOMAS

Title:    OWNER _____          Date: _____ 1/2/2019

88

**FORM N-289**

# – C –

# – D –

## – S –

## – T –

# ABOUT THE AUTHORS

**Alan M.L. Yee** is the tax partner who provides oversight to the Tax Division of KMH LLP. Prior to joining KMH in 2002 Alan was the managing partner and partner in charge of the Tax Department of Grant Thornton LLP's Honolulu office. Alan has over 30 years of experience.

**Kurt Kawafuchi** is licensed as an attorney and Certified Public Accountant (CPA) in California and Hawaii (not in public practice). He is Certified Specialist, Taxation Law, State Bar of California, and a Fellow of the American College of Tax Counsel. Kurt served as Director, State of Hawaii Department of Taxation, 2003-2010, and as Supervisor, Tax Division, State of Hawaii Department of Attorney General, 1999-2002. Kurt was the President of the Western States Association of Tax Administrators, 2008-2009. In addition to being a speaker at national and state tax conferences and an instructor at the University of Hawaii, Graduate School of Accounting, Kurt currently serves as the Chair, Council of Revenues, State of Hawaii. He earned his LL.M. (Taxation) from Georgetown University Law Center.

**Duane Akamine** is currently a tax manager at KMH LLP. He has over eight years of tax experience in public accounting and consulting, with a variety of clients on tax and business issues. Duane started his career as an intern at KMH and then acquired a variety of experience with a big four firm and other local firms here in Hawaii, before returning to KMH. Duane is a certified public accountant and a member of the Hawaii Society of Certified Public Accountants and the American Institute of Certified Public Accountants.

CPSIA information can be obtained
at www.ICGtesting.com
Printed in the USA
LVHW082030230623
750627LV00003B/42